More praise for James H. Jones's *Alfred C. Kinsey*

"Jones has written an astonishing, scrupulously researched and utterly uninhibited life of the almost legendary sexologist Alfred Kinsey, who poured his life into his work and made his 'science' serve his appetites. Without aiming to be sensational, this is a sensational book."
—Peter Gay, Sterling Professor of History Emeritus, Yale University

"[Jones] is a historian with a knack for writing books about the past that are bound to be discussed in the present."   —Alan Wolfe, *The New Republic*

"Jones does full justice to the complex and ambiguous character of his subject."   —*Nature*

"Jones's biography of Alfred Kinsey is a tour de force. It sheds light not only on his extraordinary career but also on the evolution of sex research, sexual mores, higher education, and the role of philanthropic foundations in American society. What is equally impressive is that Jones has managed to integrate Kinsey's personal life and scientific career without either denigrating or exalting him. This book will be the definitive work on Kinsey."   —Gerald N. Grob, Henry E. Sigerist Professor
of the History of Medicine, Rutgers University

"It is hard to imagine any future Kinsey books trumping this one for sheer wealth of material."   —*Houston Chronicle*

"[An] impressive work. . . . Thanks to James H. Jones, we now have a study of the man that shares the courageous spirit of openness and honesty that distinguishes the original Kinsey Reports." —*Baltimore Sun*

"Jones's *Alfred C. Kinsey* is a superb book, magnificently researched, and skillful in setting Kinsey within a number of broader social and intellectual contexts. Jones is a sensitive biographer, managing to draw a portrait—warts and all—that conveys the many striking strengths of this stubborn, driven, idealistic man, and showing that Kinsey's public and private lives were inextricably interrelated. The book reads well and the cast of characters is fascinating."   —James T. Patterson,
Ford Foundation Professor of History, Brown University

"[A] magisterial account of a driven man and the repressed culture in which he had to work."   —*Independent on Sunday* (London)

"Jones has given us Kinsey with the brutal honesty of a devoted crafts-man/writer and the nuanced humanity of a dedicated historian. This book is historical love-making at its finest, a page turner, and a compassionate tour de force on the pain of twentieth-century masculinity, prudery, and their institutional power components. If Kinsey hoped his prodigious research and dogged analysis would change how we think about sex as a nation, Jones's *Alfred C. Kinsey* will forever change our thinking about how one man's agony became a vehicle for the continual struggle for human understanding."   —Susan M. Reverby,
director of women's studies, Wellesley College

"What [Kinsey] did not confide were any secrets of his own. These are revealed for the first time in Jones' biography, and they make his book as shocking as *The Kinsey Report*. Jones is everything his subject is not: humorous, patient, compassionate and moral. . . . By writing what is both a biography of Kinsey and of pre-war America, Jones allows you to make up your mind. Without being sensationalist, this is a sensational book."   —Laura Cumming, *The Guardian* (London)

"A superb biography, worthy of this powerfully influential and controver-sial figure in our history. It shows Kinsey's inner demons, including his homosexuality and masochism, even as it honors his great and liberating achievement. Above all, Jones's massively researched and judiciously argued book inspires trust."   —Paul Robinson,
Richard Lyman Professor of Humanities, Stanford University

"Jones has written a definitive work, conveying trust by handling his sen-sational data unsensationally. Readers will be riveted."
—*Publishers Weekly*, starred review

"An exhaustive, compelling portrait of a scientist hailed as both a 'genius' and a 'dirty old man.' "   —*Kirkus Reviews*

"I have never read any text quite so meticulously researched. Jones comes as near to the truth about Kinsey as anyone could, short of bringing him back from the dead to fill out one of his own questionnaires. . . . We must always be grateful . . . to Jones for illuminating the man so clearly."
—Claire Rayner, *The Observer* (London)

"Jones paints a brilliant picture of a controversial, dedicated scientist. . . . Jones has some 'shocking' revelations, but this fascinating biography provides insights into recent cultural history and a tormented man who exposed the prevailing norms of sexual conduct as national hypocrisy."

—*Library Journal*

"[Jones] has an instinct for the way in which objective 'scrutiny' can have a de-humanizing effect, and may conceal motives of less than scientific purity."   —Christopher Hitchens, *Times Literary Supplement* (London)

"A fascinating account of a man who despite, or perhaps because of, his double life, looks set to remain the most influential figure in the field of sex research."   —Veronica Groocock, *New Statesman* (London)

"My biography of the year is *Alfred C. Kinsey*. . . . Jones' revelation [is] so psychologically acute, so sensitively explained that we feel it was obvious all along. . . . Unflagging, vital, beautifully written, it is a literary masterpiece."
—Jackie Wullschlager, *Financial Times* (London)

"The truth, as James H. Jones's masterly biography of Kinsey makes clear, is that Kinsey was not so much a scientist as a campaigner for greater sexual liberation who used science as his chosen vehicle. Seen in this light, he becomes a more attractive person: driven by demons, certainly, but with a strongly-felt purpose."   —editorial, *The Times* (London)

*Bad Blood: The Tuskegee Syphilis
Experiment, A Tragedy of Race and Medicine*

Alfred C. Kinsey

ALFRED C. KINSEY

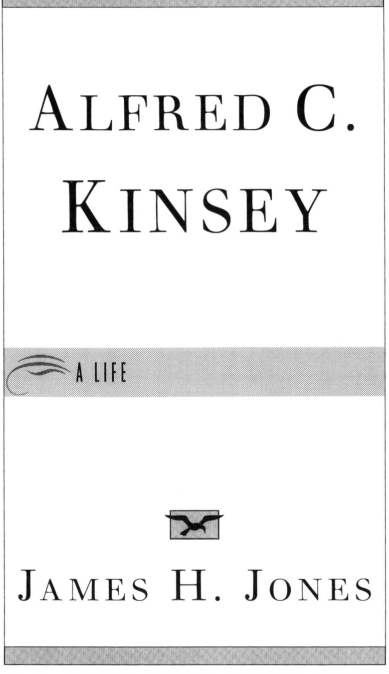

A LIFE

JAMES H. JONES

W · W · NORTON & COMPANY · NEW YORK · LONDON

For information about permission to reproduce selections from this book,
write to Permissions, W. W. Norton & Company, Inc.,
500 Fifth Avenue, New York, NY 10110.

Book design by Antonina Krass
Composition and manufacturing by the Haddon Craftsmen, Inc.

Library of Congress Cataloging-in-Publication Data

Jones, James H. (James Howard), 1943–
Alfred C. Kinsey : a life / James H. Jones.
p. cm.
Includes bibliographical references and index.
ISBN 0-393-04086-0
1. Kinsey, Alfred C. (Alfred Charles), 1894–1956. 2. Sexologists—
United States—Biography. 3. Sexology—United States. I. Title.
HQ18.32.K56J65 1997
306.7' 0973—dc21 97-27506
CIP

ISBN 0-393-32724-8 pbk.

W . W . Norton & Company, Inc.
500 Fifth Avenue, New York, N.Y. 10110
www.wwnorton.com

W. W. Norton & Company Ltd.
Castle House, 75/76 Wells Street, London W1T 3QT
1 2 3 4 5 6 7 8 9 0

FOR LINDA, AGAIN.

CONTENTS

PART THREE

PART FOUR

Photographs appear between pages 460 and 461

PREFACE

While it is by no means self-evident, Alfred Charles Kinsey was among the most influential Americans of the twentieth century. When we think about power, we usually focus on things like politics, the law, or the economy. Instinctively, we turn to presidents who make decisions about war and peace; chief justices of the Supreme Court who shape the law; and captains of industry whose technological innovations transform not merely the economy but our lives. Yet Kinsey deserves a place in our thoughts when we ponder individuals who helped change their times. More than any other American of the twentieth century, he was the architect of a new sensibility about a part of life that everyone experiences and no one escapes.

Kinsey was the high priest of sexual liberation. His power derived from the cultural authority of science. In two landmark studies, *Sexual Behavior in the Human Male* (1948) and *Sexual Behavior in the Human Female* (1953), he explored and mapped our sex lives. In addition, he used his status as a scientist in an increasingly secular society to challenge deeply ingrained moral values and legal strictures that regulated human sexual attitudes and behavior.

From the outset of his research, Kinsey correctly divined that Americans were awash in secrets. His research was designed to uncover what people actually thought and did in their private lives. Kinsey was supremely confident that he could shatter the conspiracy of silence that kept intimate matters enshrouded in taboo, and until the last few years of his life he remained optimistic that his discoveries would spell the end of what one reformer called "hush and pretend." Certainly, Kinsey need not have despaired on this account. He brought intimate matters out into the open; and by exposing their hidden lives, he forced Americans to confront the gap between prescribed and actual behavior.

Kinsey's life is a uniquely American saga, and I have several goals in telling his story. My first is to capture the man and to confront the powerful myths that surround him. During his lifetime, Kinsey carefully cultivated the image of a simple empiricist, a compiler of data who reported the facts with scientific disinterest. As I burrowed into more than a dozen archives, read tens of thousands of letters, and interviewed scores of people who knew Kinsey in various capacities, I discovered that his public image distorted more than it revealed.

The man I came to know bore no resemblance to the canonical Kinsey. Anything but disinterested, he approached his work with missionary fervor. Kinsey loathed Victorian morality as only a person who had been badly injured by sexual repression could despise it. He was determined to use science to strip human sexuality of its guilt and repression. He wanted to undermine traditional morality, to soften the rules of restraint, and to help people develop positive attitudes toward their sexual needs and desires. Kinsey was a crypto-reformer who spent his every waking hour attempting to change the sexual mores and sex offender laws of the United States.

In Kinsey's case, the personal was always political. With this thought in mind, I attempt to show how Kinsey's complex character reveals certain tensions within our culture. Of necessity, childhood and adolescence figure prominently in my analysis, because I wish to create a life that is at once factually accurate and psychologically nuanced. I devote a great deal of attention to Kinsey's youth in Hoboken and South Orange and to his university years, at both the undergraduate and the graduate levels. Similarly, I spend considerable time on his first career as an obscure taxonomist at Indiana University. I do so because his relentless pursuit of a common insect allowed him to develop both a methodology and a philosophy of science that he later applied to sex research.

In many respects, my portrait of Kinsey contains elements of tragedy. While I have attempted to avoid the pitfalls of what Joyce Carol Oates has called "pathography," I believe that many of the strange features of his personality and most of his bizarre behavior bear the unmistakable stamp of compulsion. Scarred by childhood emotional conflicts that both twisted and steeled his character, he translated his inner conflicts and anxieties into a powerful critique of Victorian morality and worked tirelessly to promote sexual liberation. Kinsey honestly believed that if people knew the facts, they would rid themselves of guilt and shame. Few assumptions better illustrate the optimism of the man or the age that produced him.

My second goal is to use Kinsey's life to explore the transition from the Victorian world to modern times, a shift that took place on several levels. It involved a moral transformation from a society dominated by a distinctive code of values known as "civilized morality" to a very different society in which many people demanded and exercised more freedom in their private lives. Many in this latter group embraced secular values, signaling a weakening of religious authority. During Kinsey's youth, religious doctrines, shaped largely by evangelical Protestantism, dictated the moral code that governed how most Americans defined sexual morality. But by the time he reached middle age, far-reaching social and economic changes had laid siege to middle class and small-town morality. Science had come to vie with religion for control over intimate matters.

In telling Kinsey's story, I touch upon several of these economic and social changes, but for the most part I focus on the power of institutions. In particular, I show how universities, scientific organizations, and private philanthropic foundations got involved in the sexual debate, and I explain how these institutions came to support Kinsey, even though a number of their officers and administrators understood that his work constituted a serious challenge to the ethos of individual restraint upon which conventional morality depended.

In recent years, there has been a tendency to argue that if science is the product of personal needs and motivations, then this somehow discredits scientific discoveries. Yet Kinsey's science was driven by needs that were not simply idiosyncratic but deeply embedded in our culture. His problems, albeit in exaggerated form, were the nation's problems. Moreover, the fact that his methodology and data were flawed in no way diminishes his stature as a pioneer—the researcher who made the public believe not only that science should and could study human sexual behavior but that social policy and the law should be reevaluated in the light of scientific data.

My third goal is to use Kinsey to explore the hidden story of sexual diversity in twentieth-century America. Better than most of his contemporaries, he understood that Americans were a people with secrets. Indeed, he himself embodied the contradictions between public persona and the hidden self. Perhaps his greatest contribution was to reveal the chasm between prescribed and actual behavior and to show the high price paid by individuals who internalized their culture's sexual prohibitions. Kinsey taught us that sexual diversity is not a recent development. It has been around for a long time, notwithstanding the jeremiads of contemporary moralists.

Like other progressive reformers who crossed cultural boundaries to study the lives of blacks, the working class, poor people, and immigrants, Kinsey explored the terra incognito of private behavior. His research provides fascinating snapshots of the incredible sexual diversity that existed just below the surface of American society. While Kinsey compiled a careful inventory of garden-variety sexual code breakers, he eagerly sought out groups whose members operated either on the margins or beyond the pale. Peering into the shadowlands, he found homosexuals, sado-masochists, voyeurs, exhibitionists, pedophiles, transsexuals, transvestites, and fetishists of various stripes. Indeed, no sex researcher, before or since, has examined human sexual behavior with such a wide lens or in such uncompromising detail.

Saul Bellow once observed, "There's nothing like a shameful secret to fire a man up. If Hawthorne had not understood this, *The Scarlet Letter* would never have been written." Much of Kinsey's spring-coil vitality can be traced to the inner conflicts and tensions that resulted from secrets he kept hidden from the world, secrets that began in childhood and have remained unknown to all but a few down to the present.

James H. Jones

Houston, Texas

April 1997

ACKNOWLEDGMENTS

It is a pleasure to thank the many people who helped me with this biography. During my graduate school days more than a quarter century ago at Indiana University, my plans to specialize in diplomatic history ended abruptly when Martin Ridge suggested that I write my doctoral dissertation on the Institute for Sex Research, the corporation founded by Alfred C. Kinsey in 1947 as an umbrella organization for his pioneering research on human sexual behavior. As the editor of the *Journal of American History,* Ridge had a commanding overview of American history. When he recommended topics, graduate students listened.

I took my first note card on Kinsey in 1970. Two years later I completed my dissertation, a straightforward institutional history that focused on Kinsey's relationship with his support structure—Indiana University, the National Research Council, and the Rockefeller Foundation. I am grateful to Ridge for his wise counsel, constant encouragement, and warm support. To the National Institutes of Mental Health, I am indebted for one year of support as a predoctoral research fellow (1971–72). Thanks are also due to John C. Burnham of The Ohio State University, who served as an ex officia member of my committee and offered many astute criticisms and suggestions. The Grant Foundation provided generous travel assistance that enabled me to interview Kinsey's relatives, former students, friends, colleagues, and university administrators, as well as foundation officers, public officials, and others who were important to his story.

Paul H. Gebhard, who succeeded Kinsey as the director of the Institute for Sex Research, kindly gave me permission to examine and cite the Institute's correspondence and clipping files. He also served on my dissertation committee. Over the years, we have had numerous conversations and he has granted me four separate interviews. Much of my understanding of Kinsey has been shaped by our conversations, both on and off tape. I am extremely grateful for his assistance. I also wish to thank Rebecca Dixon, Linda Watson, and Jo Huntington, all of whom helped me in countless ways at the Institute. A word of gratitude is also due June Machover Reinisch, who succeeded Gebhard as director. During her tenure, the Institute awarded me a summer grant that enabled me to continue my research in the Institute's correspondence files and archive. Douglas Freeman went miles beyond his duties as the Director of Information Services at the Institute to fill my numerous requests for materials. I also wish to thank William Dellenback, the Institute's gifted photographer, for granting me three interviews and for showing me his incomparable photographs.

Graduate school friends provided warm support during the initial stage of this project. For listening to my ideas and criticizing my arguments (not to mention reading all or parts of my dissertation), I wish to thank Richard Bonnabeau, Eric Gilbertson, Suellen Hoy, Howard Jones, James H. Madison, D. Scott Peterson, and Raymond L. Shoemaker. Ann Collins Nelson deserves a special word of thanks. She discussed my ideas, encouraged my efforts, and remained my friend under difficult circumstances. Although practically none of my dissertation appears in it, I am sure this book has benefited from the criticisms and encouragement I received from my teachers and friends at Indiana University.

By the time I completed my dissertation, I decided that biography offered the best genre for telling Kinsey's story. Early in the project, two research assistants provided valuable aid. Marry E. Curry tracked down Kinsey's ancestors and helped me learn about his childhood in Hoboken, New Jersey; and Terry Rugeley, a tireless and resourceful researcher, uncovered mounds of data and provided astute assessments on a variety of topics. Over the last few years, Amy Klemm, a brilliant young historian of medicine and a bear for research, has provided expert assistance, and I am grateful for her help.

Over the years, I have been aided by numerous archivists and librarians. In South Orange, New Jersey, Catherine Sullivan, reference librarian par excellence, guided me through the marvelous holdings of the South Orange Public Library, helped me locate local residents who knew Kinsey or his family, and on more than one occasion took me home for dinner. In nearby Maplewood, I also wish to thank the archivist at Columbia High School. In addition, I am indebted to archivists at the Stevens Institute of Technology, Bowdoin College, Indiana University, Harvard University, Yale University, Columbia University, Union Theological Seminary, Princeton University, Stanford University, the American Philosophical Society, the National Research Council, the Rockefeller Archives Center, the Museum of Natural History, the National Library of Medicine, the National Archives, and the Library of Congress Manuscript Division. A special word of thanks is due Susan W. Dryfoos for providing materials from the *New York Times* archive.

This biography could not have been written without oral history, and I owe an enormous debt to the people I have interviewed. Their names appear in my bibliographical essay. Each interview has its own story, many punctuated by acts of extraordinary kindness. On numerous occasions, I have been picked up at the airport or train station, taken home, fed, put up for the night, fed again, and then driven back in the nick of time to catch my flight or train. Above all, I have been privileged to witness the respect and love that people bear for history. Time and time again, I have been aided by total strangers simply because they wished to support scholarship.

Three individuals asked to be kept anonymous because of the intimate nature of what they knew about Kinsey. Although they vowed decades ago never to discuss certain aspects of Kinsey's life, they elected to answer my questions truthfully, not because they wished to damage Kinsey's reputation, but because they understood that he belongs to history and history has a right to know.

In the years since the hardback edition of my biography of Kinsey was published, all three of these individuals have died, and I am at liberty to identify two of them. All three expressed the hope that history will judge Kinsey not by his private behavior but by his efforts to promote tolerance, understanding, and acceptance of human sexual diversity. At a future date, I plan to deposit my interviews in a library or archive where they will be open to other scholars.

With two exceptions, the members of Kinsey's immediate family elected not to cooperate with me. I interviewed his widow, Clara McMillen Kinsey, and his daughter, Joan Reid. His two other surviving children, Anne Call and Bruce Kinsey, declined my requests for interviews. Following Clara's death, the family also refused to let me examine the personal correspondence between Kinsey and Clara. I was able to interview Edna Kinsey Higenbotham, the widow of Kinsey's brother, Robert. I wish to thank her for granting me permission to publish a number of photographs in her possession. In this regard, I am also grateful to Robert Kroc for allowing me to copy letters, photographs, and other memorabilia.

I am indebted to several institutions for financial assistance. In 1982, I was awarded a summer grant from the Rockefeller Archives Center to examine a variety of materials pertaining to the Rockefeller Foundation's relationship with Kinsey's research. In 1984–85, I expanded my research on these and other topics under a Senior Fellowship from the National Endowment for the Humanities. In 1988–89, I held a Senior Fellowship in residence from the Rockefeller Foundation at the Institute for Medical Humanities, the University of Texas Medical Branch in Galveston. Ronald

Carson, the director of the institute, was a warm and congenial host. I learned a great deal from discussions with the institute's talented faculty, including Mary Baker, Thomas Cole, Anne Jones, Ellen More, and William J. Winslade. I am especially grateful to Cole for his friendship and for reading and criticizing several chapters. During my tenure in Galveston, I also met Rodney D. Olsen, another fellow at the institute and a biographer in his own right. An independent thinker with a brilliant mind, a warm and generous spirit, and a penchant for seeing the best in other people's work, Olsen perused early drafts of the first half of the manuscript and improved everything he read. Over the years, we have had numerous discussions about biography, and I have learned a great deal from our talks.

The University of Houston, my home institution, has supported this biography most generously. A Research Enabling Grant paid for a summer of archival research, and a Faculty Development Grant allowed me to devote six months of uninterrupted time to writing the early chapters. I also wish to thank the University of Houston for granting me course reductions on two separate occasions that enabled me to give more time to writing.

A number of friends have always been there for me. Although they have had to listen to Kinsey stories and/or read bits and chunks of the manuscript for nearly three decades, Richard Abrams, John W. Cooke, James Hodges, Kenneth Macaluso, Charles Morrissey, Philip R. Muller, and Michael Roman have never wavered in their encouragement and support. James Reed offered keen comments on the entire manuscript. I am grateful to him for sharing his impressive knowledge of social history in general and the history of sex research in particular. His warm support meant a great deal over the years, as did the example of his formidable scholarship. I also wish to thank Dr. Douglas Appling for reading portions of the manuscript and helping me with a number of medical issues. I learned a great deal about childhood diseases from my discussions with Dr. Frederick J. Auwers.

Within my home department at the University of Houston, I received the kind of nurture that represents the academy at its best. James Kirby Martin, John Ettling, Joe Glatthaar, John Hart, and Tom O'Brien (each of whom served one or more terms as department chair during the years I have worked on this biography) supported this project in every way possible. I am grateful to them for teaching schedules and committee assignments that allowed me to pursue my scholarship with maximum efficiency. For being good listeners and for never being too busy to ask questions and challenge my thinking, I also wish to thank Norman and Hannah Decker, Sarah Fishman, Karl Ittmann, and Martin Melosi. My thanks, too, to Lorena Garcia for a thousand kindnesses.

Three of my Houston colleagues (and dearest friends) deserve special thanks. Despite repeated efforts, I never managed to be too needy, insecure, or demanding to exhaust the good cheer, intellectual curiosity, and kindness of Susan Kellogg and Steven Mintz. Sue and Steve took time from their own scholarship to read, discuss, and criticize the entire manuscript. I much admire their sweeping knowledge of social history and their generosity of spirit. In addition, I am grateful to them for encouraging me to write a bold book. The same holds true for Joe Glatthaar. A disciplined, prolific, and wonderfully gifted scholar, Joe interrupted his own work to read mine. Over the years, we have discussed this biography on countless occasions. His criticisms forced me to raise my intellectual sights several notches. Equally important, his enthusiasm for research and his love of writing have served as constant reminders of what it means to be totally dedicated to the life of the mind.

A number of friends outside the academy also sustained my efforts to complete this biography. I am grateful to Linda Shirkey for her careful reading and thoughtful criticisms of the manuscript. For their many words of encouragement and for never doubting that the book would get done, I wish to thank Bob and Carolyn Ammon, Frank and Marilyn Borowicz, Early Denison, Clara Glatthaar, Kay McCartan, Aliceann Muller, Nils and Barbara Nilsson, Michael and Susan Owens, Stephen and Linda Paine, James Tempesta, and David and Lucia Warden.

James Mairs, my friend and editor at W. W. Norton, has been a joy to work with. From the start, he recognized Kinsey's importance to American history. He encouraged me to write a book that would place Kinsey in his cultural and social contexts. Over many lunches, dinners, and drinks, he contributed insights and criticisms that have sharpened my analysis and saved me from numerous errors. Moreover, throughout the many years he waited for this book to be completed, he displayed enough patience and good humor to qualify for sainthood. Donald Lamm, too, has earned my thanks and profound respect. Despite his duties as chairman of the board at Norton, he found time to give me warm support, helpful comments, and sage advice. I also wish to thank Otto Sonntag, my amazingly thorough copy editor.

Family members provided unfailing support. James P. Jones, my late father, and Mildred Mackey, my mother, taught me the importance of hard work; Ann Grosse, my sister, always took my part; and Jewel Jones, my grandmother (deceased) assured me that I could accomplish almost anything if only I had enough "little Willie."

Our four children, Jessica, Laura, David, and Sarah have filled my life with love and joy. Over the years I have worked on this book, I watched Jessica and Laura grow into wonderful adults, and I have seen David and Sarah develop into terrific teenagers. I cherish them all for being themselves and for showing me what matters most in life.

My greatest debt is to Linda S. Auwers, my wife. She is my sharpest critic, fiercest advocate, best editor, and dearest friend. She read every word of every draft, and she paid me the enormous compliment of caring enough to argue passionately when she disagreed with what I wrote. To re- peat what I said when I dedicated my first book to her, "We alone know how much she contributed."

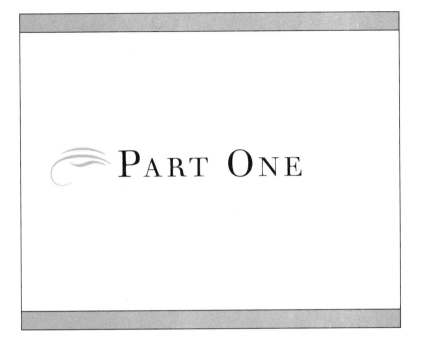

PART ONE

"The Lot of the Boy in the City"

In August 1956, Alfred Charles Kinsey, the world's most famous sex researcher, lay dying. Pneumonia had put him in the hospital, but heart disease had been grinding him down for decades. The last few years had been particularly nasty, as he waged his losing battle against chest pains, shortness of breath, and fluid buildup in his lungs, the classic symptoms of congestive heart failure. This is not a gentle death, and Kinsey was suffering greatly.

Yet far greater than his physical pain was the torment that had gripped his soul. Things had not gone well for Kinsey since 1953 when his portrait had appeared on the cover of *Time* magazine. Sales of *Sexual Behavior in the Human Female* (1953), his long-awaited sequel to *Sexual Behavior in the Human Male* (1948), had been disappointing; a congressional committee had investigated his research and all but accused him of being a Communist; the Rockefeller Foundation, his financial patron, had withdrawn its support; and financial problems were threatening to close his beloved Institute for Sex Research.

The prospect of seeing his lifework destroyed was more than Kinsey could bear. For nearly two decades, he had devoted himself to sex research, working at a feverish pace and with a single-mindedness that left everyone who knew him in awe. Together, he and his coworkers had interviewed over 18,000 people, compiling more data on human sexual behavior than any scientists before them. This was the public part of his research, the work known to the world.

Privately, Kinsey had always been more than a fact-finder. He was a social reformer, a man who waged with fanatical consistency his own private war against sexual repression and hypocrisy. Always he had been sustained by the belief that he would win. Once people learned the facts about human sexual behavior, he reasoned, they would jettison guilt and embrace their sexuality with abandonment and joy. By 1956, however, Kinsey was a broken man. He had come to despair of victory, believing he had failed to produce significant changes in the sexual attitudes, mores, and laws of the United States.

Why had Kinsey cared so passionately and worked so hard all those years? The answer lies in his private life, in the fearful things he had kept hidden from the world. Kinsey was a man with secrets, a man whose stupendous guilt had combined with his puritan work ethic to produce his spring-coil vitality.[1] Beginning with childhood, Kinsey had lived with secrets about his own sexuality, and he had spent his life deeply conflicted. Yet Kinsey understood firsthand how difficult it was to change his sexual needs, and he knew better than to expect sympathy or understanding from society. In order to help himself, he would have to help others. Thus, his messianic crusade to reform the world that oppressed him.

Kinsey's guilt about his sexuality was hardly unique. It mirrored, albeit in exaggerated form, the sexual tensions and anxieties of his generation. Many late-nineteenth and early-twentieth-century Protestants, middle-class, and small-town Americans felt anxious and guilty about sex. They simply could not reconcile their culture's demands for moral rectitude with their own sexual needs and desires. To understand how Kinsey's complex character was formed, our search should begin with his childhood, for it was then that he developed his love for science and first took up the heavy burden of self-criticism.

* * *

Flowers. As objects of beauty, they are supposed to make people happy, but they made Alfred Charles Kinsey sad. Not all flowers, to be sure. Only those that had grown in his family's tiny yard in Hoboken, New Jersey, where he spent the first ten years of his life. "He disliked Hoboken and everything connected with it," Clara Kinsey, his wife, later told an interviewer, "even the flowers that grew in the garden they had in their small backyard."[2] As an adult, Kinsey became an ardent gardener, but he would not permit marigolds, zinnias, or wisteria in his yard—the flowers his parents had grown in Hoboken. While his reaction was truly visceral, it was not the flowers he loathed but the childhood memories they triggered.[3] Not that he dwelled on these years, for Kinsey believed that bad memories should be suppressed. As an adult, he advised young people "to learn the art of *weighing down unprofitable things in our thoughts."* Referring specifically to unwanted memories, Kinsey added, "We may not be responsible for the birds (memories) that fly over our heads but we can keep them from roosting in our hair."[4]

After he gained world fame as a sex researcher, Kinsey received numerous inquiries about his past. People wanted to know his birthday, where he had been born, the names of his ancestors, whether he was married and had children, and even intimate details about *his* sex history. For a man who had become a celebrity by invading other people's privacy, he guarded his own with cool determination.[5]

Many of the inquiries came from people who wondered if they might be related. In response, Kinsey revealed only the barest details about his family. Mostly, he talked about genealogy, telling one would-be relative that Kinsey was the English version of the Scottish name MacKinsey and that his forebears had crossed the ocean with the Quaker William Penn, who founded Philadelphia.[6] Indeed, he maintained that all present-day Kinseys living in the United States could trace their ancestry back to the three brothers who accompanied Penn.[7] Nor was Kinsey above claiming distinguished personages for his family tree. He boasted that one of the original three brothers became a famous jurist in New Jersey,[8] while other Kinseys rose to the office of state treasurer in both New Jersey and Pennsylvania during colonial times.[9]

Here he must have been repeating family lore, for he offered no genealogical evidence to prove his ancestry. According to Kinsey, descendants of the three brothers who helped found Pennsylvania eventually moved out of Philadelphia into other parts of the country. One group moved to New Jersey and New York, another to Indiana and Ohio, and still a third to San Francisco.[10]

Both truth and error attended Kinsey's version of history. Men who bore his family name had indeed been important leaders in colonial days. John Kinsey (1693–1750), a brilliant Quaker lawyer, politician, and jurist, was elected the speaker of the New Jersey assembly before moving to Philadelphia, where he enjoyed even greater success, serving at different times as speaker of the Pennsylvania assembly, attorney general of the province, and chief justice of the supreme court of Pennsylvania. His son, James Kinsey (1731–1803), also compiled a distinguished record of public service, following his father into the law, winning election to the Continental Congress, and serving as chief justice of New Jersey's supreme court.[11]

By the end of the American Revolution, scores of Kinseys lived in what became the northeastern United States, but Alfred Charles Kinsey's belief that all modern-day Kinseys derived from three Pennsylvania brothers was mistaken. Numerous Kinseys immigrated from the British Isles directly to the United States in the seventeenth and eighteenth centuries, and many more followed in the nineteenth. Nevertheless, two (not three) Kinsey brothers did accompany William Penn on his journey to Pennsylvania in 1682, and it is possible (although by no means certain) that Alfred Charles Kinsey descended from one of them.[12]

Because he seldom spoke of his childhood, Kinsey's silence allowed others to speculate about his background. Before he became world famous, many of his graduate students at Indiana University had the distinct impression that Kinsey came from a well-to-do family. Perhaps it was his eastern accent, his educational pedigree (Bowdoin College undergraduate, Harvard University graduate school), and his intimidating knowledge of classical music, or maybe it was the stiff, formal bearing he often displayed. Whatever the explanation, many people found Kinsey cool and aloof, every inch a portrait of old money, with more than a sliver of ice in his heart. One of his former graduate students complained of Kinsey's "upper-class arrogance."[13]

The truth of the matter was that Kinsey's immediate ancestors, who hailed from the New Jersey branch, were plain folks whose lives paralleled those of millions of working-class families. Theirs was a tale of ordinary people in search of work, migrating from villages to towns, towns to cities, and, finally, into the orbit of the great metropolis. Kinsey's paternal great-grandfather was Charles M. Kinsey. He was listed in the 1850 census as a carpet weaver in Bergen County, New Jersey. Charles, forty-five, was married to "Margaret C.," two years his junior. Their household consisted of six children, including their youngest, Benjamin, age two. The family apparently managed to get by on Charles's wages as a craftsman, for in an era in which child labor was not uncommon, none of the older children was put to work full-time. According to census records, all of the Kinsey children over the age of three (including the girls) had attended school within the year preceding the census.[14]

Two decades later found Charles living in the same small town and still working as a carpet weaver, the trade he plied well into his seventies.[15] In 1870, his real estate was valued at $1,700 and his personal effects at $300.[16] In sum, Alfred Charles Kinsey's paternal great-grandfather was an ordinary fellow who held to his trade, who owned little beyond the means of survival, and who saw to the schooling of his children but could pass little on to them in the way of advanced education, land, a monetary inheritance, or a family business.

The same could be said about Alfred Charles Kinsey's paternal grandfather, Benjamin Kinsey. Throughout his long life, Benjamin's economic footing remained precarious, and he never managed to rise above his meager legacy. Duplicating the experience of so many other working-class youths in the nineteenth century, he married at an early age and abandoned the small farming community of his childhood to seek employment in the city. At some point in the early 1870s, Benjamin left Mendham and lived briefly in Ralston, before moving to Hoboken, across the river from New York City, where he spent the rest of his life in the shadow of America's greatest metropolis. In 1870, the census listed his occupation as "wheelwright"—certainly not a job with great prospects in an age of increasing industrialization.[17] In subsequent years, he worked as a carpenter, chair maker, "huckster," and cabinetmaker. Not until 1888 did he obtain employment as a foreman, the job he maintained until old age forced him to retire.

In the late 1860s, Benjamin Kinsey married Margaret Seguine, the daughter of Alfred and Renzila Seguine, a working-class couple whose residences had fluctuated between New York and New Jersey. As often happened among members of the working class, the marriage between Benjamin and Margaret led to an economic alliance between their families. By 1873, Alfred and Benjamin had opened their own business in Hoboken, "Seguine & Kinsey, Wheelwrights," on the corner of Ferry and Garden Streets. Two years later, the business dissolved, and Alfred found work as a laborer, while Benjamin returned to carpentry. Despite the failed business, Benjamin and Margaret Kinsey remained in Hoboken, where their growing family must have pinched their meager resources. Their first child, Alfred Seguine Kinsey, named in honor of Margaret's father, arrived on February 18, 1871, shortly before the family moved from Mendham to Hoboken. A second son followed two years later, joined within a span of eight years by two daughters and a third son. Of all the children, Alfred, the firstborn, became the most successful.

A self-made man and proud of it, Alfred Seguine Kinsey started at the bottom and worked his way up. His father, Benjamin Kinsey, like his father before him, could do no more than earn a living for his large family. His six children all attended primary school, but their prospects for additional education were bleak. Thus, when a job for a shop boy opened at the Stevens Institute of Technology in Hoboken, Benjamin jumped at the opportunity to place his fifteen-year-old son, Alfred, in this position. Alfred Seguine Kinsey would spend the next fifty-five years at the Stevens Institute.

In gaining his son an apprenticeship at the Stevens Institute, Benjamin Kinsey had the boy's best interest at heart. Manufacturing and industry had come of age in America. The new aristocrats among skilled workers were the machinists and the tool-and-die men who made and repaired the machines that kept the wheels of industry turning. As a shop boy, Alfred would have to pay his dues. At first he would sweep floors, clean machinery, and perform other menial tasks, but gradually he would also be taught to operate and repair the machines. Over time, he could reasonably hope to become a senior mechanic, a trade that would guarantee lifelong employment in a society that depended upon technology.

The machine shop was housed in the main building on campus, a three-story structure erected in 1881. The first floor contained various laboratories, the second floor the woodshop and the newly formed Department of Applied Electricity, and the third-floor classrooms and offices for the professors. As the son of a wheelwright turned carpenter, Alfred was well prepared for the woodshop. It was equipped with the usual assortment of small tools—wood lathes, wood-planing machines, band and circular saws, mortising machines, and the like. Here he remained for four years.[18]

From his first day on the job, April 12, 1886, Alfred Seguine Kinsey set his sights high. In Hoboken's city directory for 1886–87, he listed his occupation as "machinist," a considerable inflation of his job as a shop boy.[19] In the years to come, he repeated this practice again and again. At every stage of his climb to the middle class, he exaggerated his actual vocation to a higher status.

Endowed with a fierce desire to make something of himself, Alfred Seguine Kinsey wanted to escape the blue-collar world of his father by becoming a mechanical engineer. To achieve upward mobility, he confronted daunting challenges. He would have to earn the respect of his supervisors through hard work and diligent service, learn everything he could on the job, and somehow manage to advance his meager education. He moved forward on all fronts simultaneously. Blessed with great mechanical aptitude, he quickly learned all there was to know about the machines in the woodshop, and he impressed his supervisors as bright and hardworking. And most important for his future, from 1886 to 1890 he commuted across the Hudson to night classes at the Cooper Institute (later renamed Cooper Union), located on New York's Lower East Side.

That he was able to live at home with his parents helped financially, but it could not have been easy to work all day, commute to Manhattan, and attend evening classes. Still, he persevered, for he needed all the education he could get.[20] By the late nineteenth century, the professional standards of colleges and universities across the United States were rising rapidly. People without college degrees held few positions on college faculties, and the days when a bright B.A. could hope to teach at the college level had all but passed. In fact, the better schools refused to consider anyone who did not have graduate training. Owing to the rapid growth in college enrollments and the relative shortage of college teachers, many schools had to settle for candidates with master's degrees, but the strongest institutions recruited faculty who had earned their doctorates. The Stevens Institute was no exception.[21]

Alfred Seguine Kinsey was not without advantages. Added to his ambition and fierce work ethic, his four years of study at the Cooper Institute had given him a leg up on other workmen. Furthermore, he was lucky. His career at the Stevens Institute got a boost at several key junctures from fortuitous developments that would enable a former shop boy to join the ranks of the faculty.

From its founding, the Stevens Institute, in the words of one of its graduates, "emphasized a hands-on approach to the practical world of machines."[22] During their freshman year, students had to learn how to make wood patterns in the woodshop, ram greensand and molds into which molten iron was poured in the foundry, and cut castings to practical dimensions and specifications in the machine shop—jobs that fell within the domain of the Department of Shop Practice. In 1890, Alfred Seguine Kinsey was named an assistant instructor of shop work, a promotion that probably came as a reward for completing his studies at the Cooper Institute. True, his position occupied the gray area between manual arts and professional training, but no other department at the Stevens Institute offered a man of his background any chance of advancement. Since "shop" was required of all freshmen, his promotion to an assistant instructorship gave him a toehold in college teaching, and this set him apart from his fellow shop boys.

Having crossed the line from blue-collar shop boy to white-collar college teacher, Alfred Seguine Kinsey was determined to continue to improve his status. To compensate for his lack of academic credentials, he needed to acquire practical experience that would enhance his value to the Stevens Institute. His big break came in 1891, the year he transferred to the Department of Tests. There he was selected by Professor James Edgar Denton to serve as his assistant, beginning an apprenticeship that would last more than a decade.[23] As luck would have it, "Jimmie D.," as he was known affectionately to his colleagues and students, was the ideal mentor. Not only did Denton hold a chair in mechanical engineering, but he himself had been upwardly mobile, which predisposed him to look with favor on ambitious, working-class youths.[24]

From 1891 to 1902, Alfred Seguine Kinsey worked side by side with Jimmy D., learning mechanical engineering firsthand through on-the-job experience. Because his expertise was remarkably diverse, Denton's services were in great demand, assuring his assistants broad training in commercial engineering. Most of their assignments involved testing machinery for private industries, and over the years they performed tests "on boilers, pumping stations, electric plants, private yachts, ferryboats, ocean liners, locomotives, gas plants, artificial refrigeration, lubrication of machinery, metal cutting coolants, early Curtis turbines and the first Diesel motors." Of necessity, the work involved constant travel, because it was "not only done at Stevens, but all over the United States and in Europe."[25]

Thanks to his position with Jimmy D., Alfred Seguine Kinsey gained enough financial security to wed. On February 19, 1892, one day after his twenty-first birthday and a year and a half after becoming Denton's assistant, he married Sarah Ann Charles, a quiet, soft-spoken woman, two years his senior. The Reverend Charles R. Barnes performed the ceremony in the parsonage of the First Methodist Church in Hoboken, the church that would serve as the focal point of the Kinseys' spiritual lives for the next thirteen years.[26]

Sarah Charles's background is obscure. Her father was Robert Charles, a Welshman born in 1840, who immigrated to the United States as a boy.[27] In 1860, he married a Welsh immigrant named Elizabeth, also twenty. They resided in Maryland until 1863 and then headed west, finding little success but pausing long enough to have children at regular intervals along the way. Their fourth child and third daughter, Sarah Ann Charles, Alfred Charles Kinsey's mother, was born in 1869 in Colorado.[28]

The Charles family's trek to the Great American West earned an honored place in family folklore. In his high school biology textbook, *An Introduction to Biology* (1926), Alfred Charles Kinsey included a story about his grandmother's life as a pioneer. "Nine long months it took to cross the prairies and plains, and the deserts and the mountains, moving in ox-drawn prairie schooners," he wrote. "Then in time they toiled over the rugged Wasatch and down through the canyons and out into a veritable 'Land of Promise,' the valley of the Great Salt Lake of Utah. Here they planted their crops."[29]

Although the Charles family did settle in Salt Lake City, there is no evidence, other than Kinsey's story, that Robert Charles worked the land. According to another family legend, he became a printer after he reached Salt Lake City, where he was later killed by an Indian.[30] Still another version has him working as a carpenter on the Mormon temple. In the 1880 census, Charles listed his occupation as "smelter," but also stated he had been unemployed for the past year. In all likelihood, he went west to work in the mining communities, where smelters would be needed, then adopted a variety of trades out of sheer necessity, including, perhaps, those of carpenter and printer. The Kinseys' Salt Lake City neighborhood, North Temple, contained many families of similar background—English, Welsh, and Scottish immigrants who listed their occupations as plasterer, painter, ice peddler, or blacksmith.[31]

Whatever his vocation, Robert Charles needed work to feed his large family. By 1880, he had two sons and four daughters.[32] The family must have been struggling financially, for the census that year reveals that none of the Charles children had attended school the preceding year. At some point during the 1880s, the Charles family moved back East. Again, family folklore assigns Indians a role in the story. Joan Reid, Alfred Charles Kinsey's second daughter and youngest child, remembered Grandmother Kinsey saying that her family had to be escorted by soldiers part of the way because of the threat of hostile Indians.

Apart from these bare details, virtually nothing is known about Sarah Charles before she married Alfred Seguine Kinsey. The sketchy portrait that emerges reveals a young woman from a working-class family, poorly educated, with no known skills or other means of support. Although her modest fourth-grade education seldom revealed itself in her speech in later life, it was evident from her many spelling and grammatical errors in her letters.[33] Given his strong ambition and yearning for upward mobility, it is surprising that Alfred Seguine Kinsey would marry someone of this background. Over time, he would come to regret it.

The young couple wasted little time in starting a family. Their firstborn arrived two years after their marriage. Named in honor of both his father and his mother, Alfred Charles Kinsey was born on June 23, 1894. A daughter, Mildred Elizabeth, arrived two years later, followed in 1907 by their last child, Robert Benjamin Kinsey, named after his maternal and paternal grandfathers, respectively.

For thirteen years following their marriage, the Kinseys lived in Hoboken. Their son Alfred Charles spent the first decade of his life there. When he looked back on these years as an adult, he mentioned only public events, the sorts of things that make an impression on a young boy but offer little insight into his life. He recalled the first automobiles, the first paved streets, fireworks on holidays, and the like. Moreover, he claimed not to have any memories of the city after his family left when he was ten.[34]

This was a remarkable contention, as Kinsey had returned to Hoboken countless times after his family moved away. He visited his grandparents and aunts and uncles on numerous occasions and played with cousins on Hoboken's streets. Following high school, he attended college for two years at the Stevens Institute, commuting daily from the suburbs. His insistence that his only memories of Hoboken were those of a small boy suggests his time there was so unpleasant that he did not wish to remember, part of his distaste perhaps triggered by the city's poverty and crowding.

Located on the New Jersey side of the Hudson River, Hoboken (from the Indian "Hopoghan Hackingh," revised by the Dutch to Hoebuck, and later by the English to Hoboken) was aptly called the Mile Square City. Wedged between the Hudson River and the rump of the Palisades, Hoboken faced the Hudson River to the east, Jersey City to the south and west, and Union City to the north. In the early nineteenth century, Hoboken had served as a summer resort for New York City's wealthy set. On Sundays, New York's gentry would take the Fourteenth Street or Third Street ferry from Manhattan to Hoboken to enjoy the cool breeze along the River Walk and stroll through the beautiful woods in the garden spot known as the Elysian Fields. The rise of New York City during the nineteenth century, however, had transformed Hoboken into a bustling city and major transportation nexus. By the turn of the century, ten steamship lines and five railroads had converged on Hoboken, swelling its population dramatically. In 1890 Hoboken boasted 43,618 residents; in 1900 the number stood at 59,364; and in 1910 more than 70,000 people were jammed into its one-square-mile area, making Hoboken one of the most densely populated cities in the United States.[35]

The city crowded in on everyone. Except for a few postage-stamp parks and the campus of the Stevens Institute, Hoboken contained no empty spaces. Every square foot was filled with railroad tracks, industrial plants, stores, and housing, most of which consisted of cold-water tenements. At the northern end of the city, where shop fronts and tenements crowded flush with the sidewalks, smoke blackened the sky, billowing forth from factories that produced a variety of metal, chemical, food, leather, and foundry products. Running parallel with the Hudson River was River Street, the artery of the city's bawdy nightlife, described by one writer as an "almost unbroken row of saloons with cheap hotels and flats above." River Street formed the heart of Hoboken. Prostitutes solicited customers along its sidewalks lined with bars, raucous dance halls, and boardinghouses, making the city a favorite port of call for seamen around the globe.[36]

Hoboken was a rough and dirty city, and by the late nineteenth century its name had become synonymous with urban blight. When Oscar Wilde toured the United States in 1882 (his trademark lily in hand, dressed in knee britches, a flowing shirt with a wide Lord Byron collar, and a great fur-collared, green coat that hung almost to the patent leather shoes on his small feet), he was asked at every stop to define aestheticism, the strange new philosophy of beauty he had come to proclaim to Americans. It was no accident one persistent reporter mockingly asked if beauty could be found "in both the lily and Hoboken."[37]

Alfred Seguine and Sarah Kinsey experienced the same crowding as their neighbors. Unable to buy their own home, they rented a series of apartments within walking distance of the Stevens Institute. At no point during these years did they live more than a few blocks from the older Kinseys, and during at least two separate years (and probably more) the two families moved in together. "Doubling up" with relatives, as the practice was called, was by no means uncommon. Working-class families in the nineteenth century often employed this strategy in order to make ends meet. Moreover, even when they did not live together, blue-collar families often "clustered" in the same neighborhood so that they could assist one another. At least two of Alfred Seguine Kinsey's siblings (and their families) lived in Hoboken, providing a network that could offer companionship and assistance in time of need.[38]

While the streets and apartment numbers may have changed each time the Kinseys moved, the homes were much the same—low-rent housing consisting of two-, three-, and four-story cold-water tenements carved into tiny apartments that often served as multifamily dwellings. Units facing the street offered the luxury of windows, which let in sunlight year round and could be opened in warm weather for fresh air. But families who occupied interior apartments dwelled in shadows and darkness, illuminated only by artificial light. Here the air was stale and heavy, fertile breeding ground for tuberculosis and other diseases of urban blight. Hoboken was a dingy, dirty, crowded city, one that Kinsey desperately wished to escape.

For much of his adult life, Kinsey extended his hatred for Hoboken to all cities. He blamed the city for crowding in around him, shrinking his universe, and narrowing his vision. A sharp sense of claustrophobia marked his description of his childhood in Hoboken: "I was born in the heart of what was reputed to be the most densely populated square mile in the country. In lieu of woods and fields, there were the stones of the streets and the buildings, people, cats, dogs, horses, sparrows, the weeds of the vacant lots, and the frustrated plants of the mostly barren back yards. There was the cramped vision that it is the lot of the boy in the city."[39]

In addition to feeling physically cramped in Hoboken, he felt emotionally crimped there—and for good reasons. One source of pressure was religion. The man whom Billy Graham would one day accuse of doing more to undermine morality than any other American grew up in a family that was deeply religious. The Kinseys belonged to the Methodist Church, and as evangelical Protestants, they practiced a brand of Methodism that was heartfelt and fiery. Their God was no benign patriarch; neither was He a disinterested deity who had created a world that operated according to natural laws and could be left to its own devices. In spirit, if not in name, He was the God of the Old Testament—a jealous and vengeful God, a God who knew a person's every thought and deed and punished those who broke His commandments.

While Sarah had strong religious beliefs of her own, Kinsey's father dominated the spiritual life of his household. Every week, without fail, the family attended Sunday school, Sunday morning services, and Sunday evening prayer meeting. Alfred Seguine Kinsey would not allow family members to ride to church; they had to walk. Nor would he let the milkman make Sunday deliveries. One observer, who had been their neighbor as a boy, insisted that the father would not permit his family to do anything on Sunday except "go to church and eat." The same rules applied to visiting relatives. As an adult, Alfred Charles Kinsey recalled his father ordering his aunt to leave the house for playing the piano one Sunday afternoon.[40]

Religion had a profound influence on Kinsey. One could say he was reared in the "nurture and admonition of the Lord," save for one fact—his pious father admonished far better than he nurtured. Alfred Seguine Kinsey commanded dual authority: he acted as the head of the house and as God's spokesman to his family.

For his oldest child, then, there was no escaping religion. Week after week, month after month, and year after year, Kinsey sat with his family listening to sermons designed to shape his moral view of life as an unending struggle between Good and Evil. Much of what he heard was mean-spirited, hate-filled, and fearful, calculated to produce feelings of dependence and submission rather than love and trust. This was especially true of the sermons that were designed to frighten people into confessing their sins and joining the church.[41]

Kinsey heard many stories that chronicled God's wrath, but for its sheer power to terrorize young minds, none could match that staple of fundamentalist theology—the Judgment Day, the moment of reckoning when every man, woman, and child, living or dead, had to stand before the throne of God and hear His verdict. On that most terrifying of days, the Book of Life would be opened and mankind would be divided into saints and sinners. Verily, this would be the day of truth, a time of fear and trepidation. When it was over, the righteous would be raised to heaven, the wicked banished to hell. As they ruminated over mankind's fate, however, ministers did not tarry over the blissful paradise awaiting the righteous; they described with flinty severity the horrors in store for those wretched souls who had been weighed and found wanting.

Like all children who belong to deeply religious families, Kinsey had to ponder his religious instruction in order to arrive at his own understanding of spiritual matters. His God may have taken any shape or form. Perhaps he saw God as a benevolent figure, an omnipotent ally who would take his side, an omniscient friend who could be summoned in time of need. But more than likely his view of God was less benign. The sermons he heard dwelled more on God's wrath than on his love. Moreover, Kinsey's family's peculiar dynamics and distinct personalities must have worked their way into his image of God, shading his understanding of what God demanded and what would happen if he strayed from the straight and narrow path. In particular, his father, the man who loomed large in his son's imagination, offered a heralding image of patriarchal authority, the sort that could easily influence how a boy viewed God. Given his harsh religion and overbearing father, young Kinsey must have suffered in full measure the pain and agony to which seriously religious children can fall victim.[42]

He had more time than most children to contemplate an afterworld. As a child, Kinsey suffered a series of illnesses, some life-threatening, that put him to bed for extended periods. First, he developed a severe case of rickets, producing a kyphoscoliosis, or double curvature of the spine, which twisted his posture into a permanent slouch, leaving him hump-shouldered for life. Rickets also accounted for his swaybacked appearance, making him appear slightly potbellied, even when he was slender and the rest of his body looked fit.[43]

His second major childhood illness was rheumatic fever, which doctors feared damaged his heart. Long months of bed rest were required to survive this wasting disease, as the fever kept recurring. Nor was Kinsey allowed to resume normal activities after the disease passed. Convinced he had a serious heart condition, his parents treated him like an invalid and would not permit him to run and play with other children.

Kinsey's final and most life-threatening childhood disease was a severe case of typhoid fever. According to his wife, he "was in a coma and ill for weeks and weeks. They really despaired for his life." Though the disease nearly killed him, Clara Kinsey credited typhoid fever with curing his recurring bouts of rheumatic fever: "I have always felt that all this high fever probably killed off these germs."[44] As an adult, Kinsey rarely spoke of his childhood illnesses, but he did slip a reference to his struggle with typhoid fever into his high school biology textbook. "Years ago, as a small child," wrote Kinsey, "I spent nine long weeks in bed with that affliction. I have known something of the delirium, the long fight with failing strength, the full years that were required for the recovery."[45]

Moral reflection must have formed an integral part of Kinsey's struggle for survival. Like most children who suffer serious illnesses, Kinsey no doubt asked himself, "Why me?" Prolonged periods of bed rest gave him many hours to review his short life with utmost intensity. He had so much time to ask questions, so much time to think, and so much time to remember and to scrutinize his transgressions. Perhaps he sought reassurance by reminding himself that no one is perfect, but as likely as not, young Alfred found little comfort in such rationalizations.[46]

Still, even if Kinsey's childhood illnesses did not precipitate spiritual ruminations, they marked his life. Not only did he have to endure the pain and the discomforts of the sicknesses themselves, but he had to cope with the restrictions his parents placed on his behavior. Of the two, the latter left a far deeper imprint on his personality. For in addition to changing how he was treated by others, his many sicknesses altered his view of himself. Along with the city's physical density and his family smothering religiosity, childhood illnesses exacerbated Kinsey's feeling of being crowded.

The first tangible consequence of his poor health involved school. "As he described it," recalled Clara Kinsey, "he missed school as often as he attended."[47] Part of the difficulty may have involved the physical layout of the school. From kindergarten through third grade, Kinsey attended Grade School no. 2, a three-story brick building constructed in 1862 on land donated to the city by Edwin A. Stevens, the Stevens Institute's benefactor.[48] According to the terms of Stevens's bequest, the school was intended to offer primary education to working-class children. The fact that the building had three stories probably explains Kinsey's poor attendance, because his doctors almost certainly would have advised him not to climb stairs.

Since his illnesses kept him at home for extended periods, Kinsey had little opportunity to escape parental surveillance and authority. Assuming they followed standard medical advice of the day, Kinsey's parents made him stay indoors, take frequent rests, and keep calm and quiet. In addition, they must have placed strenuous games and roughhousing off limits. These restrictions cannot have been easy for Kinsey. Maintaining a positive self-image under these conditions would have been difficult for a child of either sex, but it was doubly hard for a male, as cultural norms could accommodate a sickly girl more easily than a sickly boy. Many turn-of-the-century parents believed that young girls had to be treated with kid gloves—reared, as it were, in hothouse environments, since they were thought to be by nature frail and illness prone. Boys, by contrast, were expected to be hale and hearty, blessed with strong constitutions. As a sickly child, Kinsey could not fit the picture of robust health his culture prescribed for young males. After he reached middle age, he told a friend that he had felt inferior to other boys during his childhood.[49]

As a result of his poor health, Kinsey had to rely on his wits. He often spoke of an episode from his youth when he had barely escaped a thrashing by neighborhood toughs. Walking down the street one day, still weak from rickets, he was suddenly surrounded by a group of bullies. As the menacing gang approached, Kinsey threw a handful of pennies into the air and escaped while the boys scrambled after the money.[50]

To compensate for his poor health, Kinsey badly needed something in his life at which he could excel—something he could use to build confidence. Social and academic success at school might have boosted his morale, but his frequent absences and restricted activities precluded such victories. As a result, there was little he could do to feel good about himself.

As an adult, Kinsey invented a fictional boy named Johnny Jones to illustrate various points in the textbook he wrote for high school students, and the same character appeared in the manual he wrote for teachers. In Kinsey's words, this imaginary student served as "the model of proper behavior."[51] As the ideal boy, Johnny Jones had many sterling qualities. He was an excellent student; he listened to classical music (and abhorred jazz); and he found joy in life's simple pleasures, such as sitting in the sunshine or catching a ball. What Kinsey admired most about Johnny Jones, however, was his eagerness to explore the world around him firsthand and his fierce sense of independence, as marked by his iron-willed determination to rely on his own judgment—one shaped not by whimsy but by systematic reasoning. As Kinsey described this amazing lad, Johnny Jones "was born with a considerable disposition to use the scientific method. He first learned about things by grasping them, by tasting them, by looking at them. He first learned the properties of matter by bumping into it. His early respect for energy was learned by direct contacts with it. His first generalizations were based on his own and not on anyone else's experience."[52]

But little Johnny's independence of thought had not come easily. Although Johnny was blessed with innate curiosity and the courage to explore, his childhood had been one continuous struggle against powerful adults who tried to limit his freedom by making him accept their authority and adopt their views. "Johnny Jones would have learned more, in the scientific manner, if his mother had not taught him that there are substitutes for observable data," explained Kinsey. "When he fell down stairs, he was thrashed because he had not taken her word that he would hurt himself." Nor was an overly protective mother the only check on his behavior. "He was introduced at an early age to 'they' and 'it' as sources of authority. 'Respect due his elders' was inextricably associated with an acceptance of their observations, their imaginings, their desires—things that small boys were supposed not to question."[53]

The similarities between Kinsey and Johnny Jones are striking. Little Johnny was an excellent student; after his health improved, Kinsey became a model student. Little Johnny adored classical music; Kinsey developed a lifelong love affair with classical music. Little Johnny hated jazz; so did Kinsey. But their most telling similarity involved their shared sense of childhood as a period of intense struggle for independence. Little Johnny had to battle against a mother and other adults who tried to impose non-scientific ways of thinking; Kinsey grew up in a deeply religious household at a time when science and religion were at war over Darwin's theory of evolution, the problem Kinsey later selected as his lifework. Little Johnny was eager to explore the world around him and tried to learn by tasting and touching, but he was thwarted by an overly protective mother and un-specified, older adults who demanded unquestioning obedience; Kinsey had a mother and grandparents with whom his family frequently "doubled up" who may have filled identical roles.

The story of Johnny Jones's struggles suggests that Kinsey may have re-sented the control his own mother exercised over him. Certainly, he had cause. However much she had her son's interests at heart, Sarah served as both his caregiver and his jailer. It was her job to enforce the doctor's or-ders, much as she strove to follow her husband's instructions about man-aging the home during his many absences. In all probability, Kinsey considered his mother too strict and too protective, a parent who failed to give him the space he needed to develop independence, a parent who made him feel crowded.

Sarah Kinsey was shy and soft-spoken, possessed of a personality at once retiring and diffident. From all reports, she was a loving woman with a sweet disposition, the sort of parent who could be expected to temper dis-cipline with love and punishments with forgiveness. Clara characterized her mother-in-law as "a very easy person to get along with,"[54] and once called her "the sweetest person I have ever known."[55]

Sarah's lack of education and passive personality inhibited her relations with people outside her family as well. Apparently, the Kinseys did not have much of a social life with other faculty members at the Stevens Insti-tute, which may have had as much to do with her husband's peculiar sta-tus at the college as with her withdrawn personality.[56] Nor is there any record of Sarah's involving herself with Hoboken's women's clubs, the or-ganizations that played such important roles in urban life at the turn of the century. Apart from being white and Protestant, she had little in common with the middle-class, college-educated women who typically joined these organizations. For Sarah, then, the world shrank to her household. Isolated by background and by personality from the concerns that drew other middle-class women into the community, she looked inward to her home and family, finding her identity in the cult of domesticity that sanctioned her roles as wife and mother.

As an adult, Kinsey told a story about his mother that appeared to touch a deep nerve. She collected an early version of "green stamps," and even though stores near their home had all the items they needed, she made her son tramp across town to a store that gave trading stamps. Insisting this was characteristic of his mother, Kinsey would become angry every time he told the story. In fact, the episodes angered him so deeply that he would not accept trading stamps as an adult from any store that issued them.[57]

Viewed in isolation, Sarah's request could not have produced such anger, as it was neither harsh nor unreasonable. The strength of Kinsey's resentment and its staying power in his memory suggests that he harbored deeper complaints against his mother. Perhaps he blamed her for his lack of freedom and power, for not only did he have to follow her orders at home, but he had to do exactly what she said when he was allowed to go outside. In other words, Kinsey may have disliked what he regarded as a pattern of control his mother exercised over him during his childhood in Hoboken—and beyond.

Kinsey resented his mother for subjecting him to public humiliation over their family's lack of money. Within the intimate economy of the Victorian family, money (who controlled it and how it was used) often served to underscore patriarchal authority, and this rule held true in the Kinsey household. Aware that money was power, Alfred Seguine Kinsey exercised complete control over the family's finances. He gave Sarah a weekly allowance to finance the household, and on those occasions when it proved inadequate, she did not dare ask for more money. Instead, she sent her oldest child to the store to pay the merchant what she could against their account, requesting an extension for the balance. While merchants were accustomed to working out such arrangements for their customers, Kinsey found these episodes embarrassing and humiliating, as he resented her for making him bear the public onus of his family's strapped finances. As an adult, he refused to incur debts he could not discharge immediately.[58]

More than strains with his mother or his family's austere religion, even more than his enervating childhood illnesses, the principal source of Kinsey's unhappy memories about his childhood was his father. From all reports, Alfred Seguine Kinsey was a hard man who imposed his will on others with ruthless finality, dominating everyone over whom he had authority, both in the workplace and at home.

Alfred Seguine Kinsey's professional advances did not come without steep personal costs. Part of the problem stemmed from his ambiguous status at the Stevens Institute, a situation that could easily produce insecurity in a man. "Shop practice" was not a popular subject at Stevens. As one former student explained, it "was considered to be a minor subject which most of the freshmen had taken in high school."[59] Most students held the Department of Shop in contempt and viewed shop practice as a bad joke,

and many of Alfred Seguine Kinsey's former students found it difficult to
separate their memories of him from their recollections of the Department
of Shop.[60]

"Kinsey was neither popular nor unpopular," one student declared. "He
simply was too far away from the difficult courses to evaluate that way. As
I recall it, he did not even have a nickname in an era when all professors
had nicknames."[61] Yet, whatever his status on the faculty, former students
agree that Alfred Seguine Kinsey was "very well groomed."[62] In fact, one
observer tagged him "a very natty dresser. The best of all the instructional
staff."[63] While most former students commented on his apparel and left it
at that, one particularly perceptive Stevens alumnus thought that Alfred
Seguine Kinsey dressed well as a badge of his recent elevation to the middle class. "I remember he was a rather large man, though not very tall and
[he] was very proud to have become a department head after years of supervising freshmen in the shops," he recalled.[64]

The head of shop practice "was very proud of his monstrous pocket
watch which he carefully laid out on his lectern before his weekly 1 hour
lectures."[65] Another student remembered him "constantly flaunting his
gold watch and bragging about his new Cadillac, which only geniuses of
his caliber could afford."[66] This formidable timepiece ("the famous watch,"
as it was dubbed by the *Stevens Indicator,* the alumni association's bulletin)
made a lasting impression on two generations of Stevens men.[67] According to *The Link* (1939), Alfred Seguine Kinsey's favorite teaching chestnut
was to use "his watch as an example of a piece of machinery that was kept
running in a vertical position for so long that . . . it cannot be turned into
the horizontal without losing time because the bearings are elliptically
worn."[68] But the watch in question, identified by another former student
as "a big railroad watch" with "a big chain prominently displayed on his
vest," was more than a teaching prop.[69]

After World War I, Alfred Seguine Kinsey had relatively little contact
with students, lecturing only one hour each week. Shop instructors supervised students at the machines, offering the kind of instruction he had
provided a generation earlier. Still, given the small amount of time they
spent in his presence, it is remarkable how much students disliked him. Basically, they were put off by his blatant egotism. "Kinsey was a great 'I' man
and after we caught on to that fact, we would make count of the number
of times we boys heard 'I' in a one-hour lecture," remarked one former student, who took shop practice in the late 1920s. "I do not recall the number week by week," he added. "Probably it really was not all that large but
it was fun to keep count."[70] Another former student agreed that he "used
lots of 'I's' and students counted the number of 'I's' he used." This man,

however, did recall the hourly count. "I think they got up to 100," he declared.[71]

Many students considered the "great 'I' man" worse than egotistical. One Stevens alumnus called Alfred Seguine Kinsey "a rather pompous individual,"[72] while another used even stronger language, insisting that he was "in the eyes of most students of that era, a pompous ass."[73] The latter student was especially distressed by the way Alfred Seguine Kinsey bullied people. "In the shop he was a dictator, who wouldn't get his hands dirty for anyone," the student declared.[74] Apparently, the head of shop practice was civil to students, but his shop instructors felt the force of his domineering personality. As another veteran of the shop practice class recalled, Alfred Seguine Kinsey "was hard on the shop technicians. He insisted they handle shop work according to his instructions. He would at times walk around a shop, observe what and how we were doing the work. If displeased, he would seek out the technician and tell him off."[75]

Alfred Seguine Kinsey ran his home the way he ran his shop, steamrolling any family member who dared to question his authority. Sarah knew better than to even try. "Kinsey's mother was a browbeaten hausfrau who simply did not play a large role in his life and was under the thumb of his rather tyrannical, puritan father," declared a close friend.[76] As Clara Kinsey remarked, "She couldn't stand up to her husband. She was more interested in peace than trying to assert her rights. If she felt that he was unreasonable, she would just acquiesce [rather] than try to push it."[77]

The first decade of young Kinsey's life coincided with the period when his father was struggling to make a place for himself at the Stevens Institute. During these years, Alfred Seguine Kinsey worked incredibly hard to advance his career, yet in many respects this must have been a frustrating period in his life. Although he was making progress toward the middle-class status he coveted so fiercely, his job did not carry much status. He worked as an assistant to an engineer, not as a professional man in his own right. Fourteen years is a long time to stand in the shadow of another man, even someone as supportive and kindly as Jimmy D. Consequently, when Alfred Seguine Kinsey went home at night or returned from his many trips, he may have been seeking to exercise power over his family that he lacked in the workplace. At any rate, whatever the cause, his behavior toward his family was always authoritarian and frequently selfish.

Slow to praise and quick to find fault, Alfred Seguine Kinsey knew how to reproach and how to issue orders, but he did not know how to show affection. Knowing her husband's personality only too well, Sarah tried to enforce his rules during his absences, but she never seemed to satisfy his expectations. As a result, his homecomings from his many trips brought more tension than joy to the household. As one of his daughters-in-law explained things, "Dad [Kinsey] would go off and wasn't home very much, and then when he did come home, things would never please him."[78]

Alfred Charles Kinsey tried to cope by doing his best to meet his father's expectations. Admonished by a severe God and a demanding father, he imposed a strict moral code on himself. Outwardly, he became a model child—the sickly boy who fought gallantly against poor health, the obedient boy who followed his mother's directions, the righteous boy who obeyed God's commandments, and the dutiful son who did his father's bidding. Yet, try as he might, Kinsey fell short of the mark. The only way to please his father was to follow his orders to the letter.

By attempting to live up to his father's demands, Kinsey was following a cultural script. The whole purpose of Victorian child rearing was to place children inside "a prison of expectations."[79] Middle-class parents at the turn of the century believed that children could be taught to control themselves. All they had to do was internalize the values and wishes of their parents. This accomplished, the need for external surveillance would vanish. Children would monitor their own thoughts, deeds, and wishes. And whenever transgressions arose, their tender consciousness would bury them beneath an avalanche of guilt, inflicting mental punishment with a brutality that would make hardened prison wardens blanch.

Kinsey's upwardly mobile family, the family that yearned for middle-class respectability and reached out to embrace Victorian morality, achieved this goal with a vengeance. Early in childhood, Alfred Charles Kinsey shouldered the heavy burden of self-criticism. Throughout his life, he would be haunted by a voice from within, a judge who saw his every move, knew his every thought, evaluated his every effort, and condemned his every failure. From childhood forward, Kinsey's harsh conscience would drive him to be the best at everything he did, would constantly accuse him of not working hard enough, and, above all, would condemn him soundly whenever he failed to move mountains or broke rules.[80]

The area of his life that most revealed his inner turmoil was his sexuality. Hidden from the eyes of the world, Kinsey felt his first sexual stirrings during his family's last few years in Hoboken. Like all children, he was curious about sex and wanted to explore others and himself. "The only homosexual thing that he ever mentioned in this early part [of his life] was in his childhood when there was preadolescent sex play with a neighborhood group," recalled Kinsey's colleague Paul Gebhard. The episode involved the sort of self-exploration and exploration of others (you show me yours; I'll show you mine) common to child development: "There's a somewhat older girl and there was Kinsey," explained Gebhard, "and I got

the impression there were about six kids and they would go in the basement and look at one another, poke straws in various apertures, stuff like
that, and that made him feel very peculiar and rather guilty."[81]

Gebhard's characterization of the basement incident as "homosexual"
strongly suggests that Kinsey used this term to describe the incident to
him. Although an older girl participated, her presence apparently did not
contribute to the erotic power of the episode in Kinsey's memory. Because
of her sex and age, the feelings she elicited in Kinsey may have been closer
to guilt than to arousal, as the presence of an older girl may have forced
him to recall the Victorian demands for restraint and prohibitions against
the debasing of females. At any rate, instead of attempting intercourse, the
children apparently engaged in acts of exhibitionism. Their sole attempt at
penetration seems to have involved poking straws into "various apertures"—most likely the vagina, rectum, and penis.

After he became a sex researcher, Kinsey reported that adults almost invariably remembered their first sexual encounters as children. In addition,
he argued that early experiences often played a pivotal role in shaping lifelong behavioral patterns—not according to some crude form of "imprint-
ing," to be sure, but in a less rigidly behavioral sense. People who found
their early experiences pleasurable, explained Kinsey, tended to repeat
them. With repetition came reinforcement until a pattern gradually took
shape. Kinsey's theories suggest that he traced his own adult sexual interests to this incident in Hoboken.[82]

For most children, exhibitionism and voyeurism are harmless rites of
passage, episodes that may cause momentary worries about getting caught
and punished but do not grow into the kind of obsession that can produce
debilitating guilt feelings. Kinsey was not this fortunate. According to
Gebhard, the basement episode left Kinsey feeling "very peculiar and rather
guilty." How could Kinsey have felt otherwise?[83] As the last generation of
Victorians, many middle-class Americans of his day felt anxious about sex.
While Kinsey carried parental demands for moral perfection to extremes,
Victorian culture required rigid self-control. Kinsey took these demands seriously and could not satisfy them. For him the legacy of childhood was
not psychological wholeness but emotional conflict, turmoil, and pain. In
that sense, his childhood was an object lesson in what could happen to an
earnest boy who strove for moral perfection.

At the broadest level, however, Kinsey's story underscores the problem
that confronted many boys in the United States at the turn of the century:
middle-class Americans no longer agreed on what it meant to be male. Indeed, they were locked in debate over the moral standards reformers expected men to meet in the post-Victorian world. As Kinsey moved from

boyhood into adolescence, he had to find his own answers to these questions, and the stakes could hardly have been higher. How he proceeded would guide his quest for independence and determine whether he forged his own identity. Fortunately, Kinsey got a change in venue as he was preparing to meet these challenges.

"A SECOND DARWIN"

he humor may have been roguish, but the message rang true when Mark Twain remarked, "There's something nice about Newark. I think it's the suburbs."[1] By the end of the nineteenth century, city dwellers from New York and crowded New Jersey communities like Hoboken were fleeing to the hills and valleys west of Newark in search of suburban bliss. Many settled in the four Oranges—Orange, East Orange, West Orange, and South Orange, a stretch of communities extending from the lowlands surrounding Newark upward along the slopes of the Watchung Mountains. Although these cities had separate governments and did not form a homogeneous community, their citizens shared a common identity as residents of "New York's most beautiful suburbs."[2]

In 1904, Kinsey's family joined the flight. Following the tracks of the Lackawanna railroad, they moved to South Orange, several stations west of Newark. Of the four Oranges, it was the least populated, the wealthiest, and the most beautiful. Its topography gave South Orange a rustic atmosphere, reminding visitors of the rolling English countryside, and its parklike streets, lined with huge shade trees and stately mansions, stamped the village as a prestigious address. On a clear day, the panorama from Washington Rock, the high point on Orange Mountain, included the Brooklyn Bridge and the Statue of Liberty.

From its establishment in 1872, South Orange had a population composed largely of New York and Newark businessmen and attorneys who commuted daily to the neighboring cities. As one civic-minded publication proudly proclaimed, "There is not a single factory within its boundaries."[3] By the turn of the century, South Orange's self-image had ripened into civic pride. The village newspaper assured its readers in 1903 that their community was "far advanced in material improvements and all that enters into the life of a refined and progressive suburb of the great metropolis." As proof of their rosy assessment, the editors noted, "A great many men who are prominent and influential in business and professional life have settled in South Orange, drawn hither by the refinement of the community, its beauty for situation and accessibility to New York."[4] Thanks to the village's ability to attract affluent residents, its hills and slopes contained a large number of "beautiful" and "substantial" homes.[5] Looking back on the turn of the century, one lifelong resident said, "If you told people you were from South Orange, they assumed you had money."[6]

Unable to purchase a home in this upscale community, the Kinseys rented an attractive two-story, white-frame house at 102 Roland Avenue, located in the Mellville Woods section of South Orange, near the southern boundary of the village. The house faced north, occupying the southwest corner of Roland Avenue and Academy Street. It was built and owned by Duncan Mellville, a prosperous developer who had made a fortune in real estate in South Orange at the turn of the century. Under his guiding hand, Mellville Woods had become a middle-class enclave in a prosperous neighborhood where practically all except the Kinseys owned their homes.[7]

The Kinseys' new home was distinctly different from anything they had known in Hoboken. It had ten rooms, each with a high ceiling, nine and one-half feet or more. The living room and dining room ceilings had poured plaster moldings, and the stairs leading to the second floor boasted a curved banister and newel post of black walnut. The downstairs had three fireplaces—one of white marble in the living room, and a second of white marble in the dining room, which sat back-to-back with the fireplace in the kitchen. Heat for the three bedrooms on the second floor came from pot stoves connected to a separate chimney that brought warm air up from the oil burner in the basement. The attic contained two additional rooms, completely finished with lath and plaster, and a storage room.[8]

Ten-year-old Kinsey reaped a dividend the moment his family arrived in South Orange. For the first time in his life, he had a room to himself, one of the finished rooms in the attic, which came complete with a window framing the world beyond. Here Kinsey could examine the handsome gingerbread moldings that lined the eaves of the roof and admire the bluestone sidewalk below, here he could peer at the maple and oak trees that lined the streets and gaze up at the stars at night, and here he could retreat from his family to enjoy his own private space.

To a boy who had spent his first decade feeling cramped, South Orange must have appeared wondrously open and inviting. Kinsey's section of the village sat in a valley that still contained fields and orchards, and empty lots dotted the blocks surrounding his new home. Unlike Hoboken's crowded tenements and row houses, the homes in his neighborhood occupied one-eighth-acre parcels, offering space for lawns and flower gardens.

In many respects, South Orange represented a conscious effort to reconstruct the village life of preindustrial America. Founders designed it to be a tightly knit community, a world of face-to-face relationships, a place where people knew their neighbors. Ethnically, South Orange was much less diverse than the city of immigrants Kinsey had left behind in Hoboken. Granted, a handful of Jewish families lived there, and large numbers of Irish and Italian workers arrived to build the roads and work as caretakers on the local estates, but on balance South Orange's 4,600 residents were remarkably homogeneous.[9] Residents with English and German surnames dominated the city directory.

Life followed a different tempo in the suburbs. When the Kinseys arrived in South Orange, the milkman and baker still made their deliveries in horse-drawn wagons; the local newspaper published the names of residents who bought automobiles; a village ordinance required public buildings to hoist American flags daily; Sunday school children turned out en masse every spring for the June walk in Grove Park; and the village Fourth of July celebration filled an entire day with festivities. One longtime resident described the village as "a homelike place" where parents "thought their children safe anywhere."[10] In short, South Orange provided a secure haven where Kinsey, who had spent his first decade feeling confined and controlled, could explore and engage in the task of developing his own identity.

Fortunately for Kinsey, his health improved dramatically after the move to South Orange. Rickets, rheumatic fever, and typhoid fever were behind him, and he both felt and acted stronger. Still, his new surroundings did not allow him to ignore the threat of disease. During his freshman year, a scarlet fever epidemic forced local officials to close the high school in South Orange; in his sophomore year, the senior class valedictorian died on the eve of graduation, a victim of typhoid fever.[11] Public health drives added to children's fears. During Kinsey's freshman year, two thousand schoolchildren in South Orange joined the Red Cross Christmas stamp crusade against tuberculosis, "the Captain of All the Men of Death," purchasing stamps "in quantities of five and ten cents worth up."[12] To a deeply religious boy like Kinsey, the outbreak of illness served as a constant reminder of mortality.

Alfred Seguine Kinsey made certain his son did not forget about God's judgment. Upon arrival, the family transferred their membership to the First Methodist Episcopal Church, located on the corner of South Orange Avenue and Prospect Street. Methodism had deep roots in the community, dating back to 1848 when a few Methodists living in the area decided to worship "under their own vine and fig tree." Others were attracted by the group's "primitive mode of worship," which included "simple words, fervent prayers, and earnest songs," and a tiny congregation was born.[13] By 1904, the church boasted 110 members, a spacious new church building, and a brand new parsonage at 14 Prospect Street.[14]

The church conducted a daunting schedule of services. The local newspaper announced, "Services every Sunday at 11 a.m. and 7:45 p.m.; Sunday School at 9:45 a.m.; prayer meeting on Tuesday evening at 8 p.m.; Epworth League meeting at 8:45 every Sunday night, closing at 9:15; class meeting Sunday at 3 p.m. and Friday at 9 p.m."[15] As in Hoboken, Alfred Seguine Kinsey made his family attend services every time the church doors opened. "I know that Bob always said, 'You lived in church,'" recalled Edna Kinsey Higenbotham, the widow of Kinsey's younger brother, Robert.[16]

Church activities dominated the Kinseys' social life. In contrast to the inward-looking, blue-collar congregation they had left behind in Hoboken, South Orange's middle-class and upper-middle-class Methodists leavened their religion with culture. Accompanied by a magnificent organ that cost over $1,000, the church choir routinely performed classical works, such as Haydn's *Creation*.[17] As part of its fund-raising activities, the Ladies' Aid Society sponsored classical music recitals and art lectures at the church. Nor did the women of the church neglect the broader community. The church ladies held a variety of social events designed to raise money for the poor, including a fall fair, an annual turkey supper, an annual Sunday school picnic, and a spring strawberry festival. The Ladies' Aid Society also coordinated charity drives by Sunday school classes, whose members donated provisions every year "to cheer some poor hearts on Thanksgiving Day."[18]

The men did their part as well. The Wesley Brotherhood Society of the South Orange Methodist Episcopal Church sponsored many community activities, including programs designed to promote law and order. On one occasion, the society mailed out mock subpoenas to more than two hundred village residents. Couched in legal language, with the customary title

"County of Essex, State of New Jersey, Greeting," the summonses asked recipients to lay aside "all and singular business and excuses" and appear in church "to hear Sheriff Frank H. Sommer speak on questions of the day." Those who did not appear would be rounded up "under penalty of missing an opportunity for the serious consideration of important problems affecting your welfare."[19]

Alfred Seguine Kinsey required his family to devote considerable time and energy to church work. Setting the example, he taught Sunday school classes and was elected an officer of the church in 1908, serving as an assistant secretary in charge of the Sunday school's intermediate department.[20] According to one family story, he later served as the "Superintendent of the Methodist Church Sunday School," the officer in charge of all Sunday school classes.[21] When he grew older, Kinsey, at his father's insistence, also taught Sunday school classes, a practice he continued into college and beyond.[22] By the time Kinsey had finished high school, all those years of faithful church attendance and diligent Sunday school instruction had earned him a reputation as a devout Christian. One of his classmates, Dorothy Beugler, who later served as a missionary in Thailand, would recall that she had admired his "stand as a Christian."[23]

Other classmates shared her admiration for Kinsey. Sophie Pauline remembered him as "a youth of utmost gentleness and principle," adding, "Biblical and ethical concepts were part of the general atmosphere of that period. Sophistication was absent."[24] Elliot C. Bergen, another classmate, testified to Kinsey's uncommon maturity. "He was naturally looked upon as the wisest among us," wrote Bergen, "one to turn to for counsel."[25] Trying to convey Kinsey's place among his high school peers, the "Class Will" had Kinsey bequeathing to one Manning Stopplebein "the High School halo, which has so long adorned his fair locks."[26]

Education had provided the escape hatch for Alfred Seguine Kinsey from the working class, but he knew his children could slide back. Middle-class status could not be passed to them as their birthright. They would have to earn it for themselves, just as their father had before them.[27] The identical problem confronted virtually all middle-class families of the day. In the bureaucratic, technological society emerging in the United States shortly after the turn of the century, economic and social status did not rest solely on property or money; rather, it increasingly depended on education.

When the Kinseys arrived in South Orange, the school system was feeling pinched. In 1904 the enrollment for all grades stood at 813; by 1908, Kinsey's freshman year in high school, it had risen 25 percent, with more expansion in sight.[28] In 1908, the press reported that sixty-seven homes were under construction in the village.[29] Rapid growth created severe overcrowding in the public schools, which triggered public demands for new schools. As the local press reminded citizens, "Failure to provide the required number of class rooms to prevent overcrowding will work to the injury of the whole school, and an early solution of the problem is of the highest importance."[30]

South Orange's residents met the challenge. Only months before the Kinseys arrived, a new school opened on Academy Street, the one Kinsey and his siblings later attended. Inviting parents to inspect this model facility, the *South Orange Bulletin* proclaimed, "This building is so great an advance over former buildings erected here that citizens will be well repaid for the time spent."[31] Stressing that no expense had been spared, the editors called attention "to the lighting of the class rooms; to the large amount of stone blackboard space; to the separate compartments in the cloak rooms; to the sanitary fountains; to the toilets in the basement, which will be connected with the sewers; and to the heating and ventilating plant, which delivers 1,500 cubic feet of fresh air per minute to each class room, changing the air every six minutes, and capable of delivering 3,500 cubic feet of air per minute, when desired."[32]

But the best testimonial to the school system's quality was the patronage it commanded from the local elite. Though they often grumped about the cost and issued repeated demands for greater efficiency, the same wealthy bankers and businessmen who built gracious homes opened their wallets for public education. Instead of relying upon private schools, South Orange's best families, with few exceptions, sent their children to the local public schools. Their confidence was not misplaced. At a time when only a tiny fraction of Americans finished high school, Columbia High School routinely sent an impressive portion of its graduates to college. In 1904, seventeen members (ten boys and seven girls) of Columbia High School's senior class of twenty-eight were preparing for college.[33] Four members of the class were bound for Yale University, two were headed for Cornell University, one each for Vassar College, Brown University, the University of Pennsylvania, and Rutgers University.[34] Nearly half (thirteen of twenty-seven) of Kinsey's class, the class of 1912, went to college, winning places at Princeton University and the University of Pennsylvania, and other elite schools such as Smith, Middlebury, Barnard, and Mount Holyoke.[35]

Much of the credit for South Orange's strong schools belonged to the superintendent Henry W. Foster. When he came to South Orange in 1900, the district contained several small wooden schoolhouses, and low pay caused frequent faculty turnover. Foster reformed the system from top to bottom. He hired several new teachers, revised the high school curriculum, started a high school library, conducted detailed consultations to evaluate each student, and instituted a "tracking" system at all school levels to separate students into different classes according to academic ability.

Enamored of the new empirical psychology being taught in the education departments at the best universities, Foster pushed through several changes in the teaching methods and subject matter at the elementary school level, including the use of phonetics to teach reading. But he was also a stickler on fundamentals, insisting that the "three R's" not be neglected, and his emphasis on spelling, grammar, and penmanship bordered on the fanatical. These subjects were tested and retested at every level of school.[36] As an adult, Kinsey reflected this drilling: his spelling and grammar were flawless. Not so his penmanship, however, which was flowing and ornate, except when he printed. His printed letters were typographically perfect, a skill he must have honed through many hours of practice during his first few years in South Orange.

Above all, Foster was a warm, although by no means uncritical, supporter of the University of Chicago's John Dewey. Dewey placed great weight on practical applications, believing that students should learn by doing. While Dewey's influence was evident throughout the curriculum, his thumbprint was especially visible on the way science was taught at Columbia High School, where teachers stressed empirical observation, hands-on experiments, and field trips—approaches that helped shape Kinsey's thinking about science in adolescence and beyond.[37]

Kinsey made the schoolroom his arena for personal achievement. As one his schoolmates put it, "He was a real serious guy. Great on the books. . . . He was always reading. He wasn't a guy who would socialize. He was studying all the time."[38] His grades showed it. In 1908, Kinsey was one of two high school freshmen to make the honor roll, which required a grade of 90 or above in every subject.[39] In the fall of 1909, he was the sole sophomore and one of three students in the entire high school to achieve this honor.[40] The following spring the local paper reported that "Alfred Kinsey leads the pupils of the second year high school."[41]

Kinsey's extracurricular activities did not match his scholastic achievements. The only club he joined was the Parnassian Society. The Parnassians' activities included directing the Christmas and Memorial Day exercises, sponsoring an annual play, and bringing guest speakers to campus. In 1911, for example, the club hosted a speaker on the construction of the Panama Canal, which was then nearing completion.[42] Moreover, club members frequently contributed poems to the school newspaper, some of which were praised as "extraordinarily good" by Superintendent Foster.[43] While Kinsey tried his hand at poetry, none of his verses survived.[44]

Kinsey's main academic interest in high school was biology, taught by Natalie Roeth. A graduate of Mount Holyoke College, Roeth was a gifted instructor who insisted nature could not be approached through books. Plants and animals had to be studied directly. Roeth filled her classroom with specimens and took her students on numerous field trips. Her laboratory was the woods, fields, and ponds surrounding South Orange, where she introduced students to nature by allowing them to observe birds in flight, ants at work, and flowers in bloom. Determined to do more than impart information, she strove to nurture her students' curiosity about life.

At first it did not appear that Kinsey and biology would be a match. Nearly thirty years later, he confessed that he was still "haunted by the memory of the abandoned torso of a cat and the dissecting pan of filthy water which stood for a week in a certain high school laboratory that I knew."[45] Despite this unpleasant experience in the laboratory, Kinsey responded eagerly to field trips. Over time, he became Roeth's star pupil, and a warm relationship developed between them. As she later wrote, "Alfred's family were very hospitable and I often visited there."[46] Guided by this energetic and resourceful young woman, Kinsey dug into biology. Roeth encouraged him to ask questions and to discover his own answers.[47]

As an adult, Kinsey often preached that a teacher could make or break a student's interest in biology. Citing his boyhood idol as proof, he wrote, "Theodore Roosevelt testified that biology teachers were the ones who discouraged him from becoming a naturalist."[48] How deeply Roeth influenced Kinsey became clear with time. After he finished high school, he did not keep in close contact with his classmates or any of his former teachers except Roeth. They exchanged many Christmas cards and letters, and their correspondence continued until the final years of Kinsey's life. On several occasions, he expressed deep gratitude for the knowledge she imparted,[49] and after he had become world famous, he warmly and generously gave her the credit for turning him to science.[50]

Hard work and a keen intellect made Kinsey the valedictorian of the Columbia High School class of 1912. The inscription beneath his photograph in the senior yearbook bore testimony to his academic distinction: "Alfred is our staid and steadfast student. Dignity, learning, and ability are all written upon his unruffled brow." The official "Class Prophecy" also paid homage to a certain budding scientist. Written as a commentary on a film series of the future, it observed, "After a short intermission another film was thrown on the screen. I read this: 'Alfred C. Kinsey, a second Darwin, and his wonderful experiments. New Theory of the Origin of Species.' Pictures were shown of the great scientist in his laboratories, and microscopic views of germs under the process of fertilization were described by short, concise sentences, which appeared in Prof. Kinsey's own handwriting."[51] High school prophecies, of course, are notorious for hyperbole, but Kinsey was no doubt pleased by his classmates' vision of his future. As one who routinely set herculean goals for himself, becoming "a second Darwin" did not appear far-fetched or unattainable. Indeed, he would spend more than two decades of his life in earnest pursuit of this goal. Academic achievement also brought Kinsey a degree of social success. During adolescence in South Orange, he did not make a single close friend, at least not in the sense of having a "best friend." Nor did he form a single friendship that extended into adulthood. But he did obtain a measure of popularity and a full complement of admiration. In the ninth grade, his schoolmates elected him class president, his only high school honor that denoted popularity as opposed to peer respect.[52] While additional praise from his classmates followed, it was in the form of either academic or character awards. In the "Class Elections" of 1912, Kinsey was selected the "Brightest" and the "Most Respected" boy in the senior class, honors that acknowledged his academic brilliance, community service, and formidable character.[53]

Kinsey was the type of boy school authorities knew they could count on in a crisis,[54] and, as fate would have it, a controversy engulfed Columbia High School two weeks before his sophomore year ended. The dispute involved the school lunch counter established by Superintendent Foster. Responding to a petition circulated by parents in 1908, Foster agreed to sell hot lunches at school "at very low prices, as there will be no profit gained by anyone." At first all went well. But on June 15, 1910, Henry Robinson, a wealthy resident of South Orange who served as president of the Imperial Machine Company of Manhattan, accused Foster and the principal of Columbia High School, W. E. Freeman, of skimming profits from the lunch program. Robinson further charged that the school lunchroom, located in the basement of Columbia High School, served unfit food; and he accused school authorities of forcing Margaret Lutz, a thirteen-year-old student from a poor family, to pay for her school lunches by waiting on tables and washing dishes several hours each day.[55]

Robinson's accusations masked his real complaint. Immediately before he aired his charges, his fourteen-year-old son, Henry, a sophomore at Columbia High, had been suspended for two weeks. Young Henry, who did not like the food in the school lunchroom, had slipped off campus to buy pies and pickles from Mrs. Maria Doyle, a poor Irish widow who operated a little shop nearby. Upon his return, a teacher asked Henry if he had left campus for lunch. He confessed, and Principal Freeman suspended him for leaving campus without permission.

The press had a field day. In addition to New Jersey papers, the *New York Times*, the *New York Herald*, and the *New York American* covered the controversy in detail. And why not. To a generation that had seen muckraking elevated to an art form, Robinson's charges (corrupt public officials, tainted food, forced child labor, and a poor Irish widow woman who, in the words of one paper, had been "deprived of the children's trade in candies and eatables") smacked of scandalous misconduct.[56]

On June 20, 1910, Robinson repeated his charges before a special committee appointed by the South Orange Board of Education. To prove he meant business, Robinson brought along his attorney, who produced sworn affidavits and promises of more to follow. Focusing on his allegation that the school served "poor food" at "exorbitant" prices, Robinson insisted he could prove the lunchroom took a dozen cans of soup purchased at eight cents a can and then converted them into 150 bowls of soup sold for five cents a piece for a daily return of $7.50. To substantiate his charge that a student had been mistreated, Robinson declared that young Margaret had been ordered by her teachers to work in the lunchroom more than three hours a day to pay for her lunch and had been threatened with imprisonment in the state reform school for girls if she refused.[57]

Other witnesses before the committee told a different story in what one tongue-in-cheek reporter called the "Pickles and Pies School War." Committee members heard the lunchroom cook testify to the quality of the food she served; and they listened to Principal Freeman present a detailed financial statement showing all profits had been returned to the school. Eager to hear from witnesses who had actually eaten in the school lunchroom, the committee called two students, Alfred Kinsey and Carroll Rodman, and one faculty member. President of his class the preceding year, straight-A student, devout Christian, and seemingly mature beyond his years, Kinsey was the ideal student to push center stage. No one could question his character. After all, sophomore Kinsey, announced the local press, was one of only twenty students in the entire high school in 1910 who "were neither absent nor tardy during the last year."[58] Kinsey, like the other witnesses called by the school, testified "that the food was excellent and the prices were reasonable."[59]

A few weeks after Kinsey's testimony, the committee issued its final report. Characterizing Robinson's accusations as "false in every essential particular," the committee ruled against him, and the South Orange Board of Education promptly dismissed all charges. There the controversy ended. No one seemed disturbed by the fact that Margaret worked more than ninety minutes a day for her nickel lunch. Charity was for people who could not work, and work itself was honorable.[60]

South Orange's town fathers were hardly unique in this regard. As Russell Sage, a prominent businessman, confessed in 1903, "Work has been the chief, and you might say, the only source of pleasure in my life."[61] In fact, a man's work defined his worth. "Work, work, whether you want to or not," the novelist David Phillips ordered his readers.[62] Not one to ignore his own advice, Phillips wrote standing up for eight to ten hours a day without interruption. Other men echoed Phillips's advice. Joseph Henry Dubbs spoke for his age when he told men, "It is better to wear out than to rust out."[63] No wonder South Orange's men were so devoted to the work ethic; no wonder Kinsey labored so hard at everything he did. He was fulfilling the responsibilities of a dutiful son of the middle class.[64]

While theater, poetry, and art enjoyed strong followings in South Orange, classical music dominated the cultural life of the village. The leading families served as sponsors for the magnificent Music Hall in neighboring Orange, and those same families patronized musical events throughout the New York metropolitan area. For example, music lovers in South Orange were thrilled when Ignacy Paderewski, the famous Polish pianist, performed in Newark's Krueger Auditorium in 1905 and again in 1907.[65] Within the village, several of the leading families hosted elegant musicales in their homes, which received enthusiastic notices in the local press from the same music critic who reviewed opera in Manhattan.[66]

South Orange's leading citizens took care to instill the proper musical tastes in village youths. The weekly assembly at Columbia High School featured lectures on musical theory and the history of classical music. Moreover, the Assembly Hall Music Fund Committee, composed of civic-minded music lovers, sponsored a rich program of evening concerts at the high school auditorium, including performances by Newark's Mozart String Quartet, New York's Kneisel Quartet, and the Hahn String Quartet of Philadelphia. The Columbia High School Orchestra routinely performed classical music at its concerts, and the Columbia High School Chamber Music Ensemble commanded an enthusiastic following in the village and in neighboring communities.[67]

Kinsey worked hard to earn a place for himself in this daunting musical environment. No less than education, music gave Kinsey a chance to shine. He brought the same dedication and capacity for work to music, practicing for hours on end at the family piano. At a time when friends and freedom were in short supply, Kinsey filled many lonely hours at the piano honing his skills. He showed a singular aptitude for practice, attacking the piano with the discipline, tenacity, and self-sacrifice that became his trademarks in life. Practice pitted the player he was against the player he wanted to be; and that kind of competition, a contest with his ideal self, always moved Kinsey to heroic feats.

After progressing as far as he could on his own, Kinsey advanced his training with piano lessons.[68] To pay for his lessons, he taught piano to younger children.[69] Welcoming the opportunity to exhibit his talent, he started holding little recitals in his home. By the time he reached high school, he had developed into a competent pianist. One of his classmates recalled that Kinsey "played the piano very well, very well."[70] Another classmate declared, "One of my vivid memories is of his playing Beethoven's *Moonlight Sonata* in the school auditorium."[71] Throughout his high school years, Kinsey played at school functions, a responsibility he shared with two classmates.[72] The three took turns throughout high school, but when school officials selected a student to perform at the graduation ceremony for the class of 1912, they bestowed the honor on the class valedictorian, Kinsey, who played a solo.[73]

Kinsey's repertoire was limited to classical music, as might be expected of a pious boy from an upwardly mobile family. In order to blend in socially, he had to guard against any lapses in taste or manners that might betray his working-class origins. The elite patronized classical music, while the working class listened to popular music. That alone gave this ardent culture climber ample reason for embracing classical music.

But Kinsey had a second motive for eschewing popular music. Along with other devout Methodists, he rejected it on moral grounds. This went doubly for ragtime, which no good Christian could fail to recognize as the devil's handiwork, pure and simple. At the turn of the century, itinerant black musicians introduced white Americans to the thrill of ragtime. With its suggestive lyrics, syncopated rhythms, and throbbing bass backbeat, ragtime was inherently sensual, if not patently sexual. Many middle-class parents feared that ragtime would lure young people into the dance halls, movie theaters, and amusement parks where temptations abounded.

Parents in South Orange shared this disdain for popular music and taught their children to reject it as base and vulgar.[74] Elliot C. Bergen, a Kinsey classmate, revealed how well children internalized these values. In a speech delivered at his high school graduation in 1912, Bergen warned that ragtime and other popular entertainments threatened to debase mankind. "In the field of music," he declared, "ragtime insolently stands face to face with the works of the great masters; in literature dime novels rest on the same shelves with Dickens and Samuel Johnson; in the drama burlesque is carried on next door to Shakespearean plays."[75] Moreover, if ragtime was morally degrading and culturally debasing, some thought it physically dangerous. Under the headline "Don't Whistle Ragtime," the local newspaper recounted in 1908 the story of a man from Queens who dislocated his jaw "trying to whistle one of the latest popular songs."[76] Small wonder that Kinsey absorbed his culture's animus against popular music. He held it beneath contempt and refused to play anything but the classics.

Kinsey set his sights high. His wife, Clara, recalled that "he did consider going into [classical music] professionally."[77] This was one ambition Kinsey could not fulfill, however, for he lacked two essential qualifications: extraordinary talent and familial support. Though he possessed a fine ear and considerable musical ability, Kinsey was not a brilliant musician, let alone a child prodigy. Children who develop into outstanding musicians usually have parents who encourage them (or in many cases drive them) to develop their musical talent to the fullest. Stage parents attach great importance to their children's musical training—enough to arrange, finance, and provide transportation for lessons, enough to furnish the right combination of coercion and encouragement needed to make their children practice four, five, or six hours a day. Kinsey did not receive this kind of support. Alfred Seguine Kinsey had other plans for his firstborn.

Despite many hours of diligent practice, Kinsey gradually abandoned any hope of a musical career. At some level, he knew he could never become a great performer. Referring to his youthful desire to pursue music, Clara recalled, "He told me it was certainly a good thing he never did, because he could never have been a top pianist."[78] Paul Gebhard made much the same point: "It used to puzzle me enormously that he had at one time been a very accomplished pianist. He had a piano in his home, yet I never heard that man lay a finger on a key. Because he couldn't be a really topnotch pianist, apparently he wasn't going to fool around with it."[79] Kinsey had to be the best at everything he did. Throughout his life, he showed a passion for complex and difficult activities, but he could never be satisfied with being merely good at something. As Gebhard observed, "This man had a real demon on his back. He had to excel, and if he couldn't excel in an area, he wouldn't have anything to do with that area. . . . He had this real obsession that he had to excel."[80] That fierce voice from within told Kinsey that anything less than excellence was failure.

With music, as with so many things in his life, Kinsey's lofty standards cost him dearly. He never recovered from the pain he suffered over not being able to play professionally. One of his adult friends, Clarence A. Tripp, witnessed this disappointment in Kinsey's reaction to the movie *Quartet,* a film based on four short stories by Somerset Maugham. The second story, "The Alien Corn," moved Kinsey deeply. George Bland, the main character, aspired to become a concert pianist, but his parents, wealthy British aristocrats, did not approve. Eventually, they agreed to support George while he studied music in Germany. George, in turn, agreed to abandon the piano if after two years a disinterested judge ruled that he lacked the talent to make the grade. Despite two years of hard work, the judge told him that at best he could hope to become a highly competent amateur. Not only was he denied his heart's ambition; the judge told George that his hard work would enable him to appreciate great playing as no ordinary person could. "Kinsey would weep at this point," Tripp declared. "I mean it was unbelievable. He was embarrassed as all [get out], he would just weep and tears would come down."[81]

It is easy to see why this story moved Kinsey to tears, for he and George Bland had much in common. Like Maugham's character, Kinsey could hear how perfect music sounded but could not play what he heard, despite constant practice. His demand for perfection condemned his musical performances. His only recourse was to content himself with developing the musical expertise that would permit him to appreciate (and judge) the talent of others. Over time, Kinsey the performer gave way to Kinsey the ardent music lover and discerning critic.

Music filled one more important need in Kinsey. Together with his work in Sunday school, his stint as a piano instructor gave him his first taste of teaching. Shortly before his death, Kinsey confessed, "I was, in actuality, a music teacher before I ever became a biologist!"[82] From the outset, teaching struck a responsive chord in Kinsey. Perhaps because he had been subjected to such rigid controls as a child, Kinsey seemed to enjoy the power he derived from teaching, because it gave him control over pupils, who, by definition, occupied subordinate positions and were obliged to defer to his knowledge and accept his authority. In short, teaching allowed him to be like his imposing father. As an adult, Kinsey not only followed his father into teaching but endeavored with remarkable success to assume the role of teacher in all his relationships.

Socially, Kinsey's musical talents and knowledge facilitated his entrance into the South Orange elite that used classical music (among other cultural weapons) to define boundaries of social class. Emotionally his skill as a pianist enhanced his self-esteem and provided a worthwhile outlet for the perfectionist tendencies in his personality. Listening to music enabled Kinsey to put aside his public persona and experience, if only for a moment and by small degrees, the entire gamut of human emotions.

Shortly after the move to South Orange, Kinsey started the first of three record collections he compiled during his lifetime. With most childhood collections, it is the parents (or other adult relatives) who get things started. They purchase the first few items of whatever is being collected, extol the fun (and virtues) of collecting, and then hope their kids get hooked. In Kinsey's case, his parents had good reason to turn him to collecting, for records provided his only means of listening to music on a regular basis.

Commercial radio did not exist during Kinsey's youth, and given the stringent dress codes and the stiff price of concert tickets, he could not have attended many concerts. But as Kinsey later explained, thanks to the miracle of "acoustically recorded, pre-electric disks" he could hear "performances by Kreisler, Paderewski, Cortot, Mischa Elman, Schumann-Heink,

Caruso, and others of the world's greats." Looking back on his first record collection, Kinsey expressed gratitude he had been born at the exact moment in history when "great music" became accessible for the first time "to those of us who were not princes or great musicians in our own right. It is to these records," he declared, "that I am first of all indebted for the fact that I have spent such a large proportion of the last half century in listening to music."[83]

Kinsey's classmates took note of his interest in state-of-the-art acoustical technology in the "Class Prophecy" in his senior yearbook. After predicting that Miss Wallace, the music teacher, would bring "Mlle. Edna Miller, the world famous prima donna" to South Orange to perform, the "Class Prophecy" declared, "Then a great Kinseola, another of Prof. Kinsey's wonderful inventions, reproduced with marvelous reality Mlle. Miller's voice."[84]

Many of his well-to-do classmates had fine record collections, and this made Kinsey eager to expand his holdings. Not that he could hope to match their bounty. As happened so often in his youth, Kinsey had to settle for what he could get. "The family finances did not allow me to hope to make a collection of the sort that my older and wealthier acquaintances were accumulating," he explained more than forty years later; "but I did manage to persuade some of my relatives and friends to give me records as birthday and Christmas gifts, and I even essayed to give piano lessons in order to obtain the wherewithal to buy more records."[85]

Kinsey traced a large measure of his adult satisfaction with music to his boyhood experience of building a record collection. As an adult, he confessed his love for collecting in the high school biology text he wrote. In warm and encouraging words, he told his young readers,

> Most of us like to collect things, and some of us have quite a dose of that instinct. Some folks collect stamps, others collect cigar bands, or autographs, a pocket full of junk, or dollars and dollars. Whatever their value or lack of money value, all collections are very real possessions to their owners. If your collection is larger, even a shade larger, than any other like it in the world, that greatly increases your happiness. It shows how complete a work you can accomplish, in what good order you can arrange the specimens, with what surpassing wisdom you can exhibit them, with what authority you can speak on your subject.[86]

Through collecting, then, Kinsey found a way to achieve autonomy, not to mention an outlet for his chronic need to be the best at everything he did. Through collecting, he could impose order on his world. Clearly, a collection said much about the boy who amassed it.

Kinsey's need for power drove his collector's mania. Just as he had to be the best at everything he did, his collections had to be the very best. To Kinsey that meant one thing and one thing only: they had to contain more specimens than any like them in the world. He neglected to mention, however, how unhappy this ethic would leave those who failed to meet its requirements.

Through his record collection, Kinsey pursued his need for perfection. He continued collecting the pancake disks that brought the world's great performances to his room. Here taste and knowledge, which Kinsey had in abundance, could offset money as a means to building the best collection. Not so with stamps, his second boyhood foray into collecting. Stamp collecting, real stamp collecting, required capital; and family finances would not permit Kinsey to become a serious collector of the most impassioned sort. For that reason, he gradually abandoned stamp collecting, consigning it to the same dustpan of adolescence into which are swept other seemingly meaningless hobbies that do not survive into adulthood.[87] But collecting itself was important to Kinsey, and in time this interest would become an obsession. The adult Kinsey would transform his collecting into a science, combining personal need and professional identity to good advantage.

Kinsey's devotion to academic excellence, religion, music, and collecting were at once socially beneficial and personally uplifting. The same held true for the final passion of his youth—his adolescent love affair with nature. Kinsey badly needed to master the outdoors, for without this victory he stood in danger of being labeled a "Momma's boy." Books, religion, music, and stamps did not allow him to demonstrate his masculinity in ways prescribed by middle-class culture at the turn of the century. The final feature of his struggle to become a model boy involved Kinsey's determined effort to transform himself into a formidable outdoorsman. Few challenges of his youth had a greater bearing on his future.

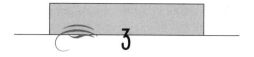

3

"THE RIGHT STUFF"

f one snapshot could capture the way Kinsey wished to be remembered as an adolescent, fixing him forever in time, it almost
certainly would be a photograph of him as an Eagle Scout.
Dressed neatly in his Boy Scout uniform, sitting on a brick wall
in South Orange on the eve of World War I, he looks at the camera with
a broad smile, sunlight glistening off his curly blond hair, a handsome
youth, every inch the portrait of the ideal American boy. He appears, in the
words of the Boy Scouts manual, "obedient, courteous, loyal, respectful,
trust-worthy, faithful, cheerful, kind to animals, patriotic, and civic-
minded."[1] His upright posture evokes outdoor skills and, most important,
leadership.

Middle-class parents at the turn of the century were concerned about the
fate of their children. They devoted enormous amounts of time and energy
to building character. Parents hoped that organizations like the Scouts
would guide young people from adolescence to adulthood. As an Eagle
Scout, Kinsey represented a success story, a boy whose uniform testified to
his character, a boy who embodied middle-class values. Both his parents
and his community could point to him with pride, as he had met every de-

mand his society had placed upon him. He had transformed himself into the kind of boy to whom the future could be entrusted.

In many respects, the United States of Kinsey's youth was a nation gripped by conflicts. When his family moved to South Orange in 1904, Americans stood at the end of a half century and more of frantic nation building. By the early 1900s, Thomas Jefferson's America, a land of farmers who lived in the countryside or small villages, had developed into an industrial, urban society. These changes brought numerous advances, but not without problems—political corruption, labor unrest, filth and misery, and abuse of power. By the 1890s, many urban, middle-class Americans decided to tally the costs and see what could be done to redress imbalances and remedy injustices. Their efforts plunged the United States into a period of reform that historians have called the Progressive Era, which began in the early 1890s and ended shortly after World War I—roughly the first twenty-five years of Kinsey's life.

Of course, earlier generations had launched crusades to battle one evil or another, but during Kinsey's boyhood reform advanced from a marginal activity to a national preoccupation. At the federal level, progressives battled corporate trusts, lowered tariffs, reformed banking, enfranchised women, recognized labor unions, abolished child labor, promoted conservation, and imposed prohibition. At the state level, progressives regulated industry, battled special-interest groups, revamped tax laws, and fought to restore power to the people by instituting the initiative, referendum, and recall. When Kinsey was a boy, New Jersey was a hotbed of progressivism, particularly from 1910 to 1912, when Woodrow Wilson served as governor. At the municipal level, reformers fought political machines, introduced the city manager form of government, and experimented with "water and gas socialism."

In South Orange, the political agenda was less dramatic. Squalid slums, uneducated immigrants, boss rule, and labor strikes might plague nearby Newark and New York City, but not this prosperous suburb. As the local paper proudly proclaimed, South Orange conducted its affairs "in a business like way," which the editors explained meant "the tax rate is low" and the community "is well governed."[2] A model of political stability, the village was staunchly Republican, routinely returning a five-to-two electoral majority for the Grand Old Party. South Orange's governing body, the Village Board of Trustees, concentrated on meat-and-potatoes municipal issues. It worked to upgrade public transportation, build new schools, construct sidewalks and curbs, connect the village sewer system to the joint trunk sewer in Newark, provide an ample supply of pure water, safeguard the public health, maintain law and order, and, not least, uphold community morals.

Publicly, the South Orange of Kinsey's youth projected businesslike, optimistic, "can do" attitudes. Its commitment to modest reforms was typical of a well-to-do, self-satisfied suburb. But despite this air of confidence, many residents harbored doubts about the strength of American culture, particularly its ability to preserve middle-class values. A glance at South Orange's newspaper during the years immediately after 1900 provides an inventory of their fears. With varying degrees of alarm, local editors informed their readers about the rising divorce rate, working women, intemperance, the race problem, unemployment, and the specter of racial suicide, the fear by many members of the middle class that recent immigrants and African Americans would take over the country by outbreeding old-stock Americans.[3] These same issues troubled middle-class citizens all across America.

In truth, South Orange was anything but a tranquil backwater. Thanks to its proximity to New York, it experienced the same intellectual currents as the great metropolis. Speakers who made the rounds in Manhattan routinely appeared in the Oranges, spreading the gospel of reform from the city to the suburbs. During Kinsey's boyhood, audiences in South Orange heard Susan B. Anthony call for women's suffrage,[4] Florence Kelly denounce child labor,[5] Benjamin Lindsey advocate a legal system tailored to adolescents,[6] Ida Tarbell attack corruption in Congress, and Booker T. Washington speak out for racial justice.[7] In suburban South Orange, as elsewhere, women's clubs led the crusade to improve the quality of life for all classes of society. Institutions like the Charities Conference of the Oranges and the Women's Club of South Orange sponsored scores of less famous speakers, who lectured on issues such as civil service reform, the temperance crusade, and programs to alleviate the plight of immigrants. Listening to such speakers, youths like Kinsey quickly came to believe that most social problems could be corrected by intelligent, purposeful action.

Following the pattern in other parts of the United States, reformers in South Orange pursued their social and cultural agendas through voluntary associations. Working as an unofficial arm of the city government, the Village Improvement Society played a prominent role in local affairs. A voluntary organization that drew its members from South Orange's "best" families, it was devoted to preserving South Orange's residential character and to enhancing the quality of life. To accomplish these goals, it organized a number of committees that galvanized community support for causes ranging from pest control to city beautification.

In 1904, the ornamentation committee of the Village Improvement Society started a garden contest, offering annual prizes "to the children of the village who keep the best looking lawns, flowerbeds, and so forth." Sponsors hoped this program, like others involving young people, would help instill proper middle-class values of order, discipline, and hard work in village youths. Competition rules limited participants to youngsters between the ages of ten and sixteen who attended public or parochial schools in the village. Well-organized and closely monitored, the contest was centered in the public schools, where teachers distributed seeds and the like to children. To attract young people, the society offered prizes in seven different categories, featuring cash awards ranging from one to five dollars.[8]

Along with many village youths, Kinsey became an avid gardener. His specialty was ferns, and he cultivated an impressive fernery along the eastern edge of his yard, bordering Academy Street. A schoolmate remembered seeing Kinsey at work there on numerous occasions, and Natalie Roeth, his beloved biology teacher, recalled with admiration the many beautiful ferns he grew.[9] As an adult, Kinsey remembered his garden fondly. While he always hated the marigolds, zinnias, or wisteria that had grown in his family's garden in Hoboken, he adored ferns, assigning these lovely plants a prominent role in the magnificent garden he created in Indiana.

Gardening gave Kinsey an outlet for his love of beauty, nurturing what his adolescent classmates called "his aesthetical temperament."[10] While the yard was part of the home and domestic sphere, it was also a gateway to what lay beyond, the world where men disappeared daily to earn their living. By removing him from the house to the yard, gardening allowed Kinsey to occupy the space between control and freedom, domesticity and masculinity. It allowed him to strengthen his grip on competence by displaying his gardening skills to others.[11]

While gardening aided Kinsey's bid for autonomy, his quest for independence received a gigantic boost from the birth of his brother. On March 11, 1907, Sarah gave birth to her third child, Robert Benjamin. If Kinsey felt jealous and resentful, he must have put these feelings behind him quickly, for the gains from Robert's arrival far outweighed the losses. A baby in the house meant more freedom for Kinsey. Robert gave Sarah another son to dote upon, and he arrived at the exact time when Kinsey no longer needed her nurturing and was eager to break free of her control. With Sarah lavishing her attention on Robert, she had less time to hover over Kinsey.

Following his brother's birth, Kinsey, then a seventh-grader, ventured beyond the family yard and began exploring the countryside around South Orange. Soon he disappeared for hours on end, roaming the hills to the west and the marshes to the east and collecting botanical specimens.[12] As Kinsey later wrote, "A new world suddenly opened before me. There were birds with colored breasts, flowers that could be picked, endless things to discover, an inexhaustible treasure chest that drew me on into the fields and over the hills. . . ."[13]

From the outset, nature held a magical appeal for Kinsey. He pored over books in natural history and became an avid collector of zoological specimens, including butterflies, which made up his first, but by no means last, insect collection. Far more than his other boyhood interests, the outdoors allowed Kinsey to indulge his need for mastery, and it provided this heretofore sickly boy with an opportunity to demonstrate his masculinity. At virtually no cost, he could spend as much time as he wanted absorbing a vast array of information, building his expertise, honing his outdoor skills, and testing himself against nature.

Kinsey displayed a special affinity for bird-watching. During his boyhood, bird-watching became a full-fledged national craze that attracted young and old alike. As Americans became conscious that they had settled the last of the western territories, many grew concerned about preserving the natural beauty of the landscape and protecting the nation's endangered wildlife. Thanks to the efforts of the Audubon Society and other organizations, birds occupied a special place in the hearts of many conservationists. In one six-year period, publishers in New York and Boston sold 70,000 textbooks on birds, while the circulation of *Birds,* a children's magazine, soared to 40,000 copies during its first year.[14]

South Orange was a nest of bird lovers. As more and more families arrived, residents worried that the community's bucolic charm would be destroyed if they failed to protect the environment and wildlife. "The suburban village or city will some time cease to reward the commuter for his daily journeys to the Metropolis," warned the *South Orange Bulletin* in 1905, "unless the conditions favorable to the continuance and increase of bird life are faithfully and vigorously conserved."[15]

Once again, the women of South Orange swung into action. During the spring of 1905, the bird committee of the Village Improvement Society launched a campaign to encourage young people to protect birds. Hoping "to stay the hand of the destroyers," the society posted signs in nearly three hundred locations, announcing a new ordinance against killing birds or disturbing their nesting places. In addition, it launched what the local editors called "a campaign of ideas," which included newspaper articles, speeches aimed at adults, and a series of talks in local schools designed to involve young people. In response to the high school talks, fifty children joined the state Audubon Society. According to the local press, ten times that number would have joined "had anybody been found to do the work involved."[16]

To keep young people interested, the Village Improvement Society announced a new contest. Beginning in 1905, the bird committee sponsored an annual competition that awarded prizes for the best birdhouses, as well as the best essays on bird-related topics. During the contest's first year, students arrayed the village with birdhouses and submitted a total of forty-nine essays. As the local editors weighed the benefits of the bird campaign, they expressed confidence it had strengthened the character of village youths, declaring "an immense educational gain to young lives preparing for the myriad activities in which they must one day take part."[17]

The bird campaign found an eager recruit in Kinsey. He approached bird-watching with the same fervor other boys reserved for memorizing batting averages of their favorite baseball stars. Kinsey taught himself to observe birds in their natural habitats, and he learned their calls, markings, and nesting places. He also discovered the power of the written word to communicate his findings, as bird-watching led to his first scientific essay. At sixteen, Kinsey wrote an essay entitled "What Do Birds Do When It Rains?" In all likelihood, he wrote the essay for the contest sponsored by the bird committee.[18] Kinsey revisited this topic decades later in his high school textbook, answering the question in the chapter called "Bird Behavior":

A bird is a peculiar creature in a rain storm. While its feathers will shed water for a time, prolonged wetting soaks them and reduces their efficiency in conserving the body heat. So most birds take to the thick shelter of the bushes and trees at such time. Only a few of them (as the robin) stay out and scold at warm rains, and a few of them (as the song sparrow) remain quite as active and cheerful as in the sunshine. But in storms that last more than a day all the birds are forced out to hunt food, and then they are a songless and bedraggled lot until the sun again shines. Parent birds usually keep their nestlings covered during a rain storm.[19]

No doubt, this passage reflected Kinsey's boyhood observations. Both the questions it raised and the methodology it employed offer a glimpse into how he approached science. In order to satisfy his curiosity, he framed simple questions that could be answered by direct observation. He did not mind paying a price (in this case, standing in the rain in soaked clothes for hours on end) to compile his data, revealing the tenacity, quest for mastery, and penchant for direct observation that later became his trademarks as a scientist.

By the time he finished high school, Kinsey was much in demand as a lecturer on birds. After noting that Kinsey at five feet eleven was the tallest senior, Margaret Craig, the class statistician for his senior yearbook announced, "If you want to see how stately and dignified he is, just come out some evening and hear him deliver one of his lectures on birds." "The Class Poem" also touted Kinsey's prowess as a lecturer: "We even have a lecturer—He talks of birds by choice; Tho' on bugs and snails and horrid things, We've sometimes heard his voice. Why, Alfred has a regular Itinerary course, And Summit, Orange, Westfield, Have joyed in his discourse."[20] Without knowing it, the class poet had offered a clairvoyant glimpse into Kinsey's future: throughout his life, he would be drawn to the lecture podium, where he could impart knowledge and exercise power over audiences.

Like his interest in gardening and bird-watching, Kinsey's adult fascination with insects can be traced to his adolescence in South Orange. For him, hiking and bug collecting went hand in hand, as boyhood curiosity fueled his interest in insects. Public health officials, in turn, drew his attention to one insect in particular, the disease-spreading mosquito. Along with other school children, Kinsey heard stories about Walter Reed's pathbreaking work on mosquitoes and yellow fever in Cuba. Indeed, Kinsey could not avoid learning firsthand about these creatures because South Orange had a horrible mosquito problem. Every summer brought swarms of the pesky bloodsuckers, which bred in nearby saltwater marshes and pools of water. At dusk, residents had to flee their yards and hide behind screened windows and doors; at bedtime, they sought refuge beneath the canopies and other coverings hanging from ceiling hooks over their beds. According to the official village historian, "when the singing, stinging creatures were abroad, sleep at night was quite impossible."[21] Moreover, those who failed to take precautions paid the price. As Superintendent Foster later recalled, when his family arrived in South Orange on a damp, hot August day in 1900, they went to bed unprepared and "looked as if they had small pox or measles the morning after."[22]

Spencer Miller, who served as president of the Village Improvement Society at the turn of the century, decided to fight back. A successful engineer and close friend of Thomas Edison's, Miller secured the help of Leland O. Howard, who served as the chief entomologist of the U.S. Department of Agriculture and a professor at Cornell University. With Miller operating the lantern to show pictures to the audience, Howard spoke at the Village Hall on May 16, 1901, on the topic "Mosquitoes and the Possibility of their Extermination."[23]

Following Howard's presentation, Miller committed himself to the battle. To combat the thirty species of mosquitoes that plagued South Orange, the Village Improvement Society formed a drainage committee, with Miller as its chairman. Armed with knowledge of the insect's life history and working under Dr. Howard's supervision, committee members destroyed mosquito breeding grounds by pouring kerosene on the surface of stagnant pools and marshes. Encouraged by their success, they then started draining bog lands, filling holes, and oiling bodies of water too big to drain or fill. In 1903, the South Orange Board of Health took charge of the oiling, and the campaign soon spread to adjacent communities.

An articulate speaker and born crusader, Miller took his message to the public schools, where he showered students, in Superintendent Foster's words, "with illustrative material and the clearest possible, succinct statements, which showed the life habits of the pest, easily understood by the youngest [student]."[24] As a follow-up to his talks, Miller enlisted the services of Dr. John B. Smith, the state entomologist. Like Miller, Smith became a familiar visitor to South Orange's schools, where he delivered many informative lectures on the insect's breeding grounds and life cycle.[25] In all likelihood, Kinsey's introduction to the fascinating world of entomology came through Smith's presentations.

Drawn by its usual interest in enlisting young people in worthwhile causes, the Village Improvement Society sponsored a mosquito eradication contest in 1906. Working under Miller's supervision, teachers put students to work scouring the countryside in search of the pools and marshes where mosquitoes bred. Teachers also asked students to prepare detailed reports on their expeditions and to map out strategies for attack. Praising the entire program as a fine example of "Practical Entomology," the nearby Newark Evening News declared, "If this subject is taught in the other schools as it has been in that of South Orange, the next generation will live in the comfort which too many of the present generation deny themselves by refusing to help exterminate mosquitoes."[26]

As a boy who loved the outdoors, Kinsey must have thrown himself with gusto into South Orange's mosquito wars, tramping the countryside in search of bogs and pools, with notebook in hand, ready to map their locations for the oil brigade. The mosquito campaign also sparked Kinsey's passionate intellectual curiosity about insects. Years later when he described them in his high school biology textbook, Kinsey spoke of insects as though they were human. While admitting that "[i]t is not easy to study such a world of Lilliputians," he insisted that anyone who took the trouble would meet creatures "whose lives are filled with love, comedies, and tragedies."[27]

In all probability, Kinsey used nature study to fill a social void. His relationship with his peers remained as difficult in adolescence as in his sickly, isolated childhood. Asked to describe how Kinsey got along, a high school classmate recalled, "He was more or less a loner."[28] Kinsey's health cut him off from the other boys. Since Kinsey was the tallest boy in his class, his schoolmates had hoped he would be interested in basketball. "We would ask him to play ball with us, but he never did," remarked one of his schoolmates. At first, the boys did not understand why he refused to play, and Kinsey had to endure the usual taunting and occasional fistfights that befall a new kid on the block. When the harassment became physical, however, adults quickly intervened, pointing out Kinsey's heart problems and, in doing so, labeling him a weakling. Two of the local boys, Girard (Jiggy) Oberrender and Don Salisbury, both fine athletes, took charge and protected Kinsey from further attacks by bullies.[29]

Kinsey's inability to engage in team sports made it hard for him to make close friends. As one of his classmates put it, "Everybody liked him, you know, but he just wasn't one of the guys, as they say."[30] In South Orange, as elsewhere, boys used team sports to forge and to validate their male identities by demonstrating skill, strength, speed, and courage in athletic competition.[31] Social life for boys in the village revolved around private sports teams at the Field Club and varsity sports at school. For residents with sponsors to nominate them, the votes to be elected, and the money to join, the South Orange Field Club (the local country club) offered tennis, golf, and lawn bowling for adults and a full complement of team sports for youths. One of Kinsey's schoolmates remembered rushing home from school every afternoon, wolfing down a snack, and then heading immediately to the Field Club to play football, basketball, baseball, or field hockey, depending on the season.[32]

School offered no relief from the culture's emphasis on sports, as Kinsey's adolescence corresponded with the rise of high school athletics in the United States. Superintendent Foster introduced organized sports to Columbia High School soon after he arrived in South Orange. Foster had no doubt that athletics built male character. The coach's task, he declared, was "to impress upon our lads the noblest lessons of real manhood."[33] Year after year, Foster pleaded for more funds for athletics. In his 1904–05 annual report, for example, he asserted, "It is not enough to supply the equipment for mental training only," and declared "that proper physical training makes possible a fine development of body, giving vigor, strength, grace, agility, and quick adaptability to sudden emergencies."[34] In response to Foster's pleas, the athletics budget was increased and Columbia High School got its first gymnasium, which opened during Kinsey's senior year.[35]

Every boy in the class of 1912 except Kinsey played one or more varsity sports. Class elections left no room for doubt that athletes were the "big men on campus." The "jockocracy" dominated the senior class offices, not to mention the leadership of most of the high school clubs.[36] Kinsey could have followed the path chosen by many nonathletic boys by serving as a manager for one of the high school teams, but supporting roles held no attraction for him. Regardless of the activity, if Kinsey could not compete well enough to win, he refused to participate.

Not playing sports set Kinsey apart from most boys of his generation. Theodore Roosevelt, Kinsey's boyhood idol and America's leading advocate of the "strenuous life," advised boys to engage in manly exercises and to develop their bodies "in the rough sports which call for pluck, endurance, and physical address." A pugilist during his college days at Harvard, Roosevelt continued to hold boxing exhibitions after he occupied the White House. As someone who had struggled to overcome nearsightedness and severe childhood asthma, Roosevelt believed that every boy should be able to hold his own in a scrap. Any boy worth his salt "should feel hearty contempt for the coward and even more hearty contempt for the boy who bullies," declared Roosevelt, while "every good boy should have it in him to thrash the objectionable boy as the need arises." Indeed, Roosevelt held boys who refused to defend themselves in utter scorn. "A coward who will take a blow without returning it is a contemptible creature," he growled. While everyone understood that exceptions had to be made for boys with physical handicaps, Kinsey simply did not measure up to what society expected of males.[37]

During Kinsey's adolescence, most middle-class Americans endorsed Roosevelt's definition of manliness.[38] Yet, if character formed the key element of manliness, self-control constituted the primary ingredient of character. In order to satisfy the cult of true manhood, a man had to bridle his instincts and rein in his passions. As breadwinner, he had to be able to balance cooperation and competition in the marketplace. As husband and father, he had to temper his aggressiveness so that he could treat his wife with chivalry and his children with benevolence.[39]

With the standard set so high, many American males had a hard time fulfilling their culture's requirements to "be a man." Everywhere there were signs of men who felt that something had gone wrong in their lives. Many had a vague apprehension that they did not measure up, as though they consistently yet inexplicably fell short of some invisible mark society expected them to meet. How could any man always be right at home, exercise perfect self-control under all circumstances, emerge the victor from every contest in the marketplace, and remain chaste but virile? Joining the ranks of those who walked around feeling anxious about their failure to meet the ideal were those who complained of a gnawing sense of disquietude, a fear that life was passing them by, that their daily experiences somehow failed to bring them into contact with the "real" world. Though voiced somewhat differently, each of these complaints registered the confusion many middle-class men felt about their gender identity, signaling a crisis of masculinity that reverberated in popular culture no less than in individual lives.[40]

Male writers flooded bookstores with tomes designed to construct suitable role models from the past. From 1894 to 1896, no fewer than twenty-eight books on Napoleon appeared in the United States, as Americans lionized the Corsican general as a heroic conqueror who had imposed his will on the world.[41] Evidence of this extraordinary personality cult reached all the way down to high school students. Speaking on the importance of "Personality" at their high school graduation, Lawrence D. Seymour, one of Kinsey's classmates, told his peers, "There have been other men with better brains, men with as much knowledge of military tactics, men of far finer character, but Napoleon's greatness and success was the sheer result of his transcendent, powerful personality."[42]

Other writers found heroes closer to home. In 1902, Owen Wister, a Harvard classmate, close friend, and great admirer of Theodore Roosevelt, published a cowboy tale, *The Virginian,* which quickly became a classic western novel. By conquering the Great West in fiction, Wister's imagination allowed men to vent their aggression in fantasy, as the nation no longer offered wilderness where men could pit their skills against nature. An instant best-seller, *The Virginian* raced through fifteen printings its first year and went on to enjoy an eight-year run as a play in theaters across the United States.[43] The *South Orange Bulletin* praised the play for reaching heights "akin to the success of the story itself."[44]

Edgar Rice Burroughs, another popular writer from Kinsey's youth, tapped the same male fantasies. After *Tarzan of the Apes* appeared in 1914, Burroughs wrote forty other novels over the next twenty years, most about Tarzan. For adolescent and adult males who felt uncertain about their identity, the adventures of a muscular and resourceful lone white man who triumphed over savages, beasts, and jungles in "darkest Africa" revived the spirit of the frontier, not to mention white supremacy and rugged individualism.[45]

Yet middle-class Americans did not have to read books to know they were experiencing a crisis of masculinity. Language itself testified to how uneasy many men felt. By the turn of the century, new epithets, such as "sissy," "pussyfoot," and, most derisive of all, "pussy," gained currency in the United States, as middle-class males voiced their contempt for weakness and their unspoken doubts about their own masculinity by creating new terms that relied upon misogynous cultural stereotypes of women for their power to embarrass and degrade.[46]

Fears about diminished masculinity extended to boyhood, prompting a flurry of advice literature designed to guide young boys through the treacherous journey from adolescence to adulthood. Teddy Roosevelt offered his formula for becoming a man in his famous essay "The American Boy." "The boy can best become a good man by being a good boy—not a goody-goody boy, but just a plain good boy," declared America's favorite Rough

Rider.[47] To Roosevelt, that meant a perfect blending of physical strength and moral purity: "He must not be a coward or a weakling, a bully, a shirk, or a prig," explained Roosevelt.[48] "He must work hard and play hard. He must be clean-minded and clean-lived, and able to hold his own under all circumstances and against all comers."[49]

Roosevelt's emphasis on clean living and competition found many supporters in South Orange, where parents worked overtime to instill masculine hardiness in their sons. The gladiatorial spirit fostered in high school and country club sports also held sway in male fraternal lodges, such as the South Orange Conclave Improved Order of Heptasophs, which supported exhibitions of jujitsu by Japanese masters.[50] Churches, too, did their part to turn boys into men. Kinsey's congregation sponsored a team called the Pioneer Club, which played basketball and football against teams from other churches.[51] His congregation also organized a "boys' battery" of "boy warriors" who conducted saber and cannon drills in the church basement on Monday nights.[52]

South Orange had a mixed record when it came to supporting the most important national groups devoted to shaping male character at the turn of the century: the Young Men's Christian Association (YMCA) and the Boy Scouts of America (BSA).[53] Drawing upon the cultural ideal expressed in the Latin phrase *mens sana in corpore sano* (a sound mind in a sound body), the YMCA sought to nurture both the soul and the body by serving its members a hefty diet of moral instruction (fortified with tips on character building) and physical education. In practice, however, the YMCA put athletics before preaching, a practice officials justified by stressing the discipline and unselfishness sports imparted. Promising to strive for self-improvement rather than selfish victory, boys and men flocked to the gymnasium, where they performed somersaults on the tumbling mats or played team sports at full throttle. According to Luther H. Gulick, who built the YMCA into a national organization with half a million members in the 1890s, the goal of all this sweat was to turn boys and men into muscular Christians. Gulick advised members to look to Jesus as their example of "magnificent manliness."[54]

Riding a wave of public enthusiasm for the outdoors, the YMCA sponsored summer camps where boys could breathe fresh air and soak up sunshine, while enjoying adventurous outdoor pursuits. Along with other middle-class Americans, parents in the Oranges equated outdoor life with clean living and moral virtue, and every spring the local newspaper reminded them the time had arrived to enroll their sons in summer camps.

The YMCA had a difficult time in South Orange. The community first organized a YMCA chapter in 1901, with quarters on South Orange Avenue. Perhaps because of the ready availability of athletic facilities elsewhere, the chapter folded for lack of funds in 1905, resumed operations in 1907, and closed shop again shortly thereafter.[55] Young people of South Orange, like Kinsey, had to join the YMCA in neighboring Orange. As a bookish, musically talented youth with a long history of illness, Kinsey was precisely the kind of boy the YMCA targeted. He had yet to demonstrate to the world any overtly masculine activity at which he excelled. Unlike competitive sports, which called for speed, physical strength, and agility, the outdoors could be conquered by anyone healthy enough to hike and curious enough to study. Kinsey was both. Beginning with his introduction to camp life at age fourteen in 1908, Kinsey returned to camps for the next twelve summers.[56] First as a camper and then as a counselor, he transformed himself from a target boy into a poster boy for the YMCA.

Sponsored by the State Executive Committee of the YMCA, the Jersey Boy's Camp was located on Lake Wawayanda, a beautiful sheet of water over two miles long and shaped somewhat like a figure eight. Nestled in the hills of Sussex County, Lake Wawayanda was the highest lake in New Jersey, some 1,300 feet above sea level. Its shores were heavily wooded, except at a portion of the northern end, where an open field commanded a view of the entire lake. The camp opened during the first week in July and operated for four weeks, each boy coming for a two-week session.

Camp Wawayanda focused on nature study. Working under adult counselors, campers learned the names of trees, plants, rocks, and insects. They also were required to record their observations on cards, a task that was supposed to foster orderly habits as much as appreciation of nature. In addition, counselors took the boys on "tramping parties" and "overnight camping trips" so they could "experience the thrill that comes in sleeping under the trees and out in the open." Summer camp was designed to give boys "not only a pleasant outing, but one that will prove a benefit physically, mentally and spiritually."[57]

Kinsey devoted his early years as a camper to mastering "woodcraft." At the turn of the century, "woodcraft" did not refer to making things from wood; it meant a knowledge of everything one needed to know in order to thrive in the wilderness without any help from civilization. As he did with everything, Kinsey attacked woodcraft methodically. Driven by his insatiable curiosity and a towering need for control, he gradually accumulated a storehouse of knowledge about the outdoors, devouring "how to do it" books on camping and natural history by the dozens. Over time, he learned the names of an amazing assortment of plants and animals, and he taught himself hundreds of tricks of the forest. While virtually everything enticed him, insects had a special hold on his imagination. Butterflies, beetles, ants, bees, wasps, or mosquitoes—it mattered not; they all had their own peculiar appeal, their own special magic. He could watch them for hours as they went about their daily routines. As Kinsey's interest in nature study deepened, he applied what he learned at camp and at the YMCA to his everyday life. Books alone could never satisfy his curiosity; he wanted to observe nature firsthand. In addition to his regular Saturday expeditions around South Orange, Kinsey started taking shorter jaunts after school. By the time he reached Natalie Roeth's high school biology class, he had developed his own empirical approach to nature study and was primed to make the most of the many field trips she led. "What I know about the sleep movements of plants, the identification of birds by flight, the identification of bird songs, the identification of trees at long distances, and many other such things," Kinsey later explained, "I have learned not from books, but from observations made in the field."[58]

During adolescence, Kinsey trained himself to notice small details in the wild, items most people passed by without seeing. Once he had hiked through a region, he knew it thoroughly. Blessed with a diamond clear memory, he could recall not only landscapes and trails but individual rocks and trees. Others marveled at this gift, for whenever he covered ground for the second time, he invariably amazed his companions with his exact recall of the terrain. Nearly a decade after he graduated from high school, Natalie Roeth wrote to ask if he remembered their high school field trips. Kinsey replied, "I can recall every single spot, I think, and each object we found on all those trips." He went on to describe the Dutchman's breeches they had photographed, the meadowlarks they had chased over the fields, and the periwinkle he had asked Roeth to identify. "That sort of memory for the utmost detail is one of the things that I find I have for the out-of-doors things I do not have for anything else, and therein lies one of the greatest charms of biology work, I think," declared Kinsey.[59]

The Boys Scouts of America knew what to do with boys like him. An offshoot of the Boy Scout movement in Great Britain, founded by General Robert S. S. Baden-Powell, the BSA was a product of society's efforts to build "real men." Even more directly than the YMCA, it reflected middle-class anxieties and fears about male character.[60] Among the mass youth movements of the twentieth century, few organizations sounded a sharper alarm about declining manliness or looked more resolutely to the past for models with which to restore the nation's manhood.

Almost to the person, the founders of the BSA regarded urban life as a cancer that was devouring the physical and moral strength of the nation. In the introduction to *Boy Scouts of America: A Handbook of Woodcraft, Scouting, and Life-craft* (1910), Ernest Thompson Seton lamented, "It is the very, very rare exception when we see a boy whose life is absolutely governed by the safe old moral standards." Only a hundred years before, Seton explained, boys had been pillars of virtue who drew their strength from the land. The typical farm boy "had all the knowledge that comes from country surroundings; that is, he could ride, shoot, skate, run, swim; he was handy with tools; he knew the woods; he was physically strong, self-reliant, well developed in body and brain." Growing up on the land virtually guaranteed that a lad would be "respectful to his superiors, obedient to his parents, and altogether the best material of which a nation could be made."[61]

According to Seton, the last few decades had all but ruined the nation's boys. Young men had been assaulted by new and insidious forces that threatened to sap every ounce of manhood from their spirit. Industrialization, urbanization, the collapse of small farms, and the decline of religion had produced "a very different type of youth in the country today." Modern-day boys had no respect for their parents or superiors, no knowledge of tools, no ability to survive in the wilderness, and no devotion to what Seton called "the safe old moral standards." Nor could their bodies match the splendid physiques of their ancestors. Neglecting their own athletic skills, they flocked to sporting events where they did "nothing but sit on the benches and look on, while indulging their tastes for tobacco and alcohol."[62]

Since so many youths suffered from diminished masculinity, Seton worried that boys would not be able to make the difficult passage to manhood: "Degeneracy is the word," he thundered. To regain the skills, self-reliance, and character farm boys had enjoyed as their birthright, modern-day boys would have to reestablish their covenant with nature. And that was where the BSA came in. According to Seton, his whole purpose in starting the BSA was "[t]o combat the system that has turned such a large proportion of our robust, manly, self-reliant boyhood into a lot of flat-chested cigarette-smokers, with shaky nerves and doubtful vitality."[63]

The BSA grew rapidly after opening its national headquarters on January 2, 1911, at 200 Fifth Avenue, in New York City. Soon BSA spokesmen were busy spreading its message in schools and churches throughout the Northeast, where concerned middle-class parents listened with alarm to strident warnings about degenerate youth. Such presentations ended with a call to arms—an invitation to organize Scout troops in every community to safeguard the nation's boys by fostering civic responsibility and masculine virtues.

Creating a local unit, a patrol, was simple and democratic. All it took was six to eight boys between the ages of twelve and eighteen (called Scouts), a patrol leader chosen by his peers or by a scout master, and the adult leader who headed up a troop, which contained three or more patrols.

(During the early years, Scouts belonged to "local councils"—"troops" did not formally appear until 1914.) By December 1913, nearly 200,000 boys, most from middle-class families, had joined the BSA, searching for ideal manhood in the virtues of the past.[64]

South Orange heeded the call to duty rather early, and whereas it showed vacillating support for the YMCA, the community stood behind the BSA. In March 1911, James McGrath, a resident of South Orange whom the local paper described as "prominently connected with the work of the American Boy Scouts," delivered a solemn warning to the members of the Home and School Association on the nation's need for "moral defense." Stressing the importance of early training, McGrath told his audience the "work of regeneration must begin with the boys," who had to be taught "respect for others, for their elders, and for authority."[65]

Alfred Seguine Kinsey endorsed this message. Few fathers in South Orange paid closer attention to the character of their children, and few could match his talent for translating moral vigilance into binding rules. As family patriarch, he imposed a long list of restrictions on his children. Dancing, card playing, drinking, and gambling were strictly forbidden, as was smoking. For Kinsey's father, then, the Boy Scouts represented a sharp tool he could use to finish shaping his older son's character. The BSA would reinforce the lessons Kinsey had learned from parents, religion, and the YMCA. He would be taught deference to authority, self-discipline, self-reliance, outdoor skills, muscular Christianity, unabashed patriotism, and a strong work ethic, traits that the senior Kinsey supported wholeheartedly, forming, as they did, a kind of catechism of middle-class virtues. Herein lay the Scouts' dual attraction for Kinsey's father: scouting would not only build character in his son but demonstrate their family's allegiance to middle-class ideals.

Soon after McGrath spoke, Alfred Seguine Kinsey helped organize several Boy Scout troops in South Orange. Eventually he was appointed to the highest local office, the president of the local council, composed of ten men who oversaw troop officers. In this capacity, he and his fellow council members supervised the work of South Orange's Boy Scout troops, conducted (through the court of honor) all examinations for promotions and the awarding of merit badges, investigated acts of heroism (particularly cases of lifesaving) to present proper documentation to the national court of honors so that medals could be awarded, and served as a final court of appeals over the rulings of scoutmasters and their assistants. While the job was time-consuming, scouting enabled Alfred Seguine Kinsey to associate with South Orange's community leaders and occupy an important position in an organization that commanded respect and support. Following her husband's lead, Sarah, too, became involved with the Boy Scouts. She served as "Second Scout Mother," one of her few ventures into "city house-keeping."

Kinsey was a junior in high school and nearly seventeen years old when he joined the Boy Scouts. Given his father's position as the president of the local council, the Scouts presented Kinsey with yet another set of patriarchal expectations to be met. He attacked scouting with all the fervor of a boy determined to demonstrate his mettle, both to his father and to the world.

During the BSA's early years, it was easy for boys to rise through the ranks because the BSA was eager to build membership. The official Scout manual freely declared, "Our policy is to get numbers."[66] Rejecting the pressure of time limits, the BSA allowed boys to take as long as they needed to earn badges, and the manual advised scoutmasters and examiners not to set "too high a standard of proficiency before awarding a badge," since the organization wanted to instill confidence in every boy by promoting "an idea of self-improvement." In other words, the BSA wanted to pit boys against themselves, not against each other. Eschewing the competition of the marketplace, the BSA hoped to foster self-esteem and self-reliance by fashioning a contest every boy could win. Primed by his earlier study of woodcraft, Kinsey knew how to play this game.

Thanks to his previous work with YMCA summer camps and his own program of nature study, Kinsey was hardly a typical "tenderfoot." It could not have taken him long to earn his badges in music, gardening, and the various outdoors skills. Working under the immediate supervision of the scoutmaster of the South Orange troop, the Reverend David DeForrest Burrell, minister of the First Presbyterian Church, Kinsey applied himself with great diligence to earning his Eagle, the highest Scout rank. Then, as now, few candidates achieved this distinction. In 1912, only 23 boys made Eagle Scout in the United States, and 54 more Eagles followed the next year out of a total population of nearly 200,000 Scouts nationwide. Alfred Charles Kinsey was among those who hit the mark in 1913, placing him among the first 77 Eagle Scouts in the United States.[67] There was only one skill he had any trouble mastering. Months after he had earned his Eagle, he had still not learned to swim, a fact duly recorded by a fellow counselor who wrote in his camp notes, "Tried teaching Kinsey to swim."[68]

The citizens of South Orange prepared a celebration banquet for Kinsey and the three other boys who earned their Eagles. Approximately two hundred people attended the awards ceremony on January 24, 1914, in the Columbia High School auditorium, freshly "decorated with the national colors and palms."[69] The principal speaker was James E. West of New York City, the chief executive of the BSA, who gave a stirring talk on the Boy Scouts of America. Nine other speakers addressed the audience that evening, including the father-and-son team of Alfred Seguine and Alfred Charles Kinsey. Kinsey's father called attention to the fact that South Orange enjoyed "the distinction of having the first scout mother in this country," and Kinsey himself delivered a brief talk on his specialty, "The Scout Afield."[70] Then, after a hearty meal, the audience erupted into applause as Kinsey and three other members of the South Orange troop received their Eagles.[71]

Kinsey took great pride in scouting. He converted the room next to his bedroom on the third floor into a den where he displayed his scouting projects, and he wore his Scout uniform almost everywhere he went.[72] It was as though he wanted others to identify him with his uniform, as every badge he earned served as a talisman of his manliness and his character. Certainly, his schoolmates sensed how important scouting was to Kinsey. The "Class Prophecy" not only foretold that Kinsey would become "a second Darwin" but predicted he would become the "Chief Scout of North America, succeeding the late Ernest Thompson Seton."[73]

Scouting gave Kinsey the opportunity to succeed in the masculine world of athletics, since the Boy Scouts awarded merit badges in both hiking and mountain climbing. Hiking had long been a popular middle-class recreation, and during the second half of the nineteenth century mountain climbing developed into a full-fledged craze, wildly popular throughout the Western world.[74] By the time he reached high school, Kinsey had developed into an outstanding hiker and climber. Year after year, he disappeared into the woods and hills around South Orange, driven by his thirst for knowledge and need to prove himself. During these expeditions, Kinsey built up his stamina, hardened his leg muscles, and honed his skills. He learned how to pace himself on uphill climbs, how to ford streams, how to make his way through underbrush, and a thousand other tricks nature yields to those who take her measure.

Confident of his skills, Kinsey was eager to lead others on nature hikes. More than a hint of challenge infused his invitations to classmates. Kinsey wanted to prove to his peers that he possessed what Teddy Roosevelt called "the right stuff."[75] At first, his classmates declined, preferring to save their weekends for team sports. Kinsey persisted, displaying the powers of persuasion he was to demonstrate often in the years ahead. Whether by pleading, cajoling, arguing, or daring, he maneuvered his schoolmates onto his turf. Following repeated invitations, several boys, including Girard Oberrender, one of the bodyguards who had defended Kinsey from bullies, finally agreed to go hiking. Besting his companions, Kinsey "walked their legs off" through more than twenty miles of New Jersey hills.[76] This outing undoubtedly marked a new phase in Kinsey's life. From then on, nature became his domain. Like the classroom, the outdoors served as his arena for competition, a setting where he could take on all comers with confidence.

Kinsey reaped a second benefit from this hike with his former bodyguard. Stunned by his supposedly sickly friend's ability to walk him effortlessly into the ground, Oberrender returned home and assured his father that Kinsey's heart had to be healthy. The senior Oberrender, struck by his son's logic, decided to discuss the matter with Kinsey's father, who in turn described how their family doctor diagnosed a heart condition following one of Kinsey's many childhood illnesses. Unconvinced, the senior Oberrender arranged (with parental consent) for the boy to be examined by a heart specialist, who gave Kinsey a clean bill of health.[77]

The new diagnosis allowed Kinsey to face the future secure in the knowledge he could plunge into strenuous activities without risking death. But reassuring as it was, the news could not undo the harm he had endured. Years of having parents hover over him at home, years of not being able to roughhouse with other boys or engage in competitive sports at school, and years of social isolation had left their mark on Kinsey. Smothered in childhood and cramped in adolescence, he had spent much of his youth feeling inferior to other boys. Nor did the news about Kinsey's heart diminish his incessant impulse to excel and to maintain perfect self-control.

Still, little by little, Kinsey had come to believe in himself. Gradually, almost imperceptibly, he had shed his image as a sickly boy and become an intrepid explorer who roamed the countryside in search of nature's secrets, a rugged outdoorsman who radiated competence and self-sufficiency. As an outdoorsman, he had automatically tapped into the public's identification of nature skills with manliness.

By the time he finished high school, Kinsey was the embodiment of the all-American boy. Outwardly, he projected an image of happiness and inner peace. One of his classmates recalled, "I can see him walking along Academy Street, preoccupied and serene, hatless as he usually was, winter and summer." Another schoolmate remembered him as "always smiling, blond curly hair, fast walking with big strides, and a nice looking young man."[78]

Yet, despite his appearance, Kinsey was a profoundly troubled young man, because the face he presented to the world was contrived. His private self bore little resemblance to the boy who was "always smiling," the boy who looked so "serene." Adolescence was the time when he became skilled at concealing his inner life. Kinsey had to master deceit, for while he had managed to satisfy nearly all the cultural requirements for the passage from boyhood to manhood, one part of the formula had eluded him.

4

"Be Pure in Thought and
Clean in Habit"

"**J**ust at present the city of Newark seems to be making a specialty of murder, suicide and sudden death," chided a newspaper editorial from the Oranges in 1909. While the editor went on to decry Newark's "mania for homicide and self-destruction," his remarks sounded more self-congratulatory than sympathetic.[1] Like the Pharisees of biblical times who prayed publicly in loud voices thanking God that they were better than other men, the editor meant to contrast the moral chaos of the city with the moral superiority of the suburbs. Yet even in the best of suburbs nothing could be taken for granted; public and private morality had to be nurtured and protected. The South Orange town fathers maintained a constant vigil against moral contamination, using the law to proscribe and eject those who would bring urban ills to their pastoral community.

In the South Orange of Kinsey's youth, the police force visibly symbolized social control. By 1908, the village employed 13 officers to preserve order in a population of 6,000—more than three times the national average of policemen per capita.[2] While any number of offenses could run a person afoul of the law, month in and month out two crimes led the field:

public intoxication and disorderly conduct. On the average, South Orange's police officers arrested a dozen citizens a month, including two for public intoxication and the same number for disorderly conduct.[3] More interesting than the numbers, however, were the residential locations of the men arrested. City records for 1909 show that 19 of the 24 inebriated offenders did not live in the village, and in the following year 23 of 27 were nonresidents.[4] At first glance, then, these figures appeared to confirm the town fathers' working assumption: the main threat to public order came not from village residents but from visitors who imported evils from the outside world into the village.

In South Orange, as across America, the struggle to control the use of alcohol pitted the middle class against the working class, particularly the urban poor and the "new immigrants" from eastern and southern Europe. Both the temperance and the prohibition movements enjoyed broad support in the village, especially among middle-class women who combated "demon rum" to protect their homes and families. Throughout Kinsey's adolescence, the Woman's Christian Temperance Union was active in South Orange, pressuring village officials to restrict liquor licenses and to regulate the sale of alcoholic beverages.

Alfred Seguine Kinsey was a staunch prohibitionist. His animus against alcohol derived from his rigid Calvinism, and he found many people who shared his views. In 1911, he and other concerned citizens organized the Inter-Church Civic League to monitor the closing time of saloons. Alfred Seguine Kinsey was a leader of this group. So was his son's scoutmaster, the Reverend David Burrell, the pastor of the First Presbyterian Church. Brandishing a petition signed by 329 villagers, the Inter-Church Civic League stoutly opposed a proposal before the Village Board of Trustees that would have changed the law to allow the six saloons and one hotel that had liquor licenses in the village to remain open until midnight, instead of closing at 11 P.M. as mandated by the existing law.[5]

The saloon controversy raged for months, becoming so heated that one trustee resigned. Unwilling to settle the issue on their own, the remaining trustees decided to hold a referendum. On February 14, 1911, nearly 1,000 village residents cast their ballots. "Some took the matter very seriously and walked to the booth as if the destiny of their country depended upon the outcome of the vote," reported the local press. This was especially true of the members of the Inter-Church Civic League, whose officers set up a command post across the street from the village hall and "showed concern about every voter in the village." In the end, their vigilance was rewarded, as the referendum yielded a victory for their league. By a scant margin of 67 ballots, voters decreed that the saloons would have to close at 11:00 P.M. In commenting on the vote, the local editors expressed the fervent hope "that there will be no further discussion, acrimonious or otherwise, on the subject."[6] South Orange's "saloon wars" formed one prong of a broad attack on behavior that violated traditional values.[7] Censorship of the movies also led to a political fight. While the motion picture industry was still in its infancy at the turn of the century, the magic of flickering images captivated many Americans. The first movies were three- to four-minute films presenting brief vaudeville turns or glimpses of everyday life. With titles such as *Fred Ott's Sneeze*, *Chinese Laundry*, and *The Gaiety Girls Dancing*, they strike our modern-day sensibilities as light and innocent. Following the release in 1903 of the first western, *The Great Train Robbery*, which ran twelve minutes, mesmerizing audiences with its violent scenes of armed robbery, movies became longer and more complex. Increasingly, movies ridiculed Victorian values such as thrift and the work ethic, or challenged sexual restraints by making premarital or extramarital sex appear attractive. As local entrepreneurs converted stores and saloons into nickelodeons, movies became extremely popular in ethnic, working-class neighborhoods, where immigrants could pay a nickel and escape the grim realities of urban life for the silent world of dreams.[8]

Alarmed by this growing threat to Victorian morality, many citizens demanded action. While the move to regulate movies began in urban areas, many parents in South Orange shared this dim view of motion pictures, as they did not want their community corrupted by immoral urban amusements. In 1909, the Prospectors' Club, a local men's athletic club, sponsored an ordinance before the board of trustees "prohibiting public exhibitions of moving pictures." The ordinance failed. The board adopted a compromise solution by "striking out the word 'prohibit' and inserting the word 'regulate.'" By opting for regulation over prohibition, South Orange's leaders pursued a moderate approach to reform, taking the position progressives usually adopted when asked to reconcile demands for censorship and artistic freedom.[9]

Still, movies did not become popular with many young people in South Orange during Kinsey's adolescence. Movies were too vulgar, too identified with the working class. Asked to comment on the nickelodeon craze, Hazel Phillips Balch, one of Kinsey's classmates, replied that she knew it existed, but added quite emphatically, "It didn't touch my life. I don't remember going to the movies."[10] Certainly, his stern father would never have allowed Kinsey to attend a movie.

When it came to protecting the morals of young people, the leaders of South Orange displayed remarkable vigilance. Village police gave parents a long arm for controlling their children. Everywhere a boy turned, a police officer seemed to be peering back at him, as even small infractions did not escape notice. In 1908, for example, Officer Kelly arrested two boys in South Orange for selling newspapers without a license. The two offenders were immediately "brought before Justice Roll and discharged with a reprimand."[11] A similar fate awaited boys who skipped school. Kinsey's adolescence corresponded with the rise of compulsory school attendance laws in the United States, and South Orange vigorously enforced the New Jersey truancy statute.[12] In 1911, the local truant officer branded Thomas McGrath, the thirteen-year-old son of a widow, "an incorrigible" and placed the case "in the custody of the probation officer, John Gascoyne."[13]

The village police took special care to protect young people from bad habits. Since one of the prime reasons families abandoned the city was to escape moral decay, the temptations of the city could not be allowed to take root in the suburbs. Parents in South Orange looked askance at pool halls, particularly those that admitted underage boys. In 1908, the judge of South Orange's police court fined Ilbarto Conderfero, an Italian barber, ten dollars "for permitting minors to play pool in the rear of his shop at 68 South Orange Avenue." The judge suspended sentence, however, "on the charge of selling cigarettes to the boys."[14]

The barber was lucky to get off on the cigarette charge, for during Kinsey's adolescence many Americans grew deeply concerned about smoking. In 1903, a coalition of religious groups, educators, temperance and prohibition crusaders, and health advocates organized the National Anti-Cigarette League. Scores of prominent leaders joined the crusade, including David Starr Jordan, the president of Stanford University, who told audiences, "Boys who smoke cigarettes are like wormy apples that fall from the tree before they are ripe," and the lecturer Elbert Hubbard, who declared, "Cigarette smokers are men whose future lies behind them."[15]

Young people in South Orange heard the same message. Dr. Krackowizer, a prominent supporter of the local Boys Club, chided both the students at Columbia High School and the members of the YMCA for "sucking on cigarettes" and advised them to develop "discipline of will as well as culture of minds."[16] To protect young people from "the vile weed," the Village Board of Trustees passed an ordinance prohibiting the sale of tobacco to minors.[17] Merchants who violated this ordinance had to worry about private citizens as well as the police. As if the community was not under tight enough scrutiny, the trustees created a position called "constable for the village without compensation," a polite title for a licensed vigilante.[18] Village constables were empowered to arrest people who broke the law.[19]

While it is not clear whether he actually received such an appointment, Alfred Seguine Kinsey certainly acted like a village constable. Drawn by his usual passion for imposing his standards on others, he became a soldier in the antismoking campaign, using his older son to entrap local merchants who sold cigarettes to minors. Alfred Seguine Kinsey's method was simple: he would send Kinsey into shops to ask for cigarettes; if the order was filled, the father immediately reported the offending merchant to the police. After he reached adulthood, Kinsey spoke of these incidents with disgust, insisting that he had hated being used as a decoy.[20]

Young people in South Orange found their behavior not only scrutinized by police and unpaid constables but also monitored by school officials. Superintendent Foster was a strict disciplinarian who refused to brook any hint of rebellion at Columbia High School. In 1904, members of the senior class, eager to display their class color, broke the dress code by wearing large yellow chrysanthemums and neckties and handkerchiefs of yellow cheesecloth. As reported in the local press, Foster told them "they must desist from wearing anything ridiculous, and must recognize his authority." To enforce his edict, Foster barred class members from the study hall for several sessions, and they quickly capitulated. Crowing over the outcome, the press observed, "This morning the members of the class attended school, all wearing neat silk ties of blue and gold." Yet Foster was not adverse to allowing the defeated seniors a small face-saving gesture. The paper added wryly, "They also wore a small yellow chrysanthemum, and as one of the school faculty said, 'made a dignified appearance.' "[21]

While school officials made an earnest attempt to uphold public decorum, students occasionally misbehaved. In 1908, four high school boys were accused of smuggling a flask of liquor into a dance at the high school auditorium. The boys, it seems, "retired to the fire escape to drink it" and "were seen by some of their school mates and thus the details of the escapade leaked out." Quick to perceive a threat to village morals in the caper, the local editors drew an association between this "disgraceful affair" and recent reports that "a boy member of the High School took a bottle of beer to a restaurant in the village and drank it with a lunch which he bought in the place." Stressing that the boys were all from "good families," the press noted with some impatience, "No punishment has yet been meted out to the offenders." The editors did seem to take some comfort from Superintendent Foster's announcement that "dances in the school hall will be discontinued for the present."[22]

Throughout Kinsey's youth, the issue of dancing divided parents. Many saw dancing as sinful behavior that would lead young people astray by arousing sexual desires. In 1908, several members of the board of education in neighboring Orange publicly criticized a Thanksgiving Eve dance held in the high school auditorium. "It is disgraceful for a public building on a main thoroughfare to ring, long after midnight, with the strains of the

'Merry Widow,' " declared three board members in a signed letter.[23] Recognizing the deep divisions within the community, the local newspaper viewed the controversy philosophically. High school dances were bound to be "something of a shock to the conservative element of the Board of Education, just as it was equally certain that other members should regard the use of the High School hall for dancing as not only not harmful, but as even meritorious in the pleasure that it gave to the young people taking part," observed the editor. Given such sharp disagreements, the editors advocated regulation rather than prohibition. Provided future dances were held "under proper chaperonage" and were "brought to a close before the hour of midnight, . . . the idea does not seem so very radical."[24]

South Orange reached the same compromise. Following the drinking incident in 1908, Superintendent Foster quickly and quietly lifted the ban on dances that he had imposed. Throughout Kinsey's high school years, dances were held in the high school auditorium. Not that he ever went to one. His father would not permit him to attend dances, a rule that apparently was not rescinded even for the senior prom. Describing what was unquestionably the biggest social event of her high school years, Hazel Phillips Balch, one of Kinsey's classmates, noted that the prom was followed by a night of theater in New York. The class went to the city by train, and her date was Norman Court, who had a reputation as a lady's man (the legend beneath his photograph in the senior yearbook read, "I am very fond of the company of ladies; I like their beauty; I like their delicacy; I like their vivacity"). "I've forgotten now what it was we saw, [but] we came home late," she declared, "and that was quite a privilege to be allowed to do anything like that." While Balch recalled many details about the evening, she added, "I can't remember Alfred being there. He may not have gone in with us."[25]

Balch's recollections offer glimpses of the social world of Kinsey's peers. In high school, Hazel became what Kinsey did not: a member of the "in crowd." Her circle of friends had eight people, five boys and three girls, denizens of the class of 1912 all. Closely knit if not inseparable, they went places together, hung out at each other's homes, and dated within the group. Balch recalled countless afternoons when the "crew" would assemble at her house after school to visit, play cards, or dance on the front porch. Asked about Kinsey, she replied, "Well, you wouldn't think about asking him to have a good time. He never fit in right. He was not asked." Pressed to explain why, she thought a moment and replied, "He wasn't the type that you would go out and have a pleasant time with. If you wanted to talk bugs maybe, but he didn't have fun." The book on Kinsey, she stressed, was that he was "very serious in everything . . . very."[26]

Balch did not overstate Kinsey's social isolation. His dearth of friends extended to the opposite sex. "He didn't go with the girls at all," recalled Balch. Asked if any of the girls had a crush on Kinsey, Balch recoiled in mock horror and said, "No. He wasn't the type who appealed to girls."[27] While there is no way of knowing whether Balch spoke for all the girls in South Orange, this much can be said with certainty: except at church services and school-related activities, Kinsey had no contact with girls in high school.

Still, this did not prompt any questions. Many boys of Kinsey's generation did not date in high school—some because they were genuinely bashful or slow maturing, many because their parents would not allow them to date, and still others because they could not afford to date. "I think he was shy," observed Balch. Another classmate agreed, calling Kinsey "the shyest guy around girls you could think of."[28] A boy of Kinsey's generation, then, could skip dating in high school without appearing odd.

American middle-class boys and girls on the eve of World War I typically had far less social contact than young people today. Parents went to considerable lengths to keep boys and girls apart and to monitor their behavior when they got together. Most youth organizations and adolescent activities were strictly segregated by sex, and chaperons kept a watchful eye over dances and parties. Still, this does not mean that young people were sexually inert, particularly the boys. After he became a sex researcher, Kinsey exposed the jarring conflict between parental demands and adolescent male behavior. His data proved that many boys of his generation became sexually active as children and that virtually all boys did so as adolescents, with masturbation serving as the chief outlet. To him it seemed almost disingenuous that society "provides a source of regular sexual outlet in marriage, in part because it recognizes the sexual need of the older male; but it fails to recognize that the teen-age boys are potentially more capable and often more active than their 35-year-old fathers." Kinsey's example fit his own history perfectly. Kinsey's father was exactly thirty-five years old when Kinsey turned thirteen, the average age at which boys of his generation entered puberty.[29]

During Kinsey's adolescence virtually all middle-class Americans believed that males had stronger sexual needs than females. Yet males had to run a gauntlet of conflicting advice. On the one hand, many people believed males would damage their health if they did not satisfy, at least partially, their sexual needs. Many adolescent boys therefore felt justified in masturbating, and many men used this same argument to rationalize sowing wild oats before marriage and visiting prostitutes on occasion after marriage. On the other hand, men were taught from childhood to control their sexual appetites, lest they debase themselves and defile decent women. The only hope was for men to marry and remain faithful to their wives.

With the help of his "better half," a man could control his sexual urges and avoid moral destruction.[30]

The specter of moral corruption hung over the family throughout Kinsey's adolescence. A profound sense of moral decay haunted many Americans on the eve of World War I. Everywhere one looked, there were threats to the nuclear family (the rising divorce rate, birth control, and abortion); evidence of declining morals (white slavery, prostitution, venereal disease, gambling, and alcoholism); and ominous demographic changes that might enable the "new immigrants" to seize power by outbreeding old-stock Americans.

Social hygienists articulated cultural fears about disease, sexuality, and moral decay. Drawing their members from medicine, education, science, business, philanthropy, social work, and government, these social reformers saw themselves as progressive defenders of traditional values. Overall, social hygienists wanted to preserve those facets of Victorian morality that rested upon discipline, restraint, and the perpetuation of WASP cultural hegemony. Their primary goal was to maintain social order (with modest modifications) by controlling human sexual behavior, a task they proposed to accomplish by confining sex to the institution of marriage.

Determined to safeguard middle-class morals and protect the bourgeois family, social hygienists called for a program of sex education to promote, in the words of one reformer, "sanitary and moral prophylaxis."[31] Social hygienists had no intention of teaching young people human reproduction, human anatomy, birth control techniques, or the like. Rather, their goal was to indoctrinate them against every form of premarital sex. Sex hygiene, like social purity, was not a plea for sexual liberation but a demand for sexual control, a major counterattack by late Victorians who were intent on holding the line against the moral chaos of the city.[32]

Many enlightened physicians rushed to endorse sex education as proposed by social hygienists. "We are dealing with the solution of a problem," declared Dr. Egbert Grandin, "where ignorance is not bliss but is misfortune, and where, therefore, it is folly not to be wise."[33] Many health officials agreed, insisting that sex education was needed in the schools to do the job abdicated by parents. By 1919, the U.S. Public Health Service threw its weight behind sex education in the schools, arguing, "As in many instances the school must take up the burden neglected by others."[34] By 1922, about half of the secondary schools in the United States offered some form of instruction in sex hygiene.

But Columbia High School was not among them, at least not during the years Kinsey attended. While Superintendent Foster was a liberal educator, he made no effort to add a sex hygiene course to the curriculum. Perhaps it was Victorian reticence that stayed the hand of this otherwise progressive man. Asked by a reporter in 1909 about the need for moral instruction, Foster declined to be drawn into a discussion, explaining somewhat enigmatically "that it was not so necessary for him to mention it to the people who were present, as they showed by their presence that they understood it, but it was for the people who did not appreciate it."[35]

Deprived of a sex education in school, Kinsey did not receive one at home, at least not in the formal sense. His mother does not seem a likely candidate to have offered explicit instruction. Nor, for that matter, does his father. Nevertheless, the religious views of both parents suffused the Kinsey household with Victorian attitudes toward sex. On the few occasions Kinsey discussed his childhood, Gebhard recalled, "he talked largely about the sexual aspects of how he was reared in ignorance and repressive things, and how he hoped . . . that nowadays people could be spared the sort of thing that he went through as a child."[36]

After he became a sex researcher, Kinsey studied very carefully how children learned about sex. According to his research, children almost never observed adult sexual behavior and their parents rarely lectured them "in regard to attitudes on sex."[37] To him, it was clear that sex education in the home was a gradual process, more subtle than explicit. Still, by the time they reached adolescence, Kinsey believed, children had absorbed enough of their parents' thinking to be turned into "conforming machines which rarely fail to perpetuate the mores of the community."[38]

Parents who did not allow their sons to date, dance, drink, smoke, or play cards sound deeply religious. Yet in Kinsey's family religion may not divulge the whole story. His parents' attitudes toward sex doubtless reflected the values and tensions of the class into which they had climbed. After all, many upwardly mobile families try to outdo the middle class at being middle class, hoping to display values that will align them with the class into which they have moved. Following the pattern of other upwardly mobile blue-collar families, Kinsey's parents probably felt pressured to embrace middle-class morality, including its vehement efforts to control sex.

Kinsey later all but said as much. After he became a sex researcher, he devoted considerable attention to the relationship between sexual attitudes and class. Furthermore, in order to accommodate social mobility, his schema allowed for movement from one class to another.[39] When Kinsey discussed upward mobility and sex education, the example he selected, moving from skilled labor to professional class, matched his own family's history exactly. Arguing that upwardly mobile fathers adopted the sexual mores of the class into which they had moved, he showed how fathers then tried to impose these new mores on their sons. "We can point to the father whose contacts with the upper level lead him to associate upper level sexual patterns with upper level success in social and business affairs," wrote Kinsey. "His contacts may not affect his own sexual performance, but they may be significant enough to lead him to encourage a pattern for his son which differs from his own." Nor did Kinsey ignore the role of the mother. "It is probable that the mother is even more often responsible for the boy's sexual restraint," he wrote. "It is often she who encourages him to associate with proper, well-behaved, and similarly restrained upper level companions."[40]

Kinsey's parents were not the only agents of middle-class morality at work in South Orange. Although sex hygiene courses were not included in the curriculum of Columbia High School, the moral agenda advanced by social hygienists was adopted by the two youth organizations that touched Kinsey's life daily: the YMCA and the Boy Scouts. Both regarded sex education as a vital part of their program for training boys to become men.[41] To safeguard Christian character, the YMCA and the Boy Scouts instructed boys to abstain from premarital intercourse and masturbation alike.

Next to premarital sex, no behavior worried middle-class Americans at the turn of the century more than masturbation, and Kinsey could not have missed the Boy Scouts' crusade against it. Among the mass circulation books of the day, none contained a clearer warning than "Chapter V: Health and Endurance," of *Boy Scouts of America: The Official Handbook for Boys* (1914 edition). After explaining everything a boy needed to do to become healthy and strong, the authors turned to "Conservation," telling their young readers,

> We should be equally concerned in saving and storing up natural forces we already have. In the body of every boy who has reached his teens, the Creator of the universe has sown a very important fluid. This fluid is the most wonderful material in all the physical world. Some parts of it find their way into the blood, and through the blood give tone to the muscles, power to the brain, and strength to the nerves. This fluid is the sex fluid. When this fluid appears in a boy's body, it works a wonderful change in him. His chest deepens, his shoulders broaden, his voice changes, his ideals are changed and enlarged. It gives him the capacity for deep feeling, for rich emotion. Pity the boy, therefore, who has wrong ideas of this important function, because they will lower his ideals of life. These organs actually secrete into the blood material that makes a boy manly, strong, and noble. Any habit which a boy has that causes this fluid to be discharged from the body tends to weaken his strength, to make him less able to resist disease, and often unfortunately fastens upon him habits which later in life can be broken only with great difficulty. Even several years before this fluid appears in the body such habits are harmful to a growing boy.

To become strong, therefore, one must be pure in thought and clean in habit. This power which I have spoken of must be conserved, because this sex function is so deep and strong that there will come times when temptation to wrong habits will be very powerful. But remember that to yield means to sacrifice strength and power and manliness.[42]

Masturbation served as a lightning rod for many people's sexual fears and anxieties. The horror and disgust with which parents viewed masturbation was revealed in the names they assigned it, such as the "heinous sin of self-pollution," the "sin of solitary self-abuse," and "secret venery." As these euphemisms suggest, many parents placed masturbation in the category of sinful behavior, giving a sharp religious edge to their moral condemnation.

Class identification served to reinforce this religious ethic. As Victorian prudery gradually took root in the United States during the nineteenth century, middle-class urbanities embraced a stringent code of sexual ethics in order to distinguish themselves from the lower classes. While it is true that Victorians routinely enshrouded sexual topics and behavior in religious taboos, their objections to masturbation also reflected their experience with the marketplace. Taught from childhood to save money in order to acquire investment capital, they condemned masturbation with special vehemence, in part because it separated sex from procreation, but also because it squandered a vital resource—namely, semen—that society depended on for its development, indeed for its very survival. The very words used to describe masturbation—"to spend" semen—underscore the marketplace metaphor.

Still, their concerns about spent semen might have been less shrill if parents had not believed that masturbation injured a boy's health, a hoary notion that had been embedded in the medical literature for at least 150 years by the time Kinsey reached puberty. Physicians traced the theory to Samuel Auguste Tissot, whose 1758 treatise claimed that all sexual activity was dangerous because it starved the nerves by rushing blood to the brain, thereby producing insanity. Tissot reached this conclusion because he theorized that the loss of one ounce of seminal fluid equaled the loss of forty ounces of blood. He further contended that unless this loss took place in the recumbent position, which he stated was usually not the case in masturbation, the ill effects were exaggerated many fold. Tissot's monograph quickly spread far and wide in translation, and his colleagues found his arguments persuasive. Over time, the medical profession adopted the view that masturbation led to serious physical and mental illnesses.[43]

In the century and a half following the publication of Tissot's book, doctors made masturbation into a full-fledged disease. In addition to endorsing the popular belief that masturbation led to general debility, doctors linked it to an astonishing assortment of illnesses, including insanity, blindness, impotence, epilepsy, vertigo, loss of hearing, loss of memory, chronic headache, rickets, and nymphomania, to name only a few. And as might be expected of a disease that could trigger so many serious illnesses, masturbation got credit for causing an occasional death. The records of New Orleans's Charity Hospital, for example, listed two men who were hospitalized for masturbation in 1872, both of whom died while under care for their illness.[44]

To combat this moral evil and psychological illness, physicians prescribed an assortment of treatments and remedies, most of which focused on prevention. Many doctors stressed moral prophylaxis, exhorting their male patients to uphold the same standard of purity they demanded of women. Others tried to frighten them into abstinence by describing all the horrible things that would happen if they masturbated. Pushing this tactic to the limit, one physician told his patients, "Masturbation is death." Most doctors, however, favored moderate remedies, such as hard work, abundant exercise, fresh air, simple diet, cold baths or cold showers, and gradually decreasing doses of opium. Other doctors preferred to treat the disease behaviorally and recommended visits to a prostitute, taking a mistress, or marriage to remove the need for masturbation. When mild measures failed, doctors prescribed more aggressive intervention, including restraining devices, infibulation, or placing a ring in the prepuce to make masturbation agonizingly painful, and circumcision to reduce tactile sensitivity. Among the surgical procedures suggested were acupuncture of the prostate, insertion of electrodes into the bladder and rectum, and cauterization of the prostatic urethra.[45]

In the most desperate cases, doctors recommended the patient be committed to an insane asylum and/or castrated. In 1898, the *Texas Medical Practitioner* reported the case of a twenty-two-year-old man, a chronic masturbator and epileptic who was castrated at the request of the county judge, with the approval of the young man's father, who reportedly said, "he would be perfectly satisfied if the masturbation could be stopped, so that he could take him home, without having his family continually humiliated and disgusted by this loathsome habit."[46] The young man reportedly faced the operation morosely, "like a coon in a hollow," but after the procedure he stopped masturbating and the frequency of his fits decreased.[47]

The medical profession's alarm both reflected and strengthened the community's concern over masturbation. In fact, any moral offense and/or disease serious enough to require commitment or castration warranted concerted community action, and the guardians of morality rose to the challenge. To save the nation's boys and girls from self-pollution, social hygienists wrote numerous advice books at the turn of the century, each designed to play upon the guilt and the fear of youth. In addition, the apostles of abstinence became mainstays on the YMCA lecture circuit. Among these moral browbeaters, none could match Sylvanus Stall, D.D., the author of *What a Young Boy Ought to Know* (1897), available, too, on phonograph cylinders. Stall had this advice for boys:

> Think for a moment of what your own parents have done for you. . . . Ever since you were born, they have been laboring to provide you every comfort.
> Nothing I am sure would bring greater pain to the hearts of Papa and Mama, than to know that their dear boy, whom they hoped to prepare for great usefulness, had turned aside into ways of sin and evil which were surely disappointing all their hopes and ruining their boy, both for this world and the world to come.[48]

Thus, boys of Kinsey's generation were under tremendous pressure to abstain from any form of sexual behavior. They were expected to fulfill the highest code of personal conduct. No one better illustrated this rigid code than Teddy Roosevelt. During his freshman year in college, Roosevelt received the following advice from his father: "Take care of your morals first, your health next, and finally your studies."[49] The fight had not been easy, but when he contemplated marriage for the first time, the twenty-one-year-old Roosevelt could still confide to his diary in 1878, "Thank Heaven, I am at least perfectly pure."[50]

Kinsey could not make that statement. During his adolescence (if not before), this indefatigable striver lost his struggle for moral perfection. Despite the injunctions of his religion, despite the vigilance of parents, teachers, and police, and despite the dire warnings of social hygienists who shaped the sex education programs of his beloved YMCA and Boy Scouts, Kinsey masturbated. Perhaps he discovered this behavior all on his own, or perhaps he learned about it from other boys, the unofficial (but in many ways most important) sex educators of youth.[51] Throughout his adolescence, Kinsey moved in a world that allowed boys far more contact with each other than with girls. Late Victorians imposed rigid sexual segregation on young people, a practice his father was happy to support. As a result, Kinsey's social life was limited to a masculine world, and it was here that he learned what boys teach one another about life.

Summer camps offered Kinsey his most prolonged opportunities for contact with other boys. Then, as now, summer camps represented a separate moral universe from the communities boys left behind. Freed from parental surveillance, supervised largely by camp counselors not far removed from their own age, and encouraged to hone their outdoor skills, boys forged their own culture, one that was quintessentially masculine. Liberated from paternal controls, many boys luxuriated in their newfound freedom, casting off the restraints of civilization with the same zeal that they shed starched collars and long pants. Physical activities dominated life in summer camps, as boys rode horses, paddled canoes, and shot bows and arrows. Camp counselors might lead morning prayers and enforce weekly attendance at chapel, but a boy's social status in camp rarely turned on Christian piety. Rather, most boys fought to establish themselves in the pecking order by demonstrating their physical prowess, or by breaking rules. (Of course, some boys did both.) They displayed their irreverence for adult authority in small, calculated outrages such as belching in the dining hall or farting in tents. In short, summer camps often spawned a jocular, male culture where boys could bend the domestic rules they had to obey at home and try out forbidden modes of behavior.

Emotions ran high in camp. While boys who preferred to be "loners" were not uncommon, most boys paired up and forged fast friendships or aligned themselves with several boys to form groups. A spirit of comradeship often developed in summer camps, as boys bonded together and became intensely interested in each other. Within this world of adolescent males, counselors occupied a special position. Part role models, part group leaders, and part parent substitutes, counselors were the objects of much admiration and careful scrutiny from their wards. Certainly, this was true of Kinsey. Recalling their two summers together at Camp Kiamesha in 1912 and 1913, one of Kinsey's fellow campers declared, "The mere facts of *who* went where or with whom on our various expeditions seemed to be emotionally colored and to warrant record." Referring to a camp diary he kept for those years, the same friend told Kinsey, "Repeatedly it is on record that you had tent No. 12."[52]

Given this potent mixture of competition, rebellion, emotion, and hormones, it is hardly surprising that the atmosphere became sexually charged in many camps. Boys told dirty jokes, recited risqué poems, composed lewd limericks, made up obscene verses to songs, and bragged about their sexual experiences, real or imagined. Many boys who thought they would be hit by a bolt of lightning if certain thoughts entered their minds or crossed their lips learned to their surprise they could venture into new territory without being burned to a crisp.

Not a few boys discovered girls in summer camp. If a sister camp happened to be nearby, there was always the possibility of a summer romance, that rite of passage that became part of the social development of so many middle-class youths. Inevitably, there would be official visits back and forth, organized social evenings, and the like, but what made the phyical proximity of boys and girls camps so alluring was the opportunity for clandestine contacts. It really did not matter whether anything serious happened when a boy sneaked over to see a girl or she stole a visit with him. The mere fact they had been together was enough to send a boy's status in the camp hierarchy soaring.

Whether they got together during chaperoned events or met in secret, boys and girls who attended summer camps frequently developed serious cases of "puppy love," plunging them into the joys and sorrows of adolescent romance. In many cases, longing glances quickly gave way to holding hands, hugging, and kissing, with precocious couples progressing to more advanced behavior. Yet even if a summer romance did not develop, a boy could always hope. Describing the diary he kept on the eve of World War I at Camp Kiamesha, Kinsey's friend wrote, "There were comments, mostly enthusiastic, on all the girls I met, and it is amazing how many even where up there in the backwoods; although relations with them all were very non-tactile as judged by the standards of these days."[53]

No doubt this complaint was common. Many boys failed to develop summer romances, and those who did often discovered that mountain air did not curtail their own inhibitions or those of their sweethearts. Then, too, there was the issue of adult control. Despite the best efforts of young people to escape adult supervision, most camps did a pretty good job of keeping tabs on their wards, as a camp's reputation depended on its ability to uphold traditional morality. Camp owners and counselors maintained a constant (and for the most part, successful) vigil to prevent unsupervised contacts between boys and girls.

Still, summer camps did offer other erotic possibilities. Preoccupied with heterosexual behavior, camp authorities paid less attention to what boys and girls did by themselves. In Kinsey's case, this meant he had thirteen summers, first as a camper and later as a counselor, to enjoy relaxed adult supervision, to be alone with other boys, and to explore his own sexuality, whether alone or with others. Like the public boarding schools of middle- and upper-class Victorian England, summer camps in the United States often became sexual schoolrooms in which more advanced peers (or in some instances their adult counselors) did the teaching. Here the prohibitive voices of preachers, parents, and teachers grew faint, as boys both observed and listened to one another. After all, boys who sat around a campfire or slept together in tents had plenty of time to talk about sex, and at this stage in their development many boys were eager to learn and ready to act.[54]

Overriding the prohibitions of parents and other influential adults, most middle-class boys of Kinsey's generation masturbated because their compulsion to do so was stronger than their will to abstain. Many campers retreated to the woods or to outhouses or bathroom stalls to masturbate, while others retired to sleeping bags or their cots. Despite his best efforts and overwhelming guilt, Kinsey succumbed to the same temptation. As an adult, Kinsey told Gebhard a poignant story. It involved one of Kinsey's guilt-ridden charges who came to him and confessed to masturbating. The boy was upset in part because he thought masturbation was sinful, but also because he believed it would hurt his health. Gebhard recalled, "Kinsey had a long heart-to-heart talk with him, and Kinsey confessed to the boy that he also was troubled by this problem, and the only thing that Kinsey could think of to do was pray. So he knelt down beside this boy's cot, and they both prayed to God that they would be relieved of this terrible vice that had seized them."[55]

Masturbation did not set Kinsey apart from other boys of his generation, the overwhelming majority of whom masturbated during adolescence. What distinguished him from his peers was the strength of his self-condemnation. Kinsey prayed, asking God to forgive him and to give him the strength not to sin again. The Boy Scout manual (along with many doctors and moral instructors) advised boys to take cold showers to improve their health and to take their minds off sex: Kinsey took a cold shower every morning, a practice he continued for life. But neither prayer nor cold showers enabled him to stop masturbating. As a result, Kinsey was consumed by guilt—not the kind that can be managed with equilibrium, but the type that recurs (both consciously and subconsciously) and diminishes a boy's self-worth. Hard on himself under the best of circumstances, Kinsey let his self-accusations soar when he failed. Confronted with evidence of his own moral imperfections, he could not muffle that voice from within. He had no ability to protect himself from self-condemnation, no ability to grant himself absolution.

As an adult, Kinsey recalled his boyhood guilt with sorrow and anger. "It is most unfortunate and one of the worst sexual crimes ever committed that this fear of masturbation should have caused so much trouble for so many people," he wrote in 1950. Significantly, a close friend used similar language to describe Kinsey's reactions. According to Gebhard, Kinsey "felt it was criminal that young people had to go through a sort of phase of guilt and concern until ultimately they learned the truth and quit worrying. For example, like agonizing for years about the deleterious effect of masturbation and only in later life discovering that it was harmless."[56]

Perhaps the damage to Kinsey's psyche would have been just as costly if his interests had been entirely heterosexual. After all, there was more than enough guilt attached to adolescent sexuality by middle-class culture to traumatize a sensitive, striving boy. In his case, however, the burden of guilt over masturbation was doubtless increased by homoerotic fantasies.

During Kinsey's adolescence, homosexuality was all but invisible in the United States. Polite society avoided it like the plague. For example, when New York's leading newspapers, the *Times* and the *Herald,* covered Oscar Wilde's legal travails arising from his libel suit against the marquis of Queensberry, both papers declined to specify the exact nature of Wilde's crime or the charges brought against him, leaving readers in the dark about Wilde's transgressions. A glance at the *New York Times* index for the first two decades of the twentieth century reveals virtually no titles or headlines referring to homosexuality (or any of the other names it was called), and the same is true for the index to the *Reader's Guide to Periodical Literature.* The same reticence prevented sex educators from discussing homosexuality, and ministers did not feel the need to add the topic to their list of sins of the flesh.[57]

Despite this official silence, however, the public's image of homosexuality was filled with opprobrium. From Puritan times forward, biblical condemnations of homosexuality suffused American culture. Men who slept with men, warned the Book of Leviticus, committed an "abomination; they shall surely be put to death; their blood shall be upon them."[58] The apostle Paul struck a similar note, condemning lustful behavior between men (and between women) as "vile passions . . . against nature."[59] Over time, of course, the world view of Americans became more secular and less God centered, but the power of religious sanctions remained strong. After he became a sex researcher, Kinsey reported that religion was "still the prime source of the attitudes, the ideas, the ideals, and the rationalizations by which most individuals pattern their sexual lives."[60] As a man who had once been a deeply religious boy, he could attest to this truth with great personal conviction.[61]

The law provided a second source of condemnation. Colonial legal codes, which drew heavily on ecclesiastical law or the religiously inspired English buggery act of 1533, prescribed the death penalty for sodomy, and upon occasion it was enforced. By the middle of the nineteenth century, most states had abolished the death penalty for sodomy, though it remained a felony subject to harsh penalties. As late as 1950, all but two states classified sodomy as a felony, preserving an animus against homosexuality that could be traced back to the ecclesiastical courts of Puritan England.[62]

Medicine was the third body of knowledge that shaped the public's attitudes toward homosexuality. During the late nineteenth century, doctors invaded the province of the law and religion by advancing a disease model of homosexuality. Doctors sharply debated whether homosexuality was an acquired disease that afflicted individuals of weak character, or a congenital illness linked to biological degeneracy. Yet, whatever their thoughts on etiology, they replaced the notion of homosexuality as a discrete punishable offense with a much more expansive definition. Under the disease model, homosexuality encompassed a whole class of people believed to have their own language, dress, emotions, behavior, mannerisms, and even physical traits. As the French historian and social theoretician Michel Foucault has shrewdly observed, "the sodomite had been a temporary aberration; the homosexual was now a species."[63]

A species, to be sure, but hardly an attractive one. Elaborating on what they learned from religion, medicine, and the law, middle-class Americans developed their own ideas about homosexuality, and their stereotypes invariably cast gays in a negative light. The press might shy away from mentioning homosexuality in headlines, but newspaper articles with different legends presented a great deal of material on homosexuality. Invariably, these stories depicted homosexuals as violent criminals, child molesters, scandal mongers, and social misfits. Small wonder that Francis Matthiessen, an Oxford student who was soon to become a Harvard don and famous literary critic, warned his male lover in 1924 that if people ever learned their secret, "we would be pariahs, outlaws, degenerates."[64]

Matthiessen could have added "effeminate" to his list of pejoratives. The public's image of male homosexuals was largely shaped by male prostitutes who crossed-dressed as women and aped feminine speech and manners. Reflecting this popular image, the Chicago Vice Commission reported in 1911 that the city contained "a large number of men . . . who mostly affect the carriage, mannerisms, and speech of women; who are fond of many articles ordinarily dear to the feminine heart; . . . who lean to the fantastic in dress and other modes of expression, and who have a definite cult with regard to sexual life." The report went on to note, "Many of them speak of themselves or each other with the adoption of feminine terms, and go by girls' names or fantastic application of women's titles."[65] Similarly, a medical student from North Carolina was terribly distressed by "creatures [who] solicited on the streets" in Philadelphia. He reported being accosted between Chestnut and Walnut Streets "by an overdressed male pervert who began his solicitation in the usual way which was more or less inferential. His mannerisms and speech were, of course, exaggeratedly feminine and his face was clean shaven and highly decorated with cosmetics."[66] Throughout his life, Kinsey made it a point to wear masculine clothes and shunned any hint of femininity in his speech, mannerisms, office decor, and home furnishings.

Other popular stereotypes held that homosexuals could not whistle and that they exhibited a marked preference for green garments, worn as much for identification purposes as aesthetic reasons. In New York, however, the color of choice for homosexuals was red. "To wear a red necktie on the street is to invite remarks from newsboys and others—remarks that have the practices of inverts for their theme," wrote one observer of cravats near the turn of the century. The man made it clear that this knowledge was widely shared by boys in New York. "A friend told me once that when a group of street boys caught sight of the red necktie he was wearing they sucked their fingers in imitation of *fellatio*. Male prostitutes who walk the streets of Philadelphia and New York almost invariably wear red neckties," he added. "It is the badge of the tribe."[67] In fact, knowledge of homosexuality, while officially repressed, had become so widespread in New York that the public had coined a nickname for homosexuals: they were called "fairies," a slang term for fellators.[68] Schoolboys of Kinsey's day also were beginning to apply the term "queer" to homosexuals, though it is not clear whether it was used it as a noun or an adjective.[69]

Throughout Kinsey's boyhood, then, middle-class Americans placed same-sex relationships beyond the pale of civilized morality. Condemned as a sin, a crime, a disease, or any combination of the three (depending on who was doing the labeling), homosexuality violated every facet of Victorian sexuality morality. Sexual relations between people of the same sex shattered gender/role definitions, made a mockery of self-control and restraint, and separated sex from procreation in ways that seemed either unnatural or immoral.

Of all these offenses, the challenge to gender/role identities may have been the most troubling to middle-class Americans. Socialized from childhood into rigidly prescribed sex-linked behavior, they regarded homosexuality as a complete inversion of the way people were supposed to look, feel, think, and act. According to cultural prescription, "normal" men were rugged, strong, and masculine, while homosexual males were weak, swishy, effeminate creatures, with regard both to their physical appearance and to personality. In short, society's image of homosexuality was unrelentingly hostile. Condemned by the Judeo-Christian tradition as a heinous sin, branded by the law as criminal, and diagnosed by physicians as pathological behavior, homosexuality, in the words of one historian, marked homosexuals "as inferior—less moral, less respectable, and less healthy than their fellows."[70]

Hidden within the middle class's rigid sexual code were important basic assumptions about human nature. The custodians of morality believed that all behavior was subject to rational control, that behavior was, in effect, entirely consensual and voluntary. Steeped in this belief, middle-class Americans thought that young people could be taught to internalize the tenets of civilized morality and control their sexual behavior.

But the guardians of morality were wrong. They could no more prevent some boys from becoming homosexuals than they could keep most boys from masturbating. Every group to which Kinsey belonged as an adolescent—his church, his schools, the YMCA, and the Boy Scouts—harbored boys who masturbated and boys whose primary sexual attraction was to members of the same sex. Yet, if homosexuals were everywhere, Kinsey had no way of knowing it. Paradoxically, they were as invisible as they were ubiquitous. The custodians of morality could not prevent homosexuality, but they could force most homosexuals to hide their feelings and behavior, leaving many alienated and awash in self-loathing and guilt.

By the time he had finished high school, Kinsey must have felt confused, isolated, and alone. Every social institution with which he had contact (family, church, schools, youth groups, etc.) had prepared him to be a heterosexual; nothing in his environment had taught him how to be a homosexual. In the middle-class world of Kinsey's youth, a boy who felt attracted to other boys could only see himself as a sinner, a criminal, a diseased degenerate, or any combination of the three.

Nothing in this binary thinking allowed a boy who masturbated or who had homoerotic desires to feel good about himself. How could he be a Christian and surrender to the "heinous sin of self-abuse"? How could he be attracted to other boys and still be both moral and masculine? Still, how could he remain pure when temptation abounded? Then, as now, there was no escaping homosexuality in American society. Beyond question, it occasionally surfaced in the male culture around him, most likely at summer camps; and in all probability, masturbation was the hook. Whether out of fear, guilt, or shyness, most boys masturbated alone. Most but not all. Goaded by adolescent curiosity, pressured by hormones, and emboldened by peer support, some boys masturbated in pairs or even in groups. These sessions served as sexual clinics where beginners could learn from more advanced boys, some of whom were eager to show their dexterity and technique.

A few of the bolder boys elaborated group masturbation into a game. Not listed in any official catalog, this most secret of camp competitions was known to generations of campers as the "circle jerk." The players formed a circle and masturbated themselves or the boy next to them, depending on the rules. The boy who ejaculated first won the prize, which typically was a pot of money formed by equal contributions from the contestants. A favorite variation was to turn the "circle jerk" into a prank. In this version, the lights were turned off, and boys who were in on the ruse would whack their fingers against their wrists to simulate the sounds of masturbation and wait for the victim to claim victory. The lights would then be turned on to examine the proof, embarrass the "winner," and amuse the crowd.[71]

Is this homosexual behavior? Maybe so; maybe not. It was not uncommon for campers of Kinsey's generation to develop strong attachments or even crushes on one another. Often couched in terms of admiration, most crushes did not amount to anything and remained secret. Some boys, of course, made the leap from silent infatuation to overt behavior. Not a few explored erotic possibilities with each other, consummating their first homosexual acts together, while others acted out their feelings by horsing around or wrestling, content, at least for the moment, to touch in "manly" ways.

Kinsey had just entered adolescence when he attended his first summer camp in 1908. Therefore, from his earliest experiences he was subject to the same rush of hormones as the other boys in camp. Yet, given his extremely repressive upbringing, it is difficult to imagine this novitiate engaging in overt sexual behavior with others. In all probability, the boy who had joined the other children in that basement in Hoboken had become an adolescent who had internalized a host of sexual inhibitions. This does not mean, however, that Kinsey was untouched by the sexually charged atmosphere of summer camps. An alert, perceptive boy with sharp ears and keen eyes, he cannot have missed what was going on around him, and the very fact that other boys were defying societal injunctions must have impressed him greatly. Dirty jokes, irreverent gibes at authority, calculated lapses in manners, and overt sexual behavior—what was a boy with his training to think?

No doubt, Kinsey's first reaction was disapproval. As a deeply moral young man, he had to condemn such behavior. Religion, parents, and middle-class culture demanded no less. Yet it is not hard to imagine disapproval giving way to other emotions over time. In all probability, the behavior of boys less rigid than he intensified Kinsey's internal conflicts, leaving him deeply unsettled. Watching others defy authority and assert their independence cannot have been easy for a boy who had been dominated all his life, but as the summers passed he may have developed a growing tolerance (if not a grudging admiration) for boys who had the courage to challenge parental constraints.

In all probability, though, Kinsey remained too conflicted to do more than watch the irreverent, insouciant boys of summer. Yet observation itself can become a form of vicarious participation. Insofar as he allowed himself to interact with others, Kinsey probably limited himself to low-intensity behaviors such as voyeurism and exhibitionism. Voyeurism would have offered Kinsey a role, albeit passive, in a world he dared not join, and the same held true for exhibitionism.

Does this mean that Kinsey peered into tents and ran naked through camp? Probably not, as neither suited his demeanor. A more plausible scenario would have him sneaking glimpses of boys while they dressed, watching them in the shower, and attaching much value to what he saw. Similarly, slow casual movements when he undressed or appeared naked before other boys would seem a better match with his personality. Pursued in this manner, voyeurism and exhibitionism would have allowed Kinsey to express, at least in subtle ways, his sexual interest in boys without arousing their suspicions. At any rate, since Kinsey practiced high levels of voyeurism and exhibitionism after he reached adulthood, it is hard to believe that these behaviors did not appear first during adolescence, if not in the manner conjectured here then in one of his own making.

What is clear is that this pious boy lost his ongoing battle with masturbation and was consumed by guilt for doing so. Given how badly he wanted to control his urges, Kinsey must have been tough on himself every time he masturbated, especially if, as seems likely, masturbation was accompanied by homosexual fantasies. How tough? Tough enough to turn masturbation itself into an act of penance; tough enough to punish himself with savage brutality. Every boy who masturbates develops his own technique, a way of performing the act that maximizes his sexual enjoyment. In secret, Kinsey found pleasure through pain.

Fourteen steps above the second floor of his home in South Orange was Kinsey's own private space, the converted attic that contained his bedroom, a storage room, and a secret hiding place.[72] There he hid from his family and the world the instrument he used to seek both sexual pleasure and physical pain. For many years his secret remained hidden. Then in the late 1960s and early 1970s, William (Bill) Gury, a lifelong resident of South Orange, who served as a ward captain in the Essex County Republican Party, got to know Kinsey's younger brother, Robert, a fellow Republican who lived in nearby Livingston. One evening at a Republican function, Gury and Robert started talking and both men were surprised to learn that Gury lived at 107 Prospect Avenue, South Orange, the house Robert's family had occupied when he was a boy.[73]

To prove he had once lived there, Robert sent Gury on a mission. Robert told him, Gury recalled, "that if I went into my attic and looked under some tin that had been nailed to the nine inch planks, the original flooring in the attic, I would find under the tiny hole burned in the wood planks." After he got home that evening, Gury had a look for himself. "I went to the attic; I did find that piece of tin; I opened it up; and sure enough there was the hole he said his 'crazy brother' had burned in it with his Bunson burner. And sure enough it was there, still charred," declared Gury.[74]

To Gury, it was obvious that the hole was a secret hiding place where a boy might put "treasures of some sort." The opening was not big, he explained, barely large enough to admit a hand, but it served as a passageway to a spacious compartment below. "I put my hand down in the hole between the beams and felt around and came up with, as I remember, a business card from some business in Newark that was very, very old," Gury explained, " 'cause I can remember that the telephone number had only three digits." He was right: the card was very old, as three digit numbers were in use before World War I in Newark and South Orange.[75]

Probing deeper into the hole, Gury pulled out a second object, a very curious item indeed. He described it as "a piece of wood that I recognized as a brush back . . . [which is to say] the back of a brush which had probably been a hand-drawn, hand-sewn brush from many years ago." How Gury came to know so much about brushes is simple: he had once been a brush salesman, and he could tell at a glance whether a brush had been made by machine or whether it was an old-time handmade brush. There was not the slightest doubt in his mind that the object he found in Kinsey's attic was very old.[76] Gury described the brush back as "just a little bit bigger than you would envision a tooth brush, with holes drilled at one end where the tufts (of whatever the brush flow was) had been sewn or, as they say, hand drawn into that brushback." A prudent man not given to speculation, Gury added, "What its purpose was I have no idea. There were no bristles, just the wooden back to the brush."[77]

Gury's inability to conceive of a use for the brush back is understandable. In a sense, he was hostage of his original premise that the hole in the floor was a hiding place for a boy's treasures. Yet boys bury more than treasures; they also hide secrets—dark, fearful things about themselves they do not want others to know. For a boy like Kinsey, a righteous boy whose sense of self-worth depended upon rigid self-control, nothing needed to be kept more hidden than the fact that he masturbated and that he did so with a foreign object inserted up his penis. Kinsey's secret hiding place was not a treasure trove but a torture chest that contained the instrument of his pain. By late adolescence, his masochism was well advanced. He had progressed beyond straws and was inserting a brush back up his penis, a practice he would continue for life, at times changing the instrument of self-torture, but never the point of attack.

Because the urethra is rich with nerve endings (as any reader who has been catheterized can testify), Kinsey's masturbatory technique must have produced exquisite pain, both while he did it and for days after when he urinated. Here his behavior was entirely consonant with his goal, for "pain" comes from the Latin word *poena,* which means "punishment" or "penalty." By late adolescence, if not before, Kinsey's behavior was clearly pathological, satisfying every criterion of sexual perversion.[78]

Yet, in one important sense, Kinsey was no different from other boys.

Like them, he wanted to gratify his sexual needs. What separated Kinsey from most boys was that he took an important detour on the road to sexual gratification. The overwhelming majority of boys are not permanently harmed by the guilt they feel when they violate sexual taboos against masturbation. They know masturbation is wrong, but they find ways to rationalize their behavior that allow them to keep their guilt from consuming them.

Kinsey was less fortunate. Somewhere along the line, he veered off the path of normal development and was pulled down a trail that led to tremendous emotional conflict and self-negating physical abuse. Something inside him would not let him satisfy his sexual urges without first paying a price in physical and emotional pain. Somehow, Kinsey's adolescent sexual fantasies got stuck on preliminary scenes of humiliation and punishment that his own sensibilities and peculiar needs endowed with erotic significance.

While their specific content remains unknown, there can be no doubt that Kinsey's masturbatory fantasies involved acts of violence and/or humiliation directed at him by others.[79] Originating in the vast majority of cases in childhood, such fantasies are defining features of masochism. In all likelihood, Kinsey's first appeared when his family still lived in Hoboken, perhaps during one of his many childhood illnesses when imagination was his constant playmate. At any rate, he doubtless elaborated and embellished upon his childhood fantasies many times after his family moved to South Orange.

What turned Kinsey in this direction? The most plausible explanation is that his childhood sexual stirrings filled him with terror. Lustful thoughts that other boys managed to entertain and cope with made him feel tense and anxious because they tapped into something in his unconscious. At the deepest level, sex frightened Kinsey. Subconsciously he was afraid of something he associated with sexual thoughts and behavior, particularly the sex act itself.

What did he fear? The best guess is punishment. Apparently, at some point in his development, most likely in early childhood, Kinsey came to attach a huge load of guilt to his erotic feelings. Perhaps he feared the wrath of God and the loss of spiritual salvation or the loss of parental love. Maybe he feared both. During his adolescence, strictures from the outside world doubtless exacerbated Kinsey's internal torment. Puberty must have fallen on him like an avalanche, burying him beneath tons of guilt. For puberty brought the need for sexual release, and, wet dreams excluded, masturbation was the only solitary outlet open to him. And every time he succumbed to temptation, masturbation must have brought every authority symbol in the world crashing down on him. After all, the moral teachings of his family, religion, purity crusaders, YMCA officials, and Boy Scout leaders—indeed of the whole sexually anxious middle-class culture that dominated urban life in the United States during his boyhood—told Kinsey that "masturbation was death." Having internalized the moral constraints of his society, he felt compelled to punish himself with savage brutality every time he failed to satisfy those demands.

But how could inner turmoil of this magnitude remain hidden from public view? Only with great difficulty. Kinsey had to struggle to keep his inner life secret, but he managed to do so. Not only was he above suspicion; he was admired and approved.

By the time he graduated from high school, then, Kinsey was trapped within two separate and conflicting identities: a public boy who met his parents' every wish, and a private boy who secretly violated their most basic moral strictures and punished himself for doing so. Although it must have taken enormous energy to keep these identities in equilibrium, Kinsey accomplished this task with remarkable success. Still, it was a precarious balancing act, requiring constant reinforcement by success in the public world and rigid control over the self he showed others. Unfortunately for Kinsey, the success that he had enjoyed in school ended the moment he entered college.

5

"FINALLY, HE JUST REBELLED"

 very year at the close of spring semester, proud parents, joined by relatives and friends, pack hot, crowded auditoriums to watch young men and women walk across the stage and receive their high school diploma. It is a time for joy and celebration, a ceremonial passing of the torch from one generation to the next. Kinsey's high school graduation took place in June 1912, in the auditorium of Columbia High School. Following the invocation by the Reverend George A. Hahns, rector of the Church of the Holy Communion, the Glee Club performed several vocal selections. Sandwiched between their singing and the conferring of diplomas by Charles G. Fielding, president of the South Orange Board of Education, were brief addresses by five graduating seniors who spoke at the invitation of the faculty.

As class valedictorian, Kinsey had an assured place at the podium. Instead of proclaiming the optimism of youth, however, his remarks struck a more embattled note, as though he expected life to be filled with struggle. "Often we shrink from a farewell," Kinsey began. While partings "seemed cruel," they should be viewed as "a rich experience" because "in farewells only are goals touched." "In our farewell," he told his classmates, "we reach the goal of our High School course."[1] Following his opening, Kinsey took the opportunity to direct traditional thanks to teachers and parents, and then to remind younger students of the need to work.[2] He then exhorted himself and his comrades to arms: "Classmates: we look, and behold a nation calling; it rots in graft, it sinks in paganism. Our youth burns in zeal for truth. We *will* fight!" he shouted. "As the years go on, let our aspirations still ring true, that at the end we may say, 'we have fought the good fight, we have finished our course, we have kept the faith.' "[3]

If Kinsey's address struck a familiar chord, it was because he was following a cultural script that could have been heard in thousands of high schools in the United States on the eve of World War I. As an ode to the molding powers of education, as a declaration of gratitude, respect, and deference to parents, as an affirmation of the work ethic, and as a civic-minded pledge to save the nation, Kinsey's speech placed him among the dutiful, pious sons of the middle class. Precisely because his remarks were so predictable, they signaled he was prepared to embark on the final stage of the difficult voyage from boyhood to manhood. Graduation from high school marked a watershed in a boy's life. Following graduation, many middle-class youths immediately made the transition to manhood by entering the work force, often by joining the family business or by entering the employment of family friends. Because the new industrial order had grown more technical and bureaucratic, however, middle-class youths increasingly attended college.

Young men who pursued higher education entered a period of extended adolescence in which they remained dependent on parents for financial support. Yet most college students enjoyed more freedom than they had known in high school, especially those who went away to college, where they could escape parental surveillance. For those who remained at home and commuted, college could be depressingly similar to high school, as parental authority and family routines still ruled their lives. This was Kinsey's predicament. Instead of marking a new beginning, college brought him little freedom. For two years following his graduation from high school, he remained at home, fulfilling his father's commands and expectations.

Kinsey applied to one college and to one college only, the Stevens Institute of Technology, and for the first time in his life his academic skills appeared to fail him. The trouble began with his college admissions examination. Stevens tested students on two groups of subjects: candidates had to pass all the subjects of Group I, which included algebra, geometry (plane and solid), arithmetic, trigonometry, physics, chemistry, English, and U.S. history; and they had to pass at least four subjects from

Group II, which featured modern foreign languages, Latin, Greek, ancient history, medieval history, English history, shop practice, drawing (mechanical or freehand), physiography, and physiology.[4] These requirements were less formidable than they appeared. Stevens offered the examination twice annually, first in June and again in September. To pass, a candidate needed only a score of sixty points out of a hundred in each subject, and applicants could take each group separately and retake any subject they failed. Moreover, results from the tests in algebra, geometry, trigonometry, physics, and chemistry could be applied to an applicant's credit for sixteen months, and the results from the tests over the remaining subjects remained valid for three years. In effect, this allowed candidates to stockpile passes over one group of subjects against the day they could conquer the second group.[5]

Kinsey took the test covering the subjects in Group I in September 1911, the beginning of his senior year in high school. He passed all four, scoring 81 in arithmetic, 74 in chemistry, 80 in Latin, and 74 in ancient history. If these numbers sound decidedly undistinguished for a straight-A student from an excellent high school, his performance on the second part of the test was even more puzzling.[6]

Kinsey did not attempt the subjects in Group II until June 1912, the month he completed high school. He passed physics and French by the skin of his teeth, with scores of 60 and 61, respectively; he squeaked by in U.S. history and English, scoring 65 in both; but he posted failing marks in geometry (54), algebra (46), and trigonometry (55). Following a summer of preparation, he repeated the latter three examinations in September 1912 and managed to score 85 in geometry, 74 in algebra, and 85 in trigonometry.[7]

How could a boy who had done so well in high school perform so poorly? His preparation in science and mathematics cannot have been weak, as he had earned top honors in these subjects in an extremely competitive school. And what are we to make of his scores in English and history, when he had excelled at both subjects in high school? It is difficult to avoid the conclusion that Kinsey deliberately performed poorly. Apparently, he did so on the admissions test because he did not want to attend the Stevens Institute. Inspired by Natalie Roeth, his high school biology teacher, and drawn by his love of nature, he had his heart set on a career that would allow him to combine biology and the outdoors. Certainly, his classmates knew his ambitions. Had not the class prophecy predicted he would become "a second Darwin"?

But Kinsey's father had other plans. The "great 'I' man" ordered his son to attend the Stevens Institute to study mechanical engineering. As Clara Kinsey later remarked with obvious sarcasm, "everybody except his father knew he wanted to be a biologist." Clara had no doubt about her father-in-law's motivation: "[Kinsey's] father was an engineer, and he wanted his son to be an engineer." Of course, money also played a role, she added, since "sons of faculty could attend without paying tuition, and that was a factor too."[8]

No doubt, money was an issue. In 1912, tuition at the Stevens Institute ran $225 for the academic year, rooms ranged from $84 to $168, board ran $210, and incidental fees added another $60, bringing the yearly total to about $600, a tidy sum. Since Kinsey did not have to pay tuition and since attending Stevens allowed him to live at home and commute by train to campus, the cost for his freshmen year was reduced to the $60 incidental fees, plus the cost of commuting.[9]

But, as Clara suggested, easing the strain on the family budget was not the primary reason Kinsey's father pushed him into engineering. As a self-trained engineer, he wanted his elder son to follow in his footsteps. Alfred Seguine Kinsey found much to commend in his profession. Engineers were the architects of the Industrial Revolution, the builders of urban civilization, and the self-proclaimed best problem solvers in the world. From the age of fifteen, he had devoted himself to training engineers, and if he was not teaching engineering he was busy practicing it, consulting with factories and shops that paid handsome fees for his services. Why shouldn't he want his son to be an engineer? It was a career that offered important work, financial security, and prestige.

Yet more was at stake than a career. It was predictable that Alfred Seguine Kinsey would dictate his son's occupation because the issue of control colored every aspect of their relationship. Telling a son what to do with his life came easily to a man who placed little premium on independence in his children. Alfred Seguine Kinsey had a heavy psychological investment in Kinsey's choice of careers since he saw his son as an extension of himself. Despite his professional mobility, Alfred Seguine Kinsey had not satisfied his own ambitions. Though he belonged to several professional engineering societies, served as a consulting engineer to many factories and shops, headed a department in a strong college of engineering, and functioned as an engineer in everything except academic pedigree, his accomplishments could not obscure the fact that he had never acquired the formal education his profession required. In ordering his son to study engineering, Alfred Seguine Kinsey was using him to take care of his own unfinished business.

For Kinsey, the thought of becoming an engineer was abhorrent. His desire for a career that could combine biology and the outdoors was heartfelt and pressing. It rested on intense curiosity, intellectual passion, and much more. Just as nature study had allowed Kinsey to separate himself physically from his parents, it had filled important emotional needs. Through his mastery of the outdoors, he had been able to demonstrate competence, control, and masculinity, traits his father routinely quashed at home. Attending Stevens would end Kinsey's bid for independence. There he could become an engineer but not a naturalist, as biology was not part of the curriculum.[10] Despite his passion for biology and his desperate need for independence, Kinsey did as he was told. He felt bound by the same cultural script that he had articulated in his valedictory address. All his life, Kinsey had been taught to obey the rules, to measure his worth by how well he satisfied what God, his parents, and his community expected of him. "So, since his father wanted him to be an engineer," explained Clara, "he went to Stevens Institute for two years, and he hated it."[11]

Kinsey entered the Stevens Institute in the fall of 1912, one of ninety-one freshmen whose survivors eventually composed the class of 1916. The school was tiny. It had fewer than forty full-time faculty members and barely three hundred students, providing a student/faculty ratio of eight to one. Stevens prided itself on the close academic community its small size made possible. As the school catalog boasted, "It is the policy of the Institute to have the Professors come in personal contact with the students so that each Professor shall know, as far as possible, the characteristics of every one of his students, and each student shall be impressed with the personality of his Professors."[12]

The faculty tried to do more than train engineers. Freshmen who enrolled at the Stevens Institute stood on the threshold of adulthood. Over the next four years, they had to complete the transition from boyhood to manhood, and Stevens aimed to see that they did. Like all colleges, it served as a cultural transmitter, a kind of finishing school, where deans and professors (patriarchal figures all) polished the character traits prescribed by Victorian culture for turning middle-class sons into middle-class men. In the words of the *Stute,* the beloved school paper, "from the moment of his entrance," the newcomer at Stevens embarked "upon the serious preparation for life."[13]

Freshmen were constantly reminded how fortunate they were to attend Stevens. "Stevens is a name to conjure with in engineering," the *Stute* assured freshmen in 1912, adding with obvious pride, "Indeed, it may well be doubted whether any other school of engineering can boast nobler or more splendid traditions."[14] And everywhere they turned, students were told that engineering was the world's most important profession. They heard it from professors, they repeated it to each other, and they absorbed it from the distinguished engineers who came to campus to lecture. While most guest speakers focused on technical topics, rare was the engineer who did not seize the opportunity to proclaim his profession's seminal contributions to the history of world civilization or its unique standing in the new industrial order.

During his first semester at Stevens, for example, Kinsey heard Willard Beahan deliver a lecture entitled "Engineering of Men," a sweeping overview of the profession. Beahan began with the birth of engineering from ancient wars and moved quickly to the rise of civil engineering in the Industrial Revolution. The bulk of his talk, however, was devoted to labor unrest and the need for industrial peace.[15] A progressive member of his profession, Beahan assigned engineers a key role in restoring harmony to the nation's factories and shops. In essence, he envisioned a hierarchical workplace presided over by paternalistic professionals, who would rule by technical expertise and reason, tempered by compassion. "An engineer must stand behind his employees," asserted Beahan; "he must give them transportation, loan them money, help them along, for an employer is big and strong, while the employee is weak." Indeed, Beahan's basic rule, which joined the golden rule neatly to Christian stewardship, was "Do unto others as you would they should do unto you and then a little more."[16] A noble fellow, Beahan was the kind of speaker deans bring to campus to inspire students and send them scurrying to the library to burn the midnight oil.[17]

Offering its own sermons on success, the *Stute* stressed the importance of competition and hard work. Under the heading "Freshmen! Here Is Some Good Advice," the student editors echoed their parents when they told freshmen in 1912, "First of all, you must work diligently and consistently and maintain a high standard of scholarship."[18] Freshmen the following year heard the identical message. Under the legend "Freshmen! You Are Now in Stevens," the *Stute* declared in 1913, "We most earnestly advise you to do your work day by day. As time goes by you will realize the wisdom of this course; and the early formulation of regular habits of study will help you materially in later years."[19] Students encountered the same message in the unofficial school poem, a ditty entitled "Work with a Will," which consisted of six stanzas, five of which ended with a repetition of the title.[20]

Kinsey did not need to hear this message, as he had long since internalized the work ethic. In keeping with school requirements, he signed up for a heavy load in the fall of 1912, enrolling in seven classes. His performance that semester, however, was mediocre, not to say poor. He posted a 76 in German, a 68 in mechanics, a 67 in descriptive geometry, and a 66 in chemistry. Kinsey did somewhat better in his other subjects, earning a combined average of 86 in English and logic, an 81 in mathematics, and an 85 in mechanical drawing.[21]

Predictably, Kinsey did his best work in shop practice, which his father taught. The course met for an hour, four times weekly for fourteen weeks. Kinsey made a 91 for the semester, a clearly superior performance.[22] Yet how he must have detested sitting at the feet of the man who had destroyed his dream of studying biology, the man he had to please in a subject he despised. Nor can Kinsey have enjoyed the hours they spent together commuting, which gave his father added time to stress the importance of engineering and to demand diligent study.

Kinsey's grades declined in the spring term. His scores in chemistry and in mechanics rose slightly, and he was able to hold his own in English and logic, but his marks dropped in mechanical drawing and in mathematics. Moreover, he failed descriptive geometry, with a score of 46 (he repeated the final examination during the summer, scoring 86), and squeaked by in physics, with a score of 61. Most telling of all, Kinsey's grade in shop practice—paradoxically, at once his easiest and most difficult course—fell to 85. While the drop was only six points, it might as well have been a hundred for what it said about his state of mind.[23]

Summer offered an opportunity to catch up, pass the courses he had flunked, and, most important, regroup away from home while he earned the money to finance his education. During his college years, Kinsey worked in a variety of YMCA and BSA summer camps, each of which offered an endless supply of younger boys eager to learn about nature. At college, he was barely hanging on; at camp, he was a born leader, respected and admired. "He was always soft-spoken and informal," recalled Joseph K. Folsom, a fellow counselor who worked with Kinsey for several summers; "what he had to say was listened to eagerly because it came as from someone who had no axe to grind, no personal vanity or desire to show off his knowledge, but whose eyes and ears and mind were so keen that anything he had to say seemed to make the world a more interesting place to live in." While stressing that Kinsey had "many of the earmarks of what we called a 'genius,' " Folsom insisted that Kinsey "participated in almost everything and was thoroughly enjoyed as a companion by everyone."[24]

College was a different story. Kinsey's sophomore year brought no more success than his first. During the fall term in 1913, he did well in English and logic (89), but his other grades ranged from average, a 78 in both German and chemistry, to awful, 51s in descriptive geometry and in mechanics. All told, he failed three courses, each of which he passed upon reexamination, with a 70 or better.[25] In the second term of his sophomore year, Kinsey's grades improved slightly, but overall his performance remained shaky. While he scored a 97 in English and logic, he flunked two more engineering courses, mechanics and mathematics.[26]

What had happened to Kinsey? From the time his family had moved to

South Orange, he had excelled in school. Thanks to hard work and a keen mind, he had compiled an outstanding record, resulting in peer respect, praise from teachers, and parental approval—the kinds of positive reinforcement every boy craves. Kinsey's high school honors had also benefited his father, the man he most longed to please. During Kinsey's freshmen year at Stevens, his father ran for a place on the South Orange Board of Education, winning a three-year term. As a self-made man, Alfred Seguine Kinsey no doubt campaigned squarely on his record. Was he not well qualified, this college professor, church leader, purity crusader, Boy Scout booster, and perennial do-gooder? Still, his candidacy cannot have been hurt by standing for election less than a year after his son had earned top academic honors in that very school system. Any voter who doubted his qualifications had only to look at his son.

At least until his son entered Stevens. How it must have pained Kinsey to show his grades to his father. Kinsey was tired of doing his father's bidding, bone tired. Years of feeling cramped, years of feeling suffocated by parental domination, and years of feeling that he somehow did not measure up had left Kinsey angry and bitter. So he rebelled in the only way he knew how. He made bad grades. He could have done the work, had he applied himself (after all, the second time around he passed all the courses he failed). He chose not to succeed. For the first time in his life, education had become an ordeal for Kinsey, something to be suffered and endured.

Kinsey's social life offered little relief. He remained the same loner at Stevens he had been in high school. While students who reside at home and commute to college often miss out on college life, Kinsey's social isolation derived from his personality more than from his residence. No less than in high school, he had great difficulty making a place for himself in a male culture where status rested not merely on academic performance but on active participation in student government, athletics, and social clubs, along with a veneer of worldly sophistication and calculated forays against authority.

Still, if student complaints can be taken seriously, social life at Stevens was sparse for everyone. While professors routinely took students on field trips, they visited power plants and factories, not art galleries or museums. The curriculum contained few humanities courses, and guest speakers lectured almost exclusively on topics related to engineering. Speakers on current affairs rarely found a place in the hour assembly students had to attend weekly. One of the *Stute*'s few references to national politics during Kinsey's freshman year was a story covering President-elect Woodrow Wilson's surprise visit to the campus on January 26, 1913. Unfortunately, Wilson came on a weekend when many students were away. But when he entered the dining hall of the Castle, the most elegant building on campus, "the Tech men rose and gave a 'Long Yell' for the President-elect."[27] Lectures on music and art were rare. During Kinsey's two years at Stevens, students heard only one public lecture on music. Devoted entirely to the physics of sound, it bore the title "Sound Waves."[28] The single lecture on art during Kinsey's tenure was also technical in nature. When John W. Lieb, Jr., class of 1880, showed lantern slides of Leonardo da Vinci's art, sketches, and manuscripts, he focused on the great artist's "extensive studies in the realm of mechanics."[29] In short, the Stevens Institute was a trade school. Students came not to pursue the life of the mind but to prepare for a career. According to the *Stute,* they shared one paramount interest, "a job."[30]

Although Stevens set a meager cultural table, it did feature a variety of social activities. On the eve of World War I, a dozen or so organizations and clubs flourished on campus, most of which solicited new members among entering freshmen at the beginning of the fall term. Beyond question, sports dominated the social calendar. Football ruled the roost, but Stevens also fielded teams in baseball and lacrosse. Moreover, various nonathletic organizations vied for student support, including three distinct music clubs, a drama society, a debate club, an engineering society, and the YMCA, which was extremely active on campus.[31]

Throughout Kinsey's years at Stevens, the *Stute* promoted athletics like a religion. The editors placed enormous emphasis on winning. When the football squad got off to a bad start in 1912, the editors flatly asserted, "The team is not really doing its best." In fact, they thought they detected a lack of commitment and toughness in their gridiron heroes. The chief problem with the players, complained the *Stute,* "is that they do not practice conscientiously. They do not come out enough to become hardened, with the result that they are soft when they go into the game, and every little knock bothers them."[32] At Stevens, as elsewhere, there was a pervasive fear that young men could not compete successfully in contests of strength and physical prowess.

Hoping to restore the gladiatorial spirit, the *Stute* constantly urged freshmen to participate in athletics. In 1913, the editors importuned new arrivals, "If you can play football we want you out on that field every blessed day; if you want to play lacrosse, now is the time to learn and the upper classmen are here to show you how, and if you are a baseball fiend, get your arm in trim for next spring." Almost as an afterthought, the editors added, "If you have musical ability, join the music clubs."[33]

It was no accident that music came dead last. At the time Kinsey entered the Stevens Institute, the "jockocracy" was so strong on campus that nonathletic students or those whose tastes ran to the aesthetic had been placed on the defensive. Students who preferred music to sports freely confessed their second-class status in the competitive world of males, acknowledging that they faced an uphill battle attracting boys to the band. Fearing sports might eclipse music altogether, one music lover at Stevens wrote anxiously in 1913, "Just at present football is occupying a great deal of undergraduate attention. This should not, however, cause the music clubs to remain in the background. The physical prowess of all is not as great as that required for football, and it is from these men that the musical talent for Stevens must be supplied."[34] During his freshman year, Kinsey heard much the same appeal. In 1912, the *Stute* pleaded, "As it is not very difficult to make a position in the various clubs all those upper and lower classmen who have any musical talent should come out."[35]

Kinsey answered the call his freshman year, auditioning for the Orchestra, one of three music clubs on campus. Although the Orchestra already had a pianist and had lost only two men to graduation in 1912 (a light blow compared to the Glee Club and the Mandolin Club, which lost five men each), it offered Kinsey a place and he accepted. As before, he looked to music for social acceptance, a goal that would prove even more elusive in college than in high school.[36]

During Kinsey's freshman year, the music clubs launched a drive to revive music at Stevens. (The *Stute* complained that the enthusiasm shown by the music clubs the preceding season "was considerably below what it had been in the past.")[37] In October 1912, about sixty men, including a strong contingent of freshman, met in Jimmy Denton's old room to discuss plans for the upcoming year and to meet the new music coach, Harry W. Weber. Described as "an enthusiastic worker of wide experience," Weber was hired for the express purpose of revitalizing music at Stevens.[38] Yet the best idea for reviving the music clubs came not from the new coach but from the music club's manager, Mr. Wellman, class of 1913. Recognizing the difficulties they were having securing off-campus books, Wellman promised to pay five dollars to any man who could arrange "contracts for concerts on the Hudson or in the southeastern part of Connecticut."[39] Sadly, there were no takers. A few months later, the *Stute* reported that the music clubs were sitting idle in March and April, ordinarily busy months, owing to "the inability of the management to secure any engagements . . . although the manager, Mr. Wellman, did his best."[40]

A hard taskmaster, Coach Weber worked diligently to bring his troops up to speed, holding three practices a week. By the end of the fall term, the *Stute* judged the school's musicians "well-trained" and boasted, "The music clubs will not fear comparison, either as to their 'repertoire,' or the quality of their work, with the clubs of any of the 'big' colleges."[41] In February 1913, the music clubs appeared at the Cranford Casino, in Cranford, New Jersey, where "the demand for encores almost exceeded the supply." While the *Stute* complained that "all three clubs were ragged in spots," it concluded that "the 'breaks' were neither frequent nor serious and the concert may certainly be classed as a success." Best of all, the concert was accompanied by a dance, where the Stevens men "were treated royally by their hostesses." During the ten dances that evening, "the Stevens men were able to fill as many as they cared to, being introduced to fair young ladies galore."[42]

At Stevens, then, music exposed Kinsey to a social life he had not known in high school. The music clubs at Stevens, including the Orchestra, played mostly popular music. It was aimed at the new consumer society, particularly its incipient youth culture that was beginning to emerge in America's urban centers on the eve of World War I. Like it or not, Kinsey had to play music that was frowned upon in communities like South Orange.

Kinsey's distaste for popular music ran so deep that he honestly could not understand what other people saw in it. Conversely, his love for classical music was so strong that he longed to share it with others, especially when doing so gave him a chance to make friends, earn respect, and demonstrate his musical talent and formidable knowledge. Throughout his freshmen year, though, Kinsey had to bide his time. As a member of the Orchestra, there was no way for him to shine. But all that changed the following year.

As a sophomore, Kinsey seized center stage. No longer reduced to playing as one of many, he frequently performed as a soloist, one of two orchestra members so honored. Ironically, his debut took place in Hoboken, on December 12, 1913, at the high school auditorium, the site of the musical clubs' first concert of the season. The Orchestra led off with "The Whip March"; the Glee Club sang "About Clocks" and "There Are Women"; the Mandolin Club, which the *Stute* complained "made the poorest showing," performed several selections from *Pinafore;* and the quartet rendered "Old Man Moses," described by the music reporter as "a venerable vender of nosegays, who was afflicted with a gay nose," followed by "a coon song as an encore." Saving the best for last, the *Stute* declared, "One of the greatest surprises of the evening was the remarkable rendition of the piano solo by Kinsey, [class of] '16. Before playing, he tried to lead us in an imaginary flight over the mountains and into the valley of the home of the birds. Although a 'bird' of a speech, our anchor caught in the first tree top and we lost sight of him until he came back to earth and began to play."[43] Kinsey was lucky the ridicule was so light. No other member of the music clubs presumed to lecture his audiences, not that evening or any other. The thought probably never would have occurred to anyone but Kinsey.

Yet if Kinsey had any inkling his behavior struck others as odd, he did not show it. In January 1914, the music clubs traveled to Brooklyn, New York, for their second concert of the season. They played at the Ridge Club at what the *Stute* called "an informal dance."[44] Kinsey again was featured as a soloist. And once again he preceded his performance with "an impromptu speech," at the conclusion of which he "favored the audience with Moskowski's 'Polonaise.' " Though he had to overcome "the disadvantage of being compelled to use a rather poor upright piano," Kinsey "played with all the vigor and force that the composition required, and in response to [demands for] an encore, gave Chaminade's Scarf Dance."[45]

Kinsey's next solo performance followed the same pattern. When the music clubs offered their home concert at the Castle in March, Kinsey delivered "a verbal description of Chopin's remarkable Polonaise, A Flat Major," and then proceeded to give "a very capable performance of this work." "As an encore," reported the *Stute*, "he played most delightfully Grieg's Birdling."[46] While the school paper had no praise for his lecture, its reporter added, "For the performer's consolation, may it be said there were some discriminating ones in the audience who appreciated his delicate interpretation of this charming composition."[47]

Traveling to Newark, the music clubs gave their final concert of the season in May. "Kinsey's solo was well received," the *Stute* observed, "and he was forced to encore twice by playing one of Chopin's Waltzes and finally Grieg's 'Birdling.' "[48] Kinsey's fondness for the "Birdling" cannot have been lessened by the openings it offered for nature discussions, which, together with its beauty, probably explains why the piece appeared so often in his repertoire. At any rate, it became a Kinsey trademark to lecture his audience before each performance and, in later years, before each program of recorded music he assembled for students or friends.

Still, Kinsey continued to shun most features of the youth culture that enthralled his classmates. College is a time for maturation, a period for loosening family ties and relaxing parental controls. Unlike many of his classmates, Kinsey did not patronize the bars, dance halls, penny arcades, and amusement parks of nearby New York. In college, as in high school, he presented an image of unsullied virtue. Kinsey did not drink, smoke, dance, or heed the siren song of popular music. Nor did he date, a fact which was starting to look more peculiar than it had in high school.

Apart from music, debate was Kinsey's only other extracurricular activity. On April 10, 1913, near the end of his freshman year, about twenty students met in Room D at the Castle to organize a debate club. Juniors dominated the meeting, as the other classes supplied no more than one man each. Representing the faculty, Professor Charles O. Gunther (mathematics) stressed "the need of more practice at Stevens in public speaking." The students then elected temporary officers, established criteria for membership, and agreed to hold the club's first debate on April 22, 1913. Their first topic was an issue that was being debated all across the nation: "Resolved, that it is desirable that the [recently completed] Panama Canal tolls should discriminate in favor of American ships."[49]

Kinsey joined the Debate Club during his sophomore year, but little evidence has survived regarding his performance. The one debate in which we know he participated focused on one of the most popular traditions at Stevens: the Flag Rush, a contest that pitted freshmen against sophomores. Unlike many athletic events, the Flag Rush required little special equipment. Every fall, representatives of the two classes fashioned a pole, eight inches in diameter and sixteen feet in length. To this pole they attached two cross arms. A canvas flag displaying the numerals of the sophomore class was fastened to the top of the pole, and the pole was driven four feet into the earth, leaving twelve feet above ground, the bottom six of which were carefully smoothed and padded.

Divided into two eight-minute halves, the contest had but one objective: capturing the flag. Members of the sophomore class defended the flag; members of the freshman class attempted to seize it. The rules stipulated, however, that the sophomores be allowed to surround the pole before the contest began. Together with the manner in which the flag was attached to the pole, which made it all but impossible to tear loose, this gave the sophomores an enormous advantage, as they routinely placed their heaviest and strongest men close to the pole and surrounded them with additional bodies to repel attackers. Indeed, the freshmen counted it a victory just to reach the second crossbar before being knocked or dragged back to earth.[50]

More donnybrook than sport, the Flag Rush was an occasion for bloody noses, broken bones, and bruised bodies, a raucous ritual that allowed combatants to demonstrate their masculinity by brute force. Tradition demanded that members of both classes throw their bodies into the melee with great abandon, and despite an occasional editorial criticizing the unfair advantage given the sophomores, the *Stute* supported the contest wholeheartedly. It viewed such contests as opportunities to display "class spirit" and praised the combatants for "parading around the track and arousing each other's combativeness by endearing salutations" during the warm-up period.[51] Most students responded to this peer pressure by joining the battle. No fewer than eighty-four freshmen from Kinsey's class rushed the flag, though five members had to be excused, the *Stute* explained, "because of being football men or of physical inability to take part."[52] Though the latter groups had valid excuses for not participating, the *Stute* still included them on its "Black List," the revealing name the paper assigned to its final tally of freshmen and sophomores who did not participate in the carnage.[53]

As a long-term recipient of medical dispensations, Kinsey was a two-time member of the "Black List." No doubt, he would have favored abolishing the contest. Yet, when the opportunity to debate the Flag Rush arose near the end of his sophomore year, Kinsey and his opponent were not given that option; rather, the proposition read, "Resolved, that the Flag Rush should include the total enrollment of both classes and that the rules should provide equal possibility of winning to each, regardless of numbers."[54]

Kinsey argued the affirmative; his opponent, the negative. According to the *Stute*, "both sides of the question were excellently given." Certainly, the judges shared this assessment. After deliberating twenty-nine minutes, they returned with a split verdict, giving the nod to Kinsey on the first part and to his opponent on the second.[55] It was the last time Kinsey ever had to share any part of victory in a formal debate.

Kinsey's willingness to join the debate team at Stevens was a good sign. Whether motivated by loneliness, a desire to make friends, or the need to assert himself, he was willing to expose himself to the risk of personal defeat in one-on-one verbal combat. It showed that two years of personal misery and academic floundering had not crushed his spirit, that he still possessed a measure of self-confidence. Yet it appears that Kinsey had been drawn to the power of language long before he entered the Stevens Institute. Decades later, a friend recalled Kinsey's saying that he had discovered as a boy that winning verbal contests could help make up for his lack of physical prowess. As an adult, Kinsey believed that developing these skills in boyhood had later helped him persuade people to give their sex histories.[56]

Kinsey needed self-confidence. As his sophomore year drew to a close, he stood at the crossroads. For two years, he had been a square peg in a round hole, a young man whose heart belonged to biology but whose mind had been mortgaged to engineering. Filial duty required him to finish his degree at Stevens, but he wished fervently to leave. Ironically, two guest lecturers spoke on campus that spring as Kinsey pondered his future, and their talks framed the choice he confronted: whether to stay at Stevens and complete his degree in engineering, or transfer to another college and prepare for a life of public service working with young people.

Kinsey heard the case for public service first. At the beginning of the spring term of his sophomore year, the assembly hosted a talk by a Mr.

Estes, a YMCA representative. According to the *Stute*, "he showed that Y.M.C.A. is purely a 'man' proposition and worthy of consideration from men." This accomplished, Estes turned to the task at hand, which was to ask for volunteers to teach immigrants. Were they aware, he asked his audience, that only two years earlier three men from Stevens, working under the auspices of the YMCA, had taught citizenship to a group of Italians living in Hoboken? Surely others, he pleaded, would be inspired by their example to donate their services to this worthy cause. Seconding his request, the *Stute* declared, "We get out of life exactly what we put in it, and time spent helping others is well spent. Doing things gives a fellow ability and makes him more sure of himself."[57] Kinsey did not have to be told that the YMCA did God's work. He had spent six summers in "Y" camps and knew the organization well. Nor did he have to be reassured that the YMCA deserved the attention of real men. His own sense of masculinity had been built in no small part in programs sponsored by the YMCA and the Boy Scouts.

A week later, a second speaker offered Kinsey the chance to contrast the YMCA's message with a blueprint for the future that represented his father's vision of utopia. The man who articulated that vision was one of the Stevens Institute's most famous alumni, Frederick W. Taylor, class of 1883. A brilliant engineer in his own right, Taylor had done important work on the process of heat treatment of tool steel. But that was not how he had earned a towering reputation as one of the most influential leaders of his day. In an age that proclaimed the "Gospel of Efficiency," Taylor had devised a formula to promote efficiency, raise production, and impose order on labor.

Taylor was obsessed with efficiency. While industry had long experimented with time and motion studies, the development of piece work, "scientific" approaches to labor relations, and other proposals for raising productivity, Taylor was the man who brought these concepts to the attention of American business. On the basis of careful studies of workers in factories (he actually used a stopwatch to time how long it took to perform different tasks), he worked out a program for centralized planning, systematic analysis, and detailed instructions. By giving management all the information and knowledge that workers and foremen had acquired through years of experience, Taylor was confident he could raise profits and place employers in firm control of the workplace. An extraordinarily gifted advocate of his views, he carried this message to businessmen all across the United States.

When Taylor visited Stevens on January 13, 1914, he came, in the *Stute*'s words, as "the father of scientific management." If anyone in America could make a young man want to become an engineer, surely it was he.

Standing before an admiring audience of faculty and students, Taylor described a world of rationalized markets, efficient factories, and contented workers, indeed a world of industrial order, prosperity, and peace. Presiding over it all were Taylor's fellow engineers, the true architects of the new industrial order. While admitting that some might think him narrow-minded for saying so, Taylor told his listeners "that the principles of Scientific Management are applicable to any kind of management and any undertaking where there is co-operation between employer and employee."[58] No skepticism greeted this pronouncement. Everyone in the audience knew that Taylor spoke for his age. Not only was he a first-rate engineer and consultant to titans of industry, but he was also a man's man, a fact that did not go unnoticed by the *Stute*. Praising his "great interest in athletics," the paper reminded its readers, "At school he was very active in sports and in 1881 he was one of the National tennis champions for doubles at Newport. He is now a very enthusiastic golfer."[59]

Taylor represented the world of Kinsey's father, while Estes embodied the world Kinsey loved. Perhaps listening to both men forced Kinsey to think about his own future with a clarity not possible when he had just finished high school. Or perhaps he simply took stock of his performance at Stevens, added up two years of failure, and came up with zero. Whatever the process, Kinsey made the most important decision of his young life in the spring of 1914: he resolved to leave the Stevens Institute and enroll in the fall at Bowdoin College, a small liberal arts school in New Brunswick, Maine.

For Kinsey, independence day fell a week early, on June 26, 1914, commencement day at the Stevens Institute. Kinsey and his family attended the exercises. While they were on campus, he went to the Registrar's Office, withdrew from Stevens, and asked to have his transcript sent to Bowdoin College, where he planned to transfer in the fall. Kinsey selected Bowdoin because he had heard it had a strong biology department.

Choosing a new school was the easy part; telling his father was the real challenge. Leaving Stevens meant defying his father, and that was something that Kinsey had never done, at least not in public. In all likelihood, he had postponed notifying the registrar until the last possible moment as a way of putting off delivering the news at home. But once he had withdrawn, Kinsey could delay no longer, as it was only a matter of time until word got back to his father.

Everything pointed to a cataclysmic explosion. There could be no negotiation, no give-and-take, no effort to find a middle ground, for his father did not know the meaning of compromise. No, Kinsey would have to present his decision as a fait accompli and then deal with the consequences. At a minimum, there would be angry shouts and emotional bullying. Since delay could only hurt his cause, Kinsey mustered his courage and delivered the news immediately after they arrived home from graduation. As Clara put it, "Finally, he just rebelled. He said he absolutely wouldn't go anymore."[60] But he did not stop there. The days of doing as he was ordered were over, Kinsey told his father: henceforth, he would be his own man and do as he pleased.[61]

Alfred Seguine Kinsey was shocked, stunned, and furious. To his authoritarian mind, Kinsey was guilty of filial rebellion, domestic treason most foul. Instead of crushing his spirit, all those years of keeping silent and doing as he was told had left Kinsey emotionally hardened and defiant, a boy whose outward compliance masked a strong will of his own. It was almost as though Alfred Seguine Kinsey did not know the defiant young man who stood before him. How could a boy who had always been so obedient, so perfect in every way, suddenly turn into a rebel?

If he could not run his son's life, Alfred Seguine Kinsey did not propose to finance his freedom. Kinsey's father refused to put another dime into his son's education. As he prepared to leave home, the only support Kinsey received from his family was a suit of clothing—worth twenty-five dollars.[62] Henceforth, Kinsey was on his own. Over the years ahead, there would be occasional visits home, largely to see his mother and siblings. But never again would Kinsey ask his father for assistance, and never again would he seek his permission or approval for anything, at least not consciously.

Kinsey had only a few weeks to find a way to finance his education. In midsummer he wrote to Kenneth Charles Morton Sills, the dean of Bowdoin College, inquiring about financial aid. "It is necessary for me to earn a part of my expenses, and a scholarship would naturally be of great help," declared Kinsey. He promised to help support himself in college and vowed to make good in his studies. "I am earning a good sum by camping this summer, specializing in Nature Study," he informed Sills. "I want to work throughout the college year. . . . I feel sure I can make good in scholarship." Kinsey then revealed his choice of careers: "After college I expect to enter Y.M.C.A. boy's work. I have worked with boys for several years, as Sunday School teacher, acting Scout master of our town troop of 65, Eagle Scout, as Vice President of the LaRue Homer Nature League, etc."[63]

The *Stute*'s parting advice to the men who were leaving that spring held a special meaning for Kinsey. Evoking the language of social Darwinism, the school newspaper told the members of the class of 1914 they would have to work hard and do their best because they were entering a world where "only the fittest survive." As he left home to resume his quest to become "a second Darwin," Kinsey had every reason to agree. Twenty years old and seasoned beyond his years, he had tasted life's struggles and had learned what it costs to survive.

"Loosen Up a Bit More, Al"

n the eve of World War I, Bowdoin College had an enviable reputation as "a nurturer of men." Located in Brunswick, Maine, five miles inland from the coast and twenty-eight miles northeast of Portland, Bowdoin possessed a proud heritage. Its graduates included President Franklin Pierce; General Joshua Lawrence Chamberlain, who held the Union line against the Confederates along the Little Round Top during the second day of fighting at Gettysburg; General Oliver Otis Howard, the commander of the Army of the Tennessee and head of the Freedman's Bureau; Robert E. Peary, the reputed discoverer of the North Pole; and Henry Wadsworth Longfellow and Nathaniel Hawthorne, two giants of American literature. Of course, Bowdoin could not claim to be the equal of schools such as Harvard or Yale, but for a young man like Kinsey, who wanted a respectable academic pedigree, Maine's premier private college had much to offer.

The campus itself was gorgeous. As one longtime admirer of the college remarked, "To walk through the Bowdoin campus is to walk through the history of American architecture." The central quadrangle, in particular,

ranked among America's most handsome, weaving examples of Federal period, Greek Revival, Gothic Revival, and Victorian architecture into a natural setting of great beauty. Connecting these buildings were paved
sidewalks where a man could stroll at sunrise, listening to the cries of seag-
ulls and breathing in the salt air from the ocean, a scant five miles away.[1]

At first glance, Bowdoin did not appear that different from the Stevens
Institute. Both schools had all-male faculties, all-male student bodies, and
tiny enrollments. Slightly larger than Stevens, Bowdoin employed 29 full-
time faculty members in the fall of 1914, who taught an undergraduate
student body of 384 students, including 81 juniors, the class that admitted Kinsey along with 4 other transfer students.[2] At 13 to 1, Bowdoin's
student/faculty ratio was higher than Stevens's, but low enough to enable
teachers to know all their pupils by name. Both institutions, moreover,
drew their student bodies overwhelmingly from their home states, suggesting reputations more regional than national.

Like Stevens, Bowdoin preached that the purpose of college was to
"mold a man," the "Bowdoin man."[3] And Bowdoin, too, supported a virile male culture, including a full complement of varsity sports—rowing,
baseball, field and track, football, tennis, hockey, fencing, and golf. Bowdoin had its own annual "Flag Rush" between sophomores and freshmen,
who also fought pitched battles on the streets of Brunswick in an event
called Parade Night. According to the college's official historian, Parade
Night became so rowdy it had to be banned in 1913 because school officials feared "that some one might be killed."[4] Apparently, the concern was
short-lived, as the freshmen and sophomores renewed their warfare the following year. Describing the melee in the fall of 1914, the *Bowdoin Orient*,
the school paper, reported that a student who toured the battlefield the
next morning "picked up a bucketful of broken noses."[5]

Yet, despite these superficial similarities, Stevens and Bowdoin had little in common. Stevens was a trade school; Bowdoin a liberal arts college.
This difference alone gave the schools different missions and approaches.
In place of narrow, technical training, Bowdoin offered a liberal arts curriculum of sciences, humanities, and fine arts. The college had its own art
museum, the Walker Art Building (1894), a fine example of classical revival
American architecture. Bowdoin also boasted an unusually strong library,
housed in Hubbard Hall (1903). It contained over 113,000 volumes
(more than ten times Stevens's holdings), including one special collection
that must have thrilled Kinsey, the complete works of Louis Agassiz, the
great Harvard zoologist-geologist. Moreover, Bowdoin set a rich cultural
table for its students, sponsoring a speakers series that brought distinguished lecturers in the sciences, humanities, and fine arts to the campus.

In short, if Stevens sought to meet the needs of an industrial, urban society, Bowdoin sprang from a philosophy of education that originated in the preindustrial world of rural America.[6]

Like many schools in New England, Bowdoin traced its roots to the eighteenth century, when the district of Maine belonged to Massachusetts and was something of a wilderness. As part of their struggle to tame the region and bring civilization to the frontier, the Great Proprietors, a group of wealthy land speculators in Maine, founded a college to educate a number of their sons as Congregational ministers. In 1794, the Massachusetts legislature passed an act "to establish a College in the Town of Brunswick and the District of Maine, within this Commonwealth." Samuel Adams, the new governor, signed the bill on June 24, 1794, and Bowdoin College, named in honor of James Bowdoin, a former governor of Massachusetts, took its place among the new republic's institutions of higher learning.[7]

Throughout the nineteenth century, Bowdoin College struggled to fulfill the ambitions of its founders, mirroring in many respects the history of higher education in New England. Over time, Bowdoin shed its seminary image, abandoned its classical moorings, and developed into a secular institution. The shift from a religious to a secular college was most evident in the curriculum. Bowdoin broadened its course offerings, instituted the elective system, and established a new program leading to the bachelor of science degree. But the act that best symbolized Bowdoin's transformation into a modern liberal arts college came in the late 1890s when Greek was dropped as a requirement for admission, a reform that passed only after three years of debate by the trustees. Still, the college never abandoned its evangelical Protestant fervor. Many Bowdoin graduates continued to enter the ministry, and the college encouraged its students to uphold public morality and to improve society through voluntary associations and individual acts of Christian charity.[8]

The man who presided over Bowdoin's transformation was the Reverend William DeWitt Hyde, who in 1885 became the college's seventh president. Like five of his six predecessors, Hyde was an ordained Congregational minister. While he struggled to preserve the college's heritage of producing Christian gentleman, Hyde was committed to completing Bowdoin's transition from an old-fashioned school with a narrow curriculum based on the classics and mathematics into a modern institution of higher learning. Furthermore, he demanded and received first-rate teaching from his faculty. At a time when many college presidents pressured professors to publish, he proclaimed vital teaching as Bowdoin's primary mission.[9] Moreover, Hyde had a clear idea of who should receive a liberal education. An ardent admirer of the stamina and pluck of Maine boys (particularly those who hailed from small towns and villages) and a firm believer in the value of a small, tightly knit college community, he nearly persuaded Bowdoin's board of trustees to limit enrollment to Maine residents![10]

Under Hyde's capable leadership, Bowdoin College earned an excellent reputation throughout New England. Indeed, its praises could be heard as far away as New Jersey. In 1907, Kinsey's hometown newspaper, the *Chronicle,* published a laudatory article on Bowdoin, noting that the college "has preserved its high standing from the first."[11] Certainly, it was Bowdoin's quality that had attracted Kinsey. After he arrived in Brunswick, he told a fellow student he had transferred to Bowdoin because of the high reputation of its faculty in biology.[12]

By the eve of World War I, President Hyde was in the twilight of his career, and the school's day-to-day administration fell pretty much to Dean Kenneth Charles Morton Sills, the man to whom Kinsey had addressed his request for admission and financial assistance. A classicist by temperament and by training, "Casey," as Sills was called by faculty and students alike, was himself "a Bowdoin man," summa cum laude, class of 1901.[13] Following graduation, Casey did graduate work at Harvard and Columbia and then returned to his alma mater in 1906 as an adjunct professor of Latin, rising quickly through the faculty ranks before moving into administration. As dean of Bowdoin College (1910–17) and later president (1917–52), Casey maintained a lifelong passion for Dante and a fierce dedication to the principle that liberal arts colleges should teach a comparatively few courses extremely well.[14]

More than most deans, Casey was a hands-on administrator who made a point of getting to know every student and faculty member. Each fall, he met individually with every student in the college. No doubt, Kinsey heard a great deal about hard work and the need to set goals when he met with Casey. Casey was appalled by how little thought students gave to the future. "In talking over the plans of students," he wrote in 1914, "it is surprising to find how very few of them have any idea of what their life work will be."[15] Casey used these counseling sessions to urge students to strive for academic excellence. He never tired of reminding students that their alma mater's success rested on intellectual achievement and that they bore equal responsibility with the faculty for building Bowdoin's reputation. Therefore, freshmen got an earful about the need to develop sound study habits, while upperclassmen were told to view their remaining years in college as a piece and to work single-mindedly toward their goals.[16]

Kinsey cannot have taken Casey's advice lightly, as he knew full well he owed his admission to the dean. He also knew that Casey played a big role in handing out scholarships at Bowdoin. In those days, colleges did not have multiple layers of bureaucracy, so Casey wore a number of hats, including those of director of admissions and director of financial aid. His concerns about character came to the fore where money was concerned. Casey headed the faculty scholarship committee that met during the spring term, usually in February, to evaluate requests and assign student aid. Though he shared Hyde's almost transcendental faith in the flinty character of Maine boys, Casey worried that their moral fiber might be damaged if colleges awarded scholarships prematurely. Therefore, Bowdoin developed a firm policy of promising no financial aid to first-semester students. This policy also reflected Bowdoin's limited financial resources. In 1916, for example, Bowdoin distributed a paltry $12,000 in scholarships to 155 lucky students selected from a field of 223 applicants.[17] Bowdoin's scholarship policy also mirrored Casey's commitment to the work ethic. He believed that students should be forced to earn financial assistance by performing well in their first semester of college work. In his view, proving one's mettle provided a wholesome tonic to those who made the grade. "It is not well for recipients of any form of beneficiary aid," he averred, "to be without such a tonic."[18]

Indeed, Casey's daunting standards were the stuff of legends at Bowdoin. During Kinsey's senior year, the *Bugle,* the college yearbook, contained a mock scholarship application form that listed twelve questions students had to complete. Typical questions included: "Have you any rich uncles who would be liable to leave money to the college, if you were granted this scholarship?" "Have any of your ancestors left criminal records?" and "Do you solemnly swear to return all money given you by a scholarship with interest at nineteen per cent within two years from graduation?"[19]

Bowdoin College in 1914 represented a good educational buy, with or without financial aid. Tuition was a flat $100 per year, which together with all other items (listed in the school catalog as incidental fees, rent for a double room, lighting, board, books and stationery, and washing) created a grand tally that ranged between $350 and $400 for most students.[20] This was less than two-thirds of the charges at Stevens.

In all probability, Kinsey paid part of his expenses during his first term at Bowdoin with money he had earned as a summer camp counselor. His letter to Sills requesting aid did not arrive until the end of July, months after the college normally distributed its funds.[21] Moreover, Casey's policy of not offering new students assistance until they proved themselves almost certainly applied to transfer students, and Kinsey's grades from Stevens hardly seemed strong enough to warrant aid. To supplement his own funds, he received financial assistance from Mrs. C. P. Mayhew, a wealthy widow whose husband had been active in community affairs in South Orange. Mrs. Mayhew recognized a deserving young Christian gentleman in

Kinsey and subsidized his college expenses after his father disowned him.[22] Kinsey came to Bowdoin to study biology, and he was not disappointed. Bowdoin had a solid scientific community, with its own building, traditions, and strong personalities. Bowdoin's science program began in 1864 when the college received a gift from Josiah Little of Newburyport to expand the teaching of science. Four years later, Bowdoin created the Josiah Little Professorship, an endowed chair dedicated to "the promotion of practical science."[23] While its first two occupants left little to mark their passing, Leslie Alexander Lee, the third Josiah Little Professor, became a legendary teacher in an institution where every faculty member was expected to teach well.[24]

In addition to the Josiah Little Chair, Bowdoin boasted a state-of-the-art science building.[25] Anyone who saw Searles Hall got a message: in an age when size denoted standing and power, this imposing three-story Elizabethan-style edifice built in 1894 underscored how highly Bowdoin valued science. Chemistry occupied the north wing, physics the south wing, and biology the third floor, each with its own separate entrance and stairway. Significantly, each entrance was lighted. Commenting on the brightness of those lights, the *Orient* complained that they would ruin the campus's beauty on moonlit nights. Glaring or not, those lights were needed. The day of the gentleman professor who dabbled in scholarship was passing. A new breed of scholar was taking his place—professors who returned to their laboratories at night to tend experiments, tabulate data, and write scholarly papers and books. The night lights at Searles Hall signaled that Bowdoin wanted a science faculty that had internalized this new work ethic, a faculty that would be driven by heroic ideals peculiar to science, such as the pursuit of truth and the quest for discovery.[26]

By the time Kinsey arrived at Bowdoin, first-rate biologists occupied Searles Hall. Lee's successor was Manton Copeland, who joined the faculty in 1908 as an instructor and sole member of the biology department. A graduate of the Lawrence Scientific School (1904), in Cambridge, Massachusetts, Copeland received his M.S. (1905) and Ph.D. (1908) from Harvard University. Copeland climbed the academic ladder quickly, rising to the rank of full professor in 1910.[27] Two years later, Bowdoin ended his professional isolation by hiring a second biologist, Alfred Otto Gross. A native of Atwood, Illinois, Gross received his bachelor's degree from the University of Illinois (1908) and his Ph.D. from Harvard University (1912). Both men spent their entire careers at Bowdoin (Copeland retired in 1947, followed six years later by Gross), and they eventually shared the Josiah Little Chair in natural science.[28]

When they arrived at Bowdoin on the eve of World War I, Copeland and Gross were Young Turks on a faculty ripe with age. Both were bright and energetic, yet each traveled a different road over the decades that followed. In many respects, Copeland was the more typical liberal arts college teacher. Thanks to his Harvard connections, he received frequent invitations to join the colony of marine biologists who descended every summer on Woods Hole, at Buzzards Bay, Massachusetts, to research, write, and exchange information. Bowdoin College stoutly supported these expeditions. In announcing Copeland's plans to work at Woods Hole during the summer of 1915, for example, the *Orient* proudly declared, "The College has obtained a table at the Woods Hole laboratory for this year."[29] Copeland worked on animal physiology throughout his career, but he published very little. Teaching interested him far more than research and writing, so he devoted himself to preparing strong courses in introductory zoology, botany, vertebrate ecology and behavior, organic evolution, and special laboratory and field investigations.[30]

Of the two professors, Kinsey was more drawn to Gross. Kinsey and Gross met at a student reception the week Kinsey arrived at Bowdoin. Gross was only eleven years older than the reserved young transfer student, with no trace of academic stuffiness. A little conversation quickly showed they had much in common. Not only was each the first member of his family to attend college, but each could trace his interest in birds back to boyhood. "He revealed a great interest in ornithology so I invited him to go on a 'Bird Hike' early the next morning," recalled Gross. Once they entered the woods, Gross witnessed the results of the many hours Kinsey had spent reading books and studying nature firsthand. "He knew his birds thoroughly and exhibited great enthusiasm for every bird seen," declared Gross. "This initiated regular week-end trips in quest of bird lore."[31]

Within a matter of months, Kinsey and Gross developed a close student-professor relationship. Seeking sympathy and support, Kinsey told Gross about his troubles with his father. Half a century later, Gross recalled learning how Kinsey's "parents wished that he would become a mechanical engineer but his interests were too deeply rooted in biology." In fact, Kinsey practically attached himself to Gross, seizing every moment he could with his esteemed young professor. Eager to repay Gross's pedagogical attention and personal kindnesses, Kinsey used his musical talent to entertain Gross and his family. Referring to their early-morning bird patrols, Gross declared, "Many times he would arrive at our home before we were up and we would be pleasantly awakened by beautiful classical music he played on our piano down stairs. In those days our house was never locked and was open for students who never needed to knock or ring the door bell."[32]

Gross was a bear for scholarship. When he died in 1970, he had 265 scholarly publications to his credit, including books as well as articles.[33] Gross's scientific interests plunged him into political activism, demonstrating how a life in science could lead a scholar beyond the borders of his cloistered campus. During the early 1920s, he fought a losing battle to save the New England heath hen from extinction (campus folklore had it that the last one in North America died in his arms). Gross also donated his time to many organizations, serving as president at one point or another of the New England Bird Banding Society, the Massachusetts Audubon Society, and the Maine Audubon Society. Happily, he lived to see admirers give his name to a newly discovered bird, to an island in the Arctic off Baffin Land, and to a trail in the jungles of Barro Colorado Island, in Panama.[34]

It was scientists like Gross who fulfilled the promise of Searles Hall, putting those night lights to regular use. His devotion to science was absolute, his work ethic fierce, his curiosity boundless, and his energy bountiful. Of course, when Kinsey arrived at Bowdoin, most of Gross's accomplishments lay in the future, but he was already displaying the drive and devotion to scholarship that shaped his career. The epitome of a high-octane young scientist, Gross offered the perfect role model for Kinsey.

Gross was impressed with Kinsey. Calling him "very versatile in his biological interests," Gross noted that Kinsey was particularly "fascinated with snakes and at one time had more than twenty of the reptiles of assorted species and sizes." To learn more about hibernation in snakes, Kinsey designed an experiment that involved direct observation, the scientific method he believed had the greatest validity. According to Gross, "when late autumn arrived he buried [the snakes] in a hole four feet deep in our back yard. He was delighted to find them dormant but all alive the following spring. He took detailed notes of the experiment."[35] By verifying things by direct observation and keeping careful notes on his research, Kinsey was starting to think and act like a scientist. Soon his interest in science became common knowledge at Bowdoin, particularly his fascination with snakes. As the *Bowdoin Bugle* remarked, "on entering his room one never knows whether Mr. Kinsey or a large, able-bodied snake is going to greet him."[36]

Kinsey made the most of Bowdoin's rich curriculum in biology. One of his classmates, who described Kinsey as "a brilliant student," believed he "took about every course in Zoology and Biology which the College offered."[37] Perhaps this was exaggeration, but not much. Kinsey took sixteen hours of zoology during his junior year, plus a four-hour general biology course and courses in psychology and sociology.[38] During his senior year, Kinsey took fifteen more hours of zoology, and his name appeared both semesters on the "Straight A Men" list published in the school paper.[39] In 1916, the school yearbook contained some good-natured kidding from his classmates about Kinsey's pursuit of academic excellence: Nickerson, coming out of a philosophy exam,—"How did you hit it?" Kinsey—"I hit it pretty well. I hope I get an A in that course. All I got was one B last semester." Nickerson—"That's all I got, too."[40]

Kinsey lived for biology. Putting those entrance lights at Searles Hall to nightly use, he displayed the strong aptitude for sustained work that became a defining feature of his adult personality. As another classmate recalled, "He spent hours on end, days and evenings, in the laboratories and in soaking up the knowledge of professors Copeland and Gross."[41] Kinsey's hard work paid handsome dividends. In the spring term of his junior year, the *Orient* announced, "Kinsey [class of] '16 has recently been chosen as assistant in Zoology."[42] Bowdoin named about fifteen student assistants a year, generally one per department. By tradition, these awards went to the outstanding junior or senior in each discipline.[43] That Kinsey received an assistantship after only one semester suggests that he had rapidly eclipsed his peers.

Kinsey was assigned to Copeland, who immediately put him to work reorganizing the college's biology museum.[44] According to the school paper, the various collections "lacked systematic arrangement" and needed special efforts "to remedy this defect." Labor-intensive and tedious, the project involved arranging synoptic and local collections of invertebrates, amphibians, reptiles, birds, and plants in cases; building new cases to house the college's collections of mammals of Maine; and building another case to exhibit embryological specimens. Tracking this mammoth project, the *Orient* reported in April 1915 "that nearly all specimens are now labeled and indexed. Kinsey '16 is museum assistant and with other students is carrying out Dr. Copeland's excellent plan of organization and systematic arrangement."[45]

Eager to prove himself, Kinsey attacked his duties with dispatch and diligence, investing as much time as it took to produce outstanding exhibits. Mounting specimens, labeling them properly, and arranging them for display required close, careful work—precisely the type of tasks at which he excelled. Copeland was particularly pleased by Kinsey's organization of the department's insect collection. Kinsey prepared an exhibit, and the finished product was exquisite. "I used it on my lecture table for several years," Copeland recalled decades later.[46]

Kinsey's duties also included field trips to the woods of northern Maine to trap live animals for the Bowdoin Museum. On one expedition over Thanksgiving recess, he and the classmates who accompanied him were walking across a beaver pond when Kinsey fell through the ice. His clothes froze stiff in the bitter cold Maine air, and he singed the bottom of his long johns trying to dry them over a campfire. His sodden shoes posed an even greater problem, but Kinsey devised a solution. He filled them with oatmeal (a breakfast staple on the trip), removed it, dried the oatmeal over the campfire, and then repeated the process until all the moisture was absorbed. History does not record whether the young campers subsequently ate the oatmeal.[47]

Outside the classroom and the museum, Kinsey devoted himself to the Biology Club, one of several social organizations created to promote academic excellence on campus. Founded in 1913 with Professors Copeland and Gross as faculty sponsors, it boasted thirty-one members when Kinsey joined in 1914. The club sponsored nature hikes (including overnight field trips), volunteer work on the biology museum's collections, informal seminars in which members presented papers, and formal lectures by distinguished scholars from other institutions.[48] The Biology Club drew its members from the ranks of biology majors, the best of whom went on to graduate school. Directing students to the program that had trained them both, Professors Copeland and Gross sent their prize students to Harvard, establishing a pipeline between Bowdoin and one of the nation's top graduate programs in biology.[49] Doubtless this message was not lost on Kinsey: if he excelled, Harvard was within his grasp.

Kinsey quickly established himself as a leader in the Biology Club. At the start of his second semester at Bowdoin, he delivered before it a paper entitled "Cross-Pollination." During his senior year, he joined Professor Copeland and a fellow student (and chief rival for top honors in biology), Lawrence Irving, in leading a discussion on the theme "The Nature of Study in Summer Camps."[50] Kinsey capped off his senior year by serving as president of the Biology Club, succeeding Irving.[51]

Because of his growing expertise, Kinsey was able to earn money by teaching off campus. During the second term of his junior year, the *Orient* reported that Kinsey had been hired to teach nature study in a nearby private school the week after Easter vacation.[52] Summers brought Kinsey additional opportunities to turn his outdoors skills and knowledge into cash. Bela W. Norton, a classmate, recalled that Kinsey "traveled extensively among summer camps while in college and gave talks and demonstrations on Nature Study which were much in demand at that time." Describing Kinsey as "a generous man, most considerate and friendly," Norton added, "He helped me obtain a job as a counselor in a first rate boys' camp in Maine for three summers while I was in college."[53]

Although biology consumed the lion's share of his time and energy, Kinsey threw himself into several other extracurricular activities at Bowdoin. Picking up where he had left off at Stevens, he joined the Debate Club his first semester and went on to earn a seat on the Debating Council, the governing body of student officers that coordinated and managed the college's debate program.[54] At the time, debate was the most popular nonathletic student activity on campus.[55] The *Orient*'s editorial welcoming freshmen that fall assigned athletics and debate equal value, a rare parody on college campuses of the day. In contrast to those at Stevens, where the school paper implied that real men played sports, Bowdoin's editors simply told newcomers that a student "should engage in some one of the various things for which he has a liking."[56]

Bowdoin supported a strong debate program. On campus, the contests included a freshmen-sophomore debate, a debate restricted to juniors enrolled in English 5, and the Bradbury Prize Debate, the competition that determined the best team debaters at Bowdoin, regardless of class standing. The stars of these contests joined Bowdoin's varsity debate team, which represented the college in the Intercollegiate Triangular Debating League, a three-way competition among Bowdoin, Hamilton, and Wesleyan. Finally, Bowdoin's most articulate students competed for individual prizes in public speaking. On campus, they battled for the Class of 1868 Prize, a prestigious award at Bowdoin; off campus, they participated in the New England Intercollegiate Public Speaking League, composed of the finest orators from Amherst, Bowdoin, Brown, Wesleyan, and Williams. The school paper followed each contest and league in detail, tracking the winners and losers with the same enthusiasm it brought to athletics.[57]

Kinsey's first outing came in English 5, a required course students took in the fall of their junior year. In November 1914, two teams faced off to debate the topic "Resolved, That Bowdoin College should be limited to about 400 students." Kinsey and his partner took the affirmative, and they won.[58] The following month Kinsey, teamed with two partners, debated an opposing three-man team on the subject "Resolved, That laws should be enacted in the various states establishing the so-called indeterminate sentence." Again, Kinsey's team took the affirmative and, again, won.[59] The following week, the Debating Council selected Kinsey to serve as the presiding officer at the freshman-sophomore debate, a clear sign he had impressed his professors and peers.[60]

Kinsey's strong performance resulted in his first prize at Bowdoin. The *Orient* announced in February 1915, "The members of English 5 voted to award to Kinsey '16 that portion of the Hiland Lockwood Fairbanks Prize which is given annually for excellence in debating."[61] Though the cash award was modest, Kinsey no doubt appreciated both the money and the recognition.

Buoyed by his initial successes, Kinsey charged into the next level of competition. On January 25, 1915, he and twenty-two other students spoke at the tryouts for the Bradbury debates.[62] Two weeks later, the school paper announced the names of the twelve men selected for the first and second teams, each composed of six members (three for the affirmative; three for the negative), and Kinsey earned a spot on the affirmative squad of the second team. The paper also announced the debate topic for the year, a subject that weighed heavily on the nation during the early months of World War I: "Revolved, That the armament of the United States should be materially increased."[63] Kinsey's team won its match, earning second-place honors in the debate.[64] More important, he was one of eight men invited to join the varsity team to represent Bowdoin in the triangular debate with Hamilton and Wesleyan.[65]

In March 1915, Bowdoin's varsity team traveled to Middletown, Connecticut, where they went head-to-head with the team from Wesleyan College, debating the topic: "Resolved, That the naval strength of the United States should be materially increased." Once again, Kinsey's team took the affirmative, but this time the judges, who included a former governor of Connecticut, Henry Roberts, ruled for the negative. Overall, the triangular league debates ended in a draw that year, with each school "winning a debate and losing one."[66]

For Kinsey, however, the season ended in triumph. In May, the Debating Council met in Hubbard Hall to adopt a new constitution and bylaws, and to elect new officers for the 1915–16 academic year. It elected Kinsey president, the first of two club presidencies he won at Bowdoin (biology followed in the fall).[67] Kinsey had every right to be proud of this honor, as few club presidencies at Bowdoin carried more prestige than debate.

Kinsey's senior season was busy, if less eventful. As president of the Debating Council, he presided over two freshman-sophomore debates, and he devoted considerable time to coaching high school teams under the auspices of the Bowdoin Interscholastic Debating League, a program designed to foster debate in Maine's high schools.[68] When not presiding or coaching, Kinsey took his turn at debating. In the Bradbury Prize competition in 1916, contestants debated the topic: "Resolved, That Secretary Garrison's plan for reorganizing the military system of the United States should be adopted."[69] This time, Kinsey's team argued against the proposition, and won.[70]

It was no accident Bowdoin's debaters tackled the issue of preparedness. That topic dominated the college debate circuit because it was a question preoccupying the nation. When World War I erupted in Europe, most Americans supported President Woodrow Wilson's declaration of neutrality. But as time passed, the president came under intense pressure to build up the nation's military and navy, forcing him to give reluctant support to the very measures students at Bowdoin debated. Yet Wilson's own party was deeply divided over this issue, as many Democrats, led by William Jennings Bryan, remained strongly opposed to a military buildup, lest it hasten the drift to war. Many of Wilson's opponents, however, insisted that the best way to preserve peace was to prepare for war. Some took this position as a matter of prudence, while others, like the fiery Theodore Roosevelt, did so because they favored war. World War I cast a shadow over college life during Kinsey's years at Bowdoin. The fall he arrived, a major official of the Peace Society spoke on campus, arguing that the United States must remain neutral. Over the months that followed, Bowdoin students teamed with Princeton students to raise supplies and money for the Belgian relief project; Bowdoin professors lectured on the war in area high schools; Bowdoin men donated cigarettes to Canadian soldiers in the trenches, in the words of the school paper, "to help pass the weary hours"; and Bowdoin officials considered but declined an invitation by Henry Ford to send student representatives on the Peace Ship, Ford's private effort to end the slaughter in Europe. Still, as the months passed, Bowdoin men heard less and less about peace and more and more about preparedness.[71]

Bowdoin's resolute dean followed the war with the utmost urgency. "Outwardly every thing seems to be the same here," Casey wrote a friend in 1915. "But in reality the war is leaving its marks. A number of lads who used to make the summer merry are at the front, and nearly forty boys have gone from the village."[72] In truth, Casey was appalled by student apathy, and not without reason. When an enterprising newsboy began hawking papers every morning at chapel, the boys who bought them, observed a faculty member in disgust, "turned to the sports page rather than to the news from Europe or Washington."[73]

In November 1915, students recommended starting a public forum at Bowdoin to discuss current events, and the matter was referred for study and development to a student committee chaired by Kinsey.[74] Before his committee could act, however, the dean decided to ascertain how much Bowdoin's students knew about events in Europe. In December 1915, Casey gave his Latin I class an informal examination on current affairs, asking questions such as "Where is Gallipoli?" "Who is Prime Minister of England?" and "Who is [Aristide] Briand?" While one student (a freshman at that) made a perfect score on the twenty-question test, the class average was 55. Many of the questions were not easy ("What countries bound Serbia?" "Who is [Eleutherios] Venizelos?" "In what country is Salonica?"), but Casey was in no mood for excuses. While admitting it would not be entirely fair to call the test results "a bombardment of unfortified brains," he added pointedly, "Where there is such ignorance is not there something the matter somewhere?"[75]

Ironically, Casey's test produced a storm. Somehow the Associated Press picked up the story, and it inspired comment in the editorial columns of the *Literary Digest* and the *New York Times*, not to mention the *Yale News*, the

Harvard Crimson, and the *Pennsylvanian,* student newspapers that had a field day at Bowdoin's expense.[76] "More notoriety for Bowdoin," groaned the *Orient* as it reported a new round of editorials. If the faculty expected students to know about current affairs, argued the school paper, the college should offer "courses in present day happenings, with the leading newspapers and reviews for text-books."[77] Unmoved, Casey blithely replied that it did not seem unreasonable to expect college men to read newspapers on their own.[78]

Though deeply pro-British in his private views, Casey saw no need for his students to prepare for the mechanics of fighting. He told the Boston chapter of Bowdoin alumni in April 1916, "Our students must be trained in patriotism and in good citizenship, as in other things; and they must be taught that they are not to look forward so much to being cared for by the State as to doing something for the State."[79] Casey had enough faith in his students to believe that, if Congress declared war, they would volunteer for duty and maintain Bowdoin's proud Civil War tradition. Till then, he thought the college should devote itself to the business of training young men to think clearly and calmly in emergencies.[80]

Despite Casey's sage counsel, Bowdoin's students found it increasingly difficult to keep their minds on books. For a generation that harbored doubts about its masculinity, World War I offered a proving ground. By performing heroic deeds in battle, soldiers could demonstrate their patriotism, bravery, and valor—in a word, their manhood. As the martial spirit rose, Bowdoin's student body supported a bellicose foreign policy. When a straw presidential election was held in the spring of 1916, the pugnacious Teddy Roosevelt, who demanded war with Germany, easily defeated Charles Evans Hughes, Elihu Root, and Woodrow Wilson, the other candidates on the ballot.[81]

No less than their grandfathers who had served in the Union Army, Bowdoin's young men stood ready to defend their country. Two Bowdoin men were among the first group of volunteers at the army training camp established in Plattsburgh, New York, in the summer of 1915, and in the spring of Kinsey's senior year the school paper predicted that "there will doubtless be a large representation from here at the camps this summer."[82] That same spring, ninety-three men joined the newly organized Rifle Club on campus, founded with the aid of the National Rifle Association, which donated firearms and ammunition.[83]

Of course, not everyone believed preparedness was enough. A few Bowdoin students left college to join the American Ambulance Corps in France. (Ernest Hemingway later made such service known to generations of Americans through his writings on his experiences as an ambulance driver in Italy.) But Casey had no wish to see a mass exodus of Bowdoin students for the blood-soaked fields of France. Ever the voice of reason, he quoted David's words in 1 Samuel: "For as his share is who goes down into battle, so shall his share be who stays by the stuff." Translated into the language of duty, he was asking Bowdoin's men to remain in college, to strive for academic excellence, and to stand ready if called for service.[84]

However large World War I loomed in the imaginations of other young men, Kinsey spent his two years at Bowdoin pursuing a different image of masculinity, one that sought fulfillment in meeting the duties of a Christian gentleman. In December 1915, he joined the First Congregational Church, or, as it was known at Bowdoin, "the church on the hill."[85] Whatever his motivation, Kinsey's new religion was less rigid than Methodism. To be sure, Congregationalism required an intense act of conversion, but by the early twentieth century it had largely purged itself of fundamentalism's emphasis on punishment to frighten people into self-denial and obedience. Perhaps Kinsey was drawn to Congregationalism because it represented a more tolerant, less anxious brand of Christianity; perhaps he was more confident of meeting its standards. Or perhaps he simply wanted to fit in. While Bowdoin was no longer a church school, it retained its historic ties to Congregationalism. Approximately fifty Bowdoin students belonged to the "church on the hill," a large enough number that the congregation voted in 1915 to elect one deacon from its student members. More than half of Bowdoin's faculty, including President Hyde, Dean Sills, and Professors Gross and Copeland, worshiped there as well. By switching churches, Kinsey broke with his past and joined the company of men he needed to impress in order to succeed at Bowdoin.[86]

Kinsey immediately became active in church affairs. The same month he joined, he spoke at the college men's supper, held in the First Congregationalist Church vestry, where he joined President Hyde, who also addressed the audience that evening.[87] Kinsey must have made a favorable impression on Bowdoin's leader because Hyde later invited him and a friend to a baseball game, and they accepted.[88] As far as is known, it was the only sporting event Kinsey ever attended at Bowdoin.

Kinsey devoted the bulk of his leisure time to YMCA activities. The YMCA commanded strong student support at Bowdoin. In the fall of 1914, it boasted 255 members in a school with 383 students.[89] That spring, 325 out of 397 students belonged.[90] Governed by a cabinet of officers elected by students and a general secretary appointed by the faculty, it conducted programs through student committees that reported back to the association at regular intervals.[91] Functionally, the YMCA sponsored two types of activities: programs for students by students; and programs for the community by students.[92] More than any other student organization on campus, the YMCA preserved an evangelical Protestant spirit, giving Kinsey an opportunity to prove his character through community service and individual acts of piety.

On campus, the YMCA aimed many of its programs at freshmen. It sponsored a social reception for freshman; a special freshmen meeting in which the YMCA distributed handbooks explaining college life; an employment bureau to help newcomers secure on-campus and off-campus jobs; a textbook loan library for needy students; a tutoring bureau for nonfraternity men (fraternities were expected to tutor their own); and a Thanksgiving Day dinner for students who could not go home.[93] For wider student audiences, the YMCA conducted Bible and missionary study classes, and a guest lecture series that brought prominent speakers to the campus. During Kinsey's first year at Bowdoin, President Hyde headed the team of instructors who taught the junior-senior Bible study class, which met every Sunday from noon till twelve-thirty at the First Congregationalist Church.[94]

The YMCA also sponsored numerous outreach programs. These included a variety of charitable activities, a deputation program that sent young men to outlying communities, and several programs designed to involve privileged college youths with the working class, including recent immigrants. On the charity front, for example, the YMCA took up donations to support a Bowdoin mission in India; collected magazines and books for distribution in the state prison at Thomaston; raised money to provide a Thanksgiving dinner for the poor; and organized the partnership with Princeton mentioned earlier to collect money and clothing for Belgian relief. Among its programs for the working class, Bowdoin's YMCA operated night schools for mill workers, English classes for recent immigrants, and boys clubs to teach blue-collar urban youths how to become real men.[95]

Kinsey joined the YMCA during his first semester at Bowdoin. He was a mainstay in its deputation work. Inspired by evangelical Protestantism's long tradition of sending itinerant preachers to carry God's word to the hinterland, the deputation program dispatched pious college men to small villages across the state to preach the gospel and offer religious instruction to young people.[96] During Kinsey's junior year, more than a dozen Bowdoin men fanned out to twenty-two communities, including four academies.[97]

Kinsey was a workhorse in the Brunswick Boys' Association, a YMCA project that offered local youths lectures to shape good character, gymnasium classes to build strong bodies, and social activities for fun. The Boys' Association was one of a number of the Bowdoin YMCA's programs designed to rescue urban youths. More than any of its other activities, these programs showed how evangelical Protestantism's social meliorism, moral righteousness, and spirit of voluntarism shaped the Progressive Era's approach to problem solving. Reformers honestly believed that once people learned about a problem, they would confront and solve it through voluntary means. At the Boys' Association, Kinsey was in charge of social activities for the boys, and he also taught a class in first aid.[98] Kinsey doubtless enjoyed the work, as it placed him in a position of authority, the only role he found congenial.

Somehow, Kinsey also found time to teach English to local mill workers, a YMCA program designed to uplift the urban poor and recent immigrants. The town supplied both a schoolhouse and books, and the college provided tutors. Kinsey was one of twenty-five student volunteers who taught night classes for thirty-five immigrants. While the program got off to a rocky start, it eventually yielded heart-warming results, fostering close relationships between the tutors and the men.[99] At Christmas, for example, the YMCA donated a tree, and the college men got together with the workers, accompanied by their wives and children, for a joyous celebration. The *Orient* praised "the spirit of social equality" that graced the occasion, calling it "one of interest and happiness."[100] A few weeks later, one of the workers who attended the night school, the president of the local Weavers' Union invited several Bowdoin men to attend the installation of union officers in his mill.[101]

Kinsey's service to the YMCA did not go unrewarded. In the spring term of his junior year, he was invited to join Bowdoin's delegation to the seventh annual student conference of the YMCA of Maine, which met for three days at Bates College, in Lewiston, Maine. Following a brief welcoming ceremony, two hundred fervent young Christians, accompanied by the Bates College Band, formed a parade and marched to the Pine Street Congregational Church. There they were greeted by Mayor Robert J. Wiseman, treated to a banquet, and, in the words of the school paper, given "the great pleasure of listening to Rev. A. D. Leavitt [lecture] on 'Moral Repairs.' "[102] Kinsey impressed his fellow delegates favorably and was appointed to the resolutions committee at the conference. The following month, he earned a place on the Bowdoin delegation that attended the boys club convention in Portland.[103] Despite his outstanding service, however, Kinsey could not muster the votes to secure a major office in the YMCA and had to settle for that of director of community services, an appointed position in the YMCA cabinet.[104] Still, his participation in the YMCA was exemplary. He had served as itinerant preacher, boys club teacher, mill workers' tutor, YMCA student delegate, and cabinet member.

At Bowdoin, Kinsey encountered secular evangelicalism in its purest form—with its intense moralism, its stress on personal character, its staunch commitment to social engagement, its potent belief in the power of education to mold and to uplift, its insistence on good works, and its dedication to social reform. He responded by becoming a model youth, donating countless hours to programs designed to salvage the individual and to elevate society. His belief in social meliorism, his commitment to moral regeneration, and his sense of personal mission marked Kinsey as a loyal son of the Progressive Era. His record of service at Bowdoin also revealed one of the central paradoxes of reform—its fundamental conservatism. In contrast to the New Deal reformers of the 1930s, with their freewheeling pragmatism, most earlier reformers did not wish to increase the power of the state. Rather, they wanted the private sector to reform society through voluntary associations. Though committed to social uplift, these reformers retained a firm belief in individual responsibility. They expected the objects of their concern to work to improve their position in society.

While Kinsey devoted himself wholeheartedly to reforms, he remained conservative in his political views. He was in no way radicalized by his contacts with immigrants or the urban poor. Kinsey had no bone to pick with America's class structure or the capitalistic system upon which it rested. Along with other reformers, he believed the best way for immigrants to improve their lot was to become thoroughly Americanized; the best way for the working poor to climb the social ladder was through hard work and education, the tools his family had employed to achieve upward mobility. Ironically, the man who was destined to become one of the twentieth century's most influential critics of established sexual mores embodied mainstream values.

All that separated Kinsey from his classmates was the strength of his commitment to good works. Despite the YMCA's large membership, most Bowdoin students did not engage in its work. Less pious students poked fun at the YMCA. As part of a student questionnaire, the *Bugle* asked, "What has the Y.M.C.A. done for you?" Though offered tongue in cheek, many of the answers had a sharp edge: "Many [were] frank enough to admit nothing gained from the Y.M.C.A.," declared the *Bugle*, adding that others replied, "Kept out of my sight," and "Got rid of Hiwale [Bowdoin's missionary to India]." Even nastier answers came back when the *Bugle* asked, "What has the Y.M.C.A. done you for?" "Some more nothings" headed the list, but other replies suggested that at least some students thought the dues they paid the YMCA had been wasted, while others indicated they were fed up with the endless collections for worthy causes: "Few financial statements. '$1.00 Freshman year.' '$1.50 more than it ever will again.' '$3.00 to that guy out near the equator.' 'A fur coat for Hiwale.' 'My best suit went to Labrador by my roommate's generosity.' "[105]

The YMCA was more respected than liked on campus. Religion was losing its grip on Kinsey's generation, as least to the extent that it ordered most people's lives. Despite its impressive numbers, the YMCA attracted mostly armchair supporters, the type who join an organization but do not put their backs into its work. Not one member in ten participated in the deputation program. Kinsey personally accounted for 20 percent of all YMCA deputations during his junior year. Scant participation also plagued the tutoring program. Most Bowdoin men preferred to participate in the youth culture that was emerging in America's cities, a culture in which personal restraints were crumbling. Secular values, not religious precepts, held sway at Bowdoin, a fact that can be confirmed by reading student publications. While the school paper was fairly sedate, carrying only a sprinkling of risqué material, the *Bugle* printed a plethora of humorous references to drinking, smoking, and voluptuous women.

On many nights, more Bowdoin men could be found in Brunswick's movie theater than in Hubbard Hall, the college library. The school paper was filled with complaints about low attendance in daily chapel, but many students went on a Gilbert and Sullivan toot, turning out in droves to watch *H. M. S. Pinafore* on campus or traveling miles to see it performed elsewhere.[106] On weekends, Portland beckoned like a siren song, offering music, theater, food, and dance. How could Brunswick's "ten-cent shows" compete with Portland's Jefferson Theater, where audiences saw the hottest plays of the day? Nor did Brunswick have anything approaching Portland's Western Promenade or Deering Oaks, where college men could "go perambulating" on Saturday nights.[107]

To dissuade their charges from pursuing the wrong kind of fun, the faculty devoted careful attention to moral instruction. All students were expected to attend daily chapel, where sermons on individual responsibility and personal restraint formed familiar refrains. Freshmen had to take a full-semester course called "Hygiene," which featured the standard anti-sex education of the day; and the YMCA sought to reinforce this message with guest lecturers. One of the most famous spoke during Kinsey's junior year, Richard C. Cabot, a prominent Boston internist and public health official who was widely regarded as the father of social work in medicine. A familiar face on the lecture circuit, Cabot delivered an address entitled "Your Part in the Difficult Team Work of Men and Women."[108] That same year Bowdoin's men heard a member of their own faculty speak on the topic "Jesus and the Social Problem," a euphemism for prostitution.[109] As far as his classmates knew, Kinsey had no reason to worry. After all, he was an excellent student and dedicated to a variety of volunteer activities. Moreover, it looked as though Bowdoin would end Kinsey's social isolation as quickly as it cured his academic problems.

During his first semester at Bowdoin, Kinsey pledged Zeta Psi, one of eight fraternities on campus.[110] He and nine freshmen were initiated that fall, bringing Zeta Psi's Bowdoin chapter up to thirty-five members. In 1914, approximately 60 percent of Bowdoin's students belonged to fraternities, and Kinsey was happy to be among them.[111] "Fraternity life at Bowdoin has long been the all in all of College life," declared the school paper the fall Kinsey arrived.[112] The editors believed that fraternities offered "social advantages in college and out, association with a congenial body of men, pleasing interfraternity relations, comfortable, well-equipped homes, excellent dining facilities, and so on. Fraternities here are a helpful and wholesome thing, and the man who becomes a member is indeed fortunate."[113]

Housing headed the practical advantages of fraternity life. Bowdoin had an acute shortage of dormitory space during this period, forcing independents to take rooms in private homes or boardinghouses. Fraternity men, by contrast, did not have to scrounge for housing. Backed by liberal support from alumni, all the fraternities owned or rented chapter houses near the campus, with full facilities for boarding.[114] The Zeta Psi house, built in 1903, was home to Kinsey both years he attended Bowdoin.[115]

Despite the successful first step in pledging a fraternity, Kinsey's social life never got off the ground. True to his pattern, he had trouble fitting in. One of his fraternity brothers, Bela Norton, who described himself as "a good—although not intimate—friend," stressed that Kinsey was not "gregarious but on the contrary modest, somewhat shy and reserved."[116] Classmates who knew him less well put the matter more bluntly. After describing Kinsey as "a dignified, non-committal individual, who stalked about the campus with little to say to anyone," the brief sketch in the *Bugle* concluded with this advice: "If you loosen up a bit more, Al, you will make quite a man."[117]

Kinsey did not know how to "loosen up." His aloof, loner image was captured in detail by Paul K. Niven, another classmate and fraternity brother. Niven attributed Kinsey's social difficulties in part, to the fact that he was a transfer student, which meant that "he lacked the intimate association which his classmates and fraternity brothers had formed during their first two years at Bowdoin." While this was definitely a disadvantage, Niven also blamed Kinsey's personality, which stood "in considerable contrast to that of the average member of his class and fraternity."[118] "At that period," observed Niven, "the majority of Bowdoin undergraduates were from State of Maine homes, with relatively limited knowledge of the 'outside' world and, for the most part, the average carefree, irresponsible, purposeless college lads of those years." By contrast, "Al was somewhat more mature, and certainly more studious, and he knew what field he wanted to enter following graduation in 1916." As a result, explained Niven, "he had little in common with the rest of us." Indeed, the "rah-rah" of college life left Kinsey cold: "In the college boy antics of his college and fraternity associates, Al took little interest," continued Niven; "for example, a pre-football game student rally with its cheers, bonfires, etc. was simply not his dish! Neither were college dances, fraternity houseparties and other social occasions." A young man who had no interest in athletic events and refused to participate in fraternity dances, houseparties, and other social events was not going to win any popularity contests on campus.[119]

Not that Kinsey was an outcast. "Despite all of this, Al was by no means unsocial," asserted Niven. "Far from it. He had an excellent sense of humor and even wit. We all enjoyed bantering with him and we believed that he did, too. He'd take part in the 'bull sessions' of that day." Kinsey's willingness to join in his fraternity bull sessions shows that he wanted to be "one of the guys," that he wanted to fit in.[120] Nevertheless, the young man whom classmates remembered at Bowdoin sounded remarkably similar to the Kinsey people had known at Columbia High School and the Stevens Institute.

Despite his social problems, Kinsey benefited from belonging to a fraternity. Fraternity life offered him the companionship of men who otherwise might not have befriended him. Like the other Greeks, the Zeta men took their meals together, which automatically gave Kinsey messmates with whom he could converse, assuming, of course, he did not talk shop. "Because of the depth of his college work, it was far beyond the comprehension of most of his friends," confessed Niven. "Perhaps Al may have wanted to discuss his courses with us, but most of us were not up to it. In that area, then, he pretty much went his own way."[121] Kinsey did display a trait that would mark his future social intercourse. Niven recalled that whenever Kinsey engaged his fraternity brothers in conversation, he "displayed a wealth of general information."[122] People who knew Kinsey many years later considered this one of his strongest personality traits. But the young man who so impressed others with his store of knowledge was anything but self-confident. Unsure of himself socially, ill at ease with others, Kinsey found it virtually impossible to make small talk. And that explains, at least in part, why he peppered people with facts. His encyclopedic knowledge enabled him to talk without groping for words, to put himself forward, and to earn respect, if not admiration. Kinsey's conversational style may not have been smooth or engaging, but at least it allowed him to participate in social discourse, albeit as a self-appointed authority on everything.

Kinsey also enjoyed other aspects of Greek life. He liked the traditional pie for breakfast and the access to the chapter's record collection. Best of all, the Zetas had their own piano. Had he been able to overcome his aversion for popular music, Kinsey might have parleyed his musical talent into popularity. "Following dinner each evening, it was customary for the fraternity members to gather around the piano and sing," recalled Niven. "But the pianist was what we would call a 'ragtime' player and the selections were the popular songs of the day or songs of college or fraternity. In such sessions, Al just plain preferred not to join."[123]

Nevertheless, Niven had clear memories of Kinsey at the piano. At mid-evening or sometimes at midday, when no one was around the large living room, "Al would sit down at the piano and play classical music. To the rest of us there was little interest in such 'stuff,' " confessed Niven, "but frequently we would gather around him in sheer admiration." Apparently, Kinsey loved the attention and put on a show. "There was indeed an aura about him as he played," recalled Niven. "His eyes mirrored the deep enjoyment he got from the selections he was playing. With his shock of wavy, blond hair, his soulful expressions, and his artistry at the piano, he was indeed a magnificent figure."[124] Another fraternity brother told much the same story. According to Bela Norton, Kinsey played only on those "occasions when we wished to hear something better than jazz or 'popular' music," at which time he would perform "more serious 'classical' works which he played most skillfully."[125]

Music remained very important to Kinsey. At Bowdoin, as in high school, music allowed this closed, controlled young man to explore and express his emotions.[126] To pursue this passion, Kinsey arranged to have access to a second piano, one far removed from the ears of his Philistine fraternity brothers. The music department, which was housed at the back of the school chapel, had its own separate entrance and its own grand piano. During his first year at Bowdoin, Kinsey obtained a key to the music department, plus permission to use the piano whenever he liked.[127]

Unbeknownst to Kinsey, he had an audience in Austin MacCormick, class of 1915, who lived in South Maine Hall. MacCormick's dormitory window overlooked the chapel and the entrance to the music hall. "I saw [Kinsey] frequently letting himself into the building, usually late in the afternoon," recalled MacCormick. "Then, for an hour or more, I would hear him play the piano. He was an excellent musician and played classical music for the most part. The main thing that impressed me was that he often played tempestuously, and I was quite sure that this was the way he took of relieving the tensions which must have been built up in him by the long hours he spent on laboratory work in his courses."[128] Perhaps this was accurate, but Kinsey had other sources of tension.

A youth with a punishing secret, Kinsey must have struggled to maintain his equilibrium at Bowdoin. By this time, he must have admitted to himself that he was sexually attracted to men. Still, in the middle-class world of college life, homosexuality was virtually invisible. The young man sitting next to him in chapel could have been homosexual, and Kinsey would never have known it. Buffeted by cultural condemnation, ignorant of their numbers, and paralyzed by fears of exposure, most homosexuals endured desperate lives. Rare was the homosexual who did not feel alienated and anxious, terrified his secret would be discovered. Convinced of their own depravity, most homosexuals struggled valiantly to suppress or deny their desires. But try as they might, most failed. Driven by desperation and emboldened by desire, at least some homosexuals in large cities ventured outward, hoping to locate kindred souls without being discovered. Some managed to find partners with whom they could have emotionally satisfying relationships, but many had to settle for furtive sex with strangers or paid sex with homosexual prostitutes. It seems unlikely that Kinsey had many, if any, such opportunities in Brunswick.

Kinsey's predicament was exacerbated by his housing arrangement. For two years, Kinsey ate, bathed, and slept under the same roof with fraternity brothers who had no idea of his feelings, no hint of his longings. Though his reputation as a loner offered some protection, Kinsey probably had to fend off attempts by well-meaning friends to fix him up with dates from nearby women's colleges. Doubtless, his fraternity brothers felt a certain obligation to help him, in part because of his social ineptness and in part because a fraternity's prestige on campus was often enhanced by its members' popularity with the opposite sex. Kinsey's reputation as a serious student and his meager funds offered ready excuses for his peers. The fact that the campus had no coeds also helped shield his lack of interest in women. By whatever means, Kinsey managed to survive another two years without dating.

How Kinsey coped with day-to-day fraternity life is less clear. Assuming the Zeta Psis acted like most fraternity men, the chapter house must have been charged with sexuality. There were no doubt blue jokes, tales of sexual conquests (real, invented, or imagined), and declarations of love for sweethearts and fiancées. Perhaps Kinsey's stern propriety shielded him, as his fraternity brothers may have been hesitant about broaching certain subjects in his presence. But given the ubiquity of sexual banter in most fraternities, it is hard to believe Kinsey made it through college without hearing sex discussed. Kinsey himself suggested that he simply learned to wait for the conversation to turn. Decades after leaving Bowdoin, he wrote, "The college male who continuously talks about girls does so with a certain consciousness that the other persons in his group are also going to be aroused by such conversation, and that they accept such arousal as natural and desirable." He added, "The homosexual male, and the heterosexual male who does not approve of such deliberately induced eroticism, considers this public display of elation over females as a group activity which is more or less artificially encouraged."[129] When fraternity brothers bantered about girls, athletics, dances, parties, and the like, Kinsey could only bide his time until he found a subject (or could change the discussion to a topic) that allowed him to hold forth. Then, and only then, could he join in.

Whatever his private turmoil over his sexuality, Kinsey's years at Bowdoin ranked among the happiest of his youth. Unlike his classmates who saw college as an opportunity for fun, Kinsey arrived in Brunswick determined to redeem himself. Serious-minded, intellectually focused, and addicted to work, he approached college as a time for study and community service. Bowdoin introduced Kinsey to the life of the mind, and no undergraduate internalized this ideal more fully. At Bowdoin, he got his first real taste of academic life, a world where people concerned with research and ideas could find kindred spirits who shared their passion for learning.

As far as the world could see, Kinsey flourished at Bowdoin. Christian gentleman, scholarship student, prizewinning debater, Debate Club president, star biology student, biology assistant, Biology Club president, and YMCA cabinet member—the list of his accomplishments showed what a good mind harnessed to a fierce work ethic could accomplish in two short years.

Kinsey's diligence paid off, creating opportunities that opened a future different from the one he had envisioned upon entering Bowdoin. Encouraged by Professors Gross and Copeland, Kinsey raised his intellectual sights several notches: instead of getting a degree in biology and working at YMCA camps, he decided to prepare for a career as a research biologist. Not surprisingly, his mentors recommended Harvard.

Bowdoin's biology program had a banner year in 1916. Kinsey's class produced four biology majors, and in May the *Orient* proudly announced that two of them, Kinsey and his chief rival, Lawrence Irving, had been accepted for graduate study in biology at Harvard.[130] Copeland and Gross had come through for their prize pupils. Still, only decades later did Kinsey learn how highly he was regarded at Bowdoin. In 1945, Paul Nixon, who later served as the dean of Bowdoin College, wrote Kinsey, "I recently asked Alfred Gross who his best Biology students of all time were. Al Kinsey headed the list."[131]

During his last term at Bowdoin, Kinsey entered one final contest. In March 1916, about the time the first straw hats appeared on campus announcing the arrival of spring, he was among twenty seniors who submitted essays in the competition to select commencement day speakers.

Unlike most colleges, Bowdoin did not import distinguished guests to perform this duty. Instead, the honor went to outstanding seniors. Kinsey earned a place as one of the four winners.[132] Overall, the speakers delivered the kinds of speeches one would expect: "Justice to the Uncivilized"; "The Metamorphosis of Faust"; and "Poe: A Poet of Unrealities."[133] Kinsey's speech was different. Far more than his high school valedictory, his remarks at Bowdoin were deeply personal. He entitled his talk "Art and Science—Companions." At one level, it told a story of friendship and loneliness; at another, it exposed his search for a new inner balance, in which science and art would supersede religion as the integrating principles in his life.

Kinsey began by introducing his friend, "a gray squirrel, yonder." "We met first by chance. I had no thought of making as lowly an acquaintance, and he on his part showed little liking for my presence. When I threw an acorn at him, he perched on an upper limb and scolded in a dozen ways. He coughed and choked with invective; he mispronounced all he said." From this inauspicious beginning, however, something unusual developed. "But my squirrel and I found, as time went on that our paths were often to cross. We talked; we confided our troubles. Each was a mystery to the other, but we were friends."[134]

At this point, Kinsey shifted gears. What had started as a story about an unlikely friendship suddenly switched to a meditation on individuality, a theme that weighed heavily on a lonely young man who wanted to make sense of himself. "Art, the guardian of beauty, had individualized my squirrel, had taken it out of a disorderly superabundance of things, had made it a unit," explained Kinsey. "Science, seeking a different end, individualizes the squirrel in a different way." Proclaiming the scientific materialism that shaped so much of his thinking in later years, Kinsey asserted that science "seeks the physiology of the tooth, it shows the perfection of microscopic tissues, it applies psychological principles and interprets the animal's behavior, and working thus it learns laws and classifications of all knowable things." "Art and science each employ correct methods," he told the audience. "But neither is sufficient alone." Left to is own devices, art "fails to see the universe as a whole, stops at small considerations." Pursued in isolation, science "fails to find the inspiration from a prolonged contemplation of individuals."[135] Here was the theme of his talk—the need to meld science and art to form a complete individual.

Kinsey had good reason to seek a new self-synthesis. From his childhood onward, he had been taught to seek self-understanding through religion. The Bible, he had been told, contained the answers to life, all one needed to know to comprehend the world and one's place in it. Despite the break with his father, Kinsey had remained deeply religious, as his membership in the Congregational Church and his work for the YMCA bore witness. Yet religion was conspicuously absent from his commencement speech, as though Kinsey was groping for something new, something beyond religion that would allow him to develop a sense of self that integrated all the features of his personality. Each individual, he seemed to be saying, had qualities that combined elements of the artistic and the scientific. And more important, each individual needed both to become a well-functioning whole. "Art alone develops weaklings, science alone, monsters," declared Kinsey. "Somewhere, somehow, we must combine the two."[136]

Kinsey's talk closed on a note of tragedy. "Great laws of creation and life I learned from my squirrel. . . . Great truths of trust and fear, of troubles and delights, of delightful peculiarities, of friendship, I learned from my squirrel, the individual of beauty," he said. "And when, one morning, I found that the car had struck the life from the gray thing, I felt the loss of a particularly personal possession I had cherished. I was glad for the laws it had taught, glad for the love it had inspired."[137] How strange these remarks must have sounded to his audience; how jarring the contrast between his words and those of his classmates. Even after three quarters of a century, it is impossible not to feel Kinsey's loneliness or to be unmoved by the isolation that could prompt a young man to invest so much time and affection in a squirrel. The squirrel, however, allowed him to express his dedication to reconciling art and science, and he would return to this question often in the years to come.

As Kinsey went back to his seat, he could not survey the audience and find the approving eyes of his parents. He had no family member to hear his talk or applaud when he finished—no one to share his pride when President Hyde handed him his diploma and announced that he had graduated magna cum laude, one of only two members of his class to achieve that honor. But Kinsey was truly his own man now. He had proven he could succeed without his family's help. And while the past continued to shape the image he showed the world, he was headed in new directions. Having selected science as his life's work, he was bound for Boston, "the hub of the universe," and for Harvard, the nation's greatest university.

"AH, I PERCEIVE THAT YOU ARE
AN ENTOMOLOGIST"

t first glance, Boston in 1916 looked like a typical East Coast city crowded against its port. Venerable buildings and functional new edifices sat side by side in the factory and mercantile districts and along the waterfront. Beacon Hill, home to the Brahmins, Boston's established elite, had stately mansions that dated back to colonial times, and Back Bay its fashionable town houses and apartment buildings. Yet the old walking city of the past was quickly giving way to suburban sprawl, as families followed the streetcar lines to live in the bedroom communities that sprang up around Boston, leaving behind a city that appeared increasingly blighted.[1]

Wooden tenement houses, painted dreary shades of yellow, brown, or gray, dominated the landscape of Greater Boston and Cambridge. Ironically, many wealthy residents painted their homes the same dismal colors. "Those yellows looked like vomit to me," declared a man who entered Harvard in 1913. Nor was the city pleasant to the nose. "As you entered it," the same man recalled, "Boston became smellier and smellier," largely because indoor plumbing for the poor was scarce and the working classes bathed infrequently. "The odors were powerful in the trolley cars and along the city streets. In almost every city block," he continued, "there was a saloon. The smells of the people and the beer and the horse manure were powerful." Dead horses frequently littered the city streets, waiting to be collected by city workers who spirited them off to an island in Boston Harbor, where the carcasses were burned.[2] But if Boston triggered unpleasant memories of Hoboken in Kinsey, he did not show it. He never complained of feeling crowded in Boston, either physically or emotionally. Overall, his mood during his three years in Boston stayed upbeat, like that of a man who had set goals for himself and was succeeding. Twenty-two years old and completely self-sufficient, Kinsey had fought his way to America's premier university. If he performed well, he could expect to emerge from Harvard a rigorously trained scientist with a bright future.

Then, as now, Harvard attracted students from across the nation and around the world, making it one of the country's most cosmopolitan institutions of higher learning. When Kinsey arrived in the fall of 1916, Harvard College boasted an enrollment of 4,998,[3] and graduate programs added another 255 students to the tally.[4] Of this latter figure, fifteen were enrolled in the Bussey Institute, the tiny academic fiefdom where Kinsey received his graduate education.[5]

Located in the Jamaica Plain Forest Hills section of West Roxbury, in South Boston, the Bussey Institute had a checkered past. From its opening in 1871, its endowment proved inadequate, forcing faculty to lead a hand-to-mouth existence. (At one point, they had to resort to truck farming on the grounds to supplement their budget.) As a result of paltry salaries, turnover was chronic, and in less than two decades the faculty dwindled to four. And as frequently happens when groups compete for resources, the institute became something of a stepchild. No science department at Harvard offered to come to its rescue. In the words of Harvard's official historian, the Bussey Institute was "impartially detested by them all." While it rebounded briefly after the turn of the century, the old Bussey Institute ceased to exist in 1907.[6]

In 1908, the Bussey Institute reopened as the Graduate School of Applied Biology, a free-standing component of the Graduate School of Applied Sciences. As before, it had its own dean and its own separate faculty, who operated independently from their counterparts in the College of Arts and Sciences at Harvard. After the remaining undergraduates completed their degrees in 1910, the Bussey Institute dropped undergraduate education entirely. Henceforth, it offered only a master of forestry degree and the master and doctor of science, the latter two in several subjects of applied science.[7]

Thanks to fresh transfusions of funding from Harvard University, the revived Bussey Institute managed to assemble a distinguished faculty. William Morton Wheeler, a towering figure in embryology, cytology, and the taxonomy and behavior of insects, arrived in 1908, the same year that William E. Castle, a pioneer in the new science of genetics, moved his laboratory from Cambridge to Jamaica Plains. Soon thereafter, Edward M. East, a distinguished plant geneticist, accepted a chair in experimental plant morphology, followed in 1909 by Charles T. Brues, who was appointed instructor in economic entomology, giving the institute a one-two punch in entomology. In 1914, the Bussey Institute underwent yet another reorganization. Wheeler became dean, the Department of Forestry was shifted to the Bussey Institute (a plum that brought additional faculty and staff under the institute's control); and Irving W. Bailey came aboard to teach plant anatomy. Finally, Oakes Ames, an expert in economic botany, joined the Bussey faculty in 1916, where he remained until 1926, when he moved his laboratory to Cambridge following his appointment as curator of the Botanical Garden.[8] All these changes occurred just in time for the Bussey Institute to become a major center of what came to be called the New Biology.

Progress in the biological sciences has always depended on the introduction of new ideas, and Charles Darwin's *Origins of Species* (1859) was a conceptual powerhouse. His theory of evolution through natural selection offered the first non-teleological explanation for the existing characteristics and peculiar adaptations of all living organisms, including man.[9] Following Darwin's lead, a number of researchers concentrated on natural history, with its emphasis on data collection and historical reconstruction. But more and more biologists turned to experimental research, employing statistical methods to test Darwin's theories. The challenge was to ascertain how heredity and variation worked, because Darwin had described a process, not the actual mechanics of evolution.

In a series of papers published in the 1870s, 1880s, and 1890s, August Weismann, a specialist in cytology at the University of Freiburg, Germany, advanced his "germ plasm" theory of heredity, which he tested in a number of laboratory experiments designed to show that each somatic trait in all sexually reproducing species could be traced to what he called germinal cells (or determinants). In 1900, three European experimentalists, Hugo de Vries, Carl Correns, and Erich Tschermak von Seysenegg independently "rediscovered" Gregor Mendel's laws of inheritance (his publications decades earlier had gone virtually unnoticed by the scientific world). Briefly, Mendel proved that each parent contributes to each segregating character a single genetic unit, later named a gene. His "rediscovery" at the turn of the century allowed biologists to use statistics to study heredity. Dazzled by the magic of numbers, researchers hoped to devise mathematical formulas, precise measurements, and controlled experiments to create a New Biology that would rival the physical sciences in its explanatory power and in its ability to develop natural laws. Within the span of a few decades, the foci of research at universities across the land shifted from fieldwork in natural history to experimental work in laboratories, as researchers used breeding experiments and statistical methods to study natural processes at the bench.[10]

Experimental biology gave rise to a new spirit of optimism and confidence. With numerous independent studies confirming Darwin's evolutionary hypothesis, nothing seemed beyond the reaches of the New Biology. Jacques Loeb, the distinguished physiologist at the University of California at Berkeley, boldly proclaimed in 1904 that the recent discoveries in biology marked "the beginning of a real theory of heredity and variation."[11] Many evolutionary biologists thought they were on the threshold of understanding heredity. This was heady stuff, for if biologists could understand the mechanisms of heredity, it followed that they might one day be able to control it. Science was envisioning a world without inherited diseases or undesirable traits.

The rapid growth of research opportunities in the United States nurtured the New Biology. Evolutionary biology developed at the exact time when the expansion of higher education opened many new positions for scientists in American universities. In the past, science had been dominated by gentleman scholars, individuals whose family wealth freed them from the need to enter the market economy.[12] By the late nineteenth century, however, the number of new academic positions was greater than the upper class could fill. This change offered upwardly mobile youths the opportunity to enter a profession that had been largely restricted to the upper class. By the twentieth century, science drew its members overwhelmingly from the middle class; and somewhere between one-fourth and one-third of each new crop of scientists came from the working class.[13]

Research universities provided a home for scientific enterprise. Most liberal arts colleges did not require faculty members to conduct research, nor could they offer the diverse curriculum, large libraries, or well-equipped laboratories needed to support experimental biology. Only heavily endowed private universities and well-supported state universities had the resources to become major players in modern science. By the turn of the century, capitalists who had made fortunes in the Industrial Revolution, such as John D. Rockefeller and Leland Stanford, began donating huge sums to higher education, and their philanthropy enabled the leading private universities to support graduate schools and research programs.[14]

Under William Morton Wheeler's leadership, the Bussey Institute developed into a major center of the New Biology. In 1901, William Castle became the first American to publish an article on Mendelian genetics. Also remembered as the first scientist to use *Drosophila* (the fruit fly) as an experimental animal, Castle quickly shifted his interests to mammalian genetics. His laboratory at the Bussey Institute was filled with rats, guinea pigs, and rabbits, which he used in breeding experiments designed to study inherited characteristics. The institute's 1915–16 annual report noted that Castle was especially interested in exploring "the constancy and interrelations of Mendelizing characters." Personally quiet and unassuming, frequently stubborn in his convictions, and totally devoted to his work, Castle had the reputation of being the best teacher at the institute and a close mentor to his students.[15]

Though originally trained as a chemist, Edward East made his mark in plant genetics. An expert on corn, he studied the percentages of protein, carbohydrates, and fats in this hearty plant with an eye to improving its nutritional value through selective breeding. East moved on to other plants of direct value to farmers, such as potatoes and tobacco. In addition to conducting work of great commercial value, he made important contributions to genetic theory. His experiments demonstrated that, contrary to the belief of most scientists, genes were extremely stable, a discovery that pointed to the significance of mutations in heredity. Not surprisingly, the commercial and theoretical importance of East's work attracted numerous graduate students to work under his supervision.[16]

Wheeler, by contrast, demonstrated that biologists who had strong roots in natural history could still hold their own in the academy. A specialist in taxonomic entomology, Wheeler was the world's leading authority on the social behavior of insects, particularly ants. Described by friends as "a man of encyclopedic learning," Wheeler churned out scholarship with machinelike regularity, producing a bibliography of 465 publications, including 9 books. Although he delighted in discovering minute details, a trait that established his kinship with other descriptive biologists around the globe, Wheeler seldom lost sight of the big picture. He was forever seeking patterns in the creatures and events he studied. In fact, his intellectual curiosity reached far beyond biology. Fluent in Latin and Greek and several modern languages as well, he thought nothing of asking graduate students to read articles in whatever language they appeared. Endowed with a wide-ranging intellect, Wheeler followed developments in psychology and sociology with intense interest. So keen was his curiosity and so vast his learning that Alfred North Whitehead, the Harvard philosopher, once described Wheeler as the only man he had ever known "who would have been worthy and able to sustain a conversation with Aristotle."[17]

By the time Kinsey matriculated in 1916, the Bussey Institute had entered its golden age, providing a wonderfully stimulating environment for the handful of students fortunate enough to study there. The atmosphere for faculty and students alike was cordial and relaxed, much more so than in the corresponding departments in Cambridge. Faculty offices were only slightly larger than graduate student offices, several of which were located on the top floor of the institute's three-story stone building. Unfortunately, heat did not always rise this high in the building, forcing graduate students to keep a pot of tea constantly brewing in a vain effort to stay warm.[18]

The housing arrangements added to the Bussey Institute's closeness. Most graduate students lived in the Bussey Dormitory, a large house located on the grounds. The rent ranged from $6.00 to $15.00 a month, depending on the accommodations, and board at the student's mess ran to an additional $5.25 a week.[19]

Kinsey could not afford to live in the dormitory. Instead, he had to settle for room and board from Miss Elizabeth Weld, who owned a grand home in Roslindale, a nearby suburb in South Boston. A relative of L. H. Weld, a distinguished entomologist, Miss Weld routinely recruited a student to live in her home, offering room and board in exchange for light housework and yardwork.[20] While this arrangement saved Kinsey money, it also had a down side. Throughout his graduate school years, Kinsey was cut off from his peers, continuing the pattern of social isolation that had dogged him earlier.

Nor was housing Kinsey's only problem. Tuition at the Bussey Institute ran $200 a year,[21] and, as usual, he had to scramble to raise the money. But at least he could count on the support of a sympathetic institution. "Harvard will always take care of a student who will work," Wheeler once reassured an anxious graduate student.[22] Harvard lived up to this pledge with Kinsey, who managed to cobble together enough assistance to finance his graduate education. He served as a laboratory assistant in general zoology at Radcliffe College, a laboratory assistant in beginning botany at Harvard, and an instructor in field botany in the Harvard Extension Division.[23] In addition, Kinsey was the second recipient of the Anna C. Ames Scholarship, created in 1917 by one of his professors, Oakes Ames, in memory of his mother.[24] Finally, Kinsey supplemented his income by working as a counselor every summer, a job that returned him to the camps he found so enjoyable.

University routine dictated Kinsey's first year at Harvard. Beginning students at the Bussey Institute had to discuss a degree plan with Dean Wheeler.[25] While candidates for the master of science degree had to fulfill two consecutive terms in residence and attain either an A or a B in at least four full courses, the institute tailored requirements for the doctor of science degree (the institute did not confer the doctor of philosophy degree) to meet each student's needs.[26] Wheeler also used these counseling sessions to survey each new crop of graduate students, though, in truth, they interested him but little. He avoided students unless they worked directly under his supervision. Those who wrote their dissertations under other faculty members found Wheeler aloof and hard to approach.[27]

During their first year in residence, graduate students at the Bussey Institute concentrated on course work. Although it operated on a trimester system and remained open year round, the institute offered few courses in Jamaica Plains during the fall and spring terms, partly because its sole building, with its high ceilings and long glass windows, was cold and drafty. As a result, the faculty conducted mostly laboratory courses at the Bussey Institute and taught lecture courses in Harvard Yard, where Bussey professors routinely gave undergraduate classes. Fortunately, Boston's new subway system (opened in 1913) made the commute from Jamaica Plains to Cambridge both easy and inexpensive.[28]

Kinsey arrived at the Bussey Institute without a specialty in mind. His biological interests were broad and diffuse, ranging from birds to insects and plants—things that would attract a schoolboy with a passion for natural history and a penchant for direct observation. In that sense, he was a throwback to the nineteenth century, to the old-fashioned naturalists who wanted to drink in nature in great gulps. During his first year at Harvard, he took from Dean Wheeler a two-semester sequence of courses, "Zoology 7a: Morphology and Classification of Insects" and "Zoology 7b: Habits and Distribution of Insects." In each instance, Kinsey was one of only three students who completed the course. He received an A in both courses (the others could manage no better than a B).[29]

Wheeler devoted considerable time in these courses to insect morphology, which he followed with detailed discussions on physiology, embryology, taxonomy, paleontology, distribution, and insect social habits and behavior. Scattered across nearly every page of Kinsey's class notes are elegant, hand-drawn illustrations, proof he studied Wheeler's musings on insect structure and development thoroughly. These illustrations also reveal considerable artistic talent; and one particular drawing suggests that Kinsey occasionally brought a touch of humor to his work. Included in his notes on insects that bite, sting, and scratch was a description of ants that coil their bodies and squirt poison at their enemies. Adjacent to this entry is a delightful, cartoonlike drawing of a "pismire" (commonly called a pissant) rearing back its head, arching its body, and spraying poison out of its bottom.[30]

Wheeler loved taxonomy, and his lectures showed it. They were based not on "book learning" but on firsthand observations. An avid collector, he pursued ants energetically in the field. Everywhere he went, Wheeler collected specimens of the local ants and did his best to observe them in nature.[31] After his death, his ant collection, composed of more than a million specimens drawn from around the world, was donated to Harvard's Museum of Comparative Zoology, commonly called the Agassiz Museum, where it remains today, a prized treasure.[32]

Wheeler opened the course by discussing the importance of taxonomy to entomology. Taxonomy was crucial, he explained, because insects were represented in nature by "an abundance of species." By Wheeler's estimation the animal kingdom included at least 2,000,000 insect species—approximately twenty times as many as all other animal species combined. Since only a quarter of the known insect species had been classified to date, and since the business of taxonomy proceeded at a crawl (the rate was 500 to 600 new species described each year), Wheeler calculated that it would take another 500 to 700 years to complete the job in descriptive entomology. "Plenty of work yet to do," beamed Wheeler, adding, "Without attention to classification, [the] entomologist would be lost in minor details."[33]

The latter remark must have had special meaning for Wheeler's young graduate students. Middle-class Americans of the day abhorred inefficiency or chaos in any form.[34] Taxonomy, stressed Wheeler, was science's primary tool for imposing order on the incredible diversity of nature, because classifying and naming represented the first step toward reducing nature to an intelligible system. Who could doubt that every biologist owed a debt to the noble taxonomist?

The science of classification found an eager recruit in Kinsey. After taking Wheeler's course, he decided to work in taxonomy, with special emphasis on entomology. This was a fateful decision, in both the short and the long term. Intellectually, biology was a Janus-faced discipline, with one faction of its practitioners looking optimistically to the future, while the other stared longingly at the past. The Bussey Institute's faculty illustrated this division beautifully. The geneticists Castle and East embodied the New Biology, with its devotion to experimentation and to statistics, while Wheeler's work (and to some extent that of Brues) had strong roots in natural history.

By World War I, most bright young scientists were casting their lots with experimental biology, electing to work in genetics, physiology, biochemistry, and the like. Only a relative handful became descriptive biologists, who relied upon empirical observation to test hypotheses. By deciding to study under Wheeler, Kinsey chose field biology over experimental biology, a decision that shaped his professional career, determining both the questions he asked and the methods he employed to answer them. Yet who was to say in 1917 whether experimental or descriptive work would shed more light on heredity, the central problem of evolutionary biology?

Kinsey had sound reasons for going with taxonomy. Topping the list was his love for nature. No laboratory could ever match the appeal of the outdoors to this careful observer of wildlife, this ardent admirer of forests, hills, and streams. Much of Kinsey's private identity had been forged in nature; he could never find the same professional satisfaction or draw the same emotional support from bench science.

Intellectual arguments reinforced his private predilections. When Kinsey entered graduate school, genetics was in its infancy, and despite the recent triumphs of the New Biology, history appeared to favor field biology. Darwin had based his theories on his perusal of earlier work by animal breeders and on his own empirical observations in the field. Might not a life devoted to taxonomic field studies yield information and insights that could be molded into new theories—concepts that might rival or eclipse those of the Darwinian revolution? And what better way to become "a second Darwin" than to follow in Darwin's footsteps?

Then there was the question of Wheeler's influence on Kinsey, both intellectual and personal. William Morton Wheeler was a walking advertisement for natural history, the sort of man who could lure bright young students into a life of field biology. Widely lauded as the greatest American zoologist since Agassiz, he was one of the most celebrated biologists of his day. The University of Chicago awarded him his first honorary doctorate the year Kinsey arrived at Harvard, and by the time of his death Wheeler held honorary degrees from the University of California at Berkeley, Harvard University, and Columbia University. The Academy of Natural Sciences of Philadelphia awarded him its Leidy Medal, the National Academy of Sciences its Elliot Medal, and the French Academy its Legion of Honor. The National Academy of Sciences (and numerous lesser-known societies) elected Wheeler to membership, and he became an honorary member of several foreign societies as well. He was in constant demand as a lecturer, both at home and abroad. A gifted writer of clear, forceful prose, Wheeler was that rare breed of scholar who managed to interest lay readers in science. Major commercial publishers, including W. W. Norton and Alfred A. Knopf, vied for his books. And if academic greatness can be measured by how often a scholar's work is cited, Wheeler was in a class by himself. Even today his books and articles appear in more bibliographies than those of any other American entomologist, living or dead.[35] In short, if Wheeler's career did not prove that a field biologist could earn a place of distinction in the academy, Darwin never sailed on the *Beagle* and the Galápagos Islands were barren of life.

Intellectually, then, it would be difficult to imagine a better match for Kinsey than Wheeler. Both men approached biology as naturalists rather than as experimental scientists, both had an interest in insects, and both were compulsive collectors. Avid researcher, student of insect behavior, taxonomist, prolific writer, and defender of natural history against the Young Turks in genetics, Wheeler was a prototype workaholic who served as a strong role model for his students.

Yet as much as his scholarly credentials, it was Wheeler's persona that drew Kinsey to him. If it is true that opposites attract, Kinsey must have found Wheeler irresistible. Despite the things they shared, the contrasts between these men could hardly have been more jarring, as Wheeler was everything Kinsey was not. Classical scholar, gifted linguist, and man of letters, Wheeler was every bit the portrait of a sophisticated, urbane man. More to the point, he was a worldly man, the sort of figure who could put a goody-goody like Kinsey to thinking. Wheeler made no bones of the fact that he did not believe in God, and his personal vices underscored his secular beliefs. Addicted to tobacco in several forms (the pipe was his favorite, though he enjoyed a good after-dinner cigar and would smoke cigarettes on occasion) and fond in equal measure of fine whiskey, beer, and wine, Wheeler was a man's man, a raconteur who in the appropriate setting would tell blue stories with rare facility.[36] No less a scoundrel than H. L. Mencken found his company delightful. Over the years, Wheeler often took the train from Boston to Baltimore to attend meetings of the infamous Saturday Night Club, where he and Mencken indulged impressive thirsts and sparred intellectually.[37]

No, Wheeler was living proof that a distinguished scholar could be a red-blooded man. His brand of biologist would not be caught dead having tea with the vicar, but he could be found discussing some godless theory of evolution over brandy and cigars at the men's club. By example, he showed Kinsey values that were fundamentally at odds with small-town Protestant morality. And Wheeler's influence may well have cut even deeper.

In the academy, it is not uncommon for graduate students to refer to their major professors as "my father in scholarship" or to hear major professors call their students "my boys" in return.[38] The father-son relationship suggested by such language may have been especially appealing to Kinsey. Bitter conflicts with his own father had left him vulnerable to the appeal of an authority figure whom he had some hope of pleasing and from whom he could derive some measure of approval and support. Whether consciously or unconsciously, Kinsey probably regarded Wheeler as a father figure. After he left Harvard, Kinsey continued to cherish this relationship. He was forever quoting Wheeler to his own graduate students. It was "Wheeler said this" and "Wheeler said that," and Kinsey made numerous references to Wheeler in his own scholarly writing.

Many years after leaving Harvard, Kinsey also told his graduate students how much he had enjoyed studying with Merritt Lyndon Fernald, the noted botanist of the Gray Herbarium. Somehow, Kinsey found time to write a book on edible wild plants under Fernald's supervision. During the time he worked on the book, Kinsey wrote Natalie Roeth that the final work would be "of interest to the camper and suburban dweller possibly more than to the strict scientist," and added, "I appreciate it, not only for the out-door fun it involves but also for the chance it offers for a training under Prof. Fernald, and publishing with him."[39] Since no credit was given for this work, it was very much a labor of love.

Kinsey's single-minded devotion to his studies placed him at odds with most students at Harvard, many of whom were preoccupied with World War I. Just as the preparedness campaign had dominated student life during his two years at Bowdoin, the Great War cast a long shadow over his years at Harvard. In January 1917, only months before the United States entered the war, the *Crimson* (the student newspaper) announced that many Harvard men were leaving school to serve in the ambulance service in Europe.[40] That same month, Harvard students voted overwhelmingly in favor of military training in the United States.[41] In February, the university added a reserve officers' training program to the curriculum.[42] The response was disappointing. By the middle of February, the *Crimson* was complaining, "Harvard men have not yet proved that the red blood of the heroes of 1861 and 1898 still runs in the veins of the present generation." Noting that only six hundred students had signed up for the officers' training program, the *Crimson* chided, "The more privileged youth of our colleges are supposed to foresee dangers and prepare for them, but we in the crisis are disgracefully failing to justify our advantages." Urging their classmates to enroll in the military science course, the *Crimson* editors cried, "The need of the hour is for action, action, action."[43]

After the United States entered the war in April, the *Crimson* urged Harvard men not to leave school to enlist. "The work of the hour for most of us is to learn to be good officers that we may train good privates," it declared.[44] Like many college newspapers across the country, the *Crimson* saw the Great War as a proving ground, an opportunity for men to demonstrate their patriotism, courage, and manhood under fire. Throughout the war, the *Crimson* kept the student body informed of the heroic deeds of the Harvard men who fought in Europe. Those reports included the "Roll of Honor," a running tally of the men who had died in the war. By September 1918, a few months before the armistice, the figure stood at 136; by early January 1919, a few months after the war had ended, reports placed the figure at 261.[45]

But what of those Harvard men like Kinsey who did not serve in World War I? The *Crimson* could not imagine anyone being pleased to miss the action. In September 1917, the beginning of Kinsey's second year at Harvard, the *Crimson* explained, "Those who remain here at school are for the greater part men who tried to get into the service and failed, or men who were beneath the declared age limitation for service." Confessing its pity for such men, the paper observed gravely that "it will be very hard to continue the usual course of cultural and disciplinary studies, which apparently . . . bear no apparent relation to life as men are living it, and dying it."[46] Later that fall, the editors insisted that the only way those who had stayed in school could justify their existence was to perform voluntary work and to labor extra hard at their studies. "The loafer in peace times should be pitied, in war times he should not be endured," they declared. "Our only excuse for being here instead of in France or at a training camp is that we are left to carry on the nation's intellectual work. It is then up to all of us to seize every opportunity the Faculty offers; if we do not we have no business in a war-time University."[47]

Kinsey did not need anyone to tell him to work hard; nor did he have to be reminded of his duty to perform good deeds. As it had for years, his social life at Harvard revolved around church affairs, particularly those involving young boys. During his second year in Boston, Kinsey helped organize a boys club at the Bethany Methodist Episcopal Church in Roslindale. Previously, the community had supported a youth group called the Boys Cadets, a paramilitary organization whose members drilled in smart blue uniforms patterned after the Grand Army of the Republic's dress blues. The Boys Cadets, recalled a former Roslindale resident, "reflected the temper of those times, when close order drill and precise military movements taught discipline and respect for authority."[48] But by the fall of 1917 the Boys Cadets had ceased to exist, and the boys of the Bethany Church were eager for new ways to learn leadership and discipline, the twin pillars of masculinity.

Howard Q. Bunker, a member of the Bethany Church, was thirteen when Kinsey volunteered his services, and forty years later Bunker still remembered the excitement generated by Kinsey's arrival. Bunker described him as an "enthusiastic leader" and "a vital, dynamic young man with a friendly smile and a crop of sandy hair." Using the Boy Scouts as his model, Kinsey built the club around hiking, taking the boys on Saturday treks and weekend overnight camping trips to Milton and then on to Ponkapoag Pond, located in the Blue Hills Reservations. Remembering how much he had enjoyed raiding his family's pantry for supplies for those trips, Bunker added, "I also recall my boyish pride in a khaki knapsack and my feeling of achievement when I learned to pack a blanket roll wrapped in a poncho; and how to make a sleeping sack out of blankets." Bunker could still sense "the thrill of hiking over woodland trails and the joy of looking out over the valleys after we had climbed each of the Blue Hills in Milton." Reflecting, too, on "the comradeship of the campfires on these trips," he added, "All of these experiences were wonderful to a boy of thirteen. And behind it all was a young man in his early twenties who had assumed the responsibility for these boys who were experiencing the excitement of camping and woodcraft for the first time."[49]

Still, Kinsey's social life was sparse. He remained a loner, a straitlaced young man whose puritanical demeanor stayed visibly in place. He neither smoked nor drank, and he had no interest in sports. Outside the classroom or the laboratory, he had little contact with his fellow graduate students or former classmates from Bowdoin. The graduate and professional schools at Harvard were loaded with Bowdoin men (the class of 1916 alone had sent eight men to Harvard, including Irving in biology). Yet Kinsey made no effort to cultivate ties with former classmates.

Despite his good looks, Kinsey remained aloof from women. Many, if not most, college men of his generation enjoyed dancing (the *Crimson* reported in 1919 that the one-step, the fox-trot, and the waltz were the favorites on campus),[50] but Kinsey was nowhere to be found when the music started. At Harvard, as before, he did not date. This was by choice. Had he desired female companionship, however, Kinsey would have had plenty of takers. "My wife, who was then a scientific assistant to one of the professors [at the Bussey Institute], tells me that he was a favorite topic of lunch-hour conversation for the secretaries and female lab assistants," recalled Edgar Anderson. "Towards them he was charmingly courteous but tantalized them with his air of ultimate inaccessibility," added Anderson.[51] Kinsey's aloofness did not raise any suspicions. Graduate school is a time of genteel poverty, big workloads, and single-minded concentration, a period when many students are forced to adopt monastic lifestyles. No doubt, his acquaintances assumed that this was the case with Kinsey.

Everyone agreed that he came across well. Recalling his first impression of Kinsey, Anderson described "a lithe, slender, almost athletic young man more often in field khaki than in tweeds, with the yellowest hair I remember having seen, an engaging smile, [and] a twinkle in the eye."[52] Anderson was the only real friend Kinsey made at Harvard, and their friendship lasted for life. They met a few weeks after Anderson entered the Bussey Institute in the spring of 1919, two and a half years after Kinsey had arrived at Harvard. As a beginning (and several years younger) graduate student, Anderson was someone Kinsey could mentor, a role he found congenial.

The two young scientists quickly discovered they had a mutual interest in natural history, and soon they were spending many hours together in the field. One expedition that stood out in Anderson's memory was a day-long excursion to Hobscot Hill, in Sudbury. They planned their trip on field maps, left at the crack of dawn, traveled by streetcar, and hiked some fifteen or twenty miles, and then returned late in the evening on the train that ran from Worcester to Boston. "At noon [Kinsey] deftly built the smallest cooking fire I had ever seen, heated tomato soup in its own can, mixing it with evaporated milk, and there was tomato bisque to go with our sandwiches," declared Anderson. "The few remaining coals were extinguished to the last spark, the cans were flattened and tucked away under a rock, our sandwich papers were collected and folded up. In less time than it takes to be served in a restaurant, we had a pleasant meal and no scar was left on the landscape." A keen observer of people in general and Kinsey in particular, Anderson added, "This almost professional perfectionalism in everything he did was a characteristic of the man."[53]

Anderson was one of the few people who knew Kinsey from his graduate school years right up to his death. "In those days Kinsey's tremendous drive was pretty well hidden," recalled Anderson. "He walked rapidly but without hurrying, his high gait was quietly relaxed. He had gentle manners and considerable charm," Anderson continued, "only when he was aroused by something about which he felt very deeply were there strident overtones in his mellifluous speech." Typically, Kinsey appeared easygoing and "only occasionally did the steel within show through the surface." Yet while Kinsey presented a calm image, Anderson was quick to add, "Complete relaxation . . . was something I never knew him to achieve." The only time he saw Kinsey attempt to do nothing was on a sailboat ride with friends. "Long lazy hours in the bright sunshine with the sails flapping idly overhead did not appeal to him," recalled Anderson. "He tried to break his boredom by reading the only available book, Conrad's *Youth,* and it left a bad taste in his mouth." Anderson added that Kinsey frequently complained of this fortnight "as time which might have been much better spent in climbing mountains or collecting insects."[54]

If recreational pursuits had little claim on Kinsey, it was because he came to Harvard to become a scientist, and nothing was going to keep him from his goal. By the end of his first year in graduate school, he had decided to work with Wheeler in entomology. Kinsey's only chance at impressing this busy and aloof professor was to write a strong dissertation, the surest way for any graduate student to distinguish himself from his peers. And that is precisely what Kinsey hoped to do. Toward the end of his course work, he started casting about for a dissertation topic. First, he considered a particular variety of beetle, but abandoned the topic after a little work left him dissatisfied with its potential.[55] His second choice was more promising. In the fall of 1917, Kinsey collected his first specimens of the insects that were to occupy the next twenty years of his life—American Cynipidae, or gall wasps, as they are commonly called.[56]

Galls wasps are tiny insects, no larger than a small ant. They live almost exclusively on roses, blackberries, goldenrods, and oaks, their favorite host. Along with other gall makers (such as gall lice, gall flies, and certain species of moths, beetles, and mites), gall wasps take their name from the galls they produce on their host plant—the plant on which they live and feed. Galls are the abnormal growths on plants caused by these parasitic insects. Anyone who has held an oak apple or oak ball or has noticed the rounded balls on the stems of goldenrods or the large swellings that occur on blackberry stems has seen a gall.[57]

The gall itself is, in Kinsey's words, "a monstrosity." Some are as tiny as a pinhead; others may reach five or six inches in diameter. They are composed of plant tissue—tender, succulent tissue that grows faster than any normal part of the plant. Galls begin when the insect bores a hole in the plant structure and deposits an egg. On oaks, for example, the gall wasp stands on its hind legs, drills into the plant, deposits a single egg, and then hurries along to another spot on the plant and begins anew, repeating the process many, many times to ensure the survival of their species. The gall forms at the point of entry, becoming in Kinsey's words, "a dining room and a bed-chamber for the creature during its larval life." Nothing injected by the parent insect is responsible for this growth; rather, it is apparently caused by something produced by the larva, though scientists still have not isolated that substance or learned how it works. All they know is that the larvae develop into pupae; the pupae feed on the gall tissue; the pupae then develop into winged adults; and the adult insects force or chew their way out of the galls.[58]

Soon after emerging, gall wasps copulate and then immediately begin searching for a place to lay their eggs. Almost without exception, particular species of gall wasps seek out particular species of plants in which to deposit their eggs. Only if two different plants are closely related will a gall wasp favor both with its offspring. Because each species of gall wasps produces distinct gall structures, trained botanists can identify some plants by their galls as easily as by their normal plant parts.[59]

Interestingly, the quest for the right species of plant often entails stupendous feats. In gall wasps that breed on oaks, the gall from which they emerged often becomes detached from the tree and then gets carried away by the wind. In such cases, the insects must run (though they have wings, they almost never fly) across the ground, negotiate thickets of grasses and weeds, and make their way to a particular species of oak, ignoring along the way all manner of trees (including other species of oaks) that do not match their genetic programming. Once they find their host species, gall wasps deposit their eggs—usually within a few hours, days, or weeks from the date they emerged from their galls, depending on the species. This accomplished, they die, having reached the end of their life cycle.[60] Once he dug into the material, Kinsey became enormously excited about his research. In March 1918, the *Crimson* reported that he was far enough along to present a paper entitled "Interesting Problems with Gall Wasps" to the Harvard Zoological Club.[61] A fellow graduate student at the Bussey Institute had vivid memories of Kinsey's "enthusiastic earnestness about his research with gall wasps."[62] Similarly, when one of the boys in the Bethany Church Boys Club expressed some interest in his research, Kinsey could not wait to show off his work. He took the boy on a Saturday morning tour of the Arnold Arboretum, where he explained how gall wasps damage trees. "We then went through some of the laboratories at the Bussey Institute where Mr. Kinsey was doing his graduate work," the man recalled. "I can remember the thousands of insects on display. I was impressed by these strange laboratories."[63]

As an evolutionary biologist, Kinsey was excited by the vivid contrasts gall wasps presented. Some species resembled each other so closely they were hard to tell apart, while some individuals of a species differed so markedly they appeared to belong to separate species. By studying each species, Kinsey expected to learn something about evolution, as variation offered unmistakable evidence of change over time, and change over time was but another term for evolution. From a biological standpoint, then, gall wasps were ideal for study. Abundant in nature, characterized by a plethora of species, wide-ranging in distribution, and easy to collect, gall wasps offered a lifetime of fruitful work to any entomologist with the will to persevere and the stamina to see a job through. And, of course, perseverance and stamina were Kinsey's strong suits.

Kinsey was also attracted to gall wasps because of their fascinating life histories. Some species had alternating generations, relatively rare in animals, though common enough in plants. As described by Kinsey, the distinguishing feature is that the offspring of one generation "bear no more resemblance to their parents, for instance, than a sheep bears to a goat, or a squirrel to a groundhog. The third generation of wasps looks like the first, and the fourth looks like the second, and so on, each of the two forms alternating in regular succession."[64] This problem puzzled and confused naturalists for many years. Not only did alternating generations produce offspring dissimilar in shape, size, and color; they could even differ in how they reproduced. For example, if the first generation included males and females that produced fertilized eggs, as was true of most animals, then the second generation would be agamic, or composed of females only. Although the eggs of the agamic generation could not be fertilized, they nevertheless grew into larvae, pupae, and insects, a puzzle Kinsey was quick to admit "no biologist thoroughly understands."[65]

As he confronted these and other questions, Kinsey drew upon the conceptual and technical tools of his day. Both the methods he employed and the ideas he used came from earlier investigators. He began by reviewing the literature on gall wasps and by examining gall wasp collections in various museums. He was indeed fortunate to be studying at Harvard, as the local libraries had virtually all the printed material on gall wasps, and the Museum of the Boston Society of Natural History and the Agassiz Museum housed several important gall wasp collections donated by earlier researchers.[66]

His review of the literature left Kinsey particularly impressed by the work of Hermann Adler, a physician and student of natural history from Schleswig, Germany.[67] In his dissertation, Kinsey sought to study American gall wasps in much the same manner Adler had studied the European species, focusing particularly on alternating generations. Early in 1918, he informed Natalie Roeth that he was enjoying himself immensely, largely because he was devoting all his time to his experiments.[68]

Kinsey's reference to experimentation was important, as it signified his determination to elevate his research to the standards of the New Biology. Unlike earlier students of natural history, he intended to base his work not merely on field observations but on breeding experiments. Explaining how he conducted the experimental portion of his work, Kinsey declared, "It involves the gathering of the galls by the thousands and tens of thousands, and breeding the adults out and putting them on the trees to form the next generations of galls." But he made it clear he had no intention of becoming a bench scientist. "You can appreciate that it means a great deal of field work, and detail[ed] observation of the tiny things—a job that is much more to my liking than the laboratory work which would be required if the problem were concerned solely with histology or anatomy," he declared.[69]

During the two years it took to complete his dissertation, Kinsey devoted countless hours to his breeding experiments. Through trial and error, he learned that mature insects could be raised successfully from hard, solid galls that had been stored for months in the laboratory. Conversely, he discovered that efforts to raise mature insects from soft, spongy, or hollow galls consistently failed if the galls were kept more than a week (or in some instance more than a few days) in the laboratory. The trick was to provide the proper environment. The best way to rear mature adults, he explained, was "to place the galls on an inch or more of moist sand in a low glass jar at least four or five inches in diameter."[70] This preserved just enough moisture to prevent the galls from drying out, but not enough to allow mold to form. Mold, he learned to his dismay, was a constant problem, which one could best avoid by placing the galls in earthen flower pots instead of glass jars, though the insects were easier to spot in the jars when they emerged.

The most important issue Kinsey confronted, however, was not alternating generations but the species problem. The lowest level of classification above the individual, species are the different kinds of organisms that make up life on earth. As scientists use the term, "species" refers to the building blocks of taxonomy, the lowest level of discontinuity in nature. As such, species are the basic units scientists assemble into genera, families, orders, classes, phyla, and finally kingdoms. Ironically, no single concept in the history of biology has caused more controversy among scientists than the species concept.[71] As Charles W. Johnson, an eminent taxonomist and contemporary of Kinsey, once remarked, "the way to start a hopeless and endless argument is to ask any group of taxonomists the simple question: What is a species?"[72]

Taxonomists of Kinsey's day came in two principal varieties—"lumpers" and "splitters." The two camps held opposing views on the species problem. Lumpers, who constituted the majority of taxonomists, responded to nature's infinite variety of life forms by assigning individuals that look alike to existing categories, often ignoring the subtle (and sometimes not so subtle) differences that existed among the specimens under study. Splitters, a highly vocal minority of taxonomists, gazed at those same variations and insisted they saw separate species. Therefore, lumpers tended to hold down the number of species by creating huge, comprehensive taxa, while splitters routinely expanded the number by emphasizing individual variation.[73]

The lumpers traced their intellectual heritage to Plato, who had extolled the timeless power of fixed forms. Noting that the shape of a triangle never varied, regardless of the combination of angles it possessed, Plato had theorized that the natural world was merely a reflection of a fixed number of eternal forms, which he called *eide,* later to be renamed essences by the Thomists during the Middle Ages.[74] Taxonomy felt the full weight of Plato's essentialism. The idea that things could be classified by the degree to which they resembled an ideal form dominated taxonomy until the second half of the nineteenth century. As Stephen Jay Gould has noted, classical taxonomists "viewed the world as a series of pigeonholes, each housing a species." Traditional taxonomists treated variation in nature, in Gould's words, as "a kind of accidental splaying out around the essential form, and serving only to create confusion in the correct assignment of pigeonholes."[75]

The most significant challenge to Platonic essentialism came from Charles Darwin, a formidable opponent indeed. Everywhere he looked,

Darwin saw evidence of changes in the world's life forms. While his research uncovered numerous examples of natural selection, adaptations,
progress, and descent, Darwin and his followers found nothing in nature
remotely resembling fixed essences. Rather, they explained evolution in
terms of infinitesimal gradation, with diversity as life's only irreducible
fact. And since nature was constantly changing, it followed that species had
no fixed essences, only a range of variations. Antiessentialists regarded immutable essences as illusionary, something man had created as a classificatory convenience. Variations, by contrast, were real. To see them, one had
only to open one's eyes. They existed everywhere; they were nature's only
given.[76]

Darwin's theories did not make a dent on many traditional taxonomists.
They went about their business as usual, creating new species for unmis-
takably "new" organisms and assigning everything else to previously
agreed-upon species. But systematists who sought to apply the concepts of
evolutionary biology to the species problem approached their work with
a new respect for the complexity of the task at hand. In contrast to traditional taxonomists, they became sensitive to the importance of variations,
large or small, within and among species.

Along with other evolutionary biologists, systematists were thrilled by
the rediscovery of Mendel's laws. Arguing that new species are the result
of mutations, Mendel's followers focused on the species problem with a
new sense of urgency. Many attempted to discover subspecies, which the
Mendelians called "races" and other taxonomists labeled geographic variants or varieties—all of which were widely recognized as incipient species.
One school of extreme reductionists even went so far as to deny the existence of species altogether. According to this group, the individual was the
only true category in nature, whereas species existed solely in the minds of
scientists as convenient concepts for classification.[77]

Philosophically, Wheeler was an antiessentialist, as are all splitters. Predisposed to look for variations in nature, he saw diversity as evolution's
handiwork. Wheeler had no more tolerance for immutable forms than for
fixed ideas. Change was the only constant in nature; and change was what
Wheeler saw and documented in his finely graded taxonomic studies. Writing to a colleague in 1917, he remarked that "in taxonomy it seems to be
important to recognize even the finest divisions of species . . . when practical to do so. The main danger seems to be that in continually splitting,
one tends to magnify the importance of the finest categories and to detach
them from the whole." Having acknowledged this pitfall, Wheeler added
perceptively, "If we could only carry on our classifications to minute detail
without losing the connections, we should, I believe, be doing useful
work."[78]

But that was the rub. Many splitters had great difficulty making the proper connections, and Wheeler himself did not escape this trap. His taxonomic work on ants suffered from excessive splitting, for he had a tendency, in the words of his biographers, "to describe many trivial variants as varieties and subspecies." Moreover, his practice of using a pentenomial system of nomenclature forced him to create "an unusual number of names that have since been relegated to synonymy."[79] The upshot was that much of his taxonomic work could not stand review and later had to be redone.

As Wheeler's student, Kinsey learned to follow Darwin and to reject Plato, becoming a splitter, not a lumper. Antiessentialism was an integral part of the scientific world view he absorbed at Harvard, as evolutionary biology was the only biology taught at the Bussey Institute. Like his mentor, Kinsey approached fieldwork expecting to encounter rich diversity, and that is what he discovered in the gall wasps he studied. But, during his graduate school days, his position on the species problem remained tentative. While he did identify sixteen new species, thereby significantly expanding the gall wasp catalog, he did not take a position on the issue beyond choosing Wheeler, a well-known splitter, as his adviser.

Upon its completion in 1919, Kinsey's dissertation, "Studies of Gall Wasps (Cynipidae, Hymenoptera)," ran to 250 pages and was distinguished by three things: the size of its sample, its meticulous attention to detail, and the quality of its prose. In contrast to most taxonomists, who based their studies on a few dozen specimens, Kinsey examined thousands of gall wasps and galls by the tens of thousands. This was an impressive effort. Similarly, his classifications rested on careful fieldwork and painstaking microscopic examinations in the laboratory, where he studied morphologic characters with uncommon rigor. Unlike many graduate students who break down at the writing stage, he was able to pull things together. In clear, concise prose, he laid out his proof of alternating generations and his discovery of new species, accompanied by detailed descriptions of each. In the years ahead, huge samples, detailed character examinations, and serviceable prose would become defining features of Kinsey's work.

His friend and fellow graduate student Edgar Anderson recalled vividly the reception of Kinsey's dissertation. "I was working in Dr. East's laboratory one morning when Dean Wheeler . . . came in with Kinsey's thesis in his hands. 'It's a remarkably fine piece of work[,]' he said to Dr. East, 'he is really of very high caliber.' " Anderson went on to explain, "All of the Bussey professors left the students pretty much to their own devices but Wheeler as a matter of principle carried this policy to greater lengths than any of the others. He really had seen so little of Kinsey that he had not sized him up until the graduate years were practically over."[80]

Wheeler's reaction marked a watershed in Kinsey's life, guaranteeing him a future in science. Kinsey had come to Harvard with one burning ambition—to become a scientist. And not just any scientist, either, but a great scientist. He had learned from Wheeler that science still had room for gifted naturalists who could write descriptive biology in clear, expository prose. In essence, Wheeler had taught him to believe in historical reconstruction over experimental biology.

Kinsey received his doctor of science degree from Harvard in September 1919; and he immediately reaped a reward for writing a strong dissertation. Thanks to Wheeler's recommendation, Kinsey enjoyed a year of financial security as the recipient of a Sheldon Traveling Fellowship (1919–20). A prestigious postdoctoral award reserved for Harvard's top graduates, it carried a stipend of $1,500, a princely sum in those days.[81] It enabled Kinsey to delay going on the job market for a year, giving him the opportunity to expand and deepen his research. "My last few weeks at the Bussey were such busy ones that I hardly had time to express to you and the others my deep appreciation of what you did for me, and of all that my years at the Bussey have meant to me," a grateful Kinsey wrote Wheeler on the eve of leaving Boston. "I shall think very often of the Bussey, and of the good friendships made there!" Describing his preparations for his year in the field to Wheeler, Kinsey added, "I have taken some time to prepare, as completely as possible, the details of equipment, etc., for my trip. And I anticipate that, in consequence, my time will be very largely free for actual collecting."[82]

Since his dissertation had been based largely on material from the eastern United States, Kinsey headed west. He traveled on foot with a rucksack, using trains to move from one collecting spot to the next and shipping his specimens back at regular intervals by mail to the Bussey Institute. A week after leaving Boston, he wrote Wheeler, "Collecting has begun very satisfactorily." Indeed, it had. At this point, Kinsey's itinerary had taken him into southern New Jersey, Cape Charles, Virginia, and the western slope of the Alleghenies in West Virginia. "I am managing to keep ahead of the frost," declared Kinsey. "I am traveling so far as possible at night, getting off at small country stations very early in the morning, and hiking all day," he continued. "My suit case with extra equipment I send ahead by train, but all my equipment necessary for a few days I carry on my back, in my pack," he explained. "I do quite a little of my own cooking, which is great fun, and makes it possible for me to get a considerable distance into the woods and mountains." While he camped many nights, Kinsey noted, "Sometimes I have stopped in small towns over night, where I find private houses that give me very nice board, much nicer than at the country hotels, and considerably cheaper." Pleased by how well the year had begun, he added, "I estimate, roughly, that if I continue collecting at this rate I shall obtain several hundreds of thousands of specimens by the end of the trip."[83]

From West Virginia, Kinsey headed to North Carolina and Georgia, and then worked his way down into Texas. Greasing the wheels before his intrepid student, Wheeler asked his old friend Carl Hartman at the University of Texas to provide a table in his laboratory for Kinsey and to show him places around Austin where he could study oaks and their galls. "He [Kinsey] has done a most remarkable piece of work on Cynipids, and you will find him a very delightful young man and extremely appreciative of anything you may do for him," wrote Wheeler.[84]

By the time Kinsey reached Texas in December, he had collected in fifty-four different locations and was hungry for the company of other scientists. Thanks to Wheeler's introduction, Kinsey received a warm reception at the University of Texas. He and Hartman spent a pleasant afternoon together exploring the hills around Austin and some profitable hours in Hartman's laboratory discussing oaks. "I found my way into some good collecting territory due to Dr. Hartman's direction," Kinsey wrote Wheeler. Noting that this was the first chance he had had to discuss his work with another scientist since leaving Boston, Kinsey confessed that "it was very pleasant to have some company."[85]

As Kinsey resumed his westward trek, Wheeler continued to open doors before him. Wheeler arranged for him to receive a table for a few weeks at the Desert Botanical Laboratory in Tucson, Arizona. Talking up his boy, Wheeler told the laboratory's director that Kinsey had done "a remarkable piece of work on gall wasps," adding, "He has made himself a thorough master of his subject in an incredibly short time and has thrown quite a new light on several of the obscure problems connected with the oak gall makers, their alternations of generations, etc."[86] As before, Wheeler's letter produced the desired results, and Kinsey reaped the professional benefits that only students who work with distinguished major professors are fortunate enough to enjoy.

The rest of the year brought more of the same, with Kinsey gradually making it all the way to California. It was a tribute to his careful planning that things went as well as they did. Still, there were a few mishaps, not all of which occurred in the field. On at least one occasion, the galls Kinsey mailed back to Boston hatched unexpectedly. Not until twenty years later did he learn how upset one of his professors had become when the cynipids filled the building.[87]

Thanks to his fellowship, Kinsey was able to spend fifteen months in the field. Carrying everything he took with him in a backpack, he visited thirty-six states and traveled a total of 18,000 miles, more than 2,500 on foot.

His bug-hunting took him to remote mountain ranges in the far north, where he went for days at a time without seeing another living soul.[88] Kinsey accomplished more than research during his fellowship year. Ever since boyhood, nature had been his proving ground, the arena in which he pitted himself against the earth and the elements in order to demonstrate competence and to build self-confidence. His travels during 1919–20 were his greatest challenge to date. Collecting in remote areas required superior outdoor skills, courage, and self-reliance, and Kinsey possessed each in full measure. Several years later, he told the story of the time he lost the trail one night in the deserts of New Mexico. While a goat rancher and a forest ranger waited anxiously for him to come out of the mountains, Kinsey had to make his way as best he could. "I . . . had to drop into the canyon and climb down for weary miles, over the boulders and through the water, hitting cactus thorns that made my hands fester for a month; and the two waiting men used profanity; but I had found some very fine specimens in those mountains!" recalled Kinsey.[89] Thus, with every mountain he climbed, with every desert he traversed, and with every forest he harvested, Kinsey was proving his mettle to the scientific community and to himself. In that sense, his year as a Sheldon Traveling Fellow was very much a private pilgrimage for him.

Anderson remembered talking with Kinsey shortly after he returned from his year of fieldwork. "He noted many things besides insects," observed Anderson. "Like a certain kind of newspaper reporter he customarily looked at mankind with a kindly but quizzical eye and was immensely curious about how people spent their lives and what they did and why." Kinsey encountered many people during his travels—some appealing, some appalling. "I remember . . . his telling a group of us about a fascinating old bum he had met on a refuse dump in the outskirts of Butte, Montana," Anderson recalled. "The man was living there quite happily in a hut put together from odds and ends of salvage. He had begun the conversation by saying in a cultured voice, 'Ah, I perceive that you are an entomologist. What kind of insects might you be searching for here?' " Anderson then related how Kinsey sat down and spent the afternoon exchanging technical information on Cynipidae "for an inside view of life as a penniless squatter on city dumps." Shelter was not a problem, and neither, it seems, was food, but Kinsey heard an earful about the old man's difficulties in keeping himself stocked in alcohol.[90]

Kinsey cherished the things he learned during his year as a Sheldon Traveling Fellow. After he became a professor, he often drew upon these experiences to explain to students the thrill of being a biologist. "I have put up with lumberjacks and miners, slept with permit prospectors whose blankets were undescribable and unforgettable [indeed!], met cattlemen and sheep herders, and folks of many other sorts, even including a few out-laws; have crossed cattle- and wolf-spotted deserts, and lived once for days without seeing another human being in the mountains of Southern Arizona," declared Kinsey. "In all those days I collected insects. I also collected memories of trails of hundreds of camps, of such folks as are to be met, and of stretches of glorious countries." Reflecting on those memories, Kinsey added, "I am not certain which of my collections is the more precious."[91]

Conducting fieldwork, wearing khaki, getting close to nature, surviving in the wild, meeting people from different backgrounds, and dealing with them in their own habitats—these were experiences no bench scientist could expect to know. Kinsey had made a good decision. For a man with his interests, taxonomic entomology was the right choice.

Overall, everything about his graduate education had worked out well for Kinsey. For the remainder of his life, he would look back on his Harvard years with fondness and be grateful he had worked with Wheeler. Kinsey had learned many things at the Bussey Institute. First and foremost was an unshakable faith in science. In the years ahead, Kinsey would never question science's ability to discover truth. His faith in the scientific method was absolute. It brooked no doubts, allowed no misgivings. Nor would Kinsey question the value of seeking truth. "Anything true is worth discovering," he would later write, adding, "Much of our most valuable knowledge has come through work which, at the time, was done in order to discover truth, with no thought of a practical application."[92]

Kinsey would always approach scientific questions with the skills he had honed at Harvard. Eschewing bench work and only grudgingly committed to experimental research, he would steadfastly believe, as he declared a few years after finishing graduate school, that "the best proofs are to be obtained by direct observation" and, as a corollary, that human senses "furnish the best means of observations."[93] He would teach his students the importance of observation, by ridiculing monks in the Middle Ages who were so steeped in Platonic theorizing that they engaged in endless debates about how many teeth horses had instead of examining and counting them![94] And he would be just as categorical about the virtue of skepticism. Explaining what it means to be scientific, he would later tell his students to question everything, to accept nothing at face value, and to doubt everything they heard or read unless it was supported by hard evidence.[95]

Kinsey had also learned not to measure success by wealth. After leaving Harvard, he wrote, "There are 'successful' men, as the world rates them; men at the heart of big business, storing up means for enjoying the years that lie ahead of them. But when they ultimately draw the financial rewards which the world can give them, the homes, the leisure, and the other comforts that can be purchased, will they find it a worth-while world into which they are retiring?" Kinsey thought not. They might possess great wealth, but they would never know what he called "the soul-feeding aspects of the biologic sciences."[96]

In large measure, Kinsey's antimaterialism stemmed from his boyhood struggles. Affluent South Orange, it seems, had left Kinsey resentful of wealthy people. Several years after leaving Harvard, he devoted a book chapter to parasites. Parasites, he explained, "must reap not only the ill-fortune that may come to one individual, itself, but in addition all of that which is coming to its host." To illustrate the point, Kinsey cited the fate of bird lice when their host bird is killed. Then he added pointedly, "The poor little rich boy who has always had servants do things for him would find himself in an awkward circumstance if his servants should expire and there were no means in the wide world of ever getting other ones." There it was: compared with self-reliant boys like himself, "poor little rich boys" were social parasites.[97]

Kinsey's heroes were scientists, and the scientists he admired most were taxonomists. In his mind, taxonomists could be likened to the intrepid conquistadores of the age of exploration. "If, in making a collection, you should discover an undescribed and wholly new insect or plant or other such thing," Kinsey later told high school students, "then you might properly become as excited as though you were Columbus finding a new continent, or Balboa discovering the Pacific Ocean."[98] To Kinsey, taxonomists were adventurous interlopers who kept wanderlust alive. There was, he insisted, "no country, no wild and rugged region, that has not been invaded by the taxonomist." His "own small list of friends," boasted Kinsey, included taxonomists who had collected in Central America, Australia, China, Newfoundland and Labrador, and the Guianas, as well as "one who has crossed and recrossed the wilds of the African jungles." Ultimately, all scientific research, he asserted, "is done mainly because scientists like to do it. For the fun of it!"[99]

Kinsey was proud to enter a profession so widely admired in the United States. A few years after leaving Harvard, he would shrewdly remark, "There are few subjects in the curriculum which do not wish to be rated as sciences." Economics and sociology had become social sciences; pedagogy preferred to be called the science of education; and even history claimed it had become more scientific. Things had reached the point that science's imprimaturs had real advertising value, making it imperative, he noted tongue in cheek, that "underwear and yeast be endorsed by a great scientist."[100] It is easy to see why Kinsey, as one who had worked long and hard for upward mobility and had struggled to earn approval through acts of piety and community service, would enjoy his newfound status.

At the Bussey Institute, Kinsey also learned that science should uplift mankind. Several of his teachers pointed to the social potential of the new secular religion—psychoanalysis. But eugenics was their favorite cause, in part because it claimed to be rooted in theories of heredity. Wheeler's preferred medium for advancing reforms was the satirical essay; and his masterpiece in this genre (and the best-known of his many essays) was an article entitled "The Termitodoxa, or Biology and Society," which originally appeared in *Scientific Monthly* in 1920. In this essay, he conjured up an imaginary termite kingdom whose members had granted absolute authority to biologists. Relishing their newfound power as social engineers, the biologists instituted many reforms. They crushed the anarchists in their midst and abolished the professions of priests, pedagogues, politicians, and journalists. In addition, they instituted rigid eugenics and birth control programs.[101]

Because these issues were very much in the air in 1920, friends and admirers showered Wheeler with praise for this essay. Many remarked on its humor and erudition, while others endorsed its exalted opinion of biologists, secure in the belief that they should rule society. In an age when scientists announced that they were on the threshold of understanding heredity and controlling human behavior, it seemed only right that biologists should step to the front and shape policies that could reform society and improve mankind. Intelligent, disinterested, selfless, objective, hardworking, and inherently moral, biologists deserved to be the new social engineers of the twentieth century.

No one admired Wheeler's essay more than Kinsey. It became one of his favorite pieces; and though he read it many, many times, he never seemed to tire of it. Years after he had departed Harvard, the essay still amused him. "He would chuckle over it at his desk and periodically lend a reprint of it to some graduate student with the admonition that he treasured it," recalled a former Kinsey student. And whenever it left his hands, the student added, Kinsey always said, "Please do not forget to return it."[102]

His delight in Wheeler's satire was a benchmark of how far Kinsey had come. When he had entered Harvard, Kinsey would probably have condemned without a second thought Wheeler's vision of a brave new world run by biologists. How could any Eagle Scout and Christian gentleman read disparaging remarks about priests, educators, political leaders, and journalists and not be angered to his bones? Attacks on vested authority were highly disrespectful if not downright heretical. But four years at Harvard had changed Kinsey. After hanging around Wheeler and other godless scientists, he had grown less rigid morally and had become more skeptical of authority. Policymakers no longer seemed infallible merely because they claimed to speak for God or the state, and public policy seemed misguided unless it rested on sound science. Thanks to Wheeler's influence,

Kinsey left Boston believing that biologists should become social engineers, shaping public policy and altering private attitudes on a variety of issues, ranging from eugenics to private morality.

In short, Kinsey emerged from Harvard a changed man. At some point during his graduate education, his belief in God began to weaken. Why remains unclear, since he left no records on the subject. Still, what happened to Kinsey was a familiar story. Many deeply religious young men of his generation entered graduate school in the sciences only to emerge agnostics or atheists because they were unable to reconcile the conflicts between science and religion. Undoubtedly this was what happened to Kinsey. After four years of rigorous scientific training, he had learned to think independently and to reevaluate his world view. Somewhere along the way, the young Christian gentleman had started losing ground to the hard-nosed young scientist who demanded proof for everything.

Kinsey's religious crisis was accompanied by a surging faith in science. As his belief in God waned, science rapidly became the integrating principle of his life, the thing that got him up in the morning and put him to bed at night. Not that Kinsey had grown less interested in morality—far from it. Rather, he had been drawn to a new sensibility, one that reflected his culture's growing faith in science. If anything, his devotion to research bore the unmistakable stamp of displaced religious fervor. It was as though science was his new religion, the academy his new house of worship, and research the method by which he proposed to discover truth. Immersed in the culture of science, he was becoming totally absorbed in securing his status within an elite corps, one whose rising cultural authority rested on brilliant ideas and impressive discoveries. That is why Wheeler's article delighted Kinsey: he identified with its heroes, the biologists. Harvard had given him a new identity: Kinsey was a scientist.

And with his new identity came one final bequest from Harvard—a job. While Kinsey was off exploring the Great American West, Wheeler and other professors at the Bussey Institute were busy trying to place him in a teaching position. In April 1920, Wheeler attended a scientific conference in Washington, D.C., where he talked with Carl H. Eigenmann, the chairman of the zoology department and dean of the Graduate School at Indiana University, the flagship campus of the Hoosier State. Eigenmann mentioned that his department had an opening, and Wheeler immediately nominated Kinsey.

The problem was that no one knew where to reach Kinsey. While he was thought to be working his way back East, his last shipment of galls had come from Colorado and his current location was anybody's guess. But Wheeler had no intention of letting this opportunity slip away. After returning to Boston, he informed Eigenmann, "I have forwarded to Mr.

Kinsey's father an account of the position you spoke about at the University of Indiana, begging him to telegraph his son as I do not know his exact whereabouts."[103] A week or so later, a persistent Wheeler contacted Eigenmann again, asking if he had been able to reach Kinsey and letting it be known that another school was in the running. Syracuse University, he told Eigenmann, "is very desirous of getting hold of Kinsey."[104]

But fate had no intention of consigning Kinsey to the East. When news of the job at Indiana finally caught up with him, Kinsey was visiting at Ohio State University, only a skip and a hop from Indiana. Early in May, he went to Bloomington for an interview. Following this visit, Eigenmann recommended to William Lowe Bryan, the president of Indiana University, that Kinsey be appointed. As beginning jobs go, this was a good position, offering considerable responsibility and plenty of room for advancement. Kinsey, explained Eigenmann, was "to take charge of the introductory course in Biology for the Home Economics students and develop this into a general course for art students." In addition, Kinsey was "to have charge in Entomology during the spring term and develop the work in Entomology" and "to assist in the laboratories where he is most needed."[105]

In describing the candidate's qualifications to Bryan, Eigenmann emphasized Kinsey's ten years of work in boys camps, as well as his experience as a laboratory assistant and instructor at Harvard. Above all, Eigenmann stressed Kinsey's academic excellence, noting, "His research work in insects has been done with M. W. [sic] Wheeler of Harvard who pronounces him the best student he has had."[106] This was all Bryan needed to hear. A few days later, he formally notified Kinsey that he had been elected by the board of trustees to a position as an assistant professor in the Department of Zoology at Indiana University. The position carried a salary of $2,000 and began on August 1, 1920.[107]

In July 1920, at the age of twenty-six, Kinsey left the golden East, following a trail blazed by generations of young scholars who had ventured to the nation's heartland to seek their academic fortunes. But Kinsey got more than he bargained for. In addition to launching his career, he fell in love soon after arriving in Bloomington.

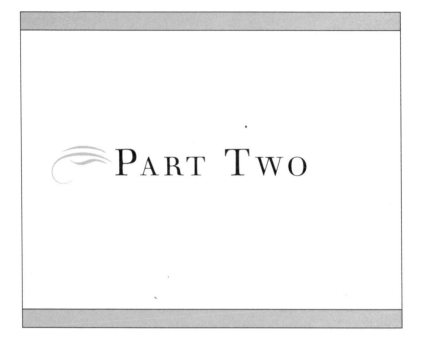

PART TWO

"We Sort of Migrated Together"

 insey arrived in Bloomington in August 1920. Since classes did not begin until early September, he had free time on his hands for the first instance in many years. Not entirely free, though. He had books and bugs to unpack and an office to set up. His office was located in Biology Hall, a ten-year-old building with handsome woodwork, high ceilings, and huge, double-hung glass windows. The zoology department's main laboratories and offices were located on the top floor, with additional office space in the west end of the basement. Kinsey was assigned a basement corner office.[1]

If Boston was "the hub of the universe," his new home presented a striking contrast. Bloomington was a backwater. One longtime resident described it as "a hick town," while another called it "a hotbed of indifference."[2] The seat of Monroe County, it had a population in 1920 that did not exceed 20,000 residents, including the college students.

Kinsey did not need anyone to tell him that his new home was off the beaten track. Then as now, Bloomington was isolated from the major urban centers of the Midwest. Indianapolis lies about fifty miles to the north; Cincinnati, nearly a hundred miles to the southeast. Trains were the usual mode of travel, but service was slow and infrequent. Less than a decade before Kinsey's arrival, a departing senior from Indiana University complained that the train consisted of a "neurasthenic engine, [and] three prehistoric passenger coaches which will stop at the least provocation."[3] Of course, the automobile helped relieve the sense of isolation, but Indiana's roads in the 1920s were notoriously poor, making travel a real adventure. Besides, Kinsey did not acquire a car until several years after he arrived in Bloomington.[4]

As a dyed-in-the-wool easterner, Kinsey must have been struck by the regional differences he encountered. In many respects, his new home was a blend of the South and the Midwest. While residents celebrated national holidays with religious conviction, the town's pace and spirit seemed more southern than northern. The monument in front of the county courthouse to the Confederate soldiers who died in the Civil War stood as a reminder that the people who had settled Bloomington in the nineteenth century had close ties to the Old South, and Hoosiers were quick to point out that all of southern Indiana bore the nickname Kentuckiana.

The weather reinforced this southern image. Bloomington sits in a valley surrounded by heavily wooded, gently rolling hills. The hills are limestone, which holds heat and humidity with grim efficiency. As a result, Bloomington's summers tend to be hot and muggy, a vivid contrast to the cool weather he had enjoyed working at summer camps in New England.

Compared with bustling Boston, Bloomington was a sleepy college town. It had one hotel (the Grove), one picture show, and few good restaurants. Bloomington was "dry" long before the days of prohibition, and even during the Roaring Twenties local ministers had enough pull to close the movie theater on Sundays. Those same ministers promptly visited congregation members who missed church on Sunday.[5]

Visitors from the East frequently commented on the town's air of southern hospitality. Monroe County's "plain folk" deepened Bloomington's provincial image. All they had to do was speak, and their words did the rest. Their accent was heavy, with a thick twang, flat *a*'s, and grating nasal tones. "It was quite a shock coming from the East," declared one faculty wife who moved to Bloomington in the 1930s after growing up in Princeton, New Jersey. "I couldn't even understand some of the natives." Visitors frequently voiced the same complaint and wondered if the region's plain folk were throwbacks to the nineteenth century.

Many were. Within five miles of town, farmers still lived in log cabins and read the Bible by kerosene lamps. On weekends, they left the hinterland and came to town. As late as the 1930s, many farmers made the journey on horseback or in horse-drawn wagons, swelling Bloomington's normal population by the thousands as they congregated at the town square to shop and visit. Their favorite gathering spot was the grounds of the county courthouse. On Saturday mornings, stone cutters, who toiled in the nearby limestone quarries, mingled easily with tobacco-chewing farmers, discussing the weather, crops, and politics, while their womenfolk sat nearby on curbs and benches, some nursing babies as they chatted. Joining them was the usual assortment of "town dog" loafers and sages who lived in the city but enjoyed gabbing with their country cousins. If conversation lagged, people turned their attention to the "snakeoil men" who worked the crowds on the courthouse grounds, plying concoctions with strange-sounding names that guaranteed miraculous cures for any ailment.

No doubt, the weekend spectacle at the courthouse made Kinsey feel as if he had stepped onto another planet. Granted, he had known farmers in New England, but Monroe County's plain folk were different. They were not as well educated, and easterners had difficulty understanding them when they spoke. They represented a way of life that was vanishing. In the past, every federal census had shown that most Americans lived in the countryside, but the census of 1920 revealed an important change: for the first time in American history, the majority of Americans lived in cities. Rural folk represented the nation's past; city people, its future. And Kinsey had urban leanings. He loved libraries, universities, music—in short, the cultural life that cities offered. As a professor, he would have great difficulty relating to Hoosier children from poor schools who did not share his devotion to highbrow culture.

Still, Kinsey's impressions of his new home cannot all have been unfavorable. Bloomington was a handsome community, and most residents enjoyed living there. Lined with beautiful maple and poplar trees, the major streets were clean and paved, and people took pride in their lawns, shrubs, and flower gardens. Certainly, Kinsey must have admired the town's physical beauty. There was none of the urban blight associated with an industrial city, nothing to stir up his childhood memories of Hoboken.

Bloomington was a world of face-to-face relationships, a tightly knit community where everyone knew everyone else's business. Local merchants called customers by their first names, and it was the sort of town where people sat on the porches in the evenings and visited with neighbors. Crime was rare; the cost of living was low (housing, in particular, was a real bargain); and recreation was plentiful. Nearby state parks offered outdoor enthusiasts beautiful streams and lakes for fishing and swimming. A scant sixteen miles to the south lay the hills of Brown County, home to a flourishing colony of rustic landscape artists.[6]

Academic families clustered in the eastern part of town, in neighborhoods close to the university. Located just a few blocks from the town square, Indiana University and its surrounding neighborhoods formed a classic academic enclave. In the words of one resident, it was as though Bloomington harbored two separate worlds "very sharply divided by Walnut Street between the west side and east—and never the twain shall meet." Kinsey arrived at special time in the university's history. Established as a state institution in 1820, Indiana University was celebrating its one hundredth birthday in 1920. At the beginning of the fall term, it had approximately 2,350 students and 100 faculty members. The university—with its books, its professors, its concerts, and its speakers—was an oasis of culture and learning.[7]

Like most faculty members, Kinsey elected to live near the university. He boarded with a faculty family on East Third Street, within easy walking distance of the campus. While his living arrangements were less than ideal, Kinsey was lucky to find a room anywhere, as housing was scarce. In 1920, the city had few apartment buildings and even fewer dormitories, so students and unmarried junior faculty typically boarded in private homes. But it really did not matter where Kinsey slept. He spent most of his time at Indiana University.

As a nature lover, Kinsey must have admired the campus. Though its area was huge, encompassing nearly 2,000 acres, Indiana University looked like a manicured park, with sculptured shrubs and neatly trimmed lawns. Red brick walkways, dating to the 1880s, crisscrossed the campus, connecting buildings of different ages and designs, some pleasing to the eye, others undistinguished. Several were of Gothic design—large and imposing, with menacing gargoyles on their roof corners. A few buildings had red brick exteriors, but most were covered with limestone cut from the nearby quarries.

Trees gave the campus its special beauty—maples, oaks, poplars, hickories, sweet gums, pines, and spruce—the variety seemed endless. Many had been standing when Indiana was still a territory, giving parts of the campus the look and feel of a virgin forest. Lovely the year round, they were truly spectacular in the fall, setting the campus ablaze with fiery reds and splashes of orange, crimson, purple, and yellow.

Nestled among the trees was the Jordan River. Named in honor of David Starr Jordan, the distinguished scientist who had served as president of Indiana University during the late nineteenth century, the Jordan was a clear, shallow creek with a glistening bed of white stone. It flowed from east to west across the campus, gradually broadening as it reached the grassy plain called Dunn Meadow. Another campus landmark, Dunn Meadow was deeded in perpetuity to the students of Indiana University by a local farmer, with the provision that title would not pass until the last cow grazing in the meadow had died.

As he walked around campus, Kinsey could congratulate himself. As first jobs go, Indiana University was a good placement. He was a college professor, a junior professor to be sure, but a professor nonetheless, with a beginning salary of $2,000.[8] Still, Kinsey's private life remained troubled and confused. He also had to endure the pain of being emotionally isolated, a man who felt at odds with the people around him. Other men his age were marrying and beginning families; he had never dated. And he had to live with the fear that he was different, that he might never fit in.[9]

Increasingly, he must have had a hard time with guilt feelings, doubts about his masculinity, and conflicts regarding his sexual orientation. How could he be secure when his sexual attraction to other men placed him outside the bounds of civilized morality? Religion, the law, and medicine told him that his sexual desires were sinful, criminal, and pathological.

Whatever his inner conflicts, Kinsey kept them hidden. Outwardly, he did not arouse suspicions, since he did not fit any of the stereotypes of homosexual males. Besides, the whole question of homosexuality was all but invisible in American culture. Physicians and a few other "experts" might know a little about it, but the general public remained woefully ignorant. Largely because homosexuality remained enshrouded in taboo, newspapers and magazines generally ignored it. Absent clear evidence to the contrary, people assumed that everyone was heterosexual. Certainly, no eyebrows were raised when Kinsey arrived in Bloomington unmarried. Partly for economic reasons and partly because graduate school demanded total dedication, many men completed their advanced education before wedding. One biologist who was trained in the late 1920s remarked that graduate students "led a fairly monastic life in those days." As far as the rest of the world could tell, Kinsey fit this mold perfectly.[10]

Yet from the moment he arrived in Bloomington, Kinsey acted like a man who wanted to make important changes in his life. While the habits of a lifetime could not be erased overnight, he made a conscious effort to meet people and to start building a social life, items he had neglected in the past. "Folks are very congenial here," he wrote a friend soon after arriving, "and I've found a great many friends already."[11] Kinsey was exaggerating. While he did join some groups that enjoyed camping and nature hikes, the relationships he formed were casual or superficial.

All that changed when he met Clara Bracken McMillen. In many respects, she was the ideal mate for Kinsey. While he was eager to begin a female relationship, it had to be with a woman who was secure and unafraid to make the first move; a woman who could look beyond his awkwardness to see his merit. Clara fit the bill. Not only was she friendly, confident, and self-possessed; she was strongly attracted to Kinsey from the first. Photographs from the period show a high-waisted, slightly plump, round-faced young woman. Her eyes were bright and lively, with a nice twinkle, and she wore her thick, dark hair in a Dutch bob, as was the fashion for college women in the 1920s. Had she worked on her appearance, Clara might have turned some heads. But she seemed oblivious to her looks. At a time when Madison Avenue was telling young women to use eyeshadow, face powder, lipstick, and rouge, she wore virtually no makeup. If anything, Clara looked downright boyish. More than her physical features, her style of dressing was masculine. Her taste in clothes—untailored pants, loose-fitting blouses, and baggy coats—was frumpish. It was almost as though she worked at dressing unattractively.

Kinsey and Clara had met during his interview at Indiana the preceding spring. Though only a junior, Clara was recognized as the university's best chemistry major and was introduced to Kinsey just before he delivered a lecture to a meeting of Sigma Xi, the national honor society in science. In later years, Clara would recall that she had found Kinsey "a very interesting young man" and would take special delight in noting that they had met under "very scientific circumstances."[12] They did not see each other again until the fall, but during the summer she occasionally thought about the young entomologist from Harvard, even if she could not remember his name.[13]

Clara was a native Hoosier, the only child of Josephine Bracken McMillen and William Lincoln McMillen. Born on October 2, 1898, in Brookville, Indiana, she had spent her childhood in this small canal town on the Whitewater River. Clara's father, the son of a country doctor, completed his degree at Indiana University, then taught English there for a few years before becoming a teacher in Fort Wayne.[14] There he climbed the public school career ladder, eventually serving as the chairman of the English department at Fort Wayne High School and the supervisor of English curriculum for the entire Fort Wayne school system. Clara's mother, a skilled musician who had studied at the College of Music in Cincinnati, Indiana University, and Harvard University, devoted her life to making a home for her husband and family.[15] Though she had taught school briefly to help finance her education before she was married, Josephine did not return to the classroom until Clara was grown and William had died.[16]

As an only child whose maternal grandparents lived in the same small town, Clara got plenty of attention. Both parents took an active role in her rearing, and her grandparents doted on her. On the material level, her life was equally secure. While her father did not earn enough money for family vacations in Europe or private schools for Clara, they owned their own home and always seemed to manage well with what they had. Nevertheless, as befitted the daughter of a schoolteacher and a Scot, Clara grew up knowing the value of a dollar. The entire family had a strong work ethic, and her mother taught her to cook and sew, not to mention the fine art of canning vegetables. But the fear of God did not intrude on her childhood, for the McMillens wore their religion lightly. As an adult, Clara would describe her parents as "inactive Protestants."[17]

Unlike Kinsey, Clara had a good relationship with her family and felt happy as a child. Nothing in her religious training, moreover, resembled the harsh faith of Kinsey's childhood. Nor did Clara suffer any traumatic illnesses. She was healthy and robust, excelled at team sports, and developed into a strong swimmer.

Still, other features of their backgrounds were similar. Each grew up in a household with a traditional division of labor. In both families, the men worked outside the home and the women worked inside it. In terms of their immediate role models, then, Kinsey and Clara both had parents who conformed to middle-class gender roles. Each had a housewife for a mother and a teacher for a father. Moreover, each was taught to value academic achievement.

Kinsey and Clara also shared a love of nature. As a child, Clara was something of a tomboy. She enjoyed hiking and was keenly interested in insects. She spent her summers stalking butterflies in her grandparents' garden, lurking beneath streetlamps to ambush cecropia moths (she kept her own killing jar at the neighborhood drugstore), and advertising in the local paper for caterpillars to add to her collection.[18] After graduating from Fort Wayne public high school, Clara studied for a year with her uncle who taught high school chemistry in Fort Wayne. Her background in science strengthened, she enrolled as a freshman at Indiana University in the fall of 1917.

It was only natural that she should pick Indiana. Her father and two of her uncles were Indiana alumni; and she had visited both the town and the campus frequently as a child. Her career plans, however, were unusual for a woman of her day. "I came here with the full intention of majoring in chemistry," she later explained, "and I sort of thought that I might become a research chemist."[19]

Clara's performance quickly validated her ambitions, as she compiled a brilliant undergraduate record at Indiana University. Her honors included Phi Beta Kappa, Sigma Xi, and graduation with high distinction. Though she minored in physics and mathematics, chemistry remained her passion. During her junior year, Clara was selected by Professor Robert Lyons to represent Indiana University in the national chemistry contest sponsored annually by Alpha Chi Sigma, the honorary chemistry fraternity. By tradition, this honor went to the school's top undergraduate chemistry major. Clara took first place. The national chapter of Alpha Chi Sigma awarded her a medal; the local chapter gave her a dozen red roses.[20]

Clara's success was no accident. Like Kinsey, she had a strong desire to excel, and as an undergraduate, she put her studies first. "I always lived in a private home, and I always had a private room," she explained, "so that I didn't have anyone to disturb me when I wanted to study." But good grades came easily to her; in fact, she seemed to take everything in stride. "There were none of these conflicts of what should you do, and who you were," she later explained. "I never thought about who I was, I knew who I was, I was Clara McMillen!"[21]

And Clara McMillen was a woman who knew how to have fun. Despite her many honors and outstanding record, she was not a grind. Unlike Kinsey, she could relax and enjoy herself without a trace of guilt. She played intramural sports (one friend recalled her as a fierce competitor in field hockey) and earned her "I.U." letter sweater from the Women's Athletic Association.[22] Clara was an avid hiker, well into old age. "I started hiking around Bloomington almost as soon as I arrived," she recalled. "I go cross-country," she later boasted, "over fences and streams and . . . through briars."[23]

The outdoors brought Clara and Kinsey together. Early in the fall, they both attended a zoology department picnic at Spring Hill in Mitchell, Indiana, about thirty-five miles south of Bloomington. Having taken his ornithology course the preceding spring, Clara was on friendly terms with Will Scott, one of Kinsey's senior colleagues. In fact, she adored Scott as a teacher, and when he told her about plans for the picnic, she finagled an invitation to come along. "I sort of invited myself," she later confessed. The reason for her maneuvering was transparent. Kinsey was the only unattached male, and she was the only unattached female. So, as she put it, "Naturally, we sort of migrated together."[24]

Actually, Clara did most of the migrating. Everyone else huddled around a common campfire, but Kinsey, as was his habit, split off from the group. He had brought his own food and built his own immaculate campfire. Clara joined him. "I helped him cook, and I had a wonderful time," she exclaimed.[25] It was an omen of their life together—Kinsey striking out on his own, Clara casting her lot with him and doing all she could to assist.

At the end of the department picnic, the Scotts started gathering persimmons, and Kinsey and Clara helped. "Mrs. Scott made persimmon pudding," Clara explained, "and she asked some of us over for dinner, and so I saw him [Kinsey] again then."[26] (Persimmon pudding later became Clara's standard dessert for guests.) In addition to Kinsey and Clara, the Scotts invited another single woman that evening. "He took the other woman home," Clara declared, "which disappointed me very much."[27]

She had better luck when they met again at a Phi Beta Kappa meeting a few weeks later. This time, Kinsey asked to walk her home, and Clara happily consented. Though he was definitely interested now, their first real date did not follow until November, when he invited her on a picnic with friends. They went to the hills of nearby Brown County, where Kinsey told stories around a campfire about his volunteer work with the Bethany Boys Club during his years at Harvard. Clara was not impressed. She considered herself something of a freethinker and feared that Kinsey was, in her words, "too churchy."[28] Clara need not have worried. The fact that he was pursuing her bore testimony to his waning religiosity, as she made no bones of her lack of religious conviction. At any rate, she decided to accept his next social invitation, and more dates followed.

Soon their relationship became serious, so much so that Kinsey bought Clara a Christmas gift. His lack of experience with women showed. Instead of choosing something personal, he gave Clara a compass, a hunting knife, and a pair of Bass hiking shoes, gifts that reflected their common interest in the outdoors but might have been exchanged by male friends.[29] Despite his awkwardness, however, Kinsey proved to be an eager suitor. "I have heard a lot of things about his being very shy," Clara later confessed, "but I didn't find him particularly so." On the contrary, she found him very direct, and their attachment progressed rapidly.[30]

To Kinsey, Clara was someone who shared his interests and might be willing to share his life. In a letter to his high school biology teacher, he described Clara as "a graduate student working in chemistry at Indiana University." Kinsey proudly proclaimed, "She is a very brilliant scholar; is one of the best athletes in the place. She knows the birds better than I do, knows flowers and trees, etc., is a capable hiker and camper, a champion swimmer."[31] The pride in these words fairly trumpeted his conviction that he had found the perfect woman.

Clara's looks and taste in clothes may have enhanced her appeal to Kinsey. He probably preferred a woman who did little to accentuate her femininity. Still, Kinsey must have been warmed by Clara's character. She was poised and self-confident, in equal measure direct, honest, and utterly devoid of pretensions. She was also highly competitive and, most important, calm and unflappable, a woman of great inner strength.

Nor is it difficult to understand what Clara saw in Kinsey. Handsome and athletic looking, he was a bright-faced young man with a shock of thick blond hair and a broad smile. Kinsey was obviously brilliant, and he gave every indication of knowing what he wanted in life. Above all, he was a devoted scientist, a man whose life revolved around the world of work. While Clara recognized early on that he was extremely serious about his profession, she did not see this as a problem. If anything, his devotion to work underscored his ambition, which in turn suggested that he would be a good provider.

Barely two months after their first date, Kinsey proposed. He popped the question at the end of January while they were hiking. Clara kept him waiting for two weeks for her answer, and the delay upset him greatly. It had taken courage for him to court her, and more courage still to propose. How could she be so heartless and cold? He accused her of "being mean," Clara later confessed, adding, "I guess I was."[32]

But meaness did not cause Clara's silence. She wanted time to think, for Kinsey was not her only suitor. She had received a proposal from another admirer and had to decide between them. Very few stars obscured her vision as she weighed her options, for Clara viewed marriage as a lifetime partnership between equals. No doubt, her decision turned in part on romantic attraction, but it also reflected her judgment as to which man would make the better match. In the end, she chose Kinsey.[33]

By Valentine's Day 1921, they were formally engaged. As a sign of their affection, they now addressed each other by nicknames. He called her "Mac," an abbreviation of her surname, with a note of masculinity; while she adopted "Prok," the contraction of "Professor" and "Kinsey" his camp boys had invented. As explained by Clara, it was simple: "They took off the *f* and added a *k*."[34] The names stuck. For the rest of their lives, they would be Prok and Mac to each other and to close friends.[35]

To all appearances, their courtship was a happy time. They made no effort to conceal their engagement, and in a community as closely knit as Bloomington they probably could not have kept it secret had they tried. Besides, there was no reason to hide their romance. It was perfectly acceptable for a professor to marry a student; it happened all the time. As long as they conducted themselves with propriety, they could count on a warm reception from the academic community.

Kinsey took care to observe all protocols. Immediately after Clara accepted his proposal, he dutifully informed Carl H. Eigenmann, the chairman of the zoology department, about their engagement. Half a century later, Clara delighted in telling how relieved Kinsey had been by Eigenmann's reaction. "Well, Prok went up to his office and there he was. He was about to photograph some fish," she explained, "and he had his head under this black thing. Prok said to him, 'Dr. Eigenmann, I thought I ought to tell you that I'm engaged to Miss McMillen,'" she continued, "and he said, 'Oh yes, I thought so, come on over and see—this is the most wonderful catfish scale you ever saw."[36] If his initial reaction seemed nonchalant, Eigenmann's official response was warm and generous. The Eigenmanns hosted a Sunday dinner to celebrate the young couple's engagement, and Clara later recalled that "all of the Zoology Department was very nice to us that spring before we were married. . . . So I felt acquainted with all of them."[37]

Clara, too, conducted herself with decorum. While she had planned to take Kinsey's course in entomology that spring, she immediately dropped the idea. As she later explained, "I didn't think it would be right for me to take a course from the man I was going to marry."[38] As befitted a proper young couple, they did most of their courting in public view. They often dined together at the school cafeteria, and many evenings Kinsey played the piano for Clara. Moreover, they attended several concerts that spring, signaling a devotion to classical music that later became their principal form of relaxation together throughout their marriage. In addition, they went hiking with friends and took long walks together on campus. Kinsey took Sundays off so they could spend more time together, and he even took Clara to a few basketball games. Much to her disappointment, however, they would not attend another game after they were married.[39]

Kinsey and Clara's private behavior matched their public decorum. Both were virgins when they started dating, and their chastity remained intact throughout their courtship. Nor were they unusual in this regard. While the Roaring Twenties are often associated with a sexual revolution, the image has been overdone. True, a great deal of sexual experimentation occurred during the decade, but it is often overlooked that most people who engaged in premarital sex had only one or two partners, one of whom they wound up marrying. Moreover, many people (approximately half of the women and a third of the men) demonstrated their support for traditional morality by remaining chaste.[40]

Yet, in Kinsey's case, traditional morality had an ally. His restraint probably had as much to do with sexual conflicts as with moral rectitude. His behavior fits the pattern of many homosexual males forming a heterosexual relationship. Recent studies show that gay men who become engaged often fail to make any efforts at seduction. This is especially true of men with little or no prior experience with women, as they tend to feel anxious about their ability to perform in what is essentially a new and difficult role. Describing his five-year engagement as "very platonic," one homosexual told researchers, "During the engagement I never tried to be alone with her to become more intimate. On the contrary, on the rare occasions I was with her, I was unhappy."[41] While Kinsey's feelings toward Clara may not have been this troubled, it seems doubtful whether he made serious intimate advances. Because of his lack of experience with women, his intense moral inhibitions, and his confusion about his sexual identity, he probably shared the ambivalence many homosexuals feel about having intercourse with their fiancées.

Whatever the explanation, Kinsey apparently confined his physical advances to hugs and kisses. It is unlikely that Clara suspected anything was amiss. Society expected young people (especially women) to remain sexually naive before marriage. As late as 1931, one marriage expert insisted that the typical bride approached marriage "in a profound general and technical ignorance, compensated for by elaborate ceremony."[42] Although Clara had dated other men, she was not sexually sophisticated.

Clara's lack of sexual experience was in no way mitigated by sex education. She once told a reporter that her premarital knowledge of sex could be summarized in one word, "None."[43] Here Clara matched the profile of contemporary women who marry homosexuals. The majority of such women tell scholars that they were "sexually naive at the time of marriage."[44] Not that she would have learned much by taking one of the sex education courses of the day. As one distinguished sex researcher complained bitterly, "the books that purport to instruct on sex matters are priggish apologies, two generations behind the times."[45]

What, then, was a woman of her background to make of a fiancé who behaved like a perfect gentleman? On the basis of her initial fears that he might be "too churchy," Clara must have known that Kinsey had high moral standards. In all likelihood, she attributed his sexual restraint to his personal code. If anything, Clara probably felt lucky to find a man who could fulfill the new single standard of morality demanded by the middle class. As defined by one social historian, the new sex role for men required that they be "powerful yet pure, virile yet virginal."[46] To all appearances, Kinsey satisfied this prescription.

It seems doubtful that Kinsey and Clara discussed their sexual histories prior to marriage. While an exchange of such intimacy would have been extraordinary for people of their generation and class, in Kinsey's case it would have been all but unthinkable. First, he would have risked driving her away; second, candor of this degree would have required a level of self-understanding he did not possess.[47]

Almost certainly, Kinsey did not consider himself a homosexual or a masochist. These are labels that subsume a wealth of knowledge and self-understanding, and in the 1920s each carried an enormous burden of guilt and self-rejection. Sin, crime, and mental illness were the only labels the culture provided for approaching homosexuality; and masochism was, by definition, pathological. To confess one's homosexuality (even to oneself) was to stand condemned; to confess one's masochism was to move beyond the pale. The pertinent issue, therefore, may not be whether Kinsey deceived Clara but how well he knew himself. Two powerful defense mechanisms—denial and repression—may have shielded him from the truth, enabling him to rationalize his homosexual longings and masochistic fantasies in order to preserve his self-esteem.[48]

Not that Kinsey and Clara's situation was unique. He was by no means the first man who harbored doubt and confusion about his sexual identity yet decided to marry.[49] Social pressures to wed were so great that many men who did not know what to make of their homoerotic urges (and many who did) elected to marry. Studies some half a century later estimated that from 10 to 25 percent of all male homosexuals (most studies put the figure at 20 percent) either are or have been married.[50] Since homosexuality has become more acceptable during that time, it seems reasonable to suggest that Kinsey's generation of homosexuals were under much greater pressure to wed, with the result that a higher percentage did so. The fear of exposure, which meant punishment and ostracism, forced many homosexuals to live their entire lives in the closet; and for many, including Kinsey, the closet came furnished with a spouse and children.

Certainly there were compensations. Clara promised to fill the void in Kinsey's life left by years of loneliness. She would end his solitude. Their marriage would permit him to assume the prescribed roles for adult males, those of husband and father. Nor should the fact be overlooked that Kinsey was in love. However confused his personal identity and private behavior, he felt true affection for Clara. By asking for her hand in marriage, he was behaving honorably. Young people in love were supposed to wed.

Kinsey may have had an additional motive for marriage: he may have believed that Clara would solve his problems, that she would be his salvation. For many years, he had felt guilty and anxious about his sexual desires. These conflicts led him to seek help by reading the literature on human sexuality, a search that apparently began during his undergraduate days at Bowdoin College. Whether he read about masturbation or homosexuality, the prescription was the same. Convinced that masturbation and homosexuality were diseases, physicians routinely prescribed marriage to cure both.[51]

By the 1920s, a few enlightened physicians had begun to regard masturbation as harmless, but the medical profession's stance on homosexuality remained unchanged. Homosexuality was a disease that required treatment, and marriage was the remedy of choice. Conjugal relations, physicians insisted, would drive any desire for homosexual contacts from the patient's mind. As late as the 1970s, it was common for homosexuals to tell sex researchers, "I told the doctor, and he said to me, 'Oh, that's nothing. All you need is a girl you like very much. You get married and it's all over.' "[52] Kinsey doubtless nurtured the same belief prior to his wedding.

Kinsey and Clara were married in a simple ceremony at her grandparents' home in Brookville, Indiana, on June 3, 1921. They took their vows at high noon, standing in front of the parlor mantle, beautifully decorated with ferns and roses. In keeping with her simple taste, Clara carried a bouquet of wild roses and wore an unadorned dress of white organdy. Kinsey donned a dark three-piece suit. Immediately after the ceremony, the wedding party, accompanied by a small group of relatives and close family friends, adjourned to the dining room, where all enjoyed an elegant dinner served on tables decorated in yellow and white.[53]

Kinsey did not have a best man, and no member of his family attended the wedding. Nor did he have a single friend in the wedding party. The guest list was limited to Clara's family and a few of the McMillens' close friends.[54] Clara allowed her mother to make the arrangements, later confessing that she was "not interested in the details."[55] She did not even pause to collect the academic honors she had earned in college. Despite the advice of friends who assured her she would later regret it, she skipped the graduation exercises with her classmates. Instead of returning to Bloomington, the newlyweds left immediately on their honeymoon. Forgoing her graduation was an omen of Clara's shifting priorities. Within a year, she would abandon her dreams of becoming a chemist in favor of becoming the homemaker and helpmate of the research scientist she had married.

Kinsey and Clara's honeymoon began on a traditional note. Following the wedding, her parents drove them from Brookville to Cincinnati, where the young couple caught a train and headed east, ensconced in the privacy and comfort of a Pullman car. Their first stop was Niagara Falls. Like millions of newlyweds before and since, they began their lives together by gazing upon the thunderous power of the crashing water. Then it was on to East Orange, where Kinsey's parents had moved from South Orange. Judging from the infrequency of his visits, Kinsey must have hated going home. His childhood hurts had not healed; the chasm between him and his father remained deep. But Clara had not been introduced to his family, and simple politeness required a visit. Besides, he was eager to show her off. After all, she was intelligent and personable. Equally important, her presence in his life signified he was no longer the penniless rebel who had left home seven years earlier. He was now a college professor, the head of his own household. If Kinsey felt obliged to introduce his bride to his family, however, he did not feel compelled to remain under his father's roof a moment longer than necessary. The newlyweds left New Jersey immediately after discharging this duty.[56]

With Niagara Falls and East Orange behind them, the real honeymoon began. To commence their lives together, the newlyweds planned an extended camping trip through the White Mountains of New Hampshire, covering the same territory where Kinsey had introduced hundreds of youngsters to nature. Since the outdoors had helped bring them together, it was not surprising they chose to spend their honeymoon camping. Nor were they unusual in this regard. Convinced that modern life had been stripped of intense physical experiences, Americans of their generation had become fascinated by the cult of the primitive, a passion many allowed to shape their honeymoons. As one expert who had studied 1,000 American marriages noted, "In these histories early marital lovemaking wants to get back to elemental things." It was this "desire to invent something original for the honeymoon, especially for the first mating," he explained, that led newlyweds to follow the example of primitive men and women who had their "first coitus outdoors, before a fire, among trees, upon a mountain top, and by the sea."[57]

Nature was Kinsey's element. Apart from the library or his laboratory, it was the one setting where he felt totally in control. Clara might be an enthusiastic hiker, but she could not match his skills as an outdoorsman. He knew how to survive in the wilderness, live off the land, and trek through uncharted territory. These were talents his countrymen admired in frontiersmen, talents that were considered quintessentially masculine.

The trip Kinsey mapped out was challenging, if not grueling. First, they would travel by boat from Boston to Portland, Maine; then they would hike the mountains on the border of New Hampshire from the northwest, beginning with Bethel, Newry, and North Ridge and then moving quickly on to Mount Moriah and the Presidential and the Franconia Range. As was his habit, Kinsey planned the trip with great precision. They made up separate food packages, each containing carefully prepared food (prunes, for example, were pitted to make them lighter) for four days on the trail. The packages were then mailed ahead to strategically placed "drop" spots (inns and lodges, for the most part) along the route. The same care went into the choice of clothing. Kinsey made certain they packed exactly the right items, in exactly the right quantity.[58]

Logistically, the trip went according to plan. At the beginning of each leg of the journey, they picked up fresh supplies and marched bravely off into the mountains, only to reappear four days later safe and sound. Not that nature failed to exact a price. Often they had to battle inclement weather, with nothing but a lean-to shelter to protect them from the wind and rain. And as luck would have it, June was unseasonably cold that summer, even for the mountains of New England. To keep warm, they had to sleep huddled beneath blankets, dressed with all the extra layers of clothes they could muster.

Though Clara was a seasoned hiker, she was unprepared for the paces Kinsey put her through. They climbed Mount Washington in a snowstorm, taking a fire warden's trail that, in Clara's words, went "straight up."[59] Kinsey led the way, pausing periodically to allow Clara, who trailed behind, to reappear. The moment she caught up, however, he would strike out again. Clearly, Kinsey was establishing a tone for their relationship. By setting up challenges for her to meet, he placed her in the position of striving to please him. But Clara persevered. She knew she was being tested, and she wanted to meet the challenge. Apparently, she was content to accept his leadership and follow.

As the days passed, Kinsey seized every opportunity to serve as her teacher. He dictated every detail of their arrangements. Campfires had to be built to his specifications, meals cooked following his recipes, and backpacks packed according to his directions. Not only did he share his knowledge of plants and animals, but he showed Clara how to pick up and handle a snake.[60] In short, Kinsey adopted (albeit unconsciously perhaps) a teacher-pupil relationship with his bride. The teacher's role was the one he knew best and the only one that gave him a firm sense of control.

But one thing eluded Kinsey's control. Their marriage was not consummated on their honeymoon, nor for several months thereafter. Kinsey later confided to a friend that the problem involved both inexperience and physiology. "Kinsey wasn't altogether clear how to go about this," explained the friend, "and secondly, Mac was quite apprehensive. She was completely inexperienced as well. I think on a couple of their early attempts it hurt physically, which one would expect, and so he would stop."[61] Small wonder that Kinsey led Mac up mountainsides and taught her to handle snakes. If their marriage could not be consummated, at least he could demonstrate his prowess in other areas.

These were minor consolations at best. Kinsey's honeymoon was supposed to mark a new beginning in his life. By consummating his marriage, he hoped to put his sexual problems behind him. Instead, the sexual part of their honeymoon was a failure. In all likelihood, Kinsey blamed himself, for in 1921 virtually everyone agreed that men bore the primary responsibility for making the honeymoon a success. Men were supposed to orchestrate the sexual union. All the marriage manuals said as much, and on this point the experts and the general public were in agreement. It was the husband's duty to initiate foreplay, to adjust the tempo and the techniques to the woman's emotional and physiological state of receptivity, and, above all, to be sensitive and gentle.[62] On the basis of what he told his friend, Kinsey was both gentle and considerate, but because of Clara's physical discomfort and their mutual lack of knowledge and experience, they did not succeed in having intercourse. Given Kinsey's deep-seated anxieties about his sexual identity, he must have been dismayed.

Clara, too, surely felt awful. As a virgin, she was not supposed to be skilled in the art of making love, but she was expected to be a willing partner. By the 1920s, marriage advisers were proclaiming that women should enjoy sex as much as men. "The ideal is for a woman to look forward to the physical experiences of marriage with the same eagerness as a man," intoned one marriage expert, "and to be equally frank in the admission of a desire for sexual pleasure, so that the burden of 'immorality' will not have to be shouldered entirely by the husband."[63] If a woman could not manage this degree of enthusiasm, she still had to submit to her husband's passion. Whether as a result of sexual inhibitions, lack of experience, or the physical pain that made her cringe at their attempts at intercourse, or perhaps a combination of all these, Clara either could not or would not accept intercourse.

For the Kinseys, then, the honeymoon had exposed the thorns on the rose. In the world of dime novels and romance magazines, popular writers depicted the honeymoon as a period of conjugal bliss. Marriage counselors, by contrast, knew that many newlyweds were not prepared to perform smoothly. Marriage manuals started discussing the sexual agenda of the honeymoon in the 1870s. In contrast to the popular culture's helium-filled expectations, these works, in the words of one historian, "sketched a uniformly alarming scene."[64] Doctors heard a rising chorus of horror stories. Typical was the lament of the woman who told her physician, "The first night was a nightmare; I shall never forget it." As a result of such reports, marriage experts started cautioning young people to be concerned about the honeymoon and not to be crushed if things went badly. One popular expert, Eliza Duffey, the author of *What Women Should Know,* warned that "the consummation of marriage is frequently attended with inconvenience, and even physical prostration."[65] After the turn of the century, the advice literature toned down such warnings and simply cautioned couples against expecting too much too soon. A good sex life, advised the experts, had to be built at home rather than discovered in a honeymoon cottage.[66]

Far from being unique, Kinsey and Clara's experience illustrated what critics had been charging all along: society was not preparing young people for marriage. In theory, husbands were supposed to teach wives, but in practice men often did not know enough to fulfill their duty. As one authority noted, husbands "are naturally educators and initiators of their wives in sexual matters, yet they often lack, not only the qualifications of a leader and initiator, but also those necessary for equal mutual partnership."[67] Other experts made the same point. Commenting on the failure of many newlyweds to develop satisfactory sexual relations, Robert L. Dickinson, a prominent New York gynecologist and sex researcher, suggested that, in the cases he had studied, the husband's "lack of aggressive charm breeds suspicion that he does not know enough to be interesting."[68]

How Kinsey and Clara coped with their honeymoon remains unknown. That they would have discussed the problem candidly is unlikely. No doubt, it took time for them to work through their inhibitions and embarrassment. Still, they did not allow their sexual problems to end their marriage; and the fact that they stayed together relieved a great deal of pressure. It was a sign that each wanted to work through their problems, that each valued the relationship more than he or she feared the pain of the moment. In order to remain together without consummating their marriage, Kinsey and Clara had to agree—not in so many words perhaps, but at least by their actions—to compromise what most couples considered fundamental. That kind of resilience and flexibility was to become a salient feature of their marriage. Even greater challenges awaited them in the years ahead.

9

"A LITTLE IMPERFECT— TOO INTOLERANT"

L ike most beginning teachers, Kinsey faced daunting tasks. There were courses to plan, lectures to write, and mounds of papers to grade. Yet Kinsey had a leg up on most beginning professors. Thanks to his stints as a Sunday school teacher, assistant scout master, camp counselor, and teaching assistant at Bowdoin and Harvard, he had considerable classroom experience. Poised and self-confident before groups, he knew how to organize his material into coherent lectures, and he spoke in a loud, clear voice. Best of all, as the first entomologist to join the faculty in Bloomington, he had an open field.[1] He was free to develop new courses and to cultivate a student following. Kinsey dreamed of building his own empire, boasting to Natalie Roeth that entomology could well become "a separate department at Indiana if I can build it up to that degree." Kinsey relished the challenge. "It all depends on what I can do," he declared, adding, "There will be no one ahead of me if that day comes."[2]

Despite his initial optimism, Kinsey found it difficult to adjust to his new environment. He discovered in short order that he and the school had different academic values and conflicting approaches to higher education. Kinsey had spent his entire academic career in the Northeast, where he had attended elite colleges and universities. Indiana University, by contrast, was a down-at-the-heels state school in the nation's heartland. In 1920, it was probably the weakest academic institution in the Big Ten, with a student body that came mostly from small towns and from rural areas, which provided poor academic preparation.

Nothing in his training prepared Kinsey for what he encountered in Bloomington. He truly did not know what to make of many of the students who appeared in his classes. Nor was he ready for the internecine academic warfare he encountered at Indiana. The school was celebrating its one hundredth birthday when he arrived in the fall of 1920, and any institution that old has a faculty with numerous complaints, including the usual gripes about low pay, heavy teaching loads, onerous committee assignments, and lazy or dull students. But Indiana's professors had a more serious grievance. Their discontent was focused on the aging William Lowe Bryan, president of Indiana University since 1902.

A native Hoosier, Bryan had grown up on a farm only a few miles from campus. Much of his early education had come from working the land, where he learned the meaning of hard work, thrift, and sacrifice. After receiving his undergraduate degree from Indiana University, Bryan had traveled east to Clark University, in Worcester, Massachusetts, where he earned his doctorate under G. Stanley Hall, the pioneering child psychologist. Following graduate school, Bryan had returned to Indiana University, quickly establishing a reputation as an excellent teacher and a productive scholar. After rising rapidly through the faculty ranks, he was named vice president in 1892, the position he held when he accepted the presidency a decade later.[3]

In many respects, Bryan was the kind of man Kinsey had been taught to emulate as a youth. Taller than average, with a round face, Roman nose, and high forehead, Bryan had a posture as straight as a ramrod. He dressed meticulously, if conservatively, with nary a hair out of place. His personal code reflected the values of civilized morality, establishing his kinship with the purity crusaders who had shaped the values Kinsey had imbibed in South Orange. Bryan refused to hire any professor who drank (he also declined to hire any married faculty member without first meeting the spouse), and he often stopped students whom he caught smoking on campus to lecture them on the evils of tobacco. Bryan forbade faculty members to smoke in public, and those caught in the act got a tongue-lashing on the spot.[4] New faculty members quickly discovered that Bryan would not tolerate profanity or any display of personal vulgarity. Nor did this unbending Victorian have any difficulty spotting the devil's hand in dancing. Aided by a series of morally stringent deans of women (hand-picked to keep Indiana's female students on the straight and narrow), Bryan struggled for decades to hold the number of dances on campus to a minimum.[5]

Bryan's authority was rooted in patriarchy. The university was his family, and he was its head, demanding and receiving obedience from everyone, including the faculty. Rather than delegate authority to his deans, Bryan presided over faculty meetings in person; he reviewed every course in the curriculum; and he imposed his will on matters of academic policy, whether large or small. As one longtime faculty member observed, "President Bryan was the Grand Mogul, the Geheimrat, he did everything," adding, "If we had had spittoons, he would have been the cleaner of those."[6]

By the time Kinsey joined the faculty in 1920, Bryan ruled the university through a "headship system," composed of the deans of the various colleges, the department chairs, and an inner core of approximately twenty faculty members—all quite senior, and all fanatically loyal to the president. In exchange for their support, Bryan allowed them to dominate other members of the faculty. As long as their judgment mirrored his own, he permitted his deans and chairs to handle faculty appointments and promotions, and he gave them control over the curriculum. Together, they dominated the affairs of the university, rewarding those who shared their values and punishing those who did not.[7]

Not everyone at Indiana University accepted Bryan's domination without a struggle. By the time Kinsey arrived, a modest revolt was under way. A group called the New Lights began to criticize (quietly at first but more openly over time) Bryan's brand of academic feudalism. The New Lights were mostly young faculty members who had been trained at elite universities in the East. It was only natural they should oppose the headship system, since it stifled them daily. As professional underlings, they were not allowed to introduce new courses, alter the content of existing courses, change a laboratory manual, or select their own textbooks.[8] Reformers all, the New Lights demanded greater input into university policies and more freedom in their personal and professional lives. Above all, they wanted to be judged by their academic qualifications and achievements rather than by their length of service, personal loyalties, and pious behavior.[9]

Given his elite academic training and high personal standards, Kinsey should have been a ready recruit for the New Lights. Instead, he preferred to go his own way, and it is doubtful whether Bloomington had ever seen a young professor quite like him. Almost from the moment he set foot on campus, Kinsey struck people as headstrong, willful, stubborn, and highly opinionated. The devotion to cooperation and community service demonstrated in his youth had apparently given way to a pent-up need for independence and self-assertion, if not power and control. While he had much in common with Bryan's critics and quickly came to share their low opinion of the president, Kinsey was too jealous of his independence to join their ranks.

From the outset, Kinsey thought he knew everything about teaching. He adored biology and was supremely confident he could make it come alive for his students. His goal was to help students regain the intellectual curiosity they had known as children, to somehow recapture their sense of awe about nature. As one of his former students recalled, "He wanted to inspire the student with the wonders of nature—with the marvel of just being alive."[10]

During his first few years at Indiana, Kinsey gradually assumed full responsibility for the general biology course, as well as for the advanced classes in entomology and insect taxonomy. By 1933, working in cooperation with the School of Education, he had developed a teaching-methods course for high school biology teachers; and in 1941 he designed and taught a special summer field course for elementary school teachers who wished to "mainstream" biology into existing courses. His most intellectually challenging course, however, was Zoology 233, "Evolution," which he taught for the first time in the fall of 1936. Developed in large measure from his own research and background reading on gall wasps, it distilled his thinking on two decades of work.[11]

Throughout his first decade in Bloomington, though, general biology remained Kinsey's bread-and-butter course. He believed everyone should have at least an elementary knowledge of biology, and he challenged his fellow teachers to design courses that would appeal to ordinary people. "Don't forget that you are always training average citizens and only rarely a future biologist," he advised. "Keep the viewpoint of the average man, whose evaluation of science must depend upon his understanding of its relations to the other affairs of life."[12] In contrast to professors who were bored by teaching beginners, Kinsey liked working with freshmen and sophomores because he viewed them as a special challenge. As one of his colleagues recalled, "he felt if you could interest them, you could interest anyone."[13] Kinsey believed in the general biology course, he once explained, because for most students it was "all that they can get of biology to carry them through their lives."[14]

Kinsey proposed to teach introductory biology as he had observed it. "Beginning students need a picture of the whole," he declared. "Specialized study of the small parts of the whole will not serve them as well."[15] Without minimizing the differences between plants and animals, Kinsey tried to stress the similarities between their structures and processes. His goal was to help students develop what would later be called a holistic view of nature.[16]

Not everyone agreed with Kinsey's "unified approach." After reviewing his proposed course outline for general biology, the zoologists found Kinsey's ideas exciting, but the chairman of the botany department refused to read it, declaring that no one was qualified to teach both botany and zoology. Ordinarily, such a split would have sealed the fate of any new course, but in this instance Kinsey prevailed. Siding with their junior colleague, the zoologists attributed the disagreement to the long-standing feud between the two departments, and Kinsey was allowed to teach the course. Throughout his career, he remained convinced that biology should be taught through his "unified approach."[17]

The man who made the decisions about zoology at Indiana University was Carl Eigenmann. A native of Flehingen, Germany, he moved to the United States in 1880, at seventeen, accompanying an immigrant uncle who settled in Rockport, Indiana. Eigenmann enrolled in Indiana University in 1882 intending to study law but changed his major to zoology in his sophomore year. He received his A.B. from Indiana in 1886, and his M.A. the following year. After teaching as an instructor at Indiana for one year, Eigenmann went east to earn his doctorate at Harvard University. Unfortunately, Harvard refused to award him a Ph.D. in taxonomy, so he returned to Indiana, where he received his doctorate for the work that he had completed at Harvard. Eigenmann rejoined the faculty at Indiana in 1891 and went on to head the zoology department for thirty-five years.[18]

Eigenmann had earned a national reputation in ichthyology, eventually compiling a bibliography of over two hundred titles. Thanks largely to his work, Sigma Xi, the national honor society in science, awarded Indiana University a chapter in 1904. Over time, Eigenmann became one of the most powerful professors on campus. In addition to chairing the zoology department, he was appointed as the first dean of the Graduate School in 1908, holding both positions until his retirement in 1925.[19] According to Fernandus Payne, who succeeded him as the zoology chair and as dean of the Graduate School, Eigenmann "kept research alive at this University."[20]

Yet Eigenmann failed to make Indiana nationally prominent in zoology. Zoology may have been one of the strongest departments on campus, but it was no match for the best departments in the East, or even the top programs in the Big Ten. For decades, Indiana's zoology department continued to emphasize taxonomy and morphology, while the nation's leading departments built strong programs in experimental biology, with special emphasis on genetics, cellular biology, and endocrinology. As a result, Indiana's best students had to go elsewhere for their graduate training.

By the end of World War I, Eigenmann had entered the twilight of his career. Once an asset, he had come to symbolize what was wrong with Indiana University. His days as an effective dean and chair were over, and his productive scholarship was long since behind him. If anything, he had devolved into the kind of colleague whom the New Lights held privately in contempt but publicly had to court if they wished to remain at Indiana.[21]

In the early 1920s, the ablest member of the zoology department was Fernandus Payne. A short, slender man with a shiny bald head, sharp cheekbones, and a straight, prominent nose, Payne was one of the few faculty members respected by the old guard and the Young Turks alike. A native Hoosier who took his A.B. degree (1905) and his M.A. degree (1906) from Indiana, Payne had served as Eigenmann's laboratory assistant and protégé. Unlike Eigenmann, however, Payne made a successful pilgrimage to the East. He earned his Ph.D. in 1909 from Columbia University, which at that time had one of the best zoology departments in the United States, if not the world. There he studied with two giants: E. B. Wilson, a distinguished cytologist, and Thomas Hunt Morgan, who later won a Nobel Prize for his work in experimental zoology. After completing a dissertation on the genetics of drosophila (fruit flies) under Morgan's direction, Payne returned to Indiana in 1909 as an assistant professor. A rigorous researcher and prolific writer, he quickly earned his "star" in *American Men of Science*, awarded largely for his work on the genetics of *Drosophila* and chromosomal analysis in Hemiptera and *Gryllotalpa*.[22]

After rejoining the faculty at Indiana, Payne quickly emerged as a leader of the New Lights. Described by a colleague as "very, very forthright," Payne was a man of great integrity. Though somewhat cool and restrained in his professional relationships (graduate students called him "the Buddha" because his facial expression almost never changed), he was direct, honest, and evenhanded.[23] Each of these qualities shaped his behavior when he succeeded Eigenmann in 1925 as dean of the Graduate School and chair of zoology. As a senior administrator, Payne sought chiefly to elevate Indiana's zoology department to national prominence and to improve the university's overall academic quality as well.

Will Scott was Kinsey's third senior colleague in the department. Scott's specialty was limnology. He, too, was a native Hoosier and, like Eigenmann and Payne, a product of academic inbreeding. Scott took all his degrees at Indiana University (A.B., 1907; M.A., 1908; and Ph.D., 1911), and Eigenmann was his major professor. Scott joined the faculty as an instructor in 1908 and attained the rank of full professor in 1921, at the end of Kinsey's first year at Indiana. Neither a dynamic teacher nor a first-rate scholar, Scott was the weakest but perhaps best-liked member of the department. He was soft-spoken and gentle. Students adored him, particularly those who took his small classes and got to know him well. Theodore W. Torrey, one of his colleagues, called him "one of the kindest, most generous and thoughtful men I have ever known."[24]

In many respects, then, the zoology department during the 1920s was a microcosm of the university. It was far from distinguished, its morale was generally low, and major divisions lurked just beneath its calm surface. Given the inherent tensions in the department and the larger fissures within the university, there was plenty of opportunity for a young, strong-willed professor to get into mischief. And that is exactly what Kinsey did.

From the outset, Kinsey participated vigorously in faculty meetings. Unlike most junior professors, he refused to defer to his senior colleagues and insisted on speaking his mind. "Although I was five years older than Dr. Kinsey," observed F. Lee Benns, a prizewinning European historian, "I was always an admirer of his ability to get on his feet and talk vigorously and well on many points—in meetings of faculty, Phi Beta Kappa or ordinary committees—when most faculty members were inclined only to sit quietly and listen."[25] Benns did not know that Kinsey was incapable of remaining silent. Assistant professor or not, Kinsey prided himself on his independent judgment, and he found it difficult to defer to anyone unless he was convinced the person was right, which was seldom the case.

Almost from the moment he arrived at Indiana, Kinsey took a strong dislike to President Bryan. Publicly, Kinsey managed to keep his views to himself. His silence revealed a healthy instinct for self-preservation, as Bryan was not disposed to accept criticism from his faculty—and certainly not from a beginning assistant professor. In private, however, Kinsey's remarks were scathing. He resented Bryan's autocratic manner, complaining that Indiana University would never become a first-rate school until it had new leadership. As one of his colleagues put it, Kinsey thought Bryan "was a fossil."[26]

While simple prudence prevented clashes with Bryan, Kinsey frequently found himself at odds with members of his own department. From the moment he hit the campus, Kinsey acted like a born full professor, saying what he thought about whomever he thought. "When 'K' first came on the I.U. faculty," Payne recalled, "he was very critical of his associates that he did not feel measured up to his standards." The first colleague to be scrutinized and found wanting was the limnologist, Will Scott, whom Kinsey denounced—not without cause—as a poor lecturer. Payne remembered vividly a department meeting during Kinsey's first year at Indiana in which plans for the upcoming year were being discussed. Scott, an associate professor, was up for promotion to full professor. With Scott sitting in the room, Kinsey, an untenured assistant professor, criticized his teaching and recommended that he be replaced.[27]

No one was safe from Kinsey's stern judgment, not even the venerable Eigenmann. A tired, old lion by the time Kinsey arrived, Eigenmann had effectively withdrawn from teaching, turning those responsibilities over to his junior colleagues. His roles as the graduate dean and the department chair were winding down, too, as Payne, at Eigenmann's request, had quietly assumed those duties. Yet Eigenmann still demanded respect, if not deference, from his colleagues, and Kinsey refused to give him either.

Kinsey had a low opinion of Eigenmann's scholarship. Although both men were taxonomists, Eigenmann was of the old school. Portions of his research focused on heredity, but he was primarily a classifier who saw nothing wrong in generalizing about various species on the basis of limited samples. Eigenmann was also a neo-Lamarkian (he believed that acquired traits were inheritable) long after the rediscovery of Mendel's laws in 1900 prompted most scientists, including Kinsey, to reject Lamarkian teachings.[28] According to a colleague, Kinsey was "highly critical of Eigenmann and was not very bashful about expressing these criticisms."[29] Another colleague put the matter more succinctly, declaring that Kinsey thought Eigenmann "was a dinosaur."[30]

During his second year at Indiana, Kinsey denounced Eigenmann's scholarship to his face in front of colleagues. "Dr. Eigenmann was at this point probably well past his prime as a research scholar," Payne observed, "and [Kinsey's] more recent training in the field enabled him easily to criticize the older man's work."[31] Incensed, Eigenmann told Payne, "I think we're going to have to let Kinsey go. He just won't accommodate and adjust."[32] Payne disagreed, electing to support Kinsey, as he was to do many times in the years ahead. Payne calmed Eigenmann, and, following a lengthy discussion, they decided to give their brash young colleague another chance. Relating the incident many years later, Payne stressed that it was definitely "a close call."[33]

Throughout the many years of their association, Payne maintained a balanced perspective on Kinsey and defended him against critics. While Kinsey was fortunate to have Payne as his advocate, the two men never became friends. One of their colleagues noted that "both had extremely strong personalities" but added that "when they clashed . . . it was the clashing of sincere and well-intentioned people."[34] According to another colleague, however, Kinsey was personally critical of Payne. "Kinsey felt that Dean Payne was very didactic and limited in his view on things," he observed, "though I did think that Kinsey felt that Payne strove to be fair."[35] One of Kinsey's former graduate students put the matter more bluntly, insisting that Kinsey considered Payne "a stick in the mud."[36]

Armed with a freshly minted doctorate from Harvard, Kinsey acted as if he was going to show the locals in the provinces a thing or two. But more was involved than hubris. Despite his youth, Kinsey had grown opinionated and domineering, pressing his views on anyone who disagreed with him. As a former college debater, Kinsey was a formidable verbal opponent. Colleagues who differed with him did so at their peril, since he rarely took a position without first being sure of his facts. Once engaged, Kinsey gave no quarter. "He could just blast you if you were a little tentative about some of your facts," declared William Breneman, Kinsey's colleague for many years. If Kinsey sensed any hesitation or weakness in an opponent, he would say things like "You just don't know what your talking about" or "How could you be such an imbecile," recalled Breneman. And when he got someone on the defensive, Kinsey immediately went for the kill.[37]

At Indiana, it became clear that Kinsey's verbal skills were harnessed to an iron will. Robert Bugbee, who took his Ph.D. under Kinsey, described his mentor as "very fixed in certain respects," a man who "just wouldn't give in for any reason at all."[38] While intellectual arrogance undoubtedly stiffened Kinsey's neck, his stubborn streak also reflected his need for power and control. Whenever disagreements arose, Kinsey invariably went on the attack if the dispute involved older, powerful males.

Authority figures remained a problem for Kinsey throughout his life. During his early years at Indiana, he made few friends and virtually none with older men. "I and my fellow graduate students had the definite impression that Kinsey was a prickly individual for fellow faculty members to live with," recalled Herman T. Spieth, a former student who worked under Kinsey in the mid-1920s.[39] Time did little to improve Kinsey's relationship with colleagues. "He was one of the most unpopular men there," remarked Homer T. Rainwater, who left his native Mississippi to study under Kinsey's supervision in the early 1930s. While stressing that "everybody recognized [Kinsey's] ability," Rainwater recalled that people "stayed away from him," including "all the professors."[40]

No less than the senior faculty, junior colleagues found Kinsey troublesome. At Indiana, junior professors had to serve a kind of apprenticeship, assisting senior professors in large courses. After he rose through the faculty ranks, Kinsey had several assistants over the years in the general biology course. Most emerged from their experience with a great deal of respect for Kinsey, but few liked him. On the contrary, they found him domineering and harshly critical. Though he personally detested arbitrary authority (as well he might, given his treatment by his father), Kinsey expected his junior colleagues to defer to him on everything, and from all reports he was not an easy man to please.

One of the few junior colleagues who felt close to Kinsey was Robert Kroc, an endocrinologist who joined the zoology department as an instructor in 1931. (His older brother Raymond Kroc would later become world famous as the driving force behind McDonald's restaurants.) Kroc assisted Kinsey with the general biology course and deferred to him on everything. Decades later, Kroc recalled that he could tell from their first meeting that Kinsey "would be a real taskmaster." Aware that he was not a field biologist, Kroc understood that he would have to learn from Kinsey, "just like the students."[41]

On one occasion, however, Kroc turned the tables on Kinsey. They were talking in Kinsey's backyard, and frogs started croaking. With obvious pride, Kinsey proceeded to identify the different kinds of frogs by the sound of their voices. Kroc immediately asked Kinsey if he knew what a frog's vocal cords looked like. When Kinsey admitted that he could not remember, Kroc offered to show him. The next day, they went to the laboratory and dissected a frog together. "I think it made him aware that while he knew the species and knew their sounds, he really didn't know the organ that helped make the sounds," Kroc recalled. This kind of spirit appealed to Kinsey, and he and Kroc became friends.[42]

Theodore Torrey, who joined the department in 1932 with a Ph.D. from Harvard, had trouble with Kinsey from the start. When Torrey came to the campus for an interview, Kinsey invited him to dinner. No sooner had he arrived than Kinsey asked him what he knew about the flora and fauna of Indiana. While it was clearly cricket to ask a job candidate in biology such a question, Kinsey's manner troubled Torrey. He felt that Kinsey was attempting to put him on the defensive intellectually, or perhaps even trying to humiliate him.[43]

Throughout his adult life, Kinsey seemed to relish testing people. The strategy he used with Torrey was the norm. The trial usually came very early in his relationship with someone, often on the first meeting. Kinsey selected the topics, and he posed the questions. Typically, he would make a point-blank query that required a factual answer. He might request someone to identify a bird by its call, or point to a plant and ask its name in Latin, or play a classical record on the phonograph and demand the name of the composer. The topics all had one thing in common: they were subjects on which Kinsey was an expert, which naturally put him in the catbird's seat. In fact, it maneuvered him instantly into the role of a teacher; and it placed the other parties immediately on the defensive. Even if they came up with the right answer, Kinsey was still the winner. They had been forced to play his game on his terms.

Torrey passed the test and was hired to assist in the general biology course, with the understanding that he would one day take it over completely in order to free Kinsey to concentrate on his fieldwork and advanced courses. Once the course began, Kinsey lost no time establishing who was boss. On one of their first field trips, they explored McCormick's Creek, a beautiful state park not far from the campus. After the class broke for lunch, Torrey turned on his car radio to listen to music. Poor man. Without meaning to, Torrey had broken three rules with a single turn of the knob: first, he had done something without asking permission in a situation where he was very much the underling; second, he had mixed pleasure with work, which offended Kinsey's work ethic; and third, he had his radio dial tuned to popular music, which Kinsey could not abide. Even in a situation that invited relaxation, Kinsey insisted on running the show; and he was neither gentle nor subtle in doing it. "All of a sudden Kinsey got up and walked over and leaned in the car and turned that radio off and stalked away without [so much as a] by-your-leave [or] any explanation or anything of the sort," Torrey later recalled, adding that the incident "embarrassed me mightily."[44]

Over the next few years, Torrey continued to serve as Kinsey's assistant in the general biology course, an apprenticeship that became an ordeal. "I was very hesitant to make any suggestions about how we might do something differently than he had done for a long time," Torrey later admitted. "He just ran it . . . he just called the shots, and we did things the way he wanted to do them."[45] Had Torrey been one to hold grudges, his relationship with Kinsey might never have recovered from these stings, but over time he came to hold Kinsey in high regard. "There were times he made me madder than hell and there were times he was cruel to me," confessed Torrey, "but I personally was very, very fond of him and admired him and respected him tremendously."[46] Another man might not have been so forgiving.

Kinsey's clashes with colleagues resulted from his confidence in his own judgment and his determination to have his way. He treasured his independence and tried to minimize the authority the university had over him. Kinsey refused to ask for raises, as he felt his work made his case. Similarly, he felt put upon by the university's annual requests for a statement of his year's research activities. If administrators could not see he was a hard worker, they were beneath contempt and beyond persuasion.

But the university was not his sole source of income. To bolster his independence, Kinsey turned to writing. Though he had never been a high school teacher, he believed that his extensive experience with young people would enable him to write a useful and successful high school biology textbook. During his second year at Indiana, he started pulling together material for the book, and the work continued off and on for the next five years. His goal was to offer students what he called "a bird's-eye view" of the seven fields he regarded as essential to a basic understanding of biology—taxonomy, morphology, physiology, genetics, ecology, distributional biology, and behavior.[47] Early in 1926, he mailed off the finished manuscript to J. B. Lippincott in Philadelphia, which published the first edition of *An Introduction to Biology* that October.[48] The following year, Lippincott published the accompanying volume, *Field and Laboratory Manual in Biology,* and, a decade later, his final venture into textbook writing, *Methods in Biology,* written for high school teachers who adopted his textbook.[49]

An Introduction to Biology was unlike any other textbook on the market. Written as a narrative, with numerous first-person asides, its prose was straightforward and simple, with a minimum of technical terms. Its tone was informal, even friendly, as though Kinsey were chatting with students around a campfire. Reinforcing this personal quality were numerous photographs of students in the outdoors, including several of the author surrounded by young people he had led on field trips.

What made the book truly distinctive, however, was Kinsey's insistence that students learn biology through direct observations and hands-on experiments. Drawing on his childhood, he exhorted young people to go into the field and observe nature, while the accompanying field and laboratory manuals gave teachers hundreds of simple exercises and experiments designed to show students how nature works and, more important, how to make the scientific method part of their daily lives. Because he knew how difficult it was for urban youths to travel to the countryside, Kinsey included a host of experiments that required no special equipment and could be performed in vacant city lots. Others were designed to demonstrate the practical value of science. One exercise, for example, showed students how to protect themselves against the fraudulent claims of Madison Avenue by applying a series of scientific questions to commercial advertisements, while another had students prepare menus for two days of balanced meals.[50]

Kinsey's textbook was also noteworthy for the strong position it took on evolution, an issue that had divided the nation only a year before the textbook was published. In 1925, the Tennessee legislature passed a bill that prohibited the teaching of evolution in the public schools, and soon thereafter John Scopes, a biology teacher in Dayton, Tennessee, provoked a test case by declaring publicly that he taught biology from an evolutionary viewpoint. Scopes was brought to trial in the summer of 1925. Since Scopes admitted he had broken the law, the trial's outcome was never in doubt. What gave the trial its drama was the clash between Clarence Darrow, who assisted the defense, and William Jennings Bryan, rural America's defender of the faith, who aided the prosecution. As one observer remarked, the trial "was a battle between two types of mind—the rigid, orthodox, accepting, unyielding, narrow, conventional mind, and the broad liberal, critical, cynical, skeptical and tolerant mind."[51] Scopes, of course, was convicted and fined $100, though Tennessee's supreme court later rescinded the fine on a technicality. In the end, the so-called monkey trial was significant for stirring up a national controversy over evolution that showed how little tolerance secular groups and fundamentalist groups had for each other.

In his textbook, Kinsey laid out the basic facts of evolution in a matter-of-fact manner, as though he were discussing the life cycle of the fruit fly. Under the general heading of "Genetics," he included chapters entitled "Heredity," "New Kinds of Organisms," "Further Evidence of Change," and "Fossils." The chapter called "Further Evidence of Change" was especially blunt. With admirable simplicity, Kinsey defined "evolution" as "the scientific word for change," and while he acknowledged that "there are some people who think they don't believe in evolution," he tried to show his students the folly of such reasoning. To find proof of evolution, students had only to look at things they used daily, such as clothing made from improved varieties of cotton, bread that came from improved wheat, and varieties of corn and fruits unknown to previous generations. Kinsey ridiculed the man who denounced evolution but owned a new breed of dog or smoked a cigar made from a recently improved variety of tobacco, declaring, "When he says he doesn't believe in evolution, I wonder what he means!"[52]

As a scientist, Kinsey felt that it was his duty to take a stand. He knew firsthand that biology often clashed with traditional beliefs and value systems, and he was eager to take biology's side. Kinsey had lost any trace of his boyhood faith in revealed dogmas. Instead, he approached mysteries with intense curiosity, with questions and doubts, and with an unerring commitment to attack problems with theories that could shift in the face of new facts. If Darwin's theory of common descent could not be reconciled with biblical accounts of man's creation, the Bible defenders would have to yield to science. Yet the casualness with which Kinsey framed the conflict represented a tactical ploy. The matter-of-fact tone of his writing was a polemical stance, intended to leave the impression that nothing remained for discussion. Religion had lost; science had won. Still, Kinsey was enough of a realist to understand that biology instructors could get into trouble with parents and local school boards, so he offered concrete advice in his teacher's manual on how to convey material on evolution without raising a storm.[53]

Kinsey made no effort to conceal his desire to politicize young people. Like many middle-class Americans who had grown to maturity at the turn of the century, he believed that education would enable people to make the right choices. Once the public understood the issues, wise policy decisions would follow. By educating students about nature, Kinsey hoped to encourage them not only to enjoy nature but to preserve and defend it. In the section "Ecology," he included chapters entitled "Forests" and "Fresh-Water Biology" that could have been written by the Sierra Club. In a ringing endorsement of conservation, Kinsey called for the protection of America's wild plants and animals "under natural conditions."[54] A firm proponent of reforestation, he recommended a scientific program of tree harvesting in which younger trees would be spared and protected from falling timber.[55] Similarly, Kinsey was a strong advocate of clean water. After stressing the importance of lakes, rivers, and streams as habitats for wildlife and as recreation sites and sources of drinking water for humans, Kinsey declared, "So, of course, we want the fresh waters of America saved. To serve us in all possible ways, they must be conserved, usually with their natural ecologic conditions."[56]

Kinsey tried to encourage students to think independently. He was constantly touting the virtues of skepticism and urging others to do likewise. "Don't get a notion that things are true because they are in print," he declared. A wise person had to "remember that even authorities sometimes publish things that aren't so" and to bear in mind "that what experts believe to be true may be found incorrect upon further investigation." Nothing was written in stone. As Kinsey put it, "We continually have to change our opinions of things in the sciences."[57]

Still, Kinsey regarded scientists as the best hope of mankind, the one group that could be counted on to discover and defend the truth. When asked to give a lecture in a popular undergraduate course called "Life Views of Great Men," Kinsey selected Thomas Huxley, the British biologist and lecturer. According to the *Daily Student*, Indiana University's school newspaper, Kinsey praised Huxley as the author of science's "declaration of independence" because he refused to accept any argument that could not be proven scientifically, regardless of whether the proposition came from the church, the state, or from other scientists.[58] By making Huxley a hero, Kinsey was underscoring his belief that scientists should be prepared to challenge authority, whatever the costs, a position he would uphold in his own life in the years ahead.

Kinsey's textbook allowed him to preach to a generation of students. He used it to proclaim his love for nature, to champion his "unified approach" to teaching biology, to advance policies he held dear, and to testify on behalf of the scientific method as a guide to life. But Kinsey also had a practical reason for writing his textbook. He wanted to make money. Spieth, his former graduate student, once asked him why he did not publish a college text. "He replied that his time was precious and, if he were going to do that sort of thing, he wanted to make money out of it." Spieth explained that "it was much more profitable to publish a high school book which would be used by thousands of students than a college text which could have only limited sales."[59] Kinsey's textbook projects gave him considerable financial independence. Advertised extensively by Lippincott, the books sold quite well. *An Introduction to Biology,* in particular, appeared in a second, enlarged edition, called *New Introduction to Biology,* and eventually sold nearly half a million copies. The income from these writings provided a measure of financial security unknown to most academic families without independent means. The royalties paid for the family's first automobile in 1927, financed at least part of the costs of building a new home, and helped pay college tuition costs for their three children. Throughout the 1930s, textbook income shielded his family from the hard times of the Great Depression when academic salaries remained stagnant or declined.

Yet this revenue also made Kinsey a target. A number of his colleagues envied his success and financial independence.[60] Others no doubt looked down their noses on his commercial writings. University professors often regarded textbooks, particularly those for a high school audience, as diversions from the important tasks of original research and scholarly writing. Kinsey himself admitted to a friend that he considered his textbook "in some ways a side issue," largely, one suspects, because he begrudged the time it took away from his gall wasp research.[61]

The suspicion lingers that Kinsey also resented teaching for the same reason. For a man who prided himself on being practical, he had little interest in working with less gifted students. His high standards made him extremely demanding and sharply critical. As a result, Kinsey never developed a large following among Indiana's students, though he did earn a reputation as a challenging teacher. While one former student called him "the most stimulating lecturer and teacher" he had ever known, the majority of students found him resistible.[62] Another former student, who admired him greatly, freely confessed that Kinsey "was not a very popular teacher at all."[63]

One student who did like Kinsey was Louise Ritterskamp Rosenzweig, who attended Indiana in the late 1920s. She knew him better than most students did, because she not only took his courses but served as his laboratory assistant for three years. She drew a vivid portrait of Kinsey in the classroom. The man she remembered was a commanding presence. Both in appearance and in demeanor, he was all business. Rosenzweig described him as "a tall man" who wore his blond hair "closely cut in a pompadour, his shoulders somewhat stooped." Peering out from behind horn-rimmed spectacles were "large eyes with lids that drooped slightly over them." His dress was conservative, as befitted a professor—a dark suit, white shirt, and a black bow tie. (Others recall that Kinsey normally wore wool socks knitted by his wife but often forgot to wear a belt.) He arrived "on the dot of the hour," entering through "a side-center door with a long, measured, rather brisk step." Upon appearing, he looked "neither to right nor to left," but walked immediately to the blackboard, where "he wrote, in print-like letters, an outline of the important topics, with subheadings, to be covered in the day's lecture."[64] And then, without further ado, he would begin to speak.

Kinsey's lectures were models of clarity and precision. Rosenzweig remembered his command of language. When he talked, she explained, "he had a precise manner of enunciation, richly modulated, as though he enjoyed using the English language." Rather than move about, he stayed in one spot for most of the hour except when he turned to refer to the outline on the blackboard. His restrained manner made him seem "aloof and shy," but once he got going "his enthusiasm . . . warmed the rather awesome atmosphere of the room."[65]

Rosenzweig described a young professor. Over time, Kinsey grew as a teacher. By the late 1930s, he had developed into quite a performer. One of his colleagues portrayed him as "a dramatic lecturer" who "obviously enjoyed it," while another recalled that Kinsey taught "beautifully" and "was a real showman." One of Kinsey's favorite teaching chestnuts was to stride into class and immediately make an outrageous statement, something like "Anybody who believes in Darwin is insane!" Then he would launch into a discussion of Darwin's theories and, over the next fifty minutes, draw his students into a stimulating analysis of evolution.[66] Not everyone praised his classroom performance, to be sure, but in a university that tolerated mediocrity, Kinsey built a rock-solid reputation as a forceful, demanding, and rigorous teacher.

Kinsey also matured as a public speaker. Ever since his days as a college debater and public orator, he had been fascinated by the power of language. This interest grew apace at Indiana. Kinsey spoke to faculty discussion clubs, civic groups, and high school teachers associations. Eager to polish his skills in the art of persuasion, he was constantly looking for ways to improve his effectiveness. Over time, he mastered a variety of rhetorical devices (raising and lowering his voice, changing intonations, poignant pauses followed by rapid-fire delivery, etc.) designed to spark an audience's interest and keep people leaning forward in their seats. His trademarks were clarity, tight organization, and total mastery of his material.

Kinsey's classroom reached beyond the lecture hall. He never doubted that students could learn more from nature than from any laboratory. "It is not a laboratory science, but an out-door biology that they need," he declared, "a science that can be translated in terms of the living world through which they move."[67] Kinsey relished this challenge, as he enjoyed field trips far more than classroom teaching. Observing nature at first hand, he believed, would show students things they could never learn from books. "One of the best things about this position here is the opportunity to get out into the open country," he wrote Natalie Roeth during his first year at Indiana.[68] To illustrate particular points, he routinely took his classes to the small ravine in the woods behind Biology Hall. There they conducted simple exercises designed to show students they did not need fancy equipment or exotic settings to learn biology.

Kinsey took the students in his general biology course on one or two longer field trips each term. Typically, he and an assistant would lead a group on Saturday mornings to the nearby hills of Brown County or to the virgin woods near Mitchell, Indiana. Kinsey's personality seemed to expand in the outdoors. It was as though nature released an energy and inner joy in him that the classroom stifled. His clothes changed, too. "I have been able to conduct a large part of my work in the field, wearing khaki, sleeves rolled up, collar open," he told Natalie Roeth. "Think of that for a University job! Nothing but biology could offer that!"[69]

During field trips, Kinsey relied upon student curiosity to generate topics for discussion. "He expected his students to pick out and comment on the things they observed," Rosenzweig recalled, and then "he would add his experience and knowledge."[70] Kinsey defended this practice, explaining that a "teacher's function in the field is not that of a demonstrator, but that of an instigator of independent exploration by the students."[71] As the years passed, his style of drawing students out on field trips, like his classroom lectures, became more animated. "He was a real showman," recalled a colleague who observed Kinsey in action in the 1930s.[72] Another colleague marveled at his ability: "Well, Kinsey would be down on his knees, and he would open up things and he was awfully good."[73]

At bottom, Kinsey was an elitist teaching in a nonelite university, and he abhorred the lowering of academic standards. "Chief among Dr. Kinsey's concerns was the trend toward what he called 'softness' in American education," wrote a colleague. "He was convinced that youngsters wanted to work and to learn if they were challenged by good teachers, good textbooks, and solid subject matter."[74] Because he took it upon himself to carry academic virtue on his shoulders, Kinsey had no sympathy for students who could not keep pace.

Phi Beta Kappa was especially dear to Kinsey's heart. Owing to its overall academic weakness, Indiana University was not granted a chapter of Phi Beta Kappa until 1911. Shortly after joining the faculty, Kinsey, who had been elected to the Bowdoin chapter a year after his graduation, was asked to serve as its adviser. He took the job seriously, donating hundreds of hours to advising students and other duties. In recognition of his service and ability, Kinsey was appointed to the executive board of Phi Beta Kappa and later served as the vice president and then president of its local chapter.

Because Kinsey believed in hard work and individual responsibility, he had little tolerance for anyone who did not share his work ethic and devotion to self-reliance. "Success isn't an accident," declared Kinsey. Rather, it came "only after long hours of hard work."[75] On one occasion, he told an audience of Young Women's Christian Association members that too many young people wanted something for nothing and were unwilling to earn their way through hard work and self-sacrifice. In his judgment, this lack of character explained why few young people attempted to become scientists and seekers of truth.[76]

Elitism also shaped Kinsey's politics. During the 1920s, he supported a new immigration policy for the United States. Along with many white, old-stock Americans, he wanted to limit immigration from eastern and southern Europe because he feared the "new immigrants" would damage the American gene pool. The spigot had to be closed, Kinsey explained, because "the melting pot cannot blend diverse materials that pour in too rapidly." Consequently, he endorsed the bills passed by Congress in 1921 and 1924 to establish a quota system. "Whether homogeneity is a biologic virtue or not," he declared, "statesmen have shown themselves good taxonomists in their insistence that we cannot become a true species until barriers are erected to protect us from continued contributions of parental stock."[77]

The same faith in science drew Kinsey to the eugenics movement. He had heard a great deal about eugenics during his graduate school days at Harvard, and during the 1920s and 1930s eugenics (from the Greek *eugenes,* meaning "well born") commanded wide support among liberals and conservatives alike. Promising to improve society through science, the eugenics movement in the United States had two branches. "Positive" eugenicists believed that intelligent, prosperous, well-educated people should be encouraged to procreate because their genes would improve human stock. While agreeing with this recommendation, "negative" eugenicists took the issue an important step further by insisting that whole classes of people (the feeble-minded, alcoholics, epileptics, the deaf and blind) should be discouraged from having children or, in some instances, prevented from doing so through sterilization by the state.[78]

In his high school textbook, Kinsey speculated that intelligence is hereditary, observing that "human behaviors, the character of one's nervous control, the way one *thinks,* a good or bad memory, quickness or dullness in seeing the point of a thing, and other such characters may be influenced by the genes of the ancestors."[79] He also backed a program of positive eugenics. "We cannot control the set of genes which we possess," he wrote. "But in the choosing of our mates we decide what other set of genes shall be passed on to our offspring."[80] To Kinsey, it was obvious that positive eugenics offered "the best hope of an improved race of mankind."[81] A few years later, he embraced negative eugenics as well, writing approvingly of the need to discourage what he called "hereditary defectives" from having children, through either "complete isolation" or "sterilization."[82]

Kinsey's lack of sympathy for those with fewer advantages was evident in his reaction to the New Deal. "Dr. Kinsey was a conservative," remarked a colleague. "He had little use for the WPA [Works Progress Administration]. He had no use for FDR [Franklin Delano Roosevelt]. He didn't believe in milk feeding, spoon feeding anybody, and that of course was reflected in his attitudes toward his graduate students."[83] Similarly, he despised Keynesian economics. Raised on the thrift ethic, he thought people should pay as they went or do without.[84] This conservative outlook carried over into international politics. In Kinsey's view, the Soviet Union was doomed to failure because communism itself was a bankrupt philosophy. "Revolutionary Russia hasn't got far, for it tried to secure wealth and leisure without working for them," he averred, "and the millions who have consequently starved to death in that country bear testimony to the truth of the scientific conviction that we can't get something for nothing."[85]

Time did nothing to mellow these views. Throughout his life, Kinsey called himself an independent, but he usually voted Republican; and more often than not, he sided with conservatives on the major issues of the day.[86] A friend from the 1940s and 1950s recalled that Kinsey complained about "how prices were going up, and how he felt people were demanding exorbitant salaries and how house prices were inflated, and he actually once said, 'What this country needs is another good depression to straighten it out.' "[87]

Kinsey had little sympathy for mediocre or poor students; his heart lay with the academically gifted. "Dr. Kinsey was impatient with mediocrity. He thought that many of the Midwestern farm boys and girls had no business trying to be college students," recalled a former student. "Why didn't they stay on the farm where they could make a practical contribution instead of pretending to be students of topics they did not have the ability or background to grasp." Confessing that she idolized Kinsey, the same student added that she saw him "as just a little imperfect—too intolerant."[88] Perhaps this tendency explains why he never won an outstanding-teacher award on campus, a prize conferred annually to recognize and honor professors who inspired students to love learning.[89]

Kinsey had neither the patience nor the desire to work with weak students. His job, as he defined it, was to teach college-level biology. Opposed in principle to remedial education, he refused to lower his standards to accommodate students who were not up to speed. Robert Kroc recalled that if a student asked "a silly question [Kinsey] could be rather strident in his comment."[91] That was an understatement. Kinsey was an ogre. On one midterm examination alone, he failed sixty physical education majors. "He flunked them out," exclaimed a colleague. "They were not to return to class, their work was so poor." The same colleague noted that the physical education department retaliated by dropping Kinsey's course as a requirement for its majors.[91]

A stickler on correct pronunciation, Kinsey often chided students for their Indiana twang, ignoring the fact that his own speech betrayed a distinct eastern accent. "He got on us midwesterners all the time," complained William Breneman, a colleague who had once been Kinsey's student. Breneman recalled one confrontation in particular when Kinsey "gave us a raking over the coals one day about our pronunciations in class." To illustrate how midwesterners abused the language, Breneman explained, Kinsey told the students that they said "Toosday" instead of "Tuesday." Tired of taking his ridicule, one student summoned the courage to hit back. Michael Johnson, a soft-spoken young man who also happened to be an outstanding student, raised his hand and asked Kinsey how to pronounce "idea," knowing full well he always said "idear." The whole class held its breath to see how Kinsey would respond. "Kinsey got a little bit red in the face," chuckled Breneman, "but there was never any resentment about it at all. I think he rather admired Johnson for speaking up."[92]

No less than his undergraduates, Kinsey's graduate students found him difficult and intimidating. The zoology department's doctoral program dated back to the 1880s, but it attracted relatively few students until after World War II. That suited Kinsey fine. He made no effort to recruit graduate students to work under his supervision. "I have never baited any grad student into taxonomy," Kinsey once wrote a friend, "for I want him to work where his interests are greatest."[93] Perhaps he was wise to assume this position. Few students wanted to work under his supervision.

Like his own mentor, William Morton Wheeler, Kinsey impressed most graduate students as distant and unsympathetic. Despite his frenetic energy, high standards, and devotion to scholarship, he never had more than one or two graduate students in the pipeline at any given time, and he directed only six dissertations during his career at Indiana. It seems doubtful he wanted more. "I sometimes had the feeling that students were something that he wished he could get along without, because he was so dedicated to his research," complained Robert Bugbee, one of his former graduate students. "But on the other hand," added Bugbee, "he was always willing to give us time when we wanted it. I always felt that I could walk into his office and ask him questions or talk about anything."[94]

As a graduate mentor, Kinsey was, in the words of Herman T. Spieth, one of his former graduate students, "very hard on his students, requiring near perfection."[95] Kinsey expected students to be self-starters, insisting that they bring to their work a strong background in biology. Spieth recalled that Kinsey "was frank to state that most of the graduate students were poorly prepared, and I remember one time when he said he thought many youngsters who were graduated from small colleges should not aspire to the Ph.D. degree."[96] Breneman got the distinct impression that Kinsey looked down his nose at certain students because of "the cultural background of the individuals."[97] Spieth agreed. He described Kinsey "as infuriating to his graduate students." Asked to explain, Spieth replied, "He denigrated us in a sense. I mean, it wasn't the kind of denigration that was done deliberately, but it was the fact that he came from an eastern, upper-class family, and most of his graduate students at Indiana came out of rural, small-town backgrounds."[98] To some extent, then, Kinsey made them feel like country bumpkins. "It wasn't a question of the overtness," Spieth added; "it was just in the air." He attributed his mentor's difficulty in relating to students, at least in part, to Kinsey's "upper-class arrogance."[99] Of course, Kinsey did not hail from the upper class at all. It was his intellectual arrogance and cool manner that made students think so.

Kinsey often used oral examinations. It was not enough to know the right answer; students had to be able to defend their answers and stand up for themselves. William R. Breneman recalled his final examination in the entomology course he took from Kinsey in the mid-1930s. It was a bittersweet memory, for Kinsey's method bordered on the sadistic. The entire test consisted of Kinsey's opening a box of gall wasps and asking him how many species it contained. Before Breneman was done scrutinizing the insects, Kinsey snapped the box shut and demanded an answer. Breneman replied that he saw three species. Kinsey then opened his desk drawer and removed a reprint of an article in which he had insisted that this particular group of insects contained only two species of gall wasps. After relaying what the article said, Kinsey demanded to know if Breneman thought he knew more than his professor. Kinsey then told him to look at the box again and decide whether he wished to change his answer. The young graduate student studied the specimens a second time and replied that the box contained three species.[100]

Kinsey was delighted. He reached into his desk and took out a reprint of a second article, in which he had corrected himself to say that the sample contained not two but three species of gall wasps. Kinsey then congratulated Breneman for standing his ground and announced that the examination was over. Breneman received an A+ for the course. Unfortunately, few students offered this much resistance. "He could be awful tough on them. They could come out just like they'd gone through a wringer after they'd had a session with him," declared Breneman, adding that a personality as strong as Kinsey's could be "very corrosive."[101]

Another student, Shelby D. Gerking, found an easier way to survive Kinsey's inquisition. Decades after the fact, Gerking could still recall shaking in his boots as he waited for Kinsey to come to his office to give him an oral examination. (Kinsey's own office was under repair at the time.) Ordinarily, confessed Gerking, his office was a disgrace. It was cluttered with fish bottles, and his "desk was unkempt and littered with paper." As luck would have it, Kinsey was thirty minutes late for their appointment, and knowing what a stickler he was about tidiness, Gerking used the extra time to put things in order. "Upon entering his eyes strayed to all corners of the room and particularly to my desk," recalled Gerking. "He commented that I was very neat, and he was glad to see a graduate student who took pride in his office. The interview about my report . . . proceeded, but it was obvious from the start that I had 'passed' without answering a question."[102]

Gerking read his professor right. Kinsey's own need for order and control made him unusually sensitive to the habits of others, a preoccupation that invariably prompted him to offer advice and form judgments. In the manual he prepared for laboratory and field workers, Kinsey declared, "Finally, I would add that an orderly desk in a laboratory, clean and well-cared-for equipment, and a neat—and a not too wordy notebook—seem to me some indication of orderly thinking. The way in which you do things may be of as much value to you as the actual information you obtain from your observations."[103]

Kinsey placed great emphasis on training his graduate students in his methods of fieldwork. His research on gall wasps was ongoing, and he made it a practice to take two or three graduate students (and an occasional undergraduate) with him on field trips. The field trips were an integral part of their graduate training, and Kinsey carried his classroom manner into the field. The routine was harsh, and Kinsey did not coddle students. He was the kind of teacher who always appeared to be sitting in judgment. As a result, Kinsey made students feel defensive, and many feared they would not make the grade.

No, Kinsey "was not popular with the graduate students in the thirties. They were scared of him, very frankly," recalled Breneman.[104] Their fears were well founded, for Kinsey could be extremely acid. As much as his gruffness, arrogance, and drive, it was Kinsey's intensity that made many people feel ill at ease. "He was tight as a banjo string most of the time," declared Theodore W. Torrey, one of Kinsey's few colleagues who actually claimed to like him.[105] Kinsey's letters reveal a man who had precious little good to say about his students. Upon returning from a collecting trip to Louisiana and Mississippi in the fall of 1934, Kinsey complained to Ralph Voris, whom he considered to be an excellent field-worker, that two of the four students who had accompanied him were "the slowest, least biologic of any I have ever gone in the field with." Instead of hustling to collect more galls, they had frittered away their time discussing philosophical questions. "They discussed infinity, and the possibility that matter was not real, but all an illusion for two whole days," Kinsey groaned, "without seeing a thing of the biology of that intensely interesting La. & Miss. country. Then I told them to butt their heads against a stone wall, and bring me the answer concerning the reality of matter."[106]

Kinsey had no tolerance for students who did not share his passion for nonstop work. Bluntly outspoken and harshly judgmental, he was not a supportive mentor. Nurture had always been in short supply in Kinsey's life, both as a child and in his own graduate training. Apparently, he found it hard to give what he had been denied.

Yet students knew exactly where they stood with Kinsey. Though quick to anger, he was equally quick to forgive and forget. Kinsey might snap someone's head off, but once the explosion was over, that was it. The incident was closed. Furthermore, Kinsey had a gentle side. However gruff the exterior, he had the ability to wipe away the hurt of past wrongs with sudden flashes of warmth, and he could be wonderfully generous with praise to those who had earned it. "Kinsey was, of course, an extraordinary human being," wrote Spieth. "Like others, I was often discouraged, sometimes humiliated, but always stimulated by any contact with this dynamic individual whose brusque impatience could suddenly change to a radiant kind of sweetness and charm."[107]

The beleaguered band of students who worked with Kinsey did so because they respected his scholarship. Whatever his personal shortcomings, he was a dedicated scientist, and no one questioned his devotion to research. Anyone who learned field biology from Kinsey received excellent training and a powerful role model.

Kinsey worked hard for his students following graduation. Once judged worthy, they were inside his circle of confidence, and he stood behind them for life. While careful not to recommend his students for positions beyond their qualifications, he worked tirelessly to place them professionally and equally hard to move them to more attractive positions. His files contain numerous letters of recommendation, each skillfully crafted to highlight an individual's strong points while offering enough critical comment to protect his credibility as a referee.

Moreover, Kinsey kept in touch with his former students long after they left the university. Surprisingly, his letters reveal a tolerance and warmth that remained hidden while they were working on their degrees. He listened patiently to their complaints about the pains of writing lectures, the intellectual numbness that attends prolonged exposure to lazy colleagues, the frustrations of dealing with self-serving administrators who inflated their own salaries and starved their faculties, and the mental drudgery of teaching dull students—in short, all the usual complaints of young professors who are paying their dues and working their way up the academic ladder.

It must have been hard for someone with Kinsey's disposition to hear such complaints. Yet he understood only too clearly what they were saying, for their experiences mirrored his own. His replies invariably offered soothing words of comfort laced with ringing exhortations to excel. To Kinsey, that meant only one thing—to publish.

Kinsey thrived on scholarship, and he advised his students to plunge into research as soon as they started teaching. When students complained that they could not do research surrounded by weak colleagues, Kinsey would have none of it, insisting that Indiana University had only a handful of professors who were doing important research and that even his friends at Harvard complained about their environment. Aware of how badly his students wished to move, however, Kinsey promised to recommend them for better jobs, provided they advanced their research.[108]

In a sense, Indiana University brought out Kinsey's worst features. Had he secured a position in an elite institution with excellent students, he might well have developed into an outstanding teacher. As it was, he found little pleasure in the task. By dint of work and will, Kinsey made himself into a strong teacher of excellent students, but he was decidedly less successful with those of average or poor abilities. He did not enjoy working with the majority of Indiana's students, and they certainly did not relish having him for a teacher.

10

"My Primary Interest Remains with Research"

oung professors sort themselves out rather quickly after graduate school. The first ten years are a decade of decision, setting the pattern for the remainder of their careers. The vast majority become teachers—respected on their campuses, but unknown one step beyond. Because they do not contribute to scholarship, they quickly sink into academic obscurity. A relative handful of young professionals, say, 10 to 20 percent, become scholars as well as teachers, and they regard themselves as the natural leaders of the academy because they not only teach but write the books and articles that shape their disciplines.[1]

Kinsey's path was never in doubt. Trained in an elite institution under distinguished scholars, he had been taught how the system worked and understood what was expected of him. He knew that the academy's number one rule was publish or perish.[2] Inspired by Wheeler's example at Harvard, Kinsey charted his course to become a contributing scholar, and he never looked back. He arrived at Indiana University determined to publish.

Any trace of humility or deference vanished from Kinsey's personality moments after he received his doctorate. Soon after he began teaching, Kinsey started speaking out about his chosen field, and his voice was critical. "For the better part of a century taxonomy has been losing caste," he declared in 1924. "It is time we admit this and try to discover the why of the situation." He averred that the reasons "must lie in the way in which we systematists have been doing things, and the sooner we learn to do them differently the sooner taxonomy will engage the interest and esteem of other biologists."[3]

The scholarship on gall wasps offered a perfect illustration of where taxonomy had gone awry. In one of his earliest publications, Kinsey lamented, "Students of the gall wasps have been few, and from large areas of the world practically no collections of this family have been made."[4] The sparse scientific literature did not take him long to review. In addition, he studied the private collections of numerous amateur collectors. He also examined the gall and gall wasp collections in many museums and natural history societies. By the time he joined the faculty at Indiana, he had encountered nearly 90 percent of the holotypes and paratypes on which the existing gall wasp classifications rested.

What he observed appalled Kinsey. "The majority of the species placed by both Europeans and American authors in Cynips," he wrote in 1922, "do not belong to that genus."[5] He laid the blame at the feet of his fellow taxonomists. In particular, he cited their careless methodology. His predecessors had failed to produce reliable data on the life cycles of gall wasps, because they had not exercised sufficient care "to keep separate the several species collected any one time."[6] Instead of storing individual specimens in separate containers (one gall to the container, properly labeled as to the host plant, date, and location of collection), they had placed "galls of several species into a single receptacle."[7] This carelessness had led to "hopeless confusion" when those same scientists later attempted to distinguish one species from another or tried to identify the host plant of a particular gall.[8] "A large part of museum material is rendered worthless by such methods of collecting," he declared.[9]

More distressing still, insisted Kinsey, was the lack of rigor with which his predecessors had examined individual insects. He found that scholars had paid scant attention to insect morphology and even less to gall structures. In one of his earliest scholarly articles (1920), he criticized his colleagues for placing many species in groups "based on the most meager of morphological characters" and constructing genera that "are not confirmed by a more careful examination of the morphology and a study of the biology of the species concerned."[10] Later that year, he complained that "no student has employed gall characters of any large scale in classifying the Cynipidae." This was a serious error. Meticulous examinations of thousands of galls had convinced Kinsey that they could yield valuable information. "I shall give great consideration to lines that the gall characters may indicate," he pledged in 1920.[11]

If sloppy methods distressed Kinsey, puny samples truly offended him. "Some years ago," he wrote in 1922, "I heard Dr. W. M. Wheeler remark that what we needed was not longer, more detailed descriptions, but pointed comparisons of related forms. These comparisons are possible only when much material is available."[12] Since leaving Harvard, however, Kinsey had learned that taxonomists had failed to collect enough material to support meaningful comparisons. "Too many systematists attain their objectives when each species is 'represented' by a half-dozen specimens pinned in their cabinets," he complained in 1930.[13] The classifications built on such anemic samples had placed individuals of different species into the same species, and taxonomists had compounded these mistakes by using erroneously identified species to construct equally flawed genera.

But lax methodology and tiny samples paled in importance when compared with scholarship's conceptual timidity. As early as 1920, Kinsey observed that these insects were "poorly understood" because other scholars had cataloged them "without much attempt to discover an arrangement which would indicate evolution" and had established genera composed "in large part [of] unnatural groups containing large numbers of unassorted, diverse organisms."[14] Two years later, he renewed the attack, fuming that much of the published work rested on "careless taxonomy" perpetrated by investigators who showed "a charming lack of knowledge of faunal areas and possible factors of distribution." What passed for fieldwork in the United States, he thundered, was "no credit to the taxonomy we have been doing."[15]

Over time, Kinsey sharpened his criticisms into a comprehensive critique, rebuking his fellow taxonomists for not matching the rigorous methodology and high intellectual standards of experimental biologists. Stressing that his differences were "not with taxonomy but with taxonomists," he declared in 1930, "If taxonomists have too often made species-descriptions and catalogs and nomenclatorial inanities the end of their efforts, it is no proof that the science cannot rise above its technique and concern itself with biologic problems."[16] Kinsey was so fed up that he considered writing a three-volume critical work on taxonomy, with special attention "on the phylogenetic method, on distributional biology, and on the nature of species."[17]

Thus, from the beginning of his career, Kinsey saw taxonomy as a beleaguered discipline. Relegated to a secondary status by the New Biology and discredited by its own simple tasks and lackluster methodology, it had lost status. During the 1920s and 1930s, only a handful of field biologists were still struggling to test Darwin's theories on evolution by studying living creatures in nature. One of Kinsey's colleagues at Indiana, Robert Kroc, who did his graduate work at the University of Wisconsin, a major center of the New Biology, recalled that he had never seen a flesh-and-blood scientist who was studying evolution outside a laboratory until he met Kinsey.[18] Kinsey must have felt as though he belonged to an endangered species.

Many scholars might have felt discouraged, but taxonomy's plight brought out the fighter in Kinsey. Taxonomy offered another battlefield on which he could demonstrate competence and control, two salient features of his personality. And he welcomed the challenge, as it appealed to his sense of mission. Who better than a secular evangelist to rescue taxonomy from academic oblivion?

But how to accomplish this feat? Kinsey's answer was simple: taxonomy would have to be leveled and built anew. It would have to improve its methodology, correlate its findings with those of other disciplines concerned with heredity, and, above all, ask important biological questions. Kinsey never doubted he was the man for the job. Increasingly, his language betrayed the passion of a man who had embarked on a personal crusade. Science was not merely his profession; it had become his religion. Science was a moral issue, a matter of right and wrong. When he vowed to uphold the highest canons of scientific rigor, with no thought to the cost in time or labor, Kinsey sounded like some born-again Christian dedicating his life to Christ.

Increasingly, Kinsey spoke in absolutes. As early as 1923, he acknowledged that the experimental determination of the life history of gall wasps was "a long and difficult matter," but added, "If we are ever to know these histories, we may not reject any clue as to just where to look for information."[19] Kinsey observed in 1928, "I have tried to utilize every method known to modern taxonomy to make this a critical correlation and genetic interpretation of all the biologic data available on the . . . genus."[20] For Kinsey, no clue could be ignored, no stone left unturned. He demanded perfection of himself. Nor was he alone in imposing this standard on himself, as society expected no less of its scientists.[21]

Kinsey drove himself to excel. Having triumphed over his father, he entered a new competition with Wheeler. Soon after arriving in Indiana, Kinsey began to distance himself from Wheeler's approach to taxonomy, becoming a pioneer of what came to be called the new systematics. "I have no interest in taxonomy per se," he declared in 1922, "for it is not a science concerned with questions of cause and effect." By "cause and effect," Kinsey meant the ultimate causes in nature, those that explain the existing characteristics and peculiar adaptations of modern organisms. Never one to shrink from a daunting task, he proposed to lay the foundation of cynipid taxonomy, in his words, "to build the structure of cynipid biology."[22] Writ large, his ultimate goal was to shed light on evolution, the central issue of natural history.

Kinsey asked large and important questions. Not content simply to name or to classify, he pondered issues such as natural selection, adaptation, progress, and descent. He wanted to know how new species are created and how (and why) species change over time. "Thru an intensive study of the nature of the species, the life-histories, host relationships, geographic distribution, and gall production in this group of insects," he wrote in 1929, "we should secure data . . . on the nature and origin of plant and animal species in general."[23] Kinsey thought taxonomy should analyze and explain, not merely classify and describe. Ultimately, taxonomy's goal should be nothing less than the "interpretation of biologic phenomena by the comparison of related species."[24]

By placing evolution at the center of his research, Kinsey hoped to transform taxonomy from a descriptive discipline into a science with strong explanatory power. In the right hands, he insisted, "a classification becomes one of the most powerful tools available for the evolutionary interpretation of biologic phenomena." In contrast to Darwin and his immediate followers, who pioneered theories such as common descent, natural selection, and survival of the fittest, Kinsey belonged to a new generation of systematists who sought to crystallize and refine concepts such as classification, species, higher category, and the like. In order to test these concepts, he proposed to collect specimens, examine them carefully, and then compare his specimens with each other and with those previously cataloged by other taxonomists.[25]

During his first year at Indiana, Kinsey promised "a thorough revision of the classification of the Cynipidae."[26] Several years later, an even bolder Kinsey announced in a grant proposal that he would attempt a new "formulation of the philosophy of taxonomy, its usefulness as a means of portraying and explaining species as they exist in nature, and its importance in the co-ordination and elucidation of biologic data." Ultimately, he hoped to "bring the fields of taxonomy and genetics into closer understanding of their common problem of the nature of species."[27]

Not that Kinsey thought of himself as a theoretician. He would have been the first to admit that he had no startling new concepts about the origin of species. Rather, Kinsey was banking on his methodology. He truly believed that methodology, what one scholar has called "the soul of science," could be used to test hypotheses and conclusions and, in turn, to formulate valid theories.[28] And for Kinsey, rigorous methodology could be reduced to one thing: direct observation of a creature in its natural habitat. The New Biology might rest on experimentation, but Kinsey placed his faith on careful observation.

A tireless perfectionist, he constantly searched for ways to improve his field and laboratory techniques.[29] As Edgar Anderson, his friend from Harvard days, observed, Kinsey meant to conduct his research "with such precision that it would illuminate the mechanics of evolution."[30] Indeed, Kinsey proposed to ferret out and analyze every knowable fact about gall wasps. His burning need to be the best at everything he did demanded no less. No shred of evidence, however minute, could be ignored, for, as Kinsey explained, "a good classification must be based on all the available data."[31] Toward this goal, he resolved to study not just the insects themselves but the galls they created and the insects that parasitized them. In addition, Kinsey strove to correlate his data with the findings of the New Biology by drawing upon the work of cytologists, comparative anatomists, embryologists, paleontologists, and, above all, geneticists. While this approach is standard operating procedure for modern-day systematists, Kinsey was way ahead of his time.

Another thing that set Kinsey apart was the huge number of specimens he collected. He called for tens of thousands, even millions, of specimens. As Anderson put it, Kinsey was determined to collect gall wasps and galls "in quantities never dreamed of by any previous investigator."[32] Why the huge sample? Part of the explanation lies in the fact that Kinsey had inherited the nineteenth century's passion for numbers. Just as the champions of the New Biology labored to make their fields as mathematical as possible, Kinsey wanted to reform taxonomy by expanding its database. In addition, he collected huge numbers of gall wasps because this particular insect happened to have a large number of species. In 1923, Kinsey estimated that there were "many thousands of varieties of Cynipidae in the world (most of them as yet undescribed.)"[33] Even if he had been willing to rely on two or three dozen specimens to establish each species (a figure he would have rejected as unacceptably low), he would have needed tens of thousands of specimens in order to complete the joint tasks of classifying the different species of gall wasps and establishing higher taxa. Besides, if Wheeler had managed to collect more than a million ants, Kinsey had to gather at least a million and one gall wasps. How could he settle for less? A man who measured his worth by his deeds, he collected because he had to collect.

Over time, Kinsey developed a new and compelling reason for his collector's mania, one that grew directly out of his field techniques. At first, his published articles had little to say on the question of varieties in species. While he dutifully reported morphological differences within and among different species of gall wasps, he assigned no special significance to variations. After carefully examining thousands upon thousands of insects, however, Kinsey noticed different varieties in the specimens that supposedly came from the same species. Within the span of a few years, he became convinced that varieties in nature had to be reckoned with, and in 1922 he boldly proclaimed his discovery to the world.

"Probably the most notable departure in this paper," Kinsey declared in an article, "is the recognition of varieties." Heretofore, he explained, entomologists in the United States had refused to admit that varieties existed, while European entomologists had made only limited use of the concept. As a result, his colleagues had either dismissed closely similar forms "as haphazard variations of one species" or treated them "as distinct species." The upshot was that "much biologic data has been scrapped, not to be recovered without difficulty." Admitting that he, too, had ignored variations or tried to pigeonhole dissimilar specimens into existing species, Kinsey announced that henceforth he would pay close attention to varieties in order "to discover the character of the variations" in gall wasps. "The only possible objection to the recognition of varieties will be the less convenient nomenclature necessary," he asserted, "but this is not a great consideration in view of the advantages of the practice." Kinsey thought the nomenclature should be expanded. "The genera of Cynipidae have always needed revision," he declared, "and the introduction of two terms new to American literature is part of my program of revision of gall wasp genera."[34]

From this point forward, Kinsey's insistence on the importance of varieties and individual variation became the defining features of his work. This belief drove him to canvass huge portions of the North American continent collecting gall wasps by the tens of thousands. In place of limited samples, he called for enough specimens to establish the true range of variation within and among species. When a student inquired how many specimens would be needed for each species, she remembered Kinsey's replying that he would keep collecting "until the statistical curve can't be changed by the addition or subtraction of a few hundred random individuals."[35] Anything less, he insisted, would yield skewed, if not totally distorted, data.

To satisfy his demanding standards, Kinsey was constantly in motion. While most taxonomists limited their fieldwork to arbitrarily defined regions, Kinsey endeavored to establish the complete geographic distribution of gall wasps. This meant stalking his quarry wherever they lived. And as luck would have it, gall wasps lived practically everywhere. Their range followed their favorite host, oak trees, which enjoyed wide distribution in North America, as well as in Central and South America. Kinsey hoped to distinguish older gall wasps from those that had evolved more recently, with the ultimate goal of tracking down the species that was the ancestor of all other gall wasps in the New World. As an evolutionary biologist, he ignored local, state, and international boundaries.

Kinsey had only scratched the surface when he arrived at Indiana. He had not touched entire sections of the United States, or the insect-rich countries to the south. In 1920, Kinsey reported that previous investigators had collected "very little material from the southern and western parts of the United States, from Mexico, or from Central or South America."[36] With these words, he fashioned a blueprint for the next eighteen years of his life.

During his first few years at Indiana, Kinsey had to settle for short trips to southern Indiana and the surrounding states. Most lasted only a few days, or at most a week. Not until 1926 was he able to mount another major field trip, and it proved to be enormously successful. Accompanied by his favorite graduate student, Ralph Voris, Kinsey made a giant swing through Indiana, Kentucky, Illinois, and Missouri, collecting more than 20,000 galls.[37] Supported by funds from the Waterman Institute of Indiana University, Kinsey took to the field again in 1927, 1928, and 1929. In 1927, he hit Michigan, southern Illinois, Alabama, and Georgia; and in 1928, he collected in northern Illinois, the Carolinas, and Georgia. In 1929, he returned to some of the regions he had explored as a Sheldon Traveling Fellow, the Colorado Rockies, Utah, and northern Arizona before cutting back across New Mexico and the Texas Panhandle. By 1929, after twelve years of research and 32,000 miles of travel, Kinsey reported that he had collected 17,000 insects and 54,000 galls.[38]

Kinsey's first automobile boosted the range of his fieldwork.[39] Given his financial situation, a car had been out of the question during his college and graduate school years. Nor had he been able to afford one during his early years at Indiana. Kinsey bought his first automobile, a Nash, in 1927, when he was thirty-three. (He taught himself to drive, and Clara, too.) Although terribly proud of that shiny, new Nash, Kinsey never developed an emotional attachment to cars. Unlike his father, who drove Cadillacs as a status symbol, Kinsey took a functional view. To him, the automobile was transportation, nothing more.

By the early 1930s, Kinsey had abandoned his sedan in favor of a vehicle he had specially adapted for rough terrain. He described it as "a big coup with a small truck body built on it in place of the rumble seat."[40] Several years later, he purchased an even larger vehicle. Known to graduate students as "Kinsey's juggernaut," it was a half-ton International truck, specially modified with an extra gas tank, a water tank behind the seat with a faucet on the outside, and heavy-duty springs for cross-country travel.[41] Kinsey used it to explore vast expanses of territory where no collector of gall wasps had gone before. A quarter of a century after he bought his first car, he told an audience of fellow scientists that the greatest tool of the tax-onomist in the twentieth century "is the automobile and highways."[42]

Not content to limit his sample to the United States, Kinsey explored the western Sierra and Cordillera of Mexico in 1931 and 1932. The expe-dition required four and a half months and was financed by a $750 stipend from the grants-in-aid program of the National Research Council, a har-binger of huge grants to follow. In 1933, he canvassed Wisconsin and its adjacent states and then swung down into Ohio and Kentucky, a trek that required three weeks. The next year, Kinsey took a three-week trip across Kentucky, Tennessee, Missouri, Arkansas, Oklahoma, Mississippi, and Louisiana. In 1935 and 1936, he again ventured south of the border on a major collecting expedition that consumed nearly four months, financing the trip with a second grant-in-aid from the National Research Council, this one for $600. After winding his way through the eastern Sierra down through southern Mexico, Kinsey descended upon Guatemala.[43] The yield from these trips was enormous. All told between 1917 and 1936, he logged more than 75,000 miles in fieldwork, with more than half coming in the last six years. He collected tens of thousands of insects and more than a million galls. His final field trip came in 1939 when he retraced the 1929 expedition into the Colorado Rockies and other points west.[44]

Extended field trips required not only financial support but the full co-operation of Indiana University. The galls had to be collected in the fall, be-tween the middle of September and the middle of November. Any earlier and the insects failed to emerge in the spring and could not be bred under laboratory conditions; any later and the weather grew too cold for field-work. Since this timetable conflicted with classes, Kinsey had to plan his courses carefully and make special arrangements for the students who ac-companied him.

He was constantly asking the university to reduce his teaching load. Early in 1930, he told President Bryan, "You must believe that my primary interest remains with research. There, I believe, I may contribute in the most substantial way."[45] Later that year, Kinsey made the first of many for-mal requests for an eight-week summer research appointment, to be fol-lowed by relief from teaching duties every fall term. Two years later, Kinsey trimmed his request, indicating that he could make do with either summer support or the fall free. "I believe I can serve the University more uniquely through this research program than through the teaching, or executive du-ties, I might assume," he declared.[46] Had he been at an Ivy League uni-versity, Kinsey might have received all the institutional support he wanted. Indiana University did not grant him everything he requested, but thanks to Dean Payne's support, Kinsey managed to get into the field more years than not.

Had he not been bound by time and human endurance, there is no telling how many specimens Kinsey would have collected. Always he was driven by his fierce work ethic. In one publication, for example, he complained that he was able to take "only scant samples" and wrote wistfully of being "reduced to glancing at most of the trees with their thousands of galls which we have not time to gather." As he contemplated all those unharvested specimens, Kinsey sighed, "We fall to wondering how many inconceivable millions of individuals of this one species are on all the trees in all the fields and woodlands and mountain forests through which we journey at many miles an hour, for hour after hour, yesterday, today, and tomorrow."[47]

A modern-day scholar hearing these laments might think Kinsey suffered from an underdeveloped appreciation of sampling theory. He did. Given his druthers, Kinsey would have collected every gall wasp on the planet. But he was enough of a realist to accept the need for sampling, and his methods evolved over time. Kinsey had no formal training in statistics, and no evidence suggests that he read widely in the field. When questions arose, he sought help from friends on the faculty such as Frank Edmondson, a young astronomer who advised Kinsey on several technical statistical problems.[48] Otherwise, Kinsey plowed ahead on his own, with little knowledge of sampling theory.

Through experience, Kinsey learned that gall wasps tend to congregate on isolated oak trees or on oaks on the fringes of woodlands. These were the areas where he and his student helpers concentrated. If they failed to find large numbers in one place, they took a sample and immediately moved on another hundred yards to a half mile until they found a tree or a thicket with a dense population of galls. On the average, they collected sixteen insects and sixty galls from each site. With these numbers, two or three energetic collectors could cover a region in four or five hours. Then they would move fifty miles or so and begin again. If they discovered large gaps between finds, Kinsey intensified his search in contiguous areas, as he strongly suspected that intermediate varieties of gall wasps could be found living near the borders of gaps.[49]

In the early years, Kinsey never specified how many specimens would be needed to constitute a reliable sample of each species. He proceeded to collect insects and galls by the thousands, chiding himself all the while for not getting more. Eventually, he concluded that a sample of 100 would suffice for species that lived in regions of diverse topography, while species that lived in regions of uniform topography would require 1,000 or more specimens. In 1936, he confessed he had collected "only" 214 insects and 755 galls for each of the 165 species studied to date.[50]

Kinsey got a lot of help from other collectors. Former graduate students routinely sent him specimens, as did scholars at other universities and approximately one hundred amateur collectors, some of whom were former students. This latter group included many individuals who became high school biology teachers. They, in turn, put their students to work collecting galls. From these sources, Kinsey obtained materials from nearly every state in the union, as well as a host of European countries, including England, France, Germany, Denmark, Italy, Hungary, Austria, Czecho-Slovakia, Finland, and the Soviet Union.[51] One European offering that especially delighted him was a fossilized gall wasp in amber, a beautifully preserved specimen that he estimated to be 25 million years old.

While acknowledging that other scientists had "commended" the size of his sample, Kinsey insisted it was too small, confessing abjectly, "No one realizes better than we how inadequate these collections in actuality are." His quest would continue, he declared, until he had collected 1.5 million insects and 3 to 4 million galls.[52] Not even Wheeler aspired to such numbers! As early as 1930, Kinsey had asserted that sound conclusions on species "cannot emanate from anything short of the most extensive data that modern facilities can provide."[53] Reflecting on Kinsey's mania for numbers, Edgar Anderson shrewdly observed, "It was here that his passion for assembling every possible scrap of evidence became almost an obsession."[54]

Kinsey planned his field trips like a general preparing for battle. The trips lasted anywhere from one week to four months, and in each instance, he took along one or two graduate students and an occasional pet undergraduate. As an experienced woodsman and camp leader, Kinsey knew that careful planning yielded successful expeditions. Therefore, nothing was left to chance. Clothing items, camping supplies, travel routes, collecting schedules, and daily menus (complete with a dessert for each dinner!) were arranged weeks before he left town. For his two trips to Mexico, he carried enough food and water to last the entire time, precautions one of his colleagues said explained why Kinsey's "expeditions came through successfully."[55]

The regimen on field trips was grueling. Kinsey rousted his troops at dawn and drove them well into the night. They spent their days collecting galls—tramping up and down hills, fording streams, hiking, it seemed, until they might drop. Kinsey set the pace, and he expected his troops to keep up. Many had great difficulty doing so, for it was hard to believe that anyone could crowd so much work into a day. Kinsey collected galls like a man fighting fire.

Sundown brought no rest. To prevent specimens from different regions from getting mixed together, Kinsey decreed that the galls had to be sorted and placed in separate containers the same day they were collected. While acknowledging that paper bags would do the job, he recommended specially sewn cloth bags, explaining that they "are much stronger, take up less room, and may be more securely tied at the top than paper bags."[56] So each night Kinsey and his assistants sorted, labeled, and otherwise prepared the galls for shipment back to Bloomington. (Typically, they made a mail drop every other day.) As a result, they routinely worked until 10 or 11 P.M. Pushed to their limits, Kinsey's assistants found the schedule exhausting.[57] One graduate student recorded in his field diary that he fell into his sleeping bag at night feeling "pissed out" and "about dead."[58] Another former student told much the same story, declaring, "[Kinsey] would work you to death."[59]

No one who accompanied Kinsey into the field ever forgot the experience. The expeditions began on a high note. The anticipation would grow as they motored across the countryside, with Kinsey behind the wheel holding forth on the joys of fieldwork. Kinsey's driving, however, was frightful. Herman T. Spieth, who completed his doctorate under Kinsey in 1931, recalled that his mentor's "passengers often had sinking feelings about their safety."[60] Osmond P. Breland's diary of his expedition with Kinsey to Mexico and Guatemala in 1934 recorded numerous horror stories. One entry described an incident high in the mountains of Mexico when they were heading down a wet dirt road and the truck started sliding. Fortunately, "the wheels stopped about 2 feet from the edge," but the near-miss left everyone shaking in his boots, including Breland, who wrote in his diary, "I was really scared shitless." What bothered him as much as the incident, however, was the fact that he felt he could not complain: "Kinsey is so darn scary on roads that are . . . slick," wrote Breland. "We could go O. K. with chains, but try to tell this stubborn ass that."[61]

When not frightened, students learned a great deal on field trips. Kinsey's delight in the wonders of nature and his insatiable curiosity were infectious. Everything interested Kinsey. One day would find him enthralled by the view from a mountaintop; the next day he would pause for an hour to watch a dirtdobber build its organ-pipe nest. Breland's diary noted that they rose early one morning because "Dr. Kinsey wanted us to see the sun rise."[62]

Kinsey never lost his sense of awe, continuing to view nature with childlike wonder. And he had a gift for finding joy in the unexpected. Breland described one incident that occurred about thirty miles south of Alpine, Texas. After they encountered oaks at an altitude of 6,000 feet, the highest point to date on their expedition, Breland wrote in his diary, "Kinsey liked to have had a hissey," and acted "crazy as a loon."[63] The scene repeated itself almost daily after they entered Mexico. In the mountains of northern Mexico, just outside the town of Múzquiz, they discovered some "5 species of oak" growing at an exceptionally high altitude. "Kinsey would shriek with glee at each new find," Breland wrote.[64] And so it went for nearly four months: Kinsey would scan the landscape, point his finger, exclaim at the top of his lungs, "Oaks," and then lead the charge.

Kinsey brought the same enthusiasm and rigor to the laboratory. Building on the techniques he had developed at Harvard, he continued his breeding experiments, but this portion of his research did not go well. The long life cycle of his insects, their peculiar life histories, which in many species involved alternating generations, and their strict adherence to particular plant hosts often frustrated his attempts at laboratory breeding. Kinsey had better luck at the bench. Examining individual specimens under a microscope, he focused on insect morphology and gall structures, both of which yielded valuable data for his studies.[65]

Kinsey's office doubled as his laboratory. It was located in Old Biology Hall, in a corner of the second floor next to the elevator shaft. Kinsey packed an amazing amount of material into a tiny space. Every item was meticulously arranged; not a pin was out of place. One observer called it "an impressively orderly laboratory."[66] Visitors had to enter through a small, windowless vestibule. Shoulder-high metal filing cabinets lined the inner wall, and rows of olive-colored metal bookshelves, stacked to the ceiling with insect cases, filled most of the remaining floor space. The bookshelves were arranged library style, with narrow aisles that ran crosswise in the room. These, in turn, were separated by a single broader aisle about two feet wide that ran down the center, a path that led to Kinsey's "office proper."[67]

Kinsey's desk occupied the center of his inner sanctum, facing a window that overlooked the Well House, one of the most beautiful sites on campus. Behind the desk sat his swivel chair, with a straight-back visitor's chair to the side. Across the room in the far corner was the only other open space in this labyrinth. A work space for assistants, it consisted of a small table, with a supply shelf for the killing, mounting, and labeling of gall wasps. Commenting on the acrobatic skill required to cope with this bookshelf jungle, one of his laboratory assistants recalled that when Kinsey wanted something from the top of one of these shelves, he had to "climb up, straddling the aisle, hand over hand . . . with his feet on opposite shelves."[68]

Amid his journals, books, and insects, Kinsey sustained a relentless work schedule. He arrived at 8:00 A.M. sharp, taught an early-morning class in general biology, returned to his office, and then burrowed into his research. He almost never broke for lunch. An inveterate brown-bagger, he ate at his desk so he could use the time to read scholarly journals. As in the field, lunch consisted of nuts, milk chocolate, and raisins. Kinsey never seemed to tire of this fare. After lunch and journals, he resumed work until about 4:00 P.M., at which time he went home for dinner.

During his early years at Indiana, he and Clara had four children. When the children were young and Clara needed help, Kinsey spent most evenings at home. An active parent, he helped bathe the children and get them ready for bed. He returned to his laboratory only one or two nights a week during these years, rarely working later than 10:00 P.M. As the children grew older, however, his routine changed. Research and writing filled more and more of his life, and late evenings at the office became the rule rather than the exception. As time passed, family time took a back seat to scholarship in Kinsey's daily routine.

The work that pulled him back to his office night after night was labor intensive. As he waited for the larvae inside the galls to mature into insects, Kinsey sewed the sorted and carefully labeled galls into envelope-shaped, fine-mesh copper bags about five inches wide and eight inches long. The bags allowed the insects to mature and breed in their natural habitat, but trapped them when they bored through the galls. Kinsey stored the bags in flower boxes containing a thin layer of moist sand (not too moist, though, or the galls would rot), placing the boxes on the ledge outside his office window.[69] He (or an assistant) checked each box several times a week to see if any insects had emerged, and during the interim he delighted in showing visitors his "special flowers."[70]

After the insects emerged, the real work began. In order to establish their life histories, Kinsey had to breed gall wasps in the wild. Here again, he followed the methods he had developed at Harvard. When the first insects hatched in his laboratory, he transported a portion of his specimens in their breeding envelopes to the outdoors, placing them near the base of the species of oak or rosebush from which they had been collected. While this sounds simple enough, it was a difficult task. Breeding gall wasps on rosebushes was easy, but breeding them on oak trees was hard. Several species of nursery-grown oaks, four to five years old, had to be transplanted a minimum of one year before the experiment commenced, and to prevent wasps other than the breeding material from contaminating the experiment, the entire trees had to be covered.[71]

Anyone but Kinsey would have been delighted with his results. Over the years, he successfully bred many thousands of insects, but he was never really satisfied, largely because he doubted whether he was getting a true portrait of how his insects existed in nature. At one point, he considered going to a remote mountain area and "putting under glass a large stand of the oaks involved." Since the species that inhabited this region had a two-year life cycle, Kinsey estimated it would take "many years of selection to develop pure lines from the wild stock, and many more years to duplicate the most significant of hybrids founds in the wild." In addition, the price would come to "perhaps a hundred thousand dollars." Would the results justify this amount of time and money? Kinsey thought not. True, such a study would produce, in his words, "a genetic analysis of one species of cynipid," but he doubted whether what he learned would hold true for other species.[72]

For reasons both practical and theoretical, Kinsey decided to assign experimental breeding a lower priority than laboratory study. Like his field technique, his laboratory work followed a fixed pattern. As each insect emerged from its container, it was trapped and killed. Then each specimen was labeled, mounted, and placed in its final resting place, a special insect-proof, cork-bottomed, wooden case called a Schmitt box.

The labeling was a chore. Kinsey insisted on minute labels, no more than three-eighths of an inch by five-eighths, so as not to distract from the specimens. Inscribed in India ink in a meticulous lettering style developed by Kinsey (Superintendent Foster would have been proud) and taught with great care to his assistants, labels recorded the species, location and date of collection, date of emergence, and sex of each insect. Each letter had to be beautifully shaped, a model of precise, careful printing. According to one former assistant, Kinsey "often beamed in his pleasure at the tiny printing on the labels."[73]

After the lettering came the mounting, which was something of an art. In preparation for mounting, many of the insects had to be soaked for several days to remove enough tannin to enable the mounter to operate the tiny drill used to bore a hole through their bodies. Once the hole was made, the mounter took a set of tweezers and, being careful not to damage the specimen, picked up the insect, applied a dab of clear cement to its left side, and placed it on a clip of cardboard. As soon as the cement dried, a two-inch steel pin was carefully inserted through the hole in the insect's side and then thrust through the clip of cardboard. These tasks completed, the insect was ready for the Schmitt box. Mounted two deep on each pin and placed approximately three-quarters of an inch apart, the impaled clips of cardboard, with their insects glued in place, were set in the Schmitt boxes about a quarter of an inch apart, all facing toward the right, in rows two inches apart. A portrait of austere order, 800 insects could be squeezed into a single box.[74]

The work was mind-numbing and time-consuming. While Kinsey did his share, student assistants performed most of the mounting. At any given time, he employed two to four students who worked, on average, twenty hours a week. The student employment office quickly learned that Kinsey had a preference for bright coeds, as he thought they did detailed work better than men. Over the years, he hired more than a dozen women as laboratory assistants, but only one man, Herbert Backer, a law student.[75]

From all reports, Kinsey was a considerate, if demanding, boss. Commenting on his administrative style, one former assistant observed that "he was the unquestioned patriarch."[76] Kinsey clearly tried to balance his authority with consideration. He gave assistants keys to his office so they could set their own hours, and he found other ways to make their job attractive. To promote harmony, Kinsey allowed his assistants to hire replacements when someone left his staff. A firm believer in rewarding good work, he also made certain they received top student pay on campus. At the depths of the Great Depression, he paid his helpers thirty-five cents an hour, a wage that one former worker described as "Magnificent!"[77] Kinsey financed this cottage industry through grants from the university, and later through various New Deal programs that provided work-study assistance for students.[78]

The atmosphere in Kinsey's office was pleasant but businesslike. One former assistant remarked, "There was nothing particularly stimulating about the job; but Dr. Kinsey's office was a happy place to work." What made it nice, she stressed, were the friendships that developed among the workers. When Kinsey was not present, she explained, "we chattered quite freely." But when he was working in his cubicle, she continued, "we felt it necessary to be more quiet of course."[79] Another former assistant confirmed this description of the working conditions, stating that he could "recall no amusing incidents or anecdotes."[80] Almost to the person, they attributed the solemn atmosphere to Kinsey's personality, describing a man with little or no sense of humor.

Workers who tried to inject a little levity got a quick lesson. One year a student assistant (a mere freshman) though it would be fun to play an April Fool's Day joke on her boss. As April 1 approached, she happened upon two of Kinsey's graduate students in the library. Admitting her awe of him, she nevertheless requested their help, and they, in turn, suggested she should pretend to discover dermestids (beetles that are highly destructive to furs, dried meats, and insect collections) in one of Kinsey's wooden insect boxes! She thought the idea was fantastic, and everyone agreed that Kinsey would swallow it hook, line, and sinker.[81]

The assistant appeared in her boss's office on the appointed day. Summoning all her courage, she announced, "Dr. Kinsey, I think there are dermestids in this type box." As he frantically rushed to examine the invaders firsthand, she muttered, without daring to look up, "April Fool." Kinsey did not see the humor. "He stood looking at her with his hands on his hips, and finally said, 'Hmmph!' and turned around and went back to his seat." "He never said anything further to her about it, but several days later, he told the two of us about it," said one of the conspirators, "and he said that he did not think a young, freshman girl would have the nerve to have done that to a full professor."[82]

Most of Kinsey's assistants liked him. As a group, they decided his bark was worse than his bite. "I think all of us who worked for him were a little frightened of him and his manner; although we had no reason to be," wrote one former worker. "Beneath his briskness he was kind and considerate."[83] Another woman considered his laboratory "one of the better student jobs on campus." She also made it clear that Kinsey got his money's worth, for as she put it, "four of us girls could mount a lot of insects in a week."[84]

Kinsey reserved the important jobs for himself. While examining each insect under the microscope was a painstaking task, he refused to delegate this work or any substantive chore to subordinates. By temperament and for the sake of quality control, he preferred keeping things under his own thumb. Kinsey thrived on meticulous tasks. Among the characters he examined were wing length, wing venation, relative proportions in thoracic and abdominal structures, body sculpture, and antennal segmentation. One former assistant estimated that Kinsey made "perhaps twenty individual measurements or specific observations about each insect."[85] Since he examined over 35,000 insects during the 1920s and 1930s, simple arithmetic suggests that he recorded about 700,000 separate measurements! How could anyone get so much done? The best answer came from one of his assistants, who remarked, "Dr. Kinsey utilized every minute of the day."[86]

Kinsey derived enormous satisfaction from his work. The tiny creatures under his microscope fascinated and delighted him, and it showed in his writing. Ordinarily, the language of science is neutral and objective, forgoing personal, emotional, or subjective observations. But Kinsey peppered his articles and monographs with exclamation points. In contrast to Wheeler's classical references and sardonic humor, Kinsey's prose often appeared to have been written by an eager young boy. Who else but Kinsey would call a particular gall "a splendid thing"[87] or suggest that "attractive oak apples" could sit "demurely on the upper surface" and hang down "like Christmas tree ornaments"?[88]

People who saw Kinsey at work marveled at his pleasure. He would sit for hours, his green eyeshade in place, peering through his microscope under the lamp, a portrait of total concentration. "He worked quietly for long periods," one of his laboratory assistants recalled, "then suddenly might remark: 'Astounding!' or 'Remarkable!' 'This is something!' or 'Wow!' These ejaculations were not directed at me (the only other person in the room), but were merely expressions of his exhilaration at his discoveries. Sometimes he would smile at me, rise from his chair for a moment and then quietly continue his work again."[89] Such displays were commonplace, and if he found something really exciting, Kinsey would bolt from his office and seek out colleagues or students with whom he could share the joy of discovery. One former graduate student had vivid memories of Kinsey's "enthusiasm for his research and of his bursting into the Graduate Room on the third floor of the old Biology Building to show . . . me the results of some of his studies on Cynipids."[90]

As much as he relished research, Kinsey had no difficulty sitting down to write. In the nearly two decades between 1919 and 1937, he churned out 3,193 pages. That broke down to about 177 pages per year, or about half a page a day.[91] In broad terms, Kinsey produced two types of writing— commercial textbooks and scholarly articles and monographs. While the textbooks offered financial security for his family and a podium for advancing his pedagogical ideas, he put his lifeblood into his gall wasp scholarship. Over the years, it revealed in full measure his strengths and weaknesses as a scholar.

Kinsey's early articles were largely descriptive. Several offered loving accounts of the new species he discovered—"my creations," he once called them with obvious pride.[92] Before long, however, his articles featured sharply worded criticisms of the current taxonomic research, detailed discussions of his methodology, and somewhat tentative formulations of his thoughts on the phylogenetic position of genera. Still, these early pieces remained silent on the species problem, offering no clue on whether he would join the "lumpers" or the "splitters."

Kinsey took a stand in his seventh article, which appeared in 1922. In this piece, he announced that "varieties" were realities in nature.[93] From this moment forward, he was a splitter. At first, he sounded tentative and unsure of himself, as though he was hesitant to develop new nomenclatures. In another article published in 1922, he insisted that the confusion surrounding earlier taxonomic descriptions of gall wasps pointed to the "merits of our conception of a single species with many varieties." He went on to argue that the "more closely related varieties might be considered in groups as subspecies if we had occasion to use the terminology."[94]

A year later, Kinsey staked out a new position on the species problem. "As long as no categories but genera and species are recognized in a classification," he wrote in 1923, "it will always be difficult to show the several degrees of relationships which actually exist in nature. For that reason I have employed subgenera and varieties in addition to species and genera." Kinsey acknowledged that his use of varieties might prove confusing to his colleagues. "By employment of varieties I am open to both the charges of being a 'lumper' and a 'splitter,' " he confessed, "the former in my treatment of species, the latter in my recognition of varieties." Nevertheless, he defended his word choice, arguing that it "does portray the different degrees of relationships that actually exist." Kinsey called for "still further categories to show the actual degree of relationships," but declined to propose them, acknowledging that "further subdivision would probably destroy the convenience of the catalog and the nomenclature."[95]

Over time, Kinsey became an avid splitter. As he dug deeper and deeper, amassing huge quantities of data, he was convinced he had discovered a plethora of finely graded, subtly shaded species. Again and again, he recognized them as species, greatly expanding the number assigned to the genus. In addition, he continued to uncover variants of species, though he could not decide what to call them.

In 1929 Kinsey tried to answer all these questions in his first book, *The Gall Wasp Genus Cynips: A Study in the Origin of Species*. Finding a publisher was not easy. Unlike Wheeler, who was able to pick and choose among the nation's leading houses, Kinsey was not able to interest a commercial publisher. Nor was he able to place his work with a prestigious university press, for he had not developed a reputation in the broader scientific community. His subject matter was too specialized (and the potential audience for his work too small) to interest a general audience. Only a handful of taxonomists wrote books, and none of the previous students of gall wasps had produced a monograph on these insects. The literature was limited to articles in highly specialized journals.

Kinsey was lucky Indiana University Press agreed to publish his monograph. That his home press came to his rescue sheds light on the support universities provided for scholarly research in America. By the 1920s, even universities as financially strapped as Indiana were beginning to organize presses, both to enhance their images and to support the scholarship of their faculties. The demands of the marketplace forced many university presses to demand subsidies from their authors. This was true in Kinsey's case, as he had to agree to purchase a substantial number of copies of his book.[96]

Although systematic data filled the bulk of its pages, *The Gall Wasp Genus Cynips* was an ambitious book. All told, Kinsey examined 93 species, and while 45 had been described previously, 48 were new. His contribution was important, because identifying new species is one of taxonomy's primary functions. Moreover, his descriptions, whether of new or old species, were exquisitely detailed, averaging about four pages. What made the book truly extraordinary, however, was "Part I"—a seventy-page introductory essay in which Kinsey identified the species problem as the central issue of taxonomy and the chief focus of his work. To restore taxonomy's luster, he called for a new systematics that would compile huge samples from vast regions, conduct state-of-the-art experimental laboratory work, and correlate the findings with those of related scientific fields. Offering his own work as a model, Kinsey laid out his methodology step-by-step, recounting his efforts over the past twelve years to apply these techniques in the field and in the laboratory.[97]

Then Kinsey turned to his findings. First, he addressed the issue of what is a species. Aligning himself with the best taxonomic theorists of the day, he defined species "as populations with common heredity," a definition at once concise and theoretically potent. Rejecting the argument that species were mere "mental concepts," he insisted "that species are realities which preserve a morphologic and physiologic identity under varying conditions, over vast areas, and thru periods of time that may extend beyond the present geologic epoch."[98]

Next, Kinsey tackled the origin of species. Departing from Darwin, he denied that the gradual accumulation of small variations could explain the origin of the gall wasps he had studied with such meticulous care. Kinsey saw Mendelian genetics at work. Mutations were the most important factor in the origin of new species, he insisted, though he acknowledged that isolating mechanisms and hybridization both played important roles in creating new species. If mutant individuals were bred back into the parental type, they altered the characters and thereby extended the range of variation within the parental species. But if mutants were isolated from the parental type, they produced a new species with fairly uniform characters.[99]

At first glance, Kinsey's findings did not seem startling. His definition of a species was widely shared by other scientists and his confirmation of Mendelian genetics was not likely to cause much of a stir in scientific circles. What made Kinsey's work distinctive was his emphasis on continua—the fact that he had uncovered such a vast range of individual variations within species and such important varieties among species. "I am at a loss for a solution of this difficulty," he confessed. Hinting that a new category might need to be created between species and genus, Kinsey demurred: "I have not the temerity to propose such a name while taxonomists are as far removed from biologic realities as the codes of nomenclature and much current systematics would indicate. Consequently . . . I have adopted the term variety for the category which, after all, fulfills the species concept."[100] Here Kinsey was starting to get into trouble. His confrontation with diversity had made him believe he had uncovered bewildering continua, which in turn had prompted him to suggest, albeit timidly, a new classificatory category. Kinsey had fallen into the same trap as his mentor Wheeler. Kinsey had carried "splitting" to extreme, suggesting that he was overwhelmed by his data and was in serious trouble as a theorist.

Still, measured against his stated goals, Kinsey's first book was a success. He had set out to earn a place for taxonomy in the New Biology by conducting case studies of individual species that would provide field data for comparison with the findings from laboratory genetics. Certainly, the sheer volume of his data could not be ignored. It demanded respect from a profession that prized counters, particularly those who combined large samples with facts derived from careful observation. No previous taxonomist had constructed such a minutely detailed field study for comparison with the findings of laboratory geneticists.

But Kinsey had presented more than raw data. While his thinking was still inchoate, he was attempting to formulate a new concept that could give intellectual cohesion to all those facts. Although he insisted he was not a theoretician, his work made its own statement. By arguing that individual variation within species (and varieties among species) were realities in nature, he had directly challenged the essentialism that dominated much of taxonomic thinking. Both his definition of a species and his recognition of continua suggested that Kinsey was struggling to fashion a new classificatory category. Though he went overboard on the matter of variation, he nevertheless anticipated the "population thinking" that formed the basis of the "new systematics," the antiessentialist school that came to dominate taxonomic theory after World War II.

Despite its impressive research and significant contributions, *The Gall Wasp Genus Cynips* received little notice. Only seven reviews appeared in print, mostly in entomological magazines. Journals that specialized in genetics ignored the book, as did the premier interdisciplinary scientific magazines with national circulations. In other words, the book failed to receive any play outside entomology and taxonomy, suggesting that the broader scientific community did not find it noteworthy.

Easily the most thoughtful (and longest) review appeared in *Entomological News*. Calling Kinsey "a remarkably assiduous and discerning student," H. M. Parshley devoted the bulk of his five-page essay to a thorough and exceedingly laudatory discussion of his methodology, venturing that "[t]he taxonomic method would soon be restored to dignity if Kinsey's principles were to find general application." Hailing *The Genus Cynips* as a "magnificent piece of scientific work," Parshley concluded that "all who have published monographs of similar general character must feel a deep sense of admiration and an even deeper sense of their own short-comings." In his judgment, the book's sheer volume of data made "Professor Kinsey's work take on at once the proportions of a classic."[101]

Parshley did offer one caveat. Perceptively, he questioned whether Kinsey had truly made peace with the species problem. At issue was whether a new category had to be created to accommodate many of Kinsey's variants or whether they represented new species. As Parshley pointed out, Kinsey spoke of ninety-three "species" in the general biological discussion of his data, but that number shrank to twenty-six nomenclatorial species in his descriptive section and in his checklist, with the rest appearing as "variants." Parshley suggested that this bow to conventional taxonomic customs and codes betrayed Kinsey's reluctance to offer a new taxonomic category between the true species (which he temporarily called "variety") and the genus. Yet, despite what he bluntly labeled as Kinsey's "predicament," Parshley concluded that the temporary use of the term "variety" was justified until someone could answer Kinsey's call for a new systematics that would coordinate biological concepts with convenient taxonomic nomenclature.[102]

No other reviewer echoed Parshley's concern about Kinsey's confusing use of "variety." While different scholars highlighted different attributes, they all commended his methodology in tones suggesting they were awestruck by his investment of time and energy.[103] Not a single reviewer criticized Kinsey's methodology. No one questioned his sampling methods or his analysis of data. On the contrary, the reviewers all lauded his sample size, endorsing his argument that modern taxonomy had to draw upon huge numbers of specimens. They also praised the geographic breadth of his fieldwork, seconding his insistence on the need to trace species across their entire ranges. Seeing these reviews, Kinsey had every right to feel confident about his methods.[104] In the future, he would always believe that huge samples collected across vast distances and under dissimilar conditions necessarily yielded representative data on any subject.

Thus, though few in number, the reviews were wonderful. It is not often that a scientist gets to hear a word like "magnificent." Yet at some level Kinsey had to feel disappointed. As the subtitle made clear, he had hoped to compete with Darwin, but the book came and went without producing any impact on the public. In a curiously reflective passage in the book, Kinsey had complained that his "specimens" might seem "insignificant, the data tedious, and the dry-rot of the technique unendurable."[105] The silence that greeted his book outside his specialty suggested that the broader scientific community shared this view.

Kinsey was thirty-six when his book appeared, old enough to take stock and evaluate his career. Privately, he had longed for a position at a first-rate university and the kinds of awards and honors that lined Wheeler's walls. Where was the call to Harvard? Where were the honorary degrees? The medals and prizes? Where was his membership in the National Academy of Sciences?[106] For twelve years, he had worked incredibly hard and suffered the jeers and ridicule of those who had called him "Get a Million Kinsey." He had been sustained by the hope that he could serve as the savior of his discipline by single-handedly restoring taxonomy's status within the biological sciences. Suddenly all that hard work and personal sacrifice had been called into question. But if Kinsey was disappointed, he did not show it. Always in the past, he had responded to adversity by trying harder; he reacted to the modest impact of his first volume in the same manner.

Kinsey immediately plunged into his second book. His new project focused on the origin of higher categories of gall wasps. Initially, he expected to find a single ancestor for the whole genus. The phylogenetic maps he had compiled to date suggested that the most primitive species of gall wasps could be traced to the American Southwest, specifically to southern Arizona. This led Kinsey to believe that evolution could be visualized, both figuratively and literally, by a " 'tree of life' in which the main branches represent ancestral stock which disappeared as they gave rise by radiate evolution to the species at the ends of the tree."[107]

To test this theory, Kinsey headed south of the border. In the fall and winter of 1931–32, he and his helpers explored the Western Sierra of Mexico, which he proclaimed "a perfect gold mine."[108] On the basis of his examination of insects he later bred from this region, he predicted in 1934, "We'll easily have 700 [new species] from the Mexican trip when it is all described."[109]

As Kinsey examined this material, his thoughts on the origin of higher categories began to crystallize, signaling a break with Darwin's position. Darwin and his immediate successors had argued that a single species formed the ancestral stock that gave rise to higher categories.[110] As late as 1930, Kinsey had believed he could locate the center of origin for gall wasps, and for several years thereafter he had expected to find it near southern Arizona. As he later confessed, he had interpreted "the convergence (without union) of so many phylogenetic lines in the Southwest as evidence of the origin of the whole group near that point."[111]

The new material from Mexico changed Kinsey's thinking. It tied up all the loose ends he had traced to southern Arizona into two or three continuous chains that spread throughout the oak-inhabited portions of the continent. The "tree of life" simile, he told Voris, should be rejected in favor of "a creeping vine or a plant with runners." In Kinsey's opinion, this new image offered a major improvement on Darwin, as it allowed scientists to visualize how evolution actually worked. "The first species of the new genus is as closely related to the last species of the old, as any two species are to each other within the genus," explained Kinsey. "Higher categories arise merely as species—by mutations or hybridization and subsequent isolation—with no greater degree of difference than is involved in the origin of any other species."[112] Thus, he had significantly altered his earlier position on species. He had come to believe that higher categories were not realities in nature, but existed merely as taxonomic conventions.

Kinsey presented his new ideas at the Indiana Academy of Science meetings in November 1934. "Got a widespread response," Kinsey wrote Voris, adding that while one group was "lukewarm" another participant in his session "said some very extravagant things for it."[113] More important, Kinsey boasted that he talked until one-thirty in the morning with Thomas Hunt Morgan, the Nobel Prize–winning geneticist from Columbia University and mentor of his department chairman, Fernandus Payne. Since Kinsey wanted to build bridges between taxonomy and genetics, Morgan was the ideal person with whom to spend an evening. The great geneticist must have been encouraging, for Kinsey went out of his way in his second book to quote approvingly and at great length from Morgan's influential study *The Scientific Basis of Evolution* (1932).[114]

Kinsey drove himself hard to finish his second book, and in March 1935 *The Origin of Higher Categories in Cynips* was ready for the press. Since the market for his work had not changed, Kinsey submitted the manuscript to Indiana University Press, which had established a new "Science Series" in 1935 to publish papers and monographs by faculty and students. This time the home folks kept him waiting. Kinsey was never quite certain whether the publication committee at Indiana University had doubts about the book or whether simple neglect explained the delay. Whatever the reason, the committee sat on it for three months before sending it out for review.[115]

The manuscript got mixed reports. As Kinsey later confided to Voris, the taxonomist said the taxonomy "was O. K. and important, but the genetics unprintably bad," while the geneticist thought "the genetics sound enough, but the taxonomy certainly not in accord with current taxonomy." Confronted with divided reviews, the committee took no action for several additional months. Revealing his reaction, Kinsey declared, "I took back the MS, put it in the bank vault while I was in Mexico, and refused to give it to them for six months after my return."[116]

There was little else he could do to vent his frustration. Other publishers were not exactly beating down his door. During the months of delay, Kinsey worked overtime breeding specimens from the samples he had collected during his recent trip to Mexico and Guatemala. "Plenty of technique handling the new material," he wrote Voris. "Bad luck on breeding much of it."[117] Still, Kinsey dutifully blended his new material into his manuscript, and his hard work paid off. The committee, chaired by Payne, immediately accepted it upon resubmission, leaving a smug Kinsey to crow, "Payne was quite meek about it."[118]

The Origin of Higher Categories in Cynips contained much that was familiar, much that was new. Echoing his trademark themes, Kinsey renewed his attack on taxonomists who settled for limited samples. Denouncing taxonomic "provincialism," he argued that local studies "show us nothing but ends or cross-sections of phylogenetic chains."[119] If taxonomists meant to discover the origin of species, they would have to compile huge samples and trace species across their entire ranges. After stressing that he had collected 35,000 insects and 124,000 galls across vast regions in the United States, Mexico, and Guatemala, and after explaining his field and laboratory methodologies in great detail, Kinsey announced with a flourish that his own thinking on the origin of species had changed dramatically.[120]

Kinsey confessed that as recently as 1930 he had expected to locate the center of origin for all the complexes and subgenera of *Cynips* in the American Southwest. After examining his new material from Mexico and Guatemala, however, he had been forced to conclude "that we were quite in error in looking for a center of origin. This is the prime point in which our present study modifies our previous publication on Cynips." Kinsey told his readers to forget about the "tree of life";[121] evolution should be compared "with a chain, vine, or (better still) with a chain of connected segments in the flattened stem of a prickly pear cactus."[122]

The new symbols, explained Kinsey, posed a bold challenge to Darwin's doctrine of common descent. In contrast to a tree, a chain implied "nothing as to common characters in the series of species, and hence nothing as to the characters of the first link in the chain."[123] Whereas Darwin and his followers had theorized that a single species had given rise to the diverging types of new species, Kinsey denied that a single ancestral form had ever existed, at least not in the sense that Darwin had used that term. "There was, of course, a single species which came before any of the others in the chain," wrote Kinsey, "but it does not represent the higher category, nor do its descendants represent the lower categories."[124] Rather, each species (link in the chain) gave rise to "one or to a limited number of new types . . . without modifying the specific status or the existence of the older species, and . . . with no certainty of the survival of any of the ancestral characters through any series of derived species."[125] It followed, therefore, that each species "originates as a modification, subdivision, or derivative of a previously existing species, usually without the extermination of the older species as a consequence of the speciation."[126]

Having laid out his reasoning, Kinsey boldly announced that higher categories did not exist in nature. Higher categories, he asserted, were "a pure convention, subject to the varying interpretations of every student of the group." Higher categories might "be warranted as a matter of classificatory convenience," but they were not "a reality in nature."[127] They were real only "in the sense that a higher rank in any artificial scheme of classification includes all the lower ranks within it."[128]

Despite their artificial nature, Kinsey did not think higher categories should be abolished. As long as scientists recognized they were playing a shell game, higher categories could be preserved as "a means of cataloging knowledge." To him, the only definition that made sense of higher categories was "a connected series of lower categories" or, as he put it even more simply, "higher categories are groups of related units." While admitting that his definition of higher categories might force taxonomists to "depart from current concepts on the origin and nature of such categories," Kinsey insisted that his was the only system that made classificatory convenience subordinate to the higher goal of working out the true phylogenetic relationships among different species.[129]

Kinsey closed by calling for a new systematics that would secure taxonomy a position of respect within the New Biology. In addition to fulfilling its traditional function as namer and classifier, taxonomy had to be transformed into a powerful analytic tool for probing evolution. To accomplish this, Kinsey argued, taxonomy would need to reform its methods along the lines he had suggested, and it would have to ally itself with genetics. Alone, neither discipline could explain the mysteries of evolution. The solution was "a combined genetic-taxonomic method in which laboratory analyses are made of phenomena observed in the field, and the significance of the experimental data checked with exactly similar individuals in natural species."[130] In short, Kinsey proposed an alliance between a revitalized systematics and the burgeoning field of genetics, which he recognized was very much in the driver's seat.[131]

The Origin of Higher Categories in Cynips was warmly received by taxonomists and entomologists. Once again, however, only seven journals reviewed the book, six of which were either local or state journals or magazines aimed at specialists in taxonomy and entomology. With the exception of a half-page notice in *Science Progress,* it was not reviewed by journals that reached nonspecialists. In other words, Kinsey's second book, like his first, failed to make a dent in the broader scientific community.[132]

Kinsey claimed to be happy with the reviews. In a letter to Robert Bugbee, a former student, he described the book's reception as "more cordial than that given the first."[133] He told Ralph Voris that the reaction was "the most encouraging thing yet," adding, "The geneticists are the strongest rooters for us, but biologists in many other fields are giving it some attention."[134]

To a limited extent, Kinsey's estimate of the book's impact was correct. Soon after it appeared, he received several invitations to present his work to audiences outside his field. The most important came from the American Association for the Advancement of Science (AAAS), which asked Kinsey to participate in an interdisciplinary symposium on higher categories in Atlantic City, New Jersey, in December 1936. The symposium was sponsored by the American Society of Naturalists meeting in joint session with the Genetics Society of America. At first, Kinsey declined, pleading he had said it all in his book. But at the program committee's urging, he finally agreed to appear.[135] He was pleased and honored that the geneticists had insisted he should represent the zoologists in the session.[136]

On the eve of the conference, Bugbee warned that the session might be stacked against him. "I do hope . . . that some of these people are at last realizing how things *can* and *should* be done taxonomically," he wrote Kinsey, "and that you will find plenty of support for your ideas." Yet Bugbee was concerned that the session might turn into a dogfight, declaring, "I imagine that the 'fur will fly' aplenty."[137]

As it happened, Kinsey's paper, "Supra-Specific Variation in Nature and in Classification: From the View-Point of Zoology," got a cordial reception. His fellow panelists praised it lavishly, especially his old friend from graduate school, Edgar Anderson, of the Missouri Botanical Garden in St. Louis, whom Kinsey described as "handsome in his acceptance." The latter's support was particularly gratifying to Kinsey. "Anderson has objected for all these years that I had a very special case in these bugs—that such major mutations were not to be expected in most groups. Now he writes he is quite convinced that it is my method that is unique," Kinsey boasted to a former student. Anderson's praise allowed him to believe that he was finally starting to convince his fellow scientists that taxonomy had something to offer, provided it was done with proper attention to variations.[138]

Kinsey also received positive feedback from the audience. He noted that the paleontologists at the conference "testified that their fossil connecting links make higher categories just what I find them" and added, "Even a number of the taxonomists are enthusiastic—thou [*sic*] they as a group, offer the most objections." The most welcome support came from the scientists whose approval he most desired. "The geneticists are strong for it," he wrote early in 1937. "All [were] quite convinced."[139]

As far as anyone could tell, Kinsey was riding high. His second book had generated favorable reviews, and his conference papers had been well received. In addition, his work was starting to appear in journals that reached a broader scientific community. His AAAS paper was published in the *American Naturalist* (1937); and Kinsey quickly turned out another major article, "An Evolutionary Analysis of Insular and Continental Species," which appeared in the *Proceedings of the National Academy of Sciences* (1937), which was read by scientists from many fields.[140] Most encouraging of all, a brief summary of the latter piece appeared the same year in *Science,* the most influential scientific journal in the world.[141]

But Kinsey's burning need to be the best could never be satisfied by a few good reviews or a handful of favorable comments at scholarly meetings. Compared with his time and effort, such rewards seemed meager. Not only had he failed to win the kind of recognition that might have moved him closer to becoming "a second Darwin," but he had not even risen to the status of "a second Wheeler." As before, the phone that might have rung with offers from first-rate universities remained silent. Impressing a handful of specialists was not enough. He wanted more.

The habits of a lifetime compelled Kinsey to push on. Long before he knew how his work on higher categories would be received, he had already committed himself to a new project, one that would build on, yet ultimately surpass, his work to date. His need to ask great deeds of himself drove him to select a new insect species, one that would tax any researcher's resolve. A few days after he submitted his second monograph for publication, Kinsey wrote a former graduate student, "Immediately I have started on the next monograph—Xystoteras is the genus—a larger group than Cynips—I have perhaps twice as much material." The specimens he had collected to date, he explained, contained 150 new species, and he estimated that it would take a year to eighteen months to complete the study. He boasted, furthermore, that the new study "will cover more ground than the 2 Cynips volumes on which I spent nine years." If the public and his fellow scientists had not heard him, he would shout louder.[142]

Kinsey approached his new project with characteristic vigor. In a letter to a former graduate student, he declared, "At long last I may be able to convince some body that I have been laying a foundation in all these 18 years—on which the finished structure may now rise rapidly." He explained, "While on Cynips I had to take a year and a half to lay the foundation of the generic rearrangement of the whole family—a matter of 6 months to solve the long-wing-short-wing riddle, much time over many years to make catalogs and correlate literature—endless technique in preparing collected material for future study." But all of his painstaking work and his lovingly crafted "technique" were about to bear fruit. "Now, suddenly, it has all come to a head. Everything is ready for the new study, and I am writing thousands of specimens and ten or a dozen new species into the manuscript each week. This is the fruition of the dream I have had about building for a life time of research. But it is a dangerous program if one gets bumped off prematurely."[143]

Instead of surrendering to disappointment, then, Kinsey renewed his determination to redeem taxonomy and to establish himself as a first-magnitude scientist. From 1935 through the end of 1937, he virtually lived at his desk. In addition to the higher categories monograph, he published a volume on methods and six journal articles, and he was hard at work on two generic monographs on *Xystoteras* (the new passion that replaced *Cynips*) and *Disholcaspis*—another genus he had decided to work on.

This explosion of writing represented the culmination of nearly two decades of work. Throughout these years, Kinsey had driven himself like a man possessed. He had logged tens of thousands of miles in the field, spent countless hours at the microscope, and thought long and hard about some of the biggest questions in biology. Always he had been driven by his need to know, his relentless desire to excel, and his messianic impulse to save taxonomy from academic oblivion and restore its scientific luster. After nearly two decades of painstaking work, Kinsey badly wanted to believe that his goals were within reach. At times, he sounded like a crusader who was confident of winning, as in his 1937 boast to Voris, "You are going to see a day when taxonomic contributions will be accepted as a fundamental part of biologic science, Sir."[144] If there was any doubt that he considered himself the best man to assume Darwin's mantle, Kinsey erased it the following year when he informed Payne, "I may undertake the writing of a critical text in evolution."[145]

Kinsey was mistaken if he believed he was on the verge of a major theoretical breakthrough, even for the little insects to which he had devoted his life. The species problem was not settled during his lifetime, nor is it any closer to resolution today. With the rise of the "new systematics" following World War II, however, scientists at least clarified the nature of their disagreements. Several new concepts, such as population thinking, geographic variation, and geographic speciation, gave rise to a new science of diversity.

Among these concepts the most important was population thinking. Rooted in antiessentialism, it allowed scholars to approach species as populations of unique individuals that shared a common heredity. In population thinking, therefore, the "new systematics" developed a concept that celebrated the fact that no two individuals were exactly alike, even as it recognized their common heritage as demonstrated by their reproductive isolation.

Given the modest reception to his work, it would be difficult to assign Kinsey a major role in preparing the ground for the rise of the "new systematics." Still, he was an avid antiessentialist whose gall wasp research anticipated many of the tenets of modern population thinking. As early as 1930, he had defined species as "populations with common heredity" and had argued that while "no two individuals are exactly alike," there were "many more points of uniformity than of variation among individuals taken from a given locality and habitat."[146] By 1938, he had defined a species as "a tremendous population of individuals with more or less the same heredity."[147] What he did not do, however, was articulate a coherent statement of population thinking that would attract disciples to his banner.

Nevertheless, Kinsey deserved high marks as a taxonomist. No scientist of his day devoted more time or energy to the species problem, nor did any work more diligently to secure a place for systematics in the New Biology. His laboratory techniques and his field methods were models of tireless effort and scientific rigor, while the number of specimens he collected was monumental. Still, Kinsey was not a great taxonomist, largely because he was not a great theorist. His principal weakness lay in his devotion to the conceptual assumptions that shaped his work. Convinced that species ultimately graded into other species, Kinsey insisted on treating geographic variants of the same species as separate species, creating in the words of Stephen Jay Gould "a bloated taxonomy of full names for transient and minor local variants."[148] Thus, Kinsey carried his belief in the primacy and irreducibility of variation too far.[149]

While excessive reductionism is an occupational hazard for many splitters, Kinsey's problem was as much psychological as intellectual. Simply put, he fell victim to his need for order and control. The same compulsion that pulled him into oak grove after oak grove, that kept him at his desk night after night, and that drove him to redeem his field made Kinsey so obsessed with individual variation that he ignored common ancestry. If he meant to rival Darwin, Kinsey would have to make his mark in a field other than taxonomy, one that could generate enough publicity and recognition to convert an obscure scientist into a popular icon.

"It Was Done Very, So to Speak, Scientifically"

"I believe in marriage as an institution," Kinsey told a class of students in 1940. No testimonial to romantic love followed this declaration. He supported marriage, Kinsey explained, because "it provides for the procreation of the race and for the care of the offspring." Acknowledging that marriage also made sense on practical grounds, he praised the institution as "a mutual aid society which provides for the best development of two individuals." He continued, "It teaches one to give and take, to fit into [the] plans of others," adding that when two people live together "there are rough edges taken off, a certain amount of roughness that still sticks with the individual who is not married, the rough edges that characterize the older unmarried person." Finally, Kinsey supported marriage because it offered companionship, nurture, and support. "It is quite possible to walk through life alone," he allowed, "but not as efficiently as when there is some one else to go with you to share your plans and your ambitions, to stand by when few others will support you, and to help at every turn."[1] Who but a progressive would mention marriage and efficiency in the same breath?

Kinsey's remarks reflected recent changes in the way people approached marriage. Between the world wars, many middle-class Americans rejected patriarchy in favor of a new ideal. Reformers argued that the conjugal relationship should be based not on gender-linked duties and roles but on the emotional compatibility of husband and wife. "Companionate marriage" was the phrase most often used to describe this new ethic. Coined by Judge Ben B. Lindsey of the Denver Juvenile Court in a book of the same name, "companionate marriage" symbolized a new ideal that recast marriage along more egalitarian lines. Specifically, Lindsey and his supporters called for an explicit recognition of the sexual equality of men and women; birth control to prevent unwanted pregnancies; the separation of sex from procreation; explicit sex education for young people prior to marriage; and uncontested divorce for couples without children.[2]

While their relationship retained important elements of patriarchy, Kinsey and Clara adopted many of the values and assumptions of "companionate marriage." Kinsey wanted his marriage to be different from the one he had witnessed growing up, as he was determined not to behave like his father. Convinced that the Victorian family, with its patriarchal authority, sexual repression, and hierarchical organization, should give way to a new ideal of sharing rights and responsibilities, Kinsey hoped to fill his and Clara's need for romance, emotional growth, and sexual gratification.

Thus, from the moment he married Clara, Kinsey was struggling to achieve a cultural ideal. Confused about his personal identity and guilt ridden about his sexual needs, he entered marriage hoping to build a stable life. Kinsey wanted a home and family, to feel as though he belonged and, above all, to see himself as a mature, responsible male. Determined to bring order and stability to his private life, he had a great deal riding on his marriage.

Beneath his quest for respect and stability lay a frantic search for identity. Determined to free himself from his father, Kinsey intended to create a family life completely at odds with his own childhood experiences. Competition and rebellion shaped many of his practices in domestic life, as he strove to become a parent better than and far different from his father. But despite his best efforts, important similarities emerged between the home of his youth and the home he made with Clara. Each had its own conflicts, each its own wreckage of unfulfilled dreams.

Ironically, none of these tensions were evident to outsiders. When the Kinseys set up housekeeping in the fall of 1921, they looked like any other young couple starting life together. Because they wanted space and privacy, they never considered living in an apartment. "We looked for a house in the spring before we were married," Clara recalled, explaining that even though houses in Bloomington were hard to find, "we refused to look at a house that didn't have a fireplace." After a lot of searching, they rented a modest frame house, with small rooms, a tiny yard, and a cozy fireplace, at 620 South Fess, a few blocks east of the campus. Immediately after moving in, they started looking for a home to buy. By Thanksgiving Day they found one barely a block away, a frame bungalow on the corner of Park and University. They moved into it in June, and there they remained for the next five years.[3]

The newlyweds received numerous callers during their first year in Bloomington. "The faculty people were very much in the mold of doing things just so," recalled one faculty wife. "Newcomers would come to town, and the other faculty people [wives] would come on Sunday after-noons and leave their cards. You had to return their call within . . . two weeks or whatever was proper, or else you just weren't in their book." Like many young couples just starting out, the Kinseys had practically no furniture, which posed a problem once visitors started arriving. No sooner had they set up housekeeping than Clara returned home one afternoon and found the calling cards of two faculty wives who had arrived in her absence. "I was sort of thankful [to have missed them]," she confessed. "There wouldn't have been anything for them to sit on."[4]

Shortly thereafter, the Kinseys purchased a set of marked-down wicker furniture manufactured in nearby Martinsville. Made from hickory and designed more for a summer porch than for a living room, the sturdy set included a rocker, straight-back chairs with woven mesh seats and backs, and a settee. They painted each piece black, and no young couple was ever prouder, though a friend described the set as "very spartan and very stiff furniture."[5] Still, it was the only living room furniture the Kinseys ever owned. It arrived just in the nick of time. "I was so amused," Clara laughed; "the President's wife [Charlotte Lowe Bryan] called on us right after we were married, and fortunately she caught us ready to receive her. She said she was very hesitant about calling on faculty members because sometimes she would come in and find a diaper on the piano, and they were so embarrassed by it."[6]

Over time, the Kinseys added a massive oak library table to their living room ensemble and durable, inch-thick rugs of dyed muslin stuffed with wool or cotton scraps. Kinsey made the rugs by hand, using a twisted braid he had learned from one of his professors at Harvard. But always the room's appearance remained stark and simple, reflecting a masculine taste in decor, as though its owners had little interest in warmth or comfort.[7]

Early in their marriage, the Kinseys established their career patterns. He attacked teaching and research with boundless energy and rare dedica-tion, serving notice that the university would be the center of his life. Clara understood. "I said to somebody when we were married, I always realized that his work would have to come first," she later remarked. "You can't ask a man just to give up what is the driving force of his life because he is your husband."[8] This understanding was woven into the fabric of their relationship; it formed an integral part of their tacit contract as a couple.

At first, it appeared that Clara, too, would pursue a career outside the home. She entered graduate school that fall to study for a master's degree in chemistry. In a matter of months, however, she lost interest and dropped out of the program. "I never became a research chemist," she later told an interviewer. "I got married, instead, and raised a family."[9] There was no bitterness in this statement, no sense of a wrong turn taken. Rather, Clara spoke matter-of-factly, as though comfortable with her decision.

While Clara considered herself a freethinker, she was typical of middle-class women in the 1920s. The passage of the Nineteenth Amendment to the Constitution seemed to take the wind out of the feminist sails. Instead of shifting the battlefield from politics to social relationships and to the marketplace, Clara's generation of college-educated, middle-class women failed to build on the hard-earned victories of the suffragettes. Rare was the woman who demanded complete social equality, and rarer still the woman who achieved parity in the marketplace. Most college-educated women of Clara's generation did not pursue careers outside the home. In 1920, only 20 percent of all married women earned salaries or wages. Most women who entered the marketplace, whether married or single, were employed at unskilled or semiskilled jobs, such as domestic service and clerical positions.[10]

Professional women encountered a similar pattern of gender-typed employment. While the proportion of women in the professions rose slightly between 1920 and 1930 (from 12 percent to 14 percent), more than 75 percent of these women worked in "female" occupations, such as teaching and nursing. Between 1910 and 1930, the percentage of female architects and attorneys remained stuck at approximately 3 percent, while the total number of female physicians actually dropped from 9,015 to 6,825 during these decades. By the late 1920s, there were only 60 female certified public accountants and 151 female dentists in the entire United States. The story in the hard sciences was much the same. In Clara's field, chemistry, America's graduate schools produced approximately 191 Ph.D.'s a year between 1920 and 1924, only 7.2 percent of whom were women.[11]

Married women were not supposed to work for wages. Mrs. Samuel Gompers, the wife of the venerable head of the American Federation of Labor, attacked working wives with a vengeance, arguing that they stole jobs from men and ignored the proper role for women. "A home, no matter how small," she advised, "is large enough to occupy [a wife's] mind and time." Fearing disaster, the secretary of labor warned in 1923 that employing married women would ultimately bring the nation's economic system "crashing down about our heads." Ironically, the Women's Bureau echoed these fears. Created to protect women and to educate the public on a host of economic issues, the Women's Bureau regarded married female workers as a threat to the home. "The welfare of the home and the family is a woman-sized job in itself," declared the bureau.[12]

Women who ignored this advice could count on little support. Since most middle-class Americans expected women to find fulfillment as wives and mothers, society made few adjustments to aid married women who worked outside the home. "There can be no real homes," warned one business executive, "when women are away from them all day and every day, and return to them at night as dog-tired as their husbands."[13] One solution to this problem, of course, was for men to share family duties ordinarily assumed by wives, but not many men volunteered. And without support from their spouses, career women had not one job but two: after working all day at their jobs in the marketplace, they had to shoulder the burdens of home and family.

While Kinsey respected Clara's intellect, there is no evidence that he wanted her to have a career. Instead of encouraging her ambitions, he expected her to support his career. "I don't think he wanted any competition," observed Gebhard. "He wanted a helpmate and that's what he got." Asked to explain, Gebhard replied, "Kinsey was a nineteenth-century husband. He felt it was the wife's job to keep the house tidy, raise the children, serve healthy, nutritious meals on time, and that was about it." The husband's job, by contrast, "was to advance his career, bring home the bacon, and be a good provider."[14]

Kinsey's views on marriage bore a remarkable resemblance to his parents' relationship. While there were things from his childhood he detested and strove not to duplicate, he recreated in his own marriage the roles his mother and father had played. The same held true for Clara. Her father had been the sole breadwinner in her family. With the exception of a brief stint to earn money for college, Clara's mother did not work for wages until her only child had left home. Thus, there was no role model pointing Clara toward a career. Everything in her background supported her decision to abandon chemistry in favor of domesticity.

Like most middle-class couples of their generation, then, the Kinseys had a traditional marriage contract. Accepting the doctrine of the two spheres, they divided life into the public world and the domestic world. Kinsey's domain was the public world, Clara's the domestic. Still, this arrangement did not imply equality, as it assigned men and women different and inherently unequal roles. Clara's function was subsumed in a single word—"nurture." As the breadwinner, however, Kinsey's world had no boundaries. While he might elect to share power with his wife on issues affecting the children and the management of the home, Kinsey demanded and got the final word over his household. Moreover, by dint of his economic identity, he was a vital participant in the outside world. He had power in two spheres, while she had power in one. This starkly conventional view of male and females roles was rooted in patriarchy, and it formed an important part of their relationship. "Companionate marriage," it seemed, did not extend to the marketplace.

The Kinseys came much closer to this ideal in their attitudes toward children. The expectation that they would have a family was an integral part of their marriage contract. Yet the sexual problems that had surfaced during their honeymoon had not been solved, for their marriage had still not been consummated when they set up housekeeping. Left on their own, they might never have done so, but fortunately they sought professional help soon after they returned from their honeymoon. They consulted a local physician, Dr. Thomas Reed. After diagnosing Clara's condition as an adherent clitoris, he performed the necessary surgery, which consisted of pulling back the veil of connective tissue over the clitoris and performing a blunt dissection under local anesthetic. Years later, Kinsey confided their secret to Robert Kroc, his friend and colleague in the zoology department. According to Kroc, Kinsey regretted their failure to seek help sooner and blamed Victorian prudery for the delay.[15]

With Clara's surgery behind them, the Kinseys were finally able to have sexual intercourse. While both must have been pleased and relieved, Kinsey in particular had reason to be thankful. Consummating their marriage meant that he could respond sexually to women, an issue that had remained in doubt until he had proved otherwise.[16]

The Kinseys' union proved fertile. By the time they moved into their new home in June, Clara was nearly to term with their first child. Donald was born on July 16, 1922. Three more children followed in rapid succession: Anne arrived with the New Year on January 1, 1924; next came Joan, who appeared on October 16, 1925; their last child, Bruce, was born on November 25, 1928.[17]

A letter to Miss Roeth captured the couple's delight in their growing family following the birth of their second child: "Our home is great fun. Wish you might stop in it sometime! The second baby, a girl, came the first of January. The boy is now running all about, getting into everything, and rapidly learning to talk. So between them it is a merry house. Often it keeps several people jumping for them, but they are lots of fun."[18]

Unfortunately, tragedy struck their firstborn. At first Donald appeared to be perfectly normal, but by the time he was two years old, he had grown extremely thin and emaciated. Doctors in Bloomington and Indianapolis were not able to diagnose the problem. Finally, Kinsey himself, after consulting with Paul Harmon, a colleague in the physiology department, came to suspect that Donald had a thyroid problem. In June 1925, the worried parents took the child by train to the Mayo Clinic in Rochester, Minnesota, where they were told to take an apartment because their stay would not be short. By this point, Donald's "pop eyed" appearance was striking. Kinsey later told a friend that when they went to the store to buy food the butcher declared, "Ah, I see you brought the little one in for his thyroid condition."[19] Nevertheless, it took a battery of tests for the doctors to determine that Donald was suffering from exophthalmos (thus, his protruding eyeballs), and in September they operated on his thyroid. During his recovery period, Clara remained with Donald in Minnesota, while Kinsey, with two-year-old Anne in tow, had to return to Bloomington to teach his fall classes.

For a time, it appeared that Donald would recover completely. Following the surgery, he gained weight and his overall condition improved greatly. Within a year, however, he became sickly again, and he deteriorated rapidly. The cause was diabetes. The disease was not diagnosed, in part because his thyroid problem had masked its symptoms and in part because diabetes is often difficult to recognize in young children. In desperation, the Kinseys contacted the Mayo Clinic and were told that one of its physicians happened to be in Indiana and would come to examine the boy immediately. By the time he arrived, Donald had slipped into a diabetic coma, acetone reeking from every breath he exhaled.

Only a few years earlier, Donald's condition would have been hopeless. No one had ever recovered from a diabetic coma. But thanks to the discovery of insulin in 1921–22, there was a chance the boy could be saved. Ironically, the Kinseys appeared to be positioned well, because the Eli Lilly drug company of Indianapolis had secured the patent to manufacture and market insulin in the United States. By September 1923, for example, 7,000 physicians were busy administering insulin to between 20,000 and 25,000 diabetics throughout the United States, including Elizabeth Evans Hughes, the granddaughter of Charles Evans Hughes, the presiding secretary of state under President Warren G. Harding. But owing to the delay in diagnosis, Donald Kinsey died before doctors could help him. He was three years and nine months old.[20]

His young parents were heartbroken. As a biologist, Kinsey knew that life ends in death, but no gloss of academic training could blunt his pain. While he liked to think of himself as cool, rational, and in control, he could not contain his grief. "I saw him break down and weep when his young son died," declared Evelyn Spieth, the wife of one of Kinsey's graduate students. She had worked as Dean Payne's secretary in the 1920s, and she remembered vividly the sorrow in Kinsey's eyes when he came to their office soon after the funeral. Dressed in a black suit and still in mourning, he tried to conduct business as usual but broke down in public. Kinsey sobbed uncontrollably in the dean's office—huge, heaping sobs that seemed to come from the depths of his soul. Evelyn had the distinct impression that he had more difficulty than Clara in coping with Donald's death. "I imagine that Clara was the one who was strong and pulling him through," declared Spieth, "although she was sad, too. But she had great strength of character."[21]

Yet, in the long run, Clara may have found it harder to deal with the loss than her husband. Donald was her firstborn, and the pain caused by his death never left her. She learned to live with it, but it was always there, like some terrible hole in her life that refused to close. In the fall of 1958, she appeared on the doorstep of Mary Gaither, who lived in the Kinsey's former home on South Park Street. Clara brought a gift of persimmon pudding and asked if she could come in and walk through the house. Since they knew one another casually, Gaither agreed. Clara moved quickly through most of the rooms, but paused in the bathroom and stood staring at the sink. Then she cradled her arms and starting humming a lullaby, explaining that this was where she had bathed Donald.[22] It was a touching scene, which spoke to the depths of a mother's love. For his part, Kinsey rarely talked about Donald in later years. When he did the references were clipped and brief. Clyde Martin remembered his saying on one occasion "that they were very broken up . . . and that it took them quite some time to get over this."[23] Given Kinsey's reluctance to talk about his private life, this was an admission of terrible grief.

Mercifully, the Kinseys had two lively girls to pull them back to the world of the living. Anne was three and Joan was six months when Donald died. Since neither was capable of understanding their parents' grief, the girls behaved as usual: they laughed and they cried, and they demanded love and attention. By so doing, they helped take their parents' thoughts off Donald. While no one could replace the son they had buried, Bruce's birth three years after Donald's death must have eased their suffering, too. Kinsey, in particular, took special comfort from Bruce's birth. While most men want a son to carry on the family name, he had another reason to delight in Bruce's birth. Because his relationship with his own father had been abysmal, Kinsey wanted to build a loving relationship with his son.

Kinsey doted on Bruce when he was young. Although she was aware the Kinseys had two daughters as well as a son, June Keisler, one of Kinsey's former laboratory assistants, did not recall many references to the girls when her boss spoke about his family. "It was chiefly 'our small boy' Dr. Kinsey talked about," she declared. Lest anyone form the wrong conclusion, however, Keisler added, "I am sure now that this was because Bruce was then at that age when bright pre-schoolers do and say the kind of things that cause parents to become anecdotal."[24]

Bruce was not in the least bashful about demonstrating the deeds his father celebrated in stories. While she never got to witness the feat performed, Keisler noted that practically everybody but her in the biology department had seen Bruce "walk up the wall fly-fashion." In fact, Bruce's daredevil climbs in the family stairwell became legendary on campus. Referring to one such exploit that nearly ended in disaster, Keisler recalled that everyone had heard "about the time when the young Icarus, mounting the heights of the second story, became petrified with fear when he looked down; his father 'talked him down' safely, like a plane making a blind landing by radio."[25]

As he grew older, Bruce displayed characteristics of both parents. From his mother, he inherited dark eyes, regular features, and high coloring, while his personality reflected traits he shared with his father. As a boy, he caught bumblebees in his bare fingers, collecting them in a jar. Moreover, just as his father went hatless in the coldest weather, Bruce frequently went to school in the dead of winter dressed in shorts and a light sweater. A non-joiner, he went his own way, pursuing only those things that interested him. Yet, unlike his father, Bruce was very athletic. An excellent swimmer, he swam competitively in high school and later enjoyed an excellent collegiate career at Oberlin College.[26]

From all reports, Kinsey was a good family man. "He loved his family and took it very seriously," remarked Evelyn Spieth, a frequent visitor in the Kinsey household when the children were young. Homer T. Rainwater, one of Kinsey's graduate students from the early 1930s, shared this view. "He loved his children. He was devoted to his wife. He talked about her quite a lot, and his children. I think he was a good husband and a good daddy," recalled Rainwater. Time only served to strengthen his devotion. Earl Marsh, a physician who came to know him well, remarked that Kinsey "was fundamentally a homebody" who had "a deep love for his children and spoke of them almost with a note of reverence."[27]

Still, Kinsey found certain requirements of parenthood difficult. "Individuals at 30 are not particularly keen about learning to play with children," he told a class in 1938; and two years later he made the identical point to another class, declaring that "in relationships with their offspring, youth will learn to get along with babies much more easily than older people do." Kinsey sounded like a man speaking from experience. He became a father for the first time at twenty-eight and was thirty-four when his last child arrived. Yet, if Kinsey felt awkward about playing with his children, the problem probably had less to do with age than with temperament. He was not a playful person. Nor was he a man for whom physical displays of affection came easily. Nothing in his childhood had prepared him to be playful or openly affectionate. Somewhat stiff and formal, he was hardly what people today would call a "touch" person.[28]

Like most fathers, Kinsey devoted more time to his career than to his family. Still, he was an active, involved parent, particularly when the children were preschoolers and Clara needed assistance. He helped bathe the children, read them stories at bedtime, and delighted in teaching them about nature. In addition, he was what people were fond of calling a "competent male," a husband who could assume household tasks as the need arose.

In many respects, Kinsey's attitudes toward children were remarkably Victorian. In 1940, for example, he told a class of students that he believed in having children "not only because they are a necessary part of the procreation of the race but because they in turn help the character of the parents." In practice, however, Kinsey adopted an enlightened view toward his children, treating them with reason and respect, a far cry from the way his father had dealt with him. Above all, he and Clara tried to deal with each of their children as separate beings. Looking back on her childhood, Joan stated, "I would say the strongest feeling that I have is that each of us was treated as an individual. We weren't lumped [together] as children and all treated exactly alike. . . ." As proof, Joan noted that on different occasions each of the children felt slighted or discriminated against, but, she added pointedly, "we all felt that we were equally loved." "If they had a favorite," she said, "I am not aware of it and I don't think I was at the time."[29]

As befitted bourgeois parents, the Kinseys taught their children to be autonomous, self-regulating, and responsible individuals. If a rule was broken, a chore left undone, or an inconsiderate act committed, the offender had to accept the consequences. Neither parent tolerated excuses. The Kinseys also encouraged their children to be independent. They taught them to think for themselves, to value their own judgment, and to be self-reliant.

The Kinseys also demanded good manners and common courtesy of their children. Thanks to the income from the textbook, the family was able to afford a housekeeper even during the worst years of the Great Depression. Her name was Mrs. Francis Turrell, and she worked for the Kinseys from 1932 to 1942. Originally trained as a secretary, Mrs. Turrell was widowed early in life and had to take domestic work in order to support herself and her children during the depression. Looking back on her years with the Kinseys, she insisted, "I was never made to feel I was a servant even by the smallest child." As proof, she noted, "One day a child from across the street asked Anne why the maid did not do something, she, Anne, was doing. Anne gave her a look as only Anne could give and said, 'That is Mrs. Turrell; we have no maid.' " Similarly, Mrs. Turrell stressed that the Kinsey children were never allowed to make extra work for her. "They had to keep their own rooms in order . . . ," she declared, "much as I would have liked to have helped the kiddies out if they had other plans. . . ."[30]

What impressed Turrell most was the kindness and the great sensitivity to her situation that Kinsey himself displayed. Describing how a thoughtful man could "take the sting out of charity," she recalled, "One evening as he was taking me home, he said, 'Mrs. T. our royalties on our new book have been more than we expected, and Mrs. Kinsey and I want to *share* our good fortune with you. Will you let us fill your coal bin for the winter?' " Moreover, Mrs. Turrell received the same mixture of generosity and kindness from Clara. "Whenever Mrs. Kinsey would hand me a check with extra [money] for any occasion and I would remonstrate," recalled Turrell, "she would smile and say, 'Boss's orders.' "[31]

Both parents administered discipline. Clara did not hesitate to discipline the children on her own, but she consulted Kinsey on every child-rearing policy decision. Joan recalled that whenever she asked her mother's permission to go out on a date or take the family car out alone, Clara would reply, " 'I will talk it over with Dad, and we'll let you know.' " Following the consultation, Clara presented their decision firmly and dispassionately, even when she did not agree with it. Again, Joan described an occasion when she happened to overhear her parents in the bedroom discussing her request for permission to go out on a date. Because the family was leaving early the next morning on a trip, her father insisted that Joan should stay home, while Clara took the opposite position. In the end, Kinsey's judgment prevailed, as it did on most family matters. "So when Mother told me the decision, she said, 'Daddy and I feel that you should not go, for these reasons.' I had no hint from her answer that she had thought I should have been allowed," Joan declared.[32] Over time, she came to realize that this was the reaction her parents intended. They understood full well the game called "divide and conquer," and they were not about to be taken in. "They attempted very, very strongly to present one decision," Joan explained. "If Daddy had said no on something, you couldn't go to Mother and get her to say yes and then work them against each other."[33]

Despite Kinsey's firmness, the children became highly skilled at probing his arguments for weaknesses. Joan, who was pretty headstrong as a teenager, often clashed with her father about her social hours after she reached high school. Citing the example of friends, Joan argued that she should be permitted to date more often and come home later than her father thought proper. "But he had this marvelous argument that there was no reason why I in high school should be allowed to stay out later than the freshmen women at IU were allowed to, or to go out oftener. Well, there was just no comeback," Joan declared.[34]

In many respects, Kinsey was a strict parent, especially with regard to his daughters. As Clara put it, "He had some definite ideas as to what they should and shouldn't do." Pressed for specifics, Clara replied, "What time the girls should get in at night." She described her husband as "a little more on the stern side than I was," but softened this characterization by insisting he was not severe. Rationality might be his watchword, but Kinsey expected his children to obey. Joan freely confessed that while she was growing up, "there were times that I felt he was extremely dictatorial."[35] Although he was willing to let Clara handle the day-to-day problems of child rearing, thereby freeing him for work, Kinsey demanded and got the final word on any issue he deemed important. Anyone who disobeyed the rules felt his wrath. Indeed, Kinsey had a temper, and Clara, too, felt its fury on more than one occasion. There were times when he would "bite your head off," she remarked, "but if he did bawl you out for something, that was it; he didn't keep harping on it."[36]

If the image of a strict, domineering man brings to mind Kinsey's father, the portrait must not be overdrawn. Kinsey dominated his household, but not to the same degree (and certainly not by employing the same weapons) as his father. Instead of behaving like a tyrant, Kinsey struggled to create a more enlightened form of patriarchy. In fact, his entire approach to parenthood was largely shaped by his rejection of his father's example. Kinsey tried to base his moral authority on reason. Unlike his father, who cited Scriptures to support his power, Kinsey installed the rule of reason as the master of his household, albeit with himself as reason's spokesman and arbiter. Instead of dismissing arguments ex cathedra, Kinsey went to great lengths, both with Clara and with the children, to resolve disputes through logic and rational discourse. Instead of riding roughshod over people, he was, in Clara's words, "a considerate person of the feelings of other people."[37] Even when the children were adolescents, a stage that breeds friction in many families, he and Clara did a good job of keeping the communication channels open, letting their children know that no topic or problem was off-limits. As Joan put it, "you knew that you could always go to talk to him, [to] either one of my parents. If you had something that bothered you, you could go talk to them about it."[38] Joan felt the same way as long as her parents lived.

Grandparents were not much of a presence in the Kinsey household. Clara's parents both died a few years after her marriage. In many families, grandparents enrich the lives of their grandchildren by offering love, wisdom, and presents. In addition, grandparents often soften family disputes by serving as sympathetic figures grandchildren can talk to. Unfortunately, the death of Clara's parents denied the Kinsey children these benefits.[39] Still, Kinsey had little interest in promoting a close relationship between his parents and his children. He and Clara did take Donald to New Jersey. A family album contains a photograph taken when Donald was about a year old, showing four generations of Kinsey males (great-grandfather, grandfather, father, and son), but the same album shows no evidence of additional visits to introduce the other children to their grandparents. Nor is there any record of his parents visiting Indiana during the 1920s.[40]

A nasty divorce ended Kinsey's relationship with his father for good. On May 21, 1930, following nearly forty years of marriage, Alfred Seguine Kinsey abandoned his wife and never returned. Economically, his timing could not have been worse for Sarah, as she faced the worst depression in American history with no independent means of support. Virtually unlettered, sixty years old, and with few marketable skills, she pleaded for a reconciliation, but her husband refused, insisting that their marriage had ended. Desperate and forlorn, Sarah appeared in July on her son's doorstep in Indiana, where she poured out her grief to a man predisposed to believe the worst about his father. Soon thereafter, Sarah returned to South Orange and renewed her efforts to save her marriage, again to no avail.[41]

In August 1931, Alfred Seguine Kinsey went to Reno, Nevada, where he filed for and received a "quickie" divorce. At the plaintiff's request, the court sealed the terms of that action, but other evidence suggests that his freedom cost him dearly. Sarah retained the house on Ward Place, and he agreed to pay her $93 a month for her support and maintenance, which was no mean sum in the depths of the Great Depression. Still, Sarah was not satisfied. She filed a countersuit in New Jersey, asking the courts to nullify their divorce and put a new financial settlement in place. These court papers were not sealed; and they reveal that the man who had started work as a shop boy in 1886 had compiled a considerable estate. Sarah claimed that in addition to their home at 224 Ward Place in South Orange he owned a lot on Turrell Avenue in South Orange valued at $4,000 and personal property worth approximately $10,000. While it is not clear whether Sarah won, the documents make one point painfully clear: it was an acrimonious and bitter end to a marriage that had lasted nearly forty years and produced three children.[42]

Alfred Seguine Kinsey did not stay single. After his divorce, he started dating Antoinette Van Duyne, a singularly attractive woman who was many years his junior. She took him by storm, and at first love seemed to mellow his disposition. He called her Towey, and during their courtship he lavished attention and gifts on her.[43] "But after they were married, things changed," declared Edna Kinsey Higenbotham, Robert's widow. Over time, Edna and Antoinette became close friends, and Edna got the distinct impression that Antoinette felt she had made an awful mistake in marrying the senior Kinsey. All too quickly, it seems, he reverted to his domineering manner, treating Antoinette much as he had Sarah. "Some men only want a housekeeper and cook," Edna asserted, making no bones of her opinion that Kinsey was such a man. "She was really a lovely person," said Edna, shaking her head from side to side, "but he gave her an awfully hard time."[44]

Each of the children opposed the divorce and blamed their father for abandoning their mother. Robert alone managed to preserve a tenuous relationship with his father. Robert did not speak of the divorce often, but Edna recalled that he "was hurt very badly . . . because he didn't think that his mother deserved that at all." As he had throughout his life, however, Robert refrained from criticizing his father, either to his face or behind his back. Moreover, unlike his older brother and sister, Robert continued to see his father following the divorce, and he alone was willing to give his new stepmother a chance. In time, Antoinette, who according to all reports was a warm and generous woman, won Robert over by coming to his aid when misfortune struck. Following the death of Robert's first wife, who died in childbirth, Antoinette offered to care for his son. Robert gracefully accepted, since he was beside himself with grief and did not know how to care for an infant.[45]

Once Robert and the baby moved under his father's roof, things did not go smoothly. Though willing to open his home to his son and grandson in their hour of need, Alfred Seguine Kinsey did not deal gracefully with the disruptions that any infant brings to a household. "Dad [Kinsey] would get furious if his meals weren't [served] right button on the time that he thought they should be," Edna declared, "and if the baby cried and Antoinette got up to see what was wrong with the baby, he would scream about that, too." Obviously, there was room for only one baby in the household, and that role was taken. The situation improved when Robert married Edna and they moved into their own home. From a safe distance, Robert was able to maintain a relationship with his father, but it was not easy. As Edna observed shrewdly, "although he never not went to see his father, he didn't break his neck going either."[46]

Sarah lived several years after her marriage ended. Economically, she survived on her alimony and by taking in boarders. While evidence is lacking, it seems likely that Kinsey helped support her, too. Unmarried and ever the dutiful daughter, Mildred continued to live with her mother until the end. Following Sarah's death, Mildred blossomed. Of the three children, she alone had remained trapped at home; she alone had not managed to break free of her parents. While the divorce had released her from her father's orbit (at least in the sense that she had little to do with him after he left her mother), it took her mother's death to free her totally. Soon thereafter, Mildred married D. E. Garrabrant, a man who had boarded in the Kinsey home. After their marriage, she continued to work as a secretary in New York. Well into her forties when she married, Mildred never had children.

The divorce did little to alter Kinsey's relationship with his mother. Instead of moving closer to her emotionally, he apparently kept his distance, as he had ever since leaving home for Bowdoin. Kinsey found it hard to relate to his mother. It was not that he was cold; rather, there was simply too much pain, pain he could neither articulate nor expunge. Ever since his childhood, his feelings toward her had been deeply conflicted. At some level, Kinsey must have held her partly to blame for his suffering. Nor was he wholly wrong to do so. How could she stand idly by and watch her husband bully and badger her children and not intercede? How could she place domestic peace above their well-being?

Similarly, Kinsey kept his distance from his sister and brother. While it is true that suffering can forge a lifelong bond among siblings, it is also the case that childhood traumas can produce unresolved tensions and hurts that leave siblings deeply ambivalent, if not openly alienated and estranged. At any rate, something in Kinsey would not allow him to reach out. From the moment he left home, he had little to do with his siblings. There were occasional visits, to be sure, but nothing like the kind or number of contacts that occur between siblings who are close.[47]

Following his parents' divorce, Kinsey severed all contact with his father. There was no reason to see him, no reason to maintain the polite fictions that civility imposes on people who really do not like each other. In truth, Kinsey despised his father, as only a person who has been deeply wronged can, and the divorce freed him to act accordingly. Perhaps Kinsey even took a perverse satisfaction at seeing his father exposed as a hypocrite. While attitudes were changing, divorce still carried a stigma in the United States. Public opinion did not look kindly on a man who abandoned his wife, especially one who had given him three children and had stood by him for nearly forty years. At any rate, Kinsey walled his father off completely. Without ranting or raging, he reduced the old man to the psychological status of a nonentity.

Like figures in a Greek tragedy, Kinsey and his father remained true to character. Neither had solved the basic conflicts that fathers and sons must resolve in order to see each other as autonomous individuals, with strengths and weaknesses that denote flesh-and-blood human beings. Instead, they stood hostage of their old roles as antagonists, and that is where they would remain—the father looming over the son as the domineering, judgmental, unforgiving, menacing patriarch; the son outwardly strong, proud, and defiant, but inwardly frightened, submissive, and guilt-ridden.

Following the divorce, Alfred Seguine Kinsey became less than a ghost in Kinsey's household. No one told stories heralding his heroic climb from a shop boy to a professional man; no photographs of his handsome face adorned the family's walls. He was not welcome in Bloomington, and Kinsey refused to take his children to see their grandfather when they went east to visit Grandmother Kinsey. It was as though the old man had never existed.

Unlike his father, Kinsey made a conscious effort to relax with his children. The outdoors was their principal playground. Over the years, there were numerous hiking expeditions to nearby state parks and several family vacations devoted to camping. And thanks to Clara, swimming became an important activity. Kinsey had not learned to swim until he was virtually grown (and never developed into a strong swimmer), so Clara took charge of this aspect of their children's recreation. The entire family swam in the university pool and enjoyed outings in Brown County, where they picnicked and swam.[48]

Kinsey definitely managed to outstrip his father as a provider. Whereas Kinsey's boyhood had been spent in a series of rental houses, a few years before Bruce was born and while Anne and Joan were still small, the Kinseys built their dream home. They could never have financed the project on Kinsey's salary, but Clara had recently come into some money of her own. Her parents had both died a few years earlier, leaving her a modest inheritance.

Armed with these funds, the Kinseys started looking for a lot. As luck would have it, Carl Eigenmann (Kinsey's department chairman) and two other senior professors at the university had some attractive land for sale. Eager to profit from the booming land sales during "prosperity's decade," Eigenmann and his partners had become speculators, purchasing an old farm on the southeast edge of town. Not that the land was much to look at. It was largely barren save for a few fruit trees, the remnants of a worn-out orchard. But the location was ideal—only a ten-minute walk from campus. For the tidy sum of $2,000, the Kinseys bought a prime lot in what quickly became one of Bloomington's most desirable neighborhoods.

They planned their new home down to the last light switch. A strong believer in cross ventilation (a real necessity in the Midwest in the days before air-conditioning), Clara wanted so many windows that Kinsey had to plead with her, she later recalled, "to leave room for a few bricks." But once they had agreed on the basics, Kinsey went to work on the blueprints, drawing upon the draftsman skills he had acquired at the Stevens Institute of Technology, one of the few times he ever put what he learned there to use. The final plans called for a two-story house with a basement. It was to be built in an L shape around one of the few mature trees on the lot, a persimmon tree that provided the fruit for Clara's signature dessert for guests—persimmon pudding.[49]

It never occurred to Kinsey to build the house himself, but he personally supervised the construction. He had definite ideas about everything, including the peculiar look he wanted for the house's exterior. After a great deal of searching, he finally settled on rough-faced, overburned bricks, purchased in nearby Martinsville. The brickyard reduced the price $2.00 per thousand because that particular run had been overdone in the kiln. The bricks' knobby surface and rangy shades of color guaranteed that the walls would look uneven, but to enhance this effect even further Kinsey had the masons lay them in a highly unusual fashion. Masons pride themselves on laying bricks in straight courses, with the joints wiped clean, which makes the finished walls look straight and smooth. (The most popular joint is formed by cleaning out the excess mortar with a piece of rebar, so that the joint appears slightly convex.) Though it took some doing, Kinsey finally persuaded his masons to leave the excess mortar behind, spilled over on the outer edge of the bricks. The result was startling, giving the exterior a singular appearance unlike that of any other home in town.[50]

On the day it was completed, the Kinseys' new house looked old and gnarled. Indeed, its overall appearance was strangely masculine, like the weather-beaten face of an old seaman. Some of the neighbors found the house's façade fascinating, even attractive, but others pronounced it ugly. As Clara later remarked, visitors to their home invariably uttered one of two remarks, "That's the craziest house!" or "I'm crazy about that house."[51]

The yard also bore its master's thumbprint. During their first decade in their new home, the Kinseys used his textbook royalties to purchase several surrounding lots, expanding the size of their property to about two and half acres. On this mini-estate in the heart of Bloomington's nicest academic enclave, Kinsey created a garden paradise. He built a lily pond, rock gardens, and terraced slopes; and he planted a great variety of flowers, shrubs, and trees. Hoping to spark their interest in nature, Kinsey assigned each of his children a small plot. Kinsey also used the garden to teach his children about biology. When Bruce was four or five, he joined his father in the garden one day. Spotting a pretty flower, Bruce told his father that God had made it. Gently but firmly, Kinsey asked his son to reconsider. Correcting himself, Bruce admitted the flower had come from a seed.[52]

If the garden occasionally served as a family classroom, Kinsey preferred to think of it as his own private art studio where he could create beauty. The shovel was his paintbrush, the earth his canvas, and flowers his colors. Long before it became fashionable, Kinsey was a nontraditional gardener. The idea was not to fashion grounds that looked formal and manicured; rather, he strove to create something wild and beautiful. Beneath an assortment of native and nursery-bred trees, Kinsey planted flowering weeds, poke, goldenrod, snakeroot, wild asters, and Queen Anne's lace, all of which formed a natural setting for the flowering bulbs and later perennials that added brilliant splashes of color.[53]

While Kinsey made abundant use of daylilies, irises reigned supreme. He admitted that irises sparked his "collector's mania," and he pursued them with characteristic avidity. At its height, the garden boasted over 250 varieties of these lovely flowers. To help finance his collection, he sold iris bulbs to other collectors. During the early 1930s, a local printing house prepared his price list, which generated orders from forty to fifty gardeners. Traffic in this commerce became part of the Kinsey folklore. "We graduate students gradually came to the conclusion that Kinsey was very astute in money matters," recalled Herman T. Spieth. "It was our understanding that the monies gained from selling the fine iris in his garden more than paid for all that he invested in them and actually netted him some additional income." Here Kinsey's reputation apparently outstripped his performance. According to Clara, he never earned as much as he spent on iris plants. But Kinsey was not out to make money. He grew irises because they were beautiful.[54]

As befitted a biologist's creation, Kinsey's garden evolved, requiring more than a decade to be completed. Though he read books and visited scores of other gardens searching for ideas, it did not follow a grand design. Rather, he made it up as he went along, following the simple rule "Straight is the line of duty but curved the line of beauty." Still, Kinsey knew the look he was after, as it reflected his own private vision. He wanted to make an artistic statement, using flowers, shrubs, and trees to paint, in his words, "garden pictures." Attacking the challenge section by section, he constructed a series of vistas for visitors to encounter, each with an open space of lawn as a vantage point, each with its own delights and surprises. Echoing his long-standing distaste for the idle rich, Kinsey insisted that beautiful gardens could never be created by "fat purses alone." Rather, they were "the issue of love."[55]

Kinsey's garden filled important emotional needs in his life. He freely admitted that he loved gardening because it offered a respite from the demands he associated with the world of work. "Irises do provide material for scientific study," he wrote, "but we, as biologists, need our garden as a hobby, not as a continuation of our books and our laboratory." Irises stood outside the male sphere; they had nothing to do with the world of work. In fact, they served no practical purpose whatsoever. As Kinsey put it, there is "little excuse for an Iris except as an element of individual beauty, or a contribution to the beauty of landscape gardens."[56] In other words, gardening allowed him to indulge his love of beauty, a need that his culture defined as "feminine."

Yet Kinsey must have felt a certain ambivalence about gardening. Still, he spoke of it "as a hobby," he was hardly a casual gardener. The only way he could be at ease with flowers was to convert gardening into a vigorously male activity. "He was not willing to 'putter' with his plants," observed a friend; "he strenuously and scientifically applied himself to this recreational activity." If anything, this was an understatement. Kinsey worked like a galley slave.

Gardening offered Kinsey a showcase for his perfectionism. As Paul Gebhard put it, "instead of just simply having a diverse garden, a damn good second-rate garden," Kinsey had to have "the very best iris collection in the whole Midwest." To achieve the look he desired, Kinsey left nothing to chance. No professional landscape architect ever fretted more about backgrounds, color combinations, and placement. Nor was one ever more critical of his own work. If Kinsey did not like his creation, he tore it apart and started over, with no thought to the cost or labor. Describing his quest for perfection, Kinsey declared, "No variety is allowed to stand until it is correctly placed in relation to its background and all of its flowering neighbors. Six times in six years we have moved some of them, still not despairing of finding their right use in some future move." This Darwinian process would continue, he explained, "until we perfect this piece of the picture."[57]

Small wonder, then, that Kinsey's yard was, in the words of one admirer, "a showplace." One visitor deemed it more lovely than the famed Shaw Garden of St. Louis. Such reactions pleased Kinsey because he regarded approval as validation for his labor. "We measure the result by our own satisfaction," he confessed, "[and] by every reaction we get from those who come to our garden." As he showed friends around, Kinsey enjoyed watching their faces as they moved from one vista to the next, and he took equal delight in reciting the scientific names of every flower, shrub, and tree. Not that he restricted access to friends. On special days, he placed a sign in the front yard that read "The Garden Is Open."[58]

Gardening brought out Kinsey's civic-mindedness. Since Bloomington did not have a village improvement society like the one he had known in South Orange, he took matters into his own hands. "I remember Dr. Kinsey and a group of students taking baskets of iris bulbs and other plants to beautify the grounds of the Court House and other public places," wrote a friend, "and the students being paid by him."[59]

Yet Kinsey's generosity did not stop him from criticizing gardens he considered second-rate. For a man who claimed he gardened to relax, he was remarkably intolerant of other people's creations. "If we are not too enthusiastic about the state of Iris growing it is because we have, in the past few years, traveled several thousand miles visiting Iris gardens," declared Kinsey in a 1933 article in the *Bulletin of the American Iris Society*. Kinsey went out of his way to heap abuse on ordinary gardens. "In the score of other gardens which we have visited," he wrote, "we find hopeless mixtures of good, bad and indifferent flowers, messes like those of an artist's palette, confusion like that in a basket of broken pottery, discord such as one might get out of a symphony if it were played backward, or up the page instead of across it." Such gardens could lay no claim to beauty, because they were "a hash of doubtful validity."[60]

What could explain such a heated response? Perhaps Kinsey's attack was nothing more than aesthetic pique, laced with the bile that often tainted his remarks when he spoke of the banal, mindless masses who failed to uphold the finer things of life. But in this instance, his snobbish remarks masked deeper complaints. Kinsey's reaction was visceral. "Gardens must be made with some respect for . . . art," he wrote, "or frankly, they hurt some of us when we go into them." His word choice was telling. While Kinsey used "hurt" in an aesthetic sense, common gardens appeared to touch a raw nerve in his psyche. Gladys H. Groves, who met Kinsey during the 1940s, described an incident that offers a clue about why he reacted so strongly to certain gardens. "We were all having breakfast outdoors under the wisteria vine we like so much in our front yard," Groves recalled. "K[insey] just mentioned casually and so gently that we were not hurt, 'I don't like wisteria, never have; I guess it goes back to my boyhood when we had one.' "[61]

Lurking in his early recollections of gardens was someone he wished to forget. In his 1933 article on gardening, Kinsey all but revealed that person's identity. "Irises do provide some relief for a collecting mania," wrote Kinsey, "but we question the moral right of any one to collect things of beauty if he intends to store them and treat them like so many nuts and bolts in a machinist's supply room—often in a mass, at best in straight rows with a chronologic or alphabetic scheme of classification." Here Kinsey sounded suspiciously like a man attempting to settle an old score. He meant to contrast himself with his father, the only important figure from his youth who possessed "a machinist's supply room."[62]

Viewed in this light, Kinsey's quest for the perfect garden reflected deep tensions. By transforming gardening into a moral issue, he had made it yet another battlefield on which to confront the man he could never please. Yet, try as he might, Kinsey could never win this contest. Regardless of how hard he worked, his garden seldom seemed to satisfy him. Kinsey demanded perfection, and it eluded him. Parts of his garden invariably failed to meet his standards, so he was forever ripping sections apart, all the while blaming himself for not getting things right. He never understood the link between his drive for perfection and his childhood conflicts. Kinsey failed to realize that behind his lifelong quest for perfection stood an injured child who had been made to feel unworthy by an accusing, judgmental father, a child whose sense of personal worth did not extend beyond what he was able to accomplish. All Kinsey knew was that he had to do better. Nothing less could protect him from his harsh conscience.

No less than gardening, music filled important aesthetic needs in Kinsey, as it had since childhood. Happily, marriage in no way diminished the importance of music in his life, as Clara shared his love of classical compositions. During their first few years together, he often played for her in the evenings, and the couple seldom missed campus concerts. In addition, he gave his children piano lessons when they were preschoolers. Anne, it seems, had little aptitude for music. Aware that her practicing grated on her father's nerves, she made every effort to confine her playing to periods when he was absent. "Once when he was at home while she was playing," wrote a friend, "he called out from the other room, 'That's wrong.' She answered, 'No it's not; that's the way it's written here.' 'Well, then it's written wrong,' was his immediate rejoinder."[63]

In contrast to his own parents, who seldom had visitors and rarely entertained, Kinsey opened his home to students. During his first decade at Indiana, he started inviting a select group of students over on Saturday evenings to hear him play the piano, much as his professors at Bowdoin had welcomed him into their homes. Later, the performances were moved to Wednesday nights. Ever the teacher, Kinsey conducted his home recitals like a classroom. Reviving the format he had followed in his college solos, he opened with a brief lecture on the composer or composers whose works formed the evening's program. Then he would play select pieces and offer closing remarks summarizing the lesson and performance. Throughout this rigid schedule, Kinsey made certain his young students learned the etiquette of proper listening. Aware that audiences had to be taught the virtue of silence, he insisted that everyone remain absolutely still and quiet until he gave Clara the signal to serve ice water and dessert, indicating that the program was over and people were at liberty to speak.

Not every student enjoyed Kinsey's one-man show. Herman T. Spieth attended one (and only one!) such performance in the late 1920s and could not stand it. Perhaps because he had grown up on a farm in Indiana and had no knowledge of classical music, Spieth found the experience oppressively stilted. Worse yet, he came away from the evening feeling hurt and humiliated. He regarded Kinsey as an eastern snob who enjoyed showing off his musical talent and knowledge.[64]

As time passed, Kinsey played the piano less and less. "He had no way of practicing anymore, nor time to do it," explained Clara. Without sufficient practice time, his performance could not match his expectations, so Kinsey stopped playing for guests altogether. With music, as with everything else, he had to excel or he felt frustrated.⁶⁵ Yet Kinsey could never abandon music completely, because it was too important to him. As he gradually withdrew from performing, he devoted more and more time to listening. A revolution in sound reproduction eased the transition. In the late 1920s, audio engineers developed electrical recording, a vast improvement over the old acoustically recorded, pancake disks Kinsey had collected as a youth. Improved turntables and receivers followed, inching the quality of sound reproduction closer and closer to live performances. As a result, many of the world's greatest musicians began recording, and in less than a decade an unbelievably rich array of classical music became available to discerning collectors like Kinsey.

His second record collection drew upon this new technology. Kinsey purchased the finest equipment money could buy, amassing 78 rpm records with the same enthusiasm that he collected gall wasps and irises. Over time, he built what was reported to be the largest private record collection in the Midwest. It included music for orchestras, instrumental groups, quartets, violinists, cellists, pianists, harpsichordists, and singers, and he kept adding to it.

Not that just any recording would do. Kinsey trained himself to engage music critically. He chose records with the same care as equipment. Giving free rein to his perfectionism, Kinsey listened to the same compositions performed by different conductors and musicians in order to find the arrangement and performance that best suited his ear. His taste was decidedly catholic. One night might find him listening to Bach or Mozart, the next night Sibelius or Bartok. But always the thrust was toward new listening experiences. Kinsey constantly expanded his repertoire, as though each piece of music, each conductor, and each artist (or performing group) was a challenge to be mastered or, better yet, a sensual conquest. Gradually, almost imperceptibly, he transformed himself from a frustrated pianist into a self-styled critic.⁶⁶

Beginning in the early 1930s, Kinsey began inviting small groups of friends into his living room on Sunday evenings for music, establishing a tradition that persisted until his death. To friends and foes alike, these Sunday concerts were known as musicales. Their format was virtually identical to the home recitals he had performed for students in the 1920s. The only difference was that Kinsey played records instead of the piano. He spent a good portion of his Sunday afternoons preparing the program—

choosing the selections, listening to them in advance, and musing about the comments he would make.

Kinsey devoted equal care to seating. "When you entered the living room," observed a friend, "it had already been set up for the guests to listen to the music, in rows to look towards Dr. Kinsey [who] would be standing beside his carefully selected and operated audio equipment." That configuration, however, was used only for large groups. On most occasions, Kinsey arranged the chairs in a circle; and as one "regular" recalled, "we would seat ourselves in usually very similar places each time."[67]

The musicales began at eight o'clock sharp. From beginning to end, Kinsey behaved, in the words of a friend, "very much like a teacher with a class." He opened each program with introductory remarks. Then he darkened the room and started playing records. In a scene striking for its air of domesticity, many of the wives, following Clara's example, sat with little wicker baskets on their laps and darned socks while they listened, the only nonmusical activity Kinsey would permit.

That he was entertaining peers in no way softened Kinsey's manner. Each and every guest was policed into polite passivity. "You didn't interrupt and you didn't make any noise if you could possibly help it during the playing," observed one guest. Explaining what prompted people to observe such strict rules of decorum, another guest declared that "any lady who was evil enough, or man either, to talk much during the record didn't get invited back." At precisely ten o'clock, Kinsey announced an intermission, and Clara served dessert and ice water (her favorite beverage), signaling that talking was permitted. But Kinsey both led and monopolized the discussion. "He was the expert," remarked one guest, stressing that the discussions took place in an atmosphere "with Dr. Kinsey really being domineering." The break lasted for approximately twenty minutes, and then Kinsey played the last selection of the evening. Following a few concluding remarks, he handed guests their hats and coats and showed them to the door. The musicales ended at ten-thirty on the dot.[68]

About half a dozen couples attended regularly, a group composed for the most part of professors and their spouses. In addition, Kinsey invited a few favorite students and out-of-town guests. The "regulars" obviously enjoyed these evenings. They did not seem to mind Kinsey's monologues or the formal decorum. Frank and Margaret Edmondson, for example, started attending the musicales immediately after he joined the astronomy department in 1937. "Frankly I enjoyed meeting a man who had strong opinions he was willing to defend," declared Edmondson. "I learned a great deal about music from him." Margaret shared this assessment, stressing that she, too, "learned a tremendous amount about music." In fact,

Margaret considered it a great honor to be asked to join Kinsey's audience. "We were really quite young, but we apparently managed to meet the standards of the group," she declared proudly.[69]

Others, including many students, found the atmosphere stiff and imposing. When June Keisler, who began working as Kinsey's student assistant in 1936, received an invitation, she asked a friend what to expect. The friend replied:

> You'll have to go, once, and see for yourself. It's kind of nice. Everybody just sits around in a circle and listens to music. You know, classical music. Records. Dr. Kinsey tends the record player. He's very particular about it. He always uses a cactus needle of a certain kind and I think he counts the number of times he uses it. Nobody talks. Some of the graduate students try to be dreadfully highbrow and appreciative. There's always at least one not very pretty girl wearing glasses who listens with eyes closed and her mouth soulfully open. . . . And afterwards Mrs. Kinsey serves refreshments on the Mexican plates. It's really rather nice. You'll like Mrs. Kinsey.[70]

She decided to take her friend's advice. Keisler attended one musicale, but never went back for seconds. Though she found the experience "rather nice," she felt out of place. Acknowledging that "youth is self-conscious," Keisler declared, "I was not educated enough to make high-brow remarks and I would not be one of the soulful, mouth-open listeners."[71]

Many of Kinsey's colleagues had a similar reaction. Kate Mueller, for example, found the view from Kinsey's feet less than inspiring. As the dean of women at Indiana University for many years, she came to know Kinsey well. Because she and her husband, John, who was a sociologist and a trained musician, shared a keen interest in music, they were delighted when Kinsey invited them to join his Sunday group. Their joy, however, did not survive the evening. Mueller described the affair as "very formal" and explained their decision not to go back by saying, "My husband being a performer of music just didn't care for that kind of dictatorship, shall we say, about the programs he would listen to."[72]

Henry Remak, a professor of German, was even more appalled. Though he admired Kinsey, and once called him "a great man," Remak could hardly believe the evening he spent with the Kinseys. "Frankly, the atmosphere was much too formal, much too frozen, much too strict for my liking," he declared. He was stunned by Kinsey's insistence that his guests listen "in complete silence and reverently stiff attention." In Remak's view, "there was not enough communication among the listeners, not enough 'letting-yourself-go'; it was too unrelaxed." Indeed, he found the whole experience deeply unsettling. While he was "impressed" by the experience, Remak confessed that he also felt "somewhat horrified and never went again."[73]

Kinsey was oblivious to such reactions. He had his coterie of devoted followers; people who wanted a democratic listening experience could go elsewhere. He ran his musicales as he pleased. Indeed, it was no accident that most couples invited to join his listening group were younger than the Kinseys. He had to be the teacher. With music, as with everything else, Kinsey had to exercise authority. Something in his personality made him want to control everyone he met. As a friend remarked, whenever Kinsey entered a room, "he dominated the assembly small or large, because he was he."[74]

If the musicales showcased his chronic need for control, they also revealed another feature of his personality: beneath the teaching and the listening ran a strong undercurrent of exhibitionism. Simply put, the musicales allowed Kinsey to show off before an audience. Like so many of his seemingly bizarre performances, Kinsey's autocratic behavior on Sunday evenings smacks of compulsive behavior. He had to instruct guests on the proper way to listen to music and the correct way to interpret what they heard; he had to reduce his audience to passivity, as their silence fed his need for power.

Yet, much as he tried to dominate his guests, Kinsey struggled even harder to control himself. Unlike listeners who have an oceanic experience with music, losing themselves completely in its sounds and rhythms, Kinsey held back. He could never give himself over entirely. Rather than melding with music, he analyzed it from every conceivable angle. He wanted distance, not absorption; control, not surrender. Any other response might tap into a torrent of emotions. In music, as in most other aspects of his life, Kinsey struggled to keep a tight grip on himself.

Keeping his emotions under control allowed Kinsey to concentrate on two things—the music and the reactions of his guests. Once the lights were dimmed and semidarkness fell across the room, Kinsey was free to listen and to observe, converting the musicale into a visual as well as audio experience. Secure in his position of authority next to the record player, his eyes went from guest to guest, searching their faces for expressions that would offer windows into their emotions.

Kinsey was sensitive to what he saw. In "Music and Love," an article published a month before his death, he explained that he had been inviting the same listening companions into his home for decades, stressing that these evenings had permitted him to "share something of their emotional responses to the full panoply of musical moods." Calling music "a great emotional experience," he declared that he and his friends "share something that is ours for the rest of our lives." In short, sharing music with others was important to Kinsey, at least in part, because their reactions enhanced his enjoyment. By searching their faces he could experience, if only vicariously, the full range of emotions music elicits from the human spirit, feelings he sought to control in himself.[75]

Overtly sexual emotions lay just beneath the surface of Kinsey's interest in music. Much of the music he played was deeply sensuous (particularly the works of Hugo Wolf), forcing Kinsey to maintain a constant vigil against sexual arousal. One member of his group had to take special precautions in this area. Margaret Edmonson recalled Kinsey's telling her about a man "who reacted so strongly to music and to rhythm and to excitement in general that he had a sexual reaction." Because the gentleman in question "was a very mild and rather elderly professor," Edmonson confessed, she was surprised to learn he "had to wear a special guard because he would go into an erection when listening to these things." Aware that Kinsey had shared a real confidence with her, Edmonson hastened to add, "Of course, I never let on that I knew."[76]

No, musicales satisfied a variety of needs in Kinsey. As a ritual of hospitality that brought guests into their home on a weekly basis, musicales unquestionably constituted his and Clara's principal social activity. Through these evenings, they could indulge their love of music while enjoying the fellowship and company of cultured, urbane friends. What a contrast from the sparse social life his father had with his colleagues at the Stevens Institute!

The best evidence of Kinsey's private struggles, however, was neither the garden nor the musicales: rather, his inner turmoil surfaced most clearly in his strident rejection of the twin touchstones of his childhood—religion and sexual repression. Each was connected to the other; each was a source of ongoing conflict; and each played an important role in how he acted as a husband and father, shaping his behavior in ways at once subtle and profound.

As the head of his own family, Kinsey rejected the intense religiosity of his childhood. Soon after he moved to Indiana, he turned his back on religion. During his first year in Bloomington, he attended services at the First Presbyterian Church, largely because the minister, the Reverend Charles Schwartz, a former Rhodes Scholar, attracted large groups of the university's faculty. At the year's end, however, Kinsey stopped going to church, and after his marriage he abandoned religion altogether.[77]

Unlike his father, Kinsey did not push religion on his children, either by teaching or by example. Quite the contrary, he encouraged his children to adopt thoroughly secular attitudes. Clara, too, assigned religion a low priority. Still, Anne came close to joining the church. Highly involved in the youth activities of the First Presbyterian Church, she attended the communicants' class at age twelve. When she was about to be confirmed, however, her parents, as she phrased it, "put their foot down." Convinced she was too young to make such an important decision, they refused to let her join the church, though they made it clear she could do so when she got older.[78]

Perhaps because she never threatened to join the church, Joan felt she had been allowed to make up her own mind about religion. "As far as their attitudes were concerned, this was fine if we wanted to go to Sunday school," Joan recalled. "Had we chosen to join a church, I am sure we could have." Joan did not join the church, in her words, because she "didn't feel inclined to, or feel the need to."[79] Yet she seemed unaware of how much her parents had influenced her decision. After all, they had voted with their feet every Sunday. Their message was clear: young people needed to be exposed to religion as part of their cultural heritage, but thinking people had no need to join a church.

As she grew older, Joan noticed a dramatic shift in her father's attitude toward religion. By the time she had reached high school, he had come to despise religion. It was as though the religious fervor of his youth had been transformed into passionate atheism. "Daddy felt very strongly about . . . the need for no religion," Joan declared. "It was not a passive attitude toward it . . . ," she explained. "He really had no use for it. It was an active, almost on occasions aggressive dislike for religion."[80]

Over time, Kinsey made no effort to conceal his disdain for religion. By the late 1920s, the man who had taught Sunday school classes himself barely a decade earlier all but belittled one of his laboratory assistants for doing the same thing. "Dr. K. learned somehow that I was teaching a Sunday School class," wrote Louise Rosenzweig many years later. "He asked why I bothered. When I explained that I enjoyed the group of bright little girls, a number of whom were faculty children, he acquiesced—'If you really like doing it.' " Similarly, Homer T. Rainwater, a former graduate student, recalled Kinsey's animus toward religion in vivid detail. "He wouldn't go to church, and he didn't believe in God, and he believed that this was it," declared Rainwater. "If there was any heaven you'd better make it right now, and you could make it hell also."[81]

Colleagues who knew Kinsey in the 1940s told similar stories. Asked by Wardell Pomeroy if he believed in God, Kinsey replied, "Don't be ridiculous. Of course not." When Pomeroy pressed him about the afterlife, Kinsey explained, "I believe that when you're dead, you're dead, and that's all there is." Paul Gebhard heard similar statements from Kinsey. They often discussed religion, and as Gebhard reviewed their conversations in his mind he had no hesitancy in declaring that Kinsey "was not only irreligious; he was anti-religious as I knew him."[82]

It is tempting to attribute this sea change to science. Certainly, Gebhard thought that Kinsey's loss of faith was "a result of science," for as he noted "it's hard to be a good objective, hard-nosed scientist and still hold any religious beliefs." But Gebhard knew Kinsey too well to leave it at that. He theorized that Kinsey's break with religion also stemmed from his "being overdosed on religion as a youth in his home."[83] Joan agreed. She considered her father's fight against religion a reaction to the "extremely religious upbringing which he had had." It is indeed hard not to see rebellion implicated in Kinsey's loss of faith and subsequent hostility toward religion.[84]

Even more than religion, sexual repression was the issue on which Kinsey broke most dramatically with his past. In a sense, this was hardly surprising, because sex seemed to serve as the lightning rod for his inner conflicts. It was clearly the area of his life that caused him the most grief. Certain that he personally had been deeply harmed by the sexual repression that had marked his childhood, Kinsey thought the best way to produce well-adjusted adults was to rear children who did not feel guilty about their sexuality. He placed his hopes on sex education, a solution that was at once rational, positivistic, and progressive, registering his strong agreement with the public's faith in the power of education to mold individuals and to reform society.

Between the world wars, a few junior high schools and a growing number of high schools in the United States started offering classes in sex education. Some school districts tucked the material into biology courses, while others stuck it in classes with names like "Mental Health" or "Social Hygiene." Taking their texts from the earlier sex education programs associated with the social hygiene movement during the Progressive Era, educators advised young people to channel their energy into wholesome activities, such as hobbies, school plays, and team sports.

Self-control was the cornerstone of these early classes. Insisting upon the single standard of morality, educators touted the virtues of self-restraint and bombarded young people with moral exhortations laced with grim warnings. Venereal diseases and unwanted pregnancies, cautioned the custodians of morality, were almost certain penalties for those who strayed. Instead of answering young people's questions about their bodies or discussing the difficulties adolescents faced in a society that made absolutely no provision for sexual contacts before marriage, educators and public officials censored any discussion of topics such as reproductive anatomy, petting, premarital intercourse, and birth control. If educators mentioned masturbation at all, they did so only to decry its deleterious effects on health and character. In short, what passed for sex education might better be called anti–sex education.

Knowing full well the consequences of ignorance and moral blackmail, Kinsey wanted something different for his children. He favored sex education that would shield the young from debilitating guilt. As was his wont, Kinsey did not attack the problem unprepared. He thought long and hard about different approaches, and left a rich record of his musings in a lecture he gave at Indiana University in 1940 entitled "Sex Education." He offered his lecture as a blueprint, stressing that his recommendations reflected his practices and experiences with his own three children, all of whom were adolescents at the time.

Sex education, argued Kinsey, had to begin at home, and it was clearly the duty of parents. Like successful teachers, parents would have to find the right words to communicate ideas effectively, and they would have to win the confidence of their children. Parents who shirked this duty, he warned, ran the risk of injuring and alienating their children, as failure to answer questions could open a gulf that never closed. In what sounded very much like an accusation directed at his parents, Kinsey insisted that parents who refused to educate their children about sex were deeply conflicted about their own sexuality.[85]

Autobiographical echoes can also be heard in Kinsey's discussion of how children learned about sex. The man who had experienced his first sexual encounter when he was seven or eight in a basement in Hoboken told his students that, sometime between the ages of seven and ten, children found answers to their questions. Since most parents ignored sex education, many young people got their information from peers. Unless they wished to condemn their children to be taught by other children, parents had to act. Children should be told the facts of life at an early age, certainly by the time they reached five or six.[86]

Here Kinsey was speaking from experience. This was the plan he and Clara had followed with their children. As the homemaker, Clara did much of the teaching. Adopting a low-key approach, she answered questions as they arose. When one of her children asked where babies came from or inquired about their bodies, Clara replied with matter-of-fact statements at a level of specificity appropriate to the child's age and ability to understand.[87]

A good teacher in her own right, Clara reinforced her points with clear illustrations. When pregnant with Bruce, for example, she let Anne and Joan put their hands on her stomach so they could feel the baby kicking. The lesson worked. Soon thereafter the family went for a drive, and Clara, seated in the front, turned around and found Anne standing on her head in the backseat. Told to sit down, Anne replied, "But what's the matter with this . . . that's the way I was inside your stomach!"[88] Joan, who was only three, got the lesson, too. "I do remember when my brother was born," she declared, "and I am sure that they must have made it all seem very natural to me, because I have no questions about it."[89]

Kinsey assumed much of the responsibility for educating his children about sex and, according to Joan, handled it very skillfully. "I was not aware that it was specifically sex education," she recalled with obvious amusement. Since the family often worked together in the garden, Kinsey used this natural setting to explain how plants, fish, frogs, birds, and dogs reproduced. "It was all just part of your education in that whole area of the way the world works," she declared. "And it was done so naturally that you weren't aware, 'Alright, this part is sex education.' "[90] In describing how things should be handled, Kinsey advised students to include sex education "as part of the average dinner table conversation, as part of the average discussion of an average day." Above all, parents had "to take matters of sex as normal and proper."[91]

As their children grew older, the Kinseys made certain the instruction became more detailed and explicit. One day after school, when she was ten, Joan and her mother had a long talk about the changes that were occurring in her body. They discussed Joan's breasts, which were beginning to develop, and the fact she would soon begin menstruating, with her mother offering a thorough discussion of the anatomy and physiology involved. A year or so later, after Joan had gotten her first period, both parents took her into the living room one evening. Her father sketched the male and female reproductive organs, explained sexual intercourse, and described how the sperm fertilizes the egg. According to Joan, "he made a point of going through it as you would . . . diagram any other part of the human anatomy, and it was done very, so to speak, scientifically." Joan was thankful for their candor, declaring that her mother and father made her "feel free to come discuss with" either of her parents if she had questions. That included behavioral questions. Looking back on her adolescence from the vantage point of middle age, Joan recalled having several conversations with her parents about premarital intercourse.[92]

By the mid-1930s, the Kinseys had developed a reputation in Bloomington as parents who gave straight answers to hard questions. According to Keisler, both Kinsey and Clara were regarded as local "authorities in the field of sex education." Keisler heard stories about neighborhood mothers asking Clara "what and when to tell their children," and there were reports "that the Kinsey children also did some 'educating' among their less knowledgeable playmates."[93]

An occasional adult even asked for help. In 1940, Kinsey told students about a pregnant faculty wife who could not bear to tell her two older children the facts of life. According to Kinsey, she came to Clara and said, "I want you to tell your children so your children can tell my children." Making no effort to conceal how much this incident pained him, Kinsey added, "I hope we are raising a generation of parents who do things differently."[94]

Kinsey did not stop with giving his children basic facts about anatomy and reproduction. Haunted by memories of his painful and guilt-ridden youth and convinced that attitudes formed in childhood molded a person's behavior for life, he wanted young people to grow up with healthy views toward sex. The responsibility for developing healthy attitudes fell to parents, Kinsey told his students, and the instruction had to begin early. It was only natural for children to explore their own bodies and those of other children, as they were innately curious about their own genitals and the anatomical differences between the sexes. In what may well have been an autobiographical reference, Kinsey added a sharp warning against interfering with a child's self-exploration, noting that such restrictions might foster sexual inhibitions that could later cause problems in marriage. Children should be taught that it was as acceptable to touch the genitalia as other parts of the body. Parents who thought otherwise, he scolded, were prudes. For Kinsey, then, parents had a duty to demystify sex. The time to begin was when children were young.[95]

With his own children, Kinsey taught by example. In order to communicate positive attitudes about the human body, he both practiced and encouraged a good deal of nudity in his household. Joan recalled numerous mornings as a child when she would join her father as he shaved in the bathroom. She would sit on the toilet seat, and he would stand naked before the mirror, making up "silly sing-song rhymes" to entertain her while he shaved. Explaining why these mornings were so special, Joan declared, "I had him as a captive audience."[96]

Joan also had memories of the entire family frolicking in the buff. In 1934, for example, when Anne was eleven, Joan nine, and Bruce six, the Kinseys took a family vacation in the Smokey Mountains. The cabin they rented "was off from the other cabins and there was a nice mountain stream nearby," Joan explained, "and so we would all go down the hill and bathe in that mountain stream in the nude." Furthermore, she recalled another vacation in New England when the family bathed together nude in a mountain stream.[97]

Nor was family nudity restricted to vacations. Thanks to the dense foliage surrounding their home, the backyard was not visible from the road or to neighbors on either side. The Kinseys took advantage of their privacy. "Once or twice I remember on extremely hot nights in the summertime, this was long before home air-conditioning was economically feasible at our level," explained Joan, "going out in the backyard and playing in the sprinkler, when the whole family was in the nude." Reared by parents who acted relaxed and uninhibited about their own bodies, Joan grew up viewing household nudity as "something that was just accepted." If anything, she regarded it as perfectly natural. During her senior year in high school, Joan had a two-hour lunch period, and she often came home for lunch and sunbathed in the nude on the back porch. Still, her parents taught her to be discreet. As Joan explained, "you were aware of the fact that you didn't want to offend other people by their seeing you in the nude."[98]

Nothing better illustrated the distance Kinsey had traveled from his childhood than the sex education he and Clara gave their children. Determined to banish ignorance and shame, the twin legacies of Victorian repression, he hoped to demystify sex by treating it as natural and healthy. The contrast between his approach and that of most middle-class Americans could hardly have been more jarring.

Yet Kinsey did not fall under suspicion. If anything, his experience in Bloomington convinced him that some people wanted their children to have more information about sex, provided that information came from those qualified to speak. Moreover, a ready-made defense shielded Kinsey from those who considered his behavior odd or morally objectionable. By the 1930s, the stereotype of the "eccentric professor" was a familiar feature of American popular culture, with more than enough explanatory power to keep friends and neighbors from devoting much thought to his behavior. After all, it was not as though Kinsey had a reputation for being liberal or progressive on other issues.

And even if a few skeptics were shocked to see parents discuss sex candidly with their children, most people were not prepared to think ill of an otherwise staid and respectable couple. Regardless of their views on Kinsey as an individual, his status as a family man protected him from serious scrutiny. Then, too, the fact that Clara was so sensible and so well liked in the community shielded the couple from doubts.

To a remarkable degree, then, Kinsey appeared to achieve his quest for bourgeois respectability. Honored professor, loving father, devoted husband, and civic-minded citizen, he seemed to fulfill all the requirements of the cult of true manhood. Yet, like so many married men of his generation who were sexually attracted to other men, Kinsey reluctantly embarked on a secret life. At great risk to everything he held dear, and despite the iron will that made his public persona a model of rigid self-control, he sought sexual satisfaction outside marriage.

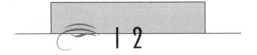

12

"POSITIONS, WIGGLING, AND PARASITES"

arriage did not end Kinsey's summers at camp. Following their honeymoon, he and Clara worked as counselors in the summer of 1921 at Camp Aloha close to Fairlee, Vermont.[1] Ever since his days as a Boy Scout, Kinsey's social world had centered on counseling, which he truly enjoyed. It took him outdoors, the setting where he felt the most free and alive. Hiking and camping had always been more recreation than work. He relished the opportunity to show young people nature's wonders.

Yet the summer job that followed their honeymoon was a departure for Kinsey. Camp Aloha was a girls camp, and his decision to work there may have reflected his determination to focus on his relationship with Clara, a resolve that continued the next summer. With Donald's birth in June 1922, he stayed in Bloomington for the summer.[2] Not so the following year. In 1923, he returned to camp, working part of the summer at Camp Laikila in Fairlee, Vermont, and then shifting over to Camp Aloha, where Clara joined him for the remainder of the session.[3] At the end of the summer, they visited a campsite near Milan, New Hampshire, to inspect a plot of land where they hoped to build a boys camp of their own. They had examined the same property two years earlier following their honeymoon, which suggests they had given the matter serious thought.[4]

Owning his own camp would have forged an important link between Kinsey and his past. For reasons that are not clear, however, nothing came of the plan. Instead, Kinsey settled for another round of counseling. In 1924, he returned to the East, where he spent the summer at Camp Winona, a boys camp in Maine.[5] Clara remained at home in Bloomington, tethered to their two small children.[6] It cannot have been easy to watch her husband go off to camp while she stayed home. This was the last summer Kinsey devoted to counseling, the final chapter on the most satisfying part of his youth. But instead of giving up his close relationships with young men, Kinsey turned to his students.

Among the first students to win his friendship was Ralph Voris, who enrolled at Indiana after earning a bachelor's degree at Southwestern College in Winfield, Kansas. At first glance, Voris's background did not make him a likely candidate to become Kinsey's confidant. Southwestern College hardly bestowed a distinguished academic pedigree. It was a blue-collar school, the sort of institution Kinsey routinely criticized for having low academic standards and weak faculties. Ordinarily, he had little use for the graduates of such institutions, as many could not compete in top-notch graduate programs. They were the poor souls he ridiculed in class, mocking their accents and posing questions he knew they could not answer.

Voris was different. He arrived at Indiana University in the fall of 1925 with sound undergraduate training in biology. His professors at Southwestern College, it seems, had given him solid instruction, further enhancing his education by naming him a teaching assistant during his last year in college, the same honor Kinsey had earned at Bowdoin. And much as Kinsey's teachers had steered him to Harvard, Voris's professors had pointed him to Indiana. In short order, even Kinsey had to admit that Voris came with a "well balanced zoology training."[7]

During his three years at Indiana, Voris turned in a respectable, though hardly brilliant, performance. His studies in zoology included course work in cytology, general entomology, and taxonomy. In addition, he took a total of sixteen graduate hours in botany. Inexplicably, he also enrolled in one course in philosophy. With the exception of a single C, he earned all A's and B's, with the A work predominating.[8] He earned his Ph.D. in zoology in 1928, the first graduate student to complete a doctorate under Kinsey's supervision.

Voris lacked the motivation to become an outstanding scientist. Friends remember him as good-natured and easygoing, the sort of man who knew how to relax and have fun. While still an undergraduate, he married his college sweetheart, Geraldine, who was a year behind him in school. In order to complete her degree, she remained in Kansas during his first year in graduate school, which means that Voris was alone his first year in Bloomington.[9] According to Herman Spieth, a fellow graduate student and close friend, Voris was a genuinely nice man, "very warm, very friendly, very outgoing."[10] Spieth was particularly impressed by Voris's sense of humor, describing him as "jovial and fun."[11]

Kinsey noticed these qualities, too. He was struck by Voris's lightheartedness and personal warmth. In a letter of recommendation written after they had known one another for several years, Kinsey commented on Voris's "rather happy, cheerful disposition."[12] On another occasion, he lauded Voris's "rich store of humor."[13] If these remarks sound less than ebullient, it must be remembered that Kinsey had great difficulty expressing or demonstrating affection. Certainly, it took a lighthearted soul to tolerate Kinsey.

Voris was born on June 23, 1902, in Newkirk, Oklahoma. His family moved to Kansas when he was still a boy. Growing up in the middle of America's heartland, he developed a keen interest in nature. He enjoyed hiking and collecting insects, and he emulated Teddy Roosevelt's passion for asserting dominion over nature. An avid sportsman, Voris developed into an excellent hunter and fisherman, blood sports that repelled Kinsey. Physically, Voris fit the image of a great hunter, standing over six feet tall and weighing about 200 pounds.[14] Blessed with dark, wavy hair, a broad forehead, and full lips that came together in a boyish smile, he was literally tall, dark, and handsome.

Voris showed more promise as a teacher than as a scholar, displaying an aptitude for the classroom that did not go unnoticed by his professors. During his four years in graduate school, he assisted with a variety of courses. Kinsey deemed his lectures "rather good," calling his presentation "not at all wearisome."[15] Coming from a man who considered himself a master teacher and who often criticized the classroom performance of others, this passed for praise.

What brought Kinsey and Voris together was their love of the outdoors and their devotion to fieldwork. Voris had little interested in the New Biology, with its high-powered laboratory research. On both a personal and a professional level, he preferred the extensive fieldwork that Kinsey hoped to make the foundation of the "new systematics." Because Voris wanted to become a field biologist, he decided early in his graduate career to specialize in taxonomy. He took several courses under Kinsey, who liked his work and agreed to supervise his dissertation. Voris came up with his own dissertation topic, electing to work on beetles of the family Staphylinidae.[16]

In Voris, Kinsey found a man whose delight in fieldwork rivaled his own. "I wish I could be in the field all the time," he once wrote Kinsey "I've thot [*sic*] a number of times that I had reached the height of thrill in collection but I guess it is still ahead of me. Every time I go out there is something that peps me up."[17] These words warmed Kinsey, who saw a kindred spirit in Voris, the sort of man who might be willing to hit the trail at a moment's notice. He was also impressed by the social skills Voris displayed on field trips. As Kinsey put it, Voris "was adept in meeting the back-country natives with whom scientific expeditions have to make contact."[18]

Among all his pupils, Voris alone satisfied Kinsey's idealized notion of how a scientist should perform under field conditions. But then Voris had an advantage—he had been present at the creation of those standards. His years at Indiana corresponded exactly with the period in which Kinsey was refining his field techniques, and in a sense they had forged those standards together. In a rare admission of indebtedness to another, Kinsey wrote Voris a few years after he left Indiana, "You helped me establish certain traditions in our field work which I have had to maintain."[19] During Voris's graduate school days, he was Kinsey's constant companion on field trips. Describing their travels to a colleague, Kinsey noted that Voris had accompanied him on "field work in eastern and western Kentucky, the Missouri Ozarks, southern Illinois, eastern Tennessee, through the state of Georgia, northern Florida, and one line which we cut across the state of Alabama."[20]

Somewhere along the way, the relationship between Kinsey and Voris changed. It was hard for Kinsey to preserve his emotional distance, as only eight years separated them in age. Nor did Voris's personality make it easy to keep him at arm's length. Voris's warmth and his easy way of relating to people eroded the air of formality Kinsey built into his relationships with students in order to buttress his intellectual authority. Gradually, a bond of friendship formed between the men.

Their letters reveal the changes in their relationship. Their correspondence began in the summer of 1926 and continued until Voris's death in the spring of 1940. At first, their letters were stiff and formal, as befitted exchanges between a young graduate student and his mentor. The tone quickly changed. After Voris finished his dissertation, he landed a job at Southwest State Teachers College in Springfield, Missouri, where he spent his entire career. As Voris struggled to establish himself professionally, he remained in constant touch with Kinsey. While Kinsey addressed Voris as "Dear Ralph" or "My Dear Ralph," Voris continued to his death to address his letters "Dr. Kinsey." Despite Voris's formality, however, their correspondence became more frank, more relaxed, more wide-ranging, and decidedly more personal, at least on Kinsey's part.

From the outset, work-related matters dominated their correspondence, with Kinsey assuming the role of helpful mentor and Voris cast as the grateful pupil. Certainly, he was wise to curry Kinsey's favor. Voris's professional situation was far from ideal, and he needed help moving to a better institution. Dejectedly, Voris described Southwest Missouri as "a teachers college with the characteristics of a teachers college." This meant low pay, heavy teaching loads, poorly prepared students, and a dearth of colleagues who conducted research. Confronted with a future so bleak, Voris started job hunting his second year at Southwest College. Kinsey recommended Voris for the few jobs that opened, and he did his best to boost Voris's spirits with assurances that better times lay ahead.

Voris tried to repay this support in a variety of ways. As the years passed, Voris became Kinsey's alter ego. Kinsey used him as a sounding board for his taxonomic theories, and Voris settled into his role as devoted partisan. Knowing the words his mentor longed to hear, Voris became a one-man cheering squad, praising Kinsey's work lavishly. In response to Kinsey's second monograph (the work on the origin of higher species), Voris beamed, "This is the best yet and it is so far reaching in its scope that I hesitate to hazard an estimate of its value."[21]

Voris also contributed data to Kinsey's research. Part of the explanation for Kinsey's success in amassing huge samples was the help he received from others, and former students became important links in his chain of collectors. None proved more valuable than Voris. After he moved to Missouri, he funneled gall wasp material year after year back to Bloomington, no doubt to the detriment of his own work on beetles.

Kinsey gave him little choice. Voris had no sooner moved to the Ozarks than Kinsey started intimating how helpful it would be to know more about the galls of that region. Dutifully, Voris marched into the field, collected galls, and shipped them back to Bloomington. The specimens delighted Kinsey, who praised the material and sent Voris a check to cover his expenses.[22] Voris respectfully returned it, insisting that he had sent the galls not for money but to show his appreciation for everything Kinsey had done for him.[23]

Kinsey made sure additional field trips followed. In most mentor-student relationships, the parties see less of one another after students graduate. In Voris's case, however, Kinsey refused to let go. Their correspondence shows that he was by far the more eager of the two to keep their relationship close. Indeed, Kinsey did everything in his power to keep Voris in his orbit. After Voris moved to Missouri, Kinsey issued yearly invitations for him to come on field trips, arguing that they would both benefit from additional work together.[24]

Voris frequently disappointed his mentor. At times, he pleaded lack of funds; on other occasions, he argued that his beetles required him to visit locations Kinsey's gall wasps did not inhabit. The first obstacle Kinsey dealt with by paying for as many expenses as his funds and Voris's pride would allow. But there was no solution to the second problem. All Kinsey could do was lament the fates, telling Voris, "It will always be one of my regrets that your bugs and mine do not always live in exactly the same places."[25] Although he accompanied Kinsey on several field trips after moving to Missouri, they made only short trips together, the last in 1934.

To supplement their visits, Kinsey tried to get Voris to come to professional meetings. Year after year, he pleaded with Voris to attend the American Association for the Advancement of Sciences (AAAS) annual meetings, suggesting that they room together to save money. Voris declined most of these invitations, citing lack of funds. The December 1930 AAAS meeting, in Cleveland, was an exception. Thanks to a small travel grant from his college, Voris happily accepted Kinsey's invitation to room together, declaring, "It will be grate [*sic*] to have that time with you."[26] Delighted, Kinsey replied, "I, too, shall be very glad to be with you and have much to talk about at that time."[27]

When the AAAS met in Pittsburgh in 1934, Kinsey tried to ease Voris's concerns about money by working up a detailed estimate of the expenses, assuring Voris that the trip would not cost more than ten or twelve dollars. He also invited Voris and his wife to spend several days in Bloomington after the meetings, sweetening the offer with promises of additional instruction in music.[28] Voris accepted. "Your letter overwhelmed us. You offer so much. Grateful. Happy and everything," replied Voris. "Your offer makes it next to impossible for us to refuse."[29] Following the visit, Voris was effusive, calling it "a grand and glorious time we had."[30]

Despite protestations of how much he enjoyed seeing his mentor, Voris declined Kinsey's invitation to room together at the AAAS meeting in December 1937, in Indianapolis. Voris chose to stay instead with a friend who lived in Indianapolis. Still, he did ask if he might use Kinsey's room as his base at the meeting. Clearly disappointed, Kinsey nevertheless agreed to let his room serve as Voris's headquarters. But Kinsey expressed the hope that he would not have to take in Voris's friend as well.[31] Voris's reply was reassuring. "No, I don't expect to have Sid [Esten] with me all the time," he wrote, "for I want to do a lot of things."[32] Apparently, both men enjoyed their Indianapolis visit immensely, though Kinsey later complained that it had been too short. "It was fine to see you at Indianapolis," he wrote Voris the following March, "but hell to have so little time with you. Let's hope for something better another time."[33]

More than business filled the nights when Kinsey and Voris were reunited at professional conferences. Chiding his former student for not attending the annual meeting of the AAAS in New York City in December 1936, Kinsey regaled Voris with a breathless description of a strip show, a spectacle that Kinsey claimed had left him hot and bothered.[34] While the letter is missing, Kinsey sent a similar description to another former student, Osmond P. Breland. Breland responded that he had received "with great glee your recent letter about positions, wiggling, and parasites [a reference to material in the letter that concerned entomology]." He continued,

> I personally think that the correct [way] to run a Burlesque would be to have two side rooms for the patrons; one labeled: "For men who are on the verge of exploding." In this room should be large quantities of damsels who would aid said gentlemen by contact wiggling! The other room should bear the rather ignoble sign: "For gentlemen who have exploded." In this room should be nothing but a shower, and several pairs of underwear and trousers! Alas, I fear me that I would never have use for the first named room![35]

Such exchanges underscore how far Kinsey had traveled from the ideals of genteel morality. He had inched away from the staid familiarity and emotional security of traditional family life and had started to explore sexual underworlds, subcultures that offered illicit behavior outside the home.

As he inched away from Clara, Kinsey longed for a closer relationship with Voris. Since field trips and professional meetings did not offer enough opportunities for visits, he made stronger appeals. After Voris moved to Missouri, Kinsey issued yearly invitations (and sometimes two or more in the same year) for Voris and Geraldine to come back to Bloomington. For the first few years, the invitations were low-key, but as time passed, they assumed a different tone, at once more cordial and urgent. The Vorises accepted as many of these invitations as their budget would allow and reciprocated by asking the Kinseys to visit them in Missouri, which they did on several occasions. As a result, Kinsey managed to see Voris during many of the years in which they missed getting together on field trips or at conventions.

But despite numerous visits, correspondence provided the bulk of their contact from the late 1920s until Voris's death. At first glance, the portrait that emerges from their surviving letters is first that of mentor-student and later that of mentor-friend.[36] Nevertheless, the letters reveal feelings and tensions overtly erotic in nature. Kinsey used their correspondence to discuss topics and experiences, like the burlesque show, that were more reminiscent of conversations between adolescent campers than mature professional colleagues. Almost without exception, Kinsey initiated the topics, and much of what he wrote concerned his quest to improve his sex life with

Clara. His letters were sprinkled with references to his efforts to acquire more information on human sexual behavior, information Kinsey was eager to share with Voris in the hopes that he, too, could achieve a robust sex life.

In December 1932, for example, Kinsey sent Voris a book that in all likelihood was a marriage manual, perhaps Robert L. Dickinson's recently published *A Thousand Marriages* (1931). In recommending the book, Kinsey praised the author's honesty and candor, admitting that he and Clara had benefited from the information it contained.[37] When he returned the book a few months later, Voris agreed that it had real merits and could be read with profit.[38]

Over time, Kinsey and Voris developed a great deal of trust in one another, giving them a bond of intimacy Kinsey shared with few others. "Now, from Kinsey's account," stated Clyde Martin, a colleague who knew Kinsey well, "somewhere along the line he and Ralph Voris had discussed their own sexual histories with one another." That Kinsey found these discussions fascinating was clear to Martin. "I think one of the things that impressed Kinsey was their many differences as well as their similarities of experience,"[39] Martin recalled. "I remember his mentioning that Voris was telling about how listless he would feel the next day after masturbating. [Voris] was one of the few people where sexual activity is kind of exhausting."[40]

Apparently Kinsey and Voris often discussed intimate details about their marital sexual relations. Immediately after returning from a four-day trip together in the fall of 1934, Kinsey thanked Voris profusely for educating him about coital positions, a subject Kinsey was eagerly exploring with Clara. "The Voris's [*sic*] have shared much of our thoughts in the last week," wrote Kinsey. "Many thanks for letting us. It is worth more than most folks can realize to have friends whose thinking is so nearly our own. The back position has suddenly proved simple—and we have the others still to try. What damned foolishness it is that actual experience is not more often passed on among friends—what blundering amateurs we can be without it!"[41]

At one point, Kinsey attempted to interest the Vorises in nudism. While no direct evidence has survived that links the Kinseys to nudist camps, the suspicion lingers that he was speaking from experience. In the fall of 1934, Kinsey sent Voris two books on nudism. "Are the Voris's [*sic*] shocked?" asked Kinsey with mock solemnity. "Mrs. Kinsey and I agree [the books] have been a healthy part of our children's education."[42] Of course, by this point in their relationship, the two men had held numerous discussions about sex, and Voris's reply registered neither surprise nor embarrassment.

But he did slam the door shut against any participation in either nudism or group sex, which he appeared to interpret as the unspoken message of Kinsey's overture. After acknowledging receipt of the books, Voris wrote, "Extremely interesting to us but I'm afraid that we are both in the second group 'not interested' in the camps etc. for the simple reason that we are not interested in groups either with or without clothes. Thanks a lot. Will comment further at a later date."[43] For his part, Voris returned Kinsey's confidences in kind. After he and Geraldine had spent the Christmas holidays with the Kinseys in 1934, Voris wrote, "It was a grand and glorious time we had. Thanks. I believe that our technique is improving. Many thanks to you both."[44]

While these exchanges show that the Kinseys and the Vorises exchanged information about their sex lives, their letters conceal as much as they reveal. It is clear, however, that their discussions as couples centered on heterosexual behavior. That Kinsey and Voris may have branched out to other topics when they were alone is entirely possible, but their surviving letters offer no evidence they were lovers. Still, both men exercised discretion in their letters. When inquiring about Kinsey's field trip to Mexico in 1931–32, for instance, Voris pleaded, "How we'd like to hear all about the trip, especially those portions one doesn't put in letters."[45] Kinsey's reply was to the point: "I have much I want to gossip with you, but this must be brief."[46] In keeping with Kinsey's preference for discussing private matters in person, no gossip followed.

So it went for years. Often Kinsey's letters portray a man with paternal feelings, a role he executed with rare dedication. Over the years, Kinsey kept up a steady drumbeat of professional encouragement, including countless exhortations for Voris to publish. Voris's letters to Kinsey are filled with expressions of gratitude and promises to excel, the sort of things that dutiful sons often say to demanding fathers. At any rate, those who knew Kinsey best insist that his relationship with Voris was one of the most important of Kinsey's life. "Voris became the closest friend Kinsey ever had," wrote Wardell Pomeroy, Kinsey's friend and associate; "their relationship probably meant more to him than any other."[47] Another staff member reinforced this judgment by taking note of the "close bond between them."[48]

In his personal relationships, Kinsey usually felt a strong need to dominate, especially where men were concerned. Voris brought out other emotions. Kinsey wished to please Voris. According to Paul Gebhard, Kinsey once confided that Voris was the only man who could make him do what he wanted.[49] When Gebhard met Kinsey, Voris had been dead for at least six years. "I know that [Kinsey] had a picture of Voris, which [Kinsey] kept on his desk, which struck me as unusual because when I first saw it I thought that it must be a son that I didn't know about or a relative or something like that. So obviously there was a considerable emotional tie between them."[50]

Two people who knew Kinsey well in his later years insist that Kinsey fell head-over-heels in love with Voris. "He was in love with Voris from day one," declared Clarence A. Tripp, a former friend and confidant.[51] Another close friend, who admitted having homosexual relations himself with Kinsey on numerous occasions during the last decade of Kinsey's life, declared, "I think the first H[omosexual] contact he had of any significance was with his graduate student [Voris]."[52] The friend stated that Kinsey told him that Voris was the second great love of his life, Clara being the first.[53]

At what point Kinsey's feelings shifted is difficult to determine. Still, Voris's importance to Kinsey can hardly be overstated. Falling in love with another man is a defining moment in the life of any homosexual. Until it happens, many men can deceive themselves about their true sexual identity. Unable to reconcile the contrast between the cultural images of men as tough and aggressive and the popular images of homosexuals as soft and effeminate, many men deny that their sexual attraction to other men has anything to do with homosexuality. Instead, they rationalize their needs, insisting they simply enjoy fantasizing about men when they make love to women or getting together with other men for masturbation. But once a man falls in love with another man, self-deception becomes more difficult.[54]

What is certain is that Kinsey sought intimacy with several male graduate students who followed Voris. While Kinsey never got as close to another student, he still desired young male companions. On his many collecting trips, some lasting only a matter of days, others consuming weeks and even months, Kinsey seldom went alone. Typically he took along one or two male graduate students and an occasional undergraduate. No one gave it a second thought when Kinsey disappeared into the wilderness with students in tow. After all, taxonomic research required fieldwork, and Kinsey was a taxonomist. He needed helpers, and his students needed instruction. One of his laboratory helpers came closer to the truth than she knew when she observed, "When Dr. K. prepared for a collecting expedition, he displayed the excited anticipation of an adolescent."[55] Indeed, Kinsey enjoyed these field trips not only because he loved the outdoors but because these outings mimicked his camp days.

Homer T. Rainwater had vivid memories of the field trip he took with Kinsey. A native of Mississippi, Rainwater entered the graduate program in biology at Indiana University in 1931, hoping to study under Kinsey.

In October 1934, Kinsey took Rainwater and Osmond P. Breland on a field trip to the Ozark Mountains in Arkansas and Missouri. It was Rainwater's first collecting expedition with Kinsey, and it was not what Rainwater expected.

Rainwater was immediately struck by Kinsey's immodesty. Describing conditions in the field, Rainwater declared, "He would go naked if we were in a campground where there was a bathhouse up the way a little ways. . . . He just plain didn't give a damn. He didn't care if we saw him naked." Nor did Kinsey show any inhibitions about his bodily functions. As Rainwater put it, "you'd see him naked around the camp and going to the bathroom, and all that sort of thing. . . . [He'd] just take a leak right there in front of us or stride off down toward the camp naked." Kinsey's behavior struck Rainwater as odd, for, as he explained, "most professors, if they had graduate students out, they'd probably come out in a bathrobe." Still, Rainwater could not bring himself to suspect anything was amiss. "I don't believe he had any sexual motive. As I think back over it." He continued, "it never occurred to me that he considered himself to be an exhibitionist, just deliberately showing himself off. My idea was that he just didn't give a damn about what you saw. That was him."[56]

Although willing to dismiss Kinsey's exhibitionism as eccentricity, Rainwater found it harder to explain his mentor's preoccupation with sex. Every evening when they assembled in cheap motor lodges to sort and label the day's collections, Kinsey invariably turned the conversation to sex. The discussions seemed to begin without any logical justification. "He'd just bring it [up] right out of the blue," declared Rainwater.[57]

After several nights, however, Rainwater saw a pattern. Kinsey would begin by sharing intimate details about his own private life. "He'd just talk about his wife, and what a good sex partner she was, and then he'd go from there. The conversation just wound around his relationship and how happy he was with his setup, and he hoped that we were," explained Rainwater.[58] "He had a pretty wife, and apparently she was very accommodating, and he talked about that to us, I thought, more than was appropriate," Rainwater confessed. "Maybe I was just too old-fashioned, and the subject was more or less taboo as far as I was concerned," he remarked. "I thought that was something that people just kept private to themselves and just didn't talk too much about."[59]

To justify his behavior Kinsey told his graduate students he wanted to share information that would help them build a better sexual relationship with their wives. "I wasn't particularly interested in his sex life at home," complained Rainwater, "but I'm sure he tried to give some points about how to be successful in sex, and how you could be more congenial with your wife, and he talked about that, I thought, too much." Kinsey's suggestions were explicit. He talked about "positioning and the whole bit," declared Rainwater.[60]

Kinsey also held forth on birth control. He "was very anxious that we didn't get our wives pregnant while we were [in graduate school], because of finances," said Rainwater. Turning to specifics, Rainwater recalled that Kinsey discussed withdrawal and talked about sterilization in some detail, though he did not recommend it. Most of his comments concerned another form of birth control. According to Rainwater, Kinsey "talked about condoms and how to use them, and how to preserve them, how to clean them up, and [how] to use them one time right after another, and then we wouldn't have to buy so many." Here, too, Kinsey shared personal information. Rainwater recalled Kinsey describing how he "washed them and then preserved them in alcohol," adding "I believe it was a certain percentage of alcohol that he told us about." Rainwater was grateful for this information, for as he explained, "we were depression kids . . . . [Franklin D.] Roosevelt had just come in, and the New Deal hadn't gotten started yet, and our little old paycheck was very small. . . . And [Kinsey] knew that we might not have money to go out and buy condoms just whenever we wanted them."[61]

If Rainwater appreciated the information on birth control, he found other parts of Kinsey's conversation intrusive. Much to Rainwater's embarrassment, Kinsey inquired about his sex life. "I told him just like it was," he recalled, "I told him that our sex life was satisfactory, as far as I knew." At the time, though, Rainwater's marriage was failing, and after considerable prodding he confessed as much to Kinsey. Rainwater's wife had her heart set on becoming an actress and wanted to move to Hollywood, and he had a hard time convincing his adviser that sex was not the root of his marital problems. Kinsey "figured it was a sexual mismatch," explained Rainwater. "He figured that was the case in most divorces."[62] Eventually, Rainwater persuaded Kinsey differently, but only after sharing the most intimate details of his marriage.

Rainwater's discomfort rose several notches when Kinsey maneuvered their evening discussions to masturbation. Again, Kinsey shared confidences about himself in order to elicit information from others. He admitted that he had felt terribly guilty about masturbation as a boy, though in retrospect he claimed he could see that his behavior was normal. "But at the time I think he sort of felt like it was a taboo subject," declared Rainwater, "something that was unnatural and something that was not to be talked about." Making the point more strongly, Rainwater stated, "He felt guilty about doing it."[63]

Confessing his childhood guilt gave Kinsey an opportunity to reassure

Rainwater that masturbation was perfectly normal, both for boys and for men. "Well, as I remember it," declared Rainwater, "he said that was a natural phenomenon, there wasn't anything wrong with it at all, that it was universal, that everybody did it, males and females alike, and that there was nothing in the world wrong with it." Asked if Kinsey told him it was all right for him to relieve his sexual desires by masturbating on field trips since he was far removed from his wife, Rainwater replied, "Oh, yes." Pressed on the point, Rainwater stood his ground, declaring, "Sure did." Indeed, Kinsey not only lauded masturbation as healthy but offered a detailed discussion of how to masturbate efficiently and effectively. Kinsey held forth on "the anatomy of the penis" and how "it took a certain amount of erotic irritation to bring climax," explained Rainwater. "And I remember him telling us something about the physiology of masturbation and the mechanics of masturbation," Rainwater continued, "the irritation, the erotic sort of thing that was necessary to bring it on." Asked if Kinsey ever volunteered to demonstrate masturbatory techniques, Rainwater replied, "No, he never went that far, but he went just about that far."[64] Queried if Kinsey ever suggested that they all masturbate together, an anxious Rainwater answered, "No, he didn't go that far. He almost did, but didn't."[65]

All this sex talk left Rainwater feeling uncomfortable and embarrassed. Certainly, it was not the kind of behavior he expected from a college professor. "I've never had another one talk to me like [that], talk openly," he declared. "Of course, we were out in the Ozarks, and we were way away from people and stuff. . . . But I had never heard that sort of thing, and to me it wasn't exactly appropriate."[66]

Another person might have asked Kinsey to stop or at least tried to change the subject, but Rainwater was unwilling to jeopardize his relationship with Kinsey. Looking back, Rainwater mused, "If I'd said, 'Dr. Kinsey, I don't think that's any of your business at all,' I think his reaction would have been that he'd have clammed [up]. I would have been with him the rest of the trip, but I don't believe Dr. Kinsey would ever have gotten over it. And I think that would have been it for me." Rainwater added pointedly, "I knew Dr. Kinsey well enough to know what he wanted to hear and what he didn't want to hear."[67]

Rainwater felt more relaxed when a fourth man joined their party. Kinsey had arranged in advance for Voris to accompany them for a few days to help train the newcomers in fieldwork. Rainwater was surprised that Kinsey would interrupt collecting long enough to team up with Voris, declaring that Kinsey "made a special effort for us to go by." From the moment his favorite student joined the expedition, Kinsey seemed totally preoccupied with Voris, taking the pressure off his dealings with Rainwater and Breland. "[Kinsey] and Voris were pretty close together, and their conversation sort of excluded us," recalled Rainwater.[68]

So did the sleeping arrangements. Breland and Rainwater bunked in separate cabins, but, according to Rainwater, "[Kinsey] and Voris stayed together." Still, Rainwater did not think anything about it. At no point did he wonder if Kinsey was homosexual. Nor was Rainwater aware of any gossip among other graduate students regarding Kinsey's sexual orientation. It was not that Rainwater and his fellow graduate students were naive. Rather, their reactions underscore the power of the cultural presumption that everyone is heterosexual, unless proven otherwise. All Kinsey's talk about coital positions and what a wonderful sex life he had at home clearly had the desired effect. Rainwater believed "he was too happy with his home sex life for him to ever be interested in something else."[69]

Why was Kinsey unable to suppress his preoccupation with sex? The answer seems obvious: only a man who was experiencing enormous internal pressures would have dared to broach sexual topics so brazenly or repeat the performance so often. Professors simply did not engage in that sort of behavior with their graduate students. Yet Kinsey seemed totally oblivious to sexual taboos. It was as though he considered himself above such petty concerns; better yet, it was as though he was determined to flaunt them.

Kinsey's behavior showed that he had undergone a metamorphosis. Years of sexual repression and inhibition had made him an ardent foe of traditional sexual morality and restraint. Gone forever was the clean-cut camp counselor who had knelt in prayer pleading for strength and forgiveness with the boy who had confessed masturbating. Kinsey had become a sexual rebel, a man who could be manipulative and aggressive, a man who abused his professional authority and betrayed his trust as a teacher. In addition, a man who placed himself in enormous jeopardy. Only a desperate man, indeed a compulsive man, would have taken such risks. If Rainwater had aired his complaints, Kinsey's reputation would have been seriously damaged, if not destroyed.

Osmond P. Breland has left us additional glimpses of Kinsey's sexual agenda on field trips. Breland and an undergraduate student named James (Jim) Coon accompanied Kinsey on a 1935 expedition south of the border, a trip that extended through southern Mexico into Guatemala. Breland kept a daily diary of their entire trip. Apart from a single page torn out from the rest, the diary is complete. In addition to recording the distances they traveled and the places they camped, Breland wrote vivid descriptions of the countryside, weather conditions, and people they met along the way, including some evocative portraits of rural Mexico as its politics swung to the left under the administration of President Lázaro Cárdenas.

Yet the bulk of Breland's diary chronicles his interaction with Kinsey, and seldom has a graduate student found more to criticize in a mentor. If Bre-land's diary is any indication, he loathed Kinsey, an assessment supported by at least one other graduate student from that period. As Herman Spi-eth put it, "Breland thought [Kinsey] was a horse's ass."[70] Whatever his true feelings, Breland had to bite his tongue. Prudence required him to pre-serve a positive relationship with his mentor, for Kinsey held a great deal of power over his career. In their face-to-face dealings, he treated Kinsey with respect and deference. But his diary revealed his true feelings. It was filled with complaints about Kinsey's foul language, domineering person-ality, lack of patience, bad temper, and "know it all" manner. At different points, Breland called Kinsey an "old wind bag," an "impatient bastard," an "idiot," a "thick headed shrimp," a "damn fool," a "damn conceited stubborn headed jackass," an "unhealthy wart hog," and a "selfish pis-sant."[71]

Ignoring his own salty language, Breland was sharply critical of Kinsey's profanity. When they encountered an awful stretch of road in Mexico on the way to Saltillo, Breland wrote, "K. of course swore all the way. I don't see what he came down here again for anyway. Although he expected bad roads he swears every time. He sure has an awful temper, and would it do me good to sit on him!"[72] Other references to profanity abound, suggest-ing that Kinsey had jettisoned the polite discourse of his youth in favor of a blue vocabulary. Why would a man with his education want to curse so fluently? Most likely, Kinsey was registering his contempt for moral re-straints and trying to act like a he-man.

Far more than his mentor's swearing, Breland resented his domineering personality. A keen observer, Breland was quick to spot Kinsey's efforts to exaggerate his own toughness while denigrating the masculinity of his companions. A series of entries in Breland's diary show Kinsey presenting himself as a model of he-man behavior, an image that he sought to estab-lish both by deeds and by contrasting his own ruggedness and stamina with the tenderfooted softness of his students. When Coon cut his finger one day, Breland noted that "Jim . . . nearly fainted during the process & was kidded considerably over it."[73] According to Kinsey's code, out-doorsmen were supposed to be unaffected by the sight of blood.

The same code made Kinsey eschew soft, warm beds in tourist camps in favor of sleeping on the ground in a tent beneath the stars. Breland's diary is filled with complaints about Kinsey's disdain for tourist camps and his romantic celebration of the great outdoors. On one occasion when they had reached a town too late to find a camping place, Breland gloats, "We put up in a hotel, much to K's disgust." Another entry finds an exasperated Breland declaring, "Wish to hell Kinsey would have to sleep out with the coyotes for a year or two since he hates so much to sleep in a bed."[74]

As the trip progressed, Kinsey's efforts to establish his dominance became more blatant. On one evening when the temperature plunged, he ridiculed his students for taking added precautions against the cold. Breland wrote, "Sure was cold during the night. Jim & I had our hunting coats over us much to K's disgust, but before morning he got cold as h[ell] himself." Similarly, Kinsey tried to prove his superiority through direct competition. Breland described a day of mountain climbing in which Kinsey tried to bait him by implying he could not keep pace.[75]

For four and a half months, Kinsey did not see his wife, just as the young men who accompanied him did not see their girlfriends. To combat the loneliness, Kinsey designated in advance a series of towns in Mexico where letters could be sent. As the months passed, Breland received a mound of letters from home, including many from his sweetheart, Nellie, whom he later married. When the group reached Monterey, for example, there were nine letters waiting for him, five from his girlfriend and four from his parents. "Gosh, sure was glad to hear from my sweetie," a delighted Breland wrote in his diary. "K. went right up in the air because he didn't get a darn thing—tickled me."[76]

Still, letters from Nellie arrived sporadically, and Kinsey proved highly adept at exploiting Breland's loneliness. Repeating the behavior that had upset Rainwater, Kinsey initiated a series of graphic discussions about sex. Judging from Breland's diary, he knew which buttons to push. A few weeks after they had left Bloomington, Breland and Kinsey spent the afternoon together in Nuevo Laredo (Coon stayed behind in camp), where, according to Breland, they "had quite an interesting conversation." Breland provided few details of their discussion, other than saying, "I was amused at K. speaking of tasty morsels and explosions."[77] From the context, however, it is clear that "explosions" meant ejaculations. Apparently, Kinsey had evoked the widely held notion that male sexuality could best be understood as a closed plumbing system, a system that obligated men to vent their sexual urges periodically or risk orgasmic explosions. Demonstrating how well he had learned the lesson, Breland wrote Kinsey the following year, "I have heard that a large amount of pressure can be created within various organs if they are deprived of their regular exercise for three months!"[78]

Breland's diary suggests that the three engaged in sexual activity, with Kinsey and Breland showing Coon the way. In a reference at once tantalizing and elliptical, Breland described what happened one evening: "After supper told 'bed time' stories & initiated Jim. Some party!" Later in the week, Kinsey orchestrated another sexual discussion, presumably to stir up interest in a second "party." A hot and bothered Breland confessed that he "liked to have gone up in smoke during our bull session before going to bed, but didn't." While Breland's diary does not say whether another "party" extinguished his fire, two days later found him fully recovered, so much so, in fact, that he was able to replace Kinsey as the interlocutor. His entry for the day in question concluded with the line "I read the boys a bed time story about our recent escapade."[79] Breland's reference to his companions as "the boys" strongly suggests that Kinsey had succeeded in his effort to re-create the adolescent atmosphere of summer camps.

On at least one occasion, Mexican storytellers titillated "the boys." Toward the end of their journey through Mexico, Kinsey's party loaded his truck on a boxcar and headed south toward Guatemala by train. Just before they reached Tapachula, a man who "talked English" entered their car and struck up a conversation, boasting of his sexual exploits and assuring them "that some of the females around here were sure too hot for him!" The conductor seconded these reports. Just as they were preparing for bed, the conductor "came back & started a bull session," wrote Breland. "He talked for about 2 hours & really did tell us some interesting things," including "his experiences in Tehauatepec." According to Breland, the conductor said that "if a mother liked your looks, if you were a healthy specimen & preferably white that [*sic*] the parents would ask you to screw their daughter as they wanted to improve the race." The conductor boasted that during a trip to Guatemala a few years earlier "he and several others had 'served' the daughters of the communities." Even more remarkable, the conductor explained "that if you were to see a girl that you would like to screw that you would go to her mother & strike a bargain with her & as long as you were in town you could keep her!" Apparently, the conductor also told them stories about prepubescent girls, for as Breland wrote in his diary, "He told us other things about things lacking hairs!"[80]

Breland's diary also chronicled the bathing customs in rural Mexico. At one point, they stopped to bathe in a river only to find a group of women already in the water. Breland described the bathers as being "in various stages of nudity—except, unfortunately none were completely nude." One woman "even pulled off her dress down to the very thing she was wearing in bathing without the least hesitation." "That sure was bad on me!" Breland moaned. Yet, instead of leaving the river to the women, the men plunged right in. "We went down to the river apiece & bathed in full sight of several females but that didn't bother us," wrote Breland, "Cause we sure were dirty."[81]

A few days later, Breland explained how river bathing could position them to look up the skirts of peasants who did not wear underwear. Noting that they swam under a bridge earlier that day "with the market women going across above," he called the view overhead "Some stuff!"[82] Though his companions had no way of knowing it, Kinsey was no doubt taking advantage of the same sort of situations to observe them. Not that

Kinsey was lacking in opportunities to see his young companions naked. He made certain of that.

Long before this expedition, Kinsey had instituted a strict policy of daily baths on field trips, a practice he himself had followed since his days as a Boy Scout and no doubt had learned from the Boy Scout manual. Over time, Kinsey had become a fanatic on this point. Whenever he took students into the field, he ordered them to shower daily. And the shower had to be cold, not hot. Here Kinsey was preaching what he practiced. Ever since his Scout days, he had taken cold showers in the morning, a habit he continued for life. During his field trips with graduate students, he began each day in the field with a cold shower or, if they were camping, bathed in a stream or in a lake. He forced the young men who came along to follow his example. "I don't know why, but he was a stickler for taking a bath at least once a day," declared Rainwater. "And it was just about a requirement. And he'd get mad with you if you didn't."[83]

Unless the weather was freezing, no one was exempt. During a field trip to West Virginia, Herman T. Spieth and a student named Ramon Kessler tried to skip a day. Describing the incident to Voris, Kinsey wrote, "You may know of the scrap I had with Kessler and Spieth one day in West Virginia. When I discovered they had side-stepped the bath, I sent them back to their room, and like good boys they disrobed & took to the water."[84] As this incident suggests, some (perhaps all) of Kinsey's students disliked being treated like children. "His insistence upon a shower, even on the coldest mornings, always meant that we were wide awake," recalled Robert Bugbee, another former student, "even though we sometimes felt that it was something of an injustice in unheated motels in late October or early November."[85]

Those who refused to bathe paid the price. During a field trip through the Southeast in 1931, Kinsey finally encountered a student, Ancil Holloway, who would not obey the rules. Over a five-day period, Holloway skipped three baths; and when Kinsey confronted him, he calmly stood his ground. "After all due warnings," wrote Kinsey, "I left him in southern Tennessee—at Columbia," a mountainous region hundreds of miles from Bloomington. Abandoned by his professor, Holloway had to make his way home alone.[86]

For his part, Kinsey felt nothing but righteous indignation. Defiance of this magnitude could not go unpunished. After describing the incident to Voris, Kinsey justified his stern treatment of Holloway: "Discipline man!— what with our difficulties in keeping decent in field work anyway." Kinsey also stressed that Holloway would not be included in the upcoming expedition to Mexico unless he apologized and promised to mend his ways. Smugly, Kinsey expressed the hope that Holloway would learn something from their "scrap," explaining "perhaps we can teach him some hygiene and discipline before we are done trying to make a taxonomist out of him."[87]

Once people on campus heard about what happened, the Holloway affair caused a flap. The zoology department's annual picnic followed the incident by a mere week, and Kinsey and Holloway found themselves at the center of a staged event. One of the professors, George W. D. Hamlett, an embryologist and native Texan described by a colleague as "a character" with a "Texan idea about free and easy dealings," presented Holloway with a pair of roller skates and a washcloth, declaring that he might need one or the other if he ever accompanied Kinsey on another field trip. Not backing down an inch, Holloway replied, "Thanks for the gift and I'll use which one I damn please."[88]

The Holloway affair quickly became part of the Kinsey folklore at Indiana University. Most observers saw it as an example of Kinsey's authoritarian manner and rigid standards. But the affair also exposed his intense need to dominate his students. Holloway had challenged his authority, and Kinsey dealt with him summarily.

In all probability, Kinsey's avid interest in his students' personal hygiene reflected deep undercurrents of voyeurism and exhibitionism. For Kinsey not only ordered his students to bathe; he routinely checked while they were showering, ostensibly to make certain they were complying with his orders. Nor was he hesitant about putting his own body on display. Instead of maintaining his privacy, Kinsey bathed with his students.

Like Rainwater, Breland did not suspect Kinsey of exhibitionism, but Breland, too, found his mentor's behavior odd. Most college professors did not display their bodies in public, even when removed from civilization and limited to the company of men. Breland's diary contains numerous references to outdoor baths, including one that read, "Took a bath in some rancher's watering tank. Some sight of a college professor."[89] As the weeks passed, however, he apparently grew accustomed to seeing Kinsey naked. Breland stopped mentioning the topic in his diary. For his part, Kinsey went right on striding about camp naked. In fact, he enjoyed exhibiting himself so much that he apparently asked (or at a minimum allowed) a student to take a photograph of him in the raw during another bathing episode. Among the surviving photographs from Mexico is a picture of Kinsey standing knee deep in the river, shot at a profile with his flaccid penis in stark relief, while one of his students looks directly at him from shore.[90]

Like their predecessors on field trips, Breland and Coon eventually got their fill of Kinsey's orders to bathe. "Such a mania for baths I've never seen," groaned Breland to his diary. By early November, the weather had grown bitterly cold. Breland complained, "Cold as mischief. Tried to piss & could hardly find the faucet!" Every morning they arose to frost and ice. Even their camp bucket "had a skin of ice on it." Describing what happened when they came upon a large crater lake, Breland snarled, "K. the jackass wanted a bath so down we went. Was it cold! I hardly got wet when out I came again & the others did too."[91]

A few days later, the group encountered another crater lake, but Coon balked at bathing. "K & I took another bath," wrote Breland, "but Jim said it was too cold & didn't. Surprisingly K. hardly said anything, but I guess because Jim has been puny lately." Nor was Coon alone in feeling under the weather. "Well, all three of us have a blinking cold now," added Breland in a huff. "Every day I think mine is going away, but each time it succeeds in coming back. Damn it anyway!"[92]

The evening they reached Tampico, Breland noted that Kinsey acted "the usual damn fool." Breland was certain that Kinsey's foul mood was prompted by his grudging decision to allow them to sleep in a hotel. "Griped and sulked about everything, I guess because he couldn't sleep in his damn, prick nibbling tent, the son of a bitch!", Breland conjectured. Assuming that "prick nibbling tent" means what it says (and Breland was a man who usually meant what he said), we begin to understand Breland's hostility and anxiety toward his mentor. It is hard not to suspect that oral sex was going down under canvas tops. At any rate, Breland's diary strongly suggests that he felt increasingly uncomfortable about Kinsey's sexual interests.

By the end of the trip, Breland clearly did not want to be alone with Kinsey. His mentor had other plans. They traveled by boat for part of the trip back to the United States, and the day before their departure the two men spent the evening sitting on the dock talking. Breland noted in his diary, "He gave me instructions in various things." No doubt, Breland knew what was coming, as he was wise by then to Kinsey's tactic of talking about sex in order to pave the way for some sort of sexual activity. The following evening, they boarded the boat, and Breland recorded what happened: "K. & I unfortunately got in the same cabin. . . . Went to bed about 10:30 & K. amused himself by giving me instructions in technique."[93] While Breland did not spell out what happened, it seems likely that Kinsey masturbated, forcing his student to become a captive audience.

Following their return to the United States, Breland finished his Ph.D. and left Bloomington in 1936 to begin his teaching career at North Dakota State College. Like Voris, he kept in close touch with Kinsey following graduation, and they wrote often during the first four or five years after Breland left Indiana. Most of their correspondence centered on their careers, the focus one would expect. Typically, Kinsey would discuss his most recent theories and discoveries and the professional response to his publications; and Breland, in turn, would keep Kinsey abreast of his research and writing, all the while beseeching his mentor to help him secure a position at a better university. And Kinsey did precisely that. Thanks to Kinsey's strong support, Breland secured a position in 1938 at the University of Texas in Austin, a first-rate institution, where he spent the rest of his career.

Yet work was by no means their only topic of discussion. Kinsey sent Breland erotic books and poems and passed along gossip about the department and the university. Like his evening talks with students on field trips, Kinsey's letters to Breland (and to others) were awash in juvenile banter. All the references dealt with heterosexual topics, a fact that is entirely in keeping with Kinsey's approach.

Most of Breland's letters to Kinsey have survived, and the image they convey is that of a horny adolescent who felt compelled to voice his every erotic fantasy and urge. Perhaps this portrait matched the man, but the image seems overdrawn. Breland, it must be remembered, was under strong pressure to preserve a good relationship with his mentor. Though he had finished his degree, he still needed Kinsey's professional support to win fellowships, to secure a position at a better university, and to publish. In other words, he had much to gain by currying his favor and much to lose by alienating him. Thus, the suspicion lingers that Breland, like Rainwater, took his cues from Kinsey, in effect saying what he thought his mentor wanted to hear.

With few exceptions, Kinsey was cautious about what he put on paper. Copies of many of Kinsey's letters to Breland are missing, either because Kinsey destroyed them or others did so later. Moreover, when he did write something he did not want known publicly, Kinsey instructed former students to destroy his letters. Their replies proved that they dutifully executed his orders. Nevertheless, the following excerpt from a letter from Breland leaves few mysteries regarding the contents of Kinsey's missing letter or his motives for wanting it destroyed:

> I think it as a good thing that you sent only half of the "Diary of the on again, off again boys." By gad, that is one of the best I ever read. What did Mrs. K. say when you came home with your pants ruined after copying it? Or did there happen to be a suitable quiff around to receive a deposit? Speaking of deposits, has [Bugbee] managed to deposit any "ears of corn" within a certain pudding that I mentioned last time? I think said pie would make very nice dessert, especially if it were chewed thoroughly. Yep, you can be sure that all incriminating evidence is destroyed. I'll bet Uncle Samuel would bite the end of his joy stick if he knew how we defamed the mails. I haven't destroyed

said diary, however. Since it does not have any incriminating marks on it, think I'll frame it! And incidentally, I think I will be sufficiently recuperated to take some more of it when you can find time. That surely was a humdinger.[94]

Over time, Kinsey became quite skilled at this game. He made a practice of doling out erotic material in pieces to titillate his former students and build their interest in future installments. On another occasion, he sent Breland half an erotic poem. Breland replied,

> And speaking of appendages, by all that's holy, I'm glad that I didn't read the little "private" message in one of my coed sections. I'm afraid that the next day the paper would have come out with headlines, "Zoology instructor castrated for biting coed's tit!" Unfortunately, I have a few students who make me feel like doing things described in the poem. Damn it, sometimes I wish I were in a boy's school. Darn it, after reading the missive, I had to wait quite a while before I could trust myself to go to class. The middle leg for some unknown reason kept hitting me in the face! Don't be so blooming stingy—let's have the rest of it! This was only a teaser. But I warn you, the consequences might be bad! But I'll be willing to take the chance.[95]

This passage is typical of the adolescent prattle that runs through Breland's letters. When not discussing entomology, he and Kinsey sounded like naughty boys in a locker room. During his first term at North Dakota, for example, Breland wrote inquiring after Jim Coon, the undergraduate whom they had "initiated" during their trip to Mexico the preceding year. "I hope that Jim doesn't become overly educated from reading my letters," snickered Breland. "You know, we would feel terrible if, because of our influence, several sets of quintuplets would shout 'popa' when Jim passed. At any rate, please tell him that I wish him the best of luck in his 'tom cat[ting]' around!" Breland concluded with the postscript "Tell him never to pay over $3.00."[96]

Breland returned again and again to what he had learned from the experiences they shared in Mexico. On one occasion, Breland reminded Kinsey of the freedom they had enjoyed in Latin cultures to exhibit their naked bodies publicly. Responding to a letter from Kinsey that has not survived, Breland wrote,

> I can assure you, sir, that I will keep all strings out to their fullest extent—except of course those strings that happen to be attached to my person. These, except under rare circumstances, such as bathing conditions in Mexico and Guatemala, are not for public consumption or observation. Although I'll admit that at times I see certain members of the female populace, whom I would like to have absorb certain appendages![97]

Not all of Breland's sexual musings came in response to Kinsey's initiatives. On occasion, Breland took the lead. In one letter, he pleaded with Kinsey to send him more juicy tidbits, complaining, "I haven't heard any I.U. gossip in so long that I feel like an outcast." Breland was especially keen to learn more about a particular graduate student, a man who had recently married and whose wife must have been very attractive. "I'll bet he has learned that he won't have to go very far from home to do his tom catting," declared Breland. "Something tells me that his old lady could screw the horns off a billy goat!!"[98]

For his part, Kinsey was constantly stoking the fire. In addition to stories and poems, he recommended recent scholarly books in the field. In the fall of 1937, he sent Breland a reference to Bronislaw Malinowski's *The Sexual Life of Savages in North-western Melanesia* (1929). Breland replied, "I haven't has [*sic*] yet had the opportunity to see the book you mentioned, but I would surely like to. I'll bet this Malinowski person got more kick out of working for his LLD than most people do! Wonder if the Harvard people meant this degree to imply that he was a 'Lingering Lascivious Dabbler?' At any rate, I envy him his dabbling!"[99]

In addition to maintaining an intimate correspondence with Breland, Kinsey bombarded him with invitations for field trips and visits to Bloomington. Although Breland tactfully declined all the field trips, he and his wife, Nellie, were guests in Kinsey's home on at least one occasion, in June 1937. Save for a brief reference to this visit in one of Kinsey's letters, their correspondence sheds no light on what happened. Yet this much can be stated with certainty. Nellie Breland hated Alfred C. Kinsey. More than half a century after her husband finished his Ph.D. at Indiana University, she adamantly refused to be interviewed about Kinsey. "He was a dirty old man," she declared over the telephone. "He really hurt us. We were just kids from Mississippi. We didn't know anything."[100] There were no more visits to the Kinseys' home.

Kinsey's behavior with his graduate students showed the risks a sex-obsessed man would take in exchange for a modicum of erotic satisfaction. By the mid-1930s, he had succeeded in reconstructing the adolescent male world of his summer camps, where sexual conduct often slipped the reins of civilized morality. Not only was he able to suffuse his field trips with sexual discussions and sexual behavior, but he managed to keep at least two of his prize students, Voris and Breland, in his orbit long after they had finished their degrees. How much warmth, support, and emotional sustenance Kinsey drew from these relationships is unknown, but the effort he put into them tells us something of the value he attached to them.

Something akin to compulsion drove Kinsey to take risks with his students, as though part of him thrived on danger. Tripp, who knew Kinsey during his final years, noticed this trait. Commenting on the photograph of Voris that Kinsey kept on his desk, Tripp remarked that it "was the most daring thing imaginable." Yet risk taking, he explained, was "absolutely Kinseyesque because he loved to skate very near the edge of the cliff." It all came down to the fact that Kinsey "liked to shock people" in order to demonstrate that he was "absolutely . . . unconstrained by moralistic forms."[101] Put somewhat differently, Kinsey courted danger to show he had freed himself from the moral restraints of his childhood. Locked into a permanent state of rebellion, he wore calculated acts of defiance as a badge of independence.

Bearing in mind this proclivity, one can make sense of a host of Kinsey's puzzling behaviors. Consider the matter of his counseling graduate students on sexual matters. At a time when most college professors would not have dared to discuss sexual issues explicitly with their students, Kinsey all but advertised his services.[102] He let students on campus know that if they had any questions or problems of a sexual nature, he was the man to see. According to Robert Bugbee, Kinsey "told his graduate students that if they ever wanted any advice or wanted to talk to him about any problems—and he mentioned specifically sexual problems—to feel free to come to him."[103]

In all probability, these invitations began in the late 1920s. Certainly, by the mid-1930s, Kinsey was putting out the word that students who wanted to talk about their private lives should see him. Many did, giving Kinsey vital information in his search for knowledge about human sexuality, a quest never far removed from his own need for self-understanding. Even in these early conferences, Kinsey was acutely aware of the importance of preserving confidentiality. One of his laboratory assistants recalled, "We girls were asked to take our work into an adjoining room after a sudden lowering of voices in the course of a routine sort of conversation with a graduate student."[104]

While Kinsey targeted graduate students for his sexual talks, he had similar discussions with at least one colleague, Robert Kroc, the young endocrinologist. From the moment Kroc arrived, his field seemed to fascinate Kinsey. During Kroc's first few years in Bloomington, he and Kinsey gradually became friends. Kroc often joined him at noon for a brown-bag lunch in Kinsey's office, where they discussed their mutual interest in endocrinology.[105] No doubt, part of Kinsey's attention could be explained by the thyroid imbalance his son Donald had developed before his death, but Kinsey had another reason for keeping abreast with developments in the field. Endocrinology promised to shed light on human sexual behavior. As one of the hottest new fields in science, endocrinology spawned a school of "glandular psychologists" who argued that research on the ductless glands might one day yield important data that could help explain human behavior, including sexual behavior. Significantly, not a few endocrinologists suggested that homosexuality might be caused by some sort of chemical imbalance. Not surprisingly, then, Kinsey followed developments in the field closely. He subscribed to the *Journal of Endocrinology* soon after it began publication in the 1930s and read every issue immediately after it appeared in print.

During their brown-bag lunches, Kinsey often discussed how sex research might be improved. More than half a century later, Kroc remembered Kinsey's puzzling over how a scientist might go about devising methods for compiling valid data on people's sexual behavior. Kroc also recalled "trading information and asking each other questions and learning each other's case histories." "I learned as much about Kinsey's own case history as he did of mine," Kroc related.[106] These discussions add one more piece of evidence suggesting that by the mid-1930s Kinsey was intensely interested in human sexuality and was extremely knowledgeable about developments in sex research. More important, Kroc's recollections also demonstrate that Kinsey was pondering how to develop a methodology for collecting reliable data on human sexuality years before he officially became a sex researcher.

Indeed, by the early 1930s, Kinsey was exploring sexuality in a variety of ways. Among all the Kinsey folklore in Bloomington, none has been more enduring than the stories about his gardening apparel. Family members, friends, neighbors, and strangers who happened to pass by his house and saw him at work in his garden offer strikingly similar descriptions of his clothing. Robert S. Tangeman, a music professor and Kinsey neighbor, described his outfit as "abbreviated garb—scanty shorts,"[107] while his daughter Joan called it "a loincloth type of thing, as brief as possible so that he had a minimum of clothing on so that it wouldn't offend people if they saw him."[108]

In September 1934, Kinsey wrote Voris, "Following your lead, I have adopted shorts—nothing more—as the garden costume, and have the best tan, even more than I ever thought a bleached blonde could have. And the most glorious live feeling that my skin has ever known." Preening his feathers, Kinsey boasted further, "Incidentally, I weigh just 20 pounds less than I did in February—from 162 to 142—and practically all that came off the waistline. Had all my trousers let out last February and now every pair is in folds at the waist. I shall see to it that something or other keeps that winter damage off of me this year."[109]

Kate Mueller, who served as dean of women at Indiana University in the

1930s and 1940s, recalls seeing Kinsey in his garden during the summer she arrived in Bloomington. The year was 1936. Her parents had come to visit, and she and her husband had taken them to church. On their way home, they walked by Kinsey's house, dressed in their "Sunday best," as she put it. In his front yard, they spotted a sign saying "The Garden Is Open," which was Kinsey's way of inviting neighbors to share the beauty of his creation. According to Mueller, the following scene repeated itself many times: "There would be Kinsey in his bare feet and nothing on him at all—brown as a berry—except what we referred to as the G-string, which was, I suppose, a kind of male bikini. He would stop and want to be introduced and would be very affable and tell you more about the garden and where to go and so forth. But it was . . . kind of [a] shock to [my] parents."[110]

At least one observer thought she understood what Kinsey was up to. June Keisler, who served as one of his laboratory assistants, recalled that he would burst into his office and proclaim to everyone at large how he had spent the morning in his garden "as always stripped to bathing trunks" and then would proceed to speculate about how he thought his neighbors "were possibly getting used to seeing him so, although a few years ago he had used to shock them." To Keisler, it looked as if Kinsey was playing a game. "I think he rather enjoyed 'shocking' people," she observed. "When he spoke thus he was always, to me," she explained, "rather like a small boy using a new word which he suspected might not meet with approval and then waiting rather hopefully for an explosion."[111]

Kinsey's loincloth was a uniform of rebellion. By donning an outfit that violated community standards, he was hoisting the flag of defiance. Kinsey was testing the boundaries of community tolerance, even as he registered his contempt for community controls over his behavior. The fact that he often chose Sundays to work in his garden and open it to the public made his choice of clothing all the more telling. The contrast between his appearance and that of passersby and visitors to his garden was acute, juxtaposing, as it did, a seminaked middle-aged male and people dressed in their "Sunday best."

If Kinsey's gardening outfit denoted defiance, it was also a warning signal. His inner tensions had sharpened his taste for danger, and those needs were beginning to spill over into unlikely places, producing behavior that was calculated to shock. Less bold but just as telling was the manner in which Kinsey used his intellect to combat his anxieties. More and more, he put his powerful mind to work learning everything he could about human sexual behavior from the scientific literature. He was beginning to see science as his best hope for liberating himself from the guilt of his childhood. Through science, he could learn to become a skillful, uninhibited lover. In addition, he could escape narrow-minded, wrong-headed, and mean-spirited sexual repression and develop a weapon for combating the prudery he despised. Yet when Kinsey turned to the scientific literature on human sexual behavior, he did not like what he found. The scientific literature on human sexuality was in worse shape than the mindless dribble that passed for taxonomy. And Kinsey knew what to do about that.

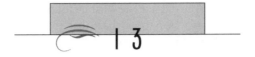

"There Isn't Much Science There"

arriage is a science," wrote Honoré de Balzac.[1] In the decades between World War I and World War II, many middle-class Americans endorsed this proposition. They wanted to believe that couples could build strong marriages by approaching their differences with intelligence and reason, making the compromises and adjustments that would enable people of good will who cared for one another to remain together. Few couples of their generation tested this proposition more severely than the Kinseys.

Over the years following their honeymoon, the Kinseys sought to combat their ignorance and guilt with knowledge and reason.[2] They were not alone. By the 1920s and 1930s, many middle-class Americans were eager to discuss a variety of issues raised by social hygienists and sexual reformers. Should sex be restricted to procreation, or was it a good thing in its own right? Was masturbation harmful? Would petting lead to premarital intercourse? Would premarital intercourse spoil a couple's chances for finding happiness in marriage? Was oral sex perverted? In keeping with other areas of their lives, middle-class Americans expected experts to come up with answers. How else could the public resolve the conflicts between prescriptive morality and private behavior?

In the 1920s, the literature on human sexuality contained little that appealed to Kinsey. At first, he probably consulted the traditional marriage manuals, as his immediate goal was to achieve a mutually gratifying sex life with Clara. Most marriage manuals mirrored the attitudes of purity crusaders and sex hygienists, many of whom were ambivalent about sex. More interested in controlling passion than in promoting pleasure, they either ignored sexual technique or approached it in euphemistic terms.

A handful of writers challenged the ethic of restraint and control that undergirded traditional morality. As a group, they were distinctly positive about sex, focused on experience, and stressed the importance of mutually satisfying sexual relationships. Conspicuous among these advisers was Robert Latou Dickinson, the author of *A Thousand Marriages: A Medical Study of Sex Adjustment* (1929).[3] Dickinson was in the vanguard of a small group of sexual reformers who pioneered what the historian Paul Robinson has called a modern approach to human sexuality.[4] Beginning in the late nineteenth century and continuing into the twentieth, these reformers mounted a potent attack on rigid controls. Arguing that sex was neither morally depraved nor physically debilitating, they struggled to change the public's thinking. On the one hand, they served as theorists of a new sexual ethic designed to promote tolerance and diversity; on the other, they became apologists, in Robinson's words, for "those apparently deviant forms of sexuality that the Victorians, with their exclusive commitment to adult, genital, heterosexual intercourse, had been reluctant even to recognize."[5]

Most sexual reformers were meliorists who sought to balance civilized morality and individual happiness. Realizing that few Americans wished to abolish all social and legal restraints on sexual behavior, reformers set out not to destroy conventional morality but to soften some of its harsher aspects. Consequently, they concentrated on loosening restraints on married couples. Reformers told couples to enjoy sex without guilt—not all sexual acts, to be sure, but the list was fairly inclusive, provided nothing "abnormal" occurred.

In practically every other area of life, middle-class Americans were being told they had a right to be happy. Why should sex be different? Everywhere the austere values seemed to be in retreat. Instead of preaching prudence and thrift, businessmen in the 1920s, aided by professional advertisers on Madison Avenue, were pushing instant gratification, telling people to satisfy their needs at once by buying goods on credit. And as the rules of economic life changed, so did the restraints on private behavior. Passion, like capital, was to be spent, not husbanded.

Over time, many Americans had come to regard a good sex life as crucial to their happiness. Urban experiences and values shaped much of this transformation. The anonymity of the city weakened the bonds of family life, encouraging many urbanites to experiment with their private behavior. This was particularly true of the working class, which by the 1920s included large numbers of immigrants, as well as old-stock, blue-collar workers. Many young and unattached workers—male and female alike—ignored middle-class warnings about the wages of sin. At night, they congregated in parks, dance halls, saloons, penny arcades, and movie shows to relax and have fun in the company of the opposite sex. Shocked by such casualness and freedom, middle-class alarmists accused the lower class of moral laxity. Sex researchers later confirmed their suspicions, at least with regard to men. Writing in the 1940s, Kinsey reported (perhaps with some exaggeration) that working-class adolescent males learned "that it is possible to josh any passing girl, ask for a simple social date, and, inside of a few minutes, suggest intercourse."[6]

Reformers used the rising divorce rate as proof of the need for change. Between 1870 and 1920, the divorce rate rose fifteenfold, and by 1924 one marriage out of seven ended in divorce. Many reformers blamed these figures on poor sexual adjustment in marriage. The best way to save the institution of marriage, they insisted, was for couples to enjoy more and better sex at home.[7] Sexual enthusiasts like Dickinson abolished the controls on passion, ended restrictions on experimentation (albeit within marriage), and acknowledged the sexual equality of men and women. Removed from the shadows and rescued from euphemisms, sex had become, in the words of one manual writer, "the foundation of marriage."[8]

By touting a good sex life as the key to happy marriage, Dickinson and other reformers put science on record as supporting vigorous, mutually satisfying sex. In addition, they offered people detailed instructions on how to improve their sex lives. In place of sexual inhibitions, they suggested openness and candor; in place of ambivalence, enthusiasm; in place of ineptness, well-honed skills. A new set of attitudes toward human sexuality had made its debut, championed by experts claiming the authority of science.

In addition to Dickinson's *A Thousand Marriages*, Kinsey must have come across another popular book, the American edition of Theodore Van de Velde's *Ideal Marriage: Its Physiology and Technique*. Although he claimed to write for other physicians, Van de Velde, a Dutch gynecologist, also hoped to reach intelligent laymen. His book was aimed at husbands in particular, he explained, because "they are naturally educators and initiators of their wives in sexual matters, and yet they often lack, not only the qualifications of a leader and initiator, but also those necessary for equal partnership."[9]

Published originally in the Netherlands in 1926, *Ideal Marriage* was the ultimate "how to do it" book. The English translation appeared in 1930 in the United States, where it became an instant hit. Its candid, demystifying treatment of human sexuality, its wide tolerance for sexual experimentation, and its celebration of passion struck responsive chords in many middle-class Americans. In place of ambivalence about sex, Van de Velde offered unblushing enthusiasm; in place of restraints, he offered freedom. Warmly received by professional and lay readers alike, *Ideal Marriage* remained the best-selling marriage manual in the United States until Dr. David Reuben published *Everything You Always Wanted to Know about Sex, But Were Afraid to Ask* (1969). Still, as late as 1951, *Ideal Marriage* was kept under the counter in many bookstores, even in cosmopolitan New York.[10]

In large measure, Van de Velde's success stemmed from his candor. *Ideal Marriage* was not a book for the fainthearted. His goal was to make every couple expert lovers, and he did not shrink from showing them how. Van de Velde devoted 321 pages (not counting the illustrations) to analyzing the sexual impulse in men and women and describing with astonishing detail the various sexual acts. His discussion of techniques alone filled five chapters, complete with explicit drawings of male and female physiology.

Van de Velde endorsed a variety of behavior. "Ideal Marriage," he declared, "permits normal, physiological activities the fullest scope, in all desirable and delectable ways; these we shall envisage without prudery, but *with deepest reverence for true chastity.*"[11] He specifically recommended the "genital kiss," condemned as sexual perversion in many texts, "to overcome frigidity and fear in hitherto inexperienced women who have had no erotic practice, and are as yet hardly capable of specific sexual desire."[12] Clearly, Van de Velde was at war with a system of morality that produced the ignorance that bedeviled the Kinseys on their honeymoon.

At first, the Kinseys may have taken heart from the words of marriage advisers like Dickinson and Van de Velde. So long as he thought there was any hope of finding sexual fulfillment with Clara, Kinsey had much to learn from experts who presented human sexuality in positive terms and offered candid discussions of physiology and techniques. Given his need to excel and his dogged determination, he probably tried hard to become a great lover. And assuming he spoke the truth when he boasted to graduate students about Clara's responsiveness, she was a willing partner. It is easy to imagine the two of them devouring marriage manuals, discussing what they read, and trying out what they learned in a joint effort to free themselves from guilt and inhibitions.

In short order, however, Kinsey became sharply critical of the marriage manual literature. On a professional level, he questioned its scientific validity. First, the samples were puny. A man who collected insects by the tens of thousands was not likely to be impressed by a physician who based his advice on a thousand marriages. As he read the marriage manual literature, Kinsey's sharp mind also detected vestiges of traditional morality masquerading as objective facts. In the final analysis, though, his objections were as much personal as professional. The advice literature on marriage had little to offer a man whose sexual needs could not be satisfied by heterosexual intercourse. Nothing he read addressed his need to come to terms with his own sexuality.

Consequently, marriage manuals constituted a mere way station in Kinsey's reading. What began as an effort to improve his marriage evolved into a quest for self-understanding. Over time, Kinsey broadened his reading to include the European sexologists. They appealed to Kinsey because they claimed to be men of science who would provide reliable information. Moreover, their focus on abnormal behavior offered data and theories Kinsey could test against his own experiences, offering the hope of increased self-understanding.

The scientific study of human sexuality originated in Europe during the second half of the nineteenth century. Sexologists concentrated on sexual deviancy rather than on ordinary behavior. From the outset the field was dominated by physicians who applied the methods that they had learned in studying human disease. For religious categories such as "right" and "wrong" and "moral" and "immoral," they substituted a new medical model that drew upon the language of science, employing terms such as "pathology," "deviants," and "cure." Instead of referring to debauched sinners and criminal degenerates, they spoke of diseased patients.[13] To Kinsey, this change of terminology represented progress, but he did not like where it stopped.

Before the disease model of sexual disorders could make headway with the public, physicians had to drive other claimants from the field. In effect, they had to appropriate for science issues that had belonged to religion and the law. Drawing their authority from the public's respect for science, doctors boldly asserted the exclusive right to define disease. Sexual disorders, they announced, fell squarely into the disease category. Writing in the 1880s, one physician proclaimed that "conditions once considered criminal are really pathological, and come within the province of the physician."[14]

G. Frank Lydston, a prominent Chicago physician, left no room for doubt that science would ultimately replace religion as the public's source of understanding about sexual deviance. "The subject has been until a recent date studied solely from the standpoint of the moralist," lamented

Lydston in 1889, a fact he attributed to "the indisposition of the scientific physician to study the subject." As a result, he continued, an "unfortunate class of individuals who are characterized by perverted sexuality have been viewed in the light of their moral responsibility rather than as the victims of a physical and incidentally of a mental defect."[15]

Such pronouncements served notice that medicine intended to assert its authority over sexual disorders. Though it would take decades to complete the process, doctors were dealing from a position of strength. Beginning in the second half of the nineteenth century and continuing well into the twentieth, the status of medicine rose dramatically compared with that of other professions. Among other developments, improvements in public health, the founding of research laboratories, the rise of modern hospitals, the triumph of the germ theory of disease, improvements in aseptic and antiseptic surgery, reforms in medical education, higher licensing standards, and the growth of specialization within medicine all combined to improve the quality of health care physicians gave their patients. And as their ability to diagnose and treat illnesses improved, the prestige and income of physicians rose accordingly.[16]

Over time, the public's faith in doctors increased dramatically. Because they commanded an esoteric body of knowledge vital to the public's well-being, physicians demanded and received deference and professional autonomy, particularly in the United States, where medicine developed a virtual monopoly on health care. Not that this pattern was peculiar to medicine. By the turn of the century, the United States had developed an urban, industrialized, bureaucratic society in which experts of all kinds were able to translate knowledge into cultural authority. Everywhere one looked, the experts stood tall. Economists, engineers, city planners, architects, investment bankers, stockbrokers, and lawyers all commanded knowledge that made the public seek out their services and defer to their judgment.

But physicians stood apart. As the experts who alone could divine the mysteries of illness and apply the magic remedies of science, they became America's new secular priesthood. They, and they alone, defined diseases and health. By and large, their edicts encountered remarkably little resistance. The same faith in science that made Americans look to the laboratory and the test tube to solve problems also made them defer to medical authority.

Once they placed sex under medicine's purview, physicians began surveying the terrain of sexual diseases. Much as physical scientists had mapped out the periodic table of the elements, physicians chartered the varieties of sexual behavior, creating a kind of sexual taxonomy. No form of behavior—masturbation, homosexuality, masochism, sadism, fetishism, transvestism, exhibitionism, necrophilia—escaped professional notice. Physicians created a huge literature on homosexuality in particular, producing more than one thousand publications on this topic in the single decade between 1898 and 1908.[17]

Most of the literature on homosexuality described individual cases, as physicians struggled to construct a new disease entity from behavior they regarded as threatening and bizarre. Much of what they wrote was confused or contradictory, and for decades physicians could not agree on a name for what they were studying. Some physicians spoke of "tribad," "invert," or "urning," while others used labels such as "third sex," "homosexual," and "invert." Nor could they agree on what caused sexual disorders. Many were biological determinists who thought that human behavior was largely shaped by heredity, which led them to explain behavioral disorders in somatic as opposed to psychological terms.

The tilt toward somatic theories reflected important changes within medicine. Appearing at a time when the medical profession was fragmenting into numerous specialties, sexology was profoundly influenced by physicians who had studied mental illnesses. The various sexual disorders were all considered forms of insanity. Just as alienists and neurologists (the two medical specialties most concerned with mental illness in the late nineteenth century) tried to discover somatic explanations for mental disorders, sexologists searched for biological causes for sexual deviance. Rejecting the moral perspective, which stressed free will and personal responsibility, many sexologists considered sexual deviance beyond the control of the individual. One school led by Havelock Ellis, the distinguished British sexologist, argued that homosexuality was congenital, while a few doctors contended that homosexuals were actually hermaphrodites—mistakes of nature who embodied elements of both sexes. Edward Carpenter and Magnus Hirschfeld later advanced a version of this theory, arguing that homosexuals could best be understood as an "intermediate sex."

Other sexologists held that sexual deviance was an acquired illness. The leading proponent of this view was Richard von Krafft-Ebing (1840–1902), the most influential sex expert of the late nineteenth century. A professor of psychiatry at the University of Vienna, he published his masterpiece, *Psychopathia Sexualis,* in 1886. The first edition, which was only 110 pages, rested on 45 case histories, but by 1903, when the twelfth edition appeared, the book had grown to 437 pages, citing some 238 cases. Employing a sober, Baconian approach, Krafft-Ebing argued that homosexuality was an acquired form of insanity, a degenerate disease (in the sense of falling away from the genus) whose onset was triggered by some form of sexual excess—typically masturbation. His reliance on degeneration theory betrayed his indebtedness to an evolutionary model of social development. For him, sexual morality and social development were organically linked.[18]

Prompted by deeply moral concerns, Krafft-Ebing worried that the savage behavior of lustful degenerates threatened "civilized morality." Since culture rested on a foundation of self-control, "civilized" sexual behavior, by definition, had to be limited to intercourse between a man and a woman within a loving marriage. Motivated by "noble and ideal sentiments," such behavior had procreation as its sole purpose. He considered all other forms of nonprocreative sexuality perversions, serving only to gratify lust. By reducing "civilized" man to a primitive savage or, worse yet, to a rutting beast of the field, nonmarital sex threatened the moral order on which civilization itself rested.[19]

Krafft-Ebing branded homosexuality a mental illness. In his case histories of homosexuals, he sought to document a family record of insanity, hysteria, epilepsy, and the like. He drew a similar portrait of sadists and masochists, two groups he studied at length (it was he who coined the terms). Convinced that the common link between sadism and masochism was the association of pain with sex, he argued that both illnesses involved gender roles. Sadism was a pathological exaggeration of the male's normal aggressive behavior and need to dominate, while masochism represented a pathological amplification of the female's urge to submit. Faced with a male masochist or a female sadist, he surmised that he was in the presence of a homosexual.[20]

Krafft-Ebing's interest in sexual pathology went beyond research. As a physician, he wanted to cure emotional disorders. He urged society to approach sexual perversions as illnesses. Calling sexual deviants "step-children of nature," he pleaded with judicial authorities in Austria to show leniency when victims of sexual compulsion appeared in court. While Krafft-Ebing's views were humane and enlightened for his day, they would not have offered Kinsey any peace of mind. Krafft-Ebing called for compassion and sympathy; he said nothing about tolerance or acceptance. There was little in his message that would have given Kinsey any comfort—unless, of course, he liked being labeled diseased, degenerate, and feminine.[21]

Nor was Krafft-Ebing's scientific method likely to impress someone with Kinsey's training in taxonomy. The Viennese doctor's sample of sexual deviants was small and select. Because he saw only people who sought medical help, his knowledge about the behavior of the general public was meager. This failing left him vulnerable to a criticism that applied with equal force to his entire field: instead of collecting enough case histories from the general population to know how people actually behaved, sexologists had labeled certain behaviors pathological on the basis of tiny, unrepresentative samples.

Sigmund Freud, the best-known theorist of sexual deviancy, shared Krafft-Ebing's belief that sexual disorders were acquired. Determined to separate psychology from biology, Freud argued that human behavior is psychologically determined. But he did not regard sexual deviants as degenerates. Rather, he saw them as victims of faulty development. Freud was too good a biologist not to acknowledge the role of heredity in human development or to recognize the possibilities in the interaction of heredity and environment.[22] Still, by locating the origins of sexual disorders in the patient's failure to resolve the Oedipus complex during childhood, Freud's theory of sexual pathology assigned primary importance to mental processes. In Freud's view, homosexual boys became overly attached to their mothers and gradually identified with them rather than with their fathers. Instead of finding a substitute self in women who would love them as their mothers once had, homosexual males turned to masculine sexual objects.

There Freud let the matter rest. He did not write extensively on homosexuality, and the little he said was generally sympathetic. With few exceptions, he refrained from labeling homosexuality as pathological. Indeed, over time, Freud became convinced that homosexuality was linked to an innate bisexuality embedded in the human psyche. Virtually all children, he insisted, went through a phase (often around puberty) of being sexually attracted to members of the same sex. "I have never carried through any psychoanalysis of a man or a woman," wrote Freud in 1905, "without discovering a very significant homosexual tendency."[23] For most people, these tendencies were "deflected" from their original targets and were channeled into social instincts, such as friendship and "the general love for mankind."[24] However, a few people fixated at this stage and became homosexuals because they failed to resolve Oedipal tensions.

Freud's theory of sexual pathology assumed a model for "normal" development, one that rested squarely on heterosexuality. As he put it, "one of the tasks implicit in object choice [for sexual desire] is that it should find its way to the opposite sex."[25] But in Freud's hands this model never acquired the prescriptive tyranny it held for others. Nor did he insist that psychotherapy offered much promise of curing homosexuals. On the contrary, Freud cautioned, "in general to undertake to convert a fully developed homosexual into a heterosexual is not much more promising than to do the reverse, only that for good practical reasons the latter is never attempted."[26] In contrast to the master, many of Freud's disciples used his theories to label homosexuality pathological. American analysts, such as Karen Horney, Harry Stack Sullivan, and Lawrence Kubie, insisted that homosexuality was a disease that required medical treatment.

Freud's explanation of sadomasochism drew upon the same theory of sexual pathology. In broad terms, he agreed with Krafft-Ebing's view that sadism in men was a pathological exaggeration of the male's aggressive nature and need to dominate, while masochism involved the feminine need to surrender. Yet Freud added his own psychological twist to this explanation. He saw sadism as a defense against the fear of castration—a kind of preemptive strike, by a person who did not possess enough ego strength to feel safe in a mature sexual relationship. Similarly, the masochist, seeking reassurance for a weak ego, invited punishments and humiliation as a substitute for imagined injuries of far greater magnitude. While Freud stressed that normal people possessed sadomasochistic tendencies, he placed sadomasochism squarely in the camp of pathology.

There is no way of knowing when Kinsey first encountered Freud's work, but by the 1920s Kinsey was obviously familiar with his ideas. Freud's theories (albeit in distorted forms) entered America's popular culture through the "new psychology." While much of Freud's subtlety, complexity, and intellectual elegance was lost in the translation, his popularizers succeeded in placing his theories, however imperfectly understood, in the public domain. Portraying Freud as a scientific folk hero, they made Freudian concepts such as the Oedipus complex, the unconscious, the pleasure principle, and, above all, the sexual instinct part of the language. In his manual for high school teachers (1933), Kinsey complained that too many biology texts were becoming cluttered with extraneous notions such as "Freudian complexes," the first of many potshots he would aim at Freud.[27]

Over time, Kinsey became sharply critical of Freud.[28] Freud was unquestionably the best theoretician among the sexologists, and Kinsey was instinctively wary of such men.[29] In part, Kinsey's animus derived from his own limitations, for, as Wardell Pomeroy has noted, "new theoretical concepts were not his forte."[30] According to Pomeroy, Kinsey "found himself uncomfortable in the presence of men who were extemporaneous theoreticians, as though he felt himself inferior."[31] But Pomeroy revealed another reason for Kinsey's dislike. "He once told me that before he got into sex research he had been afraid of them," declared Pomeroy. "Unbelievably, considering that he was a scientist himself, he had the layman's vague belief that psychiatrists were omniscient and could even know his inner thoughts. He felt uneasy with them."[32] In his later years, Kinsey often acted defensively toward psychiatrists, the majority of whom he regarded as enemies. It was not in his nature to submit to psychiatrists. His instinct was to criticize and belittle them, in part because he hated their theories and in part because he was jealous of their cultural authority.

Apart from personal animus, Kinsey's mistrust of theoreticians reflected his peculiar scientific specialty. As early as the 1920s, he was announcing that theory was no substitute for facts. His training in taxonomy made him demand empirical data before accepting any theory—however elegant and encompassing. Kinsey called this quality "scientific doubt." As he once explained to students, "a scientist doesn't believe things unless he has good proofs for them. He is something like the famous gentleman 'from Missouri' who 'has to be shown' things."[33]

Freud formulated his theories from a careful reading of the literature, exchanges with colleagues, self-analysis, and his own clinical practice. Kinsey was not impressed. Although he regarded Freud as a great theoretician, he considered him a poor scientist. Freud's database was simply too weak to support a large theoretical edifice. Theories had to be proved by hard data, Kinsey insisted, and hard data could be compiled only through painstaking research. And that was his forte.

There was another reason for Kinsey's dislike of Freud. Kinsey could not read Freud and feel good about himself. Freud labeled masturbation as adolescent behavior and thought that homosexuals were victims of arrested development, and he consigned sadomasochism to the world of pathology. At bottom, Freud's theories supported traditional middle-class morality. He was utterly conventional in arguing that heterosexual, genital union was the only mature form of adult sexual behavior, while his theory of "sublimation" could easily be read as one more addition to the long list of rationalizations about the need to restrict premarital sex.[34]

From Kinsey's perspective, then, Freud and the other sexologists were much the same. Though they tried to approach their research as disinterested scientists, their writings were hardly value-free. Sexologists understood the world not simply as scientists but as white, middle-class men who reflected the values of their class, gender, and race. With few exceptions, they both accepted and defended the gender/role arrangements of their society—arrangements they insisted were based on immutable biological differences. In broader terms, sexologists saw sexuality as reflective of female and male roles. Women were gentle, nurturing, receptive, and innocent; men were aggressive, competitive, and worldly.

Gender roles also influenced how sexologists approached sexual deviance, particularly homosexuality. Their earliest works spoke not of homosexuality but of sexual inversion, which they defined as assuming the gender role of the opposite sex, including, of course, the sexual role. As George Beard, a prominent American physician and popularizer of medical theories, explained in 1884, when "the sex is perverted, they hate the opposite sex and love their own; men become women and women men, in their tastes, conduct, character, feelings, and behavior." A male patient (who in all probability was a transsexual misdiagnosed as a homosexual) told doctors, "My feelings are exactly those of a woman. . . . As near as I can explain it, I am a woman in every detail except external appearances."[35]

At the turn of the century, sexual inversion had a much broader cultural meaning than homosexuality. It encompassed not only sexual attraction between members of the same sex but the social roles of men and women. As one doctor wrote, a trained observer could always spot lesbians by their "male characteristics," explaining that "they wear strictly tailor-made clothing, low shoes, and they seldom wear corsets. The hair is usually bobbed." Another doctor noted that a homosexual man "never smoked and never married; [and] was entirely adverse to outdoor games," while another team of researchers labeled a man perverted because (among other things) he was "fond of looking in the mirror" and spoke "in a squeaking, effeminate voice."[36] Small wonder many homosexuals constantly worried about their appearance. Some, including Kinsey, spent their adult lives eschewing anything (clothing items, mannerisms, voice inflections, speech patterns, and interior decorating styles) that might arouse suspicions.[37]

One of the few sexologists whose writings Kinsey might have found congenial was Havelock Ellis (1859–1939), an apostle of sexual tolerance. Though he often wrote as though he believed homosexuality was linked to gender roles, Ellis argued that not all homosexuals adopted the social roles of the opposite sex. Ironically, he was as guilty as most sexologists of reinforcing the popular image of lesbians as "mannish maidens," but he bent over backwards to show that the majority of male homosexuals were not "womanly males." Ellis insisted that a man could invert his sexual behavior by having sex with another man yet still be "masculine in his nonsexual habits." Thus, his definition of homosexuality was narrowly sexual.[38]

In his first major work on sexuality, *The New Spirit* (1890), Ellis praised sex as "the chief and central function of life . . . ever wonderful, ever lovely." For him, it represented "all that is most simple and natural and pure and good." To those who saw sex as a health threat and therefore something to be controlled, he replied, "Why . . . should people be afraid of rousing passions which, after all, are the great driving forces of human life?"[39] As one scholar has explained, Ellis's message was simple: the world needed "not more restraint but more passion."[40]

Among his many writings, Ellis is best remembered for *Studies in the Psychology of Sex,* a six-volume work that appeared over a thirteen-year period (1897–1910). Each volume was a scientific compendium of everything known on its subject. Drawing upon the literature in at least six languages,

Ellis cited more than two thousand authors in the *Studies*. Yet, despite its encyclopedic quality, empirical contributions to the field, impressive command of the literature, copious documentation, and other trappings of scholarship, Ellis's work was essentially moral and categorical. A naturalist in the grand tradition of the "English amateur," he was more artist than scientist, more polemicist than scholar.

Sexual Inversion (1897), the first volume of the *Studies,* was, as one historian has explained, "in essence an apology for homosexuality—a classic example of Ellis's lifelong effort to broaden the spectrum of acceptable sexual behavior."[41] Aware that most people considered erotic contacts between people of the same sex "a crime against nature," Ellis sought to normalize homosexuality, depicting it as common mammalian behavior. Far from being limited to human beings, homosexuality could be found in several species, including dogs, sheep, cattle, white rats, and monkeys. This strongly implied that homosexuality was normal animal behavior. Since human beings were animals, it followed that homosexuality was bound to appear in people.[42]

Taking his cue from cultural anthropologists, Ellis attempted to weaken moral sanctions by citing numerous foreign cultures, both ancient and modern, in which homosexuality was tolerated, if not celebrated.[43] Ellis's meaning was clear: condemnation of homosexuality was neither innate nor universal; it involved socially constructed mores and laws subject to cultural change. Ellis also assembled a veritable Who's Who of homosexuals who had made outstanding contributions to Western culture.[44] Again, Ellis's point was obvious: far from being degenerates, homosexuals included some of the finest specimens of mankind.

Ellis sought to destigmatize homosexuality by challenging the idea that it was an acquired vice. Homosexuality, he insisted, was neither degenerate nor volitional. It was hereditary. To support this view, Ellis turned to personal testimonials. Several of the homosexuals in his study believed they had been born with their sexual orientation. In one of Ellis's cases, a fifty-year-old physician, declared, "I knew from my own very clear remembrance of my own development that my peculiarity was not acquired, but inborn; my great misfortune undoubtedly, but not my fault."[45] Few arguments held out more sympathy for homosexuals, for how could people be blamed for something they inherited?

Shrewdly, Ellis worked to weaken the disease model even as he claimed to support it. Though he stopped short of arguing that homosexuality was normal, he employed statistical reasoning to suggest that it was far more widespread, and therefore far less bizarre, than people thought. Homosexuality should be regarded not as pathology, he maintained, but as an "abnormality" in the statistical sense that it involved fewer people than heterosexuality.[46] Drawing upon the work of Magnus Hirschfeld in Germany, Ellis estimated the incidence of homosexuality at about 2 percent, which placed "the homosexual population of Great Britain at somewhere about a million."[47]

Much was at stake in this numbers game. As long as homosexuality was considered rare, it was easy for middle-class moralists to brand same-sex eroticism as sexual deviance. But if science could prove that homosexuality was widespread, the custodians of morality would be hard-pressed to treat it as a rare illness. Perhaps they might even respond with tolerance. But Ellis wanted to go beyond attitudinal changes. He meant to affect public policy. He thought that no one could contemplate the power of his numbers without changing how he or she treated homosexuals. Ultimately, his goal was to undermine the notion that homosexuality was a disease and to promote an ethic of tolerance.

He employed the language of pathology, one suspects, not because he believed that homosexuality was a disease but because he suspected the public was not prepared to accept a more enlightened view. At least for the time being, the disease model offered the best hope for winning tolerance for homosexuals. For in Ellis's hands, disease itself became a part of life— neither bizarre nor disgusting, and certainly not beyond the pale of science. "Pathology is but physiology working under new conditions," he intoned. "The stream of nature still flows in the bent channel of sexual inversion, and still runs according to laws."[48]

Ellis's very words were designed to soften the disease model. Employing the most neutral terms of his day, he referred to homosexuality as "a 'sport,' or variation, one of those organic aberrations which we see throughout living nature, in plants and in animals."[49] A not very subtle challenge was at work in this language. By inching away from the disease model and by calling homosexuality a "sport or variation," Ellis was suggesting that sexual behavior was a continuum. This, in turn, implied a measure of equality between homosexuality and other forms of behavior on the continuum. Ellis went no further, but decades later Kinsey made this argument a key point in his crusade to normalize attitudes toward homosexuality.

Finally, Ellis tried to humanize homosexuality by bringing to life flesh-and-blood people. He devoted the bulk of *Sexual Inversion* to case histories, allowing thirty-three male homosexuals and six lesbians to tell their own stories in first-person narratives. Most of Ellis's male subjects were highly cultured individuals who appreciated fine music and read widely. Several noted that they had acquired considerable insight into themselves by reading Plato. Unlike the neurotic, depressed, guilt-ridden wretches who haunted most medical texts, Ellis's subjects held down jobs, paid taxes, and tried to live their lives as responsible citizens—fighting all the while to maintain human dignity in the face of what one man called the atmosphere of "Pariahdom" that surrounded homosexuals. Moreover, they not only accepted their sexual desires but defended their behavior. "I cannot regard my sexual feelings as unnatural or abnormal, since they have disclosed themselves so perfectly naturally and spontaneously with men," said one man. Another man declared, "I believe that affection between persons of the same sex, even when it includes the sexual passion and its indulgences, may lead to results as splendid as human nature can ever attain to."[50]

A few of Ellis's men challenged society's right to condemn them. One man demanded to know, "How long are the western moralists to maim and brand and persecute where they do not understand?" Two others, whom Ellis described as "ardent for social reform," denounced the laws on homosexuality as "absurd and demoralizing." Yet another man, who Ellis insisted had "no wish to injure society at large," believed that he should have "the same right to be himself that anyone else has." Ellis gave the final word on the subject to a "Mr. O," who "believes that no moral stigma should be attached to homosexuality until it can be proved to result from the vicious life of a free moral agent—and of this he has no expectation."[51]

Sexual Inversion closed with a thoughtful discussion of how homosexuals should be managed by society and the law. Ellis saw little chance of preventing or treating homosexuality. Instead, he advocated legal reforms and urged society to tolerate its homosexual members. In place of the current patchwork of sex offender codes, the law should concern itself with people's private behavior only "to prevent violence, to protect the young, and to preserve public order and decency." In Ellis's view, certain private behavior was "a matter of taste, of esthetics; and, while unspeakably ugly to the majority, it is proclaimed as beautiful by a small minority."[52] Among consenting adults, he declared, "the law cannot be called upon to interfere."[53]

At first glance, one would think that Kinsey would feel a certain kinship with the sexologists, especially with Ellis. As a group, they offered a ray of hope to sexual deviants. By appropriating sexual disorders for science, they placed the whole notion of sexual deviation in flux. As long as sexual behavior remained under the authority of religion and the law, sexual mores were not likely to change, since few legislators or men of the cloth were eager to associate themselves with reforms aimed at removing controls on private behavior. By appropriating sexual disorders for science, however, sexologists established a countervailing authority. For the first time, there was a new variable in how the public approached sexual disorders. "Unmentionable acts" could not only be mentioned but also be studied, named, and cataloged. Symptoms could be recorded, cases described, causes debated, treatments prescribed, and cures proclaimed amid great fanfare, only to be challenged when improved therapies came along.[54] Revealed truth and reified codes would have to compete with the give-and-take of scientific dialogue. What one group of scientists defined today as illness could be redefined tomorrow as something less serious or even normal. All it would take was another group citing new theories or improved data.

From the moment he read their works, however, Kinsey was sharply critical of the sexologists, including Ellis. According to Kroc, Kinsey dismissed the lot of them with the terse statement "You know, there isn't much science here."[55] Kinsey made this remark not as a casual observation but as a considered verdict, one that reflected his personal assessment of the literature. By the mid-1930s, he had given the matter enough attention to pull his thoughts together in a formal lecture. In a paper entitled "Biological Aspects of Some Social Problems," presented to his faculty discussion group on April 1, 1935, he delivered a passionate discourse on the importance of sex in human affairs.

Kinsey began by walking his audience through the recent scientific literature on human sexuality, indicating that he commanded the latest research from a variety of fields. As a Darwinian and scientific reductionist, he opened with a discussion of recent studies on anthropoid behavior. Such studies were absolutely imperative, explained Kinsey, because the biological record for human beings had to "be derived from a study of the primates most nearly ancestral to man (i.e., from the anthropoid apes), or from comparative studies of human and other mammalian structures and physiology." Kinsey was adamant in his belief that phylogenetic studies had direct relevance to human beings. Noting that the first significant study of anthropoid apes did not appear until 1914, he stressed that the recent flurry of studies on apes "are largely a result of our increasing realization of the importance of phylogenetic data in interpreting human behavior." Like his graduate adviser Wheeler, Kinsey challenged society to use scientific research to formulate the rules of human conduct. "Modern biology . . . is willing to accept the facts without finding an excuse for them," he declared, "and inclined to recommend the consideration of these facts in the shaping of human conduct." Quoting at length from an article entitled "The Primate Basis of Human Sexual Development," by G. S. Miller, Kinsey stressed that human sexual behavior "is merely a common type of primate sexual behavior with a few specialized characteristics."[56]

In addition to his tantalizing, if highly selective, discussion of anthropoid studies, Kinsey summarized recent developments in anatomy and physiology. Among the investigations he considered noteworthy were studies that examined fertilization, sex determination, sex reversals, and sex inter-grades. Physiological and morphological investigations had made impor-tant contributions to scientific research on human sexuality in the 1920s and 1930s. These studies clearly fascinated Kinsey. He was intrigued by any research that could shed light on the current theory that homosexual-ity might have an organic explanation or that homosexuals might consti-tute some sort of sexual intergrade between men and women.

Kinsey also displayed a keen interest in endocrinology. Researchers in this burgeoning field, he reported, had recently isolated estrogen, the "spe-cific compound which is the female hormone," a discovery he shrewdly noted would be utilized by human beings "in surprisingly diverse ways." Optimistic that the discovery of the male sex hormone would follow soon, Kinsey predicted that the explanation for "such age-old problems as sex-ual maturity, birth-control, and sterility" might well "find their solution in such remote corners as the cortex of the adrenal, the thyroid, the anterior lobe of the pituitary," or in other ductless glands, "which acting upon the gonads, are responsible for the normal course and at least some of the aberrations of the physiology of sex."[57] While Kinsey failed to mention it, many scientists of his day expected to locate the cause of homosexuality in some sort of malfunction of the endocrine glands.

From developments in endocrinology, Kinsey turned to research spon-sored by birth control advocates in the United States. Displaying a gen-erosity toward the medical profession rare in his later years, he praised the "forward-looking physicians" who were conducting "fundamental investi-gations" under the auspices of the privately endowed National Committee on Maternal Health, the organization founded by Robert L. Dickinson, to foster research on birth control, human fertility, and the like.[58]

While Kinsey was impressed with developments in physiology and en-docrinology, he had only qualified praise for the small group of scholars who had attempted to survey human sexual behavior. Citing the work of Katherine B. Davis, G. V. Hamilton, and Dickinson, Kinsey noted that scholars had recently compiled "four or five thousand case histories which, while inadequate statistically, are significant in their agreement." More to his liking was the research conducted by the Johns Hopkins University bio-metrician Raymond Pearl, surveys that Kinsey predicted "should be, sta-tistically, more sound."[59]

Kinsey found the work in other fields woefully deficient. He brushed aside anthropological studies with a wave of his hand. Primitive societies, he argued, could teach science little about the origins of human society, be-cause the vast majority of such societies had "already traveled ninety-nine per cent of the way from apes to man." Furthermore, anthropological studies suffered from their authors' regrettable habit of distorting data "thru the glasses of our mores."[60] Psychiatrists, Kinsey charged, were even less reliable. He dismissed psychiatrists en masse as moral conservatives who based their teachings on mindless traditions rather than on science. Psychiatrists had absorbed "[so] 'many superstitions and prejudices, which are at the base of the accepted mores that they have contributed little if they have not actually impeded our progress.' "[61]

Kinsey denounced sexual prejudices and superstitions for inflicting untold damage on people. The cultural ideals surrounding human sexuality, he charged, had induced "psychic conflicts" responsible for a series of biological maladjustments, including "ignorance of sexual structure and physiology, of the technique fundamental in the normal course of sexual activities, and the prudish aversion to adequate participation in the one physiologic activity on which society is most dependent."[62] Kinsey blamed religion for these problems. "There is abundant reason for placing the break-down of our modern home at the door of the Christian Church," he declared. Through its relentless hostility to passion and its strident efforts to control sexual behavior, Christianity was responsible for creating " 'psychic conflicts' of such magnitude as to constitute probably the most serious threat against the home." Indeed, Kinsey considered the church the family's worst enemy.

Kinsey concluded with a frontal attack on traditional morality. In his view, no true scientist could endorse definitions of perversions that rested on moral prescription. "The current use of the term, especially in regard to sex, for activities which are not approved by the mores of the day has no application in a scientific consideration of the problem," he declared.[63] Acts the custodians of morality labeled "crimes against nature" were nothing of the sort. For example, masturbation, mouth-genital contacts, and homosexuality were common practices among many mammals. Society might condemn such practices in humans on moral grounds, but they could hardly be deemed unnatural, at least not from a biological perspective.[64] Not content merely to defend the biological normalcy of most sexual perversions, Kinsey attempted to stand conventional morality on its head. "Judged by the departure from the physiologic normal and the damage wrought on the home and society," he scolded, "the great distortions of sex are the cultural perversions of celibacy, delayed marriage, and asceticism." In conclusion, Kinsey asked, "If these are the biologic data, how will the social scientist apply them in safe-guarding the home and the quality of our society?"[65]

Kinsey's lecture demonstrated how far he had progressed toward constructing his own scientific view of human sexuality. Despite his grueling work schedule on gall wasps, he had found the time to read widely on sexual research and to distill his thoughts. Because he had little aptitude for theory and because his was not an original mind, Kinsey had not formulated a coherent theory of human sexuality. Nor would he ever. Rather, his ideas reflected little more than the materialistic, mechanistic concepts of scientific positivism.

Even though much of his thinking remained tentative and inchoate, several themes emerged in this lecture. First of all, Kinsey asserted the irreducible fact that human beings are animals, an argument he would make again and again in the years to come. It followed, therefore, that people could learn something about themselves by studying the behavior of other mammals. Second, by insisting that human behavior must be approached phylogenetically, Kinsey strongly implied that society was wrong to expect human beings to jettison selective parts of their biological heritage. However repugnant certain behaviors might seem, society might just as well ask leopards to change their spots.

But Kinsey was not content to leave things at that. By insisting that human beings shared certain patterns of sexual behavior common to other mammals, he was arguing that biology had to be reckoned with when people formulated sexual mores and codes of conduct. Granted, society could tell its members what to do, but people paid a high price when social restrictions violated human nature. Kinsey thought it tragic that people should be condemned by social convention for engaging in behavior that was part of their biological inheritance.

To resolve the tension between social prescriptions and human nature, Kinsey favored sexual codes that recognized biological realities. In his view, religion had to be deposed as the arbiter of sexual conduct. In place of religion, Kinsey believed, science should guide people's sexual behavior, not in the sense of formulating mores but in furnishing reliable information that would enable secular experts to construct behavioral standards more in keeping with human nature. Just as he had turned to science for self-understanding, he wanted the public to consult science to discover "the biological bases of society." Science, and science alone, would reveal the truth about human sexuality, allowing people to satisfy their needs as nature intended.

If Kinsey's lecture was a bold challenge to conventional morality, it was also very much in character. Once again, he had taken the part of a rebel, a man at odds with the thinking around him. And, once again, he had surveyed a field and found it wanting. It was characteristic that he should question the scientific rigor of researchers whose methods he did not condone and whose conclusions he did not affirm.

But the most remarkable thing about his lecture was its tone of anger. For decades, Kinsey's life had involved a careful balancing act between rigid self-control and calculated acts of rebellion. His lecture suggested that the balancing was becoming more difficult. Years of hiding his pain from society had left Kinsey angry and combative. By the mid-1930s, he was having difficulty remaining silent. Inner tensions he had managed to keep hidden from the world were coming to the surface; private issues were starting to become public. Kinsey's 1935 lecture to his faculty discussion group showed how badly he wanted to use science, the greatest weapon he commanded, to attack the conventional morality that had caused him so much pain.

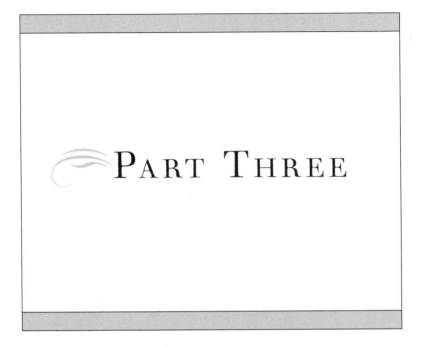

PART THREE

"You Can Work Out
Your Own Solution"

By the late 1930s, Kinsey was in a box. Professionally, he felt frustrated and undervalued, as conditions at Indiana University had become intolerable. In a letter marked "Very confidential, Sir! Destroy it," he poured out his disgust in 1935 to his old friend from graduate school, Edgar Anderson: "The whole University is in a mess, we get nothing done apart from the ancient routine—I would leave at the first opportunity offering comparable recompense and research opportunities."[1] Kinsey blamed the state of the university on the aging William Lowe Bryan, declaring, "All this [g]oes back to the fact our President is 75 years old and unwilling to settle any question, large or small."[2]

In the spring of 1937, the Victorian age suddenly, if belatedly, released its grip on Indiana University. President Bryan retired in June, ending thirty-five years of feudal rule on campus. His departure, coupled with a newly approved state-supported retirement system for college professors, triggered a mass exodus among the senior faculty. With Bryan gone and the headship system teetering on the brink of collapse, everyone sensed the dawn of a new beginning. The board of trustees appointed the dean of the

business school, Herman B (the "B" did not stand for anything) Wells, acting president.

The most noticeable feature of this remarkable man was his youth. His
investiture at the age of thirty-five made Wells the youngest president in the
university's history. A native Hoosier, Wells cut a striking figure. A short,
rotund man with a barrel chest, massive shoulders, and a huge head, he had
dark, wavy hair, a smartly trimmed mustache, a booming laugh, and a
smile that could melt ice. Hearty and engaging, he exuded the warmth and
charm of a born politician.

Wells was reared in Lebanon, Indiana, where his father was a banker and
his mother taught school. Following graduation from Lebanon High
School, Wells briefly attended the University of Illinois, but left at the end
of his freshman year to enter Indiana University, where he earned both a
bachelor's degree in business administration and a master's degree in economics. Next, he entered the doctoral program in business administration
at the University of Wisconsin. In 1931, he left Wisconsin without completing his degree, and returned to Indiana University as an instructor of
economics. Had he been riding a rocket, he could hardly have shot through
the ranks more quickly. Within a few years, this boy wonder had risen to
become dean of the School of Business, the position he held when the
trustees named him acting president, a scant seven years after joining the
faculty.[3]

On a personal level, Wells presented a vivid contrast to Bryan. Wells
was a bachelor with a reputation for enjoying a good time. As a undergraduate, he had joined Sigma Nu and was elected eminent commander his
senior year. "I suppose I had a natural affinity for fraternity life," he later
admitted.[4] Here Wells was referring to his fondness for fellowship and co-
maraderie, to be sure, but he also confessed a weakness for the endless cycle
of parties that formed such a prominent feature of Greek life. At the height
of prohibition, Wells and his fraternity brothers frequented nearby
speakeasies, where he consumed his share of home brew and white lightning. In addition, he often joined the weekend safaris to Chicago to hear
jazz in South Side night spots. Owing to his reputation as a fraternity
man, Wells later found it necessary to write in his memoirs, "Contrary to
the vivid recollections of fellow alumni, who have a great propensity for remembering things that were not so, I had neither a Stutz Bearcat nor a
coonskin coat in my undergraduate days."[5]

Still, for a man who enjoyed a good time, Wells's social life suffered one
curious omission. In his autobiography, *Being Lucky,* he mentioned dating
and going to dances in high school, but no similar references appeared for
his college years. Similarly, Wells's account of his life into old age was silent
on the subject of romance. After his father died, he shared the president's

house with his mother, who served as his official hostess at university affairs. Apparently, he was the kind of bachelor who preferred the company of other men.

Whatever his private interests, Wells was a born leader. Decisive, energetic, and jovial, he brought definite ideas to his office. Since the board thought enough of him to name him acting president, Wells acted like president. Thanks to the recent law passed by the state legislature creating a long-awaited retirement program for college teachers, Wells assumed power when the stalwarts of the previous generation could finally afford to take their leave. Their departure created an opportunity to hire bright young scholars. That was what Wells did. Allying himself with the strongest members of the faculty, he got directly involved with faculty searches in order to guarantee high-level appointments.

From the moment he assumed power, Wells distanced himself from Bryan's academic feudalism. Instead of rewarding seniority and personal loyalty, he emphasized scholarship and vital teaching. Fiercely devoted to academic freedom, he saw the university as a center for learning and the development of ideas, a place where faculty members could frame questions and seek answers. Wells was also an astute politician who recognized the need to build alliances with diverse groups. Aware that a university president must balance a number of equities, he sought to represent honestly and fairly the various components of the school's constituency. When choosing faculty members to serve on important committees, for example, Wells made it a point to appoint liberals, moderates, and conservatives, so all views were represented.[6]

Overall, the faculty supported Wells's appointment. Everywhere there was a sense of optimism and hope, reflecting the widespread belief that the young president had the ability to lead Indiana University into a bright future. Eager to put the frustrations of the Bryan era behind them, professors stepped forward with a variety of proposals to move the university ahead. Kinsey's own department, for example, showed unmistakable signs of revitalization. During the final months of President Bryan's administration, federal building funds had become available from the Works Progress Administration (WPA) and the Public Works Administration (PWA), two of the New Deal's better-known initiatives for putting men back to work. Sensing that the time was right, Kinsey and his colleagues had pressed Dean Payne to apply to these agencies for funds to renovate their dilapidated quarters in Old Biology Hall.

Indiana University got the grants. By the spring of 1938 the renovations were under way. "I have had to supervise," Kinsey wrote Voris, explaining that Dean Payne had been away for much of the spring term. In loving detail, Kinsey noted that the zoology and botany libraries had been combined in the old zoology lecture room, that the old botany lecture room was now for joint use, and that several other important changes in space allocation had been made. In addition, the department had reaped a windfall of new laboratory equipment, including a "glorious lot of new soap dishes, waste baskets, towel racks, tables, chairs" and "$1,800 of new microscopes." Kinsey added, "It does pay to hammer at things, and strike for big things, instead of accepting small gifts. We finally moved Dr. Payne to the point where he actually went after these things—and was surprised to get them."[7]

Wells had a talent for building alliances with the strongest faculty. One of his first actions was to announce a special committee to conduct a self-survey of the university to provide accurate information about the school's current status and needs. Word quickly spread that Wells intended to staff the committee with the best minds on campus. Upon hearing about the proposed committee, Robert Kroc wrote Wells and recommended Kinsey. Kinsey should be invited to serve, Kroc explained, "because of his incessant objectivity and ability for collecting and handling great masses of factual information" and "for his well-known wide variety of interests." Noted Kroc, "I have disagreed with him strenuously on many issues, but admire and respect his great energy and objectivity." An honest man, Kroc hastened to add, "Inasmuch as he has a certain bluntness, and is sometimes accused of tactlessness, it is important that, if picked, he be in a desirable combination."[8] While Kinsey was not appointed to the committee, he followed its work with keen interest. "We have a faculty 'Survey Committee,' " he wrote Voris, "and it is going to [the] rock bottom of everything, no regard for precedents—men of my age—consequently our generation ride [sic] strong in this reorganization."[9]

Kinsey was right to have faith in the committee. Its final report hit the campus like a bombshell. A searing indictment of the Bryan era, the report enumerated the many ways in which Bryan's leadership had been a disaster. By every criterion the committee devised, Bryan had assembled a weak faculty. According to the committee, only forty-eight of their colleagues appeared in *Who's Who in America* in 1938, and several of those whose names did appear were no longer with the university, having resigned or retired the preceding year. Among other schools in the Big Ten, by contrast, the University of Wisconsin had placed 155 on the list and the University of Michigan 153.[10]

Equally disappointing was the verdict on Indiana University's graduate programs. Reviewing the 1934 report of the Committee on Graduate Instruction of the American Council of Education, the Self-Survey Committee found that Indiana had only ten departments with sufficient academic strength to support doctoral programs. Of these departments, not one had earned the ranking "well qualified"—all were deemed "acceptable." The low ratings were predictable, since the strength of research activities determined a school's qualifications for training doctoral students. And if research meant publication, Indiana's professors were not doing their share.[11]

In concluding its report on the faculty, the Self-Survey Committee acknowledged that Indiana University had many competent and several distinguished professors. "When considered as a whole, however," the report noted bleakly, "it is a fact . . . that the faculty of the University is far from distinguished. Indeed, from whatever data one draws inferences, it is clear that Indiana University does not deserve to be classed with the other state institutions in the midwest (except Purdue), much less the leading endowed schools of the country." If Indiana University was to have any hope of improving its status, asserted the committee, it had to take "drastic steps . . . to obtain and retain for the University a faculty of distinguished and productive scholars and to provide adequate facilities and incentives for scholarly work." The message was clear: unless the new administration worked to keep and support its strongest faculty members and to recruit active researchers, Indiana University would remain huddled in the academic cellar of the Big Ten.[12]

As Wells labored to build alliances and to assemble information on the school's needs, Kinsey maintained a "wait and see" attitude. "I am not yet certain that I want to fix my future here," he wrote Voris in March 1938. "If it comes out right in this shuffle, I. U. will be a good place to stay; if it is screwed up as some things threaten to be, I shall be in the market for another job. Some place where there is active genetic work, and a graduate program that allows a better grounding for taxonomic-cytologic-genetic studies. Perhaps we can build that here."[13]

From Kinsey's perspective, everything depended on whom the trustees named the permanent president. Of course, opting for mediocrity would be easy. The trustees had only to appoint a Bryan clone, a man who would maintain the status quo. If they meant to improve the university, however, they would turn to a bold leader—someone with vision, high standards, sound judgment, the exact mixture of tact and courage required to build a genuine meritocracy on campus, and the political skills needed to pry additional funding from a state legislature justly renowned for its penury.[14]

On March 22, 1938, after an eight-month search, the trustees named Acting President Wells the eleventh president of Indiana University. The vote was unanimous, reflecting their strong conviction that the thirty-six-year-old bachelor was the right man for the job. "You have youth, ambition, courage, ability, and intelligence of a high order," the chairman of the board wrote Wells, "and with these qualities you cannot fail. You must, you will succeed."[15] In accepting the appointment, Wells confessed that he felt "wholly inadequate to undertake this important task," but promised, "I shall do my best—I shall give all my thought and energy to this work."[16] Wells radiated confidence and energy. Using the University of Wisconsin and the University of Michigan as his models, he set out to build what might be called the modern mega-university—a large, publicly supported, multifaceted, research-oriented institution staffed by distinguished professors who were not only strong undergraduate teachers but publishing scholars and demanding graduate mentors. To achieve his goals, Wells needed the support of students, faculty, alumni, and the trustees. He took steps to earn their backing.[17]

Wells announced that he would welcome new ideas. Aware that many matters had gone unresolved during Bryan's final (some would say moribund) years, Wells was eager to establish his credentials as a "doer," a leader who could facilitate the efforts of faculty and students alike to build a better university. Taking the new president at his word, a small band of reform-minded undergraduates immediately put Wells to the test. Weary of strict social controls and determined to explore subjects the previous administration had considered improper, they asked the university to engage a number of social problems, including venereal disease.

Shortly before Wells's appointment as president, the school newspaper launched a crusade to require Wassermann tests of all students at Indiana University. Responding to a plea for nationwide testing by Surgeon General Thomas Parran, the *Daily Student* announced on February 15, 1938, "its campaign for compulsory Wassermann tests of all Indiana students."[18] As self-styled members of "a forward-looking, liberal press" working toward "a greater and more progressive University," these young journalists boldly proclaimed that it was their duty to "lead the way." They insisted that "universities should aid the cause," because they were "the laboratories that shape future generations." While conceding that syphilis was probably not a major problem on campus, they insisted that the real issue was whether Indiana University would "join the parade to stamp out syphilis by adopting a frank and fearless attitude toward the disease."[19]

Instead of joining the parade, the faculty, with few exceptions, ran for cover. Kinsey maintained a prudent silence, as did most of his colleagues. Still, one professor did make a supportive gesture. Harvey J. Locke of the sociology department, whose liberal attitudes on many social issues were well known on campus, told a student reporter that he was conducting a survey of the venereal disease problem in the United States and abroad, with particular emphasis on the laws requiring premarital blood tests. While Locke stopped short of endorsing the student crusade, he gave it tacit support by drawing attention to his own work in the area.[20]

A local health official did endorse the campaign. Dr. J. E. P. Holland, a member of the city health department, told a reporter for the *Daily Student* that he supported making Wassermann tests available to students, noting that a large number of universities, ranging from Harvard University to the neighboring University of Illinois, already provided this service. "I think it is a fine idea," he wrote the student editors, declaring, "even if it fails, it will have served a great educational purpose. However, I hope you succeed."[21]

Victory was by no means guaranteed. Immediately after the editorial appeared, the *Daily Student* was deluged with complaints. Some critics accused the editors of sensationalism or of attempting to smear the university's reputation, while others insisted that the tests were unnecessary. Instead of backing down, the editors rebutted their critics and repeated their demands for Wassermann tests. The turning point came when powerful allies in the medical community endorsed the program and offered to help. When word of the crusade reached Indianapolis, the State Board of Health volunteered to test free of charge as many blood samples as the university cared to send. In fact, the board member Dr. Verne K. Harvey revealed that Purdue University, Indiana's arch rival, had been taking advantage of free testing for years. By May, Indiana University had a testing program in place, and the *Daily Student* proudly reported, "More than 1,000 students have taken the free Wassermann tests."[22]

A success on its own terms, the Wassermann campaign broke a logjam of student demands on other controversial issues. "I was proud to see *The Daily Student* initiate its campaign for compulsory Wassermann tests and to read the discussions—in frank language—of the syphilis Scourge," wrote one student. "But I feel that the next thing *The Student* well could put its editorial force behind would be the addition of a psychiatrist to the University's staff," the student continued. "Too many University students fight worry, fear, anxieties, depressed moods; too many succumb to hate, inferiority, self pity and superiority."[23]

Painfully aware that sexual conflicts left many of their number feeling anxious and fearful, other students called for a modern sex education course at Indiana University. Just one day after the *Daily Student* launched its crusade to make Wassermann tests available on campus, the editors started receiving letters from disgruntled students decrying the sorry state of sex education. "Hygiene . . . is the most useless course in the University when it could be the most useful one," a dejected student complained. Instead of learning something about health, students wound up "hating the course for its useless medical terms and debunking and rambling lectures."[24] Another student agreed. "In my entire four years here, I have taken one health course—the one-hour Hygiene course," he moaned.

"That in spite of the fact that I always have wanted to know something about what keeps the human body running. But at Indiana, the cause is lost."[25]

Such complaints did not overstate the case. In keeping with President Bryan's views, Indiana University's sex education course was decidedly proper. What passed for sex education was the one-hour, required course called "Hygiene." Actually, two versions of the class were offered—one for men, the other for women. Looking back on his undergraduate days, Wardell Pomeroy recalled, "As a sophomore, I took it [Hygiene] along with other bored boys (no girls were admitted) and we heard the usual slightly blue jokes at which no one laughed, along with the customary bumbling array of misinformation that was so typical of such lectures in 1932."[26]

The female version was no better. Cecilia Wahl, who suffered through the class in the 1930s, declared, "Everybody loathed the course, thought it was a total bore, and made all manner of jokes about it."[27] She recalled one funny incident in particular. President Bryan, it seems, delivered a key lecture to the women entitled "Concentration and Relaxation," or what today might be called "Tension Management." His recommendation for shedding the day's worries was simple. "When I find myself unable to go to sleep promptly," he sighed, "I lie and think of all the Johns I know." Wahl added with a chuckle, "Dear Dr. Bryan couldn't understand why the auditorium exploded with laughter, the gentle, erudite, correct-spoken scholar that he was."[28]

President Bryan was indeed the problem. Both a prig and a prude, he felt duty bound to block any class that treated human sexuality with candor. But, then, Bryan had always kept a watchful eye on campus morality. For example, when a young woman accused Robert Shelton, a medical student, in a paternity suit in 1915, Bryan acted immediately. Without attempting to learn the facts or waiting for the court to act, he expelled Shelton. As far as Bryan was concerned, the mere accusation of sexual impropriety was sufficient proof of wrongdoing. Sex had occurred outside of marriage; a woman's reputation had been destroyed; and the male culprit had refused to do the honorable thing. Therefore, expulsion was the appropriate response.[29]

Bryan applied the same standards to faculty members. When Samuel Bannister Harding, a full professor in the history department, filed for a divorce in 1916, the local newspapers in Bloomington treated the suit as a major story. Apparently, this was the first time a faculty member at Indiana University had ever sought a divorce. At first, Bryan took no action on the matter, even though he was both saddened and outraged. His restraint came to an end, however, when Harding remarried two years after his divorce. Bryan then received several letters from a local do-gooder alleging that Harding had conducted an affair prior to his divorce with the coed he subsequently married. Harding knew he was in trouble when he received a stern letter from Bryan condemning his behavior. After lambasting Harding for abandoning his wife and son, Bryan declared, "Your subsequent marriage constitutes a grave wrong. . . . For the University, the question is not a technical one. The question is as to what moral principles and moral influences the University will assume responsibility for and commend to its students and to society." A few weeks later, without giving him the opportunity to answer the charges, Bryan recommended to the board of trustees that Harding's appointment not be renewed. In 1918 Harding left the university. It did not seem to matter that Harding, who held a doctorate from Harvard University, was an excellent teacher and a productive scholar. Nor was Bryan's judgment tempered in any way by the fact that he was fond of Harding, who had been at Indiana since 1895.[30]

Time did nothing to relax Bryan's moral rigidity. During his final years in office, he imposed his personal moral code on those around him. "In loco parentis" remained his policy toward students, and his posture toward the faculty was only slightly less paternalistic. Many of his colleagues saw him, in the words of one historian, "as an unbending puritan who could instantly be repelled by a profane word, a glass of beer, or an uncouth personal act."[31] Of course, Bryan could not force others to adopt his values, but he cast a long shadow. Looking back on the atmosphere of the 1930s, one faculty wife with a gift for understatement recalled that Indiana University was "rather dominated by William Lowe Bryan's ideals of maybe a previous generation."[32]

Dated as they were, Victorian ideals dominated sex education in the United States. The first college courses in the United States on marriage and the family appeared in the early 1920s, many sponsored by the educational arm of the social hygiene movement. Over the next two decades, such classes became a familiar part of the curriculum at many colleges. A few were truly innovative, offering useful information on taboo topics such as venereal diseases, birth control, and human anatomy. Most, however, followed the script provided by the American Social Hygiene Association, which historically had demonstrated more concern for preserving traditional morality than for preventing diseases. As a group, these offerings might better be called "anti-sex" classes. Preaching the gospel of restraint, they avoided explicit discussions of human sexuality in favor of Victorian euphemisms that kept young people in the dark about it.

Many health officials looked at what was being taught and threw up their hands in disgust. "The Sex Hygienists, with their irrelevant gabble about dahlias and phio-progenitive bees," snapped one health reformer, "only make the essential mystery more mysterious, and hence more baffling."[33] Nor was this complaint limited to health authorities. Writing in the *American Mercury,* a popular critic lamented that "in Puritanical America, babies are still brought by storks, decent people copulate only in wedded antisepsis, and the pubic region is mentionable nowhere except in alleys and medical colleges."[34] Thus, however quaint Indiana University's hygiene course may appear today, it was probably representative of similar courses at other institutions.[35]

Kinsey supported student demands for a more candid approach to sex education. With Bryan safely in retirement and Wells promising to back reform, Kinsey sensed an opportunity to use sex education to advance his private war against traditional morality. Unofficially, of course, he had been teaching students about sex for many years, whether by slipping sexual material into his general biology course or by conducting private discussions with his graduate students. A formal sex education class, however, offered him both an excuse and an opportunity to proclaim publicly his own ideas on sexual morality and behavior, with every word protected by academic freedom. Kinsey was primed to speak out. He was eager to transform his hidden war against Victorian morality into a socially acceptable public crusade. Tired of suffering in silence, he wanted to fight the sexual codes that had bedeviled him since childhood.

Seizing the moment, Kinsey stepped forward and volunteered to develop a new class on marriage and the family. In the spring of 1938, he met several times in his office in Old Biology Hall with leaders of the Association of Women Students (AWS) to discuss plans for improving the quality of sex education at Indiana University. A master at manipulating others to do his bidding, he recommended that the AWS petition the university to offer a new course on marriage and the family.[36]

Simultaneously, Kinsey maneuvered to be appointed head of the course. Aware that other disciplines had strong claims to sex education, he preempted them by assuming direct responsibility for organizing the course. Acting like the man in charge, he invited colleagues in the psychology department and in the medical school to recommend readings and topics for discussion. Politically, this was a shrewd move, as it enabled him to co-opt potential rivals through consultation. In addition, he contacted the registrars of all the colleges and universities in Indiana (and several schools outside the state), asking if they had a course on marriage and requesting course syllabi. Kinsey also inquired if the courses had caused any problems on campus, a strong indication that he planned to be prepared if opposition arose. Faculty members at several schools revealed that they did offer such a course. Kinsey learned a great deal from their experiences.

The response from Purdue University was particularly helpful. According to Professor O. F. Hall, a sociologist, Purdue had offered a marriage course for the last eight years. It consisted of noncredit lectures for senior men and women (together), with no assigned readings but a reference list of twenty-two volumes on reserve in the library, which dealt "with marriage and the mingling of the sexes" and were "used most generously." As for criticism, Hall reported that two or three older professors had opposed the course in the beginning, adding, "One Dean came to me personally and said that he considered it unwise, believing that colleges have no business to instruct young people in these extremely personal matters."[37] During the past five years, however, the opposition had disappeared, approximately two-thirds of all graduating seniors had taken the class, and students routinely sang its praises.

The word from nearby Franklin College was also instructive. William G. Mather, Jr., who taught the marriage course there, offered Kinsey some practical advice on how to structure an interdisciplinary course with multiple instructors. His recommendation, which Kinsey adopted, was to invite specialists from other departments and from the community as well, including lawyers, judges, doctors, and the like. To avoid confusion, Mather stressed, it was imperative for one instructor to "dominate the course and thus set the emotional tone so to speak"; he explained that "the attitude of the instructor is of even greater importance than the material which he presents."[38] Kinsey could not have agreed more.

The reply from Colgate University was both detailed and encouraging. Professor Norman E. Himes revealed that there had been "no adverse criticism of the course here and a great deal of approval even from conservative sources." On the basis of his experience, Himes predicted that Kinsey would "find the students appreciative and sensible in their attitudes." Himes also recommended that the course be taught by scientists, a situation all too rare as such classes proliferated in colleges and universities. "Courses of this nature are going up so rapidly all over the country that there is grave danger that they will be given by crack-pots or by those of pious intentions and little information unless we can develop special teachers in the field," he declared. Still, Himes specifically warned Kinsey against including too much biological material and closed by offering his own course as a model, complete with a class syllabus and recommended reading list.[39]

Kinsey's reply was revealing, for it showed how carefully he had followed the recent literature on human sexuality. He claimed to have in his private library much of the reference material on Himes's reading list. In addition, Kinsey stated that he had followed for many years Himes's work with the National Committee on Maternal Health, one of the leading sponsors of research on birth control and other issues involving human sexual behavior. Leaving no doubt about his sympathies, Kinsey praised the committee warmly for its contributions to the field.[40]

Indeed, Kinsey credited the committee with inspiring him and other faculty members to develop a sex education course at Indiana.[41] "While I have had contact with problems of human sex behavior in my teaching for many years," he observed, "it has been the work of the Committee on Maternal Health that convinced some of us several years ago that whenever we arrived at a course in Marriage in this institution, it should be given on a scholarly basis with an adequate amount of objectively presented biology in it."[42] In a subsequent letter, Kinsey reiterated his determination to push a biological perspective, even though Himes had specifically cautioned against it. "Thanks for your warning against an overemphasis on the biological backgrounds," wrote Kinsey. "As biologists we want them [the students] to get adequate biological material, representing the best of recent developments in the biological field." Of course, what Kinsey considered adequate, many people found shocking, as time would demonstrate.[43]

As plans for the marriage course went forward, Kinsey could not resist telling Breland about the proposed class. Although Kinsey's letter could not be located, Breland's response offers a sense of how his mentor described what was afoot: "By golly, I believe they will be having copulating schools at Indiana before long. And when that happens, somebody will have to move over, because I'm moving in! Certainly seems that the new administration is changing things for the better. Best of luck to you all in the new course. I think something like that should be on every campus."[44]

By the end of the spring term, Kinsey was ready to move. Aware that everything turned on the administration's support, he directed his efforts to winning President Wells's approval. While Kinsey personally dominated every phase of planning, he was careful to involve representatives of the AWS as well. Together they had worked out details of content and presentation before drafting a formal petition to the administration, which the officers of the AWS then presented to President Wells.

Their petition called for a noncredit course, open only to seniors, that would cover legal, economic, biological, sociological, and psychological aspects of marriage. Asserting that no purpose would be served by offering the class separately to men and women, it asked that the two sexes be allowed to take the course together. To reassure the administration that students would not attend only the lectures they found titillating and skip the rest, the petition further stipulated that lectures would follow a strict se-

quence. Students who missed a class would be required to come to Kinsey's office and read the instructor's lecture notes. Hoping to demonstrate
widespread support, the petition also included signatures of leaders of
other student organizations.[45]

The marriage course petition presented Wells with both a problem and
an opportunity. On the one hand, he knew that the request for sex education represented a break with tradition. This was awkward for him. He had
studiously avoided any criticism of Bryan, for whom he had the highest
personal regard. On the other hand, Wells knew he had been named president with the expectation that he would bring new leadership and badly
needed changes. Adding a course on marriage and the family would signal a modern stance on sex education at Indiana University. It would show
that he was willing to break with the past and that he was open to requests
that had widespread support among student organizations, especially one
that had the sponsorship of a senior and highly respected faculty member.

Wells was inclined to support the request for several reasons. First, he
was eager to ally his administration with strong faculty members who
wanted to build a better university. Despite his prickly personality, Kinsey
certainly filled that bill. Second, Wells viewed his responsibility to students
differently from his predecessor. Whereas Bryan had enforced "in loco parentis," Wells preferred to let students assume responsibility for their own
behavior, with a minimum of direction from the university. He endorsed
in principle the short list of student regulations David Starr Jordan had allegedly adopted during his presidency of Indiana University. Wells was
fond of saying (with obvious approval) that Jordan had "done away with
all student rules except two: students were not permitted to shoot the faculty or to burn any buildings."[46]

Finally, when it came to the curriculum, Wells did not share Bryan's preoccupation with orthodoxy and decorum. Instead of limiting courses to the
tried and the true, Wells thought universities should encourage innovation.
"Provide for the esoteric, exotic, and impractical in the curriculum," he
once wrote; "the practical and pedestrian will take care of itself."[47] If that
meant raising a few eyebrows, Wells was equal to the challenge: on June
9, 1938, he presented the marriage course petition to the board of trustees,
with a recommendation for approval.[48]

Fortunately for the petitioners, Wells was in the honeymoon phase of his
relationship with the trustees. Nevertheless, they discussed the proposed
course thoroughly, indicating that they did not regard it as a routine addition to the curriculum. In the end, Nellie Showers Teter, the only female
board member, moved that Wells's recommendation be approved, William
A. Kunkel, Jr., seconded the motion, and, with one member requesting "to

be recorded as absent," the board approved it. Still, the trustees must have considered the class a daring innovation, for they stipulated "that no publicity would be given to this course."[49]

Following the board's vote, Wells gave Kinsey permission to form a faculty committee to organize and to plan a new course on marriage and the family. "I shall be glad if you will act as chairman of this committee," Wells told Kinsey.[50] Kinsey had been acting like the man in charge for months, and he happily acknowledged the announcement that made his appointment official. "Thanks for all the support which you have lent to the consummation of this program," he wrote Wells; "I trust that history will justify its existence." In one sense, Kinsey's appeal to history seems ironic. He had no way of foreseeing how the class would change his life or how it would bind his destiny to that of Herman Wells. Still, the reference was in character. It conveys Kinsey's sense of anticipation as he started the class. He somehow expected great things to come of it.[51]

With the board's approval in hand, Kinsey put the finishing touches on the course. Aware that opponents of sex education would pounce on the slightest impropriety, he took steps to eliminate several potential trouble spots. Working with Wells, he made certain that only tenured, highly respected faculty members were invited to teach the course.[52] To minimize differences in their knowledge (and attitudes), Kinsey asked every instructor to complete a common reading list before classes began. Furthermore, in order to preview content and delivery, he put the instructional staff through a dress rehearsal.[53] "We met ahead of time and gave our lecture to the other members of the committee, who . . . pointed out . . . ambiguous statements and so forth," recalled Dr. Edith Schuman, a physician who was asked to lecture on the topic "Pregnancy, Birth, and Venereal Disease." The purpose of this exercise, she explained, was to make certain "there would be no controversy." Asked whether Kinsey submitted his lectures to the same review, she replied in the affirmative but stressed that he remained impervious to their comments. "My impression is that nothing ever reached him," she declared. "If he had an idea that he wanted to get across, he had an answer for every, every bit of criticism."[54]

Kinsey's determination to do things his way became more evident with each passing day. As the beginning of summer school approached, he ignored the board's injunction against publicity. Late in June, the *Daily Student* announced that a new noncredit course (admission by permission of the instructors only) covering many aspects of marriage would begin classes on June 28, 1938. Ninety-eight students enrolled for the class, seventy women and twenty-eight men. Despite Kinsey's assurance that admission would be limited to seniors, this restriction, too, went by the boards. Course records reveal that forty-nine of the students who enrolled in the class were postgraduates, twenty-five were seniors, and seven were lowerclassmen, with faculty and their spouses accounting for the remaining twelve. Twenty-two were married, twenty-six engaged, and forty-six single. As a group, they no doubt enrolled in the course hoping to obtain useful information, but none could have anticipated what lay in store.[55]

The syllabus of the marriage course was impressive. An interdisciplinary class taught by a team of subject specialists, it consisted of twelve lecture topics, including the legal aspects of marriage and divorce, the economics of marriage, the sociology of the family, pregnancy, birth, and venereal disease, the ethical aspects of marriage, the endocrinological basis of human sexual response, and human reproduction and sterility. Of course, Kinsey reserved the last three topics for himself. Determined that students should absorb his biological principles, he delivered three lectures (more than any other staff member), covering the biological bases of society, reproductive anatomy and physiology, and, his favorite theme, individual variation.[56]

"The Biological Basis of Society," the opening lecture, set the tone for the course. Repeating much of the material he had delivered before his faculty discussion group in 1935, Kinsey challenged convention, insisting that human societies rested squarely on sexual attraction between their individual members. To support his argument, he shifted the discussion to infrahuman species, a tactic that was to become his standard operating procedure in the years ahead. Following a few cursory remarks on the rarity of social organization in the animal kingdom, he paused for a more detailed discussion of insect societies. Next, he turned to the behavior of anthropoid apes—chimpanzees, orangutans, baboons, and gorillas. "It is the sexual attraction which holds the male and female together, and . . . the anthropoid family breaks up as soon as the sexual attraction wanes," he declared.[57] In Kinsey's view, sexual attraction not only brought members of the opposite sex together but was responsible for the bond between the female and her offspring. Labeling the mammalian breast "a sex organ," he described how "the nerves in that breast are continuous with the nerves of the reproductive organs, and stimulation of that breast by the feeding babe brings a sexual response which is the basis of the thing that the poet calls 'mother love.' "[58]

Having deposited humans securely in the animal kingdom, Kinsey attacked the regulation of human sexual behavior by orthodox religion. While acknowledging that society had the right to curb individual freedom in order to benefit the group, he warned that "society in its regulation of the individual has gone to the point of threatening its own foundations." Rather than limit themselves to mores, customs, and taboos that were "necessary to protect the society as a whole," the custodians of morality had adopted many regulations that "lie far out-side of the fundamental needs of society."[59] Mincing no words, Kinsey told the young people in his class that they bore the brunt of those restrictions. By the time they reached adolescence, he noted, their bodies had matured. They were physically ready to begin sexual activity. Instead of marrying early in life, however, young people had to remain at home with parents who imposed moral and religious sanctions forbidding sexual activities of any kind. Why? Because the demand for prolonged education precluded economic independence for most youths. While there were good reasons for delaying marriage, he insisted that "it interfered with the biological relationship which was fundamental."[60]

In Kinsey's view, the danger to society from misguided efforts to control human sexuality was immediate and serious. Instead of protecting the family, Victorian morality threatened to destroy it. "It is the development of ideas as to what is proper and what is not—what is fine and what is not," he warned, "which interferes with the consummation of the biological relationship in marriage." To drive home the point, he cited figures to the effect "that in eighty or ninety percent of all the divorce cases that come to court there is a sexual maladjustment involved." The danger to the family, then, lay not in sexual freedom but in sexual repression. It was "prudish ideas," he declared, that had done "more than any other single factor to undermine the home."[61]

Next, Kinsey attacked the appalling sexual ignorance that Victorian morality imposed on young people. Most newlyweds, he insisted, knew next to nothing about sexual anatomy and physiology, contraceptives, and copulatory techniques. "In an uninhibited society," he thundered, "a twelve-year-old would know most of the biology which I will have to give you in formal lectures as seniors and graduate students." Their ignorance had to be corrected, he insisted, because it produced the sexual maladjustments that threatened marriage.[62] The marriage course, he promised, would provide reliable information and valid perspectives; their job was to decide what worked best for them. As Kinsey put it, the course would "provide the material by which you can work out your own solution."[63]

This was the sort of disclaimer one would expect from a man of science. By offering a biological perspective, Kinsey was arguing that people should learn the facts about human sexuality and decide for themselves which behaviors to embrace and which to eschew. It all came down to what worked for them. Kinsey stuck to this position for the rest of his life—at least in public. By the late 1930s, he had become fiercely individualistic where sexual behavior was concerned. An ardent student of individual variation in nature, he knew full well that people had different sexual interests and needs. With few exceptions (most notably, rape), he did not believe society should concern itself with people's private behavior. It followed, therefore, that no individual, religious group, or political body had the right to tell a person how to behave sexually or what one's sexual attitudes should be.

While he hoped to liberate his students from sexual repression, Kinsey was shrewd enough to realize that he had to adopt certain precautions. Putting on the protective mantle of science, he based his right to discuss sexual matters on his status as a scientist. Moreover, as a man skilled in the art of camouflage, he grasped at once that he could maintain his authority only by appearing to preserve his moral neutrality. He had to appear disinterested, his pronouncements value-free. That meant avoiding any semblance of special pleading. For once he was suspected of ulterior motives, his claim to scientific objectivity would be forfeited, his voice discounted. Like those whom he criticized, he would stand convicted of issuing moral prescriptions (indeed immoral prescriptions), and he would lose any chance of using science as a tool of social reform. To be effective, he had to cast himself in the role of the detached scientist, a seeker of truth who merely reported verifiable facts.

Besides, Kinsey did not think he needed to tell people what to do in order to modify their attitudes or change their behavior. As a seasoned teacher and forceful debater, he knew how to build a case that allowed only one conclusion. Once people understood how much damage sexual mores had inflicted on their lives, once they became aware of the huge gap between prescriptive morality and actual behavior, and once they understood that increased sexual freedom would not harm anyone, he was confident of the outcome. Facts would lead to understanding, and understanding would lead to reform.

Kinsey's second lecture before the marriage course, "Reproductive Anatomy and Physiology," expanded his covert attack on Victorian morality. At a time when most sex education courses preached the gospel of chastity and tiptoed around controversial topics, he approached his subject with astonishing candor. After opening with a cursory review of asexual reproduction and sexual reproduction in lower animals, Kinsey plunged into a discussion of human reproductive anatomy. Like the Sunday visitors who entered his garden, students in the marriage course received the surprise of their lives: Kinsey showed a series of slides tracing the development of the male and the female genitalia from the embryo through the adult. Then, using a sagittal section that was even more graphic, he compared the reproductive organs of the two sexes, pointing out structural similarities between the clitoris and the penis, the ovaries and the testicles, the labia majora and the scrotum, and so on. Males and females, he insisted, were essentially alike in their sexual anatomy, an argument that was clearly intended to blur the distinction between men and women, a favorite strategy of those who wished to gain acceptance for homosexuals by undermining the binary thinking that buttressed rigid moral categories. All this was presented in such a straightforward manner that the topic under discussion might as well have been the life cycle of the fruit fly.[64]

The same matter-of-fact tone marked Kinsey's treatment of coitus. Determined to reduce intercourse to a mechanistic model, he began by outlining what he called "the six stages of the coital sequence." These he identified as stimulation, lubrication, erection, increased sensitivity, orgasm, and nervous release. Both sexes, he stressed, experienced all six stages. Provided that people followed this pattern faithfully, intercourse would largely take care of itself. Since sexual intercourse was impossible in what he called "the normal position of the genitals," Kinsey proceeded to apply the anatomy material he had just delivered to the mechanics of sexual intercourse, describing in great detail the process by which humans prepared for intercourse "by specific stimulation."[65]

Having set the stage for intercourse, Kinsey did not flinch from telling students how to perform it. Again, his tone was one of utter detachment, as though what followed was standard fare in sex education classes across the land. Moreover, in keeping with his practice of illustrating material with slides, he showed a slide of a penis penetrating a vagina: "The actual adjustments which are made in the male and female genitalia are shown on this slide," he began. "The vagina must be spread open as the erect male organ penetrates." Commenting on the coupling of male and female genitalia, Kinsey achieved an air of detachment that was almost deadpan. "You will see that as the male organ penetrates, the clitoris at this point is stimulated, thus providing the erotic stimulation necessary for the completion of the act on the part of the female," he observed. "You will see by the same area that this point on the penis, which is the most sensitive point, is similarly stimulated."[66] His matter-of-fact approach to handling this material buttressed his message that he was just giving the facts.

Kinsey's final lecture dealt with fertilization or, more specifically, with how to prevent it. This was a controversial topic, as Americans had long been divided over whether sex should be separated from procreation. From the nineteenth century forward, large segments of the American public, led by physicians and purity crusaders, had condemned birth control as immoral and radical. In 1873, Congress had passed the Comstock Act, which, among other things, outlawed sending birth control information or devices through the mails. Despite such opposition, however, throughout the nineteenth century many couples had used coitus interruptus, douching, continence, rhythm, diaphragms, condoms, and the like to prevent unwanted pregnancies.[67]

In the twentieth century, women's continuing desire to control their fertility had created a strong demand for birth control information and for safe, reliable contraception. Beginning in World War I, Margaret Sanger led the crusade to make birth control morally acceptable. She and her supporters organized protests, published birth control manuals, established birth control clinics, and spread the gospel of contraception to anyone who would listen. By the 1930s, Sanger had won important victories. In addition to opening clinics in many major cities, she and her medical counterpart, Robert Dickinson, had worked tirelessly to persuade America's physicians to support birth control. Thanks largely to their efforts, the American Medical Association in 1937 had passed a resolution permitting its members to offer birth control as a family service.[68]

Still, many Americans regarded birth control as an attack on the family. They did not believe sex should be separated from procreation. To the male custodians of morality, birth control represented a frontal assault on patriarchy. It would also permit wives to escape what many conservatives regarded as their "biological duty" to bear children, thus transforming the family from an institution for child rearing into a sensuous union of partners who valued sex for its own sake. Many women condemned birth control just as soundly. Taught from childhood to embrace the cult of domesticity, they accepted childbearing as their highest calling and rejected birth control as immoral and radical. Moreover, many people of both sexes shared the concern that birth control would encourage promiscuity, promoting premarital and extramarital affairs that would undermine the family and render venereal diseases epidemic.

As one who had been injured by the sexual restraints society imposed on its members, Kinsey supported contraception. In his own marriage, he and Clara had used birth control to space their children and, after Bruce's birth, to prevent further pregnancies. Kinsey wanted to share his knowledge with others, especially since his discussions with students had revealed a crying need. Thanks to these little talks, he had discovered that the depression had forced many young couples to delay marriage and to postpone having children after wedlock. In addition, he had learned (not to his surprise) that many young people were woefully ignorant about contraception. Finally, despite the AMA's grudging recent approval, Kinsey knew that many doctors still opposed birth control, making it difficult for young couples to secure adequate counseling and effective devices.

Students in the marriage course heard a discussion of birth control that was both thorough and practical. Kinsey began by examining the pros and cons of surgical sterilization for men and women, but he recommended this procedure only in special cases. More to his liking were condoms, which he touted as being "practically 100% effective," provided that the condom was "of a reliable make, and this in turns means that they must be secured at a reliable drug store." He further suggested "that before using, the condom should be tested by being blown up like a balloon." Nothing that condoms frequently interfered with normal lubrication, Kinsey offered a solution. A practical soul, he told the class, "The most convenient substitute is saliva."[69]

The only other contraceptive device to earn his enthusiastic endorsement was the uterine diaphragm. Covering the tip of the uterus with a rubber membrane to prevent the sperm from reaching the egg was, in his words, "nearly 100% effective." But, warned Kinsey, a "diaphragm is not adequate unless it is fitted by a physician." Acknowledging that he had not exhausted the list of birth control methods, he flatly refused to discuss the rhythm method or techniques such as coitus interruptus. As he explained, "none of the other means are anywhere near as effective, and there is no point in giving them consideration."[70]

Kinsey's final lecture in the marriage course was titled "Individual Variation," a theme that had great resonance in his life. Quite apart from serving as the main focus of his research on gall wasps, it formed the cornerstone of the ethic of tolerance upon which he hoped to erect a new system of sexual morality for himself and for others. Kinsey began by declaring, "One of the most startling and most significant biologic phenomenon is . . . that no two individuals are alike." While every individual is distinct, however, nature could always be counted on to display "a certain rhyme and reason to distribution of variation within any population," a fact which could be readily observed in a statistical device called "the normal distribution curve." To illustrate how it worked, Kinsey referred to a chart on the blackboard tracking the onset of menstruation in a study of 50,000 women. A small number of women, he noted, got their first period "somewhere near 10 years of age, a larger number at 11, and a sudden jump at 12, with the peak of the curve at 13," adding that the same curve "begins to go down just as rapidly as it came up on the other side." The crucial point, he stressed, was that "you get this same sort of wide variation and distribution that piles up chiefly in the center and then spreads out later, in anything studied."[71]

Next, Kinsey moved deftly into a discussion of individual variation in female and male genitalia. The clitoris, he noted, varied "from slightly over 1/10″ in diameter to about 1/1″ in diameter," with the peak of the curve "at about 1/4″ in diameter." The erect phallus, by contrast, varied "from non-existence to a maximum length of 13″," with the "peak in this curve at 6″." Kinsey then offered facts and figures on the size of hymen perforations, the range in the size of the opening of the distended vagina in virgins, and the range in the size of the opening of the vagina in women who had had intercourse or who had given birth.[72]

From genitals, Kinsey shifted the discussion to social mores, asking his students to ponder the significance of the variation curve as it applied to human sexuality. "The way in which it has too often been judged," he cautioned, "is to brand a portion as normal and a portion as abnormal." This was particularly true with regard to sexual matters, he noted, because "people are very much afraid of being classified as abnormal in any such distribution curve, and so the data necessary to build a curve are not ordinarily available." Up to this point, his focus had been on morphological data, but suddenly, without warning or logical coherence, he made the leap to behavior. "I might remark once [and] for all," he declared, "that nearly all of the so-called sexual perversions fall within the range of biologic normality. It is very difficult to find any of them that fall in the range of abnormality."[73] Hence Kinsey was attempting to substitute a biological definition of normalcy for its social counterpart. He meant to abolish subjective notions of morality in favor of a new moral calculus in which the issue of "normal" and "abnormal" would be influenced by behavior.

"If the phenomenon is represented in only a small proportion of the population," Kinsey explained, "you may call it abnormal in that sense, but if the phenomenon involves most of the population it cannot be abnormal."[74] He also insisted that the physiological consequences of a particular form of behavior had to be taken into consideration. "If a phenomenon results in physiological maladjustments," he observed, "biologists may label it as abnormal." As far as he was concerned, however, few forms of behavior actually harmed anyone. Standing the ethic of restraint on its head, Kinsey referred with approval to an unnamed gynecologist (Robert Latou Dickinson) who "said there are only three kinds of sexual abnormalities: abstinence, celibacy, and delayed marriage. Think about this."[75]

Kinsey's remarks revealed the depth of his rebellion. Concepts such as normal and abnormal no longer held validity for him. Not only were they unscientific, but they reeked of moral approbation and condemnation. In place of arbitrary categories created by the church and the state, Kinsey proposed the morally neutral concept of individual variation, which would allow people to view behavior as a continuum, thereby eroding rigid notions of right and wrong. Ever the taxonomist, Kinsey thought that people should be able to classify themselves, with the clear understanding that every point on the continuum had equal value in nature. This, in turn, would enable people to accept themselves more readily, or, if they felt the need to change or "adjust" their behavior, they would know the full range of options and be able to choose accordingly. "If we indicate to you the limits between which the major portion of the population lies," he explained, "we can in a relatively few words indicate the sorts of adjustments that need to be made to allow for the variation in one direction or the other. If you know what that range and variation is, then you can classify yourself in any such curve and know what sort of adjustment you need to make."[76]

At this point Kinsey appeared to have set the stage for a discussion of sexual deviancy. Instead, he pulled back and discussed solutions for a number of sexual problems that confronted heterosexual couples.[77] His remarks were anything but conventional. A male with a penis of 7 inches or longer posed difficulties, he observed, because the "depth of the vagina shows a variation from 1.7″ to 3.5″ to 5.4″." In keeping with his mechanistic approach to problem solving, Kinsey then recommended a remedy that suited his purpose nicely. Noting that the missionary position allows the maximum penetration, he declared, "The reverse of that position, the female above and the male below, will allow for any length of the penis."[78]

Kinsey offered equally direct suggestions for solving other sexual problems. Adherent foreskin on the penis, which could make intercourse painful, could be solved by circumcision or by the simple method of stretching the foreskin. For women, the corresponding condition (the foreskin of the hood adhering to the clitoris—the problem which had pained Clara) could be corrected through simple surgery. Kinsey also noted that people varied greatly in their ability to produce lubrication. Again, his solution was "to use saliva."[79]

Near the end of his lecture, however, Kinsey dropped the aura of disinterest and grew reflective. While no one would have guessed he was speaking from personal experience, he told the class that newlyweds should begin their lives together with the clear understanding that it takes time to develop a good sex life. "The tragic thing that happens too often is that after the failure to make mutual adjustments within the first two months, without a realization of how difficult it may be to make such adjustments, too often the people conclude that it is impossible to make adjustments," he declared. To illustrate his point, Kinsey told a story. When the marriage course was being planned, he began, he went to a young couple who had sought his advice on sexual matters prior to their marriage, a year and a half ago. Kinsey asked them what was the most important advice they would offer other young couples preparing to wed. They promised to think about it and return with an answer. "When they came back they had boiled it down to this: Try to impress upon them in some way or another that these adjustments take time and that one does not achieve complete adjustments even in 1 1/2 years," reported Kinsey. As if to offer a word of assurance, he added in conclusion, "After many years of a marriage one of the most worthwhile things is that these adjustments may become more and more complete, apparently without end."[80] Certainly, this was what he wanted others to believe about all marriages, including his own.

Viewed from any angle, Kinsey's lectures before the marriage course were revealing. In later years, he went to great lengths to avoid any appearance of telling people how to manage their sexual behavior. In the marriage course, however, he offered a remarkably coherent statement of the biological perspective that guided his analysis; his criticisms of how society regulated sexual behavior; the consequences of those mistakes to people's lives; and the changes he felt were needed to develop a more rational and less harmful system for regulating human sexual behavior. Yet these lectures revealed more than Kinsey's thoughts; they offered a window into his feelings. His language throbbed with anger; his indictments were scathing; and his recommendations were nothing short of revolutionary. Despite his claims to scientific objectivity, Kinsey sounded very much like a man with a mission, a secular evangelist who had weighed how society managed human sexuality and found the results not only wrongheaded but harmful.

Kinsey's lectures were painfully personal, forming a map of his own sexual odyssey. Instead of crushing his spirit, however, his hidden struggles had forged a rebel, an angry man, a man who intended to use science, the greatest weapon at his command, to liberate himself and others from sexual repression. Characteristically, the zealot who had once taken it upon himself to reform taxonomy had set his sights on Victorian sexual morality. What's more, he planned to use the same concept that had served him well in the past. Two decades of research on gall wasps had impressed upon Kinsey the importance of individual variation. He was confident that the same concept applied to human behavior could rescue people from the pious priests whose ignorance of biology had spawned a punitive system of sexual morality.

Thus, the marriage course permitted Kinsey to transform his private struggle against Victorian morality into a public crusade. No longer content to rail in secret, he used the course to protest issues that had bedeviled him privately for decades. Boldly exploiting the academic freedom that protected his every word, he turned his classroom into a soapbox from which to attack Victorian sexual morality. Instead of extolling self-control, Kinsey denounced repression as the root cause of most sexual problems. His lectures pounded home the argument that most sexual problems resulted from repression, which he blamed on society's mindless dependence on religion and its concomitant refusal to be guided by biology.

Kinsey was certain his diagnosis was accurate. His reading of the sex literature, his numerous conversations with students and friends, and, above all, his own experience had convinced him that repressive mores and attitudes had inflicted untold damage on humanity. Too many people, he believed, had been made to feel tentative or guilty about their sexuality. Therefore, the difficulties he and Clara had experienced on their honeymoon were part of a larger social pattern in which young people routinely entered marriage burdened with attitudes that hindered their efforts to develop healthy sex lives. For Kinsey, then, the solution was for society to heed nature. Freed from religiously prescribed notions of right and wrong, people would be at liberty to act upon their sexual needs, without fear or guilt, provided, of course, their behavior did not harm others. In short, Kinsey was preaching a new sexual morality, with respect for diversity at its center and himself as its prophet.

Yet if Kinsey entered the marriage course determined to proselytize, he was no less eager to learn. From the outset he viewed the course not only as a pulpit but as a laboratory. Indeed, months before the course began, he had started making plans to use the class to collect additional data on human sexual behavior.

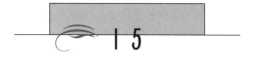

"A Very Strong Regard for Individual Variation"

t the end of the summer of 1938, Kinsey felt encouraged. The marriage course had gone well, and he was eager to repeat it. Pressing the case for future offerings, he turned directly to the man whose support mattered most. In mid-September, Kinsey sent Herman B Wells a summary of student answers to a questionnaire on the marriage course, explaining that their remarks could stand as "something of a report on what we did during the semester."[1] It was a risk-free accounting, since most of the comments ranged from supportive to glowing. Indeed, short of free tuition, it is difficult to imagine what could have generated more enthusiasm among students. The marriage course was a hit.

"Biggest event on campus for decades," proclaimed one student. "A splendid piece of pioneering work," raved another. "I personally feel that it is the best course I have ever been privileged to take," gushed a third. "Fills a significant need that should have been met long ago on this campus," agreed yet another partisan. Stressing the inherent importance of the subject matter, another student declared that the class filled "a genuine need for instruction in a thing which affects the lifetime happiness of so many people."[2]

Turning to the particulars, many students praised the class for shattering the conspiracy of silence that had kept them ignorant about human sexuality. Calling the lectures "very valuable," one student explained, "Many persons have wanted to know the information obtained, but didn't know where to get it and did not want to ask." A student who considered sex education "much needed" felt sorry for students who did not have access to the course, complaining, "Such important information about such an important subject and yet the majority of young people have no opportunity to hear it presented objectively and in such a scholarly manner." A classmate, who judged the course "the finest thing instituted by this University since I entered in 1928," announced, "Its value is inestimable to those who have scarcely any knowledge of the subject."[3] Instead of being shocked or offended, then, many students endorsed explicit and detailed discussions of human sexuality, confirming Kinsey's judgment that young people could handle sensitive material, provided it was presented factually and without a hint of embarrassment.

Aware they had been exposed to more than facts, several students applauded the marriage course for encouraging less rigid thinking. "I think the lectures have been extremely valuable and interesting, partly for the information in them, but mostly for the splendid attitudes they fostered," testified one student. Another student remarked, "It has given me confidence in the information I have acquired. I have also acquired a more healthy attitude." Given his desire to abolish guilt and to alleviate suffering, Kinsey had to be pleased by the student who confessed, "The course has helped me immensely, making clear many things which have bothered me a great deal. It gave me a new understanding of life." Ascribing even greater benefits to the marriage course, a classmate told Kinsey, "You have presented in a concrete manner the greatest problem confronting the youth of today and to a very great extent helped them to solve it."[4] Heady praise indeed, the sort that would not be lost on a man who sought self-validation, even as he struggled to help others.

Eager to point the university in different directions, Wells was clearly impressed by these remarks. The students' comments, he replied, offered "sufficient proof of the worthwhileness of the course, if there were no other substantiating evidence." Proclaiming himself "very much interested in the data you gave me," Wells asked Kinsey to send more details "at your first opportunity."[5] Since the president's backing was critical, Kinsey no doubt responded promptly.

Wells showed considerable courage in supporting the marriage course. Fortunately for the young president, at least one prominent alumnus called openly for sexual reform. A week after he assured Kinsey of his keen interest in the course, Wells received a letter from John R. Frank, a physician who practiced in Valparaiso, Indiana. Frank urged Wells to abandon the rigid morality of the past. He had advised the trustees, he confessed, to appoint "a liberal in education, a broad-minded man," to succeed Bryan, who seemed unaware of the sexual difficulties confronting young people. "Your predecessor, whom I knew, believed in repression, or ignoring this problem," declared Frank. The solution, he asserted, was to consider "allowing and encouraging our youth to marry earlier, using contraceptive devices until children are desired."[6]

Kate Mueller, the dean of women, thought the university had a clear obligation to prepare students for marriage. A broad-minded, forward-thinking educator, she had arrived in Bloomington near the close of the Bryan era when the atmosphere of moral prudery had precluded candid instruction on sexual matters. From the first, she had felt frustrated by the old "Hygiene" course because it failed to meet students' needs. As she explained several decades later, "In the dean of women's office, we had always been interested in having on the campus a good marriage course, because it was the thing that we were reading about and working on in our national conferences and discussions."[7]

Mueller's memory served her well. By the late 1930s, approximately 250 colleges and universities in the United States offered formal sex education courses.[8] Most were taught by one or two instructors, rather than the large staff of specialists Kinsey had assembled. The vast majority of these courses had a decidedly conservative bent, reflecting the social hygiene movement's emphasis on self-control as the proper goal of instruction. Still, not all universities were content to teach sexual restraint under the guise of sex education. After returning from a Panhellenic Conference in Louisville, Kentucky, in October 1938, Mueller informed Kinsey that several of her counterparts at other institutions had inquired about his class. "I found them very much interested in our marriage course," she wrote, "and after I described it to them, they asked if I would send them the list of lecture topics, the departments cooperating, etc."[9] Seizing the opportunity to advertise his course and to make points with another influential administrator, Kinsey immediately furnished the information and materials.

Mueller returned the favor by backing Kinsey wholeheartedly, at least at first. When a church group in Bloomington requested a speaker on what was delicately called "The Home," she immediately referred the matter to him. Confident other inquiries would follow, she recommended he establish a policy with regard to off-campus invitations for lectures. Deferring to his expertise, Mueller assured Kinsey her office would not interfere.

"Amateurs like myself who have nothing to do with either the church or the university marriage course should not speak in such a course at the church, and thus seem to represent the university's course, when they are not really representative of it," she declared.[10] Armed with the administration's tacit approval for off-campus presentations, instructors from the marriage course committee accepted several speaking invitations over the next few months, including one from the staff of the Bloomington hospital, which Kinsey handled personally.

The class itself, however, remained his primary focus. Thanks to the firm backing of students and his careful cultivation of administrators, Kinsey was allowed to teach the marriage course again in the fall of 1938. In response to student requests, he expanded the format to sixteen lectures—two seventy-five-minute classes per week, held in the chemistry auditorium, the only large classroom on campus equipped with a blackboard and slide projector.[11] Registration confirmed the wisdom of reserving a big classroom. The staff had to extend enrollment beyond the regular period to accommodate student demand. Even though it carried no credit, 200 students, 110 women and 90 men, enrolled for the marriage course, an unprecedented expression of student interest. Kinsey assured his fellow instructors that the students had given "nearly unanimous approval of our program."[12]

Throughout the fall semester, Kinsey threw himself into the class like a man with a cause. Ever the perfectionist, he revised his old notes and added a new lecture on sex education for children, a discussion that drew heavily on the approach he and Clara had followed at home. After the term ended, he sent Wells another radiant report. "You will see," boasted Kinsey, "that the students continue in their enthusiastic approval of the program."[13] Kinsey also enclosed separate evaluations for each lecture, allowing Wells to judge for himself how students responded to different topics and instructors. As a strategy for self-promotion, the ploy worked to perfection. Overall, the evaluations showed strong support for the class in general and praise bordering on adoration for one professor in particular. Their general tenor was nicely captured by the student who declared, "I think Dr. Kinsey is the most excellent leader and deserves lots of credit."[14]

These comments thrilled Kinsey. For the first time in his career, he had managed to relate to his students. In contrast to the arrogant and gruff image he had routinely projected in biology classes, Kinsey impressed pupils in the marriage course as earnest and sympathetic. It was as though discussing sexual issues brought out a softer side in his personality, exposing a warmth and compassion that had never surfaced before in the classroom. Struck by his ability to empathize, many students thought he truly cared about their problems. "Sincerity of course clearly established," observed one student. Echoing this point, another student confessed that Kinsey "made me feel as if attempt was sincere."[15]

Still, important features of his teaching style remained unchanged, including his precise use of language and his no-nonsense, businesslike approach. Commenting on Kinsey's peculiar ability to discuss human sexuality dispassionately, one class member described his manner as "serious, scientific, straight forward," while another remarked, "Dr. Kinsey always speaks well, presents in a scientific manner well organized material. He is convincing." Even students who found his ideas unorthodox acknowledged his persuasiveness. With words that underscored how well Kinsey had retained the skills of a college debater, one student confessed, "While unusual in views, the logic of the discussion is not to be denied." Indeed, students agreed that Kinsey put the other instructors to shame. As one admirer put it, "If all the lectures were patterned on Kinsey's, we would have an excellent class."[16]

Everyone marveled at Kinsey's candor. Unaware of the price he had paid to be able to talk so forthrightly, students praised his ability to discuss, without a trace of guilt, subjects that many people found awkward, embarrassing, or downright distasteful. "I admired his ability to speak so freely," said one student. "Dr. Kinsey was just the person to lecture," agreed another. "I admire his frankness." Bemoaning his own upbringing, another student averred with a twinge of sadness, "If parents would instruct their children as suggested in this lecture, many of the problems of adolescents would never appear. I wish my parents had treated the matter of sex instruction in such a natural way to me, instead of telling me little or nothing about it." One female member of the course, who described Kinsey's approach as "perfect," spoke for many of her classmates when she observed, "More people with the frankness and understanding of Dr. Kinsey are needed today."[17]

Even his use of slides earned kudos. Not many educators of his day would have dared to illustrate their lectures with anatomically correct pictures and drawings of genitals and coitus, but Kinsey considered these materials essential.[18] How could young people be expected to learn, he reasoned, if their instructors acted embarrassed? In his view, prudery had no place in the classroom. It hampered understanding. Furthermore, he was convinced middle-class moralists had underestimated young people's ability to handle sexually explicit illustrations without blushing or becoming aroused.

Judging from students' comments, Kinsey was right. "The pictures helped a great deal," declared one man, who considered this particular presentation "probably the outstanding lecture of the series," stressing that the slides had made the material "understandable to everyone." "The best lecture in the series," concurred another man. "I think the idea of using slides was very good. They should be used as much as possible. Liked frankness and openmindedness of lecturer." Another male student remarked that the slides had "put before us the actual pictures" and were therefore "invaluable to our knowledge." Specifying what he had learned, a fellow student declared, "This lecture gave an insight to genitalia which was well presented." A few men in the class encouraged Kinsey to go even further. "I believe the best idea would be motion pictures here," suggested one man. Another man made the identical recommendation, declaring that "a film would have been better than the slides."[19]

Despite widespread concerns about female delicacy, several women in the marriage course applauded Kinsey's use of slides. Calling his lecture "very interesting and very necessary," one woman considered them "a good addition," while another declared, "The use of the slides made the explanation very clear." Commenting on a more personal level, another female member of the class confessed with unblushing candor, "It is a satisfaction to see so many of the things one has wondered about so graphically explained. To me the behavior of the penis was already awe inspiring, now it seems even more wonderful. This was one of the highlights of the course. I had never had a complete understanding even after a dozen years of married life."[20]

Overall, such comments bolstered Kinsey's faith in his judgment. He had long suspected that a growing gulf separated students from their parents, and he, better than most, appreciated the bind young people found themselves in. While middle-class morality demanded chastity until marriage, young people heard a different message everywhere they turned. Novels, magazine articles, advertisements, songs, jokes, and, above all, movies celebrated Eros. How could young people be expected to kiss and say good night after watching Rhett Butler carry Scarlet O'Hara up the stairs or after hearing a sultry Mae West groan, "Come up and see me sometime." What were they to do when the guardians of morality said one thing and popular culture another?

Many students in the marriage course praised Kinsey for stretching their values and challenging their assumptions. "Avoid 'prudish' attitudes—point well taken," declared one student. "I liked especially the part on prudishness and harmful attitudes built up by older people," remarked another. "Particularly, I think should be stressed the riddance of prudish ideas," agreed a third. One impressionable student noted how skillfully Kinsey had "set us to thinking with the right set of mind." And what was the proper mental state? One that accepted Kinsey's overtly biological view of human sexuality. To appreciate how well he succeeded in bending young minds to his way of thinking, consider the comment of the student who confessed that listening to Kinsey "caused one to stop and compare man with other animals."[21]

Nor did students balk at Kinsey's radical ideas. Responding warmly to his lecture on individual variation, many students thanked Kinsey for calling their attention to individual differences, which, in turn, increased their tolerance for people whose sexual needs and behavior differed from their own. "It is best to let students know of the great variation in humans and that there are many individual problems," declared one student, while another testified that learning about individual differences helped clarify "many heretofore unexplainable things." Now that she understood how greatly people varied, a female member of the class promised to "think twice before I start to bite the head off of someone." Touched by the instructor's transparent desire to alleviate guilt and reduce anxiety, another sensitive soul expressed the hope that Kinsey's lecture "may relieve some of our members from undue worry." Yet another concerned student asked Kinsey to prepare an additional lecture devoted entirely to "a discussion of important psychological variations." Moreover, at least one student commented directly on the issue closest to Kinsey's heart—the need for society to develop an ethic of tolerance for individuals whose needs and behavior violated middle-class notions of civilized morality. Commenting on Kinsey's impassioned defense of individual variation, a male student judged this particular discussion "the most important lecture of the group with its stress of objective attitudes in regard to so-called 'abnormality.' "[22]

By themselves, such comments would explain why Kinsey found the class so satisfying. The marriage course earned him the kind of praise every professor craves but few obtain. Yet Kinsey had even better reasons to be pleased. Continuing his pattern of skating near the edge, he had revealed a great deal about himself in his lectures. Indeed, he had taken enormous risks in the marriage course. His attacks on Victorian morality had been sharp and his biological perspective and plea for tolerance nothing short of heretical. He had come perilously close to disclosing how much he despised sexual repression in general and society's treatment of homosexuals in particular.

Yet somehow Kinsey had gotten away with it, at least for the time being. Despite his sharp attacks on Victorian sexual morality, students had not bolted for the doors. Neither had irate local citizen groups stormed the campus. His secret life had not been exposed; nor had the custodians of morality run him out of town. If anything, his boldness had been rewarded. Thanks to the protective mantle of academic freedom, the marriage course had allowed him to discuss publicly many of the issues that had bedeviled him privately since childhood. Kinsey had used the class to test his ideas, and his audience had proved surprisingly receptive. Many had responded like true believers who had found their prophet.

The latter accomplishment, in particular, was important to Kinsey. In words that captured his own odyssey, he had used science to combat his guilt feelings. The marriage course had confirmed his faith in science's ability to help others. Determined to demystify sex, he had talked candidly about issues seldom broached in a college classroom. Displaying to full advantage his extraordinary powers as a secular evangelist, he had taught young people to regard their sexual desires as healthy and natural, rather than sinful and depraved. And if their remarks were to be believed, they had responded warmly.

Small wonder Kinsey was upbeat. He told Bugbee that the marriage course "was a huge success," and he boasted to Voris that the reactions from students and from others across the state were "superb."[23] Apparently, Kinsey sent a similar report to Breland, who shot back with characteristic humor, "Am glad to hear that the course on 'legalized frigging' is coming along nicely. Things certainly picked up at Indiana when Old Shrivel Balls [former President Bryan] got off the pot!"[24]

Emboldened by his success, Kinsey disregarded the trustees' instructions about restricting admission to the marriage course. On the eve of the spring semester 1939, the *Daily Student* reported, "Admission to the marriage course will be based on a liberal interpretation of the needs of the student this semester, Dr. Alfred C. Kinsey, chairman of the course said last night." To eliminate any "confusion . . . concerning admission," he explained, the staff had voted to accept "all seniors and graduate students, other students 21 years of age or older, students who are married or contemplate early marriage, other students who have especial and immediate desire for the course." Casting the net even wider, Kinsey stipulated that the course would welcome "all students who are mature enough to give serious consideration to the various aspects of marriage." In closing, he made one other announcement of interest: "In addition to the formal program of the course, the faculty is available for individual conference with students, both upper and lower classmen, who wish to discuss personal problems in the several fields represented in the program."[25]

The following day, Kinsey hinted at the importance he attached to these conferences in a second interview with a reporter from the *Daily Student*. Thanks to the marriage course, Kinsey declared, he had come to know his students more intimately than most professors would have dreamed possible, an experience he had found inspiring, instructive, and deeply satisfying. "My esteem for the student body has increased tremendously as a result of this course," he asserted. "Together we have faced problems which sometimes have been considered too personal for serious treatment. *As though the immediacy of a situation were reason for avoiding it!"* Contrasting students from the marriage course with people who "have never faced these questions without reacting emotionally," Kinsey declared, "You, on the other hand, have demonstrated your ability to consider such things objectively. For that I admire you." Then, speaking from his heart, he added, *"Reasoned solutions will get you through where supercilious and inhibited responses bring confusion and disaster."*[26]

According to Kinsey, the course was already changing the way people thought. He was delighted by reports "that fraternity courses and 'cross-campus' chit-chat become serious now when they touch on the problems of marriage. For that, again, I admire you." Such attitudes stood in sharp contrast to those harbored by many Americans, particularly those who were so steeped in Victorian morality that they could never consider sexual matters without feeling anxious and guilty. "Not all of the older generation can react as you do," cautioned Kinsey. *"Some of them are still amused. Some of them still respond with blocked emotions—that is, to say, they are shocked.* Whatever their chronological ages, you may determine the generation to which your professors belong by observing their approach to questions of marriage."[27]

Naturally, his role in the marriage course placed him squarely on the side of youth. With calculated boldness, Kinsey implied that students should be given more freedom, since they alone understood their needs and had to bear the consequences of their actions. "You who are students are, after all, the ones most deeply involved," he declared. "The complexities of the economic system into which you are asked to step, the intricacies of the legal and social systems that are imposed on you, the problems of pre-marital sexual adjustments are manmade inventions which weigh primarily upon you, and not upon the adults who have contrived and enforced them." Aware of how Victorian morality could produce cross-generational tensions and conflicts, Kinsey made certain his young readers got the message. "Few adults in consequence have any adequate conception of the difficulties that you face," he lamented.[28]

As if to prove that he was different, Kinsey stressed how clearly he understood young people's concerns and how strongly he affirmed their struggles. His understanding, he explained, was based on knowledge that no one else possessed, information that caused him to stand in awe of how greatly sexual needs and sexual behavior could vary from person to person. "For some time now you have been bringing your problems to me, personally," Kinsey observed. "In spite of my biologic background," he confessed with contrived modesty, "I am increasingly amazed at the complexities of the situations in which you are involved, *and I find that you meet them with poise, with honest frankness, with an idealism which is more important than the particular system of conduct which you work out for your selves;* with an assurance which is the great asset of youth. For all that, I admire you."[29]

Personal revelations filled this interview. After decades of rigid self-control, he was having difficulty restraining himself. Transforming private complaints into public fare, he had denounced the older generation for their prudish attitudes and had all but advised young people to formulate a new system of morality. In making these remarks, Kinsey showed a distinct talent for combining unctuous flattery with accurate insights into students and their personal problems. And make no mistake, every word he uttered took him in the direction he intended. Kinsey was distancing himself from the older generation and literally reaching out to young people. His interview was designed to serve as an open invitation for anyone with sexual questions and problems to enroll. Kinsey wanted the entire student body to know what students in the marriage course had discovered immediately after classes began: he was available to discuss their private lives and to answer any questions they might have of a sexual nature.

The truth of the matter is that Kinsey had planned from the outset to use the marriage course to explore his students' sexual attitudes and behavior. Years of querying friends and graduate students about their sex lives had whetted his appetite for additional information. He had organized the marriage course with the clear intention of expanding his inquiry. In other words, Kinsey began the class not merely to proselytize but to conduct basic research on human sexuality. Yet it seems doubtful that he meant to become a full-time sex researcher. At first, his intentions were surely more modest. Captive of his longtime preoccupation with sex, he probably wanted to learn how other people behaved. His interest also had a distinct political purpose. Determined to distinguish between prescriptive morality and actual conduct, he planned to discover what kinds of behavior could be considered normal, not in a moral sense, but in the statistical meaning of the term.

In later years, Kinsey created a myth to explain how he got involved with sex research, a fabrication that effectively put the cart in front of the horse. Whenever the question arose, he attributed the origins of his research on human sexual behavior to his classroom duties. As a teacher, he explained, many students had brought him questions about sex, but whenever he had consulted the literature the same problems arose. He was, he confessed, "struck with the inadequacy of the samples on which such studies were being based, and the apparent unawareness of the investigators that generalizations were not warranted on the bases of such small samples." Echoing the criticism he had directed at his colleagues when he had initiated his gall wasp studies, Kinsey declared, "All of the studies taken together did not begin to provide a sample of such size and so distributed as a taxonomist would demand in studying a plant or animal species, or a student of public opinion would need before he could safely describe public thinking or predict the future behavior of any portion of the population." Given such puny samples, he saw "ample opportunity for making a scientifically sounder study of human sex behavior."[30] Thus, his decision to interview students.

In sum, Kinsey presented himself as a disinterested scientist who had tried to answer his students' questions. While this explanation contains a sliver of truth, it distorts more than it illuminates. Despite his later declarations to the contrary, the impetus came from him. Students had brought him questions, to be sure, but mostly in response to his prodding. While he would always rationalize his actions by insisting he was helping others, Kinsey had a long history of using students to explore issues that had troubled him since childhood. All that had changed with the marriage course was that he had managed to construct a situation in which larger numbers of students heard his pleas for cooperation.

How he went about persuading them was both cunning and effective. In his second lecture in the marriage course, Kinsey discussed the biological aspects of marriage, with special attention to the "adjustments" couples needed to make in order to build a mutually satisfying sex life. At the end of the period, he announced office hours when he and other faculty members would be available for what he called "personal conferences." Stressing that interested parties could take advantage of this offer with impunity, he declared, "a ruling of the Trustees makes these conferences between students and the staff of this course confidential and inaccessible to the administration of the University."[31]

Kinsey spoke the truth. He had taken great pains to protect both those who sought help and his right to give it. Prior to the beginning of classes, he conferred with President Wells, asking Indiana University's board of trustees to guarantee the confidentiality of any private discussions between faculty and students that might result from the marriage course. No doubt, he informed the young president that students had been bringing him their sexual problems for years and argued that the new class was bound to generate similar conferences. At any rate, Wells supported the proposal. Since Indiana University (like most schools) did not offer psychiatric care or psychological counseling to students, he recognized the need to provide trusted advisers in whom young people could confide without fear of reprisal or betrayal.

Besides, Wells was predisposed to grant the request. A progressive administrator, he thought the university had an obligation to prepare students for life. In the same letter in which he sent word that the trustees had approved the marriage course, Wells assured Kinsey that the faculty would be given full responsibility in the course, "with the understanding that in individual conferences all material is to be considered confidential, and that it is not to be available to the disciplinary deans."[32]

In later years, Kinsey would insist he had kept the administration totally in the dark when he first started collecting data on human sexual behavior. "I think that the surest way of getting something done is to go ahead and do it," he declared, "without asking permission and without expecting cooperation. I undertook the research alone."[33] Kinsey made this claim for two reasons: first, he wanted to reinforce the myth that he had started his research almost by accident in response to student questions he could not answer; and, second, he hoped to shield President Wells from controversy by making it appear that the administration did not learn about his research until it was well under way. Once again, however, the facts do not support Kinsey's version. Before classes began, he had informed Wells about his plan to delve into the private lives of his students, albeit under the guise of counseling; and Wells, in turn, had obtained a ruling from the trustees that greatly facilitated Kinsey's ability to do so.

Armed with the administration's full support (and protection), Kinsey invited students to come in for private conferences with him or with other faculty. As the course progressed, he repeated the offer in different lectures, stressing that his interest was genuine, his concern sincere. His growing boldness in pursuing case histories can be traced in the wording of the questionnaire he distributed at the end of each semester. In the summer of 1938, it read, "How can we improve our service in personal conferences between faculty and students?" In the fall, he added, "Have you utilized the opportunity for personal conferences with the staff?" By the spring of 1939, he asked, "Have you utilized the opportunity for personal conferences with the staff? If so, indicate your reaction as to the value of the conference: If not, would you now be willing to contribute your history to our records, in order that we may secure a better understanding of student problems?"[34]

While students were free to consult any faculty member, virtually all turned to Kinsey. They selected him because they found his lectures the most stimulating, his attitudes the most sympathetic. In addition, they looked up to him as a respected scientist with a reputation for uncommon devotion to academic rigor. As a "starred scientist," president of Indiana University's Phi Beta Kappa chapter, and senior member of the Rhodes Scholarship nominating committee on campus, Kinsey embodied academic excellence.[35] Nor did his ability to command respect rest solely on his professional standing. His age and his family status made him a viable father figure. In fact, everything about the man inspired trust. The expression of understanding and concern in his eyes, his word choice when discussing sensitive topics, and the tone in his voice when he offered words of reassurance—all this and more spoke to a man who understood their problems and who cared about their confusion and pain. Kinsey was indeed definitely fishing in troubled waters. Many of the students who turned up in his class suffered varying degrees of anxiety because they could not meet their society's demands for sexual purity. Often they were troubled by questions about topics discussed in class, such as masturbation, petting, premarital sex, and birth control. While both welcoming and encouraging queries on such garden-variety issues, Kinsey took steps to entice students with less common problems into his office, particularly those whose behavior might shed light on his own.

Kinsey issued a special invitation to people who thought they might be different from the general population. In his lecture on individual variation, for example, he stressed that the adjustments in marital relationships that he covered would "extend to the major portion of the population—to 80 or 90% of it," but cautioned, "The individual who lies still further out on the curve one way or another will have to make the adjustment that individual conference(s) will bring."[36] In the years that followed, Kinsey went to great lengths to solicit case histories from individuals who occupied the margins of sexual behavior, a practice that ultimately would undermine the representative quality of his sample.

Kinsey excelled at coaxing students to his office. During the summer of 1938, 32 students met with him in private and 78 followed in the fall, bringing the total for the last six months of 1938 to 110. All negotiated the labyrinth of bookshelves and filing cabinets to make their way into his inner sanctum. There, Kinsey seated them next to his desk in the holy chair of confession, the one that had been occupied for the last decade by graduate students whom his technical assistants had occasionally overheard uttering barely audible whispers. Yet these current meetings yielded more than isolated tidbits about people's private lives. Students from the marriage course laid the foundation for what became the most important collection of Kinsey's life.

Kinsey obtained his first sexual histories in July 1938. By the end of the fall term that year, he had collected sixty-two, nearly all from the 110 students in the marriage course who had either requested his aid or accepted his invitation for private conferences. Therefore, simple arithmetic shows that he was able to talk more than half of the students who sought his help into contributing their sexual histories. This incredible success rate had not come easily. A decade later, Kinsey explained, "It took six months to persuade the first sixty-two persons to contribute histories; but our techniques were developing, and we began to secure subjects more rapidly."[37]

Far from leaving the administration in the dark, Kinsey kept Wells well informed. In the same letter in which he enclosed summaries of the students' evaluations for the summer of 1938, Kinsey told him that the interviews with students were becoming one of the most important features of the course. Supporting this claim with hard numbers, Kinsey reported that thirty-two students had sought his help in private conferences, providing hard evidence of the crying need for this service.[38] At the end of the fall term, Kinsey wrote Wells again, stating that seventy-eight individuals had met with him in private to discuss personal problems. Repeating how badly students needed this service, he volunteered to meet with Wells to discuss the kinds of sexual issues students confronted.[39]

To acquaint Wells with the range of those problems, Kinsey enclosed a summary of the case histories. Overall, it painted a portrait of young people bedeviled by sexual complaints and badly in need of counseling. Several students, Kinsey reported, had sought help for anatomical and physiological problems, which in some cases had demanded medical treatment. One student had inquired about an endocrine disturbance; eight had expressed concern over genital malformation; and three had sought information about spontaneous abortion in marriage. No fewer than eighteen married students had inquired about adjustments in techniques; three had requested information on contraception; three more had discussed divorce; and one had inquired about extramarital intercourse.[40]

Nor were single members of the class free of stress. If anything, their questions had confirmed Kinsey's fear that young people suffered chronic guilt feelings, largely because they either thought or behaved in ways that violated middle-class morality. Eight students had complained about a total lack of erotic response; thirty-six had asked about masturbation; twenty-nine had inquired about premarital intercourse; and no fewer than nine had sought information about homosexuality. While each and every case provided grist for his mill, the last group had special resonance for Kinsey. The nine students who had come to him to discuss homosexuality offered flesh-and-blood proof that he was neither unique nor alone. Intellectually, of course, he had known this for some time. Still, it must have been deeply reassuring and strangely exhilarating for him to discover students with the same needs that haunted him. That these anxious souls confided in him speaks volumes about the atmosphere of trust he had succeeded in creating.[41]

Yet trust alone does not explain how Kinsey was able to learn such intimate details. In purely mechanistic terms, he owed much of his success to the fact that he had the proper instrument. As part of his preparation for the marriage course, Kinsey had prepared a written questionnaire designed to reconstruct a person's sexual history. The questionnaire was extremely thorough. According to Cornelia Christenson, who later worked for Kinsey and apparently was allowed to see some of these early histories, the questionnaire covered "the major sexual outlets: masturbation, sex dreams, petting, and coitus." She went on to explain that coitus "was subdivided into categories based on the identity of the sexual partner," which "included premarital, marital, extramarital, or postmarital coitus, and intercourse with prostitutes." In addition, Kinsey examined "the two almost unexplored areas of homosexual relations and sexual contacts with animals."[42]

Comments Kinsey made a decade later reveal that these early histories included most of the basic points he examined after he became an experienced sex researcher. "Since the first year," he wrote in 1948, "there has been an expansion of 22 per cent in the list of items covered in each history."[43] Here it is important to emphasize that the mature interview included a minimum of 300 and a maximum of 521 items, depending on the individual's sexual repertoire. Therefore, the histories collected by Kinsey during the first few offerings of the marriage course, while less elaborate than those that followed, nevertheless covered hundreds of items, far too many to be thought up on the spur of the moment. No, they reflected careful homework on Kinsey's part, the kind of preparation one would expect from a man who had read the literature and had thought long and hard about how to frame precise questions.

Kinsey never doubted his ability to get students to cooperate. Years later, he explained that "enough success had been achieved in some of the previous sex studies to make it apparent that there were at least some people who could be persuaded to contribute records of their activities."[44] True enough. But Kinsey had reason to trust himself far more than his predecessors. After all, he had spent his whole life cultivating skills that would make him an outstanding interviewer. In South Orange, he had served as a Sunday school teacher, Boy Scout leader, and camp counselor; in college, he had developed into a champion debater and boys club leader; and at Indiana University, he had spent nearly two decades polishing his verbal skills in lectures, in the seminar room, and in private sessions that presaged his conferences with students in the marriage course.

At first, Kinsey concentrated on students who came in for private conferences, though he quickly abandoned this policy in favor of asking all class members to complete the sex history questionnaire (in addition to the one they filled out evaluating each separate lecture). To encourage cooperation, Kinsey appealed both to their self-interest and to their altruism, stressing that their histories would enable him to answer not only their questions but those of future students.

Kinsey made the same request of a select group of people outside the course. Here he targeted former students and close friends, people he could trust and influence, if not manipulate and control. For example, when Robert C. Bugbee, his former graduate student, stopped by Bloomington for a visit in the summer of 1938, Kinsey told him about the marriage course and asked for his sexual history. No doubt, Kinsey offered him the same explanation that had worked so effectively on students in the class—namely, that he needed basic data on human sexuality to answer students' questions.

Whatever the pitch, Bugbee fell in line. At the time, he was trying to secure a better teaching position. He was not about to alienate his old major professor. After returning to his home in Emporia, Kansas, where he taught at a small college he loathed, Bugbee replied, "I hope the marriage course was well received and I am returning in this letter the data which you wanted." Proclaiming his support for sex education, Bugbee added, "I believe we need more of that type of education because the more I see of young married couples the less you discover that they know about the whole situation."[45]

Kinsey's reply, which arrived a few weeks later, shows a man being drawn deeper and deeper into his new research. After assuring Bugbee that the marriage course had been "a huge success," Kinsey thanked him warmly "for all the data you gave us." In addition, he expressed gratitude for earlier discussions in which Bugbee had confided details about his own marital history, remarks that Kinsey had quickly passed along to students in the marriage course. "Quoted your advice as to adjustments taking time to learn (without names, of course); and the class was much struck by it," declared Kinsey. "We have over 50 case histories—complete questionnaires of the sort you filled out for us—already in our files," he added. "They help mightily in giving us backgrounds. We must accumulate more. If you know victims for additional questionnaires, refer them to me."[46] Clearly, Kinsey's fondness for numbers was spilling over into his new area of research.

It was not long before Kinsey began to doubt whether a questionnaire was the best instrument for the job. As he met with students, he discovered that verbal exchanges enhanced his ability to elicit the truth. In contrast to written questionnaires, interviews were dynamic and interactive, features Kinsey found highly attractive. In fact, he later regretted having used a questionnaire at all. Writing in 1942, he thanked one of the original students in the marriage course for his contribution back in 1938, but added ruefully, "I wish it might have been in a personal interview, for we soon discovered that the questionnaire data were not adequate and, except for a few of you right at the start, all of our other data have come from personal interview[s]."[47]

Despite such statements, it would be a mistake to conclude that data constituted the sole reason Kinsey switched from written questionnaires to oral interviews. Emotional needs also drew him to face-to-face meetings. As his conferences with students progressed, Kinsey found them extremely satisfying, because once again he had created a situation where he was the master and those who came to him were supplicants. Having students seek his help, prying deeper and deeper until they bared their souls, dispensing knowledge and information few possessed, and maneuvering others into a position that allowed him to offer reassurance and compassion all served to gratify Kinsey's need for authority and control. Not only did he enjoy exploring the shadowlands where people hide their secrets; he fed on the power surge that resulted from this psychic penetration.

Above all, counseling sessions afforded Kinsey the perfect cover for immersing himself in the intimate details of other people's lives. Suddenly, it was all so simple. The conferences brought everything together. Instead of his having to pursue people, they now came to him. And they came in droves, seeking information and advice from the resident sex expert on campus. In other words, the conferences allowed Kinsey to transform his private needs into professional duty. Through clever alchemy, he had converted sex into work, the lifeblood of his being.

Still, important aspects of Kinsey's complex character would be neglected if the explanation stopped here. However compelling his prurient needs, altruistic motives also came into play. A chronic do-gooder, Kinsey wanted to help his students and, by extension, to serve mankind. At the conscious level, his self-image was that of a man who had been victimized by sexual repression and had nevertheless managed to fight back. He saw himself as a soldier of science who had struggled against mighty odds to free himself from debilitating guilt, a rationalist who had waged a costly war to protect his self-esteem from attacks by ignorant priests and judgmental physicians.

Thus, despite his scientific armor, Kinsey's response to the troubled young people who came to his office was profoundly emotional. He felt close to the students who confided in him, as though their act of trust somehow created a special bond between them. In return for their faith, he answered their questions and offered advice, telling anyone who would listen not to feel guilty, because their sexual desires in most instances were neither harmful nor unnatural. For their part, students felt grateful. Typical was the young man who wrote to wish Kinsey "the greatest success with the marriage course" and who closed by declaring, "I want also to thank you for the advice you gave me at the time that I gave you my case history which was to free myself of my sexual inhibitions and masturbate more freely. Since acting on your suggestion I find myself in a more balanced state—no more feelings of deep depression; more feeling at ease with the world."[48]

Explaining the unique relationship he developed with his subjects, Kinsey later referred approvingly to a study that described sex interviews as "a communion between two deeply human individuals, the subject and the interviewer."[49] That he should embrace a religious metaphor need not surprise us. From the first, Kinsey operated like a secular priest whose knowledge and training qualified him to offer advice, to explain mysteries, and to grant absolution in the name of science. And like many holy men, he took it upon himself to help the needy.

Breland, his former student, had Kinsey to thank for recommending a treatment for a vexing problem. Praising the remedy he had recently adopted for what he called "premature spitting," Breland wrote, "This method is the very simple one that you suggested last summer, namely, having private session with no one present except you and the organ under discussion. By making him play butter milk with the thin air, one is able to throttle this gentleman much more effectively at the time when he has something more concrete to poke his nose into." After describing this treatment as "very effective" and declaring that "it should be recommended to anyone troubled in that fashion," Breland begged to have his wife kept in the dark about his therapy, exclaiming, "The better half knows nothing at all about this, so for pete's sake, don't pass it on to anyone who is likely to get it back to her. I'm afraid I would not have any more necessity for the private sessions or for any sessions at all—she would probably castrate me!"[50]

Thanks to the marriage course, Kinsey suddenly had scores of students who needed help. Indeed, he was besieged with questions. With varying degrees of desperation, former students (and their friends) sought advice on secret marriages, marriage between first cousins, the keys to marital compatibility, the remedies for sexual incompatibility, frigidity, birth control, sterility, premature ejaculation, homosexuality, and sundry other matters. A less dedicated man might have been overwhelmed by the number and the complexity of these queries, but Kinsey responded to each and every cry for help with remarkably thorough and detailed recommendations.

His letters showed that Kinsey was concerned about the people who sought his help. Nor did he break off contact when their difficulties ended. Often he kept in touch for years with former students from the marriage course. On more than one occasion, he drove to distant towns to attend their weddings; he invariably responded with warm notes of congratulation when they wrote to inform him of the birth of a child; and he was quick to offer advice and counseling when marriages ended in separation or divorce. Later, one of his colleagues would compare Kinsey at this point to "a young social worker who has not yet learned he must not become involved with his cases," adding that it took "three or four years before he learned that he had to stop this kind of case work if the research was to survive."[51] It is doubtful whether Kinsey ever succeeded in distancing himself. He identified with people with sexual problems. Their pain fed his anger, and his anger, in turn, strengthened his resolve to create a more tolerant and humane society.

Both his thoroughness and his sensitivity are captured in a letter Kinsey wrote in December 1938 to a woman who had taken the marriage course the preceding summer, without contributing her sexual history. Soon thereafter the woman married. Unfortunately, she experienced difficulty reaching orgasm, whereupon she asked Kinsey for advice. Kinsey replied, "I esteem your confidence in coming to us for information. It provides one more of the specific evidences we have of the justification for this marriage course." As if to confirm her decision to turn to him, Kinsey added pointedly, "I hope you will continue to come to us when we can help. Unfortunately not one doctor in a hundred has had any training on this end of biology, and you will have difficulty in finding one who could contribute in any sound way."[52] "It is difficult to diagnose a situation when the patient is not at hand," continued Kinsey. "If you were here, I could secure many data which might have a bearing on the situation, and thus figure out which items are involved in this particular case. Lacking that immediate opportunity, I am enclosing a couple of case-history blanks which you and your husband might fill out." As a reminder, Kinsey added, "All of our records are confidential, by ruling of the Trustees of the University, [and] that we have seen so much of the personal lives of our students that we are surprised at nothing, make no moral evaluations, and are interested primarily in the scientifically objective fact." Her data, he declared, would "add to our records, as well as giving us a better basis for judging what help might be applied to your own problem."[53]

Kinsey broached her personal problems with soothing words of reassurance. "Difficulty in reaching climax is a very common one among newly married people who have not had previous intercourse," he wrote. "It sometimes takes long practice to have nerves and muscles develop to the point of efficient response. If you cannot remedy the situation immediately, do not be discouraged, for that may still come in time." The important thing, he stressed, was "to understand that complete satisfaction is not only desirable, but very necessary physiologically."[54] Exploring the universe of possibilities, he asked whether her husband was able to postpone orgasm and volunteered "to instruct him on that point if he is not able to delay climax more or less indefinitely." Next, Kinsey inquired about her sexual responsiveness. Curiously, he did not seek to ascertain whether inhibitions might explain her inability to achieve an orgasm, concentrating on physical or mechanical impediments instead. Drawing upon his own marital experience, he raised the problem that he and Clara had encountered, underscoring his lifelong tendency to generalize from himself to others. "If the foreskin of the clitoris is adherent (so the clitoris is not free to erect and protrude entirely out of its hood-like covering)," observed Kinsey, "it may be a prime factor in preventing full climax." The solution, he explained, was to correct the problem with surgery, and he offered to recommend a doctor in Bloomington who would perform the operation for $3.00.[55]

Still looking for a mechanical fix, Kinsey turned to copulatory technique, suggesting that it might be possible to correct her problem by experimenting with new positions during intercourse. In his best clinical tone, he advised against the male superior position, because it afforded "a minimum of chance for the female to make her own adjustment." Infinitely more satisfactory was the female superior position, he explained, because it allowed women "to direct the stimulation to the particular parts of the genitalia which are most sensitive." This was particularly true, he stressed, "if the woman, in this position, lies slightly at an angle, so the two bodies are not directly super-imposed, [with] the penis pulled slightly to one side, and that makes it much simpler for the male to delay climax."[56]

Finally, Kinsey asked the woman to consider whether contraceptives might be the source of her problem. "The condom is too slick to bring adequate response from some women," he cautioned. As an alternative, he recommended the cervical diaphragm, provided it was fitted by a qualified physician. Finding a physician who was willing to provide this service, however, was no easy matter. Aware she might encounter difficulties, Kinsey offered to put her in touch with a doctor in Bloomington who would fit her "at a cost of $2.00 (a quarter of the charge which the other physicians have been making)." In Kinsey's mind, there was no question that the diaphragm was the device of choice. "It is easily inserted in the vagina after a little practice, is entirely safe, and if proper in form and fitting neither the male nor female are conscious of its presence," he declared. As a clincher, he added, "The penis can then supply the more normal stimulation, especially if the foreskin has not been circumcised."[57]

Kinsey closed by repeating his request for the woman and her husband to complete his questionnaires, pleading that if they did so "we should be able to help further." His ability to provide assistance, he added, would be greatly enhanced if they agreed to one last item. Each spouse should fill out the questionnaire without conferring with the other, he stressed, because "it then represents an uninhibited reaction of the one individual, and not the adjusted reactions of two in consultation."[58]

This letter goes a long way toward explaining Kinsey's success. It shows a master at work, a man who knew how to reassure people and how to offer them hope. It also reveals a man who understood how to manipulate people, how to trade upon their fears, anxieties, and need for help. In fact, it is easy to see why this woman (and so many people like her) cooperated. Kinsey's manner and tone were invariably warm and supportive. And however mechanistic his approach to problem solving, the candor and simplicity of his suggestions appealed strongly to individuals who were desperate for help, especially since most physicians and ministers offered little concrete advice.

As his conferences with students progressed, Kinsey found himself drawn more and more to face-to-face meetings. He was amazed by how much he was learning. Often he would make careful notes immediately after students left his office, while the details were still fresh in his memory. Later, he would review the session in his mind, looking for potential openings where he might have learned more by digging deeper. Once he reached this point, Kinsey was well on the road to switching from written questionnaires to oral interviews, and he started constructing a formal interview that would extract the information he craved.

Describing how her husband formulated his questions, Clara stated many years later, "Well, I think it was one of those things that evolved just like anything else. As he worked at it, then he realized other questions that needed to be asked, and it developed that way." Asked if she had helped, Clara replied modestly, "Oh, we talked about it. I doubt if I really helped any on it." She was less forthcoming about her husband's efforts to gain experience interviewing women by taking her sexual history. Asked if he had tried out his technique on her, Clara replied, "Yes, once." Pressed for more details, she answered, "It went all right." Urged to elaborate, she refused with a terse "No."[59]

Why did Clara agree to be interviewed? What would it be like to tell one's spouse everything—not in a moment of tender intimacy, either, but in response to systematic questioning in which every revelation represented in some measure a gift of trust, if not an act of psychological surrender? Kinsey, of course, would not have thought anything about asking Clara to contribute her sexual history. He would not have recognized the need to preserve her privacy; nor would he have felt awkward about the control and power he exercised over Clara by interviewing her. Nor did Kinsey doubt his right to interview his children. In response to their father's request, Anne, Bruce, and Joan each contributed a history. Had he been asked to justify his behavior, Kinsey probably would have answered with one word, "Science!" But his children were not responding to the call of science; rather, they were complying with a request from their father.

During the months Kinsey devoted to constructing his oral interview, he asked Robert Kroc, his friend and colleague in the biology department, for advice on what questions to ask, the order in which issues should be broached, and the like. Kroc agreed to be used as a sounding board, despite feeling somewhat embarrassed. His objections were not moral. Rather, he felt uneasy because Kinsey appeared to be abandoning science for what Kroc considered "a sociologic and psychologic field." Still, when his friend's thinking had progressed to the point that he had worked out his questions, Kroc readily consented to a formal interview. Thanks to their numerous brown-bag chats about their sexual histories in the past, he did not find the interview itself awkward. As Kroc later explained, "long before that he was pretty familiar with my history."[60]

Kinsey received help of a different kind from Raymond Pearl, a distinguished biologist and pioneering biostatistician from the Johns Hopkins University. During the fall term of 1938, Pearl spent six weeks as the Patten Foundation lecturer at Indiana University, where he delivered five public addresses on the general topic "Man the Animal." In addition, Pearl gave numerous seminars and several less formal talks to various groups on campus, including an appearance before the marriage course. To express his thanks, Kinsey invited Pearl and his wife, who had accompanied him to Bloomington, to a Sunday musicale.[61]

Additional social occasions followed, and Kinsey was delighted by these contacts. In a letter to one of his former graduate students, he described Pearl as "a very pleasant individual to get along with" and Mrs. Pearl as "charming and most brilliant." Kinsey added, "I begin to suspect that much of the pep in the *Quarterly Review of Biology* [for which Pearl served as editor] is due to her editing. His hobby is music, and so we are seeing a good deal of him at our house." But since work was never far from Kinsey's thoughts, he seized the opportunity to seek Pearl's help on a puzzling problem involving his current gall wasp research. Describing the situation in his letter, Kinsey noted that much of his current research was "going to be a purely biometric study of individual variation, and there is no one in the world better equipped to guide me on that than Raymond Pearl. He seems very much interested in my research."[62] Kinsey was particularly pleased by Pearl's advice on sampling. "When I told him that someone else would have to handle the mathematics of the material, he told me that when one has such quantities of material as I have it needs very little manipulation," beamed Kinsey. "[Pearl] points out that statistical theory is largely a substitute for adequate data," he continued. "All this encourages me greatly."[63]

Kinsey had every right to value Pearl's advice, as he was the current president of the American Statistical Association. To have someone of Pearl's stature endorse his methodology was wonderfully reassuring for Kinsey, particularly since gall wasps were not the only research problem occupying his attention.[64] His discussions with Pearl help explain why Kinsey later felt so confident about transferring his taxonomic methodology to sex research. His dogged efforts in the years ahead to compile a huge collection of sex histories demonstrated how strongly he placed his faith in sample size as opposed to statistical theory.

But Pearl did more than bless this mania for numbers. At a crucial juncture in Kinsey's life, Pearl encouraged him to become a sex researcher. Kroc remembered a conversation in which Pearl said that Kinsey had showed him his notes on conversations with students from the marriage course. "Pearl told me when he looked over these, he said to Kinsey, 'This must be published; this is important data. You must formalize . . . your interviews. Don't do it in such a way that you have to record it afterward, because that may bring in some errors.' And that's what Pearl told me," Kroc repeated for emphasis. Kinsey must have relished this advice as much as Pearl's remarks on sampling. Scientists need to have their research certified by fellow scientists, and Pearl's opinion carried considerable weight. His book *The Biology of Population Growth* (1926) included data on the frequency of marital intercourse that made it of considerable interest to sex researchers.[65]

Throughout the fall and spring terms 1938–39, Kinsey picked up speed. In a letter to Voris written in mid-January 1939, Kinsey claimed to have added seventeen case histories since New Year's, and he enclosed a summary of the cases, complete with orders to destroy it. Then, in an obvious reference to their close relationship and their many conversations about sex, Kinsey acknowledged Voris's role in preparing him to handle a number of these cases.[66]

As he met with students, Kinsey worked simultaneously to develop an oral interview that could serve as a reliable tool. To make certain he was not omitting anything of importance, he consulted the literature. "The more recently published research provided a considerable basis for deciding what should be included in a sex history," he later explained, "and our background in both psychology and biology made it apparent that there were additional matters worth investigation." It was his interest in "additional matters" that led Kinsey to examine areas of behavior about which previous sex researchers knew little, largely because most had not dared to ask.[67]

No previous investigator had ever attempted what he had in mind. Kinsey meant to recover every knowable fact about people's sex lives and erotic imaginations. He intended to learn how people thought and behaved, how frequently they engaged in such thought and behavior, and with whom or with what they did so. Because he believed that people routinely hid the truth about their private needs and behavior, Kinsey was determined to strip away denial, to get at the hidden side of life, to discover what people actually thought and did behind closed doors, safe from the scrutiny of judgmental others. To retrieve this information, he relied upon his interview, a research tool that he believed could uncover every facet of a person's sexual history.

Kinsey's confidence rested on his gall wasp work. As a longtime student of variation, he expected to find differences in sexual behavior, both between individuals and among and within groups. Explaining how his background in taxonomy shaped his approach to sex research, Kinsey wrote in 1940, "My own training has been broadly biological, and my research in the field of taxonomy. There I have been involved with individual variation in a group of insects, and it is with a very strong regard for individual variation that I have approached the study of the human."[68]

Kinsey also believed that his experiences as a field biologist had prepared him to deal with people from different backgrounds. Looking back on his development as an interviewer, he wrote in 1948, "We had had enough contacts with persons of other social levels, in city communities, in farm areas, in the backwoods, and in the remote mountain areas from which we had collected gall wasps, to lead us to believe that we might be able to secure cooperation from a wide variety of people."[69] Once again, however, Kinsey told only part of the story, leaving an important reason for his confidence unspoken: he knew he could persuade students to confide in him because several had already done so. Long before the marriage course, he had displayed a talent for prying into other people's sexual secrets.

Kinsey used the marriage course to improve his skills as an interviewer. "It was a slow matter learning how to secure subjects and learning what interviewing techniques were most effective," he later confessed. Textbooks on interviewing, he lamented, "did not prove effective." Again, in place of books, Kinsey drew upon what he had learned in the classroom and in the field. "Our experience in teaching and in meeting people in entomological field-work," he noted, "was a better guide toward winning confidences and securing honest answers."[70]

Kinsey's concern for confidentiality deepened his dissatisfaction with written questionnaires. Early in his research, he decided that his ability to earn people's trust and cooperation would be greatly enhanced if he could guarantee confidentiality. From a security standpoint, written questionnaires exposed subjects to serious risks, particularly if the records fell into the wrong hands, forming, as they did, a paper trail of evidence. Written sex histories could be used by the authorities to violate people's right to privacy and to incriminate those who confessed to illegal behavior. Perhaps because he understood so clearly why people might wish to conceal their sexual secrets, Kinsey developed his own private system for recording sex histories, rendering his records unintelligible to anyone who did not know the code. To enhance security, Kinsey refused to produce a written key for his system. Instead, he memorized all the questions, both in sequence and in any possible combination or order.

This required a nimble mind. If a subject gave an answer that opened up a new area for discussion or closed another, Kinsey had to be able to stop on a dime and leap to another battery of questions (all the while keeping the items in each section straight in his head). Even though it took many hours and much work to commit everything to memory, Kinsey reaped benefits that more than repaid his labor. Not having a written questionnaire guaranteed that he alone knew the items covered in a history and the answers people gave to his questions. This approach also permitted him to move smoothly through the hundreds of items covered in each history, without losing eye contact and without any of the other delays or disruptions that consulting notes would have entailed.

In a matter of months, Kinsey developed his own system for recording sex histories. Composed of two interrelated parts, his record system consisted of a specially designed form and a secret code. The form allowed him to record an entire sexual history on a single, ruled sheet of paper, divided into more than twenty separate blocks. Describing how the position code worked, Kinsey later wrote, "Each aspect of the sex history is recorded in a particular block or portion of a particular block. The significance of any symbol depends, consequently, upon its position in a particular block on the page."[71]

Kinsey's pride and joy was the code itself, the heart of his system. Employing elements of a crude shorthand he had developed to record measurements and field notes on his gall wasp research, the code was created, Kinsey later explained "with the help of an experienced cryptographer" who gave serious thought to developing "several devices designed to complicate possible decoding." The code consisted of symbols that "included various mathematical signs . . . and numbers for recording ages, the years involved, frequencies, and still other items." In addition, the code employed "numbers, letters, [and] symbols derived from standard practice in biology, chemistry, physics, and the other sciences, and some unique symbols developed especially for this study."[72] In later years, Kinsey delighted in handing visitors a single sheet of paper with a bunch of odd-looking symbols. Invariably, he would explain that the paper contained a complete record of a subject's sexual history, and he would challenge his guests to decipher it. None could. The system worked.

From the early days of his research, Kinsey made his devotion to confidentiality the cornerstone of his pitch to volunteers. Much as he assured students in the marriage course that the trustees had agreed to respect the sanctity of private conferences, he told other potential subjects that his system of recording sex histories ensured security. With great pride, he would describe his record system, emphasizing that not even people's names appeared in his files. Then came the clincher. Kinsey would conclude by stressing that individual records would be subsumed into a mass of data, rendering subjects totally anonymous. Impressed by the sensitivity he had demonstrated to the need for confidentiality and reassured by the system he had designed to guarantee it, many people agreed to be interviewed. His record system elicited precisely the responses he intended—confidence and trust, which, in turn, translated into cooperation.

Kinsey treated his correspondence with equal care. Aware of Kinsey's reputation for preserving the sanctity of any and all sexual information, one former student remarked, "I am writing you as I know anything I tell you is confidential."[73] Despite such expressions of trust, a few individuals were reluctant to discuss their sexual problems in their letters. One young man, who had contributed his sex history when he was a student in the marriage course, later wrote to inquire if he could return to Bloomington and confer with Kinsey, explaining, "I do not like to put such things in writing, as writing is so dern permanent."[74] Eager to reassure the young man, Kinsey replied, "Whatever you care to write me can be kept perfectly confidential. No one else sees my correspondence except myself."[75] Over the next few years, Kinsey shifted ground on this issue, advising his correspondents to refrain from putting sensitive issues in writing and to wait whenever possible until they could meet to discuss such matters in person.

At the same time he was designing safeguards, Kinsey was working to develop his skills as an interviewer. Through trial and error, he taught himself the tricks of the trade. He learned how to read people's eyes and body language for signs that they might be holding back or lying. He also discovered a lot about language. To prevent confusion and misunderstanding, he taught himself to phrase questions in a straightforward manner, avoiding euphemisms that could obscure meaning. Over time, Kinsey also learned to adjust his vocabulary to the appropriate level, selecting words that banished ambiguity and enabled people to understand his questions perfectly. In addition, he mastered the art of framing direct and precise follow-up questions, both to sharpen discussion and to overcome resistance to further revelations.

Kinsey quickly discovered that people could be inveigled into admitting a greater variety of behavior if they bore the burden of denial. He assumed that everyone had engaged in forbidden behavior unless she or he said otherwise, and he phrased his questions in such a way as to facilitate con-fession. For example, instead of asking people if they had ever masturbated, he would inquire how old they were when they started masturbating. Un-abashedly directive, his approach proved particularly effective with regard to illegal behavior. In later years, when he compared his data with pub-lished reports based on written questionnaires, there were irreconcilable discrepancies. This led Kinsey to believe that people often failed to put in-formation on paper that might be legally incriminating. Yet these same in-dividuals, he learned, frequently were willing to reveal compromising information in an oral interview, provided they believed the investigator would guarantee confidentiality.[76]

Over time, Kinsey also developed an arsenal of subtle skills. Through ex-perience, he discovered that a change in the tone or inflection in his voice, the expression on his face, or the look in his eyes communicated the as-surances many people required. He could use these same devices to chal-lenge subjects who appeared to be lying or covering up. Although he would later be accused of pressuring people into saying what he wanted to hear, Kinsey would always insist that effective interviewing required human interaction. The large number of people who could be encouraged to tell the truth by a reassuring nod or a disbelieving scowl, he argued, far out-weighed the risk of distorted data from a few individuals who might be un-duly influenced (pronounced overwhelmed) by such gestures.

Far more troubling were the folks who deliberately lied. Here Kinsey had to rely on his instincts, on his ability to read people correctly. And that was precisely what he did. To skeptics who wondered, in his words, "how it is possible for an interviewer to know whether people are telling the truth, when they are boasting, when they are covering up, or when they are otherwise distorting the record," Kinsey snorted in rejoinder, "As well ask a horse trader how he knows when to close a bargain! The experienced interviewer knows when he has established a sufficient rapport to obtain an honest record, in the same way that the subject knows that he can give that honest record to the interviewer. Learning to recognize these indica-tors, intangible as they may be, is the most important thing in controlling the accuracy of an interview."[77]

But Kinsey was too rigorous to leave it at that. While he would always profess faith in his powers of perception, he developed a number of tech-niques to enhance his ability to uncover the truth. Over the years, Kinsey taught himself to employ a staccato method of asking questions, which re-duced the time a subject had to think up false but plausible answers. He also made a point of maintaining eye contact, believing it would be harder for people to lie to someone who looked them straight in the eye. Still, Kinsey knew that some individuals were addicted to lying, and he developed his own peculiar method for handling these prevaricators. Once he became suspicious, he would stop the interview, denounce the person severely, and order the culprit to tell the truth or get out.

Kinsey also built a number of trip wires into the interview. Among these were a series of interlocking questions designed to break down resistance in the reticent, strip away denial from the self-deceivers, and trap the foxes. For example, he asked no fewer than twelve indirect questions about homosexuality at different points of the interview before the first direct query on the subject appeared. In each instance the inferences were so subtle that only a psychiatrist, or a person with similar training, could have grasped their significance. As a result, it was difficult for subjects to keep their answers straight if they were being less than honest.

As he became more experienced, Kinsey fine-tuned the order of topics within the interview. It helped, he discovered, if he began with biographical and socioeconomic questions, as these were relatively impersonal and nonthreatening. Then, as subjects became more relaxed, the discussions could shift to behavioral issues. Experience also taught him to vary the order of questions when dealing with men and women. Topics raised early with men had to be broached later with women, he concluded, because women seemed to require a little more time before they felt comfortable discussing sensitive issues.

Over the next several years, Kinsey also became remarkably fluent in the patois of various sexual subcultures, both to show their members he could speak their language and to force them to reveal forbidden behavior. "For instance," he later explained, "when one asks a female subject 'how many years she has been in the life,' she must betray an honest confusion and inability to understand, or else she identifies herself as a prostitute." The same ploy could be used to trap the members of other furtive groups. "There are special argots for practically all of the socially taboo activities," he added; "and they may provide checks on many of the persons who must be included in a human case history study."[78]

As Kinsey struggled to master his new craft, he never lost sight of the need to maintain human contact with his subjects. His greatest asset as an interviewer was his gift for establishing rapport. Over time, he became a master of putting people at ease and of earning their trust. As people told their stories and asked their questions, he somehow found the right words to bathe them in warmth and compassion. Invariably, his language resonated to their individual predicaments and conveyed his approval of them as human beings. Not that words were his only means of communication. Again, a nod of the head here, a smile there, a hand placed kindly on the shoulder in response to some shameful revelation, all served to get the message across.

In retrospect, it is amazing how rapidly things progressed. Describing the feverish pace at which he had worked, Kinsey wrote in 1948, "By the end of the first nine months the scope of each history, the form of the record, and the techniques of the interview had been developed to very nearly their present form."[79] In other words, it had taken Kinsey less than a year to develop both his system and his method, a feat that would have been impossible if his life to this point had not prepared him in multiple ways for the task at hand. Also in place by the end of that first year were the scientific theories and philosophical assumptions that shaped his approach to the study of human sexual behavior, a fact that suggests how nicely his new area of research united the scientist with the man.

Without using the word "sex" a single time, Kinsey articulated these views in a lecture entitled "Variation," delivered early in June 1939, to fifteen newly elected members of Phi Beta Kappa. From beginning to end, the talk was an ode to the biological concept that had preoccupied him for two decades, with one new twist: instead of sticking with gall wasps, he quickly switched to his new area of research.

Kinsey opened by telling his young listeners that his primary concern was to explain how variations accounted for individuality. As an evolutionary biologist and radical antiessentialist, he had no hesitancy in announcing that the concept of individual variation was not only fundamental to biological reasoning but of far-reaching importance. After assuring his audience that individual variation was universal in nature, Kinsey challenged anyone to find two individuals from any of the millions of species on earth that were exactly alike.[80]

Warming to his audience, Kinsey revealed that he had recently started to apply the principles of evolutionary biology to a new study of individual differences involving human behavior. Unlike his gall wasp work, he stressed, this research allowed him to apply biological concepts to human behavior that most people found interesting.[81] Without specifying the nature of the activity, Kinsey disclosed that his research entailed interviewing people about more than 250 types of behavior. Already it had become clear, he stressed, that the data he had compiled presented a portrait of diversity that challenged facile classifications and rendered meaningless a variety of social conventions, legal restrictions, and moral codes.[82]

Turning to the causes of behavioral differences, Kinsey struck a sensible pose. For decades, scientists and social scientists alike had debated the relative importance of heredity and environment in determining human behavior. Early in the century, heredity was widely regarded as the stronger influence, but by the late 1930s many scientists and social scientists leaned toward environmental influences. Instead of choosing sides, Kinsey looked for middle ground in the nature/nurture controversy, a position that was intellectually prudent and entirely consonant with his desire to promote an ethic of tolerance. "The origins of these differences between individuals are both genetic and acquired, the outcome of the hereditary equipment with which the individual came into the world, and the product of all the environmental circumstances to which that hereditary gift has been subjected," he declared. Arguing that society was wrong to condemn individuals whose behavior violated narrowly constructed social norms, Kinsey insisted, "As far as it is genetic, variation is hardly the fault of the individual concerned; and one's environment is more often a happenstance than community gossip and the courts care to acknowledge."[83]

Barely disguising his target, Kinsey then proceeded to attack unspecified social conventions that sounded suspiciously like Victorian sexual mores. "Prescriptions are merely public confessions of prescriptions," he sneered. "Argumentation *ad hominem* is bad argument, however moral the purpose of its advocate, because it is based on unique, unduplicable experience." Then Kinsey made the leap from biology to society, arguing that the concept of individual variation required people to embrace moral relativism. In words pregnant with personal meaning, he proclaimed, "What is right for one individual may be wrong for the next; what is sin and abomination to one may be a worthwhile part of the next individual's life."[84]

Society's failure to understand the primacy of individual variation, asserted Kinsey, had caused great harm to countless people. Again, without identifying his subjects, he referred to a group that sounded like people who engaged in forbidden sexual behavior. American laws, he charged, rested on the erroneous assumption that society was divided into two groups: respectable citizens and criminals. Ethical evaluations reflected the same fallacy. The public tended to frame issues in black and white, never pausing to recognize the endless shades of gray that characterized much human activity. In Kinsey's view, psychologists were the worst offenders because they labeled people either normal or abnormal, ignoring the fine gradations between these polarities.[85]

Determined to challenge conventional notions of right and wrong, Kinsey proposed a different way of defining social norms. "Biologically, I see only two bases for the recognition of abnormality," he declared. "If a particular type of variation is rare in a given population, it, perhaps, may be called abnormal." To illustrate his point, he chose physical characteristics, noting that adults who were under three or over eight feet in height could be considered "abnormal." Still, the term left such a bad taste in his mouth that he felt compelled to add, "I should prefer to call them 'rare.' "[86]

Kinsey cited "physiologic malfunction" as his second test of abnormality. "In that sense cancers and tumors may be called abnormal," he allowed. Then, without explanation, Kinsey suddenly shifted ground and switched from physical properties to human behavior. Moving danger-ously close to the issue nearest to his heart, he insisted that "popular judg-ments of normality more often represent measures of departure from the standards of the individual who is passing judgment—an admission that 'only thee and me are normal, and thee, I fear, is a bit queer.' " While this was an old Quaker expression, by the late 1930s the term "queer" was among the most popular slang words for homosexual.[87]

Unable to control his bitterness, Kinsey blamed one profession in par-ticular for fostering binary thinking. "The psychologist's more presump-tuous labeling of the abnormal is, too often, merely an attempt to justify the mores, a reassertion of society's concept of what is acceptable in indi-vidual behavior, with no objective attempt to find out, by actual observa-tion, what the incidence of the phenomenon may be, or the extent of the real maladjustment that the behavior will introduce." To remedy such sim-plistic thinking, Kinsey again suggested, society should embrace the con-cept of individual variation, an idea with potent social ramifications. "Scholarly thinking as well as the laymen's evaluation still needs to be tem-pered with the realization that individual variations shape into a continu-ous curve on which there are no sharp divisions between normal and abnormal, between right and wrong," he observed.[88]

In his final remarks, Kinsey closed the circle, stating with unmistakable candor how his belief in individual variation ordered his thinking about human affairs. Tying this idea directly to evolutionary theory, he spoke as a loyal son of Darwin when he praised individual differences as "the ma-terials out of which nature achieves progress, evolution in the organic world." Human beings, he noted, would be well advised to remember this fact and to ponder its meaning for human society. For by celebrating the great diversity among their species, people might be able to comprehend an important truth: "In the differences between men lie the hopes of a changing society." In closing, Kinsey added slyly, "I trust that our Univer-sity has not put any standard imprint on you who have gone through it. In fact, from what I know of some of you who are the newly elected mem-bers of Phi Beta Kappa, you are a strange assortment of queer individuals; and that is why I respect you, and believe in your future."[89]

Since his conferences with students in the marriage course were com-mon knowledge on campus by this time, the students who attended this talk were able to listen between the lines and comprehend many of his opaque references to sex research. In addition, many were able to catch his meaning when Kinsey discussed social policies, correctly concluding that he was referring to sexual mores. And among those who had contributed their sex histories, a few may have smiled knowingly at the double enten-dres Kinsey slipped into his talk at the end. Still, unless one knew his private history, it was possible to hear this talk and have no inkling about how much light it shed on his hidden life. In that sense, the lecture was vintage Kinsey. In the years ahead, he would find numerous opportunities to indulge his habit of saying things in public that his listeners had no way of linking to him personally.

A few weeks after delivering his Phi Beta Kappa speech, Kinsey embarked on a bold journey. Bolstered by student and administrative support for the marriage course, armed with freshly developed interviewing techniques, sustained by a philosophy of science that celebrated individual differences, and driven by compelling personal needs, he left his cloistered campus and traveled to the giant metropolis two hundred miles to the north. His goal was to see whether he could persuade total strangers to be interviewed. Yet Kinsey did not covet just any sex histories. Rather, he was answering the call of his own private sirens. He journeyed to Chicago to interview a group of people who specialized in keeping their sexual preferences secret, a challenge he understood only too well. Convincing them to cooperate would tax all of his formidable powers of persuasion.

"WHY HAS NO ONE CRACKED THIS BEFORE?"

O n a Friday afternoon in June 1939, Kinsey taught his last class of the week, got in his car, and left Bloomington on a new kind of field trip. Up to this point, he had interviewed mostly college students, family members, and friends. Yet, even within this small circle, he had managed to concentrate on certain groups by spreading the word that he would be happy to counsel people with sexual problems or individuals who considered themselves on the margins. Kinsey was eager to target more specialized histories still. Consequently, he paid no attention as he sped by the stands of oaks teeming with gall wasps in the surrounding hills. Specimens of a far more intriguing species beckoned him to the Windy City. Awaiting him was a man who had promised introductions to Chicago's gay community.

The birth of urban homosexual subcultures in the United States was closely tied to the growth of the market economy and to the rise of big cities in the late nineteenth and early twentieth centuries.[1] As the United States developed a mature industrial economy, manufacturing, commerce, and trade concentrated jobs in cities, drawing people from abroad and from the hinterland alike. In a matter of decades, many small cities grew into big cities and many big cities mushroomed into giant metropolises. Urban growth, in turn, spawned anonymous social relations, allowing city dwellers to relax the rigid standards of self-control associated with rural areas and villages, where family members and neighbors maintained a watchful eye and everyone knew everyone else's business.

In large cities, young adults often lived apart from their families. Most of the people they met on the streets were strangers. Separated from kith and kin, city dwellers gradually formed their own youth culture, centering largely on entertainment. After returning from work, they left their rented rooms or boardinghouses to congregate in various nights spots, seeking other unattached young people with similar interests. Freed from the intense moral scrutiny of family members and neighbors, they often developed relationships, some casual, others serious, in which they engaged in behavior that violated the sexual norms of their time.

All this could be said as easily of heterosexuals as homosexuals, linking, as it does, important shifts in private behavior with broader economic and social changes. The creation of a homosexual identity and the emergence of gay communities in America's largest cities were part of the larger, ongoing, if slow-motion, collapse of Victorian sexual morality. Much as heterosexuals tested the boundaries of sexual behavior and birth control practices, many homosexuals waged clandestine struggles against sexual repression. The boldest somehow found the courage to act with varying degrees of stealth upon sexual needs that the dominant culture thoroughly despised and soundly condemned. Still, finding partners often proved a daunting task. Because they had to hide their sexual identity from those who would persecute them, homosexuals had to move with extreme caution in their social relationships until they learned whether their interest was reciprocated.

For these reasons, the sheer size of large cities proved helpful. Since homosexuals constituted a small percentage of the population, large cities provided both the social anonymity and the critical mass of people required for a viable, if furtive, sexual subculture to coalesce. By the turn of the century, major American cities had their own secret sexual underworlds where homosexuals who were in the know congregated to find relaxation, acceptance, and sexual partners. Gay life revolved around a system of cafés, clubs, and bars—institutions that paralleled those of the dominant culture. Tucked away in neighborhoods and commercial districts not frequented by members of "polite society" after dark, most of these establishments catered to men. Within this all but invisible world, homosexuals created a social milieu that allowed them to drop their double lives, if only for a few hours at a time, and be openly gay.[2]

Chicago had such a community decades before Kinsey arrived. As early as 1908, a seasoned urban observer included Chicago on his list of metropolises where "certain smart clubs are well-known for their homosexual atmospheres." The same man went on to note that "steam-baths and restaurants are plentifully known—to the initiated." Already, authorities employed stereotypes that later generations used to denigrate homosexuals. Police reports stressed that many of the patrons who frequented these night spots were decidedly effeminate, illustrating how gender often conflated the issue of sexual identity. For example, vice investigators in 1911 described with disgust men who "mostly affect the carriage, mannerisms, and speech of women [and] who are fond of many articles dear to the feminine heart."[3]

Kinsey reached Chicago bent upon learning everything he could about its gay community. He checked into the Harrison Hotel, located on Harrison Street, just off Michigan Boulevard. It was a grand structure with 400 rooms, each of which came equipped with a radio, circulating ice water, and its own bath or shower. On subsequent trips over the next several months, Kinsey made the Harrison his headquarters, conducting many interviews in his room. But on this, his maiden research voyage, he abandoned his room for the field.

His quarry was a group of young homosexual males who lived together in a boardinghouse on Rush Street, not far from the so-called Village in Chicago, a district filled with cafés and cafeterias where people drank coffee into the wee hours of the morning. Because a friend of the group had vouched for him, the young men were willing to be introduced to Kinsey and to hear him out. After that, he was on his own. To secure histories, he would have to sell himself and win their confidence—no easy tasks with men who had good reasons to suspect and fear outsiders.

Overall, things went well. Because he emitted not the faintest odor of moral condemnation and because he was so transparently earnest and sincere, the young men on Rush Street wanted to trust him. Still, it was difficult to put aside the habits of a lifetime. Kinsey had to use all his powers of persuasion to combat their fears and suspicions. He assured them he would never divulge their confidences, all the while stressing that whatever they told him would benefit science. Nevertheless, his harvest of interviews was relatively meager. A year later, he confessed in a letter to one of his subjects, "It took us five days to get the first three histories out of the city."[4]

Kinsey was not discouraged. On the contrary, the trip had been a real eye-opener. He was excited about everything he had learned. Near the end of June, he returned to Chicago for a second visit, taking up where he had left off. Showing his usual tenacity, he pressed forward, meeting new people, answering their questions, explaining his research, asking for their histories, and interviewing those who stepped forward. When not interviewing, Kinsey concentrated on making contacts, as he realized that friendship networks would carry him ultimately to all parts of the city, yielding a bonanza of sex histories. Future events quickly demonstrated the soundness of this strategy. Within a year, Kinsey would tell a friend that penetrating Chicago's gay community had largely "been a matter of building up many friendships which bring introductions to their friends."[5] "Snowball interviewing" was the term social scientists applied to this method. As a means of securing histories, it worked quite well, but would the results provide a representative sample of the population? Time would tell.

Following his second visit, Kinsey peppered Chicago with thank-you notes. These invariably ended with fervent requests for help in securing additional histories. Indeed, for the remainder of his life, Kinsey's success would turn in large measure on follow-up work, as he made a point of observing social niceties. Aware that his research depended on the trust and cooperation of others, he crafted these epistles with care, filling them with expressions of gratitude that made their recipients feel as though their contributions to his research were not only crucial but unique. Indeed, he tried everything in his power to give his subjects the sense that they were partners in an enterprise of great importance. Writing to the man who had introduced him to the group on Rush Street, for example, Kinsey declared that the young men he had interviewed "gave a most valuable addition to my understanding of the problem. They are nice boys, . . . very different sorts of people, and all of them most cooperative in helping me secure data. It would have been [a] tragedy if you had failed to introduce me there."[6]

Kinsey learned an important lesson from these early trips. In large measure, he had been welcomed by the young men on Rush Street because someone they trusted had vouched for him. Acknowledging his indebtedness, he observed in a letter to one of his subjects, "Of course you had . . . [Mr. X's] word for it that I was safe, but I realize that it was asking a good deal to ask you to disclose all the details of your history. You have helped materially by so doing."[7]

In the years to come, Kinsey routinely used what he called a "contact man" to gain entry into whatever group or sexual subculture he had targeted for interviews. Acknowledging their importance, he later wrote, "Practically all of the contacts at lower levels, and many of those at other levels, have depended upon introductions made by persons who had previously contributed their own histories. One who has not already given a history is not usually effective as a 'contact man.' Contact men and women have often spent considerable time and have gone to considerable pains to interest their friends and acquaintances."[8]

Throughout the summer and into the fall, Kinsey labored to explain his research to interviewees who recommended him to their friends, both to thank them and to enlist their help for future trips. To underscore the importance of these contacts, Kinsey noted that science would not get the story straight until hundreds of people with different backgrounds were interviewed. Distinguishing himself from those professors who were interested only in knowledge for the sake of knowledge, he made no bones of his desire to change people's attitudes about homosexuality. As he wrote one of his Chicago contacts, "The histories that we have gotten convince me that we can get folk to thinking straighter on these matters, by continuing exactly the sort of conferences I have been having. So you are contributing mightily by accepting me in your circle, and introducing me to the others." Kinsey added with a note of urgency, "There are some others to whom you introduced me whose histories I do not yet have, and whose histories I need. They must contribute. It is for them and the rest of you, not for me alone that it is worth while."[9]

Nor did Kinsey ignore the parents of his subjects. Because he wanted to explore the cause (or causes) of homosexuality, he was keen to learn everything he could about their home life. He told the mother of one of the young men, who, as it happened, accepted her son's homosexuality, that she had provided unique assistance and that her contacts were precisely those that were needed to advance the study.[10]

People who extended themselves on his behalf received detailed reports of his progress, as though he were offering them a balance sheet to see what they got in return for their efforts. In a letter to a man he had interviewed on his second trip, Kinsey wrote, "It was good of you to give us your own story, and to help us contact the other men. We now have the histories of eight of the men from Chicago. Each is quite different; added to what we have from our own students it gives us the beginning of an understanding of the phenomenon. We now have 60 cases of people with homosexual experience." Of course, hundreds more would be needed, Kinsey confessed, but he promised that the day would come when his research would "speak with the combined wisdom of the experience of all of you." Only scientific data, stressed Kinsey, had the power to reform society's views on homosexuality, which was why each and every history was so precious. "If we are ever to be able to answer the questions of those who have met the experience, or if we are to have any influence in directing society's attitudes on this score," he declared, "you will have contributed to it."[11]

Kinsey collected more than sex histories in Chicago. Determined to build a reliable data bank on male sexual anatomy, he put the same request to these subjects that he made of the men in the marriage course. Following the interview, each man at his earliest convenience was to measure the circumference and length of his penis in both a flaccid and an erect state, and then mail him the results. To speed compliance, Kinsey followed up his requests with friendly reminders. "Will you send us the measurements which we need to complete your history?" he asked one subject, noting that he was enclosing "an addressed envelope to take care of that."[12] Kinsey's persistence paid off. After receiving a second reminder, the man finally returned the measurements, remarking sheepishly, "As you can see I am no Goliath. Probably that is the reason why I have been holding them back for such a long time." Ruefully, the man added, "I feel I've been short-changed in the deal."[13]

Through his subjects, Kinsey learned to keep his eyes open for a variety of materials that could shed light on human sexuality. One of the men had kept a sexual diary and love letters from an affair; another had a collection of erotic photographs; and a third claimed to have access to a cache of highly revealing letters written by a priest. While Kinsey already had the nucleus of a library on human sexuality, these materials raised the possibility of building an archive, providing additional material for study and yet another outlet for his collector's mania.

Kinsey pursued every lead with a vengeance. While prurient desires may have spurred his interest, he was too good a scientist not to recognize valuable source materials when he saw them. Reading the man's diary, for example, gave him a different perspective on their interview. "I am struck by the fact that I didn't get very deeply into your thinking in the few hours I had with you," Kinsey confessed to the man. "This diary does that so much better. It is an invaluable look-in for one making the sort of study I am attempting. If these studies do anything to reduce the homosexual problems to frank, unemotional consideration, you will have helped materially in that outcome."[14]

Within a few years, Kinsey would avoid making any comments that betrayed his desire to influence social policy. His restraint was self-imposed, as he had gradually come to realize that his ability to shape thinking, mores, and the law rested entirely on his image. If people perceived him as a social reformer, his influence would be diminished. If the public saw him as a disinterested investigator, his pronouncements would carry the moral authority of science, resting, as they did, on cold, hard data. During his first year of interviewing in Chicago, however, Kinsey had yet to learn this lesson. His letters from this period freely admitted his desire to influence policy.

Kinsey's faith in his ability to promote change reflected the mind-set and values of the Progressive Era, that remarkable reform period that had shaped so many of his boyhood experiences in South Orange and beyond. This was particularly true of his approach to problem solving. Like many progressives, he believed that purposeful action could carry the day, solving whatever issue was at hand; and he had an almost childlike faith in the power of reason to transform human affairs. Once he had discovered the truth, he would share it with the public, and the public in turn would use his data to reform attitudes and to shape policy. As he told one of the young men, "I am interested in discovering the fact(s) and believe the world's thinking can be made more tolerant only if the facts are known."[15] In order to change the world's attitudes, however, Kinsey realized he had to compile a huge body of data. "We will get somewhere if we have a large enough sample of the world; but it will take a good many histories to do that," he assured another man.[16]

Kinsey truly believed things would turn out well in the end, provided the public learned the truth. "We can make public opinion more sensible and work out solutions only as folk of your intelligence pool their understanding through this sort of scientific study," he told one of the young men who had contributed his history.[17] Proclaiming his belief in progress to another interviewee, Kinsey declared, "I am very sure that a better understanding of these things will make it better for all folk."[18]

If Kinsey's letters reveal a reformer who thought he could win, they also show a man who cared about people and was not afraid to let his emotions show. He did not approach the young man's diary that summer as a coolly objective scientist. Rather, he read it as a partisan, a man who both understood and identified with the young man's pain. Thus, Kinsey's response was intimate and tender. "Your capacity for love is the thing that stands foremost in my thinking of you," he confessed. "Your question is a fair one—if love is extolled by poets and teachers, then what can be wrong about it in any form that remains fine and real. Perhaps we can put that question to society in better form because I have had this look-in on your thinking thru this diary." As for the present, added Kinsey gloomily, "The only answer I can give that seems at all sense [*sic*] is that [homosexuality] happens to be out of fashion in the society thru which you have to move."[19]

Often Kinsey got caught up in the lives of the men whose stories he heard. Touched by the pain and conflict one of his subjects had suffered, he wrote sympathetically, "I should give more than you believe to see things turn out right for you."[20] To another youth who had struggled to make the kinds of "adjustments" every homosexual must achieve in order to survive in a straight society, he offered this prayer: "I hope you can find the utmost of happiness in the way most worthwhile to you."[21]

Kinsey quickly realized that homosexuality was not the only problem in the lives of these young men. Mired in the Great Depression, many had not been able to find jobs, and he was saddened by their lack of economic opportunity. "I realize that the whole gang of you need a new economic world in which you have a more decent chance at jobs," he wrote one of the young men. "I fear I cannot do very much to take care of the whole situation, but perhaps I can be of service in some way."[22] Actually, Kinsey did what he could. He paid many of the subjects a few dollars for contributing their histories, not to bribe them, but to try in some small way to offer a respite, however brief, from poverty's brutal grasp.[23] In later years, Kinsey's critics would object to these payments, arguing that any study that included data from subjects who had to be paid to cooperate was seriously flawed. Of all the objections leveled against his research, this one doubtless concerned him the least.

Had Kinsey not had other duties, he probably would have spent even more time in Chicago. As it was, he had to fit his early pilgrimages to the city into a packed teaching schedule that first summer. In addition to the marriage course, he was teaching an entomology class that met three hours a day and a class on evolution that met two hours daily. Nor was teaching the only demand on his time. Kinsey was a divided man. Despite his growing fascination with sex research, he still felt the pull of his gall wasps. In July, he wrote Voris, "This has been the busiest 6 months, I think that I have ever spent. I have measured some thousands of bugs and gotten a series of variation curves and correlation maps that is startling."[24]

As luck would have it, Kinsey's research in entomology had taken an interesting turn. For the past year, he had studied a Utah species that presented startling variation in wingspan. Seeking help in handling the statistical measurements, Kinsey had asked Raymond Pearl for advice the preceding fall. Because the two men had hit it off, Pearl invited him to spend the 1939 fall term at Johns Hopkins working in his laboratory, where they could confer at will.[25] This was a generous offer. Kinsey's response, written only days after he returned from his second trip to Chicago, reflects his growing fascination with his new research. "I fear that I shall not get to your laboratory this next fall," he replied. "I have a bad habit of carrying several strings along at the same time; ultimately it all gets done, but there are too many things that need attention here right now to allow me to get away for any time."[26]

Turning to the strings in hand, Kinsey revealed his plans for a bug-hunting trip to the Southwest later in the summer. Its purpose was "to make a second collection of this variable-winged Utah material," he continued, noting that the expedition would fall some "10 years after the original collections, and will give me a chance to make comparisons." His second reason for declining, Kinsey confessed, was his new area of research. "As I pointed out to you last fall we are securing an invaluable lot of material on the sexual behavior of our own students in connection with our marriage course," he wrote. "We have systematized our records and are getting something like 250 items on each student. We have over 350 complete histories so far. This should be of some scientific interest some day."[27]

Kinsey was more candid with Voris. Early in July 1939, he wrote his beloved former student a long letter, describing the marriage course's development with a glee that bordered on euphoria: "In the first four semesters we have had 100, 200, 230, 260 = 790 students. A few flurries with unfavorable criticisms from older faculty who had no first-hand knowledge—but even that is gone." Confident of his support, Kinsey boasted, "The students would do anything to defend us, their appreciation is so great." Nor did opposition appear to be building outside the class. "Following your suggestion," continued Kinsey, "we have tapped fraternity house gossip and find the course treated most considerately. The Gridiron banquet brought only one reference to it—a reprimand to a couple of the boys for having engaged in biologic activities 'without benefit of Kinsey's course in connubial calisthenics.' "[28]

Turning to the interviews, Kinsey reported that he had collected 280 histories between February and June. As preoccupied as ever with numbers, he calculated that he had collected 350 histories to date, predicting the number would rise to 1,000 within the next year and a half. Noting that he had just presented a paper to his faculty club, Kinsey boasted that his colleagues were nearly bowled over by his data but nevertheless encouraged him to continue the research.[29]

Kinsey wasted no time on that account. The following month, he made back-to-back field trips that allowed him to pursue the two areas of research he increasingly felt torn between. Near the end of August, he wrote Voris, "Mac and I went to Chicago to send Anne off to camp, and I spent another four days collecting histories. This is the third trip now with something like 18 histories from the city. I wish I could tell you about them." At this point, a growing sense of urgency crept into Kinsey's words, as though he desperately needed to confer with Voris. Kinsey lamented in a postscript, "A letter is such a poor means of talking together. There are worlds to tell you—when we can get together."[30]

A few days later, Kinsey, Clara, and Bruce (the two girls were in summer camp) left Bloomington on a field trip, retracing the 1929 expedition Kinsey had made with Voris to Colorado, Utah, and northern Arizona. For three weeks, they drove across the American Southwest, stopping periodically when Kinsey saw a stand of oaks that looked familiar. Reporting that the trip had been "highly successful," he wrote Voris, "Much to my surprise I was able to go to precisely the spot where we had previously collected in every case." Describing the field conditions in the twenty-one cities they had visited, Kinsey added with a hint of glee, "More than half of these were made in cold rain so Mrs. Kinsey and Bruce got a typical introduction to our bug collecting."[31]

Perhaps revisiting these old haunts stirred memories in Kinsey; or maybe it was the growing pressure he felt to discuss his Chicago trips with the one man to whom he could reveal his feelings with total candor. Whatever the reason, Kinsey did something extraordinary on the drive back to Bloomington. Although he knew the Vorises had travel plans, he drove hundreds of miles out of his way in the faint hope of finding them at home. But sure enough, they were gone. Describing his failed effort, Kinsey confessed to Voris, "I had not expected you to be there knowing your previous plans but we took a chance and tried to get in touch with you anyway. We telephoned and telegraphed, and after spending the night in [a] tourists' camp on the edge of the town I went around to the college the next morning to check my memories as to when you would be back." Disappointed, Kinsey could only renew his plea for a face-to-face meeting, declaring, "It will take me days of a visit with you to discuss all that we should concerning many things."[32]

During the 1939 fall term, Kinsey plunged deeper and deeper into sex research. As it happened, he discovered an invaluable contact man right on campus. The young man was upset because he could not reconcile what his political science professor was saying about local government with his firsthand knowledge of conditions in his hometown, an industrial city in northern Indiana. During their interview, he regaled Kinsey with stories about the city's sexual underworld, replete with accounts of commercialized vice. Kinsey accepted the student's offer to visit his hometown and check out things for himself.

Over the next few months, Kinsey succeeded in interviewing a number of unsavory characters, the first of many he would meet in the years ahead. Fascinated by their histories, he returned again and again on weekends to interview their friends, financing the trips with his own funds. These expeditions helped Kinsey grow as an interviewer, as he had to sell himself to madams, prostitutes, and pimps—characters who bore little resemblance to freshly scrubbed college students. Already, his search for diversity was taking Kinsey far afield, beyond the watchful eyes of the custodians of civilized morality. And always, beckoning like a beacon to the north, was Chicago.

During the fall term, Kinsey picked up where he had left off in the summer, returning to Chicago as often as his busy teaching schedule permitted. He would finish his last class on Friday, drive to Chicago, spend the weekend, and return to Bloomington just in time to teach his Monday morning classes. While histories remained the official reason for his visits, Kinsey spent much of his time observing gay life. Thanks to his previous visits, the Rush Street boys now accepted and trusted him. They outdid one another finding ways to assist him. Serving as his private guide to their hidden world, they introduced him to their friends, got him into gay parties, accompanied him to the theater, walked him through the city parks and public urinals where gay men "cruised" in search of anonymous sex, and ushered him through the network of gay nightclubs and coffeehouses, pausing long enough at each spot for him to establish contacts that ensured that a new group of men would start the process all over again. Indeed, anyone who did not know better would have thought Kinsey was socializing, not researching.

In truth, Kinsey *was* socializing. Each trip back to Chicago increased his fascination with gay life. He liked what he saw. As a man who had kept his homoerotic desires locked in the closet, he was thrilled to find a colony of men who had the courage to be openly, unabashedly "gay," if only with each other. From firsthand knowledge and from the histories he had taken to date, Kinsey understood the self-loathing, confusion, and pain that was the lot of many homosexuals. The Rush Street subjects, however, showed him a world that provided a haven from social isolation and psychological marginality, a hidden community where group acceptance could magically transform pariahs into human beings. In a society that spurned them, they were somehow managing to laugh, to dance, and to love. From them, Kinsey got his first intimate view of gay life. It warmed his heart.

Kinsey did everything he could to repay their gift. Openly and without a moment's hesitation, he let each subject know that he considered him a fine individual. Indeed, at a time when the news media were attacking homosexuals as sexual psychopaths, and even moderate people considered them diseased and degenerate, Kinsey seized every opportunity to affirm their worth and dignity as men.[33]

True to his philosophy of science, Kinsey celebrated his subjects' individuality. "Hurried as my visit was to Chicago this last week-end, your contribution stands out in my mind as particularly valuable," he wrote one young man. "You are a distinctive creature, and one with whom I should like to maintain contacts in the future."[34] Kinsey addressed virtually the same remarks to another man, declaring, "You are a distinctive individual, with considerable intelligence and force, and I am therefore particularly glad to have made contact with you."[35] After thanking him for his history, he told yet another man, "There is no one else quite like you, and I shall be particularly interest[ed] to follow your history in later years."[36] However welcome these comments, the surge of pride the Rush Street men felt about being called unique might have been diminished had they stopped to compare notes.

Despite these lapses into boilerplate, there was a purpose to Kinsey's word choice. Again and again, he used words like "decent," "noble," "quality," "brave," "distinctive," and "intelligent" to describe the young men he had interviewed. A simple matter of currying favor? Hardly, though Kinsey was not above this to get what he wanted. Keenly aware of the power of language, he was standing old-fashioned morality on its head. By assigning virtues to homosexuals that the dominant culture reserved exclusively for heterosexuals, he was granting gays not only absolution but approval. He was restoring their dignity, their pride, their masculinity, and their self-respect—all the things the custodians of morality had stripped them of simply because they were homosexuals. In effect, he was saying, "You're okay," which, in turn, carried the unspoken corollary "And so am I."

No wonder these young men liked Kinsey. It was not simply that they felt flattered by his attention, though this was undoubtedly true in some cases. Their attraction to him ran deeper. From the moment they had known they were homosexual, they had been taught to regard themselves with either pity, disgust, or contempt. And then suddenly they met this mild-mannered, soft-spoken, middle-aged scientist who learned their secrets and made it clear he approved of them as people. What with his baggy suit, bow tie, and gray-flecked, sandy hair, Kinsey must have appeared to many of these youths like an approving father.

Not surprisingly, many of them found their interviews with Kinsey therapeutic. In fact, it would be tempting to compare an interview with him to a religious confessional—tempting but wrong. Unlike a religious priest, he did not combine absolution with an admonition to sin no more. Instead, he listened, recorded, and registered his approval, telling people to let up on themselves, because their activity was neither harmful, unnatural, nor wrong.

Many of these young men went all out to show their gratitude. A neutral or dispassionate observer could never have elicited as much support as Kinsey. Not only did they outdo one another in recruiting subjects for interviews; they granted him their absolute trust, perhaps the highest compliment they could bestow. Indeed, having found such an understanding friend, many were reluctant to take their leave of Kinsey. "If there were more people like you who cared to find out and write about their fellowmen and their innermost self this would be a better world to live in," declared one thankful youth. After promising to line up his friends for interviews the next time Kinsey returned to Chicago, the young man pleaded, "I know and realize that you are terribly busy but I would appreciate it so much if you could write to me occasionally. I would like to correspond with you. I sincerely hope that it will be possible."[37]

No less than his work with the marriage course, Kinsey's contacts with

Chicago's homosexual community generated numerous cries for help. In a few cases, he was not able to help as much as he would have liked. Dejectedly, he had to confess to one youth, "You have the sort of problem of which I feel so incapable of helping because I am so far away."[38] Similarly, when another member of the group was arrested in a police raid on a homosexual bar, Kinsey could do no more than try to cheer him up with a letter. "The stuff of which you are made is so unusual that I shall always consider that you have contributed to our studies in a fashion that very few other people could," he wrote. "It was very decent of you to have helped out as nicely as you did, and I am, consequently sorry to know of the trouble you have now had. If I get to the city before you are out of jail, I shall come to see you there."[39] He enclosed a small loan with the letter.

While there were limits to what he could do, Kinsey offered his services to anyone who would accept them. Given his own childhood experiences, it was perhaps predictable that he would volunteer to intercede for young men who were trapped in parental conflicts, offering the kind of third-party intervention he had needed but not received with his own father. Responding more like a village priest than a disinterested scientist, Kinsey told one of his subjects who was strapped financially, "I have even thought about the possibility of my writing your parents and telling them that I think highly of you and your determination in the midst of these handicaps." Aware the young man might not welcome this offer, Kinsey hastened to add, "Of course, I should never write your parents unless you propose it, but if you ever think that it would be of any use, let me know."[40]

Yet, despite his best efforts, Kinsey's harsh conscience constantly accused him of not doing enough. Indeed, his letters are filled with expressions of regret over his failure to do more. Casting about for ways to show his appreciation, he sent several of the boys copies of his high school biology textbook, while others received cordial invitations to visit in his home. After interviewing a young artist, Kinsey promised to introduce him to the colony of artists in Brown County, if only he would come to Bloomington. Pressing, Kinsey added, "I want you to see my own home, some of the things we have in it, hear music with me, see my garden, meet the family, etc., etc. Be sure to come."[41] Several young men accepted his invitation and visited Bloomington, the first of many who followed in the years ahead. Each was given a seat at his table and treated like an honored guest, much as Kinsey hoped his work would one day result in homosexuals everywhere being offered a seat at society's table.

It was as an adviser, however, that Kinsey provided his most valuable service to his Chicago friends. Responding to his repeated offers, many of these young turned to him for help, laying a variety of problems at his door, most of an intimate nature. In many instances, Kinsey could offer no more than a shoulder to cry on, all the while encouraging them to look to the future. Even in the midst of misery, though, he used their inquiries to learn more about various aspects of homosexual life. For example, when a heartbroken youth wrote to complain about a lover who had disappeared abruptly during a brief but intense affair (stealing a watch when he left), Kinsey replied, "Don't lose faith in human nature." The incident, he explained philosophically, was part of a larger problem—the brief duration of so many homosexual relationships. "The difficulty of maintaining long-time friendships is one of the things that has puzzled me in this whole study and one I should like to discuss with you in more detail on the next trip," he declared, adding with a note of sadness, "I wish these friendships could be maintained for longer periods of time."[42]

As a counselor, Kinsey was at his best when people sought his advice on how to deal with their homosexuality. He received a particularly heartrending letter from a man who had left the protection and emotional support of his gay boardinghouse and returned to college. "I have suddenly become aware of my maladjustment with my fellow men," the youth confided. "I fear I am fast developing an inferiority complex—I am always afraid I will give myself away every time I speak or move," he continued. "I want the companionship and friendship of the fellows I meet and live with, but knowing their attitude toward homosexuals I keep to myself for fear they will find out." Framing a key question that confronted others in his predicament, he asked, "What do you suggest? Should I remain a 'lone wolf' or should I try to pretend all the way through?"[43]

Kinsey's answer was compassionate. The decision about whether to remain a homosexual, he stressed, rested entirely with the individual. Convinced it was possible for homosexuals to transform themselves into heterosexuals through a rigorous program of conditioning (a belief he would later recant, at least in part), Kinsey proceeded to outline a step-by-step therapy program for the young man.[44] In keeping with his stated policy of strict neutrality, he devoted equal time to advising the young man on how he could learn to live more comfortably as a homosexual. "If you decide to continue with the homosexual," Kinsey declared, "you can at least associate with heterosexual groups. Friends should be chosen for all of their qualities, not merely for their sexual patterns, else you cut yourself off from many worthwhile folk in this world." Kinsey also recommended a survival strategy that had served him and other homosexuals well. He urged the youth to remain in the closet for his own protection, stressing that homosexuals who successfully concealed their identity "need have no inferiority complex, just because other people are incapable of understanding what the homosexual really means."[45]

Not that Kinsey was completely free of prejudices. From his adolescence forward, he had displayed a strong aversion to effeminate behavior of any kind on the part of men, underscoring the extent to which he shared the public's belief that sexual identity was defined by gender-linked behavior. With brutal candor, he advised the young man to completely overhaul his public presentation, with an eye to eliminating certain behavioral traits the public associated with homosexuals. "In your case, you will have to unlearn a lot of your mannerisms: your walk, your pitch of voice, your hand flings, your other affectations," Kinsey asserted. "I am quite convinced that you learned them in the first place, and that you can, therefore, unlearn them now. Above all, you will have to avoid such arm and shoulder contacts with males as happen to be not in style in our particular civilization."[46]

If Kinsey sounded supremely confident in this exchange, he was. At the time he wrote this letter, he had been involved with sex research for two years, and he had been interviewing homosexuals in Chicago (and elsewhere) for more than a year, compiling a large inventory of homosexual histories. He was certain he knew more about human sexuality in general and homosexuality in particular than any other scientist, living or dead. Indeed, after only two years of research, Kinsey had pretty much formulated his basic theory of human sexuality, one that appeared to accommodate nicely both his own history and those of his interviewees.

Kinsey set forth his theory in the same letter in which he advised the anxious young man who felt inferior because of his homosexuality. He prefaced his advice with a declaration of his objectivity and professional authority. Stressing that he had "the histories of about 450 males who have had homosexual experience," Kinsey asserted, "My generalizations do not agree with current psychologic theory or psychiatric practise [*sic*], but there is no published study which has a quarter as much material as I already have on the subject."[47] "It is my conviction that the homosexual is biologically as normal as the heterosexual," declared Kinsey. "There is absolutely no evidence of inheritance being involved."

In essence, Kinsey argued that sexual identity was largely the result of how people responded to their early sexual experiences. "After one has had a pleasurable first experience, of either sort," he explained, "he looks forward to a repetition of the experience with such anticipation that he may be aroused by the sight or mere thought of another person with whom he can make contact." Reminding the young man of his own history, Kinsey argued that "unsatisfactory experience, of either sort, will (as in your own early contact with the heterosexual) build up a prejudice against any repetition of that experience." Therefore, it seemed clear that sexual identity followed the pleasure principle. "Whether one builds a heterosexual pattern or a homosexual pattern depends, therefore, very largely upon the satisfactory or unsatisfactory nature of his first experiences," Kinsey declared.[48]

Aware that this explanation omitted a crucial factor, Kinsey addressed culture. "Finally," he noted, "social factors do a great deal to force an individual into an exclusively heterosexual or homosexual pattern. Most of the social forces encourage the heterosexual, but society's ostracism of the homosexual similarly forces him into the exclusive company of other homosexuals and into an exclusively homosexual pattern." Along with Freud, Kinsey believed that human nature was basically bisexual, possessing in equal measure the capacity for relating to the same sex or to the opposite sex. In Kinsey's judgment, restrictive sexual mores alone prevented people from acting upon their bisexuality. "Without such social forces," he declared, "I think most people would carry on both heterosexual and homosexual activities coincidentally."[49]

Chicago's homosexual community would always have a special hold on Kinsey, largely because it was the first he studied in depth. Like a thirsty man in need of water, he traveled there again and again. And the more trips he made, the stronger the bond he felt to the men he interviewed. Over time, he came to regard them as members of his family.[50] Interestingly, Kinsey used the same metaphor in later years to express his disappointment following a visit to Chicago when he tried to look up one of the men he had interviewed in 1939, only to find no one at home when he knocked on the door. Expressing his regrets, Kinsey confessed he felt homesick thinking about the men who had provided such crucial help at the beginning of the study.[51]

Kinsey had good reason for feeling close to these men. Through them he found himself. A decade later, he confided to a close friend that interviewing gay men had not been his sole activity in Chicago. Revealing Kinsey's secret, his friend declared that "before [Kinsey] got well known, he was having sex with men at the homosexual hangouts." While Kinsey had always enjoyed skating near the edge, didn't this behavior place him in danger of falling through the ice? Not necessarily. "In those days, you see," explained his friend, "no one knew him."[52] Chicago, in common with other cities, had at least two separate and distinct gay communities, whose members did not really know one another. First, there was the subculture consisting of friend/lover networks and a variety of social institutions that catered to men who defined themselves as homosexual. Basically, this was the world the Rush Street group showed Kinsey, and it delighted him.

Then there was the other homosexual subculture, at once more furtive and hidden. It consisted of men with homoerotic desires who acted upon those needs without constructing the friend/lover networks or the social institutions to support a sense of homosexual identity as something separate and distinct from straight society. This group consisted of married and single men alike, many of whom did not think of themselves as homosexual, preferring to attribute their occasional episodes with men to liquor, cold wives, experimental urges, or the like. As a group, they tended to limit their meetings with other homosexuals to brief, anonymous sexual contacts in dark places.

Married men, in particular, had a difficult time participating in this sexual underworld. Basically, they had to make up excuses for their wives to buy a few precious moments of freedom before disappearing into the night. They were drawn to certain city parks, public urinals, bathhouses, seedy all-night movies, and the like in search of sexual partners. In such places, sex was quick and anonymous. One man might stick his penis through a "glory hole" in the wall separating stalls in a public urinal for a quick "blow job," another might accept or give anal intercourse in the bushes behind a park bench, and still others might engage in mutual masturbation sitting next to each other in a dimly lit movie house that catered to homosexuals. Yet all of these men had two goals in common: satisfying their desires while remaining virtual strangers to their partners. In many instances, if not most, they could pass one another on the street the following day without a hint of recognition.

During his many visits to Chicago, Kinsey learned all about this world, both as an observer and as a participant. This was the segment of the Chicago gay community he went to for physical release, as it contained the only group with whom he could enjoy sex with a minimum risk of recognition. Although it is highly unlikely that he abandoned himself to these outings very often, Kinsey must have relished this arrangement. In a sense, it gave him the best of everything. He had his family, with all the comforts of home and all the emotional support that entailed; he had homosexual friends with whom he could go to parties and bars to observe and to socialize, all the while preserving the perfect cover; and whenever the urge became too powerful to resist, he could slip away and engage in furtive, anonymous sex with the crowd that patronized Chicago's "tea rooms," slang for the public urinals frequented by homosexuals interested in quick, impersonal, faceless sex. In sum, his life had become a circle, within a circle, within a circle, offering enough danger and spice to complicate his balancing act.

Kinsey was practically bursting with excitement when he returned to Chicago in December 1939. It was his sixth trip in as many months. He stayed for eight days, an indication of the growing importance he assigned to these visits, both professionally and personally. Eager to tell someone about his discoveries, Kinsey again reached out to Voris. While scrupulously avoiding any mention of his own participation in Chicago's homosexual underworld, he drew a vivid portrait of a man becoming totally obsessed with a new field of research.

Confessing that his interviews were interfering with his gall wasp work, Kinsey declared, "Could never have afforded that time if it had not been the source of a research project that grows constantly more exciting." When they had met the preceding Christmas, he reminded Voris, there were only 75 histories in his files. A year later, he had "about 590—which means we will have accumulated over 500 in the year from Xmas to Xmas." Nor were these the inadequate written questionnaires Voris had seen earlier. Rather, these new records documented oral interviews that averaged one and a half hours, with some stretching to three hours. "It is the most complete, exhaustive record ever had on single individuals and already two and one half times as much in quantity as the best published study has," boasted Kinsey, adding that the psychologists, psychiatrists, and sociologists to whom he had shown his data were impressed. "We will prove to these social scientists that a biological background can help in interpreting social phenomena," he asserted defiantly.[53]

Yet, overall, Kinsey's tone was more earnest than boastful. "Wish so much that you could go over this material with me," he implored. "You are among the *very, very* few individuals to whom I can ever tell all of the story—the part that has too much dynamite to get into even the most objective scientific print. Your reactions would mean much to me—as your common sense has so often before."[54]

Saving the best for last, Kinsey concluded with a three-page addendum marked "Personal." He was, he confessed, unsure how much to put on paper, and he warned Voris to decide for himself whether his wife, Geraldine, should be allowed to see any or all of what followed. "I have wanted to tell you more about these Chicago H[omosexual] histories," Kinsey began. After impressing on Voris how hard it had been to persuade the first few Rush Street youths to be interviewed, he reported, "Now I can pick them up at 5 to 7 per day—as fast as I can get time to make the records. Each case leads to other introductions. There are half a dozen centers from which I am making contacts on this trip."[55]

Operating from multiple centers, Kinsey explained, allowed him to tap into the homosexual community's incredible diversity. "Am trying to get cases in all classes, from the most cultured and socially-economically best to the poorest type of professional street solicitor," he continued. The latter group interested Kinsey mightily, as he would always exhibit a profound sympathy for underdogs, particularly those whose sexual behavior brought them into conflict with the law. To date, he had managed to interview a number of male prostitutes, ranging "from beginners to those with 30 years active experience—a total now of about 40 histories out of Chicago who have had first-hand experience with a total of about 12,000 [customers]." Astounded by these numbers, Kinsey declared, "You can figure the average. Several with 2,000 and 3,000 each."[56]

Suddenly, everything was starting to fall into place. Thanks to hard work, he had been able to interview homosexual men who exhibited the "most marvelous evolutionary series—disclosing as prime factors such economic and social problems as have never been suggested before, and a simple biologic basis that is so simple that it sounds impossible that everyone hasn't seen it before."[57] Ever the biologist, Kinsey put his vast experience studying how and why changes occur to good use by drawing associations between the Chicago group and his students at Indiana University. "These Chicago histories are merely extensions of what I am getting on I.U. campus," he observed. "The campus gives me a better series of incipient cases, with all of their evolutionary significance," he continued. "Several extreme cases also from the campus, with small town and sophisticated variations that Chicago does not give so well." Jubilant over the size of his sample, he added, "Now have a total, from all sources, of 120 H— histories."[58] Here it is worth remembering that Kinsey had collected a total of 590 histories at this point, which meant that homosexual cases composed approximately one-fifth of his sample, clear evidence of how the targeting of homosexuals would skew his sample in the years ahead.

Yet Kinsey was too busy luxuriating in the joy of discovery, both personal and professional, to worry. Exploring this sexual subculture, he explained, had taken him to places his straitlaced childhood had not prepared him for. "Have been to Halloween parties, taverns, clubs, etc.[,] which would be unbelievable if realized by the rest of the world," he declared. "Always they have been most considerate and cooperative, decent, understanding, and cordial in their reception." Since by his estimation Chicago alone had 300,000 homosexuals, he was moved to ask, "Why has no one cracked this before?"[59]

Kinsey was elated with the results of his study. "I have diaries from long years—I have whole albums of photographs of their friends, or from commercial sources—fine art to putrid," he declared. Describing his art collection as "gorgeous," he pleaded, "I want you to see it. When do we get together again?" To sweeten the invitation, Kinsey taunted, "I think you would be interested in such I.U. campus matters as invade officialdom even the goings on in the former President's precincts (to his complete unawareness). Etc. Etc." Further details would have to wait "until we can visit for enough hours."[60]

As he had for the past fifteen years, Voris provided the support his mentor needed. "I've read and reread your letter there was so much of interest in it," he began. After careful thought, Voris had decided not to show "all of it" (that is, the addendum on Chicago's homosexual community) to his wife, out of "fear that she would not be able to comprehend." Indeed, she appeared "to have a distinct horror of the unusual and especially of talking about it."[61]

Turning to Kinsey's research on the homosexual community, Voris declared, "I am still surprised that you are able to get these cases to talk. Do any of them seem inclined to brag?" Then he put his finger on an extremely important point. "With the number of cases so many times larger than previous work it would seem that you will have to check that point sometime for you will have to defend yourself after publication," he cautioned. Responding to Kinsey's urgent requests for them to get together to discuss these matters, Voris replied, "I want to hear more about this but I have no idea when I will be able to see you." This year was out of the question, he explained, because he and Jerry were pinching pennies in case his summer leave came through.[62]

As fate would have it, the two men never met again. Early in January 1940, Voris wrote to say that a bad cold and severe cough he had contracted over Thanksgiving had turned into bronchopneumonia, leaving him exhausted and bedridden. Aware that Kinsey would soon be attending a professional meeting in nearby St. Louis, Voris invited him to Springfield, pleading, "I hesitate to insist but we certainly would enjoy the sight of you not to mention the good times for gab feast."[63] Troubled by the severity of her husband's condition, Geraldine penned a note at the bottom of his letter seconding the invitation. "A sight of you would do us both good and I don't need to tell you what it would mean to Ralph," she wrote. "He truly has been miserable and has given us a good scaring— seems weakened and I hesitate to urge him to come to you. If you could spare us some time you've no idea how welcome you would be—or have you? And I guarantee to let you talk to wee hours or all night without my interruption!"[64]

Unfortunately, their entreaties fell on preoccupied ears. Kinsey had asked one of the Chicago students, it seems, to refer him to homosexual friends in St. Louis, where he hoped to establish a second urban beachhead.[65] The plan worked, as it would again and again in other communities in the years ahead. The young man introduced Kinsey to friends, and he spent his extra time there repeating the script he had followed in Chicago—making contacts, interviewing gay men, going to parties, and the like—all of which left no time for his ailing friend.[66] Following his return to Bloomington, Kinsey told Voris, "I still feel guilty in not having come out to Springfield when I was in St. Louis. It was impossible without putting an end to the

study that I had underway in St. Louis. But, I am worried about your illness, and should have come to see you last month."[67]

Over the next few months, Voris's condition worsened. As Geraldine's
letters grew more anxious, Kinsey wrote early in March to say that he was
"very much disturbed" by the recent reports. "There is no time for it in my
schedule, but if I can be of real use I will come out to Springfield or any
where else to help you," he assured his friend. Then, characteristically, Kinsey launched into a detailed discussion of his work, as though Voris was
hanging on every word. "I have settled down almost to a constant schedule of being out-of-town the last few days in the week," he wrote. "It is this
research on human sex behavior that has piled in the extra work." Noting
that at first "it was a problem to get contributions to our histories," Kinsey declared that "now it is a scramble to find time to record all of those
that are offered." On campus, two fraternities had recently volunteered 100
percent of their members, a development Kinsey welcomed as a possible
solution to his sampling problem. As he explained, "that is invaluable because it gives us the nearest substitute that seems possible for a random
sample."[68]

Off campus, things were progressing swimmingly, too. "Every day's
mail brings requests from the outside for conferences whenever I travel
their way," observed Kinsey. In the last month alone, he continued, he had
lectured in a small town at the request of a clergyman and picked up ten
histories the following day. In addition, he had delivered a series of three
lectures to a group of 180 parents at Anderson, Indiana, "staying over in
the town for a day following each lecture, and getting histories of every variety from parents to high school boys and girls." Indeed, Anderson's high
school authorities were so enthusiastic, he boasted, "that they promise me
1,000 histories there if I want to take the time for them." Best of all, his
work of a more specialized nature was flourishing, allowing him to learn
more about homosexual culture than any investigator before him. "My
Chicago and St. Louis connections are spreading like the branches of a
tree," reported Kinsey. "We now have over 700 histories, and our tabula-
tions, curves, correlation charts, etc.[,] are beginning to be impressive."[69]

If the contents of this letter appeared strangely impersonal, it was probably because Kinsey did not want to show how worried he was and retreated to the familiar male dodge of talking shop. Still, he allowed his
emotions to show a little at the end. "Take care of yourself; mind Geraldine, for I know she will do all she can to help you come through," he advised. Then Kinsey offered a glimpse of the depths of his concern,
pleading, "Tell me what I can do."[70]

A week or so later, Voris was moved to St. Louis's Barnes Hospital, where the death watch began in earnest. Geraldine corresponded almost daily, with each report growing more despondent as her husband fought for life. Early on Wednesday morning, May 9, 1940, she wrote, "I nearly go mad thinking about a future without him. . . . Ralph is having horrible days now & I can't ask him to stay if he can't get better."⁷¹ He died later that morning, less than two months short of his thirty-eighth birthday.⁷²

Too busy to come during his friend's illness, Kinsey rushed to his side in death. On Saturday, he and Clara drove to Springfield, where they comforted Geraldine as best they could. Immediately after the funeral service on Sunday, Kinsey attended to some very important business. Under the cover of darkness, he entered Voris's office and removed certain items, including copies and originals of their private correspondence.⁷³ This accomplished, Kinsey and Clara returned to Bloomington, without staying for the internment two days later.

During the months that followed, Kinsey and Geraldine remained in close touch as she struggled with her loss. One of his letters in particular meant a great deal to her. "Scientific thinking does help," she wrote. "It was good of you to explain your reactions to me. I find great help in your attitude."⁷⁴ Yet, however rational his views on death, they provided little comfort for Kinsey's grief. A week after Voris's death, he wrote Breland, "It is a very great loss to me. I had traveled more miles with him than anyone else. I so regret the fact that there were not more contacts in the last ten years. It has greatly broken me up."⁷⁵ The pain abated in time, as it does for most people, but part of him was buried with Voris. Half a year after the funeral, Kinsey told Geraldine, "The loss of Ralph will always be a major tragedy in my life."⁷⁶ Until he joined his beloved friend in death, Kinsey kept a photograph of Voris on his desk.

Voris's death forced Kinsey to look elsewhere for support. In the same letter in which he poured out his grief, Kinsey pleaded with Breland to become his new confidant. "I never had a chance to discuss with Ralph the endless things that this new study of mine has developed. He would have understood so much better than almost anyone else," lamented Kinsey. "Now it becomes increasingly imperative that you help in my thinking on this." Explaining that he planned to devote his vacation to collecting histories in Chicago and St. Louis if he could find the funds, Kinsey beseeched Breland to come for a visit at any other time in the summer, declaring, "Our home is yours if you will use it."⁷⁷

Although they remained in close contact for several years, Breland did not fill the special role Voris had occupied in Kinsey's thinking about his research. Nor did Breland replace Voris as a love interest. That position was already taken.

About a year before Voris's death, Kinsey had met a young man on campus whom he found intriguing. Since time and distance had limited his opportunities to be with Voris, it was perhaps inevitable that Kinsey should become vulnerable to another intense relationship. At any rate, he found one among the troubled young men he interviewed on campus.

Clyde Martin was nineteen years old when he enrolled as a freshman at Indiana University in the fall of 1937.[78] A handsome young man with thick hair, broad shoulders, and a quick smile, he was not exactly what one would call "a man's man." Rather, he was warm and soft-spoken, projecting the kind of innocence and openness some people consider attractive and others find irresistible. In his personal relationships, Martin tended not to be very aggressive, as he was by nature a gentle man. In fact, many traits that society typically defined as "masculine" were alien to his character. "I don't consider myself very competitive," Martin once remarked. Nor was he particularly interested in the things society considered manly. He was, by his own description, "oriented toward the aesthetic" and "interested in the arts."[79]

Although he had doubtless seen him before, Martin's first real memory of Kinsey was watching him stride across campus on a rainy day sporting a whaling hat. Not the least bit intimidated, Martin walked right up and asked Kinsey about the hat, inquiring where he had purchased it. Insouciance always piqued Kinsey's interest, and he later reminded Martin of this exchange when they became better acquainted. For his part, Martin was impressed by Kinsey. Many years afterward, he would recall that he found him "a personable[,] friendly guy, youthful and boyish looking."[80]

The circumstances that brought them together, however, were less than pleasant. Chronically strapped for funds, Martin was miserable during much of his sophomore year. "I felt that the lack of dating and so on was pretty rough to take, and I was thinking of dropping out of school," he confessed. "I felt very lonely and wondered whether it was all worthwhile."[81] Questions of a sexual nature intensified his angst. There were things in his past that had left him troubled and confused. Consequently, like so many of his schoolmates, he took his problems to the man on campus who seemed to have all the answers. On December 17, 1938, Martin gave Kinsey his sex history, an event that would change his life forever.[82]

Kinsey knew exactly what to do with troubled young men. "I found the interview itself extremely useful," Martin declared. "I was very naive in those days. He put my mind at ease with respect to certain sexual questions."[83] As a rule, Kinsey declined to discuss his own sexual history with subjects. Indeed, if pressed on the matter, he would stoutly refuse, explaining that he would preserve their right to privacy as fiercely as he protected his own. Yet there was something about Martin that drew Kinsey closer. In large measure, Kinsey succeeded in reassuring him, Martin later disclosed, "by citing similar examples from his own history."[84]

Nor did Kinsey ignore the young man's economic plight. As someone who had worked his way through college, he sympathized with Martin. The upshot was that Kinsey offered him a part-time job working in his garden. Martin accepted, grateful for the opportunity to earn extra money. Apparently, Kinsey had no difficulty persuading Martin to wear his gardening attire. "They worked in very abbreviated garb—scanty shorts," recalled an observant neighbor.[85] Looking back on the many hours they toiled side-by-side, Martin remarked, "Here's where we really became much better acquainted."[86]

Indeed they did. As the days turned into weeks and the weeks into months, Kinsey reached out to Martin. The middle-aged professor and anxious undergraduate drew closer and closer. No doubt aware that sharing secrets would eventually narrow the gap that separated them because of age and positions, Kinsey gradually revealed additional details about his own troubled past, including a failed relationship from which he had never recovered. "I learned a great deal about his problems with his father," Martin noted.[87]

Greater intimacy brought further revelations. Of course, Kinsey knew all about Martin's private life from taking his history, while Martin, in turn, had learned a little about Kinsey's sexual history from his remarks during their interview. As they worked together in the garden, Kinsey maneuvered their discussions toward sex and their exchange of confidences expanded. "I'm really kind of astonished what kind of a moral prude Kinsey was in his very early years," confessed Martin many years later. "I think in part this helped prepare him because his [upbringing] in his younger years made him realize what a tremendous contrast there was between what was actually going on and what people often weren't aware was going on. And I think he always had kind of a chuckle in his own mind [about this]."[88]

In time, Kinsey expanded Martin's duties along lines that followed their conversations. The interviews were piling up, and Kinsey needed help tabulating his data. By the spring term of 1939, he had come to know Martin well enough to trust him. Kinsey asked him to assist with his sex research. Significantly, Kinsey's assessment reflected a favorable appraisal of Martin's attitudes as well as of his abilities. "Well, the way he put it," explained Martin, "[was] that I was educable. I really didn't have much of an opinion as to whether sex between two men was good or bad or right or wrong; I'd never thought of it."[89]

Since Martin was not the first young man Kinsey had "educated," and since he already knew Martin's sexual preferences, Kinsey had a pretty good idea how to proceed. After all, the power relationship between Kinsey and Martin was not exactly equal. Kinsey was older, well established professionally, and Martin's employer. Kinsey worked hard at seducing this insecure, anxious, and financially strapped young man, and Martin became the third and final love of Kinsey's life.[90]

According to Clarence A. Tripp, who knew both men well, Kinsey's behavior during his "courtship" of Martin was never "unfair or unkind." Rather, Kinsey relied upon guilt and covert pressure to woo young Martin into bed, which proved to be far more effective than bullying. "Sweet fatherly figure sort of expects it and you don't want to disappoint him and you don't want to make waves and so on," was how Tripp described Kinsey's approach. Not that he blamed Kinsey for lusting after Martin. "Martin was a very good-looking boy in those years," he declared.[91]

But Kinsey was much more interested in having sex with Martin than Martin was with Kinsey. For a time, Martin was able to be sexually responsive, but homosexuality was not his inclination. He was much more interested in women. "Kinsey got Martin into all kinds of things, but Martin didn't like it," Tripp explained.[92] In fact, it really was a case of Martin's "being dragged against his will into it."[93] Asked about the duration of the sexual phase of the relationship between Kinsey and Martin, Tripp replied, "I'm not sure . . . how long it lasted. I know that Kinsey was quite frustrated that Martin sort of wanted out of that. . . . I know it wasn't Martin's scene at all."[94] Still, the fact that Martin did not return his feelings in kind did little to dampen Kinsey's attraction or hope. As Tripp put it, Kinsey stayed "after him for years."[95]

Yet Martin did seize the initiative in a different relationship, one that developed not long after his dealings with Kinsey became intimate. Perhaps hoping to deflect Kinsey's attentions and place himself back on track, Martin asked Kinsey's permission to approach Clara for sex. According to Tripp, Kinsey replied, "I have to tell you that the idea never occurred to me." Still, once he thought about it, Kinsey readily agreed, as he was eager to strengthen his hold on Martin even if he had to use Clara as bait. Besides, Kinsey was far too liberated in his thinking to take offense. Forty-two years old and hardly a femme fatale, Clara was not only pleased but flattered when she learned of Martin's interest. She happily consented. Kinsey and Clara teamed up, as one friend put it, "to teach Martin about sex."[96] Asked point-blank if Clara and Martin had sex, another close friend replied, "Absolutely."[97] Nor was it a one-shot affair. They maintained a sexual relationship long after Martin managed to hold Kinsey at arm's length. "I'm sure she liked it," Tripp declared. "Besides liking the sex, . . . it was certainly participation of some kind on the wild edge of the research background. Right?"[98]

Since Clara was a strong person, we can assume that she went to bed with Martin freely. Yet marriage often has a way of bending one partner to suit the other partner's will, as every relationship has its peculiar dynamics, its own not so subtle power struggles that eventually determine patterns of deference and accommodation. By the late 1930s, the Kinseys had been together for nearly two decades, more than enough time to forge their own style of interaction. Clara seems to have been content to yield to her husband's wishes and to adapt to his needs.

Nevertheless, it seems doubtful that she would have considered going to bed with Martin an act of submission or self-sacrifice. On the contrary, she probably welcomed the opportunity to have sex with a handsome, younger man who desired her, as a means both of reassuring herself that other men found her attractive and of demonstrating her sex appeal to her husband. Indeed, she would have been less than human had she not relished the idea of being pursued by the man her husband found so appealing. One takes power (and revenge) where one can.

Not that Clara necessarily viewed sleeping with Martin as a slap at her husband. Her real motive may have been quite the opposite. Ironically, Clara may have slept with Martin, at least in part, to get closer to Kinsey She was desperate to fashion a place for herself in his research and in the new life it was opening. After all, the danger was very real that Kinsey would become so absorbed in his new research, and in the new sexual opportunities it provided, that he would distance himself even further from Clara. Here the key is to remember that the Kinseys regarded marriage as a partnership, a contract she had worked hard under difficult circumstances to fulfill.

Many people close to Clara considered her an equal partner in her marriage, and there is every reason to believe that this was how she saw herself. Subscribing to the cult of domesticity, she had sought and found her identity as a woman by fulfilling the duties of a wife and mother. Yet, unlike many faculty wives whose interests did not extend beyond the home, Clara had been able to share her husband's intellectual life. Thanks to her intelligence, her interest in hiking and in the outdoors, and her undergraduate training in science, she was a helpmate who could do more than type Kinsey's manuscripts or keep the home fires burning while he was away on field trips (both of which, of course, she did). Because she was confident of her intellectual faculties, and because she both understood and shared his enthusiasm for science, Clara was willing and able to discuss ideas.

Partnership also defined the contours of their intimate relationship. Despite the strains his sexual needs placed on their marriage, the Kinseys managed to preserve a strong emotional bond. While his attraction to men no doubt vitiated his sexual interest in Clara, Kinsey was able nevertheless to maintain a sexual relationship with her until near the end of his life. He remained deeply devoted to her throughout their marriage. Indeed, with no disservice to language, he never stopped loving her. Nor she him. Yet to say that Clara both loved and respected her husband diminishes the strength of her feelings. From all reports, she revered Kinsey—enough to accompany him on a journey that left Victorian morality far behind.

By the late 1930s, Clara, too, had become a sexual rebel. Moving on parallel tracks with her husband, she had read marriage manuals, perused nudist magazines, and experimented with different sexual positions. She had developed a local reputation as a sex expert, dispensing advice and information to neighbors and their children, not to mention her own offspring. More to the point, she had remained in her marriage, actively participating in a relationship that most women would have found unacceptable. Under circumstances that must have tested her sorely, she had learned first to tolerate and then to accept her husband's sexual needs—desires that she herself could not fulfill and society condemned.

What was the glue that held the Kinseys together as they made the transition from a respectable middle-class couple to sexual rebels? Love? Their children? Social pressures that condemned divorce? Unwillingness to admit failure? Fear of being alone? Economic considerations? To be sure, each probably had played a role. Yet, in the end, these factors probably would have failed to preserve their marriage if they had not managed to talk. Somehow, they had managed to develop a relationship that kept the channels of communication open between two people who, whatever their problems, cared deeply for one another and wished to remain together.

How early those talks began is anybody's guess. At some point, though, Kinsey made Clara his confidante, sharing his thoughts and confessing his needs as soon and as clearly as self-understanding and faith in her allowed. And while it cannot have been easy for her to learn about his interest in men, he probably took steps to cushion the blow. Doubtless, he reassured Clara of his love, insisting that he continued to find her sexually attractive. In addition, he may have sought to explain and defend his homoerotic interests by advancing arguments that reflected both his own case history and what he was learning from his ongoing research on human sexual behavior.

But, again, whatever the content of their discussions, the crucial point is that they managed to talk. Given his powers of persuasion, and given Clara's vulnerability to his appeals, it does not stretch credulity to think that Kinsey found the words to reassure her of his love, to convince her of the importance of his new research, and to enlist her in the struggle for sexual liberation. Nor does it exhaust our empathy to understand how Clara could accept whatever arguments he advanced, offering, as they did, rationalizations for the present and hope for the future.

Ironically, then, partnership, love, duty, science, sexual liberation, and her own private needs all compelled Clara to remain with Kinsey and to accept Martin as her lover. Given the nature of her marriage, she had to claim for herself the same right to sexual freedom that Kinsey seized for himself and advocated for others. And in the years ahead, Clara would welcome other men to her bed, as she struggled to preserve her relationship with a man whose devotion to research and sexual needs threatened to pull him further and further away.

For his part, Martin kept his role hidden from the world. Decades later, he categorically refused to discuss his personal relationship with Kinsey, other than to say, "We were very good friends."[99] When asked the same question about Voris and Kinsey, Martin used the identical words, remarking, "I knew they were very good friends."[100]

In 1940, the nature of Kinsey's relationship with Martin remained secret, and Kinsey, in particular, was pleased with the arrangement. Although he had suffered as a result of Voris's death, he had found a new love, albeit unrequited, and he had managed to pursue Martin with Clara's consent and cooperation. And best of all for the work-centered Kinsey, his new research had melded his public and private identities as no other endeavor could have. In fact, it had developed into a consuming passion, promising more than enough challenges and rewards (professional and personal) to fill a lifetime.

As it happened, Kinsey would need every ounce of strength he could muster. For just when he seemed to have fashioned his own satisfactory adjustment, he had to confront a serious threat to his research, one whose outcome would set the course for the remainder of his life.

17

"THE ONLY CHOICE THAT HE COULD POSSIBLY MAKE"

I n the spring of 1940, the sun shown brightly on Alfred C. Kinsey. He had fashioned a new field of research for himself, converting his personal needs into work. Not only could he interview people about their sexual thoughts and behavior, but he could do so while proclaiming his scientific objectivity in public and offering advice that advanced the politics of sexual liberation in private. Kinsey had become a secret reformer in pursuit of the great cause of his life. Sex research had given him a way to conduct a public crusade for private reasons, a way to join his outer and inner identities. And it appeared that Kinsey had accomplished these things with remarkable ease—that he had spent the last two years pushing against an open door.

Yet the truth was not that simple. From the outset, Kinsey had misread the situation on campus. Ebullient with his own sexual liberation and giddy with the flush of discovery, he had placed too much faith in student support, and he had consistently underestimated the strength of the opposition. He had acted as though middle-class morality could be swept from campus by edict, that the marriage course by itself could liberalize sexual attitudes and behavior. Kinsey was wrong. The marriage course was vulnerable, and so was he.

Although it took time for the opposition to organize, a number of critics with sharp knives had their own motives for wanting to cut Kinsey down to size. Students who had taken the course and were shocked, faculty members who had heard rumors about what was being taught and did not like what they heard, physicians who had turf to protect, and ministers who had moral objections—all joined the attack. By late spring, he was under siege, as these and other critics campaigned to remove him from the marriage course, a crusade that had started only months after the class began.

Kinsey's fulsome reports to President Wells notwithstanding, the marriage course had always generated opposition on campus. A few students had grumbled about the contents of particular lectures, while others had objected to Kinsey's agenda. Detecting a note of special pleading in his impassioned talk on individual variation, one student wrote, "I question the real value of the material presented in this lecture to the group as a whole." Another student strongly disagreed with Kinsey's advice about starting sex education early, asserting, "I feel that some matters concerning sex should be reserved until puberty," while a classmate insisted that all boys really needed to learn about sex was "more chastity." And a few students recoiled in horror from Kinsey's repeated emphasis on sexual freedom, including the angry soul who accused him of advancing arguments that were "definitely intended to destroy marriage as we know it."[1]

Nor was the support of the instructional staff unanimous. John H. Mueller, a sociologist who lectured on the history of the family to the marriage course, quickly developed second thoughts about his role in the course. Thinking back on her husband's objections, Kate Mueller, who had followed the marriage course closely because she had served as the dean of women at Indiana University, recalled that the students were interested in only a few topics and wrote "rather scathing comments in many cases . . . about the preceding lectures."[2] Her husband's presentation, it seemed, was among those that had been savaged, and it had pained him to see his efforts ridiculed and dismissed, especially since the entire instructional staff saw the evaluations. "He refused to give the lecture again," she explained, "because he just didn't want to be window dressing for Mr. Kinsey and the others who were giving the real meat of the course which the students wanted."[3]

A more serious defection occurred when Dr. Edith Schuman resigned. A physician who worked in the university's student health center, she had lectured on pregnancy and childbirth and on venereal diseases, important topics both. Yet, to some extent, her objections echoed those of John

Mueller. "I always had the feeling, from a medical standpoint, that they [the students] were less interested in what I had to say, because most of them knew what I had to say," she later confessed. Her material, she complained, "was chiefly padding for [Kinsey's] presentation of his lives and his intense discussion of sex and so forth."[4]

Schuman also bore a grudge against Kinsey over an incident that had occurred early in the marriage course. On a day she was scheduled to lecture, she failed to show up for class. "Well, the fact was that I had a sick girl," she explained. "I had to take care of her; I had to dispose of her; and I was late and I couldn't make it." Unfortunately, Kinsey's reaction to her excuse was less than gracious. "He felt that I should have made it at all cost no matter what happened," she complained, adding that he was not "very friendly from then on."[5]

But Schuman had another objection to the marriage course, one that ran deeper than any personal dislike she may have had for the man. From the outset, she had strongly resented the private conferences with students, primarily because Kinsey conducted the overwhelming majority of them. Here Schuman was defending turf, as she thought he had no right to advise students on subjects over which the medical profession had claimed exclusive authority. "From a medical standpoint I did not feel that he should counsel them," she explained. "That, I think, is a natural feeling on a medical person's side." Challenging Kinsey's competence, she added, "I felt that he emphasized certain statements, such as increase in blood pressure, more than he should, being a nonmedical person."[6] In the years ahead, Kinsey would hear similar charges again and again from physicians who resented his encroachments on their professional hegemony.

For Schuman, the final straw involved complaints from her staff. Two of her nurses, its seems, were interviewed by Kinsey, after which they came to her and charged that "he could provoke any answer that he might want from the students involved."[7] Since Schuman had long suspected as much herself, she believed these reports and punctuated her disapproval by refusing to be interviewed when he asked. Later, she would join a group of her colleagues at Indiana University's School of Medicine in Indianapolis in demanding Kinsey's removal from the marriage course.

John H. Mueller, the sociologist who had resigned in a huff from the course's instructional staff, added his voice to the growing chorus of critics. Warning that the pressure of unfavorable public opinion had to be met, he declared, "When teaching proceeds too rapidly for customs and mores, or when it takes a direction that calls it into question, some one person or group must decide whether it should continue or be modified." Mueller thought that this job belonged to President Wells, and Mueller wanted him to know why so many members of the marriage course committee had resigned. It all came down to Kinsey and his private conferences with students. Mueller charged that one woman who had been asked to come in for a conference "protested to faculty members and inquired whether she would be obliged to go." Another student, Mueller reported, had been advised at the end of a conference, "You should go out and find a healthy male and have relations with him." Yet another female student who had refused to have sex with her fiancé was told by him (after hearing Kinsey lecture) "that the best advice was not to resist." Moreover, Mueller told of a mother who withdrew her daughter from the marriage course because she "did not like the things that were going on at Indiana." He also cited by name four faculty wives who, after taking the marriage class, had made "much unfavorable comment," some of which was "very bitter."[8]

Saving the most serious matter for last, Mueller charged that Kinsey was exploiting students for his own purposes. "Mr. Kinsey has pressed the students for conferences more than they wished," Mueller declared. "He has used the course to collect data for studies of his own."[9] There, someone had finally said it: Kinsey's interest in the course had less to do with sex education than with sex research.

As student criticisms and faculty resignations mounted, the administration came under increasing pressure to act. When rumors about the marriage course reached Mrs. Nellie Showers Teter, the only female member of the board of trustees, she went directly to President Wells. Mrs. Teter was one of the richest people in town and one of the most cultivated and gracious, in Wells's words, "[a] gentle, well-bred, Victorian, but humane kind of individual." Tastefully but firmly, she asked whether the marriage course was "proper." In response, Wells suggested that she take the course and see for herself. At this point, Mrs. Teter hesitated, stating that she feared Kinsey might take offense. So Wells telephoned Kinsey, who immediately consented. According to Wells, she returned to his office three weeks later, pronounced the class "wonderful," and declared, "I wished I could have had such a course when I was in college."[10]

Thanks to Mrs. Teter's support, Kinsey had the board's backing, and the pressure subsided, at least temporarily. Then, another member of the medical professional took it upon himself to investigate the marriage course. Before the air cleared, Kinsey had learned a bitter lesson about how much cultural authority physicians exercised over American society.

Dr. Thurman B. Rice worked for the Indiana State Board of Health as the chief of its Bureau of Health and Physical Education. He was described by a colleague as "a jolly, sort of happy-go-lucky, big man," but someone who was also "a little crude."[11] Over the years, he had delivered numerous lectures on sex education to various groups across the state, and he considered himself an expert in the field. Consequently, his ears perked up when he heard certain rumors about the marriage course. In February 1939, Rice paid Kinsey a visit on campus. At the time, the meeting seemed cordial enough. The two self-styled experts spent hours reviewing the course syllabus, discussing the contents of various lectures, looking over Kinsey's slides, and exchanging viewpoints about their respective approaches to sex education. Yet, if he thought he had won Rice over, Kinsey was mistaken. Later that month, he received a four-page, single-spaced letter in which the good doctor gave substance to criticisms and concerns that had been whispered on campus for months.

Rice began by insisting that his was "a friendly letter," adding, "I know that you will not regard me as being inimical to yourself and the course." Still, Rice felt compelled to speak out: "I am extremely anxious about such matters and want the maximum of good for yourself, for the University, and for the young people concerned." After stressing how much he admired the course's organization, he confessed, "I was a little bit surprised at some of the content."[12] At this point, Rice cut to the chase, leveling criticisms against the course that grew shriller as he progressed.

"I wonder if the course is too long and too complete," he ventured. While he acknowledged the temptation to try to cover everything, Rice held firmly to the view that marriage was too large and too complicated a subject to be covered adequately by any college course. Of necessity, students would need to read additional books and pamphlets after completing the course, and they would have to supplement these with the kinds of experience that would come only in marriage. "I am somewhat afraid that sixteen lectures may have the effect of making the students think they know all about the eubject [sic] and in some instances serving as too long and too intense a stimulation," he observed.[13]

And "stimulation" was to be avoided at all costs. Knowing young people as he did, Rice worried that scholarly interest was not their only motive for taking the marriage course. "As a matter of fact," he charged, "95% of those young people in that class don't give a tinker's damn about marriage as a social or biological fact. They just want to know about it for their own personal satisfaction. They are tremendously enamored of its possibilities for personal enjoyment." Because marriage was "not principally an objective experience," people were bound to approach it subjectively. This was especially true of young people, he warned, because they were sexually deprived and easily excited. Instead of recognizing this problem and avoiding material that might ignite their passions, the marriage course poured gasoline on open flames. "For example," confessed Rice, "the pictures which you showed me, particularly the one showing coitus in sagital section, was even stimulating to me, though I think I have much less reason to be excited than have these students. I have been married for nearly thirty years, and have given the subject real objective study. The picture is just *too* good."[14]

As a venerable practitioner of the conspiracy of silence, Rice was adamant that certain matters "should be touched only in general." Cheerfully admitting that his views left him "open to the criticism of being Mid-Victorian," he nevertheless insisted that such topics "as position in intercourse and a detailed study of reasons for failure" were "out of place in a class of that sort." There was plenty of time for couples to learn about such things after they got married. If they developed any difficulties in bed, declared Rice, "they should be encouraged to go to their physician or someone who is informed in that sort of thing."[15]

Rice begged Kinsey to consider the welfare of the university. "Let us suppose that a little rosebud of a girl from the 'sticks' arrives on the campus," he intoned. "She, in the opinion of her parents and the local minister, is as pure as a drop of dew. As she comes into the new environment," he continued, "she is likely to be stimulated sexually and may very easily, in the course of the next few years acquire sex habits not to her credit and not unlikely may acquire a baby." Damaged goods, she would have to go home "in disgrace," whereupon her outraged parents would immediately "look around for a 'fall guy.' " When this happened, predicted Rice, "they are going to put the blame, not on themselves or on the girl, but on you and the University and the whole idea of sex education. And some of these days they are going to make that blame stick!"[16]

Rice offered a terrifying vision of what would follow. "I know legislators who would raise holy hell about this course," he declared. "All that an enemy of yours, or of the University, would need to do would be to demand that you show the legislature the pictures that you are showing to this class and an outline of the lectures which you are giving on contraception, coitus, and the biological problems of Marriage. God only knows what would happen to the University if that were done!" he exclaimed. Just in case Kinsey was not able to divine what the deity alone knew, Rice added, "I am very much afraid that they would raise such a fuss as would overturn the administration of the University."[17]

Aware he had treaded heavily, Rice again attempted to balance his criticisms with expressions of friendship. "Now, I am personally a great admirer of martyrs," he declared, hitting closer to home than he knew, "and as I know you have no hope of personal gain in this, I want you to believe that I feel a respect for your sincerity of purpose which I hold for very few people."[18] Still, Rice felt compelled to dispute Kinsey's naive assumption that Indiana University would be able to protect him against all comers.

"You assured me that President Wells and the trustees approved heartily of your course. I wonder, though, if the trustees know the details," challenged Rice. "I am absolutely sure that there are many influential members of the faculty down there who would be extremely opposed." After acknowledging that these same individuals would probably disapprove of his course, he quickly added, "But I have been getting by with it for fifteen years and have back of me now that experience and the approval of some of the most powerful forces in Indiana. Yet I would not for a moment consider attempting anything so frank."[19]

Rice's closing remarks were nonetheless true for their disarming candor. Admitting he might be "wrong about all this," he confessed, "Maybe I am just another old grandma. Maybe I am jealous because I wasn't asked about the content of this course, when it seems I really should have been asked, because of the fact that I have been doing it for a long time, am on the faculty and was indeed asked by the students to come and give a course myself this year." After repeating that he might be "just 'all wet' about this whole subject," Rice ended by urging Kinsey to give the matter "serious consideration."[20]

A man different from Kinsey might have treated these warnings as a wake-up call, for despite his self-deprecating tone, Rice's reactions were not isolated. Indeed, Rice had provided a reality check. He had expressed precisely those concerns that many people would have voiced had they known what was going on in the marriage course. In addition, he had sent a clear signal that a professional rivalry was brewing between Kinsey and the university's medical community, a constituency he could ill afford to alienate. Over the last century, physicians had laid claim to human sexuality. Any investigator who was not a member of the club could expect fierce opposition if he challenged their professional hegemony. Kinsey recognized this danger. Asked how her husband had interpreted Rice's position, Clara replied, "I think he may have thought it was partly professional jealousy. After all, Rice was an M.D., and M.D.'s don't always like to have somebody who is not an M.D. telling them anything that they think is connected with their field."[21]

Yet Kinsey was too caught up in what he was doing to recognize an omen when he saw one, let alone consider making changes in how he was proceeding. While the tone of his response was cordial, Kinsey elected to stonewall. The marriage course, he told Rice, was "the product of the staff of nine, and not of any one of us." He promised to pass along Rice's suggestions to the instructional staff, stressing they were always willing to make changes in the course that "experience has shown desirable." Still, Kinsey made no effort to conceal his contempt for the rumor mill, professing that he was "at a loss to know how to weigh the reactions of those who have not heard the course."[22]

This last remark offered a hint of Kinsey's pique, as it had the kind of snappy, one-liner quality he often employed to shut off further discussions. Once again, though, Kinsey had badly underestimated his critic's resolve. Rice had no intention of being dismissed like a schoolboy. Proclaiming himself much encouraged by the "spirit" of Kinsey's reply, he reaffirmed his support of the marriage course, declaring, "I sincerely hope the time has come when the subject can be handled as you are doing it." His reservations stood, however, as he doubted whether that "time had yet come."[23]

Rice was adamant that his concerns had not been addressed. He was, he warned Kinsey, still worried that if an innocent girl lost her virtue on university time "the university might be made the scapegoat, inasmuch as in such a case a scapegoat of some kind will be badly needed by her family." Nor was he impressed with Kinsey's argument that there had been no serious criticisms from people who had taken the course. The danger, stressed Rice, came not from that group but from those who had received garbled, secondhand reports. Repeating one of the stories he had heard, Rice charged that Bloomington's high school students were "quite excited" about the marriage course because they had listened to reports from students in the class who described it "in very enthusiastic and favorable terms, but with the emphasis put where you would not wish it to be put." Determined to make Kinsey see reason, Rice warned, "The course has set up a chain of circumstances over which you have no control, being responsible only for the first link." Already, one angry citizen "was directly laying the blame for the excessive interest in the subject among the high school students upon the course given in the university."[24] Due to the university's acute concern about town-and-gown relations, the board would have to act to protect the school.

Rice closed on a collegial note. "I want very much for you to succeed because if you should fail, my own work, in which I am so much interested, would also probably fall under suspicion," he explained, "because I am in the University and am teaching sex education on a very wide front. Be sure you have my continued interest and good wishes."[25]

Rice's "good wishes" quickly turned into bile. By spring 1940, he was pressuring President Wells to remove Kinsey from the marriage course staff. Decades later, Wells described Rice as "vociferous in this," adding that he was "a man of passionate beliefs of all types." Moreover, Wells charged that Rice "was jealous of [Kinsey] because he gave a different kind of marriage course than Kinsey did." Denying that their rivalry was in any way unique, Wells added philosophically, "And, of course, this is not unusual among scientists. They get jealous of each other like all other human beings."[26]

Rice was not the only physician who pressured Wells to remove Kinsey from the marriage course. Joining the firing squad were Dr. Edith Schuman from the campus and several influential faculty members from Indiana University's School of Medicine in Indianapolis, including the retiring dean, Dr. Burton Dorr Myers; his successor as dean, Dr. Willis D. Gatch; and Dr. David A. Boyd, head of the Department of Mental and Nervous Diseases.[27]

Robert Kroc discovered to his dismay how much these physicians despised Kinsey's creation. Many years later, Kroc recalled a telephone conversation with Dean Myers, whom Kroc described as "an impressive man" with a "rudy face, white hair, and a deep, impressive voice." During their discussion, explained Kroc, the marriage course came up, and Dean Myers "referred to it [as] that 'smut session.' " As someone who had helped design and teach the course, Kroc was stunned by this remark. "Wait a minute, sir," he remembered saying, "I cannot allow you to make that expression in my presence without my challenging it." When Myers refused to retract it, Kroc was so upset he made an appointment to meet with him in Indianapolis to discuss the matter. On the day of their appointment, Kroc discovered that Myers had invited Schuman to their meeting. A well-known critic of Kinsey, she was, in Kroc's words, "on the prudish side." He immediately interpreted her presence as a trouble sign. His instincts proved correct. Try as he might, Kroc could not persuade Myers to revise his opinion of the marriage course; nor could he persuade him to gather additional information by sitting in on some classes. As Kroc put it, his discussion with Myers "got nowhere."[28]

By 1940, Kinsey was under attack not only from physicians in Indianapolis but from preachers in Bloomington. That spring, President Wells received a visit from representatives of the local Ministerial Association Alliance, an interdenominational organization of pastors. As Bloomington's official custodians of morality, these men voiced grave concerns about the marriage course's social and moral implications, both for the city's young people and for the university's students. They pressured President Wells to ask the trustees to investigate the class and recommend modifications where appropriate.[29]

According to Wells, his visitors "got excited about it." Among the most agitated, he recalled, was Dr. Frank O. Beck, whom Wells described, not without irony, as "quite something of a liberal around this place." Ordinarily, Beck was "dedicated to maintaining a liberal posture, and stirring up liberal concerns," stressed Wells. But in this instance, Beck was "a little shocked by it." Contradictions of this sort were not so puzzling as they seemed, mused Wells, explaining, "He was a political liberal, I think, more than a liberal in this field. He was after all . . . a product of the Victorian Era, having graduated here in '92."[30]

In May 1940, Albert L. Kohlmeier, chairman of the University Committee on Religion, notified Wells that the members of his committee "requested that a note be forwarded to the trustees of the University expressing the attitude of the committee, as being one of serious concern regarding the moral and social implications of the present methods of conducting the non-credit course on marriage." While stressing that the course had "real merit," Kohlmeier urged Wells to conduct "an objective appraisal of the present methods of conducting this course."[31]

With various foes converging on Kinsey, Wells had no choice but to intervene. After conferring with Mrs. Teter and other advisers, he decided to offer Kinsey a choice: he could either "(1) Continue to give the lectures, with certain sections modified, the individual conferences to be held by the Medical Center," or "(2) Sever his connection with the course and go ahead with individual conferences, attracting to himself such persons as he could for the conferences but not integrating them with that course."[32] In other words, Kinsey could be a sex educator with clipped wings, or a sex researcher with the entire world outside the marriage course as his laboratory.

No part of Kinsey's character had prepared him to accept the choice he was asked to make without putting up a fight. He was not able to grasp that President Wells had fashioned a Solomon-like compromise that balanced his right to do research against the community's right to defend its moral standards, however benighted they might appear to Kinsey. Still, he knew better than to bite the hand that protected him. As a result, Kinsey hid his anger beneath a patina of civility, using reason as his weapon of choice. With great self-control, he drafted, but never mailed, a detailed reply to Wells, rebutting his critics and pleading with the president to remain steadfast in his support. Kinsey's arguments were revealing, for the light they shed both on his strategy and on his self-image.

By 1940, Kinsey had come to understand that academic freedom offered the best protection for his research. It was on this principle that he based his appeal. In his mind, he was an embattled scientist besieged by the forces of ignorance, prejudice, and superstition. His reply revealed a man who identified with science's great martyrs of the past, a man who believed that his research forced him to play a grand role in history.

Kinsey interpreted the marriage course's soaring enrollment figures as prima facie evidence that students both needed and wanted his brand of sex education. Pointing to student demand, he noted that enrollment had grown "from less than 100 on the first presentation to about 400 during the past semester," with a grand total of 1,432 students to date for the class's two-year history. To Kinsey, it seemed clear that the students had voted with their feet. No one had forced them to enroll, he stressed, since the course was an elective. Those who did, he argued, had "ample opportunity to determine the nature of the course before they enroll in it." Therefore, it was obvious that there existed "a great body of students who are biologically and legally adults, who are legally entitled to marry even without parental consent, who are interested in the course and want its continuation as it is now organized."[33]

Students' need for the course went beyond the classes and material. Over the last two years, he reported, some 1,000 students had come in for private counseling, making use of a service that followed "the best practice of other institutions." As many as a third of this group, he explained, were older alumni and other mature adults "who look to the University for such leadership."[34]

Then Kinsey abruptly shifted ground. Instead of discussing how the conferences helped students, he emphasized how the conferences could benefit science. Lecturing the young president on the crucial role universities were expected to play in modern society, Kinsey argued that the university's primary mission was research. "The invaluable body of data which we have acquired through these contacts constitutes research material which is already attracting national attention," he boasted. Thanks to his private conferences with students, he declared, "we are in a position to provide leadership which should serve our state and contribute to universal knowledge."[35]

Kinsey claimed the right to conduct his research as a matter of academic freedom. "Objection to a scholarly analysis of the problems of marriage is a challenge to the University's right to engage in research, and to transmit the results of such research to our students," he declared. Unable to resist a dig at religion, he maintained that Bloomington's clergymen were acting out of "fear that some of the problems which have hitherto been considered theological may become matters for legal criticisms, for sociologic study, and for biologic investigation." Of course, this was not the first time religion had clashed with science. Placing himself in the company of scientific giants of the past who had been forced to battle ignorance and superstition, Kinsey reminded Wells, "The right to investigate the shape and rotation of the earth, the nature of organic evolution, the forces which are basic in our social and economic organization have been challenged by one or another group ever since the founding of universities." Yet, in the long run, he insisted, "matters that are legal, economic, or physiologic will be submitted to students of law, economics, or biology for study. We have arrived at a day when these aspects of marriage are being subjected to that sort of investigation."[36]

In closing, Kinsey admitted it was only proper that clergymen should handle the ethical aspects of marriage. Nevertheless, he warned defiantly, "interference from clergymen with studies by students in these other fields is a challenge to the University's right to provide the scholarly leadership which people of this state have a right to expect."[37] This was a potent argument, one he would invoke often in the years ahead.

It is not clear why Kinsey did not send this letter to Wells. Certainly, its tone was rational, if combative. In fact, friends remembered a man who was much more upset than this letter betrayed. Describing what he called one of his "most vivid memories of Dr. Kinsey," Robert S. Tangeman, a neighbor, recollected a hot summer evening when both men were working in their gardens at dusk. Kinsey invited Tangeman in for a cool drink and for music, and he accepted. "Almost before we reached the house he began talking in a very excited way about action against his Marriage Course," Tangeman recalled. "It seems that earlier that very day the Bloomington ministerial association and the university administration had agreed that in the future Dr. Kinsey must choose between giving the course and/or interviewing students and members of the university community," Tangeman explained. "He resented this action deeply and did not hesitate to say so. He also did not hesitate to compare himself with such historical pioneers in science as Galileo," Tangeman declared. "I recall that I felt sorry for him but also felt that he was not reacting too sensibly."[38]

Aware of his isolation, Kinsey made a concerted, albeit belated, effort to mend his fences with the medical community. In July 1940, he asked Rice to come to Bloomington to discuss their differences. Although Rice agreed, he missed their appointment. "After receiving your invitation to come to your office yesterday, I fully intended to do so; however things happened in such a way that I did not get to make it," he explained lamely. While he assured Kinsey once again of his "great respect and admiration," Rice repeated his warning: "I still am of the opinion that if the legislature should learn the exact nature of the marriage course the University would be embarrassed." He continued, "We have different views on this extremely controversial subject, and both of us would be quite untrue to the tremendous convictions that both of us have if we permitted friendship or anything else to stifle our vigorous advocacy of our personal belief(s)." Having said that, Rice left the door open for further discussion. "I would welcome hearing you express in the most convincing manner your own views on this subject," he wrote.[39]

Kinsey pressed hard over the next few weeks to persuade Rice to come to Bloomington. "In our laboratories, we have what is probably the largest body of scientific data on record on human sexual behavior in existence," he boasted. "Can we not get together to look at this material?"[40]

Rice was not buying. "I feel sure that the data which you have will be less convincing to me than it is to you because it is my belief that this subject cannot be handled in a statistical way and that it is incapable of scientific analysis by present methods," he replied. Rice explained that he found most studies "extremely unconvincing because they have attempted to put into objective and non-emotional data subjects which are primarily objective and basically emotional." This was, he stressed, a critical difference of opinion that separated them. "Such being the case," he added gloomily, "it does not seem likely that either of us will convince the other."[41]

Kinsey had nothing but contempt for Rice's views. Privately, Kinsey confided to a friend, "I have not much use for a sex education program that does not give them [students] specific material on sex." Still, he had to admit he had underestimated the opposition. "I suppose there is some truth to Rice's attitude," he confessed, noting that pressure from the local ministers had reached the point that the administration was prepared "to consider restrictions or abandonment of the course." As he analyzed the situation, there was only one hope. "The students are so aroused over this that I think we may save the course," he declared, "but it shows that a great many of these people who talk about sex education really don't want information passed on."[42]

Whether at Kinsey's request or of their own initiative, several former students from the marriage course did rally to his defense. Typical of their responses was a letter signed by two young women and their mother. "The biological lectures by Dr. Kinsey are unembarrassingly objective, dignified, not in the least destructive of any sound idealism," they declared. "Without this factual biologic basis the marriage course would be a vague emasculated travesty of its original self," they protested. Indeed, without Kinsey's contribution, "the course would lose all force of appeal, all pertinence of service." Insisting that students had "a right to sexual information," Kinsey's defenders asked, "How can they better get it than from a dependable, socially approved marriage course?"[43]

No less spirited was their support for Kinsey's private conferences. Everyone they knew had found the conferences "personally helpful" or simply looked on them as a "mere recording of data in a needed scientific investigation." Furthermore, for "students with complex and insistent problems," the marriage course and Kinsey's conferences offered "not only vital information but also a very real safety value for psychological stresses." In sum, Kinsey had provided wonderful leadership for the marriage course and "Indiana University should proudly sponsor his doing so."[44]

Buoyed by similar endorsements from other former students, Kinsey decided to negotiate directly with President Wells. In early August 1940, he informed Wells that the staff of the marriage course had met the preceding day "to consider your proposal concerning my resignation from the Course." Attempting a ploy he hoped might switch the focus from himself to the course, Kinsey asked if Wells "would consider the appointment of a qualified faculty committee which could investigate the Course and make recommendations to the whole faculty as to the continuance, discontinuance, or modifications of the program."[45]

Wells would have none of it. While he truly supported his headstrong colleague, he also had a firm grasp on reality. The truth of the matter was that Kinsey had far more detractors than defenders on the faculty. Consequently, Wells held his ground. Rejecting the call for an investigation by a faculty committee, he reminded Kinsey, "I am sure the chairman of the present committee will remember that the course was not instituted in the beginning by faculty action, but rather, at his request, was inaugurated by action of the Board of Trustees. It therefore seems to me inappropriate for the matter at this late date to be referred to the faculty." Nor was this Wells's only reason for rejecting Kinsey's request. "I am convinced that it would be unfair to the marriage course at this time to submit it to the general faculty for discussions," Wells declared. "It is in such ill repute with the members of the faculty that unquestionably it would be eliminated by overwhelming vote." Because he believed "such action would be unfortunate," he had no choice, he explained, but to hold firm in his demands. His only concession was to offer to submit the marriage course to a general session of the faculty "after the course has been reconstructed and the members of the faculty have gained greater confidence in it."[46]

How could Kinsey have overestimated his support among the faculty so badly? The answer is simple: for the last two years, he had lived in a fool's paradise. Powerful needs and desires had obscured his normally acute vision. True, he had known from the start that some of his colleagues were leery of sex education and that others opposed it completely. Yet, somehow, he had grossly underestimated the size of both groups. Nor had he appeared to notice that their concerns had hardened over time, as word of the course's breadth, candor, and sexual ideology had spread across campus. No, Kinsey had been too preoccupied with his own agenda to track the storm clouds gathering around him.

Wells knew all about Kinsey's critics on the faculty because they brought their complaints to his office. Decades later, he stressed that Kinsey's critics had not been limited to physicians and preachers. "Well, of course you must remember that not all of the opposition to this was outside of the university," he explained. "Believe it or not, a tremendous amount of it was within the university." Looking back on the controversy, Wells declared that "some of the most vociferous critics of this were in the faculty itself."[47]

More isolated than he had known, Kinsey finally abandoned hope that students or colleagues would save the day. Following a month's delay, he made his decision. Asked to choose between the marriage course and the case histories, he picked the case histories. In September 1940, he tendered his resignation to Wells.[48]

As a matter of simple prudence, most professors would have stopped there. Because he had such a strong need for self-justification, however, Kinsey took it upon himself to scold Wells, explaining that it was impossible to teach the class without disseminating information that he was uniquely qualified to impart. In Kinsey's judgment, no scholar worth his salt would agree to such terms.[49]

To protest Kinsey's forced departure, Robert Kroc resigned as well. A great admirer of Kinsey, Kroc felt that his friend had been slandered, abused, and sold out. Decades later, he was still angry at President Wells for capitulating. "I resented very, very much that [Wells] would not stand up to B. D. Meyers and the ministers and call B. D. Meyers in to meet with Kinsey."[50] What Wells should have done, Kroc insisted, was "bring these people face to face and settle these criticisms and gossip."[51] Kinsey should have been given the opportunity to confront Dean Meyers in particular, Kroc explained, because Meyers was telling "students that there must be something strange about a man who would go into the behavior of other people, the sexual behavior. There must be something abnormal about such a person, especially since he's not an M.D. and doing it professionally."[52] Of course, Kroc had no way of knowing how hard Meyers's remarks hit home.

The vehemence of these attacks set Kinsey to thinking. For the last two years, he had taken incredible risks with the things he had said. The controversy that engulfed the class switched on a warning signal in his mind. His resignation was an attempt, at least in part, to lower his profile on campus and calm his critics so that he could continue his research with less scrutiny. Moreover, whatever his private fears, Kinsey was the soul of wounded innocence in public. Asked if he knew how Kinsey reacted to being forced out of the marriage course, Kroc replied, "Yes, we talked very considerably on it, and he felt like he was Galileo."[53]

President Wells took no joy in Kinsey's resignation. A firm believer in academic freedom, he saw the academy as a marketplace of ideas where people should be free to speak and do research on whatever topics they choose. Still, he was enough of a realist to know that preserving this ideal often required compromise. In controversial cases his task was to devise solutions that would protect both the faculty and the university. Decades later, Wells defended the choice he had put to Kinsey, arguing that "to give academic freedom you have to take certain protective mechanisms in order to maintain it."[54]

The hardest criticism to defend Kinsey against, explained Wells, was "that he was a propagandist for a particular point of view which he hadn't yet sustained by his research." To Wells, it was clear that if Kinsey "separated his research from the teaching angle," this would "put him and put us in the strongest possible position to protect the research."[55] Essentially, then, Wells's argument came down to this: it was easier to defend a scientist's right to conduct unfettered research than it was to uphold freedom of speech, especially when the words appeared to represent impassioned personal views masquerading as established scientific facts—ironically, the very charge Kinsey was so fond of leveling against his critics.

Wells never doubted he had made the right decision. Defending his judgment, he stressed that he had acted to defend Kinsey, arguing that "this was a way of separating him from the kind of criticisms which was the most difficult to deal with." It was, Wells explained, "part of this protective mechanism to protect the research." Asked how Kinsey had responded, Wells replied with a slight smile, "I think sometimes he probably was a little restless over this."[56]

Actually, Kinsey was bitter, although he did not blame Wells personally. "Well, I am sure that he felt that Dr. Wells had been put in such a position that that was all he could do," declared Clara. "I think he was a little surprised that Dr. Wells didn't know immediately which choice he would make," she continued. "That being a research scientist first, that that would be the only choice that he could possibly make in such a situation."[57]

In place of Wells, Kinsey directed his anger at his critics. Since he had expected opposition from the ministers, he devoted little emotional energy to denouncing them. Medical antagonists, however, were a different matter. Not long after his resignation, Kinsey told a friend that the attacks from the medical school were "a pure case of professional jealousy," adding that his critics all suffered from a common disease—"the usual medico attitude that no one can deal with human biology unless he had an M.D." As a group, he charged, physicians approached sex education with a "moralistic sentimentality devoid of the science which they pretend to be dispensing." Nor did he shrink from naming names. "Rice, Boyd, and Gatch, to my definite knowledge," he snarled, "have given student groups in the last six months such erroneous biology as would not be acceptable from an undergraduate student in the field."[58]

Kinsey took considerable comfort in the hope that the marriage course would collapse without him. "I did resign from the Marriage Course and

I am in the interesting position of watching their difficulties from the side-lines," he wrote a friend a few days after departing. "[Herman T.] Briscoe has been asked to pull together a staff," he continued. "It remains to be seen whether they can do it. The students are not quite aware yet what has happened but there are rumblings already and some rather interesting letters have been sent in to the President."[59] The fate of one specific area of the course was of particular interest to Kinsey. A month after resigning, he told another friend, "I do not know what arrangements they will effect for the biology, but they are talking now of bringing Gatch and his crew of physicians down from Indianapolis to handle it." If that happened, predicted Kinsey, "they will get a moralistic brand of human anatomy with no real discussion of the social problems."[60]

Kinsey's fears were well founded. Somehow he managed to obtain a copy of the biology lectures that his successors gave and sent it to Fowler Harper, a law professor who had been a member of Kinsey's instructional team in the marriage course. After perusing the material, Harper replied, "If these notes represent accurately the content of the lecture, I must confess that I am most unfavorably impressed with it. It sounds more like a lecture on Victorian morality than a realistic presentation of the problems which worry these kids."[61]

Yet, for a man who had been squeezed out of a course into which he had poured everything but his blood, Kinsey sounded surprisingly upbeat. After telling his friend all about his forced resignation, student rumblings, and the like, he added cheerily, "Meanwhile, I am delighted to have the additional time this gives for the case history studies."[62] Filling in another friend on the same topic, Kinsey reported, "My case histories are going on and the students are continuing to come in to contribute."[63] From where he sat, it was clear that "the ministers were more afraid of these conferences than of the lectures in the course and they thought to threaten the conferences by my expulsion from the course." Thanks to Wells's support, however, Kinsey was confident about the future. "I think everyone understands that they can not interfere with the research project and the President has publicly stated that he will defend my right to do the research. Nevertheless, most of them (for instance, those who do not know me) thought I would choose the lectures and stop the research."[64]

Actually, Clara was right. While Kinsey had bitterly resented the decision he was forced to make, the choice itself had been easy. As a vehicle, sex education had carried Kinsey far, but it was not his primary interest. First and foremost, he was a research scientist. Sex research filled too much space in his life for him to give it up. By the summer 1940, the marriage course was expendable. Thanks to his expanding network of contacts, which, as he was fond of saying, were "growing like the branches of a tree," Kinsey was now in a position to get all the sex histories he could take. He no longer needed the course. It had served its purpose.

Yet Kinsey would always be indebted to the marriage course, and not merely for getting him started. He learned an important lesson from his experience with the opponents who had forced his resignation. In the marriage course, he had become careless. His attacks on Victorian sexual morality had been blatant; and he had been candid about the reforms he wished to promote. Having discovered how hard society could bite back, he would learn from his mistakes and make the necessary "adjustments." Henceforth, he would take care not to reveal his agenda. Editorial comments that might reveal his sexual ideology and recipe for cultural change would be avoided. Instead, he would become a secret reformer, pressing as hard in private, but with infinitely more caution in public.

Thus, Kinsey emerged from the marriage course a bit bruised, but wiser. As 1940 drew to a close, his next order of business was to transform his research from a solitary operation to a team enterprise. In order to build a staff, however, he would need money, lots of money. Fortunately for Kinsey, a committee of scientists with access to Rockefeller Foundation funds was waiting in the wings. If they could be persuaded that his research had merit, they would show him where the gold was buried.

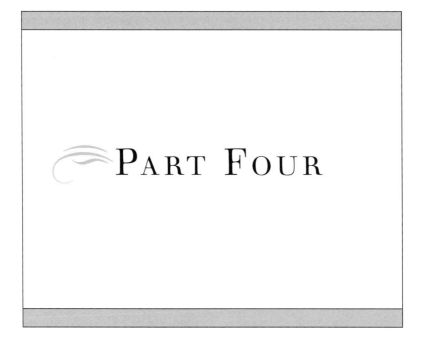

PART FOUR

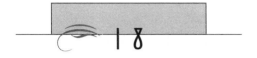

"UNLIMITED FUNDS FOR THE EXPANSION OF OUR PROGRAM"

hrough 1940, Kinsey financed his new research out of his own pocket. He was fortunate to have his salary as a tenured professor, not to mention the royalties from his high school text and manuals, which provided discretionary income. Individually, his off-campus trips were not that costly, but the expenses added up. They included oil and gas for his automobile, hotel rooms, meals, and entertainment costs, as he made a point of reimbursing the people who hosted parties in order to introduce him to prospective interviewees. Over time, Kinsey became an accomplished check grabber. Friends recall that he insisted on picking up the tab for lunch, dinner, drinks, and the like. In addition, he paid the prostitutes and many of the young men in Chicago and elsewhere a dollar or two to grease the wheels of cooperation.

Although Kinsey's circumstances were complicated, his need for funding was in no sense unusual. However sordid it may sound, "big science" usually costs "big bucks." Despite the popular image of the researcher as a solitary figure, science by 1940 was largely a cooperative enterprise, a game for team players. The size and complexity of many projects required staffs to conduct the day-to-day tasks of research, data analysis, bibliographical searchers, and the like. Of necessity, many distinguished scientists had to become academic conquistadores, empire builders who developed their own research institutes, in part by drawing upon the resources of their universities but in large measure by attracting grants from outside patrons, be they wealthy individuals, philanthropic foundations, or state and federal agencies. Thus, if Kinsey had any hope of becoming a major player in sex research, he first had to win his spurs in grantsmanship.

A fortuitous meeting pointed him in the right direction. In March 1940, Kinsey discussed his new research with Edgar Allen, a distinguished endocrinologist from Yale University who happened to be visiting Indiana University. Describing their exchange to Voris, Kinsey reported that Allen responded with words of encouragment and immediately recommended "several foundations that would be glad to cooperate with the resources."[1] Allen was not blowing smoke. A major figure in sex research in his own right, he was also an influential member of the Committee for Research in Problems of Sex (CRPS), far and away the most important source of funding for sex research in the United States from the 1920s through the early 1960s.

Established in 1921 as a product of the Progressive Era's penchant for bringing together reformers and experts to attack social problems with a potent blend of moral fervor, money, and research, the CRPS was a standing committee of the National Research Council (NRC), created by Congress in 1916 as the working arm of the National Academy of Sciences. The CRPS owed its existence to social hygienists, reformers who stood at the center of the debate about sexuality around the First World War. On the eve of that war, in one of those coincidences that happen to change history, the social hygiene movement came to be supported by one of the largest industrial fortunes in American history. This connection, in turn, served to promote the cause of scientific research on human sexuality in the United States for the next half century.

In 1910, John D. Rockefeller, Jr., served as foreman of a grand jury in New York City that conducted a sensational investigation of the "white slave traffic," the alleged business of kidnapping respectable young women and forcing them into prostitution. Deeply disturbed by what he learned on the jury, Rockefeller decided to do something. In the winter 1911, he and several other influential leaders organized the Bureau of Social Hygiene (BSH). Its purpose was to study prostitution, venereal disease, and related topics. In short order, it sponsored a number of worthwhile studies, most of which were grounded in either history, the social sciences, or the law.[2] Recognizing how little was known about the biological and psychological bases of human sexual behavior, the BSH decided to ask scientists from a wide range of disciplines to conduct basic research on human sexuality, broadly conceived. Not that social hygienists had a great affinity for pure research per se. What they had in mind was much closer to applied research. Basically, they were looking to science to explain why people behaved as they did sexually, thereby furnishing reformers with the data needed to understand and control human sexual behavior. Ultimately, however, the joke would be on the social hygienists. Just as the shattering of the conspiracy of silence had led to a public dialogue on a host of sexual questions, with far-reaching consequences no one could have foreseen, the decision to impress science into the service of social control eventually backfired. Social hygienists failed to recognize that scientific data could be used to support sexual liberation as easily as social control, a point that Kinsey would demonstrate repeatedly in the decades ahead.

Following World War I, the American Social Hygiene Association approached the NRC to see if it might be willing to try to interest scientists in sex research if the BSH, which was supported by the Rockefeller Foundation, put up the money. This request landed on the desk of Robert Mearns Yerkes, the director of the NRC's Research Information Service. After consulting with colleagues both inside and outside the NRC, Yerkes decided to accept the challenge. It was he who agreed to form and chair the CRPS.

In many respects, he was well-suited to the job. While his name never became a household word, Yerkes was one of the most important scientists of the twentieth century, in part for his scholarship but mostly for the influence he wielded on a variety of disciplines as a result of the funds he commanded; the disciplines, problems, and causes he championed; and the relationships and connections he cultivated in a long and remarkably rich career.

Yerkes was born in 1876 on a prosperous farm in Bucks County, Pennsylvania. In many ways, the similarities between his boyhood and that of Kinsey were striking. Like Kinsey, he grew up in a family steeped in religion. His parents were devout Presbyterians.[3] Yerke, too, abandoned religion for science after he reached adulthood because he found religion incompatible with science. In his "Testament," as he revealingly called his unpublished autobiography, Yerkes wrote that "the assumptions, methods, and daily experiences of the natural scientist make for objectivity, disinterestedness, breadth and independence of mind, whereas those of the religionist make rather for subjectivity, bias, limitation of view, authoritarianism, and an attitude of dogmatic certainty."[4] Searching for spiritual peace, Yerkes read widely in comparative religion during his later years but remained convinced that science offered what he called a "way of life"[5] superior to any moral system religion had to offer. He devoted several meaty chapters of his "Testament" to explaining why he considered science more moral than religion. The passion with which he advanced his arguments suggests that he, like Kinsey (and so many other late Victorians), suffered considerable inner conflict as he made the transformation from a God-centered to a man-centered universe.

The parallels to Kinsey's life went beyond religion. Yerkes, too, had to contend with an overbearing patriarch. In addition, he shared Kinsey's boyhood discomfort around girls, although for different reasons. Yerkes's "Testament" freely confessed that when it came to members of the opposite sex he was "bashful and backward."[6] Indeed, he admitted that his contacts with them were both "relatively few" and "distressingly awkward and discouraging."[7] Unlike Kinsey, however, Yerkes did not feel that his adult relationship with women had been harmed in any way by his boyhood experiences. Instead, as he put it, "I was both bound and protected by my girl-shyness and natural reserve."[8]

As a youth, Yerkes both internalized and accepted Victorian sexual morality. He was thankful he was bashful because it had enabled him to remain chaste, which in turn laid the foundation for his strong adherence as an adult to the middle-class ethic of self-control. Instead of feeling deprived or abused, Yerkes was glad he had managed to fulfill the requirements of manhood as prescribed by the proponents of civilized morality. Looking back on his adolescence from the vantage point of old age, he declared, "It was my rare good luck not to fall under the influence of an experienced and sexually uninhibited older girl or woman. Had that chanced to happen, the history of my sexual-social development and relations probably would have been entirely different. For this good fortune I can claim no credit, since it was the natural result of my girl-shyness rather than of preference and conscious choice."[9]

Thanks to financial support from a generous uncle, Yerkes was able to escape the drudgery of farm life and attend tiny Ursinus College, in Collegeville, Pennsylvania, graduating in 1898. The following year, he earned a second A.B. from Harvard, where he remained to complete a Ph.D. in psychology in 1902. Unlike Kinsey, Yerkes spent his entire career on the academic fast track. He joined Harvard's faculty immediately after completing his doctorate. In 1916–17, his last year in Cambridge, Yerkes was elected president of the American Psychological Association, a signal honor. By this point in his career, he had become deeply involved with mental testing, spending half his time at the Boston Psychopathic Hospital. As a result of this experience, he was asked to head the Army's psychological testing program during World War I, the first large-scale demonstration of psychology's ability to develop tools that touched society at large. Throughout the war, he demonstrated extraordinary organizational skills and a singular ability to sell his discipline to civilian and military leaders alike who initially did not hold psychology in high regard. In 1917, Yerkes secured a position with the NRC in Washington, D.C. He flourished in this appointment, as it allowed him to demonstrate his administrative skills and facilitate the work of others, something he both excelled at and enjoyed. In 1924, he left the NRC to resume his academic career, accepting an appointment in Yale's newly organized Institute of Psychology. In the decades that followed, Yerkes matured into a highly versatile and prolific scholar, publishing six major books and scores of articles. His main interest was primatology, a field he helped shape with the publication in 1929 of his classic work, *The Great Apes: A Study of Anthropoid Life*. That same year, he established his credentials as an empire builder, founding an experimental station on the edge of Orange Park, Florida, later designated the Yerkes Laboratories of Primate Biology. It, in turn, grew into the nucleus of the present-day Yerkes Regional Primate Research Center, one of the premier centers of its kind in the world.[10]

Yerkes accomplished all this despite being burdened with a personality that in no way advanced his career. The problem was that his boyhood shyness matured into a lifelong curse. "My earliest memories reveal uncomfortably disagreeable results of shyness, or as the folks called it, bashfulness," Yerkes wrote in his "Testament."[11] He remained excruciatingly shy throughout his life, prompting him to admit that his "behavior often was mistaken for a pose or affectation."[12] Responding to the perception that he was a bloodless, humorless, stuffed shirt, Yerkes once wrote a friend, "An estimable gentleman, I am told, once seriously remarked of me: 'I cannot really believe that anyone can be as serious as Yerkes looks.'"[13]

If his shyness shaped how other people perceived him, it also hindered his ability to communicate. "Even after decades of experience in social situations," Yerkes wrote in his "Testament," "I find it unpleasantly difficult to speak in public and I never have been able to command my intellectual resources as well before an audience as in conversation with an individual or when sitting at my desk." Students who had to suffer through one of his classes bore witness to the truth of this confession. "Yerkes . . . was the worst teacher that I have ever, ever, encountered or can imagine. He was, God bless him," remarked Vincent Nowlis, one of his former graduate students. Nowlis adored Yerkes as a mentor but had no illusions about his competence as an instructor. "He had tremendous integrity," Nowlis continued, "he had tremendous sincerity, but he had absolutely no fluency with respect to discourse about ideas. He just didn't have it." Moreover,

Nowlis noted that when Yerkes became flustered, which happened not infrequently, "he not only couldn't talk but he turned beet red."[14]

This, then, was the man who headed the CRPS. Intelligent, ambitious, hardworking, steeped in scientific thinking, mildly antireligious, intellectually curious, a gifted administrator, a proper Victorian in his moral values, and personally shy and self-effacing, Yerkes was the ideal man to recruit his fellow scientists to conduct sex research. After all, who better to fight prudery in science than a shy, straitlaced prude, particularly one with his talents.

From the day he assumed leadership of the CRPS in 1921, Yerkes was determined to focus on social problems. He knew that reformers were looking to science for answers. "I am convinced," he told his colleagues, "that we should not ignore the practical social need which brought our Committee into existence." Eager to enlist in the same crusade, his fellow committee members supported Yerkes, announcing that the CRPS's primary objective would be to "promote and support those researches which give the most promise of contributing to an understanding of the human aspects of sex."[15]

Implementing this goal proved to be difficult. Only a handful of investigators who worked on human sexuality applied to the committee during its early years. Instead, the committee was led in another direction. When the CRPS began, the study of hormones was in its infancy, and the majority of grants during the 1920s and early 1930s went to investigators in this exciting and rapidly developing field.[16] Most of these projects dealt with infrahuman species. Yerkes regarded this development as both necessary and useful. "Almost certainly work on the infrahuman problems will anticipate and pave the way for that on man," he explained.[17] Yet Yerkes found it difficult to push the committee in this direction. Hormonal studies, which had consumed the majority of its budget, had proven so successful that the NRC established a separate committee in 1937 to fund them, freeing the CRPS to strike out in new directions. By the late 1930s, the CRPS was deeply involved, in Yerkes's words, with "studies of neural and behavioral mechanisms as facts in the control of sexual activity and reproduction."[18] Once again, however, infrahuman studies predominated, leaving nagging questions about human behavior unsettled. This disappointed Yerkes, as he had never abandoned his goal of using the CRPS to support scientists who could provide reliable data that would help society understand and control human sexual behavior.

Rockefeller Foundation officials shared his disappointment. In 1931, the CRPS's budget was shifted from the Bureau of Social Hygiene to the Rockefeller Foundation. From the outset, the foundation's officers pressured Yerkes with little success to concentrate on human problems. Yerkes, of course, wanted to oblige, but few capable investigators stepped forward to conduct the kind of wide-ranging behavior studies reformers wanted. By the early 1940s, the foundation had lost patience with the committee's failure to deliver the goods. Consequently, Alan Gregg, the director of the Rockefeller Foundation's medical division, decided it was time to increase the pressure. In January 1941, he informed Yerkes that the board of trustees had approved a three-year renewal grant of $150,000 to the CRPS, with the understanding that another resubmission "would be sympathetically considered in the winter of 1943–44." This grant, he stressed, would likely be presented to the trustees "as a terminating grant since the purpose of securing recognition for the subject will have been achieved, thanks to your very much appreciated work."[19]

These kind words masked a seasoned officer's strategy for terminating an honored grantee. Instead of criticizing the CRPS's poor performance on the human front, Gregg elected, quite literally, to kill the committee with praise. He had, Gregg assured Yerkes, recommended the CRPS's application strongly to the trustees, presenting its work "as an excellent example of the exploration and development of a hitherto neglected field." Gilding the lily, Gregg added, "I told the Board what I should like to repeat to you, that we are indebted to you and to your committee for the establishment of research in sex problems on a basis to which such research was a total stranger twenty-one years ago when the committee began."[20]

Since Yerkes was near the end of his career at Yale, he recognized a retirement speech when he heard one. Yet he had no intention of vacating the field without a fight. His "Twentieth Annual Report of the Committee for Research in Problems of Sex" called for a new role for the committee. "Henceforth," he began, "we have concerned ourselves with knowledge and its extension through research. Scant attention has been given to the effects of current knowledge of sexual and reproductive phenomena on [the] individual and society." To date, the CRPS had limited itself to promoting "the extension of knowledge disinterestedly, in accordance with the scientist's ideal, and almost regardless of social values, applications, and risks."[21] Much of the knowledge that scientists had accumulated with such pains would become useless, he warned, unless some way was discovered to apply it with wisdom and insight to society. Many scientists, he continued, believed that disinterestedness was a menace. They insisted that "biological engineering" should become the teammate of research. "Lifting our eyes from the details of vital processes," he declared, "we discover that life itself needs guidance."[22]

Of course, no investigator was more eager to provide guidance to others than Kinsey. In December 1940, he made an inquiry to the CRPS that arrived at the exact moment when Yerkes and Gregg were negotiating the committee's future.[23] Kinsey's request for funds offered Yerkes an opportunity to marry the human studies sought by the Rockefeller Foundation with the behavioral focus favored by the CRPS in the 1930s. Kinsey promised nothing less than the most extensive and intensive fact-finding survey ever attempted by science, and he touted his record in taxonomy to show that he could handle a job of this magnitude. As proof that a case history approach to sex research was feasible, Kinsey noted that he had compiled 1,700 histories to date. Although Yerkes had doubts about the reliability of data based on interviews,[24] he agreed to talk with Kinsey at the annual meeting of the American Association for the Advancement of Science (AAAS) in Philadelphia later that month.[25]

This encounter offered both a singular opportunity and a severe test for Kinsey. Up to this point, he had operated as a solitary figure in a third-rate university, financing his research out of his own hip pocket. His obscurity had protected him from the scrutiny of established figures in the field of sex research. Now he was asking the most knowledgeable experts on sex research in the United States to evaluate and finance his work.[26] If he could win Yerkes over, grants would follow. If Yerkes was underwhelmed, Kinsey knew, he would have difficulty securing financial support, because the CRPS represented his best hope.

Kinsey hit Philadelphia like a hurricane, presenting not one but three papers before different groups at the AAAS meetings. Still feeling the pull of entomology, he spoke on local populations of gall wasps before the Genetics Society, boldly articulating his taxonomic research to scientists who approached evolution from a very different perspective. His second talk, by contrast, reflected his interest in sex education. It grew directly out of his experience with the marriage course. Appearing before the National Association of Biology Teachers, Kinsey spoke on the topic "A Scientist's Responsibility in Sex Instruction." Arguing that scientists had a duty to present facts rather than moral indoctrination, he delivered a scathing attack on what passed for sex education in the United States.

Pleased with his performance, he later told a friend, "My theme was to the effect that the current sex instruction was morals masquerading under the name of science and that it had no right to a place in our science class rooms."[27] Yet, as Kinsey reflected on his efforts to reshape the contents of sex education, he questioned the wisdom of getting too involved, lest it sidetrack him from his larger mission. "I am inclined to practically ignore the application of any of our results at his stage and spend our time validating our scientific data," he confided to a friend. "When we get that job done the people who ignore it will look very foolish." Sounding more like an avenging angel than a disinterested scientist, he added bitterly, "These people have been doing damage for several hundred years, and I suppose they cannot do much worse damage in the course of the next few years until we are ready to snow them under with our scientific data."[28] Kinsey's third paper marked his national debut as a sex researcher. Given the richness of his data, he could have spoken on any of a score of different topics, but there was really only one choice for Kinsey. He spoke on homosexuality. His paper, "Criteria for a Hormonal Explanation of the Homosexual," delivered before the psychology section and subsequently published in the *Journal of Clinical Endocrinology*, was a frontal attack on the theory that hormonal imbalance caused homosexuality, an idea that enjoyed broad support at the time in medical and scientific circles.[29]

As his point of entry into the debate, Kinsey attacked an article entitled "Sex Hormone Studies in Male Homosexuality," which had recently appeared in *Endocrinology*, the premier journal in its field. The authors of this article had purported to show a causal relationship between glandular imbalance and homosexuality. As proof they had offered a comparison of urine samples from thirty-one "normal" males and seventeen "abnormal" men who were known homosexuals. According to the authors, homosexuals as a group had significantly lower androgen-to-estrogen ratios in their urine, which in turn, the authors argued, caused homosexuality.[30]

Kinsey would have none of it. Scientists who wished to understand human sexuality should study people's behavior, not their urine, he argued. Seizing the opportunity to tout his methodology, Kinsey described how he had conducted and recorded his interviews. Then he attempted to impress his listeners with the sheer volume of his data. He had, he reported, obtained more than 1,600 case histories to date, most of which had been subjected to careful analysis. "Elaborate analysis of these data suggest[s] that they provide a fair basis for estimating the frequency [of homosexuality] in our American population as a whole," he declared.[31] It need hardly be added that this was the most exalted claim a researcher could make for his data.

Kinsey rejected the notion "that homosexuality and heterosexuality are two mutually exclusive phenomena emanating from fundamentally, at least in some cases, inherently different types of individuals." Binary thinking of this sort, he insisted, could not accommodate the variations he found in human beings. Among people thought to be "normal," he reported, somewhere between a quarter and a half "may in actuality have had homosexual experience at some time in their lives; and . . . it must be similarly recognized that there are very few 'homosexuals' who have not had at least some, and in many cases a great deal of heterosexual experience." Among his interviewees, he noted, were individuals whose only homosexual contacts had come during preadolescent sex play; people whose homosexual experience had been limited to one partner on a single occasion; individuals whose homosexual behavior was prodigious, involving as many as 20,000 homosexual contacts; people who had moved back and forth between heterosexual and homosexual behavior at different periods of their adult lives; and people who had maintained a bisexual balance throughout their lives. The portrait of human sexuality that emerged from his research was an intricate mosaic, rich and diverse, Kinsey argued. And while he stopped short of denying hormones any role in the matter, he assigned much greater weight to cultural and behavioral factors, including early sexual experiences, psychic conditioning, social pressures, and the availability of sex partners.[32]

Kinsey's paper was a bold performance. As a profession, psychologists were hopelessly divided on the origins of homosexuality, with glandular psychologists, Freudians, and behaviorists all advancing their own pet theories. Kinsey's remarks placed him squarely in the rising kingdom of the behaviorists. If he was any judge, his paper was well received. "I had the most profitable session with the psychologists at the Philadelphia meeting," he later told a friend. "They seemed interested, asked many questions and raised no objections. They seemed tremendously impressed by the amount of data."[33] Still, there was one psychologist whose reaction mattered more than the rest, and Kinsey went to Philadelphia determined to win him over.

As arranged, Kinsey and Yerkes met at the conference to discuss Kinsey's application. Few people could be more persuasive than Kinsey in one-on-one discussions. He put everything he had into selling himself and his work. For several hours, Yerkes listened intently as Kinsey explained his methodology, the items covered in the interview, the method of recording each history, and the overall goals of his research. Certain the meeting went well, Kinsey boasted to a friend, "I had a nice long session with Yerkes, head of the National Research Council's Committee on Sex. He immediately talks in terms of a large program, well staffed, and a long time proposition." Yerkes was "completely sold on our program, and while it will take some months to get a decision it begins to look very certain."[34]

Kinsey misjudged Yerkes's response. Although impressed, Yerkes was not prepared at this point to commit major funds. As a prudent administrator, he wanted more information about Kinsey and his work; and as a skillful consensus builder, he planned to consult with his colleagues on the CRPS. Consequently, after he returned to New Haven, he wrote Kinsey not to pledge large sums but to encourage him to revise his original request based on optimal, long-term aid and to submit three separate estimates: the first for minimal backing for one year, the second for optimal support for the same period, and the third for optimal financing for a second and a third year.[35]

Yerkes also offered some valuable suggestions. During their meeting, Kinsey had stressed repeatedly that he planned to collect 20,000 case histories (later he would raise the figure to 100,000). What Kinsey presented as a strength, Yerkes saw as a weakness. He was convinced that collecting 20,000 histories would be both time-consuming and costly, without improving the study's reliability. After mulling this over, Yerkes asked Kinsey to consider reducing the sample. This could be accomplished, Yerkes explained, "without corresponding loss in results, by varying the age magnitude of subject classes." At this point, Kinsey was calculating his frequency figures (the number of sexual outlets that led to orgasm) on an annual or "current rate" basis. Yerkes suggested that this method be scrapped in favor of a more streamlined system. He recommended that the one-year interval be retained for people between the ages of 10 and 39; that five-year intervals be adopted for people from 40 to 59; and that ten-year intervals be used for people over 60. This approach, Yerkes argued, would permit the greatest analytic stress on the three decades in which people were most sexually active (10–40), with less emphasis on the decades in which sexual activity declined.[36]

On the surface, Kinsey appeared to deal well with Yerkes's suggestion, stating it was "essentially in line" with what he had in mind.[37] Nevertheless, it took more than a year for Kinsey to modify his methods. When he did, he went to five-year groupings, rather than the breakdowns Yerkes had recommended.[38] Headstrong and stubborn, he naturally tended to resist changes. Having defined the scope and methodology of his research, he was resistant, if not hostile, to outside suggestions. Still, if pushed hard enough, Kinsey usually would compromise. His goal was to conduct his research and to place his data before the public. If that meant adjusting his methods to satisfy a benefactor, he was willing to do so, albeit grudgingly. Following Yerkes's suggestion, Kinsey requested a minimum of $1,600 and a maximum of $6,500 for the first year, to be followed by two additional yearly grants, each at $6,500. These sums, he stressed, represented only a fraction of the money needed.

Early in May, Yerkes informed Kinsey that the CRPS had approved a grant of $1,600, for the fiscal year beginning July 1, 1941, explaining that the committee wished to become more familiar with his research before awarding larger sums. Yerkes strongly advised him to acquaint the committee with his methodology over the next several months through personal discussions or printed material.[39] Kinsey replied that he would be delighted to have any or all of the committee members come to Bloomington and observe his operations.[40]

Modest as it was, the NRC's grant was immensely important to Kinsey. It represented recognition and tacit endorsement of his work by the most respected national organization of scientists involved in sex research. The good offices of the CRPS would almost certainly lead to contacts with other workers in the field. Their ideas and criticisms (assuming he would accept them) could help Kinsey in a variety of ways. Nor was the public relations value of the grant to be ignored. The NRC enjoyed an excellent reputation among well-educated groups familiar with the world of science. This was an important asset because Kinsey planned to collect many more histories from college-educated subjects. Henceforth, he made it a point to tell people that the NRC supported his research. To educated people, conditioned to admire science, its imprimatur conveyed instant respectability.

The NRC's grant greatly strengthened Kinsey's standing at Indiana University. The official notification of the award went to President Wells, who in turn sent Kinsey a congratulatory note, declaring that he was "very happy to learn of this fine contribution toward your studies."[41] Since independent and distinguished scientists had supported Kinsey's work, Wells and other officials at the university deemed it safe to follow suit. Indiana University awarded Kinsey $1,200 for the 1941–42 academic year.[42] It also gave him permission to travel anywhere the research required, provided that most of the expenses came out of the NRC award, rather than the faculty research grant.[43]

To punctuate the university's support, Herman T. Briscoe, the dean of faculties, furnished Kinsey with a letter of introduction on official Indiana University letterhead. It identified Kinsey as a professor of zoology who was "engaged in an important project on Human Sexual Behavior" that had been "recognized by the National Research Council's Committee on Research on Sex," which was "supporting the research by substantial grants." Kinsey's work, the letter continued, had "considerable significance to the army, to penal authorities, and to other groups and organizations which deal with social problems." Briscoe closed by explaining that Indiana University had furnished Kinsey with this letter "in the event that the nature of his research takes him into localities where the purpose of what he is doing might not be clearly understood."[44]

This letter was a necessary tool of the trade, as Kinsey had discovered a few months earlier during a field trip to Gary, Indiana. Describing what happened, he wrote a friend, "I secured 71 histories of [N]egroes, nearly half of whom were females at Gary. I also had my first brush with the police, who went wild upon hearing rumors of our collection of histories in the colored neighborhood." Once he realized that it was no use talking to the policemen who had detained him, Kinsey spoke with the night captain. "He called up Briscoe at the University, and as soon as identification was established, they were completely satisfied without further information, and had no objection to our continuing the work," declared Kinsey.[45] Thus, Briscoe must have been only too happy to give Kinsey a letter of introduction to prevent additional night calls from police attempting to see whether his story checked out.

As Kinsey struggled along on his shoestring budget, Yerkes wrote in February 1942 to request a report on his project, along with an estimate of his needs for the coming year.[46] Kinsey responded with a glowing account of his progress, accompanied by a new budget request of $7,500. Stressing what a great return the CRPS had received on his first grant, he noted that he had collected nearly 1,000 histories over the last year, while a helper had added 50 adolescent cases, bringing the total to date to 2,800 histories. After stressing that earlier sex researchers had relied too heavily on college-educated, middle-class histories, Kinsey reported that his case histories were drawn from all social levels. In fact, he had devoted much of his time to interviewing members of the underclass, including drug addicts, alcoholics, male prostitutes (both homosexual and heterosexual), female prostitutes, pimps, gamblers, and the like.[47]

Kinsey was proud of his ability to win the confidence of groups most sex researchers had ignored. His data, he informed Yerkes, included the histories of 300 Negroes and 800 prison histories, yielding invaluable material on the sex lives of prisoners. In addition, he noted, his records already contained 350 sex offender histories, and he announced plans for a comprehensive, long-term study of sex offenders in Indiana.[48]

Turning to his laboratory work, Kinsey reported that he and his staff had enjoyed a busy and productive year. Determined to use state-of-the-art technology, they had transferred his case histories from record sheets to punch cards, so they could be processed by a type of counting apparatus called a Hollerith machine, the forerunner of the modern-day computer. Ideally suited to his needs, this machine could run tables, figure frequencies, and calculate correlations on cases by the thousands. In the world of sex researchers, this placed Kinsey at the cutting edge in the use of technology. Indeed, few investigators of his day generated enough data to warrant machine-assisted analysis.

All told, announced Kinsey, he and his helpers had punched 15,000 Hollerith cards, involving five sets of data on as many separate topics. "All supplies and equipment have come from University funds," he stressed, "and the work in the Hollerith laboratory is contributed by the University." Kinsey made it clear that President Wells and Dean Payne had been wonderfully supportive, which, in turn, explained how he had been able to spend so much time away from Bloomington and still keep his position. "I have been relieved from a considerable part of my teaching, in order to pursue the research," he declared; "and during the next year I shall, in addition to part time relief from teaching in one-half of the year, have full time available for research during the other half of the year."[49]

Kinsey's course reduction had come not a moment too soon, because his frequent travel was starting to interfere with his teaching. "He was continually rescheduling classes at strange times," Kroc recalled. There were so many postponements that Kinsey was reduced to asking students to vote to see how many could "come at this or that time and so on." On a campus as small as Indiana's, problems of this sort did not go unnoticed. As Kroc remarked sadly, "the word had gotten out to others, because the students were talking to other faculty members about it and complaining." Decades later, his face looked pained and his voice dropped to a whisper when Kroc confessed, "It hurt me to see . . . that this man was now becoming the subject of undesirable gossip, not only among students but to other faculty."[50]

By reducing his teaching schedule, university officials did more than support Kinsey's research. They saved him from himself. For once the research really got rolling, Kinsey refused to let anything stand in the way of securing more histories—not the criticisms of opponents, not his teaching duties, and certainly not the war. In fact, Kinsey tried to turn the war to his advantage. "It seems to me," he wrote Yerkes with characteristic single-mindedness, "that the present National emergency calls for more intensified work on this project and for publication for immediate use. If there are funds available through your committee, I hope you will consider the need for pushing this project now."[51]

In April, the CRPS approved an appropriation of $7,500 to support Kinsey's research, a fourfold increase over his first grant.[52] Kinsey was ecstatic. In a letter addressed to family and friends, Kinsey proclaimed,

> And what do you think of the research council grant? Wow! That means increased support from every quarter. Just because the NRC Committee has approved to this extent! . . . The doubting Thomases may sit up and think again. . . . It is the largest single grant ever made for a year of research at IU. For a job they all predicted would be stomped on by the Trustees, by any and everybody. We'll prove to them yet that this is the most important piece of research ever undertaken at IU. I felt so four years ago when there were damn few of them who were not ready to knife it. I am sure of it now—and this is only the beginning of the recognition it will bring.[53]

While the $7,500 award testified to the CRPS's growing confidence, it also reflected Yerkes's eagerness to place its resources behind the study of social problems. Yerkes had always wanted to back investigators who worked on human behavior, and Kinsey was far and away the most productive researcher the committee had encountered.

As a seasoned officer of the NRC and director of his own research institute, Yerkes was not the sort of man who thought small. His scientific milieu was the academic fast lane, a world in which capable scientists routinely built centers devoted to research and recruited and trained able assistants. Yerkes had funneled money to investigators who founded major research programs in endocrinology at several universities. If Kinsey could pass muster, Yerkes was willing to underwrite the creation of a center devoted to research on human sexual behavior at Indiana University.

Kinsey, too, was thinking big. From his first year at Indiana, he had dreamed of heading his own center devoted to taxonomic research. The same ambition gnawed at him in 1942, only then he wanted to build an institute for sex research. He knew that the committee had funded research institutes at universities in the past, and he saw no reason why his research should not be so favored. In his view, Yerkes and his colleagues on the CRPS had been nibbling at the bait long enough. It was time to set the hook. Consequently, when Yerkes proposed a site visit in Bloomington to review data and plan for the future, Kinsey accepted happily.

From Yerkes's perspective, this was a make-or-break affair. Before recommending larger grants, he wished to assess Kinsey's project and to evaluate how well he had used previous awards. In addition, he wanted to talk with university officials to gauge their support for Kinsey. To help with these evaluations, Yerkes invited two scientists to accompany him, Dr. George W. Corner of the Carnegie Institution, in Baltimore, and Lowell Reed, the dean of the School of Public Health at the Johns Hopkins University. A physician, world-class endocrinologist, and fellow member of the CRPS, Corner was the heir apparent to head the CRPS when Yerkes retired. Unassuming and soft-spoken, short in stature and round in girth, Corner was a handsome man, with rosy, round cheeks and pale blue eyes that twinkled when he spoke. But, of course, Yerkes did not invite Corner on the trip because he looked like the kindly grandfather in a Norman Rockwell painting. Everyone who knew Corner recognized him as a man of great integrity, sound judgment, and unquestioned brilliance. Yerkes valued his opinion highly, often consulting him before making important decisions.[54] Reed, too, was an accomplished academician. Described by a colleague as "a professional, perfectionist statistician," Reed was a gifted scholar-administrator who had helped pioneer the field of public health statistics.[55] His role was to evaluate Kinsey's statistical analysis of data and to make concrete suggestions for improvement.

In early December 1942, three wise men from the East, traveling separately, made the pilgrimage to Bloomington, as Corner put it, "to get fully acquainted with Dr. Kinsey and his methods of work." Corner was the first to arrive. Kinsey met him at the station and took him home for supper, stopping by his office on the way to retrieve a package containing a shipment of records. "When we got to the house I was astonished to see [that] the whole wall of one side of the living room [contained] case after case of records, the largest private collection of classical music on records that I ever saw," Corner recalled. What happened next caught him completely off guard. "Well, after introducing me to his wife and without waiting for anything more in the way of social contact," continued Corner, "he undid his package and put a record on the machine and played it. . . . Then he turned to me and said, 'Who is the composer?' " Although he was hardly an expert on classical music, Corner made an educated guess, replying that the music sounded like a piece by Henry Purcell. Describing Kinsey's reaction, Corner stated, "He turned to his wife and said, 'Listen to that. Dr. Corner knows a lot about music.' To me he said, 'It isn't Purcell, Dr. Corner, but it's early [Franz Joseph] Haydn, and Haydn was influenced by Purcell. You made a very good diagnosis here.' "[56]

Corner was both pleased and relieved at this response, as he had the impression Kinsey was testing him. "I had a definite feeling that after this episode he had more confidence in me in general than he had shown before," declared Corner.[57] Be that as it may, the real victory in this exchange belonged to Kinsey, who had behaved in character. Once again, he had succeeded in assuming the role of teacher, reducing his guest to a schoolboy eager to please, a taste of what was in store for Corner and his colleagues over the next few days.

Unfortunately, Yerkes's mood was less than pleasant when he arrived. Owing to a mishap in communication, Kinsey failed to meet him at the train station in Indianapolis. Writing in his diary on the night he reached Bloomington, Yerkes grumped, "All day on the train or bus, with missed connections and inconveniences. It was novel to stand for an hour and a half in a bus between Indianapolis and Bloomington." Although this was hardly an auspicious beginning, Kinsey did his best to salvage the situation. "Kinsey met and carried me off for dinner with my colleagues from Baltimore and with the Kinseys," Yerkes noted. Ordinarily, dinner would have been followed by music or by a work session, as Kinsey routinely took visitors back to his office to show them his data and library, often remaining until after midnight. But the aging Yerkes opted for an early evening. "I excused myself after dinner for a night's rest to recover from my trying trip," he noted in his diary.[58]

The next morning found Kinsey raring to go. Aware his visitors had come on a fact-finding mission, he buried them in facts. For an entire day, he talked nonstop about his methodology for taking and recording histories and about his statistical treatment of data. In addition, he engaged Reed in a critical discussion of sampling theory, in part to defend his methods but also to seek suggestions. Since Kinsey was not a trained statistician, it took nerve for him to stand toe-to-toe with Reed. The remarkable thing was that Kinsey held his own. Describing Reed's reactions, Corner later recalled, "Whatever reservations he had I can't formulate now in a technical way, [but] they were slight. He was never sufficiently worried or troubled about Kinsey's statistical methods to object to a grant, for example."[59]

Yerkes, of course, followed these discussions with keen interest, jumping in from time to time to ask questions or offer suggestions. At day's end, he wrote in his diary, "All at work. Eyes and ears open, and taking in the form and promise of an unusual investigation." Indeed, after spending just one day in Kinsey's laboratory, Yerkes had seen enough to form a judgment. "He is doing well what has many times been bungled. Already he has gathered nearly 3500 sex pattern histories. His goal is 10,000. I hope he may be able to achieve it."[60]

Day two of the visit brought a curious role reversal. Although his visitors had come to Bloomington to ask questions and to collect information, Kinsey turned the tables, insisting he should interview them. Persuaded by his argument that the proof of the pudding was in the eating, Yerkes, Corner, and Reed agreed to give Kinsey their sex histories so that they could evaluate his ability to secure accurate data. Kinsey relished the opportunity. By this time, he had taken literally thousands of histories, honing his skills to a razor's edge. He knew that once the door shut and the interview began he would be in control. But there was more. Kinsey understood that the interview itself was a transforming event that would forever alter their relationship to his research. Skillfully and relentlessly, he would ask his questions, and they would give their answers. In essence, he would control; they would react; and at the end of the interviews, he would possess their secrets, but they would not know his.

Kinsey had built a life on the principle that knowledge is power. He understood full well that taking their histories would give him leverage. They would become part of his data, direct contributors to his work. Indeed, they would have a special relationship to his research, unlike any they had ever forged with a fellow scientist. Once they contributed their histories, they would surrender their privacy, an act of trust that would force them to rely on his pledge of confidentiality. With so much at stake, would their critical faculties be compromised? Would they be able to perform objectively the evaluative aspect of their role as patrons? Or would they be looking for ways to confirm their decisions to confide in Kinsey? After all, who would want to admit that his innermost secrets had been surrendered to anyone but a completely trustworthy scientist?

Events bore out Kinsey's self-confidence. After their interviews, his judges were sold. "I am agreeably surprised to find the picture much better than I had hoped or expected," Yerkes confided to his diary. "Kinsey in the course of one to three hours of interview questioning gets a history which he records by code on a printed form," he continued. "A single page carries a [great] deal of information—no copying is necessary: only coding and Hollerith transfer. It is a very well planned system."[61] Corner, too, was sold. "I was astonished at his skill in eliciting the most intimate details of the subject's sex history," he later wrote in his autobiography.[62]

Although Reed returned East after just two days, Yerkes and Corner remained in Bloomington to dig deeper into Kinsey's work. Determined to impress his visitors with his ability to handle all classes of people, Kinsey arranged a little demonstration. For the past two years, he had been taking histories in the state's penal institutions. Kinsey drove his guests to the men's prison, to the women's prison, and to a black house of prostitution in the slums of Indianapolis. At each stop, he interviewed a subject, while Yerkes and Corner observed. Four decades later, Corner described the subject at the men's prison as "a major offender of some sort, I think murderous assault or something like that." With Corner and Yerkes looking on in disbelief, Kinsey's demeanor underwent an amazing transformation. He abandoned the vocabulary and persona of a college professor and became a streetwise hustler, fluent in the language of the gutter. "We sat through this, and I was enormously impressed with Kinsey's technique," Corner declared. In fact, Corner had precisely the reaction Kinsey intended. "The contrast between the way he handled me, with some pretensions to being an intellectual, and this prisoner, representing next to the lowest grade of humanity, was very instructive," remarked Corner. In the years ahead, he was immune to critics who questioned Kinsey's ability to obtain accurate data in interviews. Those doubters, he asserted, had never been interviewed by Kinsey. "He made me talk, and he made a Negro criminal talk, and I thought he could deal with [anyone]," declared Corner.[63]

The demonstrations had a similar effect on Yerkes. Writing in his diary at 2 A.M. that night, a bone-weary Yerkes noted, "He [the prisoner] was not embarrassed by us. The demonstration was impressive."[64] Several years later, Yerkes would describe Kinsey as "an extraordinarily gifted interviewer," remarking that "[h]is success in overcoming individual and social mistrust, timidity, and prejudice relative to studies of sex behavior patterns, and in obtaining voluntary subjects for this inquiry, is truly amazing."

Every aspect of Kinsey's research—the sampling techniques, the interview procedures, and the recording system—struck Yerkes as first-rate. "Without reservation," he declared, "I characterize this plan as the best of which I have knowledge in recorded human history." In his estimation, Kinsey was "a genius in this extremely difficult field of inquiry."[65]

While Corner returned to Baltimore following these demonstrations, Yerkes remained in Bloomington for another day to confer with university officials. From Kinsey's standpoint, this was a golden opportunity for Wells to reassure Yerkes of the university's support. Ironically, Yerkes had a similar goal for his meeting with Wells. "I wished to give him our reaction on Kinsey's work and stir his interest and appreciation," wrote Yerkes in his diary. Consequently, when the two men met, it was a love feast. Delighted and charmed by Wells, Yerkes noted that the president had been "courteous, gracious, and responsive. I felt that my time had been well spent." Indeed, Yerkes left Bloomington completely sold. As he rode the rails home, he wrote in his diary, "My opinion is that my committee is here supporting the most important investigation of human sexual behavior yet undertaken anywhere at any time. I am most pleased and optimistic. We must press forward."[66]

And press forward Yerkes did. As soon as he returned to New Haven, he requested and received reports from Corner and Reed as a prelude to increased funding. Corner's assessment was glowing, praising Kinsey's research as "decidedly the most thorough, careful and original investigation of human sex behavior of which I have any knowledge. I think our Committee ought to obtain support for it as generously as possible."[67]

Reed, too, was impressed. "From the point of view of quantitative science," he declared, "I think he is doing an excellent job. His methods of taking the observations are objective to an astonishing degree when one realizes the complexity of the problem he is undertaking. His very method of recording not only assists in keeping the information confidential, but also yields observed material that is capable of quantitative analysis, which very often is not the case in studies of this type." Reed did offer suggestions, but they were more practical than statistical. He strongly recommended that Kinsey write out a key to his code and place it in a safe-deposit box, with the understanding that others would have access to it if anything should happen to him. Since many of Kinsey's items would need to be analyzed with some type of score, Reed also suggested that Kinsey be urged to study recent developments in scoring systems. As Reed put it, "one or two techniques that he is employing at the moment would be subjected to criticisms with regard to his treatment of unanswered questions, or of questions with which the individual had no experience." In closing, Reed declared, "My impression of the project in general was very favorable indeed, and I certainly hope that nothing will come up to interfere with the continuation of a study as valuable as this one."[68]

In light of the controversy that would later erupt over Kinsey's sampling technique, Reed's report is noteworthy more for what it omitted than for what it said. Significantly, he did not mention the issue of sampling. He raised no objections to Kinsey's selection process, use of volunteers, or efforts to secure 100 percent samples from various groups. In his annual reports to the CRPS, of course, Kinsey had insisted that random sampling, which was in its infancy at the time, was not possible in sex research, because of the high declination rate that sex researchers routinely encountered. In all probability, Kinsey made the same argument to Reed. Assuming he did, Reed's silence on this point suggests that he agreed with Kinsey and had decided not to hold him to an ideal standard no sex researcher could meet.

Overall, then, the CRPS's site visit was a triumph for Kinsey. For the better part of five days, he had worked his magic, persuading his visitors that he was the scientist for whom the CRPS had been searching for more than two decades. And he had done so without encountering any serious objections to his methodology or raising any suspicions about his personal motivation. His public persona had worked to perfection: the mask had not slipped; his secrets had remained hidden. Kinsey, by contrast, had learned everything he needed to know from his visitors. Having picked their brains and heard their suggestions, he could press forward, confident of where he stood with the committee.

Equally important, Kinsey had obtained intimate knowledge about the sexual attitudes and behavior of Yerkes and Corner, the men who controlled the purse strings. Everything he had learned underscored the need for caution. Although Yerkes and Corner strongly supported sex research, neither had engaged in private behavior that told Kinsey he had found an ally in his clandestine campaign against Victorian sexual morality in general or the repressive treatment of homosexuals in particular. On the contrary, each had presented a sexual history that struck Kinsey as limited and conventional. Henceforth, he would know exactly what to say and what not to say in their presence.

Still, Kinsey found it hard to disguise his disappointment over Yerkes's stiff moral rectitude. In fact, he once told Corner that he thought Yerkes was "sex shy," which, as Corner explained, was Kinsey's pet term for people he considered "prudish" or "oversensitive about the mentioning of sex matters." According to Corner, Kinsey believed that Yerkes had become involved with sex research "in spite of an almost subconscious reluctance, because of a sense of duty to get at the bottom of any scientific problem." Still, Corner was certain Kinsey felt the same way about most people.

"Yerkes was sex-shy; I believe he thought I was," declared Corner. Reflecting on this trait, Corner continued, "He had a general air of being a little superior. He gave me the impression from the start and until the day of his death that he felt that he knew all about sex behavior and that the rest of us, while we might be fine people and interested and helpful, could never really see it with the same clear vision." If anything, he explained, Kinsey "could never quite realize that other people might feel as free to be interested in sex problems as he was."[69]

Like so many before them, then, Yerkes and Corner found Kinsey a troublesome property. Although they never had any inkling about his secret life, they saw from the beginning that Kinsey's peculiar personality was a problem. Never before had they encountered anyone so frightfully focused, so suspicious and contemptuous of the work and opinions of others, and so unnervingly sure of himself. "To use a common, old-fashioned term, he became hipped on the subject," declared Corner. "I think he thought about his work during every waking hour, and he talked about it during every hour in which he was talking." With acute insight, Corner described Kinsey as "the most intense person I ever knew outside of an institution for psychiatry. He was absolutely wound up."[70]

In the wake of the CRPS's site visit, Kinsey was optimistic. "It is my private opinion that the trip was worth a hundred thousand dollars to us," he boasted to a friend a few days after his visitors departed.[71] In a letter to Dean Briscoe, Kinsey was even more ebullient, declaring, "We think we shall have unlimited funds for the expansion of our program as a result of the visit of these three men."[72] Obviously delighted to be cast as a man of destiny, Kinsey told a friend that Yerkes, Corner, and Reed "everywhere made it apparent that this is the study they have been waiting for more than twenty years."[73]

Yerkes was indeed sold. Buoyed by his colleagues' evaluations and certain of his own judgment, Yerkes decided that the CRPS should go all out for Kinsey. In January 1943, he traveled to New York to brief Dr. Alan Gregg on Kinsey's work, with the hope of persuading the Rockefeller Foundation to approve long-term funding, both for Kinsey and for the CRPS. Setting aside the cool demeanor and reserved manner for which he was justly renowned, Yerkes was unstinting in his praise, offering detailed, enthusiastic remarks about the importance of Kinsey's research. After listening to Yerkes's assessment, Gregg found himself in full agreement, noting in his desk diary that he thought Kinsey was "doing an extraordinarily comprehensive and effective study on human sex phenomena." Consequently, when Yerkes inquired whether the CRPS grant would be renewed, Gregg declared that he favored continued support for Kinsey and saw no reason why grants for the CRPS should not be renewed.[74]

As a result of Gregg's assurances, Yerkes encouraged Kinsey to ask for more money, with the understanding that the CRPS would approve his request. In May 1943, the NRC announced a $23,000 grant in support of Kinsey's research. This grant, which represented nearly half of the CRPS's annual budget from the Rockefeller Foundation, was only the beginning. Over the next decade, the NRC would give Kinsey hundreds of thousands of dollars, rapidly increasing his awards to $40,000 annually. Compared with the grants in biochemistry and molecular biology being handed out by the Rockefeller Foundation's natural sciences division to investigators at places like the California Institute of Technology and Harvard University, the awards to Kinsey were relatively modest. But in the field of sex research, which was a small, underdeveloped area of science, they were huge.[75]

The CRPS's support for Kinsey was not limited to money. Yerkes became Kinsey's sponsor and advocate. When he inquired in April 1943 if it might be possible for the CRPS to arrange for him to confer with experts on ape behavior,[76] Yerkes was delighted at the prospect of introducing Kinsey to what was informally known as the monkey fraternity. The CRPS's purpose, he told Kinsey, was "to be of service to you."[77]

In August 1943, the CRPS hosted a primate conference for Kinsey's benefit at the Hotel Pennsylvania in New York City. Among the sixteen scientists who attended were five members of the CRPS. In addition to Yerkes and Corner, they included Karl S. Lashley, a psychologist who held a joint appointment with Harvard University and the Yerkes Laboratories of Primate Biology, in Orange Park, Florida; Carl R. Moore of the zoology department at the University of Chicago; and Adolph Meyer, the pioneer in American psychiatry. Among the prominent experts who attended as guests of the committee was Frank A. Beach, the chairman and curator of the animal behavior department in the American Museum of Natural History, New York City. This was the first of many times that Kinsey would be asked to coordinate his research with experts from numerous technical fields, each with its own esoteric body of literature.

In his opening remarks, Yerkes expressed his fervent hope that the conference would inspire further research "which would contribute to the understanding and wise control of human sex behavior."[78] He then turned the podium over to Kinsey. As he had with so many groups before, Kinsey spoke at length and with great passion. His presentation stunned his listeners, most of whom had little prior knowledge of his research and were not prepared for his remarks about individual variation or group patterns of sexual behavior. Kinsey presented facts so at odds with current beliefs that many of his listeners must have thought they were being introduced to a new science. Many years later, Frank Beach confessed that his own reaction had been "one of shock."[79] And this from a scientist who was widely recognized as an expert on sex research!

Beach was even more astounded by what happened at the end of Kinsey's talk. Kinsey did what he always did when he lectured to a group about his research: he asked for volunteers. "He had structured the situation in such a way that it was very difficult to say no," declared Beach, a curious mixture of admiration and irritation evident in his voice. "Here we were sitting around a large table, perhaps sitting right next to a member of the sex research committee, a committee which was supporting our own work, and we knew that they were supporting Kinsey. It would have been extremely difficult to say no." Although he had, in his words, "some understandable reluctance," Beach agreed to be interviewed. "I thought this meant sometime in the future," he explained, "but lo and behold in a very short time I was up in Kinsey's hotel room, and he was starting to fire from a sheet with machine gun–like rapidity." By the end of the session, Beach was convinced that Kinsey was "an extremely adroit interviewer."[80]

Following Kinsey's remarks and call for volunteers, Yerkes opened the conference to a wide-ranging discussion. Among the topics examined were masturbation, nocturnal sex dreams, heterosexual behavior, same-sex behavior, interspecific sexual activity, and the phylogenetic backgrounds of these activities in human behavior.[81] Although Yerkes had sponsored the conference to give Kinsey a chance to pick the brains of the nation's leading experts on mammalian sexual behavior, Kinsey did most of the talking. Despite his pleas for help, he had already read most of the scholarly literature in the fields represented by the experts who participated in the conference, and he dominated the technical discussions about the phylogenetic origins of many human sexual activities.

Still, the conference was important to Kinsey, both as an ego booster and for the contacts he made. Writing to Breland, his former graduate student, he described his trip to New York as "most successful" and declared, "Big folk in biology, medicine, psychology, psychiatry, sociology, and other fields were all enthusiastic and ready to back us."[82] The conference served to deepen Kinsey's ideological commitment to his materialistic approach to human sexual behavior. The discussions reinforced his belief that many human sexual activities had their origin in lower animals and constituted normal mammalian behavior. After all, if masturbation and same-sex behavior were common in lower animals, it was hardly surprising to find the same behavior in humans.

Finally, Kinsey made fresh converts at the conference, several of whom contributed their histories and returned to their institutions singing his praises. Beach was the prize catch, for he became Kinsey's friend and chief consultant on the sexual behavior of lower animals.

Yerkes, by contrast, emerged from the conference somewhat troubled. By this point, he had seen enough to feel uneasy about some potential problems with Kinsey's research. Even though he had difficulty translating his fears into words, Yerkes was troubled by the ardor with which Kinsey presented his material and pressed his points. Yerkes also had misgivings about the size of the sample Kinsey proposed. Surrendering to the temptation, as he put it, "to offer a gratuitous word of advice," he wrote Kinsey, "You are engaged in an extraordinarily difficult and hazardous undertaking. So far as reasonably possible, minimize your risks. Avoid spreading too thin and being, or even seeming to be, over-ambitious, lest you ruin all." Getting down to specifics, he advised Kinsey to limit himself to presumably "normal" male and female whites between the ages of twelve and seventy who belonged to what Yerkes called "our U.S.A. culture and education." Hoisting the flag of conformity, he added, "Postpone inquiry into human variants—racial, cultural, degree of typicalness, etc., etc.,—until you have completed your primary task, then let them come as extensions or specialized inquiries."[83]

Morally tinged advice was exactly what Kinsey expected from someone he considered "sex shy." By telling him to concentrate on middle-class WASPs whose private behavior presumably embodied sexual restraint, Yerkes was asking Kinsey to skew his research in support of a cultural norm. Kinsey had no intention of becoming an agent of social control. Instead, he was determined to document (and celebrate) human sexual diversity, offering people an entirely new way of comprehending both their own behavior and that of others.

Kinsey's response gave no hint of his contempt for Yerkes's advice. "I am very much in sympathy with the idea of getting a picture of the usual portion of the population, before we attempt to analyze the unusual," replied Kinsey, "although such a picture has meant to me, as a taxonomist and a student of variation, securing the picture of the population as a whole." Therefore, explained Kinsey, it would not be wise to restrict the scope of his investigations. Not content to leave it at that, he attacked Yerkes's underlying assumption, arguing that what most people considered normal was actually rare. "There is no modal portion of a population in curves which are shaped as most of ours," insisted Kinsey. As proof, he informed Yerkes that among the eighteen people who had attended the primate conference in New York no more than two or three would fit any one person's notion of normal or modal sexual behavior. "I speak with some knowledge, for I have the histories of most of that group," declared Kinsey. Stressing that he did not wish to be misunderstood, he reiterated that his first and foremost concern was to get at "the usual picture." He was pursuing "special groups," he explained, only "because they are, in a way, the experimental material which elucidates the normal controls."[84]

To his credit, Yerkes conceded Kinsey's point and immediately attempted to smooth over their disagreements. Assuming a fatherly tone, Yerkes wrote, "You took very well my recent critical remarks about [the] scope of undertaking, and I may say . . . that I fully appreciate the fairness and wisdom of your defense." Attempting to reconcile their perspectives, Yerkes observed philosophically, "The situation is so complex that one must be pragmatic always, and also so far as practicable, logical!"[85]

Impervious to Kinsey's resentment, Yerkes continued to treat him like a protégé. While Kinsey was attending the animal behavior conference in New York, Yerkes arranged for him to meet Alan Gregg, the director of the medical division of the Rockefeller Foundation. Yerkes hoped that Gregg would be sufficiently impressed with Kinsey to consider making an open-ended commitment to the CRPS, so that it, in turn, could support Kinsey. From Yerkes's viewpoint, the odds for success appeared excellent. No one was better at selling himself and his research than Kinsey, as Yerkes knew from experience. A few hours alone with Kinsey would convince Gregg that the CRPS had finally located the scientist they had all been seeking.

19

"To Deal Directly with the Rockefeller Foundation"

Few foundation officers of his generation were more widely admired than Alan Gregg. A graduate of Harvard College and of Harvard Medical School, he had joined the Rockefeller Foundation at the end of World War I. During the 1920s, Gregg spent several years at the foundation's Paris office, which he used as a base of operations for visiting various medical schools and research institutes across Europe. These experiences gave Gregg a unique perspective on medical education and research in many of the world's best institutions, knowledge he later drew upon to enrich medical education in the United States. In 1931, he became the director of the Rockefeller Foundation's Division of Medical Science. As medical director, Gregg focused the foundation's resources on psychiatry and neurology, fields that he felt had enormous potential for improving the quality of human life. His interest in psychology was deeply personal. As one of his colleagues noted, Gregg was committed to "making medicine more humane."[1]

By the early 1940s, Gregg had established four criteria for evaluating the scientists who walked into his office. First, he considered the man, who, as Gregg put it, "should be intellectually gifted, curious, unsatisfied, persistent, preferably healthy, though not necessarily young." Second, he looked for a "good problem or a promising field of interest or curiosity," which he defined as "a question which offers in the present state of knowledge and methods a promising lead or chance of development." Third, he scrutinized the researcher's plans for recruitment, by which Gregg meant "the continuation, through training of the coming generation, of advances already obtained, and the possibility of bringing fresh minds and energies to the resolution of problems still unsolved." The fourth, and final, item he considered crucial was "favorable circumstances," which entailed "support of a financial sort for the payment of salaries, supplies, instruments, housing, and the opportunity of keeping in contact with the work and ideas of others."[2]

Researchers who could satisfy these criteria earned Gregg's patronage. He made certain they got the grants needed to endow their chairs, build their institutes, and conduct their research. Widely admired for his elegant writing, a talent he had demonstrated in his undergraduate years at Harvard, Gregg was also an eloquent speaker. His superb communication skills made him extraordinarily persuasive, a quality he used to full advantage when presenting his recommendations to the foundation's board of trustees. What stood out most about Gregg, however, was the warmth of his personality. In a professional world characterized by detached, formal dealings, he routinely cultivated close personal relationships, to the point that some of his colleagues feared he became too identified with the scientist he supported. This concern was well founded. No foundation officer was more fiercely devoted to his grantees or did more to protect and promote their interests, and few officers were Gregg's equal when it came to defending turf within the foundation or persuading the trustees to accept recommendations. Brilliant, confident of his own judgment, passionate in his advocacy, fiercely partisan in his views, and persuasive to the point of being virtually irresistible, Gregg was a formidable champion of the scientist who earned his favor. To his grantees, he was the next-best thing to a rich uncle.

Kinsey arrived at Gregg's office on the morning of September 3, 1943. While Gregg was expecting nothing more than a "courtesy visit," Kinsey had no intention of making small talk, kissing the great man's ring, and departing. A great storyteller with a great story to tell, Kinsey was there to win Gregg over. For hours, Gregg listened as Kinsey described his graduate training at Harvard, his gall wasp research and methodology, his critique of the current state of sex research, his transfer of methodology from gall wasps to human sexuality, his techniques for training staff members, the magnificent support he was receiving from Indiana University, and his plans for expanding his research in the future. Had he been following a script specially drafted for the occasion, Kinsey could hardly have done better. By the end of their meeting, he had addressed each of Gregg's criteria for determining whether or not to support a project.

Gregg's reaction was strongly positive. In his desk diary, he described Kinsey as "attractive in manner and impressive in his account of his work—pupil of Wm. Morton Wheeler and with an established reputation I judge as an entomologist." Like so many others before him, Gregg was especially taken with Kinsey's methodology, noting with approval that Kinsey used the "same form of analysis of records which he devised for studying speciation in wasps for the psychological study of sex phenomena in human beings." Convinced that this methodology yielded an accurate portrait of human sexuality, Gregg observed, "The correlations and the statistical validity of the results are impressive." Moreover, his tone sounded decidedly favorable when he called the project "a long term undertaking" that would eventually require 15,000 to 20,000 histories. He also praised Kinsey's methods for training staff members, noting that the case histories taken by Kinsey and his coworkers yielded "virtually the same results." In Gregg's judgment, Kinsey had brought the foundation a "quite extraordinary program on the whole."[3]

It is easy to explain Gregg's enthusiasm. For decades the Rockefeller Foundation had pumped hundreds of thousands of dollars into sex research, hoping to find solutions to a host of human problems. The results had proven disappointing, as the CRPS had failed to locate an investigator who could fill the bill. Kinsey, by contrast, promised to provide these data. He had an excellent academic pedigree, a proven track record as a scholar, an ambitious research plan, a promising methodology, the leadership ability to head a big project, the support and protection of his university, and the dedication and drive to finish what he started. Nor was there any question about his character. A middle-aged family man, Kinsey presented a portrait of respectability.

Kinsey left the meeting confident of Gregg's support. Reporting to Wells, Kinsey boasted, "As an outcome of our conference, Dr. Gregg assured me that the Rockefeller Foundation would support our work on an unlimited scale for an indefinite time." "Dr. Gregg has personally been interested in seeing this sort of project pursued for some period of time," continued Kinsey. "He tells me that the Rockefeller Foundation has been disappointed that Yerkes' Committee did not push the human end of their work."[4]

Following his trip to New York, Kinsey began to cultivate Gregg and to distance himself from Yerkes. Although careful to keep Yerkes well informed, Kinsey routinely took items large and small to Gregg. Moreover, he rarely went to New York without arranging an appointment with

Gregg, ostensibly to keep him abreast of the research but also to schmooz with his patron. Again, part of the attraction was personal. Kinsey was drawn to Gregg's warmth and outgoing personality. But power politics also entered the picture. Once he understood who controlled the purse strings, Kinsey made a cold and calculated decision to cut out the middleman. Henceforth, whenever possible, he would deal directly with Gregg.

Kinsey seized every opportunity to trade upon his association with the Rockefeller Foundation. Instead of identifying his research with the National Research Council, he now told people that the Rockefeller Foundation was his patron. In letters and in public appearances alike, Kinsey made this point so often that it became a refrain. From his standpoint, this name-dropping made good sense. Most people were more familiar with the Rockefeller Foundation than with the NRC. From the foundation's viewpoint, however, Kinsey was out of line. As a rule, the Rockefeller Foundation shunned publicity regarding its awards. Its officers made certain that this policy was strictly applied to grants that in any way could be considered controversial. Funding sex research through the NRC had enabled the Rockefeller Foundation to remain safely in the shadows, but Kinsey's announcements threatened to throw a spotlight on the foundation's efforts to involve itself with social policy.

The issue was joined in July 1944 when officials at the Rockefeller Foundation received a complaint from Dr. Frank Milam, who worked for the Rockefeller Foundation's international health division, in Chapel Hill, North Carolina. Milam had recently been in New York, where he visited with Frank S. Hackett, headmaster of the Riverdale County School, in the Bronx. Hackett was in a complete uproar. He had just attended the annual meeting of the Headmasters Association, where the featured speaker was Alfred C. Kinsey, who gave a lecture entitled "A New Research Program Supported by the Rockefeller Foundation and Indiana University."[5] Following the lecture, Kinsey, as usual, asked for volunteers to give histories, and Hackett stepped forward, hoping to learn more about the research.

The experience left him badly shaken. "Though I could understand the reason for perhaps the bulk of the questions, I am still writhing under others which seem nothing less than revolting," Hackett complained to Milam. Fearful that the so-called facts Kinsey discovered were accompanied by attitudes that were "thoroughly unwholesome," he asked the foundation to "consider carefully every question which he is asking, to determine whether or not it has scientific validity."[6] In forwarding Hackett's letter, Milam joined the attack, registering his disgust over "the revolting nature of the subject matter of this research." To Milam's mind, "it was not a proper subject for the program where it appeared," because it "was concerned entirely with some three thousand interviews of various people on the subject of sex techniques and perversions."[7]

If he expected the foundation to dump Kinsey, Milam was in for a disappointment. Substituting for Gregg, who was away on vacation, Robert A. Lambert, a fellow officer, handled the complaint in a low-key manner. After recapitulating the history of the foundation's support of the CRPS, Lambert simply repeated the foundation's long-standing policy on publicity. "I am sure you know that the Foundation has consistently disapproved the use of its name on buildings or in designating projects regardless of subject, to which financial support is given," Lambert declared. The foundation, he explained, had always maintained that "investigators and their institutions should receive the credit for work done," adding, "This policy applies equally to research on malaria, nutrition, and sex behavior."[8]

In his memo to Gregg, however, Lambert was critical of Kinsey's sampling technique, confessing that he did not see the need for interviewing thousands of boys and girls. Lambert wondered if a few hundred carefully selected interviews "wouldn't reveal pretty much all there is to know through that technique." In his view, a larger sample was both unnecessary and unwise. "My point," he wrote, "is that such mass enquiries not only cost a lot of money, but they put a value on numbers which is unsound. Furthermore in the sex field it is almost inevitable that widespread questioning will stir up trouble." Bearing this in mind, Lambert advised Gregg to caution Kinsey "about the Foundation's name, which he is obviously using protectively."[9]

Upon his return from vacation, Gregg called Lambert's reply "perfect." Making no effort to conceal his contempt for Kinsey's prudish critics, Gregg observed to a fellow staff member, "Sex research is so great a subject of taboo and hypocrisy that we shall never learn much more about it unless the Hacketts and the Milams are given a cautious but deliberate amount of disregard." Still, Gregg agreed that to deter critics "the essential point" was "that Kinsey would do best not to use the Foundation's name even if it were a direct grant (which it isn't, but via the N.R.C.)."[10]

Gregg could have dealt with the problem directly. Instead, he turned to Yerkes, hoping to use the incident to restore the proper relationship among Kinsey, the NRC, and the foundation. Gregg asked Yerkes to make Kinsey understand that his use of the foundation's name had three consequences, all bad: "it omits any reference to the National Research Council Committee which is the immediate source and the original (and present) sponsor of financial support for his research; it directs to us the matter of complaints which we can't handle with equal directness with Kinsey; and such a title suggests that Kinsey seeks protection in advance, and thus weakens his position personally." Attempting to get the NRC back out front, Gregg declared, "I think Kinsey would do better to refer to the NRC Committee for Research In Problems of Sex, and then if the winds still blow we are all at our stations and much better qualified to perform our proper functions." In closing, Gregg authorized Yerkes to use as much of his letter as necessary, but added, "The main thing is that I do not want Kinsey to be troubled in point of the confidence I have in him."[11]

Yerkes was plainly irritated by Kinsey's attempts to tie his work directly to the Rockefeller Foundation. With ham-handed bluntness, Yerkes confronted Kinsey with the title of his paper and demanded an explanation. "We had not known that the Rockefeller Foundation was supporting the work," observed Yerkes tersely. "If it is, information to that effect and the time and nature of the grant should be reported immediately to the National Research Council." Offering Kinsey a convenient out, Yerkes stated that he assumed this was all a misunderstanding and suggested that perhaps someone else had chosen the title without Kinsey's permission. Still, Yerkes made it clear that the issue was serious and had to be settled fast. "From our point of view," he wrote, "this matter is more important than you might naturally suppose, since so far as my Committee is concerned and so far as my personal knowledge of the relations of your project is in point, the Rockefeller Foundation has neither responsibility nor special knowledge."[12]

Kinsey's response was swift and unrepentant. Seizing the excuse Yerkes had provided, Kinsey categorically denied that he had selected or approved the title in question. Instead of leaving it at that, however, Kinsey declared, "Reference to the Rockefeller Foundation as a source of support for the work is, to my knowledge, correct." The foundation's support of the CRPS was common knowledge in medical circles in New York and Philadelphia, he insisted. Twisting the knife, Kinsey added, "What special knowledge the Rockefeller Foundation may have about the research is the result of your recommendation to me that I meet with Dr. Gregg last September. On that occasion, and on subsequent occasions, Dr. Gregg has had an opportunity to learn a good deal about the research."[13]

Stressing that he was conveying his "official reaction," Yerkes rejected any tie between Kinsey and the Rockefeller Foundation. This issue had to be settled once and for all, Yerkes told Kinsey, or else the NRC would not be able to handle the "requests for information, critical comments, etc., etc., resulting from oral or printed statements relative to your work," nor would it be able to safeguard the research "against undesirable misunderstandings."[14] Yerkes wanted Kinsey to realize that, in the event of a storm, it was to the advantage of all parties concerned for the NRC to be acknowledged as his sole sponsor. The Rockefeller Foundation must not be mentioned, because it was far more subject to shifts in the political winds. At this point, most scientists would have let the matter drop. But Kinsey had not come this far without being a fighter, and he was ready to do battle again. Although he had not chosen the title for that particular talk, he had evoked the Rockefeller Foundation's imprimatur on numerous occasions, and he had no intention of stopping. Yerkes, of course, had made his position clear, but his was not the only opinion that mattered. As Kinsey knew full well, the final word belonged to Gregg.

It was part of Kinsey's genius to know how to read people and to know when and how hard to push, and he had long since mastered the art of drawing people to him, in part by impressing them with his dedication and zeal but also by finding the right words to make them identify with his research and bend to his will. To say that he used these skills to full advantage on Gregg would be an understatement. Actually, it was a case of an irresistible force meeting a movable object.

In his appeal, Kinsey sounded less like an anxious supplicant than an embattled crusader who wondered where his allies had fled. Barely able to conceal his anger, he asked Gregg whether he, his division, "or the Rockefeller Foundation as a whole, wishes to have its connection with this work repudiated."[15] Kinsey then proceeded to argue the importance of the foundation's support to his work. Its name, he explained, had opened doors that otherwise would have stayed closed, particularly in regard to the medical profession. As Kinsey put it, "the medical profession is skeptical of research which is done by other than medical groups, and the known connection between our research and the Rockefeller Foundation has, without question been a considerable factor in giving us access to these groups during the past year."[16]

Aware that Gregg was a desk-bound bureaucrat whose idea of excitement was to make occasional site visits to various institutes and universities, Kinsey offered a stirring account of what it was like to open a field of science that spawned opposition at every turn. Indeed, his self-portrait was heroic, combining in equal measure elements of struggle, self-sacrifice, courage, and dedication, with a touch of martyrdom to boot. "The research has been more difficult than any one except two or three members of the immediate staff can realize," he declared. "It has involved meeting tens of thousands of people of all social levels, winning their confidence, and persuading them to confide histories, which, in eighty-five per cent of the males, involved possibility of legal action if the confidences were divulged." Hundreds of people, he complained, had gone "out of their way to interfere with the work for no other reason than their desire to prevent all scientific investigation of sex." Sounding more than faintly oppressed, he continued, "We have been arrested, investigated by sheriffs, and repeatedly stood up by the police." Yet, in nearly every case, they had come through "these thousands of obstacles," he boasted, "without having to refer to the University or anyone back of us for support."[17]

For the research to go forward, Kinsey stressed, all parties concerned had to stand up and be counted. "We are ready to assume all the difficulties and responsibilities for the way in which individual problems should be met and solved; but any source of support for the work must, on occasion, be willing to defend it when particular questions are raised," he declared. Kinsey closed by pleading, "There is no organization that can support us better, in most cases merely by acknowledging its support, than your own Rockefeller Foundation."[18]

Gregg was moved by the substance and the passion of Kinsey's arguments. "I hasten to answer, and let me say at the very outset," he replied, "that neither I personally nor this Division of the Foundation nor the Foundation as a whole wishes to have or has thought of any repudiation of your work." Gregg followed these reassuring words with a three-page (typed), single-spaced review of foundation policy, articulating with admirable clarity the two principal methods by which the foundation distributed its funds. He explained that one type of award was made directly by the foundation for projects chosen and overseen by the foundation; the second type went to other institutions that were charged with responsibility for selection and oversight. Kinsey's funding fell into the second category. While agreeing that the foundation's name might be better known in some quarters, Gregg nevertheless insisted the NRC had to be acknowledged. As he put it forcefully, "There would be no honesty whatever in my stating or tacitly being allowed to be understood that the support you have received from that Committee is to be credited directly to the Foundation."[19]

Yet Gregg looked for and found a way to split the baby. "I have no objection whatever to your saying that the grant comes from the National Research Council and that that Committee is supported by the Rockefeller Foundation," he conceded, "and in any discussion I have no objection to your saying that the Foundation officer involved approves of what you are doing." Closing on a kindly note, Gregg engaged in a bit of therapeutic hand-holding. "Please don't believe that I am unaware of the complexities and difficulties and the constant struggle it is to do work that you are engaged on," he entreated. "What troubles me is that I apparently have not made you realize that I do understand these difficulties and that I do very highly value the tenacity and energy that you use in meeting these difficulties. If I could say anything that would set your mind at rest on this point I would do so, and the more gladly since it is so sincerely felt by me."[20]

At first, Gregg's skillful diplomacy appeared to satisfy all concerned. Yerkes, who received a copy of the epistle, expressed "hearty thanks" for what he called Gregg's "tactfully informing and morale-strengthening message to Kinsey."[21] Kinsey, too, signed off on the compromise Gregg had offered, declaring, "Your interpretation is entirely agreeable to us." And well it should have been, as Gregg had left him plenty of wiggle room. While Kinsey pledged to acknowledge the NRC as his sponsor in "any printed statement and for any technically trained audience," he took full advantage of the huge loophole in Gregg's instructions, insisting that "in some situations it will be advantageous to add that the Rockefeller Foundation is supporting the work in accordance with the statement which you make in your letter."[22]

Kinsey's courtship of Gregg continued unabated. In March 1945, Kinsey was in the East interviewing, and at Gregg's invitation they had lunch. For three hours, Kinsey talked nonstop, giving Gregg and Robert S. Morison, Gregg's assistant, a complete update on the research. Among other things, Kinsey reported that to date he had 8,500 histories, an astonishing figure by any standards. Doubtless because he knew of Gregg's special interest in mental health, Kinsey stressed the importance of his data to psychiatrists. Taking Kinsey's remarks at face value, an impressed Morison wrote in his diary, "Psychoanalysts think Kinsey's work will advance the status of psychoanalysis by 50 years. I am inclined to think that it will change a good many things." Nor did Morison foresee any danger of Kinsey's fading in the stretch. "Having examined and taken 18 measurements of 152,000 wasps," he wrote, "Kinsey is not daunted by a rather large order of detail work."[23]

As the interviews piled up, Kinsey's data became at once a precious commodity and a source of concern to his patrons, who worried what would become of these materials if something happened to him. In May 1945, Yerkes suggested to Gregg that they should discuss "ways of insuring ourselves against accident to Kinsey," explaining, "as things now stand, if anything should remove him from the picture the loss to research would be enormous."[24] Gregg suggested that Kinsey should be asked to write down "in some fashion, using the utmost secrecy, a key to his coding system." In addition, Gregg thought it would be a good idea for Kinsey to "write out, also only to be used in the case of his death, an account of what he has in mind as the course to pursue in preparing the studies."[25]

Armed with Gregg's suggestion, Yerkes met with Kinsey in Philadelphia in July 1945. While Kinsey appeared willing to cooperate on some matters, he dug in his heels on others. For example, he promised to consider writing out a code for the interview, provided the Rockefeller Foundation agreed to take possession of it in a sealed package and promised to honor his explicit instructions governing the circumstances under which it could be opened. Kinsey refused to commit himself on the matter of a subject identification code, however, because neither he nor Yerkes could think of a way to preserve confidentiality. Nor would Kinsey agree to draft a general outline for the future, explaining that he considered this a waste of time. The information could be easily extracted from his annual reports to the NRC. On a happier note, however, Kinsey and Yerkes were able to concur on the need to increase the size of Kinsey's staff, and they discussed the possibility of seeking a ten-year commitment of funds for his research from the Rockefeller Foundation.[26] In the end, then, this meeting accomplished little, as no agreement had been reached about safeguarding Kinsey's data.

What did result from the meeting was a new resolve on Gregg's part to resist Kinsey's attempts to draw the Rockefeller Foundation deeper into his research. After learning about Kinsey's desire to make the foundation responsible for his code, Gregg informed Yerkes, "We have no special or unique method of safe storage here." Confessing that he had no suggestions to offer regarding the subject identification code, Gregg cautioned, "Obviously it is a subject with many potentialities for abuse and such a code so directly involves Kinsey's personal undertakings to people interviewed that his own wishes must have the predominant weight." Shifting responsibility back to the NRC, Gregg promised that "any recommendations from your Committee would be sympathetically considered here."[27]

Determined to resolve the issues at hand, Yerkes met with Kinsey again in December 1945, this time in George W. Corner's private laboratory at the Department of Embryology of the Carnegie Institution. They were joined by Lewis H. Weed, the director of the NRC's medical division. As they discussed the code issue, Kinsey became extremely agitated because he was worried about security. "I remember the meeting well," recalled Corner decades later, explaining that Weed and Kinsey were so anxious to confer "incognito, so to speak, that my wife actually came over from our suburban home and cooked some kind of a luncheon" so the group could eat in the privacy of his office, thereby precluding any verbal slips in public. "It was all as secret at that," declared Corner.[28]

The issues that had been raised in Philadelphia proved no less intractable in Washington. In the end, nothing was agreed upon but Kinsey's need for more funds. By this point, Kinsey was receiving more than half the committee's budget. With the war over, everyone expected that the CRPS would receive more applications, which in turn would increase demands on the committee. Moreover, Kinsey argued forcefully that although his current budget of $28,000 was enough to meet his present requirements, his needs for the coming year would rise to somewhere in the neighborhood of $32,000 to $35,000, with the possibility of still larger sums to follow. Consequently, the conferees asked Weed, who had routinely handled budget requests in the past, to confer with Gregg to see how high the Rockefeller Foundation was prepared to go.

On January 9, 1946, Weed and Gregg met for several hours at the foundation's headquarters in New York. As reported by Weed, Gregg agreed that Kinsey would need more money in the coming year (1946–47), and he invited the NRC to apply "for a special grant to take over the financing of Kinsey's program."[29] Specifically, Gregg proposed a $120,000 three-year grant, to be paid at the rate of $40,000 a year beginning July 1, 1946. Gregg assured Weed that a term award for Kinsey would in no way interfere with any subsequent budget requests from the CRPS in support of its total program. In other words, Gregg made it clear that he was proposing a two-track program involving one grant for the CRPS and an entirely separate grant for Kinsey. This was a bold and generous proposal on Gregg's part, one that altered fundamentally the relationship between the foundation and Kinsey. An appropriation this large would have to be approved by the foundation's board of trustees, and its decision would place the foundation on record regarding Kinsey's work.

To help sell his proposal to the trustees, Gregg asked the CRPS to furnish "interesting background materials." In response, Weed suggested that Corner might be willing to furnish a report of his impressions of Kinsey's interviewing technique. Weed and Gregg further agreed that Yerkes should do likewise, taking care to include materials describing "Kinsey's ability to interview members of diverse social groups."[30] The following month Weed submitted a formal application to the Rockefeller Foundation requesting $120,000 over a three-year period "in support of the important research program of Dr. Alfred C. Kinsey." Aware of Gregg's reluctance to assume direct responsibility for Kinsey's work, Weed stipulated that "the Committee for Research in Problems of Sex would continue to supervise Dr. Kinsey's project."[31] Weed also reported that Yerkes had circulated this proposal among the members of the CRPS and had "the concurrence of all the members of the group."[32]

This was not true. Whether by accident or design, Yerkes had misinformed Weed, because at least two CRPS members had refused to approve a larger appropriation for Kinsey. The psychologist Karl S. Lashley expressed reservations about what he considered Kinsey's mindless pursuit of numbers. "I have always felt a little skepticism concerning the magnitude of Kinsey's project," Lashley confessed. "He was known at Harvard, I believe, as 'Get a million' Kinsey because of his insistence on large samples," continued Lashley. "I am not convinced that it is necessary to have as many cases from each of his groups as he plans to get. He has never given us figures showing range of variation for any group, from which we can judge the number required for reliable figures."[33]

Yerkes received an even stronger dissent from a newly appointed member of the committee, John Romano, professor of psychiatry at the University of Cincinnati's College of Medicine. Romano wrote, "It appears to me that the interview is the tool of the investigation; thus, the adequacy of the tool determines the validity of the total investigation." As the sole psychiatrist on the committee, Romano felt obliged to remind Yerkes of the complex and devious workings of the human mind. "All of modern psychology indicates the subtlety and variety of defenses against revealing truths about one's self," he declared. "When one considers the personal and cultural forces inherent in talking about sexual experience, the problem becomes more complex," he continued. "Unconscious emotional factors may bring about serious distortions in the interviewee through mechanisms of rationalization, guilt feelings, compensatory needs, etc.," he warned. Implying that no one could be as objective as Kinsey claimed, Romano added, "Emotional blind spots in the interviewer are frequent sources of distortion." On the basis of these concerns, Romano declared gravely, "I am afraid that my impression leads me to believe that the study consists of accurate recording of inaccurate data."[34]

As he assembled materials for Gregg to present to the board, Yerkes felt both exhilarated and more than faintly hassled. In the past, the committee's business had generated few fireworks, but Kinsey had changed all that. The sheer size and ambition of his undertaking, his unvarnished biological perspective, his controversial methodology, and his personality quirks were bound to spark disagreements. "Kinsey and his great task are very much in my mind," Yerkes wrote Gregg, "for he and it create more interesting problems of administration and more research leads than all the other committee projects combined! I am not complaining."[35]

When the Rockefeller trustees met in April 1946, it was their first opportunity to hear about Kinsey's work. There was no way of telling how they would react. Early in the foundation's history, the trustees had seldom taken an active role in determining policy or in evaluating recommendations for awards. That situation had changed dramatically in the 1930s, however, when the foundation started appointing prominent business leaders, public officials, and university presidents to its board. By the mid-1940s, the trustees had become more assertive and involved, routinely asking officers to explain or defend their recommendations, especially with controversial projects or those that raised policy questions. And because they were accustomed to grilling subordinates, poking holes in arguments, and getting their own way in disputes, the trustees expected the officers to defer.

Occasionally, this led to spirited exchanges. As a rule, officers tended to identify with their grantees. After all, officers had advanced academic training in the areas they supervised. They saw themselves as experts who were in a unique position to advance the disciplines they served. As a result, they did not always welcome challenges and objections from the trustees, most of whom were laymen. Yet astute officers tried to avoid conflicts and to build consensus among the trustees, and, more often than not, careful preparation was the tool of choice. Typically, officers assembled detailed informational packets on controversial projects as part of their efforts to educate the trustees and earn their support. Again, this was why Gregg had asked Yerkes and Corner to supply detailed evaluations of Kinsey's work. Needless to add, their testimonials were glowing. Not that Gregg intended to rely solely on the printed word—far from it. He knew he would be given an opportunity to address the trustees and answer their questions, and Gregg had confidence in his ability to argue Kinsey's case with clarity, conviction, and verve.

Gregg's careful homework paid off. Kinsey's appropriation sailed through the meeting. On April 3, 1946, the Rockefeller Foundation trustees approved a $120,000 three-year grant.[36] Kinsey was delighted. Despite Gregg's and Yerkes's efforts to the contrary, he had succeeded in drawing the Rockefeller Foundation deeper and deeper into his research. His success rested in equal measure on his skillful wooing of Gregg and on the particular circumstances and needs of his project that had worked to his advantage.

Over the next two years, Kinsey's relationship with the NRC, by contrast, went from bad to worse, strained at every turn by a series of misunderstandings and disagreements about various administration problems. The first involved complaints from the NRC's financial officer to Indiana University regarding the large amounts of money Kinsey spent on entertainment. Irritated by what he interpreted as unwarranted interference, Kinsey reminded Yerkes of the discussion they had at their very first meeting, during which he had explained that it was necessary to pay certain individuals a few dollars to secure their cooperation and to entertain people as a means of making contacts for generating more histories. This explanation satisfied Yerkes, who took care of the matter promptly, but the episode left a bad taste in Kinsey's mouth.

The second issue was more serious. Over time, Kinsey had built the core of a research library on human sexuality, purchasing books, articles, and pamphlets with his own money. By the end of 1946, he had invested approximately $10,000 in his library. As he started making plans to create a permanent organization, Kinsey asked Yerkes if the NRC would agree to pay him for transferring his library to the new entity, suggesting that the money could come from unexpended funds in his budget from the NRC. Yerkes was supportive, but Weed, his superior, rejected this proposal, insisting that the ownership of books purchased with their funds had to revert to the NRC. Throughout 1946 and well into 1947, Yerkes and Kinsey tried to break the impasse, but every solution they floated was shot down by Weed or other higher-ups at the NRC. This angered Kinsey, who failed to credit Yerkes with either good will or hard work in trying to resolve the matter.

The most important bone of contention, however, involved disagreements over the precise form Kinsey's proposed research organization should take. The Rockefeller Foundation and the NRC were not the only organizations Kinsey had to satisfy on this matter. Indiana University was a vital party to the discussions as well, a development that bore the unmistakable political touch of its president.

Herman Wells saw distinct advantages in incorporating Kinsey's research. First, it would put the university in a stronger position to help preserve the confidentiality of the records, which, as Wells put it, "was an extraordinarily important thing from Kinsey's standpoint." Since the state board of accounts or the legislature could demand to examine any property owned by the university, Wells thought that Kinsey should create a separate, free-standing corporation. Thus, if any state official or body demanded access to Kinsey's files, explained Wells, "you could say no." To his mind, this was the perfect solution. "By giving the Institute this degree of autonomy . . . ," he declared, "you could insure the confidence of the interviews," a protection that also carried "over to the library."[37]

The second reason Wells favored incorporation involved public relations. He wanted Kinsey to incorporate his research for precisely the same reason that the Rockefeller Foundation wanted to preserve the NRC as a buffer between itself and Kinsey. In other words, Wells knew that a separate corporation would distance the university, if only in a legal sense, from direct responsibility for Kinsey's research. As Wells later explained, a corporation gave the university the opportunity to say, "Well, . . . while Dr. Kinsey is a full professor at the University and has full professorial rights and is a member of the faculty and so on, the Institute itself has its own autonomy and has its own funds and operates independently."[38]

After consulting for many months with lawyers and administrators at Indiana University, Kinsey finally agreed to create a private corporation with broad powers. Once again, however, senior officials of the NRC balked, explaining that the council preferred to do business with universities and would not feel comfortable dealing with a private corporation. For months, the parties went back and forth on this issue, with Yerkes offering soothing words of encouragement while Kinsey rapidly ran out of patience.

Yerkes did not agree with the policies he was forced to defend. "I am deeply disturbed by the seeming possessiveness of [the] NRC and I fear that Kinsey may have sensed it," Yerkes confided to Corner. "Certainly we have no right to dictate to a cooperating investigator." Yerkes also worried that his relationship with his prize grantee had been seriously damaged. With more insight than he knew, Yerkes told Corner, "Kinsey is a person who is both capable and determined to manage his own affairs and I should fear that such differences as have recently appeared, if they prove to be symptomatic, might presently result in his estrangement from our organization and decision to go it alone."[39] Yerkes was right. In the end, the squabbling over entertainment expenses, compensation for his library, and the form of his proposed research organization eroded what little faith Kinsey had left in the NRC. As a result, he decided to look elsewhere for solutions.

Repeating what by now had become a habit, Kinsey turned to the Rockefeller Foundation. On December 19, 1946, he met with Gregg at the foundation headquarters in New York. According to Gregg's desk diary, Kinsey came directly to the point, declaring "that he would prefer to deal only with the University of Indiana and the RF." Stressing how difficult his dealings with the NRC had been over the last few years, Kinsey rehashed the squabbles involving his library. It was imperative, he told Gregg, that his library be preserved and expanded because it was a unique collection, the sort no other group or institution had dared to build, including the nation's largest and most famous library. "K says it is the policy of the Library of Congress to destroy such materials as it considers [them] too erotic," wrote Gregg.[40]

Kinsey was even more upset about the NRC's position on incorporation. He accused Weed of threatening to cut off funding if articles of incorporation were filed. Furthermore, Kinsey, Gregg noted in his desk diary, complained that it had become all but impossible to do business with the NRC because there were "too many executives and authorities to be consulted" and because there appeared to be "divided authority in the committee, neither Corner nor Yerkes being a final authority." In addition, Kinsey charged that the CRPS was no longer in a position to be helpful. As a result of recent resignations and new appointments, the current roster of committee members, Kinsey complained, did not "know much about human sex phenomena." In this regard, Kinsey singled out Corner, the chairman elect, insisting that he was "not very well informed." Picking up on the real source of the problem, Gregg observed, "Kinsey thinks that most of the committee members are limited by their prudishness."[41] Although Kinsey left the meeting with no promises or guarantees, Gregg made no effort to conceal his sympathy or his desire to be of service. While taking care not to commit the foundation to direct support, Gregg remarked that the NRC's position on the issue of "property control" was "of doubtful value in certain cases and probably a rule more honored in the breach than in the observance."[42]

That was all the encouragement Kinsey needed. Immediately after returning home, he informed Yerkes of his meeting with Gregg, making clear his future intentions. "Frankly, it becomes increasingly a question whether it would not be more efficient to deal directly with the Rockefeller Foundation," wrote Kinsey.[43] Privately, of course, Yerkes was terribly upset by Kinsey's ingratitude, but his official response was low-key and coolly professional. "I have nothing to say at the moment in comment or reply on your remarks," he wrote Kinsey. "As you know, my efforts throughout the years have been to try to facilitate your project through the instrument of our research-promoting committee of the National Research Council. The decision, naturally, as to financing of your work and its organizational relations must be yours primarily." Having said this, however, Yerkes advised Kinsey to preserve his ties with the NRC at least until the period of his special grant had expired.[44]

Leaving Yerkes to stew, Kinsey importuned Gregg to come to Bloomington. "I would like to have you meet our staff here on the project. I should like to have you get some time with the President and Vice President of the University and with Dr. Payne, who is Dean of our Graduate School," he implored. "I want you to get to know my wife and my home," Kinsey continued. "I want you to see the way in which our data are kept. . . . I want you to see our library and our collections of erotic materials in sufficient detail to understand what bearing they have on the research project as a whole."[45] This was Kinsey at his best—betting on himself, willing to stake everything on his extraordinary powers of persuasion.

Much to Kinsey's delight, Gregg accepted the invitation and made the pilgrimage to Indiana. On the morning of February 6, 1947, he arrived in Indianapolis, where he was met at the train station by Kinsey, accompanied by his wife and two assistants. After listening to Kinsey talk a mile a minute during the drive back to Bloomington, Gregg was grateful, no doubt, for the few moments he had alone after checking into his room in the Student Union, a mammoth building used as a student center with guest rooms for visitors. Then it was back to business over a working lunch, followed by a brisk walk to Kinsey's laboratory on the second floor of Biology Hall. Since part of his mission was to size up the physical facilities, Gregg paid close attention to Kinsey's working quarters, which consisted of an office, a secretary's room, and what Gregg described as "a fairly large size but very much over-crowded single room" that housed the records and library. Kinsey took obvious delight in showing his visitor various books, photographs, and drawings, all the while stressing how utterly unique and invaluable these materials were. For his part, Gregg apparently accepted this assessment at face value, writing in his diary, "In the light of policy at the Library of Congress I should presume that Kinsey's collection was unexampled in the U.S." Gregg placed the library's value "in the neighborhood of $10,000," noting that Kinsey estimated another $4,000 would be required annually to maintain it "in an effective working state."[46]

As an experienced circuit rider (the name foundation officials used for officers who made inspection trips), Gregg was eager to learn as much as he could about the university's commitment to Kinsey's research. On the basis of his previous discussions with Kinsey, Gregg was satisfied that the administration's past support had been "very satisfactory and staunch." That evening, Kinsey arranged for Gregg to investigate the matter further over dinner with President Wells, Dean Payne, and other university officials, a strategy that worked to perfection. Noting that he was "agreeably impressed" by Wells and his colleagues, Gregg wrote in his diary, "They clearly understand the nature and implications of K's work."[47]

Following dinner, Kinsey invited his guest home for refreshments and a few hours of conversations with his colleagues and their wives. As a man of the world, Gregg was amused by the beverage Kinsey served. "I was introduced to a new and harmless temperance drink—a mixture of tea, orange juice and plenty of cinnamon served hot—and all the effect of mulled wine except the after-effect," he wrote in his diary.[48] Here, Kinsey's longstanding aversion to alcohol served him well, as his abstinence helped reinforce his image as a sober, even stodgy, figure. Moreover, like so many visitors before him, Gregg must have been struck by the austere simplicity of Kinsey's home, particularly the simple decor of the living room, which contained the wicker ensemble and the hand-braided rugs that seemed to underscore Kinsey's puritanical nature. Nor could Gregg have failed to draw the proper message from observing Kinsey and Clara together. Like so many other guests before him, Gregg saw exactly what Kinsey intended, a middle-aged couple who appeared genuinely devoted to one another.

Yet if Gregg thought the night would end on a domestic note, he was mistaken. At what should have been the end of the evening, Kinsey dragged him back to the laboratory, in Gregg's words, "for further conversation and a clearer understanding of the library and what the collections contain."[49] There they remained until after midnight, at which time Gregg retreated to the Student Union.

Barely giving his visitor enough time to roll in one side of the bed and out the other, Kinsey escorted Gregg bright and early the next morning to visit again with Wells. During the meeting, Gregg gave off strong signals that the site visit had gone well. Addressing the impasse over Kinsey's library, he announced that the foundation would consider making a special grant to Indiana University, which, in turn, could hand it over to Kinsey, but not until he had formed his own research corporation.[50] Delighted by this proposal, Wells, of course, promised to submit an application in the near future.

Then, Gregg and Kinsey had one last conference alone, during which Kinsey was at his messianic best, announcing that he planned to collect up to 100,000 histories in the years ahead.[51] Coming from most researchers, such ambition might have given Gregg pause, but he did not think it odd of Kinsey. Over the years, Gregg had come to regard Kinsey as larger than life, a man of superhuman energy who dreamed big and delivered what he promised. Everything Gregg saw in Bloomington had only served to deepen his respect and admiration for Kinsey.

Gregg was no innocent. He knew that some researchers might be attracted to sex research for personal reasons, using science to conceal their private needs, agendas, and designs. Some might even have prurient interests in the field, and the danger existed that those interests might be perverted. Consequently, Gregg had arrived in Bloomington determined to evaluate Kinsey's character, as well as his research. The visit had erased any suspicions or doubts. Deeply reassured by Kinsey's image as a family man, by a laboratory that looked all business, and by Kinsey's unbridled enthusiasm, Gregg confided to his diary, "I do not have the impression that K. or any of his associates have any morbid or pathological preoccupation with any particular aspect of sex." Gregg found only one fault in Kinsey. Referring to the recent squabbles with the NRC, Gregg observed, "K's considerable immersion in the subject makes him rather sensitive to even small degrees of prudery and very intolerant of it in scientists who are also controlling the funds on which his activities depend."[52]

Gregg's final diary entry was no less acute. Expressing his sense of irony over finding a man like Kinsey in a backwater like Bloomington, he wrote, "My general impression of the U. of Indiana was that it was one of the largest small-town universities that I have ever seen. It is isolated in point of travel and a simple, unselfconscious Hoosier University, perhaps the last place in the world that one would expect the kind of work K is doing to originate and perhaps one of the best places imaginable for it is proceeding uninterrupted and without effective interference."[53]

Following Gregg's visit, it was as though Jacob's ladder came down for Kinsey. The organizational and bureaucratic issues that had plagued him for the past few years rapidly vanished. On April 8, 1947, George W. Henley, a prominent attorney who was both a trustee of Indiana University and an influential member of the state legislature, filed articles of incorporation with the Indiana secretary of state creating a new scientific organization called the Institute for Sex Research, with headquarters in Bloomington, Indiana. The new corporation effectively solved Kinsey's organizational problems by providing a legal entity with the power to conduct research; to accept and expend income; to acquire and administer research materials, libraries, case histories, and the like; to obtain and to sell real estate and personal property; and to do "all things reasonably incidental to the corporation's general purpose which are permitted by law." Significantly, the articles of incorporation also contained a provision that solved the long dispute with NRC officials over the ownership of Kinsey's data and library. Article 11 authorized the corporation to assume ownership of the case histories and the library holdings. In the event the corporation ceased to exist, the case histories, library, and other materials were to be tendered and delivered up to the Rockefeller Foundation, which was free to accept or reject them.[54]

On April 10, 1947, the Institute for Sex Research conducted its first official act of business. For the sum of one dollar and other considerations not expressed, Kinsey gave the institute title to the case histories, research materials, and his library. After mailing copies of the articles of incorporation to Gregg, Kinsey sent Yerkes several copies for distribution among the committee members, declaring, "I think this settles many issues in the most satisfactory way."[55] When Yerkes asked what influence the incorporation would have on accounting, Kinsey replied that Indiana University would continue to keep the books "as usual," adding that all future grants, like those in the past, would be made to Indiana University "for the use of the Corporation."[56]

The creation of the Institute for Sex Research also broke the logjam over the library. At Kinsey's request, Wells applied for a $14,000 grant from the Rockefeller Foundation to support future growth for the library and to compensate Kinsey for the personal funds he had invested in to date.[57] While the application did not arrive in time for the spring meeting of the trustees, Gregg presented it in the fall. Wells's request was approved.[58] Thus ended a long and bitter dispute that had produced more ill will than it was worth.

Alfred C. Kinsey as he appeared in the
South Orange High School *Senior Year
Book, 1912.*

Class of 1912 from the South Orange High School *Senior Year Book, 1912.* Kinsey is in
the top row, second from the left.

The Stevens Institute Orchestra as it appeared in *The Link, 1914*. Kinsey is in the second row, second from the right.

Kinsey and his brother, Robert, in 1918. *Courtesy of Edna Kinsey Higenbotham.*

From left to right: Kinsey, Robert, Sarah, and Mildred. *Courtesy of Edna Kinsey Higenbotham.*

From left to right: Kinsey, Mildred, Sarah, and Alfred Seguine Kinsey. Robert is in front. (Note Kinsey's Phi Beta Kappa Key). *Courtesy of Edna Kinsey Higenbotham.*

Kinsey's senior photo at Bowdoin College. *Bowdoin Bugle,*
1916.

Kinsey (second row, center) was president of the Biology Club at Bowdoin College.
Bowdoin Bugle, 1917.

Kinsey was president of the Debate Team at Bowdoin College. *Bowdoin Bugle, 1916.*

Kinsey (first row on left) was an officer of the Y.M.C.A. Cabinet at Bowdoin College. *Bowdoin Bugle, 1917.*

The Searles Science Building at Bowdoin College. *Bowdoin Bugle, 1916.*

Zeta Psi Lamba House at Bowdoin College. *Bowdoin Bugle, 1917.*

From left to right: Benjamin Kinsey, Alfred Seguine Kinsey, Alfred Charles Kinsey, and Donald Kinsey. *Courtesy of Edna Kinsey Higenbotham.*

Clara Kinsey, 1927. *Courtesy of Edna Kinsey Higenbotham.*

Alfred Kinsey, 1927. *Courtesy of Edna Kinsey Higenbotham.*

A close-up of mounted gall wasps.
Courtesy of Robert Kroc.

Mounted gall wasps in a Schmitt box.
Courtesy of Robert Kroc.

Kinsey sorting galls in Mexico, 1935–1936. *Courtesy of Robert Kroc.*

Alfred C. Kinsey in 1939, one year after the marriage course and the sex research began. *Courtesy of Robert Kroc*

Herman B. Wells, president of Indiana University and staunch defender of Kinsey. *Courtesy of Indiana University archives.*

Fernandus Payne, chairman, Department of Zoology, and dean of the graduate school at Indiana University. Payne defended Kinsey's right to do research. *Courtesy of Indiana University archives.*

Robert M. Yerkes, chairman of the Committee for Research in Problems of Sex. *Courtesy of the National Academy of Science.*

George W. Corner, Yerkes' successor as chairman of the Committee for Research in Problems of Sex. *Courtesy of the American Philosophical Archive.*

Dean Rusk, president of the Rockefeller Foundation. *Courtesy of the Rockefeller Archive Center.*

Warren Weaver, director of the Natural Science Division of the Rockefeller Foundation. *Courtesy of the Rockefeller Archive Center.*

Alan Gregg, director of the Medical Science Division of the Rockefeller Foundation. *Courtesy of the Rockefeller Archives Center.*

Robert S. Morison, associate director of the Medical Science Division of the Rockefeller Foundation. *Courtesy of the Rockefeller Archive Center.*

Clara Kinsey in a domestic moment, 1948. *Courtesy of UPI/Corbis-Bettmann.*

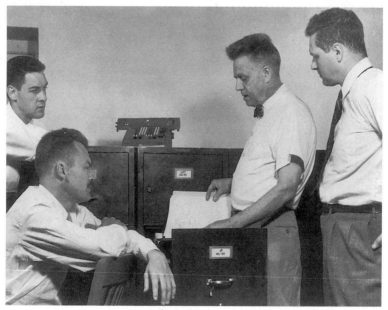

Members of Kinsey's senior staff and inner circle. From the left: Clyde E. Martin, Paul H. Gebhard, Kinsey, and Wardell B. Pomeroy. *Courtesy of UPI/Corbis-Bettmann.*

Thousands pack the gym at the University of California, Berkeley, to hear Kinsey speak following publication of *Sexual Behavior in the Human Male*. *Courtesy of UPI/Corbis Bettmann.*

Kinsey and Clara in March 1954. The strain and fatigue are starting to show. *Courtesy of UPI/Bettmann.*

All that remained was to clarify once and for all the relationship between the NRC and the Rockefeller Foundation regarding Kinsey's research. By negotiating his own separate budget and by securing a special library grant from the foundation, Kinsey had made two successful end runs, raising the possibility he would succeed in his goal of attaching his research to the foundation and severing his ties to the NRC. To prevent this from happening, the CRPS had to find a way to rein Kinsey in. This would not be easy. The committee itself was in a state of flux, with a new generation of members coming on board and Yerkes poised to resign as chairman.

For Yerkes, this was a bittersweet time. As he made the journey from New Haven to Washington, D.C., to attend his twenty-fifth and final meeting as chairman of the CRPS, he could not help worrying about the future, even as he reflected on the past. "Momentous days internally, these, for I am completing . . . my retirement from the active phase of my research career," he wrote in his diary. "Henceforth I shall be on the side lines as coach or observer." Small wonder there was an air of excitement as the committee convened in April 1947. As the first item of business, the committee accepted Yerkes's resignation, with what he described as "a skillfully worded note of appreciation." Then, following the script agreed to by all, the committee immediately elected George W. Corner to the chairmanship. "I am delighted by this action," confided Yerkes to his diary.[59] And well he should have been. Corner was a worthy successor, a man who brought to his duties as chairman sound judgment, great personal integrity, and superb human relations skills.

Although his term did not begin formally until July, Corner moved with dispatch and purpose to reach an understanding with Kinsey. "I had the feeling that he was turning from the committee in hopes of finding a more solid rock at the foundation," Corner later explained.[60] He decided to force the issue. Two days after being elected chairman, he wrote Kinsey, "I should like very much to have a general chat with you about plans, in order that we may understand each other fully when I become chairman."[61]

Kinsey agreed, and in May he traveled to Baltimore to confer with Corner in person. Returning the hospitality he had enjoyed four years earlier in Bloomington, Corner invited Kinsey home for supper the night before their meeting. The evening was a disaster. Instead of treating it as a social occasion, Kinsey monopolized the conversation with a nonstop monologue on his research. Corner, of course, was not surprised by this performance, but his wife and daughter were stunned. "Their comment after Kinsey paid his respects and left for the evening was that he talked too much about sex," recalled Corner, adding for good measure, "And this from two relatively emancipated women."[62]

Nor did things go better the next day. For more than an hour, Kinsey and Corner discussed the issues that separated them. They parted without having settled anything. Describing their meeting to Yerkes, Kinsey made it clear that his feelings about the NRC had not changed, despite Corner's candor and open-mindedness. "I am not at all clear what service it can render at this stage in the process," declared Kinsey, "and if it is going to cause difficulties of the sort that came up . . . last year, it can interfere with efficient management."[63] Still, Kinsey promised not to act hastily, admitting that it might be wise to remain with the NRC for the remainder of his present grant.

Not long after his conference with Kinsey, Corner requested a meeting with Gregg to ascertain where the committee stood with the foundation. "In particular," wrote Corner, "I shall need to understand your thoughts as to the Committee's future relationship to the work of Dr. Kinsey and his associates."[64] Gregg readily agreed, and in late May 1947 the two men met at the foundation's headquarters. Gregg moved swiftly to repair the damage to the foundation's relationship with the NRC. "I explained our principal intention was to have the committee feel free to select what they thought was best," wrote Gregg in his desk diary, "and I added that I thought the record of the committee had been an extremely good one, and for various reasons." Turning to Kinsey, Gregg continued, "I told Corner that we would want to continue the support for K's work through the Committee," adding, "My impression is that Corner has a better temperament for dealing with Kinsey than either Yerkes or Weed, and Corner himself thinks things will straighten out in his relationships with Kinsey."[65]

Corner, too, left the meeting feeling reassured. Two days after his talk with Gregg, he reported to his superiors at the NRC that the Rockefeller Foundation "wants the Committee to go on handling the Kinsey grant." In addition, Corner stated that the foundation's habit of "by-passing (or seeming to by-pass) the NRC and the Committee . . . was made at least partly plausible to me by Gregg, who had taken Kinsey's misinterpretations a little too much at face value." The bottom line, stressed Corner, was that Gregg "promised, in effect, to play ball in the future." As a result of these assurances, Corner agreed to tackle what he considered the most daunting challenge of his chairmanship. "I am willing to see, for a year, whether I can handle Kinsey, before I throw up the sponge," he declared.[66] For his part, Yerkes was far from confident that Corner would succeed. Early in July 1947, as he prepared to leave New Haven for his summer home in New Hampshire, he mailed his files on the CRPS to Corner, thereby passing the torch of leadership. "What a relief to feel that I need no longer think about the problems of that committee and its success," Yerkes confided to his diary. "I wonder how much longer it will survive."[67]

Nor did everyone at the Rockefeller Foundation share Gregg's and Corner's confidence about the future. Robert Morison, a Harvard-trained physician who was Gregg's second in command in the medical division, was gravely concerned about the foundation's relationship with Kinsey. Like his boss, Morison knew that the foundation frowned on becoming publicly identified with its grantees, especially those who were identified with controversial projects. As a result, Morison had grown progressively more irritated and apprehensive as he watched Kinsey manipulate Gregg into violating that policy. "The relations between Kinsey and the Committee are ticklish enough so that an unusual move in supplementation of the Committee's support might be taken as a demonstration of lack of confidence and upset things generally," he wrote Gregg late in June 1947. Turning to the real source of his concern, Morison cautioned, "I am also not very happy about giving Kinsey the impression that he can always draw on us if the Committee disapproves a request."[68]

While Morison's arguments merited serious consideration, Gregg was in no condition to heed the warnings. By 1947, he was hooked. He saw Kinsey as a man of destiny, a scientist whose work would forever change the world. Consequently, when an expert on sex education wrote to inquire about Kinsey, Gregg replied, "I have visited Professor Kinsey and believe that he is doing most valuable research in the study of sex phenomena in human beings." Going even further out on the limb, Gregg opined, "I personally regard his approach to such matters as an excellent one despite the fact that it will involve, in all probability, a great deal of criticisms and disillusionment because it concerns a field which is not very far removed from powerful emotions and taboos."[69] Although Gregg knew better than to put the foundation's imprimatur on a scientist, this amounted to an official endorsement.

As 1947 drew to a close, then, Kinsey was riding high. From his timorous beginnings as an obscure researcher, he had managed to place his research on firm financial ground. He was the head of his own research institute, and his support structure was firmly in place. In addition to that of Indiana University, he enjoyed the backing of the Rockefeller Foundation, which gave him access to seemingly unlimited funds—funds he could use to build a staff, to travel, to purchase books and other materials for the library, and to do whatever else he liked in order to advance his research. Kinsey's success in landing this patron had turned in part on historical circumstance, as he had emerged at precisely the right moment to capitalize on the foundation's desire to use science as a tool for controlling human behavior. Yet, in large measure, Kinsey had succeeded because he appeared to be the right man for the job. He had come to the foundation with a well-developed methodology, the soul of science. That methodology, in turn, had yielded data, more data on human sexual behavior than the world had ever seen. What's more, Kinsey had dazzled his patrons by promising to collect more data still, case histories by the tens of thousands, erotic books and magazines, material artifacts ranging from the crude to the sublime, and much, much more—as long as the money poured in.

Still, it had taken more than vision, methodology, and data to spring open the foundation's vault. Kinsey had triumphed in no small measure because he had managed to sell himself to Gregg, and Gregg was no pushover. As a senior officer of one of the richest foundations in the world, he was accustomed to dealing with first-rate scientists. Supremely confident of his judgment, Gregg was the sort of man who could walk into a laboratory and say, "That man is a scientist; that man is not." Yet Kinsey had not only impressed this discerning judge; he had played Gregg like a fiddle.

Finally, as 1947 drew to an end, Kinsey had managed all this without severing his ties to the CRPS. Although he had denounced their prudishness and had questioned their scientific knowledge, Kinsey did not have two stronger supporters than Yerkes and Corner. In truth, he owed them more than he knew. His snide remarks notwithstanding, both were respected and knowledgeable experts on human sexuality, and both had played a crucial role in securing and expanding his support from the Rockefeller Foundation. Their steadfast loyalty was a monument to how far scientists would go to support a difficult colleague whose work they respected.

The irony, of course, is that Gregg, Yerkes, and Corner were not able to see beneath the surface. In Kinsey, they thought they had found a metric-minded, Baconian scientist. They saw him as an instrument, a collecting machine who would compile the data others would use to develop social policies and programs designed to control human sexual behavior. Instead, they had been co-opted by a genuine revolutionary, a man who intended to use science to attack Victorian morality and to promote an ethic of tolerance.

"We Cannot Use Anyone Who Is Afraid of Sex"

"**I**t was heart warming to see you settling down into what I suppose will be your real life work," Edgar Anderson wrote Kinsey following a visit to Bloomington in July 1941. "One would never have believed that all sides of you could have found a project big enough to need them all. I was amused to see how the Scotch Presbyterian reformer in you had finally got together with the scientific fanatic with his zeal for masses of neat data in orderly boxes and drawers. The monographer Kinsey, the naturalist Kinsey, the camp counselor Kinsey all rolling into one at last and going full steam ahead."[1]

Anderson hit the mark, for Kinsey had found his calling. From his childhood, the desire to serve others had been a defining element of Kinsey's personality. Time had done nothing to diminish this trait. Astute observers like Anderson were quick to perceive that sex research was more than a job to Kinsey. It was a mission, a grand cause that filled his every waking moment. People who visited Kinsey during the 1940s encountered a secular priest, a man whose laboratory was his temple. It was not so much that he preached, which, of course, he did. Rather, it was the strength of his messianic impulse, the sense of urgency that filled his voice. Sex research had given this chronic do-gooder a new way to do good, and he attacked it with religious fervor.

The essence of Kinsey's gospel was simple: sexual morality needed to be reformed, and science would show the way. To date, the public had been kept in the dark about the facts of life. Intimate matters had been governed by moral prescription and superstition, with little regard for the way flesh-and-blood human beings thought and behaved. Consequently, society had constructed a system of sexual morality strangely at odds with human behavior. Kinsey hoped to change this. If people knew the facts about human sexual behavior, he reasoned, one day they would jettison attitudes that had put them at war with their nature and embrace values that treated sexual desires as healthy and wholesome.[2]

To provide these data, Kinsey believed, researchers had to divorce science from morality, studying sex with the same rigor that investigators brought to the hard sciences. From his perspective, this meant only one thing—amassing a sample so vast that people would be bowled over by its sheer volume. In the early 1940s, Kinsey set his goal at 100,000 histories. This was an astounding figure. No one in the history of sex research had approached this number. In fact, no previous survey had compiled more than a few hundred case histories. Still, Kinsey had made a career of doing the unprecedented. Challenging himself to collect 100,000 histories was very much in character for the man whom graduate school classmates had called "Get a Million Kinsey."

While Kinsey had an almost childlike faith in the redemptive power of data, he did not expect attitudes to change overnight. He was enough of a realist to understand that current sexual attitudes and mores had taken centuries to form, reflecting religious teachings and legal strictures that had been socially constructed and modified many times over the centuries. Nor did he underestimate the complexities and difficulties that awaited any reformer who challenged the system. Kinsey knew that the public's thinking on these matters was highly resistant to change. "Social reactions are realities which have to be accepted as realities whether they are what we like or not," he once wrote a friend. "I differ from you primarily in believing that social changes come very slowly and as the result of greater complicity of processes than we academic people usually realize."[3] Still, Kinsey never doubted that facts and reason would ultimately prevail. His task, therefore, was to collect those 100,000 case histories and then publish his data in a form that allowed only one set of conclusions.

Not even a man with Kinsey's drive and stamina could do this alone. To accomplish his goals, he had to build a staff. He needed interviewers, legal advisers, translators, and secretarial and clerical help. Yet his timing could not have been worse, as the competition for able bodies was fierce. Labor in any form was at an absolute premium throughout World War II. Economic growth associated with the war created 17 million new jobs at the same time as 15 million men and women entered the armed services, causing unemployment virtually to disappear. And, unfortunately for Kinsey, workers with the skills he needed were in especially high demand. The armed services snapped up people with scientific backgrounds, as the medical, intelligence, and communication units, to mention only a few, demanded professionally trained workers in unprecedented numbers. Because of his age and previous health problems, Kinsey was exempt from military service, but the draft was a serious threat to young professionals who had just completed their graduate training and were looking for their first real jobs. In addition, it seriously handicapped Kinsey's effort to recruit academics who already held teaching positions, as many professors were reluctant to change jobs, because they feared losing their occupational deferments.

Not that Kinsey was the only sex researcher who felt pinched by the war. Shortly after hostilities erupted, the Rockefeller Foundation asked the NRC to study how the war was affecting sex research. After reviewing records and polling grantees, Yerkes reported that both the number of applications for aid and the sums requested had dropped by 50 percent during 1941–42. Yerkes also discovered significant reductions in institutional support, manpower shortages caused by conscription, difficulties in obtaining certain materials and apparatuses, shortages of labor and technical assistance, and reductions in the time available for research as a result of increased teaching loads. Yerkes also found the political winds shifting. Several grantees of the CRPS had complained of interference with their work, while others expected difficulties in the near future.[4] In sum, Yerkes's report painted a grim picture, predicting that fewer scientists would be chasing the CRPS's resources. From Kinsey's perspective, however, less competition spelled better odds when he sought budget increases from the NRC.

Kinsey began the difficult process of staff building by turning to someone he knew well, Clyde Martin. Martin, of course, had started out as a part-time yard boy and technical assistant on the gall wasp research, producing high-quality insect sketches that demonstrated considerable artistic talent. He had also shown an aptitude for statistical analysis and painstaking, tedious calculations. Consequently, as Kinsey's interests had shifted, so had Martin's assignments. By his junior year, he was preparing tables and charts on human sexual behavior, and Kinsey had come to rely heavily on him for the statistical side of the work.[5] This was where things stood when Martin finished college.

Kinsey used his first grant from the NRC, in 1941, to hire Martin on a full-time basis. In no sense was he a strong appointment, as his degree was in economics and he had no formal graduate training. Still, his appeal to Kinsey did not turn on professional qualifications; it was deeply emotional. Martin knew Kinsey's secrets, had been intimate with both Kinsey and Clara, and could be trusted to keep quiet. Martin also provided an ongoing, if unrequited, romantic interest for Kinsey. For although their brief affair had ended, Kinsey was still in love with his handsome, young assistant and could not bear to part with him—modest professional qualifications and all.

For his part, Martin elected to stick with Kinsey, despite the sexual tensions that continued to complicate their relationship. Martin felt bound to the older man, in part because of the force of Kinsey's personality but also because Martin believed in the research. By this point, he had absorbed much of Kinsey's missionary zeal, for, like so many leaders who dedicate their lives to a cause, Kinsey had the ability to infect others with his passion. "We did feel sort of being on the forefront of something and doing something of a real contribution," Martin later remarked. "So, I was very proud of what we were doing, very enthusiastic."[6]

Martin's youth and meager education posed problems for Kinsey, especially in his dealings with officials from the NRC and the Rockefeller Foundation. Men like Yerkes and Gregg were accustomed to seeing projects staffed by promising young scholars with advanced academic training. Aware of Martin's shortcomings, Kinsey constantly tried to stress his assets. Writing to Yerkes in 1941, Kinsey described Martin as "a painstaking technician, accurate and efficient in his statistical handling of material and an artist of most unusual ability." Kinsey also lauded Martin's "thorough dependability," explaining that it had been possible to give him access to "the records without any danger of their betrayal." Kinsey noted that he had taught Martin the position code, enabling him to transfer data from history sheets to punch cards. "His combination of qualifications has made it possible to hand him the raw data represented on our histories, and, with a minimum of direction, get from him the finished results in the forms of curves and graphs which, he, with his ability as an artist, is able to turn out in unusually fine form," reported Kinsey.[7]

Yet, as he himself was quick to admit, Kinsey's most pressing need was for interviewers. Since Martin was still wet behind the ears, unmarried, and without advanced education, Kinsey hesitated to train him for this assignment, fearing that many people would not feel comfortable confiding in an interviewer so young, uncredentialed, and presumably inexperienced. Wedding bells, however, soon changed Kinsey's mind. While still an undergraduate, Martin met his future wife, Alice, in a sculpture class, and their romance developed quickly. When Martin revealed their plans to marry, Kinsey replied, "Fine, but it will have to be done in our garden."[8] Although the young couple had intended to marry in August 1942, they changed the date at Kinsey's insistence to May, the month the garden was at its best.

Following the wedding, Kinsey moved quickly to expand Martin's assignments. "His youth is against him, but he is now married, and I shall train him to secure histories as rapidly as possible," Kinsey wrote Yerkes. Insisting that "the qualifications necessary for an interviewer are such as is not to be found in one person in many thousands," Kinsey went on to assure Yerkes that Martin had the right stuff. "He has that rare combination of polish, obvious culture and democratic comradeship which will take him into any social level," raved Kinsey. "He is not only absolutely honest, but deeply sympathetic with the other person's problem." That last trait, Kinsey stressed, "is the one thing that is most difficult to find in prospective interviewers." The ideal interviewer had to "be absolutely without judgment, pro or con, on any item of human sexual behavior, or the subject will never expose his full and complete history."[9]

Ever the demanding taskmaster, Kinsey put Martin through a grueling training program. First, Martin had to memorize the questions, a chore that required months. Then, he had to learn how to interact with people during the interview—just as Kinsey had before him, but with one important difference: Kinsey did not have a hypercritical perfectionist evaluating his every word, look, and action. Convinced that practice made perfect, Kinsey had Martin take his sexual history again and again. Hour after hour, day after day, Martin toiled away, with Kinsey delivering copious criticism at every juncture. Among other things, Kinsey stressed the importance of proper word choice in framing questions, of pursuing leads with bulldog tenacity, and of following the same procedures. In essence, Kinsey was attempting to clone himself in order to produce staff members who would obtain uniform results. Anything less, he feared, would undermine the integrity of the data.

But Martin was no Kinsey. Although Martin worked diligently, he never developed into anything more than a competent interviewer of young people. One former colleague described him as "a very quiet, self-effacing interviewer."[10] He never redeemed Kinsey's early hopes. All told, Martin took approximately 1,100 histories, fewer than any other member of Kinsey's inner circle of associates. Not that this bothered Martin. He was relieved not to have to do more interviewing. "I really never saw myself as a professional person," he later confessed.[11] Essentially artistic in temperament, he preferred the routine and serenity of laboratory work.

Martin spent much of his time punching cards. "We have made our first venture into the use of the Hollerith statistical machine and other calculating instruments in our new Bureau of Statistics," Kinsey wrote a friend in February 1941. "I immediately see that it will save us endless hours of work in analyzing our data. It will be possible for us to run correlations of an indefinite number of factors, at least eight in any one problem—a thing which is utterly impossible by any hand calculation."[12]

Over the next fifteen years, Kinsey would ask innumerable questions of his data, but the first topic he analyzed was telling. In the same letter in which he discussed the Hollerith machine, Kinsey reported, "We have just completed our first set of punched cards which covers the heterosexual-homosexual formulae for the entire lifetime of the individual," including "such correlative items as age, age of adolescence to frequency of outlet per week, etc." Encouraged by the machine's capabilities, Kinsey believed he could assert control over his data and give the world its first accurate portrait of what he visualized as the heterosexual/homosexual continuum. "I had despaired of every analyzing these formulae by hand techniques," he confessed. "The machine will do it for us at the rate of 400 cards per minute." Kinsey did not exaggerate when he exclaimed, "The new equipment is a godsend to our particular problem."[13]

Early in 1941, at precisely the time he was learning to use technology to process his data, Kinsey hired Glenn V. Ramsey, the second addition to the staff. An educational psychologist, Ramsey had completed his doctorate at Indiana University only a few months earlier. As it happened, Kinsey was not really looking for someone at this point, since the large grants from the NRC had not started arriving. He spent his own money to hire Ramsey because he had just been fired, and Kinsey felt responsible, a situation that requires further comment.

Ramsey's relationship with Kinsey dated back to the marriage course. Like so many of his fellow students, Ramsey answered the call for volunteers to be interviewed, but with one big difference. When he arrived for his appointment, he surprised Kinsey. An incipient sex researcher in his own right, Ramsey slapped a stack of questionnaires on Kinsey's desk involving the sex education of adolescent boys. According to Ramsey, Kinsey was "astounded and taken aback that a young twerp of a graduate student would come in and place so much data in front of him at that particular time."[14]

The material came from a sex education questionnaire Ramsey had administered to approximately 350 boys in Peoria, Illinois, where he taught health education courses in a large public high school. Unlike Kinsey, Ramsey had been careful to separate his teaching from his research. Instead of using his students, he had turned to boys in churches, the Young Men's Christian Association, and other organizations that had agreed to cooperate. This was the kind of resourcefulness Kinsey admired, and he agreed to help Ramsey plan and organize his dissertation.

As happened so often when he offered to help, Kinsey insisted that things be done his way. "He had me expand my own study from that of sex education to include aspects of sexual biology, and sexual behavior," explained Ramsey. Looking back on this experience, he did not feel resentful. Rather, he regarded Kinsey as a mentor, both helpful and wise. Admitting he was "influenced in a very major way by him [Kinsey]," Ramsey declared, "I was really taught the canons of scientific research based upon empirical evidence."[15]

Without being aware of what was happening, Ramsey quickly found himself transformed into Kinsey's assistant. During the period Ramsey worked on his dissertation, Kinsey trained him thoroughly. "I followed his system as closely as possible, because the data was going to go into his general body of data," explained Ramsey. His instruction included memorizing the position code for recording histories, which, in turn, allowed him "to decode all of the histories that [he] had taken on boys so that they would fit into the Kinsey data and become an integral part of the basic research data."[16] In fact, Kinsey cited Ramsey's data in his article on hormones and homosexuality.[17]

By the fall of 1940, Kinsey was calling Ramsey "an important cog" in his research. He was particularly impressed by his young collaborator's success in using various organizations to generate volunteers. "You are clever and deserve distinct congratulations on your ability to contact so many civic groups," wrote Kinsey. "Perhaps I should take more time to meet more people personally in such connections," he continued, "though I hate to take time away from the research study itself."[18] Over time, Kinsey overcame this reservation and made it a point to work with civic groups whenever possible, a tactic he learned from Ramsey. By midsummer 1941, Kinsey was paying Ramsey thirty dollars a week to collect adolescent male histories in Peoria, and by the fall they were discussing the possibility of his joining the staff full-time at the end of the school year 1942, provided the NRC came through with a second and larger grant.[19]

At Kinsey's request, Ramsey also served as a "contact man" in Peoria, where he arranged for Kinsey to speak at Bradley University, with the understanding that he also would collect histories from fraternity boys there. Anxious to provide feedback, Ramsey reported following Kinsey's visit, "One of the common answers on the Bradley campus to the question 'Where are you going?' is the response 'I'm going home and jerk off a quickee—Kinsey says its O.K.' "[20]

Yet, if they thought that sex research had played well in Peoria, Kinsey and Ramsey were mistaken. Late in 1941, a group of Catholic mothers stormed the board of education in Peoria, demanding Ramsey's dismissal for interviewing their sons. They objected strenuously to the fact that Ramsey was dispensing sex information to young people in Peoria. Decades later, Ramsey made no effort to deny this charge, freely confessing that he had answered questions that arose during the interviews with "factual information about sexual biology and sexual behavior."[21]

In December 1941, the school board held an emergency session to consider these charges. In the end, the board voted to suspend Ramsey without a hearing. Immediately thereafter, it launched an investigation, not to learn the truth but to build a case for dismissal. Reporting to Kinsey on the witch-hunt, Ramsey charged that lawyers for the board were "canvassing the town for boys that I have interviewed and getting affidavits from them on the 'worst items' that the boys can remember." Ramsey complained that some of those items were "frame ups, [such] as 'Mr. Ramsey took my penis and measured it.' "[22]

Kinsey, of course, sided with his young protégé. Denouncing the board's actions as an attack on "the validity of the whole research program," Kinsey declared, "We feel a great responsibility for your own personal future and certainly should be able to do something to help you on that score. Do not worry about that."[23] Over the next few weeks, Kinsey moved on several fronts. First, he sought legal advice from a friend in the law school. Then he sent a letter to the North Central Association (an accrediting organization) demanding a full investigation. For him the issue was simple. As he told a friend, "if we let them get away with this in Peoria now . . . this precedent will encourage Catholics elsewhere, perhaps here in Bloomington or anywhere else, to try the same tactics against us here and against the entire research program."[24]

Hoping to convert the critics, Kinsey appeared before the school board to plead Ramsey's case. While his arguments were forceful and clear, the judges were not persuaded.[25] Recognizing that the situation was hopeless, Kinsey advised Ramsey to leave Peoria. To make this financially feasible, Kinsey offered to employ him at the same rate as before. "While $30 a week is not much," wrote Kinsey, "it would allow you to live, and it is all that our funds will allow for the immediate use." Had his mentor stopped there, Ramsey hardly could have asked for more, but Kinsey was not finished. "In addition," he continued, "Mrs. Kinsey and I are ready to back you financially whenever you need it. Do not hesitate to call on us." Explaining why he was willing to go to such lengths, he declared, "You are being penalized for doing scholarly research and all of us should defend you on that account. Inasmuch as the research was largely at my instigation and under my direction, I feel doubly responsible for your difficulties."[26]

Ramsey's firing, coming as it did on the heels of his own ouster from the marriage course, gave Kinsey pause. Both incidents were chilling reminders of the dangers inherent in sex research, prompting Kinsey to redouble his efforts to deny critics ammunition. Consequently, after Ramsey moved to Bloomington, Kinsey laid down the law. "Well," recalled Ramsey, "he flat [out] stated that he didn't want anybody involved in any kind of behavior which would cast question, reflection, or discredit upon the project."[27] Ramsey readily agreed to abide by this condition, for he understood Kinsey's motive. "It was not that he cared so much about our personal life as he did about avoiding any kind of questioning from people outside who were looking for some way to get a knife into the study," Ramsey explained.[28]

Following their heart-to-heart discussion, Kinsey put Ramsey to work. "My first assignment was to go through all the literature that we could put our hands on which dealt with any aspect of human sexuality," Ramsey recalled. For the next six months, he made "a fine-tooth combing of the literature" and examined "every crumb of data," preparing detailed abstracts for Kinsey's perusal. Yet, as Ramsey thought back on this work, he was certain that Kinsey "had read all the significant research first before I came along." The major sexologists and "scores of other writers were old hat to him," declared Ramsey. In fact, it was clear that Kinsey knew much more about human sexual behavior than any of his predecessors, largely because he had more data. As Ramsey put it, "Kinsey was far ahead of any of the published research by the time I met him."[29]

As the months passed, Ramsey was struck by what he called Kinsey's "very high work morality." Admitting that he had never seen such "a hard-driving researcher," he noted that his boss "spent hours and hours at that laboratory," often working until one or two o'clock in the morning. No one could match Kinsey's power of concentration, as nothing else in the world seemed to matter except the work before him. He even begrudged the time it took to eat. "In order to save time at noon," recalled Ramsey, "we often had a meeting in his office and each brought our own lunch." Yet, if Kinsey was "a very hard taskmaster," Ramsey also stressed, he "set a harder pace for himself than he ever did his staff." Kinsey demanded excellence not by edict but by example, because "he was never someone that would order you to work," Ramsey explained. "You just knew the implicit standards of complete devotion to the research cause."[30]

Ramsey's regard for Kinsey bordered on hero worship, a quality that seemed to be shared by all the assistants Kinsey hired. "I admired him as a scientist," Ramsey confessed. "He was dedicated to [the] canons of science as no one I know. This was his religion."[31] Moreover, Ramsey was proud of his part in Kinsey's grand mission to use science to combat ignorance, superstition, and repression. Thirty years after he left Kinsey's staff, he declared, "I still feel that it was one of the great research efforts of my lifetime."[32]

There is no evidence that Ramsey knew about Kinsey's private sex life. Not that Ramsey was unusual in this regard. In the years ahead, most of the people who worked for Kinsey did not have a clue. Within the staff, that knowledge would always be restricted to a handful of close associates whom Kinsey swore to secrecy, both with regard to what they learned about his sex life and what they learned about each other's. Extremely careful about whom he admitted to this inner circle, Kinsey waited until he was certain his trust would not be betrayed or his sexual overtures rejected.

Apparently, things never reached this point with Ramsey, because World War II intervened before Kinsey had had enough time to size up his young assistant. Despite Kinsey's efforts to secure him a deferment, Ramsey was forced to enlist in the Air Force to avoid being drafted into the army. He left Bloomington in the summer of 1942, only months after joining the staff. Ramsey's departure was a serious blow to the research, as Kinsey was already shifting him into interviewing. Still, there was one bright spot. While he lost an interrogator, Kinsey gained a wonderful observer. For the remainder of the war, Ramsey sent back a stream of letters describing life in the military, including the intimate exploits (both homosexual and heterosexual) of his comrades in arms.[33]

World War II threatened other members of Kinsey's staff as well. During the war years, Kinsey employed no fewer than five draft-eligible men, and he fought to keep them out of the armed services. It was a testament to his single-mindedness that he considered his research more important than the nation's need for conscripts. To secure deferments, Kinsey assured local draft boards that his project was crucial to the war effort, arguing that sex research would uncover information that would benefit the armed services, penal authorities, and public health organizations. He also stressed that the special qualifications and extensive training required of his coworkers made them difficult, if not impossible, to replace in a tight job market. To strengthen his position, he persuaded officials from Indiana University, the NRC, and the Rockefeller Foundation to write similar letters to his staff members' draft boards. Their support doubtless contributed to Kinsey's success. Ramsey was his only loss to the draft.

For an educated man who had lived through the Great War, Kinsey showed remarkably little interest in World War II. The thousands of letters he wrote during the war make no reference to geopolitics, political personalities, battles, military leaders, or the like. Nor do his friends and colleagues recall any discussions of a political or philosophical nature with him about the war. Except on those occasions when the war impinged on his research, he paid it no mind. Kinsey was too obsessed with work to think about anything else. While the free world fought to survive, he waged his own private war against Victorian morality. He put everything he had into collecting data, his weapon of choice in the great war he had fashioned for himself.

Still, staff recruitment and retention were not the only areas in which World War II impeded his research. To collect histories, Kinsey had to travel, and, like other Americans, he had to contend with rationing. Thanks to relentless petitioning, backed by strong letters from university officials, Kinsey managed to secure extra allotments of gasoline and tires. To stretch these, he and his coworkers traveled by train whenever possible. As a result, Kinsey was able to work around wartime rationing, though it certainly did not make his life any easier.

Other inconveniences proved more difficult. Like everyone else, Kinsey and his associates had to cope with crowded cities when they journeyed to the East Coast. Throughout the war, tens of thousands of servicemen on leave poured into cities like Washington, Philadelphia, and New York, packing trains, restaurants, and hotels. As a result, reservations of any kind were hard to get. On the plus side, jammed cities offered Kinsey thousands of histories for the taking, many from unattached people who were sexually on the make.

Despite these war-related problems and inconveniences, Kinsey refused to get sidetracked or discouraged. From the day the grants from the NRC started arriving, he devoted considerable time to recruitment. His correspondence is filled with letters to distinguished professors in a variety of disciplines requesting nominees, and he was in constant communication with Yerkes and Gregg, asking for leads or seeking their advice on particular candidates.

As a result of his experiences in training Martin and Ramsey, Kinsey felt he had a better idea of what to look for in interviewers. "At the start, I should have thought that it would have taken someone trained in Psychology, Sociology, or Biology to have made a good interviewer," he wrote Yerkes in June 1942. "Now I am certain that we can give enough information on those items to any prospective interviewer, whatever his background, if he works for six months or a year handling the data in our own laboratory. What is much more important than academic equipment is personality, sincerity, and an abundantly sympathetic viewpoint in the interviewer."[34]

Age was another factor. Writing to a job candidate, Kinsey noted that interviewers should be "preferably in their thirties or early forties."[35] Individuals in this age group had completed their professional training, had some work experience, and possessed the maturity and poise to put subjects at ease. Kinsey was wary of candidates beyond their forties. Explaining his reservations to a friend, he insisted that "too many older people are interested in directing behavior rather than in a completely objective acceptance of the facts."[36] What Kinsey did not say, however, was that few people who had reached an advanced stage in their careers were eager to serve as junior assistants. Nor were they willing to accept the control he exercised over his staff members.

Kinsey also insisted that interviewers be, in his words, "happily married."[37] Commenting on a prospective candidate, he told a friend that the man "is out if he is not married."[38] Kinsey had to toe the line on this point, because it was central to his strategy for protecting the research. In his mind, image was everything. Aware that his status as a family man had shielded him from suspicions, he made it a firm rule to recruit only married men. Actually, he preferred men with children, as they completed the portrait of wholesome family life. He once told a reporter that the interviewers on his staff had to be "virtual saints as well as scientists," with private lives beyond reproach "so as not to attract criticisms or suspicion."[39]

Yet many family men did not want to work for Kinsey. Several candidates refused his offer, expressing concerns about the strains that constant travel would place on their marriages. Noting that it was precisely because he was "happily married" that he was declining Kinsey's offer, one applicant wrote, "I must admit that the prospect of being apart from my wife and family for half of the next twenty years is not pleasant."[40] Unlike her husband, Clara both understood and sympathized with such complaints. As she later remarked, Kinsey "was asking for something that was a contradiction in terms." On the one hand, he "wanted somebody that was happily married," but, on the other hand, he wanted a man whose "wife didn't object to him being out of town for long periods of time."[41]

Kinsey fretted over how to prevent unhappy wives from damaging the research. His solution, which derived from experience and evolved rather quickly, was to screen wives with the same care as husbands. "The wives are a very important part of our research," he told one applicant. "If they do not thoroughly believe in the project and if they are not as objective as we want our staff to be on these questions, it can cause considerable difficulty." Assuring the candidate that this requirement was not pro forma, Kinsey added, "We have been held up in our thinking of you because we have not met your wife, do not have her history, and do not know what her attitudes would be on matters of sex."[42] In other words, he expected the wives of job candidates to join their husbands in contributing sex histories—yet another example of the control and power he exercised over his staff.

Kinsey pressured wives to be team players, and he offered Clara as a model. No one put in more hours at the office or stayed away from home longer on trips than Kinsey. Consequently, if anyone had a right to complain, it was Clara. Instead, she backed her husband at every turn. One of his interviewers recalled Kinsey's stressing "on several occasions that he was sure that Mrs. Kinsey understood and that she didn't resent the fact that he was away a good deal."[43]

Kinsey was mistaken. After the sex research began, he all but disappeared from the home as he devoted more and more time to work. Consequently, Clara saw less and less of him. Referring to her husband's interviewing trips, she declared, "There were never any of them [who] was gone as long as my husband. He often went first, and he was usually last to finish up." Explaining that he tried to arrange things "so that no one else was ever gone for more than, say, three weeks at a time," she added with a hard edge to her voice, "but that didn't mean that he wasn't." In truth, Clara felt abandoned. Many years later, when she was asked to name the biggest adjustment she had to make after her husband became a sex researcher, her reply was chilling: "Being alone a lot."[44]

Still, Clara could not bring herself to complain. Because she was part of a generation of women who had been taught from childhood to help advance their husbands' careers and because she affirmed his research and goals, Clara responded like a good helpmate. "I realized how important it [the research] was to him," she later declared, "and I felt that it was important work." Thus, even in the face of rising neglect, she never surrendered to the temptation to ask him to spend more time at home. "I just couldn't do that to him," she explained.[45]

Rather than fuss or demand more attention, Clara tried to create a niche for herself in his work. Once the research really got going, hundreds of people offered Kinsey their notebooks, diaries, and letters. Many were outright gifts, while others came with the understanding that the items would be copied and the originals returned. Since these were the days before photocopying, every piece had to typed or copied by hand. This was Clara's job. Over the years, she typed numerous notebooks and diaries, yet another example of how hard she struggled to remain close to Kinsey even as he pulled further and further from the domestic sphere. When not helping her husband, Clara built a life for herself, filling her days with her children, hiking, Girl Scout work, and the like.

Kinsey was too busy to notice Clara's feelings. Completely caught up in his research, he looked for people who shared his enthusiasm. When one job candidate inquired about salary, Kinsey's reaction was swift and brutal. "The work is too difficult for anyone who does not have an enthusiastic conviction that it is worth doing whatever the obstacles," he growled. "I am skeptical of the man who says he will be interested if the salary is not less than thus and so. That is the wrong point from which to begin."[46] Yet, if Kinsey expected applicants to be excited about the research, he also went out of his way to assure them that the work was special. He once told a candidate from his alma mater, "If you find people interesting, I think we could convince you that even a Harvard University faculty position is humdrum in comparison."[47] It had taken him decades, but Kinsey had finally proclaimed victory in his competition with Wheeler.

Kinsey was particularly keen on hiring applicants who could deal effectively with the working class. Unlike most of the earlier sexologists, Kinsey included the lower classes in his sample, as he was eager to examine (and tout) their behavior as a counterpoint to middle-class restraint. Consequently, he needed interviewers who could establish rapport with people from different backgrounds, including criminal elements.

Finding academics who could fit the bill proved difficult. Confiding to a friend, Kinsey revealed that he had hesitated to pursue one candidate because the man had "a quiet and careful way." While acknowledging that the applicant could relate well to "educated and cultured people," Kinsey mused, "I am wondering what would happen when he is called upon to meet people, both frequently and in numbers, and sell himself in a matter of minutes with them. The qualities of Fuller brush men would seem more effective at such a moment." Above all, Kinsey questioned the man's "ability to meet lower level groups and rough and criminal characters." To be effective, he insisted, an interviewer not only had to "be aggressive in meeting these people, but he must be able to dominate when they talk and attempt deliberate cover-up, double-crossing and damage." Returning to the theme of domination, he declared, "Unless one can so dominate, the rough lower level and underworld does not have much respect for one."[48]

In Kinsey's mind, the ability to relate to members of the lower class was a direct result of personal experience. "It is going to take someone who has some wide acquaintance with the variety that the world offers," he told one candidate. "It takes somebody who can like folk of any sort or at least some of their qualities, and make them feel that we are sincerely interested in them," he continued. "It is going to take someone who is ready to listen to the record of any sort of sexual activity without making any sort of criticism in his own mind."[49] It followed, therefore, that prudish attitudes could disqualify a candidate. Explaining why he had decided not to offer him a position, Kinsey told one young applicant, "There are some attitudes in your history which would need modification before you were acceptant of everything in human sex behavior to do a good job in taking histories."[50] At a minimum, Kinsey expected interviewers to be nonjudgmental. "They will have to be individuals particularly adapted to meeting people and capable of exploring for the facts without any concern with the evaluations," he told a friend. "Otherwise they can never win the confidence of individuals on items which are socially taboo."[51] What Kinsey really wanted, however, were individuals who were very accepting, both of others and of themselves. In dismissing one candidate, Kinsey complained that the man's "whole attitude is restrained and reserved on matters of sex. He insists that he is neutral on everything, but . . . academic neutrality is one thing and thorough acceptance is another."[52] Describing the ideal candidate, Kinsey told another applicant, "Obviously, it would be someone who is not afraid to face the realities of sexual behavior in the human animal, and someone who is poised and balanced in relation to his own sexual life."[53]

To learn whether applicants were "sex shy," Kinsey required them to submit to an interview. "I need a sexual history from the person under consideration and long contact with him in order to become acquainted with his attitudes on a variety of things," he told Yerkes. Aware this was an extraordinary requirement, Kinsey explained, "It might easily take a year or two to train some quirk out of the thinking of a collaborator, before he would be worth anything as an interviewer of histories that contained the particular sexual items on which his thinking was not objective."[54]

Last but not least, Kinsey was an absolute fanatic on the subject of confidentiality. Exquisitely vulnerable himself, he understood that the vast majority of human beings at one time or another had done or fantasized about things of a sexual nature they did not wish revealed. Some secrets were large, others small. Whether significant or trivial, these hidden truths needed to be discovered if science had any hope of mapping human sexuality. And that was why confidentiality had to be preserved at all costs. Without it, subjects would fear betrayal and withhold their trust and their cooperation.

Yet, in reflecting on what he called Kinsey's "basic rocklike integrity," a close friend said a mouthful when he remarked, "I think he liked secrets, that their possession gave him a sense of power." Over the years, the friend continued, Kinsey interviewed "political, social, and business leaders of the first rank." Had he been inclined to reveal what he had learned, "Kinsey could have figuratively blown up the United States socially and politically."[55]

Publicly, then, Kinsey insisted upon a formidable list of qualifications for interviewers. Candidates had to satisfy age, educational, and marital requirements, not to mention careful scrutiny of their interpersonal skills. No wonder one of his associates later observed, "Kinsey was never more arbitrary than when he was considering hiring interviewers."[56] Yerkes made the point even stronger, telling Kinsey, "There is no use denying that your specifications would discourage about 99% of possible candidates."[57]

And Yerkes did not know the half of it. In addition to the qualifications Kinsey made public, there was a secret yardstick. Kinsey wanted more than mere workers. Like all messiahs, he was looking for disciples, true believers who would work until they dropped, follow his instructions to the letter, and accept his highly autocratic style of leadership. And there was more. As a covert revolutionary, he wanted interviewers who shared his conviction that sexual mores should be brought into line with how people actually behaved.

Not surprisingly, then, sexual politics also shaped and restricted Kinsey's choice of interviewers. Simply put, Kinsey did not want coworkers with orthodox sexual values. By requiring applicants to give their sexual histories, he did his best to limit the pool to candidates who shared or who he believed could be taught to endorse his biological, materialistic attitudes about human sexuality in general and homosexuality in particular.

Nor were attitudes his only concern. As his hiring of Martin made clear, Kinsey had a preference for coworkers with certain behavioral items in their histories. Homosexual experience was a definite plus, as Kinsey identified with any man who had this in his record. In fairness to Kinsey, however, he was willing to hire heterosexuals with little or no homosexual experience, provided they had jumped a few fences in their heterosexual behavior and were not homophobes.

Given his agenda, Kinsey encountered the ideal candidate in Wardell Pomeroy, a young psychologist who had received both his bachelor's and his master's degrees from Indiana University. In contrast to Martin and Ramsey, Pomeroy had not taken any classes with Kinsey, though their paths had occasionally crossed on campus. They did not meet formally until several years after Pomeroy had left Bloomington.

In 1941, Kinsey delivered a lecture in South Bend, Indiana, where Pomeroy worked as psychologist for the Department of Public Welfare. Pomeroy thought he knew a great deal about Kinsey's topic, "Sex in Prisons." Prior to moving to South Bend, Pomeroy had been employed by the Indiana Reformatory at Pendleton, so he was curious to learn what Kinsey had to say. "After I heard Kinsey's lecture it was clear to me that I didn't know as much as I had imagined," Pomeroy later confessed. The lecture left no room for doubt that Kinsey "had been in the field and knew what he was talking about." Calling Kinsey's presentation "brilliant," Pomeroy added, "I was deeply impressed by his knowledge of both prisons and sex."[58]

Pomeroy hung around after the lecture to chat, and Kinsey did what he always did: he asked Pomeroy to contribute his sex history. A day or two later, Pomeroy arrived at Kinsey's hotel for an early-morning appointment, knocked on the door, and heard a voice from the distance say, "Come in." What happened next was vintage Kinsey. Upon entering, Pomeroy was surprised to find his host undressed and shaving before the mirror. Ordinarily, Kinsey kept his appointments with military punctuality, so there was something odd about his not being ready. The suspicion lingers that he wanted to be caught in the nude, perhaps for the delight he took in shocking others or perhaps because he was making a sexual overture. Pomeroy was of medium height, with dark, wavy hair, a stocky build, and a face that always made him look years younger than his age. In truth, Pomeroy was handsome enough to be a movie star, with a confident and engaging personality. Disarmingly smooth and outgoing, he was a born extrovert, a man who thrived on human contact.

After Kinsey apologized for running late, Martin, who was with him, excused himself and left the room. Then Kinsey got dressed, and the interview began. Pomeroy was impressed by the deftness and persistence of Kinsey's technique. "I found myself telling him things I had never dreamed of telling anyone else," Pomeroy later wrote. "When we were finished," he continued, "Kinsey told me he was impressed by my attitudes about sex. I appeared to be relaxed, he said, and without fear or unwarranted modesty."[59]

But then Pomeroy was not a modest man, least of all where sex was concerned. Close friends conjured up an image of Pomeroy as a kind of equal-opportunity Don Juan. With something approaching unanimity, they described a man of magnetic charm and a prodigious sexual appetite, utterly relentless in his pursuit of sexual partners of both sexes, though with a decided preference for women. Several claimed that Pomeroy kept a "little black book" (in code, of course) of his sexual conquests.

Other sources close to Pomeroy concurred with the sexual aspects of this characterization but found his personality less than appealing. While no one accused him of concealing a hideous self-portrait in the attic, they insisted that his handsome, eternally youthful face masked a character of little substance. Clarence A. Tripp remarked, "There's something extremely light and shallow about Pomeroy." They described a man whose charm was superficial, whose vanity was immense, and whose main goal in life appeared to be sexual conquest. Stressing that Pomeroy had bedded literally hundreds of people, Tripp, who had once declined a proposition from him to join a ménage à trois, declared, "He just fucks everybody and it's really disgusting." Recalling a conversation in which Pomeroy had summarized his attitude toward sex, he continued, "He says, 'Well, sex is fun, why not?' " Repulsed and bewildered by such thinking, Tripp added, "It's some kind of lightness that escapes you it is so trivial. I can't make it sound as trivial as it is."[60]

Kinsey viewed Pomeroy in a different light. Following their interview, Kinsey asked Pomeroy to serve as his "contact man" in South Bend. Over the next few months, they kept in touch through correspondence and met occasionally for lunch when Kinsey visited South Bend. During these contacts, Kinsey discussed his research and constantly complained about his need for "more hands,"[61] the telling phrase he used to convey both his chronic need for assistants and his attitude toward anyone who joined his staff.

In February 1942, Pomeroy wrote to inquire about the possibility of coming to work for Kinsey. At Kinsey's insistence, they met for an entire weekend to discuss the matter, at the end of which Kinsey offered Pomeroy a job at a monthly salary of $300. After considering the offer, Pomeroy declined, explaining that it was only a little more than he was currently making. Yet money was not the sole reason. "As a freshly graduated psychologist with a career ahead of me," Pomeroy later wrote, "I could not visualize myself tied to sex research, and to a single project at that."[62]

In less than a year, Pomeroy changed his mind and again approached Kinsey for a job. After mulling the matter over for more than a month, Kinsey offered him a position and Pomeroy accepted. In February 1943, Pomeroy reported for work in Bloomington, and his wife and children arrived a few weeks later. Since interviewing was his top priority, Kinsey pushed Pomeroy to learn the code as quickly as possible. In addition, Kinsey devoted at least two hours daily to Pomeroy's training. "I could not help being impressed from the beginning with Prok's supreme dedication," Pomeroy later wrote. "He was a fired-up human being, full of a driving resolution which he communicated to me and the other staff members."[63] And no less than the others before him, Pomeroy felt he had joined an important project. "I knew this was untrodden territory; we were pioneers," he recalled. "I was convinced from the beginning that this would be an important contribution to knowledge and science."[64]

Since office space at Indiana University was in short supply, Kinsey was fortunate to secure a large room right across the hall from his own for his growing staff. His plan was to divide the space into three separate cubicles—one for Martin, one for Pomeroy, and one for a secretary to be shared by the two men. To meet the peculiar needs of the research, Kinsey arranged with the Office of Buildings and Grounds to have these rooms soundproofed to eighty decibels, the level required to permit his assistants to conduct interviews without being overheard. When the time came to inspect the remodeling, however, Kinsey was disappointed. Sounds above forty decibels could be heard plainly. As a result, he refused to accept the offices, insisting that the soundproofing had to be raised to his original specifications. When officials protested that this would require them to tear out their work and start from scratch, Kinsey held his ground. "His insistence was characteristic; he was a perfectionist," Pomeroy later observed. "Time and again we were to see and marvel at his unflagging attention to every detail, his dogged insistence on coming as close to perfection as a human being could."[65]

Despite the office flap, Pomeroy's first few months in Bloomington were, in his words, a time "of extreme elation." Driving himself night and day, he learned the interviewing code in two months flat. Then, without permission, he taught himself a second code that served as the master key for identifying subjects whose histories were in the files. Pomeroy then proceeded to identify Kinsey's history and those of Clara and their children, not to mention those of half a dozen other people about whom he was apparently curious. "I told him at once what I had done, and at first he appeared irritated, but then was quickly pleased because I had shown myself so anxious to absorb everything as quickly as possible," Pomeroy declared. Still, he noted that Kinsey "prudently changed the coding of the names so that no new person coming to the project could do it as easily."[66]

Pomeroy's curiosity, it seems, also extended to the sex history of his wife, Martha. Soon after she arrived in Bloomington, Kinsey asked her to contribute her history, and she agreed, albeit with some reluctance. On the eve of the interview, Pomeroy realized that Martha's history would soon be in the files and that he would have access to the complete record of her private past. Apparently, it never occurred to him that he could refrain from examining his wife's history. Instead, he suggested that they swap histories. "We told each other everything we could remember, and this honesty was at once refreshing, amusing and strengthening to both of us," he later wrote. Martha's interview with Kinsey also went well. "Kinsey made the experience so easy that she could not help having a warm feeling toward him," wrote Pomeroy.[67] In the years that followed, Kinsey would test the depths of those feelings on numerous occasions.

Kinsey put Pomeroy to work as soon as he had memorized the code. The first person he interviewed was a young male college student. "Prok called these 'baby histories,' " Pomeroy later explained, "because the young men were like lambs jumping after each other and their histories were innocuous by comparison with, say, those of the inmates he had interviewed in prisons."[68] More interviews followed in quick succession, as Kinsey strove to bring his new assistant up to speed. Reporting on Pomeroy's progress, Kinsey wrote Yerkes in April 1943, "It has been a very interesting experience training him. He has just begun to take histories independently, and I have every expectation he will fit into that splendidly." Still, Kinsey sounded a note of caution. "It has become apparent, however, that it is a long time proposition to train a man to take histories, independently," he wrote, "and it may be wise for us to expand our staff not only cautiously but slowly, so that each person can be absorbed into the spirit and technique of our labor."[69]

As Pomeroy gained experience and improved his interviewing technique, Kinsey gradually exposed him to individuals whose histories presented special challenges, including prostitutes, sex offenders, and underworld figures. Pomeroy not only proved to be a quick study; he was a natural. A high-energy man with a personality a colleague once described as "zip and zap and snap-crackle-pop,"[70] Pomeroy had an interviewing technique that was penetrating and forceful, like a man digging for gold. Furthermore, he worked rapidly and had great stamina, characteristics that served him well on field trips where grueling hours were the norm. Highly competitive by nature, he pitted himself against Kinsey, refusing to stop until Kinsey broke for the day. A year after Pomeroy joined the staff, Kinsey proudly reported to Yerkes, "Pomeroy has doubled our intake."[71]

Kinsey's next hire was Robert E. Bugbee, a former graduate student who had accompanied him on extended field trips collecting gall wasps. Through correspondence, chats at professional conferences, and occasional visits back to Bloomington, Bugbee had kept in touch with Kinsey, though in truth the two men were never close, as Kinsey did not have a high opinion of Bugbee's work. Still, in January 1942, Kinsey wrote to inquire if Bugbee would agree to serve as a "contact man" at Fort Hays Kansas State College, in western Kansas, where he taught biology. Eager to escape this dead-end job and aware that he needed Kinsey's recommendation to move, Bugbee readily consented to arrange for his mentor to lecture and take histories on campus. Sensing that there might be objections from the college's administration, Kinsey cautioned, "If I can get the histories, it does not matter to me what the college authorities subsequently think about it, but I don't want to get you into trouble by any subsequent complaint from your superiors for your part in it."[72] As it happened, Kinsey's visit did not stir up any opposition, though the trip itself yielded fewer interviews than anticipated. "People in western Kansas are a bit conservative," Bugbee later explained, "and I just don't think that they offered to [give them]."[73] Still, Kinsey did manage to persuade a number of people to contribute histories, including Bugbee's wife.

Bugbee's second effort to facilitate Kinsey's research was more successful. Utilizing local contacts, he was able to put Kinsey in touch with a black minister who lived in Nicodemus. A tiny hamlet in the windswept hills of western Kansas, Nicodemus was founded by former slaves after the Civil

War. Prior to this trip, Kinsey had taken several hundred black histories, far fewer than he thought were needed to provide a reliable sample. Hoping to entice the minister to serve as his "contact man" in Nicodemus, Kinsey wrote, "We can offer one dollar to each person who contributes a history, and we can offer an additional one dollar to the contact man who is responsible for securing the history." Anyone who accepted these terms "would have the responsibility of persuading the persons who contribute that they may do so fully and completely, without fear of disclosure." Stressing that he hoped to get 150 to 200 histories in Nicodemus, Kinsey added, "This would mean that the contact man would earn quite a little money." But there was one issue that Kinsey felt obliged to raise. "If you were to help," he wrote, "I wonder if your position as a clergyman would interfere with your helping us get the histories of nonreligious persons, including prostitutes, pimps, gamblers, bootleggers and others whom we also need in our histories."[74] From the minister came the swift reply "I will do all I can to help you."[75]

In April 1943, Kinsey, accompanied by Martin and Pomeroy, arrived in Nicodemus, where they spent five days interviewing. Thanks to the enthusiastic support of the minister, they managed to collect 131 black histories on the trip, all from residents in or around Nicodemus. "There is no question that the . . . [minister] was the ideal contact man for us," Kinsey later wrote. "Without him we could never have gotten into one half the [N]egro homes we did get into."[76]

Once he had the opportunity to analyze the histories, Kinsey was struck by the wholesome portrait of the black family that emerged. "The totals and averages on all of our data are distinctly different from those of our Eastern City [N]egros, and this makes it especially valuable in our study," wrote Kinsey. Asserting that the contrasts were "obviously the result of the distinct background which these people have had," he reported that marriages in Nicodemus "have been much more stable and infinitely more successful than the marriage of the average city [N]egro. We were pleasantly surprised at this."[77]

Pomeroy, too, got a surprise during the trip. It involved a thirty-five-year-old man who was a visitor in a home where Pomeroy was conducting interviews. Before departing, Pomeroy asked the man for his history, and he consented. To ensure privacy, they got into Pomeroy's car and drove a little way into the country. Then Pomeroy stopped the car, turned off the engine, switched on the dome light, and commenced the interview. Pomeroy quickly discovered that the subject was a homosexual. "We had switched seats so that he sat behind the steering wheel, leaving me free to write," Pomeroy later wrote. "Fortunately that gave me freedom in both directions, since I found myself able to fend him off with my left hand and write with the other." Aware that this problem might occur again, Pomeroy turned to Kinsey for advice. "Kinsey taught us that the best way to handle this situation was to remain completely impassive, neither making any motion forward in an interested way, nor backing off in an obvious disinterest," Pomeroy wrote. "Nothing cools sexual ardor more than impassivity, he told us, and he was right," added Pomeroy.[78]

Several months after the Nicodemus trip, Kinsey offered Bugbee a job.[79] This was a sign of desperation, for, again, Kinsey had often been critical of Bugbee's work habits. Still, Kinsey must have felt reassured by his former student's response, as Bugbee said all the right things. Describing himself as "a firm believer," Bugbee confessed that he considered Kinsey's research "one of the greatest projects that has ever been undertaken in connection with the Human animal," and he went on to declare that he "would consider it an honor to be considered for the position."[80]

Bugbee joined the staff in the fall of 1943. He spent the first few months learning the code, reading in the library, helping out in the laboratory, and learning to take histories. Many years later, Bugbee noted that the interview training had stretched him in ways he had not expected. "I had to make some rather drastic changes in my thinking and my attitude," he declared. "I was raised in a fairly liberal Methodist minister's family, but sex was not something that we talked about," continued Bugbee. "I found that at first I was embarrassed by some of the questions and some of the information, especially that [which] was coming from many of the interviews."[81]

Because he was taught that effective interviewers had to develop "a kind of poker face," Bugbee struggled to overcome his reservations. "I tried to accept it just as another approach to a problem of biology," he explained, "and I think this helped, because I was a biologist to start with." Moreover, Bugbee had a ready answer when friends asked why he had joined Kinsey's staff, or argued that sex research was morally wrong. "I tried to explain to them that, after all, this was a pretty important part of human behavior and [that] it didn't seem to me that it was right to know more about the sex life of a drosophila [fruit fly] than about the sex life of a human."[82]

But filling a lacuna in scientific knowledge was not his sole reason for supporting the research. From numerous discussions with Kinsey, Bugbee came to understand that their work had a social purpose. "We felt this might help people, help in counseling, in keeping people together and making adjustments, marriage counseling, student counseling," he explained. Emphasizing one group in particular, Bugbee insisted that Kinsey "was very much concerned about the attitudes of people, for instance, toward the homosexual, and he felt that the homosexual never had an even break." Kinsey was driven by the hope, continued Bugbee, that "maybe if we understood them better they could find a place in society." Bugbee insisted that everyone connected with the research had "the feeling that if the real nature of human sexual behavior could be learned that a new attitude or a better attitude towards it might develop, might be an outgrowth of the study." Still, while he considered Kinsey a reformer in everything but name, Bugbee understood why his mentor always claimed to be an objective, disinterested scientist. The reason, explained Bugbee, was that Kinsey did not want people saying, "You are setting yourself up as a judge here. You are making decisions. You are deciding this person is wrong [or] this person is right."[83]

Yet Bugbee also realized that Kinsey's desire to reform social attitudes was not his only motive for becoming a sex researcher. Something deep inside made Kinsey yearn for public recognition and acclaim, needs his scholarship on gall wasps had failed to satisfy. "He once said that studying gall wasps might make some important contributions but [that] it would have never caused people to beat a path to his door," declared Bugbee.[84] And occupying the limelight was very important to Kinsey. How else could he rival Darwin? How else could he change the world?

Like other members of the staff, Bugbee was awed by Kinsey's work ethic. He was always the first to arrive at the office and the last to leave, often returning in the evening to work until after midnight. Brooking no excuses, Kinsey pushed forward even when ill. Bugbee remembered driving to the penal farm one day when Kinsey "was so sick, literally, he could hardly hold his head up." "It was the flu of some kind," Bugbee continued. "He was running a temperature, his eyes were watering; but he was going to put in a full day in spite of it." Admitting that he could not match Kinsey's dedication, Bugbee added, "And this, I think, was the problem that I faced the most with him."[85]

Often it was Bugbee's family that paid the price for the commitment Kinsey demanded. Bugbee and his wife, Peggy, had three small children when he went to work for Kinsey, and Bugbee came to dread the time away from his family he spent on field trips. Many years later, he described a trip to Philadelphia that had filled him with remorse. The outing was supposed to last only a week to ten days, but Bugbee confessed that he had left Bloomington "with a very guilty conscience," explaining that two of his children "were down with the measles, and my wife was just about frantic."[86] Unfortunately for Bugbee and his family, the interviewing went exceptionally well, and Kinsey decided to extend their stay. He was aware, of course, that Bugbee had sick children at home, but refused to cut him any slack. The work came first.

Eventually, Bugbee decided to leave. Decades later, he made no mention of sex when discussing his reasons. Instead, he stressed his desire to return to teaching and his own research. In addition, he cited family concerns, explaining that he wanted more time with his wife and children. Bugbee also complained about the social isolation he and his wife had suffered. Since he was neither a faculty member nor a graduate student, they were outside the usual friendship networks that universities provide. Although socializing with other staff members might have filled this void, his wife preferred to keep her distance from Kinsey. Bugbee later put his finger on what made her feel uncomfortable. "She always felt as though she was being kind of sized up," explained Bugbee. "She always felt a bit strange, I know, around him."[87] In August 1945, Bugbee resigned to accept a one-year, replacement job teaching beginning biology at the University of Rochester. The fact that he was willing to trade a secure position for a temporary job was a sign of how badly he wanted out. For his part, Kinsey was glad to see Bugbee go, as he had not developed into a forceful interviewer and was not a particularly hard worker in the laboratory.[88] Bugbee eventually wound up at Allegheny College, where he had a long career as a respected teacher.

Vincent Nowlis was another wartime hire who did not remain long on Kinsey's staff. A man of brilliant intellect, first-rate academic credentials, and a firm commitment to research, he had attended Bowdoin College on scholarships, pledging Zeta Psi and graduating at the top of his class in 1935 with a double major in psychology and biology, just as Kinsey had a generation earlier. But Nowlis's next stop was not Harvard but Yale, where he had earned his doctorate in psychology in 1939 under Robert Mearns Yerkes. For the next two years, Bugbee had worked at Yerkes's institute in Orange Park, before landing a teaching position at the University of Connecticut. In the spring of 1943, a colleague recommended Nowlis to Kinsey, who immediately asked Yerkes for his assessment. Eager to place one of his students on Kinsey's staff, Yerkes answered with a glowing report that filled three pages.[89]

Soon thereafter, Kinsey, with Martin and Pomeroy in tow, appeared at the front door of the converted barn that was home to Nowlis and his family. While somewhat amused by what he called Kinsey's "foolish crewcut," Nowlis found him an imposing figure, later recalling that he "looked rugged but not athletic" and "had piercing eyes." What struck him most, however, was Kinsey's "twenty-four-hour-a-day aura of authority."[90] They spent the afternoon talking, and Nowlis was impressed by Kinsey's remarks on the local flora and fauna.

Even more amazing was the enthusiasm and openness with which his visitors discussed their work. "Kinsey and the other two had a calling," explained Nowlis. "They had a mission." Their goal, he continued, was to document the infinite variety of human sexual behavior. "These guys were full of this, this vision of nobody's like anybody else," observed Nowlis.

When it came to sex, Kinsey "wanted to be the guy who knew, the guy whom other people could depend upon for knowledge"—indeed, the guy who was as "close to how God sees it as we humans can attain."[91] Before the day was over, Nowlis gave his history, joining the long list of people who surrendered to Kinsey's powers of persuasion.

In the fall 1943, Kinsey tendered an offer and Nowlis accepted, though he did not actually move to Bloomington for many months, because of uncertainty about the draft. Despite his strong academic credentials, Nowlis was an odd choice. From a personal standpoint, his was not the sort of history that appealed to Kinsey. Nowlis had been reared a Catholic, and although he had left the church by the time he entered college, he had never abandoned the moral codes of his youth. In fact, Nowlis remained deeply religious throughout his life. In no area was his moral decorum more apparent than in his private behavior. In sexual matters, Nowlis was straight as an arrow. "I didn't have premarital intercourse," he told an interviewer, noting that this was one of several revelations that did not earn him any points when Kinsey took his history. Nowlis described Kinsey as "disappointed with the fact that even though my first wife and I had an extremely intense, two-and-one-half-year courtship, we didn't have any premarital intercourse in our record," confessed Nowlis.[97]

Nor was Kinsey encouraged by Nowlis's attitude toward homosexuality. Prior to joining Kinsey's staff, his only exposure to homosexuality had occurred during his college years when a gay sailor had propositioned him. "I said, 'No, thank you,' and I shook his hand and ran home and washed my hand," recalled Nowlis. As might be expected, such homophobia concerned Kinsey. "I didn't have any indications either indirect or direct of homoerotic arousal or interest, and he was worried about that with respect to my ability," Nowlis declared.[93] Under ordinary circumstances, Kinsey would not have considered an applicant with Nowlis's sexual history and attitudes, but he was a unique case. Nowlis was a Yerkes student, and Yerkes controlled the purse strings. Kinsey had little choice but to hire him and hope for the best.

Nowlis arrived in Bloomington in June 1944, accompanied by his wife and their two young sons. Through diligent effort, he memorized the code in record time. This accomplished, Kinsey put him to work interviewing college students, the usual assignment for beginners. Socially, Kinsey tried to make him part of the team. In what amounted to command performances, Nowlis and his wife were invited to musicales at the Kinseys', as were all the senior staff members and their spouses. Because he adored classical music, Nowlis found these evenings enjoyable, despite the fact that he considered Kinsey "an authoritative, overbearing person" where music was concerned.

Yet Nowlis could not help noticing how neatly Kinsey tied his interest in classical music to his research. "One of the first questions he ever asked me when we were discussing music was 'Which music have you heard that aroused you erotically?' " recalled Nowlis. As his thoughts returned to those Sunday evenings, Nowlis painted a vivid portrait of thinly veiled voyeurism: "in those musicales, with this piercing glance of his, he would scan the intimate audience for potential signs of responsiveness at times when he thought there ought to be responsiveness." And whenever people displayed the proper reactions, added Nowlis, "he'd be delighted."[94]

Nowlis's wife, Helen, found these evenings dreadful, mainly because she wanted nothing to do with Kinsey. Like Bugbee's wife, she sensed something odd in Kinsey, something that gave her pause. "She had her concerns about him," declared Nowlis. A Ph.D. in psychology in her own right, she was the only staff wife who refused to give Kinsey her history, "not because of the substance of it," explained Nowlis, "but [because] in principle she just didn't agree with his getting this information on all of the staff members and their [spouses]." Sharpening his point, Nowlis observed, "she didn't like the . . . degree of control which somehow or other he felt he needed over his colleagues."[95]

Both at the office and on field trips, Nowlis had ample opportunities to observe the power Kinsey exercised over his staff. Not only did Kinsey find it difficult to delegate responsibilities, but he constantly checked and rechecked work he had assigned others. In addition, he expected every moment to be devoted to sex research. Nowlis recalled Kinsey's getting angry with him once during a field trip for reading a novel in the evenings instead of perusing the scientific literature or doing something else to advance the research. Interests that detracted from the research, Nowlis stressed, were "jealousy rejected."[96]

Having served as a junior member at Yerkes's research institute, Nowlis knew what it was like to be the low man on the totem pole, but nothing in his background had prepared him for the deference Kinsey demanded. It did not matter whether the issue was large or small; Kinsey had to call the shots. And one staff member in particular seemed to bear the brunt of his need to dominate and control others. "Martin was really servile," recalled Nowlis, "and Kinsey demanded that he be." Nowlis did not know what to make of what he called "this hyperdominance thing with Clyde," but he repeated that Kinsey was "very domineering."[97]

Nowlis's bewilderment reflected his total ignorance of the powerful sexual undercurrents that swirled within Kinsey's staff. Granted, there were hints Nowlis appeared not to notice. Many years later, he would recall that Pomeroy was constantly engaging in sexual banter. Then, too, there was the issue of Kinsey's inordinate interest in the private lives of his staff members. "Kinsey would very often talk to me about the sexual activity of others on the staff," Nowlis revealed. Nevertheless, he had no inkling that Kinsey or anyone else on the staff might be gay, let alone that they might be having sex with one another. "They talked about it a lot, in a kind of nonprofessional way as well as a professional way, but it never occurred to me that there was homosexual activity going on," insisted Nowlis.[98]

About six months after he joined the staff, however, Nowlis's innocence came to an abrupt end. In October 1944, Kinsey, accompanied by Martin, Pomeroy, and Nowlis, made a field trip to Columbus, Ohio, where they collected histories from juvenile delinquents at the Ohio Bureau of Juvenile Research. In the course of one such interview, Nowlis became visibly nervous and broke out in a sweat, unable to disguise his distaste for the subject's behavior. Word of his reaction got back to Kinsey, who apparently decided that the time had come to "educate" him. That evening Kinsey asked him to come to his hotel room, where Martin and Pomeroy had already assembled.

Decades later Nowlis grew tense and somber when he told what happened. Kinsey did all of the talking, while Martin and Pomeroy "were simply kind, passive observers at this point." Describing what he considered a blatant sexual overture, Nowlis declared, "Kinsey very definitely seemed to be setting up some kind of homosexual activity." As near as Nowlis could tell, his boss was offering to provide "seductive instruction" that would involve "learning plus pleasure." Freely admitting his confusion, Nowlis continued, "I didn't know what it was going to be, but it obviously would involve some kind of sexual activity on my part. And I didn't see my wife or any desirable partners, shall we say, around, and I wasn't interested." At the time, he recalled, only one thought was racing through his head: "Jesus, I'm getting out of here!"[99]

At this point, Nowlis politely declined, bolted for the door, and retreated to his room. Too upset to sleep, he spent the night pondering what to do. By sunrise he had made up his mind to leave Kinsey's staff. Allowing himself no time for second guesses, he announced his decision that very morning, and Kinsey made no effort to dissuade him. Decades later, Nowlis still felt sad about the circumstances that had prompted his resignation. The episode in the hotel room, he explained, had provided his first intimation that Kinsey was not what he seemed, that more was involved in his research than "sheer scientific outreach and enlightenment and helping all these people." The more he thought about it, the more Nowlis was amazed at how completely Kinsey and the others had managed to keep him in the dark. Nearly a year and a half had passed since their first meeting, and for six months of that time Nowlis had been on Kinsey's staff. Yet, prior to that evening, Kinsey and the others had been waiting and watching, uncertain whether to take him into their confidence. "I must have really been on probation," Nowlis explained. Still, he had the feeling that Kinsey's invitation that evening was neither spontaneous nor accidental. "He probably planned this," Nowlis mused. "It took him a year and a half to get around to it. And I said, 'No.' "[100]

In the past, Kinsey's habit of skating near the edge had often placed him in jeopardy, but somehow he had always managed to keep his balance. The failure to anticipate Nowlis's reaction, however, threatened to wreck Kinsey's career. If Yerkes got wind of what had happened, the NRC and the Rockefeller Foundation would drop Kinsey cold, as neither organization was willing to support a sex researcher whose private behavior was controversial. And no other patron would have taken their place. Kinsey's reputation would have been ruined, his days as a respected scientist ended.

Yet, amazingly, Kinsey made no effort to muzzle Nowlis. Although badly in error about Nowlis's interest in sampling homosexual sex, Kinsey apparently thought he could rely on his discretion. Instead of asking Nowlis not to tell anyone, Kinsey never broached the subject. As Nowlis put it, "He assumed I was that kind of person."

Fortunately for Kinsey, Nowlis kept his mouth shut. In his letter informing Yerkes of his resignation, Nowlis omitted any reference to Kinsey's sexual advance. "My training and background have proved to be in sharp conflict with the requirements for history-taking in this project," he wrote. This point had been driven home during a recent trip to Columbus, Nowlis explained, "when it became very clear that the complete role of interviewer as developed, so effectively, by Kinsey was basically incompatible with any role I am prepared to assume and maintain." To preclude any hint of suspicion, Nowlis offered words of reassurance, declaring, "I remain as certain as ever of the importance of this research and of Kinsey's extraordinary skill in getting histories and organizing data." Addressing Yerkes as his "friend, teacher, and colleague," Nowlis added, "As chairman of the NRC committee you will note that my decision to leave is intended in no way whatsoever to reflect on the value of the very fine work being done here."[101]

Terribly concerned about Yerkes's reaction, Kinsey, too, struggled to put the best light on the situation. Professing that he was "much disappointed" by the resignation, Kinsey went out of his way to say how much he respected Nowlis's ability and admired his "fine grasp of psychology." Kinsey also underscored Nowlis's faith in the research, insisting that his departure in no way implied criticism. In fact, he argued forcefully that Nowlis had decided to leave because he had come to realize he was not the right man for the job. The basic problem, explained Kinsey, was Nowlis's lack of experience, which made it difficult for him "to make up to the many other groups from which we are getting histories." And since it would take many years to make Nowlis feel comfortable with diverse groups, it seemed "wiser, both for him and for the research, not to spend more time on his training."[102] Yerkes was shocked and saddened by the resignation. Confessing disbelief over what he called "our failure of prophecy," Yerkes wrote Nowlis consolingly, "It does seem that among the three of us we should have been able to make safer judgment or at any rate that some one of us might have been right! This misadventure is expensive from every point of view, but I hope that it may not unfavorably penalize any of us." Acknowledging that Nowlis undoubtedly would wish to leave Bloomington "as soon as practicable," Yerkes declared, "I shall be glad to do anything possible to help you in relocating."[103] Reassured by his mentor's support, Nowlis responded like a trooper. "Everything points to a mutually satisfactory conclusion to what might have been a sorry affair, and I am keenly aware of the fact that you and Dr. Kinsey have confidence in my continued loyalty to the research. This you can depend on absolutely," Nowlis replied.[104]

Unfortunately for Nowlis, he took more than a year to find a suitable position. This was, to say the least, an awkward situation for all concerned. Dropped from the interviewing team, Nowlis spent the remainder of his tenure squirreled away in the laboratory, where he worked closely with Martin on statistical problems.[105] "To our pleasant surprise," Kinsey wrote Yerkes, "Nowlis has proved very definitely valuable to us in the process of analyzing our data for publication."[106] By and large, the months that followed were uneventful for Nowlis. Certainly, there was no repetition of what had happened in Columbus, as Kinsey avoided any hint of sexual impropriety. "He recognized something very negative and that was the end of it; never anything like that again," declared Nowlis.[107]

Early in 1946, Nowlis accepted a position at the Iowa Child Welfare Research Station at the University of Iowa. In a warm letter to Yerkes, he said that he was leaving Indiana "with sincere regret." Indeed, Nowlis was nothing if not gracious. "My two years here have been most valuable in many ways," he declared. "I know of no other place in the world where I could have learned so much in so little time, and found so many intimations of great things that are coming to enrich biological and social sciences and medical and applied arts."[108]

After Nowlis left the staff, he and Kinsey not only stayed in touch but remained on good terms. The incident in Columbus, Nowlis stressed, "was never, never referred to by either of us."[109] In the years that followed, Kinsey twice attempted to persuade him to return to the staff, but in both instances Nowlis politely but firmly declined. Eventually, he landed a job at the University of Rochester, where he spent the rest of his career.

Decades after he left the staff, he was remarkably generous when he reflected on Kinsey. "I liked Kinsey," Nowlis confessed. While Kinsey's intellectual curiosity, work ethic, loyalty to staff members, devotion to family, and love of music all appealed to Nowlis, one feature of Kinsey's character overshadowed all the rest: "I admired him because of his guts," explained Nowlis.[110]

For his part, Kinsey would be much more cautious with staff members, never again making a sexual advance without first being sure of the outcome. In addition, a new phrase appeared in the boilerplate letter he sent to prospective candidates: "We can not use anyone who is afraid of sex."[111]

While the loss of Bugbee and Nowlis within months of each other had left Kinsey shorthanded, the prospects for replacing them looked bright. The war had ended, and millions of soldiers had been discharged from the military, increasing the pool of qualified applicants. Seeking to capitalize on the situation, Kinsey worked overtime to recruit interviewers who could satisfy his stringent requirements, both personal and professional.

But as Kinsey stepped up his efforts to hire interviewers, one thing or another always seemed to prevent him from making offers. He rejected one applicant because the man's wife had a drinking problem, while another applicant failed to get the nod because he had a record of supporting labor unions and civil rights for blacks. In this latter case, Kinsey's reasoning was pragmatic, though hardly noble. Sex research was sure to generate enough critics of its own, he reasoned, without his hiring staff members who were involved with other controversial crusades.

Often Kinsey objected to the training that applicants presented. When a friend recommended a candidate with advanced degrees in education, Kinsey replied, "Frankly, I am skeptical of people who have done their work in Education, for ours is a very definite scientific problem and the people in education usually have had a minimum of contact with scientific research."[112] Similarly, Kinsey responded coolly to applicants in psychiatry. Psychiatrists, he told a friend, were trained in an interviewing technique that was "inadequate for obtaining an overall picture of sexual behavior in any large number of persons." Kinsey once boasted that his methods could obtain in a few hours nearly all of what it took psychiatrists several hundred hours to learn. Privately, he also questioned whether many psychiatrists would be willing to put in the hours required of his staff.[113]

Of course, Kinsey's objections to psychiatrists ran deeper than any doubts he may have had regarding their interviewing technique or work ethic. He regarded most psychiatrists as thinly disguised moralists who served as agents of social control. With few exceptions, he considered them the competition, the professional group he would have to unseat in the battle for cultural authority. Psychiatrists (particularly Freudians) had raised their professional banner over sex, and their definitions of normal and abnormal behavior were precisely what Kinsey meant to change. As he scoured the nation's leading universities for candidates, Kinsey's first choice was an anthropologist. A scholar trained in anthropology, he told a friend, "may have learned how to deal with people belonging to cultures other than the one in which he himself was raised." This sort of preparation struck Kinsey as particularly useful for sex researchers, since "in a way he would be doing anthropology in a diversity of cultures here at home." Among the anthropologists he contacted was Clyde Kluckhohn of Harvard University. He, in turn, suggested Paul H. Gebhard, a twenty-nine-year-old graduate student who was completing his dissertation at Harvard. Stressing that Gebhard was the only member of their current student crop whom he could recommend with confidence, Kluckhohn declared, "He has shown great capacities for adjusting himself to the most varied situations and to individuals of the most varied backgrounds." Speaking directly to the issue of attitudes, Kluckhohn assured Kinsey, "Mr. Gebhard is not afraid of sex and has certainly learned to accept any type of human behavior without judgment in terms of our own culture."[114]

Gebhard was born in 1917 in Rocky Ford, Colorado, the son of a prosperous cattle buyer father and elementary school teacher mother. After attending public schools in Denver, Gebhard spent two years at the Univeristy of Arizona before he was suspended for cutting too many Reserve Officers' Training Corps classes. Among the schools to which Gebhard then applied was Harvard College. To his surprise he was accepted. Confessing that his first days in the East involved "a little culture shock," Gebhard later recalled, "When I arrived in Boston I came wearing a velveteen Navaho shirt, a Navaho bracelet, and high heel cowboy boots. You can imagine how well I fitted in for the first few weeks."[115] But settle in Gebhard did, receiving his B.S. in anthropology, cum laude (1940), and his Ph.D. in physical anthropology (1947), with fields in archaeology and social anthropology. Along the way, he married Agnes West, a graduate of Radcliffe College.

Acting on Kluckhohn's recommendation, Kinsey wrote Gebhard in May 1946. It was the usual boilerplate letter describing his staff needs and the research, complete with the warning "We can not use anyone who is afraid of sex."[116] As it happened, Gebhard already had a job offer from another institution. Still, he was fascinated by Kinsey's description of the research. "It is high time for sexual behavior to be taken out of the mysticism of Ellis and the archives of psychopathology and subjected to a broad and truly scientific scrutiny," he told Kinsey. "My main value to you," Gebhard continued, "would lie in interviewing since I have had considerable experience interviewing both normals and psychoneurotics at the Psychiatric Laboratory of the Massachusetts General Hospital." Proud of his personal maturity and professionalism, he asserted, "I am not, as you put it, 'afraid of sex' and I have largely outgrown the vicarious pleasure which many experience in discussing sexual matters." Then Gebhard said something that must have been music to Kinsey's ear: "Abnormal sexual behavior does not repel me . . . in fact, I'm beginning to suspect that our concept of the norm is too restricted when applied to actuality."[117]

Suddenly, it was Kinsey's turn to be intrigued. As it happened, he had a trip planned to the East, and he arranged to interview Gebhard the following week. In June 1946, they met in Kinsey's room at the Astor Hotel in New York City for an evening appointment. Naturally, Kinsey asked Gebhard for his history, and he agreed. "I remember being very impressed by the way in which he established rapport, put me at ease, and then tenaciously went after the information that he wanted," declared Gebhard. As an interviewer, Kinsey never engaged in "free association or rambling," continued Gebhard. "He was in control every second. But he did it in such a clever and unobtrusive way that you were scarcely aware that you were being controlled as to the subject matter throughout the interview." Commenting on the look in Kinsey's eyes, Gebhard observed that "one got the impression of great interest, and not only interest but sympathetic interest," which made it "very easy to talk to the man."[118]

Following the interview, they began to discuss sex research, and Kinsey asked what he thought about homosexuality. "I pontifically told him that I considered it some disturbance of the hormones, some endocrinological dysfunction or imbalance," Gebhard recalled. Uttering not a word of remonstration, Kinsey then asked what he thought about the incidence of homosexuality. Gebhard replied that it was "quite rare."[119] At this point, Kinsey suggested a little fieldwork, and he took Gebhard to Grand Central Station. On the way, Kinsey asked if he had ever used the rest room there, and Gebhard replied that he had done so many times. Then Kinsey inquired if he had ever observed any homosexual activity in the rest room, and Gebhard's response was negative.

What happened when they reached Grand Central Station was a real eye-opener for Gebhard. Like a teacher with a schoolboy, Kinsey marched him to the head of the stairs leading down the basement to the public urinal. Instead of descending to the bottom, however, they stopped about halfway, just far enough to be able to see everyone in the room. At this point, Kinsey turned and asked Gebhard how long he thought it took for a man to urinate. "Oh, I don't know. A couple of minutes, I guess," Gebhard remembered saying. Kinsey suggested that they should just stand there and watch.

To Gebhard's amazement, a world he had never noticed appeared before his eyes. Eight or nine men were migrating from one urinal to another, washing their hands, drying them, milling around, and then coming back to the urinals. Describing what happened next, Gebhard declared, "He [Kinsey] said, 'Gebhard, those are homosexuals. They are looking for partners. So, now what do you think about the incidence of homosexuality?'" Shamefaced, Gebhard confessed that he had been to that rest room a dozen times without seeing a thing. "You never looked," he remembered Kinsey's replying. "As an anthropologist you should have observed this." Looking back on this exchange, Gebhard observed, "I felt very humiliated that I hadn't."[120]

At this point, Kinsey and Gebhard returned to the hotel to talk some more. Around 3:00 A.M., Gebhard suddenly realized the hour was late, offered his apologies, and prepared to leave. Asked if he had a place to stay, Gebhard replied that he had failed to make a reservation. Remarking that his hotel room had double beds, Kinsey then invited him to spend the night, and Gebhard accepted. "We both went to bed, and I must say I didn't sleep very much, because Kinsey snored," Gebhard later recalled. The next thing he knew Kinsey was shaking him, saying it was 8:00 A.M. and the first morning appointment would be there soon. Groggy from lack of sleep, Gebhard dressed, staggered to the door, said good-bye, and left for Boston, as he put it, "very impressed, [and] thinking about all he told me."[121]

Within a few weeks, a letter arrived inviting Gebhard and his wife to Bloomington for a job interview. Feeling he had nothing to lose, Gebhard accepted. "For four days he and Pomeroy and Martin . . . put me through a real interrogation," Gebhard declared. "I was aware of this because when one of them was talking to me, the other two were always watching me. I had this feeling that they were noting all of my reactions and that sort of thing." His wife was "also examined," he stressed, though she was "subject to a somewhat lesser scrutiny."[122] The grilling came to a halt during a midnight conference in Kinsey's office when he abruptly offered Gebhard a job at the generous salary of $4,400 per year, which was $400 higher than his other offer. Without a moment's hesitation, Gebhard shot back, "You've got yourself a man!"[123]

Reflecting on Kinsey's motives decades later, Gebhard explained that he was hired "because as an anthropologist I had been thoroughly imbued with the idea of cultural relativism, that other people did not necessarily behave like I did or that other people in my culture behaved." With an opaque reference to Nowlis, Gebhard also stressed Kinsey's need for someone who could deal with lower social levels. "He [Kinsey] had had some difficulty with prior people on the staff who had spent all of their lives in the ivory towers of academe, and hence couldn't relate very well to lower social levels," observed Gebhard. In his case, he continued, this was not a problem, "because having been brought up in the West [he] had rubbed shoulders with ranchers and hardrock miners and Mexicans."[124]

Despite Kinsey's urgent need for interviewers, Gebhard remained in the East for two months, mostly to complete the requirements for his degree, but also to take a brief vacation before reporting for work. Writing from a cabin in the piney woods of Maine, where he was putting the finishing touches on his dissertation, Gebhard sent reassurances of his devotion to the project. "I'm anxious to join you and begin my training," he told Kinsey. "The sooner I can become useful to the project the better, and I hope I prove an apt pupil." Gebhard was sincere, as he was completely sold on the research. With obvious pride in his voice, he later observed, "I felt frankly that I had gotten in on the ground floor of research that was going to have far-reaching implications for the study of human behavior." Not everyone agreed with his decision to work for Kinsey, however. His parents, admitted Gebhard, "were definitely embarrassed by my being in sex research, and concealed this for many years from their friends."[125]

Traveling alone because his wife and young son had to remain in the East for a few months to tie up loose ends, Gebhard arrived in Bloomington in mid-August 1946. His training commenced immediately. "The first thing I had to do, which was an incredible job, was memorize the interview," he recalled. As it had for those before him, this entailed memorizing the questions, the alternate forms in which the questions could be phrased, the exact spot on the code sheet where the information was to be placed, and so on. Kinsey and Pomeroy really put him through the wringer, administering thorough examinations almost daily. Commenting on these sessions, Gebhard later remarked, "If I didn't have the phraseology right or if I got out of sequence, I heard about it immediately."[126]

Once he had memorized the questions, Gebhard graduated to simulated interviews. "Kinsey and Pomeroy would pretend to be a person of some particular type or social level or something, and then I would interview them and record," explained Gebhard. "At the conclusion of this then they would mercilessly pick me apart," he winced, "showing me where I hadn't recorded it properly or where I had goofed in the thing." Decades later, Gebhard's face grew pained when he added, "It was equivalent to having a final examination every few days. One couldn't help but feel that one's competence was at stake."[127]

After a few months, practice runs gave way to the real thing—interviews with college students, with Kinsey sitting in. Confessing that he found these even more stressful than the mock interviews, Gebhard recalled that Kinsey would remain silent while the sessions proceeded, but once they concluded, the criticism began. "If you had done things almost perfectly," explained Gebhard, "he would say grudgingly, 'Well, you are much improved.' But that was about the highest praise one could anticipate. Ordinarily, he would mercilessly pick out each error and bring it to your attention."[128]

As he gained experience and confidence, Gebhard shifted to more difficult interviews. Still, he did not work with lower-class subjects until two years after joining the staff. "It wasn't until three years that they'[d] let me interview special groups like prostitutes or homosexuals," he recalled.[129] Over time, Gebhard developed into a resolute interviewer, described by one colleague as "dogged, persistent and low-keyed."[130]

Of all his associates in sex research, Kinsey probably respected Gebhard the most professionally, as he alone was well trained and possessed a scholar's soul. Moreover, Gebhard was a very likable man. Six feet tall, with a mustache and reddish hair that receded into a widow's peak, he wore his double Ivy pedigree lightly, largely because he was blessed with a terrific sense of humor. If anything, he was relaxed and witty, as comfortable making small talk as Kinsey was ill at ease.

And Gebhard was definitely not "sex shy," a fact he punctuated by having an affair almost immediately after he moved to Bloomington. He was not interested sexually in Kinsey or the other male staff members, for Gebhard was decidedly "straight" in his private life. Because his sexual attitudes were liberal, however, he felt drawn to the free and easy sexual atmosphere Kinsey had fostered among his senior staff members and their wives. Explaining that his wife and son were not able to join him until November, leaving him alone for three months, Gebhard later confessed with a chuckle, "I was ripe for a little extramarital activity if it were available."[131]

Within days after arriving in Bloomington, Gebhard started an affair with Alice Martin. "Kinsey had no objection to interstaff sex. In fact, he sort of encouraged it," revealed Gebhard. The problem in this instance was that the relationship quickly started to heat up, threatening to become serious. "He [Kinsey] felt that Alice was getting too involved with me because at that particular moment she was having some trouble with Clyde," continued Gebhard. To prevent things from escalating, Kinsey spoke with Gebhard, telling him "to cool it" because Clyde and Alice's marriage was being damaged. An apostle of sexual freedom, Kinsey took no joy in ordering the affair ended. According to Gebhard, "He made some remark about he didn't like to interfere. He put this rather gently, but his eyes were brimming."[132]

Decades later, Gebhard denied that the affair had damaged his relationship with Martin. Describing Martin as "a tolerant person" and "kind of a gentle person, too," Gebhard declared, "If it caused any hard feelings toward me he never expressed them."[133] Gebhard was badly mistaken, because Martin was emotionally crushed. In retrospect, Martin called his wife's affair "very brief but very intense" and confessed, "[It] was very upsetting to me, and I thought my world was crumbling."[134] While Martin feared for his marriage, this may not have been his only concern. Given his lowly status on the staff, he must have felt deeply humiliated by the ease with which a fresh recruit who was higher in the pecking order could move in on his wife. Martin had lost face, as sexual prowess counted mightily within Kinsey's inner circle.

By the end of 1946, then, Kinsey had assembled his team—Martin, Pomeroy, and Gebhard, three fiercely loyal men who shared his sexual attitudes, knew his secrets, and supported his plan for using science to reform the sexual mores of American society. At first glance, they appeared to have little in common. One was a lowly factotum, another a covert Don Juan, and the last a free spirit who saw human sexuality as anthropology's next great frontier. Yet in hiring these men, Kinsey knew exactly what he was doing. The survivors of a process of attrition that had seen one interviewer trainee depart for every one who stayed, Martin, Pomeroy, and Gebhard would stick around to the end, providing Kinsey with the "hands" he needed, and the loyalty he demanded.

From Kinsey's perspective, they were ideal. Awed by the force of his personality, inspired by the depth of personal commitment, and intoxicated by the heady brew of sexual liberation, they could be counted on to follow him anywhere. Ironically, it was Nowlis who struck the perfect metaphor, likening their demimonde to "a submarine, moving in a self-contained world with a commander directing every movement, and the crew utterly dependent on him and on each other because the craft was so vulnerable. No one could afford to make a mistake."[135]

They had good reason to feel in jeopardy. As they steamed toward the publication, Kinsey's scientific curiosity, private sexual needs, and penchant for courting danger drove him to take risks that threatened to destroy both him and his crew. To shift the metaphor slightly, it was as though Kinsey had become Ahab, tossing his quadrant into a troubled sea and hurling his crew against his personal Moby Dick, Victorian morality. Dangerous waters lay ahead.

21

"A REPORT ON WHAT PEOPLE DO"

T he last interview was over and night had fallen, Kinsey's favorite time of day. With the return of darkness, he could pursue the research he found most satisfying, even though it had to be hidden from the public. Everything had been arranged. At Kinsey's request, Wardell Pomeroy had made an appointment to have sex with a female friend who had agreed to let others watch. The exhibition promised to be memorable. Pomeroy's sexual prowess was a matter of record, and his partner for the evening, a professional woman by training, was said to be highly responsive. Equally important, she was known for her discretion, a quality demanded by Kinsey, who required Pomeroy (and every other member of the inner circle) to seek advance approval before having extramarital sex with anyone. This condition was hardly pro forma. As Gebhard later explained, "if Kinsey had had any qualms about any of the female partners he would have simply said, 'No, I won't allow it.' "[1] Pomeroy, of course, was only too happy to play by the rules. He enjoyed having sex with a variety of partners, and he relished these opportunities to demonstrate his virtuoso techniques before an audience.

Over time, Kinsey had become astonishingly bold about inviting people to these demonstrations. In the 1940s and 1950s, he asked a number of trusted friends outside the staff to join him as observers, ostensibly to pick their brains, but also, one suspects, to enhance his own pleasure. Watching others have sex satisfied both the scientist and the voyeur in Kinsey. Emphasizing the essential paradox of a man whose interests in sex ran at right angles, one former staff member, Vincent Nowlis, described Kinsey's reactions as "orthogonal." Kinsey's complex personality, Nowlis explained, brought him down on both sides of the equation, "high on the scientific-objective and high on the prurient."[2]

On this particular evening in the late 1940s, Kinsey's guest was Frank Beach. As their acquaintance had deepened into friendship, Kinsey had taken Beach into his confidence, at least to a point. Together, they had explored Times Square, visited gay bathhouses and bars, and hung out in various parks and tea rooms (public urinals) where homosexuals congregated to find partners for anonymous sex. It was easy for Kinsey to justify this fieldwork. A lifelong naturalist with a keen appreciation for what could be learned by the naked eye, he knew that direct observation has probably led to more discoveries than any other method in history. He was also the last researcher in the world who would allow prudery to prevent him from observing human sexual behavior. Beach shared these values. As a fellow scientist, he believed that researchers should not limit themselves to books and interviews but must observe human behavior whenever possible, recording their observations with scientific detachment and personal disinterest.

Cold objectivity was the ideal. It was also difficult to achieve, as Beach quickly discovered when he accompanied Kinsey to watch Pomeroy and his friend perform that evening. Decades later, Beach admitted that his façade of professional disinterest quickly gave way to passion, making him feel more like a Peeping Tom than a scientific observer. In his words, Pomeroy and his partner "really got after it," and before Beach knew it, he found himself becoming sexually aroused.[3] Embarrassed, he checked to see how Kinsey was reacting. To his amazement, Beach suddenly realized that Kinsey was virtually on top of the action, his head only inches removed from the couple's genitals, close enough to smell body odors and hear the squish of juices. And above the groans and moans, Kinsey could be heard chattering away, pointing out various signs of sexual arousal as the couple progressed through the different stages of intercourse. In Beach's estimation, no observer had a keener eye for detail. Nothing escaped Kinsey's notice—not the subtle change in the breast's skin tone that accompanied tumescence during arousal, not the involuntary twitch of the muscles in the anus upon orgasm—Kinsey saw everything. At one level, it was all very analytic and detached. As Beach looked closer, however, he was certain he detected a gleam of desire in Kinsey's eyes, a look that grew more intense as the action built to a climax.[4]

The beauty of sex research was that it allowed Kinsey to transform his voyeurism into science. Former staff members recall that Kinsey started observing live sex fairly early in the research. Offering his version of how it began, Pomeroy described an incident involving a black female prostitute in Indianapolis. In the course of her interview, noted Pomeroy, the woman mentioned that her "spur tongue," the term she used for her clitoris, was two inches long. Skeptical, Kinsey challenged her on the spot. For an additional dollar (he had already given her a small sum for her interview), she agreed to undress and let Kinsey see for himself. "This observation of anatomical differences—and it typified the kind of research Kinsey knew would be attacked if it was known—was the first step toward observing actual behavior," wrote Pomeroy.[5]

Other steps quickly followed. Nowlis recalled hearing Kinsey talk about "sex shows that [Kinsey] got some of his contacts in Indianapolis to put on."[6] Martin adds that Kinsey and Pomeroy "went to steam baths on occasions and they saw sexuality going on there."[7] Decades later, of course, research scientists and clinicians would be able to observe and photograph human sexual behavior openly, with little opposition from the public. Researchers such as William Masters and Virginia Johnson of Washington University in St. Louis, would become famous for their groundbreaking work in this area. But the real pioneer was Kinsey.

Over time, he developed a remarkable network of individuals who were willing to perform while others watched. In any of half a dozen cities, he could pick up the telephone, contact trusted confidants, and stage sex that evening. Many of these individuals Kinsey recruited personally. Others came to his attention through various "contact men" who knew people with more than a trace of exhibitionism in their case histories.

Among these "contact men," none worked harder for Kinsey than Robert Latou Dickinson, a retired New York gynecologist and pioneering sex researcher. After receiving his medical degree in 1882 from Long Island College Hospital, Dickinson began his professional career in Brooklyn Heights. By the late 1890s, he had built a lucrative practice shaded toward obstetrics and gynecology, with patients who included many socially prominent women. Financially secure, he retired early in the 1920s, only to begin a second career as a sex researcher and the medical profession's most influential advocate of birth control. At the same time that Margaret Sanger was fighting to make contraception both available and acceptable to the American public, Dickinson led the crusade to persuade physicians to make birth control available to their patients. Close medical friends recalled that he could bring any conversation around to birth control in ten minutes or less. Dickinson's crowning achievement came in 1937 when the American Medical Association passed a resolution stating that physicians should follow their patients' wishes with regard to dispensing birth control information.[8]

Personally, Dickinson was a Christian gentleman and a habitual do-gooder who sprinkled his conversations with the acclamation "Glory to God." As a vestryman of Holy Trinity Episcopal Church, he supported lib-eral clergymen who advocated the social gospel, demonstrating his own commitment to the poor by assuming a heavy load of charity cases. Nor was he afraid to dirty his hands in politics. Plunging into the political fray, he served as a Republican ward captain in the campaign to reform Brook-lyn government.

Dickinson's interest in women's issues sprang from his medical specialty. Constitutionally incapable of inaction when he spotted something wrong, he devoted much of his energy to fighting social conventions and gender roles that confined women. Aghast at the fashion world, Dickison soundly condemned corsets, arguing that they restricted women's movements and deformed their bodies. During the 1890s, he dove headfirst into the great cycling debate. At a time when many of his colleagues condemned the new fad of cycling as unladylike or, worse yet, a practice that might "beget or foster the habit of masturbation," Dickinson urged women to take up "wheeling." Bicycle riding, he insisted, was both innocent recreation and good exercise.[9]

Dickinson's interest in sex research, it seems, grew out of his efforts to combine the roles of physician and marriage counselor. A resolute Victo-rian who routinely referred to his wife, Sarah, as "my dear lady," he was completely devoted to the preservation and promotion of marriage in a changing world. Yet Dickinson was also one of those Victorians who helped change his times. As a result of numerous conferences with pa-tients, he believed that sexual ignorance was at the root of many marital problems. Convinced that a healthy sex life was the key to happy marriage, he was determined to educate the public about sex and to promote new at-titudes that celebrated sex as healthy and good.

Dickinson practiced what he preached. Not only did he shatter the con-spiracy of silence by discussing and writing about sexual matters in plain language, he was unabashedly enthusiastic about sex. A proponent of more and better sex within the institution of marriage, he demanded complete equality in erotic pleasure for both sexes. Every sexual union, he main-tained, should end in mutual bliss: any husband who did not leave his wife sexually satisfied had failed to perform his manly duties. And like Kinsey's, Dickinson's approach to sex was at once materialistic and mech-anistic. In sexual relationships, he intoned, "harmony must come, or a reason [be] found." Some adjustments might require changes in technique, but in many cases "patience and desire and the use of vaseline will overcome all difficulty."[10]

Like Kinsey, Dickinson was a master at inspiring trust. Sensing a sympathetic spirit and a kind soul, many of his patients poured out their woes to him. "I don't know by what magic RLDism you broke my inability to take care of my particular problem . . . ," wrote one grateful woman. *"Before,* I'd gotten it entangled with all the inter-personal highly emotive values I have always connected with a love relation, but putting it in purely physiological terms . . . gave it a whole different semantic meaning, and one I can happily accept."[11]

This ability to win confidence enabled Dickinson to persuade women to answer questions and to participate in studies few physicians dared to conduct. By the late 1920s, he had compiled 5,200 heavily illustrated case histories (he was an anatomical artist of great skill) and 1,200 detailed sex histories. In addition, he had completed numerous scientific experiments, some of which required him to handle female sex organs. In one such study, Dickinson sought to learn if popular reports of the vagina's gripping the penis during coitus could be confirmed. To measure the pressure exerted by the levator ani muscle during contraction, he inserted a wax phallus into the vagina of his subjects (domestic servants), who were instructed to contract the muscle firmly. Captured in indelible impressions, the data showed that the levator ani gripped the penis with powerful contractions. This finding was important, he argued, because it altered medical science's understanding of how conception occurred, suggesting that the rubbing of semen against the os played a key role in the sperm's journey to the mucus of the cervix.[12]

Their mutual interest in sex research eventually brought Kinsey and Dickinson together. When Kinsey published his article in 1941 debunking the theory that homosexuality was a glandular disorder, Dickinson was impressed. In a warm, handwritten letter, he praised the article's scientific rigor, declaring with characteristic exuberance, "You see I do not even wait for a stenographer before greeting the discovery of a discoverer." Kinsey's reply was gracious: "It was your own work which turned my attention to the purposes of research in this field some 10 or 12 years ago although circumstances were not propitious for starting the work until three years ago."[13]

More letters followed, leading to a meeting between the two sex researchers in New York in January 1943. After spending the better part of two days with Dickinson, Kinsey was captivated. And well he should have been. A geriatric marvel, Dickinson radiated energy, carried himself erect as a flagpole, dressed smartly, and sported an immaculately groomed

Vandyke. His speech was animated and rapid, as if to keep pace with his nimble mind and the brisk clip at which he walked, and his body language was remarkably agile, testifying to decades of vigorous exercise as an avid walker, cycler, and sailor. As one historian has noted, Dickinson at the age of eighty-five "could still do a flip across two canoes into New Hampshire's Squam Lake. Dickinson himself took an impish delight in being elderly, remarking to a friend, "There's nothing like a gray Van Dyke and crow's feet to each temple . . . to get you past the people who are hired to keep you out."[14]

Ordinarily, no one could outtalk Dickinson, but Kinsey was no ordinary man. During their meetings in New York, it was Kinsey who dominated the discussion, describing his research with riveting passion and admirable clarity. Impressed by what he heard, Dickinson decided then and there to anoint this earnest professor from the Midwest as his successor. He offered to open his research files, to provide advice, and to plug Kinsey into his vast network of contacts. "I am overwhelmed at your willingness to give me access to your materials, to give me the benefit of your own experience, and to actively cooperate at certain angles," wrote Kinsey. "Of course I shall take advantage of this on a very extensive scale," he continued. "The research is not for myself but for the elucidation of a badly neglected field, and I am capable of considerable immodesty in asking for help in pushing the research." Turning to the issue that was always at the top of his list, Kinsey added, "I do want to get your help on the intersex [homosexual] study."[15]

Dickinson was as good as his word. Whispering in ears that mattered, he assured the Rockefeller Foundation's Alan Gregg in January 1943 that Kinsey's sex histories were not only "the largest in numbers and the most varied for range of intelligence and social status, but the most important and fullest for detail, of any series so far gathered or analyzed." Expressing his personal pleasure that Kinsey had arrived on the scene, Dickinson added, "I think you can imagine what it means to an Ancient to find someone who would be willing to shoulder a frayed mantle."[16]

In December 1943, Dickinson visited Bloomington as Kinsey's houseguest during the Christmas holidays. Mindful of his opportunity to cement their relationship, Kinsey gave his distinguished visitor "the treatment." This consisted of a dinner party and musicale in Dickinson's honor, accompanied by four days of nonstop sex talk, most of it in Kinsey's suite of offices at the university. With the intensity of a zealot, Kinsey discussed his methodology, findings, and research goals, and showed him the library. The results were predictable: Dickinson was completely won over and contributed his history before leaving town.

After he returned to New York, Dickinson worked hard to advance Kinsey's research. During his long career as a sex researcher, Dickinson had encountered many remarkable characters, some with case histories of the sort sexologists reported in scholarly journals. These were the prizes he bestowed upon Kinsey. With Kinsey in tow, Dickinson rushed around New York digging up people with unorthodox sex histories for interviews. They included homosexual males with vast knowledge of gay culture and extensive friendship networks in New York and beyond; lesbians who fit the same description; heterosexual females who were willing to engage in a variety of sexual activities while scientists observed; and several individuals with sexual interests that would have taxed a taxonomist to classify.

For sheer perversity, the jewel of Dickinson's collection was a man we shall call Mr. X. His bizarre sexual behavior, it seems, was a family legacy. The product of a home poisoned by cross-generational incest, he had sex with his grandmother when he was still a young child, as well as with his father. In the years that followed, the boy had sexual relations with seventeen of the thirty-three relatives with whom he had contact. And this was just the beginning. After he reached adulthood, Mr. X was obsessed with sex, a walking id with polymorphous erotic tastes. By the time Dickinson brought him to Kinsey's attention, wrote Pomeroy, "This man had had homosexual relations with 600 preadolescent males, heterosexual relations with 200 preadolescent females, intercourse with countless adults of both sexes, with animals of many species, and besides had employed elaborate techniques of masturbation."[17] Mr. X had also compiled a sizable collection of erotic photographs, and he had made extensive notes on all his sexual activities, chronicling not only his behavior and reactions but those of his partners and victims.

These notes included a detailed record of his life as a tireless and unbelievably resourceful voyeur. College educated, Mr. X had held responsible positions with the government that required considerable travel. On each trip, he had carried along a special kit of tools that he used to drill holes through hotel walls to spy on the guests in adjacent rooms. For hours on end, he would peer through these peepholes, recording in minute detail every sexual act he observed. Together with his written remarks about his own sexual exploits, Mr. X's hotel materials did for Americans what Samuel Pepys did for the seventeenth-century English court—they pulled back the sheets and provided the kind of firsthand observations scientists coveted but rarely obtained.

Armed with an introduction from Dickinson as his entree, Kinsey began his courtship of Mr. X in the fall of 1943. A genius at manipulating people, Kinsey seemed to know which buttons to push. In this instance, he correctly divined that Mr. X longed for recognition and approval. From the beginning, therefore, Kinsey treated him like a colleague, a fellow seeker of truth who had compiled valuable scientific data. In a letter that combined flattery and praise, Kinsey wrote, "I congratulate you on the research spirit which has lead you to collect data over these many years." Stressing that he was "very much interested in your account of hotel observations," Kinsey asked, "Do you have more case history material of the sort which you tabulated for Dr. Dickinson? Would it be possible for us to see a series of the photographs which you sent to Dr. Dickinson?" Then, in the best tradition of collegial support, Kinsey added, "There are difficulties enough in this undertaking to make it highly desirable for all of us who are at work to keep in touch. I hope we can keep in touch with you."[18]

Much to Kinsey's delight, the materials arrived by return mail, the first of many shipments over the next several years. "Your instant willingness to cooperate, and your comprehension of the problem involved in these studies, make me all the more anxious to meet you," replied Kinsey. Entreating his quarry to come to Bloomington, he declared, "Mrs. Kinsey and I should be glad to entertain you in our home."[19] When his invitation failed to produce a houseguest, Kinsey did not lose heart. Instead, he concentrated on prying loose additional data, reassuring Mr. X again and again that his experiences were scientifically valuable and had to be preserved for posterity. "You must not, under any condition, destroy your materials," pleaded Kinsey in May 1944. "It is unique in its value. There is nothing else quite like it and nothing that has been published in the scientific literature. Everything that you accumulated must find its way into scientific channels."[20]

As the months passed, Kinsey became more and more anxious to interview Mr. X. Pressing hard for a meeting, he renewed his invitation for Mr. X to come to Bloomington and offered to travel to the Southwest if necessary. "If expense is any factor in limiting your trip East, we can cover a good part of that expense for you," wrote Kinsey. "We really ought to have two or three days, and preferably more, in which to discuss our material and to work out further plans for cooperating with you; so wherever we meet, I hope it will allow us time enough to really cover the ground."[21]

Finally, Mr. X consented, agreeing to rendezvous at a site about fifty miles from his home so that the meeting would go unnoticed. In June 1944, Kinsey and Pomeroy traveled some eighteen hundred miles to interview Mr. X, their longest trip ever to take a single history. "At the time we saw him," wrote Pomeroy, "this man was sixty-three years old, quiet, soft-spoken, self-effacing—a rather unobtrusive fellow." Despite his unprepossessing appearance, it took a record seventeen hours to record Mr. X's case history, which as Pomeroy put it, "astounded even us, who had heard everything." Equally amazing was the little demonstration that occurred partway through the interview. In response to the questions on masturbation, Mr. X described his various techniques, casually mentioning that he could still start at a flaccid state, achieve an erection, and ejaculate in ten seconds flat. "Kinsey and I, knowing how much longer it took everyone else, expressed our disbelief," Pomeroy later wrote, "whereupon our subject calmly demonstrated it to us."[22]

After the interview, Kinsey went after Mr. X's materials in earnest. Like so many others before him, Mr. X agreed to cooperate. Over the next few years, he kept the postal service to Bloomington hot, shipping materials that included diaries, case histories of some of the people with whom he had had sex, his private collection of erotic photographs, and a large collection of penis measurements. Each batch whetted Kinsey's appetite for more. Over and over, he played to Mr. X's vanity, praising these materials as unique and extremely valuable to science. "I rejoice at everything you send," he wrote after the arrival of one particularly large shipment, "for I am then assured that that much more of your material is saved for scientific publication."[23]

A less ardent and more careful researcher might have hesitated to embrace these materials, but not Kinsey. In his search for data, he was like a human vacuum cleaner, sucking up everything in his path. As a result, he was often uncritical and at times even careless about the data he collected. Anyone who had material on human sexual behavior was fair game, and he usually succeeded in persuading people to turn over what they had. Then, following the same procedure he employed with Mr. X, Kinsey would translate as much of these materials as possible into his own code, making it part of the Institute's aggregate data. Former staff members recall that Kinsey often remarked, "Our data shows such and such," when referring to materials that only recently had been subsumed into his own data after being contributed by someone else.

Owing to the criminal nature of many of the sexual acts Mr. X had committed and had chronicled with such care, Kinsey handled these materials with even greater caution than usual. Keeping the clerical staff at arm's length, he personally opened the packages from Mr. X and entrusted the copying to Clara alone. When one shipment appeared to get misplaced, Kinsey gave a timely reckoning the minute it was found. "It arrived while I was in New York," he explained, "and my wife put it in a hidden place in order to protect it. . . . You may be interested to know that my wife is very much interested in the research and has cooperated to the absolute limit."[24] A few months later, Kinsey again underscored the precautions he was taking, as well as Clara's contributions. "My wife has started in copying the case material," he wrote, "and we will return copies to you with the originals."[25]

Perusing these materials only increased Kinsey's determination to exhaust Mr. X's collections and personal expertise. In March 1945, Kinsey offered to pay Mr. X's salary if he would take a leave from government and pull together his materials.[26] When Mr. X declined, Kinsey peppered him with additional questions. Confessing that his own data on preadolescent orgasms were "definitely scant," Kinsey wrote to Mr. X in March 1945, "Certainly you have very much more material than we have in our records." Specifically, Kinsey asked for information about the average age at which orgasm occurred in preadolescent boys, their capacity for multiple orgasms, and the earliest age at which orgasms have been observed in boys. So vast were Mr. X's records that it took months for him to search his files and pull this material together. Kinsey was delighted by the results. "This is one of the most valuable things we have ever gotten, and I want to thank you most abundantly for the time you put into it and for your willingness to cooperate," declared Kinsey. "We have carefully gone through all of the published literature, and there is nothing on this preadolescent story in the published histories," he continued. "We have several hundred histories who have given record of preadolescent climaxes but your material fortifies this so abundantly that it will make a very definite contribution. Anyone who is scientifically trained must comprehend how valuable the data are."[27]

By 1946, Kinsey was at work on his first book on human sexuality, and he asked Mr. X to read and criticize those portions of the manuscript that dealt with preadolescent development and behavior. After several written requests failed to produce results, Kinsey decided that a second visit was in order and made a special trip to Mr. X's hometown. As requested, Mr. X gave the manuscript a careful reading, and his critique pleased Kinsey. Upon returning to Bloomington, he wrote on Christmas Eve 1946, "I very much appreciated your reading of the manuscript. It helps very much to have one with your experience going over the material." Emphasizing how much he valued Mr. X's contributions, Kinsey added almost wistfully, "I wish our paths could cross more often. It would be most profitable for science."[28]

Science would have been better served had Kinsey not allowed his lust for data to obscure his judgment. Viewed from any angle, his relationship with Mr. X was a cautionary tale. Whatever the putative value to science of Mr. X's experiences, the fact remains that he was a predatory pedophile. Over the course of his long career as a child molester, he masturbated infants, penetrated children, and performed a variety of other sexual acts on preadolescent boys and girls alike. Betraying a huge moral blind spot, Kinsey took the records of Mr. X's criminal acts and transformed them into scientific data. Indeed, prior to publication Kinsey expressed his disappointment over not being able to acknowledge publicly Mr. X's contributions, telling him, "I wish I knew how to give credit to you in the forthcoming volume for your material. It seems a shame not even to name you."[29]

Kinsey's debt to Mr. X was indeed great. Chapter 5 of the finished book, "Early Sexual Growth and Activity," offered a finely graded discussion of preadolescent male sexuality, and much of this chapter was based on materials Mr. X had provided.[32] In presenting this material, Kinsey adopted a tone that was candid and matter-of-fact, whether discussing his sources or the boys themselves. He made absolutely no effort to soft-pedal anything. The boys under consideration, Kinsey reported, ranged from fifteen-year-old adolescents all the way down to two-month-old infants. His data, Kinsey stipulated, came from adults who answered questions about their childhood and from "older subjects who have had sexual contacts with younger boys." Further into the chapter, the text and charts suggested that infants less than a year old had been stimulated (pronounced "molested") and observed for as long as an hour at a stretch; four-year-olds for as many as twenty-four hours. Referring to an unidentified source who sounded very much like Mr. X, Kinsey even reported that one of his subjects had had sexual "contacts with certain males over long periods of years (as many as sixteen years in some cases), from their early pre-adolescence into their late teens and twenties."[31]

On the basis of these sources, Kinsey calmly proceeded to describe orgasms in children in graphic detail. In one category of boys, he noted, "the legs often become rigid, with muscles knotted and toes pointed, muscles of abdomen contracted and hard, shoulders and neck stiff and often bent forward, breath held or gasping, eyes staring or tightly closed, hands grasping, mouth distorted, sometimes with tongue protruding; whole body or parts of it spasmodically twitching, sometimes synchronously with throbs or violent jerking of the penis." These same individuals, Kinsey continued, experienced "a gradual, and sometimes prolonged, build-up to orgasm, which involved still more violent convulsions of the whole body; heavy breathing, groaning, sobbing, or more violent cries, sometimes with an abundance of tears (especially among the younger children)." Another group experienced "hysterical laughing, talking, sadistic or masochistic reactions, rapid motions (whether in masturbation or in intercourse), culminating in more or less frenzied movements which are continued through the orgasm." Other individuals had orgasms "culminating in extreme trembling, collapse, loss of color, and sometimes fainting of subject." Some boys suffered "excruciating pain and may scream if movement is continued or the penis even touched." Members of this latter group, he noted, "will fight away from the partner and may make violent attempts to avoid climax, although they derive definite pleasure from the situation."[32]

Children gasping for breath, sobbing, screaming in pain, fainting, and desperately struggling to fight off the assailants Kinsey dignified as "partners"—these were descriptions of hapless victims. Informants like Mr. X may have convinced Kinsey that their victims derived "definite pleasure from the situation," but how reliable was the testimony of pedophiles about the children they molested? Not very. As one Kinsey critic observed decades after his death, "Looking to sexual molesters for information on childhood sexuality is like drawing conclusions on the sexuality of adult females from the testimony of rapists."[33]

Kinsey was not able to grasp this point. In his eagerness to combat prudery and to celebrate Eros, he found it increasingly difficult to maintain moral boundaries. Until his death, he continued to hold that rape was wrong because it involved force or coercion, and he condemned petty offenders like flashers and Peeping Toms as public nuisances. But as Kinsey moved deeper and deeper into his research, most sex offenses, like most sexual taboos, struck him as arbitrary and harmful, the legacy of anxious Victorians who cared more about self-control than about satisfying erotic needs.

By the mid-1940s, Kinsey had come to believe that many sexual perversions, however repugnant to the public, were basically harmless in the sense that they did not pose a threat to public safety. He even questioned society's condemnation of pedophilia. Kinsey understood that "the possibilities of coercion there are certainly great," recalled Gebhard. Yet Kinsey was prepared to believe, continued Gebhard, "that some child-adult contacts were not harmful and possibly even beneficial." Elaborating, Gebhard explained, "Once in a while we'd run across an occasional incest thing or an occasional child-adult contact that seemed to work out favorably, and [Kinsey] would always tell us about this and let us know that pedophilia wasn't as black as it was painted, that it could be, under proper circumstances, beneficial or something like that—which would be heresy nowadays. Well, it was heresy then!"[34]

Taken alone, however, Kinsey's benign view of pedophilia does not fully explain why he was so taken with Mr. X. To fathom their relationship, one must understand that Kinsey considered Mr. X not merely a sexual phenomenon but a scientific treasure. Privately, Kinsey had long believed that human beings in a state of nature were basically pansexual. Absent social constraints, he conjectured, "natural man" would commence sexual activity early in life, enjoy intercourse with both sexes, eschew fidelity, indulge in a variety of behaviors, and be much more sexually active in general for life. To Kinsey, Mr. X was living proof of this theory. Describing Kinsey's joy in discovery, Nowlis declared, "This was like finding the gall wasp which would establish not a new species but a new genus." Mr. X, continued Nowlis, "was way off the line, way off the scale, beyond anything else that [Kinsey] knew about."[35] It was as though "the second Darwin" had discovered his "missing link."

Yet Kinsey's fascination with Mr. X transcended the thrill of discovery. It was as much personal as professional. Having spent so much of his life feeling guilty and constrained, he admired Mr. X for refusing to conform or be controlled. As Nowlis put it, Kinsey looked upon Mr. X as "a hero" because "the guy had the courage and the ingenuity and the sexual energy and the curiosity to have this fantastic multi-year odyssey through the Southwest and never get caught."[36]

Nowlis saw things differently. He regarded Mr. X as a monster pure and simple and thought it was wrong to use data that came from immoral research. Decades later, he recalled telling Kinsey, "Look, that material on timing infants and youngsters to orgasm—I don't think that belongs in this book."[37] But Kinsey was adamant, insisting that science needed data regardless of their source. As a researcher, it was not his job to pass moral judgment on the sources of his data.

Intellectually, this argument has always presented problems, but never more so than in Kinsey's case. However much he talked about science's need for data, this was not his primary motivation. Again, his research sprang from a private agenda shaped by personal politics. Decades of inner turmoil had transformed Kinsey into a rebel, a man who rejected the sexual mores of his age. He meant to change the public's thinking on sexual matters. Convinced that cold, hard facts alone would persuade the public to develop more tolerant sexual attitudes, Kinsey was determined to provide those data. And if that meant trafficking with someone like Mr. X, then so be it. The end justified the means. As Pomeroy put it, Kinsey "would have done business with the devil himself if it would have furthered the research."[38]

That same single-mindedness occasionally got Kinsey into trouble on campus. In January 1945, for example, Kate Mueller, the dean of women, received an anguished letter from a woman whose daughter, a freshman at Indiana University, had been recently interviewed by Kinsey. Declaring that she felt "fortunate my daughter has always felt close enough to me to discuss these things," the anguished mother confessed that she was deeply concerned about Kinsey's counseling during the interview. "When he tells these young girls that 60% of college graduates are no longer virgins—and when he tells them that 75% of the divorced women are women who have never had any necking, petting or kissing relations before marriage—he creates an unhealthy state of mind for these youngsters," she complained. "Also," she continued, "to tell them that 90% of happy marriages are made up of women who have done this considerably with other men before marriage—that seems to be going too far." Stressing that she did not consider herself "narrow minded or old fashioned," the woman declared that her family was "quite wrought up over this."[39]

Mueller, whose dislike of Kinsey went back to her strong criticisms of his handling of the marriage course, immediately referred the matter to President Wells.[40] To garner support for decisive action, she also sent copies of the letter to Herman T. Briscoe, dean of the Graduate School, and Ross Bartley, the director of the News Bureau at Indiana University. As the official in charge of the school's public relations, Bartley was upset. Declaring that there could "be no doubt of the truth of the statements made in the letter," Bartley warned Wells, "The incidents related indicate that the University is sitting on top of a volcano which may errupt [sic] any time— and when it does no explanation will calm public indignation. I can think of hardly anything that will react as quickly or as disasterously [sic] on the name of the University."[41]

For her part, Mueller had been worried about Kinsey's behavior for some time. In addition to fretting over the information and permissive attitudes he conveyed during interviews, she was concerned about the persistence with which he pursued female histories on campus. She had heard complaints on this score in the past, and she had no reason to doubt that the future would bring more. As she put it many years later, "It was one thing if you invited Mr. Kinsey to come and talk to a small group, and you voluntarily attended, and it was quite another thing if you were drawn by the mere fact of your attendance into the giving of your own history." The basic problem, she maintained, was that Kinsey put too much pressure on students. Women's groups would issue invitations, or he would volunteer to go to various sororities or female dormitories on campus and lecture on marriage and the family. At the end of each presentation, he would ask people to contribute their histories. But Kinsey would not leave it at that, as he did not wish to take "no" for an answer. As Mueller explained things, "he would work very hard to get everybody in the hall, because that was his particular method of collecting data. If he got some members of a complete group, he wanted all of them."[42]

In her judgment, Kinsey crossed the line between soliciting and badgering when he attempted to draw in girls who were either reluctant or simply did not wish to give their histories. When he pursued them, Mueller declared, "he ran into difficulties with parents and girls who objected, girls who were really scandalized, you see." Some of the young women who objected "were actually interviewed and didn't like it and were surprised by the very intimate questions which were asked," while others balked because they "knew they were going to be asked" and resented being pressured. Both groups complained to their parents or turned to their dorm coun selors. "Of course, the counselors would support the girls in their desire to avoid giving the interviews, and, of course, we supported the counselors in my office as dean of women," declared Mueller. "So, this was the conflict, quite simply, which Mr. Kinsey and I found each other facing," she sighed.[43]

Hoping to resolve their differences, Kinsey made an appointment to confer with Dean Mueller. Despite his efforts to win her over, the meeting did not go well, to say the least. "We talked first very affably about his work," she recalled. "Then he asked me if I wouldn't change my attitude about supporting the girls who did not want to be interviewed." She refused. "I felt very strongly that I could not ever ask the girls to give him interviews when they did not voluntarily want to do so," she explained. "As we discussed this a little further," she continued, "Mr. Kinsey became very angry with me, emotionally angry, and he shouted. Perhaps I shouted too," she allowed, "but he did shout at me." As their conversation became more heated, Kinsey underwent a physical transformation. "His face changed; he became more pale," she declared. "He was really shaken by my refusal, because I think that the one thing that he could not endure was to be thwarted in his need for getting more cases."[44]

Thirty years after that encounter, Mueller made no effort to conceal how strongly she had reacted to Kinsey's menacing demeanor. "I was quite frightened by this, and I remember feeling that I was glad he could be overheard by Mrs. [Lottie] Kirby, associate dean, who was in the next office, because I thought if I can't get him out quietly at least she can rescue me." After a brief silence in which Kinsey appeared to be struggling to regain his composure, another outburst ensued. "He shouted at me [again]," declared Mueller, "and I had nothing more to say."[45]

Kinsey, however, was not done. As nastily as he had treated her, he could not resist the temptation to add insult to fear before leaving. "He did tell me I was unsuited for the job I had; he thought I ought to give him my own history," she said with a grimace. Choking back tears, she added, "He went so far as to say I should have some treatment by a psychiatrist to correct my bad attitudes and so forth." Asked whether Kinsey had shown any empathy whatsoever for her position, Mueller replied, "Oh, not at all, but I wouldn't be surprised at that, because he was such an intense person." Then she made a most perceptive observation: "I think that he was not thinking of me as a person; he was thinking of me as an obstacle that somehow had to be surmounted."[46] In the years to come, Dean Mueller would not be the last to comment on Kinsey's intensity or on his tunnel vision in regard to his research.

Given the complaints from students and their parents, administrators at Indiana University needed to find a way to minimize the contact Kinsey had with students. Fernandus Payne, the chair of the Department of Zoology, found a way to accomplish this and to strongly support Kinsey's research at the same time. A few months after the flap between Kinsey and Dean Mueller, Payne recommended to President Wells that Kinsey "be made a Research Professor, without teaching duties." Noting that Kinsey's work was attracting widespread interest from a variety of groups, Payne declared, "Even now I feel that we cannot envision the possibilities and the values of these researches. They certainly are far-reaching."[47] The appointment was granted, and Kinsey had only minimal contact with students at Indiana University after 1945.

The same passion that propelled Kinsey as a researcher drove him to get his data before the public. No one familiar with his research thought that it would be easy to organize his material and present it coherently. The huge volume of data precluded a single volume, and the issue of what subjects to include in separate volumes was an organizational nightmare. Early in the research, Kinsey considered doing separate volumes on a variety of topics, including "sexual factors in marriage," "the incidence and frequency of homosexuality," "patterns of sexual behavior at different social levels," "sex education and consequent behavior patterns," "the heterosexual-homosexual balance," "sexual adjustment in prison," "sex offenses and sex offenders," and the like.[48] By the mid-1940s, however, he projected a total of nine separate volumes, covering the following topics: "1. Sexual Outlet in the Human Male," "2. Sexual Outlet in the Human Female," "3. Sexual Outlet in the Negro (including both male and female, and with comparisons for the white male and female)," "4. Sex Offenses and Sex Offenders," "5. Sex Factors in Marital Adjustment," "6. The Heterosexual-Homosexual Balance," "7. Sexual adjustment in [penal] Institutions," "8. Sex Education," and "9. Prostitutes [both male and female]."[49] Of these, Kinsey would live to complete only the first two.

It was no accident that Kinsey elected to treat men first. As late as 1944, he had collected roughly twice as many male histories as female histories, a skewing that said a great deal about which sex he found more interesting, from both a scientific and a personal standpoint.[50] Whether researching or writing, he preferred males.

Kinsey started on the male volume in the summer of 1945, following a hectic spring of traveling. Offering his prize grantee some well-intentioned advice, Yerkes wrote, "I am ignorant of the summer climate of Bloomington, but most heartily hope that if it is not reasonably favorable, you will migrate to some spot which is and there write in comfort."[51] As it happened, Bloomington's weather was mild that summer, but the cool conditions did not prevent Kinsey from paying the price for the pace he had maintained for the last few years.

Shortly after the writing began, Kinsey collapsed, a portent of the recurring health problems he would suffer for the remainder of his life. Was his breakdown physical or psychic? A case could be made for both. Certainly, Kinsey had been working long days and even longer nights. Yet it also is tempting to see emotional strains at work. Just as Charles Darwin had suffered immobilizing ailments on the eve of publishing his earth-shattering *Origin of Species,* Kinsey suffered health problems as he prepared to do battle against Victorian sexual morality. As he rushed to confront the greatest challenge of his life, the task of controlling his long-suppressed anxieties, fears, and anger may have been momentarily overwhelming. Whatever the answer, Kinsey himself attributed his collapse to physical fatigue. "I have been exhausted and in bed part of the time for the last several weeks and I am glad that my traveling is over for the first half of this year," Kinsey wrote a friend. "Bloomington is remarkably comfortable this summer, and I can settle down and spend most of the rest of the summer on the first book," he continued. "It has taken three years of continuous calculation on the statistics, and there is a tremendous amount of detail to work into the text that I hope will be rather easy reading. There are endless charts and diagrams for those who want to examine minute details of the data."[52]

Despite warning signals from his body, Kinsey refused to delegate any of the writing. Instead, he returned to his desk as soon as possible and proceeded to write every word himself. His approach was unorthodox. Rather than review the secondary literature before plunging in, Kinsey analyzed his data and wrote it up. Only then did he consult what others had written. In those instances in which his data disagreed (and there were many), he dismissed the literature out of hand. His response to critics was equally firm. Although he asked the staff to read the manuscript, he rarely accepted their criticisms. Furthermore, while Martin was in charge of all the graphs and charts, Kinsey planned and checked every detail.[53]

Concerned that Kinsey might be pushing himself too hard, Yerkes wrote at the end of the summer, "I hate to think of you as slaving on the manuscript of your book all summer long and I am saying so in the hope that you may break away at some opportune time for a real vacation." Kinsey's response was predictable. "I am feeling very much better than I did at the beginning of the summer," he replied reassuringly. "I have gotten some outdoor exercise in my garden and caught up a bit on sleep. I will live through very well without any other vacation."[54]

All told, it took Kinsey more than two years to complete the writing. For parts of this period, of course, he and his staff were away interviewing, but every moment he could steal in Bloomington was reserved for writing. Week after week, month after month, he pounded out the pages, displaying the work ethic that was his trademark. Once he had a draft, he really got down to business, for he was a firm believer in the old adage "There is no writing, only rewriting." Changing a word here, reworking a line there, reorganizing a section someplace else, he crafted his prose with the care of a man for whom words are weapons. He even read his prose out loud, so that he could listen to the cadence and render his work more pleasing to the ear. The results were gratifying. While it would be stretching things to call Kinsey a stylist, he wrote with clarity and verve, producing prose that communicated exactly what he meant.

A less dedicated reformer might have written with less care, but Kinsey was sustained at every juncture by his devotion to the cause, his intense intellectual curiosity, and his fierce dedication to the canons of science. Yet sexual politics also fueled the fire in his belly. From his childhood, Kinsey had known firsthand the pain and anxiety that sexual guilt can inflict, and his research over the last several years had demonstrated that he was not alone in his suffering. Finally, after all those years of painstaking research, Kinsey had the chance to show the world his data, to use science to fight back. And strike a blow he did!

It is hard to imagine a book that looked more imposing than the male volume. It had all the trappings of heavy-duty science. Topical headings in bold print announced subjects, 173 graphs and 162 tables laid out the evidence in mind-numbing detail, and an impressive bibliography commanded the literature. In fact, everything about the book was designed to impress the reader with the richness of Kinsey's empirical data. In case anyone missed the message, however, Kinsey announced on page 6 that the male volume rested on no fewer than 5,300 histories. And this, he boasted, was only a fraction of the 12,000 histories he had collected to date, a figure that represented "forty times as much material as was included in the best of the previous studies."[55]

Touting numbers was a key component of Kinsey's attempt to inspire confidence in the male volume. His strategy was to shout "Science!" at every turn; to proclaim the need for caution in attaching too much emphasis to his findings (followed by assurances that his data were both representative and reliable); to assert over and over his objectivity; and to disavow again and again any thought of influencing social policy. "This is first of all a report on what people do," he announced near the beginning of the book, "which raises no question of what they should do, or what kinds of people do it." His goal, he explained, was "to accumulate an objectively determined body of fact about sex which strictly avoids social or moral interpretations of the fact." Such matters, he insisted, should be addressed only by philosophers, theologians, and others who possessed the appropriate special training. His approach to what he delighted in calling "the human animal" was "agnostic."[56] Despite his claim of cool disinterest, Kinsey was nothing of the sort. He had definite ideas about how people should behave sexually, and these preferences were only too transparent in his writing. Anything but a bloodless treatise, the male volume was packed with special pleadings, thinly disguised opinions, and polemical stances, all designed to challenge conventional morality and to promote a new social ethic.[57]

Decades after the male volume appeared, Gebhard pointed to the essential paradox that was Kinsey, acknowledging that the man who postured as an objective scientist was actually a passionate reformer. Dismissing the protestations of disinterest, Gebhard noted that Kinsey turned his prose into a weapon for combating sexual repression. "Now, you had to really twist his arm to get him to admit to this humanitarian impulse," observed Gebhard, following the company line, "because ordinarily he was the objective scientist without any ax to grind, without any crusade to pursue. But underneath there was this powerful streak of crusading humanitarianism which, despite his attempts to cover it, show up in between the lines in everything he ever wrote." Elaborating, Gebhard repeated, "Kinsey tried to be completely objective, but he couldn't succeed, because this thing was too much a matter of heart and emotion with him to keep it out of his writings."[58]

Gebhard was certain he understood the source of Kinsey's passion. "[Kinsey] had led such a wretched, sexually inhibited life himself as a young man that he was determined that he was going to promulgate a more rational approach to sex so that people would be happier," explained Gebhard.[59] Undergirding this "more rational approach" was a new sexual ethic, the essence of which was simple: sex was good. In keeping with this ethic, Kinsey applauded practically every kind of sexual activity, and he disapproved of sexual abstinence. "I think he felt that the human animal, as he would say, was basically pansexual—that everybody would be a mixture of hetero and homosexuality, about a two on his Kinsey scale," noted Gebhard. "And he felt that neither male nor female was inherently monogamous, and he thought sex was a wonderful thing, and it was just a pity that it had to be constrained and unnecessarily restricted."[60]

This enthusiasm for sex was a fundamental tenet of Kinsey's thought, and it rang out loud and clear in his writing. From start to finish, the male volume was an ode to Eros, a celebration of the "human animal's" ability to find sexual outlets in a society obsessed with controlling and restricting sexual freedom. In the broadest terms, Kinsey showed that Americans were awash in sexual activity, only a small fraction of which was confined to behavior sanctioned by society. In addition, he identified and evaluated the factors that determined the number and the kinds of sexual outlets in which Americans engaged, bemoaning those that restrained sexual activity and celebrating those that propelled people to act upon their sexual needs and desires.

If the male volume provided a compendium of sexual behavior, it also offered a prayer for further liberation. Kinsey looked for signs of hope anywhere he could find them, duly reporting the little victories people had achieved in their struggle to loosen the reins of rigid conformity. For example, when he discussed young boys who had somehow found the courage to defy the sexual morality of their parents, Kinsey spoke not of wicked or evil children but of youngsters who "triumph over the parents." Elsewhere, he praised members of the lower class for overriding social restrictions against premarital intercourse. Despite their meager education, he noted, "even they recognize that nature will triumph over morals," adding, "They may 'know that intercourse is wrong,' but 'they expect to have it anyway, because it is human and natural to have it.' "[61] This was the language of defiance, hope, and redemption.

Yet no book that bore Kinsey's name could ignore the suffering and pain that had cast such a shadow over his life. "Sexual histories," he reported from experience as well as from his research, "often involve a record of things that have hurt, of frustrations, of pain, of unsatisfied longings, of disappointments, of desperately tragic situations, and of complete catastrophe."[62] Other parts of the book betrayed his private angst as well, particularly those passages that described the lot of sexual minorities forced to live in a society whose sexual mores had been fashioned centuries earlier by religious zealots.

Reflecting on the issue of motivation, Gebhard thought that Kinsey had two overriding goals for his research. "One was he felt that knowledge would prevent tragedies, upsets, frictions, guilt—bad things of this sort," revealed Gebhard. "In other words, it is almost like the biblical saying 'The truth will set ye free.' If he could only get the facts and the truth to people," he explained, "life would be a lot happier and less guilt [ridden]. That was motivation number one." Motivation number two was that "he was a great champion for tolerance and liberality." Kinsey believed "that it didn't much matter what you did sexually as long as it didn't hurt anyone else and it made you and your partner happy." Added Gebhard, "Both of these motivations showed up in his writings despite his efforts to be clinical and objective."[63]

Tolerance was the central message of the male volume. To show the need for forbearance, Kinsey bombarded his readers with the theme of sexual diversity. "There is no American pattern of sexual behavior," he boldly declared, "but scores of patterns, each of which is confined to a particular segment of our society." An accomplished debunker, Kinsey delighted in showing that many forms of sexual behavior labeled criminal, immoral, and rare were actually quite common. Indeed, he argued that "at least 85 per cent of the younger male population could be convicted as sex offenders if law enforcement officials were as efficient as most people expect them to be."[64] How could a single, rigid moral code accommodate so much variation? For Kinsey the answer was simple: none could. In the face of so much diversity, tolerance was the only sensible and humane response.

Kinsey divided the book into three sections. "Part I: History and Method" contained four chapters designed to convince readers that he and his associates were rigorous scientists. Offering the official version of how he got involved with sex research, Kinsey related how students had brought him questions he could not answer, how his search of the literature had failed to uncover much reliable information, and how he had launched his own investigation to fill a hole in science. His sole motive, he insisted, was to provide accurate data on how human beings behaved sexually. After explaining how the taxonomic approach was ideally suited to this task, Kinsey discussed by name nineteen earlier sex surveys, each of which, he argued, rested on inadequate samples and failed to meet other standards associated with high-caliber research.[65] Anyone who had read Kinsey's attacks on taxonomists during his gall wasp days would not have been surprised by his critique of earlier sex researchers.

Next, Kinsey walked his readers through the interview, offering a detailed discussion of its content and a ringing defense of its rigor and reliability. Pride of authorship dotted these pages as he described the evolution of the interview and how he had learned the tricks of the trade that had enabled him to develop into a master interrogator. Then Kinsey discussed the daunting statistical problems inherent in sex research, followed by a cogent, if somewhat defensive, justification of his sampling technique. Part I closed with soothing reassurances about the validity of the data, with Kinsey outlining the various safeguards he had adopted, such as retakes, comparisons of interviews provided by spouses, 100 percent samples, and the like. Although he repeatedly vouched for the accuracy of his research, Kinsey ended with an official disclaimer, cautioning readers that "the data are probably fair approximations, but only approximations of the fact."[66]

If this qualification sounded uncharacteristically modest, it was because Kinsey was playing games. By striking just the right note of caution and humility, he hoped to win trust and inspire confidence in his data. Still, Kinsey could not go long without touting his research. Interspersed with the qualifications were passionate statements defending the reliability of the data and subtle reassurances that his research had yielded a representative sample of how white American males behaved sexually.[67]

Yet, for all his posturing and bluster, Kinsey was chronically unsure of himself as a statistician. This was not without irony, given the fact that he had set himself up as the scientist with not only the most data but the most reliable data. Indeed, his criticisms of previous sex researchers had centered not just on the size of their samples but on how they had collected their data. Most researchers, he charged, had relied upon written questionnaires, which were notoriously unreliable for getting people to admit illegal or allegedly immoral behavior. Their data, he stressed again and again, rested on puny samples that should not be used to generalize. Yet the reliability of Kinsey's sample was no less problematic. Despite the huge number of histories he had compiled, his sample was far from random and therefore far from representative—too many of his histories came from prisoners, too many from college students, and too many from subjects he knew in advance to be gay.

In Part II of the male volume, Kinsey devoted nine chapters to the topic "Factors Affecting Sexual Outlet." These factors included age, marriage, religion, and social class. To learn how each of these factors operated, Kinsey used the orgasm as his basic unit of measurement. Intellectually, there were compelling reasons to do so. Most men could tell whether or not they had an orgasm, and orgasms could be counted. It was all so straightforward. Yet, whatever its intellectual justification, Kinsey's emphasis on orgasms was also a brilliant tactical maneuver. No approach could have been more deeply subversive of traditional morality, as orgasms reduced sex to quantifiable physiological events. This, in turn, only served to demystify sex, which was exactly what Kinsey intended.[68]

According to Kinsey, the average male in his study group between adolescence and thirty years of age had precisely 2.88 orgasms per week. Returning to the theme that had provided the backbone of his research for the last quarter century, Kinsey cautioned that "no mean nor median, nor any other sort of average, can be significant unless one keeps in mind the range of the individual variation and the distribution of these variants in the population as a whole." To illustrate this point, he cited two individuals who represented polar opposites. The first man, who was apparently healthy, had ejaculated only once in the last thirty years, while the second man, whom Kinsey described as "a scholarly and skilled lawyer" (and whom the press later turned into an instant hero), had "averaged over 30 [orgasms] per week for thirty years."[69] In round figures, the second man had produced 45,000 times as many orgasms as the first.

To Kinsey, the irreducible fact of individual variation had great social importance. "The publicly pretended code of morals, our social organization, our marriage customs, our sex laws, and our educational and religious systems are based upon an assumption that individuals are much alike sexually, and that it is an equally simple matter for all of them to confine their behavior to the single pattern which the mores dictate," he observed critically. With thinly veiled sarcasm, he accused the custodians of morality of "overlooking the fact that one individual may be adapted to a particular, perhaps relatively inactive, sort of sexual adjustment, while the next would find it practically impossible to confine himself to such a low level of activity."[70] Rigid standards that required everyone to behave alike were at once unrealistic and doomed to failure.

Kinsey's analysis of the factors affecting sexual outlet contained biting social commentary. At bottom, he saw civilization as the enemy of eros. Society, he argued, began its efforts to inhibit and control the sexuality of its members in childhood, with the prohibitions and restrictions continuing for life. Yet Kinsey detected a delicious irony at work in how the story played out. By making youngsters feel guilty and anxious, society could make them less sexually active, but the goal of complete abstinence remained elusive. The sexual urge was simply too strong. Kinsey's histories revealed that most boys had sexual experiences before reaching adolescence. His only regret was that children did not have more, and he blamed society for making it hard for youngsters to explore their sexuality. He even went so far as to argue that "half or more of the boys in an uninhibited society could reach climax by the time they were three or four years of age, and that nearly all of them could experience such a climax three to five years before the onset of adolescence."[71]

Memories of his own unhappy youth haunted Kinsey's portrait of childhood as a period of great conflict, with children pitted against their elders. Despite society's best efforts, however, children learned about sex, just as he had in that basement in Hoboken. Kinsey located the origins of adult sexual behavior in childhood experiences, arguing that children engaged in most if not all of the activities they would later perform as adults. "Nevertheless," he wrote, "at a very early age the child learns that there are social values attached to these activities, and his emotional excitation while engaged in such play must involve reactions to the mysterious, to the forbidden, and to the socially dangerous performance. . . ."[72]

Those activities, Kinsey stressed, included widespread experimentation with one form of behavior in particular. "On the whole," he wrote, "the homosexual child play is found in more histories, occurs more frequently, and becomes more specific than the pre-adolescent heterosexual play. Approximately 48 percent of the older males and 60 percent of the boys who had contributed their histories when they were still adolescents recalled engaging in homosexual activities before reaching adolescence. Specifically, their homosexual play included exhibitionism, manual contacts, anal intercourse, oral sex, and one more activity Kinsey deemed it necessary to list—urethral insertions.[73]

In his discussion of early sexual development, Kinsey went out of his way to belittle Freud. Relying on data obtained at least in part from child molesters, Kinsey rejected Freud's theory on the development of erogenous zones. Many of the male infants and young boys in his study, Kinsey reported, had either manipulated their genitals to orgasm or had obtained orgasm as a result of being manipulated by others. Either way, they had experienced orgasms that, "except for the lack of an ejaculation, [were] a striking duplicate of orgasm in an older adult." Similarly, Kinsey rejected with scorn Freud's theory of sublimation, noting that his case histories showed no trace of a period in which children or young adolescents channeled sexual energy into creative activities.[74]

Among the factors that affected sexual outlets, Kinsey assigned the greatest importance to age. With the sovereign authority of biology, age was instrumental in determining when sexual activity commenced, when it peaked, and when it stopped. Most males, he reported, began sexual activity early in life, reached their sexual zenith between the ages of sixteen and twenty, and remained sexually potent well into old age, with a gradual tapering off of overt behavior as the decades passed. Never one to minimize the "human animal's" capacity for sexual expression, Kinsey celebrated the human male's capacity to remain sexually active into old age. Although he was careful to stress that sexual activity declined with age, he proudly informed his readers, "There is the history of one 70-year old white male whose ejaculations were still averaging more than 7 per week."[75]

It was the young, rather than the old, who concerned Kinsey. Aware that the sexual cycle he had described condemned males to experiencing their greatest need during a period when society made absolutely no provision for their sexual satisfaction, Kinsey could not contain his sympathy for youth. "This means," he lectured with barely disguised anger, "that the majority of the males in the sexually most potent and most active period of their lives have to accept clandestine or illegal outlets, or become involved in psychologic conflicts in attempting to adjust to reduced outlets."[76] It need hardly be added that Kinsey knew the consequences of those conflicts firsthand.

Of all the factors affecting sexuality, none had more personal resonance for Kinsey than religion. Although he reported that religion was less important than other factors, such as age and social class, in determining conduct, he directed his most pointed barbs at religion. At times, he attempted to belittle the role of religion. When it came to the choice of sexual outlets, for example, devoutly religious men did not seem to behave differently from nonreligious men. At least not with regard to the types of behavior in which they engaged. Broadly speaking, both groups indulged in the same kinds of activities, although true believers paid a price for their piety. Positing a direct relationship between religious fervor and reduced orgasms, Kinsey reported that "devout acceptance of the church's teaching is correlated with sexual frequencies which are two-thirds or less than two-thirds of the frequencies which are found among males of corresponding age and educational levels who are not actively connected with the church." Rejecting the notion that pious people channeled their sex drive into other interests, Kinsey observed that "devoutly religious individuals have repressed rather than sublimated sex histories."[77] If religion could not change people's sexual tastes, it could and did cut back on how often they engaged in those outlets.

Kinsey considered religion the source of much human misery. Although he was careful to include deeply religious Protestants (the tormentors of his youth) and Jews among the sexually repressed, Catholics struck him as the most wretchedly conflicted group around. In words tinged with both anger and pathos, he noted that the Catholic Church "has always emphasized the abnormality or the perverseness of sexual behavior which occurs outside of marriage."[78] Having been taught from childhood that sex was for procreation and must be restricted to marriage, many Catholics grew up feeling ambivalent. Some even believed that sex was dirty. As a result, many Catholics had difficulty making satisfactory sexual adjustments. "Devout Catholics," reported Kinsey, "are restrained in regard to the frequencies of their total outlet, and in regard to their acceptance of any variety of sexual outlets."[79]

Kinsey had not the slightest doubt that religion was the root cause of sexual repression. A better scientist than historian, he insisted that sexual mores had not changed appreciably since ancient times. Moreover, he showed no awareness that sexual restrictions might involve something more than mean-spirited attempts to deprive people of pleasure, that they might in fact serve beneficial purposes such as preserving a group's cultural identity.

Nor was Kinsey a fan of modern-day sexual mores. As far as he was concerned, contemporary sexual mores were mindless relics of the priest-ridden past. The enemy of everything that was natural and spontaneous in human nature, they were intended to thwart, restrict, deny, and control. Therefore, to reform sexual mores and the sex offender codes, science had to displace religion as the arbiter of what was moral or immoral, normal or abnormal. The male volume was Kinsey's effort to reshape the debate and change social definitions.

Of all his findings, Kinsey was perhaps most surprised by what he discovered about the relationship between social class and sexual behavior. He learned that males of different educational and occupational levels presented markedly dissimilar sexual histories. Young single males who went to high school but not beyond had the highest total of orgasms, reported Kinsey, while those who went to college had the lowest. Moreover, members of these groups differed not only in the number of orgasms but in how they achieved them. Broadly speaking, those in the less-well-educated single group obtained most of their orgasms through intercourse (often with prostitutes), while those in the better-educated group relied heavily on masturbation.

After marriage, the contrasts were no less striking. Working-class men had very little masturbation in their histories, did not go in for petting, achieved most of their orgasms through intercourse, shunned oral sex, were somewhat limited in the number of positions they utilized during intercourse, and tended to have most of their extramarital affairs early in their marriages, settling into fidelity in most instances later in married life. Husbands with college educations, by contrast, were likely to continue masturbating after marriage, to indulge in petting, to engage in oral sex, to experiment with different positions during intercourse, to be faithful early in married life, and to have extramarital affairs later. Finally, Kinsey reported that differences in the incidence and types of homosexual activity separated members of the two groups at every stage of their lives.[80]

Seizing the opportunity to editorialize, Kinsey spelled out the social significance of his findings. "Each social level is convinced that its pattern is the best of all patterns," he observed. And since different groups believed what they did was right, they tended to be intolerant of groups whose behavior differed from their own. Members of the educated group, he explained, were more likely to accept or reject behavior on the basis of whether they considered it moral or immoral, while members of the less-well-educated group defined morality on the basis of what they considered normal or abnormal. What made the situation unfair, however, was that educated groups had all the power in society and routinely imposed their sexual mores on those below. It was almost as though they spoke different sexual languages. "Most of the tragedies that develop out of sexual activities are products of this conflict between the attitudes of different social levels," Kinsey declared. "Sexual activities in themselves rarely do physical damage, but disagreements over the significance of sexual behavior may result in personality conflicts, a loss of social standing, imprisonment, disgrace, and the loss of life itself."[81]

In the past, charged Kinsey, certain groups had been too quick to impose their values on others. "The physician who mixes moral advice with his medical prescription should realize that the applicability of his advice will vary with the social level from which the patient comes," warned Kinsey. Addressing marriage counselors, he cautioned, "The sexual techniques which marriage councils and marriage manuals recommend are designed to foster the sort of intellectual eroticisms which the upper level esteems." Most of what they wanted to impose, noted Kinsey, "would be anathema to a large portion of the population, and an outrage to their mores."[82] The same warnings, he argued, should be heeded by social workers, college administrators, public school teachers, and administrators of institutions with inmate populations. Because they came mostly from the middle class and commanded men who hailed mostly from the lower class, officers in the armed services also had to be aware of these differences.

But Kinsey saved his most impassioned remarks for the legal system. "Anglo-American sex laws are a codification of the sexual mores of the better educated portion of the population," he began. "While they are rooted in the English common law, their maintenance and defense lie chiefly in the hands of state legislators and judges who, for the most part, come from better-educated levels." Those same legislators and judges decided issues of sexual morality according to the mores of the group from which they originated. As Kinsey put it, "their severe condemnation of sex offenders is largely a defense of the code of their own social level."[83]

Predictably, this left members of the lower class at once bewildered and vulnerable. "Lower level individuals simply do not understand the bitter denunciations which many a judge heaps upon the lower level boy or girl who has been involved in sexual relations," he lamented. "They cannot see why behavior which, to them, seems perfectly natural and humanly inevitable should be punishable under the law." Here Kinsey was unable to conceal his sympathy. "For them, there is no majesty in laws which are as unrealistic as the sex laws. Life is a maze," he continued in one of his most deeply autobiographical passages. "The sex laws and the upper level person who defend them are simply hazards around which one has to learn to find his way. Like the rough spots in a sidewalk, or the traffic on a street, the sex laws are things that one learns to negotiate without getting into too much trouble; but that is no reason why one should not walk on sidewalks, or cross streets, or have sexual relations."[84] In the years ahead, Kinsey would return repeatedly to this theme, sharpening his attack on the sex offender codes in the United States and, by inference, pleading for reform.

Part III of the male volume examined the theme "Sources of Sexual Outlet." Devoting a chapter to each, Kinsey discussed masturbation, nocturnal emissions, heterosexual petting, premarital intercourse, marital intercourse, extramarital intercourse, intercourse with prostitutes, homosexual outlets, and animal contacts. The point was to identify what portion of the white, male population engaged in these activities and to stipulate what percentage of the total number of orgasms each group derived from these outlets.

Whether viewed individually or collectively, these chapters were bombshells. Not only did they reveal that Americans were falling short of prescribed standards of behavior; they showed that sexual morality in the United States was in shambles. Acts expressly forbidden and assumed to be rare were actually quite common, while marital intercourse, the only officially sanctioned form of sexual behavior, accounted for less than half of the total number of orgasms most men obtained during their lives. Among the findings Americans would find most shocking, Kinsey reported that more than 90 percent of the males he had interviewed had masturbated, about 85 percent had engaged in premarital intercourse, something between 30 and 45 percent had had extramarital intercourse, another 59 percent had indulged in mouth-genital contacts, some 70 percent had patronized prostitutes, another 37 percent had had at least one homosexual contact that produced an orgasm, and finally (and doubtless most disturbing to many) no less than 17 percent of farm boys had had sexual relations with a lower animal. Because he abhorred the hypocrisy and deceit that were the stock-in-trade of middle-class morality, Kinsey made certain his readers would never be able to look at each other again in quite the same way. "The persons involved in these activities, taken as a whole," he declared with a flourish, "constitute more than 95 per cent of the total male population."[85]

Because his findings were so sensational, it was easy to lose sight of how skillfully Kinsey presented his material with an eye to challenging conventional morality. His decision to treat all orgasms as equal, for example, was not without polemical value. In the past, most sexologists had insisted that orgasms achieved through marital intercourse were the only legitimate sexual outlet open to men and women.[86] Kinsey, by contrast, refused to elevate any outlet above another. In place of moral judgments, he offered evenhanded acceptance, treating all orgasms as equal.

Yet, if Kinsey's views were amoral, they also reflected a strong dose of common sense. Convinced that sexual repression had forced the men he had interviewed to make the best of a bad situation, he saw outlets like masturbation, petting, and animal contacts as substitutes for heterosexual intercourse. Marital intercourse might be the only sexual act sanctioned by society, but it was only one of nine means by which American men achieved their orgasms. And at different points in a male's life, it accounted for far fewer climaxes than those obtained by other means. During adolescence and early adulthood, for example, masturbation was the primary outlet for most males.

Kinsey's approval of unsanctioned behavior was obvious. No condemnation flowed from his pen when he described the various sexual outlets his subjects had utilized, only words of sympathy, understanding, and support. Nowhere was this more evident than in his chapter on homosexuality.

At a beefy fifty-six pages, Chapter 21, "Homosexual Outlet," was the longest chapter in Part III. Although homosexual outlets accounted for only 6.3 percent of the orgasms for the single and married males in his study between adolescence and old age, Chapter 21 was more than twice as long as the chapter on marital intercourse, which accounted for somewhere between 85 and 62 percent (depending on age) of the orgasms of men between adolescence and old age. Indeed, not only was Chapter 21 the longest chapter in Part III; it was one of the longest in the book.

Most of what Kinsey wrote was fresh and original, displaying a point of view that drew in equal measure on biological reductionism and on personal experience. Never one to avoid a fight, he dove headfirst into the contentious debate regarding the origins of homosexuality. Kinsey rejected any connection between endocrinological imbalance and homosexuality, bluntly declaring, "No work that has been done on hormones or any other physiologic capacities of the human animal justified such a conclusion."[87]

Kinsey dismissed psychological explanations of homosexuality with equal firmness, insisting that theories of deviance and pathology should not be mentioned in the same breath with this behavior. "Psychologists have been too much concerned with the individuals who depart from the group custom," he declared. "It would be more important to know why so many individuals conform as they do to such ancient custom, and what psychology is involved in the preservation of these customs by a society whose individual members would, in most cases, not attempt to defend all of the specific items in that custom. Too often the study of behavior has been little more than a rationalization of the mores masquerading under the guise of objective science."[88]

Kinsey's explanation for the origins of homosexuality was complex and finely layered, involving the same forces he saw behind all forms of sexual behavior. "The sexual behavior of the human animal is the outcome of its morphologic and physiologic organization, of the conditioning which its experience has brought it, and of all the forces which exist in its living and non-living environment," he wrote. "In terms of academic disciplines, there are biologic, psychologic, and sociologic factors involved; but all of these operate simultaneously, and the end product is a single, unified phenomenon which is not merely biologic, psychologic, or sociologic in nature."[89]

Kinsey saw both nature and nurture at work in homosexuality, but he had difficulty deciding how much weight to assign either. At times, he appeared to come down on the side of nature, as when he relied on the argument *de animalibus*. Nothing better illustrated his rhetorical style or revealed more fully his polemical skill than his repeated reference to "the human animal." The phrase runs the length of the book, and one can almost sense the delight Kinsey derived from using it. He knew how deeply referring to humans as mammals would offend and upset people who refused to believe that human beings were members of the animal kingdom. Homosexual behavior, insisted Kinsey, was part of the human mammalian heritage. As a member of the animal kingdom, the "human animal" possessed the capacity for same-sex eroticism. Homosexuality was, as he put it, "a part of the pattern of the human animal."[90]

Yet Kinsey stopped short of arguing that homosexuality was biologically determined. Whether or not people became involved with homosexual behavior, he explained, turned in large measure on experience and conditioning. For most people, basic sexual preferences were already formed by adolescence. If their early childhood experiences happened to be with members of the same sex and if they happened to be enjoyable, then there was a good chance the individual would repeat these experiences, gradually forming a pattern that culminated in adult homosexual behavior.[91]

Along with early experiences, Kinsey emphasized individual preference. In keeping with his efforts to demystify sex, he likened the issue of one's taste in sexual partners to a variety of mundane decisions people make about routine matters. "This problem is, after all, part of the broader problem of choices in general; the choice of the road one takes, of the clothes that one wears, of the food that one eats, of the place in which one sleeps, and of the endless other things that one is constantly choosing," he wrote. "A choice of a partner in a sexual relation becomes more significant only because society demands that there be a particular choice in this matter, and does not so often dictate one's choice of food or of clothing."[92]

Significantly, Kinsey denied that homosexuality was a valid marker of identity. As he put it, "the heterosexuality or homosexuality of many individuals is not an all-or-none proposition." While admitting that some people had sexual histories that were exclusively heterosexual or purely homosexual, Kinsey reported that there was "a considerable portion of the population whose members have combined, within their individual histories, both homosexual and heterosexual experiences and/or psychic responses." Nor were patterns of behavior within a individual's life

necessarily static. "Some of the males who are involved in one type of relation at one period in their lives," he noted, "may have only the other type
of relation at some later period."⁹³ Still others engaged in both types of sexual activity simultaneously, moving back and forth between partners of
the same and opposite sex with apparent ease.

For Kinsey, then, labels such as "homosexual" and "heterosexual" did not
make sense. People engaged in homosexual acts; they were not homosexuals. Therefore, the only proper use for the word "homosexual" was as an
adjective, not as a noun. Pressing this point vigorously, he declared, "It
would encourage clearer thinking on these matters if persons were not
characterized as heterosexual or homosexual, but as individuals who have
had certain amounts of heterosexual experience and certain amounts of homosexual experience."⁹⁴

This argument served to buttress Kinsey's efforts to present human sexual behavior as a continuum. Rejecting facile categories or rigid classifications, Kinsey depicted human sexual behavior as fluid and diverse, an
argument he advanced forcefully with his six-point scale. Offered as a finely
tuned instrument for measuring the rich continuum of individual variation,
the scale was designed to blur distinctions and to find common ground
that united people in the sexual behavior they shared. The individuals who
registered "0" were exclusively heterosexual (how interesting that he should
assign this no value), while those who rated a "6" on his scale were strictly
homosexual. Polar opposites, they were meant to be seen as uncommon
and rare, if not isolated and alone. Most people blended nicely into the categories in between, with private lives that combined both heterosexual
and homosexual elements. Their differences were matters of degree rather
than kind. A "2" and a "4" were measurably different one from the other,
yet they shared many of the same sexual experiences.⁹⁵

Binary labels such as "homosexual" and "heterosexual," argued Kinsey,
could never capture the rich diversity and overlapping experiences of
human beings. "Males do not represent two discrete populations, heterosexual and homosexual. The world is not to be divided into sheep and
goats," he preached. "Not all things are black nor all things white." As an
antidote to such rigid thinking, Kinsey delivered a hearty dose of his own
brand of evolutionary naturalism. "It is a fundamental of taxonomy that
nature rarely deals with discrete categories," he declared. "Only the human
mind invents categories and tries to force facts into separated pigeonholes." Echoing the radical antiessentialism that had been a defining feature of his gall wasp research, Kinsey continued, "The living world is a
continuum in each and every one of its aspects. The sooner we learn this
concerning human sexual behavior the sooner we shall reach a sound understanding of the realities of sex."⁹⁶ When read today, these lines sound as

if they were written by a scolding preacher rather than a disinterested scientist.

Kinsey closed with a plea for tolerance based upon understanding. "Viewed objectively," he wrote, "human sexual behavior, in spite of its diversity, is more easily comprehended than most people, even scientists, have previously realized." The nine types of sexual outlets he had described in such rich detail might "seem to fall into categories that are as far apart as right and wrong, licit and illicit, normal and abnormal, acceptable and unacceptable in our social organization," but in reality "they all prove to originate in the relatively simple mechanisms which provide for erotic response when there are sufficient physical or psychic stimuli." From the standpoint of the individual, he stressed, "the significance of any particular type of sexual activity depends very largely upon his previous experience." Once an individual became conditioned to a particular sexual outlet, regardless of its nature, "these activities may seem to him to be the only things that have value, that are right, that are socially acceptable; and all departures from his own particular pattern may seem to him to be enormous abnormalities."[97]

In the end, then, whether a person got involved with one sexual outlet or another was largely a matter of chance. Just as Kinsey could trace his own sexual journey back to his repressive childhood, he thought that most people could locate the origins of their adult sexual interests in early childhood experiences. His data, he noted, suggested "that, if circumstances had been propitious, most individuals might have become conditioned in any direction, even into activities which they now consider quite unacceptable." As a son of the Enlightenment, Kinsey never doubted that knowledge would bring understanding. As he put it in his best fatherly tone, "most human sexual activities would become comprehensible to most individuals, if they could know the background of each other's individual behavior."[98] In other words, people had only to learn the truth, and understanding and tolerance would follow. Few propositions reveal more fully the values and assumptions of the Progressive Era, whose optimism and naïveté had shaped Kinsey's life so profoundly in youth.

Kinsey ended the male volume with the usual disclaimer. "The social values of human activities must be measured by many scales other than those which are available to the scientist," he declared. "As scientists, we have explored, and we have performed our function when we have published the record of what we have found the human male doing sexually, as far as we have been able to ascertain that fact."[99] What Kinsey did not say, however, was that he raised serious questions about the reliability of his sample.

All that remained was for Kinsey to secure a publisher. That task would prove to be surprisingly complicated, for, as happened so often in his life, he managed to make the birth of his book a tale of control, manipulation, and intrigue.

2 2

"Properly Placed before the Public"

ong before Kinsey had finished writing the male volume, he started casting about for a publisher. Since his high school biology textbook had been a financial success, it was only natural that he should explore the possibility of signing with a commercial house, preferably one that boasted an established line of medical books. As early as 1941, Kinsey put out feelers to Farrar & Rinehart, but the project was not far enough along to generate anything more than a polite expression of interest.[1] By the mid-1940s, however, Kinsey had given enough talks up and down the eastern seaboard for the major houses to get wind of his work, and publishers started checking him out.

In 1945, a senior editor from McGraw-Hill contacted Alan Gregg of the Rockefeller Foundation, requesting an assessment of Kinsey's work as a publishing venture.[2] In Gregg's absence, his associate, Robert S. Morison, offered a strong endorsement, volunteering that Dr. Gregg had not only "followed very closely the work of Dr. Kinsey" but "approves of its objectives and the way the work is being carried out." Venturing an opinion about the project's commercial prospects, Morison observed, "I should be very much surprised if it does not excite a good deal of discussion both in medical and sociological circles," adding, "There may be some material which runs the danger of being played up rather sensationally by the daily press, but I think this can be avoided by careful handling."[3] Inquiries from other publishers followed, and the answer was always the same: Gregg or Morison invariably endorsed Kinsey.[4] With officers of one of the world's great foundations vouching for his research, publication of his work looked like a no-lose proposition. After all, how often does a scholar with solid credentials come along with something new and important to say on a topic as commercially viable as sex?

From 1945 to 1947, Kinsey received dozens of feelers from publishers, all of whom fell over themselves trying to explain why their houses were uniquely positioned to present his material to the American public.[5] Although delighted by their interest, Kinsey recognized that commercial houses carried political risks. The prudent choice was to sign with a staid medical publisher that catered to a professional audience. That way critics would not be able to accuse him of commercialism, sensationalism, or attempting to influence public opinion.

But Kinsey was deeply conflicted on this issue. While his head accepted the wisdom of signing with a medical publisher, his heart pulled him in the opposite direction. Kinsey had not labored long and hard only to hide his light under a bushel. Rather, he meant to reach as broad an audience as possible. Since most medical houses offered limited distribution, he preferred to publish a trade book that could be purchased in any quality bookstore. Toward that end, he talked throughout 1946 and well into 1947 with publishers as diverse as the J. B. Lippincott Company (the publisher of his high school biology texts), the McGraw-Hill Company, and W. W. Norton and Company.

In many respects, Norton's efforts to sign Kinsey typified these negotiations. Following months of correspondence, Kinsey met with Norton's president, Storer B. Lunt, in the company's offices in New York. Taking the same tack he had followed with other publishers, Kinsey dazzled Lunt with plans for a series of books that would explore various aspects and problems of human sexuality. Although Kinsey made it clear that political considerations might dictate signing with a medical publisher, Lunt was not discouraged. After their meeting, he wrote an extremely upbeat letter, stressing Norton's track record of producing quality books that reached a broad readership. Admitting that his company had "no department devoted solely to medical books," Lunt declared, "But it seems to me that in view of . . . your own great wish to reach a wide intelligent nonprofessional audience, you would find it advantageous to place the books with a serious, non-fiction, general publisher." Noting the advantages of signing with a house with a small list that included works that had topped

500,000 copies in sales, Lunt asserted, "Our books do not get lost in the shuffle, and we do print for permanence and re-advertise over the years— a practical expression of our publishing aims, which are borne out in our slogan Books-that-Live."[6]

Seeking an honest edge over the competition, Lunt joined the growing line of publishers outside Gregg's office. While admitting it might seem unorthodox for a publisher to solicit aid from a foundation officer, Lunt explained, "I hate to leave any stone unturned in presenting our case."[7] Gregg's response was polite but firm. Pleading that it was "a little awkward for us to make any comment on the matter of Kinsey's choice of a publisher," he declared with an air of finality, "I do not believe that there is anyone so competent to decide how his work shall appear as Professor Kinsey himself."[8]

Not everyone agreed. As the competition to sign the male volume neared the home stretch, President Wells became concerned that Kinsey's desire to reach a vast audience might cloud his judgment. A consummate politician, Wells knew that the male volume was certain to ignite controversy, and he understood that defensive measures would have to be adopted. Consequently, Wells took steps to shield Kinsey from critics and to protect Indiana University's relationship with the state legislature.

First, Wells pressured Kinsey to sign the male volume with a medical house rather than a commercial press. A medical publisher, reasoned Wells, would handle the book in a dignified manner and not attempt to exploit it commercially, thereby holding publicity down to a minimum. "We assumed that if they published it that it would go into the hands of the reputable people, people who needed it for scientific purposes, and it wouldn't be very widely used outside of that and misinterpreted," Wells later explained.[9] Second, he asked Kinsey not to publish the male volume (or any other major work in the field of sex research) during the sixty-one days the state legislature remained in session each year. Defending his strategy, Wells observed slyly many years later that "things which happen in the midst of the Assembly get dealt with in the heat of the moment, which if they happened 15 days after the session was over they would never be heard of again."[10]

Finding a medical publisher proved easy. As it happened, the W. B. Saunders Company of Philadelphia, a respectable (if not stodgy) publisher of medical textbooks and monographs, was among the throng of publishers vying to sign Kinsey's book. In the spring 1944, Lawrence Saunders, the company's president, heard Kinsey lecture. Several months later, Kinsey's interviewing schedule took him back to Philadelphia, and he asked Saunders to contribute his history, stressing that practically everyone who had heard the lecture earlier that spring had agreed to be interviewed.[11] Saunders consented, and soon thereafter he started making inquiries of his own about Kinsey.[12]

In April 1946, Saunders paid a visit to Robert Morison at the Rockefeller Foundation. Determined to uphold the reputation of his press, Saunder sought reassurance that Kinsey was a proper scientist. Without a moment's hesitation, Morison replied that the foundation stood behind Kinsey. Moreover, when Saunders inquired about the audience for Kinsey's work, Morison opined that it would not be limited to the medical profession but would include the fields of sociology, psychology, penology, and social anthropology. Saunders was also pleased to learn something he had not known previously—namely, that Kinsey's work was supported not only by the Rockefeller Foundation but also by the National Research Council's Committee for Research in Problems of Sex. Saunders had long been familiar with the committee's work, and he was reassured to learn that the NRC stood behind Kinsey's research. Morison, too, found the meeting comforting. Writing in his diary, he mused, "Offhand it seems desirable to have a well known and conservative house like Saunders sponsor the publication since it does not seem desirable to push a wide public sale with the accompanying possibility of arousing unfortunate publicity." On a more personal note, Morison added, "S[aunders] struck me as a very pleasant Philadelphia gentleman with a high degree of pride (but not hubris) in the excellent reputation enjoyed by the family business."[13]

Saunders's next step was to telephone Lewis Weed, the chairman of the NRC. Stressing that he was delighted to learn of Saunders's interest, Weed, too, endorsed Kinsey's research. In addition, Weed encouraged him to contact Kinsey directly, which Saunders promptly did.[14] The discussion went well, and Kinsey promised not to sign with anyone until he had met with Saunders. Shortly after Labor Day 1946, Kinsey traveled to Philadelphia, where he inspected the Saunders Company's facilities and had what Saunders described as "a very satisfactory talk" with senior editors.[15]

A month later, however, Kinsey had still not reached a decision, and Saunders paid another visit to the Rockefeller Foundation. Fearful that Kinsey might sign with McGraw-Hill or some other publisher, Saunders asked if Gregg or Morison might be willing "to put in a word in favor of S[aunders]." Amused by Saunders's ardor, Morison observed in his diary, "His doubts and hesitations of last year have given way to a gentlemanly Philadelphian enthusiasm."[16] Abandoning the hands-off pose Gregg had struck when other publishers had made similar requests, Morison responded favorably, assuring Saunders that the Rockefeller Foundation had a high regard "both for him as an individual and for the high standards of his house and would be willing to say so if asked."[17] Gregg promptly redeemed this pledge. A few days before Christmas 1946, Kinsey informed a senior editor at Saunders, "I had a recent session with Dr. Gregg and he again spoke very highly of your company."[18]

Throughout spring 1947, Saunders pursued Kinsey in earnest. As the negotiations progressed, however, Saunders learned that Kinsey was considering publishing not one book on male sexuality but two—one designed for a professional audience, another aimed at the lay public. In late April and again in early May, Saunders telephoned Morison to voice his fear that Kinsey would embark on a joint publication venture. Wary of the problems that mass publicity would create, Morison invited Saunders to meet with Gregg and him the following week at the Waldorf Hotel in New York, where, as luck would have it, they all had plans to attend a professional dinner.[19]

Although careful to preserve a low-key demeanor, Saunders was quite forthcoming at this meeting. According to Gregg's diary, he cited two or three things which indicated that Kinsey "may be over-interested in immediate efforts to reach a wide lay public." Saunders was also disturbed about something that had long troubled the officers of the Rockefeller Foundation. "S[aunders] feels it would be better not only from his own standpoint but from that of Kinsey's scientific reputation—not to mention the prestige of the RF—to direct first attention to the professional and educational market," wrote Morison. It was not so much that the Philadelphia gentleman was opposed to reaching a wide audience. To him, the crucial issue was timing. Plans for a popular edition, Saunders believed, should be delayed until after the work had established "a sound reputation."[20]

In the end, Kinsey elected not to pursue a joint publication venture. Pressured by Wells and Gregg to sign with a medical press, he informed Saunders on May 9, 1947, "Our group is inclined to give you first chance to discuss final terms with us."[21] Wasting no time, Saunders immediately traveled to Bloomington, where he closed the deal and mapped out his company's plans for the male volume in meetings with various university officials, including Dean Payne and President Wells. Informing Gregg of his contract with Saunders, Kinsey wrote, "We decided that there was definite advantage in being associated with a company known to the public as distinctly medical publishers. We think we will have a very dignified treatment, both in the way the book is put up and the way in which it is presented to the public."[22] An obviously pleased and relieved Gregg replied, "I am inclined to think you have made the best choice and certainly the appearance of the book exclusively as a medical publication very greatly protects it and you from the charge of sensationalism, etc."[23]

Once the contract was signed, things moved rapidly. Near the end of May, Kinsey submitted a hefty chunk of the manuscript, accompanied by a cover letter that testified to his determination to maintain control. "You will find the manuscript in such good order that I think your editorial work will be materially reduced," he boasted. That statement set the tone for what followed. After indicating that he was not inclined to eliminate statistical material from the book, Kinsey let out a primordial growl over the text itself. "You will understand that there will be no modification of material, even if it offends," he declared, "as long as the material is a precise statement of fact which is adequately authenticated by our data."[24]

Still, Kinsey was eager to accept any and all suggestions for pruning unsupported editorial comments. Stressing his determination to make the volume, in his words, "so consistently scientific that no one can charge that we have been biased and have interpreted facts on the basis of a bias rather than on any strictly scientific basis," Kinsey declared, "We should be glad to have the editors point out any point at which we have made interpretations on the basis of moral or social significance or anything else except strictly logical interpretations of causal relationships."[25] This was, of course, a prudent posture. Still, there can be little doubt that Kinsey believed he had presented the evidence in such a manner as to support his position at every turn, and he was eager to place his message before the public as fast as humanly possible. Kinsey informed Saunders's production manager at the end of August, "My staff has worked terrifically long hours, including overtime every time without exception and every weekend and holiday. I have worked 14 and 15 hours every day since you saw me in Philadelphia, including every Saturday and Sunday, without exception."[26]

The task of editing Kinsey's manuscript fell to Lloyd G. Potter, vice president and senior editor. Throughout the summer and into the fall, Potter was in constant touch with Kinsey, negotiating modest changes in the text and cleaning up inconsistencies in tables and graphs. Although he failed to point out a single instance in which Kinsey had editorialized, Potter's critique of the manuscript anticipated many of the criticisms that dogged the book after it was published. By far the most serious involved statistics.

Potter asked Kinsey for assurances that the statistical method and data in the male volume were, in his words, " 'bullet proof' insofar as major statistical attack is concerned." Sharpening his point, Potter continued, "The assumption is, of course, that your findings can be applied to the United States population as a whole, but the data seem preponderantly to be collected in the eastern part of the country, and very little relates to the west and the south."[27] Nor was Potter satisfied with Kinsey's disclaimers. While acknowledging that Kinsey had repeatedly warned that his records were too incomplete to represent much about the population as a whole, Potter worried that the tables that often followed such statements might give the opposite impression, leading many casual readers to believe that the data applied to the whole population.

Although thoroughly professional in tone, Kinsey's response did not engage Potter's most important criticism. Instead of addressing the issue of whether or not his data were representative, Kinsey answered blithely, "Calculations are always subject to the adequacy of the sample on which they were based and this is stated repeatedly, both in Chapter III and elsewhere in the book."[28] While this response may have satisfied Kinsey, it left Potter far from reassured.

Unbeknownst to Kinsey, Potter turned to Gregg for advice on "certain editorial problems that we have not yet been able to resolve ourselves." Although such a request was admittedly unusual, Potter thought it appropriate, noting that both the NRC and the Rockefeller Foundation "may be called upon to duck some of the brickbats leveled at us." And Potter was certain the fusillade would commence the moment the book appeared. Since everyone in his company expected Kinsey's book to arouse "most heated controversy," the prudent course was to anticipate as many of the criticisms as possible and attempt to deal with them prior to publication.[29]

Just as he had with Kinsey, Potter asked Gregg for assurances that both the data and the methodology were " 'bullet proof' insofar as major statistical attack is concerned."[30] His most anguished questions, however, centered on the "ethical considerations" raised by Kinsey's book, particularly those questions that impinged directly on the Saunders Company. Ignoring the pleas for tolerance and the criticisms of Victorian morality that ran the length of Kinsey's manuscript, Potter focused on the political issue of how to protect his company from irate critics. He had not the slightest doubt that the male volume would immediately earn a place on the Vatican's *Index Librorum Prohibitorum*. And although he conceded that science had the right and the duty to publish its findings on all subjects, Potter wondered whether his company should consider the reactions of religious groups or other interested parties.[31]

In view of these concerns, explained Potter, the Saunders Company was struggling to decide how to handle the book. Nothing in its past had prepared the company to know how to market a controversial trade book. At present, the editors were in agreement "that the distribution of this volume should be controlled." The problem, explained Potter, was Kinsey. He wanted to reach the educated lay public and opposed any effort to limit the book's distribution to professional groups. Thus, Potter allowed that it might be necessary to offer the book for sale to the general public. "I suppose it would be all right for us to have copies of the book in book stores," ventured Potter, "but I would like your opinion as to whether we should attempt to promote the sale of the work through advertisements in, for instance, the New York Times, the Saturday Review, and other such media, which seems to be Dr. Kinsey's plan." The moment it was released, there was bound to be "an immediate and very large demand for the book, the bulk of which would come from the so-called 'educated' layman group who could only be served through book stores." It thus seemed wise "not to attempt to place restrictions on that source to any considerable degree."[32] Still, the prospect of having a blockbuster book that was bound to rain controversy on the house of Saunders left Potter feeling more than a little uneasy.

Apprehensive about the storms ahead, Potter had prepared a foreword he hoped would protect his company, and he asked Gregg to comment. The foreword read, "This volume is presented as an objective, factual study of sex behavior of the human male, based on surveys made under the sponsorship of Indiana University, and supported by the National Research Council's Committee for Research on Problems of Sex and by the Medical Division of the Rockefeller Foundation. It is intended by the publishers primarily for professional workers in the fields of biology, medicine, psychology, sociology, anthropology and allied sciences, and for others professionally interested in problems of human behavior."[33]

Under normal circumstances, a man of Gregg's sophistication probably would have been amused at the spectacle of an editor who was worried about having a controversial best-seller on his hands. But Gregg both understood and shared Potter's concern. Gregg feared that the male volume might embroil the Rockefeller Foundation in controversy, because he correctly foresaw that Kinsey's findings would produce a storm of protest. Since it was foundation policy to shun publicity, even when favorable, Gregg wanted the volume handled in a dignified fashion, with every effort to avoid sensationalism. Yet he also worried that Kinsey's publisher might wilt under pressure. Convinced that the Saunders Company needed a little steel added to its backbone, Gregg not only defended Kinsey but proceeded to lecture Potter on why publishers bore a special responsibility to support science in its long struggle against ignorance, superstition, and repression.

Gregg assured Potter that Kinsey's statistics had been carefully reviewed by Lowell Reed of the Johns Hopkins University, whom he described as "a competent referee."[34] In fact, Gregg did not seem terribly concerned about any of the statistical questions Potter had raised. Instead, Gregg focused on the social issues posed by Kinsey's work. But, incredible as it seems, he, too, failed to question Kinsey's scholarly objectivity. Gregg's reply indicated that he saw Kinsey as a disinterested scientist who had pursued the truth with unswerving dedication and cool detachment.

Ignoring the social commentary that suffused Kinsey's manuscript,

Gregg focused on "the general issue of freedom of scientific inquiry." In his judgment, the problems surrounding Kinsey were no different from those that had plagued scientists who had worked on contraception and venereal disease. The important thing was to keep things in perspective. "I have no doubt that the book will stir up criticism," declared Gregg. "Psychoanalysis did and yet it has now become the subject of numerous books that encounter no great risk of suppression and occasion no storms."[35]

While he did not comment on whether or not the book should be advertised, Gregg advised Potter to accede to Kinsey's desire to make the book available to "educated laymen," declaring, "You would not be able to restrict or control it anyhow." The educated public, argued Gregg, had as much right to scientific truth as any of the high priests, be "they clerical, scientific or political." Turning to the opponents of sex research, Gregg observed wisely, "The people who won't like Kinsey's records and the inferences wouldn't want them even compiled, much less printed. So you can count on their criticizing you for publishing it at all. But why throw away the support of all the others who would respect your courage? They would think you hypocritical for trying to 'control' the readers. And so you'd satisfy neither group if you tried to restrict sales of what you publish." Gregg closed by observing, "Experience in the past suggests to me that the period of disillusionment may be stormy but that we shall do well to meet it with equanimity."[36]

While fortunate to have a patron as staunch as Gregg, Kinsey was prepared to fight his own battles. With his goal so close, he had no intention of allowing anything or anyone to stand in the way of placing his message before the public. Throughout the summer and fall of 1947, he pressured his publisher to agree to a large printing, to market the male volume in bookstores, and to advertise the book widely in learned journals and the popular press alike. But Kinsey did much, much more. Whereas most authors leave promotion to their publishers, Kinsey took charge of public relations himself. From the outset his thinking was guided by a single issue—control.

Kinsey was one of the first American scientists to confront the problem of dealing with the modern media, and his story constitutes a fascinating chapter in the history of journalism.[37] Because of his subject matter, journalists had pursued him from the early years of the research. On a personal level, Kinsey found this deeply satisfying, as he had long coveted public recognition and felt that he had not received the attention he deserved. From a professional standpoint, however, he saw danger in the press's interest. Fearing that no good could come from premature publicity, Kinsey was determined to bide his time. Hard work would add to his store of case histories, and the more data he possessed, the stronger his defense against critics.

Consequently, Kinsey shunned publicity during the early years of the research. When he was invited to address the National Conference of Social Workers in May 1944, for example, he told an official who requested an advance press release, "I agreed to present the material to the Conference on condition that it was not to be published in the proceedings of the Conference, or that any other publication of the data would be made at this time." Explaining, Kinsey noted that since his research was "of prime importance to human welfare . . . it would be disastrous if opposition developed to the work as a result of premature publishing of the tentative results."[38]

To avoid publicity, Kinsey routinely asked officials at the scholarly conferences at which he spoke to omit any reference to his session in press releases.[39] In those instances in which reporters showed up, he declined to be interviewed, all the while assuring journalists that he would be happy to cooperate at a future date when his data were ready for publication. Kinsey also declined requests for sneak previews of his data. For example, when *Harper's Magazine* got on his trail in 1942, Kinsey refused to cooperate. "You will understand why we must see to it that publication of our results does not occur before thorough scientific establishment of our conclusions, and why it is fundamental that only accurate and adequate accounts of our work be made available to the public," he explained.[40]

When the *American Mercury*'s Lawrence E. Spivak made a similar inquiry the following year, Kinsey begged off, pleading, "Give me another year or so to get this material in better shape before I attempt this."[41] By 1946, Kinsey had made a firm decision not to cooperate with any newspaper or magazine until the book was in print. Explaining his position to Norman Grieser, the managing editor of the *New Republic*, Kinsey declared, "Our conclusions are too new and too important socially to venture publication until the full body of technical material is in print somewhere to satisfy the people who will object to our conclusions. It would put any magazine, and it would put us, in a very bad situation to publish material which could not go into all the details before the volume was in print."[42]

In truth, Kinsey was wary of the press. "With a few exceptions he didn't like the press, because he felt always on guard," recalled Gebhard. Kinsey worried constantly about being misquoted or quoted out of context, and he also feared the press would distort or sensationalize his work, reporting only those findings that made good headlines while omitting any discussion of the size of his database or the rigor of his methodology. Then, too, he was afraid he might get caught in inconsistencies or factual errors, particularly where the numbers were concerned. Noting that Kinsey "disliked being recorded or quoted," Gebhard explained, "He felt that if he made a statement and perhaps for pedagogic reasons he made it too simplistic or if he exaggerated, then if it were recorded either by a reporter or on a tape . . . then he could be held accountable for this and criticized."[43] What Gebhard did not say is that Kinsey often inflated his numbers for dramatic effect, because he enjoyed shocking people.

To protect the research (and himself), Kinsey made it a point to keep the press at arm's length, accepting speaking invitations only if his hosts promised to exclude reporters. In addition, he required groups or organizations that invited him to speak to agree not to publish his remarks in conference proceedings.[44] Overall, Kinsey was pleased by the results of his efforts to control the press. Stressing that he had "lectured publicly on this subject six or eight hundred times in the last few years," Kinsey told a friend in the summer of 1946, "Remarkable as it may sound, I have persuaded all the newspapers, and all other sources, never to publish any statement concerning the results of our data, and I repeat that we have had many hundreds of contacts with both scientists and the general public."[45]

Kinsey also proved adept at persuading magazine writers and editors to contribute their histories, an experience he felt confident would make them more favorable when they did write about his research. For example when Fredrick Lewis Allen, the editor of *Harper's Magazine,* expressed an interest in doing an article on the research, Kinsey renewed his promise to cooperate at a future date and then turned the tables. "We have already spent quite a little time with the editors of a number of the other magazines and several dozen of them have learned more about the study by contributing their own histories to the series," revealed Kinsey. Noting that this experience had been "of definite value to them in giving them an idea of our approach," Kinsey added pointedly, "We should be very glad to get together with you on that score."[46]

Yet, long before he published the male volume, Kinsey had come to resent journalists, in part because he worried about their ignorance and penchant for sensationalism. In the mid-1940s, there were only a handful of journalists specializing in science, most of whom were freelance writers. Most newspapers and magazines did not have science reporters per se. Fearing that the average journalist would not be able to handle the explosive material in his book with balance or sensitivity, Kinsey felt he had no choice but to deny access to his data until he was prepared to present his evidence in full.

Then, too, Kinsey had come to resent the press because reporters made too many demands on his time. More and more, he saw journalists not merely as pests but as obstacles that impeded his great cause. When a writer for *Magazine of the Year* kept bugging him early in 1947, an angry Kinsey thundered, "Drop the whole thing until fall. I have told you before that if you and one hundred other magazines do not leave me alone there will not be a book to write about. You have no comprehension of how serious a matter this is; with telegrams, long-distance telephone calls, and endless letters to try to answer."[47] Against this backdrop of suspicion, mistrust, and exasperation, Kinsey resolved to make the press play by his rules.

After months of careful thought, Kinsey devised a plan for exercising a remarkable degree of control over the press. Instead of dealing with journalists on an ad hoc basis, he would issue a blanket invitation for them to come to Bloomington. There they would receive a detailed summary of the male volume prior to its release date, or, if they preferred, they would be permitted to read the proofs. Either way, they would be free to write whatever they liked, pro or con. In exchange, however, they would have to sign a thirteen-point, written contract. Among other things, it bound reporters not to publish their articles until the December 1947 issue of their publications, which was roughly one month before the book was scheduled for release. In addition, they had to consent to submit copies of their articles prior to publication to Kinsey, who would review them for factual accuracy, with the understanding that any errors would be corrected.[48] Although basically a gentleman's agreement, the contract worked surprisingly well.

Not content, the Saunders Company urged Kinsey to place even greater restrictions on reporters. Responding to his requests for comments on the contract he had prepared for reporters, Potter wrote early in September 1947 to say that their attorneys were in agreement that he should keep reporters away from the book until after it was published. Part of their concern focused on adverse publicity, to be sure, but they also worried that too many (or too lengthy) quotations would almost certainly infringe his copyright.[49] "Tell your lawyers to forget it," barked Kinsey in reply. "Their proposition that we withhold all publicity until after the book is out is utterly unrealistic. It is too late now anyway, because the contracts are all signed and the articles are written."[50]

Kinsey told the truth. By summer 1947, dozens of reporters and feature-story writers had accepted his terms in exchange for access to his data, and despite their annoyance, the overwhelming majority had done so with little grousing. Apparently, all those years of being kept at arm's length had instilled a powerful curiosity, and journalists were anxious to see what Kinsey had learned. And who could blame them? If his findings turned out to be controversial, as seemed likely from the few titillating comments he had dropped along the way, the story was bound to make good copy.

Not surprisingly, then, Kinsey's press policy worked exactly as he had planned. Beginning in the late summer and continuing throughout the fall of 1947, an orderly procession of feature-story writers and reporters made the trek to Bloomington. Most spent two or three days at the institute, where the more energetic plowed through the page proofs and the less ambitious contented themselves with perusing the press summary. Either way, Kinsey had them on his home turf, which was exactly where he wanted them. For not only did they read his words, but they met the man, and that gave him a chance to work on them.

Kinsey knew exactly how to proceed. By this time, he had guided literally scores of important visitors through the Institute, polishing the routine to perfection. Few people who got the grand tour emerged unimpressed, for together the man and the setting made a powerful statement. From the instant Kinsey greeted them to the moment he said farewell, he was all business, and the physical plant of the Institute itself, with its crowded rooms and austere furnishings, conveyed the image of a shrine devoted to work. Like so many visitors before them, then, these journalists allowed Kinsey to present himself only as he wanted to be seen. To the person, they felt as though they were in the presence of a middle-aged family man and a dedicated scientist whose sincerity, devotion to research, and passion for objectivity were beyond question.

The truth was that they had encountered a man who could have sold snow to Eskimos. With groups of journalists sitting at his feet like so many schoolchildren, Kinsey delivered his version of how the research got started, rapturous odes to the taxonomic method, brilliant explications of how the interview worked, and deftly chosen remarks on the reliability of the data. Significantly, he also persuaded many of these writers to give their sex histories, which, of course, allowed him to satisfy their curiosity about the questions and banish any doubts about his skills as an interviewer. Doubtless Kinsey enjoyed putting them in a double bind. He relished the power that knowing their secrets gave him, with all the implications for compromising their objectivity that this entailed.

Nor did Kinsey neglect to give his guests brief but fascinating tours of the library and archive, showing them things that few of their number knew existed. In short, he gave them the "treatment." As a result, even those journalists who walked into the Institute as skeptics left singing his praises. After returning home, one journalist wrote to say, "I can't tell you how much I enjoyed my visit with you and your associates. . . . One rarely comes in contact with a group of scientific explorers blazing so important a trail as you people are, and I count my contact with you and your work as a very rich experience."[51] Summarizing the feelings of many of his colleagues, another journalist declared, "I'd like to say, before you read my article, that I think no man could do real justice to your magnificent study in the relatively small space at my disposal."[52]

Kinsey quickly came to share this opinion. When the first batch of drafts started arriving in September for his review and approval, he was not pleased. Although most writers got the facts right, their manuscripts amounted to little more than bald listings of sensational disclosures. Despite his best efforts to force-feed them what to write, these writers had made almost no effort to discuss the history of the research, its social implications, or the context and arguments that supported the conclusions they cited. On the contrary, most had fulfilled Kinsey's worst fears, behaving like yellow journalists who deliberately attempted to shock the public by airing a long list of findings they knew would give offense. Dismayed at the manner in which they had handled his "delicate material," Kinsey scolded one journalist, "This can do irreparable damage to the whole future of the research."[53]

To prevent this from happening, Kinsey pressured journalists to revise their articles in ways that would inspire confidence in his research and faith in his professional and personal integrity. Ignoring his pledge to comment only on factual accuracy, he moved to shape the contents of their stories. Again and again, Kinsey urged them to focus on the origins of the research, his struggle to win support from the NRC and the Rockefeller Foundation, his brilliant methodology, the far-reaching social implications of his research, and, finally, no more than one or two of his conclusions that they could develop in detail. Nor were these the only changes he brokered. Setting his sights squarely on content, Kinsey wrote the editor of *Science Illustrated*, "We have checked all the figures and suggested an occasional change of wording where I thought it would stir up unnecessary trouble. I have already discussed the possibility of toning down the suggestion that there is anything shocking about the work that we have done."[54]

What was surprising was the success he enjoyed. Persuaded by his obvious dedication and zeal, feature-story writers and reporters bent over backwards to accommodate his suggestions. Viewing these developments from Philadelphia, Lawrence Saunders found Kinsey's skill at handling the press little short of miraculous. In October, Saunders reported to a friend at the Rockefeller Foundation, "It is amazing the interest which has been expressed by the lay magazines. A number of them have been out to Bloomington to get the story and have taken innumerable pictures. . . . Dr. Kinsey is handling personally all the releases to the lay press. It seems to us he is doing extremely well and is getting wonderful cooperation from them." Elaborating, Saunders observed with only slight exaggeration, "He has them all sign a contract by which he has the right to delete any material he does not think appropriate."[55]

Kinsey justified his press policy by citing numbers. As he explained to a writer for the Associated Press, "We have had so many requests for press material that we are having to handle the arrangements uniformly for everybody."[56] Yet, whatever the practical reasons for his actions, Kinsey was attempting to preserve control and to maximize publicity. Treating everyone alike allowed him to impose uniform conditions and restrictions. Furthermore, by coordinating the release date of the articles for December, he hoped to orchestrate publicity that would build to a national climax by the time the book was released.

Indeed, Kinsey was confident of the outcome. Early in September, he wrote his editor, "The people who have been here in the last week represent magazines that will give us a total of more than ten million circulation, and this should be worth a great deal to us in advance publicity." Underscoring his determination to cultivate friends in the press, Kinsey added, "Our relations with them have been extraordinarily fine. They are all absolutely for us and can mean a great deal to us in publicity if we keep them in that mood."[57] In October, Kinsey was even more optimistic, telling a friend that by the time the book was published in January, he would "hear about it from 101 quarters, beginning with the December issues of the magazines."[58] For his part, Lawrence Saunders was delighted. Passing along a remark he knew would please Kinsey, he wrote, "My favorite reaction so far on the book comes from one of my publishing friends. He said, 'I think it is probably the most widely publicized unpublished book on record.'"[59]

By November, Kinsey was predicting that the male volume would make a huge splash. Writing to George Gallup, whom he was trying to persuade to write "a series of surveys on the development of public knowledge and public reactions to our own research," he declared, "My guess is that right now there are perhaps 100,000 people in the country who know something about our research. By the last week in November, several million will have seen magazine articles, and by the middle of January there should be a very high proportion of the total population that has had information about it." Confessing that it had been "a most interesting experience to try to keep control of our public relations," Kinsey asserted with unblushing self-promotion, "It is a wonderful chance to study the way in which public opinion develops around an issue which is going to get such violent divisions of opinion."[60] A few months later, when Kinsey's name was appearing everywhere in print, Gallup agreed to conduct the poll.

Among the staff members, Kinsey alone predicted that the book would sell well. Decades later Gebhard recalled, "Kinsey asked me how many copies I thought should be printed, and I said I thought that 8 or 10,000 would be ample, that this would cover most of the main libraries and textbooks for a few classes. But I thought that 10,000 would be an optimistic estimate. At this point, he said, 'Don't be ridiculous, Gebhard. We'll sell at least 20[,000].' "[61] Although this struck Gebhard as a wildly optimistic, events would soon demonstrate how woefully both men had underestimated the book's appeal. On the basis of advance orders and its reading of the potential market, the Saunders Company decided on a first printing of 100,000 copies, an extraordinary number for a work of fiction, hence an unbelievable figure for a scientific report.

Saunders was wise to project huge sales. While the book's subject matter assured high public interest, Kinsey had also taken steps to make certain that the male volume would be launched to a chorus of favorable notices and reviews. Through careful maneuvering, he had placed himself in a position to largely shape the first wave of stories that presented him and his work to the world, and he had made the most of it. The articles that hit the newsstands at the end of November and throughout December followed his script to the letter, demonstrating how well he had succeeded in impressing journalists with the social importance and scholarly integrity of his research. In fact, Kinsey had displayed a talent for public relations any politician would have envied. His reward was one of the greatest publicity coups in American history.

"Today, on the campus of a Midwest university, a soft-spoken, keen-eyed man is quietly at work—producing a social atom bomb," announced *Look* magazine. The first of many who evoked the symbol of a new scientific age to describe Kinsey's research, the writer continued, "His task, like the conquest of the atom, holds large promise for humanity. For in half a million years of mankind's history, it is to be the first, adequate, large-scale inquiry into man's sex life." Nor could there be any doubt regarding the validity of his data. "Leading American statisticians have examined and approved the statistical basis of the Kinsey study," reported *Look*. "In fact, Kinsey's entire technique and procedure for the survey have been highly praised by experts in fact-finding and scientific research."[62] Offering its readers the same assurances, *Harper's Magazine* vouched, "Experts who have closely scrutinized the interviewing techniques of Kinsey and his associates endorse their scientific validity and state further that the people so far interviewed represent a fair cross section of the American population."[63]

If anything, these magazines hailed Kinsey's methodology as a milestone. Lauding his research as "one of the finest examples of co-operation among the physical and social sciences known to date," *Science Illustrated* proclaimed, "His encyclopedic work is being hailed as one of the great sociological labors of our age, a frame of factual reference in a field which up to now has been disorganized, chaotic, and filled with dangerous misinformation." Awed by the volume of Kinsey's data, *Science Illustrated* predicted, "The end of 1947 may well be marked down in sociologists' calendars as the great turning point in the struggle to bring broad mass facts into the social sciences."[64]

Reader's Scope was no less effusive, calling Kinsey's work "the most complete and objectively scientific report ever assembled on the sex life of American men." Asserting that Kinsey's revelations were certain "to astonish even other scientists" and to "shock millions of Americans," it correctly forecast, "One thing is certain: this report will create nationwide debate."[65] *Harper's Magazine* struck a similar note, declaring, "Many of our most deep-rooted concepts of sex and marriage are about to be blasted by a soberly documented report of a group of University of Indiana [*sic*] scientists, following a nine year survey of the sex habits of the American people." After assuring its readers that the 12,000 Americans who had been interviewed by Kinsey represented "a scientific cross-section of the population," *Harper's* cut directly to the book's social impact, boldly announcing, "Age old ideas about sex embedded in our legal and moral codes are revealed as myths and delusions under the searchlight of this important investigation."[66]

How Kinsey must have delighted in the social messages these articles attributed to his research! *Science Illustrated* reported that his facts showed "a great schizophrenic split, a chasm between what Americans do and what they believe they do, what they practice and what they preach." Indeed, the Americans in Kinsey's study came off "as furtive, self-righteous, unobjective, and intolerant in their sexual beliefs and practices." Nowhere was this more true than in their attitudes toward homosexuals. Whereas most Americans thought homosexuality was rare, Kinsey's data showed it was quite common. Arguing that his report "must stimulate thinking men to a consideration of this problem," *Science Illustrated* challenged Americans to "ask themselves if it is still enough to say that homosexuals are 'bad' and should be punished. Is not more understanding required?"[67]

Nor did the need for reevaluation end there. In words that must have warmed his heart, *Look* proclaimed, "Perhaps the greatest lesson to be gained from Kinsey is the realization of the tremendous variation in sex behavior between peoples, educational levels, other groups—and between individuals themselves in identical levels."[68] Insisting that Kinsey's survey "explodes traditional concepts of what is normal and abnormal, natural and unnatural in sex behavior," *Harper's* drew precisely the conclusion he intended when it declared, "Implicit in the revolutionary Kinsey report is a plea for greater public and private tolerance of the vast differences in the sex habits of Americans. Such terms as abnormal, unnatural, oversexed, and undersexed, as used in our legal and moral codes, have little validity in the light of Professor Kinsey's revelations. There is a tremendous variety in the frequency and type of sexual behavior in normal Americans."[69]

Yet these articles did more than trumpet the importance of Kinsey's research: they introduced him as a person to the American public, creating a profile that would follow Kinsey to his grave. All the ingredients of the image that soon shaped the public's understanding of Kinsey were present, exactly as he had fed them to the writers. One writer called him "a great modern biologist,"[70] while another described him as "a hard-working, meticulous, and courageous scientist."[71] To another journalist, Kinsey seemed "a happy, tolerant, easy-mannered, but implacably scientific Indiana University professor," a man who had used "his charming personality to excellent advantage in getting men, women, and children from all social levels to confide to him secrets that most of them certainly never have told to any other person."[72]

Reinforcing this portrait, another journalist called attention to Kinsey's "out-going, tolerant, easy-to-talk-with personality that permitted him to gain quick contact with people and speedy confidence of all kinds and conditions of men and women." This last writer, who admitted that he had given Kinsey his sexual history, offered a personal testimonial, declaring, "I am as inhibited as the next fellow about sexual matters, but to my great surprise I experienced no embarrassment in giving intimate details of my personal life to this amazingly skillful interviewer."[73] In short, the Kinsey who emerged in these articles was a father figure—likable, hardworking, dedicated, disinterested, and trustworthy. Impervious to criticism, he was also someone who could be counted on to stay the course. As *Look* told its readers, "You will hear a good deal about Kinsey in the months ahead. Some of it will be condemnation from the conclusion-jumpers, some will be praise from the thoughtful. But whatever the reaction, Kinsey will go right on wading into his big job," seeking out facts "entirely with their social implications in mind, and with the undeniable conviction that discovering new truth about a subject too long in the dark can bring mankind nothing but benefit."[74]

Like the flattering image he had cultivated, Kinsey's version of history found a prominent place in these articles, laying the groundwork for what quickly became the official canon surrounding his work. Partly fact and partly fiction, it was a tale of one man's struggle to conduct controversial research in the face of great obstacles.

"The saga of Kinsey," declared *Look*, "begins somewhat like a Gary Cooper movie." Parroting the script Kinsey had provided, *Look* went on to explain how students had asked sexual questions of a quiet, mild-mannered zoology professor in Indiana; how the professor, unable to answer those questions, had searched the literature for data, only to be appalled by what he had found; and how he had started interviewing his students to find answers to those questions. When the campus started to buzz over his controversial research, however, Kinsey was summoned to the President Wells's office. "One session with that clear-headed, fact-hungry scientist convinced the president," declared *Look.* "He sent Kinsey off with a pat on the back," pledging that "the University would defend his right to do objective research that was obviously going to be of benefit to mankind." Armed with this assurance, Kinsey had spent the last nine years conducting his research with total dedication, all the while battling a variety of opponents who threatened "legal action, political investigation, and censorship."[75] In other words, Kinsey's research had involved both conflict and struggle, adding another chapter to a time-honored tradition in Western culture—the scientist as embattled hero.

While the lay press kept him busy, Kinsey also had to worry about scholarly reviews. His publisher, of course, had been concerned about adverse publicity from the outset. In June 1947, Lawrence Saunders met with Robert S. Morison at the Rockefeller Foundation to discuss how to handle the scholarly and professional advertisements for the male volume. Saunders suggested placing ads in professional journals about two weeks before the announcements in the lay press, and Morison readily agreed. Morison's primary concern was not advertising but the timing of the scholarly reviews. The problem, he explained, was that the lay press published reviews much faster than the professional journals, and in Kinsey's case it was terribly important "to have a solid background of professional opinion before the newspapers get a chance to start things off on the wrong foot."[76]

As work on the book progressed, Saunders informed Kinsey of Morison's concerns. A less resourceful man might have accepted this problem as an unavoidable fact of academic life. Kinsey, by contrast, saw it as another challenge to be overcome. Instead of despairing, he involved himself in one of the academy's most sacred rituals: the process of peer review.

Most scholars place their fate in the hands of the gods, since they have no control over who reviews their books. As a rule, the editors of reputable scholarly journals assign books to reviewers without consulting authors. They do this for a good reason: authors tend to recommend people they believe will write favorable reviews. To make certain a chorus of favorable reviews launched his book, then, Kinsey had to devise a way to corrupt a system of peer review designed to operate without input from authors.

Kinsey's solution was as clever as it was effective. Rather than defer to editors, he decided to pick his own judges by requesting luminaries in various fields to contact the editors of specific journals and volunteer to review the book. In the fall 1947, he asked a number of scholars to review the male volume, including Clyde Kluckhohn (the professor at Harvard who had encouraged Gebhard to join Kinsey's staff) in anthropology, Carl Hartman in reproductive biology, and Joseph K. Folsom in sociology, whose friendship with Kinsey dated back to summer camps in New England. With regard to Folsom, some scholars might have found it awkward to ask this favor of someone they had known since boyhood, but not Kinsey. As he told Folsom, "I realize this is imposing on an old friend, but you will understand that it is particularly important to have this sort of thing properly placed before the public."[77]

At first glance, it seems almost unbelievable that Kinsey was able to plant so many reviews in leading academic journals. Upon closer examination, though, it is clear that he succeeded for three reasons. First, he chose people with the professional clout to place reviews wherever they wished; second, he stressed that newspaper reviews would almost certainly damage the book and had to be counterbalanced by scholarly reviews; and third, he did a great job of flattering the people he approached. For example, in his letter to Bentley Glass, a distinguished zoologist at Johns Hopkins whom he asked to write a review for the *Quarterly Review of Biology,* he declared, "We are particularly anxious to counter-weight this public review of our book with technical scientific criticisms of it." Explaining why speed was of the essence, Kinsey added, "We are not looking for publicity or advertising, but I think in the interest of scientific advancement on a subject that has to be handled carefully, it will be well to get scientific evaluations of our book in print at an early date."[78]

Again, only a shrewd psychologist and a master manipulator could have pulled this off. Implicit in every invitation to write a review was a compliment in the form of a huge vote of confidence. In effect, Kinsey was telling these scholars that he trusted them to handle a difficult task with distinction. Small wonder that several scholars actually submitted drafts to him for comment before their reviews were published.

Nor would Kinsey take no for an answer. In his letter to Glass, for example, he wrote, "We should be delighted if you yourself would care to review the book, but would trust your judgment to choose someone else." When Glass replied that he did not feel qualified and suggested Frank Beach as a substitute, however, Kinsey refused to let Glass off the hook.[79] The negotiations that followed underscored not only Kinsey's ability to persuade scholars to write reviews but his knack for shaping what they said. "Frank Beach could do a good job on the review, but I think you would see more of the significance of the tie-up of scientific data and social problems which is involved throughout the book," insisted Kinsey. "It is time that the scientists have their attention drawn to the possibility of applying our methods to social problems. That is why I would be delighted if you decided to write the review yourself."[80] In the end, Glass gave in to this potent mixture of flattery and pleading. His review, which took the exact approach Kinsey had suggested, appeared in March 1948 as the lead review in the *Quarterly Review of Biology*. A master at the game, Kinsey followed up with a thank-you note, a practice he pursued with all reviewers who pleased him. "You did a magnificent job in accurate reviewing," praised Kinsey. "We much appreciate your friendly and commendatory review. It is nice to know that the biologists are approving as they evidently are everywhere."[81]

As Kinsey perused the popular and scholarly articles that appeared in print as the new year approached, he had one last reason to be pleased with himself. It involved an achievement of no little import. During Gregg's visit to Bloomington back in February 1947, Kinsey had made a momentous request. He asked Gregg to write the introduction to the male volume.[82] This request, which Kinsey pressed with impassioned conviction, placed Gregg in an awkward position. As a senior officer, Gregg understood full well the foundation's aversion to publicity, and he correctly foresaw that Kinsey's work would generate controversy. Indeed, the two men had clashed on this issue on several occasions, with Gregg all but ordering Kinsey to credit the NRC with financing his research and to cease his public proclamations about the Rockefeller Foundation's support. Since a preface was tantamount to an endorsement, Gregg could not agree without identifying himself and the Rockefeller Foundation with Kinsey's research. In short, foundation policy required Gregg to say no.

And for a while it looked as though Gregg would do precisely that. Despite Kinsey's importuning, Gregg returned to New York without accepting, promising only to give the matter serious thought.[83] Surprisingly, Gregg decided in the end to do it, allowing his faith in the research and his belief in Kinsey to override foundation policy.

Once he agreed, Gregg took the assignment very seriously, producing a preface that would have graced any book. He even went so far as to send Kinsey a draft, with the friendly note—"I submit it for criticism or rejection, not for acceptance. In other words if you don't like all of it, don't take it—or if you want part but want something more or less, tell me and I'll try to catch and rephrase your idea."[84]

Gregg's draft was a ringing endorsement of Kinsey's research. While the opening was majestically philosophical, Gregg quickly adopted a partisan tone, lauding Kinsey's findings "for their extent, their thoroughness, and their dispassionate objectivity." Kinsey, he noted, had "studied sex phenomena of human beings as a biologist would examine biological phenomena, and the evidence he has secured is presented from the biologists' view, without moral bias or prejudice derived from current taboos." Gregg went on to characterize Kinsey's studies as "sincere, objective, and determined explorations," insisting that they had required of Kinsey and his associates "very unusual tenacity of purpose, tolerance, analytical competence, social skills, and real courage." In closing, Gregg pleaded, "I hope that the reader will match the authors with an equal and appropriate measure of cool attention, courageous judgment, and scientific equanimity."[85]

Yet Gregg's preface was also a carefully crafted political document, one that omitted any mention of the Rockefeller Foundation's role in supporting Kinsey's research. Instead, Gregg gave sole credit to the NRC's Committee for Research in Problems of Sex, an organization that had sponsored, in his words, "a more significant series of research studies on sex than has been accomplished perhaps by any other agency."[86] In this manner, Gregg doubtless hoped to endorse Kinsey's research, to acknowledge the NRC, and to keep the Rockefeller Foundation safely in the shadows. Although he succeeded on the first two points, Gregg failed on the third. Directly beneath his name, which appeared at the end of the preface, was printed his affiliation: "The Medical Sciences, Rockefeller Foundation, New York City."[87] Given his position, there was no way he could separate his personal and professional identities. Anyone who read his preface would have assumed that the Rockefeller Foundation had placed its imprimatur on Kinsey's research. Despite everything Gregg had argued in the past, then, Kinsey got what he wanted.

And just as he had planned, the first wave of magazine articles and scholarly reviews emphasized that the NRC and the Rockefeller Foundation had supported his research, with much greater stress on the latter than the former. This was no coincidence. When these same journalists had visited Bloomington, Kinsey had shouted his affiliation with the Rockefeller Foundation and whispered his relationship to the NRC. Not that this was anything new. Again, from the moment the grants had started arriving, Kinsey had traded shamelessly on the Rockefeller Foundation's name, attempting to use its prestige and reputation to convince the public and other scientists that his research was rigorous and valid. All that changed in 1947 was that he commandeered a host of reporters to help him broadcast this message to the nation.

"So startling are its revelations, so contrary to what civilized man has been taught for generations that they would be unbelievable but for the impressive weight of scientific agencies backing the survey," declared *Harper's Magazine*. It went on to identify Kinsey's patrons as the NRC, which it called "the most authoritative scientific body in the land," and the Rockefeller Foundation, which it stressed had supported Kinsey's work with a steady stream of grants. In addition, *Harper's* emphasized that the preface to the male volume had been written by the medical chief of the Rockefeller Foundation, Alan Gregg, whom *Harper's* praised as "one of the wisest of medical statesmen." Quoting directly from his preface, it appealed to the public "to receive Kinsey's findings with 'cool attention, courageous judgment, and scientific equanimity.' "[88]

Decades later, Robert S. Morison called his boss's decision to write the preface "unwise," largely because the preface was "so likely to be misinterpreted." Morison continued, "The theory under which we were operating was that we made every effort to investigate projects and programs and people before we gave them grants, but that after that they were responsible for what they did." Without citing names, Morison observed with remarkable understatement, "There were people who felt that it was fuzzing up that relationship a bit to write that introduction."[89] In Morison's view, Gregg wrote the preface partly because he "liked and admired Kinsey" and partly because he hoped that Kinsey's work "would have some sort of an effect on improving the attitude of the American people toward sex." Not that Gregg's reform instincts were limited to sex. The Gregg whom Morison knew "wanted to promote more humane attitudes in almost anything."[90]

Whatever misgivings others might have had, Kinsey was elated. "If you knew how far back we began to hope that you would write this Preface, you would understand that this is a day of considerable importance to us, now that you have done it," he wrote Gregg.[91] Although careful to say how much he liked the preface, he did not allow his approval and gratitude to prevent him from gilding the lily. Gregg's eloquence notwithstanding, Kinsey made three or four minor corrections on the draft, being constitutionally incapable of doing otherwise.[92]

Thus, as the publication date approached, Kinsey had done everything in his power to orchestrate a favorable reception for his book. Whether handling journalists or his fellow scholars, Kinsey had demonstrated his characteristic instinct for manipulation and control. No scientist of his day had schemed harder to stage the publication of his work as a national event or to influence its reception by the public and the academy alike. Yet Kinsey was far from alone in his efforts to smooth the way for the male volume. In the fall of 1947, each of the key figures who had supported his research took steps to shield him and their organizations from the storms ahead.

For President Wells, the task was complicated by the fact that he had to manage things from abroad. From November 1947 through May 1948, he was on leave of absence from the university, serving as a personal adviser to General Lucius Clay, who was in charge of the U.S. Military Government in Germany. Given the simulated rank of a two-star general, Wells was to advise General Clay on educational and cultural matters, in which capacity he played a key role in founding the Free University of Berlin.[93] But despite his busy schedule, Wells took steps to leave Indiana University in a strong position to defend both itself and Kinsey from critics.

Prior to his departure for Europe, Wells turned his prodigious administrative talents to tucking Kinsey's forthcoming volume safely under the protective mantle of academic freedom. Convinced that those who were forewarned would be forearmed, Wells briefed the university's trustees on Kinsey's research, all the while reminding them that a scholar's right to publish his findings was the essence of academic freedom. In Wells's judgment, Kinsey's research offered the perfect test case for academic freedom. "So frequently when issues are raised over academic freedom, the cases are not clear-cut, and so you have many problems with them that are not involved with the issue itself," observed Wells many years later. "But here is a recognized scientist, a man who is a starred man of science, a man that other scientists have judged to be one of the few of that quality who is not exploiting his field for any personal gain or anything of this sort, his motives are entirely pure and scientific." Wells remembered telling the trustees, "You will either back him, and back him completely if you want to have a university. If you can't take that, you might as well recognize what you are doing. You are liquidating the essence of the university."[94]

Wells also moved to shore up the university's defenses in the state legislature. "In those days the budget committee . . . was all-powerful in the legislature, . . . and made an annual or a biannual visit to the university of two or three days in which they looked at a great many things," recalled Wells. "We always insisted that they go over and have a session at the Kinsey Institute, go in it and look around and look at the material that was available and talk to Kinsey and his people," he continued. "The Institute was always so clinical in its appearance, so dry and unerotic that they always came away convinced that this was a serious scientific endeavor." Describing Kinsey's skill at selling his research, Wells exclaimed, "Oh, magnificent, magnificent! Just magnificent!"[95]

George W. Corner, too, prepared his troops for battle. In October 1947, he gave the members of the CRPS a detailed briefing on the publication plans for the male volume, noting that he had arranged for each of them to receive a copy of the book "as early as possible." Reminding his colleagues that Kinsey's research would "augment to a revolutionary extent the scientific knowledge of human sex behavior now available," Corner cautioned, "A great deal of comment is likely to occur, and in some quarters there may be reactions of surprise, even of shock." Still, he was confident that everything possible had been done to present the book tastefully.

Complimenting Kinsey on his astute guidance of the specialized journalists who had prepared articles on the forthcoming volume, Corner concluded, "In my opinion it is better for this enlightening work to be introduced to the public by trained science writers under Dr. Kinsey's control, than by uncontrolled, ill-informed, sensational journalism."[96]

No less than Wells and Corner, Alan Gregg conducted last-minute maneuvers. Although his confidence in Kinsey remained firm, Gregg, too, worried that the going might get rough. Kinsey's research, Gregg confided to a friend, was bound to produce "a great deal of criticism and disillusionment because it concerns a field which is not very far removed from powerful emotions and taboos."[97] To prepare for the storms ahead, Gregg adopted pretty much the same strategy for handling the foundation's trustees that Wells used with the university's trustees. At their annual meeting on December 3, 1947, Gregg gave the trustees a thorough review of the foundation's relations with Kinsey, though he evidently failed to mention he had written the preface for the male volume. What is certain is that the trustees followed his presentation closely and asked a number of questions, as the first group of magazine articles had just hit the newsstands and Kinsey's research was being much discussed across the nation. "Their attitude was sensible and encouraging as well as interested," Gregg later wrote Kinsey. Gregg also noted that he was contacting the Saunders Company "to place an order for copies to be sent to our Trustees."[98]

A day after Gregg delivered this upbeat report, Arthur Hays Sulzberger, publisher of the *New York Times* and one of the most influential members of the Rockefeller Foundation's board of trustees, wrote a testy letter to his good friend Raymond Fosdick, president of the foundation. Sulzberger, it seems, had read one of the magazine articles on Kinsey that had just appeared, and the publisher did not like what he saw. "I am afraid some unpleasantness may develop because of the Rockefeller Foundation's backing of the project," he declared. While admitting that the Saunders Company was "a presumably reputable publisher of medical books," he passed along rumors that the advance orders for the book numbered 100,000 copies, and he accused the firm of "trying to cash in on some 'hot stuff.' "[99]

As proof, Sulzberger enclosed samples of advertisements the Saunders Company had submitted to the *New York Times,* notices he found grossly offensive. Not only did the advertisements contain descriptive materials and the table of contents from the male volume, but they splashed the Rockefeller Foundation's name all over the copy, announcing that the foundation had provided financial support and that Alan Gregg had written the preface. The *Times* flatly refused to publish these advertisements. Furthermore, Sulzberger questioned the publisher's decision to make the manuscript widely available to the press, although he did acknowledge that Kinsey had attempted to minimize sensationalism by stipulating "that any articles written from the proofs must be submitted to him and passed by him." Still, Sulzberger made it clear he was less than pleased, telling Fosdick, "The whole situation is creating no little flurry." Admitting he was personally caught up in the controversy, he noted that he was currently involved in discussions "as to how we should review the book."[100] His complaints offered the first hint that trouble might be brewing on the board.

The preface produced bewilderment, disappointment, and concern at the NRC, whose officials faulted Kinsey far more than Gregg. Decades later, Corner described Yerkes as "a little disappointed" that the invitation had gone to Gregg in the first place.[101] "Yerkes had expected to write the preface. He had every reason to feel that he had staked his reputation for judgment on backing Kinsey's work, as indeed Gregg had," explained Corner.[102] Yerkes, of course, was too much of a gentleman to complain publicly, but he did criticize Kinsey in private, telling Corner, "I am more than a little humiliated and embarrassed by the special acknowledgment made to me personally when it should instead have been to the committee." Sharpening his criticism, Yerkes continued, "After all our organization assumed certain risks and took very considerable pains to try to help Kinsey forward and his acknowledgments make one feel that he has largely forgotten it or for some reason feels that all of his blessings should be credited to the source of funds instead of to the agency which was charged with responsibility for deciding how they should be used and for the wisdom of their use. This is not as it should have been and I am disappointed."[103]

Corner shared this view. "Like you, I have not been altogether happy over Kinsey's way of doing things," he confided to Yerkes. "It seems to me that he let himself forget, as you can say, that the Committee was the effective agent in getting him large-scale support, and came to feel that the Committee and the NRC, as organizations, were to some extent in his way." Trying to soothe Yerkes's hurt feelings, Corner added reassuringly, "There are plenty of people who realize that you took the brunt of backing Kinsey when his work really needed support and that the Committee strongly backed you. In the long run I do not think that this will be forgotten."[104]

Reflecting on this episode decades later, however, Corner made it clear that Yerkes's sadness over being snubbed was nothing compared with his concerns about how the Rockefeller trustees would react. "Now, up to this point the Foundation had been very careful, it seemed to me, not to have its name introduced into this," explained Corner, who insisted that the foundation "did not want to be dragged into this in any way which would make it seem responsible for the work." In Corner's judgment, Gregg had made a tactical mistake by writing the preface, as it "drew public attention onto the Rockefeller Foundation."[105]

On December 9, 1947, Fosdick, with copies of the offending advertisements in hand, descended on Gregg's office with orders to put out the fire.[106] That same day, Gregg telephoned Saunders, explained the foundation's position, and asked him to change the offensive advertisements.[107] Defensive and embarrassed, Saunders was mortified by the whole affair and immediately agreed to Gregg's demands. Writing in his desk diary, Gregg described their conversation as "entirely satisfactory," adding, "He agrees to show us copy of any advertising for the newspapers."[108]

To underscore the seriousness of the matter and to establish a paper trail, Gregg followed up with a strong letter, stating that he was "disturbed" by the newspaper advertisements for Kinsey's research because the tone was "not in keeping with what we hoped from Kinsey's selection of your firm as medical publishers." Turning to the red button issue, Gregg declared, "The use of the Foundation's name . . . would not have had our sanction had your advertising division consulted me in advance. We are prepared for the misunderstandings and disfavor that may attend the support of a scientific study of a taboo subject but not prepared to be used in a kind of advertising that can hardly fail to discredit an undertaking we wish to help." The challenge facing them all, Gregg lectured, was to advertise Kinsey's book with "dignity and candor and without a trace of commercialism" so that Kinsey's study would "not suffer."[109]

But Gregg did not stop there. Opting for a two-prong attack to reinforce the message, he telephoned Corner and asked him to hit Saunders with the same complaints. Corner, too, found Saunders the soul of contrition. When they spoke by telephone, Corner had barely finished greeting him before Saunders interrupted to say that he agreed with Gregg's criticisms and would see to it that the advertisements were changed. Saunders promised to suppress the inappropriate copy and to replace it with advertisements that would be, in Corner's words, "dignified and proper."[110]

True to his word, Saunders got back immediately to Gregg with a conciliatory note and a revised copy that dropped the table of contents. The only problem was that the new copy retained the references to Gregg's preface, complete with his Rockefeller affiliation.[111] In response, Gregg praised the revised copy as "much more satisfactory" but requested additional changes. Noting that he had explained his position "more than once to Dr. Kinsey," Gregg told Saunders, "I think the credit for the National Research Council's support of his [Kinsey's] study belongs to the N.R.C. Committee for Research on [sic] Problems of Sex, and I do not quite like any presentation that ignores or minimizes the credit I think that Committee deserves." While some might interpret his position as "an oblique way of dodging responsibility," Gregg argued, "the long term result of this whole study will be greatly to the credit of all of the members of that Committee, and in as much as in the earlier stages of Kinsey's work we were not even aware of it [,] it seems a little shabby for it to be presented as something which the Foundation had discovered." Gregg was equally firm about his role. "As to the use of my own name," he wrote, "I would, of course, much prefer to have it not made a point of advertising, though I don't have any regret nor qualification for the support I gave personally by writing the preface." So that there would be no mistaking his meaning, he added, "I would, of course, be glad to have my name left out and certainly very grateful indeed if you did not use it at all."[112] This letter produced the desired results, and the third version of the advertising met with Gregg's approval.

All that remained was to deal with Kinsey, who everyone knew would not be pleased by the changes in the advertising. As a courtesy, Gregg had sent him a copy of his first letter to Saunders. By mutual agreement Gregg and Corner had decided that Corner should be the point man with Kinsey. Corner did his best to head off the expected explosion. Stressing that he and Gregg were in complete agreement, Corner informed Kinsey that the newspaper advertisements for the male volume "had come all too close to the kind of commercial, irresponsible advertising of books on sex physiology, erotica, etc., that are sold without honest scientific and educational intentions." Advertising of this ilk was dangerous, he warned Kinsey, because it was "likely to give the wrong impression of your attitude and standards." Corner also reported that he and Gregg had discussed the matter with Saunders and that Saunders had agreed to revise the advertising plan.[113]

Anyone else would have backed off, but Kinsey was incapable of remaining silent. Just as he had bypassed Yerkes in previous disputes, Kinsey ignored Corner and went directly to Gregg, professing not to understand the foundation's objections. "The statement that The Rockefeller Foundation has financially backed the research has, of course, been publicly made ever since that became a fact; and that statement is made, in a form which I understood you approved in the book," declared Kinsey. Conveniently ignoring that he had boasted about the foundation's support to the press at every opportunity, Kinsey added innocently, "The magazine and newspaper writers have, inevitably, laid emphasis upon that fact, and that is beyond our control as long as it is part of the fact."[114]

Kinsey also attempted to reassure Gregg that the male volume would be well received. Among the hundreds of letters that had poured in, he reported, most had expressed "enthusiastic approval." Nor was the university wavering. "Our Administration is taking a very staunch stand in its determination to defend the whole project, and its present publication," asserted Kinsey. "Personally I do not expect any particular difficulty."[115]

Gregg made one last effort to try to explain his "misgivings." Arguing that publicity of this sort was both unnecessary and unwise, he declared, "Frankly I think the advanced orders indicate that the magazine articles are going to be the best form of advertising and that any sensational stuff put in the newspapers would injure the status of the book rather than aid it and perhaps affect the Saunders Company's reputation as well." Repeating what he had often said, Gregg insisted that the credit belonged to the NRC. Moreover, he was, he noted with great restraint, "a little troubled" over seeing his name played up "in such a conspicuous position" in some of the first advertisements. "I realize that the subject is not one that can be left to the medical profession alone but the magazine articles have taken care of that, and I think the wise course from now on is to be firm and decorous and cautious lest the suspicion arise that there are lively commercial motives involved with the publication," he counseled Kinsey.[116]

Thus, on eve of the male volume's publication, it appeared that the last-minute flap regarding undignified publicity had been brought under control. Still, Gregg had been right to worry that some people might think there were "lively commercial motives involved with the publication." That suspicion had disturbed Sulzberger, and at least one officer in the Rockefeller Foundation knew where to point the finger. Writing to his boss, Morison told Gregg, "The only comment I would like to make . . . is that I am sorry the idea is getting about that Saunders is trying to exploit Kinsey's book for his own financial gain." Morison thought otherwise. "It has certainly been my impression that Saunders has been very wary of the whole thing from the start, and on several occasions he has expressed his obvious distress that Kinsey was thinking in terms of advertising to the general public," he declared. In his view, Saunders had done his best to resist but had been forced "to make some concessions in order to insure that publication rights would not go to some other house."[117]

If Gregg felt troubled by this assessment, he did not show it. Foremost in his mind was the contribution he felt certain Kinsey's book would make. Writing to his brother on January 4, 1948, he declared, "Tomorrow the much heralded Kinsey report on Sexual Behavior in the Human Male comes on sale. It will be something of a landmark I think and though the going has been a little rough in spots I am glad to have been connected with the support given these studies." Showing how deeply he had drunk at Kinsey's well, Gregg continued, "The most interesting and significant fact revealed is the extraordinary variety in the patterns of different individuals. Together with the taboo involved this extraordinary variety could well cast light upon the passionate differences of opinion that have grown up and made such monkeys of Western culture in this field." Anticipating the slings and arrows ahead, Gregg ended with a quotation at once apt and ironic: "As Oscar Wilde neatly observed, 'All criticism is a form of autobiography.' "[118]

Kinsey would have agreed, as his complaints against society had sprung from his life. But after a decade of disciplined, relentless, and altogether fascinating research, Kinsey was about to get his wish. On January 5, 1948, the male volume would hit the stands. From the moment it went on sale, the world would beat a path to his door.

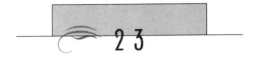

"Successor to Darwin?"

ot since *Gone with the Wind* had booksellers seen anything like it," exclaimed *Time* magazine. Despite its three-pound weight, hefty price of $6.50, and 804 pages packed with "a dreary morass of technical jargon and statistical charts," Americans seemed drawn to *Sexual Behavior in the Human Male* the way they "had once taken to the Charleston, the yo-yo and the forcing two bid," raved *Time*.[1] *Newsweek* agreed, calling the book "the season's most sensational best seller."[2]

"The Kinsey Report," as the public quickly dubbed the book, was a blockbuster. During the first two months of 1948, Americans purchased more than 200,000 hardback copies, with the W. B. Saunders Company running two presses around the clock to satisfy demand. To keep the orders coming, Saunders doubled its original advertising budget and placed consecutive ads in many scientific journals and metropolitan newspapers, particularly those with Sunday issues that included book review sections.[3] Kinsey saw the book's success as vindication. "People have wanted a study of this kind," he told a reporter. "I think scientists have completely underestimated the public's desire to get a really unemotional, scientific book on sex." Unable to resist tooting his own horn, Kinsey added, "There are an awful lot of timid people in the world. If we'd been as timid as the rest, we'd never have done the study."[4]

Favorable reviews drove the sales of *Sexual Behavior in the Human Male*, with the nation's most important newspaper leading the way. On January 4, 1948, one day before the book's official publication date, the Sunday edition of the *New York Times* published a lengthy, serious, dignified, and altogether glowing review by Howard A. Rusk, which appeared on the fourth page of the book review section. A physician and the founder and director of New York University Medical Center's Howard A. Rusk Institute of Rehabilitation, Rusk wrote a weekly medical column for the *Times* from 1946 to 1969. More important, he was the newspaper's favorite medical book reviewer. Correctly predicting that Kinsey's book would be "sure to create an explosion and to be bitterly controversial," Rusk left no doubt about where he stood. Among the hundreds of books that littered the field, *Sexual Behavior in the Human Male*, he told his readers, was "by far the most comprehensive study yet made of sex behavior."[5]

Like so many reviewers who followed, Rusk lauded the sheer volume of Kinsey's data, data that seemed absolutely reliable. In his judgment, Kinsey's research could be trusted because it rested on sound methodology. "The approach of this specific study is the taxonomic one of the trained scientist, and is based on over 12,000 personal interviews, each encompassing over 300 questions," reported Rusk. For those readers who might be unfamiliar with science, he explained that the "taxonomic approach" involved the "measurement of the variation in a series of individuals that represent the species." The ease with which Rusk embraced terms such as "variation" and "species" reflected the degree to which he and Kinsey spoke the same language, a language that reflected shared values regarding the biological basis of human sexual behavior.[6]

Much of Rusk's review focused on Kinsey's findings. Rusk ticked off shocking data on premarital intercourse, homosexuality, and the like. The essential point, he argued, was that Kinsey had revealed the extent to which Americans of different ages and classes routinely violated prescribed behavior. In other words, Rusk told Americans that most of what they had been taught about human sexuality had been disproven by Kinsey. People who transgressed, it seemed, were neither deviant nor unusual. Instead of a fixed pattern, sexual behavior was a mosaic of individual variation, a fact that raised important questions about "what is 'normal' and 'abnormal,' and where such terms fit in a scientific study."[7]

Aware he was handling political dynamite, Rusk devoted fully half of his review to the social implications of Kinsey's book, arguing that its data required a thorough reevaluation of the meaning and control of human sexuality in America. Armed with Kinsey's facts, declared Rusk, "we can reorganize some of our attitudes [later in the review he spoke explicitly of "moral concepts"] and methods of sex education on the basis of need as dictated by experience rather than preconception, and we must surely re-examine the legal criteria by which we renounce and condemn sex behavior." Kinsey's research, Rusk insisted, "should promote tolerance and understanding and make us better 'world citizens.'" Implicit in this message was a plea: groups that engaged in uncommon behavior should neither be ostracized nor punished. Recognizing that many Americans would feel threatened by any challenges to conventional morality, Rusk closed by quoting Gregg's preface beseeching readers to match Kinsey's scientific rigor and scholarly detachment "with an equal and appropriate measure of cool attention, courageous judgment and scientific equanimity."[8]

The *Times*'s review was a godsend to Kinsey. No other newspaper in the country commanded more respect or had more power to influence public opinion.[9] Kinsey was thrilled by the review, boasting to President Wells that the *Times* had "finally done big things for us."[10] Interestingly, despite its reference to Gregg, the review was warmly received in some quarters of the Rockefeller Foundation. Calling Rusk's review "a masterpiece," Raymond B. Fosdick, the president of the foundation, told his friend Arthur Sulzberger, "It set the tone and pattern for public discussion, and I think it will prove a very useful thing. You couldn't have found a wiser or abler man to do the job."[11]

The *Times*'s review did establish the tone for the nation, at least initially. In the beginning, Kinsey got a fantastic press, as journalists (and many scholars) showered him with praise.[12] They endorsed his methodology, lauded his data, and assured their readers that the nation was in for a major overhaul of its sexual mores. Echoing the prepublication pieces (accounts *Time* magazine correctly characterized as "excited drum-beating by science writers"),[13] journalists described Kinsey as a dedicated scientist—focused, hardworking, serious, dispassionate, and objective. The *New Republic*, for example, hailed *Sexual Behavior in the Human Male* as "a triumph of sanity and reason in a field of the highest human consequences,"[14] while the prim and proper *Good Housekeeping* gave Kinsey its official seal of approval, deeming his book "the most important report of the kind ever attempted."[15] All across the land, in newspapers and magazines large and small, journalists commended Kinsey's methodology, sample size, and analytic rigor, agreeing that his research had far-reaching social implications that required a thorough review of sexual mores, sex education, and sex offender codes.

Aware that the public regarded Kinsey as a scientific jack-in-the-box who had appeared to pop out of nowhere, journalists went to great lengths to humanize the Hoosier sex researcher. Most began by assuring their readers that he was a reputable, well-established scholar who was backed by organizations that could be trusted. His research, they noted, was supported by Indiana University, the CRPS of the NRC, and the medical division of the Rockefeller Foundation, with particular emphasis on the latter. Announcing that this foundation was contributing $40,000 annually, *Life* magazine reported, "Before the grant was made both the research program and Kinsey himself were carefully scrutinized by the foundation, which concluded that he was not merely well but superbly qualified for his undertaking."[16]

In the months following the book's release, Kinsey became a national celebrity. As an entomologist, he had been a major player in a minor field, producing research that seldom got noticed by scientists outside his specialty and remained virtually invisible to the public at large. Following his shift in 1938 to sex research, of course, Kinsey had gradually become known to a wider circle, but a decade of frantic work had failed to make most Americans aware of his research. The publication of *Sexual Behavior in the Human Male* changed all that. Suddenly, and for the rest of his life, Kinsey would be familiar to most Americans, and eventually his fame would extend worldwide. Journalists, clergymen, physicians, psychiatrists, psychologists, attorneys, judges, social workers, marriage counselors, criminologists, penologists, birth control workers, youth organization administrators, and public school teachers (to name only the most obvious groups)—all took an avid interest in Kinsey's research. As well they should have. No scientist in history had served up more data on human sexual behavior to the endless line of experts who badly needed these facts.

Nor did the book's audience stop with professional groups. No scientific book of this century became more widely known to the general public than *Sexual Behavior in the Human Male*—even if it was more often mentioned than read. In the months following its publication, Americans could scarcely pick up a newspaper without seeing Kinsey's photograph or reading ruminations about his work, and magazines and other periodicals conspired to keep Kinsey before the public long after the newspaper stories had dropped off. The two years following its publication saw more than five hundred magazine and journal articles about *Sexual Behavior in the Human Male* or about Kinsey personally.[17] In short, the Kinsey report became that rarest of publishing events: a book that becomes a news story. As *Cue* magazine put it, the winter of 1947–48 would "undoubtedly be known as the year of the big snow and the Kinsey Report."[18] A scholarly reviewer was even more effusive, predicting that Kinsey would be the "man from whom an era would take its name."[19]

Journalists outdid themselves writing positive personal sketches to feed the public's craving for details about Kinsey's life. *People* magazine told its readers, "Dr. Kinsey has few conventional vices," adding, "The professor does not swear and he does not smoke." Even when they seemed on the verge of penetrating Kinsey's congenial façade and uncovering the domineering, driven man who lurked just beneath the surface, journalists usually softened implied criticisms, as was the case with the *People* article, which reported, "Conversationally, Kinsey is brisk, direct, sure of himself. He smiles readily and has a nice turn of humor, which saves his self-assurance from bordering on the obnoxious. A faculty friend calls him, 'one of those men who are always right about everything.' "[20] A little more digging would have uncovered faculty members who made the same point with considerably less charity.

Kinsey must have been particularly pleased by the tributes to the purity of his motives. At a time when social critics were bemoaning the crass materialism of American society, journalists depicted Kinsey as an otherworldly scientist, a completely selfless man who derived no financial rewards from his research—none whatsoever. "All royalties go into a fund for continuing Dr. Kinsey's work in what is called the Institute for Sex Research, Inc.," reported *People* magazine. "Kinsey could add to his income by writing for magazines or giving an occasion public lecture," it continued. "He has been offered more than his yearly professor's salary for one article (the editor wanted to call it How I Do It) and as much as Winston Churchill for a single talk. . . . Thus far he has resisted commercialisation [*sic*]."[21]

Polishing her husband's halo, Clara bristled at the suggestion that they were getting rich off the royalties. "I get so furious at those who mistakenly think we've made a lot of money out of this book!" she told an interviewer. "Why, it's cost us money!" she fumed. "Prok has no time to revise his biology textbook and such a revision would insure us a small income. Every nickel made by *Sexual Behavior in the Human Male* goes to the Institute for Sex Research to be reinvested in further work. . . . If people think we're rich I wish they could take a look at Prok's wardrobe. He's only got one decent suit to his name."[22] Kinsey himself repeatedly stressed that it was not for personal glory or private gain that he had undertaken the study. His sole motivation, he insisted, was to give the public badly needed information. "Think of the tens of millions of people who for the first time have seen open discussion of sex in magazines," he told a reporter.[23]

If Kinsey enjoyed the comments about his personality and character, he must have loved the physical descriptions. Ironically, the man who had been such a sickly youth and the only boy in his class not to play a single team sport was cast in robust, masculine terms. In its most widely read section, "The Talk of the Town," the *New Yorker* described Kinsey as "a big, husky fellow, appearing to be younger than his fifty-three years."[24] *Life* considered Kinsey "a rugged, tweedy man,"[25] while *People* magazine described him as "a husky, hardy man in his mid fifties, with . . . a powerful square-cut jaw."[26] To *Time* magazine he appeared "burly,"[27] while *Cue* magazine described him as "a big, husky man looking much younger than his fifty-three years and resembling a football player rather than the zoologist he is."[28] *Cosmopolitan* magazine thought Kinsey looked "like a truck driver."[29] "Burly," "husky," "hardy," "football player," "truck driver"—Kinsey could hardly have asked for more flattering tributes to his masculinity.

As part of their background research, many journalists investigated Kinsey's private life. Those who hoped to dig up any dirt were disappointed, as they quickly discovered that Kinsey was an adoring husband and devoted father, the perfect family man. "Everyone who knows the Kinseys reports that they are not only happily but ideally married," announced *Life* magazine. "At parties Mac and Prok usually behave as though they had just met and are trying to impress each other," *Life* continued, "and unless the conversation is pretty stimulating Kinsey is apt to devote his whole attention to his wife."[30] Striking the same note, *People* magazine gushed, "In any casebook, the Kinsey marriage would have to be set down not only as 'happy' and 'successful' but probably as 'ideal.' After nearly 30 years they still seem in love with each other."[31]

Several magazines included brief sketches of Clara, each describing a devoted mother and a wife who served as the perfect helpmate. Still, the nation's curiosity about her was far from satisfied. A cartoon in the *New Yorker* showed a woman seated in a comfortable chair looking up from her copy of *Sexual Behavior in the Human Male* with a quizzical look on her face and asking, "Is there a Mrs. Kinsey?"[32] Playing off that cartoon, *McCall's* published an article in July 1948 entitled "Yes, There Is a Mrs. Kinsey." From start to finish its portrait of the Kinsey family was wholesome. Clara came off as warm and loving, a homebody who cooked and sewed, entertained the many visitors her husband brought home, and never, ever complained about his long workdays or the many field trips that kept him away from Bloomington. Commenting on the unqualified support she gave her husband, Clara beamed, "What I'm doing is a privilege. I believe so thoroughly in Prok's survey."[33]

With journalists vouching for his home life and testifying to the historic importance of his research, Kinsey was a shoo-in for stardom. Suddenly, the man who had longed to do great things all his life heard his book mentioned in the same breath as *Principia Mathematica*, *The Wealth of Nations*, and *Das Kapital*. He saw himself added to a pantheon of scientific heroes that included Galileo, Copernicus, and Freud. But the historical figure to whom most writers likened Kinsey was Charles Darwin. Thirty-six years had passed since his classmates at Columbia High School had labeled him "a second Darwin," and in the ensuing decades Kinsey had worked frightfully hard to redeem their faith. Beginning in 1948 and for the rest of his life, he heard many thoughtful adults make the same comparison, and they were serious.

Astounded by the phenomenal sales of *Sexual Behavior in the Human Male, Life* magazine assured its readers, "To find another purely scientific book with a record which even approaches this, it probably is necessary to go back to Darwin's *On the Origin of Species,* published in 1859."[34] Under the heading "Successor to Darwin?" *Time* magazine reported that reviewers all across the country had "hailed Kinsey as one of the greatest scientists since Darwin."[35] Even a critical reviewer acknowledged that "to parallel the immediate impact of a scientific book, one would probably have to go back to 1859, and the publication of Darwin's *Origin of Species,* and even then the sales were not comparable."[36] Of course, not everyone who compared Kinsey to Darwin intended it as a compliment. After reading *Sexual Behavior in the Human Male,* the reviewer for the Catholic periodical *Commonweal* remarked, "The book brings to mind Darwin's *Origin of Species* which mixed science, philosophy, and theology in a most unwholesome fashion."[37]

Ordinarily, scientists are unlikely candidates to become folk heroes, but Kinsey was an exception. Within months following the publication of *Sexual Behavior in the Human Male,* he became an icon of popular culture, even celebrated in music. Although many radio stations censored her record, insisting it was too racy to be aired, Martha Raye, that lovable, zany, big-mouthed singer cum comedian, produced a jukebox hit for Discovery Records when she recorded Phil Moore's "Ooh, Dr. Kinsey."[38] Julie Wilson also put his story to song, delighting nightclub audiences with a little ditty called "The Kinsey Report." And Tin Pan Alley, not to be outdone, churned out a batch of catchy tunes with titles like "The Kinsey Boogie" and "Thank You, Mr. Kinsey."[39] Folk poets, too, took turns lionizing and vilifying Kinsey in verse. An anonymous master of that inherently indecent verse form known as the limerick wrote,

> There was an old phoney named Kinsey
> Whose ideas of fucking were flimsy
> He knew how to measure
> A penis for pleasure,
> But he came much too quick in a quim, see?[40]

Quick to discover that references to Kinsey got laughs, playwrights worked his name into their scripts. In Detroit, an enterprising producer of an off-color play even went so far as to mention Kinsey in newspaper advertising, promising "the bare facts about the subject Dr. Alfred Kinsey discussed in his book." Nor did radio ignore Kinsey. In one episode, Sam Spade, the top-rated sleuth, investigated a murder of a chauffeur named "Kinsey Martin Pomeroy."[41]

Movie moguls thought they spotted dramatic potential in Kinsey's work. An Indianapolis attorney representing a film executive tried to purchase the movie rights to *Sexual Behavior in the Human Male*,[42] while a Hollywood producer ordered his minions to scrutinize the book for clues "to mass male sex appeal."[43] And in an open letter to Kinsey published in *Cosmopolitan*, Mae West offered to compare notes, one sex expert to another. "Your approach is scientific: observing, investigating, classifying, statistical," she wrote. "Mine involves at least the first two of those methods, but, when it comes to statistics, I'm afraid the only figure I employ is my own. And that figure, which has become internationally familiar, stands for sex—just as your report of facts and figures does."[44] America's aging sex symbol was right. In popular parlance, Kinsey quickly became known as "the Dr. Gallup of Sex" or simply as "Dr. Sex." Booksellers who were asked the book's price often quipped, "Sex-fifty."[45]

Assuring Kinsey he had "inspired some new phrases for the English language," Vance Packard wrote to say, "I have followed with fascination your rise to the position of America's Most-Talked About Man. Did you have any idea the book would create such a hullaballo? I overheard one of my students at NYU refer to another student sarcastically by saying, 'Oh, he's Kinsey-crazy.' "[46] While Kinsey relished every line of inquiries like this, he managed to feign modesty, replying, "I knew, of course, that there was going to be considerable public interest, but I had not realized that it would develop into quite so large a proposition."[47]

Professional comedians had a field day with Kinsey. Nightclub jokers specialized in "blue" one-liners, while radio comedians, wary of censors, had to settle for tame gags such as "If it's OK with Kinsey, it's okay with me"[48] and "He's at the awkward age—you know, too old for the Bobbsey Twins and too young for the Kinsey report."[49] Folk humorists, too, explored the comic potential of Kinsey's research. Expressions such as "hotter than the Kinsey report" and "Kinsey-crazy" entered the language. Meanwhile, back home in Indiana, many Hoosiers started calling Kinsey's base of operations at Indiana University "The Sex Center,"[50] students on campus circulated a mock petition proposing to change the name of a popular necking spot from the "Passion Pit" to "Kinsey Hall," and a campus publication published a cartoon showing a solitary girl's snow tracks leading to a women's dormitory late at night, beneath which appeared the caption "Evidently she doesn't read Kinsey."[51] And the student chorus at Harvard University, where Kinsey had once walked the "yard," crooned,

I've looked you up in the Kinsey report
And you're just the man for me.[52]

Fearing that Kinsey might be offended by such levity, J. A. Lutz, the director of public relations at W. B. Saunders, wrote reassuringly, "I feel that they do not hurt the sale of the book any more than the Ford jokes some forty years ago interfered with the sale of the Ford car."[53]

For a time, it seemed that everyone was attempting to cash in on Kinsey's name. Citing Kinsey as her inspiration, a prominent fashion designer brought out a new line of dresses "designed to influence behavior in the human male"; steamy novels were touted as "fictionalized Kinsey reports"; a Newark psychiatrist's survey of teenage morals was advertised as a "bobby-sox Kinsey report"; *Clinical Sonnets,* a book of poems by a Boston psychiatrist, was heralded as a "Kinsey report in verse"; a scholarly book on bird life was hailed (no doubt to Kinsey's delight) as an "ornithological Kinsey report"; and a marriage manual, out of print for two decades, was resurrected in a new edition as a "pre-Kinsey sex report."[54]

Even a liquor company got into the act. When its customers started mailing in labels and bottle tops requesting free copies of *Sexual Behavior in the Human Male,* the Kinsey Distilling Corporation of Philadelphia, distiller of Kinsey Whiskey and Kinsey Gin, took out a newspaper ad explaining that the company had no relationship to the famous sex researcher, but wished him and his research well.[55] Aware that publicity could work both ways, Lloyd G. Potter, Kinsey's editor at Saunders, told him that a number of people "thought it was a very clever 'plant' of ours."[56] Joking with his wife, Robert Kinsey (Kinsey's brother) quipped, "Well, you either read it or you drink it."[57]

Politicians jumped on the bandwagon, too. At the Republican National Convention in 1948, in Philadelphia, delegates appeared with campaign buttons bearing the inscription "We want Kinsey, the people's choice." That same year, Kinsey got one vote to Harry S Truman's twenty-seven and Dwight D. Eisenhower's twenty-six at the annual Cherry Blossom presidential poll in Washington, D.C.[58]

Kinsey was thrilled by the book's reception. When a reporter asked how it felt to be the author of a best-seller, Kinsey replied with characteristic bluntness, "Hell, is there anyone who wouldn't like to have written one?"[59] Naturally, his newfound celebrity status included the usual nuisances that accompany fame. Because his photograph had appeared in so many newspapers and magazines, Kinsey's face was familiar to millions, making it difficult for him to walk down a street or enter a restaurant without being recognized. "He pretended to be irritated by this sudden attention, and complained that he was no longer free to observe people without being observed," wrote Pomeroy, "but he would have been less than the very human man he was if he had not been pleased and proud to be recognized."⁶⁰ Commenting on Kinsey's vanity, Dr. Frances Shields, a longtime friend and supporter, observed, "I remember one sparkling day when I drove him from San Francisco to Big Basin to sit among the giant Sequoias. We ate lunch at the cafeteria in the park and he was so pleased when the cashier recognized him. He never seemed to outgrow this ego-satisfying experience."⁶¹

If Kinsey enjoyed being recognized, he loved being contacted by old friends, particularly those who had been important to him. Soon after *Sexual Behavior in the Human Male* went on sale (and for the rest of his life), he heard from high school classmates, Boy Scouts from his troops, campers he had taught in summer camps decades before, and former teachers at Bowdoin College. Included among these voices from the past was a warm letter from his beloved high school biology teacher, Natalie Hirschfeld (formerly, Roeth). "Dear Alfred: For old time's sake, if I may so address the Great Dr. Kinsey," she began. "Hardly do I take up a magazine, *Time, The Atlantic* and others without seeing the above name emblazoned in bold type. My! How you have 'rise[n]!'" Of all the photographs, the one in *Time,* beamed Hirschfeld, "seems more like my 'boy.'" The remainder of her letter discussed her retirement from teaching and their mutual interest in gardening, and ended with the plea "How I'd love to see you all and especially *my* renowned boy and his wife. . . . Am I proud?"⁶² Graciously and affectionately Kinsey replied, "I shall always consider that you did more than anyone else at the very crucial age to turn me to science. That is saying a good deal."⁶³ Later that summer of 1948, teacher and prize pupil enjoyed a pleasant reunion over lunch in New York, where Kinsey was attending a conference. It was the last time they saw one another.

Hundreds of letters poured in from people he had interviewed. Former students from the marriage course wrote to express their pride and support, as did scores of students from other campuses he had visited. But the letters that seemed to mean the most to Kinsey came from the homosexual men he had interviewed in Chicago during the early years of the research, the men who had introduced him to his first urban gay community. One member of the Chicago group wrote, "I need not tell you how exciting it has been to read of late the many articles about it. I am proud to have been an early 'interviewee' in the project, which appears to be more monumental than I ever dreamed it was intended to be back in 1940."⁶⁴ Kinsey replied, "There is no one whose approval of our work we appreciate more than those who were brave enough to cooperate in the early days of its history."⁶⁵

Thousands of letters arrived from total strangers. Surprisingly few came from people who condemned the research, and only a handful could be described as crank letters. Many people wrote to thank, congratulate, praise, and bless Kinsey, feeding his self-image as the leader of a crusade of historic importance. Others wrote volunteering to be interviewed, accompanying their offers in many instances with enough personal information to give Kinsey a good idea of what their histories would reveal.

Despite his busy schedule, Kinsey answered each and every letter, except the ones from cranks. While some of the well-wishers received personal notes, most had to settle for a form letter thanking them for their interest and support. The majority of readers who condemned or criticized the research also got form letters thanking them for their interest and promising to keep their concerns in mind as the research progressed. In many instances, however, strangers who raised substantive criticisms received detailed responses, many of which ran on for two or three single-spaced typed pages. It was as though Kinsey, ever the teacher, believed that if he just tried hard enough, he could convince anyone.

The immediate impact of Kinsey's work was to heat up cultural wars of long standing. In the months and years following its release, *Sexual Behavior in the Human Male* precipitated the most intense and high-level dialogue on human sexuality in the nation's history. Prior to Kinsey, Americans had debated a variety of sex-related issues, including prostitution, venereal disease, birth control, sex education, and Freud's theories. But the cultural debate that greeted *Sexual Behavior in the Human Male* was far more important. It swept away the last remnants of the taboos that had inhibited Americans from engaging in public discourse about their erotic lives. In boardrooms, in barbershops, in cafés, in grocery stores, and on street corners Americans could be heard reciting his findings on the incidence of masturbation, homosexuality, premarital and extramarital intercourse, and the like. And wherever this happened, these and other topics became fair game for polite conversation. However awkward, prurient, or naughty they might feel, Americans suddenly had permission to talk about sex. Kinsey gave them that right, and he did so in the name of science.

Kinsey had to be confronted, for there was no escaping him. A cottage industry of Kinsey critics and defenders sprang up overnight and flourished for years, filling the nation's college campuses with symposia, debates, and lectures. Nor was the interest limited to academe. As *Life* magazine told its readers in August 1948 (eight months after the book had appeared), "Far from subsiding with the passage of time, the initial excitement created by the Report has been stimulated by an astounding number of reviews, critiques, summaries, interviews and 'think pieces,' which have saturated every level of journalism from the tabloids to the most recondite scientific publication." Added to these, *Life* continued, were "innumerable forums, round tables and debates, both on and off the radio," not to mention "a respectable library of satellite subreports, or keys to Kinsey."[66]

The response to Kinsey's work among professional groups was phenomenal. Overall, the reviews in medical journals were positive, as many physicians believed that Kinsey's research would enable them to answer their patients' sexual questions with better data. Surprisingly, the same held true for clergymen. Most religious leaders praised Kinsey's research and welcomed his data, arguing that it was better to have the facts than to remain ignorant, even if that meant society would have to reevaluate its sexual mores.[67]

Kinsey's strongest supporters, however, came from the new class of highly educated, white-collar professionals whose business it was to analyze, explain, and mediate between conflicting human values. This class included sexologists, sociologists, anthropologists, physicians, psychologists, educators, marriage counselors, journalists, and lawyers who wanted to reform sex laws. Although they were direct descendants of the moral reformers and "uplifters" of the Progressive Era, Kinsey's advocates displayed certain differences. They were less doctrinaire, less devoted to the "genteel tradition" and its moral absolutes. While older reformers had appealed to the public primarily through moral imperatives, nationalism, efficiency, and racial solidarity, the new social professionals began a shift toward appeals based on personal fulfillment. *Sexual Behavior in the Human Male,* with its emphasis on individual variation, proved congenial to this group. To some, Kinsey was a champion of truth. To others, he was a pioneer in the application of social science research techniques to important social problems. And to still others, he was a disinterested scientist who had provided objective data for the revision of laws and the liberalization of social relations. To all, he was an apostle of progress.

Of course, no one expected the rave reviews and popular kudos to go unchallenged, least of all Kinsey. He had known from the start that his work would be controversial, and he had done everything in his power to shore up his defenses. Apart from his efforts at manipulating the press and orchestrating favorable reviews, however, Kinsey could do little to control the response to his book in the months following its release. Still, just as he had tried to use student support to protect himself from opponents of the marriage course, Kinsey remained hopeful that public support for *Sexual Behavior in the Human Male* would shield him from critics. A few weeks after the book's release, he wrote to Yerkes, "The great advantage of this wide-spread approval is the fact that the bickering critics are snowed under, and we have so far not had to give any time to meeting them. If objections do arise, they will have to be on a more serious level which will be more worth our attention."[68]

It did not take long for serious challenges to emerge. Once it entered the marketplace of ideas, *Sexual Behavior in the Human Male* had to stand or fall on its own. After newspapers and journals assigned it to reviewers of their choosing (not his), the entire tenor of the book's reception changed. While many of the reviews continued to be highly laudatory, others ran the gamut from skeptical to scathing. The critics were sharpening their claws and waiting to pounce.

Many of the naysayers believed that Kinsey had attempted the impossible, an error that prompted one skeptic to accuse him of "trying to make an objective study about something about which we cannot be objective."[69] Other critics were shrill and vituperative, comparing Kinsey, in the words of one reviewer, to "a combination of Jack the Ripper and Cagliostro."[70] To more rational foes, Kinsey seemed less a monster than the bearer of bad news, if not a scientist whose research was in singularly poor taste. The wife of a high official of the *Washington Post*, remarked, "We all know that there is too much sexual promiscuity, marital infidelity, and homosexuality in our country. What does it add to our knowledge to know the exact percentage in each of these three areas?"[71] Angered by this sort of reasoning, a friendly Kinsey reviewer countered, "One of the constantly recurring behavior patterns of primitives is the custom of attempting to murder the bringer of bad news. Many of Kinsey's severer critics, it is to be feared, are exhibiting a reaction more suitable to skinclad savages than to civilized men."[72]

Kinsey's most vociferous critics were deeply religious people who feared that his work would undermine traditional morality. He had anticipated a rough reception from conservative Catholics, and he got one. The Right Reverend Monsignor Maurice Sheehy, of Washington's Catholic University of America, denounced *Sexual Behavior in the Human Male* as "the most antireligious book of our times," charging that it "has made the most devastating inroads on Christian morality in this century,"[73] while an editorial in the *Catholic Mind* denounced Kinsey for being "at war against purity, against morality, against the family."[74] Evangelical Protestants were no less harsh. *Awake,* a Jehovah's Witnesses publication, insisted that the report "engenders scorn for the moral code, and leans toward tolerance for delinquency that guilt complexes may lessen."[75] Kinsey did not lose much sleep over religious critics on the right, as he knew there was nothing he or any other scientist could do to satisfy their objections.

The critics who most worried him were the professional groups, particularly his fellow scientists, many of whom were self-proclaimed religious liberals and humanists who shared his desire for greater freedom in private behavior. As the *New Republic* told its readers, the specialists were "heating the cauldron in anticipation of the feast at which Kinsey will be the main dish."[76] Their reviews cut the deepest precisely because their criticisms did not involve a priori objections to his research. Rather, they attacked Kinsey on scientific grounds, demonstrating the talent for textual exegesis, methodological scrutiny, and theoretical criticism that are the stock-in-trade of reviewers from academe and the professions. Still, it would be wrong to conclude that they were all totally objective. As one reviewer said of his fellow critics, "Much of the criticism, though often disguised as methodological, is actually moral dyspepsia caused by the results that Kinsey got."[77]

While no single reviewer crystallized all the objections, the academic and professional critics of Kinsey's work tended to raise one or more of the following criticisms: first, Kinsey was a poor statistician (he did not understand statistical theory, his numbers did not always add up, some of his cells contained too few cases to be meaningful, etc.); second, his sampling technique was unrepresentative (volunteers skewed his data, too many people from the Northeast and Midwest, too many college-educated subjects, too many prisoners, etc.); third, his interview technique was faulty (human memory was unreliable, rapid-fire questions did not give people time to think, placing the burden of denial on a subject could produce false answers, sympathetic looks and words from the interviewer were not neutral, etc.); fourth, Kinsey approached human beings as animals; fifth, he lacked the conceptual tools needed to study human sexual behavior (he was a crude empiricist, he was a rank biological reductionist, his behaviorism was too blatant, his understanding of Freudian psychology was too unsophisticated, etc.); sixth, he ignored the emotional or social context of sex (there was no discussion of love, he made sex appear joyless, he "atomized" sex, etc.); seventh, he had no appreciation of how culture works and the role that certain necessary restraints play in the preservation of culture (the "normal" vs. "abnormal" problem); and finally, he was a crypto-reformer who promoted permissiveness under the guise of science.

Had these objections been made by minor people in obscure journals and magazines, Kinsey could have sat comfortably in his chair, but his critics read like a Who's Who of American intellectual life. They included the theologians Reinhold Niebuhr and Norman Vincent Peale; the anthropologists Margaret Mead, Ruth Benedict, and Geoffrey Gorer; the historian Bernard De Voto; the psychologist Lewis M. Terman; the psychiatrists Eric Fromm and Lawrence Kubie; and the cultural critic Lionel Trilling—to name only a few.

Outraged by what he called "Kinsey's proposals of anarchism in the field of sex," Reinhold Niebuhr, the great Christian theologian, deplored Kinsey's "absurd hedonism" and "consistent naturalism," arguing that Kinsey had made "the achievement of orgasm . . . the *summum bonum* of his value scheme."[78] Norman Vincent Peale, the minister of New York City's Marble Collegiate Church and soon-to-be author of the popular book *The Power of Positive Thinking*, rejected Kinsey's implied argument that numbers rendered behavior normal. Contributing to a lopsided symposium entitled "Must We Change Our Sex Standards?"—published in the *Reader's Digest*—Peale gave this answer to young people who wondered if there was no place for the word "abnormal" in a scientist's vocabulary: "No matter how many murderers there are, murder will never be normal."[79]

Kinsey did not anticipate a hostile reception from social scientists, but he got one just the same. Renowned for their internecine warfare, their inability to reach a consensus on whether they should do applied or pure research, and their failure to integrate their perspectives, theories, and methodologies, the scholars in these disciplines typically had little but disdain, if not contempt, for outsiders. In large measure, their opposition to Kinsey was a matter of turf. They saw him as the quintessential outsider, a biologist who had invaded territory claimed by the social sciences. In the face of such insolence, they could hardly be expected to remain silent. At stake was cultural authority—which disciplines could claim to speak on questions pertaining to human sexual behavior.

Thus, although Kinsey had given specialists, in the words of one reviewer, "grounds for complaint and criticism as well as much to be grateful for,"[80] many of the social scientists who reviewed his work kept their gratitude to themselves but roared out their complaints. In retrospect, many of their criticisms seem petty and trivial. Indeed, more than a few critics appeared mean-spirited and churlish. Not that the reason for their ill temper and lack of intellectual generosity was a mystery. It was as obvious as their iridescent green glow: they were jealous of the publicity he had received and wanted to take him down a peg.

Others were simply doing their jobs. Neither mean-spirited nor jealous, they wrote conscientious, fair reviews, mixing praise and criticisms as their judgment warranted. They attacked Kinsey because he had attempted an enormous undertaking of great social importance, producing a work that deserved to be engaged critically. As one critic (who commended Kinsey and his associates for "endeavoring energetically, even frantically to study all aspects of human sexual behavior in the whole United States of America") remarked, "They have a bear by the tail and, unless they study the animal from every conceivable angle and take suggestions from others, they must expect to get clawed up a little."[81]

Anthropologists spearheaded the attack on Kinsey. In a review in the *New York Herald Tribune* entitled "A Statistical Study of Sex," Geoffrey Gorer, a British anthropologist, challenged the reliability of Kinsey's data, charging that "the sampling is so poor that the only reliable figures are those for college graduates in six of the northeastern states." The basic problem, explained Gorer, was that sound sampling procedures required "some carefully planned system of randomization which avoids bias on the part of the investigator." At a minimum, he insisted, Kinsey should have used "stratified sampling," a system that rested "on the calculation that the distribution of characters being studied is directly correlated with other criteria, such as age, education, religion, region, economic level, etc." Instead, Kinsey had relied upon volunteers at college lectures and "on personal introductions from interested individuals, which are obviously statistically invalid; and in consequence his population is completely distorted." According to Gorer, Kinsey's sampling technique was so flawed that adding "cases may well considerably increase rather than lessen whatever distortions there are in the present study."[82]

Margaret Mead, a close friend of Gorer's and one of America's most distinguished cultural anthropologists, broadened the attack. Speaking at a symposium on *Sexual Behavior in the Human Male* in New York City, she criticized Kinsey for upsetting the balance between ignorance and knowledge upon which social restraint depended, for atomizing sex by taking "sexual behavior out of its inter-personal context" and reducing it "to the category of a simple act of elimination," and for his flagrant puritanism. "Nowhere have I been able to find a single suggestion that sex is any fun, not anywhere in the book, not a suggestion," she declared. What most disturbed her, however, was Kinsey's failure to offer young people guidance. Through his many graphs, tables, and other paraphernalia, Mead charged, Kinsey had purported to give the norms and ranges for the sexual behavior of men, allowing them to find out where they and their spouses belonged. In her view, Kinsey's "atomization of sex," "quantification," "justification by numbers," "Puritanism," and tendency to separate sex from interpersonal relations had left young people without a clue about how to handle sex. As she put it caustically, "the book suggests no way of choosing between a woman and a sheep."[83]

The Gorer and Mead critiques upset Kinsey, all the more so because he suspected ill will and collusion. Kinsey told Corner, "We have information that it was Margaret Mead who sponsored the article and got Gorer to write it."[84] Writing to another supporter, Kinsey snapped, "The Gorer review either represents stupidity or deliberate maliciousness. He criticizes us as though our technique had been that of proportionate sample, and ignores the careful and elaborate explanation which we made of stratified sampling technique."[85] He complained to yet another friend that Gorer's review "had a vicious slant which indicated animus that antedated his actual acquaintance with the book." Speculating on the reason for Gorer's opposition, Kinsey continued, "I think this is due in part to the association

with Gregory Bateson and the fact that Margaret Mead objects strenuously to the materialism of masculine sexuality this book deals with."[86]
Kinsey was right. Mead and Gorer were in cahoots. As long-standing
friends, staunch cultural determinists, and avid admirers of Freud, they
had little but contempt for Kinsey, whom they regarded as a doctrinaire biological determinist and crude reductionist. In Mead's case, however, jealousy probably aggravated spite. Two decades had passed since the
publication of her classic study, *Coming of Age in Samoa* (1928), and none
of her subsequent works had matched its success. It was Mead, not Gorer,
who was the *New York Herald Tribune*'s first choice to review Kinsey's
book, and it was she who recommended Gorer to the newspaper after declining the assignment herself,[87] knowing full well that he would trash the
book in print, just as she later did in person. So great was her distaste for
Kinsey that several years later she refused to let her editor use a quotation
that mentioned the Kinsey report for the dust jacket of a new edition of
one of her books.[88] For his part, Gorer enjoyed the misery he caused Kinsey. Referring disparagingly to "Old Doc Kinsey," Gorer later gloated to
Mead, "I'm still amazed at what one review will do."[89] In the case of Gorer
and Mead, then, Kinsey had walked into a one-two punch, and there was
little he could do about it.

Still, Kinsey's instinct was to fight back. Ironically, the man who loved
to dish out criticism had little appetite for taking it. The lavish praise he
had received did nothing to ease the pain he felt over negative reviews. As
the months passed, Kinsey became obsessed with his critics. Thin-skinned,
aggressive by nature, and quick to anger, he got upset by every negative review, including those that operated at highly professional levels. To him,
all criticism was personal, and it cut him to the core.

People who did not know Kinsey had no way of comprehending how
badly negative reviews wounded him. All they could see (at times with be-
musement, at times with grim concern) was the ferocity of his responses.
In private (and sometimes in public), Kinsey would explode in anger, denouncing critics with a fury that bordered on rage. Friends and supporters often accused him of overreacting. Yet Kinsey saw his critics as obstacles
to the sexual revolution he hoped to precipitate. As he told a friend, "I
worry about these supercilious criticisms only because I think they may
confuse the public, and delay their utilization of our material."[90]

In the end, Kinsey wound up opposing all critical assessments of his
work, whether based on moral bias or on disinterested intellectual assessment. It was not that he considered himself above criticism—though opponents sometimes accused him of this. For him, the issue was political.
Kinsey saw himself as the great hope, the one scientist in the world who
had uncovered the facts about human sexual behavior and had placed the

truth before the public. Fellow scientists, he thought, should abstain from criticizing his work in print, lest they play into the hands of those who would censor science to prevent the public from learning about sexual diversity, with all the challenges to conventional sexual morality this entailed.

Kinsey pressed this argument on a number of critics, hoping to persuade them to write favorable notices or to change reviews that he saw prior to publication and considered hostile. Occasionally, he was successful; more often he failed. At bottom, Kinsey was asking his fellow scientists to suspend critical judgment (at least in public or in print). Most balked at his request. However accurate his assessment, his arguments reeked of special pleading. Reviewers insisted they were evaluating a book, not undermining a cause.

Despite his need to engage his critics in print, Kinsey was under enormous pressure to resist the temptation. His publisher, university officials, and friends all advised against it. Better to maintain a dignified silence, they told him. Concentrate on the research and let others fight your battles, they advised. For the most part, Kinsey heeded this advice, at least with regard to answering his critics in print. What Kinsey refused to do was to ignore his critics. Just as he had worked behind the scenes to manipulate the press, he tried his best to get others to defend his research in public. In the case of Gorer, Kinsey turned for help to the CRPS, a group that he had frequently slighted of late.

"There are a number of people who now feel that the Gorer review has done us considerable damage," Kinsey wrote Corner. Articulating his concerns, Kinsey warned that "the acceptance of the research and the public dependence on it for translation into social affairs could be retarded for a good many years if none but the objectors record their so-called scientific evaluations of the work." Explaining that the people at Saunders had strongly advised him not to answer his critics in print, Kinsey declared, "We are of the opinion, however, that this Gorer criticism must be answered by somebody. Personally, I think the appropriate party to answer the criticism is the National Research Council's Committee."[91]

Kinsey's request put Corner on the spot. Hesitating to commit the CRPS, he polled his fellow members, seeking advice on whether it would be wise to defend Kinsey's work publicly. Their replies revealed sharp disagreements and a certain coolness to Kinsey, much of which he had earned. "I am . . . obliged to point out that prior to the publication of his book, Kinsey successfully resisted any suggestion that the committee should have a chance to read his book and pass judgment upon his methods and he gave every indication of wishing to avoid mention of the committee whenever possible," responded Wallace O. Fenn. "Now that the book is published and under fire, he is clamoring for support. This does not make a very good impression upon me and I think we should continue to keep our hands off."⁹² Agreeing that the committee "should not take responsibility for public defense of Kinsey's work," Karl S. Lashley declared, "The book was published with a splurge of publicity for which I suspect that Kinsey was in part responsible and I think he should face the consequences. The reviews that I have seen were just as much distorted in his favor (Time, 'a second Darwin') but he has not complained about them." Only one committee member responded sympathetically, and his support was tepid. "Kinsey may be overly exercised, but again perhaps not," replied Carl R. Moore, who added that "if this review should be deemed sufficiently damaging, especially if it handicapped Kinsey's further operations in obtaining histories, a dignified 'letter to the Editor' might be appropriate, helpful, and worthwhile."⁹³ In the end, Corner decided not to issue a press release, though he did agree to speak before the symposium sponsored by the American Social Hygiene Association, where he strongly defended Kinsey's methods and findings.⁹⁴

Kinsey was still reeling from the anthropologists' attacks when he came under fire from Lawrence Kubie, one of the nation's most prominent psychoanalysts. Affiliated with Columbia University, Kubie was a Freudian whose rigid views on homosexuality were well known in psychoanalytic circles. Kinsey and Kubie had met a few years earlier during one of Kinsey's trips to New York, and Kinsey regarded him as a supporter. Consequently, while the book was still in press, Kinsey had asked Kubie to review it for one of the psychoanalytic journals and to recommend other psychoanalysts who might be favorably disposed.⁹⁵ Kinsey issued this invitation, of course, assuming that Kubie's review would be favorable. Before the review was published, Kubie sent Kinsey a copy, along with the warning "It is a two-fisted review, I am afraid."⁹⁶ This was a gross understatement. Hands down, it was Kinsey's least successful effort to rig a review.

Kubie's piece, which appeared in the March–April 1948 issue of *Psychosomatic Medicine,* began on a positive note, praising Kinsey's courage, patience, humility, and broad humanity. But there the sweet talk ended. The ten pages (in double columns and in fine print) that followed more than redeemed Kubie's promise of "a two-fisted review." If anything, he seemed to be going for a knockout. Weaving back and forth between technical criticisms and theoretical objections, Kubie attacked Kinsey for faulty statistical procedures that inflated the incidence of taboo behavior, for failing to comprehend and correct for the bilateral deceptions and other psychodynamics inherent in oral interviews, for his blind faith in and imperfect understanding of human memory, for consistently ignoring or discounting the importance of psychological forces in human sexuality, for his biological definition of normality that was elastic enough to include a variety of sexual perversions, and, last but not least, for his gratuitous, ignorant, and wrongheaded criticisms of psychological theory and his demeaning characterizations of the psychiatric profession. As Kubie put it testily, "At times it almost seems as though the authors are trying to caricature the psychiatrist by attributing to him ideas which are patently absurd."[97] Kubie was not content merely to criticize. Instead, he also chided the individuals who had served in an advisory role to Kinsey at the start of his research "for their failure to insist that it be a combined operation, in which all that is known from the study of sick individuals would constantly be used in the evaluation and interpretation of the statistical data in large groups." To correct this deficiency, Kubie recommended that Kinsey's study be redesigned "to make intensive individual physiologic, anatomic, psychiatric, and social studies of individuals who would constitute a statistically adequate random sample of each form of sexual behavior," a suggestion that would "require the cooperative effort of teams of psychoanalysts, clinical psychologists, neurophysiologists, endocrinologists, cultural anthropologists, and psychiatric social workers, as well as biologic taxonomists." Failure to make these changes would only compound past errors and perpetuate bad science, warned Kubie. As things stood, Kinsey's methodology was so flawed that his entire study was in danger of becoming "an example of accurate recording of inaccurate data."[98]

Kubie's criticisms were powerful, and whatever hope Kinsey may have had that they could be confined to psychoanalytic circles proved to be short-lived. Not long before it appeared in print, *Time* magazine gave Kubie's review big play. Calling his criticisms "the most devastating scientific attack on the report yet," *Time* declared, "Dr. Kubie stuck a scalpel into the heart of Zoologist Alfred C. Kinsey's whole project: the interviews."[99] *Time* then proceeded to summarize the review in detail, stressing that Kinsey had incurred the wrath of psychiatrists.

The review both surprised and angered Kinsey. Another scientist might have mined it for constructive criticisms, but his response was hostile and defensive. "Kubie is on the warpath," Kinsey complained to a friend. Defending biology against psychology, Kinsey continued, "He would like to connect everything that the human animal does to its previous experience, as it is passed on through the subconscious, and I see no attempt on his part to pay attention to the phylogenetic basis of these things."[100] Certainly, Kinsey saw no need to accept Kubie's criticisms. "If Kubie's review is scientific, then I have never had any contact with science," he sniped to another friend.[101]

Still, Kinsey was concerned that Kubie's criticisms might give the Rockefeller Foundation and the NRC second thoughts. To prevent this, Kinsey went on the offensive, assuring Gregg that jealousy was behind Kubie's efforts "to take the project out of our hands and put it in the hands of psychoanalysts who can do the job properly." Pleading that this must not be allowed to happen, Kinsey declared, "The emotional intensity of the moves against us needs to be understood and everyone concerned with this project needs to stand firm on the scientific and social desirability of this study and our right to make the results available to the public."[102] Kinsey adopted a different tactic with Corner, resorting to ridicule. "First, they dismiss it all by saying that the analysts knew this all 25 years ago, and that we have nothing new," he complained. "Secondly, they call upon the Rockefeller Foundation, the National Research Council, and us to make amends for the gross negligence in not having an adequate staff of psychoanalysts on this project, and they insist that each case must be studied by a psychoanalyst before we can recognize the subconscious backgrounds which are always involved in any person's behavior." According to his calculations, Kinsey estimated, "it would take 223 analysts to do the sort of thing that they demand on the population which we are handling. That is one-half of the entire supply of analysts in the United States."[103]

Kinsey was right to take Kubie seriously. Kubie was a formidable opponent, and he was determined to press the issue. To make certain he got results, Kubie sent a copy of his review (months before it appeared in print) to Gregg at the Rockefeller Foundation, hoping to persuade Kinsey's principal backer not to put more money into his research unless it was changed along the lines Kubie had recommended. Making no bones of his goal, Kubie told Gregg, "I am on a crusade to induce Kinsey to make the rest of the work fulfill the great opportunity that it has created and missed."[104] Despite his keen interest in psychiatry and great admiration for Freud, Gregg was not impressed by Kubie's arguments. In his reply, he stressed that Kubie's criticisms boiled down to the fact that Kinsey had not covered every angle. In fact, Gregg not only answered Kubie's criticisms but played down their importance. "In a field of such lively concern," he calmly told Kubie, "I am not surprised that there is a good deal of difference of opinion and feeling."[105]

Privately, Gregg was dismayed. In his estimation, the hostile reception to Kinsey's work in psychoanalytic circles was a turf war, pure and simple. Gregg was convinced that professional jealousy and the desire to preserve their cultural hegemony were the real reasons psychoanalysts opposed Kinsey.[106] Shrewdly summarizing the situation in his notes, he wrote of Kubie's criticisms, "The nearest analogy is the emotion of a gamekeeper on seeing a poacher getting a rather handsome bag. It is not particularly edifying."[107] Kubie was distressed by his failure to win Gregg over and stepped up the campaign. Despite additional letters and a conversation over dinner, however, he could not shake Gregg's confidence in Kinsey.

Shortly after he had started lobbying Gregg, Kubie went to work on Corner in a vain attempt to open a second front with the NRC. In his dealings with Gregg, Kubie had been careful not to attack Kinsey personally, no doubt because Gregg's preface to *Sexual Behavior in the Human Male* had left little doubt where he stood. No such reticence marked Kubie's approach to Corner. Mixing professional concern and scientific reservations in equal measure, Kubie added a new reason the project had to be redesigned: Kinsey was showing signs of stress that raised doubts about his emotional health.

According to Kubie, his review had smoked out unpleasant qualities in Kinsey. When Kinsey had first asked him to review the book, Kubie was excited, as he expected big things. Once he had started reading it, however, the book disappointed him greatly, a fact that he communicated to Kinsey, along with an offer to send him a copy of the finished review. "This brought him [Kinsey] to my office . . . to talk it over," Kinsey wrote Corner, "but I found him in such a disturbed and almost agitated state that I felt considerable concern for him, and the talk did not get very far." He offered to meet with Corner to provide more details, declaring, "If this work is to achieve its worthy goals the whole approach to the task and the organization behind it will have to be basically changed." Stressing that he did not speak just for himself, Kubie revealed that he had discussed this matter with several men who had known Kinsey for years. "They share both my disappointment in the report, and my concern for Kinsey himself, and for any future reports," asserted Kubie. "I think it would be well for your committee to consider this whole matter fully."[108]

Kubie's timing was acute. His letter arrived only weeks before the CRPS was scheduled to evaluate Kinsey's latest application. Yet, far from being swayed by Kubie's criticisms, Corner remained squarely in Kinsey's corner. He confided to a friend, "My first reaction to all the difficulties and criticisms concerning the Kinsey book and his work in general is that after all it is extremely important work and on the whole thoroughly scientific in its methods. To get it done, we have to back Kinsey for there is no one else who can do it."[109] Nor was Lewis H. Weed, the Chairman of the Division of Medical Science of the NRC, impressed by Kubie's review. "I should not take too seriously any opinion expressed by Kubie as he has been jealous of his specialty and is the person who alone knows the real answer," Weed wrote Corner.[110] Still, Kubie's standing in the psychoanalytic community guaranteed him a hearing before the full membership of the CRPS, which was scheduled to meet at the end of April 1948.

Kinsey was extremely fortunate that Kubie did not have a soulmate on the committee. John Romano, the committee's sole psychiatrist, had recently resigned, and there were no plans to replace him with another psychiatrist in time for the upcoming meeting. In fact, Romano had totally alienated his colleagues, leaving behind little sympathy for his specialty. Confessing that he was "delighted to hear of Romano's resignation," Karl Lashley, the lone psychologist on the committee, complained to Corner, "He was anti-everything except psychoanalysis."[111]

A few weeks before the meeting, Corner predicted to Gregg "that smoke from the battle between Kinsey and the psychoanalysts will be drifting into the committee room at our Meeting on April 29."[112] In the end, however, the review of Kinsey's work (the first since his book appeared) was a cakewalk. The committee voted unanimously to renew his annual $40,000 grant.[113] Still, Kubie and other critics hoped that they had found a soft spot. The following year, the NRC would have to seek a new appropriation for the CRPS and for Kinsey from the Rockefeller Foundation. Who was to say whether the foundation would renew its support?

In spring 1948, however, Kinsey was riding high. Buoyed by his new grant, he felt that he had taken the best his critics could dish out. In his mind, the unflinching support of the Rockefeller Foundation and the NRC was tantamount to vindication, proof that he was right and the critics wrong. To a friend, Kinsey wrote, "I have tried to analyze the attacks on us, and, within the limits which any scientist must make as he obtains more information and polishes his data, I am increasingly sure that we have an approximation to the fact in our volume. It will be accepted as so in the future. It will be interesting to see who of the so-called scientists were the ones who tried to dodge the fact."[114]

Kinsey's victory dance was premature. The April issue of the *Partisan Review* brought a brilliant, keenly analytic, sharply critical, and, paradoxically, intellectually generous review by Lionel Trilling. A literary scholar, cultural critic, and mainstay of the circle of writers and polemicists known as the New York intellectuals, he taught at Columbia University. Together with the other members of his circle, who included Hannah Arendt, Saul Bellow, Sidney Hook, Irving Howe, Mary McCarthy, and Philip Rahv, Trilling wanted to arbitrate the intellectual life of the nation. Consequently, any cultural event of importance was fair game for his scrutiny.

Trilling declared at the outset that *Sexual Behavior in the Human Male* was a cultural event of the first magnitude. In the past, he explained, sex had been inseparable from morality, and its guardians had been drawn from religion, ethical philosophy, and literature. "But now science seems to be the only one of our institutions which has the authority to speak decisively on the matter," he observed. While Freud had prepared the way, Trilling freely admitted, "Freud, in all the years of his activity, never had the currency or authority with the public that the Report has achieved in a matter of weeks." To Trilling, the fact that science had to sort things out was a symptom of the degree to which modern society had isolated itself in sexual ignorance and had weighted down individuals in socially created fears. The popular reaction to Kinsey's work revealed that, in Trilling's words, "we must assure ourselves by statistical science that the solitude is imaginary."[115]

Much to Kinsey's consternation, Trilling approached *Sexual Behavior in the Human Male* as a humanist and man of letters. His review was sprinkled with references to Aristophanes, Rabelais, Malory, William James, and, especially, Freud, to whom Trilling, in common with the other New York intellectuals, prayed nightly. Trilling took Kinsey to task for his view of human nature, which never transcended the argument *de animalibus;* for atomizing sex (failing to comprehend that sex involves the whole of an individual's character); for his seemingly willful misrepresentation of Freudian psychology; for allowing the notion of the natural to develop into the idea of the normal; and for advancing his own peculiar views while simultaneously proclaiming his objectivity. Although the Kinsey Report purported to be "only an accumulation of objective data," Trilling correctly charged, "it is full of assumptions and conclusions; it makes very positive statements on highly debatable matters and it editorializes very freely."[116]

Above all, Trilling criticized Kinsey for his oversimplified thinking and reliance on absolute concepts. He not only exposed Kinsey's logical fallacies but laid bare his intellectual limitations. He saw Kinsey for what he was: a biologist who could not transcend narrow, materialistic thinking. Stressing that "awkwardness in the handling of ideas is characteristic of the Report," Trilling declared, "It is ill at ease with any idea that is in the least complex and it often tries to get rid of such an idea in favor of another that has the appearance of not going beyond the statement of physical facts." Indeed, the Kinsey Report betrayed "an extravagant fear of all ideas that do not seem to it to be, as it were, immediately dictated by simple physical fact."[117]

Still, Trilling found much to praise in the motives behind the Kinsey Report. Commenting on "how very characteristically American a document it is," he explained, "I have in mind chiefly the impulse toward acceptance and liberation, the broad and generous desire for others not to be harshly judged." Correctly divining Kinsey's central message, Trilling insisted that the book should be viewed "as a recoil from the crude and often brutal rejection which society has made of the persons it calls aberrant." To accomplish this goal, the book sought to habituate "its readers to the idea of sexuality in all its manifestations, to establish, as it were, a democratic pluralism." Trilling called this a "good impulse," one that reflected America's "generosity of mind."[118] On balance, however, his assessment was decidedly mixed, an ambivalence that was captured nicely in the closing remark, "It is impossible to say of the Report that it does not bring light, and necessary to say of it that it spreads confusion."[119] Kinsey, of course, tried to discount Trilling's review, but Gregg wrote to say that he considered it "valuable," a clear message that he wanted Kinsey to address its substance.[120]

The summer brought another round of criticisms in popular magazines and scholarly journals alike. In its June issue, *Reader's Digest*, the magazine with the largest circulation in the world, published a symposium entitled "Must We Change Our Sex Standards?"[121] *Reader's Digest* was famous for its ultra-conservative position on many social issues, including sex. Its article on Kinsey was a hatchet job. It consisted of excerpts from the letters of eighteen prominent Americans, all of whom felt compelled to attack Kinsey's alarming portrait of private behavior in the United States, although not one of them mentioned him by name.

Despite bad publicity over the summer, Kinsey was feeling secure enough by September to tell Gregg, "We think that the major wave of adverse criticisms of our work has passed its crest, and the increased cooperation we are getting from professional people everywhere indicated that they do esteem the work that we have done."[122] Once again, however, Kinsey had underestimated the opposition. His most determined critic proved to be Lewis M. Terman, a retired psychologist from Stanford University who was near the end of a long and distinguished career. A past president of the American Psychological Association, a father of intelligence testing, a sex researcher who had received substantial grants in his own right from the CRPS, and a close friend of Yerkes, Terman was the caliber of reviewer Kinsey wanted on his side.

Terman worked on his review for a solid month. Much of his time and energy was devoted to reading the book at a highly critical level. In particular, Terman pondered its tables and graphs, trying to ascertain how much data supported Kinsey's analysis. Aware that he had strong feelings about the book, Terman struggled to keep them from creeping into his writing, a challenge that required several drafts. Describing his labors to Yerkes, Terman confided, "I am trying very hard to take out of my comments anything that might wound his [Kinsey's] amour propre too much. However, there are a lot of things about the book that get me down. Of course, it is an extremely valuable collection of data, but just how representative his facts are for the U.S. population it is utterly impossible to find out from the facts he presents." But this was not Terman's sole objection. "I react very unfavorably, too," he told Yerkes, "to many of his slanted interpretations. It was a mistake to include them. His data are so valuable that they can be left to others to moralize over."[123] Later Terman would describe his review to another colleague as "without exception the most difficult . . . that I have ever attempted."[124]

What Terman did not tell friends, however, was that he (like so many others) had a personal score to settle with Kinsey. In the first chapter of *Sexual Behavior in the Human Male*, Kinsey had delivered an almost uniformly ungracious assessment of the books by earlier sex researchers. While many of his criticisms were justified, Kinsey had given needless offense to a group of scholars that included several prospective reviewers for his own work. Characteristically blunt in his assessment of Terman's book *Psychological Factors in Marital Happiness* (1938), Kinsey had faulted him for using a group-administered questionnaire in place of face-to-face interviews. And while admitting that Terman's "statistical treatment" was "better than in most studies," Kinsey had ended on a negative note, declaring "the conclusions would have been totally different at certain points if the analyses had been confined to particular educational levels."[125] Apparently, these criticisms stung Terman, for it is difficult to read his review without getting a whiff of revenge.

Terman's review appeared in the September 1948 issue of the *Psychological Bulletin*. From start to finish, it was a vigorous, if gentlemanly, attack on *Sexual Behavior in the Human Male*. Terman chided Kinsey for failing to provide sufficient information about the wording of the questions used in the interview; for placing the burden of denial on the subject; for failing to distinguish between remote recall and memories dealing with current or near-current activities; for neglecting to address the representativeness of the various segments of the total population interviewed; for making numerous sweeping statements that lacked sufficient support in the tables; and, finally, for including "numerous passages in which recklessly worded and slanted evaluations are expressed, the slanting being often in the direction of implied preference for uninhibited sexual activity." Insisting that *Sexual Behavior in the Human Male* was packed with judgments (and he cited half a dozen examples to bolster the point), Terman declared, "Some of them are closely akin to moral evaluations, although Kinsey time and again disavows any intention to pass moral judgment or any competency to do so."[126]

Kinsey was furious over the review. Corner, who discussed the review with Kinsey, described his reaction as "one of pained surprise at what he considers a hypercritical attack."[127] Privately, however, Kinsey dropped his posture of wounded innocence and resorted to ad hominem attacks. "I think we are objective and fair when we say that the animus of the whole review is jealousy and a considerable prudery," Kinsey told a friend. "Terman was one of the 20 or more people to whom the National Research Council appropriated money over a long period of years to get this survey on human sex behavior done," Kinsey continued. "All of them failed, or stopped short." In his judgment, Terman was "among those who failed, and who, in consequence, have opposed and criticized us from the beginning of our own research."[128]

Like Kubie, Terman hoped his review would prompt the Rockefeller Foundation and the NRC to take Kinsey in hand. And like Kubie, Terman was destined to be disappointed, at least in the short run. His review failed to provoke a response one way or the other from Gregg,[129] and it was a total flop with key figures at the NRC. Defending Kinsey against Terman's criticisms, Corner wrote Yerkes, "My own reaction includes, I must confess, an element of irritation. I find it difficult to understand how an experienced psychologist could commit the ineptitude of frankly writing comments solely on the shortcomings and inadequacies of a fellow scientist's work. With this approach he could not possibly avoid the appearance of ungenerosity, in spite of his disclaimers."[130] In the end, the committee sided with Kinsey, concluding that Terman had acted out of jealousy and spite.

But Terman was not through. After his review was published, he pursued a personal vendetta against Kinsey. A retired scholar with a high energy level, time on his hands, and a long and unforgiving memory, Terman busied himself with academic intrigue. He bad-mouthed Kinsey in conversations with friends, attacked him in letters, and mailed copies of his review to anyone he thought might be interested. (He had five hundred printed.) For example, Terman sent a copy of his review to President Wells, declaring in a follow-up letter, "I am strongly of the opinion . . . as are also my psychological colleagues at Stanford, that Dr. Kinsey should take account of some of the criticisms in preparing his later volumes."[131]

This was just the beginning. For several years following the publication of *Sexual Behavior in the Human Male,* Terman directed a growing chorus of Kinsey's detractors in the social sciences—cheering on his fellow critics, critiquing drafts of their reviews, and recommending journals that might welcome negative assessments. And because he was perceived as a Kinsey foe, Terman became a clearinghouse for tales, criticisms, and gossip that his fellow academics were not willing to air in print.

In January 1949, Terman received a long letter from Albert Ellis, a psychologist without academic affiliation who wrote extensively on human sexuality and related topics for popular consumption. Ellis's review of *Sexual Behavior in the Human Male* had recently appeared in the *Journal of General Psychology,* where he had defended Kinsey strongly against the methodological criticisms that were coming to dominate reviews by social scientists. In fact, Ellis had gone out of his way to attack Kinsey's critics, arguing that they had blown minor objections all out of proportion. In his letter to Terman, however, Ellis admitted that in its original form, the piece was similar to Terman's review, but that version never got published.

It seems that Kinsey was up to his old tricks, only with a new twist. "After my review had been accepted for publication, I happened to meet Kinsey at a meeting of the American Association of Marriage Counselors, and I told him about its contents," revealed Ellis. "He asked to see a copy, so I sent one to him," continued Ellis. "He was apparently quite disturbed by my criticisms, and wrote me that it might well provide deadly ammunition for Fulton Oursler, Dorothy Thompson [journalists who had written articles criticizing Kinsey], various prelates, and other anti-sexological forces who, at that time, were ganging up against the Kinsey study." Kinsey's argument, Ellis explained, "was that, no matter how well meant my critical review might be from a scientific standpoint, these puritan-minded individuals and groups would be certain to use it for their purposes, and against the general cause of sexual science." After reading a number of reviews, Ellis had, he confessed, come to believe that Kinsey was right to worry that "negative criticism of his book might easily, when it appeared in print, be misconstrued and distorted by anti-sexological sources, and the future scientific study of sex might thereby possibly be endangered."[132] Terman was not persuaded that the press was ganging up on Kinsey. Describing to a friend how Kinsey had hoodwinked Ellis into changing his review, he declared, "My personal opinion is that Kinsey's conspiracy story was made up and that Ellis was played for a sucker."[133]

Terman also heard from Kate Mueller. A longtime Kinsey foe at Indiana University, she had done battle with him on more than one occasion in her capacity as dean of women, particularly during the years of the marriage course. "There are many of us who have read your 'Comments' with admiration because they state so clearly the things that we suspected but could not specify," she wrote.[134] Mueller was happy to share local gossip about Kinsey. After describing in a mildly shocked tone the erotic art objects Kinsey was collecting, she confided, "There has been a good deal of discussion as to whether or not Mr. Kinsey's interest in his collection is scientific and objective or emotional, and pretty general agreement that it is the latter." Members of the art department who had consulted with Kinsey, she revealed, thought that he was weird. "The one thing which impresses these artists who have given Mr. Kinsey their time is: 'How can he continue to work day after day, week after week, on this subject?' " Mueller then quoted a letter from an artist friend, who observed, "We were glad to discuss the whole problem, to express ourselves on the subject, and learn something. But after the first day we were through. We were thoroughly satiated. It didn't take us long to reach that point, and then we were just bored. He can go on and on, but we were very very bored."[135] Delighted by this tidbit, Terman replied, "It looks to me as though Kinsey were running a certain amount of risk in building the type of art collection you mention, especially if many of the articles can be purchased only illegally. He certainly takes more chances that I should want to take if I were in his place."[136]

The more Terman thought about Kinsey's research, the more troubled he became about a problem he had alluded to but had not fleshed out in his review. It concerned the ages of the boys whose sexual behavior Kinsey had discussed, and the circumstances under which he had obtained this information. "It is strange that nowhere does he [Kinsey] give the age distribution of the subjects when they were interviewed," Terman wrote to Mueller. "I am wondering whether his failure to tell us that he interviewed children as young as 12 or 11 or 10, or 9 or 8 (if he actually did) would get him into legal difficulties," he continued. "I have wondered too whether the persons he calls informers or something like that are the ones who gave him the data on orgasms induced in infants by adult masturbation, and if he got the data from the informers on the number of orgasms of which teen-age boys are capable under what I take to have been homosexual contacts. It seems to me he was taking chances in publishing such data without making it absolutely clear that he had nothing to do whatever in the collection of such data."[137] Terman repeated these concerns verbatim in a subsequent letter to Mueller, with the thinly veiled warning "I hope [Kinsey] doesn't get the university into too much trouble."[138] As it happened, none of Kinsey's other critics raised this question in print—at least not during his lifetime.

Still, Terman had been right to worry about the university. Of all the elements of Kinsey's support structure, Indiana University was the most vulnerable to political retaliation. Ironically, it was also the best protected, thanks in no small part to the careful planning and the astute leadership of Herman B Wells. Wells had correctly foreseen that Kinsey's research would provide the most severe test to academic freedom in the university's history, and he had worked with Kinsey, the university's board of trustees, fellow administrators, and others to devise a defensive strategy. The incorporation of the Institute for Sex Research, which allowed the administration to claim that Kinsey's research was not formally part of the university, was an important element of that plan.

Moreover, Wells had made certain that the governor's office and important members of the state legislature received careful briefing on Kinsey's work before it appeared in print. Wells had also seen to it that the book was not released until shortly after the state legislature adjourned, thus assuring a lengthy cooling-off period before the state's elected officials reconvened and had an opportunity to discuss what action, if any, should be taken regarding Kinsey's work.[139] Following the book's publication, the administration had also arranged for copies to be sent to the governor and to key legislators, allowing them to judge its scientific merits for themselves.[140] (No doubt, Wells was confident that reading a few pages would dampen the ardor of all but the most determined readers.) Finally, Wells had relied heavily on members of his board of trustees, who, in his words, "spent endless hours . . . explaining the Kinsey project to irate friends, alumni, and legislators, and absorbing a considerable amount of personal abuse." Looking back on these hectic struggles, Wells declared, "I am proud to record the fact that, although the individual members of the board and the board as a whole were harassed and subjected to all manner of pressure, they never once wavered in their support of our policy toward the Kinsey Institute."[141]

Kinsey helped the university protect him, playing Hoosier politicians with the same skill that he managed the national press. By the time his book was published, he had hosted so many visitors at the institute that he had the routine down pat. Consequently, when delegations of legislators appeared at his door, he showed them his operations, explained his research, and fielded their questions with a unique blend of candor and tact. Above all, Kinsey looked, talked, and acted like a scientist, a man whose earnest demeanor testified to the seriousness of his research. While acknowledging that Kinsey did not suffer critics gladly and could be "dogmatic and bitter in his counterattacks," Wells later wrote, "I am confident that Dr. Kinsey's willingness to cooperate in various ways in handling the delicate public-relations problems posed by the study was a major factor in winning the battle. Without his help it could not have been done."[142]

But the battle that Kinsey could only watch from a distance, and the one that most concerned him, was raging at the Rockefeller Foundation's headquarters in New York. From the moment the news stories and reviews started appearing, his book was linked in the public's mind to its principal patron. Again, Kinsey had guaranteed this would happen by touting his relationship with the foundation in his public lectures, by emphasizing the connection in his talks with reporters, by thanking the foundation profusely for its support in the book's acknowledgments, and, above all, by persuading Gregg to write the preface. From Kinsey's perspective, this had been a brilliant strategy, as it had served to legitimize his research for many. Indeed, it had allowed him to bask in the foundation's prestige, even as its power had offered him a degree of protection. Yet, as Gregg had been arguing for years, this strategy was extremely risky.

Gregg's warnings proved prophetic. Kinsey's book turned the spotlight of national publicity on a foundation renowned for its low profile. Over the weeks and months following the book's publication, the Rockefeller Foundation found itself drawn deeper and deeper into the controversy that swirled around Kinsey's work. Popular magazines and scholarly journals alike played up the foundation's sponsorship of Kinsey's research—some with approval, others out of curiosity, and many with disdain. The one point that fans and foes agreed upon, however, was that the foundation shared the responsibility for Kinsey's work. For example, in an otherwise highly favorable article, *Good Housekeeping* was sharply critical of the mass publicity the book had received. Wondering out loud whether the forth-coming volume on women would be similarly exploited, the magazine de-manded, "Does the Medical Division of the Rockefeller Foundation want it to be?"[143]

Scores of critics took their concerns directly to the foundation. People wrote, telephoned, and made personal appointments to denounce Kin-sey's research (whether for moral or scientific reasons) and to register their disapproval or concern that the Rockefeller Foundation had supported him. Henry C. Link, the vice president of the Psychological Corporation in New York who contributed a piece to the one-sided *Reader's Digest* symposium on Kinsey,[144] complained to an officer at the foundation, "This study so far is a half-baked and highly regrettable piece of work. Kinsey is not a social scientist, to begin with; he is a zoologist. Psychologists, psy-chiatrists and sociologists should have been called in to help with the tech-niques of this study. . . . I wonder what is the ethical responsibility of the Foundation in a matter of this kind?"[145]

Faced with a host of similar complaints, the Rockefeller Foundation, like the nation, found itself pulled into a great debate about Kinsey's work. Chester I. Barnard, who became president of the foundation in the sum-mer of 1948, following Raymond Fosdick's retirement, moved quickly to bring himself up to speed on the Kinsey controversy. Talks with Gregg and his assistant Robert S. Morison revealed strong support for Kinsey within the medical division's professional staff, but also a willingness to consider the foundation's options, up to and including pulling the plug. Conse-quently, foundation officials, acting under orders from Barnard, weighed the pros and cons of Kinsey's methodology, spent the next several months reading his reviews (both favorable and critical), conducted lengthy cor-respondences with his critics and supporters, and debated whether or not the foundation should continue to back his research.

As the review proceeded, Barnard was especially eager to take the board's temperature. In a letter requesting a candid assessment of Kinsey's book, Barnard told his friend John S. Dickey, a trustee and the president of Dart-mouth College: "I have not gotten over the belief that we should not have been involved in an introduction to the book, and I have been more than peeved at the popular exploitation of it by the publishers." Barnard also confided that one of the board's most prominent trustees, Harold Dodds, the president of Princeton University, was very upset by *Sexual Behavior in the Human Male* and had given him in person "a most adverse statement about it," adding that a second trustee, Henry P. Van Dusen, the president of Union Theological Seminary, was "also adverse."[146]

Barnard was wise to be troubled on this score, because a dangerous situation was brewing. Like most organizations, the foundation preferred to operate on the basis of consensus. Kinsey's work, however, threatened to pit the officers, who were highly trained professionals, against the trustees, many of whom were not in a position to evaluate the scientific merits of the research. The danger was very real that the terms of this debate would place Kinsey in a no-win situation: the officers would defend his work with scientific arguments, while individual trustees would seize upon scientific criticisms to disguise moral objections to his work. In the face of such opposition, there was really very little Kinsey could do, short of abandoning the research, to satisfy his critics.

It did not take long for the foundation's split to spill out in plain view. Dodds felt so strongly that he went public. In the September issue of *Reader's Digest* (in the second of two back-to-back symposiums attacking Kinsey's work), Dodds delivered a sweeping denunciation of sex researchers: "We laymen shall be wise if we pay serious attention to the scientists who question the methodology of the reports and the significance of their findings. Perhaps the undergraduate newspaper that likened the reports to the work of small boys writing dirty words on fences touched a more profound scientific truth than is revealed in the surfeit of rather trivial graphs with which the reports are loaded."[147]

Henry P. Van Dusen shared this sentiment. In a letter to Dodds, Van Dusen called the *Reader's Digest* piece "first-rate" and expressed the hope that someone would challenge the foundation's support for Kinsey at the next board meeting. Explaining why he was hesitant to do so himself, he declared, "As a parson, I should be suspected by some of being a professional moralist; more important, the R. F.'s support of this project was undertaken long before I joined the board." Still, Van Dusen found "something very disheartening about the prospect of the Foundation's continuing to pour money into the project without the issue of both the scientific validity and the moral consequences of the project even being faced by the Board." Moreover, Van Dusen was angry that the money spent on Kinsey was not being used on more important matters, such as promoting morality as an antidote to the spread of communism abroad and the threat of internal subversion at home. "I have sometimes thought that if I were asked (as I know I shall not be) to advise the Foundation how to spend a million dollars more effectively in implementation of their newly declared program for 'moral and spiritual values,' I should recommend the use of $500,000 to counteract the influence of Kinsey's work, not of course by direct refutation but by a second, constructive interpretation of the nature and meaning of sex and the widest dissemination of such material. Isn't our appropriation of $25,000 to some trivial church commission a rather absurd gesture in view of the demoralization of moral standards and practices which is flowing widely from the Kinsey book?" Correctly sensing that he had found a soulmate in Dodds, Van Dusen added, "Forgive my vehemence. It is good to have someone to whom one dares to say exactly what he thinks. In these crucial times, I am finding it increasingly difficult to appreciate a complacent 'objectivity' when the destiny of human lives is involved."[148]

Given the heated opposition of trustees like Dodds and Van Dusen, Bernard must have been relieved by Dickey's response. Influenced, no doubt, by Gregg's strong advocacy, Dickey made a compelling case for standing firm. "Just think what they'd be saying about the Foundation if it had built even the most cock-eyed telescope for Mr. Galileo, and yet today we bask in the glow of universal acclaim for having made possible the biggest and most perfect one the world has ever known,"[149] declared Dickey. While time alone would determine the ultimate value of Kinsey's work, Dickey thought, science's patrons had to remember that progress in science was often incremental, with each generation of scientists standing on the shoulders of their predecessors, including those who had made some errors.

With the trustees sharply divided, Barnard asked Gregg to cut through the debate and prepare a recommendation to the board of trustees. From summer 1948 through spring 1949, Gregg collected information. In addition to talking and corresponding with Corner, Yerkes, Wells, and Kinsey, he conferred with a rather large cast of characters from outside and inside the foundation. Gregg concentrated on three issues: statistical criticisms, the fear that Kinsey's rigid personality might prevent him from addressing his critics in a constructive fashion, and the matter of need—specifically, whether the huge sales of *Sexual Behavior in the Human Male* had brought in so much revenue as to obviate additional grants. This last question weighed heavily on Gregg. In December 1948, he told the NRC's Lewis H. Weed that "the question of a grant to Kinsey involved the rather unusual circumstances of a grantee receiving royalty income from a publication which was larger than the grant which had made the publication possible." Given this peculiar situation, Gregg felt "inclined to think that our Board would not feel that further aid was needed."[150]

Privately, Gregg was leaning toward cutting Kinsey loose, as well as tapering support for the CRPS, with an eye to phasing it out completely.

Gregg was worried that Kinsey might be too stiff-necked to address his critics. "I know that in addition to some pretty dubious personal attacks," Gregg told one of his fellow officers, "Kinsey has had to take a good deal of rather pertinent and well-based criticisms from the statisticians. Just how much Kinsey can stand without becoming irritated and unreasonable, I do not know."[151]

Then, too, Gregg was pessimistic about the chances of securing another round of financing. As winter 1948 turned into spring 1949, he continued to send out signals that Kinsey's grant would not be renewed. As late at March, Gregg told President Wells, who had telephoned to lobby for additional funding, to advise Kinsey not to submit another application until all the royalties from the male volume had been completely exhausted, with the additional understanding that every penny would be plowed back into the research.[152] In short, Kinsey's budget was in deep trouble, placed in jeopardy by statistical and methodological criticisms, his perceived unwillingness to make changes, and, ironically, by the financial success of his book.

Throughout Gregg's deliberations, Corner proved to be Kinsey's staunchest ally. Putting aside whatever disappointments and pique he may felt over Kinsey's shabby treatment of the NRC in the past, he pressed Kinsey's case with great resolve. Through persistence and skillful diplomacy, he was able to secure a unanimous vote from the committee approving Kinsey's request for $40,000 for the coming fiscal year. Aware that the foundation would welcome an opportunity to distance itself from Kinsey, Corner and Weed put a new proposal on the table, recommending that the original relationship between the foundation and the committee be restored. The current grant from the Rockefeller Foundation to the NRC had provided $40,000 a year to be spent at the CRPS's discretion, and another $40,000 a year earmarked for Kinsey. Corner and Weed proposed to replace this two-track budget with a single appropriation of $60,000, a $20,000 reduction. Technically, the committee was to have complete discretion over how it was spent, but Corner made it clear the committee would reserve $20,000 for all comers and award $40,000 to Kinsey, thereby preserving his current level of support. The beauty of this proposal, of course, was that it restored the committee's claims to autonomy and shielded the foundation from direct responsibility for Kinsey's research. While this solution was less than perfect, Corner hoped that it offered the foundation enough protection to enable Gregg to accept it. In Corner's opinion, Gregg was their only hope. If he stood firm, the odds of winning the board over were good.

Corner had no doubts that Kinsey was worth saving. In a letter to Yerkes (with a copy to Gregg), Corner insisted that his confidence in Kinsey remained unshaken, despite a year-long bombardment by critics. Admitting with remarkable candor how a hard-nosed scientist like himself could be co-opted by familiarity, Corner confessed, "I find that I tend to judge Kinsey's work on the basis of my knowledge of its overwhelming qualitative superiority, and perhaps to be too lenient toward his quantitative expression." "As for Kinsey himself," he added, "if I judge his temperament correctly, he will regularly be hypersensitive about unfavorable reviews, however well-meant, but will consciously or unconsciously guard himself with respect to the debatable points in subsequent publications."[153] Of all the information that reached Gregg's desk, none had a greater impact than Corner's declaration of faith that Kinsey would learn from his mistakes and not repeat them.

Still, Gregg wanted to hear this message directly from Kinsey. Few things could have been more odious for a man as proud, stubborn, and deeply insecure as Kinsey. It was hard for him to admit his errors and even more difficult for him to agree to modify his study along the lines proposed by critics. Kinsey's instinct was to bare his teeth at opponents, whatever their objections. Had he followed his nature and snapped away, Kinsey would have forfeited any chance of getting his grant renewed. Instead, he did what he had to do to get the money. As the May meeting of the Rockefeller Foundation's board of trustees drew near, Kinsey swallowed his pride, sat on his anger, concealed his contempt, and agreed to address his opponents' criticisms—at least those he could not talk his way around.

How Kinsey went about this was clever. Aware of the concerns about his resistance to criticisms, the seriousness of the methodological and statistical points raised by his critics, and the size of the war chest he had built with royalties, Kinsey formulated a plan to address all three issues at once. In a long letter to Gregg, he outlined his blueprint for the future, stressing that he intended to improve his handling of statistical data and to pay more attention to psychological issues. To implement these changes, he announced plans to expand his staff to include a statistician, psychologist, and perhaps even a psychiatrist. Of course, changes of this magnitude would cost money, a great deal of money. And while royalties would be used to cover part of the expenses, Kinsey insisted that outside grants would be needed. But he did not stop there. Years of dealing with Gregg had taught Kinsey what needed to be said, and he said it. With characteristic overkill, Kinsey listed no fewer than thirteen reasons why the foundation should not terminate its support. Reason number one was that the public would interpret the foundation's actions "as a vote of no confidence in the research."[154]

In the end, Kinsey's concessions to his critics, the towering importance of his research, the sheer force of his personality, and the timely administrative changes proposed by Weed and Corner won Gregg over. Summoning the argumentative skills and powers of persuasion for which he was famous, Gregg made an eloquent presentation in May 1949 to the executive committee of the board. He recommended an annual grant of $80,000 (restoring $20,000 to the budget) for each of the next three years to the CRPS, with the understanding that the committee intended to award $40,000 annually to Kinsey. A long and animated discussed followed. Van Dusen, an alternate member of the committee, argued strenuously that a number of trustees opposed any additional grants to Kinsey. In the face of his objections, the committee debated whether the issue should be held over for consideration by the full board at its regular meeting in June. In the end, however, Gregg carried the day. The committee approved the recommendation unanimously, with Van Dusen abstaining.[155]

Yet Kinsey's troubles were far from over. The trustees who had opposed him felt that they had been bulldozed by colleagues who had given scant attention to his scientific deficiencies and even less thought to the moral consequences of his work. Dejected and bitter, Dodds complained to Barnard a few days after the executive committee vote, "I still think that the Foundation got snarled in something in which its name was abused."[156]

For the moment, however, Kinsey had won a stunning victory. Despite a year and a half of perpetual controversy, he had stood firm and kept his cool, at least publicly. Although critics had challenged his sample, his interviewing techniques, and his claims to objectivity, he had managed to keep his support structure intact. Indiana University, the NRC, and the Rockefeller Foundation (the latter after considerable soul-searching) had stood by him, providing the vote of confidence he badly needed to reassure the public that his work was basically sound, despite the attacks of critics.

Important as their imprimatur was to the public, it meant even more to Kinsey. The last year and a half had worn him down. It was as though the favorable reviews had no ability to shield him from the hurt he had suffered at the hands of critics. Often he had felt persecuted and betrayed. That was why he needed his patrons to stand firm. Their support sustained his faith in himself. As long as people like Gregg and Corner, not to mention Wells, backed him, Kinsey was able to hold himself together. With large elements of the public and many of his fellow scientists hailing his achievements, he could and did see himself as a great scientist who was conducting research of tremendous social value. Steeped in the ethos of science, Kinsey believed he had followed the canons of his profession. After all, had he not fruitfully applied the taxonomic method (the tools of his trade) to sex research? Had he not uncovered more data on human sexual behavior than any other scientist in history?

In the long run, Kinsey hoped that his data would change how society viewed and governed the sexual behavior of its members. In the meantime, all he had to do was keep working and not fly apart. By 1949, however, his private behavior was becoming more bizarre. There were signs that his carefully orchestrated balancing act might collapse. His habit of skating near the edge was getting worse, as Kinsey was taking more and more risks. Had he been able to talk, his boyhood idol, Teddy Roosevelt, might have helped Kinsey understand what was happening. A wise man, Roosevelt often parted from friends with the prayer that God might keep them from the werewolf and from their heart's desire. With the publication of *Sexual Behavior in the Human Male,* Kinsey had moved close to achieving his heart's desire, obtaining recognition and fame few scientists ever taste. In the wake of this success, however, came a host of problems—loss of anonymity, critics scrutinizing his every word and chart, and the growing fear that success in the public sector might not give him peace. Paradoxically, as his fame increased, Kinsey was finding it more and more difficult to maintain rigid self-control—and his private behavior showed it.

24

"I HOPE THE BLINDS WERE CLOSED"

He looked tired when he stepped off the bus early that morning to visit his brother Robert's family in Livingston, New Jersey. Kinsey was low on sleep, having spent the night walking around Times Square, observing gay pickups and talking with the many hustlers he knew by name. "He was exhausted when he came to see us," recalled his sister-in-law Edna, "so he fell asleep on the bus and rode all the way to the end of the bus line and had to come back. Poor guy." They were living on a farm then, and Kinsey took his nephews for a walk in a big field, where he identified different flowers and grasses for them. All too soon, he was back on the bus for New York, slumped in his seat with his head against the window, a middle-aged man looking older than his years, as though he bore the weight of the world on his shoulders. It was the last visit she could remember his making to their home, Edna lamented, adding, "That may be the only one we ever had."[1]

The battles with his critics were taking a heavy toll on Kinsey. Restless and irritable, he was having trouble sleeping. The fatigue was starting to show on his face; his jowls were beginning to sag, and his eyes had lost their sparkle. His response to pressure was to drive himself harder, stretching the hours he spent at the Institute in the evening and staying up later the nights he was on the road. Edgar Anderson was alarmed by Kinsey's appearance when the two old friends met in the spring 1949. "As for me I am deeply concerned about the future of your program," wrote Anderson. "It hinges on you, more than I think you can realize. Unless you mend your ways you cannot carry on in this fashion for very much longer." Pleading with Kinsey to get some rest, Anderson advised, "It is time you let your Scotch-Presbyterian conscience drive you into taking a real vacation for the sake of your most important program. I am not an M.D. but I am a trained observer and I have been observing you for some years. It is later than you think."[2] Clara was worried, too. When a reporter asked what her greatest concern was, she replied, "Prok's health. He is so very tired."[3] In rare moments, when he paused long enough to take stock, Kinsey knew that he reacted so strongly to critics, at least in part, because he was exhausted. In a letter to Yerkes, Kinsey confessed, "When I can get enough sleep, however, I realize that this has been a handsome reaction to our work."[4]

But restful nights were becoming all too rare. Chronically short on sleep, Kinsey was finding it harder and harder to maintain his internal equilibrium. Ever since childhood, his life had been a delicate balancing act between his private persona and his public one. By the late 1940s and early 1950s, Kinsey appeared to have melted the two. Publicly, he was hailed as the disinterested scientist who had penetrated the secrecy enshrouding human sexual behavior; privately, he had managed to function as a covert revolutionary who had used science to lay siege to middle-class morality.

Yet Kinsey was far from happy. The pressure was getting to him. He was like the mainspring of a watch that was being wound tighter and tighter. In what should have been his finest hour, Kinsey was at once angry at his critics and fearful they would bring him down. It was as though the controversy surrounding his work had sapped his confidence, unleashing insecurities and anxieties never far from the surface. Not the least of these worries involved his long-standing fear of death. A close friend from this period in his life recalled that Kinsey was plagued by a "constant sense of mortality," adding that "a great many decisions and a great deal of the spirit of the research was because he was haunted by the brevity of his life."[5] In other words, Kinsey lived in fear that his health would fail and that he would die before his life's work was completed.

Anxious, driven men often behave irrationally. Kinsey was no exception to that rule. As his level of frustration rose, his private behavior became more erratic and compulsive. How erratic and compulsive? Enough to elevate sharply the risks he took in his hidden life.

Following the publication of *Sexual Behavior in the Human Male,* Kinsey attempted to build a private world that would provide the emotional support he needed. Within the inner circle of his senior staff members and their spouses, he endeavored to create his own sexual utopia, a scientific subculture whose members would not be bound by arbitrary and antiquated sexual taboos. What he envisioned was in every sense a clandestine scientific experiment, if not a furtive attempt at social engineering: unfettered sex would be the order of the day. Although he excluded children categorically (again, there were no pedophiles at the Institute), Kinsey decreed that within the inner circle men could have sex with each other, wives would be swapped freely, and wives, too, would be free to embrace whichever sexual partners they liked. Kinsey further ordained that a handful of trusted outsiders would be taken into their confidence, admitted to their scientific subculture, and given full membership privileges.

Bringing in outsiders was absolutely essential for Kinsey to achieve sexual satisfaction, as no other member of the inner circle could fulfill his masochistic or homosexual desires, though Pomeroy was willing to playact to meet Kinsey's needs. The problem, though, was that the sex between Kinsey and Pomeroy had gradually lost its erotic charge. A man who knew both Kinsey and Pomeroy intimately, declared, "Wardell [Pomeroy] is fundamentally not s/m; he's experimental."[6] Thus, Pomeroy's performances, however well intentioned, were staged and unconvincing, lacking the erotic power of the genuine article. Kinsey had to look elsewhere for sexual partners who could meet his peculiar needs, and locating them was no easy matter. "Kinsey thought sadomasochists were the most frustrated people in the world because of their difficulty in finding each other," wrote Pomeroy.[7] What Pomeroy did not say, of course, was that Kinsey was speaking not just from his research but from experience.

But find suitable partners Kinsey did, and one of these outsiders, who asked not to be identified and whom we shall call Mr. Y, gave a detailed account of their relationship and Kinsey's relationship with other members of the inner circle as well. It was Dickinson who introduced Kinsey to Mr. Y, a handsome young professional with a diverse sexual history that included sadomasochism and extensive homosexual contacts. When Kinsey took his history, Mr. Y was awed by Kinsey's gift for putting people at ease. Years later Mr. Y recalled, "You were instantly . . . at peace with yourself with him," adding, "You just knew whatever you had done he was on your side."[8] Some time later, during one of Kinsey's visits to the West Coast, where Mr. Y lived, the two men were visiting in Kinsey's hotel room when something extraordinary happened. "I told him I had a fantasy of having sex with him, with no idea in mind except to report it," Mr. Y later recalled, "and he sort of said, 'Take off your clothes.' So I did and we started right there. So every time we met from then on, we had sexual contact."[8]

Mr. Y, at Kinsey's invitation, made several trips to Bloomington for consultation and sex. Referring to the Institute's senior staff, Mr. Y declared, "I also had sex with everybody else around there too." That included members of both sexes. Mr. Y had fond memories of copulating with Clara and Martha (Pomeroy's wife) and equally warm recollections of his contacts with their husbands. "We all sucked one another," he declared. Kinsey, of course, was an eager participant in these sessions, but not at the expense of ignoring the women. "[Kinsey] had sex with the wives, too," stressed Mr. Y. "It wasn't all 'H[omosexual].' "[9]

During his visits to Bloomington, Mr. Y always stayed at the Kinseys'. A keen observer, he quickly divined that while Kinsey's relationship with Clara was no longer passionate, their emotional bond remained strong. "I don't think they were sexy to one another, just deeply appreciative and deeply loving," he declared. "They slept in different bedrooms," he continued. "I don't think he had sex with Mac to have sex, but if I was there we'd all have sex." Elaborating, Mr. Y revealed, "Kinsey and I'd be having sex upstairs and I'd go down[stairs] and have sex with Mac in the same house. She accepted what went on, you know." Indeed, Mr. Y was surprised by how liberated Clara was sexually. "Mac was tremendous," he declared. "She looked like she was a little pip-squeak, you know. Her hair was straight and she didn't look like she was all loose or open and she was open as hell."[16] Looking back on those encounters, Mr. Y was struck by the total absence of possessiveness and jealousy in the Kinsey household. Awed by what he called "the real durable love between the two of them," Mr. Y observed, "They totally accepted what the other one did, totally."[17] Not that Clara had much choice, not if she wished to remain with her husband. "Kinsey once said, 'The reason she does [accept everything] is that she knows when I make up my mind to do something I do it,'" recalled Mr. Y. "And he didn't say that threateningly," added Mr. Y. "It was just a fact."[10]

Mr. Y's recollections of Kinsey as a sexual partner were somewhat ambivalent. Mr. Y revealed that while Kinsey enjoyed oral sex (both giving and receiving), he "loved anal intercourse," particularly when he functioned as the active rather than the passive partner. As the sadist member of the team, however, Mr. Y found Kinsey's performance as a masochist a trifle disappointing. "He was kind of a punk when it comes to s/m," complained Mr. Y, explaining that "he liked [for me] to beat him with a cat-o'-nine-tails but not very hard." Nor was Mr. Y pleased with Kinsey's meager use of props and his total neglect of staging. While confirming that Kinsey "put ropes around his testicles," Mr. Y added somewhat wistfully, "he didn't dress up in clothes and he didn't establish scenes, you know." More troubling still were Kinsey's facial expressions when they had sex. Ironically, the secular evangelist who advocated joy and abandonment in sex did not appear happy. Mr. Y recalled that Kinsey would "get kind of a long-suffering look on his face when he was having sex," noting that "some of the [other] sex partners and I used to kind of smile about it because he looked gross," like a man who seemed weighted down with some awful burden. Reflecting a moment longer on his sad expression, Mr. Y remarked that Kinsey "looked almost grotesque."[11]

There was something grim in the way Kinsey was approaching sex, not only in his private life but in his research. In both areas, he was becoming more compulsive, like a man who had become addicted to risk taking. The sexual escapades in his attic were political dynamite. If the press had gotten wind of what was happening, Kinsey's career would have ended then and there. Yet not only did he go right on staging these sessions but he compounded the danger by creating a visual record. Unbeknownst to all but the participants, Kinsey filmed many of these sessions in his attic.

Flatwork photography had been going on for some time at the Institute before the publication of *Sexual Behavior in the Human Male*. A good amateur photographer, Gebhard was assigned to photograph erotic drawings, art objects, or photographs that collectors were willing to have copied but did not wish to donate to the Institute. "Since we looked upon this as an extremely touchy thing, the existence of our collections and the fact that we did photography was a deep state secret," Gebhard later explained. "Consequently, we set up a little amateurish darkroom in Kinsey's basement, down in his fruit cellar," he continued. "So for a couple of years I was down there with the paper cartons and whatnot with a few bottles of chemicals, and an enlarger and a few trays, developing and printing the photographs that I had made of collections."[12]

Gebhard's tenure as a photographer was short-lived. Sometime in 1948, Kinsey met William (Bill) Dellenback, a superb commercial photographer in New York City. They were introduced by their mutual friend, Clarence Tripp. A few months earlier Tripp and Dellenback had become partners in a photographic business in New York. Tripp had telephoned Kinsey out of the blue shortly after the publication of *Sexual Behavior in the Human Male* to express his delight with the book, but also to argue some points. Pleased by the young man's interest, Kinsey invited Tripp to Bloomington, and he accepted. The visit went beautifully, marking the beginning of a fast friendship. From then on, whenever Kinsey visited New York, he usually managed to see Tripp for dinner. On one such occasion, Tripp brought Dellenback along, and he, too, became Kinsey's friend.[13]

It was not long before Kinsey hired the partners to do a variety of photographic work in New York, though in truth Dellenback handled most of the load as Tripp's interests were already shifting from photography to psychology, the field in which he eventually made his career. One of their more interesting assignments stemmed from a disagreement Kinsey had with the current medical literature on male orgasms. Most of the urologists of the day maintained that fertilization depended on the squirting of semen into the cervix. Kinsey's data suggested otherwise. A substantial majority of the men he had interviewed reported that their semen "dribbled" rather than "squirted" out. To settle the dispute, Kinsey announced that he needed to film two thousand men masturbating to climax. Delighted to be of service, Tripp volunteered to arrange everything, an offer Kinsey readily accepted, even though he suspected Tripp of boasting. Aware it would not be easy to meet the quota, Tripp enlisted the aid of a friend who was having an affair with a young hustler. Decades later, Tripp described the seventeen-year-old youth as "a beautiful German boy prostitute" who had "practically organized Forty-second Street and Bryant Park at that time." Working together, Tripp and his friend devised a plan to enlist the young prostitute's help. They got Kinsey to agree to pay everyone who masturbated two dollars and to give the German boy two dollars for every person he brought in.[14]

The scheme worked like a charm. When the night for the filming arrived, Dellenback and Tripp looked out their window and saw a line in front of their brownstone that stretched all the way around the block. Recalling the scene decades later, Tripp noted that men kept arriving in such numbers and with such speed that the sidewalk looked "like the box office at Radio City Music Hall." Dellenback, who tended to be a little on the fastidious side, viewed the mob with some trepidation. Their office, it seems, had wall-to-wall carpet, and Tripp remembered Dellenback saying, "Mercy, whatever is going to happen to the rug." Recalling his answer with a chuckle, Tripp declared, "And I said, 'Nothing, because we'll put a big sheet there.'" In the end, added Tripp, they filmed so many men masturbating they had to spread "two sheets to keep it [the semen] from leaking through." Kinsey was thrilled by their success. Although they failed to reach their goal of two thousand, the data from the filming showed that the vast majority of the men (over 70 percent) "dribbled" rather than "squirted"—just as Kinsey had predicted.[15]

In March 1949, Kinsey offered Dellenback a job as a permanent member of the Institute's staff, and he accepted. Kinsey put aside a budget of $10,000 for photographic equipment and started Dellenback off at an annual salary of $4,400, raising the sum to $4,800 at the beginning of the new fiscal year in July 1949.[16] Since Kinsey was eager to film as much live sexual activity as possible, the camera started rolling almost immediately after Dellenback arrived in Bloomington, with staff members and their wives cast in the starring roles. Everyone was sworn to secrecy. To further maximize security, most of the filming was done at Kinsey's home in one of the finished bedrooms in the attic, a private setting that could not be viewed from the street. Stressing that they all were "extremely sensitive on this whole film matter," Gebhard later revealed, "The filming was a deep, dark secret. Only the staff members and their spouses, and, of course, the [other] participants in the film knew this." The Institute's secretaries and clerical staff, Gebhard stressed, "had no idea of what was going on."[17] Dellenback, too, recalled the tight security, noting that all the filming was done "on the q.t." and that copies of the staff films were not filed with the general film collection but were "kept under lock and key."[18]

Not all the staff members and their spouses agreed to be filmed. While Pomeroy and Martha, his wife, were not in the least bit camera shy, Martin and his wife, Alice, flatly refused to be filmed as a couple. (Although he could not remember her by name, Mr. Y recalled that one of the staff wives refused to have sex with Kinsey. Perhaps it was Alice.)[19] Martin, however, did agree to masturbate alone on camera. "I really wasn't interested, the idea kind of offended me," Martin later confessed. "I recall the one occasion that I participated, as I remember, I had a hell of a time getting an erection. I was such a failure nobody ever asked me again," he added.[20] Dellenback had a similar reaction. "The only one time I indulged in any sort of thing was [when] Kinsey had some group sessions," recalled Dellenback. "[I] didn't photograph them, but we were all around there undressed up in his bedroom there, and I remember masturbating to climax by myself in front of the others because Kinsey wanted it. Somebody else probably did it too, you see. And so I stood there on tiptoes or leaning against the wall or something." Looking back on that evening, Dellenback lamented, "I didn't enjoy it," adding that the entire experience was "against my sense of propriety, I think."[21] Agnes, Gebhard's wife, had an even stronger reaction. Complaining of "the sickening pressure" she was under to have sex on film with her spouse and other staff members, she told an interviewer, "I felt like my husband's career at the Institute depended on it."[22]

That charge would have saddened Kinsey. His self-image was not that of a man who coerced people. According to Dellenback, Kinsey had a gift for making outrageous requests appear reasonable. Kinsey accomplished this by arguing that because the Institute was investigating sex there should be no shame or guilt or repugnance attached to any sexual activity among senior staff members. In other words, he assumed his familiar role as teacher, the mentor who knew how to show less liberated souls the path to sexual freedom. Looking back on Kinsey's adroit handling of the situation, Dellenback described it "as an educational kind of thing," as though "we all had to be brought along and educated as to certain things we might have little reservations on."[23]

From Kinsey's perspective, then, these sessions were part and parcel of his ongoing struggle to banish inhibitions. One of the keys to understanding his complex personality, insisted a close friend, was that Kinsey "liked to feel that he was absolutely unconstrained by moralistic forms."[24] Yet the members of his inner circle, while technically free to enjoy the fruits of sexual liberation, had to accept limits on their behavior. Anyone contemplating an extramarital affair had to clear it first with Kinsey. Gebhard remembered Kinsey's saying, "You've got to tell me who it is and explain it all, and then I'll tell you whether you can or can't." Smiling broadly, Gebhard added, "That edict was not obeyed necessarily, but he gave that edict."[25]

Kinsey, of course, justified this demand by insisting he had to protect the Institute from scandal. Yet this was not the whole story. Whether through necessity or design, his version of sexual utopia came with restrictions. True to character, he cast himself not only in the role of sexual liberator but in that of benevolent dictator. And while there was no gainsaying his devotion to sexual freedom, his need for dominance and control remained strong. The filming occurred because Kinsey willed it; as did the various kinds of sexual activity staged. Viewed from this perspective, staff members and their wives were not so much participants in sexual liberation as pawns for Kinsey to manipulate and control.

No one felt the force of his unyielding demands more strongly than Clara. Just as she had with so many things for so many years, she went along with the filming, doing her best to throw herself into the role with the proper abandon, as befitted the wife of the high priest of sexual liberation. Clara was filmed masturbating, and she was also filmed having sex with Pomeroy. According to Dellenback, "She was wonderfully cooperative and all in the filming and such."[26] Offering his thoughts on why she agreed to be filmed, Gebhard declared, "Mac so deeply believed in the research that Kinsey was doing, I swear if he'd asked her to cut her wrists, she probably would have. She idolized the man, even though she was quite free in saying he irritated her occasionally."[27] Dellenback shared this view. Asked to explain why she would agree to masturbate before the camera and take various staff members and strangers to bed, Dellenback answered that "she just believed in him, was cooperative—anything he wanted." Reflecting at greater length, Dellenback observed astutely that "she enjoyed it because she didn't have anything else." Dellenback also thought that Kinsey brought different sexual partners home for Clara because "he was sympathetic to her needs and he couldn't [meet them]."[28] According to Gebhard, Kinsey "was already having some troubles with erectile impotence." While it would be tempting to attribute Kinsey's dysfunction to psychological problems, Gebhard thought the explanation was organic.

"As his health declined, which it was doing, particularly his blood pressure and cardiac condition," Gebhard explained, "it was more difficult for him to function."[29]

Kinsey both led and taught by example. Surrounded by devout followers who knew better than to question the sacred principle of individual variation, he was completely open. As an exhibitionist extraordinaire, Kinsey seldom passed up an opportunity to show off his genitals and demonstrate his various masturbatory techniques to staff members. One outsider, who was himself filmed masturbating, told an interviewer that Kinsey "had very large genitalia, and that means both penis and balls." The man added, "Several of the staff members used to say, 'Maybe that's why he whips the goddam thing out all the time to show you the urethra or to show the corona.' I mean he is not ashamed of what he has got."[30]

While Dellenback could not remember shooting any homosexual activity involving his boss, he often filmed Kinsey, always from the chest down, engaged in masochistic masturbation. Once the camera started rolling, the world's foremost expert on human sexual behavior and a scientist who valued rationality above all other intellectual properties would insert an object into his urethra, tie a rope around his scrotum, and then simultaneously tug hard on the rope as he maneuvered the object deeper and deeper. During one filming session, Dellenback remembered Kinsey inserting a swizzle stick, the kind with a knob on the end, up his urethra. This particular occasion stood out in Dellenback's memory, perhaps, because it offered a perfect illustration of how Kinsey could make the bizarre seem rational. Ever the teacher, Kinsey paused just long enough to give Dellenback a brief anatomy lesson that explained why the knob posed a problem. "I remember vaguely Kinsey saying to me, 'you know, there's a little flap as you go partly up the urethra there you have to bypass, so you can't just jam the thing in,' " recalled Dellenback.[31]

Kinsey's object of choice, however, remained the item he had kept hidden under the floorboards in the attic of his boyhood home in South Orange. Mr. Y described seeing Kinsey in the late 1940s and early 1950s insert "a toothbrush with the brush end first." To facilitate entry, Mr. Y noted, "He [had] cut the urethra, too, sort of wide open."[32] How many years of physical conditioning and psychic distress it had taken to reverse the ends of the toothbrush (i.e., to go from the handle to the bristles) can only be a matter for conjecture. Still, the fact that he was able to perform this feat offers an index of how far Kinsey's masochism had advanced. Explaining in purely physical terms why Kinsey gradually progressed to ever larger objects, a close friend observed, "You know how it is when you touch a sensitive part of your body; it gets a little tougher. Now all of a sudden it begins to take more stimulation to get the same effect, right?" Elaborating, the friend described how Kinsey developed from the boy who inserted straws in that basement in Hoboken into the adult who required much larger objects to obtain the desired results. "So after a while he had to use bigger objects, and he got into pipe cleaners and then larger pipe cleaners," the friend declared. "Then he got up to hard objects, round pencils and hexagonal pencils, then up to the handle of a toothbrush and then up to the brush end of a toothbrush in which he let the brush end stay in there and went like this [twirling his hands together in a back-and-forth motion] on the handle to twist it. This is the degree to which that thing grew."[33]

Not that Kinsey's situation was unique. As his friend pointed out, the human body and mind quickly grow accustomed to pain. Consequently, the stimulus required to inflict the desired degree of pain has to be increased over time, as many masochists discover. By the time he had reached middle age, of course, Kinsey had learned this lesson with a vengeance. A friend recalled Kinsey warning, "Tell your sadomasochistic friends to observe great caution. The human body adjusts rapidly and the levels are capable of escalating rapidly."[34] Again, Kinsey was speaking from experience. On one occasion, when his inner demons plunged him to new depths of despair, Kinsey climbed into a bathtub, unfolded the blade of his pocketknife, and circumcised himself without benefit of anesthesia.[35] Although Dellenback denied capturing the incident on film, he confirmed that it happened. "No, I remember he [Kinsey] must have told me something about it," recalled Dellenback. "God, it must have been damn painful. It must have bled a hell of a lot."[36]

Dellenback had no memory of filming Kinsey having sex with Clara, or for that matter with any other partner, male or female. His friends believed that his difficulties in achieving an erection explained his solo performances. Confirming Kinsey's problems, Dellenback declared, "I remember he had to go into the bathroom to work himself up."[37] Sympathetic, Gebhard observed, "It's hard enough, God knows, to function with lights and camera on you, and Kinsey would be the last person to want to 'fail.' So, I think he just didn't want to put himself to that test where it might not work out."[38]

Yet Kinsey's declining health in no way diminished his capacity to watch others perform. If anything, the waning of his own sexual powers seemed to intensify his voyeurism. In addition to staff members and their spouses, Kinsey coaxed a variety of people not affiliated with the Institute to his attic. Indeed, he was good at not getting turned down. From their histories, he had a good idea of which individuals would be willing to cooperate, and he had no difficulty defending the scientific merits of filming. Every scientist needs data, Kinsey would explain, and the direct observation of biological phenomena is one of the most reliable ways to get it. Although self-serving, this argument was not specious. After all, the history of science is filled with discoveries that can be traced to direct observation, a fact that should not be forgotten in Kinsey's case, regardless of the prurient interest he brought to many areas of his research.

As a scientist, then, it was easy for Kinsey to justify filming sexual behavior. Politically, however, the risks were enormous. Public opinion would never have tolerated sexual filming, particularly of the kinds of behavior he preferred. However much he shouted "science," the public would have answered "pornography." Consequently, Kinsey exercised great caution in casting these sessions, selecting only those individuals whom he trusted to keep their mouths shut. All told, Dellenback filmed about twenty homosexual couples, ten heterosexual couples, and approximately twenty-five men and women engaged in masturbation.[39] As happened so often in the research, Kinsey managed to mix business with pleasure. Many of the homosexual sessions he filmed involved sadomasochism.

Glenway Wescott was one of the gay men who performed in Kinsey's attic. A strikingly handsome fellow, Wescott was an accomplished and much heralded writer of the "Lost Generation." He was one of many gay men who read *Sexual Behavior in the Human Male* and felt transformed by the event. Many years later, he recalled, "I thought at once that it was the most important book that had been written in my time insofar as potential good influence—and almost revolutionizing influence—because all my life I had seen the psychological ravages of the unfavorable situation of the homosexual." In 1949, the two men met for dinner with a group that included E. M. Forster during one of Kinsey's frequent visits to New York. "It was a delicious evening," beamed Wescott many years later.[40] Kinsey was at his best, regaling his dinner companions with an erudite discussion of the sexual differences between men and women.[41] Indeed, Wescott was intrigued by this earnest scientist from the Midwest. "Kinsey is a strange man, with a handsome good sagacious face but with a haunted look—fatigue, concentration, and (surprising to me, if I interpret rightly) passionateness and indeed sensuality," Wescott confided to his diary. "With all his scientific conscientiousness, and pride of science, and faith in science," he continued, "he has the temperament of a reformer rather than a scientist: fierily against hypocrisy and repressive law of every sort, censorship, etc., and against Judaism and Catholicism and Irishy."[42]

Soon the two became friends. Wescott took it upon himself to educate Kinsey in literature, a subject Kinsey knew very little about. Wescott also introduced Kinsey to Monroe Wheeler, his longtime lover, who agreed to be interviewed as well. Like Wescott, Wheeler was a godsend for Kinsey. As the director of exhibitions and publications at the Museum of Modern

Art in New York, Wheeler knew an amazing number of artists in New York and was happy to serve as a contact man in this community. Together, Wescott and Wheeler put Kinsey in touch with hundreds of artists and writers in New York, many of whom were homosexual. Through these contacts, Kinsey was able not only to add scores of homosexual histories to his collection but to deepen his appreciation for the many ways in which homoerotic experiences and imagination inform literature and art. In return, Kinsey shared his incomparable knowledge of human sexuality with Wescott and Wheeler and gave them a standing invitation to visit Bloomington and examine materials of interest at the Institute, an offer they accepted on numerous occasions.

During one of Wescott's solo visits to Bloomington, Kinsey broached the subject of filming, and Wescott agreed. Kinsey's plan was to pair Wescott with a man who was reported to have most unusual orgasms. At the climactic moment, it seems, the man's body virtually jackknifed, twisting and thrashing in such violent contortions that he was frequently thrown out of bed. Kinsey was eager to capture this spectacle on film, and the man did not disappoint. At the critical instant he "jackknifed," and Kinsey was ecstatic. For their part, Wescott and the man were equally delighted by a surprise they received. When the filming stopped, Clara popped into the room with a tray of refreshments, along with clean towels so they could freshen up.[43] For any other woman, such a quaint display of domesticity would have seemed jarringly out of place, but Clara saw this as part of her duties as a good hostess. She also prepared dinner for her guests, inspiring Wescott to write in his diary, "Mrs. K is one of the greatest of cooks—if Alfred were not the hardest-working of men he would be the fattest."[44]

Although homosexual males figured prominently in the filming sessions in his attic, Kinsey's decided preference was for sadomasochists. "He was interested in watching s/m," recalled Mr. Y. "We had many people who came to visit who did lots of s/m."[45] Among Kinsey's favorite masochists was Samuel M. Steward, an English professor at a university in Chicago, whose case history was so rich it had taken Kinsey five hours to interview him. Decades later, Steward recalled that at the end of the interview Kinsey gave him a thoughtful look and said, "Why don't you give up trying to continue your heterosexual relationships?"[46] Steward dropped his phony "bisexuality" then and there. He also became a tireless contact man for Kinsey, persuading many of his gay friends to give their histories, too. In return, Kinsey showered Steward with attention, never visiting Chicago without first arranging a meeting. Like Kinsey, Steward was an avid record keeper (he kept a "Stud File" of his sexual partners), and by his reckoning he and Kinsey spent a total of about seven hundred hours together, pursuing a friendship that lasted until Kinsey's death.

Over time, Steward formed a close emotional bond with Kinsey. Confessing freely the transference that took place, Steward later wrote, "In him I saw the ideal father—who was never shocked, who never criticized, who always approved, who listened and sympathized. I suppose I fell in love with him to a degree, even though he was a grandfather." Like so many other gay men whose lives Kinsey touched, Steward never knew that Kinsey was gay, and there was never any physical contact between the two. Still, many of Steward's friends asked point-blank if Kinsey was "queer." When Kinsey learned about this, he asked Steward what he told them. Steward replied that he always said, "Yes, he is—but not in the same way we are. He is a voyeur and an auditeur. He likes to look and listen." Noting what happened next, Steward wrote, "Kinsey laughed, but a moment later I caught him observing me thoughtfully. I may have hit closer to the truth than I realized."[47]

The two men had known each other for about a year when Kinsey raised the subject of filming. From their interview, Kinsey knew that Steward had some sadomasochism in his history. This intrigued Kinsey. As Steward later put it, Kinsey's "interest in sado-masochism had reached a point of intolerable tension," and "he wanted to find out more." When Steward agreed to cooperate, Kinsey arranged an assignation with a freelance artist from New York named Mike Miksche, whom Steward described as "a tall mean-looking sadist . . . with a crew-cut and a great personality." The two men came to Bloomington, where Kinsey brought them together for a pre-filming chat in his backyard. To get Miksche in the mood, Kinsey got him half-drunk on gin. Steward did a little prompting of his own. Miksche, it seems, was wearing stylish brown English riding boots, the kind with lacing at the instep, and as they sat around talking, Steward leaned over, impishly tugged at one end of a lace, untied it, and declared, "Humph, you don't look so tough to me."[48]

For the next two afternoons, Steward and Miksche put on a show. A born actor with a flare for high drama, Miksche threw himself into the role with gusto. Every time he heard Dellenback's camera start to roll, Miksche would resume his attacks with renewed energy and ardor, leaving Steward after each assault, in his words, "exhausted, marked and marred, all muscles weakened." As the sessions unfolded, various members of the inner circle dropped in to watch the performance. Among these spectators, Steward was particularly impressed by Clara, whom he described "as a true scientist to the end," noting that "she sat by and once in a while calmly changed the sheets upon the workbench."[49] This was typical of Clara. "At the conclusion of many a filming session," noted Gebhard, "Mac would suddenly appear, literally with persimmon pudding or milk and cookies or something. [She would] simply come in absolutely blasé about the nude individuals or the semi-clothed individuals. Some of the participants were just absolutely dumbfounded by this, but it charmed them."[50] Another visitor who was filmed in Kinsey's attic recalled that Clara "was more like just a regular fellow."[51]

In the case of Steward and Miksche, however, it appears that Clara jumped the gun a bit, as they were not through. "At the end of the last session, when my jaws were so tired and unhinged that I could hardly close my mouth, Mike got really angry and slapped me hard on each cheek, saying that I was the lousiest cocksucker he had ever seen," wrote Steward many years later. Furious, Steward leaped from the bed, bolted for the bathroom, and sought refuge in the shower, leaving Miksche craving more action. "Later that evening," continued Steward, "Kinsey left Mike and me in separate parts of the library to do some reading, and suddenly Mike appeared, wild-fire-eyed and excited—having stimulated himself with some typewritten S/M stories—and had his way with me on the cold cement floor of the library stacks. When Kinsey heard of that encounter, he laughed and said, 'I hope the blinds were closed.' "[52]

In a sense, the blinds were always shut. Kinsey had successfully compartmentalized his public and private personas. While signs of emotional stress and the first intimations of mental collapse were starting to show in his private behavior, he nevertheless managed to keep up appearances for the many gay men and sadomasochists who came to the Institute to be filmed. Excluding the few who became his sexual partners, they did not have a clue about Kinsey's personal interest in their sexual identities. As one gay man who was filmed at the Institute later remarked, "The picture I saw was a smooth, heterosexual consistency throughout."[53] As far as most of his visitors knew, then, the man they met was a somewhat bolder version of the Kinsey who was known to the world, a fearless scholar who had the courage to collect forbidden facts, who answered their questions, and who served as sexual guru to an eager public.

If filming satisfied both the voyeur and the scientist in Kinsey, his daily mail appealed to his missionary instincts. Following the publication of *Sexual Behavior in the Human Male,* he was flooded with practically every sexual question imaginable. Many of the queries were routine (what were the best forms of birth control, when should parents start educating their children about sex, etc.); others were bizarre. People asked about everything from dirty jokes to whether too much sex could cause cancer.

Not surprisingly, it was the letters from people seeking personal advice that Kinsey found most compelling. His replies were anything but consistent. In many cases (particularly those involving complaints of sexual incompatibility in married couples), he would decline to get involved, explaining that he and his associates were research scientists, not clinicians.

In other cases, Kinsey would go out of his way to be helpful. Often he would summarize data from his research that impinged on the problem at hand, as if to say, "Stop worrying. Everything will be okay. All you need to know are the facts, and you will be able to solve your own problems." In many instances, however, Kinsey would take a definite stand on critical issues, offering advice and observations freely. His lengthiest responses appeared to be triggered by the urgency of the pleas. Simply put, he was a soft touch for a sob story. Tortured souls who described their problems in great detail and with sufficient pathos almost always received detailed replies, many of which contained important revelations about Kinsey's sexual attitudes and philosophy. Often he threw caution to the wind, offering advice on delicate social issues he would not have dared to put in his books or give to the press.

Tendering advice allowed Kinsey to expand his secular ministry. For years, he had advised individuals in private, advancing his own peculiar sexual philosophy, granting absolution to all who would listen, and loudly proclaiming in public that research scientists must stick to the business of information gathering and refrain from any practical application of their data. All that changed after the publication of *Sexual Behavior in the Human Male* was that Kinsey suddenly found himself in greater demand. From 1948 until his death, the cries for help came from a national congregation of the sexually anxious, repressed, deviant, or dysfunctional. He was deeply moved by their letters, largely because he identified with their suffering.

Kinsey did his best to succor as many tortured souls as possible. Always he preached the gospel of self-acceptance, telling people there was nothing abnormal about their behavior. Whatever difficulties they were having, he insisted, were the result of guilt feelings brought about by the clash between their behavior and rigid middle-class morality. And although he stressed that he was not qualified to pass moral judgments, Kinsey proclaimed the same message to anyone who would listen: nearly all sexual needs were biologically normal, and people should act upon them without inhibition or guilt.

Easily one of the more charming queries he received came from an elderly bard, who had been named a poet laureate of one of the southern states. Could Kinsey recommend "a harmless aphrodisiac," the man inquired, explaining, "I am approaching eighty, and though in good health and otherwise vigorous, I find that my virility is waning."[54] Kinsey answered, "I know of no aphrodisiac which is as good as good health and plenty of sleep. The only drug that is known to have any temporary effect is the Indian drug Yohimbin." Kinsey went on to say that the drug's effect was "very temporary" and that it had so many side effects that the medical establishment refused to recommend it in the United States.[55] More than a year later, Kinsey received another letter from the poet. This time, the elderly gentleman wanted to know whether a man could have intercourse with a woman of fifty who had not menstruated for a year "without fear of making her pregnant."[56] No doubt delighted to learn that the poet had a much more pleasant problem to ponder, Kinsey promptly replied that while it was exceedingly rare for a woman who had stopped menstruating to conceive, "there is some wisdom in continuing some protection against fertilization for a year or two after cessation of the menstruation."[57]

Scores of anxious masturbators contacted Kinsey. In each instance he tried to lift the burden of guilt from their shoulders. "Masturbation does no harm, but the sort of worrying you are doing does wreck the life of an individual," he wrote one troubled young man. "You have to jerk yourself up by your bootstraps, and stop worrying."[58] Similarly, when a young college man, with a history of frequent masturbation and a perfect record of impotence with women, begged for some medicine that would remedy his condition, Kinsey replied, "There is no drug which will work any permanent cure—the only remedy is for you to be able to learn to enter into sexual relations without any questions or doubts in your mind, and then you will find that it will be no difficulty."[59]

Kinsey received a number of inquiries from men who worried that masturbation might impede their ability to have sex with women. A thirty-year-old man, who admitted to being a virgin and asked if masturbation could cause impotence, prompted this response from Kinsey: "Your difficulty in sex relations with girls is probably dependent upon nothing else than the fact that you have delayed so long in arriving at such experience. If you had gone for 30 years without ever trying to walk, you would have some difficulty in walking when you first began. You can, however, contribute to the continuation of the impotency by thinking about it and worrying about it." Kinsey added, "You will be able to perform only when you can completely forget the question and concentrate your interest entirely in the girl with whom you are having your relation."[60] Responding to a similar query from another man, he declared, "If you are once able to convince yourself that masturbation is not doing you any harm, there is no reason why it should interfere in any way in your capacity to have heterosexual intercourse."[61]

While many men worried about masturbation, others were concerned about their anatomy. Kinsey received a surprising number of letters from men who feared their penises were too short. One man was so concerned that he asked if there was any way to enlarge his penis. "There is no reliable method known to medicine of lengthening the male penis," replied Kinsey. Instead of leaving it at that, however, the missionary in Kinsey drove him to say, "For your comfort I should add that you do not need to worry over this problem. It is quite certain that the effectiveness of intercourse is not determined by the size of the male organ, unless the individual worries about the question. . . . Success to you."[62] When another man pleaded for specific data, Kinsey replied, "The average length of the male penis is 6.3 inches, in erection," adding that the variation for most individuals ranged from 4.5 inches to 8.5 inches, with extreme cases both shorter and longer than this. "I should add that the size of the penis apparently has nothing to do with the satisfaction of intercourse," declared Kinsey. "No one need worry on that score."[63] Explaining why a short penis was not a problem, Kinsey told another anxious soul, "Stimulation of the female depends primarily upon stimulation of the labia (out lips) and the clitoris and this may be accomplished even with the shortest penis because it depends upon contact of the female pubic area with the male pubic area."[64]

Kinsey was equally helpful with men who feared that their penises were too long. One young man, who was only weeks from marriage, confided that his penis was 4.5 inches relaxed, 7.25 erect, and 6 inches in circumference. "I am afraid that my organ is too long for intercourse with an average women," the man declared. "Something that I have always thought would be an advantage, I now wonder whether or not it is a handicap. I am not going to marry if my worries are founded. Will you please help and advise me? What is the largest penis in your records which has been able to have sexual relations comfortably?"[65] By return mail came this reassuring, if somewhat deflating, reply, "I think we have never seen a solitary instance in which the dimensions of the penis caused any difficulty in intercourse. Certainly we have records of successful adjustment where the penis measured two to three inches more than your own." Unable to resist editorializing, Kinsey added, "Sexual relations usually work out well, unless people worry about them."[66]

Kinsey brought the same mind-set to most sexual problems, especially those that involved taboo behavior. If people would only stop worrying, he believed, they could fulfill their sexual needs and desires, regardless of how vehemently society condemned those desires as unnatural, degenerate, or abhorrent. People with forbidden needs might have to conform outwardly, which often condemned them to living double lives and pretending to be someone other than themselves. Publicly, they would need to hide their desires; privately, however, they could act upon them. As long as they were discreet and observed the proper caution, there was no reason they could not accommodate their needs and escape punishment from society. In Kinsey's view—and this was something he knew from experience—it was all a matter of making "satisfactory adjustments."

Few problems were beyond the pale for Kinsey. While most psychologists and psychiatrists considered fetishism a textbook example of sexual perversion, Kinsey took a much more benign view. In a letter to a French physician who had prepared a piece on fur fetishists, Kinsey declared, "It is difficult to see why any fetish which does not interfere with an individual's general social adjustment, or do damage to other individuals, can be thought of as a moral problem. It is to the everlasting shame of our Christian culture that such socially inconsequential things should have been considered questions of morals." Kinsey confessed that he was unable to comprehend "why female sexual partners should object to the introduction of furs any more than they do to the introduction of any other clothing, bed clothes, or the general set-up of a room in which coitus is had. It is not fur fetishism itself; it is the worry over it that is the problem that needs help."[67]

Kinsey was even more explicit in a letter to a sixty-three-year-old Congregationalist minister in New England who admitted to becoming erotically aroused at the sight of an amputee on crutches. Hoping to gain some insight into his odd attraction, the good parson asked, "Can it be that the leg-stump becomes a phallic symbol sexually?"[68] Insisting that fetishism was a normal part of human sexuality, Kinsey replied, "There isn't anything that does not become a fetish at one time or another." Yet he was not content to leave it at that. "I am much less startled at any sort of fetishism than some of the psychiatrists are," he continued. "I think everyone has fetishes for I see no difference between the male who is attracted by the female in general and the male who is attracted by her hair, shoes, or some other particular part of the female." Confessing that he would welcome an interview, Kinsey closed, "To discuss your own case would help educate us, however."[69]

Kinsey devoted considerable attention to transvestites and over time compiled an impressive number of case histories of members of this group. Like individuals in other sexual subcultures, transvestites responded warmly to Kinsey, sensing that he was totally nonjudgmental about their need to cross-dress. Unaccustomed to such acceptance, one contact man in this community asked Kinsey half jokingly whether he, too, was a transvestite. "However, I imagine you have been accused of every 'perversion' in 'The Book,' " the man added. "Each variant group probably wishes to 'claim' you to justify their own particular variance, which is quite understandable."[70] Eager to secure more histories, Kinsey replied tongue in cheek, "If it should prove that I am really a transvestite, would that secure more cooperation from your friends, or would that spoil cooperation?"[71]

Not even the most sacred taboos fazed Kinsey. When a lawyer who said that he was defending a man "charged with carnally knowing a pig by the anus" wrote asking for advice,[72] Kinsey replied that such behavior occurred "in a fair proportion of the population (17% completed acts with animals, and nearly 30% at least attempted acts)." He further noted that his research indicated "that such behavior is not merely the product of a diseased mind—that it is not a perversion as much as it is a natural consequent of quite understandable psychology."[73] A month later, the attorney wrote to say that he had succeeded in getting the original charge of sodomy, which would have carried a fifteen- to twenty-year sentence upon conviction, reduced to a minor offense. Noting that his client had received a one-year sentence, the attorney declared, "Your book was of considerable assistance to me in the preparation and disposition of this case."[74] Clearly pleased by the outcome, Kinsey replied, "I am very glad if our studies were of use to you in this particular trial. I hope they can be of increasing use to many people in regard to our sex laws."[75]

Kinsey got his wish. For the remainder of his life, virtually every week's mail brought similar letters from attorneys and judges, and in each instance he did his best to show how his research could be used to push the law toward an ethic of tolerance. Pleased by the rush of legal reformers to his doorstep, Kinsey boasted to a friend, "I think a very great many people have done a good deal of thinking about our American sex laws since our data was published."[76]

Had Kinsey been given his way, he would have overhauled America's sex offender codes completely. To his mind, they were archaic, unscientific, inhibited, mean-spirited, and punitive. "There is no scientific justification for the definitions of sex perversion which are customarily made under the law," he wrote a court official. "Almost without exception the several types of behavior which are known as perversions are basic mammalian patterns," he continued. "In non-inhibited societies and in non-inhibited portions of our own society, the so-called sex perversions are a regular part of the behavior pattern, and they probably would be so throughout the population if there were no traditions to the contrary. This statement applies to such things as mouth-genital contacts, anal contacts, the homosexual, group activities, relations between individuals of diverse age, and animal intercourse." Current sex offender laws, he explained, were based on English-American common law traditions, which in turn were "a direct continuation of the Talmudic proscriptions on such activities and not the product of scientific judgments." Still, Kinsey estimated that if these archaic laws were to be enforced, most of the male population would be in jail. As things stood, however, ubiquitous behavior all but precluded effective enforcement. "Our sex laws are so far from the normal biologic picture, and so remote from the actual behavior of the population," warned Kinsey, "that it is physically impossible to enforce them in any but the most capricious fashion."[77]

In their place, Kinsey favored codes that would not interfere with sexual behavior, unless one person used force against another. Kinsey told a prison official, "If all the sex laws were repealed, society would probably find adequate protection in the assault and battery laws." Revealing the basis of his objection, he added, "Apart from society's interest in protecting a person, as the assault and battery laws aim to protect him, our sex laws attempt to go a good deal further, and attempt to protect custom."[78]

Kinsey's deep-seated animosity to traditional morality led him to take a benign view of child molestation and incest. Among the many inquiries he received was one from a man who reported a problem with his nine-year-old nephew. It seems that the lad had spent quite a few weekends and holidays with his aunt and uncle. For the last year the boy had, in his uncle's words, "experienced quite frequent, pronounced erections always at night." Moreover, when the boy undressed for bed, he would "frequently ask us to take a look and see for ourselves that it bothers him and he can't get sleep and what causes it." Confessing that he and his wife were at a loss about what to say, the man continued, "So on numerous occasions his Aunt has massaged it with baby cream under the pretext that perhaps his clothing may be irritating him." Although orgasm was effected in three or four minutes, the man explained, two or three orgasms were required before the boy's erection subsided. "On other nights he will come into our room when we have retired, perhaps two hours after he has been in bed and climbs in with us (in the nude) telling us he can't get to sleep and would she (his Aunt) hug and cuddle him," the man continued. "She does and he then will keep changing his position so that his organ will come in contact with her hands. As soon as the desired results are apparently accomplished, he returns to his bed and sleeps soundly, but otherwise has nightmares at times." Stressing that both he and his wife wished to be "understanding and sympathetic without arousing in him fear of criticism or cause him to go underground and resort to other methods or confer his innocent confidence in others where it could lead to some hazards," the man inquired, "We therefore are wondering if we are pursuing the proper course or if we should decline, brush off the appeal and leave it to his own determination. Obviously he will seek outlet by one means or another."[79]

Following the usual disclaimers (we are scientists, not clinicians; we are here to provide information, not to give advice), Kinsey made it clear that the most important issue was preserving a sexual outlet for the boy, even if that meant leaving him in the obliging hands of his aunt. "Apparently the small boy is erotically responsive and it looks as if he is already so conditioned to the sort of contact that he has had that the chances of his getting along without a regular sexual outlet are now reduced," observed Kinsey. "If he were to be forced to go without any outlet of any sort," he cautioned, "it is probable that he would be nervously disturbed and might be difficult to handle socially." Given this assessment, Kinsey felt justified in declaring, "There are apparently no alternatives except to apparently continue the sort of contact he has had, or to have him develop with or without someone else's help, contacts with some other persons, or to have him learn to secure orgasms through his own efforts." Emphasizing that they themselves would have to decide on the best course of action, Kinsey repeated his warning (no doubt for emphasis): "We do not consider that complete cessation of the activity is a practical alternative for reasons I have already mentioned. As a matter of record for our files, I should be interested to know the ultimate outcome of your problem."[80]

Whenever possible, Kinsey provided encouragement to advice seekers, stressing that most of their difficulties would vanish if they refused to allow social taboos, prejudices, and meddlesome laws to control them. When a young man who had fallen in love with his cousin expressed concern that their children would be deformed and asked if it was wise to marry, Kinsey replied cheerily, "Cousin marriages may actually be beneficial if there are good qualities in the family which would be intensified by the mating of related individuals. It only rarely happens that undesirable or poor qualities are brought out by such cousin marriages. Certainly we wish you success in working out your problem."[81]

Still, there were issues that gave even Kinsey pause. When an anxious father who feared that two of his children were involved in an incestuous relationship turned to him for advice, Kinsey responded soberly. "We have seen cases in which such relationships have completely spoiled the possibility of a successful marriage for either individual and led to ultimate bitterness and more specific difficulties between the two parties," he wrote. To Kinsey, though, it was far from clear that such cases had to end badly. He had knowledge of other cases, many that had lasted for decades and even for most of a lifetime, he noted, that did not interfere with individual marriages. "Legal and social difficulties that might result from such cases probably complicate the issue more often than actual relationships themselves," he averred. Declining to say more, Kinsey advised, "For further guidance and advice, certainly you should depend upon the best balanced and the most liberal councilor that you can find."[82]

Vast age differences also gave Kinsey pause. He had seen enough autumn/spring unions between middle-aged men and young girls to know that such relationships occasionally worked out, but when a fifteen-year-old boy who wanted to marry a forty-five-year-old woman asked for his prognostication, Kinsey was discouraging, explaining that he had never known such a relationship to work out.[83]

Kinsey was equally direct with an Englishman who desperately wanted to have a sex change operation. "A male cannot be transformed into a female through any known surgical means. In other words, it would be very hopeless to attempt to amputate your male organs and implant a vagina," he wrote. Kinsey told the man that, instead of undergoing surgery, he should change his attitudes and adjust his life accordingly. "We humans are either heterosexual or homosexual," wrote Kinsey. "There is no disgrace to being in the latter category and a great many important successful people have been homosexual. If you cannot adapt yourself to a heterosexual existence in which you adopt the role of a male, I would certainly advise you to go to London and to find a homosexual colony, which certainly must exist there as it does in any other metropolis, and make yourself a member of it. Fighting the problem, hoping for physical transformation is certainly not a satisfactory solution."[84]

Kinsey was no less blunt with an American soldier who was considering a sex change operation. Kinsey advised against it, explaining that gender identity involved much more than anatomy. No operation, he insisted, could make a man into a woman. Moreover, people who had undergone sex change operations had great difficulty in their social relationships. In view of these concerns, Kinsey recommended that the soldier try to fashion a new social role for himself in society and offered to counsel him on how to make the necessary adjustments.[85]

Responding to another man who had the same problem and felt he had only two options, "to go crazy or commit suicide,"[86] Kinsey counseled, "You must not decide that there are only two possibilities in the world. Actually, there are thousands of possibilities and any plant or animal, whether human or some lower species, can never expect to get along in the world until they are ready to face realities and make the most of what is possible." Kinsey then scolded the man for "asking the whole world to change in accordance with your desires" and concluded with a stern admonishment, "You have made practically no attempt to fit your self into the realities of the world. Until you do you are going to be in continuous trouble."[87]

Homosexuals, by contrast, could count on unqualified support and encouragement from Kinsey, not to mention heartfelt statements of sympathy and compassion. From the early years of the research, they had formed the largest single group seeking his help (this was hardly surprising, as gays constituted the largest sexual subculture that the dominant society condemned as deviant), and the number of their letters shot up dramatically following the publication of *Sexual Behavior in the Human Male*.

Many expressed amazement and pleasure at the tone of Kinsey's book, the fact that he had managed to treat the subject without moralizing. "Nowhere have I read a report that is more fair and objective, more unbiased and unprejudiced, and which at the same time adheres strictly to the scientific method," declared one grateful reader. "Only we who are ho-mosexuals, especially those of us who are completely so," he continued, "know what it means to be a member of an unmentionable, misunderstood and despised minority." The great contribution of Kinsey's book was that it promised "to alleviate the appalling ignorance, fears, prejudice and taboo so long associated with this subject."[88] Another man made the identical point more simply, declaring, "I was more stupefied than surprised to read that a homosexual may be a human after all."[89] Other homosexual readers saw through Kinsey's façade of objectivity and correctly sensed his sym-pathy. As one man who poured out his soul in a letter confided, "You see how frankly I talk to you. I never thought I could put what I have done on paper. But somehow I felt, after reading your book, I could tell you any-thing and everything."[90]

Other homosexuals wrote to express their philosophical agreement with Kinsey's fierce antiessentialism. "To me, one of the most fraudulent schemes of Modern Science has been to reduce everything to a 'norm' in which the public is led to believe that any aberration from the conventional notions constitutes a degeneracy," declared one gay man, who continued, "Someday—I hope!—the educators of this country will realize that to love is normal and that physical union with the beloved is not only the only sat-isfying fulfillment of that emotion, but that it too is perfectly normal. It seems to me that until society is organized on principles of self-determination which include the emotional and its logical expression, democracy is a name only."[91]

Kinsey's own experience shaped the advice he offered others. Many peo-ple became homosexuals, he believed, because something in their youth pointed them in that direction. More often than not, he blamed the social prohibitions that prevented young people from premarital sex. He told one advice seeker in 1950, "Our data increasingly show that a prime factor in the development of homosexuality is the failure of our society to approve pre-marital heterosexual relations."[92] In some cases (as in his), young peo-ple were isolated from the opposite sex by strict parents who did not allow dating. Kinsey wrote one man that there were many cases where parents prevented their sons from having any contacts with girls, thereby making any sort of social adjustment impossible.[93] Such boys were thrown to-gether with members of their own sex. Consequently, when they did man-age to explore their sexuality, as youngsters were wont to do, they usually did so with members of their own sex. Need and satisfaction caused those initial same-sex contacts to be repeated over and over until a pattern was formed. Again, it is easy to see why Kinsey believed this explanation: it fit the facts of his life snugly.

Not that strict parents were the sole factor. Good biologist that he was,

Kinsey always insisted that sex was highly competitive. Anything that made a person less attractive, he reasoned, could push that individual toward homosexuality. Any sort of handicap—physical, mental, or social—could render a child less appealing to members of the opposite sex, resulting in fewer social contacts and, it followed, fewer opportunities for sexual explorations. Blindness, deafness, a withered limb, acute acne, and any number of other problems could diminish a child's attractiveness and self-confidence, resulting in diminished social popularity and fewer (and less satisfying) contacts with members of the opposite sex. Thus, the temptation to turn to members of the same sex.

While Kinsey was reluctant to state his theory quite so boldly in print, this was the explanation he gave homosexuals in his letters. Rejecting the dominant theories of the day, he told one woman who identified herself as a lesbian, "We do not know of any glandular nor any other hereditary or physical factor which causes homosexuality. It occurs abundantly among all of the other animals and biologically is a normal part of human sex behavior." While admitting that many people considered homosexuality an illness, Kinsey rejected the disease model out of hand, asserting that "it is not an abnormality like a disease which is caused by any specific factor." To his mind, homosexuality was acquired behavior, the result of conditioning and response. "Individuals learn by experience that it is possible to be aroused sexually by contact with members of their own sex," he declared. "Timid persons, physically handicapped persons and particularly persons who are morally restricted by their parents from social contacts with males are most likely to become attracted to individuals of their own sex primarily because they have not learned the satisfaction to be obtained from contact with individuals of the opposite sex."[94]

Stating the matter more succinctly (if somewhat more opaquely), Kinsey told another male inquirer, "Animals most often do things for which they receive a satisfactory reward. . . . Things which interfere with the individual's appreciation of the rewards to be had in the heterosexual, are, in a negative way contributory to the development of a homosexual which, at its initiation, often offers higher rewards than the initial source of contacts that are possible with younger girls."[95] Kinsey, of course, always insisted that this interpretation was based on his research, but it is hard not to hear an autobiographical echo in the following statement, made to another advice seeker: "Our data increasingly show that a prime factor in the development of homosexuality is the failure of our society to approve premarital heterosexual relations. This is true of both male and female."[96]

Many of the homosexuals who contacted Kinsey were desperate. By their own accounts, they suffered from acute anxiety, loneliness, depression, and low self-esteem. More than a few feared they were losing their minds and admitted to feeling suicidal or to having made failed suicide attempts in the past. Confronted with such cases, Kinsey immediately abandoned any pretense of disinterest and donned the priestly robes of advice giver to the damned, dispensing in equal measure forgiveness, redemption, and hope.

Thanks to personal experience and thousands of histories, Kinsey knew exactly how to proceed. He began by categorically denying that sexual tastes were in any way related to mental health. "You are not feeble-minded and you are not abnormal just because you have particular things in your sex history," he wrote one anxious young man. While confessing that it was impossible to pass judgment on a person's mental or physical health without first meeting and examining the individual, Kinsey nevertheless declared, "I can tell you that nothing in anybody's sex history is sufficient proof of any mental disturbance."[97] Kinsey also attacked the sense of isolation that haunted so many homosexuals, in part to offer reassurance that their situation was not hopeless and in part to stress the need for self-acceptance. He told another young man not to worry, because 10 to 15 percent of the men in the world shared his problem. The important thing was to accept himself.[98]

Kinsey advised against any effort to change a person's sexual orientation. As he bluntly wrote one man, "It is about as possible to cure a person of heterosexuality as it is to cure one of homosexuality."[99] Psychotherapists who attempted to "cure" patients of homosexuality, in Kinsey's judgment, did more harm than good. Not only were their efforts doomed to failure; they made their patients feel terrible. To a woman who inquired if the "corrective" field could offer any therapy to return a "pervert" to "normal,"[100] Kinsey replied, "I have never known any case of a person who has been exclusively homosexual over a long period of time, whose pattern has been changed as a result of their own planning, or as a result of clinical redirection." Underscoring the danger, he added, "There is both frustration and definite damage when a clinician tries to force a person to change a pattern of behavior when it is hopeless for them to do so, or even when the process costs too much in the way of self esteem and peace of mind."[101]

Not that Kinsey was above evoking the authority of therapists who shared his views, particularly when it allowed him to make his point by proxy. "Many of the best psychiatrists never attempt to change an individual's pattern of behavior," he informed one advice seeker. "They do spend their effort in teaching the individual to accept himself without worry as to his normality or abnormality and with a sufficient esteem."[102] Still, extreme caution had to be exercised in selecting a therapist. "You do need the help of a clinical psychiatrist or a clinical psychologist," Kinsey told one man, "but many of them do not understand the questions which you raise, and are not particularly helpful. Consequently, what you need is the help of someone who has helped other persons and who knows of the problems of the homosexual."[103] After advising the man to read the pertinent sections of *Sexual Behavior in the Human Male,* Kinsey proceeded to offer a full paragraph of advice. Apparently, he could think of no one better qualified to counsel homosexuals than himself.

Many of Kinsey's efforts were aimed at getting homosexuals to jettison their guilt. "The difficulty with the homosexual arrives from the fact that we happen to be in a society which disapproves of such activity," he told one advice seeker.[104] Similarly, when Dr. O. Spurgeon English, a rare admirer in the psychiatric community, argued that homosexuals were generally dissatisfied with their behavior, Kinsey took sharp exception. Homosexuals loved their behavior, he insisted, but they hated the condemnation that society heaped upon them.[105] Still, until society developed more humane attitudes, Kinsey saw no alternative for homosexuals but to remain in the closet. Offering the advice he gave again and again to homosexuals who sought his counsel, Kinsey told another young man, "Any departure from the social codes demands that an individual's behavior not become public knowledge or else it may cause difficulty. If our paths should cross, I should be very glad to go through a history with you and then I could advise you more specifically."[106]

Publicly, then, Kinsey advised homosexuals to be accommodationists, much as Booker T. Washington offered similar advice to turn-of-the-century blacks regarding race relations. But just as Washington abhorred segregation in private, Kinsey's letters reveal a pattern of fierce opposition to his culture's homophobia. In addition, he made a habit of assuring homosexuals that they could find enough wiggle space in their private lives to satisfy their sexual needs without being exposed. As a skillful practitioner of the art of avoiding detection, Kinsey saw no reason why others could not learn to adjust. He told one concerned mother, "It is a mistake for your son or anyone else to feel that the difficulties are insurmountable, even though his history may be primarily or even entirely homosexual. The difficulties are primarily dependent upon society's reaction, and it is not impossible, even though it may present some difficulties, for an individual to learn to avoid social conflicts." Sharpening his point, Kinsey declared, "It is very important that one learn to accept himself and to adjust his life in accordance."[107]

Moreover, Kinsey could be very directive when the situation warranted. Writing to a homosexual male, who admitted having effeminate mannerisms, Kinsey advised, "I think the most important thing is for you to try to overcome some of the obvious personality characteristics that are getting you in trouble with people you meet. Your chances of holding a job and avoiding conflict and insult are going to depend upon your training yourself out of the voice and body and hand movements and other characteristics which you say you have." Acknowledging that the changes he had recommended "would not be easy," Kinsey promised that if the young man made them it "would . . . be possible for you to live without carrying on in such a fashion that you come in conflict with other persons and with the law."[108]

And so it went in the months and years following the publication of *Sexual Behavior in the Human Male*. Letters from homosexuals poured in, and Kinsey continued to answer them. Eventually, he had to write shorter replies, but he hated having to do so. No group tugged at his heartstrings harder, and no other group so excited the missionary inside him. When a black male homosexual accused him of not understanding the plight of homosexuals, Kinsey seemed wounded. "We do appreciate your problems," he replied, "and we have done our best to learn what these things mean to other people." Kinsey spoke the truth when he added, "We have done our best to have the world sympathetically appreciate the problems that are present in this area."[109]

Kinsey's best was not good enough, at least not in the short run. Ironically, his plea for tolerance, the central message of his book, could hardly have come at a more unpropitious moment. *Sexual Behavior in the Human Male* burst onto the scene at a time when the backdrop of significant domestic and international events made many Americans more anxious than usual about the state of the nation's moral health. In an unpublished memorial to Kinsey, written only three days after his death, Henry Remak, a professor of German at Indiana University, recalled with disdain that the "conservative political climate, the insistence on patriotic orthodoxy, the trend toward conformism, the shying away from controversial issues which characterized the later 1940's and early 1950's . . . were really less favorable to the acceptance of so radical a departure from accepted, tolerated or simulated taboos dating many centuries back than the 1920's or 1930's might have been declared." Many critics, Remak stressed, thought that "Dr. Kinsey was undermining our morality, our belief in established values; the Communists were doing the same thing; hence Dr. Kinsey was, in fact, willy nilly, helping the Communists; to view sex the way he did was subversive, and its possible consequences were as serious to 'our way of life' as threats from the east."[110]

The national mood had turned ugly, placing Kinsey's research at risk and his private behavior in peril. It was his fate to rise to national prominence near the beginning of the Cold War and to watch with horror as both he and his work got sucked into the internal witch-hunts associated with Senator Joseph McCarthy of Wisconsin. World War II had seen Nazism and fascism go down to defeat, but communism had replaced these ideologies in the minds of many Americans as an even more sinister threat to the nation's security. The Pax Americana that was supposed to shape the post–World War II world had failed to materialize. Instead, a bellicose Soviet Union had defiantly challenged the United States's leadership in Western Europe; the Iron Curtain had descended on Eastern Europe; and Communist-led armies threatened to topple American-backed governments in Asia. Haunted by fears of internal subversion, many Americans worried that Communists had infiltrated the government of the United States and were secretly working for Moscow. The year before Kinsey's book was released, President Harry S Truman had imposed a loyalty oath on federal employees, the Justice Department had issued a list of subversive organizations, and the House Un-American Activities Committee in highly publicized hearings had alerted the nation to the threat of traitors.

Many scientists worried that the government's loyalty program would harm their research. In October 1948, the Federation of American Scientists organized the Scientists Committee on Loyalty Problems to provide information and legal advice to individual scientists with clearance problems. No doubt because of his recent fame, Kinsey was invited to serve as a sponsor of this committee and a consultant on major policy issues.[111] Although he agreed to serve, Kinsey did so with reservations. "I should make it clear at this point," he wrote, "that I am not at all in sympathy with those who would modify our American Government by force or the use of anything less than democratic procedure." Kinsey felt it necessary to make this declaration because he believed that some of the scientists who had joined the committee were, in his words, "not as clear in their understanding of loyalty to the Government." Still, he shared the concerns of the committee's organizers. "I am disturbed at the procedure which has been employed by certain Congressional groups in their examination of loyalty," he explained, "and feel, as many other scientists do, that the inevitable result will be interference with the pursuit of scientific research."[112]

Loyalty oaths were just the beginning. In the five years between the publication of *Sexual Behavior in the Human Male* (1948) and the completion of its companion volume, *Sexual Behavior in the Human Female* (1953), Communists won the bloody civil war in China; the Soviet Union exploded an atomic bomb (and soon a hydrogen one); the Alger Hiss case lent credence to charges of treason from within; Senator McCarthy orchestrated a new Red scare; the Korean conflict converted the Cold War into a shooting war; and Julius and Ethel Rosenberg were tried and executed for conspiracy to commit espionage.

But just as World War II did not distract Kinsey from his research, the rise of the Cold War and McCarthyism held little interest for him. He was so preoccupied with his own battles that he paused to take note of domestic or foreign affairs only when they threatened his work. Later, in the 1950s, ultra-conservative critics would accuse Kinsey of aiding communism by undermining sexual morality and the sanctity of the home. Not until those charges were made, however, did Kinsey spend much time fretting over the Cold War or its impact on domestic politics. This was a serious oversight, because Kinsey's rise to fame coincided with one of the worst moral panics of the century in the United States.

In the late 1940s and early 1950s, the United States was a nation besieged by fears of sex crimes. For five years running, lurid accounts of savage sex murders and assaults filled the press, fifteen states appointed commissions to study sex crimes and make recommendations about how to control sex offenders, and parents debated whether it was safe to let their children play outdoors. In truth, there was no epidemic of sex crimes. Statistical evidence showed that sex crimes had not increased. All that had changed was the amount and the nature of the publicity sex crimes received, as reports of a nation stalked by predatory sexual psychopaths flooded the press.

Soon the term "sexual deviate" developed enough elasticity to cover any sexual act that fell outside the social norm. Equating the most benign and the most harmful behaviors, press reports branded as sexual deviants people who exhibited their genitals in public, had premarital sex, raped women, masturbated, molested and murdered small children, peeped into other people's windows, or simply cast "lewd glances" at others.[113] One angry woman accused Kinsey of providing a legal defense for sex offenders. Noting that she had read a recent report "that sex criminals have gone without punishment because of your book," the woman declared, "I wonder, Dr. Kinsey, if one of your family ever falls into the power of one of these cruel beasts, if you will be proud that your book can be used as the law that frees them unpunished."[114]

Homosexuals were thought to pose a grave threat to public safety. Easy targets, they had long borne the brunt of the middle class's anxieties about sexual nonconformity. In the emotionally charged atmosphere following World War II, however, the anti-gay prejudices of the past intensified, and the public demonized homosexual males. Not only were they attacked as immoral and mentally ill, but they were widely depicted as a menace to the nation's youth. "The sex pervert, in his more innocuous form is too frequently regarded as merely a 'queer' individual who never hurts anyone but himself," cautioned the special assistant attorney general of California in 1949. "All too often we lose sight of the fact that the homosexual is an inveterate seducer of the young of both sexes," he continued, "and is ever seeking for younger victims."[115]

Trumpeting the same theme, the press created a stereotype of gay men as brutal child molesters and murderers, an image that reached its zenith in spring 1949 when reporters shocked the nation with vivid accounts of the brutal rape and murder of a six-year-old boy whose body was discovered behind a furnace in a Detroit basement. The following year, *Coronet* magazine warned, "Once a man assumes the role of homosexual, he often throws off all moral restraints. Some male deviants do not stop with infecting their often-innocent partners: they descend through perversions to other forms of depravity, such as drug addiction, burglary, sadism, and even murder." No wonder a gay man complained in 1956, "To the average parent I am a menace to warn their children against."[116] In a letter to Gregg, a man called the hysteria against homosexuals "another 'Spanish Inquisition.' "[117] For his part, Kinsey thought that the problem of child molestation was greatly exaggerated. Privately, he decried what he called "the foundless hysteria that is abroad on the subject."[118]

The Cold War exacerbated the public's fear of homosexuals. In February 1950, when the moral panic was at its peak, Senator McCarthy accused the State Department of being riddled with Communists and sexual deviants. In the wake of these charges, the State Department conducted an investigation and purged hundreds of employees who were found to be gay. In a personal letter, Kinsey's friend and attorney, Morris L. Ernst of Greenbaum, Wolf, and Ernst in New York, complained bitterly of "the outrageous behavior of government officials with respect to homosexuals." In his view, the real problem was that "our social ostracism of this pattern . . . creates a situation in our culture in which homosexuals are made subjects of easy blackmail, and hence, are truly vulnerable in sensitive areas of our government."[119]

Kinsey was horrified and disgusted by the witch-hunts. Aware of how many homosexuals there were in society, he thought that the government had blundered badly. "Certainly there is the possibility of a serious situation developing which can do considerable damage to the whole operation of the Government," he wrote a friend. "If all the persons with homosexual histories are thrown out of government employ, it will involve many persons who are of top importance in maintaining the continuity of governmental operation, and many who are recognized by the country at large as rendering unusual service."[120] But when a psychiatrist friend encouraged him to speak out about how many homosexuals were making worthwhile contributions to society, Kinsey called the request "fair and reasonable" but "completely unrealistic." If he were to do that, he warned, "the upheaval that would follow would be hardly less disrupting than [as] though the Communists were to take over the administration of the Federal Government." Stressing that the public had no idea about "the extent of homosexual histories among their close acquaintances and friends, in professional groups, among clergymen, teachers, business men, government officials, etc., etc.," Kinsey observed ominously, "What would happen if there were open disclosure of the whole thing is something that I should be very glad to discuss with you some day. Keep the present instances in the State Department in mind as an example of what can happen."[121]

Kinsey himself came under scrutiny from the Federal Bureau of Investigation (FBI). Prior to the publication of *Sexual Behavior in the Human Male,* the FBI had shown little interest in Kinsey. In 1942, Kinsey and J. Edgar Hoover, the director of the FBI, had exchanged letters about Kinsey's request for a copy of the Uniform Crime Reports bulletin (the request was denied).[122] Three years later, an FBI agent interviewed Kinsey in Philadelphia regarding a student organization thought to be subversive. According to the agent's report, Kinsey stated that he had no knowledge of the group in question and stressed "that the entire success of the research he was doing depended on his maintaining information he obtained in absolute confidence."[123] In 1946, Kinsey and Hoover exchanged a second set of letters, this time concerning the FBI's role in enforcing the Mann Act in Tennessee during World War II (Hoover again declined Kinsey's request for information).[124] Following the publication of *Sexual Behavior in the Human Male,* however, the FBI's interest in Kinsey became more personal.

Ironically, Kinsey brought this scrutiny upon himself, though that was not his intention. In March 1948, fearing that the FBI might try to interfere with the research, he asked Morris Ernst for help in obtaining a special clearance. Explaining that he stood "a chance of securing a good many histories from persons more or less associated with the Communist Movement in New York," Kinsey pleaded, "I should be very glad if you will raise the matter with Mr. Hoover . . . to make sure that they have no objection to this, and to make sure there will be no trailing of our subjects, or no attempt to secure information obtained in their interviews with us."[125] Ernst did as he was asked, writing Hoover at length on the subject.[126] Then Ernst departed for England, prompting a clearly cautious Kinsey to write his friend, "I think it is better to call off our work with groups that are distinctly communist until after you get back, when we may have a chance to visit Hoover together at Washington."[127]

Immediately after Ernst's letter reached Washington, the FBI's file on Kinsey started growing, as Hoover and his associate director, Clyde Tolson, demanded and received detailed investigative reports. The first report, filed in April 1948, provided biographical data on Kinsey, an overview of the research, and a brief description of the current controversy surrounding his work, complete with the observation that "due to his determination, energy, resourcefulness and ability to overlook such criticism, he [Kinsey] has managed to cool much of the heat engenered [*sic*] toward his study and has turned out a volume of vast interest to the American people."[128] The report the following month, however, had a different tone. It described Kinsey's book as "a rocking report of our prejudices, sexual habits, preconceptions, unheard of behavior patterns in various stratas of society, all wrapped up in a cold, analytical, 804 page book bulging with statistical charts." Turning to Kinsey, the report continued, "His sincerity to do a scientifically important study is not questioned, but exceeds his ability to accomplish the net result." While conceding "that interested legislators might glean from the book valuable data in forming more effective sex laws," the report warned gravely that Kinsey's book "could do incalculable harm in the hands of adolescents who read it as a justification for their own sexual habits." The special agent in charge of sex offender investigations had reviewed the book for any light it might throw on the subject, the report continued, acknowledging that for "this purpose the book has a limited value."[129]

Personally, Hoover found the book deeply upsetting, a fact he communicated to the world by contributing a piece to the *Reader's Digest* symposium in June 1948 decrying the moral consequences of Kinsey's work. "It is important to the very future of our national life that we hold fast to our faith," wrote Hoover. "Man's sense of decency declares what is normal and what is not," he continued. "Whenever the American people, young or old, come to believe that there is no such thing as right or wrong, normal or abnormal, those who would destroy our civilization will applaud a major victory over our way of life."[130] In effect, Hoover had come dangerously close to smearing Kinsey with a red brush, a tactic other foes would employ with increasing frequency in the years ahead.

As the moral panic over sex crimes and homosexuality in government deepened, Hoover started collecting information on homosexuals in the United States. Beginning in 1950, the FBI conducted background checks for the Civil Service Commission, and part of this operation included a broad surveillance program of homosexuals. Working with friendly police departments, the FBI compiled lists of gay bars (and other meeting places) and developed an extensive file of news clippings on gay life.[131] In addition, the FBI renewed its interest in Kinsey, the nation's leading expert on homosexuality. Early in January 1950, it received a report that Kinsey was "anti-FBI." At the bottom of the page bearing this news, Hoover wrote in longhand, "I think it would be well to . . . have someone see Kinsey & make him put up or shut up." Hoover concluded ominously, "What do we know of Kinsey's background?"[132]

A few days later, L. B. Nichols, an assistant director of the FBI, reported that he had learned that Kinsey had recently delivered a speech in New York in which he "was quite critical of the Bureau in his views on crime, homosexuality and other other matters." Asking "if it wouldn't be a good idea to tackle Kinsey," Nichols recommended sending the agent in charge of the investigation to visit with Kinsey in Indiana. Failing that, Kinsey should be asked to come in for a meeting the next time he was in New York or Washington, D.C.[133] To underscore the gravity of the situation, Hoover delivered the message himself. "I would like to have one of my assistants see you on the occasion of your next visit to New York," he wrote Kinsey in January 1950.[134] Kinsey, of course, had no desire to get on Hoover's bad side. He replied that during his next visit to New York he would be happy to meet with Nichols or with any agent Hoover might care to send to Bloomington.[135]

What happened next can only be a matter for conjecture. Vital portions of numerous documents in the FBI's file on Kinsey have been blacked-out, and many other documents have not been released. Still, it seems reasonable to speculate that Kinsey did eventually meet with FBI officials. Assuming one or more discussions took place, did Hoover or any of his minions pressure Kinsey to release the names and friendship networks of Communist Party members or sympathizers in his files? Was Kinsey also squeezed to divulge the names and friendship networks of homosexuals? If so, did he cooperate or refuse?

All that can be said with certainty is that the FBI's interest in his research worried Kinsey greatly. He knew he had huge skeletons in his closet, and who was to say that they would remain hidden if the FBI dug deeply enough into his private life? But even if the FBI did not investigate his private life, Kinsey was still a likely target because of his information on Communists and homosexuals. Given Hoover's obsession with ferreting out Communists in the United States, there is good reason to believe that he would have leaned hard on Kinsey on this score. Can anyone imagine Hoover's being deterred by academic notions like confidentiality or freedom of inquiry? Furthermore, Hoover's animus against homosexuals was legendary, a fact not without irony, given the persistent rumors (both during and after his lifetime) about his own homoerotic proclivities.[136] Consequently, it is difficult to believe that Hoover did not pressure Kinsey to open (and decode) his files.

In all probability, Kinsey stonewalled Hoover. Assuming he did turn Hoover down cold, a case can be made that Kinsey might have pulled it off. Less than a year after Kinsey's death, FBI agents tried to pressure Gebhard, who succeeded him as director of the Institute, into revealing the names of the dealers from whom the Institute purchased pornography. Gebhard refused to reveal his sources and got away with it.[137] Perhaps Kinsey did as well.

Whatever the true story with the FBI, Kinsey found at least one friend in government. In April 1950, Wayne N. Aspinall, a congressman from Colorado, asked Kinsey for information about sexual perversions, stating "that if we have a problem in this particular, certain facts are necessary for a proper evaluation thereof."[138] Specifically, Aspinall requested a definition of sexual perversion and an estimate of the ratio of sexual perverts to the total population. Moved by the "evident sincerity" of Aspinall's inquiry, Kinsey replied with characteristic bluntness, "The so-called sexual perversions are, according to Jewish and Catholic codes, any departure from a sexual activity which is not vaginal intercourse." Such departures, continued Kinsey, included masturbation, petting, mouth-genital contacts, anal contacts, animal contacts, "and all homosexual contacts by whatever techniques." Kinsey then proceeded to summarize his data on the incidence of homosexuality, stressing that "the number of persons with homosexual histories in any segment of our society, whether in some branch of the Federal Government, or in any other walk of life, is considerably higher than the number of cases that has been recognized in the State Department in recent months." Confident of his expertise, Kinsey added, "Certainly, no one has any data to show that the situation in the State Department, or in the City of Washington as a whole, is basically different from what exists in any and every other group, in any part of the country."[139] An opponent of the current witch-hunt in the nation's capital, Aspinall was delighted by Kinsey's letter and asked permission to read parts of it to Congress if the State Department's attacks on homosexuals "should flare up again."[140]

Apart from providing information to friendly politicos, however, there was nothing Kinsey could do to stop the government's persecution of homosexuals, at least not in the short run. In the long run, he placed his faith in his research, hoping, as ever, that science could change people's minds and hearts about homosexuality, with the understanding that social tolerance would eventually lead to reforms in public policy. Thus, despite his growing personal problems, the body blows he had received from critics, and a national atmosphere that was increasingly hostile to his message of social tolerance, Kinsey was determined to forge ahead. The female volume was waiting to be born, and beyond it beckoned the volume on homosexuality, the book he hoped would contribute to a public dialogue that one day would rid the United States of sexual repression, inhibitions, and prudery—and perhaps allow him to rest.

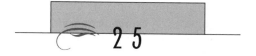

2 5

"THE OLD ATTITUDE ABOUT SEX"

s the months stretched into years following the publication of *Sexual Behavior in the Human Male,* Kinsey discovered that he was in deep trouble with the Rockefeller Foundation. Not only had he upset trustees who opposed the research on moral grounds, but he had managed to irritate Chester Barnard, the foundation's president. "I have always been unhappy about the way Kinsey's report was put out, including the fact that an introduction to it was written by Dr. Gregg," Barnard confided to Arthur Hays Sulzberger in August 1949. Explaining why it was wrong for foundations to endorse projects, Barnard declared, "Whether the results are good or bad is to be determined, so far as public expression is concerned, by the scientific and scholarly world, rather than by us."[1]

In point of fact, Kinsey's scholarly reputation was under siege. Instead of bottoming out, the controversy surrounding his work had kept building. Every month brought new attacks, as critics honed in on various problems. By 1950, half a dozen scholarly reviews focused on the statistical and methodological aspects of *Sexual Behavior in the Human Male,* and most were critical. Much to Kinsey's chagrin, a consensus was building that his work was badly flawed from a statistical standpoint. As one of the nation's most distinguished statisticians observed, "The inadequacies in statistics are such that it is impossible to say that the book has much value beyond its role in opening a broad and important field."[2]

Corner followed Kinsey's sagging reputation with the gravest concern. While his support never wavered, he gradually came to believe that Kinsey had to address his critics. Writing to Gregg, Corner explained that the situation called "for some kind of a showdown in order that such necessary backing as that of the Rockefeller Trustees may not be risked."[3] He thought that Kinsey should either answer his critics in print or seek advice from a committee of distinguished and disinterested statisticians. Gregg agreed that something had to be done. If no steps were taken, warned Gregg, "Kinsey would put himself in the apparent position of considering himself above criticism, or flawless. And that would weaken his entire position."[4]

Yet the wounds to Kinsey's reputation were not all self-inflicted. His work got caught up in the internecine battles of the Rockefeller Foundation, where the political currents were both strong and treacherous. Early in 1950, a powerful figure within the Rockefeller Foundation joined the opposition. In a lengthy memorandum to Barnard, Warren Weaver, the head of the natural sciences division, announced that he was "extremely worried" that Kinsey had no apparent plans to hire a statistician. Weaver also stated that anyone who knew anything about sampling theory had to be very disturbed by Kinsey's deficiencies, charging "that substantially more than one-third of all of Doctor Kinsey's histories have been obtained on the basis of what a statistician calls 'cluster' sampling," a flaw that all but destroyed Kinsey's claims that his data were representative.[5]

Coming from someone else, this point might have seemed less damning, but Weaver's opinion on statistical matters carried a great deal of weight. Prior to joining the foundation in 1931, he had taught physics at the University of Wisconsin. Not only did he have advanced training in mathematics, but he was a self-styled expert on statistics. A compulsive quantifier, Weaver admitted to his inability to walk up a flight of stairs without counting each step.[6] Professionally, his career had been intertwined with numbers. He had spent the last twenty years nurturing a revolution in the biological sciences. Through various grants and programs, he had encouraged scientists to apply the techniques of quantification to fields such as genetics and molecular biology. No, this man knew how to count. When he talked numbers around the Rockefeller Foundation, his colleagues listened.

Still, there was more behind Weaver's questions about Kinsey than statistics. Weaver and Gregg were arch rivals within the foundation. As directors of their respective divisions, they competed for funds and for influence over the board. Nor was the contest particularly friendly. On a personal level, their dislike for one another was acute. Ordinarily, Gregg made it a point not to speak ill of any colleague, not even within the privacy of his home. With Weaver, however, Gregg made an exception. "There was no question that Warren and Dad did not get along well," recalled Gregg's son, Michael, decades later. "I think the reason was that Warren Weaver had a very closed, channeled, conservative, and opinionated mind," ventured Michael. "Warren was just sort of a rigid steel box that just couldn't be cracked."[7] Weaver's attacks on Kinsey's work, then, signaled a major fissure among the foundation's officers. Henceforth, Gregg would have to defend Kinsey against a colleague who knew how to cloak moral objections in statistical garments.

With Gregg and Weaver pulling in opposite directions, Barnard was in a quandary. Increasingly, he had grown concerned that the foundation might be betraying the public's trust by supporting Kinsey. Aware of the influence the foundation wielded, Barnard launched a full-fledged review of the responsibilities that officers bore to the trustees and to the public for grantees. He was concerned that unless Kinsey improved his methods "it would seriously depreciate the scientific status of Kinsey's work and would greatly embarrass the officers in presenting the program for future support of the Trustees."[8]

Gregg's fears ran in a different direction. Proud of the foundation's policy of granting funds with no strings attached, he pointedly asked whether pressuring Kinsey "belies our claim that we don't tell recipients how to run their affairs."[9] Chastened by Gregg's argument, Barnard inquired of his fellow officers, "[W]here do we draw the line between legitimate concern and management or dominance of the work of others?" Giving his own opinion, Barnard declared, "It seems to me that it is clearly the duty of the officers to be reasonably satisfied of the competence of the prospective recipients of funds before we can properly recommend to the Board an appropriation." Sharpening his point, Barnard concluded, "If Dr. Kinsey, by reason of temperament or the results of his experience, is unable to accept our advice, it seems to me fair to indicate that the officers feel there is danger of jeopardizing the willingness of Trustees to continue support."[10]

Executing his marching orders, Gregg bluntly warned Corner in March 1950 that there would be trouble with the board unless Kinsey did something to satisfy his critics.[11] Corner, in turn, promised to impress on Kinsey as forcefully as he could the wisdom of hiring a statistician.[12] If Corner needed additional proof of how serious the situation had grown, it came in April when Gregg revealed that his efforts to secure a funding recommendation for the Committee for Research in Problems of Sex at the recent officers' conference "did not meet with approval and was therefore not presented to our Trustees."[13] Gregg blamed this setback on the foundation's reservations about Kinsey. Gregg, of course, was free to try to present another recommendation at some future date, but as things stood in the spring 1950, Kinsey's stock with the Rockefeller Foundation was in a free fall. Worse yet, he was threatening to take the CRPS down with him.

When he learned of Gregg's ultimatum, Kinsey reacted defensively. He had not been given a fair chance to answer his critics, he complained to Corner. "Few of the objections are well taken. Most of them are exceedingly trivial," he insisted. "A number of them call for additional work on our part which would turn us into a group doing research on statistics rather than research on sex." Hammering away at this point, he declared, "We must not, however, allow the study to become statistical. That was never our intention and a great deal of the work that we have already done, lies in other areas."[14] Small wonder that Corner later confided to a friend that Kinsey acted as though he was afraid of "an inquisition."[15]

Corner's word choice aptly described Kinsey's state. He felt persecuted and beleaguered. If the female volume was ever to be completed, he needed to give it his undivided attention. There were still interviews to be conducted, data to be tabulated and analyzed, and a manuscript to be written. The last thing Kinsey wanted was to open his records to a group of hot-shot statisticians who might ridicule his knowledge of statistical theory, pick apart his data, and second-guess his entire operation. Yet he was enough of a realist to know when to bend.

In August 1950, despite grave misgivings, Kinsey informed the American Statistical Association (ASA) that he would be willing to meet with a statistical advisory panel, provided that certain conditions were met. He insisted that the committee be composed of at least three statisticians, all of whom had to be in population studies. Determined to fight the battle on home turf, he further stipulated that the advisers be willing to visit the Institute "so that they can understand the relation of our statistical problem to other aspects of the work." Kinsey also recommended that each committee member contribute his own sex history. "There is no other way in which they can get a first-hand understanding of the way in which we have done our interviewing, and since our interviewing techniques have been questioned by our critics, we think it highly desirable that the committee have a first-hand knowledge of the interviewing." Finally, Kinsey attempted to frame the agenda. He asked the ASA to evaluate the statistical objections raised by his critics and to compare the overall quality of his methods with those of earlier sex researchers. His final request was "that the statistical committee give us an opportunity to discuss their findings in the presence of a group from the National Research Council's Committee."[16]

Once Kinsey had agreed to meet with the statisticians, Corner swung into action. In May 1950, following lengthy consultations with Kinsey and Gregg, he issued a formal request to the ASA's Commission on Standards to evaluate Kinsey's statistical methodology and to provide constructive advice that could be made available to Kinsey, with the understanding that the CRPS had set aside $4,000 to cover expenses and honoraria.[17] Corner's request initiated months of tedious negotiation to hammer out the terms of the review, a process complicated by Kinsey's efforts to insert new conditions. He not only fought to impose his original demands but added a proviso about being allowed to help select his judges. At Kinsey's request, Corner dutifully submitted a list of names to the ASA, stressing that Kinsey had expressed "special confidence" in these individuals.[18]

At first, it was not clear whether the statisticians would accept the assignment. Before deciding, Samuel S. Wilks, the president of the ASA, telephoned his old friend Warren Weaver to ask whether they should take the request seriously. Aware that Kinsey's research had been proceeding for over a decade and mindful of his reputation for stubbornness, Wilks was troubled that they were being asked to step in so late. He was also apprehensive that they would uncover major problems and might have to recommend a delay in the publication of the second volume, a prospect Kinsey could be counted on to oppose. According to his desk diary, Weaver urged Wilks to "go at the whole matter as seriously and as earnestly as possible" and to register any "piece of warning" they thought necessary.[19]

Reassured by Weaver, the ASA agreed to conduct the study. Over the years ahead, Wilks proved to be a jealous defender of the statistical committee's prerogatives. At the outset, he insisted on naming people of his choosing to the committee. In addition, he reserved the right to publish the committee's report in the *Journal of the American Statistical Association*, with the understanding that a separate report would be submitted directly to the CRPS.[20] When an official from the NRC read Kinsey these terms over the telephone, he accused the ASA of attempting to set itself up as a "policing body in statistics."[21]

Fearful of the criticisms that might arise, Kinsey reiterated his conditions for cooperating.[22] In making these protests, of course, he was scratching a line in the sand, serving notice that he planned to contest every inch of ground. Yet Kinsey was not the only one who was thinking in political terms. The officers of the Rockefeller Foundation were becoming increasingly worried about the potential fallout from Kinsey's forthcoming volume on women. To facilitate their review of Kinsey's work, Gregg decided to visit the Institute in July 1950. Prior to his departure, Barnard asked Gregg for a full report, explaining, "There may be some trouble arising out of Senator McCarthy's exploitation of the homosexuality problem, and in any event I would think we ought at least to be prepared for more difficulty on Kinsey's second book than on his first, and I would like to be able to do as much advance thinking on these possibilities as is feasible."[23]

Gregg arrived at the Institute at 9:00 A.M. on July 7, 1950. For Kinsey, the visit was a godsend, for it allowed him to discuss the foundation's concerns and lobby hard for additional support. Gregg had always served as his angel in the past, and Kinsey was counting on him to come through again. Whatever the outcome with the statisticians, Kinsey knew that Gregg was the man who would present their findings to the board. Therefore, Kinsey was determined to put the right spin on things, so that Gregg would have ammunition for his next encounter with the trustees. Thus, despite the extreme pressure he was under, the embattled scientist pulled himself together (Gregg's diary noted that Kinsey "was tired but not irritable"),[24] summoned his energy, and presented his case with fervor and conviction.

Playing to his strength, Kinsey touted the social relevance of his research. Arguing that the nation badly needed scientific data to facilitate reasoned and informed discussion in these troubled times, he insisted that the national panic over sex offenders, coupled with McCarthy's attacks on homosexuals, made his research more timely than ever. Stressing that his services were in great demand, Kinsey revealed that he had emerged as a key witness in the hearings before legislative committees in the twenty-one states (including New York, New Jersey, and California) that were reconsidering their sex offender codes. In addition, he noted that one or more important visitors appeared daily on the Institute's doorstep seeking advice and data.

These arguments played well with Gregg. Like most foundation officers, he had a soft spot in his heart for projects that addressed important social problems. Sickened by McCarthy's benighted attacks on homosexuals and convinced of the need for reform, Gregg wrote in his diary, "The current ignorance in such matters is great. It provides the emotional fuel for such persons as McCarthy. K. wants to get as much done as he can while he is still on the job." Noting that Kinsey planned to do a separate volume on sex offenders as soon as he finished the book on females, Gregg added, "I would infer from Kinsey's references . . . that he is emotionally involved by his sense of injustice at current laws and their application."[25]

Kinsey was eloquent in his pleas for future funding. With lawyers, judges, penal institutions, and state legislators clamoring for data, it was no time for the foundation to pull the plug. As for the foundation's concerns about royalties, Kinsey again stressed that while the male volume had made a lot of money, every dime had been plowed back into the research. Furthermore, he argued forcefully that outside funds were still needed to fill the gap between his current budget and the Institute's operating expenses. Summarizing Kinsey's final argument, Gregg wrote sympathetically in his diary, "Withdrawal of RF support before Volume 2 comes out would have the flavor of disavowal of Volume I even if royalty funds were sufficient to assure publication [of volume 2]."[26]

The most critical part of their discussion focused on the forthcoming evaluation of Kinsey's research by the ASA. Aware that the future of his funding hung in the balance, Kinsey was sweetness and light, promising to address his critics whenever possible. In fact, he maintained he had already adopted most of the statisticians' suggestions, with one glaring exception. Anticipating that his failure to employ random sampling would pose the largest problem, Kinsey seized the opportunity to plead his case. Random sampling, he insisted for the umpteenth time, was simply not feasible for sex research, as persons chosen at random often refused to be interviewed. Given this obstacle, he maintained, the next-best thing was the taxonomic approach—relying on huge samples to reveal the full range of individual variation in a population. Moreover, Kinsey had no intention of allowing Gregg to return to New York without first clearing up one additional matter. Aware of his reputation for stubbornness, Kinsey repeated his willingness to cooperate with the committee, though, characteristically, he could not refrain from enumerating no fewer than eight qualifications the statisticians chosen to review his work should meet. While he did not agree with all of Kinsey's criteria, Gregg was sympathetic. Mindful that his diary would serve as a report to Barnard, Gregg observed in defense of Kinsey, "My general impression is that it is now up to the American Statistical Association to meet K at least half way. Unless the statisticians can keep a common sense approach, they will lose rather than gain from their apparent offer of service."[27]

The ASA assembled a distinguished committee to review Kinsey's work. In September 1950, it announced that the committee would be composed of William G. Cochran, professor of biostatistics, School of Hygiene, the Johns Hopkins University, who agreed to chair the committee; Frederick Mosteller, associate professor of statistics, Department of Social Relations, Harvard University; and John W. Tukey, professor of mathematical statistics, Princeton University.[28] While none of these men had any expertise on human sexuality or any other aspect of human behavior, each had a wealth of experience applying sophisticated analysis to a vast array of statistical problems. Publicly, Kinsey responded graciously to this panel, promising the association "our complete cooperation, and our appreciation of the considerable debt that we shall owe to your group."[29] Privately, the thought of going head-to-head with three statisticians of this caliber must have filled him with something akin to terror.

Gregg was worried, too. Aware he would never be able to get Kinsey another dime unless the statisticians blessed his work, Gregg wrote to say that he hoped the collaboration between Kinsey and the statisticians would "be free from inadvertences, prejudices or suspicions." He added, "The ideal issue of this collaboration is so much to be hoped for that I am reminded of Samuel Butler's aphorism, 'An honest god is the noblest work of man.' "[30] For his part, Corner was hopeful that Kinsey would cooperate. Explaining his optimism many years later, Corner noted that although Kinsey's initial reaction to the statisticians "was ungraceful, . . . he was influenced by the criticism . . . and gave attention to it in the long run."[31] Time would tell how well Gregg and Corner knew their man.

In October 1950, the ASA's committee descended on Bloomington. Any thought that the meetings would be relaxed was quickly dispelled. On the morning work was scheduled to begin, Cochran, Mosteller, and Tukey walked the short distance from the Student Union to the Institute, which was housed in Wylie Hall. As they walked, Mosteller started singing a song from *H. M. S. Pinafore* and his comrades, both Gilbert and Sullivan fans, joined in. Upon arriving at the Institute, they were greeted briskly by a very businesslike Kinsey and shown to an office they could use. After Kinsey took his leave, Mosteller, hoping to lighten things up, suggested that they finish the song. "And so we started to sing this last verse, and the next thing we knew the door was being broken down and there was Kinsey and an army behind him of secretaries and others," Mosteller later recalled. Agitated and upset, Kinsey bellowed that the noise was traveling through the air ducts and disturbing everybody in the building. He then scolded them, saying that their behavior was very inconsiderate. The entire episode, confessed Mosteller, was "a little embarrassing."[32]

Things got worse. For five days running, Kinsey went toe-to-toe with Cochran, Mosteller, and Tukey, and from the outset it was clear that Kinsey did not want to change how he did things. "I thought he was a man who felt he had to do it all himself," recalled Mosteller, "that he'd invent every method and use only methods that he'd invented because he was sure they worked and that he may find it difficult to use methods that others had invented." Elaborating, he explained that Kinsey "believed that he'd learned all his stuff the hard way and he also, I think, believed that his way of doing it was likely to be better than the way anybody else wanted to do it." At bottom, Mosteller added, "he liked to be the one that was running things."[33]

In the past, Kinsey had grown accustomed to winning arguments by dint of will, personality, and debating skill. These were the assets he drew upon in his discussions with the statisticians. Yet, no matter how forcefully he argued, he did not have the expertise to support his positions. Kinsey was in over his head, and his debating skills had little effect on his visitors. As Mosteller noted, "in mathematics, we are very used to very harsh arguments in which we don't pay any attention at all to the other person's feelings." Beginning in graduate school and for the rest of their careers, explained Mosteller, mathematicians settle disputes by grabbing a piece of chalk and working out their proofs on the blackboard. Describing how this worked, Mosteller declared, "You make the proof and the other fellow doesn't like it; he shows you where you've got your mistake and you show it up or you don't and pretty soon somebody's got to give up." Because of this feature, Mosteller believed, mathematics has a real advantage over those disciplines that "don't have firm endpoints," because they lack "a natural way of handling disagreements."[34]

Not surprisingly, Kinsey lost most of the discussions when he picked up the chalk. Faced with demands for "proofs," he could not provide them. To escape this predicament, Kinsey attempted whenever possible to shift the argument. Instead of debating statistical points, he would hold forth at great length on the unique problems inherent in sex research that had prevented him from adopting statistical procedures, such as random sampling. Then he would move quickly into a defense of the procedures he had employed, insisting that they were honest, intelligent, and, above all, the only feasible alternatives.

Although sympathetic to Kinsey's problems, the statisticians remained focused on the statistical issues at hand. In exchange after exchange, Kinsey would fight like a lion, only to have to capitulate to superior knowledge in the end. And each defeat seemed to deflate him, as though someone had let the air out of his ego. A less zealous man might have lost heart, but Kinsey was sustained by a will that would not admit defeat. Time and time again, he would regroup and resume the battle with fresh ferocity. In those areas where there was any room for compromise, Kinsey more than held his own.

Things did not take a turn for the better for Kinsey, however, until the statisticians gave their sex histories. For the first time since they had arrived, Kinsey finally had them where he wanted them—on his turf. He had every confidence that they would be won over by the experience, just like countless critical subjects before them. Knowing that the statisticians would compare notes and mindful of the need to demonstrate that each of the Institute's interviewers could obtain nearly identical results, Kinsey decided against doing all the interviews himself. Instead, he shared the duties with Pomeroy and Martin. In the end, this proved a wise decision. In their final report, Cochran, Mosteller, and Tukey declared, "The KPM interview impressed us as an extraordinarily skillful performance." Moreover, they conceded a major point to Kinsey when they noted, "For what our opinion is worth, we agree with KPM that a written questionnaire could not have replaced the interview for the broad population contemplated in this study. The questionnaire would not allow flexibility which seems to us necessary in the use of language, in varying the order of questions, in assisting the respondent, in following up particular topics and in dealing with persons of varying degrees of literacy."[35]

Kinsey hoped to gain more by socializing. No doubt believing that a pleasant evening would alleviate the tensions, Kinsey asked the statisticians home for dinner. Clara prepared a delicious meal. A full program of music followed, with Kinsey, as usual, delivering remarks on each piece. Yet his attempts at winning friends and influencing people failed miserably. Recalling his host's authoritarian style that evening, Mosteller later remarked that it was obvious that Kinsey "just wanted to run things."[36] Clara's memories of the evening were even less pleasant. "I never fed any group of men that I would have so much liked to have poisoned," she later confessed. "I just felt that here we invited them out for dinner, along with the associates, and I just felt that they were not very friendly. Tukey was the worst."[37]

Clara's animus against Tukey was understandable. More often than not, it was he who argued her husband down. Like Kinsey, Tukey came at people frontally, and he refused to cut Kinsey any slack on the statistical errors and compromises he had made. Indeed, as the meetings progressed, the relations between these two strong-willed men became increasingly strained. Gebhard recalled that Kinsey "disliked Tukey enormously," largely because "Tukey was too much the purist and the theoretician to suit him."[38] At times, Kinsey would dig in his heels and refuse to budge. In most instances, however, he would concede the point, albeit grudgingly. It was as though Kinsey was forcing himself to appear reasonable, lest word get back to the Rockefeller Foundation that he had been recalcitrant. At the end of one exchange in which Tukey had won the point, Mosteller recalled, Kinsey turned to Martin and announced with a flourish that henceforth they would change the way they handled a particular statistical problem.[39]

With the possible exception of Kinsey, no one felt more beleaguered in these meetings than Martin. The last two years had been hard on him. "My wife and I weren't getting along too well," he recalled.[40] In addition to his personal problems, Martin was in the throes of a professional crisis. As the staff member who had done most of the statistical calculations, he had watched with horror as the critics had ripped his work apart. "I think a number of mistakes could have been avoided early on if we had [had] more intellectual talent," he observed.[41] Indeed, months before the statisticians arrived, Martin's strain was starting to show. "I became really quite tired of all the traveling and being away, and I began to lose my sense of self-confidence within the interview situation," Martin observed. Revealing how bad things got at one point, he lamented, "In the middle of interviews I would start losing my voice, fearing that I might forget questions."[42]

More enervating than the constant travel were his doubts about the research. "I came to feel that the quantity of interviews was never ending, that the whole inquiry was rather trivial after all," Martin later confessed.[43] "There are a number of places where things went wrong," he declared. "One was Kinsey's conviction that we needed 100,000 case histories. That's foolish." Instead of "wasting all that effort building up large numbers of case histories," declared Martin, "it would have been better to have more clearly specified what our objectives were and organized a series of studies around each of those objectives and planned our sampling to minimize wasted efforts."[44]

The problem, of course, was that Kinsey did not wish to make changes, in part because he was just plain stubborn. "I don't think he [Kinsey] was very open to new ideas," Martin later admitted. "I think he was a man of tremendous conviction to the point of harming himself."[45] Mosteller concurred, remarking that Kinsey "felt he did it right, so how could this criticism arise?"[46] Yet more important than hubris was Kinsey's fear that if he made wholesale changes the new data he acquired would not fit with the old and all his previous work would have to be scrapped. Unwilling to abandon more than a decade of work, Kinsey was hostage to the way he had done things in the past. He refused to even consider altering the way he recruited subjects, at least if that meant switching to a random sample.

Officially, though, Kinsey put up a good front. After his inquisitors left Bloomington, he assured Gregg that the session had been "very profitable."[47] And while he used nearly identical language with Corner, Kinsey pressed, "It is very important that the National Research Council's Committee (as many as can come) should meet with the statistical group when they bring their preliminary report back here to Bloomington some time within the next few weeks or month or two." He continued, "Dr. Cochran is judicial in his handling of the situation, and emphasized that he would like to have our group and the NRC group go over the material with them before that is put into a report in final form."[48] In the end, then, all Kinsey could do was agree to minor changes, wait for the statisticians to draft their preliminary report, and then pray that he and Corner could bend it in the Institute's favor before it was released to the press or published in a professional journal.

Waiting was the hard part. The report took much longer to complete than anyone had anticipated. As the months passed, Kinsey grew increasingly anxious and tense. He was right to worry. Cochran, Mosteller, and

Tukey had every intention of putting his numbers under a microscope and boosting the magnification until every error could be seen in stark relief. At the outset, they decided not to examine the research or data pertaining to the female volume but to focus exclusively on the male volume, so as not to disrupt Kinsey's work schedule. However thoughtful their motives, this put Kinsey at a distinct disadvantage. It meant that he would be judged at his worst. Thanks to the statistical criticisms he had received from reviewers, Kinsey already had a full plate of suggestions, and while it had irked him to do so, he had made a good-faith effort to correct a number of errors. By concentrating on his past mistakes, then, Mosteller, Tukey, and Cochran would not be in position to see, or credit him for, the adjustments he had already made.

The one thing Kinsey could not complain about was how hard his judges worked. In the months that followed their visit to Bloomington, Cochran, Mosteller, and Tukey stayed in more or less constant contact by telephone, and they met in Chicago (December 1950), Princeton (January 1951), Cambridge (May 1951), Baltimore (July 1951), and Princeton (October 1951). Overall, their deliberations were collegial and harmonious, though Tukey, as Mosteller later observed with considerable understatement, "was always happy to argue his point vigorously."[49] Yet as spring approached, it became clear that their report would not be ready in time for the Rockefeller Foundation's board meeting in April 1951, a fact Cochran communicated to Corner, who in turn passed along the disappointing news to Gregg.[50]

From Gregg's perspective, this was a serious problem. He badly needed an assessment of Kinsey's work to present to the board in April. At Barnard's suggestion,[51] Gregg asked Weaver to contact Cochran to see if they could learn which way the committee was leaning.[52] Before doing so, however, Weaver spoke with Tukey, thinking he would talk more freely than Cochran. In response to close questioning, Tukey gave a generally favorable report, stressing that the committee had made a good deal of progress with Kinsey, even though the going had been heavy in places. On the basis of their success at educating him on a number of statistical problems, Tukey predicted that the female volume would be substantially improved. "As an incidental point," noted Weaver, "Tukey remarked that after all of the very careful examination of this committee, he would be inclined to say that about half of the statistical criticism of Kinsey was quite unwarranted, but that most of the other half was significant."[53]

On the more basic issue of sampling, Tukey informed Weaver that no progress was possible at this stage, because the work was over and done with. Nor was Tukey sanguine that the sample Kinsey had in hand was representative of American males. "I think it is clear, from my conversation, that Tukey himself has pretty grave doubts as to whether useful and significant generalizations about the population as a whole can actually be inferred from the kind of samples which Dr. Kinsey has used," Weaver informed Gregg. "After all of this is said and done, Dr. Tukey remarked quite voluntarily that if he were in your [Gregg's] position he thinks that he would probably, although obviously reluctantly, go ahead with the project," Weaver continued. "In fact, Tukey said that if he were Dr. Kinsey himself, it is not at all clear to him that he would be willing to stop, wipe all of these years' work off the blackboard, and start over right. It was inferred in everything Tukey said that what Kinsey is doing is a substantial improvement over what anyone has produced or otherwise done in this field."[54]

As Weaver had anticipated, Cochran was more guarded in his remarks. At first, the only comment he would offer was that the committee had made a series of suggestions to Kinsey, and it was not clear whether he would accept them. Several of their recommendations, explained Cochran, were "definitely troublesome in nature" and would require " 'major readjustments' " in Kinsey's procedures. Stressing that Kinsey was "an able and experienced person," he also noted that Kinsey harbored "very fixed and determined ideas about his own work." Summarizing Cochran's position, Weaver reported, "He recognized perfectly sensibly that Kinsey has already done so much work, and that he is so deeply into this whole affair, that it is certainly hard for him to make adjustments of the sort which are at issue."[55]

Hoping to draw Cochran out, Weaver made him a proposition. He asked Cochran to pretend that he and his colleagues on the statistical committee had been appointed to the foundation's board and had to decide whether to give Kinsey more money. He further instructed Cochran to assume that Kinsey had refused to accept their recommendations and that his whole statistical procedure was not significantly modified by the minor suggestions he did adopt. Under these circumstances, would the committee vote to fund Kinsey? "Cochran said," reported Weaver to Gregg, "with all of the reticence and reserve which are characteristic of him (remember that he has a great, heavy burr), that he rather guessed that his committee would vote in the affirmative on such a question, in spite of all of the difficulties."[56]

Following his discussion with Weaver and realizing that he had no authority to speak, Cochran contacted his fellow committee members to see if they could draft something for Gregg to present to the Rockefeller Foundation trustees. After serious deliberations, Cochran, Mosteller, and Tukey sent Gregg a cautiously favorable statement, which read in part, "Without pre-judging our final conclusions, we see no factor at this stage which would make us wish to recommend against a continuation of financial support of the work of the Institute for Sex Research."[57] Relieved and pleased, Corner confided to Kinsey, "Cochran is certainly one of the most cautious Scots I have ever had to deal with. In view of his temperament I should rate the statement as almost enthusiastic."[58]

While the endorsement could have been stronger, it gave Gregg the ammunition he needed. If three of the nation's finest statisticians were not disposed to ax Kinsey, Gregg was not about to second-guess them. After all, what sex researcher in the past had been subjected to such scrutiny? Had not the statisticians conducted a review of Kinsey's statistical methodology unprecedented in the history of sex research? From Gregg's perspective, then, it seemed desirable for the foundation to continue to stand behind Kinsey, even if that meant incurring the wrath of trustees who opposed his work or making the foundation a target for politicians like McCarthy and his ilk.[59]

Gregg also had a personal stake in seeing Kinsey funded. The upcoming meeting of the trustees held a special importance for Gregg. It was to be his last as director of the medical sciences division. He had asked to be relieved of his duties as director, ending a tenure in that position that stretched back to 1931. "Dad's health wasn't terribly good," recalled Gregg's son, Michael, many years later. Explaining that his father suffered from cardiac arrhythmia, Michael added, "He was an old man at age sixty-one and sixty-two."[60] At sixty-one, Gregg was eager to clear the deck. His review of his family tree had revealed that his male ancestors did not live much beyond the age of sixty-five, and he wished to devote the rest of his life to writing.

The foundation had granted Gregg's request with reluctance, since he was among the most respected and beloved members of the staff. Rather than see him retire, however, the foundation had agreed to name Gregg a vice president at large, a position that freed him from the responsibilities for the medical division but allowed the foundation to draw upon his advice. The spring meeting of the trustees, then, was to be his swan song. The prospect of having his final recommendation rejected was not something Gregg relished. Every trustee and every officer of the foundation knew where he stood on Kinsey, and Gregg meant to go out a winner.

The Rockefeller Foundation's board of trustees met on April 4, 1951, in Princeton. From the opening remarks, the atmosphere at the meeting was pregnant with anticipation. As the trustees heard the recommendations from the foundation's other divisions, the suspense kept building. Everyone knew there would be a battle when Gregg presented the medical division's business. He did not disappoint. Included in his recommendations was a request for $80,000 annually for the next two years to support the

CRPS's budget, with the provision that Kinsey would receive $40,000 annually.

Gregg's defense of his motion was spellbinding. Summoning all his eloquence and powers of persuasion, he discussed each of the criticisms that had been raised in the 1949 board meeting about Kinsey's work. Gregg then proceeded to make the case for funding, supported at every turn by Barnard, who also threw his weight behind Kinsey. No project before the board, insisted Gregg, had greater social relevance than Kinsey's research. His work had brought the light of science to a field that had stood for centuries in the darkness of taboo, and it had done so at a moment in history when the nation badly needed hard data with which to reevaluate its legal, moral, and educational approaches to human sexuality.

No sooner had Gregg completed his presentation than a group of trustees rose in opposition. Indeed, few board meetings in the foundation's history had generated debates that could match the heat and the venom of what followed. Most of the early discussions centered on the statistical objections. Although Gregg shared the statement from the statistical committee with the trustees, Kinsey's critics on the board remained unpersuaded. Ignoring the fact that the statisticians had given Kinsey a relatively clean bill of health, several board members honed in on the alleged deficiencies in his interviewing procedures and challenged the reliability of his data. Unflappable, Gregg parried each attack with skill. Calmly and resolutely, he held his ground, undaunted by their attempts to shoot down his proposal.

"There was a good deal of discussion, and some of it was pretty far out," recalled Andrew J. Warren, the North Carolina–born and Harvard-trained physician who succeeded Alan Gregg as the director of the medical sciences division. Possessed of an understated personality and as soft-spoken as Gregg was dynamic and articulate, Warren looked back on that meeting decades later and grimaced: "There was a bit of animosity aroused in that meeting among the trustees as a matter of fact."[61]

As the discussion intensified, the debate shifted to the moral propriety of Kinsey's research, the issue that had been the real basis for most of the opposition to Kinsey all along. With the specter of McCarthyism hanging over the discussions, the debate quickly escalated into a battle between the forces of good and the forces of evil. Holding the line against immoral science was a group of leaders whom a later generation would dub the "eastern establishment," but who in a more genteel age would have been called the custodians of morality. Leading the attack was John Foster Dulles, secretary of state, chairman of the Rockefeller Foundation's board of trustees, rock-ribbed Republican, a lifelong Christian who was as Presbyterian as predestination (he had graduated from Princeton, his father was a Presby-

terian minister, and he was a deacon in the Presbyterian Church). "The
only guy who has direct contact with God is John Foster Dulles, and if you
don't think so, just ask him," sneered Robert Loeb, a fellow trustee who
could not abide Dulles.[62] The same unerring moral compass that had told
this Cold War Warrior to contain communism abroad made Dulles alert to
any threat to public morality at home. Joining him in opposition to Kinsey were other key members of the establishment who feared for the moral
health of the republic, including those who had opposed support for Kinsey in the past—Arthur Sulzberger, publisher of the *New York Times,*
Harold W. Dodds, president of Princeton University, and Henry P. Van
Dusen, president of the Union Theological Seminary.

Reflecting on this board meeting decades later, Gregg's fellow officers in
the medical division charged that several of the trustees had used statistical issues to mask moral objections to Kinsey's research. "I think that anyone who knows anything about subconscious motivations and
rationalizations and that sort of thing can come to the conclusion that
there will be some people who opposed it on semiconscious grounds or
moral grounds . . . and then cited these methodological bits of evidence in
support of a more fundamental antagonism if you like," opined Robert S.
Morison, who served as Gregg's associate.[63] Andrew J. Warren was considerably less guarded in his views. "I think it was the old attitude," he declared. "You see, most of the trustees were men, oh, [in their] late fifties
or sixties, and it was the old attitude about sex," Warren explained. "Sex
was sort of taboo," he continued, "it was just something that shouldn't be
published, something that shouldn't be discussed, something the foundation shouldn't have anything to do with."[64] Given these sentiments, it is
easy to understand why many of the Rockefeller trustees were not persuaded by the statement from the statistical committee regarding Kinsey's
methodology. In truth, there was nothing Kinsey could have done, short
of abandoning his research, to please them.

At the close of the heated debate, no one knew how the issue would be
resolved. As chairman of the board, Dulles carried enormous weight with
his fellow trustees. Nor were the views of men like Sulzberger, Dodds, and
Van Dusen held in slight regard. With opponents of this caliber lined up
against him, Kinsey's prospects appeared dim. In the end, all he had going
for him was the chance that a narrow majority of the trustees would be
swayed by Gregg's presentation, which, again, had been strongly seconded
by Barnard.

As the votes were counted, a hush fell over the room. Then, finally,
came the announcement: the vote was nine to seven in favor of Gregg's
recommendation.

In assessing the board's action, one could hardly overstate Gregg's role.

It was not simply that Gregg had gone to the wall for Kinsey, which, of course, he had. The real issue was how much influence Gregg carried with the board. He won because a majority of the board members held him in such high regard that they did not wish to hurt him, whatever their thoughts on Kinsey. As Thomas Parran, a trustee who had previously served as U.S. surgeon general, later confessed, "I felt that the proposal should be supported if for no other reason than that this was Alan Gregg's last recommendation and a vote of 'no confidence' then would have been a very real traumatic experience for him."[65]

Yet, if the vote was a personal triumph for Gregg, it was a Pyrrhic victory for Kinsey. The debate left deep wounds in the board, the kind that do not heal quickly, if ever. The exchanges had been too bruising; the divisions had cut too deep. Everyone who attended the meeting knew that Kinsey's work could not survive another review before the board, as it was extremely doubtful whether any of the trustees who had voted for Kinsey out of loyalty to Gregg would have the stomach to fight the battle again.

For their part, the losers were anything but gracious. John Foster Dulles informed Flora M. Rhind, the secretary of the Rockefeller Foundation, after the meeting that he wanted the minutes to show "that there was debate and a divided vote."[66] The same bitterness surfaced in the professional staff. A month after the board meeting, Warren Weaver sent Barnard a blistering twelve-page memorandum attacking Kinsey's research, insisting that the grant was a mistake, and arguing adamantly against future funding.[67] In short, the Kinsey debate divided the foundation as few issues ever had.

In the months following the board meeting, Barnard held a series of meetings with senior officers to decide what to do about Kinsey. Ultimately, he settled on a policy of watchful waiting. Outlining his thinking in a memorandum to Weaver, Barnard stipulated that it would be unwise to seek future funding for Kinsey from the board "unless there developed more confidence in and support for his method and unless the future publications indicated a real justification for further support that would be convincing to the Board."[68] To promote fresh thinking, Barnard informed Andrew J. Warren that he was taking over from Gregg with complete authority to consider Kinsey afresh from every standpoint. Significantly, he also advised Warren to inform Kinsey, Indiana University, and the NRC that the foundation's most recent grant did not imply a commitment for future funding.[69]

Still, Barnard refused to close the door on this possibility, telling Weaver, "It is not appropriate at this time to make up our minds or to say that we will not again aid this work." Philosophical about the statistical controversy that had raged around Kinsey's work, Barnard noted, "There are a good many fields of investigation, particularly in the social sciences, where in fact if you say anything at all it will not be scientifically justified, and yet in all the affairs of life this kind of investigation seems to be necessary and I don't think can be avoided." Unlike certain social scientists, Barnard had no difficulty understanding how people could regard Kinsey's work as "exceedingly important and useful." In his judgment, the social applications of the research were potentially enormous, particularly at a time when there was so much anxiety about homosexuality and sex crimes. A social liberal who favored fewer restrictions on people's private behavior, Barnard hoped that Kinsey's data would lead to reform. The real test of Kinsey's work, he insisted, "will be whether legislators and law enforcing authorities, reoriented to their problems by this kind of study, will appear to have constructively reorganized the legal prescriptions affecting sex behavior, etc."[70]

Kinsey, of course, was delighted to have his grant renewed, even though it came with warnings from Gregg to Corner and others that the likelihood of future Rockefeller funding was extremely remote.[71] In an effort to shore up his position, Kinsey paid a call on the medical officers in May 1951 at the foundation's headquarters in New York. Making the most of his opportunity to sell himself and his work, Kinsey was at his best. Aware that each of the officers was an M.D., he touted the contributions his forthcoming female volume was expected to make to the field of gynecology, particularly with regard to the physiology of reproduction and to issues related to sterility in women. He described his data with the precision of a scientist and the enthusiasm of a researcher who knew he had material no one else in the world possessed. Pleased by what he saw and heard, Morison wrote in his diary, "K. certainly makes an excellent impression in conversation, being to me at least rather less argumentative and defensive than he seems to be in correspondence."[72]

Hoping to cultivate the same close relationship he had enjoyed with Gregg, Kinsey also called upon Andrew J. Warren, the new director of the medical division, on this trip. Once again, Kinsey worked his magic, displaying the sincerity and enthusiasm that were his trademarks. Warren confided to his diary, "It was a pleasure to discover at the end of a visit of about twenty minutes that on the whole [Kinsey] left a very favorable impression."[73]

Kinsey also met with Gregg to thank him for his many years of support and to wish him well in his new duties as vice president. This meeting proved extremely valuable. Gregg explained in great detail the difficulties in the way of future funding, including the fear that Kinsey would not fare well when the ASA's committee issued its full report. Kinsey listened attentively, but according to Morison, who was present for part of the meeting, it was difficult to read his attitude toward the committee. He seemed upset over the time it was taking to prepare the report, noted Morrison. And while Kinsey readily acknowledged that some of the committee's suggestions had proven useful, he also insisted that in many instances his procedures were preferable to those advanced by the statisticians. "After all this is said there is still an area of unknown size in which there are varying amounts of agreement and disagreement," noted Morison. "One can only await the report with considerable eagerness."[74]

As the statistical committee labored on its report, Kinsey and Corner entered into a close collaboration. Indeed, Corner abandoned any pretense of neutrality. Over the next several months, Kinsey and Corner exchanged ideas on how to coordinate their efforts to minimize the potential damage and maximize the potential benefits from the report. In the end, they agreed on two points: first, the statisticians had to be persuaded to meet with them to discuss the preliminary report and to revise it in accordance with their suggestions; and second, the statisticians had to be dissuaded from publishing any part of the report until the problematical sections had been expunged. Making clear his position, Corner told Kinsey, "the less published the better."[75]

In December 1951, fifteen months after the ASA agreed to conduct the study, Cochran, Mosteller, and Tukey completed the preliminary draft of their report. A monument to their industry and seriousness of purpose, the report provided the most detailed technical discussion of Kinsey's work imaginable. One had only to glance at its dense, closely argued prose, supported by seven appendixes that ran to several hundred pages, to fathom why the report was so long in the making.

Corner tried to reassure Kinsey about the report. "At first sight I was upset by the tone of the first few pages," he wrote Kinsey, "but on second reading it seems that the verdict is far from unfavorable and that the statements which disturbed me are merely examples of inept wording."[76] Still, there was one major problem. Cochran had distributed copies of the preliminary report to about thirty individuals, including officials of the ASA, members of the CRPS, and a number of key officers at the Rockefeller Foundation. That meant that people who were going to decide the fate of Kinsey's funding had seen the preliminary report before he had a chance to respond to it.

Predictably, Kinsey took a hostile view of the report, as he was angry that others had been allowed to see his laundry before it was washed. Early in January, he wrote to Corner and complained bitterly about the report's being distributed before he had been given an opportunity to comment. Kinsey also voiced the fear that Weaver, who he knew opposed his work, might leak the report to the press. He even went so far as to suggest that the statisticians might be trying to renege on their promise to meet with his staff and with representatives of the CRPS to discuss and revise the report. "So far I have seen nothing in the report which indicates that the statistical committee anticipated that it was going to do any revisions of the report on the basis of a conference," complained Kinsey, "and their action in sending the report to so many persons immediately suggests that they do not want their minds tampered with since they have rendered their decisions."[77]

Kinsey's fears were far-fetched. There is no evidence that Weaver even considered leaking information to the press. Still, to prevent anyone from doing so, Corner sent a letter to everyone who had received a copy of the preliminary report, declaring, *"You are urgently requested therefore to hold your copy of the report in confidence and in particular to avoid every possibility of its getting into the hands of the press."*[78] Nor was there any basis for Kinsey's worries about the statisticians' breaking their word. Early in January, Corner received a letter from Cochran offering his assurances that the ASA would not take any "hasty action" with regard to publishing its report and saying that an "informal round-the-table discussion of our report with no holds barred might be helpful."[79]

With these issues settled, Kinsey busied himself with preparations for the meeting. Lining up his arguments in advance, he sent Corner a detailed critique of the statisticians' preliminary report late in January, itemizing nine areas in which he disagreed with their findings.[80] Then he took steps to get ready for the upcoming battle with Tukey. Aware that "random sampling" was relatively new and untried, at least on a national scale, and convinced that no scientists to date had succeeded in using this method in a large-scale study, Kinsey undertook to educate himself on probability sampling.

First, he asked Harold Davis, a distinguished mathematician at Northwestern University, if he was aware of any instances in which probability sampling had been used as a technique "in the securing of data on a nationwide scale in the United States."[81] Stressing that he knew of numerous instances of its use in small areas, such as a portion of a single town, Kinsey repeated that he was looking for examples "of such a sampling technique in the gathering of information on a national scale." From Davis came the encouraging reply that the only such study he knew about involved a national survey that had recently been completed in Greece. To learn more about it, Davis told Kinsey to contact William E. Deming, who worked as an adviser on sampling for the Bureau of the Budget, in Washington, D.C. Deming's recent book on sampling theory, noted Davis, devoted a chapter to the recent Greek survey.[82] As it happened, though, Kinsey was already aware of Deming's book and had a copy in his possession. President Wells had served as a member of the committee that had supervised this study in Greece, and Kinsey had learned a great deal from him firsthand about the survey.[83]

Next, Kinsey contacted George Gallup, who had rendered the research a great service in the past. Complaining that the statisticians who were reviewing his work insisted that all surveying employ probability sampling, Kinsey asked if he could come to New York to discuss the matter.[84] Gallup immediately agreed to the meeting, even though he confessed to being a little surprised that the statisticians were being such sticklers. "I had thought that some of our academic friends had weakened on this question," observed Gallup. "Certainly the 'random sampling' boys aren't beating the drums quite so hard these days."[85]

On February 5, 1952, Kinsey met with Gallup and his assistant William A. Lydgate, of the American Institute of Public Opinion in New York. Generously, Gallup and Lydgate spent several hours that afternoon tutoring Kinsey on sampling theory and priming him with arguments he could use against Tukey, who everyone agreed had a mania for random sampling. Hoping to calm Kinsey down, Lydgate wrote to him after the meeting, "Is it possible that the report of the statisticians is regarded as far less damaging or critical by other people than by yourself, because you are too close to the work? Maybe the reason it hasn't leaked to the press is that your detractors in the Foundation and elsewhere, many of whom may not even be aware of what probability sampling is, consider it practically a whitewash of your efforts."[86] Kinsey thought not. By the middle of February, he had drafted (and mailed to Corner) a lengthy memorandum on probability sampling, listing numerous reasons why this method was totally impractical for sex research.[87]

Kinsey was not the only person who moved at a feverish pace to prepare for the meeting. Throughout January and February, Corner worked hand in glove with Kinsey, suggesting items of strategy, points for discussion, fallback positions, and the like. At one point, Kinsey and Corner even considered inviting all the members of the CRPS to the meeting, but in the end Kinsey vetoed the idea, telling Corner, "If the group is too heavily loaded with people representing our interests, I am afraid that the statisticians will be inclined to think the meeting is too biased against them and not be inclined to compromise."[88]

And compromise was definitely what Kinsey had in mind. Academic etiquette might require a scholar in his situation to stand by and take his lumps, but Kinsey had no intention of allowing a bunch of academic purists to destroy his work. Remembering his training as a college debater, he intended to make their report rather than his work the central issue. His plan was to shift the discussion whenever possible away from the errors he had committed to the question of whether or not the statisticians had given him credit for the things he had done well. In other words, Kinsey was determined to put his judges on the defensive. He meant to transform what the ASA envisioned as a scholarly review into a political process in which criticisms would be negotiated and differences closed through the difficult art of compromise. To him, the review was not an opportunity to improve his methodology but a menace to his research. And few things were better calculated to bring out Kinsey's fighting spirit than a threat to his research.

The conference met on February 23–24, 1952, at the Institute for Sex Research. In addition to Kinsey and his senior staff members, Cochran, Mosteller, and Tukey attended, as did Corner and two additional members of the CRPS, Willard M. Allen and Carl R. Moore. In his opening remarks, Corner, who presided over the meeting, reviewed the circumstances that had led to the conference. Then, without further ado, Corner guided the group through an item-by-item discussion of the preliminary draft, focusing on the seven principal conclusions the statisticians had reached.

Kinsey, of course, knew what was at stake. Everything he had worked for and hoped to accomplish was on the line. If the final revision of the statisticians' report was damning, his scholarly reputation, already under siege, was bound to plummet and his entire support structure might well collapse. At a minimum, he was bound to lose whatever remote chance he had of securing additional funding from the Rockefeller Foundation. Furthermore, it was entirely possible that Indiana University might abandon him, as Wells might have great difficulty keeping the state legislature in line. Yet Kinsey had one enormous advantage in this contest, despite the mismatch in technical expertise. He did not have to win; he simply had to avoid losing. In a sense, he was like a champion prizefighter defending his title against a dangerous challenger: no one expected Kinsey to win every round; all he had to do was fight to a draw.

For two grueling days, Kinsey, supported at every turn by Corner, slugged it out with the statisticians. Describing the battle decades later, Mosteller recalled, "We took the whole thing we'd written and their team went over it in great detail, and we went over it line by line, so to speak. And any time he [Kinsey] wanted something changed, we would then argue about whether that was a good idea or not." In retrospect, Mosteller was impressed by how many objections Kinsey raised and how skillful he was at getting them to see his position. "One thing I think that happens in deals like this is that the person being criticized is more sensitive to nuances that the other authors are not," explained Mosteller, "so I think that Kinsey may often have detected some issue in a wording that we wouldn't have realized." Noting that this sort of thing happens all the time when people "from outside are trying to work inside," Mosteller added graciously, "I was very glad that we did go over it in that manner, so he [Kinsey] did have plenty of opportunities to point out places where we were perhaps giving innuendos in directions we didn't realize or perhaps saying something mistaken about what was going on." Stressing that the discussions "took a long time," Mosteller declared, "We fought through all those things and sorted them out."[89]

And what a bout it was! Kinsey battled like a heavyweight. Determined not to repeat the mistakes he had made in their first conference, he abandoned his defensive stance, came out swinging, pressed the attack, and never took a step backward. Kinsey meant to transform the debate from an assessment of the statistical components of his research into a critical evaluation of the report's failures to acknowledge his work's many strengths. Still, his opponents were wise to his strategy. Decades later, Mosteller recalled that Kinsey felt "beleaguered and that this wasn't really going to help and all he could do would be to minimize the damage."[90]

Part of Kinsey's attempt at damage control involved the issue of publication. For weeks prior to the meeting, he and Corner had conspired to find a way to prevent the statisticians from publishing their report, whether in a professional journal or in the press. As a fallback position, they had targeted certain areas of the report that could be published with little or no damage to Kinsey's reputation and certain areas that required changes in the event their efforts to block publication failed. According to Weaver's diary, Tukey later told him that "Dr. Kinsey and his colleagues, and also Dr. Corner of the NRC committee, objected most strenuously to the publication of this summary."[91] After spirited debate on these matters, Cochran, Mosteller, and Tukey remained adamant about their right to publish the report. In the end, Kinsey lost this point, though the statisticians did reiterate their earlier promise not to publish anything until he had been given an opportunity to read it and offer suggestions.

Kinsey had better luck with his plans for managing the press. It was just a matter of time before reporters got wind of the report, and Kinsey, as determined as ever to control the information the public received about his work, wanted to be ready for them. Consequently, he suggested that they prepare in advance a press release that would provide a brief summary of the report. Kinsey insisted, however, that the summary not be given to reporters unless it became absolutely necessary. On this point, the statisticians were in full agreement. On the day following their meeting, Cochran wrote Corner that a summary "will be held in readiness in case the Press should make an urgent request for a statement," adding, "It is not intended, however, that Dr. Kinsey, Dr. Corner or myself will take the initiative in sending such a statement to the Press without request from it."[92] Kinsey, however, had a somewhat different understanding, telling a friend that the conference participants had "agreed that no statement will be given to the press until we discover that the press does have information which it intends to publish."[93]

The sharpest exchanges of the meeting involved sampling procedures, pitting Kinsey squarely against Tukey. Describing their clashes to a friend, Kinsey noted, "On this point they did not give very much ground, but I think [they] recognize that we are going to defend a substitute method of sampling and do recognize we have considerable justice in doing so."[94] Wincing visibly as he recalled those battles, Corner charged that Tukey "was absolutely reckless in his criticisms" and "was on the warpath for exact statistical sampling." A purist on the issue of random sampling, Tukey insisted that Kinsey would have been better advised to stick a pin in a telephone book and then interview the people whose names got pierced. "Tukey was fanatical about this, and he weakened my confidence in the necessity of probability sampling," declared Corner. "He went so far, believe it or not, as to say that he would rather have a sample of three than Kinsey's kind of sample of three hundred, or figures to that effect," revealed Corner.[95] Decades later, when Mosteller was asked whether he could confirm this story, he looked embarrassed and replied, "That may be an exaggeration, maybe [Tukey] said five names."[96]

With Kinsey and Tukey, then, it really was a question of who would be left standing when the smoke cleared. "On occasion it was hideously tense," recalled Gebhard. "Kinsey felt that his neck and the neck of the research was on the chopping block, and if he didn't successfully defend himself and the research, that we would be seriously injured," Gebhard continued. "He was under one hell of a lot of stress, and it showed."[97] Mosteller concurred. Describing the atmosphere in their meetings, he later admitted, "Sometimes there was very great tension. No doubt about it." Mosteller confessed, "I think we didn't entirely appreciate the hint of threat that we represented to Dr. Kinsey and maybe to his little group."[98]

When the battle ended, however, Kinsey had much to celebrate. The revised version of the statisticians' report to the CRPS was a model of balance and fairness. Reflecting the intense pressure from Kinsey and Corner, the report's authors sounded in their opening remarks like men who were tip-toeing ever so gingerly through a minefield. Had they wished to do so, began Cochran, Mosteller, and Tukey, they could have written two factually correct yet dramatically opposed reports—one arguing, "that KPM's work was of the highest quality, the other that the work was of poor quality and that the major issues were evaded." Making clear their determination to find middle ground, they declared, "We have not written either of these extreme reports."[99]

Still, Cochran, Mosteller, and Tukey freely admitted that there was no way to prevent people who were so inclined from bending the report to partisan purposes. The academy was so divided and the assessments of Kinsey's work (both pro and con) had grown so polemical, they warned, that "a reader who is trying only to support his own opinions could select sections and topics to buttress either view." On the one hand, readers who backed Kinsey could point to "numerous problems that we feel KPM handled admirably." By quoting these sections alone, they explained, the conclusion could be drawn "that the work is nearly impeccable and that the conclusions must be substantially correct." On the other hand, readers who opposed Kinsey could cite "other problems which we believe KPM failed to handle adequately, in some cases because they did not devote the necessary skill and resources to the problems, in other cases because no solutions for the problems exist at present." By focusing only on the problems, therefore, naysayers could "find support for the opinion that KPM's work is of poor quality."[100]

Precisely because the atmosphere surrounding Kinsey's work was politically charged, Cochran, Mosteller, and Tukey felt that it was imperative to clarify where they stood. "Our own opinion," they announced, "is that KPM are engaged in a complex program of research involving many problems of measurement and sampling, for some of which there appear at the present to be no satisfactory solutions." Saying the words that Kinsey, aided by Corner, had worked so hard to wring out of them and had waited so long to hear, the statisticians declared boldly, "While much remains to be done, our overall impression of their work to date is favorable."[101]

Relegating the details and the discussions to lengthy appendixes, Cochran, Mosteller, and Tukey offered seven "main conclusions" about Kinsey's work. The first compared Kinsey's work to his predecessors' and found it "superior," noting that his team's "interviewing was of the best." The second finding was mixed, for it noted that certain of their conclusions were based on data not presented. "KPM should have indicated which of their statements were undocumented or undocumentable and should have been more cautious in boldly drawing highly precise conclusions from their limited sample," the report chided.[102] So much for Kinsey's claims that he did not interpret his data.

Not until the third conclusion did the three statisticians address sampling, the most serious of the criticisms that had dogged Kinsey's work for years. They admitted that there was no way Kinsey could have avoided the use of a nonrandom sample. Indeed, in their judgment, the peculiar problems associated with sex research made statistical analysis extremely difficult. Even with the most reliable sampling techniques, they declared, "there will be a certain percentage of the population who refuse to give histories."[103]

Where did this leave readers who wanted a straight answer about the reliability of Kinsey's sample? Significantly, the authors refused to say. Having spent more than a year studying the works of earlier sex researchers and working through Kinsey's data with a fine-tooth comb, they had become convinced that this issue was all but impossible to resolve. "These comments, which are not a criticism of KPM's research, emphasize the difficulty of answering the question: 'How accurate are the results?', which is naturally of great interest to any user of the results of a sex study."[104]

The fourth conclusion focused on the reliability of human memory. In keeping with the overall tone of their report, Cochran, Mosteller, and Tukey shook first their fists and then their fingers. While admitting the failures of memory and the risks of false reporting, they nevertheless declared, "Until new methods are found, we believe that no sex study of incidence or frequency in large human populations can hope to measure anything but reported behavior." The fifth conclusion also found a way to split the baby. True, they pointed to Kinsey's inadequate use of statistical analysis, but they also admitted that "the sort of assistance which might resolve some of their most complex problems would require understanding, background, and techniques that perhaps not more than twenty statisticians in the world possess."[105] How Kinsey must have relished this line when he thought back over the dozens of reviews by social scientists with little training in statistics who were certain they would have done better!

The sixth conclusion made a huge concession to Kinsey. Raising what should have been the most contentious issue in their report, the authors advised lamely, "A probability sampling program should be seriously considered by KPM." Instead of taking Kinsey to task on this point, they acknowledged that the benefits of probability sampling were limited to an unknown degree by "refusal rates and indirect costs, particularly by the costs of maintaining the present quality of the individual histories by KPM's approach."[106] No concession revealed a more indelible image of Kinsey's thumbprint. Tukey's efforts to make sampling the central focus of the report had come to naught.

The final finding was something of a grab bag. The statisticians advised Kinsey's group to undertake "expanded methodological checks of their sampling program, a further study of their refusal rate, some modification of their methods of analyses, further comparisons of reported vs. observed behavior, and stricter interpretations of their data."[107] Ending on a positive note, Cochran, Mosteller and Tukey reported that Kinsey had recently informed them that many of these improvements had already been adopted in the forthcoming volume on sexual behavior in the human female.

Kinsey was both relieved and pleased by the committee's report. Once again, his drive, determination, and combative spirit had enabled him to confront a seemingly impossible task and emerge triumphant. Yet Kinsey had not won single-handedly, as he was the first to acknowledge. Discharging the debt he owed to the CRPS, he thanked Willard M. Allen "most sincerely" and noted, "I am sure our success at the meeting would not have been so certain if you had not been there."[108] Kinsey's letter to Corner was even more effusive. "I want to thank you most heartily for the very considerable service that you and the two other men on the NRC's Committee contributed to our research last weekend," he wrote. "Since this was such an important event in the history of our whole research," continued Kinsey, "it would have been unfortunate if we had had anything less vigorous in support than that which you, Dr. Moore and Dr. Allen gave." Commenting on the last-minute corrections the statisticians had made on Corner's summary of their report, Kinsey gloated, "You will note they have changed only two or three sentences and we have no objection to accepting their changes. The most considerable changes concern probability sampling and I think that is so much eyewash designed to preserve Tukey's ego."[109]

Members of Kinsey's staff had not the slightest doubt about who had won. In something of an exaggeration, Martin would later declare, "The major points in summarizing their whole analysis were basically written by Kinsey." Martin elaborated, "He got them to agree to those major points because what they [originally] came up with were all these negative criticisms. What he suggested was that we also be praised for what we had accomplished, that it was superior to the work that had been done before." Boasting that Kinsey had forced the statisticians to "put the positives and the negatives all together," Martin declared with obvious satisfaction, "I think they ended up with a very balanced criticism."[110] Gebhard agreed. Emphasizing that only Kinsey could have bucked such heavy odds and eked out a victory, Gebhard later observed, "Frankly, the man was beyond his depth, but he had enough personality and drive that damned if he didn't come out rather well, so that the final report was by and large rather favorable."[111]

At least one member of the statisticians' committee was not pleased with the outcome and wanted a second bite at the apple. Meeting with Weaver in April 1952 at the Rockefeller Foundation's headquarters, Tukey gave a blow-by-blow description of the meeting in Bloomington as well as subsequent negotiations to put the final touches on the report. "[Tukey] feels confident that they have carried out no intellectual retreat with respect to any point which they consider important," noted Weaver in his diary. Weaver saw the matter differently. He had anticipated that meeting thinking that he had Kinsey by the throat, and that Tukey would be the instrument of Kinsey's demise. How had Kinsey managed to slip away? At

Weaver's insistence, therefore, they went over the new summary point by point in comparison with the first draft, and Weaver got Tukey to admit that the committee had, as Weaver put it, "definitely backed down in their new version." At this point, Tukey dropped his defenses and confessed that he did not believe that the statistical committee had "met the whole of its scientific and moral obligation by writing the report and the summary." Contrite, Tukey informed Weaver that the committee "would like very much to write a short report of a much more critical nature, but one which would be treated as definitely confidential by the only three groups who would ever see it—namely Dr. Kinsey's group, the NRC committee on research in problems of sex [sic], and The Rockefeller Foundation." When Tukey asked what he thought of the idea, Weaver replied that "it is not only proper but is a most desirable and constructive thing for them to do, if they feel that there are issues which are not properly dealt with in the general report."[112]

While Tukey maneuvered to broker yet another revision of the committee's report, Kinsey was one step ahead. After the February meeting with the statisticians, several friends, who had seen the revised report, wrote to offer their congratulations. "It seems to be quite harmless from your point of view—a statement that won't stir up any controversy," opined Lydgate, who, along with his boss, Gallup, had helped Kinsey get ready for his showdown with Tukey a few months earlier.[113] Kinsey was rapidly coming to the same conclusion. Feeling that the revised report did him more good than harm, he was reconsidering his opposition to the idea of releasing it to the press. In March 1952, he informed Corner that pressure from critics (Kinsey cited Terman by name) might force him as a matter of self-defense to quote publicly from the statisticians' report.[114] The following month, Kinsey asked Cochran, "Are we free to show this final draft of the digest to other persons?"[115] From Cochran came a gracious reply, "We hope that the final draft of the Digest really is final. You are free to show it to any interested parties."[116]

In the end, the pressure that brought the issue to a head came not from critics but from the press. Acting on a tip (the source of which was never revealed), the *New York Post* contacted Kinsey on June 19, 1952, stating that it had information that pointed to the existence of a high-powered statistical report on his work. Kinsey put them off without providing any specific comments. Later that day he got a call from Corner, who stated that he had just received an identical inquiry from the *New York Post* and had confirmed the existence of the report without providing any details. Since it was apparent that the press was going to ferret out and publish the story, and since Kinsey was convinced that the reporters would convey, in his words, "a garbled version," he advised Corner to release a prepared statement, along with the summary of the statisticians' report. Unwilling to act unilaterally, Corner immediately contacted senior officials of the ASA, who indicated that they would prefer to release the summary through their regular public relations committee directly to the Washington press corps, a process that would require several days. The mere thought of such a delay worried Kinsey greatly. For months, he had been sitting on a statement Corner had prepared in anticipation of just such an emergency. Therefore, with Corner's approval, Kinsey released the statement to the press that very day.[117] Tactically, this was a shrewd maneuver on Kinsey's part. It enabled Corner to completely upstage the statisticians.

Corner's statement, which Kinsey released to both the United Press and the Associated Press on the afternoon of June 19, 1952, was a masterpiece of public relations. From beginning to end, it managed to put the statisticians' report in the best possible light. Cherry picking his way through the summary, Corner highlighted the kudos the statisticians had bestowed on Kinsey and glossed over their criticisms. To set the proper tone, he began by announcing that the statisticians had compared Kinsey's work with the nine most important preceding studies and had found it vastly superior with regard to statistical analysis and its methods of checking and verifying figures. Corner also reported with obvious satisfaction that the statisticians had judged Kinsey's interviewing technique outstanding and had praised his care in filing the records and in preserving confidential data.[118]

Corner's handling of the criticisms was especially deft. Noting that the statisticians had made numerous suggestions for extending and improving the quality of data, Corner stressed that Kinsey and his group had already recognized the value of these suggestions and were currently using them in preparing their forthcoming volume on the human female. And while conceding that the statisticians urged Kinsey to adopt probability sampling, Corner noted that many scientists felt that this procedure had not been well tested and was not well suited to the peculiar problems associated with research on human sexuality. Declining to speculate on how much Kinsey's conclusions would be changed by adopting the suggestions the statisticians had offered, Corner emphasized instead that Kinsey had repeatedly stressed that his figures were only close approximations. If the time ever arrived when it was possible to apply mathematically ideal methods to sex research, conceded Corner, it was possible that Kinsey's figures might have to be adjusted a few percentage points up or down. Corner also acknowledged that some of Kinsey's conclusions might have to be revised from time to time as new data became available. Still, this need not give anyone pause, argued Corner, as Kinsey and his workers, like all scientific researchers, were constantly adjusting their methods and finding new ways to acquire and evaluate data.[119]

Corner's closing remarks showcased his skill as a spin doctor. Statistics, he announced solemnly, was not the whole story, or even the biggest part of the story, of Kinsey's research. The CRPS had been watching Kinsey and his associates go about their business for fourteen years, noted Corner. Its members had been greatly impressed by the vast knowledge and experience Kinsey and his coworkers had accumulated. Much of what Kinsey had learned, argued Corner, could not be expressed in figures. Nevertheless, it had a prime bearing on social adjustments, sex education, and the law. With these thoughts in mind, and a favorable review by a committee of distinguished statisticians appointed by the ASA in its possession, noted Corner, the CRPS had recently voted to continue its support for this important work.[120]

In the end, however, Kinsey and Corner could have saved their concerns over the statisticians' report, at least insofar as public opinion was concerned. Corner's statement went virtually unnoticed by the press, and those newspapers that did pick it up from the news services gave it very little play. Perhaps the response would have been different had the report been strongly negative, but the press had carried so many stories on Kinsey over the last several years that Corner's statement simply got buried. A few days after his statement was released, Corner, who was attending a conference on "population problems" in Colonial Williamsburg (which the Rockefeller Foundation had spent a fortune building and restoring), wrote Kinsey, "What glances I could make at the newspapers did not reveal anything about the statistical report, nor was anything said by the five or six Rockefeller people who were with us at Williamsburg."[121]

No doubt because of the lack of interest in Corner's statement, the ASA decided not to release a summary of its report to the press. Time passed and nothing happened. Finally, a year and a half after Corner's statement was released to the press, and more than three years after they had agreed to undertake the study, Cochran, Mosteller, and Tukey published an article entitled "Statistical Problems of the Kinsey Report" (Kinsey would doubtless have preferred a less judgmental title) in the *Journal of the American Statistical Association,* where it went largely unnoticed by the public. Nearly a year later, the ASA, agreeing with Tukey that a more candid assessment was needed, published the committee's full report as a 338-page monograph under its imprint.[122] It, too, bore the title *Statistical Problems of the Kinsey Report,* and it, too, failed to arouse much public interest, though anyone who had bothered to look would have found some sharp barbs buried in its appendixes.

From Kinsey's perspective, however, the "inquisition" had turned out well. From a professional standpoint, the ASA's review was the most serious threat to his work to date, and he had emerged largely unscathed. He had fought the statisticians to a standstill, and their report had had little or no impact on the public. Consequently, the officers and trustees who opposed his research would not be able to use it against him.

Indeed, Kinsey still thought he had a fighting chance of preserving his relationship with the Rockefeller Foundation. Despite numerous warnings from Warren and Morison, delivered to him personally, and repeated to Corner and to others, Kinsey continued to hope that he would be funded when his next application came before the board. After all, had he not been in hot water with the trustees for years, and had he not always pulled it out in the end? Kinsey would not—in fact, could not—bring himself to think that anything was impossible. Anyone else in his situation would have seen the handwriting on the wall and felt dejected. Kinsey, by contrast, meant to erase the handwriting. He willed himself to believe that if he did his part, others would do theirs. All he had to do was address his critics and make the female volume a better book than the male volume. That is exactly what Kinsey intended to do, and what the public wanted him to do. Most Americans could hardly have cared less what academics thought. They wanted to hear what Kinsey had found about American women.

2 6

"A VICTORIAN IMAGE
OF FEMALE SEXUALITY"

"I want to object to the lack of parking space on this campus," Kinsey complained to President Wells in 1948. Lesser officials could have handled the problem, but Kinsey wanted action. "I bring this question directly to your attention because it is one that concerns the efficiency of our staff," he explained.[1] In the wake of the male volume's runaway success, the need for efficiency weighed heavily on Kinsey. Ever since his childhood, when he had listened to progressive reformers preach the gospel of efficiency to a middle class anxious about personal productivity, Kinsey had always been a man who met his deadlines. In the heady days immediately after the publication of the male volume, he had planned to start writing the female volume in late 1949,[2] confidently predicting that he would have the book completed by 1950 or 1951 at the latest.[3] For the first time in his life, however, Kinsey had fallen behind schedule. To his profound embarrassment, 1950 came and went, as did 1951, with the female volume nowhere in sight. The man who valued control and order above all else was losing his grip on the one thing he had always been able to manage—his work.

It was not that Kinsey was afraid to write. Perhaps because he had produced so much as an entomologist, he never suffered from second-book curse after he switched to sex research. No crisis of confidence weakened his will, no dearth of inspiration clouded his vision, no breakdown of discipline vitiated his work ethic, and no waning of zeal obscured his mission. Kinsey was not ruined by success. His problem was time. There simply were not enough hours in the day (or night) for him to say grace over everything on his plate. Although at times he seemed totally preoccupied with his battles with critics in general and statisticians in particular, Kinsey was actually juggling with great dexterity a host of problems—some routine, others quite extraordinary.

First, there were his administrative duties. With success had come the problems of running his own show. By 1951, the Institute's annual budget stood at over $100,000. The staff had grown to seven full-time and five part-time employees. In addition to the members of his inner circle (Martin, Pomeroy, and Gebhard), Kinsey had to supervise the work of Alice W. Field, a lawyer whom he had hired to conduct a court-based study of sex offenders in New York; William Dellenback, the photographer; Cornelia V. Christenson and Dorothy Collins, research assistants; a secretary; a librarian and a part-time librarian's assistant; and a part-time laboratory assistant. In addition, he had to ride herd on several translators drawn from the faculty who contracted on a piecework basis to translate books, articles, and manuscripts into English from French, German, Latin, Greek, Japanese, Chinese, and other foreign languages.

Duties this demanding would have taxed the resources of a gifted administrator, but supervising was not Kinsey's forte. Reluctant to delegate responsibilities, he tended to micromanage everything.[4] Weekly staff meetings, supervisory conferences with individual workers, and budget preparations ate into his time, as did his recurring and seemingly endless negotiations with fiscal officers of the university to find ways to circumvent university regulations and procedures so that he could pay his staff members top dollar on campus.

Visitors also crowded his calendar. It was not unusual for people with sexual problems or questions to telephone Kinsey out of the blue or show up unannounced on the Institute's doorsteps. Then there were the expected guests. Despite the demands on his time, this chronically overextended man was generous with invitations. Friends of the research could count on being asked to Bloomington for guided tours of the Institute (and in some instances to be filmed). Moreover, the list of "official" guests was seemingly endless. Scientific consultants, scholars who wished to use the library and archival collections, state officials, foundation officers, and the like found their way to Bloomington. When Alan Gregg visited the Institute in 1950, he wrote in his diary, "K. averages about one well-qualified visitor a day: penologists, sociologists, legislative experts, psychologists, doctors of medicine, lawyers and directors of welfare and social work, ministers and teachers."⁵

Many of these interlopers were important figures, people who could help the Institute by whispering in the right ears. In such cases, Kinsey was on hand to discuss the Institute's mission and display its facilities. In his mind, these tours served an important public relations function and could not be entrusted to others. "Frankly, there were very few people that came and were not charmed, damn few," recalled Gebhard. "If he could once get at somebody, he generally sold them," he continued. "He sold them not with any con game; he sold them with his incredible sort of belief in what he was doing. The guy was so transparently honest in his own belief and the importance of what he was doing that it couldn't help but impress them."⁶

No visit was complete without a tour of the library, and Kinsey delighted in showing off its treasures. "The library really didn't blossom until after 1948, when we were able to use the large book royalties that we got from the male volume. At that point, then, the library began to just expand at an exponential rate," Gebhard later explained.⁷ The library was Kinsey's baby. It consumed huge amounts of his time, giving this chronic collector a new outlet for his passion. By March 1952, the library was valued at over $170,000, housed 13,790 volumes, and boasted an annual acquisitions budget of more than $25,000.⁸

Kinsey took personal charge of library acquisitions. Over the years, he had developed an extensive network of dealers (both in the United States and abroad) who trafficked in erotica, including rare books, manuscripts, artworks, and artifacts. Whenever he went on field trips, he would browse in their shops and secondhand bookstores, searching for anything that touched on sex, whether from a scientific or an erotic viewpoint. In addition, he would ask the book dealers to keep their eyes open on his behalf. "Since these people were businessmen," observed Gebhard, "you can be sure that they did indeed, so that they were offering us large quantities of books."⁹

Only modest discretion inhibited Kinsey's purchases. He approached books in the same manner he pursued histories; he wanted them all. "In fact, it ultimately got to the point where [the book dealers] were victimizing Kinsey, I am sorry to say," observed Gebhard. With no more than thirty minutes budgeted for each stop, Kinsey would rush into the stores, zip through the stacks, and then ask the proprietors if they had run across anything that merited a place in his library. Invariably, the owners would disappear into backrooms and then reappear with armfuls of books. "Well, poor Kinsey wouldn't have time in his half hour, you know, to appraise all of the volumes they offered him," continued Gebhard. "So, we purchased, well, not an exorbitant number, but a substantial number of things that were pretty damn peripheral actually."[10] It showed. Following a tour of the library, Robert S. Morison of the Rockefeller Foundation wrote in his diary, "It seems quite clear that K. and the others have a very vigorous drive to collect things without always knowing just why."[11]

Over time, Kinsey accumulated virtually all the works by sexologists and a wealth of books, articles, and pamphlets on topics such as abortion, anatomy, birth control, marriage counseling, physiology, prostitution, and psychology. Nor did he neglect popular culture. Works of fiction (he was particularly proud of his collection of first editions), art books, poetry books, girlie magazines, and nudist magazines all found their way to Bloomington. Determined to learn what ordinary people thought about sex, Kinsey also amassed still photographs by the thousands (ranging from cheesecake to hard-core pornography), films (from stag films to underground erotic classics), slides, prints of erotic art, and erotic objects. Among the art objects were drawings, paintings, and etchings, including an extensive collection of prison art. A small portion of his collection consisted of originals, but most were copies; a few pieces were by renowned artists, but most were by amateurs. Similarly, the erotic artifacts Kinsey collected, which included many hundreds of objects, ran the gamut from the exquisite Mochican pottery of ancient Peru to rustic hand-carved, wooden figures by American farm boys. In between were items such as gold pocket watches whose backs slipped open to reveal erotic scenes, phallic-headed statues of Catholic priests, decorative condoms with rooster head tips, and Roman wax seals of copulating figures. In short, the library and archive, as one visitor put it, contained "everything from the sublime to the ridiculous and from the highest to lowest art."[12]

The archive also had areas of special strength. It contained a treasure trove of sadomasochistic paraphernalia (handcuffs, cat-o'-nine-tails, leather hoods and masks, etc.). Moreover, the library featured an extensive collection of materials dealing with sadomasochism. With more personal satisfaction than he revealed, Kinsey routinely made it a point to show these materials to guests. During his visit to the library, for example, Alan Gregg recorded with amazement in his diary "that sales of books and pamphlets relating to sadism and masochism are larger than those of erotica."[13]

Building a research collection on sex was not without risks, as Kinsey discovered in 1950. Many of the items he had purchased over the years came from foreign book and art dealers. These materials had to be sent through the mail. This was an apparent violation of federal obscenity law, as the tariff act of 1930 prohibited anyone in the United States from importing obscene materials. In 1947, Kinsey attempted to head off any legal problems by asking Huntington Cairns, the Customs Bureau's legal adviser in Washington, D.C., to grant the Institute a dispensation under Section 305 of the tariff act of 1930. It allowed for exceptions if the erotic materials provided insight into "the significance of sex in all aspects of human activity."[14] Before a decision was announced, however, Alden H. Baker, the customs collector in Indianapolis, seized a shipment to Kinsey, insisting that a Japanese art book it contained violated the tariff act. In the end, Baker agreed to release the shipment, establishing a modus vivendi that permitted Kinsey to import erotica from abroad.[15] Still, the arrangement was inherently fragile. As Kinsey told a friend in 1949, "Someone along the line might disagree with the interpretations which we are getting and might confiscate the next lot of material."[16]

The agreement did collapse in 1950 soon after Baker retired. Eugene J. Okon, his successor, did not think it proper for the Indianapolis office to grant an exception to federal law, and in May 1950 Okon asked the Washington bureau for guidance. After looking over the enclosed samples, David B. Strubinger, the assistant commissioner of customs, replied, "All the books you have submitted are grossly obscene. The most liberal interpretation could not bring them within the statutory limitations of the discretionary authority of section 305."[17]

Convinced that the only way to resolve the issue was to forge an agreement with officials in Washington, Kinsey reached for a sharp legal blade. He sought advice from Morris L. Ernst, a renowned authority on censorship, who had represented Random House in the *Ulysses* customs case of 1934. In June 1950, Kinsey and Harriet F. Pilpel, Ernst's junior partner, met with Cairns at the Customs Bureau and tried unsuccessfully to reach an agreement.[18] When subsequent negotiations came to naught, Kinsey reluctantly decided to take the Customs Bureau to court to establish his right to import erotica. Plans for the test case were going forward when the press intervened.

On November 17, 1950, the *Indianapolis Star* published a front-page story entitled " 'Science' Says Kinsey: 'Dirty Stuff' Says U.S." In the article, Collector Baker characterized items from the shipment he had shown the press as "d—— dirty stuff . . . nothing scientific about it." Hounded by reporters, an angry Kinsey was described by the *Star* as "touchy and irritable on the whole subject." A few days later, a second customs official described material from another shipment as "so obscene that any scientific value is lost." By this point, the *Indianapolis Times* and the *Indianapolis News* had also zeroed in on the story, and the Associated Press and the United Press had spread it nationwide. The *Boston Herald* chided the Customs Bureau for its efforts to "protect Dr. Alfred C. Kinsey against too much sex," while the *Anniston* (Alabama) *Star* supported the seizures, declaring that "pictures of moral degenerates in degenerate poses hardly can reveal much of real scientific worth."[19]

The political fallout was swift. "President Wells and our Trustees have inevitably been concerned because our State legislature convenes in five weeks and the University's request for support for the next two years is involved," Kinsey informed Corner.[20] Fearing a free-for-all in the legislature, Governor Henry F. Schricker telephoned President Wells and threw a fit. Years later, Wells recalled, "He was so angry that he was beyond reason. Finally, I said, 'Governor, you're so mad that I can't reason with you. When you calm down, we'll discuss it,' and I hung up the phone on the governor of Indiana."[21] Fortunately for Kinsey, Wells and Schricker had known each other since boyhood, and Wells could take such drastic action without fear of reprisal. Still, it was clear that the governor would have to be educated about a research library's importance to Kinsey's work. Describing what happened next, Kinsey wrote a friend, "In consequence our Board of Trustees sent its medical member to survey the material with us last Saturday. He is excellent and quickly understood the scientific significance of the things. He is visiting with the Governor this afternoon to try and convince him of the necessity of the material to our research."[22] In the end, Wells, aided by key allies on the board of trustees, was able to win over the governor. Neither the university's appropriation nor Kinsey's budget suffered any retaliation from the state.

To reduce the risk of future blowups, Wells decided to do a little public relations work. At his request, the staff of the *Indiana Alumni Magazine* published a feature story (March 1951) on Kinsey and the Institute for Sex Research. From beginning to end, the article was a starry-eyed tribute, celebrating Kinsey as a dedicated, fearless, and altogether disinterested scientist whose research was backed by a prestigious foundation and a distinguished scientific organization. Its tone was captured perfectly by the legend that appeared beneath Kinsey's photograph: ". . . tolerance, skill, courage."[23] Stressing that Kinsey's research was at the cutting edge of a neglected field, the article included a detailed description of the library and its importance to science.

Kinsey adored the piece, and sent Wells a warm note of thanks.[24] After acknowledging that he was indeed responsible for the article, Wells observed shrewdly that "in public relations the offensive and precautionary measures are the most effective."[25] Realizing that the Rockefeller Foundation's board of trustees was about to review Kinsey's proposal, Wells had copies sent to the foundation[26] and to the National Research Council.[27] As usual, Wells's political instincts served Kinsey well. The article arrived just in time for Gregg and the foundation's president, Chester Barnard, to share it with board members before they narrowly agreed to fund Kinsey's research.

Kinsey's dispute with the Customs Bureau dragged on over the next several years. The lack of resolution gnawed at Kinsey. For years, he had dreamed of creating a body of scientific data that would be so vast and so compelling that it would force local, state, and federal governments to revise their sex offender codes. By confiscating his materials, customs officials had served notice that the system could strike back, forcing Kinsey to live in fear that the government would keep him from the "unfettered" pursuit of his research.

Kinsey was determined to continue the fight. If he refused to defend his right to import erotica, he told a friend, this would endanger not only his research but the work of other sex researchers because ignorant customs inspectors would be left free to confiscate any materials they considered offensive.[28] So Kinsey kept importing erotica from Europe, and the customs officials kept seizing it. Discouraged, Kinsey confessed to a friend in 1952 that the Institute had spent thousands of dollars on legal fees trying to reach a settlement with the Customs Bureau and the Treasury and Justice Departments, with no end in sight.[29]

Several times the Institute and the customs authorities came close to a compromise. On each occasion Kinsey nixed the deal. Restrictions or conditions of any kind were not acceptable. Explaining why he could never consent to an agreement to give a statement of the scientific importance of each imported item, Kinsey told his lawyer in June 1952, "It is the equivalent of asking an explorer to tell how he is going to use the material he may find on a previously unexplored continent."[30] Largely because of Kinsey's unwillingness to seek common ground, the dispute with the Customs Bureau was not settled during his lifetime.

As the staff and the library expanded, Kinsey requested and received more space.[31] In February 1950, the Institute for Sex Research moved from Biology Hall into its new quarters in the basement of Wylie Hall, the oldest building on campus. While the decor was not lavish (there were exposed pipes in some of the ceilings), the space was ample, occupying about one-third of the floor. Divided into twelve to fifteen rooms, the Institute's new home consisted of a series of long halls, offices, filing rooms, a large photographic dark room, and a library. For the first time, the library was concentrated in one room, and there was space for visitors to work without interrupting the staff. As before, however, the decor was Spartan and drab. Following a visit to the Institute soon after the move, Lawrence Saunders asked Kinsey's private secretary, in confidence, whether it would be okay to send some wooden coat hangers to replace the cheap metal hangers in the cloakroom.[32] The price tag on the new quarters was steep, both for the university and for Kinsey. The university spent $70,000 remodeling the space.[33] It took Kinsey months of vigilant hovering to get things done the way he wanted them (he was particularly concerned about soundproofing and fireproofing). In fact, the last workmen were still under foot putting the final touches on the facility two months after the Institute officially moved in. Frazzled but pleased, Kinsey wrote a friend in April 1950, "We have about twice as much space as we did in the other place. For the first time we are able to get all of our histories and punch cards in the same room, and in another big room we have all of our library together. The whole place is air conditioned, with steel wire on the windows and venetian blinds."[34]

Yet not even the lure of a new facility could overcome the habits of a lifetime in Kinsey; he still preferred fieldwork to the laboratory. Following the publication of the male volume, he found it easier than ever to attract volunteers for histories, as his fame had spread wide and far. Besieged by offers of help, he was determined to capitalize on them. Retaining his faith in numbers, Kinsey still spoke bravely of getting 100,000 histories. His coworkers, by contrast, were starting to question the taxonomic method. Increasingly, they had come to regard his pursuit of numbers as an onerous, mind-numbing, and never-ending chore.

The fact that the Institute was a man short did not make the interviewing any easier. Pomeroy went on leave in summer 1950, and again in spring 1951, pursuing his doctorate in psychology at Columbia University. Kinsey tried but failed to hire another interviewer, which put additional pressure on the staff to take up the slack. For the first time, Kinsey could not shoulder the load. Increasingly, his fatigue was betrayed in his recording, which showed signs of deterioration. Errors of fact were starting to creep into his sheets, and he omitted answers to some questions. Gebhard later acknowledged that Kinsey's "recording left something to be desired," particularly "toward the end of a field trip when he was terribly fatigued and perhaps going through a whole series of rather routine interviews."[35]

The strain was most evident when Kinsey discussed interviews he found compelling. From the early days of the research, he had done much of his interviewing in prisons. Following the publication of *Sexual Behavior in the Human Male*, Kinsey stepped up his prison work, focusing on sex offenders. The week the book was released, he and his coworkers were at San Quentin, where they received excellent cooperation from both the administration and the inmates. Kinsey had always been disturbed whenever he came across men who had been incarcerated for sex crimes, particularly prisoners jailed for minor offenses, such as exhibitionism, public indecency, and homosexual contacts.

Kinsey seemed drawn to such men, and over time his sympathy for them became almost unbearable. Gebhard recalled one incident, in particular, involving a prisoner Kinsey had interviewed in San Quentin. Kinsey felt the man had been jailed unjustly for a minor sex crime, and during the drive back to San Francisco he had tears in his eyes as he described the case to his coworkers. Kinsey was, in Gebhard's words, "visibly shaken by this." Added Gebhard, "I think this wore him down, he would be exhausted after some of these things."[36]

Dellenback, the Institute's photographer, remembered Kinsey's telling the story of a man who had had oral sex with his wife and gone to prison for it. It seems that the man's mother-in-law hated him, and when she learned from her daughter what had happened, the old woman called the police. He was arrested, tried, convicted, and imprisoned for violating the state's sodomy law. "[Kinsey] had tremendous sympathy for this kind of thing," declared Dellenback. Kinsey complained about "how terrible this was," continued Dellenback, noting that Kinsey considered it "a travesty, injustice and anachronism."[37]

Glenway Wescott also remembered how distraught Kinsey became over sex offenders he felt had been hideously wronged by the state. As they were talking one evening, Kinsey related the story of a man who had agreed to be castrated to avoid going to prison. "Kinsey would tell you that story with his eyes suffused with the beginning of tears and . . . he turned pale with the horror of it," Wescott recalled, adding, "He was so sorry for people that you felt that you'd never noticed human beings at all." Groping for the right word to describe Kinsey's emotion, Wescott said, "It's sympathy—sympathy." After a moment's pause, he corrected himself and said firmly, "[It's] empathy."[38]

Wescott was right. Kinsey identified with the sex offenders he interviewed in jail. He felt their pain and sorrow as deeply as if it were his own. The man who enjoyed shocking people by declaring that 90 percent of all American males had broken the nation's sex laws knew that he, too, was a sex offender. All Kinsey had to do was compare his history with those of many of the sex offenders he interviewed in prison. If they had been caught, who was to say that he would not be next? No, if Kinsey understood anything, it was that he, too, was jailable.

In the early 1950s, gay men were just beginning to organize to fight discrimination, and Kinsey was contacted by the Mattachine Society, a homosexual rights organization that laid the groundwork for what would eventually grow into a national gay rights movement. At first, however, Kinsey refused to have anything to do with the Mattachine Society, a posture that reflected his policy of denying that he was a reformer. His stance seemed particularly wise in this instance because the organization was widely regarded as more than a little "pink." Organized in Los Angeles in 1951, the Mattachine Society took its name from mysterious medieval figures who wore masks and were alleged to be homosexuals. Its founders included individuals who had been active in left-wing political causes, including the Communist Party and the radical fringe of the labor movement. Drawing heavily on these experiences, they created an organization with a secret cell-like structure, centralized leadership, and a hierarchical structure involving five distinct orders of membership, each with ascending levels of responsibility. In the beginning, the society's goals were to break down the isolation of homosexuals, to make gays aware of their status as a victimized cultural minority, and to organize gays into a political action group that could protect and promote the rights of homosexuals in American society. By 1953, the Mattachine Society had 2,000 members, mostly in southern California, but with a rapidly growing outpost in the Bay Area.[39]

In February, 1953, Kinsey was invited to serve on an advisory committee to the Mattachine Foundation, a nonprofit, educational organization chartered in California by the Mattachine Society the preceding summer. Created with the hope of securing heterosexual allies among professionals and public officials, the foundation planned to conduct or sponsor research on homosexuality and to use the fruits of this research to educate the public. In asking Kinsey to serve, however, the invitation made it appear that his name was already being used in letters to other potential advisers.

Furious, Kinsey fired off a telegram to Los Angeles ordering the Mattachine Society not to attach his name to any letter.[40] Following up with a letter, Kinsey explained that the Institute could be more useful to the Mattachine Society and to everyone else if it confined itself to research and objective reports. To show that he was serious, he threatened to sue anyone who used his name. And, as a parting shot, he lectured the Mattachine Society on the duties of citizenship, noting that in order effectively to advance the cause of homosexuals it had first to respect the rights of others in its publications.[41]

In the spring of 1953, the Mattachine Society fell upon hard times, confirming Kinsey's wisdom in remaining aloof. As the organization grew more public, its leaders' Communist backgrounds became a matter of grave concern to rank-and-file members. They were right to be worried. In February 1953, Senator Joseph McCarthy, chairman of the Government Operations Committee, began his infamous hearings on Communist infiltration of the State Department, its overseas programs, and the Voice of America. In March and April, the House Un-American Activities Committee, which had been investigating Communist influence in Hollywood for six years, moved its show to Los Angeles, where it staged hearings in the shadow of the film capital of the world.[41] With much of the public worried sick about subversion from within, Paul Coats, a columnist for the Los Angeles *Mirror,* picked this moment (March 1953) to publish a piece on the Mattachine Society. Not only did Coats reveal that the society's legal adviser had been an unfriendly witness before the House Un-American Activities Committee, but he pointedly reminded his readers that the State Department had branded homosexuals bad security risks. Claiming that Los Angeles had as many as 200,000 homosexuals, he warned that "sexual deviants" might organize to "swing tremendous political power" and might forge their power "into a dangerous political weapon." Added Coats, "If I belonged to that club, I'd worry."[43]

And worry many members did. Those who feared being smeared with a red brush demanded changes within the Mattachine Society. Following months of bruising battles, the founders with Communist backgrounds reluctantly decided not to run for office when the organization adopted a new constitution in May 1953. Kenneth Burns, who worked as a safety engineer for the Carnation Company in Los Angeles and wore conservative business suits, emerged as the organization's new leader.[44]

Under Burns's guidance, the Mattachine Society shifted from secret to open membership and abandoned any pretense of celebrating homosexuality as a minority culture with its own distinctive benefits and strengths. Instead, Burns fashioned a political strategy as conservative as his dress. Henceforth, the Mattachine Society would drop its emphasis on differences and concentrate on persuading the public that homosexuals were just like everyone else. In other words, Burns was an integrationist who wanted to gain acceptance for homosexuality. To promote integration, he thought that homosexuals should ally themselves with a variety of professional groups that could help to normalize attitudes. Their cultural authority, he reasoned, made them uniquely qualified to serve as agents of social reform in a society that routinely looked to experts for information with which to rationalize vexatious social problems. Convinced that vicious social stereotypes were responsible for oppression, Burns and his supporters insisted that the Mattachine Society's "greatest and most meaningful contribution . . . will consist of aiding established and recognized scientists, clinics, research organizations and institutions . . . studying sex variation problems."[45]

This was the sea change that brought the Mattachine Society back to Kinsey. On August 22, 1953, when the "K-Day" hype was at its zenith, Burns informed Kinsey that the Mattachine Society wished to cooperate with his research.[46] This time Kinsey accepted the offer. Noting that his next major project would examine the whole problem of sex laws and sex offenders, he replied, "If persons in your group care to contribute histories at any of the points in which we are working, we shall always be glad to have them cooperate."[47]

Over the next few months, Kinsey met with members of the Mattachine Society in San Francisco to work out the terms for cooperation, with Kinsey specifying that he wished to secure "the histories of persons who had had any contact with the police, whether it led to conviction or not."[48] In February 1954, the society's research chairman announced that he had lined up thirty-five members,[49] and in late March and early April 1954, Kinsey interviewed them in Los Angeles.[50] In return, Kinsey reversed himself and agreed to serve as an unofficial adviser to the Mattachine Society. Many years later, Burns recalled that Kinsey told them to eschew "special pleas for a minority group" and to limit themselves to helping "qualified research experts."[51] Significantly, this was the strategy that many leaders of the gay liberation movement pursued for decades after Kinsey's death, a strategy that played an important role in the American Psychiatric Association's decision in 1973 to remove homosexuality as a disease from its *Diagnostic and Statistical Manual of Psychiatric Disorders*.[52]

There can be little doubt that Kinsey would have preferred to follow the male volume with a major book on homosexuality or a study of sex offenders. For him, the personal had always been political. Yet he was enough of a realist to know that the public expected a volume on women to follow his book on men. The blows he wanted to strike on behalf of homosexuals and sex offenders would have to wait. Consequently, Kinsey willed himself not to collapse. If deadlines for the female volume came and went, this did not signal that he had fallen beneath his load. It simply meant that he was human. He went to work on the female volume as soon as his hectic life (and the pull of other interests) permitted.

Kinsey brought heavy baggage to the task. Despite his formidable learning and scholarly devotion to objectivity, he had developed some definite opinions about female sexuality over the years, most of which were judgmental and critical. In the male volume, Kinsey had made a number of digs that betrayed his attitude. Essentially, he had characterized women as undersexed moralists who served as willing agents of social control. Indeed, he had repeatedly discounted both their interest in sex and their capacity for high rates of sexual outlets. In many respects, then, Kinsey's attitudes toward women reflected the cultural values of his youth. He saw women as largely uninterested in sex, morally pure, and devoted to reforming men.

Gebhard later remarked that, "basically, he had rather a Victorian image of female sexuality." He elaborated that "he had the feeling that females were essentially receptive, passive individuals; and the males were the ones who were sexually active and aggressive." In Gebhard's judgment, there was no gainsaying that Kinsey was "a bit of a misogynist in that sense."[53]

Privately, Kinsey had always been deeply ambivalent about women. He had never had the same emotional investment in their sexual problems that he felt for men's, in part because he tended to regard women as agents rather than as victims of sexual repression but also because his vision of a sexual utopia rested on a decidedly male homoerotic model. To him, the evidence was unmistakable that men were far more interested in sex than women were. In fact, he was convinced that the only persons other than prostitutes who appeared to get as much sex as they desired or could handle were homosexual males who lived in gay communities in large cities. And this made Kinsey doubt the sexual compatibility of men and women. Simple arithmetic suggested that men and women were better matched with members of their own sex.[54]

At bottom, Kinsey believed that women simply were not as sexually responsive as men. Compared with women, men were more often conditioned by their sexual experiences, he insisted, and they responded to a range of erotic stimuli that had little or no impact on women. Unlike women, men seemed to have vivid erotic imaginations. They were aroused by fantasies, observing naked people, looking at erotic art, listening to erotic stories, and the like. On the basis of these contrasts, Kinsey concluded that sex had a much stronger psychological component for men than for women.[55]

One other factor may have tainted his attitude toward female sexuality. According to close friends, Kinsey did not particularly like women or feel comfortable in their presence. Perhaps because he worked so hard to repress any hint of femininity in himself, Kinsey found contacts with women strangely troubling. Musing on Kinsey's difficulties with women, Clarence A. Tripp observed, "It's something close to disgust with femininity. He doesn't trust it; he doesn't like it."[56] Dellenback went a step further. He speculated that gender prejudice might explain Kinsey's feelings, declaring that "homosexual males . . . have that sort of vicious approach to females in their nature."[57]

Whatever his overall attitude toward women, Kinsey made little effort to conceal his low estimation of their sexuality. As late as 1948, he told a journalist that the average girl under twenty engaged in sexual activity for social as opposed to sexual reasons. "She is interested because it means dates with boys, automobile rides, shows, and hilarious company," he explained. "If intercourse is part of the tax, OK, so long as the other girls in her group are similarly involved." For emphasis, he added, "The sex drive involves the boy, not the girl."[58]

Many women who had read the male volume took umbrage at his disparaging remarks. Some took the time to write, hoping to disabuse him of his misconceptions. To the woman, they insisted that females were not sexually inferior to males. A few went so far as to claim superiority. None made the case for female sexuality more forcefully than a thirty-five-year-old mother from the Midwest with two young sons. A single parent, her principal outlet was masturbation. "I have an outlet of approximately 130 a month," she wrote. Stressing that she was not alone in such behavior, the woman declared, "I know of at least 6 women whose husbands could only partially satisfy them." To fulfill their needs, she revealed, "These 6 women and myself have made penises for ourselves out of spun rubber and an inner core of hard rubber." Noting that one of the women had made hers nine inches long, the woman commented, "She said she never knew anything could be so wonderful. I'm afraid you won't believe me but she 'came' over 100 times in one evening." To make certain Kinsey got the message, the woman declared indignantly, "So don't blame it on the woman for low output! What man could stay hard that long?" Unwilling to be dismissed as peculiar, she closed, "I am in the best of health, I don't jump everytime the phone rings nor scream at other noises. I consider myself a well-oriented person."[59]

The women who defended their sexuality constituted a minority. Most of the external pressure on Kinsey ran in the opposite direction. In the consensus-minded 1950s, the mothers in television family programs such as *Ozzie and Harriet, Leave It to Beaver, Father Knows Best,* and *I Love Lucy* captured the officially sanctioned image of women. Fearful that Kinsey would reveal a contradiction between fictional women and real ones, many Americans did not want to hear what he had to say. Natalie Roeth Hirschfeld, his high school biology teacher, recognized the dangers he faced as he prepared to study what she called "the female species." Her tone was humorous, but her advice was sage when she cautioned, "Watch out! They'll rip you to pieces if you give away their secrets!"[60]

Viewed side by side, the responses Kinsey elicited from the multiorgasmic woman and his high school biology teacher captured the two faces of womanhood at midcentury. The latter was afraid he would reveal secrets that would knock women off their pedestals; the former was afraid that he wouldn't. Natalie Hirschfeld's warning betrayed her allegiance to Victorian reticence. The divorced mother, by contrast, spoke the language of sexual liberation. She wanted Kinsey to reveal that women were not only sexual but in many instances spectacularly so, a truth many people had long suspected but polite society had worked overtime to conceal. Given these divisions, Kinsey could not write about female sexuality without plunging into the fray of gender politics. Whatever he said, his findings would automatically provide ammunition for one side or the other. Kinsey, of course, knew which camp he wanted to help, and this put him in a bind. Politically speaking, his low opinion of female sexuality was counterproductive. It simply did not fit with his ideology of sexual liberation. For if Kinsey was predisposed to discount the sexual capacity of women, he placed the highest premium possible on the need for a sexual revolution. But how was the revolution to be achieved if half the troops were not at the barricades?

From a political standpoint, Kinsey needed to switch his stance on female sexuality. Instead of disparaging the sexual capacity of women, he should have been celebrating it at every turn. As he had with men, he should have been highlighting the experiences of women who were highly responsive in order to create sexual heroines. Their case histories, he could have argued, proved that women had the capacity for bountiful and robust sex lives. Highly sexed women, then, could have taken their place beside male sexual athletes (such as the outlet prodigious lawyer in the male volume) as role models to be admired and emulated. And in those areas where female performance fell below that of men, Kinsey could have fashioned a cultural explanation for their low rates. All he had to do was blame Victorian morality for any differences he discovered between the sexes.

As a political strategy, this would have worked. It had the additional advantage of fitting nicely into the cultural critique that Kinsey had long espoused. In 1948, though, it was far from clear whether Kinsey would jettison his private bias against women in favor of an inclusive ideology that would recognize the potential of females to become full-fledged participants in the sexual revolution he hoped to promote. It remained to be seen how or whether Kinsey would be able to resolve the tension between his misogyny and his life's mission.

Kinsey and Pomeroy did most of the interviewing for the female volume. The fact that no women were included among the interviewers for the male volume was not lost on female subjects. Announcing that she was "somewhat perturbed to learn that a large part of the investigation of women's sex life is being done by men," a woman from Pennsylvania declared, "I feel very strongly that this is a grave mistake. You will certainly not get a true picture of women's inner lives. Indeed, we have had far too many books written by men about women, laying down some law or other which is invalid." The woman went on to suggest that Kinsey hire female interviewers and "offer a large enough compensation to insure women's participation," demanding, "Is not the value of a woman's work in this field high?"[61] Kinsey's reply was reassuring. "We are anxious to expand our staff whenever we can find qualified persons and we will make the expansion irrespective as to whether the interviewers are male or female," he wrote.[62] In the end, Kinsey did attempt to train a few women as interviewers, but none worked out well. Consequently, he remained somewhat defensive on this score. "We do not feel that the sex of the interviewer in relation to the sex of the interviewee is of particular importance if you get the right interviewer," Kinsey wrote in 1956 to David Riesman, a famous sociologist at the University of Chicago (he later moved to Harvard). "We know several women who would have made excellent interviewers on our staff, two of whom we did attempt to train as interviewers," Kinsey continued. "We failed only because our interviewing has called for considerable travel and our demand that interviewers be happily married. It is much more difficult for a woman to stay happily married and travel away from home a good deal."[63] Friends, however, offered an additional explanation for the absence of female interviewers on the Institute's staff. One friend recalled, "[Kinsey] once complained to me, 'People say that we don't have women on the staff, and in the first place we do have some women. We don't use them as interviewers, because nobody likes women [interviewers]; men don't like them, and women don't like them.' "[64]

The absence of female interviewers did not stop women from cooperating. Indeed, despite the notoriety of the male volume, female volunteers lined up in droves to offer their histories. They volunteered for the same reasons as men. Many were curious about what the experience would be like, some had problems they hoped to find answers for during the interview, and others stepped forward because they held liberal attitudes on sex. Many cooperated, however, because they wished to support science and to expand the frontiers of human knowledge.

For the most part, the interviews with women proceeded in the same manner as those with men. Still, there were a few differences. Over time, Kinsey had come to believe that women had a greater tendency to cover up taboo behavior than men did, and he and his associates made adjustments to address this problem.[65] Moreover, questions asked early for men had to be deferred until later in the interview for women in order to give interviewers a chance to establish rapport. In addition, Kinsey and his associates often had to adapt their vocabularies in order to find the right words to put their female subjects at ease.[66] But again, apart from such minor adjustments, there were virtually no differences in the interviewing techniques.

In the summer of 1948, Martin started pulling together the statistical data on women, while Kinsey labored to broaden and deepen the research. In most respects, the questions Kinsey pursued were identical to those he had posed for men. From a behavioral standpoint, he wanted to learn what women did sexually, at what ages they started doing it, how often they did it, what they thought or fantasized about while they did it, and with whom or with what they did it. From a sociological perspective, he wished to explore how a number of variables (age, religion, education, etc.) influenced female sexual behavior. But there was one more thing. Kinsey meant to discover and to map the ways in which men and women were alike and different sexually.

In the past, Kinsey's need for power and control had driven him to conquer vast expanses of academic terrain. This time around, his quest for absolute dominion over his subject matter approached megalomania. Simply put, he meant to control the entire inventory of human knowledge on female sexual behavior. When he was preparing the male volume, he had made little effort to coordinate his data with other studies, largely because he had a low regard for the work of earlier sex researchers. With the female volume, by contrast, he was determined to correlate his findings with everything science had discovered about female sexuality.

From April 1 to July 1, 1950, Kinsey had his entire staff largely confined to the library perusing the literature and preparing material for the forthcoming volume.[67] No morsel of data escaped his notice; no study was too esoteric to excite his interest. Plumbing the depths of his energy reserves, he worked at a frantic pace, consulting with specialists in animal behavior, anthropology, biology, endocrinology, the fine arts, literature, medicine, physiology, psychiatry, psychology, and sociology. Yet Kinsey not only consulted these disciplines; he commanded them.

Kinsey started writing in summer 1951, and he continued to grind it out (with numerous interruptions) for the next year and half, against a fall 1953 publication date. Ever the perfectionist, he refused to settle for anything less than his best effort. Kinsey read passages out loud while he wrote, trying to decide whether the cadence and rhythm of his language was pleasing to the ear. He devoted even greater care to the clarity of his expression. Struggling to find the right words, he wrote and rewrote, polishing his prose until it captured his exact meaning.

The production of the female volume proceeded smoothly. Lloyd Potter repeated as the editor, and once again Kinsey left him relatively little to do. As before, the manuscript was extremely clean. Perhaps the biggest worry for all concerned was security. Just as happened with the male volume, there were a number of publishers waiting in the wings, poised to do knockoff books as soon as they could lay their hands on Kinsey's data. To guard against leaks, the staffs of the Institute and of Saunders imposed strict controls, limiting access to the manuscript to as few people as possible and drilling them with the need for tight security. Saunders also impressed the security issue on officials of Kingsport Press, Inc., of Kingsport,

Tennessee, the subcontractor that handled the actual printing. As it happened, Saunders had chosen well, for the Kingsport Press was led by a man who knew how to keep secrets. "Having had quite extensive experience during World War II as Commanding Officer in Charge of All Army printing and publishing, ranging from open to top-secret publications, I feel that I am competent to evaluate our procedures and controls on all restricted, confidential, and even secret publications," declared E. W. Palmer, the president of Kingsport Press.[68] Palmer then proceeded to lay out step-by-step an impressive list of measures his company was prepared to follow to guarantee security as the book went through production. The precautions worked. No security leaks occurred.

Taking aim at some of the most serious criticisms that had plagued the male volume, Kinsey worked hard to refine his numbers. To improve the sample, he removed prisoners and many lower-class subjects, and he cleaned up most of the minor statistical errors that had annoyed reviewers the first time. While these changes helped, it would be wrong to conclude that they constituted any sort of drastic revision. Decades later, Mosteller remarked, "He [Kinsey] did quite a lot often about things that were of very little consequence." Still, Mosteller made it clear that he was sympathetic, admitting, "The problems that Kinsey was up against are problems that everybody is still up against. If you don't have a way of drawing samples in systematic ways, it's very hard to make inferences to the population that you're pointing to."[69]

To protect his flanks, Kinsey again turned to experts for advice. Although the American Statistical Association's committee had offered a number of suggestions and recommendations, he had no intention of giving it everything it wanted. In spring 1952, Kinsey asked Mosteller to serve as a paid consultant to help decide which criticisms to address and which to ignore. Mosteller declined, pleading both a busy schedule and ethical concerns about the propriety of serving first as a judge and then as an adviser.[70] He did, however, recommend several statisticians to Kinsey, including Harold F. Dorn and Jerome Cornfield of the U.S. Public Health Service, both of whom subsequently agreed to serve.

By this time, Kinsey had become a seasoned veteran at managing statisticians. He established the ground rules at the outset. Preempting any discussion of random sampling, he informed Dorn, "Our sample, with all of its defects, has to be the basis for this volume and the material is being presented as the data on our sample without any attempt to calculate data for the total population." After stressing that their methods of calculation had been checked by other statisticians and were basically sound, Kinsey told Doran, "The chief problem will come in restricting our statements to make them a fair interpretation of what we have and do not have in our data."[71] From Dorn came the astute reply "I am not certain that this will eliminate all criticisms by statisticians and their kindred since statisticians have a long tradition of disagreeing with each other."[72] In September 1952, Dorn and Cornfield visited the Institute and spent several days going over the manuscript. Taking their marching orders from Kinsey, they focused on things he wanted done, limiting their suggestions to relatively minor problems that could be easily corrected. Pleased with the outcome, Kinsey responded, "It was exactly what we wanted and the book will be very much better for it."[73]

In addition to refining the numbers, Kinsey substantially increased the number of cases supporting the text, providing a firmer factual foundation for each cell of his data. He also broadened the empirical base by adding new sources. These entailed both "recorded" and "observed" data. The former consisted of thousands of works of art, while the latter included sexual calendars, correspondence, fiction, graffiti, and a number of clinical studies by gynecologists, obstetricians, neurologists, urologists, and the like, as well as data acquired through direct observation. Although he was careful to conceal it in the text, many of Kinsey's statements drew upon his personal observations of human sexual behavior (many of which were filmed), as well as his observations of the sexual behavior of lower mammals.

In its finished form, *Sexual Behavior in the Human Female* demonstrated once again Kinsey's talents as an alchemist: it was a potent blend of science and polemic. If anything, Kinsey spoke his mind more bluntly and directly in the female volume than in the male volume. Still, he employed fewer rhetorical devices and postures, though at times he did attempt to make his points by inference and indirection. Yet, even when he made a good-faith effort to be subtle or to avoid blanket statements and value judgments, Kinsey's views often suffused his prose. Simply put, he could not keep himself out of the text. As a secular evangelist, he had a gospel to proclaim, and he meant to preach it.

Like its predecessor, *Sexual Behavior in the Human Female* looked like a medical text. A tome with all the trappings of heavy-duty science, it had 179 tables and 155 figures in its 842 pages—38 pages more than the male volume. And like its predecessor, the book was divided into three sections, each with its own information to impart and distinct mission to accomplish.

"Part I: History and Method" consisted of three chapters. Although their ostensible purpose was to discuss the project's history and methodology, these chapters frequently revealed Kinsey's preoccupations and obsessions. Together, they show a man whose view of his critics had become more than faintly paranoid, whose self-image had become grandiose, and whose secular ministry had expanded to encompass the world. For decades, he had been a covert revolutionary, a man who had secretly rebelled against authority figures, chafed at social restraints on his private behavior, and bitterly denounced his culture's entire system of sexual control. All that had changed in 1953 was that Kinsey's private demons came dangerously close to howling in public.

Early in the first chapter, Kinsey launched an impassioned defense of his right to conduct research. Starting out low-key and unemotional, he recounted the history of the project and talked about science's need for information in areas where little or no reliable data existed. Then, his tone changed abruptly as he turned to what was really on his mind—the power of the state, as it threatened sex offenders as well as his research. Angered and frightened by the harsh laws that been passed under the shadow of McCarthyism, Kinsey declared, "We have recently seen poorly established distinctions between normality and abnormality lead to the enactment of sexual psychopath laws which are unrealistic, unenforceable, and incapable of providing the protection which the social organization has been led to believe they can provide."[74] His research promised to provide reliable data as a foundation for humane and realistic sex codes.

Kinsey refused to retreat an inch from his scientific materialism. He dismissed his critics on this score, charging that they had ignored "the material origins of all behavior."[75] Ignorant people had obstructed scientific progress for centuries, he explained, with moral philosophers opposing each discovery that had threatened their domain. "The works of Kepler, Copernicus, Galileo, and Pascal," Kinsey reminded his readers, "were in the list of condemned books some two or three centuries ago."[76] That the past was filled with knaves who had opposed scientific progress was, of course, well known. But that was not the point of this little history lesson. By putting his opponents in historical context, Kinsey meant to show that he deserved to be included in the pantheon of science's greatest heroes.

His duty was to testify, to bear witness to his faith in science and to his unshakable belief that the benighted souls who opposed it would never prevail. "There is an honesty in science which demands that the best means be used for the determination of truth," he preached. That the universe contained many kinds of truth Kinsey readily conceded. "But in regard to matter—the stuff of which both non-living materials and living organisms are made," he declared, ". . . [n]o theory, no philosophy, no body of theology, no political expediency, no wishful thinking, can provide a satisfactory substitute for the observation of material objects and of the way in which they behave."[77]

People had been led astray by leaders who in Kinsey's description sounded very much like the custodians of morality, the false prophets he had been battling for decades. Ridiculing the moralists, Kinsey sneered, "There are some who, finding the ocean an impediment to the pursuit of their designs, try to ignore its existence. If they are unable to ignore it because of its size, they try to legislate it out of existence, or try to dry it up with a sponge. They insist that the latter operation would be possible if enough sponges were available, and if enough persons would wield them." Those same moralists, charged Kinsey, had attacked him with a vengeance. Complaining bitterly of the vilification he had suffered, he wrote, "The scientist who observes and describes the reality is attacked as an enemy of the faith, and his acceptance of human limitations in modifying that reality is condemned as scientific materialism."[78]

The right of scientists to investigate, he explained, derived from academic freedom, a privilege that in turn was closely akin to freedom of speech. "Each of these privileges, however, carries with it an obligation," declared Kinsey, "an obligation, in the case of the scientist, to investigate honestly, to observe and to record without prejudice, to observe as adequately as human sense organs or the most modern instruments may allow, to observe persistently and sufficiently in order that there may be an ultimate understanding of the basic nature of the matter which is involved." Since science obtained its right to investigate from the citizens at large, every scientist was "under obligation to make his findings available to all who can utilize the data." Sex researchers had an even more binding social compact with the public. "The scientist who investigates sexual behavior," Kinsey averred, "seems under especial obligation to make his findings available to the maximum number of persons, for there are few aspects of human biology with which more persons are more often concerned."[79]

By 1953, then, Kinsey had fashioned his own convenant with the people. Just as Martin Luther and John Calvin had proclaimed the Protestant Reformation to anoint every man his own priest, Kinsey had come to proclaim a secular revolution that would wrest control of intimate affairs from religion and make people everywhere the priests of their own private parts. Again, the grandiosity of Kinsey's mission was apparent, but there was something else at work here, too. Politically, Kinsey had undergone a transformation. Ironically, the man who was such an elitist in many areas of his life had come to regard the redeeming power of science in very democratic terms.

To foment a sexual revolution, Kinsey needed to spread the gospel far and wide. Many critics of the male volume, however, had denounced the publicity it had received, decrying its wide distribution to the public. Counterattacking with a vengeance, Kinsey proclaimed his contempt for those who would restrict sexual knowledge "to a limited number of professionally trained persons, to physicians, to priests, or to those who can read Latin." These false priests had failed to serve "the millions of boys and girls, men and women who need such knowledge to guide them in their everyday affairs."[80]

Thus, by 1953, Kinsey had come to believe that only a global pulpit could provide enough scope to accomplish his mission. No longer content to limit his ministry to the United States, he pointed with pride to the fact that the male volume "was taken out of the hands of those who claimed the exclusive right to knowledge in this area and made a part of the thinking of millions of persons, not only in this country but in countries spread all over the world." Given this vast need, Kinsey felt obligated to spread the gospel "to all who can read and understand and utilize our data."[81]

Any doubts about which groups most concerned Kinsey vanished at the end of the chapter. Pausing again to revisit the current hysteria over sexual psychopaths, he mustered an impressive array of arguments to show that the number of sex crimes had not risen in recent years. Bolder yet was his bald assertion that the current sex laws were "out of accord with the realities of human behavior" and attempted "too much in the way of social control." Predictably, Kinsey used the plight of homosexuals to illustrate his point. The current sex offender codes, he argued, inflicted far more harm on society than homosexual behavior. Indeed, all that these laws really accomplished was to victimize homosexuals in countless ways. "Somehow, in an age which calls itself scientific and Christian," he scolded, "we should be able to discover more intelligent ways of protecting social interests without doing such irreparable damage to so many individuals and to the total social organization to which they belong."[82]

Kinsey devoted the second chapter to answering his statistical critics. His irritation at his detractors was transparent. Making short work of probability sampling, he insisted that it could never be used in sex research, because too many people would refuse to be interviewed. In place of probability sampling, Kinsey defended group sampling as the only feasible approach. Whereas individuals frequently refused to be interviewed, the members of various clubs, organizations, and associations, he explained, could usually be persuaded to cooperate as a group activity.[83]

Next, he delivered a discursive discourse on his statistical methods. With Kinsey as their teacher, readers learned about accumulative incidence, active incidence, frequency classes, active median frequency, median frequency, mean frequency, active mean frequency, total mean frequency, standard error, percentage of total outlet, and the like. Kinsey also discussed the statistical changes he had made, such as dropping any and all references in the female volume to the statistical calculation known as coefficient of correlation and abandoning the use of U.S. correlations (employing census data to assign national weights to his sample groups).[84] This last point was critical. To satisfy his critics, Kinsey knew, he had to concede that his generalizations pertained only to his samples and should not be applied to the nation as a whole. In the male volume, Kinsey had repeatedly denied any intention of trying to influence social policy. In the female volume, by contrast, he abandoned this fiction, admitting that his purpose was not merely to present the facts but to explore their social consequences. His research, he acknowledged, had been motivated by a strong desire to help society manage sexual matters in a more rational manner, particularly with regard to young people, married couples, and sex offenders. But in order to exert the influence he craved, Kinsey recognized, the public would have to accept his data. Consequently, despite his disclaimers about his data not being representative, he told his readers at the close of the first chapter that "the samples of high school, college, and post-graduate groups are of some size, and the generalizations drawn for the sample may not be too far from the actuality for those segments of the American population."[85] Since the samples mentioned were the only ones in the book, this was an indirect way of saying that every generalization was representative. Still, which Kinsey was the public to believe: the one who cautioned that his data were not representative or the one who winked and said they were?

In "Part II: Types of Sexual Activity among Females," Kinsey devoted ten chapters to the preadolescent and adolescent sexual development of females and the various sexual outlets they employed. Dreaded by some and eagerly awaited by many, this was the material that revealed the actual sexual behavior of women and the similarities and contrasts between male and female behavior.

Kinsey opened with a discussion of childhood and adolescent female sexual development. As always his goal was to show that sexual activity was socially beneficial and sexual abstinence socially harmful. Females, he reported, displayed the ability to respond to sexual stimuli early in life, in some cases at three months. Approvingly, he related accounts of infants masturbating and children playing sex games ("momma and poppa," "doctor," etc.), arguing that the only harm that resulted when girls explored their sexuality came from guilt feelings, not from their behavior.[86] His message, of course, was that children found their childhood sexual experiences traumatic not because of what they did but because of the heavy load of guilt they suffered.

Then Kinsey abruptly veered off into a discussion of adult-child contacts, and his remarks again made it clear that he was terribly agitated by the current sex crimes panic. His focus was not at all on little girls, but on the misunderstood and much maligned adult males who abused them. Hoping to counter the public's image of pedophiles as predatory monsters, he attempted to put child molesters in a benign light. Blaming the victims, Kinsey reported that in many incest situations children often initiated additional contacts after the first incident, and he noted that sexual contacts between children and adults who were not family members "often involved considerable affection." Kinsey also observed that "some of the older females in the sample felt that their pre-adolescent experience [with adults] had contributed favorably to their later socio-sexual development."[87] And while he admitted that "some 80 percent of the children had been emotionally upset or frightened by their contacts with adults," he likened the level of their fright to how youngsters typically reacted to "insects, spiders, or other objects against which they have been adversely conditioned."

To Kinsey's mind, the conclusion was obvious. "If a child were not culturally conditioned," he observed, "it is doubtful if it would be disturbed by sexual approaches of the sort which had usually been involved in these histories." Characteristically, Kinsey scolded the public for failing to distinguish between sexual contacts that caused harm and those that caused no harm. His definition of harm in young girls, however, was narrow enough to exclude "a very few cases of vaginal bleeding," which, he insisted, "did not appear to do any appreciable damage."[88]

Next, Kinsey examined in separate chapters the six sexual outlets in women. As they had in men, his data pointed to a wide gap between the conduct society expected of women and how they actually behaved. According to Kinsey, 62 percent of the women in his sample had masturbated; 66 percent had had nocturnal sex dreams; 90 percent had petted; nearly 50 percent had had premarital intercourse; 26 percent had had extramarital intercourse; 13 percent had had at least one homosexual contact that resulted in an orgasm; and 3.6 percent had had at least one sexual contact with a lower animal.[89]

These figures were bound to produce an uproar among social conservatives. Yet in many respects, these revelations contained few surprises, and compared with his data on men those surprises were ones of degree rather than kind. People familiar with the male volume had come to understand that there was a gap between the prescribed and the actual sexual behavior of men. Putting aside hope or hypocrisy, there was no reason not to expect similar revelations for women. By filling in the numbers, Kinsey, of course, had provided the particulars, and many Americans were indeed shocked to learn the exact percentages by which women fell short of absolute purity.

But overall, Kinsey's figures merely reinforced what people had been told all along. For in virtually every category of behavior, his data showed that women were less sexually active than men. Women had fewer orgasms from all sources than men, and they had fewer sexual partners for life. In short, while Kinsey's data made some people fear that the country had undergone a sexual revolution of massive proportions, *Sexual Behavior in the Human Female* nevertheless documented that women were less sexually active than men. In that sense, the book was at once disappointing and reassuring in its failure to shock.

Had Kinsey done nothing more than report these data, his claim to fame would have been assured. But he had not seized the national stage merely to publish the bare facts. Despite the brickbats that had been hurled at him for interpreting his data in the male volume, he used the female volume to advance arguments that denounced traditional morality and pointed to the need for sexual reforms.

To minimize negative responses, Kinsey tucked many of his most controversial ideas into the background materials that preceded his discussions of sexual outlets. As he had in the male volume, he advanced the argument *de animalibus* with relish and determination. Many of the "outlet" chapters opened with discussions of the mammalian origins of the behavior in question, and in each instance Kinsey gave numerous examples of animals that exhibited the same behavior as people. After listing a variety of animals that formed couples, for example, Kinsey observed in the chapter on extramarital sex, "Both the females and the males in these mammalian mateships are quite ready to accept coitus with individuals who are not their established mates. . . ." So that no one would miss the connection, Kinsey added, "There are obvious parallels between the situation in these other mammalian families, and the course of marital infidelity in the human species. Not all of the human problems are cultural developments or the product of particular social philosophies."[90]

Kinsey went so far as to suggest a similar link with emotions. Referring to the human male, he noted that "his jealousies so closely parallel those of the lower species that one is forced to conclude that his mammalian heritage may be partly responsible for his attitudes."[91] The point of all this emphasis on the mammalian origins of human behavior, of course, was to persuade people to embrace their biological heritage. When human beings aped it up, he believed, they were being true to their nature.

Many of the "outlet" chapters also included sections on "anthropologic data." Roaming across continents and centuries, Kinsey gave numerous examples of societies that had dealt with premarital and extramarital sex with tolerance and, in some instances, with approval. By administering a strong dose of cultural relativism, he meant to expose the sexual mores and laws of the United States as provincial, restrictive, and harsh. Nor was he above putting his views into the mouths of foreigners. Following a long and pained discussion of the legal prohibitions against premarital sex, he observed, "There is no aspect of American sex law which surprises visitors from other countries as much as this legal attempt to penalize pre-marital activity to which both of the participating parties have consented and in which no force has been involved." Pushing the point, he added that "there is practically no other culture, anywhere in the world, in which all non-marital coitus, even between adults, is considered criminal."[92]

Building on these phylogenetic and anthropological arguments, Kinsey employed his own data to attack sexual restraints. While sexual freedom was unquestionably his goal, he presented himself as a defender of marriage. Premarital sexual outlets were socially beneficial, he argued, because his data showed that women who had them made better adjustments in marriage than their abstinent sisters. Few revelations in the book would prove to be as controversial. Tactically speaking, Kinsey was wise to make marriage the centerpiece of his argument. This allowed him to cloak his revolutionary goals in very traditional garb. By repeatedly stressing how premarital sexual experiences could improve marital sex, he appeared as a responsible scientist who wished to preserve society's most important social institution.

Starting from the proposition that a good sex life was important to happy marriages, Kinsey argued that the failure of many women to have orgasms when they were single often hampered their sex lives after marriage. Conversely, women who made the best sexual adjustments in marriage were the ones who had started exploring their sexuality at an early age. To Kinsey, then, it was clear that the ability to respond to sexual stimuli was learned behavior. Far from being innate, it depended on experience. Moreover, because the ability to reach orgasm seemed to derive from practice, Kinsey thought that the trial and error should begin early in life. As he told his readers, "such learning is most effective in the early years, when inhibitions have not yet developed or have not yet become too firmly fixed." Driving home his point, he declared, "Early orgasmic experience may, therefore, contribute directly to the sexual effectiveness of a marriage."[93]

But what of those women who fulfilled the cultural prescription for purity and practiced abstinence when they were single? These poor souls had a hard time developing a satisfactory sex life after marriage. According to Kinsey, they were one-third as likely to achieve an orgasm in marriage as their sisters who had masturbated, petted, or copulated to orgasm prior to marriage. The conclusion was unmistakable: sexual abstinence harmed women and, by extension, the institution of marriage, putting the lie to the notion that virtue was its own reward. "When there are long years of abstinence and restraint, and an avoidance of physical contacts and emotional responses before marriage," warned Kinsey, "acquired inhibitions may do such damage to the capacity to respond that it may take some years to get rid of them after marriage, if indeed they are ever dissipated."[94]

Kinsey scoffed at the idea that premarital sex left women guilt ridden and remorseful. "As a matter of fact," he noted, "some 69 per cent of the still unmarried females in the sample who had had coitus insisted that they did not regret their experience." Kinsey also reported that "some 77 percent of the married females, looking back from the vantage point of their mature experience, saw no reason to regret their pre-marital coitus." Unable to conceal his glee over destroying an argument that moral blackmailers had used for centuries to pressure women into sexual abstinence, he gloated, "These figures differ considerably from those usually presented in public discussions of such pre-marital activity. They illustrate the difference between wishful thinking and scientifically accumulated data."[95]

With astonishing boldness, Kinsey found much to commend in extramarital sex. After noting that it was both more common and more often tolerated in men than in women, he mustered the usual phylogenetic and anthropological arguments to show that women, too, needed sexual variety. Then he discussed the social reasons why women had affairs. Many women took lovers to relieve sexual boredom and fatigue; others, to accommodate valued friends. More than a few did so to retaliate against a spouse who had cheated on them and yet others to assert personal independence, either from a spouse or the social code.[96] In keeping with his low opinion of the female libido, however, Kinsey had virtually nothing to say about passion.

Although he acknowledged that adultery often caused friction and not infrequently led to divorce, Kinsey made it clear that such disturbances were far from inevitable. His data included "cases of extra-marital relationships which do not seem to get into difficulties." In some instances the "sexual adjustments with the spouse had improved as a result of the female's extra-marital experience." But adultery was not for the fainthearted or for those easily intimidated by social mores. Rather, it could be handled successfully only by those who were capable of overriding social mores with will power, people who sounded suspiciously like Kinsey and his inner circle. "There are strong-minded and determined individuals who can plan and control their extra-marital relationships in such a way that they avoid possible ill consequences," revealed Kinsey. "In such a case, however, the strong-minded spouse has to keep his or her activity from becoming known to the other spouse, unless the other spouse is equally strong-minded and willing to accept the extra-marital activity."[97]

Kinsey also reported cases of husbands encouraging their wives to have extramarital sex. His explanations for why husbands would do so were among the most deeply autobiographical passages in the female volume.

"In some instances it represented a deliberate effort to extend the wife's opportunity to find satisfaction in sex relations," he explained. "In not a few instances the husband's attitude had originated in his desire to find an excuse for his own extra-marital activity," he continued, noting that this was usually true of couples who practiced "wife swapping." In other cases, "the husband had encouraged extra-marital relations in order to secure the opportunity for the sort of group activity in which he desired to participate" for, as Kinsey could likely testify, "sometimes his interest in group participation involved a homosexual element which was satisfied by seeing another male in sexual action, or which he, on occasion, had satisfied by extending his contacts to the male who was having coitus with his wife."[98] Certainly, there were several men close to Kinsey and to Clara who could confirm the accuracy of this observation.

In "Part III: Comparisons of Female and Male," Kinsey devoted five chapters to the biological and cultural differences between the sexes. This was the section of the book where he revealed most clearly his gloomy assessment of the sexual compatibility of men and women. In general, Kinsey made it clear that he believed women were less sexually responsive than men. They had fewer orgasms before marriage, he noted, and they had fewer orgasms after marriage. Kinsey also stressed that, in contrast to that of men, the sexual behavior of women did not seem to be affected much by social variables such as class, education, and geographic backgrounds, though he did stress that religion exercised a powerful inhibiting influence on women, just as on men. The more devoutly religious a woman, the more likely she was to experience difficulties with her sex life, both before and after marriage.

Kinsey also reported that many women who were not inhibited by religion often had difficulty forming satisfactory long-term sexual relationships. The internal clocks of men and women, he revealed, had different settings. Whereas men reached their sexual peak in their late teens and then gradually went downhill for the rest of their lives, women peaked in their late twenties and early thirties, maintaining this plateau into their fifties and sixties, at which point they, too, faded from the sexual picture.[99] Thus, the sexual drives of men and women seemed doomed by nature to wax and wane on different schedules. Equally troubling was the fact that even when most women were at their sexual peaks, they wanted sex less frequently than their husbands. The implication was clear: from a sexual standpoint, men and women were badly mismatched.

Kinsey's assessment of female sexuality became more positive when he discussed the female orgasm. Having enshrined the orgasm as the centerpiece of his work in the male volume, it was only natural that he should do the same in the female volume. But there was a problem. While the overwhelming majority of men both had orgasms and concluded most sexual acts with orgasms, the same did not hold for women. A small minority of women went their entire lives without experiencing a single orgasm, and relatively large numbers of women did not have orgasms every time they had intercourse or engaged in other forms of sexual behavior. Nor was the intensity of their orgasms at all comparable. For some women the sensation was extremely mild, while other women had orgasms strong enough to make them faint, with most women falling somewhere between these poles.

Kinsey's task was complicated by the fact that scientists were embroiled in heated debate on the clitoral versus the vaginal orgasm. Many (if not most) Freudian psychologists of the day took a doctrinaire stand on the subject. Dismissing sexual climaxes achieved through clitoral stimulation as juvenile and immature, they insisted that the only "mature" orgasm was a vaginal orgasm. Kinsey begged to differ. What he had learned from thousands of case histories led him to believe that vaginal orgasms were all but impossible from a physical standpoint. The overwhelming majority of women he had interviewed reported that the vagina had little, if any, feeling. They further reported that the clitoris, by contrast, was richly innervated and served as the primary locus of sexual stimulation.

Of course, Kinsey could have published his data and let it go at that, but that would have been contrary to his nature. Instead, he worked to supplement his case histories with every scrap of data he could locate. First, he consulted a number of physicians who were working on the basic physiology of sexual response and orgasm. Over a period of several years, he carried on lengthy and highly technical correspondences with physicians who had conducted (among other things) histological studies of vaginal tissues; studies of the effects of the stimulation of end organs of touch in genital and perineal areas; studies of the nerves that connect those end organs with lower portions of the spinal cord; studies of the role of hormones; studies of the distribution of nerves adjacent to the urethra; studies of the distribution of nerves into the cortex; and studies of the number and distribution of nerve endings in the labia major, labia minor, clitoris, vulva, vagina, and cervix of the human female. In addition, he consulted with a number of gynecologists, hoping their data from pelvic examinations might shed light on the issue. In each instance, Kinsey asked whether their data were based on clinical histories or direct observations. When only a few gynecologists claimed to have data based on the latter, Kinsey's response was predictable.

To secure the appropriate data, Kinsey persuaded five gynecologists to conduct sensitivity tests of the clitoris and other parts of the genitalia of approximately nine hundred females. (Naturally, he volunteered Clara and several other senior staff wives for one of these studies.) The results were enlightening. Fully 98 percent of the women could feel tactile stimulation of the clitoris (albeit with varying degrees of sensitivity), while only 14 percent had any touch sensation whatsoever in the vagina. To supplement these findings, Kinsey utilized data on female masturbation. Once again he made an interesting discovery. Instead of focusing on the vagina when they masturbated, the overwhelming majority of women relied upon labial and clitoral stimulation.[100] These data confirmed what the gynecologists had discovered by inserting various items into the vagina: for all but a small minority of women the vaginal tube was virtually a dead cavity.

On the basis of exhaustive research and an analysis of all available data, Kinsey concluded that the vaginal orgasm was an anatomical impossibility. Responding to a physician who had inquired whether clitoral stimulation deprived the vagina of sensation, Kinsey wrote in 1950, "There are apparently no nerves in the vagina except right at the anterior wall, right at the opening, and there is no way by which non-existent sensation can be robbed from the vagina."[101] Writing in the female volume a few years later, Kinsey unloaded on the psychoanalysts. After recounting their prescriptive position on the vaginal versus clitoral orgasm, Kinsey bluntly declared, "It is difficult, however, in the light of our present understanding of the anatomy and physiology of sexual response, to understand what can be meant by a 'vaginal orgasm.' "[102]

Interestingly, Kinsey had evidence that appeared to moderate his conclusions about women's sexual natures. One of his most interesting discoveries was that the decade of birth had an important bearing on behavior. Compared with women who had been born in the late nineteenth century, women who had been born after 1900 and who had grown to maturity in the 1920s (and in the decades that followed) had more orgasms from a variety of premarital sexual activities (petting, masturbation, coitus, etc.) and had more orgasms in marital coitus. The meaning of these data, insisted Kinsey, was obvious: the double standard of morality had faded significantly.[103] In effect, the United States had undergone a sexual revolution, albeit of modest proportions. Still, even though a larger percentage of women were having premarital sex, in most instances they had only one or two partners, one of whom they subsequently married.

Kinsey did not advance a cultural explanation for changes in female behavior. Ironically, the man whose life bore witness to the influence of culture on human sexuality looked to nature rather than to nurture to explain sexual differences. Ignoring the strong emphasis he had placed on socialization in many of his earlier chapters, Kinsey sounded like a hidebound biologist when he sought to explain the modest changes that occurred in sexual behavior in females born after the turn of the century.

Indeed, the book's final chapters revealed that Kinsey's thinking remained firmly grounded in biology. Patiently and thoroughly, he sorted out the issues, drew associations, and stipulated what science knew and did not know. His mastery of the scholarship on these topics was total, and he supplemented it at every turn with his own data. While he could not say so, in many instances his data included knowledge based upon direct observation. In fact, there can be little doubt that Kinsey had observed more sexual behavior, both in humans and in lower animals, than any other scientist in history. Still, however impressive intellectually, the concluding chapters of *Sexual Behavior in the Human Female* were largely bereft of answers. In the end, Kinsey could not explain why men and women differed in their sexual behavior, and he was extremely tentative about advancing any theories. The book closed on an anticlimatic note, exposing the same theoretical limitations that ultimately had brought Kinsey to a dead end in taxonomy.

Not that he was troubled by his failure to theorize. On the contrary, Kinsey undoubtedly saw his silence as a virtue. In the face of so much uncertainty, restraint seemed the only prudent posture. Nevertheless, had he been less ambivalent about women, he would probably have fashioned a cultural/behavioral argument to explain many of the differences he posited between the sexes. All the ingredients were at his fingertips; he simply elected not to assemble them.

Yet, for all its limitations, *Sexual Behavior in the Human Female* remains an astonishingly provocative and singularly personal work. It reveals in stark relief the scientific philosophy and methodology; the private passions, values, and prejudices; the social agenda; and, above all, the inner conflicts of its author.

As he entered the final stage of the book's preparation, Kinsey devoted a lot of thought to the question of who should write the preface. To him it was a political issue pure and simple, a matter of whose imprimatur would give the book the greatest boost and the most protection. Since an official of the Rockefeller Foundation was not an option, Kinsey decided on George W. Corner, who in Gebhard's words was "an enormously prestigious and impeccable name in science."[104] Kinsey, of course, hoped not only to bask in Corner's reputation but to associate the research with the NRC, whose protective mantle he regarded as a defense against hostile critics.[105]

Once again, however, Kinsey managed to turn a preface into a controversy. Remembering how hurt and disappointed Yerkes had been over being slighted the first time around, Corner declined and recommended Yerkes for the honor.[106] After giving the matter some thought, Kinsey proposed a compromise whereby Corner and Yerkes would coauthor the preface.[107] They consented, though at Corner's suggestion the two old friends agreed privately that Yerkes would do the writing.[108]

Yerkes took the assignment very seriously.[109] Despite his advanced age (he was into his eighties) and failing health, he made a special trip to Bloomington in September 1952 to bring himself up to date on the research. During his four-day visit, Yerkes read the manuscript and toured Kinsey's new quarters, spending several hours in the library. "It is an impressive, unostentatious place, which looks and feels like business all the time," Yerkes wrote in his diary. "Enlightenment, as well as information gathering, enriches the hours here."[110] Naturally, Kinsey made certain that the administration showed the colors. Commenting on his audience with President Wells, Yerkes observed, "Evidently, he has large faith in K., in what he is doing, and extraordinary courage, assurance, firmness, tact and resourcefulness in dealing with problems which threaten to become disruptive."[111]

After returning home to New Haven, Yerkes stewed for weeks. Few men have worked harder to find the right words to do a book proud. Before putting pen to paper, he even made a special trip to New York to seek Gregg's advice on what points to make, a conference that Yerkes noted in his diary resulted in "some excellent suggestions for the preface."[112] Nevertheless, Yerkes agonized for weeks trying to get something on paper. He would write, show drafts to family members and friends, and then rewrite again and again.[113] Not even this earnest effort was good enough for Kinsey. Sadly, when Yerkes sent him a draft for comment, Kinsey reacted coolly and Yerkes wound up getting his feelings hurt.[114] While the final version of the preface was more to Kinsey's liking, his perfectionism and his insensitivity to the feelings of others turned what should have been an honor for Yerkes into an ordeal.

With the preface out of the way, all that remained was for Kinsey to manage the press. As before, his goals were clear: he wanted to ensure accuracy, to put a favorable spin on the first wave of articles, and to orchestrate a publicity coup of massive proportions. Put more directly, he meant to manipulate and to control the press. His plan was to repeat on a large scale for the female volume what he had done so successfully on a small scale for the male volume, but with a few key refinements. In the summer and fall of 1947, he had met with a handful of reporters and had fed them material for articles to be released roughly a month before the male volume was published. While few in number, these articles, which had appeared in November and December 1947, had not only whetted the public's interest but set the tone for the rush of articles that followed the book's publication in early January 1948. This time around, by contrast, Kinsey, planned to hold prepublication briefings for scores of reporters, with correspondingly grander results.

Once again, Kinsey invited journalists to the Institute to read the manuscript under careful supervision. And once again he had them sign contracts agreeing to submit copies of their stories to him prior to publication for correction of factual errors. As before, Kinsey made them promise to hold their stories until an agreed-upon date, which he set at August 20, 1953—roughly a month before the book's release date. Finally, Kinsey restricted each journalist to a single publication not to exceed 5,000 words in length.[115]

By spring 1953, more than 150 journalists, some from as far away as Great Britain, Denmark, and Australia, had contacted the Institute. Because he had neither the time nor the space to accommodate everyone who inquired, Kinsey handpicked fifty or sixty journalists. These lucky souls received invitations to Bloomington, where Kinsey set aside three separate blocks of time for prepublication briefings and manuscript readings. Beginning near the end of May, journalists descended on Bloomington, filled up the local hotels, and alighted on the Institute's doorsteps. In addition to many of the nation's leading newspapers, most of the nation's best-known magazines (and virtually all of the women's magazines) sent representatives, including many of the top feature-story writers in the United States.[116]

Kinsey personally took charge of the press. This was not a good decision, because he was near exhaustion. Upon meeting Kinsey face-to-face, many of the writers grew concerned about his health. One reporter described him as looking "haggard, bleary-eyed."[117] Another noted that there was "something dogged and very tired about his face," adding, "One suspects that he has been angered, even embittered to some extent, by attacks upon his work, by attempts to discredit and question its reliability or to infer that there is something immoral about the very idea of making such a study."[118]

Though on the verge of collapsing, Kinsey summoned his energy and administered "the treatment." During the four days each group spent at the Institute (the workday began at 9:00 A.M. and ended at 5:00 P.M.), he delivered a four-hour briefing, answered questions, and gave brief tours of the Institute. In addition, he explained why he was placing so much emphasis on keeping what they heard and read under wraps until the anointed hour. According to the reporter for *Time*, Kinsey claimed he knew "of five other books trying to beat his to the bookstalls; one had been in type for months, with blanks to be filled in with Kinsey's figures as soon as they could be obtained."[119] To some reporters, the experience seemed surreal. "There was an Alice in Wonderland quality about the whole thing," recalled a writer for *Cosmopolitan*. "In the memory of the oldest reporter, there'd never been anything like this."[120] Other members of the press agreed that Kinsey's concern seemed excessive, not to say paranoid. A reporter for the International News Service remembered Kinsey's saying, "Take these proofs back to your hotel room and read them. But when you leave your room, be sure to put the proofs in your suitcase and lock it, and then lock the room door."[121]

As the last group departed Bloomington, it looked as though Kinsey's efforts to control the press would succeed. The reporters, their eyes sore from reading and their ears ringing with his admonitions, returned to their publications firm believers in his integrity. Over the weeks that followed, they abided by the rules and dutifully submitted their pieces to the Institute for corrections. (In the case of the Associated Press, it was acknowledged that the changes included "one or two amplifications").[122] Nor did they jump the gun on publication, assuring that all the articles would appear at the same time and would produce both a publicity bonanza and a financial gold mine—precisely as Kinsey had planned. "We were aware that if we did synchronize the press releases that this would attract more attention to the volume and would promote sales," Gebhard acknowledged many years later.[123] "We knew what was happening, and there we did attempt to sort of manipulate the press."[124]

Months before the book's release date, Kinsey boldly predicted a winner, repeating the message again and again, as though trying to convince himself. In February 1953, he assured Corner that the female volume would be much better than the male volume.[125] The following month, he delivered the identical message to Morison.[126] June found him telling Fernandus Payne, his old department chairman, that the staff was satisfied with the female volume, even though it was bound to provoke controversy.[127] And in July, he wrote Wells an upbeat note expressing confidence that the scholarship in the female volume was so strong that it would be sure to satisfy critics in Indianapolis who had questioned the Institute's value to the university.[128]

A few days before the newspaper and magazine articles came out, an Indianapolis reporter quipped, "You can either smile and nervously change the subject after calling a woman unfaithful, or you can get out of town." Kinsey and his entire staff, the reporter noted, had decided to take a trip. They would be out of town and incommunicado for approximately three weeks, enough time, perhaps, to let things calm down and allow cooler heads to prevail. Not that Kinsey admitted the trip was a dodge. Instead, he curtly announced, "We've given as much time to the press as we intend to for the time being," and then added quickly that "the press has been very nice." But the Hoosier reporter recognized a disappearing act when he saw one. "Operation Fade-Out," he observed shrewdly, was scheduled to commence about "three days before *Sexual Behavior in The Human Female* hits the stands and 90,000,000 women hit the roof."[129]

This prediction did not seem far-fetched. Everyone connected with Kinsey's research anticipated a major cultural earthquake, with the campus of Indiana University as its epicenter. Kinsey, too, expected a huge response. In fact, he was counting on it. Five years had passed since the publication of the male volume, and he was eager to reclaim the national spotlight. And while everyone was certain that the publication of *Sexual Behavior in the Human Female* would return Kinsey to national prominence, no one knew how the book would be received. The prophet of sexual liberation had spoken, but would the people listen? On the eve of "K-Day" (as the press took to calling August 20, 1953), all that seemed clear was that the biggest ballyhoo in the history of American publishing up to then was about to begin.

"DAMN THAT RUSK"

-Day was a publicity agent's dream. On Thursday, August 20, 1953, at 6:30 A.M. (central standard time), the news media unveiled what *Cosmopolitan* magazine called "the most feverishly awaited, most wildly speculated on, most sensationally publicized book in history."[1] As a news story, *Sexual Behavior in the Human Female* far outstripped the male volume. The Associated Press asserted flatly that it was "the biggest news prominence ever to greet a new book."[2] Delighted by all the attention, a friend predicted to Kinsey, "This advance publicity will guarantee you a sale of at least a half million copies, I am sure."[3] The actual figures would not approach this estimation.

For a moment in history, *Sexual Behavior in the Human Female* dominated the news. Many big-city newspapers reported the story in eight-column front-page headlines, where it vied for space with the other major news event that day, the Soviet Union's explosion of its first H-bomb (in many newspapers the Kinsey headlines were bigger). Five national magazines hit the newsstands in the same week with feature-length articles on the book, replete with lavish photographic layouts of Kinsey, his family, and staff. Declaring that 1953 would go down in history "as the year of the great Kinsey hullabaloo," the *New Republic* reported that some magazines had "actually changed their time of printing so that their September issues could conform to this deadline."[4] By November, Kinsey was so familiar to Americans that *U.S. News & World Report* would describe him as "the most widely noticed man in the United States at the moment, next to President Eisenhower."[5] By December, the *New York Times* would proclaim *Sexual Behavior in the Human Female* "the most widely discussed book of the year."[6] The only parallel the press could recall was the media frenzy that had marked the coronation of Queen Elizabeth II in 1952.

Kinsey's crowning moment came on August 24, 1953, when his face appeared on the cover of *Time* magazine. A flattering likeness by the artist Artzybasheff, the portrait was suffused with symbols. Birds fluttered overhead; a solitary bee hovered above beautiful pink roses with sharp thorns; and a somber-faced Kinsey, wearing a bow tie (imprinted with the mirror of Venus, the symbol for the female), peered resolutely out into space. Appropriately, his lips were tightly sealed and his eyes looked faintly sad, like a man who had seen too much.

Time's coverage of *Sexual Behavior in the Human Female* included a generally flattering biographical sketch that developed in full the official Kinsey canon. It was a saga of struggle and triumph. Americans learned of his bouts with ill health in Hoboken, his rebirth when he discovered the outdoors and academic achievement in South Orange, his undergraduate years at Bowdoin, his emergence as a scientist at Harvard, his two decades of prodigious research on gall wasps, and the story of how student questions he could not answer had turned him to sex research. Yet not everything was as Kinsey would have written it. On the darker side, readers learned about a man who could be "impatient and cutting," a man whose "attacks on scientists in other fields border on arrogance." Kinsey was an "insomniac," a man who "does not know how to relax." *Time* also raised questions about his health. Noting that Kinsey had subjected himself "to tremendous strain" over the summer "by personally handling his elaborate press relations," *Time* reported ominously, "his heart has begun to protest and doctors have warned him that he must rest."[7]

Kinsey's handling of the press become something of a news story itself. Many journalists who had not made the pilgrimage to Bloomington thought that Kinsey had hired a slick agent to manage the press. One businessman even wrote to the Institute requesting the agent's name.[8] Kinsey, of course, had a self-serving reply ready and waiting. "We did not employ any publicity or public relations organization, and our relations with the press were confined entirely to holding down their treatment of any material that they saw prior to publication," he wrote one inquirer. Sounding more than a little self-righteous, Kinsey declared, "We never asked for publicity and did nothing to encourage it." The press gave the story a lot of play, he explained, "because the subject matter concerned all human females and males and because we had accumulated, in the course of 15 years, data which had not been available from other sources."[9]

Journalists openly marveled that a Hoosier professor had pulled off such a publicity coup. "It was a press agent's dream of a journalistic mountain going to an author Mohammed," declared *Look* magazine.[10] *U.S. News & World Report* concurred, insisting that the publicity buildup for *Sexual Behavior in the Human Female* "would have done justice to P. T. Barnum."[11] *Time* complimented Kinsey for handling the advance publicity "with results a professional press agent might envy,"[12] while the *Saturday Review of Literature* quipped that Kinsey could "teach the flacks of Madison Avenue and the drumbeaters of Hollywood a few things about their own trade."[13] The *New York Times* also reported, in a mildly disapproving tone, that Kinsey "had a keen sense of publicity."[14] Yet astute observers understood that Kinsey's adroit management of the press was only partly responsible for launching the book. With its usual haughty air, the *The New Yorker* attributed the book's meteoric rise "to skillful public relations and a rather touching manifestation of national prurience."[15]

Where the press posited prurience, Kinsey saw urgent social need. He had always believed that the public both wanted and supported his work, and the evidence supported his opinion. A poll on Kinsey's research by George Gallup's American Institute of Public Opinion revealed that Americans by a ratio of nearly three to one (compared with five to one for the male volume) believed that it was "a good thing, rather than a bad thing, to have this information available." Even among women, a majority approved "of making available the information on female sex habits."[16] That view, of course, was shared by many professional groups who thought that Kinsey's data would be useful. Like the male volume, the female volume drew support (as well as opposition) from physicians, psychologists, sociologists, marriage counselors, birth control workers, ministers, lawyers, and penal officials, among others.

Kinsey's mail brought daily reminders of his support among rank-and-file Americans. Granted, he received some negative feedback, typical of which was the blast from a Virginia woman who wrote, "All my women & men friends, and I, think you're full of *Bull shit,* and I hope you rot in hell, which we figure you will in due time. You're just a frustrated old codger, who doesn't even know which 'end' is up."[17]

Yet only a tiny percentage of Kinsey's mail was critical. Women from across the country wrote to thank him personally for *Sexual Behavior in the Human Female.* A California woman, who described herself as "a grandmother of eight children, mother of four, a nurse and a farmer," wrote, "I want to thank you for the wonderful work that you are doing in teaching men and women the facts, the truth, about sex. It is the most important work, the most curative, the most constructive, the most godly, that can be done on earth."[18] A Massachusetts woman, delighted that Kinsey had revealed the "truth" about sex, declared, "I think it is about time it came out in the open and I think when people get use [*sic*] to the idea and the shock is worn off they won't be so quick to criticize. Of course, the truth always hurts. . . . The public is afraid to agree with you because they don't want the truth known. They can disagree with your statements but can't disprove them." The woman added, "This letter is for you to read and nothing else. My husband would put me through the third degree if he knew about it!!"[19]

Many of the letters emphasized the importance of knowing and facing the facts, as though data alone were needed to order life. A woman from Iowa proclaimed, "We feel electrically grateful that you and your workers have taken the lid off the Pandora Hush Box and have given us THINGS AS THEY ARE." Sharing the comments from "the rank and file" in her town of about 20,000, she reported, "Its full of curiosity, willingness to be shown, and plenty of pure downright gratefulness to you for having the intestinal fortitude to give us facts, regardless of the pulpit, law, Prudes, Inc., and anybody that we have left out." After reiterating her thanks for "this monumental work of sincerity," she told Kinsey, "You may take your seat beside John the Baptist and Darwin and Brother Freud."[20]

A woman from California was even more effusive. "I have just finished the book. To me it is the book of the century and of my life," she declared. "I feel that ultimately it will do more toward improving relationships between the sexes than any other work to date. I love you and your co-workers. Your courage in stating what you find, rather than what supports the age old myths is the mark of true greatness."[21] In what she admitted unabashedly was "fan mail," a New York woman, who profiled herself as "a 31-year old housewife, happily married, mother of one son, one and one-half years of college, second-generation Italian extraction, baptized Catholic church, married Episcopal church, connected with no church," told Kinsey, "Were it in my power, your book would become a required text in every high school in the nation. It is the most necessary, most vital 'book' that has ever 'rolled off the press,' and I sincerely mean 'ever.' " Endorsing Kinsey's meliorist vision of the future, she added, "Perhaps you've 'broken the ice' and by the time my six year old son has found my daughter-in-law she will have a much happier time of all-around living."[22]

Emboldened by the example of the thousands of women who had been interviewed by Kinsey, other women wrote to share information they hoped would help their sisters. Easily one of the most bittersweet letters came from an elderly woman who began, "Married at 19 to a fine boy 24, made love morning noon and night. He had loads of fun, I thot it was all there was to it until I found out different." Recalling the event that changed her sex life forever, the woman described kneeling one day in her bath to rinse her hair with a hose attached to the faucet. By accident, she explained, the water stream "reached the right spot, [and] I nearly fainted. I felt so good, I started all over again slowly and experienced the same thing." "Well," she continued, "I do not believe there is a human being that could replace that hose, I am still using one at 71 and never told a soul." The woman added with what must have been a sigh, "I get a thrill every time I look at the tube, and that is many times a day." In closing, the woman asked, "Why are we ashamed to admit to our husbands that we do not feel anything? We can't respond. My desire would be that all the women in the world knew about my secret and [could] share my happiness."[23]

Of course, Kinsey also received cries for help. Though less numerous than the men who had written following the male volume's publication, the pained women who wrote to Kinsey provided proof that his work was badly needed, that his secular ministry served a national congregation. The list of questions was as varied as the human condition. A woman who worried whether too much sex early in her marriage would harm her health when she entered menopause pleaded, "Please help us Dr. Kinsey, as our own local Dr. on hearing of our plight, calmly told us we were 'sex maniacs.' "[24] A woman from Tennessee inquired, "If a woman have [sic] hairs on [her] chest and breast, but seems to be normal in ever[y] other respect will she be pleasing to a husband?"[25] A New York woman, who had endured nineteen years of grief from an obsessed husband who accused her almost daily of not being a virgin when they married, wrote to express her anger over being "a target" and her sorrow over her "very unsuccessful marriage."[26]

Many of the women described failed romances and marriages, tragedies they blamed in many instances on their disastrous sex lives. Some spoke candidly of their total absence of sex education in childhood and of their lack of preparation for conjugal relations. Others complained about lovers and husbands whose libidos they found excessive or whose sexual preferences they found perverse. A Michigan housewife, who described herself as "a middle age lady past 50," inquired about some sexual interests her husband had recently developed. "To put it plainly," she wrote, "he likes to enjoy what he calls 'French' kisses, and to kiss feminine regions in this manner, and he also likes to have intercourse 'through the mouth,' if you know what I mean. He likes to place his penis in my mouth and have me fondle him that way and then have regular intercourse." Freely admitting her ignorance, she asked Kinsey, "What am I to say? Shall I agree? Or is it something wrong? I would very much appreciate an answer, because I do not know, never having heard of these things before. I want to please him, but I do not want to go against nature or do anything unnatural."[27]

Forty years after Margaret Sanger began her campaign to make birth control information and devices available to American women, Kinsey received numerous letters from women who decried their ignorance of birth control techniques, admitting they had often been left paralyzed with fear of unwanted pregnancies. These and other complaints from distressed women poured into Bloomington with each day's mail. Yet, whatever their problems, a common thread ran through their letters. Almost without exception, the women who wrote to Kinsey spoke of their ignorance of sexual matters and of keeping their pain secret. If he required additional proof that the sexual attitudes that had so filled him with guilt as a boy still stalked Americans, Kinsey had only to read his mail.

Confronted by suffering of this magnitude, Kinsey must have been saddened by how timidly the press dealt with his implicit calls for changes in sexual mores. His pleas for sex education went largely unheeded. Moreover, the few journalists who questioned conventional sexual morality stopped far short of the wholesale changes he had hoped to inspire. Not that he was totally devoid of influence. Responding to Kinsey's data on the relationship between premarital sexual experience and marital sexual adjustment, *Science News Letter* did venture to suggest, ever so discreetly, "Parents who want their daughters to marry happily and make a success of marriage may want to encourage the girls to have many dates. Some will decide to turn a blind eye on petting, even when it goes on to more than just petting."[28]

Most publications were not this bold. Instead of debating the reforms that seemed to be warranted by his data, most magazines simply credited Kinsey with shattering the conspiracy of silence. Holding that his greatest contribution might well be "conversational," *Time* declared, "No single event did more for open discussion of sex than the Kinsey report, which got such matters as homosexuality, masturbation, coitus and orgasm into most papers and family magazines."[29] *Newsweek* made the identical point, declaring, "Sexual discussions and terminology that would be taboo in any other instance rolled off presses and rolled up circulation."[30]

Overall, caution and blandness marked the national news media's analysis of *Sexual Behavior in the Human Female*. While a few journalists adopted a wide-eyed, sensational tone, the general reaction to it was remarkably staid. Many writers (particularly those who had visited Bloomington) were content to summarize the book's major findings. Most magazines either kept their editorial comments to a minimum or played it safe by running parallel statements by prominent figures who supported or opposed Kinsey's research. *Life* had the novelists Kathleen Norris and Fannie Hurst square off, with the former arguing that the book would harm the family and the latter insisting that Kinsey's work would nurture family life.[31] Attributing the restraint displayed by most magazines to "shrewd editors," the *New Republic* reported, "With few exceptions, they stood conspicuously aloof from his conclusions."[32]

Much to Kinsey's chagrin (and the nation's relief), *Sexual Behavior in the Human Female* produced remarkably little soul-searching. In fact, the response to this volume was milder than the reaction that had greeted the male volume. As one reviewer noted, the female volume "caused fewer violent convulsions among the defenders of our morals than his earlier book about the male."[33]

In the ultra-conformist late 1940s and early 1950s, Americans had little tolerance for challenges to cultural orthodoxy. Much of the public's concern centered on threats to the image of women, to the traditional family, and to prevailing gender roles. For all the talk about wanting openness about sex, many Americans found it disconcerting to learn that their growing anxiety about declining female morality had some basis in fact. Americans placed a premium on home and family. Many did not want to hear that the percentage of women who engaged in premarital and extramarital sex had increased since 1910. If anything, they were distinctly hostile to Kinsey's portrait of female sexuality. They preferred to deal with him by ignoring or denying his message.

Apart from professional groups, Kinsey did not really have a vocal constituency. In 1953, feminism was in the doldrums, depriving him of voices that might have emerged as firm supporters. For despite the confusion, contradictions, and occasional misogyny that marked the female volume, Kinsey was generally supportive of female sexuality. In a culture that remained anxious and ambivalent, placing little emphasis on women's erotic pleasure, Kinsey's approach to women can only be described as progressive. That he had accorded women the same treatment as men was extraordinary, since it implied that female sexuality should be given parity with male sexuality.

But Kinsey had done much, much more. Throughout the female volume, he depicted women as sexual beings; he resolutely separated sex from procreation; he documented the full range of female sexual outlets; he celebrated masturbation as the behavior most likely to result in orgasm, thereby deflating the importance of the penis to female sexual pleasure; he showed great concern for the stability of marriage; and he consistently depicted marriage as a partnership of equals that required sexual satisfaction for both parties. Fifteen years later, feminists would take up these and other sexual issues as part of their broader critique of gender politics, but in 1953 Kinsey was a prophet without an organized feminist reform move-ment to take up his cry.[34]

Of course, this held true for lesbians as well. A gay liberation movement for women was years in the future, because the Daughters of Bilitis (DOB) was not founded until 1955.[35] But no less than heterosexual feminists, gay women had good cause to be thankful to Kinsey. As one lesbian later wrote, "Probably the reams of material written in passionate defense of the homophile have done less to further the cause of tolerance than Kinsey's single, detached statement that 37 per cent of the men and 19 per cent of women whom he interviewed admitted having had overt homosexual re-lationships."[36]

Only a handful of journalists attempted to engage the social meaning of Kinsey's work. Those who did were critical. Not only did they spot him as a reformer, but they correctly concluded that Kinsey had launched a cul-tural war. At stake was what values would determine the sexual morality of the nation. Kinsey clearly advocated more freedom for individuals and a re-laxation of sexual codes, while the guardians of morality held that private behavior had to be tightly regulated to preserve abstinence outside of mar-riage as the only acceptable standard. Realizing that Kinsey posed a direct challenge to traditional morality, conservative journalists refused to defer to his data.

By and large, the press rose to the defense of American womanhood. While a few writers struck an alarmist note, arguing that science had ex-amined the sexual behavior of women and found little support for the cul-tural assumption of female superiority, many journalists expressed their faith in the abiding goodness of the female character. The *Indianapolis Star* declared, "We are not alarmed. . . . We do, however, strongly deny the degradation of American womanhood. We earnestly believe that our na-tion's human majority yet retains an omnipotently-inspired concept of high human moral values."[37]

As part of their defense of women, journalists adopted a variety of strate-gies to discredit Kinsey, to qualify or distort his findings, and, above all, to refute his conclusions. Some magazines charged that *Sexual Behavior in the Human Female* was incomprehensible. *The New Yorker* complained that "the ordinary reader can no more appraise its contents justly than he can appraise those of a manual on prestressed concrete." Explaining the prob-lem, it noted, "Much of the volume consists of tables and charts, whose va-lidity only a master of statistics would be fit to dispute or endorse."[38] Other magazines reported Kinsey's statistics but shifted the emphasis. Rather than dwell on how many women had violated sexual norms, writ-ers stressed the percentages of women whose private behavior had upheld cultural ideals. In an obvious effort to tame Kinsey's message, *Science News*

Letter began its discussion of the book with the cheery announcement "Married women are more faithful than married men. Only about half as many women as men commit adultery during their married lives."[39] The *New Republic* placed the emphasis on exactly the same spot, declaring, "Adultery is twice as frequent among married men as among married women."[40]

Above all, journalists hammered home the point that Kinsey had documented in great detail the fact that females were less sexually active than males. This, in turn, was taken as prima facie evidence of the moral superiority of women. As *Newsweek* told its readers with obvious relief, "The reputation of the American housewife comes out with fewer scratches than those upon her American husband."[41] The *Woman's Home Companion* agreed, declaring that "the second report will not dent the reputation of American women and will not break up the American home."[42]

What occurred was nothing less than the domestication of Kinsey's message by a press that proved hostile to threats to traditional morality. Adopting a position employed by several other publications, *Cosmopolitan* all but discounted the social relevance of Kinsey's work. While allowing that *Sexual Behavior in the Human Female* made "many interesting disclosures—and some disturbing and surprising ones," the magazine reassured its readers, "We can all breathe easier" because "for the most part, it is a technical treatise offering little that is startlingly new and much that is doubtful. It definitely does not measure up to the expectations of a shattering blast that was to upset all our sex thinking and change the whole pattern of our lives." Among those who "will be greatly disappointed," declared *Cosmopolitan,* "will be the scientists and other serious thinkers who had hopes that now, finally, we would get the full, scientifically accurate facts to guide us toward a saner handling of women's sex problems."[43]

Kinsey, who had been forced by critics to tone down his claims about the reliability of his sample, must have winced at what followed. Portraying his carefully worded qualifications as a weakness, *Cosmopolitan* declared in a heavy-handed parody, "For instead of emphatically proclaiming, 'This is the sexual behavior of American women,' the report haltingly asks, 'Is this the sexual behavior of American women?' and reluctantly answers, in effect, 'Well . . . no . . . not exactly of all women. Only of those who are like those we interviewed, and they, we admit, are not quite typical.' "[44]

In *Cosmopolitan*'s judgment, an unrepresentative sample could hardly be expected to yield reliable social policy. "Be equally wary when you read the dazzling Kinsey conclusions—that what we've been teaching our daughters about sex is all wrong, that chastity may often do more harm than good, that premarital sex relations are likely to help toward adjustment in many ways (maritally, psychologically, socially), and that girls who don't indulge in sex may be refraining less because their morals are strong than because their sex urges are weak," *Cosmopolitan* warned its readers. "These and other Kinsey conclusions may be largely theories, without scientific proof as yet to back them up, *particularly when they are applied to American women in general.*"[45]

Journalists also challenged Kinsey's scholarly objectivity. In the past, no part of the Kinsey canon had been more basic to his public image than scientific disinterest. With the male volume, he had proclaimed again and again that he was simply a fact finder, and he had reaped a rich dividend of trust and support when the press had uncritically passed this claim along to the public. With the female volume, however, Kinsey was less successful at duping journalists.

Journalists who carefully studied *Sexual Behavior in the Human Female* agreed that its senior author was not a bloodless scientist. After reporting that Kinsey himself had described the book as "a much more humane document," *Life* warned its readers that it "may be just a little too humane for some critics." The problem, stressed *Life*, was that Kinsey "makes it very clear that he considers modern sexual conventions to be mere superstitions, the uncritical acceptance of a primitive heritage from Hittite and Talmudic days." In its judgment, Kinsey had changed "from scientific observer to philosopher."[46]

Science magazine concurred. While Kinsey's study had "started out to be a biologist's analysis of actual practice, based on personal reports," observed *Science*, "it often seems to culminate in propaganda for certain sociological views: that what is common in sexual behavior must be right; that the Judeo-Christian culture imposes undesirable restraints upon normal and natural sex activities; that inhibition of sexual outlet, in some form or other, is biologically as well as psychologically unhealthy and unwise; or that certain laws ought to be changed."[47] *Cosmopolitan* shot even closer to the mark, insisting that *Sexual Behavior in the Human Female* "boldly attacks many of our existing sex standards with blistering arguments plainly slanted against chastity and in favor of what used to be called free love."[48] *Time* warned, "Kinsey's work expresses and strengthens an attitude that can be dangerous: the idea that there is morality in numbers."[49]

Discerning journalists had no difficulty identifying Kinsey as a passionate reformer. While acknowledging that he was "frequently depicted as a heartless scientist trying to reduce one of the most profound of all human emotions into a neat set of statistical tables," and while admitting that "Kinsey himself feeds this myth by insisting that he is only a dispassionate scholar in pursuit of facts," *Woman's Home Companion* insisted that the Hoosier scientist was actually "a crusader deeply touched by the needless misery arising from ignorance and striving to enhance people's chances for happiness."[50] Without realizing how right they were, a few publications detected displaced religious fervor in Kinsey. The reviewer for the *New York Times Book Review* described portions of *Sexual Behavior in the Human Female* as "essentially undisguised preaching,"[51] while *Time* quoted, with obvious approval, a friend and fellow scientist who remarked, "There is too much emotion there. He should have been a revivalist."[52]

As if having his objectivity disputed were not bad enough, Kinsey also had to contend with prudish put-downs. In terms of popular culture, his resurrection as a folk hero was at once short-lived and more hollow than before. Once again, comedians made jokes, playwrights slipped references to Kinsey into their scripts, and sex research was put to music as Abner Silver's "Pul-leeze, Mr. Kinsey" blared out from juke boxes.[53] The comments from celebrities, however, had an edge, reflecting the broader culture's efforts to discredit Kinsey and preserve a wholesome image of womanhood. Gypsy Rose Lee, the famous stripper, cautioned, "Sex and statistics don't mix!"[54] Zsa Zsa Gabor advised men not to read the Kinsey report, sighing, "The whole thing is too scientific."[55] Ann Baxter declared, "So some 6,000 women lined up and confessed. I place my faith in the 80-odd million who weren't contacted."[56] Asked for her reaction, Evelyn Margaret Ay, "Miss America of 1954," snapped, "I haven't read it yet, and I can think of other things I'd read first."[57] Frank Sinatra, one of the few male celebrities to venture a remark, quipped that the female volume should be called "From Here to Maternity."[58]

Many Americans tried to ignore Kinsey's work. Despite the unprecedented publicity accorded *Sexual Behavior in the Human Female,* many newspapers and magazines made a conscious decision to play down the story. After rejecting Kinsey's terms for a prepublication briefing in Bloomington, the *New York Times* relied upon the Associated Press's 1,000-word condensation for its information, burying its coverage of K-Day on page 15.[59]

Worse yet, from Kinsey's perspective, *Sexual Behavior in the Human Female* was widely censored. Explaining why there was so little coverage on the airwaves in New York, a journalist reported, "Radio-TV stations are leaving Kinsey be as 'just too ticklish.' "[60] Not a few newspapers followed suit. The *Oakland Tribune* and the *Christian Science Monitor* did not print a word of Kinsey's findings. Neither did the *Philadelphia Bulletin,* which informed its readers, "It is impossible to present any adequate summary of the findings without giving unnecessary offense to many in [our] larger family of readers." The *Raleigh Times* omitted any coverage, but offered to let its readers peruse the wire service accounts (provided they came to the office).[61] The *San Francisco News* refused to publish any stories about Kinsey, explaining in an editorial that they were not "proper literature" for a "family newspaper." The *Globe-Democrat* in St. Louis also nixed Kinsey, as did the *Schenectady Union Star,* whose editor called the report "an affront to womanhood." In Kinsey's home state, the *Fort Wayne News-Sentinel* kept mum, telling its readers in a front-page editorial, "If interested, buy the book."[62] Other newspapers opted for selective censorship, including Denver's *Rocky Mountain News,* which omitted the data on teenage petting. Rather than repeat Kinsey's clinical language, still other newspapers employed euphemisms.[63]

Many editors were troubled by the treatment Kinsey received. Calling the wave of censorship "one of the most remarkable developments in modern journalism," the *New York Post* scolded, "None of the censorious editors contended that Dr. Kinsey faked his findings; some simply decreed that what he found about women was an affront to American womanhood, presumably because it might be true; others said they just didn't believe their readers could bear to face the facts." While granting that "each man (or woman) has a right to his own opinion," the editors demanded, "we wonder how many of the editors who killed the Kinsey report have delivered speeches proclaiming that the public has a right to know the truth and the full truth about everything. About everything, that is, except the facts of life."[64]

Congress also made noises about censoring the book. On August 29, 1953, Representative Louis B. Heller, Democrat from New York, asked the Post Office Department to ban *Sexual Behavior in the Human Female* as soon as it was released. While admitting he had not read the book, Heller nevertheless charged that Kinsey had drawn conclusions that were "highly questionable, if not downright ridiculous," after interviewing fewer than 6,000 women, "many of them frustrated, neurotic, outcasts of society." On the basis of this sample, complained Heller, Kinsey was "accusing the bulk of American womanhood of having sinned before or after marriage." Heller further charged that "under the pretext of making a great contribution to scientific research," Kinsey "is hurling the insult of the century against our mothers, wives, daughters and sisters." Expressing his regret that Congress was not currently in session so he could move against the book immediately, Heller promised to convene a special committee to investigate Kinsey's work when Congress reconvened in January, and he pledged to call clergymen, sociologists, educators, medical specialists, and other experts to ascertain the "value of such studies, if any."[65]

Heller's call for a ban went nowhere. Pointing out the hypocrisy in the congressman's position, the *New York Post* chided, "Heller, who describes himself as a foe of censorship and a defender of 'freedom to read,' has concluded from not reading the book that, until a Congressional Investigating Committee investigates Dr. Kinsey's investigations, no one else should read them either." A spokesman for the Post Office Department put a damper on the proposed ban, stating that there was no legal authorization for barring a book from the mail until it was actually in circulation and a formal complaint had been registered.[66] The New York Civil Liberties Union also opposed the ban. In a letter to Representative Heller, George E. Rundquist, executive director of the New York affiliate of the ACLU, sounded the alarm, charging that a postal ban amounted to precensorship and would prevent the book from receiving a fair hearing about its alleged obscenity. "It is not within our province to comment on the content of the book," wrote Rundquist, "but because we believe that controversial discussion is one of democracy's most prized possessions, any action taken to curb it should be carefully studied."[67] Upon reflection, Heller must have agreed. His promised investigation never materialized.

President Wells had to worry about the political climate closer to home. Predictably, K-Day brought a number of protests from Hoosiers who were outraged that Indiana University had supported Kinsey's work. In Indianapolis, Superior Court Judge John L. Niblack accused Kinsey of "wasting the funds of my old alma mater exploring the writings on the public toilet walls." Added Judge Niblack indignantly, "What Indiana University really needs so badly are some good, stalwart halfbacks to furnish good, clean mayhem on fall Saturdays." The Roman Catholic archbishop of Indianapolis, Paul C. Schulte, declared angrily, "Every self-respecting Hoosier must profoundly regret the notoriety Dr. Kinsey has brought to our renowned university." While Archbishop Schulte conceded that there could be "no valid objection to a scientific investigation of sexual behavior," he charged that Kinsey had "degraded science." "Instead of circulating his findings among those competent to weigh their worth and apply them to the betterment of mankind," Schulte claimed, "he publicizes them like a cheap charlatan and in most unscientific fashion makes them available to the young, the unlearned, the mentally deficient—to their own great harm and the endangering of society." An angry woman from Parker, Indiana, spoke for many conservative Hoosiers when she declared, "Indiana University should hang its head in shame for permitting such rot."[68]

As he had since the days of the marriage course, President Wells erected his defense of Kinsey on academic freedom, a shaky foundation in the McCarthy era but the only one available. Wells had anticipated that Indiana University would come under pressure. He was prepared to handle it. When the United Press asked Indiana University for a statement, Wells had one waiting. With the board of trustee's permission and approval, he said, "Indiana University stands today, as it has for fifteen years, firmly in support of the scientific research project that has been undertaken and is being carried on by one of its eminent biological scientists, Dr. Alfred C. Kinsey."

Stressing that the university was proud to have the National Research Council as cosponsor of Kinsey's research, Wells ended on a high note: "We have large faith in the values of knowledge, little faith in ignorance."[69]

Less than a week after Wells's strong statement hit the press, the Indiana Provincial Council of Catholic Women asked him to clarify his position. "In the name of more than 150,000 women—most of them mothers, many of them with sons and daughters of college age," the council sought reassurance "that Indiana University is still a place fit for the educating of the youth of our State." While its members had not read the book, the council argued that press reports made it clear that Kinsey "considers our present sexual morals for the most part to be superstitious notions of an unenlightened and uncritical past." The council demanded, "Will our sons and daughters be exposed to the ideas of Dr. Kinsey? Dare we risk placing them in the charge of a university that seems to be willing to degrade science for the sake of sensational publicity?"[70]

Wells's handling of this episode illustrates why he earned his reputation as the greatest president in the history of Indiana University. Without backing off an inch from his support for Kinsey, Wells was not only reassuring and conciliatory but managed to uphold academic freedom and defend his institution's reputation. After stressing the high regard and great respect he had for the National Council of Catholic Women, he declared, "The University never approves or disapproves the research findings of its experimental scientists." Time alone, he intoned, would determine the validity of any scientist's findings, since it often took years for the profession to examine and check research. "The endorsement given by the University to the research project in question, or to any other," Wells explained, "concerns the right of the scientist to investigate every aspect of life in the belief that knowledge, rather than ignorance, will assist mankind in the slow and painful development toward a more perfect society."[71]

Turning to the issue of whether students would be exposed to Kinsey's findings in the classroom, Wells asserted, "Dr. Kinsey's research is entirely divorced from the University's teaching function and he and his colleagues are assigned full time to research duties." As for the state of student morality, Wells declared proudly that Indiana University's graduates "will stand comparison with the graduates of any institution in the country as to morals, ideals, high-minded purpose, and integrity."[72] His combination of staunch support and skillful diplomacy had the intended results. There was no further communication from the National Council of Catholic Women.

Throughout August and September, university officials held their breath, waiting to see what the political fallout would be. As it happened, Indiana University took remarkably little heat. Despite a few letters of protest to

Wells and a few irate letters to Hoosier editors, the public remained calm. With obvious relief, Ross Bartley, the director of public relations at Indiana University, told a college public relations meeting early in October, "Reaction was less than we had feared." While admitting it had received a number of calls from women who were "indignant and outraged," the *Indianapolis News* revealed, "But of women chosen at random from the telephone directory and called by the *News,* only one expressed disapproval and this only mild. The others felt the Kinsey report . . . to be in the public interest."[73]

It was Wells's nature to think in political terms. His strategy of coming out strongly in support of Kinsey and not allowing critics to place the university on the defensive reflected his unique talent for keeping ahead of the curve. And precisely because he was politically astute, Wells constantly looked to the future. Hoping to shore up Kinsey's relationship with the Rockefeller Foundation, he sent Morison a copy of the university's press release and inquired if the foundation wished to be included in the future as a cosponsor of Kinsey's research.[74] It was a good try, but Morison was not buying. While he praised the statement as "excellent," he politely declined, "I am sure none of us here would wish to make any additions or subtractions."[75]

Morison's decision reflected a hardening of the foundation's policy. Following the bruising board battle of 1951, foundation officers had been sending out signals that Kinsey should not expect further funding. A change at the foundation's helm reduced Kinsey's chances even further. On July 1, 1952, Dean Rusk succeeded Chester Barnard as president of the Rockefeller Foundation. Rusk's ascent meant that Kinsey no longer had a friend in the president's office.

Despite his low-key manner and gentle southern drawl, Rusk had definite ideas about whose judgment should rule the foundation, ideas calculated to ingratiate him with the powers that be. One of the first things he did was to read the charter and the laws that affected the foundation. "It was my view that at the end of the day the foundation is the trustees. That is, they are the ones who carry the responsibility . . . and they were the ones to make the final decisions," declared Rusk many years later. "Now, there were some staff officers who were inclined to take a different view," he continued. They thought "it was the officers who were the foundation." Acknowledging that this group believed that the "trustees ought to follow the advice of the officers on every case," Rusk said, "I was determined to try to insure that the trustees had a full and free shot at making the policy decisions and approving the grants as a matter of trustee responsibility and not just automatic endorsement of recommendations of officers."[76]

Rusk, who came to the foundation via the State Department, owed his appointment to John Foster Dulles, the same man who had bitterly opposed Kinsey's grant in 1951. As chairman of the foundation's board of trustees, Dulles had headed the search committee that recommended Rusk, and he had strongly supported his candidacy.[77] Rusk never forgot it. Although Dulles had resigned from the board to become secretary of state under President Dwight D. Eisenhower, by the time Rusk assumed the foundation's presidency, he considered Dulles an important ally. Dulles, of course, wished fervently to see Kinsey's relationship with the foundation severed, a fact duly communicated to Rusk by officers and trustees as he settled into his new position and reviewed the history of various grants.

Rusk was disturbed by the dissension Kinsey had caused. "When I became president of the Rockefeller Foundation," recalled Rusk many years later, "I found that there were some serious misgivings among some of the officers, among some of the trustees, about Kinsey's methods." As a result of their concerns, Rusk continued, "we had a lot of discussion about it among the officers and on one or two occasions among the trustees." As he remembered those talks, the core issue "was Dr. Kinsey's tendency to translate the materials he had on the particular kind of people he worked with and interviewed into generalizations about the sex behavior of the American people as a whole." Describing his own reaction, Rusk later confessed, "I had some very deep reservations about whether this sample was adequate for that kind of generalization."[78]

The upshot was that Rusk sided with Kinsey's critics. Not that he shared the moral outrage of the worst detractors. "I myself did not have any reservations about work in that field," he insisted. "I thought it was an important field. I thought Kinsey had done some important exploratory work and some pioneering work."[79] For Rusk, then, his position on Kinsey was not a moral issue but a question of restoring power to the trustees and protecting the foundation from political embarrassment.

A week before K-Day, Rusk started getting nervous that the foundation would get drawn into the controversy everyone knew was about to engulf Kinsey. He discussed his apprehensions with Huge H. Smith, the acting director of the Division of Medicine and Public Health, who in turn notified Kinsey about the foundation's concern.[80] "As the publication date for the volume 'Sexual Behavior in the Human Female' approaches there appears to be more and more public interest being fanned up by the press," Smith wrote Kinsey. "We have been approached by one or two New York papers on points they wish to raise about the support to your work from this Foundation," Smith continued. "Mr. Rusk is anxious, of course, that our relationship to your undertaking be presented to the public as accurately as possible. Whenever possible we expect to refer inquiries to the Committee for Research in Problems of Sex of the National Research Council."[81] Clearly, Rusk meant to distance the foundation from Kinsey, a policy that did not bode well for future funding. As the K-Day hype unfolded, the Rockefeller Foundation again received unwelcome publicity. Since a senior foundation officer had not written the preface for the female volume, the press did not feature the foundation so prominently in its discussions of Kinsey's research this time around. Still, a number of number of publications called attention to the relationship. *U.S. News & World Report,* for example, noted that the Institute for Sex Research was "an established research enterprise, supported mainly by the National Research Council of the National Academy of Sciences and the Rockefeller Foundation,"[82] while the *Nation* declared, "It is also not without significance that the work of Dr. Kinsey's Institute for Sex Research received financial aid from the Medical Sciences Division of the Rockefeller Foundation, which contributed its grants through a special committee set up by the National Research Council." Deeply impressed by the caliber of Kinsey's supporters, the *Nation* added, "To have two such august bodies lending guidance and support to studies of sex behavior is itself an event—an indication of how our norms have changed concerning areas of legitimate research."[83] *Glamour* magazine pushed the point even further. After telling its readers that the Rockefeller Foundation's medical sciences division had been pumping $40,000 annually into Kinsey's research, *Glamour* declared, "Naturally, before such money was granted, Kinsey and his program both underwent searching scrutiny by the Foundation and were found superbly qualified."[84]

Concerned about the publicity, Rusk contacted several members of the board to see if they had heard any complaints. "The general public seems to have taken Dr. Kinsey's report in stride," replied Thomas Parran. "I have received no inquiries or comments whatever concerning the Foundation's role in supporting these studies."[85] W. I. Myers made much the same point, declaring, "In spite of the tremendous publicity that has been given to Dr. Kinsey's books, I have never received any criticism of the Foundation for its support of this project."[86] Despite these reassurances, Rusk remained troubled.

Corner, of course, had feared for some time that a crisis over Kinsey was brewing between the NRC and the Rockefeller Foundation. Specifically, he was afraid the foundation would violate the committee's autonomy and integrity by ordering it to cut Kinsey loose. In February 1953, he told a colleague that the CRPS would "have to consider what it would do if (as seems possible) a continuation grant is offered with specific exclusion of further aid to Kinsey." Corner left no doubt about where he stood: "Personally, I should be reluctant to administer grant money under any restriction as to the recipients and would rather see the Committee retire from the field while at the peak of its reputation than go on in a limited, partially suppressed way." Corner felt certain that Alan Gregg, Andrew J. Warren, and Robert S. Morison as men of science were all "personally sympathetic," and their support allowed him to hope that "a workable formula for future support" could be achieved.[87] The difficulty, of course, involved getting Kinsey's budget by the trustees, especially now that Rusk was president of the foundation. As laymen, neither Rusk nor the trustees shared the professional knowledge and understanding that the senior officers in the medical division brought to Kinsey's work. As Corner assured a colleague at the NRC, "The scientists do not need to convince each other about the need for more research."[88]

Corner brought the issue to a head in fall 1953. In November, he and R. Keith Cannan, chairman of the NRC's medical division, journeyed to New York to meet with Warren and Morison. At their meeting, Corner asked if the foundation would welcome an application for additional funding for the committee and for Kinsey when the current grant expired on June 30, 1954. In anticipation of this meeting, Warren and Morison had met with Rusk earlier that day to discuss Kinsey's case. With Rusk's agreement, they gave their visitors extremely cautious encouragement.

The foundation would consider aid to the committee, declared Warren. As for Kinsey, Warren's desk diary noted, "It was also explained to Dr. Corner that it was very doubtful if the Foundation's Trustees would look with favor on continued aid to Dr. Kinsey's studies." Still, Warren and Morison could not bring themselves to order the NRC to drop Kinsey from its proposal. Personally, both men thought that the foundation should support him. In the end, they told Corner and Cannan that though the outlook was bleak, the NRC was free to submit a budget that included funds for Kinsey.[89]

Following the meeting, Corner gave Kinsey a thorough briefing, making no effort to sugarcoat either the committee's or Kinsey's chances for renewed support. While stressing that the prospects did not look good, Corner added, "They specifically stated however that the Foundation officers were prepared to receive and consider a request which would imply the Committee's willingness to continue making grants for the relevant part of your work."[90] Under the circumstances, this was the best Kinsey could hope for, and it was certainly all he could expect of Warren and Morison.

Corner and Cannan worked hard on the proposal. Their goal was to find language that would enable the officers to persuade the trustees to approve another three-year grant for the committee, with the understanding that the committee, in turn, would be free to expend on Kinsey whatever portion of its appropriation it saw fit. After several drafts, Corner and

Cannan had finished the proposal, and in late November the NRC formally requested a three-year "grant of $80,000 per annum." The reference to Kinsey was skillfully worded. Noting that the committee had in the past been "unanimous in its allocation of grants to the Kinsey program," the proposal stated, "The backing of the Committee has been and will continue to be desirable to Dr. Kinsey as a sign of scientific recognition. Whether the same proportion of the total resources should be allocated to the Institute for Sex Research in the future should be a matter for study."[91]

Aware that his stock with the Rockefeller Foundation was sinking, Kinsey urged Corner to stand firm. In the past, Kinsey had treated the CRPS shabbily, threatening on more than one occasion to sever their relationship in favor of dealing directly with the Rockefeller Foundation. Shifting ground, Kinsey declared, "I think first of all we are most interested in the possibility of maintaining some sort of connection with the NRC's committee. We have appreciated their professional advice, and frankly, it has meant a good deal to us and to Indiana University to have an outside group sharing sponsorship for the research."[92]

With his chances for renewed Rockefeller support in peril, Kinsey badly needed uniformly positive reviews to enhance his standing. He did not get them. Although he received his share of rave notices, the scholarly and professional reviews of *Sexual Behavior in the Human Female* mirrored the response to the male volume. They were mixed. Some reviewers praised the female volume extravagantly, announcing that it was much better than the male volume. Others demurred, insisting that methodological and philosophical flaws rendered both studies all but useless. In fact, Kinsey must have had a sense of déjà vu as he read the notices. His reviewers seized upon the same points to praise and to criticize. Still, at least he had the satisfaction, rare for an author, of seeing his work received favorably a second time by the newspaper of record. The review for the *New York Times Book Review* was positive, declaring that "this book is science, serious science, and science in the grand style." Nevertheless, the *Times*'s reviewer predicted that "the psychoanalysts and psychiatrists will howl almost as loudly as they did five years ago."[93]

Surprisingly, Kinsey had a few supporters in the psychiatric community. Bemoaning how "tiresome" it was "to hear the rather superficial carpings of our psychiatric and analytic brethren to the effect that 'love is not in the index of the book' or 'that Kinsey has neglected the psycho-dynamics of sex,' " the reviewer for the *Psychoanalytic Review* scolded, "shades of Galton, Darwin, and Freud—do we expect the poor man to psychoanalyze his females for three years to know how many times they have coitus each week?" A generous soul who worshiped data, the reviewer intoned, "Let first things come first. This book is a daring exploit, a monumental result, and a tribute to human endurance. If there be a Nobel Prize available, the authors should have it for the sheer staggering labor itself."[94]

Overall, however, psychoanalysts snarled at Kinsey. The nastiest review came from Karl Menninger, of the famed Menninger Clinic, in Topeka, Kansas, which in the early 1950s trained roughly 15 percent of all the psychiatrists educated in the United States. As a pillar of the psychoanalytic community, Menninger took it upon himself to defend his profession against what he called (and not without reason) Kinsey's "somewhat hysterical antipathy." Writing for the *Saturday Review of Literature,* Menninger accused Kinsey of repeating the errors he had made in the male volume—namely, ignoring the psychological components of sex and forcing everything into a zoological framework.[95]

Although Menninger had praised the male volume for using innovative methodology to document individual variation, he criticized the female volume for employing essentially the same methods. The difference, of course, was that Menninger, like so many other critics, felt a strong need to defend women. At times, he came close to suggesting that female sexuality was best left unstudied. In addition, he criticized Kinsey for belittling moral restraints and for implying that all sexual outlets were equally good. Nor did he agree with Kinsey's implied argument that numbers and frequency somehow made behavior normal. Adopting a prudish tone, Menninger also took sharp exception to Kinsey's efforts to alleviate guilt feelings, arguing that certain acts should make their perpetrators feel guilty, as guilt was necessary to preserve morality.[96] In short, moral objections ran the length of Menninger's review. He sounded like a pious missionary defending modern society against the corrupting influences of scientific materialism and moral relativism.[97] Kinsey, of course, dismissed all moral criticisms of his work. Projecting his own demons, he told a friend, "It is amazing what emotional disturbances there can be in this day and generation when science attempts to enter a field which has heretofore been considered primarily a matter of moral philosophy."[98]

Predictably, Kinsey suffered his worst moral condemnation at the hands of ministers. While many liberal men of the cloth argued that religion had to know the facts about human sexuality, their more conservative brethren felt obliged to hold the line against godless science. Exclaiming, "Sin is still sin!," Billy Graham, the up-and-coming evangelist, warned, "It is impossible to estimate the damage this book will do to the already deteriorating morals of America."[99]

Yet many liberal clergymen also denounced Kinsey, as traditional sexual morality had the power to override progressive political views. One of the most scathing reviews came from Reinhold Niebuhr of Union Theological Seminary in New York. "The findings of the Kinsey Report," he wrote, "are not as disturbing as the presuppositions upon which the inquiry into the sexual habits of American females is initiated and the conclusions which Kinsey thinks are prompted by his evidence." While admitting that it was "disturbing to find this further evidence of the decay of the family," Niebuhr declared, "But Kinsey's rejoicing over the result is more disturbing: as are the ruling presuppositions of his inquiry which prompt his satisfaction."[100]

Kinsey simply assumed, charged Niebuhr, "that men and women face a rather purely physiological problems in their sex life," that they "must find sufficient 'outlets' for their sexual urges," and that "traditional 'inhibitions' and restrains must be brushed aside to accomplish this emancipation." Insisting that human sexuality was governed by "a whole hierarchy of values," Niebuhr wrote that "this obvious and important fact is obscured or denied in Kinsey's consistent naturalism and its logical fruit of a crude hedonism, in terms of which the achievement of sexual pleasures becomes the *summum bonum* of his value scheme." After repeating his bitter denunciations of Kinsey's "absurd hedonism" and "moral anarchism," Niebuhr wondered out loud "whether Kinsey's approach to complex ethical problems in the sexual field is not an indication of one of the deplorable effects of the introduction of the so-called 'methods of science' into the field of the humanities."[101] While he did not question Kinsey's integrity, calling him "an honest scientist," Niebuhr made it clear that he considered Kinsey "but a single individual who does not speak for any large section of the 'scientific' community in whose name he pretends to speak." If anything, he found it disturbing that Kinsey's "abysmal ignorance of the complexities in the heights and depths of the human spirit should be cloaked and dignified by the prestige of 'science.'" Lamented Niebuhr in closing, "A culture has to reach a pretty low level for such pretenses to be at all plausible."[102]

Determined to see that Niebuhr's review reached the right hands, Henry P. Van Dusen, president of Union Theological Seminary and a Rockefeller trustee, sent a copy to Warren Weaver, Kinsey's principal detractor among the foundation's senior officers.[103] Weaver was most receptive. Stressing that he found himself "agreeing heartily with Dr. Niebuhr," he announced that he supported sex studies, but only if they were "highly factual and reasonably objective." "I suppose that Dr. Kinsey thinks that his studies are of this character," continued Weaver. "I do not agree with this, and I object most strenuously to the direct and implied interpretations which one finds throughout his two books." Betraying the moral reservations that explained the real source of his hostility to Kinsey, Weaver added, "I am not at all sure that a book of the strictly factual and objective character should receive unlimited circulation."[104]

Van Dusen also sent a copy of Niebuhr's review to Dean Rusk, who delayed reading it for a month because he was preoccupied with other problems. When he did get around to it, Rusk wrote to Van Dusen, "After reading it carefully, it is quite clear that we shall have to give it further thought, because the run-of-the-mill type of reply which one would be tempted to give to questions by the Reece Committee would not meet Niebuhr's points at all."[105]

While the reference seemed offhand, the Reece Committee weighed heavily on Rusk. In fact, it was the problem that had preoccupied him almost totally since practically the moment he had become president. In the summer of 1953, the House of Representatives passed a resolution creating a special committee to investigate tax-exempt foundations, with B. Carroll Reece, Republican of Tennessee, as its chairman. To some at least, the timing seemed curious. Only the preceding year, the Cox committee, led by Judge Eugene E. Cox, a congressman from the Second District of Georgia who served as a leader of the conservative wing of the Democratic Party, had investigated the same subject. While Cox had started out by accusing the foundations of being riddled with Communists, he had quickly changed his tune. After six months of research and public hearings, the Cox committee wound up giving the foundations a relatively clean bill of health.[106] So why have another investigation? Reece alone knew the answer.

At first glance, he seemed an unlikely candidate to lead the charge. Although he had served on the Cox committee, Reece apparently had only a modest interest in its work, as he attended only one of the committee's eighteen hearings. His change of heart was the result of a private grievance. A former chairman of the Republican National Committee, Reece had served as the southern campaign manager of Robert Taft's losing bid against General Eisenhower for the Republican Party's nomination in 1952. Bitterness over Taft's defeat, it seems, was what had turned Reece against the foundations. Many years later, Representative Wayne Hays, Democrat from Ohio, told an interviewer, "I talked to Mr. Reece when the [Reece] committee was being formed, and he told me that he believed that the foundations had conspired to prevent Senator Taft from being nominated for President, and, thereby, kept him from being secretary of state, because Mr. Taft had promised him this job."[107]

Whatever the truth of Hays's story, there can be no doubt that Reece had it in for the foundations. Long identified with some of the most conservative forces in Congress, Reece told his colleagues in the House, "Here lies the story of how Communists and socialists are financed in the United States, where they get their money." He planned to produce "evidence to

show there is a diabolical conspiracy back of all this. Its aim is the furtherance of socialism in the United States."[108]

From the middle of September through the end of December 1953, the
Reece committee built a staff of thirteen members and spent nearly
$25,000 on preparations for the investigations ahead, which included a
probe of the Rockefeller Foundation. Many years later, Andrew J. Warren
recalled that everyone was "quite disturbed" by the Reece committee,
adding that the professional staff "spent considerable time and money in
reviewing the activities of the Rockefeller Foundation in the past and what
influence it might have on the future of the activities of the foundation."[109]
As he prepared to meet the challenge, Rusk was concerned about a number of grants, but none loomed larger than the awards to Kinsey. Kinsey's
grants, Rusk feared, had left the foundation vulnerable to precisely the
kind of right-wing attacks Reece promised to deliver. After all, no single
grantee in the foundation's history had been so controversial as Kinsey.

To make matters worse, critics had recently questioned Kinsey's patriotism. In the poisonous political atmosphere of the early 1950s, it was inevitable that Kinsey would be smeared with a red brush. He received a
number of letters from private citizens attacking his loyalty, including one
from an irate critic who accused him of "aiding the Communist's aim to
weaken and destroy the youth of your country."[110] Newspapers across the
land published similar charges. For example, a woman assured an editor in
Lincoln, Nebraska, that Kinsey's research was "nothing but Communistic
destruction of American women's morals and decency."[111] A Boston editor heard from an "Ex-Kinseyite" who called the female volume "a deep,
dark, Communist plot to overthrow and destroy the American home."[112]
Adopting a tactic that became an art form in the 1950s, other critics
stopped short of calling Kinsey a Red, but implied that the Communists
were in the grandstands cheering him on. "Very Much Concerned" told an
editor in Indianapolis, "Such things must please the Communists tremendously. They would like nothing better than to wreck the morals of the
American people."[113]

Conservative Catholics echoed this charge. An editorial in the *Indiana
Catholic and Record,* a weekly newspaper published by the Indianapolis
Roman Catholic Archdiocese, charged that Kinsey's books "paved the way
for people to believe in communism and to act like communists." While
acknowledging that neither President Wells "nor his notorious sexologist"
was a Communist, the Catholic editors declared, "But we couldn't for sure
tell you in what aspect the Kinsey view of nature and human morality differs from the communists."[114] Upon learning that Kinsey had been accused of promoting communism, a friend observed sympathetically, "Well,

this is not the first time in the history of the world that scientific research has been accused by a hierarchy of being in league with the devil."[115]

Wells, of course, rose to Kinsey's defense, explaining that the Catholic editors had "failed to recognize that one of the differences between America and Communist Russia is that here a scientist is free to investigate any field . . . to investigate every phase of human activity." Added Wells, "To deny this right is to deny one of the ways by which the human race attempts to reach goals established for us by our Divine Creator!" The *Indiana Daily Student,* the student newspaper at Indiana University, also backed Kinsey. In an article entitled "Who? Are You Kidding? Dr. Kinsey? Aiding Communism?" the newspaper declared, "If society is to better itself, it can do so by correcting the situations pointed to in the research finds. And we're for the betterment of society . . . any time. We think Dr. Kinsey is, too."[116]

The faculty also stood behind Kinsey. In a strongly worded letter to Wells, the Indiana University chapter of the American Association of University Professors denounced the attempts "to tie Dr. Kinsey's methodological position to communism," calling those efforts "a deliberate and deplorable appeal to emotionalism which, if successful, could only undermine the democratic functions of the American university." The members of the organization went on to reaffirm their support of academic freedom, stressing that scholars had a duty to conduct research and every university had an obligation "to support competent research to the limit of its facilities, no matter how unpopular the findings may become."[117]

Early in January 1954, the press published rumors that the Reece committee was preparing to investigate Kinsey's financial backers.[118] Publicly, Kinsey pretended to be unperturbed, telling one reporter in a telephone interview, "I've nothing to hide." Responding to queries from another reporter, he declared, "There is nothing about the financing of the Institute that is not public record. There has never been any personal take by myself or other members of the staff." Unable to conceal his contempt, he went on to suggest that the committee could save a lot of time, effort, and money by consulting the Institute's official financial records, copies of which were on file with the university. In addition, he denied that his studies were "subversive" or a threat to morality and marriage. "We have reported factual data," he told reporters. "We have not advocated social policy."[119]

Having reaped a windfall of sensational publicity, Reece coyly told reporters that he had no plans at the present to call Kinsey to testify.[120] No one was fooled. Everyone expected Kinsey to be a target when hearings began in the spring, if for no other reason than that his research would guarantee the committee headlines. And Reece badly needed something to boost his standing in the press, as the overall response to his committee was cool. The editors of the *Washington Post* charged that Reece had demonstrated his "total incompetence to conduct the investigations" and called the committee "wholly unnecessary" and "stupidly wasteful of public funds," a probe whose sole purpose was "intimidation."[121]

If Reece did mean to intimidate the foundations, he found an easy victim in Dean Rusk. "Having been a former member of the State Department, [Rusk] was very sensitive to political activities on the hill," recalled Warren. Rusk, of course, was aware of Kinsey's checkered record with the board, a legacy that had left the embattled scientist no capital upon which to draw. Indeed, from a political standpoint, it was clear that Kinsey had long since become a liability. Why should the foundation expose itself to political risks for a controversial figure who had caused trouble on the board? Rusk asked himself the same question and decided the time had come to cut Kinsey loose. As Warren put it, the Reece committee's threatened investigation prompted the president "to look with disfavor on further aid."[122]

Within days after the press identified Kinsey as a possible target of the Reece committee, Rusk took decisive action to protect the foundation. Since Warren was ill with a bleeding ulcer, Rusk turned to Robert S. Morison, Warren's associate and the number two man in the Division of Medicine and Public Health. Rusk instructed Morison to tell Corner in no uncertain terms to drop Kinsey from the CRPS's budget.[123]

Rusk's orders put Morison in a bind. Only a few months earlier, Warren and Morison, with Rusk's consent, had informed Corner that the CRPS could make some provision for Kinsey in its budget. Now Rusk was reneging on this agreement, and Morison found this decision deeply troubling. There was no way to interpret the foundation's demands as anything but a violation of the committee's autonomy. Years later, Morison recalled feeling "uneasy about telling the National Research Council what they could and could not do." In fact, Morison feared that the conflict over Kinsey's funding might precipitate a crisis in the relations between the NRC and the Rockefeller Foundation. On a personal level, Morison felt ashamed. "I knew and admired and respected those people on the council enormously," declared Morison. Barely able to disguise his anger at Rusk, Morison added, "I knew and admired but didn't always respect, I guess, some of the people I was working for in this particular instance." For all these reasons, Morison remembered feeling certain that "the meeting with Corner was going to be a very bad show from the start." He added, "By that time, the committee was getting pretty damn agitated, and I would rather not have it blow up into a great crisis of academic freedom."[124]

On January 17, 1954, Morison and Corner had a fateful lunch together.

"[Morison] came to see me privately in Baltimore, asking that I not let out the news of his coming," recalled Corner many years later. "He acted like a spy coming into enemy territory," continued Corner, noting that the meeting took place "in surroundings of the utmost caution."[125] However personally distasteful Morison may have found his mission, he did his duty. According to his desk diary, he told Corner "quite bluntly that there is no chance of putting a proposal for the Committee before our Board if it includes provision for further allocations to Kinsey." Morison further recorded, somewhat sheepishly, that he assured Corner "that we certainly would prefer not to dictate to the Committee and that it would be very nice if they could decide as far as anything official is concerned to submit a proposal to us which does not include such a provision."[126] Corner kept his cards vested, replying that he could not predict how the CRPS or the NRC's Division of Medical Sciences would react. The best he could do, concluded Corner, was to take immediate steps to secure an answer.[127]

When the ax finally fell, Corner had not the slightest doubt that Dean Rusk was at once doing the trustees' bidding and seeking to protect the foundation from political reprisals. At no point did Corner blame the foundation's medical officers for the order to drop Kinsey.[129] Reflecting on his painful meeting with Morison, Corner later confessed that he could not help feeling sorry for the messenger. "He gave me the impression that he had been rather beaten down and that he was sorry about it and that he was a little ashamed of having to tell me this," declared Corner.[130] A keen observer, Corner had read his man right. Morison was mortified. "I wasn't very pleased about all this. And I don't think [Corner] was either," he later observed. Explaining his discomfort, Morison repeated that he did not enjoy "telling an intermediate organization like the National Research Council what they can and cannot do with their money" and admitted that he had found the whole affair "damned unpleasant."[131]

This was the moment Corner, and Yerkes before him, had dreaded. Unlike Kinsey, they had foreseen the dangers ahead. For years, they had pleaded with Kinsey to utilize the good offices, advice, and protection of the CRPS. Repeatedly, they had told him to identify his work with the NRC, to use it as a buffer and a shield, and to keep the Rockefeller Foundation safely in the shadows. They had stressed that the foundation did not want publicity, let alone controversy. Moreover, they had struggled to get Kinsey to understand that officers like Gregg, Warren, and Morison would not be able to keep the board at bay indefinitely, that the day would come when conservative trustees would overrule the professional staff and force the foundation to drop him.[128]

Two days after Morison returned to New York, Corner, accompanied by Keith Cannan, presented the foundation's demands before a meeting of the executive committee of the NRC's Division of Medical Science. Following heated discussion, the executive committee instructed Corner and Cannan to present the issue for debate to the CRPS. The following day, they took steps to convene a special meeting of the CRPS.[132] As part of those preparations, Corner informed Yerkes of the foundation's demands, calling the situation a "crisis in the affairs of the Sex Research Committee." Stressing that "the historical background of the problem is very important," Corner beseeched Yerkes to attend the meeting and advise the committee.[133]

Yerkes declined to attend, but offered advice aplenty. All those years of suffering insults and slights at the hands of Kinsey, it seems, had not filled Yerkes with the milk of human kindness. He advised the committee in no uncertain terms to do as the foundation asked and cut Kinsey loose. In his judgment, it was either Kinsey or the committee; and having devoted thirty years of his life to the committee, Yerkes found the choice easy. Calling this his "major pragmatic argument," he warned, "Rejection almost certainly would result in discontinuance of financial support of Committee activities by [the] Rockefeller Foundation, and unfavorably affect relations of the National Research Council with the Foundation." Neither possibility, he stressed, "can be faced with equanimity . . . by the officers and board of the Council." Yerkes went on to list several more reasons for dumping Kinsey, emphasizing in particular that the climate of opinion, as he put it, "definitely has changed very radically in the Rockefeller Board." In closing, he argued that the committee had "done its full duty freely and effectively in promoting the Kinsey undertaking during its early and adolescent years." Since Kinsey's work had come of age, Yerkes felt confident in predicting, "The Institute will survive and flourish without further assistance from the Committee for Research in Problems of Sex."[134]

In the end, it was Corner rather than Yerkes who carried the day. On February 2, 1954, the CRPS met to resolve the crisis over the foundation's demands. Although careful to share Yerkes's views with his colleagues on the committee, Corner refused to accept any solution that abrogated the committee's freedom to spend its funds (even though the money came from the Rockefeller Foundation) as it saw fit. Instead, he brokered a compromise.[135] Under Corner's skillful guidance, the CRPS agreed to remove the paragraph on Kinsey from its earlier application and to replace it with one that praised Kinsey's research but declared, "It is the Committee's understanding that this undertaking is now well established and in a position to carry on its program without further aid from the funds allocated to the National Research Council by the Foundation." In view of this development, the new draft explained, the committee wished to reduce its budget request from $80,000 to $50,000 per annum, with the understanding that "the Committee will continue to include in its program studies in the field of human sex behavior, and without restriction as to the institutions supported."[136]

The beauty of this compromise was transparent. On the one hand, it gave the Rockefeller Foundation what it wanted by eliminating from the committee's budget the funds that had been earmarked for Kinsey and by implying that he would no longer be receiving committee funds. On the other hand, the closing sentence left the committee technically free to grant Kinsey some portion of the funds it received.[137] Yerkes grasped this point immediately. "I can readily understand why your group seemingly offers something with one hand and withdraws it with the other," he wrote Corner after studying a draft of the language, "but I cannot imagine the responsible [Rockefeller] officers feeling happy about the proposed formulation, and if they should be willing to present it to the Board it seems to me unlikely that a majority would be willing to support favorable action if there were a few individuals strongly and affectively opposed."[138]

Miraculously, Yerkes was wrong. On February 3, 1954, one day after the committee hammered out the compromise, Cannan traveled to New York and hand-delivered the draft to Warren. Privately, Warren, like Morison, supported Kinsey's research and felt that the board had treated both him and the NRC shabbily. Consequently, Warren stuck his neck out. He accepted the new wording and agreed to present the application as written to the board.[139]

On February 8, 1954, Cannan submitted to the Rockefeller Foundation a revised version of the committee's application containing the budget reduction and the new language on Kinsey.[140] So that there would be no misunderstanding, Cannan informed Morison in a separate letter that the new proposal "should not be interpreted as an indication that the Committee is faltering in its opinion that Doctor Kinsey's work is highly significant and that from it have come important contributions to our knowledge of human behavior." Cannan declared further that while there were no plans at present to support the Institute for Sex Research within the new grant period, the committee was "unwilling to place any restriction on its freedom to develop the most effective scientific program possible." Therefore, should a member of the Institute "submit a project which, in the opinion of the Committee, is worthy of support," the committee planned "to feel free to implement its best scientific judgment." In a poignant postscript, Cannan added, "In my view, the Committee could take no other position consistent with the traditions and the mission of the National Academy of Sciences–National Research Council. I feel confident that you will agree."[141]

Corner, of course, was satisfied with the compromise, telling Yerkes, "I believe that if a grant is made on these terms we shall be in an excellent po-

sition."[142] Graciously, Yerkes replied, "There are times when it is [a] pleasure to be mistaken and your letter . . . convinces me that I sadly underestimated the courage and optimism of the officers of R.F. with whom you
are dealing. Surely, you should be encouraged by their cooperativeness."
Clearly contrite, Yerkes added, "I suppose I must have become appreciably more conservative and pessimistic!"[143] Ultimately, the board did approve the application that spring, crowning Corner's careful diplomacy
with success. Against huge odds and at considerable risk to the NRC, he
had stood behind Kinsey and achieved an honorable compromise.

In keeping with his practice of sharing information (good or bad) as
soon as it became available, Corner sent Kinsey the text of the new proposal that pertained to him. "As you will note, the last sentence is worded
in such a way that the Committee would be free at an appropriate time in
the future to consider a specific request from any member of your group
on the same basis as those originating elsewhere," wrote Corner. "I believe
that what we are now asking goes as far as possible under the circumstances," he added. "It specifically avoids any suggestion that the Committee is withdrawing favor from your work."[144]

Kinsey was too disappointed over the loss of his big grant to have more
than a scant appreciation for Corner's efforts. Despite all the evidence to
the contrary, Kinsey had continued to hope that the Rockefeller Foundation would renew his grant at its current level. Consequently, Corner's
news crushed him. For weeks on end, Kinsey boiled in anger. His good
friend Clarence Tripp, who happened to be visiting the Institute during this
period, had vivid memories of Kinsey skulking around the Institute and
muttering from time to time, "Damn that Rusk."[145]

Kinsey challenged the falsehood that his research no longer needed
grants. Early in March, he informed Rusk that while it was true that the
royalties from the male and female volumes could carry the Institute for the
next three years, those funds were not sufficient to see his current studies
on sex law and sex offenders to completion. "Moreover," he explained,
"to use up all of the visible income in the next three years would threaten
the continuation of the research beyond that point." Summoning the fighting spirit that had sustained him through so many battles over so many
years, Kinsey declared, "To have fifteen years of accumulated data in this
area fail to reach publication would constitute an indictment of the Institute, its sponsors, and all others who have contributed time and material
resources to the work. The discontinuation of support from the Rockefeller
Foundation and the National Research Council at this time makes it imperative, therefore, that we seek other sources of income before our immediate resources are gone."[146]

These words fell on deaf ears. For Kinsey, the matter was deeply personal. For Rusk, it was all in a day's work. A consummate bureaucrat, the only equity he sought to balance was the good of the foundation. By foreclosing additional applications from Kinsey, Rusk hoped to satisfy the trustees and to protect the foundation from the Reece committee.

Many years later, Rusk vigorously defended the decision to cut Kinsey loose. "When we reached the point where we were not willing to have the Rockefeller Foundation's 'Good Housekeeping Seal' put upon the Kinsey studies, it was appropriate for us to withdraw," he declared. Nor was Rusk troubled by whether or not this action violated the autonomy of the NRC. "I wouldn't think that is very much of a problem," he remarked cavalierly. "To start with, a private foundation has complete freedom of action to give or withhold funds," he explained. "The fact that it has made a grant in the past creates no obligation on renewing that grant."[147] From Rusk's perspective, then, the foundation's behavior was beyond reproach.

Rusk was right to worry that politicians would attempt to use Kinsey to get at the foundation. As the Reece committee prepared for the upcoming hearings, its staff members queried Rusk about the foundation's role in supporting the CRPS in general and Kinsey in particular. In February 1954, Norman Dodd, the Reece committee's director of research, asked Rusk pointedly to explain the switch in policy from making the fruits of research available to physicians and other specialists to "a policy of exploding findings on a public ill-prepared to receive them." In a crude attempt to bait Rusk, Dodd suggested that perhaps scientists believed "that the only way to dispense with fallacies and their consequences was to resort to as intense publicity as surrounded Dr. Kinsey's work and thereby get the subject out in the open once and for all."[148]

The NRC also received an inquiry from the Reece committee. Early in March, Karl Egmont Ettinger, a Reece staff member, paid a visit to Cannan. Ettinger was particularly interested in the NRC's relationship with Kinsey. Among other things, Ettinger inquired if the NRC intended to make additional grants to Kinsey, if the CRPS had analyzed the criticisms directed at Kinsey's work, if it had played any role in the publicity that had attended the female volume, and if it supported "the 'pornographic' museum and library" that Kinsey was reputed to possess. Troubled by the tone of the questioning, Cannan noted in his memorandum on this meeting, "There was a clear implication that the [Reece] Committee was preparing a brief to indicate that Kinsey went beyond scientific analysis and was attempting to influence legislation." While recording that Ettinger had volunteered a private opinion to the effect that Kinsey, not the NRC, was responsible for the entire matter, Cannan declared, "I had a distinct impression that the NRC was actually under scrutiny by the Committee."[149]

Of necessity, then, Kinsey figured prominently in both the foundation's and the council's efforts to formulate a defensive strategy against the Reece committee. For Rusk, the first line of defense was to stress that the foundation no longer supported Kinsey's research. In addition, he hoped to downplay the foundation's long record of direct involvement with Kinsey and to push the NRC front and center.

A cautious man by nature, Rusk erected his defenses with care. To counter the adverse publicity, Rusk arranged to feed the Reece committee favorable reviews and news clippings about Kinsey's two volumes. At the foundation's request, Corner asked Kinsey to supply these materials, a request he was only too happy to fill.[150] In addition, Rusk took steps to line up friendly witnesses. At Rusk's request, Gregg contacted Corner to see whether he would be willing to meet in person with Rusk. Musing on the reason for the request, Corner confided to Yerkes, "The rumors of a Congressional investigation of the Rockefeller Foundation seem to be causing the new president, Dean Rusk, some concern about the possibility of the Kinsey support being dragged into the limelight."[151]

Corner, of course, agreed at once to Rusk's request.[152] In February 1953, he met in New York with Rusk, who was accompanied by two prominent attorneys retained by the foundation. Describing this meeting to Kinsey, Corner observed, "Evidently [Rusk] was looking me over to see whether I would be a suitable witness before a Congressional committee, and he finally asked if I would consent to being named by him if he is asked questions relating to the work of the Sex Research Committee. I told him I would gladly testify."[153] Corner later recalled, "The session was devoted to coaching me as to what I would say if I were called on to testify." The gist of what Rusk wanted said, explained Corner, "was that the Committee for Research in Problems of Sex had backed the Kinsey work because it was regarded as a matter of scientific importance for the public good, that we had received money from the Rockefeller Foundation and had expended [it] on our own responsibility without pressure from the foundation."[154]

Since Corner had no desire to shirk responsibility, he had no problems with offering this testimony. What did disturb him, however, was Rusk's dearth of intestinal fortitude. "Dean Rusk was very much concerned; he was troubled," recalled Corner. "He was very much afraid that bad publicity for the foundation would come out of all this. I had the impression that he was really worried and that he was timid about it."[155]

The medical officers of the Rockefeller Foundation shared this opinion. Morison held strongly to the view that under Rusk's leadership "the foundation got more worried [about the Reece committee] than it should have."[156] Warren's assessment was harsher. When it came to policy issues of any kind, Warren saw Rusk as the trustees' rubber stamp. "Dean Rusk was very articulate, and he was very polite," Warren later declared. "But I would say Dean was not a leader. He is an excellent follower. . . . He would not fight for a project, I don't believe."[157] Warren's assessment would not have surprised Lewis Douglas, a Rockefeller trustee. Asked for his candid opinion when Rusk was being considered for the presidency, Douglas replied, "Dean Rusk is a capable man but I am rather apprehensive about him as President of the Rockefeller Foundation. . . . I am not at all certain that he would stand up under pressure. My experience with him has led me to believe that he bends too much to the prevailing breezes of the moment."[158] Had Douglas added that Rusk also had a tendency to pass the buck, the warning would have been complete.

Despite their recent friction over Kinsey, officials from the NRC worked hand in glove with the officers of the Rockefeller Foundation to prepare for the hearings. In March 1954, Corner approached Yerkes to see if he, too, would be willing to testify. Noting that "things are buzzing a bit with regard to the House of Representatives Committee on Foundations (Congressman Carroll Reece, Chairman)," Corner explained, "The chain of thought seems to be that the tax-free Foundations are to be scrutinized to see whether they are attempting to influence legislation. Kinsey is suspected of trying to influence legislation, therefore the Rockefeller and NRC are in turn suspected."[159]

If he expected Yerkes to leap to Kinsey's defense, Corner was mistaken. Tired and old, Yerkes had no fire in his belly for battle. In a response that was at best tepid, Yerkes declared, "If it were urgently necessary, I could, if called upon make the trip to Washington, but my own feeling is that I could do nothing for the investigators or the institutions involved which could not be as well or better done by you, Cannan, or both of you. It therefore would seem to me an inexcusable waste of time and energy for me to accept the request to serve as witness."[160] When Corner expressed his agreement,[161] Yerkes confessed that he felt both "greatly pleased and relieved." Added Yerkes bitterly, "But my dominant sentiment is one of disgust because of the obvious wastefulness of this investigative procedure. . . . There are times when I feel that our present Congress is unprecedentedly unwise and inefficient, and perhaps costing our nation more than it is worth."[162]

As the months passed and the tension over the forthcoming congressional hearings kept building, Kinsey's morale sank lower and lower. At times, his spirit would rally and he would fire off letters to Rusk, Warren, or Morison, pleading with them to come to Bloomington for a tour of the Institute, confident that if he could only get them on his turf he could work his magic, win them over, and restore his standing with the foundation.[163]

But most of the time Kinsey fell deeper into despair. Powerless to arrest the forces that threatened him, he could only worry and wait.

But Kinsey could not refrain from expressing his growing anger, if only by indirection, when opportunity arose. In April 1954, he traveled to the Biltmore Hotel in New York City, where he accepted the "Hoosier of the Year" award from the Sons of Indiana at the society's annual banquet.[164] Kinsey spoke with conviction on the hardships he had endured to obtain the same right to do research that other scientists took for granted, and he used this occasion to lavish praise and thanks on the people of Indiana and Indiana University for their many years of unwavering support. Reflecting on what he had seen that evening, Morison confessed in his diary that he felt "a little embarrassed inside to realize that this cornfed and relatively isolated state, so well represented in Washington by [William E.] Jenner and [Homer E.] Capehart, should display more courage and steadfastness in support of this controversial figure than we have."[165]

Kinsey's next public remarks were less guarded. Doing a good impression of Daniel in the lions' den, he appeared in early May on a panel at the annual convention of the American Psychiatric Association in St. Louis, Missouri. Making no effort to conceal his anger, Kinsey struck back at his critics and delivered an impassioned defense of his research. To the psychiatrists who had lambasted him for not considering love, Kinsey replied sarcastically, "I am a great lover of music, but if I were a physicist studying sound, I would be resistant to the notion I had to write a treatise on the esthetics of music." It was not that he considered love unimportant, explained Kinsey; it was simply that science had not yet discovered a way to measure love.

Kinsey also directed some sharp barbs at opponents of his methodology. Attacks on this score, he charged, amounted to "a complete denunciation of the scientific approach." Replying to critics who had accused him of "insecticizing human science," he demanded, "How many years do I have to study human behavior before I am no longer classed as an entomologist?" In what were perhaps his most revealing remarks, Kinsey identified himself with his role model, likening his battles to the struggles Darwin had been forced to wage in order to gain acceptance for his theory of evolution.[166]

Kinsey's most emotional remarks, however, pertained to his support structure. He told his listeners that he had had "to fight for funds and the right to do this study." Going public with his complaints, he charged that "considerable pressure" was being placed on Indiana University and the Rockefeller Foundation by "certain churchmen and others" to withdraw support from his work. "Things have been hurled at me as if I were the lowest of the low," he complained bitterly. And in a final shot at his critics, he lamented the "hundreds of thousands in the public whose use of my data has been impaired by this shallow criticism."[167] The frustration was starting to get to Kinsey, and it showed.

On May 10, 1954, the Reece committee finally opened its hearings. From the standpoint of public notice, the timing was not auspicious. On the domestic front, Americans were glued to their television sets watching another set of congressional hearings in a different building on Capitol Hill, where Senator McCarthy and the U.S. Army were going toe to toe. (Before those hearings ended, Joseph Welch, the army's chief counsel, had exposed McCarthy as a bully and a tasteless boor, and his downfall quickly followed.) Moreover, within a matter of weeks, the whole nation would be discussing the Supreme Court's decision in *Brown v. Board of Education of Topeka*, the most important desegregation case of the century. Foreign affairs also made heavy demands on the public's attention, as a generation of Americans followed the collapse of France's colonial fortunes in Vietnam after the Battle of Dien Bien Phu.[168]

With competition of this caliber, the Reece committee hearings needed to get off to a snappy start to capture headlines. Quite the opposite occurred. Staff members consumed the first four and one-half days of testimony delivering papers and reports on their research. Among other things, they accused the foundations of favoring empirical research in the social sciences, thereby ignoring "principles and their truth or falsity." In the end, they charged, this "wholesale acceptance of knowledge acquired almost entirely by empirical methods" could lead only to a "deterioration of moral standards and a disrespect for principles."[169] The stage was set for an attack on Kinsey.

On May 19, 1954, the Reece committee heard testimony from Albert Hoyt Hobbs, a right-wing sociologist from the University of Pennsylvania. Six years earlier, Hobbs had written a blistering review of the male volume, and time had not improved his opinion of Kinsey's research. In rambling testimony marked in equal measure by invective and by something very close to paranoia, Hobbs accused Kinsey of being "unscientific" and charged that his books tended "to undermine morals and faith."[170] Hobbs was particularly exercised about Kinsey's treatment of homosexuality, insisting that anyone who read his books would come away thinking that homosexuality "is normal and right."[171] Stressing that the research had been funded by the Rockefeller Foundation, Hobbs charged further that the foundation's prestige added undue weight to Kinsey's suggestions that "homosexuality is normal" and that premarital sex for women might be socially beneficial."[172] Adding his two cents, Chairman Reece dismissed Kinsey's work as "a bunch of claptrap."[173] The Democrats on the committee, by contrast, said nary a word against Kinsey, but they did accuse

Reece of using sex to generate publicity in order to revive a moribund committee. Bellowed Congressman Wayne Hays (whose own political downfall would later be caused by a sex scandal), "Sex is being brought in the 'back door' to make good headlines."[174] Kinsey was beside himself. In an anguished note to a friend at Penn, he demanded to know why Hobbs was attacking his research. Lamenting that he knew of no way to silence a psychopath who spewed out deliberate and malicious distortions of the truth, Kinsey expressed incredulity that attacks of this nature could occur after the Middle Ages.[175]

The hearings ground on into late June, but no official from the Rockefeller Foundation or the NRC was ever called to testify. Neither was Kinsey. All their careful preparation had come to naught, as the Reece committee's staff had no intention of telling both sides of the story. On the contrary, they had set out to stack the deck, and that was what they did. With one exception, all the witnesses who testified before the Reece committee attacked the foundations and railed against the kinds of studies they funded. The only positive remarks to be uttered before the committee came from Pendleton Herring, president of the Social Science Research Council. His defense was so powerful that the committee voted to suspend further public sessions.

Suddenly, the heat was off. For a time, observers believed that the Reece committee would fold its tent and sneak out of town. Instead, Reece invited parties that wished to make their views known to the committee to submit written statements, an opportunity that was accepted by Dean Rusk and a number of other foundation heads. As might be expected, Rusk delivered up a staunch defense of the Rockefeller Foundation and painted his organization as a bastion of academic freedom.

Over the summer, a few conservative newspapers criticized the Rockefeller Foundation for having supported Kinsey. In an editorial entitled "Shame on Rockefeller," the *Union Leader* in Manchester, New Hampshire, declared, "It is interesting to speculate what the elder Rockefeller, whose money went to create this great foundation, would have thought of spending money for Kinsey researches in sex. We don't think that is what Rockefeller had in mind when he started the foundation." The editors of the *Bristol* (Connecticut) *Press* were not as restrained. "If a foundation wants to lower its standards by supporting something like the questionable Kinsey research program, that is its privilege," they allowed. "However, when it does so and retains its tax exempt status then the situation is of concern to every citizen. Furthermore, such a foundation should be investigated and action should be taken against it if the results of the probe so indicate."[176]

But such attacks were rare. By autumn, most people in the world of foundations breathed a collective sigh of relief, confident that the danger from the Reece committee had passed. In the middle of October, Corner heard from Yerkes, who said that he assumed "that the nightmare of congressional investigation has subsided." Agreeing that the threat had "completely subsided," Corner disclosed, "The Reece Committee failed absolutely to win popular support and has apparently shut up shop." While comforting, that statement was premature.

In December, the Reece committee issued its final report. To the surprise of no one, the report, which ran to 432 pages, parroted the accusations of witnesses who had denounced the foundations. Among the witnesses singled out for praise was Hobbs, who had attacked Kinsey without mercy. Hobbs's testimony, declared the report, was "lucid, impressive and seemingly incontrovertible." Accompanying the majority report, however, was a stinging, if brief (only 15 pages), minority report from the Democrats, who denounced the Reece committee as "an ugly stain on the majestic record of the United States House of Representatives" and a "complete waste of public money." The minority report went on to attribute the attitudes of the committee's Republican majority to "the cloud of fear so evident in all phases of our national life in recent years," a kind of "fear-sickness" that infected the United States in the aftermath of World War II.[177]

The overwhelming majority of newspapers across the country endorsed the minority report, agreeing that the Reece committee had been a disgrace. "The Lunatic Fringe of the Lunatic Fringe," declared Wisconsin's *Madison Capital Times*. "Reece Report Wins Stupidity Title," announced the *San Francisco Chronicle*. "Reece Committee Report Is Completely Biased," declared the *Atlanta Constitution*. "Reece Report Insults Publics Intelligence," proclaimed the *San Antonio News*. "Attack on Free Inquiry," charged the *Washington Post and Times Herald*. "That Foundation Witch-Hunt," chided Salt Lake City's *Deseret News Telegram*.[178]

The *New York Times* was particularly forceful in denouncing the Reece committee's report. In a withering editorial, the *Times* declared, "The crime of the foundations seems to be that they don't finance research in the social sciences to support the isolationist, reactionary beliefs of Messrs. [Jesse P.] Wolcott and Reece, for whom the income tax spells socialism and anything more progressive than the right wing of the Republican party is a 'leftist' tendency." The best that could said of the Reece report, concluded the *Times*, was "The sooner forgotten the better."[179] Privately, Arthur Sulzberger admitted to Rusk that the *Times* "over-played the Reece report" and added that he personally did not plan to comment on it in public, explaining, "When somebody calls me an S. O. B. I don't think it's necessary to run home and look for my parents' marriage certificate."[180]

Rusk felt pleased by how well things had turned out. In the end, the Reece committee had gone nowhere, and Rusk felt fully vindicated by the way he had played his cards. In June 1955, months after the Reece committee had closed up shop, Rusk strongly denied that it had won a victory. "If you would care to look through the Reece Committee Report and Hearings," Rusk told a friend, "you would find criticisms of a considerable number of institutions and individuals who appear in our own publications as currently receiving support from The Rockefeller Foundation." So that there would be no mistaking his meaning, Rusk answered the "general charge that the foundations were intimidated by that Committee" by declaring, "I know that the charge is not true, as applied to us, and I do not believe that it is true in the case of other large foundations."[181]

This would have come as news to Kinsey. His name, of course, had not appeared on the foundation's list of grantees in 1955. In fact, Kinsey had been forced to remain silent and watch through clenched teeth while the NRC did the foundation's dirty work. The *New York Times* reported on August 24, 1954, "Dr. Keith Cannan, chairman of the council's Committee on Problems of Sex, said yesterday that funds for Dr. Kinsey were dropped as of midsummer, because his Institute for Sex Research did not request a renewal of support." The *Times* went on to note that "Dr. Kinsey's work was now well endowed and did not need further help from the council."[182]

For the next several years scholars and philanthropists often debated whether the Reece committee had a chilling effect on the foundations and whether it had made scholars think twice about the topics they worked on or the methodologies they employed. Gradually, a consensus emerged that the Reece committee had been little more than an annoyance. But this was not entirely accurate. There was one clear-cut casualty, and his name was Alfred Charles Kinsey. The withdrawal of the Rockefeller Foundation's support under fire threw him into a tailspin from which he never recovered.

28

"UP AGAINST THE WALL"

arly in the Reece committee hearings, Kinsey's view of the future had turned dim. Everything he had worked for was in jeopardy, and he despaired of being able to keep the Institute together. "Obviously, we cannot hold a professionally trained staff that has no guarantee of its work beyond the end of a given year," he wrote a friend. "Consequently, we are up against the problem of long-term financing."[1] But finances were not Kinsey's only worry; he confronted a crisis of confidence.

By the end of summer 1954, Kinsey finally had faced the reality that the Rockefeller Foundation would never renew his grant. Dejected and bitter, he stood in his offices in the basement of Wylie Hall one night early in August, looking up at the exposed pipes just below the ceiling. For years, he had boosted the pain he inflicted on himself with urethral insertions by tying a rope around his scrotum and tugging hard while he masturbated. On this particular evening, his anxiety must have been worse—much, much worse.

Too strong to be resisted, the compulsion could only be obeyed. Doing as his inner demons demanded, Kinsey threw a rope over the pipe. Only a man with special knowledge could have secured the knot so firmly, but this former Eagle Scout had not forgotten his boyhood training. Skillfully, he tied a strong, tight knot around his scrotum with one end of the rope dangling from the pipe overhead. The other end he wrapped around his hand. Then, he climbed up on a chair and jumped off, suspending himself in midair. For what length of time he stayed aloft, caught between heaven and earth, remains unclear. But it was long enough for this self-appointed messiah of the sexually despised to experience much pain and suffering, precisely as he had intended. His inner equilibrium had always been fragile, and the only way he could vent his anxiety was through self-torture and debasement.[2]

Immediately after the basement episode, Kinsey, accompanied by Gebhard and Dellenback, left for Peru, where they had made arrangements to photograph a fabulous collection of Mochican pottery, highly erotic in design, owned by a wealthy Peruvian banker. Soon after arriving at their host's hacienda, Kinsey took to bed, suffering from an infection in his pelvic region. As a cover story, he attributed his illness to a throat infection he had contracted earlier in Los Angeles, explaining that the infection had spread to his pelvis en route to Peru.[3] A physician friend, however, labeled Kinsey's illness orchitis, pinpointing the testicles as the site of the infection.[4]

Kinsey was not a model patient as he suffered through his painful injury. Many years later, Dellenback recalled an incident in Peru while he sat up writing letters home. Kinsey, who was sleeping in the room next door, got up to use the bathroom and then appeared momentarily in the doorway. Dellenback looked up, smiled, and nodded "hello," at which point Kinsey, in Dellenback's words, let him have "both barrels full in the face," roaring out, " 'Dellenback, what do you mean keeping the entire household awake?' " This said, Kinsey turned on his heels, stalked back to bed, and left Dellenback fuming. "I should have known the mechanism," he later confessed. "Kinsey generalized this sort of thing all the time. He actually catharticized constantly all of his internal troubles. It was rough on outsiders and staff, but it sure helped Kinsey out."[5]

With his emotions, perhaps, but not with his body. The infection got worse, forcing Kinsey to enter a hospital in Lima. During his childhood, he had suffered numerous bouts of poor health, experiences that had left him chronically impatient with any illness. Rather than surrender to sickness, Kinsey had always been a fighter. But this was one occasion when he could not force his body to obey his will. For nearly two weeks, he lay in a hospital bed in a foreign land waiting to heal.

By the beginning of September, Kinsey felt well enough to return to Bloomington, but he was not able to resume his hectic schedule. His appointments and travel plans for September had to be canceled, as he spent most of the month in bed. Among those most concerned was his close friend Glenway Wescott, who had been told to expect a visit shortly after Labor Day and had lined up a number of people for interviews. "Kinsey did not arrive . . . I called Paul Gebhard. They expect A.C.K. to pull through all right, but he was in bad condition," wrote Wescott in his diary. "Some Peruvian bug, culminating in a 'pelvic infection'—twelve days in bed in a Lima hospital?" Added Wescott with obvious embarrassment, "It did not occur to me not to, in making his excuses to people who had expected to have their histories taken, etc., not to specify the nature of illness—until someone said, 'Pelvic infection? Oh yes, of course, llamas.' "[6]

Although the effects of the injury lingered well into the fall, Kinsey forced himself back to work. Early in October, he wrote a friend, "I am steadily improving and hope to be in the field again within another week or so."[7] This was to be the pattern of Kinsey's last years: repeated bouts of illness interspersed with frenzied efforts to pursue his work.

One of the earliest signs of Kinsey's failing health was acute insomnia. As the Institute's financial woes deepened, the pressure got to Kinsey, and he had trouble sleeping. To combat his insomnia, he started taking sleeping pills, followed by stimulants in the mornings to get himself going. In the 1950s, physicians handed out barbiturates and amphetamines rather freely to their patients, as the medical community had little understanding of these drugs' addictive quality. Neither did Kinsey. Before long, he was trapped in what one of his coworkers called "an impossible cycle of drugs for tranquilizing and then for stimulation." The effects showed. "He would come to the office in the morning bleary-eyed and feeling groggy after a restless night with little sleep," recalled Christenson. "Strangely enough," she added, "he could nap easily in the daytime. His demons pursued him only at night."[8]

Edgar Anderson, his old friend from graduate school, noticed the change in Kinsey's appearance immediately. "His face is more lined than when I last saw him and his pace is being slowed down by drugs," wrote Anderson. He also observed that Kinsey had "a kind of puffiness in the face" and "a pink flush between the cheek bones and the eyes." Alarmed by Kinsey's physical deterioration, Anderson begged his old friend to get medical attention and slow down a bit. "I thought I had him but he looked at me impishly and said, 'Oh, I did talk to my doctor and you know what he told me? He said that under no circumstances must I ever let people scold me.' "[9]

Flagging stamina, accompanied by a need for frequent rests, also betrayed the fact that Kinsey was winding down. Beginning with his family's move to South Orange, he had prided himself on being able to walk most people into the ground. Well into middle age, he had moved at a brisk clip, bounding up steps two at a time. But in his final years Kinsey's pace slowed to a crawl. Pomeroy recalled starting up a hill in San Francisco with Kinsey, who quickly began panting and fell behind. Instead of asking for a moment to catch his breath, Kinsey cried out, "Pomeroy, I want to look at this marvelous window display."[10] Kinsey then commenced to hold forth on the items in the window until he could manage to resume walking. This sort of thing happened again and again. Kinsey would take a few steps up a hill or a flight of stairs and be forced to stop partway up, at which point he would pant out a few observations on one topic or another while he gasped for air. Near the end of his life, friends noticed a dramatic change even when he was not exerting himself. Margaret Edmondson, a regular at the Sunday musicales, was stunned by Kinsey's loss of mobility. "It was a real shock to come in on a Sunday evening and have him not walk across the room to meet you because his health would not allow it," declared Edmondson.[11]

Heart disease and severe hypertension were to blame. During his final years, Kinsey had to endure one heart episode after another. (Most likely, his heart ailment was related to the rheumatic fever he had suffered as a boy.) Harry Benjamin, a prominent psychoanalyst in San Francisco, witnessed Kinsey having a mild heart attack in a hotel during one of his many visits to the West Coast. Most men would have checked into a hospital immediately, but Kinsey's response, in Benjamin's words, was to become "very impatient with his own illness" because he "could not overcome this terrible handicap."[12] Other friends told similar stories. "I saw him through one of his heart attacks in New York," recalled Wescott many years later. "It wasn't a big one, but I sat with him while he was panting, panting while he was waiting for these extreme medicines to work. I was one of the first people who realized that he was almost a continuously angry man. And angry men perhaps cause heart attacks."[13]

Repeated failures to secure funding fed Kinsey's anger, and over time he expressed his frustration increasingly in public. In November 1954, he attended a symposium sponsored by the National Science Foundation at Amherst, Massachusetts, on the theme "Genetic, Psychological, and Hormonal Factors in the Establishment and Maintenance of Patterns of Sexual Behavior in Mammals." Scheduled to speak on the topic "Unique Problems in the Study of Human Sexual Behavior," Kinsey was expected to deliver a technical paper, but his talk took a different tack. His presentation was less scientific than political, if not deeply personal, and his tone was decidedly bitter.

Describing the talk to Yerkes, Corner revealed that Kinsey "chose to speak chiefly about the obstacles raised against his work by the conventionality or worse of various people and institutions," particularly the Rockefeller Foundation and Reinhold Niebuhr and Warren Weaver, both of whom Kinsey had targeted for special abuse. "Neither the scientific contribution nor the expression of alarm about the adverse conditions affecting sex research were new enough to interest the audience very much," declared Corner with obvious concern. "I heard a good deal of murmured complaint afterward because he had not taken the occasion to give us something from his vast stores of information."[14] Despite their many clashes over the years, Yerkes remained Kinsey's partisan. Confessing that he felt "dismayed as well as surprised" by Kinsey's performance, he observed, "I most earnestly hope that this does not indicate [a] change in his point of view or attitude, personal relations, etc., etc., which would almost inevitably lessen his usefulness as scientist and encourage prejudice against his work."[15]

From Kinsey's viewpoint, the only positive thing that came out of the Amherst symposium was the opportunity to confer with Corner. The two men had not talked in person since the Reece committee hearings, and Kinsey was anxious to sound Corner out for ideas about funding. Certainly, Corner knew what was on Kinsey's mind. A month before the conference, Corner admitted to Yerkes that he had avoided reopening correspondence with Kinsey for months because he expected to see him at Amherst and preferred "to state the Committee's views in private conversation," noting that this would make it "easier to explain to him the tightrope walking we have to do and to convey our continued sympathy with his work."[16]

The meeting was anything but easy, as Kinsey was beside himself with worry. In an age when scientists flourished or floundered by their ability to land grants, Kinsey was fearful that the Institute might not survive the loss of its patron. Agitated and desperate, he pleaded for ideas about possible sources of funding. "I told Kinsey that I felt sure the Sex Research Committee will give favorable consideration to well-phrased, specific requests for individual projects of his group, beginning at the 1955 meeting," Corner confided to Yerkes. "Indeed," he continued, "I think we ought to grant a few thousand dollars to the Institute for Sex Research, assuming that a suitable project reaches us, in order to define our position." As a political statement directed at the Rockefeller Foundation, this was a courageous offer. It went a long way toward salvaging the committee's autonomy and self-respect. Still, Corner had no illusion that a token grant would solve the problem. "I confess I do not know what I could do personally to help Kinsey find the large-scale support he wants and will need in a year or two," he wrote Yerkes.[17]

Meanwhile, Wells was taking steps to minimize the political damage. In

January 1955, he met with Dean Rusk at the foundation's headquarters in New York. Rusk noted that Wells "came in to discuss the position he should take with his State Legislature on the Kinsey report and to come to a meeting of minds so that he and I would not clash in any public statements on the subject of why The Rockefeller Foundation had discontinued its support." After considerable discussion, they hammered out a statement that drew heavily on the self-serving explanation the foundation had released earlier to the press. Specifically, they agreed to recycle the fiction that Kinsey's grant had not been renewed because he was now in a position to obtain support from other sources. For his part, Rusk volunteered to release another statement declaring that the foundation considered sex research an important part of the life sciences, and he promised to characterize "the aim of the Kinsey studies as a contribution to the better understanding of 'some of the elements in a complex aspect of human behavior in which parents, doctors, ministers, teachers, legislators, social workers, penologists and many others have a serious interest.' "[18] If these words fell short of an endorsement, they were the best Wells could pry from Rusk.

While Wells worked to head off problems with the state legislature, Kinsey pounded the pavement in search of money. In February 1955, he met with Yerkes in New Haven, hoping that the man who had solved his financial problems fifteen years earlier could work a second miracle. At this meeting, in contrast to his conference with Corner, Kinsey appeared calm, giving no hint of the desperation he felt. Though neither man knew it at the time, this was to be their last meeting.

Yerkes later described the visit as "very pleasant and highly informing and enlightening." As their talk progressed, Kinsey handed Yerkes a typed list of eighteen reports he hoped to publish in book or monograph form, the data for which were already in hand and awaiting analysis. All that was needed to complete these projects, insisted Kinsey, was $50,000 annually for the next decade. "I suggested that he search systematically for an angel instead of continuing to hope for institutional, governmental, or foundational backing," Yerkes wrote Corner, "but he seemed not very optimistic about finding a well disposed individual, and although federal funds might logically . . . be used for the purpose, the expediency would seem to preclude that solution of the problem which I most earnestly hope he may be able to satisfactorily resolve."[19]

Kinsey had good reason for feeling pessimistic. Ever since the Rockefeller Foundation had announced that his grant would not be renewed, he had been searching for a wealthy patron to help with his budget shortfall or, better still, to provide an endowment for the Institute to solve its money problems for good. From 1954 until his death, Kinsey hounded his supporters for introductions to their wealthy friends. Several did arrange meetings with potential patrons, with results that can only be described as painful.[20]

Among the first to discover Kinsey's brown thumb as a fund-raiser were Monroe Wheeler and Glenway Wescott, a gay couple whose friendship network cut a wide swath in New York's artistic and literary worlds. After considering the problem from several angles, they advised Kinsey to change the Institute's name to make fund-raising easier. As one possibility, Wheeler suggested "The Research Institute for Animal Behavior," explaining, "Some people might be embarrassed to mention sex to their lawyers when making their wills."[21] Kinsey, of course, vetoed the idea immediately. He had worked too long and too hard to make sex research respectable to even consider this suggestion.

Nor did Kinsey cotton to their other idea. Wescott and Wheeler both advised him to seek out wealthy homosexuals. Recalling his reasoning many years later, Wescott explained, "The only people I thought he could get money from were homosexuals." But Kinsey "was simply horrified" by the suggestion, noted Wescott, a reaction that he attributed to the pioneering sex researcher's "extraordinary fear of his being associated with homosexuality."[22] Having lost one patron, Kinsey had no intention of endangering his relationship with Indiana University. He was determined, as Wescott put it, "to keep the research impeccably respectable and austere in order to continue to have the backing of a great university behind him."[23] In the end, despite numerous attempts at persuading Kinsey to target homosexuals, Wescott and Wheeler got nowhere. "[Kinsey] was afraid of wrecking the Institute on the reef of the doomed minority," lamented Wescott.[24]

Therefore, at Kinsey's insistence, Wheeler and Wescott put together a list of prospective patrons whose personal lives would not raise questions about their motives. At first, Kinsey was optimistic. "He thought that he was such a national celebrity" that "if he went and beat on people's doors, he would get somewhere," explained Wescott. Instead, Kinsey got nowhere fast. Wheeler, who had acquired vast experience dealing with patrons in his position with the Museum of Modern Art and who felt totally at ease around wealthy people, would arrange cocktail parties with the rich and famous in Kinsey's honor. Invariably, the evenings would begin on a pleasant note and end in disaster. One explanation, noted Wescott, was that Kinsey "put people off" because he "talked down to people."[25] Members of his inner circle, by contrast, told a different story, suggesting that the real problem was his inability to ask for money.

Schmoozing is the oil that lubricates the wheels of fund-raising, but Kinsey could not do it. Whenever he attended a fund-raiser with fabulously wealthy people, Kinsey, in Pomeroy's words, "was paralyzed." The man who was a genius at persuading people to tell their secrets "simply froze up and could not ask for money."[26] Part of the problem was Kinsey's inability to make small talk. Somehow small talk invariably became big talk. Always Kinsey would hold forth nonstop about his research and its importance to science, displaying an earnestness and seriousness that were quite frightening in their purity. On occasion, he even would summon the courage to ask prospective patrons to contribute their sex histories. But, again, requests for money never left his mouth.

Pomeroy blamed this on Kinsey's inability to relate to rich people, explaining that he disliked their "arrogance" and "complete egocentrism."[27] Equally important was Kinsey's fear of failure. The man who had to be the best at everything dreaded being turned down or, worse yet, appearing self-serving. As a result, Kinsey hated going hat in hand to fund-raisers, almost all of which left him feeling dejected and bitter. Nor was he the only person who found these evenings agonizing. Friends had to suffer through only a few flops (at most) to realize that Kinsey was incapable of landing a fish. As Wescott later confessed, he and Wheeler tried to help, "and then we didn't do anything, because we didn't know what to do."[28]

Each failure took a toll on Kinsey. He would leave Bloomington in high spirits and return with his heart in his shoe. The worst part was having to face the staff. Part of being "Poppa" was bringing home the bacon, but the Institute's cupboard was becoming bare. Kinsey was not delivering the goods. Never mind that sex research was a "hard sell" to potential patrons; his personal code admitted no excuses. Kinsey blamed himself. Yet, month after month, he managed to pull himself together and project a confident air in staff meetings. Ignoring the most recent disaster, he would announce with hope and excitement a new lead on some wealthy individual who could solve the Institute's financial worries with the stroke of a pen.

Staff members admired and respected Kinsey for these performances, all the more so because they knew he was trying to keep up their spirits in the face of dwindling hope. "We knew that we were in serious condition," declared Gebhard. "But Kinsey was not a man who could admit defeats or setbacks," he continued. "He also had the feeling that he must not ruin our morale by telling us how bad things really were. In consequence, he had a tendency to conceal the acuteness of a situation from us. Since he handled these matters himself, we were often unaware of just exactly how precarious our situation was."[29]

As the Institute's financial prospects became more grim, Kinsey started charging a fee to lecture. In the past, the only recompense he would accept was an assurance that members of his audience might be receptive to calls for interviews. As the Institute's financial crisis deepened, however, Kinsey requested and received a $500 honorarium (plus travel expenses) for each lecture, a considerable sum at the time.[30] Although there were plenty of takers, the demands of his research, coupled with his deteriorating health, prevented Kinsey from delivering enough lectures to rescue the Institute from its financial woes.

In April 1955, Kinsey paid a visit to the Rockefeller Foundation, not to solicit funds but to cry on Morison's shoulder. Kinsey, whom Morison described as "looking a bit tired and worn," was brutally frank in expressing his fears about the Institute's future. During their discussion, Kinsey produced the same list of projected books he had given Yerkes. Although impressed by the number of uses Kinsey had envisioned for his data, Morison quickly perceived that nothing on the list had any chance of bringing in another gusher. "The difficulty is that most of these books will not command anything like the royalty payments which were enjoyed by the first two, and that with the termination of support from the Committee on Sex, he will really be up against the wall," confided Morison to his diary. Kinsey also poured out his fears that Wells might encounter serious problems with the state legislature as a result of the foundation's decision not to renew the Institute's grant. "President Wells," noted Morison with obvious regret, "feels a little isolated now that support from the Foundation and the Committee on Sex is terminating," continuing, "It just makes his case more difficult to make before the Legislature, and he has enough other problems so that one could hardly blame him if his strength began to flag a little." Barely able to conceal his sadness, Morison added, "K., of course knows full well the difficulties in the way of further aid from this Foundation, and RSM does not do much more than listen during the whole of this lunch—listen and express sympathy."[31]

Often Kinsey did not even get sympathy from the foundations he approached. Long before the Rockefeller Foundation had pulled the plug, he had started searching for a new patron. In addition to contacting a number of small foundations, he spent months and months trying to interest the Ford Foundation in his research. But apart from a courtesy visit with Bernard Berelson, the director of the Behavioral Sciences Program, nothing came of these efforts. Exasperated, Kinsey complained to a friend, "The surest way of not getting any money from the Ford Foundation is to ask them for it."[32] Corner, too, attempted to make inroads with the Ford Foundation, and he, too, failed.[33] These setbacks left Kinsey darkly pessimistic. In April 1956, he wrote a friend, "Unfortunately, the foundations are scared out of supporting sex research and we face imminent danger of our whole project coming to an end if we cannot raise funds within another twelve months."[34]

To Kinsey, this prospect was horrible beyond words. "I know that in the latter part of his life he broke his heart, practically, trying to raise funds, literally going from foundation door to foundation door and having it slammed in his face," Gebhard later declared. "Everyone would tell him how important his work was and how it merited support, but no one would put their money where their mouth was." A less resolute man might have given up, but not Kinsey. Miraculously, his ego would rally and he would repeat the routine. "When he came back to us from an unsuccessful venture," declared Gebhard with genuine awe, "he would always couch the report in terms of how this didn't happen to work but so and so is going to introduce me to somebody else, or we have this other foundation that might be interested."[35]

On at least one occasion, Kinsey turned down help. Early in December 1954, Russell Yohn, a sexual enthusiast who had followed the Institute's work for several years, read newspaper accounts that the Rockefeller Foundation had discontinued its support of Kinsey's research. Shortly thereafter, he approached Kinsey with "a Christmas surprise to the members of the Institute, who have contributed so much to the cause of sexual enlightenment and tolerance." To help the Institute through its financial straits, Yohn announced a plan to organize the "Friends of Kinsey," a "people's foundation for sex research," with membership dues of one dollar a year. His goal was not only to provide funds to the Institute but "to secure the renewal of the Rockefeller Foundation's support." What Yohn envisioned was a grassroots movement, an outpouring of support from ordinary people who endorsed Kinsey's call for a new sexual ethic, one that would replace guilt with enthusiasm and condemnation with tolerance. "If antisexuals can use organization to interfere to remove the financial means of sexual science," announced Yohn "prosexuals can certainly organize to protect sexual science."[36] While taking care to express his gratitude and thanks to Yohn, Kinsey rejected the offer summarily, explaining that the plan would never generate enough money to be significant and might well antagonize a great many people.[37]

Ultimately, Kinsey's search for funds brought him full circle. In February 1955, he sent Corner the same list of projects he had shown Yerkes and Morison, asking if there were any items that the committee might wish to fund. Pleading his case with great passion, Kinsey declared that it was unthinkable that sixteen years of hard work should fail to be published for lack of funds. Pointedly, he reminded Corner of how important it was for Wells and the trustees to know that the NRC supported his work. Although Kinsey failed to specify an amount, he insisted that even a token grant would benefit the Institute greatly. A grant of any size, he argued, might spell the difference between life and death for the Institute if questions arose in the state legislature.[38]

True to character, Corner took Kinsey's part, bending the rules and procedures in ways that would have reduced to envy the committee's other applicants. "Ordinarily," wrote Corner, "I avoid as much as possible influencing an experienced investigator in the choice of a problem, but this is a special situation, in which emphasis should be placed on the ready justifiability of the work to our financial sponsors." With one eye on the Rockefeller Foundation's likely response, he then proceeded to pull from Kinsey's list four projects, noting that "the Committee would be especially receptive this year to a request for funds to write up your study of Drugs and Sexual Behavior, or of Abortion, or of Juvenile Sexual Delinquency, or of Transvestism, perhaps in the order named." Promising to support whatever project Kinsey submitted, Corner stated that he would do so "with good hopes that favorable action might be secured this year to the extent of $5,000."[39]

In March 1955, Kinsey submitted a formal application to the CRPS in the amount of $5,000 to write up his material on abortion, stipulating that the funds would be "applied toward the salaries of the persons on our staff who will be directly involved in the analyses of these data."[40] It was, of course, an inside job all the way. The committee approved the grant in its spring meeting, though the amount was cut to $3,000. Aware that Kinsey might regard the reduction as a concession to the Rockefeller Foundation, Corner explained that the committee had received an unusually large number of applications. "I can tell you privately that there was no serious difference of opinion as to the advisability of the grant in the light of our relations with the Rockefeller Foundation," confided Corner.[41]

The grant pleased Kinsey. In his letter thanking Corner, Kinsey declared, "I trust that it causes no trouble in your relations with the Rockefeller Foundation."[42] Relieved to have good news to report for a change, Kinsey also fired off a note to Wells. While admitting that the sum was small, Kinsey noted proudly, "[I]t constitutes, nevertheless, an expression on the part of that Committee of its desire to continue to be identified as one of the sponsors of our research." Underscoring the symbolic importance of the NRC's willingness to stand shoulder to shoulder with Indiana University, Kinsey added, "This fact may be of considerable use to you in handling the University['s] official relationship to our research program."[43] Wells, of course, was both delighted and relieved to learn of the grant and sent "Hearty congratulations" in return.[44]

The Rockefeller Foundation reacted less cordially. In the middle of May 1955, the NRC's Keith Cannan telephoned Morison to inform the foundation of Kinsey's award.[45] Many years later, Corner described Morison as "somewhat disturbed" because he felt "that we have rather put him on the spot."[46] In early June, Cannan was summoned to New York for a meeting.[47] During the discussions, Morison complained that the NRC had shown poor judgment by awarding Kinsey a grant on the heels of public announcements that he no longer needed support, an action that threatened to expose the statement drafted by Rusk and Wells for the sham it was.

Chastened by Morison's tone, Cannan made it clear that the NRC was not prepared to endanger its relationship with the Rockefeller Foundation any further over Kinsey. The grant to prepare the Institute's data on abortion for publication had been made, noted Cannan, because it had the strong backing of the clinicians on the CRPS. "K. has much more extensive material on this important subject than anyone else has ever assembled," wrote Morison in his notes. To calm the foundation's fears about publicity, Cannan promised to make every possible effort to see that Kinsey published his material in medical journals, far from the public's view. "In addition to this [Cannan] feels that the period of great advance publicity and public interest in the Kinsey findings is probably coming to its end," wrote Morison. "The sale of the second book was much less than that of the first and he feels that any further publications from the Kinsey group will not contain enough new or exciting material to justify continued public interest," he added.[48]

By meeting's end, Morison and Cannan had reached an understanding. While the officers did not wish to question the recent small grant to Kinsey, stressed Morison, if larger grants followed, the foundation "would be in a different position."[49] According to Morison's notes, Cannan, in turn, acknowledged "that the committee may have crowded things a little" in making a grant to Kinsey so quickly after the announcements that he was in a position to secure funds elsewhere. Indeed, Morison also noted that the more Cannan thought about it, the more he questioned the committee's judgment, an issue that led him to wonder "if the time may not be approaching when it might be wise to change the chairman."[50]

Following the meeting in New York, officials from the NRC moved swiftly to pacify the Rockefeller Foundation. Acting on orders from above, Corner asked Kinsey to publish his abortion data "in an article in a clinical or clinico-scientific journal (e.g. the *American Journal of Obstetrics and Gynecology,* the *Journal of Fertility*)," explaining that this "would help us all to rebuild our understanding with the Rockefeller Foundation." Correcting an oversight, Corner sent another note advising Kinsey that in all subsequent publications that involved NRC funds "it would be . . . highly politic that the support should be acknowledged to the NRC only," because "for the present Dr. Morison would prefer not to have the Foundation mentioned."[51] Kinsey agreed to play ball, promising to publish his abortion material in a medical journal and to confine his acknowledgments to the NRC. Still, he had enough fighting spirit in him to assert that "if the

Rockefeller Foundation pushes this matter, it places them on record for future history in regard to the obstruction of medical research."[52]

This exchange marked the end of any fruitful relationship between the NRC and Kinsey. Henceforth, Kinsey and Corner remained in contact about the customs case, but they were never able to devise a workable plan for solving Kinsey's financial problems.

For fifteen years, Yerkes, Gregg, and Corner, with Wells anchoring the squad magnificently in Indiana, had made up Kinsey's support team. Yerkes, the quintessential organizational man of science, had served as the talent scout and early counselor and booster; Gregg, the philanthropoid qua risk taker and man of vision, had opened the Rockefeller vault and kept it ajar under fire longer than anyone would have dreamed possible; and Corner, a distinguished scientist equally at home in the laboratory and in the world of institutional science, had served as Kinsey's sage adviser and stalwart defender. As a group, their relationship with Kinsey had never been easy, because he was not an easy man to deal with. At times they had cooperated; often they had battled. But, like it or not, Kinsey had brought them together, intertwining their lives with each other's and with his. Together, they had pursued their common goal of expanding the store of scientific knowledge on human sexual behavior. They had done so because they believed in progress, or, more specifically, in science as a vehicle of progress. From the outset, they had shared the view that society knew far too little about human sexuality and that this dearth of knowledge had hindered social policy. And to varying degrees, each had been motivated by his belief that repressive morality had to be softened and that scientific data offered the best basis for fashioning a new sexual ethic.

Together, Kinsey, Yerkes, Gregg, and Corner had pushed the envelope of science, greatly augmenting knowledge about human sexuality. In addition, they had produced a dialogue that spilled over into the broader culture as Americans tried to resolve conflicting demands for freedom and restraint in their private behavior. Convinced that most people could not satisfy the proscriptions and strictures of middle-class morality, Kinsey had the genius to invent an instrument, however flawed, for measuring actual behavior. And it was also his genius to perceive the crucial role of institutions in fostering social reform, both as sources of funding and as legitimizing agents of cultural power and authority. Astutely, he had divined that his message stood a far greater chance of being accepted if it carried the imprimatur of the NRC and the Rockefeller Foundation. Kinsey was right. While he received all the headlines, it seems doubtful whether he could have completed the two books and built the Institute that made him world famous without the support of those faceless, but incredibly important, organizational men of science—Yerkes, Gregg, and Corner.

Kinsey and his supporters were part of a generation of scientist-reformers who had come of age during the Progressive Era, and their approach to problem solving was a product of attitudes and beliefs they had imbibed as young men. Like most progressives, they believed strongly in the possibility of human progress and had absolute faith in the power of education to uplift society. As men of science, they never doubted that scholarly research could uncover fundamental truths about human nature and that these discoveries, in turn, could be used to fashion rational social policy. They believed that once science learned the facts about human sexual behavior the public could be educated to reject harmful attitudes and behavior and to think and act in ways that would be socially beneficial. Few assumptions better illustrate the optimism of the age.

By 1956, of course, Kinsey's generation of scientist-reformers had reached old age. Their faith in human progress seemed curiously naive in the face of two world wars, the Holocaust, and the development of atomic weapons with the power to destroy the planet. Their moment on history's stage was rapidly vanishing. Society would have to look to a new generation of leaders with different assumptions and new approaches to problem solving. As if by cue, Yerkes, Gregg, and Kinsey would all die in 1956, followed by Corner's resignation as chairman of the CRPS a few years later.

Although the quest for funds preoccupied his final years, Kinsey struggled mightily to keep his research going. Horrified and angered by the repressive sexual climate of the late 1940s and early 1950s, he had decided to delay his study on homosexuality and to make sex offenders the subject of his next book, confident that his data would show that most sex offenders were harmless people whose behavior need not concern the public. Consequently, he concentrated much of his interviewing after the male volume in male prisons, where he focused on inmates who had committed sex crimes.

From the earliest days of the research, Kinsey had felt profound sympathy for these men, largely because he identified with many of them. In his judgment, most sex offenders were not a danger to society. While their behavior violated sexual taboos and offended the public's sense of propriety, they did not inflict physical harm on others. Indecency, sodomy, adultery, fornication, masturbation, homosexuality, and the like, Kinsey believed, had no place on the criminal code books. Publicly, he acknowledged that the state should penalize rape, exhibitionism, peeping, and adult-child sexual contacts.[53] Privately, he believed that exhibitionists and Peeping Toms were simply public nuisances whose behavior should not be penalized, and he was not so sure that adult-child contacts should be illegal.

The more Kinsey interviewed sex offenders, the more angry and resentful he became over their incarceration. In December 1954, he vented his feelings in a brief article written for the *San Quentin News*, a piece that reads at once like a plea for tolerance, an effort to provide absolution to most sex offenders, and, above all, an attempt at self-justification and exoneration. Noting that the United States had entered a season when many persons were reexamining their beliefs, Kinsey declared that his own faith in people had steadily grown as a result of taking prisoners' histories. "Even though some of these histories have included things which did no good to anyone, and occasionally things which may have done outright damage to someone," he wrote, "most of the things which I have seen in the histories have increased my faith in the basic decency, the basic honesty, and the basic reasonableness of human behavior."[54] Certainly, that is the way Kinsey longed for society to view him—as decent, honest, and reasonable.

Addressing his next remarks directly to the inmates, Kinsey declared, "I believe that most of you here at San Quentin have done a great deal more good than you have ever done damage in this world." There it was again, a plea for society to judge people in balance, not to seize upon an aspect of behavior and elevate this fragment to the whole. What followed sounded deeply autobiographical. "I have found that the sexual behavior of most men and women, including even their most cantankerous and socially impossible behavior," testified Kinsey, "makes sense when one learns about the handicaps, the difficulties, the disappointments, the losses, and the tragedies which have led them into such behavior."[55]

As Kinsey neared life's end, his private boundaries eroded, reaching the point that he was prepared to withhold moral judgment on incest and other adult-child sexual contacts. Wescott recalled a conversation in which Kinsey acknowledged that, when he first started the research, he considered "corrupters of children, men who had intercourse with children, beyond the pale," a group for whom "there could be no sympathy." Wescott also remembered Kinsey's saying that child molestation was the only behavior that he abhorred. Over time, however, Kinsey had tempered his views. "He used to talk quite a lot about the feeling that the parent has a property right to children," recalled Wescott, "as long as he's brought them into the world and supported them, he has the right to bring them up as he wants."[56] Apparently, the child's rights in this matter did not burden Kinsey's thinking. It was as though he was blind to the power politics (both psychological and physical) within families.

Had Kinsey been asked to explain why he changed his mind, he would have answered "data." Wescott remembered Kinsey's talking about all the people he had interviewed who had been molested and saying that while they all condemned sexual child abuse as a matter of principle, only a few felt that they personally had been harmed. From Kinsey's perspective, child molestation, like other sexual taboos, violated morals, but the actual harm it inflicted was all in people's minds. If society did not make a big deal of it, children would not be harmed. "At any rate," added Wescott, Kinsey "felt this was going to be the last taboo to be raised, if it ever would be lifted."[57]

According to Clarence A. Tripp, Kinsey believed that the public did not realize the social benefit of the pedophile. Tripp remembers his saying, "Well, most pedophiles deal with urban, low social level young males, Forty-second Street preprostitutes ideal material. This kind of male may not have any kindness or niceness in his life from any source, and the pedophile is the only source of it. And people who have a sexual motivation often bring kindness and affection into [a] life where it is found nowhere else."[58] If true, this observation was all the sadder for being so. The fact that these boys would sell their bodies for a little affection was a harsh commentary on how society treats its throwaway members. In his eagerness to dissolve restraints and to celebrate eros, Kinsey was blind to the coercion inherent in any sexual contact between an adult and a child. He failed to see that sexual exploitation of adolescents by adults was a poor substitute for nonerotic love and attention.

In the end, Kinsey had little impact on the sex offender codes, at least during his lifetime. Politicians at the local, state, and national levels in the 1950s were in no mood to relax legal controls. From a political standpoint, sex reform was too controversial. Kinsey had hoped for greater tolerance. Instead, he encountered cultural intransigence, and he regarded his inability to win greater acceptance for groups that violated middle-class morality as one more failure on his record. As a result, his frustration and desperation grew apace.

Kinsey was angry—angry about the persecution of homosexuals, angry about harsh sex offender codes, angry about the collapse of his support structure, and angry, perhaps, because time was running out. Increasingly, he directed his hostility at his heart. "To Kinsey his body was the enemy, preventing him from doing everything he wanted to do," declared Pomeroy. Kinsey "personalized the stubborn organ" and began many sentences with the complaint " 'My heart won't let me do this,' " noted Pomeroy.[59] And the more Kinsey had to struggle, the more his anger fed a related emotion. He grew bitter. "The bitterness did show up in certain facial expressions, I think, in a certain lacklusterness of the eyes, a certain drooping around the mouth, a certain grimness mixed with a bit of tiredness," recalled Henry Remak, one of Kinsey's translators. "I would not be surprised," added Remak, "if, in these last two or three years, he may not have been the easiest man to deal and live with on the part of his most intimate associates and his family."[60]

Hoping a rest might improve Kinsey's health, friends and family members finally persuaded him to take a European vacation in the autumn of 1955, his first visit to Europe and his first vacation in sixteen years. The plan called for Kinsey and Clara to spend seven weeks abroad. Yet Kinsey had no intention of relaxing on this trip, any more than he allowed himself to rest at home. Calling upon European friends of the Institute and several contact men who happened to be living abroad at the time, he planned a full schedule of fieldwork.

The first stop was Scandinavia. To his delight, the press gave him a warm reception, and he discovered that he was a celebrity in this part of the world.[61] He enjoyed this segment of the trip immensely, as Denmark and Sweden had the most liberal sex laws in Europe. In Denmark, he lectured at the University of Copenhagen and at Aarhus University. He spoke on American sex law, recording in his trip notes that the students in the audience "could hardly believe that there were such laws."[62] For two nights running, Kinsey also accompanied the chief of police and the vice squad on their rounds through Copenhagen's night spots. Working from 9:00 P.M. to 2:00 A.M., they visited eight to ten places each night. Kinsey marveled at the open and accepting sexual attitudes he observed, and he was equally impressed by the tolerance the police displayed toward male and female prostitutes alike.

From Scandinavia, the Kinseys went to Great Britain, which proved to be something of a letdown. Kinsey spent much of his time at the British Museum, examining sexual treasures (books and art objects for the most part) that the average visitor never got to see. He also visited a few penal institutions, which he was sorry to learn housed a number of homosexuals and other minor sex offenders who were every bit as pitiful as their American counterparts. Noting that fully 30 percent of the inmates had been incarcerated for sex offenses, Kinsey observed in his trip notes, "There isn't any doubt of it from all other quarters that England has become utterly rabid on the homosexual question."[63]

More to Kinsey's liking was the time he spent observing Britain's sexual underworld. Accompanied by Clara and a British friend, Kinsey went to Piccadilly Circus on a Saturday night. "I have never seen so much nor such aggressive behavior anywhere else," declared Kinsey. For a man who was supposed to be on vacation, he kept late hours, pushing himself as hard as ever. Estimating that he counted at least a thousand prostitutes there between 8 P.M. and 3 A.M., Kinsey observed that "both males and females were accosting" and that by 2 or 3 A.M. "all the prostitutes—male and female—were letting their hands dribble across the crotch of passer[s]by." Most of the girls at Piccadilly Circus, he noted, "were trim and neat," but deeper into Soho one encountered "the old worn-out hags."[64] From Kinsey's perspective, rampant prostitution could mean only one thing: sexual repression was alive and well in Great Britain, for there would be little need to sell sex in a society in which sexual attitudes and behavior were relaxed. Summarizing his opinion of the British, Kinsey wrote, "I am quite convinced at this point that we inherited a lot of our attitudes from our English forebears."[65]

The next stop was Paris. He was met at the airport by reporters, who he noted "were pretty decent and got the story right." Kinsey lectured before the medical society in Paris, speaking on concepts of normality and abnormality. But attendance was light, largely because his talk happened to fall on a holiday and many doctors had cleared out of Paris for a long weekend. The translator was another problem, as he could not keep up and had to be replaced partway through the lecture.[66]

Following the lecture, Kinsey was free to explore Paris. He took an instant dislike to the French gendarmerie, whom he considered overbearing and mean-spirited. Kinsey was also distressed by the disdain with which the French treated homosexuals. Moreover, while French males appeared to adore French females, noted Kinsey, it was obvious that they did not regard them as equals. Nor was Kinsey impressed when he and Clara attended a performance of the Folies-Bergère. While allowing that the show was a grand spectacle, Kinsey could not help noticing that the audience appeared to be as bored as he was.[67]

From France, the Kinseys traveled to Italy, where they spent three weeks. As he had throughout his European vacation, Kinsey skipped the usual tourist spots in favor of observing the sexual underworld in various cities. He adored Italy, calling it "a man's country."[68] Italians (males in particular), Kinsey believed, engaged in a great deal of sexual activity; and he was determined to observe as much of the sexual scene as possible. Never one to leave things to chance, Kinsey had arranged in advance to be shown around by several individuals who knew where to find the action.

One such guide was Kenneth Anger, an American avant-garde filmmaker who happened to be living in Italy that year. They had met in Los Angeles in the late 1940s, soon after Kinsey saw *Firecracker*, a fifteen-minute homemade movie that marked Anger's first attempt at film production. Anger was seventeen years old and still in high school when he shot *Firecracker*, a homoerotic film about gay bashing, with strong sadomasochistic undertones. Kinsey was so impressed by the film that he asked Anger for an interview and later invited him to Bloomington, where Anger was filmed masturbating.[69]

Anger served as Kinsey's guide in Rome, Palermo, and Cheflieu, the little village where Anger lived that summer. Although they visited several houses of prostitution, they spent most of their nights (often into the early hours of the morning) observing Italy's homosexual underworld. "I was his gay guide through hell, like Vergil and Dante or whatever," declared Anger decades later. In Rome, Anger took Kinsey to the Coliseum, a favorite cruising ground for homosexuals.[70] Indeed, its many dark passageways, niches, and corners teemed with sexual activity. In his trip notes, Kinsey stated that he observed two soldiers masturbating each other, a male on one side of an iron fence showing his erect penis to another male on the other side of the fence, and a priest "who was certainly cruising the Coliseum for sexual contact." Kinsey also observed that the fields around Rome were "filled with copulating couples both homosexual and heterosexual on a balmy night."[71]

As they traveled together, Anger became concerned about Kinsey's health. One could see at a glance that he was not well, yet he insisted on keeping late hours and driving himself at a frantic pace. Night after night, Anger watched Kinsey push on, trying to cram as much as possible into his visit. To make matters worse, Kinsey was having a hard time getting any rest. "He told me that he hadn't slept in years and that he had to take Nembutal sleeping pills. And I saw these pills when I was once in his hotel room," recalled Anger. The problem, explained Anger, was that Kinsey could not disengage from his work. "I got the impression that he knew that sleeping pills were not a great thing," declared Anger. "It was just that he didn't have any alternative. It was either that or not sleeping at all, and he had to turn off his mind."[72]

In addition to sleeping pills, Kinsey was taking heart medication, which Anger identified as "nitroglycerin pills, or some kind of pills." Since he could no longer manage stairs, Kinsey requested hotel rooms on the first floor. But this precaution did not stave off bouts with his heart. Kinsey had a particularly scary episode in Taromina, where he experienced considerable difficulty breathing and painful pressure in his chest. Certain Kinsey was having a major heart attack, Anger remembered following him around a room with a chair to catch him when he collapsed. "I told Mac, 'You've got to get him to rest; he's driving himself,' " recalled Anger. "And she agreed, but she said, 'He's impossible; forget it.' "[73]

Kinsey was, as Anger put it, "bullheaded." Asked not to do something, Kinsey "would do it even though he obviously shouldn't or he was tired or feeling stressed." Anger felt sorry for Clara, who struggled valiantly, but with absolutely no success, to make Kinsey slow down. "A couple of times I saw him almost lose his temper with her," recalled Anger, "and he would sort of snap at her a little bit." Furthermore, Anger could not help noticing how little time the Kinseys spent together. Granted, there were brief visits to museums, but Anger stressed that "the tourist thing was just peripheral." More often than not, Kinsey abandoned Clara. As Anger put it, "Well, she did her own thing; she let us do [ours]."[74]

The more time they spent together, the more Anger grew concerned about Kinsey's emotional health. "I did catch the depression," recalled Anger, who thought that it was caused by the attacks Kinsey had suffered in the press and by his financial woes. According to Anger, Kinsey considered the Rockefeller Foundation's refusal to renew his grant an act of "betrayal." Instead of being immobilized, however, he responded to depression by speeding up. Haunted by his memories of Kinsey's frenetic mental state, Anger later observed, "It seemed to me that he functioned too much. That he couldn't slow down or take it easy."[75] Anger was right: Kinsey was winding himself tighter and tighter, like a watch spring about to break.

The Iberian peninsula was Kinsey's last stop in Europe. "Rather tight lipped," was how he described Spaniards, insisting that they were a "silent, dull, beaten people." He blamed the Catholic Church for making Spaniards so unappealing, announcing with characteristic certainty that "there isn't any doubt they are a church ridden people." Kinsey considered Madrid one of the most sexually inhibited cities in Europe. Barcelona, by contrast, was somewhat freer, and sex there was "much more evident." Describing his experiences in that city, Kinsey noted, "Fortunately I was able to line up with a G.I. who acted as the bait that I could watch being approached and he traveled with me for two or three days."[76]

Not everything Kinsey observed pleased him. In Barcelona, he saw a male homosexual prostitute, who was openly ridiculed by the female prostitutes, sailors, and other men. "Tried to engage him in conversation but he was such a pitiable creature he wouldn't even talk to me," lamented Kinsey.[77] Still, on the basis of what he saw and heard, Kinsey concluded that homosexual contacts were plentiful in Barcelona, particularly near the waterfront, where soldiers and sailors congregated. "If I had been there longer and had people to guide me I could have found all the hypocrisy that goes with the suppression," he declared.[78]

Kinsey's reaction to Portugal was much the same. Although he did some sight-seeing, he did not enjoy his stay. "Didn't get much on sex here," he complained in his trip notes. "This is a priest ridden country." In one town, Kinsey asked a taxi driver about homosexuality. The driver replied that there was none and flatly announced, "Men are men in Portugal," an explanation that Kinsey dismissed as "a grand piece of nonsense."[79]

Overall, though, Kinsey was glad he had visited Europe. While friends and family had hoped that he would relax, he had gone abroad intent on studying human sexuality in every country he visited. In part, he was looking for data that would allow him to compare Europeans with Americans, but he was also hoping to broaden his thinking. Shortly before returning to the United States, he wrote Eleanor Roehr, his secretary, "It has been a most profitable trip, research-wise, and everything we do in the future will be colored by the new thinking I have picked up along the way, on erotic art, on sex laws, prisons, police, attitudes on nudity, church control, female prostitution, male prostitution, etc."[80] Soon thereafter, Kinsey wrote a friend, "I never realized that I could learn so much more about sex as I did in the seven weeks in Europe."[81]

Perhaps the most important thing he learned that was at least other nations had succeeded in managing human sexuality with less repression, guilt, and pain than the United States. When Kinsey went to Europe, he was unquestionably looking for hope. The McCarthy years had left him deeply pessimistic, and he badly needed to find cultures that practiced greater tolerance toward sexual diversity. Kinsey found what he was seeking. "Of all the places where we were in Europe this last year, Southern Italy and Scandinavia are the two areas I want to go back to. Both of them are remarkably freer in their acceptance of sex than anything in our Anglo-American culture," he wrote a friend.[82] Making even more explicit his joy over finding countries that could serve as models for reforming American sexual laws and mores, he wrote a Danish friend, "We should keep in touch so we understand each other better. Certainly Denmark has a great deal to teach the United States."[83]

Yet, whatever the trip's professional value, it was a complete failure as a vacation. Instead of relaxing, Kinsey had worked, and the work had taken its toll. He himself admitted as much, telling his secretary early in November that it had been an "exhausting trip so far."[84] Not surprisingly, then, when Kinsey came home to Bloomington, he looked anything but rested. Commenting on his appearance, Christenson observed, "He was short of breath, lines in his face were deepened, and his color was pallid."[85] Pomeroy offered a more chilling assessment, declaring, "Europe was Kinsey's swan song. He came home to die."[86]

"He Helped to Change the Times"

D uring Kinsey's European travels, the Institute had moved into Jordan Hall, the new biology building. Spacious and secluded, the Institute's quarters could be reached only by way of an elevator to the third floor, where it stopped directly in front of an imposing oak-paneled door. Visitors entered an outer office occupied by Kinsey's private secretary, Eleanor Roehr, who served as the gatekeeper. Beyond her were two corridors, one lined with Dellenback's handsome portraits of distinguished scientists who had befriended the Institute, the other with Dellenback's equally stunning photographs of Mochican pottery. Along the corridors were the staff offices, library, and the file room, the heart of the Institute's operations. By the spring of 1956, the file room, located next to Kinsey's office, contained more than 18,000 histories, a monument to the staff's industry.[1] Naturally, the Institute's decor was Spartan and drab (the walls were painted institutional gray), in keeping with Kinsey's instructions.

Upon his return from Europe, Kinsey resumed his normal work routine despite his fragile health. More days than not, he put in long hours, often remaining at the Institute until midnight or later. How many of those hours were productive was an open question, however, an issue under-scored by the addition of a piece of furniture to his otherwise stark office. Kinsey's new office, noted a visitor, had "a large metal desk at one side of the room and a divan and chair at the other," with huge metal cabinets lin-ing two of the walls. The divan, the first allowed inside the Institute, rep-resented one of the few victories the staff ever won over Kinsey. Members of the inner circle, in particular, knew how badly he needed rest, and they also understood how much he hated capitulating to his body. "He looked on the couch as an admission of weakness, [and] as a possible public rela-tions hazard," recalled Gebhard. Kinsey feared that people might think the couch was for sexual purposes or, worse yet, that he was literally lying down on the job. But after his wife, physician, and staff members ganged up on him, he finally relented and agreed to move the couch in. "But he didn't like anyone knowing that he was using it," noted Gebhard. "So he would have his door shut so we would never know whether he was work-ing at the desk in a period of uninterrupted quiet or whether he was actu-ally sacked out on the couch."[2]

Soon it became clear that very little was happening behind that door. Writing, analyzing data, and planning new research require energy and purpose. Kinsey was rapidly running out of both. So instead of grinding out routine work, he started holding more and more staff meetings. Sur-rounded by friendly and supportive faces, he would then fall into his fa-vorite roles as teacher and mentor. "The meetings were usually to tell the staff some experiences he had had, but those experiences were not so un-usual, so different from others that we knew about to require that much time of the staff," recalled Dorothy Collins, a research assistant at the In-stitute. Emphasizing that Kinsey held "so many staff meetings," Collins added, "I felt that they were probably as much as he could stand to work. He couldn't apply himself to other things and so was having staff meetings to give [us] a sense of working."[3]

On many such occasions, Kinsey was not able to hold his emotions in check. In the past, his eyes had merely brimmed up when he had described some poor wretch rotting in jail for a minor sex offense. In his last year or two of life, by contrast, Kinsey lost control. The dam would break and a torrent of grief gush forth. Collins remembered one episode in particular when Kinsey told a sad tale about a young man in a California prison. And as Kinsey spoke, "the tears began pouring out of his eyes." Looking back on how odd his reaction had struck her at the time, Collins added, "He had had so many experiences of this nature, I felt it unusual for him to lose his composure over this one. But he had these emotional reactions more and more frequently during the last period of his life."[4]

Gebhard knew what was happening. Years later, he recalled a man who was haunted by visions of persecution and fears for the Institute's survival; a man who aired his demons at staff meetings, often to the point of ranting; a man who was anxious and depressed; a man who was losing self-control. "Particularly in the last year of his life, he had more difficulty controlling his emotions, and he became frankly quite paranoid," declared Gebhard. "He was convinced that various people, both known and unknown, were antagonistic to his work and to him personally, and were attempting to bring things to a halt to prevent his getting funds," Gebhard continued, stressing that Kinsey became "hypersensitive and extremely defensive in his last years."[5] Gebhard could not bring himself to state the obvious. Kinsey was perilously close to a breakdown. Only a speck of emotional glue was holding him together, the residue of the muscular will that he had developed as a youth.

Troubled by his boss's bizarre behavior, Gebhard worried that Kinsey might be mentally impaired. "I don't know how much of his difficulty was due to the disease itself, and how much was due perhaps to the medication," recalled Gebhard many years later. "But I got the impression that the man had suffered a series of small strokes." Still, Gebhard would not have dared raise the issue with Kinsey. It was not simply that Kinsey was becoming increasingly irrational or that his tendency to behave like a tyrant, never far from the surface, was becoming more acute, though these considerations certainly gave Gebhard pause. No, Gebhard held his tongue out of respect for Kinsey's pride. However precipitous his emotional and physical decline and whatever the limitations imposed by his health, Kinsey was still "Poppa" and he demanded respect, deference, and loyalty from his staff. "The last thing I would have ever discussed with him was whether or not there was any intellectual deterioration," confessed Gebhard. "This would have outraged him completely. But I felt that there was."[6]

With Kinsey behaving like a wounded bear, the Institute's work all but ground to a halt. As Gebhard later remarked, "We were really marking time." Throughout the spring 1956, weeks turned into months and the situation did not improve. "It was very bad for morale," recalled Gebhard sadly. "A number of us thought about leaving, yet on the other hand we realized that this point of all times is when we should stay. One was faced with the dilemma: would you be a rat and desert the sinking ship, or would you be a staunch mate and attempt to salvage the vessel before it sank."[7] While members of the inner circle all stayed the course, at least one staff member abandoned ship. After sitting through one more pointless staff meeting than she could abide, Collins resigned her position as a research assistant at the Institute. Recalling her decision to leave, Collins confessed many years later, "I felt that I was not getting enough out of the time I spent there."[8]

Outsiders could also sense the trouble. The last time Glenway Wescott visited the Institute before Kinsey's death, he had a feeling the end was near, a premonition that began with a haunting encounter early in the morning as he walked from the Student Union to Jordan Hall. "I saw a dying thrush, a wood thrush, a beautiful little creature, with brown tassels on its creamy, white bosom," Wescott recalled. "And it was scarcely able to walk, it staggered and looked up at me in a blind sort of way, and I shooed it off the path and wondered if there was anything I could do for it." A few minutes later, Wescott was standing in the doorway to Kinsey's office. Unaware that his friend had arrived, Kinsey was staring blankly at the wall. "[I] saw him there at his desk waiting for me, and I looked at him and I realized—it came to me terribly because I had just seen this little dying animal—that he was a dying man." Kinsey's entire demeanor, explained Wescott, "bespoke self-pity," like a man waiting for death with "numb, dumb, patience." The instant their eyes met, however, Kinsey stirred, "making believe that he was doing something." As Wescott thought back on that moment many years later, the word he used to describe it was "heartbreaking."[9]

According to Gebhard, Kinsey's productivity dropped by at least 50 percent, if not more, in his last few years.[10] Even at this rate, though, Kinsey still managed to turn out an amazing volume of work. His correspondence alone was a demanding chore, but he kept abreast of it, answering most letters in a timely fashion and initiating numerous exchanges as the occasion warranted.

Somehow Kinsey also summoned the energy to look for a new publisher. Because of new directions in his research, Kinsey and the W. B. Saunders Company agreed in 1955 that he should place his future books with a different publishing house. (The parting was amicable, with Lawrence Saunders and Kinsey remaining on good terms.) Desperate for money, Kinsey devoted considerable time and energy in 1956 to the search. His goal was to find a house with deep pockets and a willingness to offer big advances and favorable royalty rates. While there was less of a feeding frenzy than the one that had greeted his search for a publisher in the 1940s, Kinsey still had some magic. Once again, he found himself being flattered and wooed by several houses. Although McGraw-Hill seemed to have the inside track, Kinsey died without having reached a decision. The issue was not resolved until several months later when the trustees of the Institute finally gave the nod to Harper and Brothers.

Unwilling to admit defeat, Kinsey continued his efforts to raise money until the last days of his life. At one point, he considered hiring Pierce, Hedrick & Sherwood, a prominent fund-raising firm. Its fee, he discovered, came to $30,000 a year, irrespective of how much it raised. Since this was a large portion of what the Institute needed to stay afloat, Kinsey decided to explore other options, telling a friend, "We are trying to see if we cannot get effective fund raising help at some lower figure than that."[11] Increasingly desperate, Kinsey hoped to strike it rich in the Lone Star State, imploring another friend, "If you find any Texas oilman who would like to contribute to the support of such research, let me know and I would go anywhere in the U.S. to discuss it with him."[12]

Kinsey's last serious attempt at hooking a patron came at the beginning of May 1956. Tripp, who had provided help so many times in the past, arranged for Kinsey to meet Huntington Hartford, the A & P heir, in New York. Believing that Kinsey would be most effective one-on-one, Tripp decided to absent himself from the meeting, unaware that Hartford had planned an elaborate dinner party in Kinsey's honor. The evening proved to be one of those rare events in human history—a perfect failure. Socially ill at ease in the opulent setting in which he found himself, Kinsey could not bring himself to ask for money. Once again he left empty-handed, having blown an opportunity that Tripp considered, quite incorrectly, to be foolproof.[13]

After the Hartford debacle, the last in a long series of spectacular failures, the fire seemed to go out of Kinsey. He returned from New York crestfallen and exhausted, looking like a man who no longer believed that things would turn out well in the end. Clara later remarked that she thought he never recovered from the contretemps in New York.[14]

A visitor to Kinsey's home in May could not shake the fear that Kinsey had seen his last spring. Hoping to find relaxation and pleasure, Kinsey arranged an outing to the opera, but the evening did not go well. "After walking up to the balcony he took one of his 'little white pills,' but he was not comfortable or relaxed all evening," the friend later wrote. "I felt then I'd probably not see him again and—as it turned out—this was the last May of his life."[15]

Another man might have heeded the warning signals, but the habits of a lifetime would not allow Kinsey to rest. Toward the end of May, he traveled to Chicago, the city that in the late 1930s had provided his first glimpse into the embryonic homosexual communities that operated just below the surface of urban life in the United States. On May 24, 1956, Kinsey took his 7,984th and 7,985th histories. They would be his last. Reflective and wistful, he wrote a friend a few weeks later, "It is a shame there comes a time that you have to work up data and publish it instead of continuing the gathering. Frankly, I very much enjoy the gathering."[16] Thus, to the end, collecting remained Kinsey's passion. It satisfied (as no other activity could) his need for power, control, and discovery.

On June 1, 1956, Kinsey had another heart attack, marking the beginning of the end. He spent a week in Room 612 of the Robert W. Long Hospital in Indianapolis. Although he seemed to respond well to rest, his doctor warned that Kinsey would not be so lucky the next time if he failed to mend his ways.[17] Writing to express concern, President Wells pleaded, "Please stay in bed until you absorb some rest. It is the best of all medicines."[18] Shortly after his release, Kinsey provided a graphic description of his problem. "There is an enlargement of the heart, constant fibrillation, an apical beat of about 140 at the time I went to the hospital and a pulse of anywhere between 40 and 80, and other such foolishment," he wrote a friend. "Failure to compensate induced the problem of water retention. My Indianapolis man was very pessimistic, but the young, local man who is following me now that I am home is gradually learning to make allowances for individual variation, and learning that I cannot so easily be put down."[19] Publicly, then, Kinsey held firmly to the intellectual guidepost that had shaped his career, insisting that the outcome would be favorable because he was a unique individual.

Kinsey should have gone to bed and stayed there until his doctors said he could move. Instead, he attended the dedication ceremony for Jordan Hall, the third floor of which provided the Institute's new quarters. Upon learning that several of his former students planned to attend the dedication, Kinsey had them come to supper in his garden on June 7. He enjoyed seeing them again and reminiscing about the gall wasp days. Yet, somehow the conversation always came back to the Institute's perilous state and his fears for its survival. As he spoke, his anger boiled to the surface and he became quite emotional. The evening was hard on Kinsey, and his guests departed gravely concerned about his health. After returning home, Breland, salty as ever, advised, "Be sure to take care of yourself, and get plenty of rest, even though Mrs. K has to tie you in bed!"[20]

That is what it would have taken to make Kinsey rest. Despite multiple signs that his health was perilous, he had no intention of heeding the warnings. As if to prove it, he forced himself to attend a dinner in Alumni Hall in honor of Fernandus Payne, the final event of the three-day ceremonies for Jordan Hall. Kinsey had many faults, but ingratitude toward his old chairman was not among them. In Payne's words, Kinsey "dragged himself" to the dinner "out of loyalty."[21] Distressed to find Kinsey looking so frail, Payne pleaded with him, "Please slow down. You'll contribute more in the long run by living longer." But Payne knew that Kinsey would not listen. Years later Payne observed sadly, "He couldn't do it; he couldn't slow down."[22]

For Kinsey, ill health was but another test of character, another obstacle to be overcome. No, he would not surrender to his failing body; he would make his body obey his will. Consequently, Kinsey ignored his doctor's warnings and made himself go to the Institute more days than not.

"It was along in June that Kinsey came to my office, and he looked like hell," recalled Torrey, his colleague of many years.[23] Kinsey had come to discuss some minor problems with the Institute's news quarters. As Kinsey stood up to leave, Torrey asked him to remain so they could talk a moment longer. Pressing the point as strongly as he could, Torrey advised Kinsey to take some time off—weeks, months, a year—whatever was necessary to regain his strength. More than a decade later, Torrey remembered Kinsey's reply, "Oh, I've got to keeping working." Torrey shot back, "But if you continue you are liable to kill yourself," and added, "If you want to commit suicide I suppose that's your business, but I believe you should give some consideration to your family and to your research colleagues and to this Institute." Unable to shut up, Torrey then repeated every word of the warning for emphasis. For a moment, Kinsey seemed shaken, but he quickly regrouped and replied, "Well, I'll think about it." As he walked toward the door, however Kinsey apparently had thought long enough. Pausing, he looked over his shoulder and said, "If I can't work, I would rather die."[24]

Did Kinsey have a death wish? Perhaps. Still, it seems just as likely that he thought he could hold death at bay with one hand and bully his body into doing his bidding with the other. But this time Kinsey was wrong. Despite his best efforts to keep going, he spent most of June in bed, though he did manage to drag himself into the office a couple of times for a few hours.

Late in June, Kinsey wrote a friend, "I have been in bed more or less continuously for the past three weeks, partly in the hospital; but there has been definite improvement in the last couple of days and today I am strangely calm and appear, for the first time, able to get some things done in the laboratory." Stubborn as ever, he added, "This encourages me to believe that I can work back into it again."[25] By early July, Kinsey informed Breland that there had been "definite improvement" and predicted pluckily, "In spite of a pessimistic doctor I shall prove to them as I have in the past 30 years, that you can do more with a physical handicap than they sometimes think."[26]

Throughout July, Kinsey's health was up and down. On bad days, he grudgingly took to bed; on good days he got up, dressed, went to the office, and worked a few hours until fatigue overtook him. "I have steadily improved, in the last week especially," he wrote a friend early in the month. "There is still lots of room to go, and I continue to need frequent rest and nap in the course of the day."[27]

Kinsey had a pretty good idea of what had caused his heart to act up. He admitted to a friend that he had been working too many hours, was not getting enough sleep, and felt tense over some problems that had developed during his recent trip to New York. Still, Kinsey predicted that he would prove the doctors wrong and be back at work soon.[28]

August opened with more of the same. On good days, Kinsey would go to the office for a few hours; on bad days, he would stay in bed. "Two or three weeks before his death I heard him say over the phone: 'I can't understand why I can't get my strength back,' " recalled Remak, noting that Kinsey had said this "in a tone of indignation," as though he believed his illness was "unfair" and "unjust" because "there was so much to be done."[29] Characteristically, Kinsey also directed his anger at his doctors. Blaine Johnson, who worked part-time at the Institute during his student days, remembered driving Kinsey to work while he slumped in the seat and complained about incompetent physicians.[30]

On August 9 and 10, Kinsey felt well enough to work on his correspondence and to begin dictating what proved to be his last attempt at writing. Assuming the muse Clio, he discussed the history of his research, as he wanted it told, as though intimations of mortality were weighing heavily on his soul. In heated, passionate, rambling, and often disjointed sections, Kinsey spoke of the need for sex research, of the damage inflicted on society by ignorance, of earlier giants in the history of science who, like him, had been forced to battle censorship and social condemnation; and of the individuals, institutions, and groups that had supported and protected his research.[31]

But mostly Kinsey talked about the hardships he had been forced to endure. Casting himself as a martyr, he unfolded a simple morality play, with daunting challenges, insurmountable obstacles, and wicked villains. For many people such an exercise might have proven cathartic, but not for Kinsey. The intensity of his emotions showed no diminution whatsoever: from beginning to end, his tone was angry and bitter, like that of a man who had remembered everything and forgiven nothing. As it happened, he was a man who was providing his own epitaph.

Kinsey delivered his last public lecture at Purdue University on August 14, 1956, less than two weeks before his death. Staff members pleaded with him to cancel the lecture, but Kinsey insisted, threatening to go by bus or by train if no one would drive him. In the end, Clara relented and chauffeured him the one hundred miles to West Lafayette, where she watched, as she had so many times in the past, her husband speak in a matter-of-fact tone about things that only twenty years earlier could not have been discussed in public. Clara knew that he did not have long to live. By this point, his complexion was ashen, more blue-gray than fleshlike in tone. Most distressing of all, he was finding it increasingly difficult to breathe, owing to fluid buildup in his lungs and around his heart, the telltale signs of advanced congestive heart failure. Mercifully, Kinsey's powers did not fail him. His lecture was a credible performance, a triumph of stupendous spirit over failing flesh. He even managed a note of humor. Addressing a training institute for college deans, Kinsey noted how the sexual activity of men declined with age, announcing in his best deadpan "and then they become deans!"[32]

Shortly after Kinsey and Clara returned to Bloomington, the customs case again demanded his attention. On August 1, the government had filed suit against the Institute.[33] Although the Institute was capably represented by Morris Ernst and Harriet Pilpel in New York, Wells decided to add local counsels to the defense team. Explaining his reasoning, Wells later observed, "I felt that [Kinsey's] flank needed to be protected by another kind of firm, which, if we could get them to get into it, would give him a broader background of understanding of the federal courts and the Indiana relationship and so forth." Indeed, Wells thought that Indiana University had a clear obligation to stand up and be counted. "Kinsey was here, he was ours," declared Wells. Consequently, Wells went to his board and announced, "I think we ought to join in this case. I think it would be wholly not only improper, but just unfair, for us not to do it. It has to be won for American scholarship."[34]

Wells persuaded his old friend Hubert H. Hickam, of Barnes, Hickam, Pantzer, and Boyd, one of the most prestigious law firms in Indiana, to take the case. Wells then asked Kinsey to give the attorneys a tour of the Institute and answer their questions. On August 18, the day of the appointment, the attorneys arrived in Bloomington only to learn that Kinsey was too ill to show them the Institute. At Kinsey's insistence, however, the meeting was moved to his home. Describing the scene many years later, Wells recalled vividly a man who was "just gasping for breath" and who "started talking with all the intensity with which only he could talk, explaining the case to them as he saw it." Horrified, Wells took Clara aside and said, "For heaven sake can't we stop this. He is just consuming himself. These men are going to take this case. He doesn't have to explain it to them." As Wells told this story many years later, Clara's response still rang in his ears. "There is nothing you or I can do," she answered. "This is just the way he is."[35]

This was the last time Wells and Kinsey met. Perhaps if Kinsey had known that death was about to overtake him, he would have thanked Wells for his help for all those years. After all, Wells was the most important member of Kinsey's support team by far. For eighteen years, he had defended Kinsey before the board of trustees, the faculty of Indiana University, the Indiana state legislature, and the public. In addition, Wells had given Kinsey an endowed chair in everything but name, providing released time from teaching and holding his other university responsibilities to an absolute minimum. He had also made certain that Kinsey had the physical plant for an institute, complete with all the costly soundproofing and other special appointments the Institute required. No, for nearly two decades Kinsey had had an angel, and his name was Herman B Wells. Not that Kinsey was unaware of his debt to the president. Many years after Kinsey's death, Wescott recalled, "I have never heard him express so much gratitude toward anyone as toward that man."[36]

As his health gradually declined, Kinsey had often told his staff members, "I'd rather be dead than not put in a full day's work."[37] He meant what he said. His work was his life. The old puritan work ethic that he had absorbed in childhood was part of the explanation, but only part. Kinsey was a self-appointed martyr. For years, he had compared himself to other great scientists who had defied cultural conventions and suffered great wrongs from the forces of ignorance. Kinsey identified with these figures and viewed his impending death as his final sacrifice to the cause. Then there was the issue of power. From the outset, he had used sex research to gain power and control over others, and he could not bear to surrender authority to anyone as long as there was life in his body. Years after Kinsey's death, Gebhard could still recall the last words his boss spoke to him: "Don't do anything until I come back!"[38]

But Kinsey never returned to the office. A few days after the meeting with Wells and the attorneys, he entered the Bloomington hospital. He was suffering from pneumonia, which in turn aggravated his heart condition. Not long before entering the hospital, Kinsey had fallen in his garden. The damage was not serious, only a slight bruise on his leg. Still, it was that bruise that produced the embolism that finally killed him.[39] Kinsey died on Sunday, August 25, 1956, at 8:00 A.M. He was sixty-two years old.

Torrey spoke at the memorial service. His words were gracious and kind, smoothing over Kinsey's rough spots in order to celebrate his considerable strengths. Although people came from as far away as New York, attendance from the community was light, a reflection both of Kinsey's modest popularity among his colleagues at the university and of the fact that it was the end of summer and many faculty members had not returned to Bloomington from their vacations. Later, the faculty passed a resolution honoring Kinsey, a gesture that meant a great deal to his family.

Clara bore her husband's death with dignity and grace. Friends who attended the memorial service recall her strength and composure. But, in a sense, Kinsey had been preparing Clara for his death for many years. Left alone for so much of the time, she had been forced to follow her own advice to the other Institute wives. Over time, Clara had made a life for herself, one that revolved around Kinsey, yet was not totally dependent upon him. No, Clara was far from devastated by her husband's death. If anything, her sorrow had to be mitigated by relief, for she had borne a great burden and was suddenly free.

Clara enjoyed a long life. She died in 1982, outlasting her husband by twenty-six years. As Kinsey's widow, she enjoyed an active life, putting her time to good use. She hiked, swam, did volunteer work for the Girl Scouts, and enjoyed her children and grandchildren. Touchingly, Clara also kept a shrine, preserving the living room where she and her husband had hosted so many musicales exactly as it was, as if Kinsey might return at any moment and take his chair. Friends who came to visit recall that they could still feel his presence in the room.

Despite Kinsey's fears, the Institute survived, too, with Gebhard as its new director. At first the times were lean, but Indiana University's support never wavered. Wells saw to it that the Institute had the necessary funds until it could attract new sources of "soft" money. Eventually, Gebhard was able to secure federal funding for a number of the Institute's projects, a switch in patrons that mirrored developments in the broader scientific community. Beginning in World War II, the federal government eclipsed private foundations as the chief benefactor of scientific research in the United States, a shift that has continued down to the present. Feeding at the federal trough, Gebhard and his colleagues over time turned out a number of studies that preserved the Institute's claims to leadership in the field of sex research, including a massive tome on sex offenders.

None of the Institute's subsequent studies generated as much publicity as the male and females volumes, and this suited Gebhard fine. Unlike Kinsey, he did not seek publicity, largely because he had a clear understanding of how seriously it had backfired. "While on the one hand it helped us and helped sales," Gebhard later explained, "it also hurt us badly, particularly with some scientific groups who felt that we were publicity seekers. [They felt] the amount of publicity, whether we sought it or not, was unseemly to scientists, and it hurt us."[40]

Despite this implied criticism, Gebhard was the first to admit that he never could have matched Kinsey's accomplishments as a pioneer. "He was an extraordinarily dogged, stubborn, and hardworking man," declared Gebhard. "He was not one to be deflected from his goals by anything." Deepening the portrait, Gebhard also confessed that Kinsey "was a bit of a showman and the con man," whose qualities were "precisely what was needed to launch a controversial research [project]." He added astutely, "It took a tough man with the gift of gab and a certain amount of oversimplification and exaggeration to really sell the thing and keep it going."[41]

Unaware of Kinsey's private demons, the press could only comment on the public man when he died. Failing to recognize the rebel who lay hidden beneath all that scientific armor, newspapers across the nation reported his passing with a sense of sadness. Most editors praised Kinsey as a dedicated scientist and a brave pioneer. In the consensus-minded 1950s, the urge to smooth over cultural differences was a salient feature of American society, and even papers that had been sharply critical during Kinsey's lifetime had nice things to say about him in death. The *Indianapolis News* praised Kinsey as "a dedicated, objective scientist" and deemed his death "a great loss to the world of science."[42] Calling Kinsey "a truly dedicated scholar," the *Indiana Catholic and Record* declared, "Few could disagree more strongly than we with Dr. Kinsey's views or deplore more deeply the evil influence such views could have on individuals and society. Yet one cannot deny that Dr. Kinsey's unremitting efforts, his patient, endless search, his disregard for criticisms and ridicule, and his disinterest in financial gain should merit him high marks as a devoted scholar." Graciously, the Catholic editors added, "While we have hurled our share of brick-bats at some of Dr. Kinsey's ideas when he was living, and still hold these ideas to be poisonously wrong, we must admit that we would welcome on our side many more scholars with something of Kinsey's devotion to knowledge and learning."[43]

The editors of the *New York Times* also lauded Kinsey, declaring "that he was first, last and always a scientist." Showing Kinsey the charity in death they had withheld during his life, the editors offered more than praise. They also took a stab at assessing his importance to history. What they chose to emphasize would have pleased Kinsey no little. To them, he was the embodiment of Baconian science, a fact-finding empiricist whose chief strength was his rigorous methodology. "In the long run it is probable that the value of his contribution to contemporary thought will lie much less in what he found out than in the method he used and his way of applying it," they wrote. After stressing that any scientific approach to sex research had to overcome "moral precept, taboo, individual and group training and long established behavior patterns," the editors declared, "Dr. Kinsey cut through this overlay with detachment and precision. His work was conscientious and comprehensive."[44]

In the decades following his death, Kinsey's name constantly resurfaced in the cultural wars over family values. Liberals lionized him as the father of the sexual revolution of the 1960s, architect of candid sex education, and patron saint of gay liberation,[45] while conservatives vilified him as a corrupter of morals, a godless scientist, or, worse yet, a charlatan and a fraud.[46] Indeed, in 1995, nearly forty years after Kinsey's death, Steve Stockman, a conservative congressman from Texas, introduced a resolution in the

House of Representatives calling for a special committee to investigate Kinsey's influence on sex education in the United States, not to mention charges that he had trafficked with child molesters or, that he was himself a child molester.[47] Neither the roses nor the brickbats would have surprised Kinsey's contemporaries. Whether they had worked closely with him or whether they had followed his career from a distance, Kinsey watchers agreed that his middle initial should have stood for "controversy."

Yet, in trying to take Alfred Charles Kinsey's measure, a few of his contemporaries had managed to render thoughtful assessments. In the spring 1956, only months before Kinsey's death, Morison found himself embroiled in yet another debate with Lawrence Kubie, who was determined to take one more shot at Kinsey, even though there was no danger that the Rockefeller Foundation would ever resume its support of his work. As before, Kubie was carping on the CRPS's failure to make Kinsey pay more attention to psychological issues.[48]

Morison's response was instructive. Commenting on what he called "the Kinsey saga," Morison offered a brief lesson on the way science works. "I find it pretty difficult to criticize a scientist for not wanting to examine all aspects of a given subject at once," Morison chided. "Granted that it would be awfully nice to see life steadily and see it whole, it is regrettably true that science has not yet found any very satisfactory way of doing it," he continued. "We will have to break our big problems down into little pieces and study the pieces as carefully as we can," declared Morison wryly. "Actually, experience shows that if we do this long enough, we end by having quite workable concepts about the functioning of systems and organisms." Reminding Kubie that scientists were also humans, Morison observed "that people are fitted by temperament to do certain kinds of things better than others." Getting his man exactly right, he concluded, "I should say that in Kinsey's case, we have a man well suited by temperament for counting and classifying."[49]

Morison's point was well taken. In most cases, scientific knowledge builds incrementally, with each investigator making a discrete contribution and with each generation standing on the shoulders of the preceding generation. If subsequent researchers managed to do the job better than Kinsey, their debt to him was nevertheless great. He was a pioneer, an explorer who blazed the trail for those who followed. It was he who convinced most Americans that human sexual behavior could and should be studied scientifically and, just as important, that scientific data should help inform discussions of social policy. More than any other investigator, Kinsey made sex research respectable. To the public, Kinsey came across as a fearless, rigorous, humane scientist who collected data and encouraged people to use his findings to make their own decisions about their private lives.

While Morison was right to pigeonhole Kinsey as a classifier and a counter, history will also remember Kinsey as a reformer, who devoted much of his life to social issues of the first magnitude. It was no accident that his emotional problems and compulsive behavior manifested themselves most graphically in sexual dysfunction. His private demons, albeit in exaggerated form, also bedeviled the nation. Born into a society that was anxious and conflicted over human sexuality, Kinsey was a product of Victorian culture's power to shape and contort character. His formative years were spent in a home and in a nation where many middle-class parents enshrouded sex in shame, heaping more than enough guilt on young people to mangle and twist them. This was particularly true of those like Kinsey who aspired but failed to achieve moral perfection. His great accomplishment was to take his pain and suffering and use it to transform himself into an instrument of social reform, a secular evangelist who proclaimed a new sensibility about human sexuality. As a friend and great admirer put it, Kinsey's secret life "was the source of his greatness."[50]

By preaching the gospel of individual variation, Kinsey meant to strike a blow for human diversity. Always he was motivated by his heartfelt desire to gain social acceptance for homosexuals and other despised sexual minorities. Privately, he unquestionably took tolerance to extremes, plunging into the abyss with regard to incest and child molestation and refusing to acknowledge that certain sexual behaviors were at once antisocial and pathological. Yet, in Kinsey's case, this could hardly have been otherwise. As Saul Bellow has observed so poignantly, "Anxiety destroys scale, and suffering makes us lose perspective."[51]

Despite his preoccupation with marginal groups, however, Kinsey compiled an unprecedented volume of data on people who engaged in the more garden variety forms of behavior, the kinds that turn up in most people's sexual histories. Both from private experience and from thousands of interviews, he knew that virtually everyone falls short of the rigid sexual code demanded by middle-class morality. And better than anyone else of his day, Kinsey understood that most Americans felt compelled to hide things about their sex lives.

Confronted by a nation awash in what Dickinson had called "hush and pretend," Kinsey pleaded for an end to hypocrisy and for a new ethic of tolerance. What people did in the privacy of their bedrooms was their own business and should not be subjected to social or legal sanctions. He was particularly adamant on this point where consenting adults were involved, though he coveted the same freedom for children and for young adults. Asked what attitude her husband would have changed first if he had been able to play God, Clara replied, "My offhand guess would be the all-too-human desire to regulate the sexual lives of other people."[52]

Reducing and abolishing rigid controls on human sexual behavior was thus the great cause of Kinsey's life, the quest that put him to bed at night and got him up in the morning. More than any other figure of his day, he set Americans to thinking about how much authority society should exercise over intimate matters. Those who believed that people's private behavior should be strictly regulated tended to view Kinsey with anger and dismay, while those who thought that people should have more freedom found his message congenial.

Like most reformers, Kinsey was sustained by the hope that society would adopt the changes he championed. Had he lived a few more decades, he would have found much to celebrate and much to abhor. As an apostle of sexual liberation, he would have applauded the sexual freedom of the 1960s; the addition of candid sex education courses to the curricula of many high schools and colleges; the pill; and *Roe* v. *Wade*. In particular, he would have been warmed by the successes of the gay liberation movement. Still, much that has happened in the decades since his death would have left Kinsey dismayed. He would have opposed the pro-life movement because he supported the right of women to control their fertility. Nor is it difficult to imagine Kinsey weeping over the moral majority's gay bashing in the 1980s and 1990s, just as he was sickened by the sexual witch-hunts of the McCarthy era. As for HIV, Kinsey's public response would have been enlightened and humane. He would have advocated more funds for research, he would demanded explicit sex education for young people and adults alike, and he would have told anyone who would listen to practice safe sex. Privately, however, AIDS might have been enough to restore his faith in a mean-spirited, vengeful God.

Of course, Kinsey's work did not cause the shifts in sexual attitudes and behavior that occurred in the United States after his death, any more than he caused the changes during his lifetime. First, those shifts had been under way for several decades before his books were published, as Kinsey himself documented so richly; and second, they were driven more by social and economic changes than by the work of sex researchers.[53] What Kinsey did accomplish was to bring intimate matters into the open so that people could discuss them with unprecedented candor. This cultural dialogue, in turn, helped shape what followed. Perhaps the fairest assessment of Kinsey's role as a social reformer came from Corner, who observed, "The times were changing anyway, but I think he helped to change the times."[54] Had Kinsey believed this during his lifetime, perhaps he would have known a little peace.

NOTES

ABBREVIATIONS

ACK	Alfred C. Kinsey
CRPS Files, NRC Archives	Committee for Research in Problems in Sex Files, National Research Council Archives, Washington, D.C.
IUA	Indiana University Archives
IUOHP	Indiana University Oral History Project
KIA	Kinsey Institute for Research in Sex, Gender, and Reproduction Archive, Indiana University, Bloomington
NRC Archives	National Research Council Archives, Washington, D.C.
Rockefeller Archives	Rockefeller Archives Center, Hillcrest, Pocantico Hills, North Tarrytown, N.Y.
SBHF	Alfred C. Kinsey et al., *Sexual Behavior in the Human Female* (Philadelphia, 1953)
SBHM	Alfred C. Kinsey et al., *Sexual Behavior in the Human Male* (Philadelphia, 1948)
Wheeler Papers	William M. Wheeler Papers, Pusey Library, Harvard University, Cambridge, Mass.
Yerkes Papers	Robert M. Yerkes Papers, Yale University Archive, New Haven, Conn.

Chapter 1: "THE LOT OF THE BOY IN THE CITY"

1 Historians of masculinity insist that the personal can become political, particularly in the case of homosexuals. See Peter Filene, "The Secrets of Men's History," in *The Making of Masculinities: The New Men's Studies,* ed. Harry Brod (Boston, 1987), 114.

2 Author's interview with Mrs. ACK, Dec. 10, 1971, 6, Indiana University Oral History Project (hereafter IUOHP). In her interview, Clara Kinsey requested that she be identified as Mrs. ACK.

3 Cornelia V. Christenson, *Kinsey: A Biography* (Bloomington, 1971), 16.

4 ACK, *An Introduction to Biology* (Philadelphia, 1926), 430. Here Kinsey was paraphrasing, with attribution, Thomas Carlyle.

5 See, for example, the correspondence with a curious astrologer, ACK to Ronald E. Storme, June 6, 1954, Kinsey Institute for Research in Sex, Gender, and Reproduction

Archive, Indiana University, Bloomington, Indiana (hereafter KIA). Storme to Kinsey, May 31, 1954, KIA.

6   ACK to Alfred Kinsey, Jan. 9, 1953, KIA ("I am delighted that somebody else can manage to bear so nearly the exact name that I have and certainly I appreciate your thought in writing me," he declared).

7   ACK to Arthur E. Bye, May 6, 1948, KIA.

8   Ibid.

9   ACK to William F. Steinberg, Nov. 7, 1953, KIA.

10 ACK to William H. Roberts, Jan. 8, 1947, KIA.

11 *The Dictionary of American Biography*, vol. 10 (New York, 1933), 421–22; and *The National Cyclopedia of American Biography*, vol. 12 (New York, 1904), 257.

12 William F. Filby, ed., *Passenger and Immigration Lists Index, 1982–1985, Cumulated Supplements* (Detroit, 1985), 2:1597.

13 Author's interview with Herman Spieth, Feb. 18, 1988, 34.

14 Prior to the 1830 census, individual names are not consistently given. The only identifiable candidate for the Charles Kinsey in question first appears in the 1830 census as either twenty-six or twenty-seven years old and lists Pennsylvania as the place of birth. Charles M. Kinsey was almost certainly the "Charles Kinsey" of Franklin Township, Bergen County, whose name reappears in the 1840 census. Since pre-1850 census reports merely list family heads and the number of males and females of various age groups residing within each household, it is difficult to offer a positive identification of the Kinsey listed in Franklin Township. The Charles M. Kinsey of Mendham Township, Morris County, in 1840, however, is definitely the great-grandfather in question, for he had a son named Benjamin who was born in 1838 in Mendham, the town ACK identified as his grandfather's birthplace. Moreover, Benjamin's birth year made him the right age for such a grandfather, as Benjamin would have sired Kinsey's father at twenty-three. *United States Census of Bergen County, New Jersey, 1830*, 108; *United States Census of Morris Country, New Jersey, 1840*, 276; *United States Census of Morris County, New Jersey, 1850*, 116.

15 *United States Census of Morris County, New Jersey, 1860*, 211.

16 *United States Census of Morris County, New Jersey, 1870*, 180.

17 Ibid.

18 *Stute* (the student paper at the Stevens Institute), April 10, 1943.

19 *Gopsill's Jersey City Directories, 1886–1887*, Hoboken Public Library.

20 The text beside his picture in the faculty section of the 1909 edition of *The Link* (the Stevens Institute yearbook) reads, "Mr. Kinsey took a four-years' special evening course at Cooper Institute, New York City, graduating in 1890." This is misleading. While he may have received some sort of technical education diploma, he almost certainly did not earn an academic degree from the Cooper Institute. According to Pomeroy, Alfred Seguine Kinsey had no better than an eighth-grade education. This, too, is a distortion of the record. His education included a combination of public school work, plus the courses he took at Cooper Union. See Wardell B. Pomeroy, *Dr. Kinsey and the Institute for Sex Research* (New York, 1972), 24.

21 Alfred Seguine Kinsey was the only faculty member listed in the 1909 *Link* who did not have a college degree—the overwhelming majority held advanced degrees. Kinsey did not include an academic degree in any subsequent school publication or in any professional publication that carried his biography.

22 Robert A. Cole to James H. Jones, Nov. 30, 1988.

23 See *Gopsill's Jersey City Directory, 1891–1892,* Hoboken Public Library, 299. This is the first year Alfred S. Kinsey listed his occupation as "instructor." In all previous directories in which his name appears, his occupation is listed as "machinist" or "laborer." Beginning in 1893, Kinsey lists his occupation in city directories as "secretary," a vocation with a connotation very different at that time from what it became subsequently. In the late nineteenth century, "secretary" was a white-collar vocation, to be sure, but it carried considerably higher status than it does today. It included college-educated men who worked in responsible capacities with the rich and the powerful.

24 *Stute,* Sept. 27, 1911, 1, 2, 4.

25 *Stute,* April 10, 1943, 1–2. How many countries in Europe they visited is not clear, but we know their work took them to Italy and to France. See *The Link* (Buffalo, 1920), 48.

26 *Kinsey v. Kinsey,* Bill of Complaint, March 10, 1932, Chancery of New Jersey.

27 In 1855, Robert Charles swore a declaration of intention and/or an oath of allegiance in the Philadelphia Court of Common Pleas. P. William Filby, ed., *Philadelphia Naturalization Records* (Detroit, 1982), 91.

28 *United States Census of the Territory of the Salt Lake Area, Utah Territory, 1880,* 17.

29 Kinsey, *Introduction to Biology,* 311.

30 Author's interview with Edna Higenbotham, Nov. 28, 1984, 6.

31 *United States Census of the Territory of the Salt Lake Area, Utah Territory, 1880,* 17.

32 Ibid.

33 Christenson, *Kinsey,* 14–15.

34 Kinsey to Arthur E. Warner, Jan. 21, 1949, KIA.

35 *New Jersey: A Guide to Its Present and Past,* compiled and written by the Federal Writers' Project of the Works Progress Administration for the State of New Jersey (New York, 1936), 262–64.

36 Ibid., 263.

37 Richard Ellmann, *Oscar Wilde* (New York, 1988), 159.

38 The city directories for Hoboken provide at least a partial record of Alfred Seguine Kinsey's residences, and the frequency of his moves points to a family in search of cheaper housing, evidence that money was scarce in the Kinsey household. In 1893–94 they lived at 611 Bloomfield Street (his parents lived one block away at 530 Bloomfield). When Alfred Seguine Kinsey and Sarah made the short move to 621 Bloomfield Street in 1895, Benjamin's family moved into the apartment they had vacated at 611. One year later, the two families were living together at 621 Bloomfield Street. In 1897–98 the two families were living together again at 161 Seventh Street. By 1899–1900, however, Alfred Seguine Kinsey had left his father's residence and moved his family to 707 Garden Street, the home ACK would later remember with displeasure. The last listing for Alfred Seguine Kinsey in Hoboken (1904–5) was at this same address. There are no listings for Alfred S. Kinsey in 1892–93, 1894–95, 1896–97, 1902–3, and 1903–4. Since the directories for this period are quite reliable, it is hard to explain Alfred S. Kinsey's absence from city directories for five years (three separate, two consecutive) between 1892 and 1904. (Benjamin H. Kinsey's name, by contrast, is absent from city directories for only one year [1896–97] from 1873 to 1907.) Perhaps Alfred S. Kinsey had his own residences during these years and got overlooked, or perhaps he lived in another city and commuted to Hoboken. A more likely explanation, however, is that he traveled so much during the years in question that he elected to have his wife and two small children live with his parents (as we know, they did in 1895–96 and again

in 1897–98) and that somehow the son's family got omitted from town directories. *Gopsill's Jersey City Directories, 1873–1907,* Hoboken Public Library.

39   ACK, *Methods in Biology* (Chicago, 1937), 5.

40   Christenson, *Kinsey,* 17.

41   For a study of children and religion, see Robert Coles, *The Spiritual Life of Children* (Boston, 1990). Though aware of the possibilities, Coles did not choose to emphasize the psychic damage that religion can inflict on seriously religious children. Mary Gordon, a reviewer of the book, pointed out this danger with terrifying clarity. See Gordon's review in *New York Times Book Review,* Nov. 25, 1990, 1, 28.

42   Coles, *Spiritual Life of Children,* 17, and 40–68.

43   Christenson, *Kinsey,* 16.

44   Author's interview with Mrs. ACK, Dec. 10, 1971, 7.

45   ACK, *New Introduction to Biology,* rev. ed. (Chicago, 1938), 358.

46   See Coles, *Spiritual Life of Children,* 98–128.

47   Author's interview with Mrs. ACK, Dec. 10, 1971, 7. It is possible that Kinsey's health led him to fall behind a year in primary school—his family moved when he was ten, yet Kinsey had only completed the second grade. The school records are not available to verify Kinsey's memory.

48   ACK to Arthur E. Warner, Jan. 21, 1949.

49   Pomeroy, *Dr. Kinsey,* 24.

50   Ibid., 40.

51   Kinsey, *Introduction to Biology,* 175. Why Kinsey chose this particular name remains a mystery, but he may have taken it from a very popular turn-of-the-century musical play by George M. Cohan entitled *Little Johnny Jones,* which drew huge crowds in Manhattan Liberty Theater in 1904. See *South Orange Bulletin,* Dec. 1, 1904, 2.

52   ACK, *Methods in Biology,* 28.

53   Ibid.

54   Author's interview with Mrs. ACK, Dec. 10, 1971, 8.

55   Christenson, *Kinsey,* 15.

56   Pomeroy, *Dr. Kinsey,* 24.

57   Ibid.

58   Christenson, *Kinsey,* 175.

59   James E. Dutton to James H. Jones, Dec. 7, 1988.

60   According to Frederic J. Meystre, another former student, Alfred Seguine Kinsey's course "was deemed to be the easiest one in the freshman year. Indeed, perhaps in the entire curriculum." Meystre to James H. Jones, Dec. 3, 1988.

61   Ibid. Similarly, the head of shop practice at the Stevens Institute failed to make an impression on Frank J. Oliver, who took his course in 1917. As Oliver put it, "Professor Kinsey was just the man in charge." Oliver to James H. Jones, Dec. 5, 1988.

62   Meystre to Jones, Dec. 3, 1988.

63   Ernest C. Lundt to James H. Jones, Dec. 19, 1988.

64   Dutton to Jones, Dec. 7, 1988. Dutton recalled, "He was very fastidious in his dress and appearance," a trait Dutton speculated was "probably a result of [Alfred Seguine Kinsey's] being a blue collar instructor for years."

65   Ibid.

66   W. E. Horenburger to James H. Jones, Nov. 27, 1988.

67   *Stevens Indicator* 60, no. 3 (May 1943): 4.

68   *The Link* (n.p., 1939), 27.

69   Edlow S. Bance to James H. Jones, n.d. (letter postmarked Dec. 18, 1988).

70 Meystre to Jones, Dec. 3, 1988.

71 Bance to Jones, n.d. (letter postmarked Dec. 18, 1988).

72 William K. Meyers to James H. Jones, Dec. 7, 1988.

73 Horenburger to Jones, Nov. 27, 1988.

74 Ibid.

75 Joseph P. Vidosic to James H. Jones, Nov. 29, 1988.

76 Author's interview with Paul H. Gebhard, Oct. 14, 1984, 12.

77 Author's interview with Mrs. ACK, Dec. 10, 1971, 8. On the basis of stories Kinsey's brother, Robert, had told her about his childhood, Edna Coulture Kinsey Higenbotham, Robert's widow, remarked, "I don't think he [Alfred Seguine Kinsey] was an easy man to get along with." Author's interview with Higenbotham, Nov. 28, 1984, 8. Perhaps the final word should be given to Clara Kinsey. Asked point blank to comment on her husband's relations with his mother, Clara described them as "very good" and added, "He thought highly of his mother." If this description made their relationship sound less than warm and loving, it nevertheless takes us as close to the truth as the evidence allows. Author's interview with Mrs. ACK, Dec. 10, 1971, 8.

78 Author's interview with Higenbotham, Nov. 28, 1984, 8.

79 Steven Mintz, *A Prison of Expectations* (New York, 1982).

80 From the standpoint of social psychology, the child-rearing practices of the Kinsey household appear to fit the pattern of the "Evangelicals" described by Philip Greven. For a provocative analysis, see Greven, *The Protestant Temperament: Patterns of Childrearing, Religious Experience and the Self in Early America* (New York, 1977).

81 Author's interview with Gebhard, Oct. 14, 1984, 21–22.

82 The basement story is remarkably consistent with the overall pattern of childhood sexuality described by Kinsey. According to Kinsey, most young boys begin their sexual activities by exhibiting their genitals to other children and by engaging in genital contacts with those same children. Kinsey reported that 48 percent of the older males and 60 percent of the boys who were preadolescents at the time they gave their sex histories admitted having engaged in homosexual activities during their preadolescent years. Specifically, they experimented with genital exhibition, mutual genital manipulation, oral or anal contacts with genitals, and urethral insertions. Kinsey reported that 1.8 percent of the men he interviewed had engaged in urethral insertions by the age of nine. If this figure sounds high, one must remember that Kinsey did not distinguish between a onetime experiment and habitual behavior. See *SBHM*, 163–72. The material on urethral insertions appears on 169–70. To obtain the figure for urethral insertions, multiple the percentage of population engaged in homosexual play by the percentage utilizing urethral insertions. The medical literature describes cases of urethral insertions serious enough to require medical attention in boys as young as seven. H. Alibadi et al., "Self-Inflicted Foreign Bodies Involving Lower Urinary Tract and Male Genitals," *Urology* 26, no. 1 (July 1985): 13. For a medical note devoted entirely to the case of a fourteen-year-old boy with "a length of plastic tubing wedged in the urethra," see B. F. Millet and S. C. W. Harrison, "An Unusual Case of Urethral Self-Instrumentation," *British Journal of Sexual Medicine* 13, no. 10 (Oct. 1986): 296.

83 Freudian psychologists who seek to explain the origins of masochism describe children who learn at an early age to associate sexual pleasure with physical and/or emotional pain. Because these children are filled at the unconscious level with fears of reprisal, they construct at the conscious level elaborate fantasies of torture, humiliation, and self-degradation. Unable to bear the tension of waiting to be punished by powerful adults who dominate them, they attempt to decrease their anxiety by rushing forward and

compulsively inflicting pain on themselves. Over time, the self-infliction of pain becomes an integral part of their sexual ritual, as they cannot allow themselves to have sexual pleasure unless they pay for it first in suffering. Moreover, absent medical intervention, masochists almost never break free of this cycle. However twisted their pattern of behavior, it works for them. It gives them pleasure, and it is the only pattern they know. For a highly readable discussion of the Freudian explanation (with certain modifications) of masochism, see Theodor Reik, *Masochism in Modern Man* (New York, 1941). Philip Greven has posited a strong correlation between strict fundamentalist child-rearing practices and the development of masochism. Certainly Kinsey appears to fit this analysis. See Greven, *Spare the Child: The Religious Roots of Punishment and the Psychological Impact of Physical Abuse* (New York, 1991), 174–86.

Chapter 2: "A Second Darwin"

1　*New Jersey: A Guide to Its Present and Past,* compiled and written by the Federal Writers' Project of the Works Progress Administration for the State of New Jersey (New York, 1936), 339.
2　Ibid.
3　Henry W. Foster, *The Evolution of the School District of South Orange and Maplewood, New Jersey, 1814–1927* (Geneva, N.Y., 1930), 159. For general information on South Orange, see *Village of South Orange: Photographic Views and a Short Historical Sketch of This Ideal New Jersey Home Community* (South Orange, N.J., 1922).
4　*South Orange Bulletin,* Nov. 26, 1903, 2.
5　Ibid.
6　Author's interview with William J. Parry, Sept. 13, 1990.
7　Author's interview with William Gury, Nov. 7, 1991.
8　Ibid.
9　The number of Italian gardeners was large enough to prompt the local town fathers to establish a night school to teach them English and to print certain local posters in both Italian and English. See *South Orange Bulletin,* Oct. 13, 1905, 6.
10　Foster, *Evolution of the School District,* 177.
11　Columbia High School Newspaper Scrapbook, April 16, 1909; June 4, 1910; *Daily Chronicle,* Jan. 3, 1911, Sec. 2, p. 1.
12　*Daily Chronicle,* Dec. 10, 1908, 7.
13　Ibid., Oct. 20, 1908, 2.
14　*South Orange Bulletin,* April 14, 1904, 3.
15　Ibid., Feb. 4, 1904, 2.
16　Author's interview with Edna Higenbotham, Nov. 28, 1984, 7.
17　*Daily Chronicle,* Nov. 28, 1908, 2.
18　For examples of these cultural and social events, see ibid., Nov. 11, 1908, 2; Feb. 10, 1909, 2; Feb. 23, 1909, 2; *South Orange Bulletin,* May 26, 1904, 3; *Daily Chronicle,* Nov. 17, 1908, 2.
19　*Orange Chronicle,* Feb. 1, 1908, 3.
20　*Daily Chronicle,* Nov. 6, 1908, 2.
21　Author's interview with Higenbotham, Nov. 28, 1984, 7.
22　Cornelia V. Christenson, *Kinsey: A Biography* (Bloomington, 1971), 17.
23　Dorothy Beugler to ACK, April 17, 1954, KIA. In 1954, following publication of the female volume, she wrote Kinsey, "Do you recall that when you graduated from South Orange High in 1912 you had a classmate named Dorothy Beugler? You went to the

Methodist Church and I to the Presbyterian and we did not know each other very well."
Beugler could not believe that the pious young boy she had known in high school had
grown into a godless scientist. "It is a terrible thing for our nation's sin to be exposed
without a challenge to turn to God," she preached, "the Holy God Who demands ho-
liness and purity." But then she had no way of knowing how completely Kinsey had
abandoned the religious beliefs of his youth.

24 Quoted in Christenson, *Kinsey,* 19.

25 Ibid.

26 "Class Will," *Senior Year Book, 1912, South Orange High School* (n.p.), 26 (hereafter *Senior Year Book*).

27 For a trenchant analysis of the middle class's fear of downward mobility, see Barbara
Ehrenreich, *Fear of Falling: The Inner Life of the Middle Class* (New York, 1990).

28 *South Orange Bulletin,* Feb. 11, 1904, 3.

29 *Daily Chronicle,* Oct. 22, 1908, 2.

30 Ibid., Nov. 19, 1908, 2.

31 *South Orange Bulletin,* March 3, 1904, 3. Another new building followed in 1913, a
year late for Kinsey's class to enjoy. David Lawrence Pierson, *History of the Oranges to
1921: Reviewing the Rise, Development and Progress of an Influential Community* (New
York, 1922), 528–29.

32 *South Orange Bulletin,* March 3, 1904, 3.

33 *South Orange Bulletin,* Sept. 22, 1904, 2.

34 Ibid.

35 *Columbian* 3, no. 1 (Oct. 1912): 14, Columbia High School Archive, Maplewood, N.J.
(hereafter CHS Archive). The *Columbian* was the school newspaper, published
monthly.

36 Foster, *Evolution of the School District,* 160–67.

37 Ibid., 194.

38 Author's conversation with William J. Parry, Sept. 17, 1990.

39 *Daily Chronicle,* Nov. 10, 1908, 2. The numerical score required of honor roll students
appeared ibid., Jan. 8, 1909, 2.

40 Kinsey's sophomore year grades were gleaned from the clipping file, CHS Archive. The
fall notice was dated Nov. 10, 1909. The name of the newspaper in which the item appeared was not given, though, presumably, both appeared in *Daily Chronicle*.

41 Ibid. The spring notice from the CHS Archive is dated April 1910.

42 *Senior Year Book,* 58.

43 Foster, *Evolution of the School District,* 183, 161.

44 Christenson, *Kinsey,* 19. During Kinsey's junior year, the students founded a school
paper, the *Owl,* but there is no evidence that Kinsey ever served on the paper's staff. See
Daily Chronicle, Feb. 8, 1911, 2.

45 ACK, *Methods in Biology* (Chicago, 1937), 120.

46 Natalie Hirschfeld (Roeth's married name) to Paul H. Gebhard, Sept. 27, 1961, KIA.

47 Ibid.

48 Kinsey, *Methods in Biology,* 12.

49 ACK to Natalie Roeth, Feb. 12, 1924, KIA.

50 ACK to Natalie R. Hirschfeld, May 28, 1948, KIA.

51 *Senior Year Book,* 9, 20. Following the publication of *SBHM,* the local paper in South
Orange reported that Kinsey may have earned "the highest point score ever recorded
at Columbia," but hastened to add that "neither the high school office nor the Board
of Education office can prove it. They have few records dating back to 1912, and no

records of Dr. Kinsey's activities, in the classroom or extracurricular." See *News-Record,* n.d., clipping file, South Orange Public Library, South Orange, N.J.

52 *Daily Chronicle,* Oct. 8, 1908, 2.
53 *Senior Year Book,* 12.
54 Christenson, *Kinsey,* 16–23.
55 *Daily Chronicle,* Oct. 24, 1908, 2; *Newark News,* June 15 and June 21, 1910; *New York Herald,* June 15, 1910; "Columbia High School Scrap Book" (hereafter CHS Scrap Book). No page numbers were recorded for the scrapbook items.
56 *Newark News,* June 26, 1910, CHS Scrap Book.
57 *New York Times,* June 21 and July 1, 1910; *Newark News,* June 21, 1910, CHS Scrap Book.
58 *Newark Evening News,* July 20, 1910, and *New York Herald,* June 15, 1910, CHS Scrap Book. Robinson ignited one more round of fireworks before fading into history. On July 25, 1910, the committee held a second public hearing. After listening to Robinson repeat his charges with renewed vehemence, the committee demanded additional proof, which he was not able to provide. Using the testimony of other witnesses to rebut Robinson's accusations, several committee members then went on the offensive and attacked his veracity. Following five hours of bitter debate in which members of the audience shook their fists and committee members pounded the table in anger, Robinson rose to his feet at 1:00 A.M. and asked for an adjournment. "Stay here and fight your battle. Don't show a white feather," challenged one angry committee member, while another shouted, "You're a bluff. You published the charges broadcast. Now you are not man enough to stay and prove them." "I will receive no consideration from you people," answered Robinson; "why should I stay." Amid jeers of "coward" and "cur" from the audience, Robinson then left the auditorium. *Newark News,* June 30, 1910, CHS Scrap Book.
59 *New York Times,* June 21, 1910, CHS Scrap Book.
60 *New York Times,* July 1, 1910, CHS Scrap Book.
61 Quoted in Peter Filene, *Him/Her/Self: Sex Roles in Modern America,* 2nd ed. (Baltimore, 1986), 73–74; Daniel T. Rogers, *The Work Ethic in Industrial America, 1850–1920* (Chicago, 1978).
62 Quoted in Filene, *Him/Her/Self,* 73.
63 Quoted ibid., 74.
64 For a general discussion, see ibid., 73–74.
65 For notices of Paderewski's performances, see *South Orange Bulletin,* March 9, 1905, 1, and *Orange Chronicle,* Dec. 14, 1907, 3.
66 For home musicales, see *Daily Chronicle,* Feb. 19, 1909, 3, and Feb. 20, 1909, 3.
67 For examples of music lectures, see *South Orange Bulletin,* Jan. 7, 1904, 3; for the names of the members of the Assembly Hall Music Fund Committee, see *Daily Chronicle,* Dec. 18, 1908, 3; for the names of village citizens who contributed money to the committee, see *Daily Chronicle,* Feb. 10, 1909, 2; for the names of the quartets that performed at the Assembly Hall concerts, see *South Orange Bulletin,* Jan. 19, 1905, 3; *Orange Chronicle,* Feb. 15, 1908, 7; and *Daily Chronicle,* Feb. 20, 1909, 3.
68 No record has survived concerning his teacher, but the two most likely candidates are Eugene Hughes, who taught piano, harmony, and theory at the South Orange Music School, founded in 1908, and Mrs. Alexander Irving, who taught students and held musicales in her residence on North Seventh Street.
69 *Daily Chronicle,* Oct. 8, 1908, 2, and Feb. 20, 1909, 3. See Christenson, *Kinsey,* 18.
70 Author's interview with Hazel Phillips Balch, March 28, 1992.

71 Quoted in Christenson, *Kinsey,* 19.

72 Sophie Gibling later recalled that all two hundred high school students gathered every morning "in the main study hall, each at his own desk; the boys and girls, of course, separated, the nine or ten faculty members seated solemnly on the platform." Once everyone was present, " 'Page 81,' Mr. Freedman, the principal would announce as the clock hands came to 8:25 exactly. Whereupon one of us—Alfred, or Anna Geiger, or I—would march up to the grand piano in front, and all would rise to sing the national anthem. Then followed a reading from the Bible, and another song, nonreligious." Ibid., 18.

73 *Senior Year Book,* 14.

74 Asked if she had been required to listen to classical music, Hazel Phillips Balch, one of Kinsey's classmates, replied, "Yes, yes. None of this jazz. . . . All good music." Author's interview with Balch, March 28, 1992.

75 Elliot C. Bergen, "Educational Value of the Stage," in *Senior Year Book,* 47.

76 *Daily Chronicle,* Sept. 24, 1908, 1.

77 Author's interview with Mrs. ACK, Dec. 10, 1971, 20, IUOHP.

78 Ibid., Dec. 19, 1971, 20.

79 Author's interview with Paul H. Gebhard, Oct. 29, 1971, 47, IUOHP.

80 Ibid., 47–48.

81 Author's interview with Clarence A. Tripp and William Dellenback, Oct. 13, 1984, 89–90. "The Alien Corn" ends on a note of high tragedy with George Bland's death. Officially, the death is ruled an accident, but Maugham leaves the strong impression that Bland committed suicide.

82 ACK, "Music and Love," *High Fidelity,* July 1956, 27.

83 Ibid.

84 "Class Prophecy," *Senior Year Book,* 20.

85 ACK, "Music and Love," 27.

86 ACK, *An Introduction to Biology* (Philadelphia, 1926), 40.

87 Asked to comment on her husband's boyhood interests, Clara later made light of his stamp collection, declaring, "I don't think he ever went into it in that big a way." Pomeroy, too, attached little importance to Kinsey's stamp collection, though he did make the astute observation that "it was the only collection he ever made that was not designed to be useful." Author's interview with Mrs. ACK, Dec. 10, 1971, 16; Wardell B. Pomeroy, *Dr. Kinsey and the Institute for Sex Research* (New York, 1972), 16.

Chapter 3: "THE RIGHT STUFF"

1 "Scout Characteristics," *Boy Scouts of America: The Official Handbook for Boys,* 11th ed. (Garden City, N.Y., 1914), 15–19; see also 5–15.

2 *South Orange Bulletin,* Nov. 26, 1903, 2.

3 Ibid., Sept. 15, 1904, 2; *Orange Daily Chronicle,* Feb. 6, 1909, 1; *Orange Chronicle,* Feb. 2, 1907, 1; *South Orange Bulletin,* Jan. 19, 1905, 3, and June 28, 1906, 1.

4 *Orange Daily Chronicle,* Feb. 9, 1907, 1.

5 Ibid., Jan. 5, 1907, 11.

6 *South Orange Bulletin,* Jan. 5, 1905, 3, and Jan. 19, 1905, 3.

7 *Orange Daily Chronicle,* Jan. 3, 1911, sec. 2, 1.

8 *South Orange Bulletin,* April 7, 1904, 2, and Oct. 20, 1904, 3.

9 Author's conversation with William Gury, Dec. 6, 1991; author's conversation with William J. Parry, Sept. 17, 1990; Cornelia V. Christenson, *Kinsey: A Biography* (Bloom-

ington, 1971), 21. I do not know if Kinsey entered the city contests or if his yard ever won a prize. No records for the Village Improvement Society could be located; and after 1907 the local newspaper went out of print. Affairs in South Orange (unless of great import) were relegated to a weekly column in the *Daily Chronicle*, published in neighboring Orange. Thus there is not good coverage on South Orange between 1907 and 1912, the most likely period in which Kinsey would have competed. Still, the competition existed during the years he lived in South Orange and beyond. In 1915, for example, three years after he graduated from high school, the South Orange School Board, which by this time included Alfred S. Kinsey, heard an appeal from several organizations (including the Village Improvement Society) "to bring the matter of gardens for the people before the Board of Education with a view to securing the co-operation of that body." *South Orange Bulletin,* March (no day given), 1915.

10   *Senior Year Book, 1912, South Orange High School* (n.p.), 17 (hereafter *Senior Year Book*).

11   In many families, gender-linked divisions of labor extend to the yard. Men tend to grass, trees, and shrubs, while women cultivate flower gardens.

12   Christenson, *Kinsey,* 17.

13   ACK, *Methods in Biology* (Chicago, 1937), 5.

14   John Higham, "The Reorientation of American Culture in the 1890's," in *The Origins of Modern Consciousness,* ed. John Weiss (Detroit, 1965), 29.

15   *South Orange Bulletin,* April 13, 1905, 1.

16   Ibid.

17   Ibid. The bird campaign bore fruit when the Bird Club was organized in the high school. See Ibid., Oct. 25, 1906, 3. During Kinsey's junior year, Clarence D. Hiker of Maplewood lectured to the students of South Orange on the topic "Birds and Their Nests." See *Orange Daily Chronicle,* April 28, 1911, 2.

18   Pomeroy states the essay appeared in a nature magazine, but does not document its publication. My explanation seems more plausible. See Wardell B. Pomeroy, *Dr. Kinsey and the Institute for Sex Research* (New York, 1972), 25.

19   ACK, *An Introduction to Biology* (Philadelphia, 1926), 505–6.

20   *Senior Year Book,* 23 and 35.

21   David Lawrence Pierson, *History of the Oranges to 1921: Reviewing the Rise, Development and Progress of an Influential Community* (New York, 1922), 519.

22   Henry W. Foster, *The Evolution of the School District of South Orange and Maplewood, New Jersey, 1814–1927* (Geneva, N.Y., 1930), 174.

23   Pierson, *History of the Oranges,* 519.

24   Foster, *Evolution of the School District,* 174–75. During Kinsey's junior year in high school, South Orange conducted a spirited campaign against mosquitoes. For a running account, see *Orange Daily Chronicle,* March 2, 1911, 2; April 14, 1911, 2; May 2, 1911, 2; May 10, 1911, 2; May 16, 1911, 2; and May 17, 1911, 2.

25   As the years passed, Dr. Smith developed a warm following in South Orange. The Village Improvement Society praised him as "the leading authority in the United States on marsh mosquitoes." *South Orange Bulletin,* July 7, 1904, 3.

26   Quoted ibid., June 7, 1906, 1; *Orange Chronicle,* Nov. 2, 1907, 4. The following year, the Village Improvement Society announced plans to renew its attack on mosquito breeding grounds. See *Orange Daily Chronicle,* Oct. 3, 1908, 2. Moreover, the campaign to eradicate mosquitoes was still being waged in the 1920s. See Pierson, *History of the Oranges,* 522.

27   ACK, *Introduction to Biology,* 285.

28 Author's notes on conversation with William J. Parry, Sept. 17, 1990. Queried about Kinsey's social relationships as a boy, Gebhard replied, "He was a real loner." Author's interview with Paul H. Gebhard, Oct. 14, 1984, 13.

29 Christenson, *Kinsey,* 17.

30 Author's interview with Hazel Phillips Balch, March 28, 1992. Asked if Kinsey played sports, Balch replied, "No, not a thing." In addition to the teams sponsored by the Field Club, South Orange boasted a second private football team called the Prospect Club, named after the neighborhood where many of the boys lived. Shortly after 1903, it was absorbed into the Field Club. See Foster, *Evolution of the School District,* 169. For a discussion of how boys used sports to gain independence from parents and forge their own masculine culture, see E. Anthony Rotundo, *American Manhood: Transformations in Masculinity from the Revolution to the Modern Era* (New York, 1993), 34–38.

31 For discussions of the cultural meaning of sports at the turn of the century, see Donald Mrozek, *Sport and American Mentality, 1880–1910* (Knoxville, 1983); Joe L. Dubbert, *A Man's Place: Masculinity in Transition* (Englewood Cliffs, N.J., 1979), 163–90; and Michael Messner, "The Meaning of Success: The Athletic Experience and the Development of Male Identity," in *The Making of Masculinities: The New Men's Studies,* ed. Harry Brod (Boston, 1987), 193–209.

32 Author's notes on conversation with William J. Parry, Sept. 17, 1990.

33 Foster, *Evolution of the School District,* 171.

34 Ibid., 172.

35 *Senior Year Book,* 75.

36 Ibid. For statistics on the football, baseball, and basketball seasons, see ibid., 66, 68, 70; for information on class officers and club leaders, see ibid., 6–10 and 12.

37 Theodore Roosevelt, "The American Boy," reprinted in *The Strenuous Life: Essays and Addresses* (New York, 1902), 156, 164, 161. The decades of Kinsey's youth have been called "the strenuous life" by two historians in their periodization of men's history. See Elizabeth J. Pleck and Joseph H. Pleck, eds., *The American Man* (Englewood Cliffs, N.J., 1980).

38 For a deft analysis of Theodore Roosevelt's influence, see Dubbert, *Man's Place,* 122–31.

39 Peter Filene, *Him/Her/Self: Sex Roles in Modern America,* 2nd ed. (Baltimore, 1986), 70.

40 Rotundo, *American Manhood;* Jackson Lears, *No Place of Grace: Antimodernism and the Transformation of American Culture, 1880–1920* (New York, 1981), also offers a keen analysis of these themes.

41 Higham, "Reorientation of American Culture," 31.

42 *Senior Year Book,* 43.

43 Filene, *Him/Her/Self,* 94.

44 *South Orange Bulletin,* Jan. 14, 1904, 1.

45 Filene, *Him/Her/Self,* 94–95.

46 Higham, "Reorientation of American Culture," 30, 27.

47 Roosevelt, "American Boy," 163–64.

48 Ibid., 155.

49 Ibid., 160.

50 *South Orange Bulletin,* Oct. 20, 1904, 3.

51 Ibid., Dec. 10, 1903, 3; March 23, 1905, 4; May 3, 1906, 1.

52 *Orange Daily Chronicle,* Nov. 27, 1908, 2; Jan. 12, 1911, 2.

53   For an analysis of the cultural meaning of these organizations, see David I. Macleod, *Building Character in the American Boy: The Boy Scouts, YMCA, and Their Forerunners, 1870–1920* (Madison, Wis., 1983).

54   Filene, *Him/Her/Self,* 75. For an excellent discussion of "muscular Christianity" and cultural notions of health in Victorian England, see Bruce Haley, *The Healthy Body and Victorian Culture* (Cambridge, 1978).

55   *South Orange Bulletin,* March 17, 1904, 3, and *Orange Chronicle,* Oct. 5, 1907, 4; author's interview with Balch, March 28, 1992.

56   Most likely, Kinsey's first camp was Wawayanda, although over the years he attended many different camps. In 1948, Kinsey wrote a nature author, "I spent thirteen summers in the New England camps as a counselor and specialist in natural history." Since Kinsey spent his last summer as a camp counselor in New England in 1921 and since he did not skip any summers, this would fix the first date at 1908. See ACK to Porter Sargent, Jan. 5, 1948, KIA.

57   *Orange Chronicle,* June 1, 1907, 2.

58   Kinsey, *Introduction to Biology,* 150.

59   Quoted in Christenson, *Kinsey,* 21.

60   See Jeffrey Hantover, "The Boy Scouts and the Validation of Masculinity," in *American Man,* ed. Pleck and Pleck, 293–99; Macleod, *Building Character.*

61   Ernest Thompson Seton, *Boy Scouts of America: A Handbook of Woodcraft, Scouting, and Life-craft* (New York, 1910), xi.

62   Ibid.

63   Ibid., xii.

64   Filene, *Him/Her/Self,* 96. By 1918, the figure had risen to 300,000; by ten years later, almost a million boys had joined the BSA. See Tim Jeal, *The Boy Man: The Life of Lord Baden-Powell* (New York, 1990), 488. At least in Great Britain, the Boys Scouts drew its members largely from the middle and lower middle class. See John O. Springhall, "The Boy Scouts, Class and Militarism in Relation to British Youth Movements, 1908–1930," *International Review of Social History* 16 (1971): 125–58.

65   Clipping file, Columbia High School Archive, Maplewood, N.J., March 21 or 22, 1911 (illegible date) (hereafter CHS Archive). For an earlier story on the Boy Scouts, see *Orange Daily Chronicle,* Feb. 14, 1911, 3.

66   Seton, *Boy Scouts of America,* 13.

67   "National Eagle Register, 1912–1925," Boy Scouts of America National Headquarters, Archives Division, Irving, Tex. My thanks to Robert Kavanaugh for his help in locating Kinsey's name.

68   Quoted in Pomeroy, *Dr. Kinsey,* 27. According to Christenson, young Alfred "worked energetically and persistently on the many tests and badges." See Christenson, *Kinsey,* 22.

69   Clipping file, CHS Archive, Jan. 24, 1914.

70   "Program for the Second Annual Banquet of the South Orange Troop Boy Scouts of America," Jan. 24, 1924, CHS Archive.

71   According to the local reporter, South Orange's four new Eagles brought New Jersey's total number of Eagle Scouts to sixteen, one more than the previous national leader, New York. The menu listed bouillon, saltines, roast turkey, dressing, cranberries, mashed potatoes, green peas, celery, olives, bread rolls, ice cream, cake, nuts, mints, and aqua pura. Clipping file, CHS Archive, (n.d.).

72   Dudley W. Rice to ACK, Aug. 17, 1953, KIA; Christenson, *Kinsey,* 19.

73 "Class Prophecy," *Senior Year Book,* 20. After he finished high school, Kinsey became an assistant scoutmaster, leading the South Orange troop of about fifty younger boys. He enjoyed working with them and found a great deal of satisfaction in the position of teacher and mentor, especially since it involved the outdoors. Author's interview with Gebhard, Oct. 14, 1984, 13.

74 South Orange leaders endorsed this emphasis on outdoor activities. As part of its speakers series, the YMCA brought James A. Cruickshank, an editor for *Field and Stream,* to the Oranges to lecture on the topic "Camping Out." See *Orange Chronicle,* May 23, 1908, 3. In 1907, Benjamin S. Comstock spoke at the Assembly Hall of South Orange High School on the theme "Camping and Climbing in the Rockies." Ibid., Dec. 7, 1907, 7. Then, in 1911, Donald B. McMillan, who had accompanied William Peary to the North Pole, delivered a talk at Kinsey's church entitled "With Peary in the Arctic." Ibid., Jan. 11, 1911, 2.

75 Theodore Roosevelt, "Character and Success," in *Strenuous Life,* 115.

76 Christenson, *Kinsey,* 17–18.

77 Ibid., 18. Clara related this story to Christenson. Kinsey did, in fact, later suffer heart disease, and its relationship to his childhood health problems is unknown but likely.

78 Quoted in ibid., 19.

Chapter 4: "Be Pure in Thought and Clean in Habit"

1   *Daily Chronicle,* Feb. 10, 1909, 4.

2   "Proceedings of the Board of Trustees," June 15, 1908, 1, South Orange Board of Trustees Archive, South Orange, N.J.

3   Jan. was the low month, with seven arrests, while April was the high, with twenty-six. Ibid., Feb. 17, 1908, 1; April 20, 1908, 1; May 18, 1908, 1; June 15, 1908, 1; July 20, 1908, 1; Sept. 21, 1908, 1; Oct. 19, 1908, 1; Nov. 16, 1908, 1; Dec. 21, 1908, 1; and Jan. 18, 1909, 1. Three of the monthly reports are missing for 1908, and in each instance the report is for the preceding month. Police records for 1909 and 1910 showed a similar pattern. In 1909, police officers made twenty-four arrests for public intoxication; in 1910, the figure rose to twenty-seven.

4   Ibid., Jan. 16, 1911, 4.

5   Ibid. Kinsey was elected treasurer of the Inter-Church Civic League. See *Daily Chronicle,* May 26, 1911, 2.

6   *Daily Chronicle,* Feb. 15, 1911, 2, 4.

7   The enforcement of other laws aimed directly at supporting the family. During the five-year period 1907–12, police officers made at least three arrests for bastardy, two for nonsupport, one for desertion, two for bigamy, one for fornication, and one for seduction.

8   Lary May, *Screening Out the Past: The Birth of Mass Culture and the Motion Picture Industry* (Chicago, 1980), 35–42.

9   "Proceedings of the Board of Trustees," Nov. 29, 1909, 1, and Dec. 20, 1909, 1. For a reference to the Prospectors' Club as an athletic association, see *Daily Chronicle,* Jan. 12, 1911, 2.

10 Author's interview with Hazel Phillips Balch, March 28, 1992, 4–5.

11 *Daily Chronicle,* Dec. 1, 1908, 2.

12 Henry W. Foster, *The Evolution of the School District of South Orange and Maplewood, New Jersey, 1814–1927* (Geneva, N.Y., 1930), 215. South Orange also complied with state

requirements for accurate statistical data on its school population. See *Daily Chronicle,* Oct. 14, 1908, 2.

13   *Daily Chronicle,* March 9, 1911, 2.

14   Ibid., Nov. 30, 1908, 2.

15   Quoted in Robert Sobel, *They Satisfy: The Cigarette in American Life* (Garden City, N.Y., 1978), 61. For a provocative discussion of how smoking became a moral issue in the Progressive Era, see John C. Burnham, *Bad Habits: Drinking, Smoking, Taking Drugs, Gambling, Sexual Misbehavior, and Swearing in American History* (New York, 1993), 89–92.

16   *Daily Chronicle,* Jan. 23, 1911, 2.

17   "Proceedings of the Board of Trustees," April 20, 1908, 1.

18   Ibid., Dec. 21, 1908, 1.

19   To be appointed, a man merely had to submit an application to the Village Board of Trustees, which in turned referred the application to the Committee on Police. Upon the latter's recommendation, the appointment was granted, and the "constable" was in business.

20   Cornelia V. Christenson, *Kinsey: A Biography* (Bloomington, 1971), 17.

21   *South Orange Bulletin,* Oct. 27, 1904, 1. Superintendent Foster was equally paternalistic with his faculty. The local press reported that he did not favor the faculty's mingling in local society, "because," he argued, "they could not afford to buy the clothes necessary to keep up with it, and besides they would not have the time." See *Daily Chronicle,* Jan. 23, 1909, 2.

22   *Orange Chronicle,* April 4, 1908, 5.

23   *Daily Chronicle,* Dec. 9, 1908, 1.

24   Ibid., 4.

25   Author's interview with Balch, March 28, 1992. Interviewed a week past her ninety-seventh birthday, Balch was a lovely woman who had grown old with dignity and grace. Married for most of her life to a prosperous businessman who manufactured screen wire for windows and doors (she proudly reported that her husband's company made the screens on the White House), she was born in 1895 to well-to-do parents in Newark, N.J. Her father was the president of a large bank in Newark, and at the turn of the century he moved his family into a gracious home in South Orange, where Hazel attended school. Captain of the girls basketball team, officer of numerous high school clubs, and blessed with a personality described by classmates as "sweet and gracious," she was well liked by everyone (the caption beside her photograph in the senior album declared, "Hazel seems to be popular with both sexes. And indeed, what wonder that she is?") See *Senior Year Book, 1912, South Orange High School* (n.p., 1912), 6.

26   Author's interview with Balch, March 28, 1992. In addition to herself, the "crew" included Donald W. Salisbury, Norman G. Cort, Pierce A. Cassedy, Girard F. Oberrender, Dudley Pierson, Vernetta M. Crooks, and Leah Thomas.

27   Ibid.

28   Ibid.; Christenson, *Kinsey,* 19. With his usual penchant for reducing matters to sex, Kinsey placed sexual development at the center of shyness. In the male volume, he wrote of adolescent boys whose newly acquired ability to ejaculate and whose body changes made them feel "awkward about making social contacts." See *SBHM,* 182.

29   *SBHM,* 222.

30   Peter Filene, *Him/Her/Self: Sex Roles in Modern America,* 2nd ed. (Baltimore, 1986), 70.

31   Ibid., 80–82.

32 Ibid., 89.

33 Quoted in Allan M. Brandt, *No Magic Bullet: A Social History of Venereal Disease in the United States since 1880* (New York, 1985), 24.

34 Quoted ibid., 26.

35 *Daily Chronicle,* Jan. 23, 1909, 2.

36 Author's interview with Paul H. Gebhard, Oct. 29, 1971, 66, IUOHP.

37 *SBHM,* 440.

38 Ibid. There were, of course, parents who gave their children explicit sex education, including horrific injunctions against masturbation. "If you do this," one father told his son, whom he suspected of masturbating, "you will never be able to use your penis with a woman." Quoted in Havelock Ellis, *Studies in the Psychology of Sex,* vol. 2, *Sexual Inversion* (Philadelphia, 1921), 124.

39 *SBHM,* 417–26.

40 Ibid., 440–41.

41 Regina Lois Wolkoff, "The Ethics of Sex: Individuality and the Social Order in Early Twentieth Century American Sexual Advice Literature" (Ph.D. diss., University of Michigan, 1974).

42 *Boy Scouts of America: The Official Handbook for Boys,* 11th ed. (Garden City, N.Y., 1914), 260–61. If the world's most famous scout master had had his way, the warning against masturbation would have been much stronger. The original draft of this section of the Boy Scout manual, written by Sir (later Lord) Robert Baden-Powell, was toned down at the insistence of the publisher. See Tim Jeal, *The Boy-Man: The Life of Lord Baden-Powell* (New York, 1990), 107.

43 H. Tristram Engelhardt, Jr., "The Disease of Masturbation: Values and the Concept of Disease," *Bulletin of the History of Medicine* 48 (Summer 1974): 235.

44 Ibid., 237–38.

45 Ellis, *Psychology of Sex,* 2:124; Engelhardt, "Disease of Masturbation," 244–46.

46 Quoted in Engelhardt, "Disease of Masturbation," 244.

47 Quoted ibid., 245.

48 Quoted in Alex Comfort, *The Anxiety Makers: Some Curious Preoccupations of the Medical Profession* (New York, 1967), 92–93.

49 Quoted in Filene, *Him/Her/Self,* 83.

50 Ibid.

51 Kinsey's own research points to the importance of peer groups in the sex education of youth.

52 Joseph K. Folsom to ACK, Feb. 5, 1948, KIA.

53 Ibid.

54 John Reid, *The Best Little Boy in the World* (New York, 1973), 27–40. Reid is writing about the late 1950s. See also the description of "fussing" in summer camps contained in Martin Duberman's poignant memoir *Cures: A Gay Man's Odyssey* (New York, 1991), 14.

55 Author's interview with Paul H. Gebhard, Oct. 14, 1984, 13–14.

56 ACK to Anonymous, Aug. 30, 1950, KIA; author's interview with Gebhard, Oct. 29, 1971, 67.

57 For an excellent discussion of the press's treatment of the trials of Oscar Wilde, see Jonathan Ned Katz, *Gay/Lesbian Almanac: A New Documentary* (New York, 1983), 258–65.

58 Quoted in John D'Emilio, *Sexual Politics, Sexual Communities: The Making of a Homosexual Minority in the United States, 1940–1970* (Chicago, 1983), 13.

59 Ibid.

60 *SBHM*, 487.

61 After he became world famous, publishers deluged Kinsey with unsolicited books, asking for endorsements or dust jacket accolades. As a rule, Kinsey declined to comment, but he made an exception for a book entitled *Dear Timothy*, published by Simon and Schuster. Writing M. Lincoln Schuster early in 1953, Kinsey judged the book "outstanding" and praised it for its "fine portrayal of an obviously kind man who shows considerable wisdom in regard to many human affairs." He was particularly impressed by the book's treatment of religion and sex, calling it "one of the best demonstrations I know of the impossibility of an individual breaking away from his Orthodoxy on matters of sex even though he intellectually decided that his Orthodox training was wrong, and believes that he has actually broken with it." In all probability, Kinsey was moved by the book because he identified with its main character, a victimized hero. Indeed, the two had much in common. As a man who had been reared in a deeply religious household and whose own behavioral pattern fit the description, Kinsey could speak with great personal conviction when he added, "His ambivalent attitude toward things like masturbation and the homosexual, provide an intelligent and penetrating insight into the impossibility of abandoning Orthodoxy after one has once been immersed in it." The task may have been impossible, but, as we shall see, much of Kinsey's life can be read as a struggle to use science to free himself from his own religious upbringing and the sexual guilt he felt as a boy. See ACK to M. Lincoln Schuster, Jan. 23, 1953, KIA.

62 D'Emilio, *Sexual Politics*, 14–15.

63 Ibid.; Michel Foucault, *The History of Sexuality,* vol. 1, *An Introduction,* trans. Robert Hurley (New York, 1978), 43, quoted in John D'Emilio and Estelle B. Freedman, *Intimate Matters: A History of Sexuality in America* (New York, 1988), 226.

64 F. O. Matthiessen to Russell Cheney, Sept. 23, 1924, quoted in Katz, *Gay/Lesbian Almanac,* 413.

65 Chicago Vice Commission, "Whole . . . colonies of these men," April 5, 1911, quoted ibid., 335.

66 Charles Nesbitt, "Sexual Perverts," circa 1890, quoted ibid., 221.

67 Ellis, *Psychology of Sex,* 2:299. Referring to homosexuals, a prominent doctor wrote, "In New York they are known as 'fairies' and wear a red necktie (inverts are generally said to prefer green). In Philadelphia they are known as 'Brownies.' "

68 See James G. Kiernan, "Chicago Has Not Developed a Euphemism Yet" (1916), quoted in Katz, *Gay/Lesbian Almanac,* 367; and Douglas C. Murtrie, "The Situation and Its Dangers" (1913), quoted ibid., 341.

69 There is some evidence to suggest that the term "gay" may have appeared as early as Kinsey's adolescence as an in-group code word homosexuals applied to each other. See Gertrude Stein, "Miss Furr and Miss Skeene" (1922), quoted ibid., 405–7.

70 D'Emilio, *Sexual Politics*, 13.

71 Reid, *Best Little Boy,* 24–25. Recalling his own boyhood in upstate New York at the turn of the century, Harry Stack Sullivan, one of the most influential psychiatrists of his generation, wrote perceptively about the sexual escapades of boys who belonged to what he called "gangs," particularly the sense of adventure and discovery with which they approached masturbation and experimented with homosexuality. By "gangs," he did not mean the modern-day urban-based, crime-oriented youth organizations; rather, he referred to any organization or group that brought boys together. Thus, both the YMCA

and Boy Scouts fall within his definition of a "gang." See Helen Swick Perry, *Psychiatrist of America: The Life of Harry Stack Sullivan* (Cambridge, 1982), 93–95.

72 I am indebted to William Gury, a former occupant of Kinsey's boyhood home, for supplying the exact number—fourteen—of steps. Author's telephone conversation with Gury, Aug. 24, 1992.

73 Author's interview with William Gury, March 28, 1992; author's telephone interview with Ruth Bowman Clapp, July 20, 1992.

74 Author's interview with Gury, March 28, 1992.

75 Ibid. Although Gury kept it for years, he eventually lost track of the card, all but precluding any modern-day effort to discover the owner's name or his relationship (if any) to Kinsey.

76 Ibid.

77 Ibid.

78 Elaine Scarry, *The Body in Pain: The Making and Unmaking of the World* (New York, 1985), 16.

79 Later, as a sex researcher, Kinsey collected data on sexual fantasies, though he did not devote a great deal of space to this topic in the male volume. "Nearly, but not quite, all males experience sexual fantasies during masturbation," he wrote. According to Kinsey, heterosexuals had heterosexual fantasies, homosexuals had homosexual fantasies, and individuals who responded in both directions alternated between heterosexual and homosexual fantasies. "There are occasional sadistic or masochistic fantasies," he added without elaboration. Yet Kinsey warned that it would be a mistake to assume that fantasies always followed behavior. As he explained it, "there may be some striking disparities between the nature of the fantasies accompanying masturbation and the overt experience of the male, and one cannot discover the history of an individual merely by finding out what he thinks about when he masturbates." *SBHM*, 510–11. Still, it is possible to gain some insight into the content of masochistic fantasies by examining those of other individuals. Havelock Ellis collected a number of sexual fantasies of masochists. A few examples will suffice, beginning with a relatively mild case and then proceeding to more advanced cases. The first involves a man who recalled a preadolescent fantasy in which he was made to work as a servant for several naked sailors. Forced to crouch between their thighs, he called himself their "dirty pig" and serviced their genitals and buttocks, which he admired and handled with glee. The second draws upon a more advanced case, a man who remembered having a distinctly masochistic dream at the age of seven and who had elaborated his urges by the time he reached thirteen. "My enjoyment now was to imagine myself forced to undergo physical humiliation and submission to the caprice of my male captors, and the central fact became the discharge of urine from my lover over my body and limbs, or, if I were very fond of him," he added, "I let it be in my face." The third example is that of a man who at age six began fantasizing about acts of violence directed against himself. He imagined that a servant girl spread his legs apart and showed his genitals to another. He used these thoughts to excite himself to masturbation, but he eventually turned to homosexual fantasies in which boys buggered one another or cut off one boy's genitals. He envisioned himself a participant in these orgies of cruelty and violence, first in a passive role and then in an active role. Over time, however, the masochistic role eclipsed the sadistic. See Ellis, *Sexual Inversion*, 140, 150; Richard von Krafft-Ebing, *Psychopathia Sexualis*, trans. from the 12th German ed. (New York, 1965), 108–9.

Chapter 5: "FINALLY, HE JUST REBELLED"

1 ACK, "Valedictory," *Senior Year Book, 1912, South Orange High School* (n.p., 1912), 41.

2 Ibid.

3 Ibid.

4 *Annual Catalogue of the Stevens Institute of Technology, 1912–1913,* 35–38 (hereafter *1912 Stevens Catalogue*).

5 Ibid.

6 Official Transcript of ACK, Registrar's Records, Stevens Institute of Technology, Hoboken, N.J. (hereafter Stevens Transcript).

7 Ibid.

8 Author's interview with Mrs. ACK, Dec. 10, 1971, 7, IUOHP.

9 *1912 Stevens Catalogue,* 84–86.

10 While the Stevens library had approximately 10,000 books and subscribed to about 150 journals in 1912, it had only a handful of titles in biology; and during Kinsey's two years on campus, it added only one book on natural history to its holdings. See the *1912 Stevens Catalogue,* 32–33; and *Stute,* Nov. 12, 1913, 2.

11 Author's interview with Mrs. ACK, Dec. 10, 1971, 7.

12 *1912 Stevens Catalogue,* 24.

13 *Stute,* Sept. 27, 1912, 2.

14 Ibid.

15 *Stute,* Dec. 21, 1912, 1–4.

16 Ibid., 4.

17 Ibid., 1.

18 *Stute,* Sept. 27, 1912, 1.

19 *Stute,* Sept. 26, 1913, 1.

20 Here is the first stanza:
Back we've come to Stevens
Back to the Old Stone Mill,
Back to these halls of learning,
Back to work with a will.

21 Stevens Transcript.

22 Ibid.

23 Kinsey's marks during the spring term of his freshman year were as follows: 86 in English and logic (the same combined score as in the fall term); 46 in descriptive geometry (down from 67 but later raised to 86); 80 in mechanical drawing (down from 85); 74 in German (down from 76); 61 in physics (a new course); 85 in sho practice (down from 91); 74 in mathematics (down from 81); 69 in mechanics (up from 68); and 72 in chemistry (up from 66). Ibid.

24 Quoted in Wardell B. Pomeroy, *Dr. Kinsey and the Institute for Sex Research* (New York, 1972), 27–28.

25 Stevens Transcript.

26 Ibid.

27 *Stute,* Feb. 15, 1913, 1–2.

28 *Stute,* Feb. 22, 1913, 1, 5.

29 *Stute,* Feb. 25, 1914, 1.

30 *Stute,* March 11, 1914, 2.

31   In 1914, students and alumni cooperated to produce a sixteen-page booklet entitled "Activities at Stevens Tech," which described social life on campus. For a summary of the booklet's contents, see *Stute,* April 15, 1914, 3. When Kinsey arrived at Stevens in 1912, sports were so "big" on campus that a student reporter felt justified in stating, "The various student activities here at Stevens may be divided into two main classes: athletic and social." See *Stute,* Sept. 27, 1912, 1.

32   *Stute,* Oct. 12, 1912, 2.

33   *Stute,* Sept. 26, 1913, 1.

34   Ibid.

35   *Stute,* Sept. 27, 1912, 1.

36   Ibid.

37   *Stute,* Oct. 9, 1912, 3.

38   *Stute,* Sept. 27, 1912, 1.

39   *Stute,* Oct. 12, 1912, 4.

40   *Stute,* April 9, 1913, 1.

41   *Stute,* Dec. 21, 1912, 1.

42   *Stute,* Feb. 15, 1913, 1.

43   *Stute,* Dec. 20, 1913, 1, 3.

44   *Stute,* Jan. 24, 1914, 1.

45   Ibid., 4.

46   *Stute,* March 25, 1914, 1.

47   Ibid., 3.

48   *Stute,* May 13, 1914, 3.

49   *Stute,* April 19, 1913, 2.

50   *Stute,* Oct. 16, 1912, 1, 4. For an editorial criticizing the rules for favoring the sophomores, see *Stute,* Oct. 16, 1912, 2. During Kinsey's sophomore year, the *Stute* criticized his class for following "a too liberal interpretation of the word 'tacks.' " Their "sophomoric version" of tacks, it seems, "were about three inches long and bore a marked resemblance to ten-penny nails," and, as if this were not bad enough, "washers were provided by these zealous ones so that the flag might tear the less easily." See *Stute,* Oct. 22, 1913, 1, 4.

51   *Stute,* Oct. 3, 1913, 1.

52   Ibid., 3.

53   *Stute,* Nov. 7, 1912, 4.

54   *Stute,* Feb. 18, 1914, 4.

55   Ibid.

56   Pomeroy, *Dr. Kinsey,* 24–25.

57   *Stute,* Jan. 10, 1914, 2. A few months later, another guest lecturer repeated this message. In March 1914, Peter F. Robert, a former Yale professor who now worked for the YMCA, tried to enlist men from Stevens to teach English to foreigners. "At the present time," declared Roberts, "men from 160 colleges are taking up this work with the manly principal of 'helping the fellow lower down,' and Hoboken, with its large foreign element, would seem an ideal place for the 161st college to exercise some of its surplus energy." See *Stute,* March 11, 1914, 1–2.

58   *Stute,* Jan. 17, 1914, 1, 4.

59   *Stute,* Jan. 10, 1910, 1, 4.

60   Author's interview with Mrs. ACK, Dec. 10, 1971, 7.

61   Cornelia V. Christenson, *Kinsey: A Biography* (Bloomington, 1971), 23. Robert Kinsey's widow, Edna Higenbotham, offered a similar account. Asked to explain the

blowup between Kinsey and his father, she replied, "I think his father was just domineering and Alfred wanted to do what he wanted to do and what's wrong with that?" Author's interview with Edna Higenbotham, Nov. 28, 1984, 10.

62 Christenson, *Kinsey,* 24.

63 ACK to Dean K. C. M. Sills, July 24, 1914, KIA.

Chapter 6: "Loosen Up a Bit More, Al"

1 Patricia McGraw Anderson, *The Architecture of Bowdoin College* (Brunswick, Maine, 1988), prologue.

2 *Bowdoin Orient,* Sept. 29, 1914, 93, 96, and May 30, 1916, 78. Near the end of the term during Kinsey's junior year, total undergraduate enrollment climbed to 397, but the number of juniors fell to 77. See ibid., Dec. 8, 1914, 175.

3 Ibid., Sept. 29, 1914, 94.

4 Louis C. Hatch, *The History of Bowdoin College* (Portland, Maine, 1927), 362, 369, 373–76, 263.

5 *Bowdoin Orient,* Oct. 6, 1914, 103.

6 Hatch, *History of Bowdoin,* 428; *Bowdoin Orient,* May 23, 1916, 73, and May 16, 1916, 67.

7 Hatch, *History of Bowdoin,* 1–5.

8 Ibid., 154–65, 185–90.

9 Ibid., 202, 199.

10 Herbert Ross Brown, *Sills of Bowdoin: The Life of Kenneth Charles Morton Sills, 1879–1954* (New York, 1964), 31.

11 *Chronicle* (Orange, N.J.), Feb. 9, 1907, 3.

12 Paul K. Niven to Paul H. Gebhard, Dec. 22, 1961, KIA.

13 Brown, *Sills of Bowdoin,* 44–45.

14 Ibid., 50.

15 Ibid., 108.

16 Ibid., 92.

17 *Bowdoin Orient,* Feb. 22, 1916, 270.

18 Brown, *Sills of Bowdoin,* 109–10.

19 *Bowdoin Bugle* 71 (n.p., 1917), 269.

20 *Catalogue of Bowdoin College & the Medical School of Maine, 1914–1915,* 106.

21 ACK to Dean K. C. M. Sills, July 24, 1914, KIA.

22 Cornelia V. Christenson, *Kinsey: A Biography* (Bloomington, 1971), 24. Little is known about Kinsey's relationship with the Mayhews. Kinsey refers to Mrs. Mayhew as "a friend" in his letter to Dean Sills. Kinsey also stated that Mrs. Mayhew had contacted Dr. Hyde on his behalf. ACK to Sills, July 24, 1914, KIA.

23 Hatch, *History of Bowdoin,* 154.

24 Ibid., 166–68.

25 Searles Hall was 172 feet long and 107 feet wide and cost over $60,000. Ibid., 459.

26 Ibid., 397; Anderson, *Architecture of Bowdoin,* 39–42. Many Americans considered scientists exemplars of morality. See David A. Hollinger, "Inquiry and Uplift: Late Nineteenth-Century American Academics and the Moral Efficiency of Scientific Practice" in *The Authority of Experts,* ed. Thomas L. Haskell (Bloomington, 1984), 142–56.

27 *Bowdoin Alumnus* 45 (July 1971): 53.

28 Ibid., 44 (July 1970): 49.

29 *Bowdoin Orient*, March 23, 1915, 286.

30 *Bowdoin Alumnus* 45 (July 1971): 53.

31 Alfred O. Gross to Paul H. Gebhard, Dec. 29, 1961, KIA.

32 Ibid.

33 *Bowdoin Alumnus* 44 (July 1970): 49.

34 Ibid.

35 Gross to Gebhard, Dec. 29, 1961.

36 *Bowdoin Bugle* 70 (n.p., 1916), 70.

37 Bela W. Norton to Paul H. Gebhard, Dec. 13, 1961, KIA. Bowdoin College would not allow me to see Kinsey's transcript.

38 Christenson, *Kinsey*, 25.

39 Ibid., 28; *Bowdoin Orient*, Feb. 15, 1916, 258, and June 22, 1916, 101.

40 *Bowdoin Bugle* 70:298.

41 Niven to Gebhard, Dec. 22, 1961.

42 *Bowdoin Orient*, Feb. 23, 1915, 252.

43 Ibid., Oct. 5, 1915, 113.

44 *Bowdoin Alumnus* 45 (July 1971): 53.

45 *Bowdoin Orient*, April 13, 1915, 13. In the spring of 1915, Bowdoin received a valuable collection of thirty new birds for its biology museum, and the New York School of Forestry donated a collection of American woods specimens. Doubtless, Kinsey was responsible for cataloging these as well. See ibid., May 4, 1915, 41.

46 Manton Copeland to Paul H. Gebhard, April 13, 1962, KIA. For a brief discussion of Bowdoin's special facilities and collections in biology, see Hatch, *History of Bowdoin*, 480–81.

47 Christenson, *Kinsey*, 28.

48 During Kinsey's senior year, the Biology Club hosted Professor G. H. Parker of Harvard University, who lectured on the topic "The Fur Seals of the Pribilof Islands." *Bowdoin Bugle* 70:219; *Bowdoin Orient*, Jan. 18, 1916, 231.

49 *Bowdoin Orient*, Jan. 26, 1915, 224.

50 Ibid., Feb. 23, 1915, 253–54, and Dec. 14, 1915, 188. Unfortunately, no records for the Biology Club have survived, but the school paper carried news of the club's activities.

51 *Bowdoin Orient*, June 2, 1916, 87.

52 Ibid., March 23, 1915, 286.

53 Norton to Gebhard, Dec. 13, 1961. Despite Bowdoin's reputation as a middle- and upper-middle-class school, Kinsey was not alone in having to work summers. An editorial in the school paper insisted that "many Bowdoin students are dependent in part upon their work during the summer." See *Bowdoin Orient*, Feb. 8, 1916, 248.

54 *Bowdoin Bugle* 71:38, 167.

55 Hatch, *History of Bowdoin*, 202.

56 *Bowdoin Orient*, Sept. 29, 1914, 94. Students in the English 5 class at Bowdoin even debated whether intercollegiate athletics should be abolished. See ibid., Feb. 8, 1916, 246.

57 *Bowdoin Bugle* 70: 178–81.

58 *Bowdoin Orient*, Nov. 24, 1914, 164.

59 Ibid., Dec. 15, 1914, 182.

60 Ibid., Dec. 22, 1914, 191.

61 Ibid., Feb. 9, 1915, 223. One of four prizes to encourage public speaking at Bowdoin, the Fairbanks Prize amounted to one-fourth of the annual income derived from a

$2,000 bequest to the college by Captain Henry N. Fairbanks of Bangor, in memory of his son, Hiland Lockwood Fairbanks, class of 1895.

62 *Bowdoin Orient,* Feb. 9, 1915, 233.
63 Ibid., Feb. 23, 1915, 251, 252.
64 *Bowdoin Bugle* 70:177.
65 *Bowdoin Orient,* March 23, 1915, 280.
66 Ibid., April 6, 1915, 1.
67 Ibid., May 4, 1915, 41.
68 Ibid., Dec. 14, 1915, 183; Jan. 11, 1916, 214–15; and March 14, 1916, 289.
69 Ibid., Feb. 8, 1916, 249.
70 Ibid., Feb. 22, 1916, 263. For some reason, Kinsey was not on the varsity debate team his senior year. See ibid., March 7, 1916, 283.
71 Ibid., Dec. 15, 1914, 182.
72 Brown, *Sills of Bowdoin,* 114.
73 Ibid., 143.
74 *Bowdoin Orient,* Nov. 23, 1915, 172.
75 Ibid., Dec. 14, 1915, 184–85.
76 Ibid., Feb. 8, 1916, 251.
77 Ibid., Feb. 22, 1916, 266.
78 Brown, *Sills of Bowdoin,* 115.
79 Ibid.
80 Ibid., 115–17.
81 *Bowdoin Orient,* May 9, 1916, 51.
82 Ibid., April 18, 1916, 11.
83 For the Rifle Club's story, see ibid., Feb. 8, 1916, 251; Feb. 22, 1916, 263; and March 14, 1916, 93.
84 Brown, *Sills of Bowdoin,* 117.
85 *Bowdoin Orient,* Dec. 15, 1914, 187.
86 Ibid., Feb. 16, 1915, 244. If Kinsey had wished to remain in his father's religion, he could have transferred his membership to the Methodist Church in Brunswick.
87 Ibid., Dec. 14, 1914, 188.
88 Joseph K. Folsom to St. Clair McKelway, Jan. 27, 1948, KIA.
89 *Bowdoin Orient,* Oct. 6, 1914, 103.
90 Ibid., Feb. 9, 1915, 234.
91 Ibid., June 4, 1915, 79–80.
92 Ibid., Jan. 11, 1916, 206–7.
93 Ibid., June 4, 1915, 79–80, and Jan. 11, 1916, 206–7.
94 Ibid., Sept. 29, 1914, 95.
95 Hatch, *History of Bowdoin,* 284; *Bowdoin Orient,* June 4, 1915, 79–80; Jan. 11, 1916, 206–7, and Jan. 19, 1915, 211.
96 Hatch, *History of Bowdoin,* 284.
97 Kinsey participated in four deputations. On Jan. 10, 1915, he preached at Falmouth, Maine; February found him in Bethel, where he spoke at Gould's Academy; in March, he appeared in South Windham; and his last deputation followed in May at Bristol. *Bowdoin Orient,* Jan. 19, 1915, 211; Feb. 9, 1915, 234; March 2, 1915, 260; and May 25, 1915, 67.
98 Ibid., March 16, 1915, 276.
99 Ibid., Jan. 11, 1916, 207.
100 Ibid.

101 Ibid., Jan. 25, 1916, 241.
102 Ibid., Feb. 23, 1915, 251–52.
103 Ibid., March 9, 1915, 270.
104 Ibid., April 6, 1915, 5, and June 4, 1915, 80.
105 *Bowdoin Bugle* 71:284.
106 *Bowdoin Orient,* Dec. 22, 1914, 193.
107 Brown, *Sills of Bowdoin,* 36.
108 *Bowdoin Orient,* Nov. 16, 1915, 165; Dec. 15, 1914, 187; Jan. 19, 1915, 211; and Jan. 11, 1916, 215.
109 Ibid., March 16, 1915, 276.
110 Listed according to when their Bowdoin chapters were founded, with the oldest first, Bowdoin's eight fraternities were Alpha Delta Phi, Psi Upsilon, Chi Psi, Delta Kappa Epsilon, Delta Upsilon, Theta Delta Chi, Zeta Psi, and Kappa Sigma. See Hatch, *History of Bowdoin,* 316.
111 *Bowdoin Orient,* Sept. 29, 1914, 94–95.
112 Ibid., Oct. 13, 1914, 110.
113 Ibid., Oct. 20, 1914, 120.
114 Hatch, *History of Bowdoin,* 228.
115 Anderson, *Architecture of Bowdoin,* 175.
116 Norton to Gebhard, Dec. 13, 1961.
117 *Bowdoin Bugle* 70:70.
118 Niven to Gebhard, Dec. 22, 1961.
119 Ibid.
120 Ibid.
121 Ibid.
122 Ibid.
123 Ibid.
124 Ibid.
125 Norton to Gebhard, Dec. 13, 1961.
126 Like Stevens, Bowdoin had several musical clubs, but Kinsey never joined one. Perhaps he was too busy with his other activities, but a more likely explanation is that he had finally concluded he lacked the talent to become a professional musician. Yet, for a man who did not play in the school orchestra, Kinsey acquired a musical reputation. The *Bugle* called him "a professional at the piano," adding that even "to the most uncultivated ear the 'Moonlight Sonata' is preferable to Niven's one finger selections." *Bowdoin Bugle* 70:70.
127 Austin MacCormick, "Personal Recollections of Dr. Alfred C. Kinsey," May 1, 1962, KIA.
128 Ibid. Overall, MacCormick's memories of Kinsey at Bowdoin were strikingly similar to those of Niven. According to MacCormick, Kinsey "had a more mature interest in his courses than most of the student body." He also described him as "an excellent scholar as well as a hard worker." And like Niven, MacCormick went out of his way to balance his portrait by insisting that, despite his maturity and hard work, Kinsey "was not considered a grind."
129 *SBHM,* 364.
130 *Bowdoin Orient,* May 16, 1916, 64.
131 Paul Nixon to ACK, Feb. 21, 1945, KIA.
132 *Bowdoin Orient,* March 21, 1916, 295.
133 Ibid., May 30, 1916, 79.

134 Ibid., June 22, 1916, 107.
135 Ibid.
136 Ibid.
137 Ibid.

Chapter 7: "AH, I PERCEIVE THAT YOU ARE AN ENTOMOLOGIST"

1 During Kinsey's first semester at Harvard, a new section of the subway opened between Washington Street and South station, part of the planned extension of the system into Dorchester. *Harvard Crimson,* Dec. 1, 1916, 1.
2 "Buckminster Fuller '17," in *Our Harvard: Reflections on College Life by Twenty-two Distinguished Graduates,* ed. Jeffrey L. Lant (New York, 1982), 8–9.
3 *Harvard Crimson,* Dec. 13, 1916, 6.
4 Ibid., Jan. 15, 1917, 5. This figure was for the 1916–17 academic year.
5 *Official Register of Harvard University* 15, no. 6 (Feb. 28, 1918): 18.
6 William M. Wheeler, "The Bussey Institute," ibid., 118; Samuel Eliot Morison, *Three
   Centuries of Harvard, 1636–1936* (Cambridge, 1936), 356. Harvard's veterinary
   school closed in 1902.
7 William M. Wheeler, "The Bussey Institution, 1871–1929" in *The Development of
   Harvard University since the Inauguration of President Eliot, 1869–1929,* ed. Samuel
   Eliot Morison (Cambridge, 1930), 513.
8 Ibid., 513–14.
9 Ernst Mayr, *The Growth of Biological Thought: Diversity, Evolution, and Inheritance*
   (Cambridge, 1982), 14.
10 Hamilton Cravens, *The Triumph of Evolution: American Scientists and the Heredity-
    Environment Controversy, 1900–1941* (Philadelphia, 1978), 37, 39.
11 Ibid., 34.
12 Ibid., 19.
13 Mayr, *Growth of Biological Thought,* 5.
14 Cravens, *Triumph of Evolution,* 19–20. That Harvard University quickly emerged as a
    major center for biological studies was hardly surprising. Its leadership in the life sci-
    ences had been firmly established in the first half of the nineteenth century by the pi-
    oneering work of Jeffries Wyman, the anatomist; Asa Gray, the botanist; and Louis
    Agassiz, the zoologist-geologist. Harvard further enhanced its standing in natural
    history and the biological sciences by establishing the Lawrence Scientific School in
    1847, by creating independent departments for the various natural history disciplines,
    and by founding the Museum of Comparative Zoology in 1859. Ibid., 20–21.
15 Mary Alice Evans and Howard Ensign Evans, *William Morton Wheeler, Biologist* (Cam-
    bridge, 1970), 240–41, 243. Unless otherwise indicated, all material on Wheeler is
    drawn from this biography.
16 Ibid., 241–43.
17 Ibid., 11.
18 Ibid., 181.
19 *Official Register of Harvard University* 13, no. 3, pt. 1, *Bussey Institution for Research in
    Applied Biology, 1916–1917* (Feb. 24, 1916) (hereafter *Bussey Register*).
20 Cornelia V. Christenson, *Kinsey: A Biography* (Bloomington, 1971), 35.
21 *Bussey Register,* 28.
22 Evans and Evans, *William Morton Wheeler,* 191.

23 Carl H. Eigenmann to William Lowe Bryan, May 12, 1920, William Lowe Bryan Papers, IUA (hereafter Bryan Papers).

24 *Official Register of Harvard University* 17, no. 7 (March 20, 1920): 107.

25 *Harvard Crimson,* Sept. 27, 1916, 10.

26 *Bussey Register,* Feb. 24, 1916, 8.

27 Evans and Evans, *William Morton Wheeler,* 188.

28 Ibid., 181; and "Buckminster Fuller," in *Our Harvard,* 7–8. According to Fuller, it only took seven minutes to travel from Cambridge to Park Street, the end of the line in Boston in 1913.

29 Notebook—Miscellaneous (includes student grades, Bussey Institute, 1909–[17]), Box 2, William M. Wheeler Papers, Pusey Library, Harvard University (hereafter Wheeler Papers).

30 Meticulously organized, astonishingly detailed, and richly illustrated, Kinsey's notes from this course have survived, allowing us to reconstruct his introduction to the field. ACK, "Entomology, Lecture Notes, Dr. Wheeler, Feb.–June 1917," 36, KIA.

31 Evans and Evans, *William Morton Wheeler,* 11.

32 Ibid., 177.

33 ACK, "Entomology, Lecture Notes," 87; Mayr, *Growth of Biological Thought,* 139. According to Mayr, modern-day taxonomists have picked up the pace considerably, describing approximately 10,000 new species each year. But even if the lowest estimates of the number of unclassified species are accepted, he notes, an additional two hundred years of taxonomic work remain to be done. Ibid., 246.

34 Their desire for an efficient, well-organized society has prompted one leading historian to characterize the entire Progressive Era as "a search for order." Robert Wiebe, *The Search for Order* (New York, 1968).

35 Evans and Evans, *William Morton Wheeler,* 302–3.

36 Ibid., 317.

37 Ibid., 248–49.

38 Laurence R. Veysey, *The Emergence of the American University* (Chicago, 1965), 156–57. Wheeler himself spoke of "an almost filial piety" he felt toward one of his professors. Evans and Evans, *William Morton Wheeler,* 205.

39 ACK to Natalie Roeth, Jan. 20, 1918, KIA. In preparing the work for publication, Kinsey took a number of photographs for use as illustrations. Their cost was partly responsible for the long delay in publication that followed, and in the end the publisher substituted line drawings for many of the photographs. *Edible Wild Plants of Eastern North America* did not appear until 1943, at the height of World War II. The book's publication owed much to the emergency atmosphere of the war, when the public developed a keen interest in the concept of survival training. The trustees of the Massachusetts Horticultural Society named it the best horticultural book of the year, an honor that delighted Kinsey no little—all the more so, one suspects, because it came so many years after the brunt of the work had been completed. M. L. Fernald and ACK, *Edible Plants of Eastern North America* (Cornwall-on-Hudson, N.Y., 1943).

40 *Harvard Crimson,* Jan. 11, 1917, 2.

41 Ibid., Jan. 25, 1917, 1.

42 Ibid., Feb. 12, 1917, 2.

43 Ibid., Feb. 14, 1917, 2.

44 Ibid., April 7, 1917, 2.

45 Ibid., Sept. 24, 1918, 1, and Jan. 4, 1919, 1.

46 Ibid., Sept. 17, 1917, 2.

47 Ibid., Nov. 1, 1917, 2.

48 Howard Q. Bunker, "My Association with and Recollections of Dr. Alfred C. Kinsey" (unpublished MS, Nov. 20, 1957), 1, KIA.

49 Ibid., 1–3.

50 *Harvard Crimson*, Feb. 18, 1919, 1.

51 Edgar Anderson, "Kinsey as I Knew Him" (unpublished MS, n.d.), 2, KIA.

52 Ibid.

53 Ibid., 2–3.

54 Ibid., 4–5.

55 Christenson, *Kinsey*, 32.

56 ACK, *The Gall Wasp Genus Cynips: A Study in the Origin of Species* (Bloomington, 1930), 13; and Kinsey to Roeth, Jan. 20, 1918.

57 My description of gall wasps is drawn from the chapter on these insects contained in Kinsey's high school biology textbook, which offers a level of detail appropriate to general readers. See ACK, *An Introduction to Biology* (Philadelphia, 1926), 329.

58 Ibid., 329–30.

59 Ibid., 334.

60 Ibid., 334–35. The revised edition of Kinsey's textbook offers a slightly improved discussion of the same material. See ACK, *New Introduction to Biology* (Philadelphia, 1933), 578–94.

61 *Harvard Crimson*, March 1, 1918, 1.

62 Anderson, "Kinsey as I Knew Him."

63 Bunker, "My Association," 2.

64 ACK, *Introduction to Biology*, 336.

65 Ibid.

66 *Bussey Register*, Feb. 24, 1916, 23. From a research standpoint, the Bussey Institute boasted strong facilities. In 1916, its library, located on the third floor of the main building, housed 3,300 volumes and 16,000 pamphlets. Supplementing this collection was the library of the Arnold Arboretum, which contained 37,000 volumes and pamphlets. In addition, Bussey students could draw upon the superb college and department libraries in Cambridge, which housed 1,700,000 volumes and pamphlets, and the libraries of the Gray Herbarium and the Museum of Comparative Zoology, both of which had outstanding biological collections, as did the library of the Harvard Medical College, located in nearby Back Bay. Finally, Bussey students could utilize the resources of the community, which included the Boston Public Library and the libraries of the Boston Society of Natural History and the Massachusetts Horticultural Society, all of which contained valuable biological collections.

67 ACK, "Life Histories of American Cynipidae," *Bulletin of the Museum of Natural History* 42 (1920): 325–26. Shortly after finishing graduate school, Kinsey admitted, "My methods have been similar to those used by Adler but involve some modifications." Ibid., 320.

68 ACK to Roeth, Jan. 20, 1918.

69 Ibid.

70 ACK, "Life Histories," 321.

71 Mayr, *Growth of Biological Thought*, 251.

72 H. M. Parshley, "Gall Wasps and the Species Problem," *Entomological News* 41 (June 1930): 191.

73 Mayr, *Growth of Biological Thought*, 240.

74 Ibid.

75 Stephen Jay Gould, "Of Wasps and WASPs," *Natural History* 91 (Dec. 1982): 12.

76 Mayr, *Growth of Biological Thought*, 38–39; Gould, "Wasps and WASPs," 12.

77 ACK, *Gall Wasp Genus Cynips*, 17.

78 Evans and Evans, *William Morton Wheeler*, 175.

79 Ibid., 315.

80 Anderson, "Kinsey as I Knew Him."

81 ACK, "Contribution outside of Indiana University Grants" (handwritten note, undated, but internal evidence suggests it was written in 1928), KIA. The note details the financial support he received for his gall wasp research from 1917 to 1925, the locations of his various research trips, etc. Also, see *Harvard Crimson*, March 30, 1917, 4. This article offers a brief description of the Sheldon fellowship program. However, the article erroneously lists the stipend as $15,000, rather than $1,500.

82 ACK to William M. Wheeler, Oct. 12, 1919, Box 19, Wheeler Papers.

83 ACK to William M. Wheeler, Oct. 22, 1919, ibid.

84 William M. Wheeler to Carl Hartman, Nov. 5, 1919, Box 16, Wheeler Papers.

85 ACK to William M. Wheeler, Dec. 9, 1919, Box 19, Wheeler Papers.

86 William M. Wheeler to Forrest Shreve, Nov. 15, 1919, Box 32, Wheeler Papers.

87 Christenson, *Kinsey*, 38.

88 ACK to Natalie Roeth, Jan. 29, 1921, KIA.

89 ACK, *Introduction to Biology*, 45.

90 Anderson, "Kinsey as I Knew Him," 3–4.

91 ACK, *Introduction to Biology*, 47.

92 Ibid., 179.

93 Ibid., 527.

94 Ibid., 519.

95 Ibid., 526.

96 ACK, *Methods in Biology* (Chicago, 1937), 6–7.

97 ACK, *Introduction to Biology*, 474.

98 Ibid., 42–43.

99 Ibid., 42, 40.

100 Ibid., 23–24.

101 William Morton Wheeler, "The Termitodoxa, or Biology and Society," *Scientific Monthly* 10 (Feb. 1920): 113–24.

102 Louise Rosenzweig and Saul Rosenzweig, "Notes on Alfred C. Kinsey's Pre-Sexual Scientific Work and the Transition," *Journal of the History of the Behavioral Sciences* 5 (April 1969): 177.

103 William M. Wheeler to Carl H. Eigenmann, April 29, 1920, Box 11, Wheeler Papers.

104 William M. Wheeler to Carl H. Eigenmann, May 12, 1920, ibid.

105 Carl H. Eigenmann to William L. Bryan, May 12, 1920, Bryan Papers.

106 Ibid.

107 William L. Bryan to Alfred C. Kinsey, June 1, 1920, Kinsey File, IUA.

Chapter 8: "We Sort of Migrated Together"

1 For a description of Biology Hall and its layout, see Theodore W. Torrey, "Zoology and Its Makers at Indiana University," *BIOS* 20 (May 1949): 87.

2 Author's interview with Theodore W. Torrey, Sept. 17, 1971, 2, IUOHP; author's interview with Robert Kroc, Nov. 7, 1987, 16.

3   Quoted in Thomas D. Clark, *Indiana University: Midwestern Pioneer,* vol. 2, *In Mid-Passage* (Bloomington, 1973), 39.

4   Cornelia V. Christenson, *Kinsey: A Biography* (Bloomington, 1971), 68.

5   The portrait of Bloomington in this and the following paragraphs is a composite based on the oral interviews cited.

6   Christenson, *Kinsey,* 41.

7   Author's interview with Torrey, Sept. 17, 1971, 2; Christenson, *Kinsey,* 53. The enrollment figures were provided by the Registrar's Office.

8   Clark, *Indiana University,* 245.

9   Wardell B. Pomeroy, *Dr. Kinsey and the Institute for Sex Research* (New York, 1972), 37. Pomeroy, Kinsey's research associate, notes that Kinsey was "shy and lonely" when he arrived in Bloomington, but he does not elaborate.

10 Author's interview with Herman T. Spieth, Feb. 18, 1988, 12.

11 Quoted in Christenson, *Kinsey,* 43.

12 Author's interview with Mrs. ACK, Dec. 10, 1971, 3, IUOHP.

13 Pomeroy, *Dr. Kinsey,* 37.

14 *Fort Wayne News Sentinel,* Oct. 13, 1924.

15 Ibid., Jan. 21, 1925.

16 Author's interview with Mrs. ACK, Dec. 10, 1971, 1–2.

17 Ibid., 2.

18 Pomeroy, *Dr. Kinsey,* 38.

19 See Thomas D. Clark's interview with Mrs. ACK, Feb. 17, 1969, 1, 6, 7, KIA.

20 Christenson, *Kinsey,* 47.

21 Clark's interview with Mrs. ACK, Feb. 17, 1969, 3.

22 Ibid., 2–3.

23 Christenson, *Kinsey,* 48.

24 Author's interview with Mrs. ACK, Dec. 10, 1971, 3–4. In her biography of Kinsey, Christenson states that Clara and Kinsey met one other time prior to the picnic. According to Christenson, Clara had a friend in one of Kinsey's courses and received permission to accompany his class on a brief field trip, but nothing noteworthy happened between them. See Christenson, *Kinsey,* 44–45.

25 Author's interview with Mrs. ACK, Dec. 10, 1971, 4–5.

26 Clark's interview with Mrs. ACK, Feb. 17, 1969, 5.

27 Author's interview with Mrs. ACK, Dec. 10, 1971, 4.

28 Ibid., 4; Christenson, *Kinsey,* 45.

29 Christenson, *Kinsey,* 48.

30 Author's interview with Mrs. ACK, Dec. 10, 1971, 4.

31 Quoted in Christenson, *Kinsey*, 46.

32 Quoted in Nanette Kutner, "Yes, There Is a Mrs. Kinsey," *McCall's,* July 1948, 92.

33 Ibid.; Pomeroy, *Dr. Kinsey,* 38.

34 Author's interview with Mrs. ACK, Dec. 10, 1971, 3–5.

35 Clark's interview with Mrs. ACK, Feb. 17, 1969, 4–6.

36 Ibid., 6.

37 Ibid., 7.

38 Quoted in Christenson, *Kinsey,* 45.

39 Author's interview with Mrs. ACK, Dec. 10, 1971, 19, 34; Pomeroy, *Dr. Kinsey,* 38.

40 Kinsey's research later revealed that approximately 33 percent of the college-educated men and approximately 40 percent of the college-educated women of their age cohort did not have sexual intercourse prior to marriage. See *SBHM,* 549–52, and *SBHF,*

293. Following World War I, sex education was on the rise, but many young people elected to use their knowledge to reaffirm traditional values. As one woman told her doctor, "During the war the widespread discussion of sex hygiene and similar problems gave me practical added information, but it also reentrenched my idea of demanding a single standard for men and women." See Robert L. Dickinson, *A Thousand Marriages: A Medical Study of Sex Adjustment* (Baltimore, 1931), 92.

41   H. Laurence Ross, "Odd Couples: Homosexuals in Heterosexual Marriages," *Sexual Behavior* 2 (July 1972): 45.

42   Dickinson, *Thousand Marriages,* 73.

43   Kutner, "Yes, There Is a Mrs. Kinsey," 92.

44   Jean S. Gochros, "Wives' Reactions to Learning That Their Husbands Are Bisexual," *Journal of Homosexuality* 11 (Spring 1985): 103.

45   Dickinson, *Thousand Marriages,* 243. It should be noted that scholars who have studied gay-straight marriages disagree sharply about the personalities of women who marry homosexual males. Sympathetic observers insist that normal, well-adjusted women often marry gay males. Women do so, explain the experts with perfect logic, because these wives do not know that their husbands are gay when they marry them. A minority of scholars, however, insist that women who marry homosexuals are neurotic wretches bent upon self-destruction. One such scholar, a Freudian analyst, reported that her entire sample of women who married gays had "marked feelings of inadequacy" and "doubts about their physical attractiveness, sexual adequacy, or capacity to relate to men." In addition, she detected "marked disturbances in the relationships between these women and their fathers," which often left them feeling "devalued and rejected by their fathers." In her view, such women harbored enormous hostility toward men and had "singled out homosexual men and had moved from one such relationship to another." Overall, every woman in the group "had a retarded psychosexual and social development and saw herself as a failure in the competitive arena of her emerging heterosexual relationships." See Myra S. Hatterer, "The Problems of Women Married to Homosexual Men," *American Journal of Psychiatry* 131 (March 1974): 275.

46   Allan M. Brandt, *No Magic Bullet: A Social History of Venereal Disease in the United States since 1880* (New York, 1985), 69. There is no reason to believe that Clara suspected his restraint might be linked to other causes. If this makes her sound hopelessly gullible, consider the case of a more contemporary woman who described a similar courtship. Following a six-month engagement during which her fiancé made no effort to touch her, this woman told herself, "Well, there's a real man! He respects me because he knows I don't feel that way towards him yet. . . . This is the way a real man should be." As it happened, the man turned out to be gay. See Ross, "Odd Couples," 45.

47   Historians know very little about the confidences couples exchange on the eve of marriage. See Ellen K. Rothman, *Hands and Hearts: A History of Courtship in America* (New York, 1984), and Beth L. Bailey, *From Front Porch to Back Seat: Courtship in Twentieth-Century America* (New York, 1988).

48   For a discussion of denial and repression, see Frederick W. Bozett, "Heterogeneous Couples in Heterosexual Marriages: Gay Men and Straight Women," *Journal of Marital and Family Therapy* 8 (Jan. 1982): 83. Scholars are in agreement that before homosexuals can tell others they are gay, they must first accept this reality about themselves. Such self-acceptance typically takes a long time. In fact, it is best understood as a process. One gay father described it as, "[a] long, difficult awareness. Trying to understand, you know." See Frederick W. Bozett, "Gay Fathers: How and Why They

Disclose Their Homosexuality to Their Children," *Family Relations* 29 (April 1980): 174. For additional examples of gays who knew they were "different" before marrying, but who did not know they were homosexual, see Ross, "Odd Couples," 43, Barry M. Dank, "Why Homosexuals Marry Women," *Medical Aspects of Sexuality* 6 (Aug. 1972): 19, and H. Laurence Ross, "Modes of Adjustment of Married Homosexuals," *Social Problems* 18 (Winter 1971): 387. Recent scholarship may also help us understand why courtship apparently did nothing to clarify Kinsey's sexual identity. Above all, this literature paints a portrait of men who are profoundly confused. While virtually all the men in these studies knew that something was "different" about their sexual orientation, and while the overwhelming majority admitted they were aware of feeling attracted to persons of the same sex before marriage, many did not comprehend the meaning of their feelings. "I didn't know I looked differently at men and at women," insisted one man. "Only when I was 26 did I understand that I was looking at men only." See Ross, "Modes of Adjustment," 387.

49   The exact percentage of homosexuals who married early in this century remains unknown. One sex researcher in the 1970s called married homosexuals "[o]ne of the most invisible groups of the homosexually oriented" and declared, "No one can estimate the number of homosexually oriented people who marry, live out their lives carrying their secret to their graves, experiencing various degrees of guilt and pain—as well as satisfaction—throughout their married life." Harvey L. Gochros, "Counseling Gay Husbands," *Journal of Education and Therapy* 4 (Dec. 1978): 6.

50   For estimates on the percentage of homosexuals who marry, see Alan P. Bell and Martin S. Weinberg, *Homosexuals: A Study of Diversity among Men & Women* (New York, 1978), 162, which puts the figure at 20 percent. Bell and Weinberg cite other studies that place the figure at 18 percent, 17 percent, and 15 percent. One scholar estimates that 25 percent of homosexuals wed. See Dank, "Why Homosexuals Marry Women," 14. Kinsey's data in the male volume are not comparable, but they do document an incidence of homosexual behavior in married men ranging from 10 percent in the 21- to 25-year-old group down to 2 percent among 45-year-old males. Admitting that the percentage of gay men who married was probably higher than his data showed, Kinsey declared, "Married males who have social position to maintain and who fear that their wives may discover their extra-marital activities, are not readily persuaded into contributing histories to a research study." In his view, it was highly probable that "the true incidence of the homosexual in married groups is much higher than we are able to record." See *SBHM*, 285, 289.

51   For the medical prescription of marriage as a cure for masturbation, see John S. Haller and Robin M. Haller, *The Physician and Sexuality in Victorian America* (Urbana, 1974), 206–7. One of the cases discussed by Havelock Ellis states that doctors advised him to marry as a cure for homosexuality. See Ellis, *Studies in the Psychology of Sex*, vol. 2, *Sexual Inversion* (Philadelphia, 1921), 138.

52   Ross, "Modes of Adjustment," 388; also see Bell and Weinberg, *Homosexuals*, 161.

53   See *Brookville American*, June 9, 1921, 1.

54   The local paper published a complete list of those who attended the ceremony. See ibid.

55   Quoted in Christenson, *Kinsey*, 48.

56   Ibid. According to Christenson's account, he introduced Clara to his mother, sister, and brother; no mention is made of his father.

57   Dickinson, *Thousand Marriages*, 74.

58   Christenson, *Kinsey*, 48–49.

59   Quoted ibid., 49.

60   Ibid. Nor did the teacher-pupil relationship cease with the honeymoon. After it ended, the couple spent the remainder of the summer working as counselors at Camp Aloah on Lake Moreoy, near Fairlee, Vermont. It was an all-girls camp, and Kinsey was in charge of camp craft and nature study. Clara served as his assistant in both duties.

61   Author's interview with Paul H. Gebhard, Oct. 14, 1984, 16. Referring to the consummation of the marriage, Gebhard could not be specific about how long it required. He stated, however, that "it took a longer time than average" and added, "I think [Wardell B.] Pomeroy said a year, but actually I don't think it was a year, I think it was less than that, but it was still a long time. It wasn't during the honeymoon or anything like that." In an earlier, more guarded interview, Gebhard alluded to Alfred and Clara's early sexual problems, stating, "All he's ever told me was that, yes, there was a fairly lengthy period of adjustment. . . . So I gather that there was a little problem in the beginning." Author's interview with Gebhard, Aug. 7, 1984, 2–3.

62   Th. H. Van de Velde, *Ideal Marriage: Its Physiology and Technique* (New York, 1930), 8.

63   See Milliard S. Everett, *The Hygiene of Marriage: A Detailed Consideration of Sex and Marriage* (New York, 1932), 121–22.

64   Rothman, *Hands and Hearts,* 281.

65   Quoted ibid., 281–82.

66   Ibid.

67   Van de Velde, *Ideal Marriage,* 8.

68   See Dickinson, *Thousand Marriages,* 84. Dickinson discussed several cases of marriages that were not consummated on the honeymoon, or in some instances for months or even years thereafter. See ibid., 81, 88, 95, 316. See also Rothman, *Hands and Hearts,* 281.

Chapter 9: "Just a Little Imperfect—Too Intolerant"

1   Unlike many assistant professors, he did not have to carry a senior colleague's briefcase for several years before being allowed to teach courses in his specialty. From that perspective, Indiana was a dream appointment, as he was the only entomologist in the department. Back in the 1880s, John C. Branner, a noted geologist, had offered a course in entomology at Indiana, and three of his students had actually gone on to become professional entomologists. But following this brave beginning, the administration had allowed entomology to disappear from the curriculum, and insect material was tucked into the general zoology course.

2   See ACK to Natalie Roeth, Jan. 29, 1921, KIA.

3   Thomas D. Clark, *Indiana University: Midwestern Pioneer,* vol. 2, *In Mid-Passage* (Bloomington, 1973), 6–7.

4   Ibid., 120, 27–29.

5   Ibid., 27, 30.

6   Ibid., 20–21; Thomas D. Clark's interview with Fernandus Payne, Oct. 12, 1968, 9–10, KIA.

7   Clark, *Indiana University,* 308, 296–97.

8   Ibid., 21.

9   Ibid., 311.

10   See Louise Ritterskamp Rosenzweig, "Reminiscences about Dr. Alfred C. Kinsey" (typed transcript of unpublished MS), 2, KIA. A revised version of this MS was later published. See Louise Rosenzweig and Saul Rosenzweig, "Notes on Alfred C. Kin-

sey's Pre-Sexual Scientific Work and the Transition," *Journal of the History of the Behavioral Sciences* 5 (April 1969): 173–81.

11 See Cornelia V. Christenson, *Kinsey: A Biography* (Bloomington, 1971), 54–55.

12 ACK, *Field and Laboratory Manual in Biology* (Philadelphia, 1927), xiii.

13 Author's interview with William R. Breneman, May 21, 1985, 10.

14 ACK to Robert Bugbee, Sept. 28, 1936, KIA.

15 Ibid.

16 "General biology utilizes both plant and animal material but it is not botany added to zoology," he explained. "It is concerned with those principles applicable to all organisms, and usually leaves for advanced courses in botany such data as apply only to plants, or to advanced courses in zoology the material that concerns only animal species." ACK, "Biologic Sciences in Our High Schools," *Proceedings of the Indiana Academy of Science* 35 (1926): 64.

17 See Christenson, *Kinsey,* 54.

18 Theodore W. Torrey, "Zoology and Its Makers at Indiana University," *BIOS* 20 (May 1949): 72–90.

19 Ibid., 81–88.

20 Clark interview with Payne, Oct. 15, 1968, 19.

21 According to Robert Kroc, this condition persisted well into the 1930s. See author's interview with Kroc, Nov. 7, 1987, 10–13.

22 Torrey, "Zoology and Its Makers," 86–87, 96.

23 Author's interview with Breneman, May 21, 1985, 3. To illustrate the point, Breneman pointed to the time when Payne informed him in person that a university committee had turned down his application for a research grant by a unanimous vote, and quickly added, "But lest you get a misconception, I agree with them one hundred percent." Breneman also challenged the image of Payne as stern and aloof, insisting that "he could be very, very warm . . . once you got through that little outer crust."

24 Torrey, "Zoology and Its Makers," 91–92. Significantly, Homer T. Rainwater, a former graduate student in the department, used nearly identical words to describe him. "Dr. Scott was one of the gentlest, one of the finest, one of the most lovable characters as a college professor that I have ever known," declared Rainwater. "I have *never* heard him speak a hard word against anyone." See author's interview with Rainwater, May 30, 1990, 11.

25 F. Lee Benns, "Alfred C. Kinsey" (unpublished and undated essay), KIA.

26 Author's interview with Breneman, May 21, 1985, 17.

27 [Fernandus Payne], "Confidential; Anonymous: As told to an IRS staff member" KIA. In a conversation with the author, Payne identified himself as the author of this document and filled in the names that were disguised as letters. "K" was Kinsey, and "X" was Payne. Eigenmann was mentioned by name, and Clara Kinsey was called by her nickname, Mac. Will Scott was the unnamed poor lecturer. Payne told the same story to Torrey. See author's interview with Theodore W. Torrey, Sept. 17, 1971, 4, IUOHP. Corroborating evidence on Scott's teaching may be found in the official history of Indiana's zoology department, which states, "He was very informal in his teaching and the students in the large introductory course . . . often found that informality, especially in lectures, something of an obstacle." Torrey, "Zoology and Its Makers," 91.

28 See Torrey, "Zoology and Its Makers," 80–88.

29 Author's interview with Torrey, Sept. 17, 1971, 4.

30 Author's interview with Breneman, May 21, 1985, 16.

31 [Payne], "Confidential; Anonymous."

32 Author's interview with Torrey, Sept. 17, 1971, 4.

33 [Payne], "Confidential; Anonymous."

34 See author's interview with Torrey, Sept. 17, 1971, 4. Breneman recalled Payne's support for junior colleagues with warm affection: "Payne was a great believer in the young men," he noted, and consistently argued that the university should "support them." See author's interview with Breneman, May 21, 1985, 4. Robert Bugbee, one of Kinsey's first graduate students, insisted that Payne had a high regard for Kinsey's scholarship. In his letter of acceptance to the Graduate School, Bugbee recalled, Payne "made the statement that he felt that Dr. Kinsey was one of the most promising young entomologists in the country." See author's interview with Robert E. Bugbee, Oct. 19, 1971, 4, IUOHP.

35 Author's interview with Kroc, Nov. 7, 1987, 22.

36 Author's interview with Herman T. Spieth, Feb. 18, 1988, 37.

37 Author's interview with Breneman, May 21, 1985, 23–24. Another former colleague who had watched Kinsey in action remarked that "no one could state a point or defend a position with his clarity and brevity." Cecilia H. Hendricks, "Memories of Dr. Alfred C. Kinsey" (unpublished essay, April 5, 1962), KIA.

38 Author's interview with Bugbee, Oct. 19, 1971, 11–12.

39 Herman T. Spieth, unpublished and undated essay on ACK, 6, KIA.

40 Author's interview with Rainwater, May 30, 1990, 58.

41 Author's interview with Kroc, Nov. 7, 1987, 12.

42 Ibid., 35–36.

43 Author's interview with Torrey, Sept. 17, 1971, 3–4.

44 Ibid., 15–16, 19–20. Torrey told the McCormick's Creek story in the context of illustrating how Kinsey "could on the one hand be so pleasant and so accommodating and on the other hand could be so ornery." Ibid., 20.

45 Ibid., 16.

46 Ibid., 21. Like Torrey, Breneman found his early dealings with Kinsey unpleasant. The two men were by no means strangers. Breneman had received his Ph.D. from Indiana in endocrinology under Payne in 1934, and as part of his graduate work he had taken two classes (taxonomy and entomology) under Kinsey, an experience that he found both stimulating and nerve-racking. Following graduation, Breneman held a postdoctoral fellowship at Wisconsin and then taught for a year at Miami University of Ohio before returning to Indiana in 1936. He took over Kinsey's general biology class in the late 1930s, and Kinsey did not approve of the way he taught it (not enough plant material). Kinsey took his complaint to Payne, demanding that the course be revised, but, just as he had once defended Kinsey from senior colleagues, Payne now took Breneman's part. A few years later, Kinsey made a big point of telling Breneman he was doing a great job in the introductory biology course. According to Breneman, Kinsey was extremely gracious, freely confessing that he had been wrong to doubt Breneman's ability. While the two never became friends, the tension between them gradually dissipated after this meeting. Apparently, this was the sort of relationship Kinsey had with most members of his department. Author's interview with Breneman, May 21, 1985, 17.

47 ACK, *Field and Laboratory Manual,* xii, 3.

48 ACK, *An Introduction to Biology* (Philadelphia, 1926).

49 ACK, *Field and Laboratory Manual;* ACK, *Methods in Biology* (Chicago, 1937).

50 ACK, *Field and Laboratory Manual,* 147, 56.

51   Quoted in Lawrence W. Levine, *Defender of the Faith, Williams Jennings Bryan: The Last Decade, 1915–1925* (Cambridge, 1987), 333.
52   ACK, *Introduction to Biology*, 196–97.
53   ACK, *Methods in Biology*, 224–25.
54   ACK, *Introduction to Biology*, 247.
55   Ibid., 269.
56   Ibid., 344.
57   Ibid., 529.
58   Quoted in Christenson, *Kinsey*, 64.
59   Spieth, unpublished essay. Kinsey may have had an unconscious motive as well. His father, it must be remembered, supplemented his income by writing manuals that were used as texts in the shop practice course at the Stevens Institute. It is tempting to see Kinsey's high school biology textbook as another example of the high-stakes competition he had with his father, a contest that saw Kinsey continually trying to one-up his old man.
60   Christenson, *Kinsey*, 58.
61   Ibid., 57.
62   Shelby D. Gerking to Paul H. Gebhard, Dec. 12, 1961, KIA.
63   Author's interview with Rainwater, May 30, 1990, 58.
64   Rosenzweig and Rosenzweig, "Notes," 173. Her sketch was penned years after his death at the request of Paul Gebhard, who solicited material on Kinsey from his former students, friends, and colleagues.
65   Ibid.
66   Author's interview with Kroc, Nov. 7, 1987, 24; author's interview with Breneman, May 21, 1985, 9–10. Other colleagues, some none too friendly, agreed that Kinsey developed into a strong teacher. Payne, not a man to hand out praise lightly, remembered Kinsey as "an excellent teacher," a view that apparently had more adherents among professors than among students. Author's interview with Fernandus Payne, March 2, 1971, 7, IUOHP. "He had a lot of charisma," remarked another colleague. "When he talked, he held you in the palm of his hand waiting for the next word. You felt bad when he quit." Author's conversation with Frank Young, May 20, 1985. Still another colleague commended his command of his material. Kinsey "used notes either at a minimum or none at all," and "had his subject matter in line, and it rolled out." Author's interview with Torrey, Sept. 17, 1971, 18. For other assessments of Kinsey's teaching, see author's interview with Frank Edmondson, Nov. 8, 1971, 27, IUOHP, and author's interview with Edith Schuman, Sept. 15, 1971, 6 and 11, IUOHP.
67   ACK, *Methods in Biology*, viii.
68   ACK to Roeth, Jan. 29, 1921.
69   Ibid.
70   Rosenzweig and Rosenzweig, "Notes," 174.
71   ACK, *Methods in Biology*, 147.
72   Author's interview with Breneman, May 21, 1985, 9.
73   Author's interview with Kroc, Nov. 7, 1987, 26. Yet not every student reacted favorably to Kinsey. One former student, who described the course he took under Kinsey as "stimulating and interesting," described him as "remarkably opinionated, often impatient, but always dynamic." Others were less generous, particularly those who found him intimidating. Some despaired being able to satisfy his standards, while oth-

ers were bowled over by the strength of his personality. "As a teacher he was forceful, as he always was," remarked a former student. "He had his own very definite opinions . . . and if you wanted to support your own point of view, you had to be quite forceful." Spieth, unpublished essay, 7. Few of Indiana's students had that much self-confidence. Most wilted before his keen intellect and direct manner, correctly sensing that he held their opinions in low regard.

74 Howard K. Bauernfeind to Paul H. Gebhard, Sept. 27, 1961, KIA.

75 KIA, *Introduction to Biology*, 529.

76 Christenson, *Kinsey*, 63.

77 ACK, *The Gall Wasp Genus Cynips: A Study in the Origin of Species* (Bloomington, 1930), 57.

78 See Daniel J. Kevles, *In the Name of Eugenics: Genetics and the Uses of Human Heredity* (New York, 1985). Kinsey's growing support for eugenics can be traced in his writings and his lectures. See ACK, "Biologic Aspects of Some Social Problems" (unpublished lecture to discussion group, April 1, 1935), 14, KIA. For a cogent discussion of where most scientists stood on the role of heredity versus the environment, see Hamilton Cravens, *The Triumph of Evolution: American Scientists and the Heredity-Environment Controversy, 1900–1941* (Philadelphia, 1978), 157–90. Kinsey strongly endorsed both positive and negative eugenics. With cool logic and chilling moral certainty, he advocated a program of "birth selection," which he defined as "a reduction of the birth-rate of the less desirable elements and—no less—an increase in the birth rate of the desirable elements." Since few people doubted the wisdom of raising the birthrate of the "desirable elements," Kinsey concentrated on negative eugenics, calling for a program of sterilization that was at once sweeping and terrifying. "The reduction of the birth-rate of the lowest classes must depend upon the sterilization of perhaps a tenth of our population," he wrote. "The nation that dares institute sterilization on this scale will be followed by its neighbors," he declared. "They cannot safely ignore the quality of their enemies." ACK, "Biologic Aspects," 16.

79 ACK, *Introduction to Biology*, 174.

80 Ibid., 184.

81 Ibid., 185.

82 ACK, *Methods in Biology*, 223. See also ACK, "Biologic Aspects."

83 Author's interview with Breneman, May 21, 1985, 34–35.

84 ACK, *Introduction to Biology*, 529.

85 Ibid.

86 Author's interview with Mrs. ACK, Dec. 10, 1971, 16–17, IUOHP. According to a close friend, Kinsey made statements during the final decade of his life "that put him to the right of Ronald Reagan." Author's interview with Breneman, May 21, 1985, 34–35.

87 Author's interview with Paul H. Gebhard, Aug. 7, 1984, 8–9.

88 Rosenzweig and Rosenzweig, "Notes," 174.

89 If Kinsey's opinion of Indiana's students was harsh, others shared it. Robert Kroc complained that many of the students from country schools "could hardly read or write." He recalled one, in particular, who "had such poor pronunciation that I advised him to use a dictionary, and he came back to me and said, 'How can a dictionary talk?' And he did not know the alphabet well enough to know that the letters were sequential in the dictionary." Author's interview with Kroc, Nov. 7, 1987, 32.

90 Ibid., 25.

91 Author's interview with Edmondson, Nov. 8, 1971, 27.
92 Author's interview with Breneman, May 21, 1985, 6, 34. Johnson later completed a Ph.D. under Payne and went on to teach at Duke University.
93 ACK to Ralph Voris, July 8, 1936, KIA.
94 Author's interview with Bugbee, Oct. 19, 1971, 2.
95 Author's interview with Spieth, Feb. 18, 1988, 14.
96 Spieth, unpublished essay, 3.
97 Author's interview with Breneman, May 21, 1985, 15.
98 Author's interview with Spieth, Feb. 18, 1988, 27.
99 Ibid., 34.
100 Author's interview with Breneman, May 21, 1985, 7.
101 Ibid., 7–8, 11–12.
102 Gerking to Gebhard, Dec. 12, 1961.
103 ACK, *Field and Laboratory Manual,* xi.
104 Author's interview with Breneman, May 21, 1985, 21.
105 Author's interview with Torrey, Sept. 17, 1971, 19.
106 ACK to Ralph Voris, Nov. 10, 1934, KIA.
107 Author's interview with Spieth, Feb. 18, 1988, 12–13.
108 ACK to Ralph Voris, Sept. 3, 1934, KIA.

Chapter 10: "MY PRIMARY INTEREST REMAINS WITH RESEARCH"

1 The faculty at Indiana University was badly divided on the importance of research versus teaching. One group whose members included many of the older professors, touted teaching, while the other faction, composed mainly of New Lights, placed scholarship on a higher plane. Since Indiana was as much a college as a university, this debate reflected the unavoidable growing pains of a university in transition. The lack of consensus obliged everyone to choose sides. Thomas D. Clark, *Indiana University: Midwestern Pioneer,* vol. 2, *In Mid-Passage* (Bloomington, 1973), 279–99, 311.
2 ACK to Ralph Voris, March 26, 1931, KIA.
3 ACK, "Review of 'MacGillivray's External Insect Anatomy,' " *Entomological News* 35 (1924): 31.
4 ACK, "New Species and Synonymy of American Cynipidae," *Bulletin of the American Museum of Natural History* 42 (1920): 293.
5 ACK, "Studies of Some New and Described Cynipidae (Hymenoptera)," *Indiana University Studies* 9, no. 53, (June 1922): 6.
6 ACK, "New Species," 321.
7 Ibid.
8 Ibid.
9 ACK, "Life Histories of American Cynipidae," *Bulletin of the American Museum of Natural History* 42 (1920): 321.
10 ACK, "New Species," 293.
11 ACK, "Phylogeny of Cynipid Genera and Biological Characteristics," *Bulletin of the American Museum of Natural History* 42 (1920): 366–67.
12 ACK, "Studies of Some New," 6.
13 ACK, *The Gall Wasp Genus Cynips: A Study in the Origin of Species* (Bloomington, 1930), 9.
14 ACK, "Phylogeny of Cynipid," 357a.
15 ACK, "Studies of Some New," 5 and 68.

16   ACK, *Gall Wasp Genus Cynips,* 9.
17   ACK, "Major Research Problems" (report to the dean of the Graduate School, Indiana University, Jan. 30, 1930), KIA.
18   Author's interview with Robert Kroc, Nov. 7, 1987, 12.
19   ACK, "The Gall Wasp Genus Neuroterus (Hymenoptera)," *Indiana University Studies* 10, no. 58 (1923): 19.
20   ACK to the trustees of Indiana University, May 23, 1928, KIA.
21   John C. Burnham, "The Cultural Interpretation of the Progressive Movement," reprinted in *Paths into American Culture: Psychology, Medicine, and Morals* (Philadelphia, 1988), 224.
22   ACK, "Studies of Some New," 6–7.
23   ACK to the Trustees of Indiana University, Aug. 1, 1929, KIA.
24   ACK, *Gall Wasp Genus Cynips,* 10.
25   Ibid., 61.
26   ACK, "Phylogeny of Cynipid," 357b.
27   ACK to the trustees of Indiana University, May 26, 1927, KIA.
28   Ernst Mayr, *The Growth of Biological Thought: Diversity, Evolution, and Inheritance* (Cambridge, 1982), 32.
29   ACK, "Phylogeny of Cynipid," 357b.
30   Edgar Anderson, "Kinsey as I Knew Him" (n.d., enclosed in a letter from Anderson to Paul H. Gebhard, Oct. 2, 1961), KIA.
31   ACK, "Gall Wasp Genus Neuroterus," 6.
32   Anderson, "Kinsey as I Knew Him."
33   ACK, "Gall Wasp Genus Neuroterus," 19.
34   ACK, "Studies of Some New," 3–6.
35   June Keisler to Paul H. Gebhard, April 24, 1962, untitled recollections on Alfred C. Kinsey, 6, KIA. Theodore Torrey also recalled a conversation he had with Kinsey on this subject. "Look, if dogs were known only by one fossil specimen which just by chance happened to be a Chihuahua, we would conclude that all dogs were constructed like Chihuahuas," Torrey remarked. And Kinsey said, "That's exactly right." Torrey argued that Kinsey stressed the importance of collecting large samples far more than most taxonomists. Author's interview with Torrey, Sept. 17, 1971, 7, IUOHP.
36   ACK, "New Species," 293.
37   See Cornelia V. Christenson, *Kinsey: A Biography* (Bloomington, 1971), 77.
38   ACK to the Trustees of Indiana University, Aug. 1, 1929, KIA; ACK, *Gall Wasp Genus Cynips,* 11, 23.
39   When the sociologists Robert and Helen Lynd launched their classic study of everyday life in the Midwest during the early 1920s, a resident of Muncie, Indiana, asked, "Why on earth do you need to study what's changing this country. I can tell you what's happening in just four letters: A-U-T-O!" The man was right. In 1900, there were only 8,000 motor vehicles registered in the United States, but by 1930 more than 25 million people owned automobiles (roughly one car for every five persons). The great American love affair with the automobile was under way. Robert S. Lynd and Helen Merrell Lynd, *Middletown: A Study in Modern American Culture* (New York, 1956), 251.
40   ACK to Voris, Sept. 15, 1931, KIA.
41   Herman T. Spieth, untitled recollections of ACK (n.d.), KIA. For the description of the automobile, see Christenson, *Kinsey,* 81.

42 Frank Young, unpublished notes on a series of lectures on evolution (1951–53), KIA. The fact that the Kinseys were able to purchase an automobile so soon after building their new house indicates that they were among those Americans who were enjoying the material bounty of "Prosperity's Decade." Perhaps they used income from his high school biology textbook, or perhaps the money came from Clara's inheritance from her parents' estate.

43 ACK, *The Origin of Higher Categories in Cynips* (Bloomington, 1936), 19–21; ACK, Jan. 30, 1931, no. 213, and ACK, March 23, 1935, no. 1326, Card File for the Grants-in-Aid program, NRC Archives. Wheeler wrote a letter of recommendation for Kinsey's first NRC grant, declaring, "Dr. Kinsey is one of three or four very brilliant young men we have trained in Entomology at Harvard during the past 22 years." Wheeler also praised Kinsey's first monograph on gall wasps, calling it "a very remarkable book, not only on account of its contribution to the taxonomy of our North American species, but because of the important theoretical considerations it contains in regard to the questions of biological species in general." See William M. Wheeler to Vernon Kellogg, Feb. 4, 1931, Box 20, Wheeler Papers.

44 ACK, "An Evolutionary Analysis of Insular and Continental Species," *Proceedings of the National Academy of Sciences* 23 (Jan. 1937): 6; Christenson, *Kinsey,* 94.

45 ACK to President W. L. Bryan, Jan. 28, 1930, KIA.

46 ACK to President W. L. Bryan, Feb. 22, 1932, KIA.

47 ACK, *New Introduction to Biology,* rev. ed., (Chicago, 1938), 422.

48 Author's interview with Frank Edmondson, Nov. 8, 1971, 4–5, IUOHP.

49 ACK, *Gall Wasp Genus Cynips,* 14, 21.

50 ACK, *Origin of Higher Categories,* 21.

51 ACK, *Gall Wasp Genus Cynips,* 13–14. After he became a sex researcher, Kinsey actively solicited the assistance of scores of professionals who studied human sexuality, not to mention hundreds of laymen whose interest in sex ranged from the mildly academic to the intensely personal. After all, he had been drawing upon the help of experts and amateurs alike for decades in his gall wasp research.

52 ACK, *Origin of Higher Categories,* 21. After he became a sex researcher, Kinsey insisted that 100 case histories were needed to provide a reliable sample for each cell of his data, offering still another example of how his experience as a taxonomist influenced his later research.

53 ACK, *Gall Wasp Genus Cynips,* 16.

54 Anderson, "Kinsey as I Knew Him." Anderson further asserted that an "almost professional perfectionalism in everything he did was a characteristic of the man."

55 F. Lee Benns, "Alfred C. Kinsey" (n.d.), KIA.

56 ACK, "Life Histories," 321.

57 Spieth, untitled recollections.

58 Osmond P. Breland, "Field Diary, 1935–1936," Dec. 3 and Oct. 28, 1935. (Thanks to Mrs. Osmund P. [Nellie] Breland).

59 Author's interview with Homer T. Rainwater, May 30, 1990, 57.

60 Spieth, untitled recollections.

61 Breland, "Field Diary," Nov. 16, 1935.

62 Ibid., Oct. 8, 1935.

63 Ibid., Oct. 12, 1935.

64 Ibid.

65 For a discussion of the difficulties he encountered in his efforts to breed gall wasps, see ACK, "Evolutionary Analysis," 6.

66 Howard K. Bauernfeind to Paul H. Gebhard, Sept. 27, 1961, KIA.
67 Ibid.
68 Keisler to Gebhard, untitled recollections; for another description of Kinsey's office, see Louise Rosenzweig and Saul Rosenzweig, "Notes on Alfred C. Kinsey's Presexual Scientific Work and the Transition," *Journal of the History of the Behavioral Sciences* 5 (April 1969): 174–75.
69 Rosenzweig and Rosenzweig, "Notes," 175.
70 Keisler to Gebhard, untitled recollections.
71 ACK, "Life Histories," 322–23.
72 ACK, *Origin of Higher Categories*, 65.
73 Rosenzweig and Rosenzweig, "Notes," 175. Kinsey later used the same precise lettering technique to record the most intimate details of people's lives.
74 Ibid.; Christenson, *Kinsey*, 72–73.
75 Christenson, *Kinsey*, 235. Christenson was able to identify the following assistants by name: Florence Flemion, Enola Van Valer, Eloise Kuntz, Louise Rosenzweig, Helen Walling, Betty Frazier, Maxine Wesner, and Betty Wray.
76 Helen D'Amico Walling, "My Recollections of Dr. Alfred C. Kinsey" (n.d.), KIA.
77 Keisler to Gebhard, untitled recollections.
78 While he was critical of much of the New Deal as one big federal giveaway, Kinsey did not hesitate to take advantage of its programs to foster his own research.
79 Keisler to Gebhard, untitled recollections.
80 Herbert J. Backer to Paul H. Gebhard, Oct. 19, 1961, KIA.
81 Christenson, *Kinsey*, 74–75.
82 Ibid.
83 Walling, "My Recollections."
84 Keisler to Gebhard, untitled recollections.
85 Ibid.
86 Walling, "My Recollections."
87 ACK, "New Species," 309.
88 ACK, *Origin of Higher Categories*, 145, 147. For examples of Kinsey's frequent use of exclamation points, see ACK and K. D. Ayres, "Varieties of a Rose Gall Wasp (Cynipidae, Hymenoptera)," *Indiana University Studies* 9, no. 53 (1922): 143; ACK, "Gall Wasp Genus Neuroterus," 23 and 65; and ACK, *Origin of Higher Categories*, 99, 145, 249.
89 Rosenzweig and Rosenzweig, "Notes," 175.
90 Robert E. Bugbee to Wardell B. Pomeroy, Sept. 11, 1961, KIA.
91 This prolific volume of writing included his high school biology textbook (1926, revised in 1933, and again in 1938); a field and laboratory manual to accompany his textbook (1927); a workbook in biology designed for students (1934, revised in 1938); a methods book in biology designed for high school teachers (1937); two major monographs on gall wasps (1930, 1936); seventeen articles in scholarly journals on gall wasps; and four additional articles on topics ranging from the content of high school biology courses to practical tips on how to create a beautiful flower garden. For a complete bibliography of Kinsey's writings, see Christenson, *Kinsey*, 231–33.
92 Kinsey, "Studies of Some New," 64.
93 Ibid., 3–171.
94 ACK and Ayres, "Varieties of a Rose Gall Wasp," 142–43.
95 ACK, "Gall Wasp Genus Neuroterus," 7–8.

96   ACK to Voris, Oct. 25, 1933, KIA.
97   ACK, *Gall Wasp Genus Cynips,* 7–10.
98   Ibid., 5 and 17–24.
99   Ibid., 25–36, 49–54, 55–60.
100 Ibid., 24.
101 H. M. Parshley, "Gall Wasps and the Species Problem," *Entomological News* 41 (1930): 192–93, 195.
102 Ibid., 193–94.
103 Proclaiming the book a "remarkable work" that "is one of the best studies in print because [it is] based on such an enormous amount of data," the reviewer for the *Annals of the Entomological Society of America* recommended it as "a book that should be studied for its methods by every student of systematic entomology." See C. H. Kennedy, "Review of *The Gall Wasp Genus Cynips,*" *Annals of the Entomological Society of America* 23 (1930): 610.
104 For a succinct statement of his approach to research in his gall wasp years, see ACK, *Gall Wasp Genus Cynips,* 16.
105 Ibid., 77.
106 Aware of his mentor's fierce ambition, Voris fed these hopes, declaring, "I will be very much interested in the way certain individuals in Washington and those others who have been none too complimentary take this work. If it doesn't make believers out of them they are hopeless and do not need to be converted." Ralph Voris to ACK, March 19, 1930, KIA.
107 ACK, *Origin of Higher Categories,* 5.
108 ACK to Voris, Sept. 3, 1934, KIA.
109 Ibid.
110 In 1902, C. C. Adams had listed several criteria for locating the center of origin of any taxonomic group. ACK, *Origin of Higher Categories,* 58.
111 Ibid.
112 ACK to Voris, Sept. 3, 1934.
113 ACK to Voris, Nov. 23, 1934, KIA.
114 ACK, *Origin of Higher Categories,* 15.
115 ACK to Voris, Jan. 31, 1937, KIA.
116 Ibid. In addition to Payne, who served as chairman, the committee was composed of Henry H. Carter, Edgar R. Cumings, Harold T. Davis, Ford P. Hall, Albert Kohlmeier, and Robert E. Lyons. See ACK, *Origin of Higher Categories,* 2 (unnumbered in text).
117 ACK to Voris, July 8, 1936, KIA.
118 ACK to Voris, Jan. 31, 1937. Kinsey apparently resubmitted the manuscript sometime in late June or early July 1936.
119 ACK, *Origin of Higher Categories,* 17–18.
120 Ibid., 21.
121 Ibid., 59.
122 Ibid., 53.
123 Ibid., 54–55.
124 Ibid.
125 Ibid.
126 Ibid., 53.
127 Ibid., 56–57.

128 Ibid., 58.

129 Ibid., 60.

130 Ibid., 64.

131 Ibid., 66.

132 The longest (and most favorable) notice appeared in the *Annals of the Entomological Society of America*. Stressing that the book was based "on an almost unbelievable amount of field work," Clarence H. Kennedy, the reviewer, thought that Kinsey had made a major contribution by giving science "a clearer picture than ever before of the nature of natural species and species groups (species-complexes, subgenera, etc.)." Kennedy strongly endorsed Kinsey's vine metaphor, arguing that "the idea of 'species-chains' " allowed Kinsey to challenge "the previous idea of radiating phylogenies." In addition, he endorsed Kinsey's definition of higher categories as "a connected series of lower categories." Kennedy, review in *Annals of the Entomological Society of America* 29 (1936): 816–17. Other reviews were favorable, if less enthusiastic. One praised the book's "excellent evolutionary discussion," noting that it drew upon "years of collecting in the field and intensive thought and study of material in the laboratory." See R. H. Davidson, review in *Ohio Journal of Science* 37 (1937): 124. Another merely summarized without comment the book's major findings and arguments, though he did convey Kinsey's repeated cautions about workers who were "too prone to speculate from restricted and inadequate data." See G. S. Walley, review in *Canadian Entomologist* 69 (Jan. 1937): 21.

133 ACK to Robert E. Bugbee, Jan. 28, 1937, KIA.

134 Ibid.

135 ACK to Voris, Dec. 5, 1936, KIA.

136 ACK to Bugbee, Jan. 28, 1937.

137 Robert E. Bugbee to ACK, Nov. 15, 1936, KIA.

138 ACK to Voris, Jan. 31, 1937.

139 Ibid.

140 ACK, "Supra-Specific Variation in Nature and in Classification," *American Naturalist* 71 (1937): 206–22; Kinsey, "Evolutionary Analysis," *Proceedings,* 5–11.

141 ACK, "An Evolutionary Analysis of Insular and Continental Species," *Science* 85 (Jan. 8, 1937): 56–57.

142 ACK to Voris, July 8, 1936.

143 Ibid. This was the first hint of what soon became a theme in Kinsey's life—the fear that death would intervene before he could complete his goals. After he became a sex researcher, Kinsey was constantly worrying (and for good reason) that his health would break before he could finish the research that he hoped would free mankind from Victorian morality.

144 ACK to Voris, Jan. 31, 1937. Kinsey made the identical boast to Bugbee, declaring, "In other words, You are going to live to see the day when taxonomy will take a place among the biological sciences." ACK to Bugbee, Jan. 28, 1937.

145 "Research Report of A. C. Kinsey: Made to Dean of the Graduate School, June 6, 1938," KIA.

146 ACK, *Gall Wasp Genus Cynips,* 20, 19. Kinsey's understanding of the species problem anticipated much of the current thinking on this timeless debate. As of 1930, however, he still refused to acknowledge that reproductive isolation was the crucial factor in the development of species. See ibid., 20.

147 ACK, *New Introduction to Biology,* 423, 422.

148   Steven Jay Gould, "Of Wasps and WASPs," *Natural History,* Dec. 1982, 12.
149   Kinsey also committed an error that afflicted other evolutionary theorists of his day—
      he failed to understand the role of isolating mechanisms. He labored under the erro-
      neous belief that geographic barriers were included among isolating mechanisms.
      Following World War II, the "new systematists" clarified the role of isolating mecha-
      nisms and correctly identified the development of reproductive isolation as a crucial
      component in the process of speciation, but, again, by this time Kinsey had aban-
      doned gall wasps in favor of his pioneering work on human sexual behavior. See
      Mayr, *Growth of Biological Thought,* 24.

Chapter 11: "It Was Done Very, So to Speak, Scientifically"

1   ACK, "Bases of Society" (lecture ms, Feb. 5, 1940), 1, KIA.
2   For discussions of the "companionate family," see Sidney Ditzion, *Marriage, Morals,
     and Sex in America: A History of Ideas* (New York, 1969), 381–83; Steven Mintz and
     Susan Kellogg, *Domestic Revolutions: A Social History of American Family Life* (New
     York, 1988), 113–31; and John D'Emilio and Estelle B. Freedman, *Intimate Matters:
     A History of Sexuality in America* (New York, 1988), 265–66. For an incisive critique
     of "companionate marriage," see Christopher Lasch, *Haven in a Heartless World: The
     Family Besieged* (New York, 1977), 44–49.
3   See Thomas D. Clark's interview with Mrs. ACK, Feb. 17, 1969, 13, IUOHP, and Cor-
     nelia V. Christenson, *Kinsey: A Biography* (Bloomington, 1971), 51–52. My portrait of
     the Kinseys' family life was also informed by interviews with Joan Reid, Kinsey's
     daughter, first in 1972 as part of the IUOHP and then in 1985. I have quoted only
     from the first interview.
4   Author's interview with Mary G. Winther, March 11, 1971, 25, IUOHP; Clark's in-
     terview with Mrs. ACK, Feb. 17, 1969, 12.
5   Author's interview with Winther, March 11, 1971, 4.
6   Clark's interview with Mrs. ACK, Feb. 17, 1969, 12.
7   For the description of the Kinseys' living room furniture, see Christenson, *Kinsey,*
     51–52.
8   Author's interview with Mrs. ACK, Dec. 10, 1971, 21.
9   Clark's interview with Mrs. ACK, Feb. 17, 1969, 1–2.
10   For a discussion of women's failure to achieve economic equality in the 1920s, see
     William H. Chafe, *The American Woman: Her Changing Social, Economic, and Political
     Roles, 1920–1970* (New York, 1972), 48–65.
11   Ibid., 58; Lindsey R. Harmon and Herbert Soldz, comps., *Doctorate Production in
     United States Universities, 1920–1962: With Baccalaureate Origins of Doctorates in Sci-
     ences, Arts, and Professions* (Washington, D.C., 1963), 52.
12   Chafe, *American Woman,* 64.
13   Peter Filene, *Him/Her/Self: Sex Roles in Modern America,* 2nd ed. (Baltimore, 1986),
     121.
14   Author's interviews with Paul H. Gebhard, Aug. 7, 1984, 6–7; Oct. 14, 1984, 26–27.
15   Author's interview with Robert Kroc, Nov. 7, 1987, 74–76.
16   Since their first child, Donald, arrived on July 16, 1922, the latest the marriage could
     have been consummated was Nov. 1921. Perhaps it occurred as early as Sept. when they
     first returned to Bloomington and sought professional advice. For Donald's birthdate,
     see author's interview with Mrs. ACK, Dec. 10, 1971, 5.
17   Ibid.

18 ACK to Natalie Roeth, Feb. 12, 1924, KIA.

19 Author's interview with Kroc, Nov. 7, 1987, 46–48; Christenson, *Kinsey*, 59.

20 The story of insulin's discovery and early distribution is capably told in Michael Bliss, *The Discovery of Insulin* (Toronto, 1982).

21 Author's interview with Evelyn Spieth, Feb. 18, 1988, 9, 16.

22 Author's telephone conversation with Mary Gaither, Bloomington, Oct. 7, 1996.

23 Author's interview with Clyde Martin, March 21, 1986, 8.

24 June Keisler to Paul H. Gebhard, April 24, 1962, KIA.

25 Ibid.

26 Christenson, *Kinsey*, 173.

27 Author's interview with Spieth, Feb. 18, 1988, 9; author's interview with Homer T. Rainwater, May 30, 1990, 21; Earl Marsh to Paul H. Gebhard, Nov. 25, 1961, 5, KIA.

28 ACK, "Biological Bases of Society" (unpublished lecture, summer 1938), 7, KIA; ACK, "Bases of Society," 11.

29 ACK, "Bases of Society," 1; author's interview with Joan Reid, Feb. 14, 1972, 6, IUOHP.

30 Quoted in Christenson, *Kinsey*, 174.

31 Mrs. Francis G. Turrell to Paul H. Gebhard, Sept. 26, 1961, KIA.

32 Author's interview with Reid, Feb. 14, 1972, 8.

33 Ibid., 9.

34 Ibid., 7–8.

35 Ibid., 7. It would be fascinating to know if Kinsey treated his son, Bruce, any differently from Anne and Joan. Unfortunately, Bruce refused to be interviewed.

36 Author's interview with Mrs. ACK, Dec. 10, 1971, 40.

37 Ibid.

38 Author's interview with Reid, Feb. 14, 1972, 7.

39 Clara's father died on Oct. 11, 1924, of pneumonia; see *Fort Wayne News Sentinel,* Oct. 13, 1924, 2. Clara's mother died less than five months later of asphyxiation; see ibid., Jan. 21, 1925, 1.

40 The photograph mentioned above was preserved in Alfred Seguine Kinsey's family album, which I viewed when it was in the possession of Edna Kinsey Higenbotham, Robert Kinsey's widow.

41 Kinsey referred to his mother's visit in a letter to a friend. See ACK to Ralph Voris, July 18, 1930, KIA.

42 Complaint, Kinsey vs. Kinsey (2nd District, Washoe County, Nev., Aug. 18, 1931); Findings of Fact, Conclusions of Law and Judgment and Decree, Kinsey vs. Kinsey (2nd District, Washoe County, Nev., Sept. 21, 1931).

43 Author's interview with Edna Kinsey Higenbotham, Nov. 28, 1984, 11–12.

44 Ibid., 1, 4–5, 11–12.

45 Ibid., 5.

46 Ibid., 4, 14.

47 Ibid., 10; author's interview with Gebhard, Oct. 14, 1984, 12.

48 ACK to Voris, Sept. 3, 1934, KIA.

49 Nanette Kutner, "Yes, There Is a Mrs. Kinsey," *McCall's,* July 1948, 92.

50 Author's interview with Fernandus Payne, March 2, 1971, 10, IUOHP; Louise Ritterskamp Rosenzweig, "Reminiscences about Dr. Alfred C. Kinsey" (n.d.), KIA.

51 Kutner, "Yes, There Is a Mrs. Kinsey," 92.

52 Wardell B. Pomeroy, *Dr. Kinsey and the Institute for Sex Research* (New York, 1972), 29.

53 Christenson, *Kinsey*, 65.

54 ACK, "Landscape Picture with Iris," *Bulletin of the American Iris Society* (July and Oct. 1933), 1; author's interview with Payne, March 2, 1971, 10; Herman T. Spieth, untitled recollections of ACK (n.d.), KIA; Rosenzweig, "Reminiscences," 11–12; Christenson, *Kinsey,* 66.
55 Rosenzweig, "Reminiscences"; ACK, "Landscape Picture with Iris," 3.
56 ACK, "Landscape Picture with Iris," 1.
57 Author's interview with Paul H. Gebhard, Oct. 29, 1971, 47–48, IUOHP; ACK, "Landscape Picture with Iris," 1, 3.
58 See Helen D'Amico Walling, "My Recollections of Dr. Alfred C. Kinsey" (n.d.), KIA; ACK, "Landscape Picture with Iris," 2.
59 Author's interview with Kate Hevner Mueller, April 1, 1971, 22, IUOHP; Turrell to Gebhard, Sept. 26, 1961.
60 ACK, "Landscape Picture with Iris," 1–2.
61 Ibid., 2; Gladys H. Groves to Paul H. Gebhard, July 22, 1963, KIA.
62 See ACK, "Landscape Picture with Iris," 1.
63 Quoted in Christenson, *Kinsey,* 172.
64 Author's interview with Herman T. Spieth, Feb. 18, 1988, 8.
65 Author's interview with Mrs. ACK, Dec. 10, 1971, 19–20.
66 ACK, "Music and Love," *High Fidelity,* July 1956, 27–28.
67 Author's interview with Dorothy Collins, Dec. 7, 1971, 19–20, IUOHP; author's interview with Margaret Edmondson, Nov. 9, 1971, 15–17.
68 Ibid.
69 Author's interview with Frank Edmondson, Nov. 8, 1971, 31; author's interview with Margaret Edmondson, Nov. 9, 1971, 16.
70 Keisler to Gebhard, April 24, 1962.
71 Ibid.
72 See author's interview with Mueller, April 1, 1971, 1–2.
73 Henry Remak, "Dr. Kinsey" (unpublished ms, Aug. 28, 1956), 1, 6–7, KIA.
74 Ibid., 7.
75 ACK, "Music and Love," 28. This article chronicles Kinsey's lifelong love affair with music, but its real purpose was to draw a parallel between what his research had done to free people to pursue the art of love and what other scientists had done to enable people to hear classical music through improved audio technology. In fact, the piece fairly bristles with clues about Kinsey's image of himself and how it changed over time. Woven into the story of his three different record collections is Kinsey's assessment of his rise from humble origins to become a world-famous scientist, who, through the miracle of modern technology, could possess "such artists presenting such a repertoire of music as no king of the past could command, and no musician of any other decade ever had." His message was clear: Kinsey considered himself a benefactor of mankind, a crusader who had used science to promote compassion, tolerance, and understanding of human sexuality, in all its manifestations.
76 Author's interview with Margaret Edmondson, Nov. 9, 1971, 16.
77 Christenson, *Kinsey,* 172.
78 Ibid.
79 Author's interview with Reid, Feb. 14, 1972, 5.
80 Ibid., 4.
81 Louise Rosenzweig and Saul Rosenzweig, "Notes on Alfred C. Kinsey's Pre-sexual Scientific Work and the Transition," *Journal of the History of the Behavioral Sciences* 5 (April 1969): 177; author's interview with Rainwater, May 30, 1990, 47.

82 Quoted in Pomeroy, *Dr. Kinsey,* 29; author's interview with Gebhard, Oct. 14, 1984, 14.

83 Author's interview with Gebhard, Oct. 14, 1984, 14.

84 Author's interview with Reid, Feb. 14, 1972, 4.

85 ACK, "Sex Education" (unpublished lecture, March 6, 1940), 1–2, KIA.

86 Ibid., 1–3.

87 For a general discussion of the sex education the Kinsey's gave their children, see Pomeroy, *Dr. Kinsey,* 30, and Christenson, *Kinsey,* 68.

88 Kutner, "Yes, There Is a Mrs. Kinsey," 92.

89 Author's interview with Reid, Feb. 14, 1972, 11.

90 Ibid., 10–11.

91 Kinsey, "Sex Education," 5. Years later, Clara told a reporter that if she had to do it over, she would not wait for her children to ask questions, but would volunteer sexual information in advance. See Kutner, "Yes, There Is a Mrs. Kinsey," 92.

92 Author's interview with Reid, Feb. 14, 1972, 11–12, 15–16.

93 Keisler to Gebhard, April 24, 1962, 10. Keisler stressed that the Kinseys had this reputation, in her words, "even before the advent of 'the marriage course,' " the class that Kinsey and his associates later insisted triggered his interest in human sexuality and marked the beginning of his research in the field.

94 ACK, "Sex Education," 4.

95 Ibid.

96 Author's interview with Reid, Feb. 14, 1972, 12–13.

97 Ibid., 12. For evidence that the Smokey Mountain vacation occurred in 1934, see ACK to Voris, Sept. 3, 1934, KIA. Kinsey wrote, "We are now leaving, tomorrow for a 10 day trip to the Smokies. The family has been there before."

98 Author's interview with Reid, Feb. 14, 1972, 12.

Chapter 12: "Positions, Wiggling, and Parasites"

1 Cornelia V. Christenson, *Kinsey: A Biography* (Bloomington, 1971), 54.

2 Recent research on gay-straight marriages underscores the hardships they face. Almost without exceptions, scholars paint a grim portrait. Most gay husbands find it next to impossible to perform heterosexually for any length of time. The overall pattern is one of waning interest in women and waxing interest in men, culminating in the end of heterosexual contacts. Irving Bieber, "The Married Male Homosexual," *Medical Aspects of Human Sexuality* 3 (May 1969): 76–84; Alan P. Bell and Martin S. Weinberg, *Homosexualities: A Study of Diversity among Men & Women* (New York, 1978), 164; H. Laurence Ross, "Odd Couples: Homosexuals in Heterosexual Marriage," *Sexual Behavior* 2 (July 1972): 46–47; Frederick W. Bozett, "Heterogeneous Couples in Heterosexual Marriages: Gay Men and Straight Women," *Journal of Marital and Family Therapy* 8 (Spring 1985): 179; Barry M. Dank, "Why Homosexuals Marry Women," *Medical Aspects of Human Sexuality* 6 (Aug. 1973), 20. Scholars found much the same pattern early in the century. Drawing upon data on fifty-two homosexual males, Havelock Ellis, the pioneering English sexologist, reported that in sixteen cases, "there has been connection with women, in some instances only once or twice, in others during several years, but it was always with an effort, or from a sense of duty and anxiety to be normal; they never experienced any real pleasure in the act, or sense of satisfaction after it." The men in four of the cases, he revealed, were currently married, "but marital relationships usually ceased after a few years." Ellis also

cited the work of a German sexologist, Magnus Hirschfeld, to the effect that fully 50 percent of married homosexuals were impotent with their wives. Havelock Ellis, *Studies in the Psychology of Sex,* vol. 2, *Sexual Inversion* (Philadelphia, 1921), 278, 142, 327.

3 Christenson, *Kinsey,* 54.
4 Ibid.
5 Ibid.
6 Ibid.
7 ACK to R. V. Chamberlain, April 24, 1930, KIA.
8 Ibid. Kinsey listed Voris's grades in this letter of recommendation.
9 *Moundbuilder* (n.p., 1925), 39. The *Moundbuilder* is the yearbook of Southwestern College.
10 Author's interview with Herman T. Spieth, Feb. 18, 1988, 24.
11. Ibid., 26.
12 ACK to Chamberlain, April 24, 1930.
13 [ACK,] "Ralph Voris" (unpublished obituary, [n.d.], KIA. While the author of this obituary is uncertain, internal evidence points strongly to Kinsey.
14 Author's interview with Spieth, Feb. 18, 1988, 24–25.
15 ACK to Chamberlain, April 24, 1930.
16 Ibid.
17 Ralph Voris to ACK, April 15, 1930, KIA.
18 [ACK,] "Ralph Voris."
19 ACK to Ralph Voris, n.d. [about 1931], KIA.
20 ACK to Chamberlain, April 24, 1930.
21 Ralph Voris to ACK, Dec. 14, 1936, KIA.
22 ACK to Ralph Voris, Nov. 22, 1928, KIA.
23 Ralph Voris to ACK, Feb. 15, 1929, KIA.
24 While Kinsey issued most of the invitations, there were times when Voris reached out to him. In the spring of 1930, Voris wrote Kinsey, "This nice weather makes my feet itch— certainly wish we were going somewhere." Ralph Voris to ACK, May 27, 1930, KIA. Finding himself in agreement, Kinsey replied, "I, too, am inclined to believe that there is some collecting to be done somewhere." ACK to Ralph Voris, June 2, 1930, KIA.
25 ACK to Ralph Voris, Jan. 24, 1936, KIA.
26 Ralph Voris to ACK, Dec. 3, 1930, KIA. Following the convention, Voris indicated that he had mixed feelings about the meeting. "I enjoyed every minute of the trip but came away with the feeling that it was an expensive trip," he wrote. "Aside from the few contacts with old friends a person does not have the opportunity to see individuals at such a large meeting." Realizing that his words might hurt Kinsey, Voris hastened to add, "Don't get me wrong the time with you well repaid me if we reduce the trip to that." Ralph Voris to ACK, April 4, 1931, KIA.
27 ACK to Ralph Voris, Dec. 20, 1930, KIA.
28 ACK to Ralph Voris, n.d. [early Dec. 1934], KIA.
29 Ralph Voris to ACK, Dec. 11, 1934, KIA.
30 Ralph Voris to ACK, Feb. 19, 1935, KIA.
31 ACK to Ralph Voris, Dec. 5, 1937, KIA.
32 Ralph Voris to ACK, Dec. 11, 1937, KIA.
33 ACK to Ralph Voris, March 11, 1938, KIA.

34 ACK to Ralph Voris, Jan. 31, 1937, KIA. Kinsey's letter strongly suggests that he had attended a similar strip show during his recent trip to Mexico.
35 Osmond P. Breland to ACK, Jan. 12, 1937, KIA.
36 Internal evidence suggests that their correspondence is not complete, raising the possibility that individual letters have been removed.
37 ACK to Ralph Voris, Dec. 30, 1932, KIA.
38 Ralph Voris to ACK, April 20, 1933, KIA.
39 Author's interview with Clyde Martin, April 8, 1971, 9, IUOHP.
40 Author's interview with Clyde Martin, March 21, 1986, 19.
41 ACK to Ralph Voris, April 20, 1933, KIA.
42 Ibid.
43 Ralph Voris to ACK, Nov. 13, 1935, KIA.
44 Ralph Voris to ACK, Feb. 8, 1935, KIA.
45 Ralph Voris to ACK, Dec. 19, 1932, KIA.
46 ACK to Ralph Voris, Dec. 30, 1932, KIA.
47 Wardell B. Pomeroy, *Dr. Kinsey and the Institute for Sex Research* (New York, 1972), 46.
48 Christenson, *Kinsey,* 79–80. Citing Clara Kinsey as her source, Christenson stated that Voris was the only graduate student "who showed personal concern for Kinsey's welfare and had an influence over him."
49 Author's interview with Paul H. Gebhard, Oct. 14, 1984.
50 Ibid., 22–23.
51 Author's interview with Clarence A. Tripp, Dec. 15, 1987, 4.
52 Author's interview with Anon. B, Feb. 17, 1988, 17. Author's interview with Tripp, December 15, 1987, 107.
53 Ibid., 74.
54 Brian Miller, "Adult Sexual Resocialization: Adjustments toward a Stigmatized Identity," *Alternative Lifestyles* 1 (May 1978): 223–27.
55 Louise Rosenzweig and Saul Rosenzweig, "Notes on Alfred C. Kinsey's Pre-sexual Scientific Work and the Transition," *Journal of the History of the Behavioral Sciences* 5 (April 1969): 176. The authors followed this observation by noting, "He would be gone for about a week, sometimes longer, and was usually accompanied by two or more male assistants."
56 Author's interview with Homer T. Rainwater, May 30, 1990, 54–55.
57 Ibid., 31.
58 Ibid.
59 Ibid., 27–28.
60 Ibid., 27, 30.
61 Ibid., 28–29.
62 Ibid., 28, 52–53.
63 Ibid., 33, 34.
64 Ibid., 32, 34.
65 Ibid., 36. Rainwater grew tense and uncomfortable during this portion of the interview. Similarly, he appeared tense when asked if Kinsey ever suggested that they should all masturbate together. Pleasant, soft-spoken, and self-effacing, Rainwater was a gentle soul who bent over backwards to accommodate others. Constitutionally incapable of tolerating conflict, he took care to adjust himself to the wishes of people who mattered most to him. Looking back on his life from the vantage point of his

eighties, Rainwater confessed, "My personality is such that I have all my life avoided controversial stuff." Ibid., 32.

66 Ibid., 30.
67 Ibid., 31, 32.
68 Ibid., 38.
69 Ibid., 38, 39.
70 Author's interview with Spieth, Feb. 18, 1988, 30.
71 Osmond P. Breland, "Field Diary, 1935–1936," Nov. 2, 9, 14, 20, 24, Dec. 22, 1935. (Thanks to Mrs. Osmond P. [Nellie] Breland).
72 Ibid., Nov. 8, 1935. For example, an entry for Nov. 7, 1935, reads, "Went through Saltillo[,] K. swearing every foot of the way because we found no oak."
73 Ibid., Oct. 13, 1935.
74 Ibid., Nov. 17, Oct. 14, 1935.
75 Ibid., Nov. 8, 14, 1935. "Coming down [Kinsey] remarked that this was awfully hard country to introduce me to mt. climbing—as though I wasn't taking it," protested Breland. "That griped me because he would stop every 10 ft. and rest or survey the land for a good path," he continued, "so I sold [sic] out in front & would get ahead & then just as he caught up would sell [sic] out again before he had a chance to rest!" Apparently, this tactic worked, for Breland added with obvious glee, "Boy was he whipped down to a nub when we got down!" Ibid.
76 Ibid., Nov. 7, 1935.
77 Ibid., Oct. 19, 1935.
78 Osmond P. Breland to ACK, Nov. 15, 1936, KIA.
79 Breland, "Field Diary," Oct. 21, 23, 25, 1935.
80 Ibid., Dec. 15, 1935.
81 Ibid., Dec. 16, 1935.
82 Ibid., Dec. 20, 1935.
83 Author's interview with Rainwater, May 30, 1990, 25.
84 ACK to Ralph Voris, n.d. [fall 1931], KIA.
85 Robert E. Bugbee to Wardell B. Pomeroy, Sept. 11, 1961, KIA.
86 ACK to Voris, n.d. [fall 1931].
87 Ibid. The incident is also described in author's interview with Spieth, Feb. 18, 1988, 22.
88 Ibid.
89 Breland, "Field Diary," Oct. 8, 1935.
90 I saw the photograph of Kinsey standing naked in the stream among a group of photographs and negatives of the Mexico trip in William Dellenback's office at the Institute for Sex Research.
91 Breland, "Field Diary," Oct. 12, Nov. 9, Dec. 6, 8, 1935.
92 Ibid., Dec. 10, 1935.
93 Ibid., Nov. 24, 1935, Jan. 4, 5, 1936.
94 Osmond P. Breland to ACK, March 23, 1938, KIA.
95 Osmond P. Breland to ACK, March 10, 1938, KIA.
96 Osmond P. Breland to ACK, Dec. 15, 1936, KIA.
97 Osmond P. Breland to ACK, Nov. 15, 1936, KIA.
98 Osmond P. Breland to ACK, n.d. [1937], KIA.
99 Osmond P. Breland to ACK, Nov. 4, 1937, KIA.
100 Author's telephone conversation with Nellie Breland, March 30, 1989.
101 Author's interview with Clarence A. Tripp, Dec. 15, 1987, 5.

102 Kinsey managed to slip more than a little sex into his general biology course. Herman Spieth, who wrote his dissertation under Kinsey's supervision and served as his teaching assistant in the course in the late 1920s, recalled that his mentor "brought a good deal of sex into it . . . which was atypical for a general biology course." Author's interview with Spieth, Feb. 18, 1988, 28–29.

103 Author's interview with Robert E. Bugbee, Oct. 19, 1971, 25, IUOHP. Asked if he interpreted these discussions with graduate students to mean that Kinsey had an interest in sex before he became a sex researcher, Bugbee replied, "Oh, I think so, yes." Ibid., 26.

104 June Keisler to Paul H. Gebhard, April 24, 1962, untitled recollections on ACK, 11, KIA. Keisler stressed that this incident occurred prior to the beginning of the marriage course, the event usually offered as the starting point for Kinsey's interest in human sexuality and the beginning point of his data collection.

105 Author's interview with Paul H. Gebhard, July 30, 1982, 3.

106 Author's interview with Robert Kroc, Nov. 7, 1987, 38. The period in question, Kroc stressed, "was long before [Kinsey] ever thought of doing research in this [area]." Gebhard confirmed that Kroc helped formulate the interview, though he labored under the impression that Kroc's contribution came after Kinsey had launched his formal study of human sexual behavior. According to Gebhard, Kroc "helped Kinsey devise his original format for the Kinsey interview." Kinsey used him "as a sounding board," Gebhard explained, and often asked him what items should be included in the interview. See author's interview with Gebhard, July 30, 1982, 3.

107 Robert S. Tangeman to Paul H. Gebhard, July 25, 1962, KIA.

108 Author's interview with Joan Reid, Feb. 14, 1972, 13, IUOHP.

109 ACK to Ralph Voris, Sept. 3, 1934, KIA.

110 Author's interview with Kate Hevner Mueller, April 1, 1971, 22, IUOHP.

111 Keisler to Gebhard, April 24, 1962, 8.

Chapter 13: "THERE ISN'T MUCH SCIENCE THERE"

1 Honoré de Balzac, quoted in Th. H. Van de Velde, *Ideal Marriage: Its Physiology and Technique* (New York, 1930), iii.

2 Commenting on Kinsey's motivation, Paul H. Gebhard mused, "It's as though he said, 'Sex has caused me a lot of problems up to now from my childhood guilt over masturbation, my sort of stunted socio-sexual career as a young man because I worried about morality and v.d. and everything, and then my delayed adjustment in marriage.' " Elaborating on his conjecture, Gebhard continued, "He probably said, 'Damn it, something ought to be done about this. I as a biologist am concerned with reproduction, I know about reproduction in other mammals, I'm going to start finding out what gives with human sexual behavior." Author's interview with Paul H. Gebhard, Oct. 14, 1984, 17.

3 Author's interview with Robert Kroc, Nov. 7, 1987, 40. Kroc stated that Kinsey read Dickinson.

4 Paul Robinson, *The Modernization of Sex: Havelock Ellis, Alfred Kinsey, William Masters and Virginia Johnson* (New York, 1976).

5 Ibid., 2.

6 *SBHM*, 265, 268.

7 Christopher Lasch, *Haven in a Heartless World: The Family Besieged* (New York, 1977), 8.

8   Van de Velde, *Ideal Marriage,* 8.

9   Ibid.

10 Author's conversation with Donald Lamm, Oct. 1, 1996.

11 Van de Velde, *Ideal Marriage,* 131.

12 Ibid., 155.

13 See Ronald Bayer, *Homosexuality and American Psychiatry: The Politics of Diagnosis* (New York, 1981), 10.

14 Quoted in George Chauncey, Jr., "From Sexual Inversion to Homosexuality: Medicine and the Changing Conceptualization of Female Deviance," *Salmagundi,* nos. 58–59 (Fall 1982–Winter 1983): 129.

15 Ibid.

16 Medicine's triumphant rise to professional hegemony is told brilliantly in Paul Starr's *The Social Transformation of American Medicine* (New York, 1982).

17 See Frank J. Sulloway, *Freud, Biologist of the Mind: Beyond the Psychoanalytic Legend* (New York, 1979), 280. For an astute analysis of American doctors' discovery of sexual disorders, see Charles Rosenberg, "Sexuality, Class, and Role," in Rosenberg, *No Other Gods* (Baltimore, 1976), 71–88.

18 For an excellent analysis of Krafft-Ebing's work, see Sulloway, *Freud,* 279–89.

19 See Chauncey, "From Sexual Inversion," 133, 130.

20 Sulloway, *Freud,* 279; Robinson, *Modernization of Sex,* 20–21.

21 Sulloway, *Freud,* 279–80.

22 Ibid., 319.

23 Quoted in Havelock Ellis, *Sexual Inversion,* vol. 1 of *Studies in the Psychology of Sex,* 3rd rev. ed. (New York, 1915), 81.

24 Sigmund Freud, "Psychoanalytic Notes upon an Autobiographical Account of a Case of Paranoia," in *Three Case Histories* (New York, 1963), 164, quoted in Bayer, *Homosexuality,* 22.

25 Sigmund Freud, *Three Essays on the Theory of Sexuality* (1905) (New York, 1962), 133, quoted in Bayer, *Homosexuality,* 21.

26 Sigmund Freud, "The Psychogenesis of a Case of Homosexuality in a Woman," in *Sexuality and Psychology of Love,* 157, quoted in Bayer, *Homosexuality,* 26.

27 Alfred C. Kinsey, *Methods in Biology* (Chicago, 1937), 76.

28 *SBHM* contains numerous digs at Freud and psychiatrists in general for relying too heavily on theory. For examples, see pp. 158, 180–81, 206–7, 211–12, 315, 456.

29 Gebhard saw this trait on numerous occasions. According to him, Kinsey used two words as pejoratives: "One was philosophy and one was theory. If he wanted to put something down and denigrate it, he would say that was sheer philosophy, or he would say that is only theory." Without speculating on the "whys" of it, Gebhard agreed that Kinsey had little use for theoreticians, or, as he put it, Kinsey "was atheoretical, and indeed, sometimes anti-theoretical." Author's interview with Paul H. Gebhard, Oct. 29, 1971, 48, IUOHP.

30 Wardell B. Pomeroy, *Dr. Kinsey and the Institute for Sex Research* (New York, 1972), 15.

31 Ibid.

32 Ibid., 155.

33 ACK, *An Introduction to Biology* (Philadelphia, 1926), 526.

34 For a trenchant discussion of the moral underpinnings of Freud's work, see Philip Rieff, *Freud: The Mind of the Moralist* (Chicago, 1959).

35 Quoted in John D'Emilio and Estelle B. Freedman, *Intimate Matters: A History of Sexuality in America* (New York, 1988), 226.

36 Chauncey, "From Sexual Inversion," 120.

37 See Paul Robinson, "Dear Paul," *Salmagundi,* nos. 58–59 (Fall 1982–Winter 1983): 26.

38 Chauncey, "From Sexual Inversion," 122. As he did with so many other disputes, Freud further clarified the matter by distinguishing between "sexual objects" and "sexual aims." The sexual aim, he explained, was a person's preferred form of sexual behavior (say genital or oral, or assuming the active as opposed to the passive role), while the sexual object was the person (or thing) of sexual desire. In mature adults, the latter was confined to persons of the opposite sex, while sexual perverts chose sexual objects that were inappropriate, such as children, animals, inanimate objects (shoes, garter belts, etc.), and persons of the same sex.

39 Quoted in D'Emilio and Freedman, *Intimate Matters,* 224.

40 Robinson, *Modernization of Sex,* 28. Like Kinsey's, Ellis's interest in human sexuality was tied to personal problems. Until late in life, Ellis suffered from premature ejaculation, as well as other sexual dysfunctions that dated from his youth. As a boy in England, he was troubled by wet dreams and by urolagnia—sexual arousal in watching women urinate. When he consulted the scientific literature on sex, however, Ellis was appalled and resolved to make sex research his life's work. "I determined," he later wrote, "that I would . . . spare the youth of future generations the trouble and perplexity which this ignorance had caused me." Quoted in Sulloway, *Freud,* 305. True to his word, Ellis studied medicine and at the age of thirty embarked on a career as a scientist and writer. He brought to the task a dedication and an intellectual passion of someone who had suffered deeply. See James Reed, *From Private Vice to Public Virtue: The Birth Control Movement and American Society since 1830* (New York, 1978), 92–94.

41 Robinson, *Modernization of Sex,* 4.

42 Ellis, *Sexual Inversion,* 4–8.

43 Homosexuality was mentioned, Ellis revealed, in the code of Hammurabi and in other ancient texts from Assyria and Babylonia "which do not on the whole refer to it favorably." Ibid., 9. Ancient Egyptians, by contrast, "never regarded homosexuality as punishable or even reprehensible." Ibid., 11. In ancient Greece, he noted approvingly, homosexuality "was frequently regarded as having beneficial results, which caused it to be condoned, if not, indeed, fostered as a virtue." Ibid., 16. Moreover, the various Indian tribes of the New World treated homosexuals on the whole rather well. "Sometimes they are regarded by the tribe with honor, sometimes with indifference, sometimes, with contempt," reported Ellis; "but they appear to be always tolerated." Ibid., 21. Moving on to modern times, Ellis showed that homosexuality could be found in countries around the globe, including Europe, where it was known to flourish in the lower classes and in penal institutions. Ibid., 25–26.

44 As in his cross-cultural survey of attitudes toward homosexuality, Ellis began with ancient history and marched forward to modern times. Among the ancients said or alleged to have been gay were Julius Caesar, Augustus, and Hadrian, while his list of Renaissance men included (with varying degrees of certainty) Muret, Leonardo da Vinci, Michelangelo, and Cellini. No less impressive was the group of homosexual notables from early modern and modern times. The list from Germany included Alexander von Humboldt and F. A. Krupp, while England contributed Francis Bacon, Lord Byron, Edward Fitzgerald, and, of course, Oscar Wilde. Ibid., 39–50.

45 Ibid., 105.

46 Ibid., 61.

47 Ibid., 64.

48   Ibid., 357.
49   Ibid., 317. Sneaking a flattering image in with the less becoming, he argued that sexual inverts "may thus be roughly compared to the congenital idiot, to the instinctive criminal, to the man of genius, who are all not strictly concordant with the usual biological variation . . . but who become somewhat more intelligible to us if we bear in mind their affinity to variations."
50   Ibid., 182, 100, 108, 96.
51   Ibid., 168, 181–82, 190, 194.
52   Ibid., 354. With a nod to Victorian values, Ellis acknowledged that homosexuality was "a disgusting abomination." Still, he was quick to remind his readers, "An act does not become criminal because it is disgusting."
53   Ibid., 355.
54   John D'Emilio, *Sexual Politics, Sexual Communities: The Making of a Homosexual Minority in the United States, 1940–1970* (Chicago, 1983), 18–19.
55   Author's interview with Kroc, Nov. 7, 1987, 41. Paul Gebhard, who heard that same criticism repeated years later, offered this explanation: "Kinsey had a certain intellectual arrogance, if you want to call it that. There were a small number of people whose opinions he respected, but he looked on no man as his mentor or his superior when it came to sex research." In part, Kinsey's determination to be his own father as a sex researcher reflected his peculiar scientific method, which Gebhard explained again as meaning, "One should do one's own research, one's own thinking, and only at that point should one turn to the pre-existing literature." Yet there was clearly more to it than this, as Gebhard understood full well. "I might add," he concluded, "at the root of his thinking was the fact he didn't have a very high opinion of what anybody else had done previously." Author's interview with Paul H. Gebhard, Oct. 29, 1971, 28–29.
56   ACK, "Biological Aspects of Some Social Problems" (unpublished lecture), 4, 5, 8, 9–10, KIA. Kinsey apparently delivered this paper before his discussion group at Indiana University in the spring of 1935.
57   Ibid., 5–6.
58   Ibid., 7. Significantly, Kinsey also commented on the agencies and groups that had funded sex research. A successful grantsman who had received funds awards from the Waterman Institute of Indiana University and two grants-in-aid from the Division of Biological and Agricultural Sciences of the NRC, he understood the importance of funding to scientific research. In the paper to his faculty study group, Kinsey mentioned by name the two most important organizations currently funding sex research in the United States. Research in endocrinology, he told his colleagues, was being financed by grants from "the National Research Council's Committee on the Biology of Sex." (The correct title was the Committee for Research in Problems of Sex.) Similarly, he noted that other investigators had been funded by the National Committee on Maternal Health, which was privately endowed. As early as 1935, Kinsey knew where to turn for grants to support scientific research on human sexuality. Ibid., 6–7.
59   Ibid., 7. In the years to follow, both Dickinson and Pearl played important roles in encouraging Kinsey's own research on human sexual behavior.
60   Ibid., 4. In later years, Kinsey would change his mind about what anthropology had to contribute to scientific knowledge of human sexuality, but it took all of Paul H. Gebhard's powers of persuasion to revise his opinion.
61   Ibid., 6.
62   Ibid., 10.
63   Ibid., 21.

64 "The currently accepted list of sex perversions are, almost without exception, rooted in primate behavior and, in that sense, natural; if divorced from their present-day social reactions most of them would have little effect on the security of the home or the propagation of the race." Ibid.

65 Ibid.

Chapter 14: "You Can Work Out Your Own Solution"

1 ACK to Edgar Anderson, Feb. 7, 1935, KIA.

2 Ibid.

3 Author's interview with Herman B Wells, Dec. 3, 1973, 1–2, IUOHP.

4 Herman B Wells, *Being Lucky: Reminiscences and Reflections* (Bloomington, 1980), 35.

5 Ibid., 40.

6 Ibid., 96–97.

7 ACK to Ralph Voris, March 11, 1938, KIA.

8 Robert L. Kroc to Herman B Wells, Jan. 21, 1938, IUA.

9 ACK to Voris, March 11, 1938.

10 Wendell W. Wright, Herman T. Briscoe, and Fowler V. Harper, "Report of the Self Survey Committee to the Board of Trustees of Indiana University," March 21, 1939, pt. 2, p. 403, table 9, IUA.

11 Ibid., 398–99. The faculty at Indiana University had published an average of .61 books and 2.0 articles per professor during the decade 1924–34. Figures released by the North Central Association placed the average for other state universities in the region by contrast at 1.7 books and 10.8 articles per faculty member for the same period. The disparity, concluded the committee members with dismay, was "so great as to be alarming to those vitally interested in the reputation and prestige of Indiana University in the field of scholarship." Moreover, the situation in the natural sciences, Kinsey's home base, was hardly more flattering. A review of *American Men of Science* (1937 ed.) revealed that Indiana University had five "starred scientists" on its faculty, while the University of Chicago boasted forty-six, the University of Michigan thirty, the University of Minnesota twenty-six, the University of Illinois twenty-two, and Ohio State University thirteen. Ibid., 415, 417, 387–88.

12 Ibid., 417–18.

13 ACK to Voris, March 11, 1938.

14 As the public awaited the board's decision, Bloomington buzzed with speculation, and Kinsey, too, got caught up in the gossip. He informed Voris that one candidate, Paul McNutt, the governor of Indiana, was "out of the picture" but that Acting President Wells was "running strong in newspaper comment." Kinsey rated Wells as "Not bad— in fact very good as an executive, but not too long on scholarship." ACK to Voris, March 11, 1938.

15 Wells, *Being Lucky*, 104.

16 Ibid.

17 Wells's story has been ably told by Thomas D. Clark in his sesquicentennial history, *Indiana University: Midwestern Pioneer*, vol. 2, *In Mid-Passage* (Bloomington, 1973), and vol. 3, *Years of Fulfillment* (Bloomington, 1977). Wells himself has offered his own assessment in his autobiography, *Being Lucky*.

18 *Daily Student*, Feb. 15, 1938, 1. While the public's interest in venereal disease had dropped off sharply after World War I, Thomas Parran, who joined President Franklin D. Roosevelt's administration as surgeon general of the United States in 1936, took of-

fice determined to reverse this trend. A few months after he arrived in Washington, D.C., he published an article in *Survey Graphic* (later reprinted in *Reader's Digest*) entitled "The Next Great Plague to Go." Shattering the conspiracy of silence that still inhibited public discussion of sexual issues, Parran told his readers that venereal disease would never be conquered until Americans abandoned the notion "that nice people don't talk about syphilis, nice people don't have syphilis, and nice people shouldn't do anything about those who have syphilis." Quoted in Allan M. Brandt, *No Magic Bullet: A Social History of Venereal Disease in the United States since 1880* (New York, 1985), 138. In contrast to the jeremiads of social hygienists, however, he did not proclaim the need to change people's behavior. "I have come to the conclusion that it is much easier to control syphilis by making Wassermann tests routinely for the age groups needing it, and seeing that treatment is obtained by all people who require it," wrote Parran, "than it is to alter the way of life of a people." Ibid., 140.

19 *Daily Student,* Feb. 15, 1938, 1.
20 Ibid., Feb. 18, 1938, 1.
21 Ibid.
22 Ibid., Feb. 17, 1938, 4; Feb. 23, 1938, 1–2; May 28, 1938, 4.
23 Ibid., Feb. 19, 1938, 4.
24 Ibid., Feb. 16, 1938, 4.
25 Ibid., March 8, 1938, 4.
26 Wardell B. Pomeroy, *Dr. Kinsey and the Institute for Sex Research* (New York, 1972), 58.
27 Author's interview with Cecilia Wahl, Jan. 22, 1972, 6, IUOHP.
28 Author's interview with Cecilia Wahl, March 8, 1972, 1, IUOHP.
29 Clark, *Indiana University,* 2:137.
30 Ibid., 291–96.
31 Clark, *Indiana University,* 2:120–21, 147.
32 Author's interview with Margaret Edmondson, Nov. 9, 1971, 3, IUOHP.
33 Quoted in Brandt, *No Magic Bullet,* 135–36.
34 Ibid., 136.
35 For a discussion of the early marriage courses, see Steven Mintz and Susan Kellogg, *Domestic Revolutions: A Social History of American Family Life* (New York, 1988), 283, n. 68.
36 Virginia Johnson, "Sex and the Scientist," Public Broadcasting Service, May 21, 1989, WTIU, Bloomington, Ind. In later years, Kinsey (and those close to him) insisted that the AWS had approached him for assistance, but there is no evidence to support this claim. Asked to clarify the matter thirty-five years after the fact, a former officer of the association replied, "I can't tell you whether AWS thought it [starting a marriage course] was a good idea or whether Dr. Kinsey had thought of it through his contacts with students and thought the AWS might be a good body to help sponsor it or work out details." While stressing she simply could not be certain who took the initiative, she added, "Maybe we didn't [approach him], . . . maybe he came to us." Author's interview with Wahl, Jan. 22, 1972, 3, 6.
37 O. F. Hall to ACK, April 15, 1923, KIA.
38 William G. Mather, Jr., to ACK, May 12, 1938, KIA.
39 Norman E. Himes to ACK, April 22, 1938, KIA.
40 ACK to Norman E. Himes, April 29, 1938, KIA.
41 In fact, his remarks raised the intriguing possibility that Kinsey had given serious thought to starting a marriage course on campus several years earlier, an idea whose time apparently had had to await President Bryan's retirement.

42 ACK to Himes, April 29, 1938.
43 ACK to Norman E. Himes, May 7, 1938, KIA.
44 Osmond P. Breland to ACK, April 11, 1938, KIA. No copy of Kinsey's letter to Bre-
    land has survived, but Breland acknowledged receipt of a newsy letter.
45 Association of Women Students et al. to President Herman B Wells, May 14, 1938,
    Marriage Course Files, IUA. Portions of the AWS petition also appear in "Minutes of
    the Board of Trustees, 1938," 259, IUA.
46 Wells, *Being Lucky,* 128–29.
47 Ibid., 145.
48 "Minutes of the Board of Trustees, 1938," 259.
49 Ibid.
50 Herman B Wells to ACK, July 9, 1938, KIA.
51 ACK to Herman B Wells, July 19, 1938, KIA. The autobiography of Wells reveals that
    he shared Kinsey's enthusiasm for sexual metaphors, indicating that they truly were kin-
    dred spirits. Wells confessed that he had some difficulty deciding what to use as a title
    for the "advice" section of his book—the maxims that he wished to share with young
    college presidents. Wells noted that he considered borrowing something from one of
    the volumes in Kinsey's library of erotica, a famous tome published in London in
    1792 under the title *Useful Hints to Single Gentlemen Respecting Marriage, Concubinage
    and Adultery, in Prose and Verse, with Notes Moral, Critical, and Explanatory.* While ad-
    mitting that an erotic theme might not be altogether appropriate, Wells added, "In one
    respect it is: if you will develop a love affair with your university, her seduction will be
    easier and more satisfying." Wells, *Being Lucky,* 142.
52 ACK to Wells, July 19, 1938; Herman B Wells to ACK, July 21, 1938, KIA.
53 ACK to Thurman B. Rice, Feb. 28, 1939. Kinsey's reading list included the following
    books and articles: Katherine B. Davis, *Factors in the Sex Life of 2200 Women* (New York,
    1929); Katherine B. Davis, "Periodicity of Sex Desire," *American Journal of Obstetrics
    and Gynecology* (Dec. 1926): 12; G. S. Miller, Jr., "The Primate Basis of Human Be-
    havior," *Quarterly Review of Biology* (Dec. 1931): 6; Paul Popenoe, *Problems of Human
    Reproduction* (Baltimore, 1926); Olga Knopf, *The Art of Being a Woman* (Boston,
    1932); William S. Taylor, *A Critique of Sublimation in Males* (Worcester, 1933); Have-
    lock Ellis, *Psychology of Sex: A Manual for Students* (New York, 1933); Robert Briffault,
    The Mothers (New York, 1927); Eric M. Matsner, *The Technique of Contraception* (Bal-
    timore, 1936). Students were also invited to read these books and articles.
54 Author's interview with Edith B. Schuman, Sept. 15, 1971, 5, IUOHP.
55 *Daily Student,* June 22, 1938, 1; ACK to Herman B Wells, Sept. 12, 1938, "Summary
    of Student Answers: Marriage Course, Summer, 1938, Indiana University," IUA.
56 ACK, "Marriage Course Outline: Summer, 1938," KIA. Fowler Harper of the law
    school (the same professor who told the *Daily Student* that he was investigating marriage
    laws) explored the legal aspects of marriage and returned later in the term to discuss the
    legal aspects of divorce; Carroll Christenson lectured on the economics of marriage; Ed-
    mund Conklin spoke on the psychological aspects of marriage; Harvey Locke discussed
    the sociology of the family; Edith Schuman, a physician who worked in the university's
    student health service, lectured on pregnancy, birth, and venereal disease; and Alfred
    Kohlmeier, a historian, analyzed the ethical questions of marriage. The final two lectures
    were delivered by Kinsey's colleague and friend in the zoology department, Robert
    Kroc, who spoke on endocrinology and reproduction and sterility. After the course had
    been taught for a year and a half and was firmly established, Kinsey added a lecture on
    sex education, which he taught, bringing his total to four presentations before the class.

57 ACK, "First Lecture of Marriage Course" (June 1939), 5, KIA. The identical point is made in the first version of this lecture given in July 1938. See ACK, "Biologic Bases of Society" (n.d.), 3, KIA. Here, however, Kinsey said that scientists had been studying anthropoid behavior for about twenty years, a decade longer than he said in 1939.

58 ACK, "First Lecture," 7.

59 ACK, "Bases of Society" (Feb. 5, 1940), 7–8, KIA.

60 ACK, "First Lecture," 9.

61 For the development of misguided ideas about right and wrong, see ibid., 11. For figures on sexual maladjustment and the divorce rate, see ACK, "Bases of Society," 9; for the role of prudish ideas in undermining the family, see ACK, "First Lecture," 10–11.

62 ACK, "First Lecture," 11.

63 Ibid., 7.

64 Ibid., 1–8. In a revised version of the same lecture, Kinsey used even stronger language to make the same point. "Fundamentally," he declared, "male and female are the same. Such differences as exist between male and female are differences in degree of development." In his view, what people called genitals were merely "external appendages which . . . provide for a means of holding male and female together while the sperm penetrate the body of the female to come in contact with the eggs." See ACK, "Reproductive Anatomy and Physiology" (Feb. 21, 1940), 4–5, KIA.

65 ACK, "Reproductive Anatomy and Physiology" (July 12, 1938), 9, KIA.

66 Ibid., 10–11.

67 For a complete discussion of birth control in the nineteenth century, see James Reed, *From Private Vice to Public Virtue: The Birth Control Movement and American Society since 1830* (New York, 1978), 3–18.

68 Ibid., 143–93. Reed does an excellent job of explaining how Sanger and Dickinson put aside their differences and worked together. In the end, it was Dickinson who played the crucial role in persuading physicians to accept birth control.

69 ACK, "Reproductive Anatomy and Physiology" (July 12, 1938), 12.

70 Ibid.

71 Ibid., 2.

72 Ibid., 3–4.

73 Ibid., 4.

74 Ibid., 5.

75 Ibid. In a revised version of the same lecture, Kinsey pushed the point even further: "I'm telling you that I say there is no basis for classifying people into normal and abnormal. There is no basis biologically for recognizing abnormal. If the individuals are so few that they lie way up on the ends of the curve you might think of them as abnormal. I should still prefer to think of them as rare rather than abnormal. Biologically, we usually recognize abnormality when a given structure interferes with physiological well-being." ACK, "Individual Variation" (Feb. 28, 1940), 8, KIA.

76 ACK, "Reproductive Anatomy and Physiology" (July 12, 1938), 5.

77 Even so, he had a hard time abandoning the issues that concerned him personally. His penchant for skating near the edge of the ice was much in evidence in his word choice. Employing a bold double entendre, he told the class that "successful physical relationships in marriage involve the adjustments of one very queer individual to another very queer individual." Ibid.

78 Ibid., 6.

79 Ibid., 7.

80 Ibid., 10.

Chapter 15: "A VERY STRONG REGARD FOR INDIVIDUAL VARIATION"

1 ACK to Herman B Wells, Sept. 12, 1938, KIA. In a cover letter he sent to staff members of the marriage course, Kinsey boasted that the questionnaire completed by students revealed "nearly unanimous approval of our program." See ACK to "Staff of the marriage course," Sept. 12, 1938, KIA.

2 ACK, "Summary of Student Answers, Indiana University, marriage course, Summer, 1938," KIA.

3 Ibid.

4 Ibid.

5 Herman B Wells to ACK, Sept. 18, 1938, IUA.

6 Dr. John R. Frank to Herman B Wells, Sept. 25, 1938, KIA. In response, Wells pointed to the marriage course as proof of his administration's progressive thinking, adding that he had referred Frank's letter to Kinsey and the marriage course committee. Quick to capitalize on Frank's letter, Kinsey wrote Wells, "I wish we could get the reactions of a large number of people in the state on these matters." See Herman B Wells to Dr. John R. Frank, Oct. 3, 1938, KIA; ACK to Herman B Wells, Oct. 8, 1938, KIA.

7 Author's interview with Kate Hevner Mueller, April 1, 1971, 2, IUOHP.

8 *Daily Student,* Feb. 2, 1939, 1.

9 Kate H. Mueller to ACK, Oct. 25, 1938, KIA.

10 Kate H. Mueller to ACK, Nov. 29, 1938, KIA.

11 *Daily Student,* Sept. 28, 1938, 2.

12 ACK to "Staff of the marriage course," Sept. 12, 1938.

13 ACK to Herman B Wells, Jan. 14, 1939, KIA.

14 ACK, "Summary of Student Comments on marriage course, Fall, 1938," KIA.

15 Ibid.

16 Ibid.

17 Ibid.

18 A decade later, Kinsey revealed where he got the slides in response to an inquiry. Referring to the marriage course, he declared, "We did use some lantern slides, based primarily upon anatomical material from [Robert L.] Dickinson's *Sex Anatomy.*" See ACK to Anonymous, March 8, 1948, KIA.

19 ACK, "Summary of Student Comments on Marriage Course, Fall, 1938," KIA. Within a decade, Kinsey would be deeply involved with filming human sexual behavior, often as the subject of the films he made.

20 Ibid.

21 Ibid.

22 Ibid.

23 ACK to Robert E. Bugbee, Sept. 20, 1938, KIA; ACK to Ralph Voris, Nov. 28, 1938, KIA.

24 Osmond P. Breland to ACK, Dec. 1, 1938, KIA.

25 *Daily Student,* Feb. 3, 1939, 1.

26 Ibid., Feb. 4, 1939, 4.

27 Ibid.

28 Ibid.

29 Ibid.

30 *SBHM,* 9. Kinsey offered the same explanation in a film interview. "There are a good many people who think that we began to study humans because they had some rela-

tion to the insects," he began. "As a matter of fact I taught the general biology course at Indiana University. Students came to me with questions concerning sex. They could get their answers from all sorts of people as to what they should or shouldn't do, but they wanted scientific data. I went to the scientific data in psychology, biology, and medicine and psychiatry," he explained, "and I discovered that there was practically nothing known about human sexual behavior in comparison with what we knew about the sexual behavior of other animals, and in comparison with what we knew about the activities of other parts of the human body. Consequently, I found a gap in our knowledge and that was sufficient for any scientist to undertake research." See "Sex and the Scientist," PBS, May 21, 1989, WTIU, Bloomington, Ind.

31 ACK, "Reproductive Anatomy and Physiology" (July 12, 1938), 1, KIA.
32 Herman B Wells to ACK, July 9, 1938, KIA.
33 "Sex and the Scientist."
34 ACK, "marriage course Questionnaire: Summer of 1938," "marriage course Questionnaire: Fall of 1938," "marriage course Questionnaire: Spring of 1939," KIA.
35 See Daily Student, Sept. 27, 1937, 2, and April 29, 1939, 1; for Kinsey's appointment to head the Phi Beta Kappa chapter, see ibid., April 29, 1938, 1; and for his appointment to the Rhodes Scholarship committee, see ibid., May 3, 1938, 3.
36 ACK, "Individual Variation" (July 19, 1938), 5, KIA.
37 SBHM, 10.
38 ACK to Herman B Wells, Sept. 12, 1938, KIA.
39 ACK to Herman B Wells, Jan. 14, 1939, KIA.
40 ACK to Herman B Wells, Jan. 14, 1939, Enclosure, KIA.
41 Ibid.
42 Christenson observed, "Such a variety of factual questions on sexual activities had never been asked systematically of any sample, much less of such a large one." Cornelia V. Christenson, Kinsey: A Biography (Bloomington, 1971), 109–10.
43 SBHM, 11, 50. Referring to these early interviews, Pomeroy noted, "They were not quite the detailed histories we eventually took in our interviewing, but they were substantially the same, needing only expansion and refinement." Wardell B. Pomeroy, Dr. Kinsey and the Institute for Sex Research (New York, 1972), 54.
44 SBHM, 10.
45 Robert C. Bugbee to ACK, Aug. 24, 1938, KIA.
46 ACK to Robert C. Bugbee, Sept. 20, 1939, KIA.
47 ACK to Anon., June 25, 1942, KIA.
48 Anon. to ACK, July 3, 1940, KIA.
49 SBHM, 42.
50 Osmond P. Breland to ACK, Jan. 24, 1939, KIA.
51 Pomeroy, Dr. Kinsey, 55.
52 ACK to Anon., Dec. 19, 1938, KIA.
53 Ibid.
54 Ibid.
55 Ibid. Several months after writing to this woman, Kinsey sent President Wells a report on the marriage course that may throw light on the physician's identity. "We should like to draw your attention to the splendid service which Dr. William C. Reed, one of our local physicians, has given us in connection with the [marriage] course," wrote Kinsey. "Upon invitation of our staff, Dr. Reed presented one of the lectures in the series this semester, giving the students valuable material from his extensive experience, in connection with childbirth. Dr. Reed has also shown an intelligent interest in taking care

of a number of student cases which have come to us in consultation, and which we needed to refer to expert medical service." ACK to Herman B Wells, May 19, 1939, KIA.

56 ACK to Anon., Dec. 19, 1938.
57 Ibid.
58 Ibid.
59 Author's interview with Mrs. ACK, Dec. 10, 1971, 35, IUOHP. Kinsey also interviewed each of his children. See Pomeroy, *Dr. Kinsey,* 107.
60 Author's interview with Robert Kroc, Nov. 7, 1987, 37–39.
61 Christenson, *Kinsey,* 103.
62 Ibid.
63 Ibid.
64 ACK to Osmond P. Breland, Oct. 8, 1938, KIA.
65 Author's interview with Kroc, Nov. 7, 1987, 60. Pearl's interest in sex research was ongoing. In 1939, he published *The Natural History of Population,* which included a chapter entitled "The Biology of Fertility," based upon the most recent studies on the frequency of human intercourse. As a token of their friendship, Pearl sent Kinsey a copy of this book, with the inscription "With warmest regards." See Christenson, *Kinsey,* 106.
66 ACK to Ralph Voris, Jan. 17, 1939, KIA.
67 *SBHM,* 10.
68 ACK to Anon., June 19, 1940, KIA. Still, nothing in his earlier work prepared him for the success he was having studying sexual variation in human beings. "I am still astounded," he confessed, "that it has been possible to get such a large body of information from so many people in such a short time. It was not until two years ago that I discovered I could get this out of people." Ibid.
69 *SBHM,* 10.
70 Ibid.
71 Ibid., 72.
72 Ibid., 73.
73 Anon. to ACK, Feb. 11, 1942, KIA.
74 Anon. to ACK, Oct. 22, 1940, KIA.
75 ACK to Anon., Oct. 28, 1940, KIA.
76 Attempting to justify this technique, Kinsey wrote in 1948, "The interviewer should not make it easy for a subject to deny his participation in any form of sexual activity. It is too easy to say no if he is simply asked whether he has ever engaged in a particular activity." Therefore, scientists should "always assume that everyone has engaged in every type of activity. Consequently we always begin by asking *when* they first engaged in such activity." *SBHM,* 53.
77 Ibid., 43.
78 Ibid., 55.
79 Ibid., 11.
80 ACK, "Individuals" (unpublished lecture delivered to the members and friends of Phi Beta Kappa, June 5, 1939), 2–3, KIA.
81 Ibid., 2.
82 Ibid., 6–7.
83 Ibid., 7. Significantly, this was as close as Kinsey would ever come to sorting out the relative importance of heredity and environment in shaping human sexual behavior. Whenever he addressed the question in the future, he made it clear that he thought

human sexual behavior resulted from the interaction of nature and nurture, with the precise contribution of each yet to be determined.

84 Ibid.
85 Ibid., 8–9.
86 Ibid., 9.
87 Ibid.
88 Ibid.
89 Ibid., 9–10.

Chapter 16: "Why Has No One Cracked This Before?"

1 John D'Emilio and Estelle B. Freedman, *Intimate Matters: A History of Sexuality in America* (New York, 1988), 226–27. For the best analysis of the development of an urban gay culture, see George Chauncey, *Gay New York: Gender, Urban Culture, and the Making of the Gay Male World* (New York, 1994).
2 D'Emilio and Freedman, *Intimate Matters,* 228.
3 Ibid., 227–28.
4 ACK to Anon., June 12, 1940, KIA.
5 Ibid.
6 ACK to Anon., June 29, 1939, KIA.
7 ACK to Anon., July 6, 1939, KIA.
8 *SBHM,* 38–39.
9 ACK to Anon., Aug. 18, 1939, KIA.
10 ACK to Anon., Aug. 18, 1939, KIA.
11 ACK to Anon., June 29, 1939, KIA.
12 Ibid.
13 Anon. to ACK, Nov. 15, 1939, KIA.
14 ACK to Anon., July 4, 1939, KIA.
15 ACK to Anon., May 25, 1940, KIA.
16 ACK to Anon., Aug. 18, 1939, KIA.
17 ACK to Anon., June 17, 1940, KIA.
18 ACK to Anon., June 14, 1940, KIA.
19 ACK to Anon., July 4, 1939, KIA.
20 ACK to Anon., Dec. 23, 1939, KIA.
21 ACK to Anon., June 17, 1940, KIA.
22 ACK to Anon., Oct. 5, 1939, KIA.
23 ACK to Anon., Sept. 2, 1944, KIA. In this letter, Kinsey wrote, "It has been several years since I have seen you. Do you remember that you met me at . . . [Mr. X's] home and that you helped me get histories for a study that we are making in human sex behavior? I paid you and the persons who contributed the histories, and you told me that if I came back to Chicago, you would be glad to help again." Explaining that he planned to return to Chicago in the near future, Kinsey declared, "We could take a good many histories at the same prices that we have paid before, if you want to make contacts for us."
24 ACK to Ralph Voris, July 6, 1939, KIA.
25 Pearl was sufficiently impressed by Kinsey after their meetings in Indiana to ask Fernandus Payne (Kinsey's department chair) to send him a list of Kinsey's most recent publications. See Raymond Pearl to Fernandus Payne, Dec. 13, 1939, Raymond Pearl Papers, American Philosophical Society Library, Philadelphia.

26 ACK to Raymond Pearl, July 7, 1939, ibid.
27 Ibid. If the latter remark sounded curiously faint, he was more forthcoming with others. In a letter to Bugbee, Kinsey provided an update on the marriage course, declaring, "The personal conferences are giving us a set of histories that are invaluable, and I begin to wonder if this is not going to account for the largest volume of research I will yet publish." ACK to Robert E. Bugbee, July 14, 1939, KIA.
28 ACK to Voris, July 6, 1939.
29 Ibid.
30 ACK to Ralph Voris, Aug. 24, 1939, KIA.
31 ACK to Ralph Voris, Sept. 19, 1939, KIA.
32 Ibid.
33 Estelle B. Freedman, " 'Uncontrolled Desires': The Response to the Sexual Psychopath, 1920–1960," *Journal of American History* 744 (June 1987): 89–91.
34 ACK to Anon., Nov. 1, 1939, KIA.
35 ACK to Anon., Dec. 23, 1939, KIA.
36 ACK to Anon., Dec. 23, 1939, KIA.
37 Anon. to ACK, June 26, 1940, KIA.
38 ACK to Anon., Dec. 23, 1939, KIA.
39 ACK to Anon., Feb. 13, 1940, KIA.
40 ACK to Anon., Dec. 23, 1939, KIA.
41 ACK to Anon., Dec. 8, 1939, KIA.
42 ACK to Anon., June 24, 1940, KIA.
43 Anon. to ACK, Sept. 27, 1940, KIA.
44 ACK to Anon., Oct. 9, 1940, KIA. Much of what Kinsey recommended would later become the standard therapy recommended by behavioral psychologists trying to convert homosexuals to heterosexual behavior. Specifically, Kinsey offered the young man the following six-part plan:

1. Associate with heterosexual men, whose daily reactions to the female will, in time, interest you in such reactions. 2. Take opportunities to make social contacts with girls in parties, movie dates, etc., etc. 3. Start the physical contacts with the simplest sort of petting, gradually build up to heavy petting to the point of actual climax. Mouth, female breast, and genitalia should be involved; they are usually added to the picture in that order. 4. Come to intercourse only after you have known definite arousal in the petting. The physical techniques of heterosexual intercourse are, in any case, more difficult to learn than the techniques of homosexual intercourse. It will take a lot of the heterosexual to equal the hundreds of contacts you have had with the homosexual. 5. Avoid sex relations with the male as far as convenient. Do not be discouraged if you continue to make occasional contacts, for it is still possible to develop the heterosexual at the same time. 6. Do not be discouraged if you find the male still arousing you more than the female: it may take time and abundant heterosexual experience to bring you satisfaction equal to what you have known in the homosexual. Sometimes, however, I have known the homosexual pattern to change almost overnight, as the result of a fortunately satisfactory heterosexual experience.

Optimistic about the outcome if his program were followed, Kinsey added, "Whether you want to put yourself through this training is up to you. I have known it to work in many cases. I have seen it fail in some. I see nothing in your history which should make it impossible for you to succeed." Here it is hard not to believe that Kinsey was speaking from personal experience, as well as from the case histories of others.

45　Ibid.
46　Ibid.
47　ACK to Anon., Oct. 9, 1940, KIA.
48　Ibid.
49　Ibid.
50　ACK to Anon., Feb. 15, 1940, KIA.
51　ACK to Anon., Oct. 14, 1949, KIA.
52　Author's interview with Anon. B, 101–2, 106.
53　ACK to Ralph Voris, n.d. (internal evidence suggests that the letter was written some-time in Dec. 1939), KIA.
54　Ibid.
55　Ibid.
56　Ibid.
57　Ibid.
58　Ibid.
59　Ibid.
60　Ibid.
61　Ralph Voris to ACK, Dec. 15, 1939, KIA.
62　Ibid.
63　Ralph Voris to ACK, n.d. [internal evidence suggests the letter was written sometime in late Dec. 1939 or in Jan. 1940], KIA.
64　Geraldine Voris to ACK, n.d. (note at the bottom of the Voris letter cited above, n. 63), KIA.
65　ACK to Anon. and Anon., Dec. 22, 1939, KIA. In this letter, Kinsey wrote, "When you next head toward St. Louis let me know, for I am very anxious to get a batch of histories out of that city."
66　In a letter thanking the "contact man" from Chicago who had introduced him to his gay friends in St. Louis, Kinsey wrote, "It was slow, as I might have anticipated, to persuade the first contacts; but that was the history in Chicago, and just as in Chicago, the whole St. Louis group is most cordial now that we have started." See ACK to Anon., Feb. 2, 1940, KIA.
67　ACK to Ralph Voris, Feb. 13, 1940, KIA.
68　ACK to Ralph Voris, March 2, 1940, KIA.
69　Ibid.
70　Ibid.
71　Geraldine Voris to Dr. and Mrs. A. C. Kinsey, May 9, 1940, KIA.
72　Geraldine Voris to Dr. and Mrs. A. C. Kinsey, Western Union telegram, May 9, 1940, KIA.
73　Grateful for the assistance, Geraldine Voris later thanked Kinsey, declaring, "Your work in Ralph's office has lifted such a load." Later, however, she indicated that others had been sharply critical of this action. "It seems they felt we had no right to enter Ralph's office Sunday night after the services," she wrote, adding that one individual "went to the Business Manager and filed [a] written complaint that the Office had been entered by someone not connected with the school & so on far into the night." See Geraldine Voris to Dr. and Mrs. Kinsey, May 29, 1940, July 18, 1940, KIA.
74　Geraldine Voris to Dr. and Mrs. Kinsey, June 14, 1940, KIA.
75　ACK to Osmond P. Breland, May 17, 1940, KIA. Kinsey may have blamed Voris for his death, at least in part. "He had not kept himself in as good physical trim as was necessary to throw off the after effects of the pneumonia," Kinsey explained. "He

fought with great suffering for four months in the hospital. Man, keep yourself in physical trim, for we must carry on with the things we have started."

76 ACK to Geraldine Voris, Oct. 9, 1940, KIA.
77 ACK to Osmond P. Breland, May 17, 1940.
78 Author's interview with Clyde Martin, April 8, 1971, 1, IUOHP.
79 Ibid., 7.
80 Clyde Martin, "Some Memories of Clyde E. Martin about the Research and Kinsey" (unpublished MS, n.d.), KIA.
81 Author's interview with Martin, April 8, 1971, 4.
82 Martin, "Some Memories," 1.
83 Clyde Martin interviewed on "Sex and the Scientist," PBS, May 21, 1989, WTIU, Bloomington.
84 Martin, "Some Memories," 1. Martin confirmed this point in an interview. "At the time of the interview [Kinsey] did mention something about his earlier background," observed Martin. "As I remember, he admitted something about his own sexual [unintelligible] but I do not recall what the content of that was." See author's interview with Clyde Martin, March 21, 1986, 2.
85 Robert S. Tangeman to Paul H. Gebhard, July 25, 1962, KIA.
86 Martin interviewed on "Sex and the Scientist."
87 Author's interview with Martin, March 21, 1986, 4–5. Among his most vivid memories was Kinsey's description of what happened when he announced he had withdrawn from the Stevens Institute to attend Bowdoin College. Repeating what Kinsey had told him, Martin declared that "there was a dramatic confrontation over it, and his father essentially disowned him." As a result, Kinsey "supported himself through conducting nature programs for summer camps." From there on out, his relationship with his father was essentially nonexistent. "I remember that he did not go to visit his father," Martin recalled. "They were estranged for many years."
88 Martin interviewed on "Sex and the Scientist."
89 Ibid.
90 Author's interview with Anon. B, February 17, 1988, 74–76, 78.
91 Author's interview with Clarence A. Tripp, December 15, 1987, 57–58.
92 Ibid., 16.
93 Ibid., 56.
94 Ibid., 16.
95 Ibid., 57.
96 Author's interview with Anon. B, 1988, 78.
97 Ibid.
98 Author's interview with Tripp, December 15, 1987, 54.
99 Author's interview with Martin, March 21, 1986, 2. Martin had a hard time leaving things at that. Like the apocryphal man who keeps his lips sealed but taps out his message with his fingers, he took an indirect route to convey his fear that people would discover their secrets and that Kinsey's place in history would be destroyed by the revelations. American society, he told me in 1986, "thrives on information and on scandal." As examples, he cited exposés regarding "the case histories of Martina Navratilova, Eleanor Roosevelt [both of whom had been unmasked recently as participants in lesbian relationships], and John Kennedy in the White House," adding, "These things became the focus of attention that tend to dominate other considerations of these individuals and for that reason I think it's counterproductive." Ibid., 13. But, then, Martin had a long history of protecting Kinsey. When I first interviewed

him in 1971, Martin was quite candid about his fear that Kinsey might become the object of crude psychological analysis. Author's conversation with Clyde Martin, April 8, 1971. These remarks were made off tape. Fifteen years later, Martin appeared more at ease. Indeed, he was relaxed enough to confess to something important. He admitted that prior to their first meeting he had walked around for days with his stomach tied in knots, anxious about where the discussion might lead and what he would say if the questioning got personal. Now he was calm and collected, Martin explained, because he knew in advance what he would say: he would refuse to answer any questions about Kinsey's sex life or their private relationship. Author's conversation with Clyde Martin, March 21, 1986. These remarks were made off tape. Martin meant what he said. Asked to respond to a probing question, he replied, "I really don't plan to discuss Kinsey's sex life." Author's interview with Martin, March 21, 1986, 21.

100   Author's interview with Martin, March 21, 1986, 13.

Chapter 17: "The Only Choice That He Could Possibly Make"

1   "Student Evaluations of the Marriage Course (Fall, 1938)," KIA.
2   Author's interview with Kate Hevner Mueller, April 1, 1971, 3–4, IUOHP.
3   Ibid.
4   Author's interview with Edith Schuman, Sept. 15, 1971, 6–7, IUOHP.
5   Ibid., 9.
6   Ibid., 8.
7   Ibid., 6.
8   "Memorandum of Conversation Regarding Marriage Course," Sept. 23, 1939, IUA. Neither the author of the memorandum nor the names of the participants in the conversation are given. Presumably, Mueller was the memorandum's author, and the conversation took place between him and President Wells. See John H. Mueller Papers, "Marriage Course, 1942/43," Folder 9081-24, IUA. Several months later, the sociologists all turned against Kinsey. In January 1940, Edwin H. Sutherland notified Wells, "The staff of the Department, by unanimous vote, has requested its staff members to resign from this course and hereby requests you to accept these resignations and to relieve these members from further duties in connection with the course." To justify this request, Sutherland explained that the sociologists had not been assigned important work in the course. In addition, he declared, "the sociologists share the increasing criticisms of the course with the other participants, although few of the criticisms are directed specifically at the lectures by the sociologists. Since Sociology deals with many delicate problems on which the public is often divided and has much emotional concern, Sociology cannot afford to participate in a venture which involved criticisms on matters which are not the primary concern of Sociology." See Sutherland to Herman B Wells, Jan. 15, 1940, "Marriage Course Files," Herman B Wells Papers, IUA.
9   Author's interview with Schuman, Sept. 15, 1971, 6.
10   Author's interview with Herman B Wells, Dec. 3, 1971, 9–10, IUOHP.
11   Author's interview with Schuman, Sept. 15, 1971, 13.
12   Thurman B. Rice to ACK, Feb. 18, 1939, KIA.
13   Ibid.
14   Ibid.
15   Ibid.
16   Ibid.
17   Ibid.

18　Ibid.

19　Ibid.

20　Ibid. A few years earlier, it seems, Kinsey had cautioned him about the repressive sexual atmosphere that existed on campus under President Bryan. Reminding Kinsey of this incident, Rice concluded by stating he only meant to return the favor in kind. "I appreciated tremendously the warning that you gave me about two years ago, when I was to speak on that subject [sex education] on the campus," he declared. "It was a friendly act and in compensation thereof, I am offering this friendly letter." Here it should also be noted that Rice was not entirely accurate in claiming that Kinsey had not consulted him about the content of the marriage course. A month before the class began, Rice gave Kinsey a number of bulletins and article reprints pertaining to sex education, materials that were sent in obvious response to a request from Kinsey. See Thurman B. Rice to ACK, May 16, 1938, KIA.

21　Author's interview with Mrs. ACK, Dec. 10, 1971, 11–12, IUOHP.

22　ACK to Rice, Feb. 28, 1939.

23　Thurman B. Rice to ACK, March 8, 1939, KIA.

24　Ibid.

25　Ibid.

26　Author's interview with Wells, Dec. 3, 1971, 6.

27　ACK to H. G. Nester, Nov. 21, 1940, KIA. In this letter, Kinsey listed each of these figures by name as "the ones responsible for forcing me out of the Marriage Course at I.U."

28　Author's interview with Robert Kroc, Nov. 7, 1987, 49–51.

29　This account is based largely on material contained in a letter written by Kinsey, in which he summarized his understanding of the demands made by the ministers when they visited Wells. See ACK to Herman B Wells, draft, n.d. [internal evidence suggests the letter was written in summer 1940], KIA. On the top left-hand corner of the first page of this letter, the following notation in Kinsey's handwriting appears: "never sent."

30　Author's interview with Wells, Dec. 3, 1971, 4.

31　A. L. Kohlmeier to Herman B Wells, May 20, 1940, "Marriage Course Files," Herman B Wells Papers, IUA.

32　HBM [Herman B Wells], "Conference with Mrs. [Nellie] Teter and Mrs. [Kate] Briscoe," June 4, 1940, IUA.

33　Kinsey to Wells, undated letter draft. Acknowledging that there had been "some criticism of the biology included in our program," Kinsey stated that these lectures constituted only 35 percent of the material presented in the marriage course, and he reported that "96.7% of the votes from those who have actually taken the course have called for as much biology, or for more biology." In fact, he denied any skewing, noting that a similar course at Vassar College devoted 23 percent of its material to biology, while courses at the University of Iowa and Colgate College assigned 33 percent and 37 percent, respectively. Of course, Kinsey conveniently neglected to mention that what the instructors at these institutions considered biology and what he called biology were not necessarily identical.

34　Ibid.

35　Ibid.

36　Ibid.

37　Ibid.

38　Robert S. Tangeman to Paul H. Gebhard, July 25, 1962, KIA.

39 Thurman B. Rice to ACK, July 11, 1940, KIA.

40 ACK to Thurman B. Rice, July 12, 1940, KIA.

41 Thurman B. Rice to ACK, July 15, 1940, KIA.

42 ACK to Lloyd Messersmith, Aug. 5, 1940, KIA.

43 Anon. to President Herman B Wells, Sept. 7, 1940, KIA.

44 Ibid.

45 ACK to President Herman B Wells, Aug. 7, 1940, KIA.

46 Herman B Wells to ACK, Aug. 8, 1940, KIA. For the terms of the original authorization for the marriage course, see "Minutes of the Board of Trustees, 1938," 259–60, IUA.

47 Author's interview with Wells, Dec. 3, 1971, 13.

48 ACK to Herman B Wells, Sept. 10, 1940, KIA.

49 Wells's reply was terse: "Thank you for your letter of September 10, in which you state your desire to continue the case history studies in connection with the marriage course. I accept your resignation from the course." See Herman B Wells to ACK, Sept. 17, 1940, KIA.

50 Author's interview with Kroc, Nov. 7, 1987, 84.

51 Ibid.

52 Ibid., 85.

53 Ibid., 103.

54 Author's interview with Wells, Dec. 3, 1971, 10.

55 Ibid.

56 Ibid.

57 Author's interview with Mrs. ACK, Dec. 10, 1971, 12.

58 ACK to H. G. Nester, Nov. 21, 1940, KIA.

59 ACK to Glen V. Ramsey, Sept. 20, 1940, KIA.

60 ACK to Osmond P. Breland, Oct. 9, 1940, KIA.

61 Fowler V. Harper to ACK, Nov. 2, 1940, KIA.

62 ACK to Ramsey, Sept. 20, 1940.

63 ACK to Breland, Oct. 9, 1940.

64 Ibid.

Chapter 18: "Unlimited Funds for the Expansion of Our Program"

1 Kinsey to Dr. and Mrs. Ralph Voris, March 29, 1940, KIA.

2 Vern L. Bullough, *Science in the Bedroom: A History of Sex Research* (New York, 1994), 113–16. For a partial history of the CRPS, see Sophie D. Aberle and George W. Corner, *Twenty-five Years of Sex Research: History of the National Research Council Committee for Research in Problems of Sex* (Philadelphia, 1953).

3 Referring to the first third of his life, Yerkes noted in his "Testament," "I followed the religious way of life in conformity with indoctrination and in the steps of my known ancestors." Robert M. Yerkes, "Testament," 378, Series VI, Box 146, Robert M. Yerkes Papers, Yale University Archive, New Haven (hereafter Yerkes Papers).

4 Ibid., 384.

5 Ibid., 371.

6 Ibid., 53.

7 Ibid., 54.

8 Ibid.

9 Ibid.

10 See John C. Burnham, "Yerkes, Robert Mearns," in *Dictionary of Scientific Biography* 14:549–51; Harry Harlow, "Yerkes, Robert M.," in *International Encyclopedia of the Social Sciences,* 16:588.

11 Yerkes, "Testament," 29.

12 Ibid.

13 Robert M. Yerkes to Alan Gregg, Feb. 16, 1935, Box 22, Yerkes Papers.

14 Author's interview with Vincent Nowlis, Jan. 18, 1988, 30–31.

15 "First Annual Report of the Committee for Research in Problems of Sex, March 1, 1923," 7, Committee for Research in Problems of Sex Files, National Research Council Archives, Washington, D.C. (hereafter CRPS Files, NRC Archives)

16 Yerkes, "Testament," 232.

17 "Exhibit A, Eleventh Annual Report of the Committee for Research in Problems of Sex, July 1, 1931 to June 30, 1932," 30–31, CRPS Files, NRC Archives.

18 Yerkes, "Testament," 232.

19 Alan Gregg to Robert M. Yerkes, Jan. 17, 1941, Series 200, Box 39, Folder 442, Rockefeller Archives Center, Hillcrest, Pocantico Hills, North Tarrytown, N.Y. (hereafter Rockefeller Archives).

20 Ibid.

21 "Twentieth Annual Report of the Committee for Research in Problems of Sex, July 1, 1940 to June 30, 1941," 1–2, CRPS Files, NRC Archives.

22 Ibid., 2.

23 ACK to Ross G. Harrison, Dec. 7, 1940, CRPS Files, NRC Archives.

24 Yerkes later wrote, "I should confess that when . . . I first read a description of the project and of the proposed method of inquiry, I was considerably prejudiced against it because of my extensive experience as experimentalist, objectivist, and naturalist with the shortcomings of the interview." Whether done in person or by questionnaire, Yerkes continued, interviewing "has serious limitations, ordinarily yields results of low reliability, and is especially subject to impressional and other types of subjective error." Robert M. Yerkes to Lewis H. Weed, Jan. 26, 1946, CRPS Files, NRC Archives.

25 Ibid. Kinsey also enclosed a copy of his first major article on sex research, "Criteria for a Hormonal Explanation of the Homosexual," which appeared a few months later in the *Journal of Clinical Endocrinology* 1 (May 1941): 424–28. This article is discussed later in the text. Robert M. Yerkes to ACK, Dec. 17, 1940, CRPS Files, NRC Archives.

26 ACK to Harrison, Dec. 7, 1940. In a similar letter to the Brush Foundation, Kinsey again dated the origins of his involvement with the field back to his adolescence. "My interest in human sex behavior originates in nearly thirty years of contact with human problems at the secondary and college level, including continuous contact with the sex instruction program in the high schools." Emphasizing the social relevance of his research, Kinsey added, "The data already obtained indicate that many of our current physiologic explanations, psychologic theories, and sociologic interpretations do not begin to fit the actuality in human behavior." See ACK to W. Greulich, June 20, 1940, KIA.

27 ACK to Osmond P. Breland, Feb. 14, 1941, KIA.

28 ACK to Glenn V. Ramsey, Feb. 21, 1941, KIA. Taking his own advice, Kinsey decided to reduce his involvement with sex education in order to concentrate on research. As he told a high school teacher in Indiana, "The demands on my time for outside lectures are so great that I have to put limitations on them. I, therefore, limit myself to accepting those invitations that are willing to pay the minimum university fee of $15, or to lecture before audiences which contribute to my case history studies in the human sex

behavior." With regard to groups that promised histories, he declared, "I can come and lecture to any group anywhere in the state that guarantees 25 or more histories." Kinsey was frank about the reason for this policy. "More important than sex education right now is further study of the facts of human sex behavior." See ACK to Elmer Weber, Feb. 10, 1941, KIA.

29   ACK, "Homosexuality: Criteria for a Hormonal Explanation of the Homosexual," *Journal of Clinical Endocrinology* 1 (May 1941): 424–28.

30   S. J. Glass, H. J. Deuel, and C. A. Wright, "Sex Hormone Studies in Male Homosexuality," *Endocrinology* 26 (1940): 590–94.

31   ACK, "Homosexuality," 425.

32   Ibid., 425–28.

33   ACK to Glenn V. Ramsey, Jan. 13, 1941, KIA. The following month, Kinsey discussed this paper with a group of psychologists at Indiana University. Afterward, he told a friend that the psychologists had "expressed considerable pleasure at our conclusions." In addition, the session apparently helped win over an administrator whose support Kinsey needed. "Dr. Payne came to hear the paper and indicated his complete agreement with my conclusions, and he went out of his way to indicate that he now understood the objectives of the study and the significance of the exploration of the fact," wrote Kinsey. See ACK to Glenn V. Ramsey, Feb. 7, 1941, KIA.

34   ACK to Ramsey, Jan. 13, 1941. Referring to Yerkes's positive reactions, Kinsey told another friend, "That has added a great deal to the awakened interest of Dr. Payne and recently of President Wells in this study, and things begin to look easier for us." ACK to Breland, Feb. 14, 1941.

35   Robert M. Yerkes to ACK, Jan. 4, 1941, KIA.

36   Ibid.

37   ACK to Robert M. Yerkes, Jan. 14, 1941, KIA. Responding to Yerkes's concern that 20,000 histories were not needed, Kinsey trimmed his sails without conceding the point entirely, declaring, "I think a program of 10,000 cases as an objective would be a good one to start with now."

38   Commenting on the importance of this change, Clyde Martin observed, "The shift was very helpful in many ways for it meant that more close attention had to be paid to securing in the interview age at onset and early, as well as late, frequencies in order to incorporate changes in frequency over time. Simply, these two statistical requirements did a great deal to focus the questioning in a way that revealed new aspects of the life history, especially the picture over the course of marriage." Quoted in Cornelia V. Christenson, *Kinsey: A Biography* (Bloomington, 1971), 121.

39   Robert M. Yerkes to ACK, May 5, 1941, KIA. It is worth noting that this grant, as well as all the NRC grants that followed, was made to Indiana University, not to Kinsey directly. Although his relations with the fiscal officers and accountants of the university were occasionally strained, this arrangement proved to be advantageous for Kinsey. Not only did it offer him excellent bookkeeping and accounting services, but it placed the university between him and the vast sums of money appropriated for his research. Since he supplied the university each year with an itemized account of expenditures, the complete financial record of his research was a matter of public record. Any balance at the end of the fiscal year reverted to the NRC. Kinsey's ability to account for every cent helped to answer public and private critics when a congressional investigating committee later threatened to review his financial operations during the McCarthy era.

40   ACK to Robert M. Yerkes, May 14, 1941, KIA.

41   Herman B Wells to ACK, June 14, 1941, KIA.

42   ACK to Robert L. Dickinson, June 23, 1941, KIA. Kinsey informed Dickinson, "The National Research Council's Committee on Sex has given us $1,600 for next year and the University has made $1,200 more available so the work will be expanded next year."

43   ACK to Herman B Wells, Sept. 16, 1941, KIA; Herman B Wells to ACK, Sept. 22, 1941, KIA.

44   Herman T. Briscoe, "To Whom It May Concern," Nov. 12, 1941, KIA.

45   ACK to Glenn V. Ramsey, Nov. 6, 1941, KIA. For another discussion of this incident, see Wardell B. Pomeroy, *Dr. Kinsey and the Institute for Sex Research* (New York, 1972), 128.

46   Robert M. Yerkes to ACK, Feb. 9, 1942, KIA.

47   ACK, "Studies in Human Sex Behavior: Progress Report, Projected Program, 1942–3," March 1942, KIA.

48   Ibid.

49   Ibid.

50   Author's interview with Robert Kroc, Nov. 7, 1987, 56–58.

51   ACK to Robert M. Yerkes, March 24, 1942, KIA.

52   Robert M. Yerkes to ACK, April 28, 1942, KIA.

53   ACK to Clara Kinsey et al., quoted in Pomeroy, *Dr. Kinsey,* 92.

54   For a charming self-portrait, see George W. Corner, *The Seven Ages of a Medical Scientist: An Autobiography* (Philadelphia, 1981).

55   Author's interview with George W. Corner, Aug. 5, 1971, 6, IUOHP.

56   Ibid., 4.

57   Ibid., 5.

58   Diary of Robert M. Yerkes, Dec. 4, 1942, Box 173, Folder 2671, Yerkes Papers.

59   Author's interview with Corner, Aug. 5, 1971, 6.

60   Diary of Yerkes, Dec. 5, 1942.

61   Diary of Yerkes, Dec. 6, 1942.

62   George W. Corner, *The Seven Ages of a Medical Scientist,* 314.

63   Author's interview with Corner, Aug. 5, 1971, 5, 6, 25.

64   Diary of Yerkes, Dec. 7, 1942.

65   Robert M. Yerkes to Lewis H. Weed, Jan. 26, 1946, CRPS Files, NRC Archives.

66   Diary of Yerkes, Dec. 8, 1942.

67   George W. Corner to Robert M. Yerkes, Dec. 22, 1942, CRPS Files, NRC Archives.

68   Lowell J. Reed to Robert M. Yerkes, Dec. 22, 1942, CRPS Files, NRC Archives.

69   Author's interview with Corner, Aug. 5, 1971, 11, 12, 28, 29.

70   Ibid., 12, 29.

71   ACK to Robert E. Bugbee, Dec. 11, 1941, KIA. Breaking this figure into annual installments, he told Bugbee a month later, "[W]e will go on a budget of twenty-to-twenty-five thousand dollars per year for an indefinite number of years in the future. That shows their estimate of the importance of what we have and can do." ACK to Robert E. Bugbee, Jan. 19, 1942, KIA.

72   ACK to Herman T. Briscoe, Dec. 11, 1942, KIA.

73   ACK to Robert E. Bugbee, Dec. 11, 1942, KIA.

74   Desk diary of Alan Gregg, Jan. 14, 1943, Series 200, Box 39, Folder 443, Rockefeller Archives.

75   The story of the Rockefeller Foundation's support for the natural sciences is ably told by Gerald Jonas, *The Circuit Riders: Rockefeller Money and the Rise of Modern Science* (New York, 1989).

76 ACK to Robert M. Yerkes, April 5, 1943, KIA.
77 Robert M. Yerkes to ACK, May 18, 1943, KIA.
78 Robert M. Yerkes, "Minutes of Conference on Patterns and Problems of Primate Sex-Behavior," Aug. 28–29, 1943, CRPS Files, NRC Archives.
79 Author's interview with Frank A. Beach, Aug. 20, 1971, 5, IUOHP.
80 Ibid., 5–6.
81 Yerkes, "Minutes of Conference."
82 ACK to Osmond P. Breland, Sept. 18, 1943, KIA.
83 Robert M. Yerkes to ACK, Sept. 25, 1943, KIA. To bolster his argument, Yerkes took a page from history. "It was one of Freud's irreparable errors to base his statements of fact, inferences, and generalizations too largely on subjects either on the psychopathic fringe or definitely abnormal," asserted Yerkes. "Safety for you, as in my opinion was true for Freud also," he continued, "lies in limiting your initial inquiry to those individuals who are modal, both structurally and functionally."
84 ACK to Robert M. Yerkes, Sept. 28, 1943, KIA.
85 Robert M. Yerkes to ACK, Oct. 18, 1943, KIA.

Chapter 19: "To Deal Directly with the Rockefeller Foundation"

1 Author's interview with Robert S. Morison, Oct. 18, 1971, 3, IUOHP.
2 Alan Gregg, *The Furtherance of Medical Research* (New Haven, 1941), 23–24.
3 Desk diary of Alan Gregg, Sept. 3, 1943, Series 200, Box 40, Folder 457, Rockefeller Archives. Following his meeting with Kinsey, Gregg wrote his fellow Harvard alum Yerkes a glowing report, declaring, "It would appear that among the excellencies of William Morton Wheeler that of having a first-rate pupil was one." Warming to the topic, Gregg confessed that he found portions of Kinsey's statistical analyses "quite remarkable" and the thoroughness of his studies "entirely exceptional." Alan Gregg to Robert M. Yerkes, Sept. 7, 1943, Series 200, Box 39, Folder 443, Rockefeller Archives.
4 ACK to Herman B Wells, Oct. 21, 1943, KIA.
5 Frank S. Hackett to Frank Milam, July 10, 1944, Series 200, Box 40, Folder 457, Rockefeller Archives.
6 Ibid.
7 Frank Milam to Dr. [?] McIntosh, July 17, 1944, ibid.
8 Robert A. Lambert to Frank Milam, July 21, 1944, ibid.
9 Robert A. Lambert to Alan Gregg, July 21, 1944, ibid.
10 Alan Gregg to Robert A. Lambert, July 25, 1944, ibid.
11 Alan Gregg to Robert M. Yerkes, July 31, 1944, ibid.
12 Robert M. Yerkes to ACK, Aug. 17, 1944, KIA.
13 ACK to Robert M. Yerkes, Aug. 21, 1944, KIA.
14 Robert M. Yerkes to ACK, Aug. 23, 1944, KIA. "The National Research Council, through its Committee for Research in Problems of Sex, is giving financial support to your work," declared Yerkes, "whereas the Rockefeller Foundation, so far as I know, has never been requested to support it and has no responsibility in connection with it."
15 ACK to Alan Gregg, Aug. 26, 1944, Series 200, Box 40, Folder 457, Rockefeller Archives.
16 Ibid.
17 Ibid.
18 Ibid.
19 Alan Gregg to ACK, Sept. 8, 1944, ibid.

20 Ibid.

21 Robert M. Yerkes to Alan Gregg, Sept. 9, 1944, Series 200, Box 39, Folder 444, Rockefeller Archives.

22 ACK to Alan Gregg, Sept. 25, 1944, Series 200, Box 40, Folder 457, Rockefeller Archives.

23 Alan Gregg to ACK, March 7, 1945, "Dr. A. C. Kinsey, RSM [Robert S. Morison]— lunch," ibid. Stressing that they had lunched at Gregg's invitation, Kinsey reported to Yerkes, "He [Gregg] has a very clear understanding of the research and seems thoroughly convinced of the importance of our expanded program." ACK to Robert M. Yerkes, March 28, 1945, KIA.

24 Robert M. Yerkes to Alan Gregg, June 12, 1945, Series 200, Box 39, Folder 444, Rockefeller Archives.

25 Alan Gregg to Robert M. Yerkes, June 14, 1945, ibid.

26 Robert M. Yerkes to Alan Gregg, July 17, 1945, Series 200, Box 40, Folder 457, Rockefeller Archives. This letter contains a detailed summary of the Philadelphia meeting between Yerkes and Kinsey.

27 Alan Gregg to Robert M. Yerkes, Aug. 30, 1945, ibid.

28 Author's interview with George W. Corner, Aug. 5, 1971, 16, IUOHP.

29 Lewis H. Weed to Robert M. Yerkes, Jan. 10, 1946, National Research Council Central File, Medical Science Division, 1946, NRC Archives.

30 Ibid. Gregg's desk diary offers a somewhat different account of what was said at the meeting: "I said that I thought we would be prepared to make an additional grant for Kinsey's work to cover his need for 1946–47 and possibly a longer period." See desk diary of Gregg, Jan. 9, 1946, Series 200, Box 40, Folder 457, Rockefeller Archives. Still, Weeds's version is the one that got enacted.

31 Lewis H. Weed to Alan Gregg, Feb. 4, 1946, Series 200, Box 39, Folder 445, Rockefeller Archives.

32 Lewis H. Weed to Alan Gregg, Feb. 5, 1946, Series 200, Box 40, Folder 457, Rockefeller Archives.

33 Karl S. Lashley to Robert M. Yerkes, Dec. 31, 1945, CRPS Files, NRC Archives.

34 See John Romano to Robert M. Yerkes, Jan. 28, 1946, CRPS Files, NRC Archives. Yerkes replied that he, too, had once doubted Kinsey's ability to obtain the truth by means of oral interviews. "Naturally those of us who have had several years' acquaintance with the work have passed through something more or less like your present state of mind," wrote Yerkes soothingly. Indeed, Yerkes freely confessed that at first he, too, "was strongly prejudiced against the method of interview, whether used direct or by questionnaire." What made the difference, he explained, was the chance to watch Kinsey perform. "As opportunity to observe Kinsey in action and to study both his method and his results critically were afforded me, my judgment changed in his favor and I am now a strong supporter of the undertaking," wrote Yerkes. "Kinsey has the best interview scheme and recording procedure that I have ever met and he is by a long way the best interviewer I chance to have known." Ignoring Lashley's objections, Yerkes noted, "Actually every member of the Committee except yourself has unreservedly approved the proposal that we recommend to the National Research Council request to the Rockefeller Foundation that $120,000 be made available for support of the Kinsey project during a three-year period." See Robert M. Yerkes to John Romano, Jan. 30, 1946, CRPS Files, NRC Archives.

35 Robert M. Yerkes to Alan Gregg, Feb. 8, 1946, Series 200, Box 39, Folder 445, Rockefeller Archives.

36 Alan Gregg to ACK, April 8, 1946, Series 200, Box 40, Folder 457, Rockefeller Archives.
37 Author's interview with Herman B Wells, Dec. 3, 1971, 18–19, IUOHP.
38 Ibid., 19.
39 Robert M. Yerkes to George W. Corner, July 12, 1946, CRPS Files, NRC Archives.
40 Desk diary of Gregg, Dec. 19, 1946, Series 200, Box 40, Folder 457, Rockefeller Archives.
41 Ibid.
42 Ibid.
43 ACK to Robert M. Yerkes, Dec. 23, 1946, KIA. Kinsey told Yerkes, "You and your committee have served us very well and deserve considerable credit for helping us along to this stage. The question now arises whether a committee constituted as the reorganized committee is in Washington can be of such importance in the future."
44 Robert M. Yerkes to ACK, Dec. 30, 1946, KIA.
45 ACK to Alan Gregg, Jan. 7, 1947, KIA.
46 Desk diary of Gregg, Feb. 6, 1947, Series 200, Box 40, Folder 458, Rockefeller Archives.
47 Ibid.
48 Ibid.
49 Ibid.
50 Ibid., Feb. 7, 1947.
51 Ibid.
52 Ibid.
53 Ibid.
54 "Articles of Incorporation for the Organization of the Institute for Sex Research," Indiana Department of State, KIA.
55 ACK to Robert M. Yerkes, April 11, 1947, KIA.
56 ACK to Robert M. Yerkes, April 23, 1947, KIA.
57 Herman B Wells to Alan Gregg, May 23, 1947, KIA.
58 Herman B Wells to Norma S. Thompson, Oct. 24, 1947, Rockefeller Archives.
59 Diary of Robert M. Yerkes, April 27, 1947, Box 174, Folder 2677, Yerkes Papers.
60 Author's interview with Corner, Aug. 5, 1971, 19.
61 George W. Corner to ACK, April 29, 1947, KIA.
62 Author's interview with Corner, Aug. 5, 1971, 12–13.
63 ACK to Robert M. Yerkes, May 7, 1947, KIA.
64 George W. Corner to Alan Gregg, May 13, 1947, CRPS Files, NRC Archives.
65 Desk diary of Gregg, May 29, 1947, Series 200, Box 40, Folder 458, Rockefeller Archives.
66 George W. Corner to Lewis H. Weed, May 31, 1947, CRPS Files, NRC Archives.
67 Diary of Yerkes, July 7, 1947.
68 "Interoffice Correspondence," Robert S. Morison to Alan Gregg, June 26, 1947, Series 200, Box 40, Folder 458, Rockefeller Archives.
69 Alan Gregg to W. D. Asfahl, Oct. 23, 1947, ibid.

Chapter 20: "WE CANNOT USE ANYONE WHO IS AFRAID OF SEX"

1 Edgar Anderson to ACK, July 16, 1941, KIA.
2 See author's interview with Robert E. Bugbee, Oct. 19, 1971, 22, IUOHP.
3 ACK to Fowler Harper, Oct. 14, 1946, KIA.

4 Robert M. Yerkes to Ross G. Harrison, July 6, 1942, KIA.
5 Author's interview with Clyde Martin, April 8, 1971, 5, IUOHP.
6 Ibid., 33.
7 ACK to Robert M. Yerkes, March 22, 1941, KIA.
8 Quoted in Wardell B. Pomeroy, *Dr. Kinsey and the Institute for Sex Research* (New York, 1972), 89.
9 ACK to Robert M. Yerkes, June 4, 1942, KIA.
10 Author's interview with Wardell Pomeroy, July 19, 1971, 23, IUOHP.
11 Author's interview with Martin, April 8, 1971, 36.
12 ACK to Glenn V. Ramsey, Feb. 19, 1941, KIA. The following month, Kinsey reported, "Martin and I are doing the most stupendous piece of work we have undertaken yet. We are transferring something around six hundred items from the histories to punched cards to be run through our statistical machine. It is a very slow process, but when we get this set of cards done, we will have all the data that will have a bearing on marital adjustment ready for instant analysis." See ACK to Glenn V. Ramsey, March 28, 1941, KIA.
13 ACK to Ramsey, Feb. 19, 1941.
14 Author's interview with Glenn V. Ramsey, March 15, 1972, 4–5, IUOHP.
15 Ibid., 6.
16 Ibid., 9.
17 ACK, "Homosexuality: Criteria for a Hormonal Explanation of the Homosexual," *Journal of Clinical Endocrinology* 1 (May 1941): 425.
18 ACK to Glenn V. Ramsey, Sept. 20, 1940, KIA. In the years ahead, this was precisely what Kinsey did. He became quite adept at using people's organizational affiliations to bring in large numbers of histories.
19 The financial terms of their arrangement are discussed in ACK to Glenn V. Ramsey, Jan. 11, 1942, KIA; for Kinsey's job offer to Ramsey, see ACK to Glenn V. Ramsey, March 21, 1941, KIA.
20 Glenn V. Ramsey to ACK, May 10, 1940, KIA.
21 Author's interview with Ramsey, March 15, 1972, 14.
22 Glenn V. Ramsey to ACK, Jan. 13, 1942, KIA. The next day, Ramsey wrote to say that the lawyers also asked the boys if he had shown dirty pictures or asked them to undress. In addition, he stated that the attorneys appeared to be especially interested in what he had said about masturbation. See Glenn V. Ramsey to ACK, Jan. 14, 1942, KIA.
23 ACK to Glenn V. Ramsey, Dec. 23, 1941, KIA.
24 ACK to Anon., Jan. 23, 1942, KIA.
25 Author's interview with Ramsey, March 15, 1972, 15.
26 ACK to Glenn V. Ramsey, Jan. 11, 1942. Acting on that sense of responsibility, Kinsey later asked Yerkes for permission to use CRPS grant funds to pay Ramsey's legal expenses ($150) in the case, stressing that he would pay the expenses himself if the committee thought best. Following Yerkes's recommendation, the CRPS approved this request, despite the fact that such an expenditure was totally unprecedented. Kinsey would take the CRPS into uncharted territory often in the years ahead. See ACK to Robert M. Yerkes, June 10, 1942, KIA; Robert M. Yerkes to ACK, July 6, 1942, KIA.
27 Author's interview with Ramsey, March 15, 1972, 21.
28 Ibid., 20. Later in the interview, Ramsey returned to this point, declaring, "[Kinsey] knew that if there was any questionable behavior on the part of any staff member that

deviated from the community standards that this would get him in trouble." See ibid., 43.

29 Ibid., 16–17.

30 Ibid., 18.

31 Ibid., 21–22.

32 Ibid., 23. Ramsey went on to explain, "I personally felt that a scientific investigation of human sexual behavior was far overdue, because as a psychologist with clinical experience I have seen many sexual tragedies, [and] as an educator I have seen many of the areas where lack of knowledge was damaging to human lives."

33 For an excellent study of how gays fared in the military during the Second World War, see Allan Berube, *Coming Out under Fire: The History of Gay Men and Women in World War Two* (New York, 1990). During the course of the war, Kinsey consulted with the military on several occasions and tried, without much luck, to influence the policy on a number of issues, including the treatment of homosexuals. Nor was he able to forge an agreement that would have allowed him to interview men and women in the military, largely because the issue of confidentiality could not be guaranteed.

34 ACK to Robert M. Yerkes, June 4, 1942, KIA.

35 ACK to Anon., Feb. 5, 1946, KIA.

36 ACK to Benjamin Gruenberg, Feb. 3, 1941, KIA.

37 ACK to Anon., Feb. 5, 1946.

38 ACK to Frank A. Beach, Dec. 27, 1944, KIA.

39 *Indianapolis Eastern Sun,* Nov. 8, 1956, clipping files, KIA.

40 Anon. to ACK, Jan. 18, 1946, KIA.

41 Author's interview with Mrs. ACK, Dec. 10, 1971, 20, IUOHP.

42 ACK to Anon., Jan. 21, 1947, KIA.

43 Ibid., 13.

44 Author's interview with Mrs. ACK, Dec. 10, 1971, 21, 17.

45 Ibid., 21.

46 ACK to Anon., Nov. 2, 1945, KIA.

47 ACK to Anon., Nov. 14, 1944, KIA.

48 ACK to Anon., Feb. 26, 1946, KIA.

49 ACK to Anon., Nov. 14, 1944.

50 ACK to Anon., May 2, 1946, KIA.

51 ACK to Benjamin Gruenberg, Feb. 3, 1941.

52 ACK to Anon., Feb. 26, 1946, KIA.

53 ACK to Anon., Jan. 6, 1949, KIA.

54 ACK to Robert M. Yerkes, April 16, 1943, KIA.

55 Pomeroy, *Dr. Kinsey,* 107.

56 Ibid., 101.

57 Robert M. Yerkes to ACK, July 20, 1945, KIA.

58 Pomeroy, *Dr. Kinsey,* 97.

59 Ibid., 98.

60 Author's interview with Clarence A. Tripp, Dec. 15, 1987, 59, 60.

61 Pomeroy, *Dr. Kinsey,* 99.

62 Ibid.

63 Ibid., 104.

64 Author's interview with Pomeroy, July 19, 1971, 3.

65 Pomeroy, *Dr. Kinsey,* 105.
66 Ibid., 107.
67 Ibid., 106.
68 Ibid.
69 ACK to Robert M. Yerkes, April 5, 1943, KIA.
70 Author's interview with Martin, April 8, 1971, 6.
71 ACK to Robert M. Yerkes, Feb. 18, 1944, KIA.
72 ACK to Robert E. Bugbee, Jan. 19, 1942, KIA.
73 Author's interview with Bugbee, Oct. 19, 1971, 6.
74 ACK to Anon., April 2, 1943, KIA.
75 Anon. to ACK, April 10, 1943, KIA.
76 ACK to Mr. W. J. Belleau, May 11, 1943, KIA.
77 Ibid.
78 Pomeroy, *Dr. Kinsey,* 126, 127.
79 ACK to Robert E. Bugbee, Aug. 24, 1943, KIA.
80 Robert E. Bugbee to ACK, Aug. 26, 1943, KIA.
81 Author's interview with Bugbee, Oct. 19, 1971, 16.
82 Ibid., 7, 16, 18.
83 Ibid., 21–24.
84 Ibid., 20–21.
85 Ibid., 10.
86 Ibid.
87 Ibid., 13.
88 Without going into details, Kinsey informed Yerkes that Bugbee "did not succeed as a field man as we had hoped he would." See ACK to Robert M. Yerkes, March 28, 1945, KIA.
89 ACK to Robert M. Yerkes, April 5, 1943, KIA; Robert M. Yerkes to ACK, April 10, 1943, KIA.
90 Author's interview with Vincent Nowlis, Jan. 18, 1988, 55–57.
91 Ibid.
92 Ibid., 61.
93 Ibid., 11–12, 62.
94 Ibid., 94–96.
95 Ibid., 85.
96 Ibid., 22.
97 Ibid., 72, 77.
98 Ibid., 109, 66, 108.
99 Ibid., 101, 67, 104–5, 116.
100 Ibid., 116, 140, 103.
101 Vincent Nowlis to Robert M. Yerkes, Oct. 21, 1944, Box 38, Folder 715, Yerkes Papers.
102 ACK to Robert M. Yerkes, Oct. 26, 1944, KIA.
103 Robert M. Yerkes to Vincent Nowlis, Nov. 24, 1944, Box 38, Folder 715, Yerkes Papers.
104 Vincent Nowlis to Robert M. Yerkes, Dec. 12, 1944, ibid.
105 Aware of Yerkes's interest in Nowlis, Kinsey went out of his way to praise Nowlis's skill at crunching numbers. "He has contributed very definitely in the analyses of our data," declared Kinsey. See ACK to Robert M. Yerkes, March 28, 1945, KIA.

106 ACK to Robert M. Yerkes, Feb. 6, 1945, KIA.

107 Author's interview with Nowlis, Jan. 18, 1988, 107.

108 Vincent Nowlis to Robert M. Yerkes, Jan. 2, 1946, KIA. Relieved to have the matter resolved, Yerkes responded with "warm congratulations," telling his former student, "You are going to a great university which undoubtedly can and will offer you incomparable opportunities." Now that Nowlis had secured another position, Yerkes felt free to request a favor. "I very much wish, for many reasons, that we might have opportunity to discuss, face to face and on the basis of our quite different but intimate knowledge, methodological and other important aspects of the Kinsey project," he wrote. The exchange he sought, insisted Yerkes, was "not a matter for correspondence since there would be too great risk of misunderstanding because of partial and incomplete statement." Instead, if they could arrange to meet, Yerkes requested "a conference appointment" anytime in the next months. It is not clear whether such a meeting ever took place. See Robert M. Yerkes to Vincent Nowlis, Jan. 7, 1946, Box 38, Folder 715, Yerkes Papers.

109 Author's interview with Nowlis, Jan. 18, 1988, 143.

110 Ibid., 98.

111 ACK to Anon., April 1, 1946, KIA.

112 ACK to Anon., Aug. 27, 1946, KIA.

113 ACK to Frederick C. Thorne, Nov. 2, 1945, KIA.

114 Clyde Kluckhohn to ACK, May 20, 1946, KIA.

115 Author's interview with Paul H. Gebhard, Oct. 29, 1971, 5, IUOHP.

116 ACK to Paul H. Gebhard, May 25, 1946, KIA.

117 Paul H. Gebhard to ACK, May 30, 1946, KIA. Gebhard's interviewing experience was extensive. During his graduate school days, he had conducted "about 700 interviews of one sort or another" at the Massachusetts General Hospital. See author's interview with Gebhard, Oct. 29, 1971, 12–14.

118 Author's interview with Gebhard, Oct. 29, 1971.

119 Ibid., 15.

120 Ibid., 16.

121 Ibid., 16–17.

122 Ibid., 17, 22.

123 Ibid., 17–18. In describing this exchange, Gebhard put Kinsey's offer at $4,500, but the official letter from the administration of Indiana University approving the offer stipulated $4,400. See H. T. Briscoe to ACK, July 12, 1946, KIA.

124 Author's interview with Gebhard, Oct. 29, 1971, 21.

125 Ibid., 20, 22.

126 Ibid., 22–23.

127 Ibid., 23, 64.

128 Ibid., 64–65.

129 Ibid., 23.

130 Pomeroy, *Dr. Kinsey,* 6.

131 Author's interview with Paul H. Gebhard, Oct. 14, 1984, 19.

132 Ibid., 6, 18.

133 Ibid., 6.

134 Author's interview with Clyde Martin, March 21, 1986, 21.

135 Pomeroy, *Dr. Kinsey,* 161–62. This quotation has Pomeroy paraphrasing what Nowlis said.

Chapter 21: "A REPORT ON WHAT PEOPLE DO"

1 Author's interview with Paul H. Gebhard, Oct. 14, 1984, 5.
2 Author's interview with Vincent Nowlis, Jan. 18, 1988, 81.
3 Author's conversation with Frank Beach, Nov. 29, 1983.
4 Ibid.
5 Wardell B. Pomeroy, *Dr. Kinsey and the Institute for Sex Research* (New York, 1972), 173.
6 Author's interview with Nowlis, Jan. 18, 1988, 79.
7 Author's interview with Clyde Martin, March 21, 1986, 24.
8 James Reed, *From Private Vice to Public Virtue: The Birth Control Movement and American Society since 1830* (New York, 1978), 163, 190.
9 Ibid., 159.
10 Quoted in ibid., 162.
11 Quoted in ibid., 157.
12 Ibid., 158.
13 Quoted in Cornelia V. Christenson, *Kinsey: A Biography* (Bloomington, 1971), 96.
14 Quoted in Reed, *From Private Vice,* 149, 167.
15 ACK to Robert L. Dickinson, Feb. 3, 1943, KIA.
16 Robert L. Dickinson to Alan Gregg, Jan. 13, 1943, Series 200, Box 40, Folder 457, Rockefeller Archives. Dickinson sent Kinsey a copy of this letter, and Kinsey was grateful. "Thanks very much for the contact you made for me with the Rockefeller Foundation," he replied. "I deeply appreciate your interest in acting for me." See ACK to Dickinson, Feb. 3, 1943.
17 Pomeroy, *Dr. Kinsey,* 122.
18 ACK to Mr. X, Nov. 3, 1943, KIA.
19 ACK to Mr. X, Nov. 18, 1943, KIA.
20 ACK to Mr. X, May 24, 1944, KIA.
21 ACK to Mr. X, May 6, 1944, KIA.
22 Pomeroy, *Dr. Kinsey,* 122.
23 ACK to Mr. X, Nov. 24, 1944, KIA.
24 ACK to Mr. X, June 12, 1944, KIA.
25 ACK to Mr. X, Aug. 1, 1944, KIA.
26 ACK to Mr. X, March 29, 1945, KIA.
27 ACK to Mr. X, July 12, 1945, KIA.
28 ACK to Mr. X, Dec. 24, 1946, KIA.
29 ACK to Mr. X, March 12, 1947, KIA.
30 Pomeroy, *Dr. Kinsey,* 122.
31 *SBHM,* 160, 180.
32 Ibid., 161.
33 Judith A. Reisman and J. Gordon Muir, "Male Child Sexuality," in Judith Reisman and Edward W. Eichel, *Kinsey, Sex and Fraud: The Indoctrination of a People,* ed. J. Gordon Muir and John H. Court (Lafayette, La., 1990), 33. Decades after his death, the authors and editors of this book, conservative critics all, revisited Kinsey's data on preadolescent male sexuality, charging that he and his coworkers may have witnessed or personally participated in child molestation under the guise of scientific research. Unless new evidence to the contrary becomes available, these charges must be considered groundless. No evidence has come to light to suggest that Kinsey or any member of

his staff ever committed child abuse or observed child sex abuse in person. All that can be safely said is that Kinsey and the members of his inner circle knew pedophiles, interviewed them, and accepted data from them. Kinsey and his colleagues, in keeping with their revolutionary social agenda, expressed tolerance for adult-child sexual contacts, arguing that cases had to be evaluated on an individual basis. Critics may fault Kinsey for not turning known pedophiles over to the police, but exposing sex offenders was not the goal of his research. Many of the subjects he interviewed had engaged in illegal behavior. As Pomeroy has noted, "Ultimately, Kinsey concluded, nearly every individual was involved—and most were regularly involved—in sexual behavior which at some point or other was contrary to the law." Pomeroy, *Dr. Kinsey,* 209. Had Kinsey exposed any of them, he would have violated his pledge of confidentiality, and no one with anything to hide would have consented to be interviewed again. In short, his sources would have dried up and along with them his research.

34 Author's interview with Gebhard, Oct. 14, 1984, 29–30.
35 Author's interview with Nowlis, Jan. 18, 1988, 168.
36 Ibid., 167.
37 Ibid.
38 Pomeroy, *Dr. Kinsey,* 198.
39 Anon. to Dean of Women, Jan. 22, 1945, Herman B Wells Papers, IUA.
40 Kate Hevner Mueller to Herman B Wells, Jan. 25, 1945, ibid. Wells wrote a note on Mueller's letter stating that he wished to meet with her, Dean Herman T. Briscoe, Fernandus Payne, and Ross Bartley. Another note on the same letter records that the meeting was held on Jan. 30, 1945. While no minutes of this meeting have survived, it seems likely that they agreed that Kinsey should be counseled on the matter.
41 Ross Bartley to Herman B Wells, Jan. 27, 1945, ibid.
42 Author's interview with Kate Hevner Mueller, April 1, 1971, 4, 5.
43 Ibid., 5–6.
44 Ibid., 9.
45 Ibid.
46 Ibid., 10.
47 Fernandus Payne to Herman B Wells, April 10, 1945, Herman B Wells Papers, IUA.
48 ACK, "Studies in Human Sex Behavior, Annual Report, March, 1942," 3–4, KIA.
49 ACK, "Studies in Human Sex Behavior, Progress Report, April 1, 1945," 16–17, KIA.
50 At the end of 1944, Kinsey had collected a total of 5,408 histories, of which 3,643 were male and 1,865 were female. Ibid., 13.
51 Robert M. Yerkes to ACK, June 19, 1945, KIA.
52 Quoted in Pomeroy, *Dr. Kinsey,* 217.
53 Ibid., 260–61.
54 Robert M. Yerkes to ACK, Aug. 27, 1945, KIA; ACK to Robert M. Yerkes, Sept. 4, 1945, KIA.
55 *SBHM,* 6.
56 Ibid., 7, 5, 8.
57 Paul Robinson, *The Modernization of Sex: Havelock Ellis, Alfred Kinsey, and William Masters and Virginia Johnson* (New York, 1976), 49–50. Robinson's analysis of what he calls the "presuppositions, tensions, biases, and implications" of Kinsey's writings can only be described as brilliant. My own discussion draws heavily on his insights and interpretations.
58 Author's interview with Paul H. Gebhard, Oct. 29, 1971, 44, 78, IUOHP.

59 Ibid., 44.
60 Author's interview with Gebhard, Oct. 14, 1984, 27.
61 *SBHM*, 445, 385.
62 Ibid., 42.
63 Author's interview with Gebhard, Oct. 29, 1971, 79.
64 *SBHM*, 329, 224.
65 Ibid., 9–11, 16–34.
66 Ibid., 35–62, 63–119, 153.
67 Ibid., 33–34, 152–53, 176, 195, 395.
68 Robinson, *Modernization of Sex*, 62–66.
69 *SBHM*, 194, 195.
70 Ibid., 197.
71 Ibid., 178.
72 Ibid., 164.
73 Ibid., 168, 170.
74 Ibid., 177, 205–13.
75 Ibid., 235.
76 Ibid., 223.
77 Ibid., 472.
78 Ibid., 483.
79 Ibid., 485. In private, of course, Kinsey was less guarded. "He felt that religions that were sexually repressive and were responsible for all sorts of unnecessary guilt feelings and problems, and, who knows, neuroses and what not," recalled Gebhard, "and he always looked on the Judeo-Christian attitude toward sexuality as being a real curse." Author's interview with Gebhard, Oct. 14, 1984, 14.
80 *SBHM*, 327–93.
81 Ibid., 384–86.
82 Ibid., 386.
83 Ibid., 389, 391.
84 Ibid., 391.
85 Ibid., 392.
86 Robinson, *Modernization of Sex*, 62–66. Robinson lists six outlets, whereas Kinsey discusses nine.
87 *SBHM*, 615.
88 Ibid., 203.
89 Ibid., 327.
90 Ibid., 414.
91 Ibid., 204, 293, 327.
92 Ibid., 661.
93 Ibid., 638, 639.
94 Ibid., 617. For an excellent discussion of Kinsey's rejection of sexual preferences as markers of identity, see Robinson, *Modernization of Sex*, 67–68.
95 For a sharp critique of Kinsey's "homosexual-heterosexual rating scale," see Robinson, *Modernization of Sex*, 73–74. Calling the scale "arguably the most pathetic manifestation of Kinsey's philosophical naïveté," Robinson argues persuasively that the scale in no way improves upon the conventional homosexual, heterosexual, bisexual three-way breakdown.
96 *SBHM*, 639.

97 Ibid., 678.
98 Ibid.
99 Ibid.

Chapter 22: "PROPERLY PLACED BEFORE THE PUBLIC"

1   ACK to James Van Toor, May 24, 1941, KIA; James Van Toor to ACK, June 3, 1941, KIA.
2   John S. Crossman to Alan Gregg, Oct. 8, 1945, Series 200, Box 40, Folder 457, Rockefeller Archives.
3   Robert S. Morison to John S. Crossman, Oct. 10, 1945, ibid.
4   For example, describing a telephone conversation he had with E. W. Bacon, who asked after Kinsey, Gregg wrote in his diary, "Said I knew Kinsey; that the RF had made grants for his work and that I thought him a dependable scientist. This was all Bacon apparently wanted to know." See desk diary of Alan Gregg, Dec. 23, 1946, ibid.
5   ACK to John S. Grossman, Feb. 8, 1947, KIA. Kinsey told Grossman, a senior editor at McGraw-Hill, "As you understand we have had dozens of publishers contact us, and we have advised three of them as we have you that we will give them all a chance to talk to us again when our manuscript is finished and we can consider definite plans for publication."
6   Storer B. Lunt to ACK, Jan. 8, 1947, KIA.
7   Storer B. Lunt to Alan Gregg, Jan. 24, 1947, Series 200, Box 40, Folder 458, Rockefeller Archives.
8   Alan Gregg to Storer B. Lunt, Jan. 28, 1947, ibid. Repeating official foundation policy, Gregg closed, "A long experience has taught me that foundations have to be very careful to give liberty along with their money, and I am sure you will understand that it is in the interest of this position that I write you."
9   Thomas D. Clark interview with Herman B Wells, Jan. 1968, 10, IUOHP.
10 Ibid., 11.
11 ACK to Lawrence Saunders, Nov. 27, 1944, KIA.
12 Lawrence Saunders to ACK, Dec. 2, 1944, KIA.
13 Desk diary of Robert S. Morison, April 11, 1946, Series 200, Box 332, Folder 2243, Rockefeller Archives.
14 Saunders described the substance of his conversation with Lewis H. Weed in the following letter, Lawrence Saunders to Robert S. Morison, April 15, 1946, ibid.
15 Lawrence Saunders to Robert S. Morison, Sept. 30, 1946, ibid.
16 Desk diary of Robert S. Morison, Oct. 10, 1946.
17 Ibid.
18 ACK to Lloyd G. Potter, Dec. 23, 1946, KIA.
19 Desk diary of Morison, April 30, 1947, and May 2, 1947, Series 200, Box 40, Folder 458, Rockefeller Archives.
20 Desk diary of Morison, May 9, 1947, ibid. See also diary of Alan Gregg, May 9, 1947, ibid.
21 ACK to Lawrence Saunders, May 9, 1947, KIA.
22 ACK to Alan Gregg, May 23, 1947, KIA.
23 Alan Gregg to ACK, May 26, 1947, Series 200, Box 40, Folder 458, Rockefeller Archives.
24 ACK to Lawrence Saunders, May 29, 1947, KIA.

25 Ibid.
26 ACK to John L. Dusseau, Aug. 30, 1947, KIA.
27 Lloyd G. Potter to ACK, June 4, 1947, KIA.
28 ACK to Lloyd G. Potter, June 7, 1947, KIA.
29 Lloyd G. Potter to Alan Gregg, May 28, 1947, Series 200, Box 40, Folder 458, Rockefeller Archives.
30 Ibid.
31 Ibid.
32 Ibid.
33 Ibid.
34 Alan Gregg to Lloyd G. Potter, June 2, 1947, ibid.
35 Ibid.
36 Ibid.
37 For a detailed discussion of Kinsey's publication strategy, press policy, press reaction to the two volumes, and minor squabbles between Kinsey and various journalists, see Robert Delbert Brinkman, "Dr. Kinsey and the Press: Historical Case Study of the Relationship of the Mass Media and a Pioneering Behavioral Scientist" (Ph.D. diss., Department of Mass Communications, Indiana University, 1971).
38 ACK to Jack Y. Bryan, May 16, 1944, KIA.
39 ACK to J. M. Hutzel, Dec. 23, 1946, KIA. Hutzel was a staff member of the American Association for the Advancement of Science.
40 ACK to "Sirs," *Harper's Magazine,* June 25, 1942, KIA.
41 ACK to Lawrence E. Spivak, Dec. 24, 1943, KIA.
42 ACK to Norman Grieser, July 23, 1946, KIA.
43 Author's interview with Paul H. Gebhard, Oct. 14, 1984, 15.
44 ACK to Bryan, May 16, 1944.
45 ACK to D. E. Minnich, July 8, 1946, KIA.
46 ACK to Frederick L. Allen, Jan. 15, 1946, KIA.
47 ACK to Jerome Ellison, Feb. 27, 1947, KIA.
48 The origins of this policy and the details of how it worked are outlined in a letter from Kinsey to the Associated Press. See ACK to Howard Blakeslee, Oct. 27, 1947, KIA. An earlier version of this agreement was articulated by Kinsey in discussions with *Harper's Magazine.* See ACK to Allen, Jan. 15, 1946. As might be expected, the author of *Only Yesterday* was not pleased by Kinsey's terms. In a letter to a friend at the Rockefeller Foundation, Allen grumped, "I am considerably dampened by the fact that there is a 'list of magazines' lined up to do the job. Especially if they include news magazines it would rob the thing of most of its interest for us." Nevertheless, Allen stated that he would not abandon the project until he had had a chance to meet with Kinsey and discuss the matter. See Frederick L. Allen to George W. Gray, Feb. 2, 1946, Series 200, Box 40, Folder 457, Rockefeller Archives.
49 Lloyd G. Potter to ACK, Sept. 4, 1947, plus enclosure, KIA.
50 ACK to Lloyd G. Potter, Sept. 6, 1947, KIA.
51 Albert Deutsch to ACK, Sept. 4, 1947, KIA.
52 Fred Myers to ACK, Sept. 10, 1947, KIA.
53 ACK to Albert Deutsch, Sept. 18, 1947, KIA.
54 ACK to Gerald E. Wendt, Oct. 1, 1947, KIA.
55 Lawrence Saunders to Robert S. Morison, Oct. 27, 1947, Series 200, Box 40, Folder 458, Rockefeller Archives.
56 ACK to J. M. Hutzel, Oct. 27, 1947, KIA.

57 ACK to Potter, Sept. 6, 1947.
58 ACK to F. S. Hirsh, Oct. 27, 1947, KIA.
59 Lawrence Saunders to ACK, Nov. 17, 1947, KIA.
60 ACK to George Gallup, Nov. 11, 1947, KIA.
61 Author's interview with Paul H. Gebhard, Oct. 29, 1971, 87, IUOHP.
62 Harold B. Clemenko, "Toward a Saner Sex Life," *Look,* Dec. 9, 1947, 106–7.
63 Albert Deutsch, "The Sex Habits of American Men," *Harper's Magazine,* Dec. 1947, 493.
64 "A Scientist Looks at America's Sexual Behavior," *Science Illustrated,* Dec. 1947, 34.
65 Fred Myers, "The Truth about Sex in America," *Reader's Scope,* Dec. 1947, 154.
66 Deutsch, "Sex Habits," 490.
67 "Scientist Looks," 34, 37.
68 Clemenko, "Toward a Saner Sex Life," 107.
69 Deutsch, "Sex Habits," 494–95.
70 "Scientist Looks," 34.
71 Clemenko, "Toward a Saner Sex Life," 107.
72 Myers, "Truth about Sex," 154, 157.
73 Deutsch, "Sex Habits," 493.
74 Clemenko, "Toward a Saner Sex Life," 107.
75 Ibid., 106.
76 Desk diary of Morison, June 13, 1947, Series 200, Box 40, Folder 458, Rockefeller Archives.
77 ACK to Joseph K. Folsom, Nov. 11, 1947, KIA.
78 ACK to Bentley Glass, Oct. 27, 1947, KIA.
79 Bentley Glass to ACK, Nov. 4, 1947, KIA.
80 ACK to Bentley Glass, Nov. 7, 1947, KIA.
81 ACK to Bentley Glass, Feb. 3, 1948, KIA.
82 Alan Gregg's field notes, Feb. 7, 1947, Series 200, Box 40, Folder 458, Rockefeller Archives.
83 Ibid.
84 Alan Gregg to ACK, March 21, 1947, ibid.
85 Ibid., enclosure.
86 Ibid.
87 *SBHM,* vii.
88 Deutsch, "Sex Habits," 491.
89 Author's interview with Robert S. Morison, Oct. 18, 1971, 36, IUOHP.
90 Ibid., 37.
91 ACK to Alan Gregg, March 24, 1947, Series 200, Box 40, Folder 458, Rockefeller Archives.
92 Ibid.
93 Herman B Wells, *Being Lucky* (Bloomington, 1980), 301–11.
94 Author's interview with Herman B Wells, Dec. 3, 1971, 11, IUOHP.
95 Ibid., 8.
96 George W. Corner, "Memorandum to the Members of the Committee for Research in Problems of Sex," Oct. 30, 1947, CRPS Files, NRC Archives.
97 Alan Gregg to W. D. Asfahl, Oct. 23, 1947, Series 200, Box 40, Folder 458, Rockefeller Archives.
98 Alan Gregg to ACK, Dec. 4, 1947, ibid. At this meeting, several of the trustees expressed the hope that they could obtain copies of Kinsey's book, as did numerous of-

ficers of the foundation. To accommodate this demand, Gregg decided to order twenty-five copies of the book, a sizable order that pointed to the keen interest in Kinsey's work within the foundation. See Alan Gregg to HW, Inter-Office Correspondence, Dec. 4, 1947, ibid.

99 Arthur Sulzberger to Raymond Fosdick, Dec. 5, 1947, New York Times Archives. Thanks to Susan W. Dryfoos.

100 Ibid.

101 Author's interview with George W. Corner, Aug. 5, 1971, 10, IUOHP.

102 Ibid., 9.

103 Robert M. Yerkes to George W. Corner, Dec. 22, 1947, Box 77, Folder 1461, Yerkes Papers.

104 George W. Corner to Robert M. Yerkes, Dec. 30, 1947, ibid.

105 Author's interview with Corner, Aug. 5, 1971, 10–11.

106 Desk diary of Gregg, Dec. 9, 1947, Series 200, Box 40, Folder 458, Rockefeller Archives.

107 Ibid.

108 Ibid.

109 Alan Gregg to Lawrence Saunders, Dec. 9, 1947, ibid.

110 George W. Corner to Alan Gregg, Dec. 10, 1947, ibid. Ever the gentleman, Corner wrote Saunders, "I appreciate your sympathetic understanding of the objections Dr. Gregg and I had to the proposed newspaper advertising," adding, "I take it for granted that the newspaper advertising will not include . . . descriptive material and table of contents of the Kinsey book." George W. Corner to Lawrence Saunders, Dec. 10, 1947, ibid.

111 Lawrence Saunders to Alan Gregg, Dec. 9, 1947, ibid.

112 Alan Gregg to Lawrence Saunders, Dec. 10, 1947, ibid.

113 George W. Corner to ACK, Dec. 10, 1947, KIA.

114 ACK to Alan Gregg, Dec. 11, 1947, KIA.

115 Ibid.

116 Alan Gregg to ACK, Dec. 12, 1947, Series 200, Box 40, Folder 458, Rockefeller Archives.

117 Robert S. Morison to Alan Gregg, Inter-Office Correspondence, Dec. 11, 1947, ibid.

118 Alan Gregg to Richard Gregg, Jan. 3, 1948. Thanks to the Gregg family.

Chapter 23: "SUCCESSOR TO DARWIN?"

1 "Manners & Morals," *Time,* March 1, 1948, 16.

2 "Kinsey Speaks Out," *Newsweek,* April 12, 1948, 51.

3 Lawrence Saunders to ACK, Jan. 19, 1948, KIA.

4 *Indianapolis Times,* Jan. 10, 1948, clipping files, KIA.

5 Howard A. Rusk, "Concerning Man's Basic Drive," review of *SBHM,* in *New York Times,* Jan. 4, 1948, sec. 3, p. 1.

6 Ibid.

7 Ibid.

8 Ibid., 3.

9 Kinsey's hometown newspaper reprinted large portions of the review, telling its readers that the *Times* placed "high value" on his book. See *Bloomington World-Telephone,* Jan. 6, 1948, 1.

10 ACK to Herman B Wells, Jan. 27, 1948, KIA.

11 Raymond B. Fosdick to Arthur Hays Sulzberger, Jan. 4, 1948, New York Times Archives. Thanks to Susan W. Dryfoos. Within the foundation, Alan Gregg received kudos from his fellow officers. For example, Joseph H. Willits wrote, "I congratulate the Medical Sciences Division on the significance of the task they have made possible in financing the work of Dr. Kinsey." Willits predicted that Kinsey's work would "lift the plane of discussion and thinking to a new level." See Joseph H. Willits to Alan Gregg, interoffice correspondence, Jan. 5, 1948, Series 200, Box 40, Folder 459, Rockefeller Archives.

12 In the months prior to the publication of his book, Kinsey had cultivated the press's good will with every means at his disposal, including entertainment, which he paid for with grant money. When Corner ran across an item labeled "Entertainment for Journalists" in the amount of $133.50 for October 10, 1947, he called the item "a peculiar one," but added, "I am not disposed to be petty with Dr. Kinsey. Everything about his project is a little different from any other grant on our list. It can be argued that his publicity is a good investment for science because his royalties are all going to support future research." Still, even the gentle-spirited Corner felt forced to admit, "I certainly would not usually approve such an item on any other investigator's voucher." George W. Corner to Lois G. Bowen, Secretary, Division of Medical Sciences, CRPS Files, NRC Archives.

13 "Medicine," Time, Jan. 5, 1948, 66.

14 James R. Newman, "The Proper Study of Mankind," New Republic, Feb. 9, 1948, 31.

15 Rosalind Ives, "The Great Topic," Good Housekeeping, May 1948, 33.

16 Francis Sill Wickware, "Report on Kinsey," Life, Aug. 2, 1948, 97.

17 Leo P. Chall, "The Reception of the Kinsey Report in the Periodicals of the United States," in Jerome Himelhoch and Sylvia Fleis Fava, eds., Sexual Behavior in American Society: An Appraisal of the First Two Kinsey Reports (New York, 1955), 365.

18 "Dr. Kinsey Continues His Report," Cue, April 24, 1948, clipping files, KIA.

19 Hugh J. Parry, "Kinsey Revisited," International Journal of Opinion and Attitude Research 2 (Summer 1948): 196.

20 "Kinsey—A Professor in Search of Sex," People, July 19, 1950, 29.

21 Ibid.

22 Nanette Kutner, "Yes, There Is a Mrs. Kinsey," McCall's, July 1948, 94.

23 Indianapolis Times, Jan. 10, 1948, clipping files, KIA.

24 "The Talk of the Town," New Yorker, March 27, 1948, 19.

25 Wickware, "Report on Kinsey," 98.

26 "Kinsey—A Professor in Search of Sex," 28.

27 "Medicine," Time, Jan. 5, 1948, 66.

28 "Dr. Kinsey Continues His Report."

29 Robert Van Gelder, "Interview with a Best-selling Author: Alfred C. Kinsey," Cosmopolitan, May 1948, 18, 118.

30 Wickware, "Report on Kinsey," 98.

31 "Kinsey—A Professor in Search of Sex," 29.

32 New Yorker, May 1, 1948, 27.

33 Kutner, "Yes, There Is a Mrs. Kinsey," 94.

34 Wickware, "Report on Kinsey," 87.

35 "Manners and Morals," Time, March 1, 1948, 16.

36 Geoffrey Gorer, "Justification by Numbers: A Commentary on the Kinsey Report," American Scholar 17 (Summer 1948): 280.

37 Harry McNeill, "Kinsey, Pomeroy, and Martin," *Commonweal,* April 23, 1948, 656.

38 Hoping to promote the record, a press agent for Discovery Records contacted Kinsey and asked if he would be willing to be photographed with Moore. See Howard Hutchinson to ACK, Sept. 3, 1949, KIA. Kinsey replied, "No! Thanks, however, for your interest." ACK to Howard Hutchinson, Sept. 8, 1949, KIA.

39 Albert Deutsch, "The Kinsey Report and Popular Culture," in Himelhoch and Fava, eds., *Sexual Behavior,* 384. I have drawn heavily on this article.

40 G. Legman, ed., *The Limerick* (New York, 1964), no. 483, p. 99.

41 Kinsey learned of this radio reference to his work in a postcard signed "Enola." See "Enola" to Dr. Kinsey, March 21, 1949, KIA.

42 Alvin C. Johnson to ACK, Feb. 26, 1948, KIA. Johnson's client was Maurice Feuerlicht, a film executive who had worked for Paramount Pictures. In reply, Kinsey agreed to talk with Feuerlicht, but confessed, "I cannot conceive how such a thing could be made into a motion picture which would have any public appeal." ACK to Alvin C. Johnson, March 1, 1948, KIA. Following Kinsey's death, Hollywood contacted President Wells with an offer to make a motion picture with the title "The Kinsey Story." See Guido Orlando to Herman Wells, Sept. 6, 1956, KIA. Orlando represented the director, Frank Tuttle. Wells was not receptive to the idea. See E. Ross Bartley (the director of public relations at Indiana University) to Guido Orlando, Sept. 14, 1956, KIA.

43 Deutsch, "Kinsey Report," 384.

44 Mae West, "An Open Letter to Dr. Kinsey from Mae West," *Cosmopolitan,* March 1949, 42.

45 Deutsch, "Kinsey Report," 385.

46 Vance Packard to ACK, July 16, 1948, KIA.

47 ACK to Vance Packard, Aug. 11, 1948, KIA.

48 "Kinsey Speaks Out," 51.

49 "Manners & Morals: How to Stop Gin Rummy," *Time,* March 1, 1948, 16.

50 Ibid.

51 Kutner, "Yes, There Is a Mrs. Kinsey," 93–94.

52 Ibid.

53 J. A. Lutz to ACK, Aug. 2, 1948, KIA.

54 Deutsch, "Kinsey Report," 384–85.

55 ACK to Lawrence Saunders, Oct. 14, 1948, KIA. On the eve of the female volume's publication, the Kinsey Distilling Corporation ran a second ad. See *New York Times,* Sept. 1, 1953, 15.

56 Lloyd G. Potter to ACK, Oct. 20, 1948, KIA.

57 Author's interview with Edna Kinsey Higenbotham, Nov. 28, 1984, 16.

58 Deutsch, "Kinsey Report," 385.

59 "Dr. Kinsey Continues His Report," *Cue,* April 24, 1948.

60 Wardell B. Pomeroy, *Dr. Kinsey and the Institute for Sex Research* (New York, 1972), 149.

61 Quoted in Cornelia V. Christenson, *Kinsey: A Biography* (Bloomington, 1971), 186–87.

62 Natalie R. Hirschfeld to ACK, May 25, 1948, KIA.

63 ACK to Natalie R. Hirschfeld, May 28, 1948, KIA.

64 Anon. to ACK, Jan. 21, 1948, KIA.

65 ACK to Anon., Jan. 23, 1948, KIA.

66   Wickware, "Report on Kinsey."

67   For a detailed study of how Christian theologians reacted to the male and female volumes, see Robert Cecil Johnson, "Kinsey, Christianity, and Sex: A Critical Study of Reaction in American Christianity to the Kinsey Reports on Human Sexual Behavior" (Ph.D. diss., University of Wisconsin, Madison, 1973).

68   ACK to Robert M. Yerkes, Jan. 31, 1948, KIA.

69   Lawrence Frank, "Educational Considerations—From the Parents' Point of View," in *Problems of Sexual Behavior* (New York, 1948), 117.

70   Parry, "Kinsey Revisited," 196.

71   Quoted in "Woman and the Male Animal," in *Saturday Review of Literature,* May 8, 1948, 20.

72   Parry, "Kinsey Revisited," 197.

73   "Kinsey—A Professor in Search of Sex," 30.

74   "Kinsey Again," editorial, *Catholic Mind,* Sept. 1949, 561.

75   "Sex-Worship Snares This Smart World," *Awake!,* Dec. 8, 1948, 8.

76   Newman, "Proper Study of Mankind," 30.

77   Parry, "Kinsey Revisited," 196.

78   Reinhold Niebuhr, "Kinsey and the Moral Problem of Man's Sexual Life," in Donald Porter Geddes, ed., *An Analysis of the Kinsey Reports on Sexual Behavior in the Human Male and Female* (New York, 1954), 68, 66, 64.

79   Norman Vincent Peale, "Must We Change Our Sex Standards?: A Reader's Symposium," *Reader's Digest,* June 1948, 4–5.

80   Newman, "Proper Study of Mankind," 30.

81   Claude C. Bowman, "A Note on the Sociological Inadequacies of the Kinsey Report," *American Sociological Review* 14 (Aug. 1949): 549.

82   Geoffrey Gorer, "A Statistical Study of Sex," review in *New York Herald Tribune,* Feb. 1, 1948, 4.

83   Margaret Mead, "An Anthropologist Looks at the Report," in *Problems of Sexual Behavior* (New York, 1948), 60–61, 67, 69.

84   ACK to George W. Corner, March 20, 1948, KIA.

85   ACK to Robert Kroc, Feb. 10, 1948, KIA.

86   ACK to Robert L. Dickinson, Feb. 10, 1948, KIA.

87   Irita Van Doren to Margaret Mead, Jan. 8, 1948, Box 19, Margaret Mead Papers, Library of Congress. In this letter, Van Doren, the editor of the *New York Herald Tribune*'s "Weekly Book Review," invited Mead to review Kinsey's book. The same letter contains Mead's handwritten note "No—Gorer will do it."

88   Margaret Mead to Geoffrey Gorer, Oct. 31, 1955, Margaret Mead Papers, Library of Congress. Thanks to Mary M. Wolfskill, head, Reference and Reader Service Section, Library of Congress, who furnished me with this letter, and to Mary Catherine Bateson for special permission to examine closed portions of her mother's correspondence.

89   Geoffrey Gorer to Margaret Mead, March 1, 1948, ibid.

90   ACK to Roland E. Mueser, March 25, 1948, KIA.

91   ACK to George W. Corner, March 20, 1948, KIA.

92   Wallace O. Fenn to George W. Corner, March 26, 1948, CRPS Files, NRC Archives.

93   Carl R. Moore to George W. Corner, March 26, 1948, CRPS Files, NRC Archives.

94   See George R. [*sic*] Corner, "The Origin, Methods, and Finds of the Report—Sexual Behavior in the Human Male," in *Problems of Sexual Behavior,* 1–19. At least one officer of the Rockefeller Foundation took Gorer's review in stride. Responding to a query from Lawrence Saunders, Robert S. Morison, Gregg's assistant, wrote, "I had

already seen the review in the NEW YORK HERALD TRIBUNE and was a little sorry that Gorer had not made a more detailed analysis of Kinsey's defense of his statistical methods. Nevertheless, it does serve to provide a little balance against the overwhelming chorus of approval." See Robert S. Morison to Lawrence Saunders, Feb. 5, 1948, Series 200, Box 40, Folder 459, Rockefeller Archives.

95 Explaining how he came to write the review, Kubie told Corner, "I have known Kinsey for several years, and in the course of the years I had had several talks with him, and an exchange of letters, in some of which we discussed many of the criticisms which are incorporated in this report. We seemed always to reach agreement about the criticisms and about my various suggestions, which was rather borne out by the fact that Kinsey phoned me personally to ask me to write a review of the book, and to choose some colleague of mine to review it in one of the other psychiatric journals." See Lawrence S. Kubie to George W. Corner, April 6, 1948, CRPS Files, NRC Archives.

96 Kubie, quoted in Pomeroy, *Dr. Kinsey,* 297.

97 Lawrence S. Kubie, "Psychiatric Implications of the Kinsey Report," *Psychosomatic Medicine* 10 (March–April 1948): 101.

98 Ibid., 97, 105, 106, 96.

99 "Dr. Kinsey's Misrememberers," *Time,* June 24, 1948, 76–77.

100 ACK to Frank A. Beach, March 6, 1948, KIA.

101 ACK to Albert Deutsch, Feb. 14, 1948, KIA.

102 ACK to Alan Gregg, April 30, 1948, KIA.

103 ACK to George W. Corner, March 4, 1948, KIA.

104 Lawrence S. Kubie to Alan Gregg, Jan. 14, 1948, Series 200, Box 40, Folder 459, Rockefeller Archives.

105 Alan Gregg to Lawrence S. Kubie, June 10, 1948, Series 200, Box 40, Folder 460, Rockefeller Archives.

106 Alan Gregg to George W. Corner, April 16, 1948, Record Group 1.1, Series 200, Box 77, Folder 923, Rockefeller Archives.

107 "Report of Interview at lunch—June 8, 1948," typed at the bottom of ACK to Alan Gregg, May 26, 1948, Series 200, Box 40, Folder 759, Rockefeller Archives.

108 Lawrence S. Kubie to George W. Corner, April 6, 1948, CRPS Files, NRC Archives.

109 George W. Corner to Karl S. Lashley, April 7, 1948, CRPS Files, NRC Archives.

110 Lewis H. Weed to George W. Corner, April 13, 1948, CRPS Files, NRC Archives.

111 Karl S. Lashley to George W. Corner, March 26, 1948, CRPS Files, NRC Archives.

112 George W. Corner to Alan Gregg, April 9, 1948, Record Group 1.1, Series 200, Box 77, Folder 923, Rockefeller Archives.

113 George W. Corner to ACK, May 5, 1948, CRPS Files, NRC Archives.

114 ACK to Anon., May 27, 1948, KIA.

115 Lionel Trilling, "Sex and Science: The Kinsey Report," *Partisan Review,* April 1948, 460.

116 Ibid., 462.

117 Ibid., 470.

118 Ibid., 475.

119 Ibid., 476. After the review appeared, Trilling became embroiled in a dispute with L. C. Dunn, a scientist who accused him of positing inherent tensions between science and the humanities. For Dunns' argument and Trilling's response, see Box 39, Folder 425, Lionel Trilling Papers, Butler Library, Columbia University. Apparently, Trilling took the matter seriously enough to ask advice from his friend Jacques Barzun, a dis-

tinguished historian. Barzun replied that Trilling should answer Dunn and made suggestions for how this should be done. See Jacques Barzun to Lionel Trilling, July 28, 1949, Box 1, ibid. Thanks to Diana Trilling (deceased) for permission to examine her husband's papers.

120 Alan Gregg to ACK, April 12, 1948, Series 200, Box 40, Folder 759, Rockefeller Archives. Kubie called Trilling's review "extraordinarily brilliant and provocative." See Lawrence S. Kubie to Robert S. Morison, July 20, 1948, Series 200, Box 40, Folder 460, Rockefeller Archives.

121 "Must We Change Our Sex Standards?" 1–6.

122 ACK to Alan Gregg, Sept. 16, 1948, KIA.

123 Lewis M. Terman to Robert M. Yerkes, May 18, 1948, Box 17, Yerkes Folder, Lewis M. Terman Papers, Special Collections 38, Stanford University Archives (hereafter Terman Papers).

124 Lewis M. Terman to D. D. Klein, Oct. 26, 1948, Box 14, Folder 31, Terman Papers.

125 *SBHM*, 31.

126 Lewis M. Terman, "Kinsey's 'Sexual Behavior in the Human Male': Some Comments and Criticisms," *Psychological Bulletin* 45 (Sept. 1948): 444–46, 459.

127 George W. Corner to Robert M. Yerkes, Dec. 1, 1948, CRPS Files, NRC Archives.

128 ACK to Howard M. Parshley, Nov. 9, 1948, KIA.

129 Terman apparently sent a copy of his review to Gregg. At any rate, it is clear Gregg read the review. A physician friend sent him a copy, declaring, "You will undoubtedly be interested in this shrewd dissection, which does not detract too much from the value of the entire report." This same letter contained Gregg's handwritten notation "I have seen [Terman's review]." See Henry W. Brosin to Alan Gregg, Sept. 12, 1948, Record Group 1.1, Projects, Series 216, Box 7, Folder 84, Rockefeller Archives.

130 Corner to Yerkes, Dec. 1, 1948.

131 Lewis M. Terman to Herman B Wells, Dec. 23, 1948, Terman Papers. A copy of this letter is in the KIA.

132 Albert Ellis to Lewis M. Terman, Jan. 14, 1949, Box 14, Folder 31, Terman Papers.

133 Lewis Terman to C. R. Carpenter, Jan. 27, 1949, ibid.

134 Kate Hevner Mueller to Lewis M. Terman, Jan. 22, 1949, ibid.

135 Kate Hevner Mueller to Lewis M. Terman, March 24, 1949, ibid.

136 Lewis M. Terman to Kate Hevner Mueller, April 4, 1949, ibid.

137 Lewis M. Terman to Kate Hevner Mueller, Feb. 3, 1949, ibid.

138 Lewis M. Terman to Kate Hevner Mueller, April 4, 1949, ibid.

139 Herman B Wells, *Being Lucky* (Bloomington, 1980), 186.

140 ACK to F. T. Reed, March 5, 1948, and F. T. Reed to ACK, March 9, 1948, Herman B Wells Papers, IUA. Reed was Wells's administrative assistant.

141 Wells, *Being Lucky,* 181, 179.

142 Ibid., 186.

143 Rosalind Ives, "The Great Topic," *Good Housekeeping,* May 1948, 302.

144 "Must We Change Our Sexual Standards?" 129.

145 Henry C. Link to Joseph H. Willits, July 23, 1948, Record Group 2, Series 100, Box 398, Folder 2685, Rockefeller Archives.

146 Chester I. Barnard to John S. Dickey, June 28, 1948, Series 200, Box 40, Folder 460, Rockefeller Archives.

147 "Must We Change Our Sex Standards?" 130.

148 Henry P. Van Dusen to Harold Dodds, Oct. 27, 1948, Henry P. Van Dusen Papers, Personal Correspondence, Harold W. Dodds Folder, Union Theological Seminary Archives.
149 J. S. Dickey to Chester I. Barnard, June 30, 1948, Series 200, Box 40, Folder 460, Rockefeller Archives.
150 Desk diary of Alan Gregg, Dec. 17, 1948, Series 200, Box 40, Folder 460, Rockefeller Archives.
151 Alan Gregg to Warren Weaver, Feb. 1, 1949, Interoffice Correspondence, Series 200, Box 40, Folder 461, Rockefeller Archives.
152 Desk diary of Alan Gregg, March 4, 1949, Series 200, Box 40, Folder 461, Rockefeller Archives.
153 Corner to Yerkes, Dec. 1, 1948. Yerkes was less sanguine about Kinsey's temperament. "I particularly regret that Kinsey is not more hospitable to adverse criticisms because as his report unfolds in volume after volume critics will become less kindly and considerate if it becomes clear that he is highly defensive and only slightly appreciative," replied Yerkes. "I wish it were the reverse because in the long run I am certain it would be immensely more profitable to him personally and to the work to which he and his staff are committed. At the present juncture he is setting a pattern which will greatly influence his younger associates and fellow workers. I do not like the pattern thus far revealed." Robert M Yerkes to George W. Corner, Dec. 30, 1948, CRPS Files, NRC Archives.
154 ACK to Alan Gregg, April 2, 1949, KIA. Armed with the ammunition he needed, Gregg showed Kinsey's letter to his new boss, Chester I. Barnard, who replied, "This letter straightens the matter out in my mind." Stating that he was willing to see Kinsey supported at the rate of $40,000 to $50,000 annually for the next three to five years, Barnard declared, "I regard this work as so important and ultimately valuable in so many different ways that I would be willing to continue substantial support, provided only that Kinsey is also using his royalty money for the same purpose." See Chester I. Barnard to Alan Gregg, April 5, 1948, Inter-Office Correspondence, Series 200, Box 40, Folder 461, Rockefeller Archives.
155 For the details of the executive committee meeting, see Chester I. Barnard to Winthrop W. Aldrich, June 2, 1948, Series 200, Box 41, Folder 462, Rockefeller Archives.
156 Harold Dodds to Chester I. Barnard, May 23, 1949, ibid.

Chapter 24: "I HOPE THE BLINDS WERE CLOSED"

1 Author's interview with Edna Kinsey Higenbotham, Nov. 28, 1984, 13.
2 Edgar Anderson to ACK, March 18, 1949, KIA.
3 Nanette Kutner, "Yes, There Is a Mrs. Kinsey," McCall's, July 1948, 94.
4 ACK to Robert M. Yerkes, May 28, 1948, KIA.
5 Author's interview with Glenway Wescott, June 27, 1972, 36, IUOHP.
6 Author's interview with Anon. B, Feb. 17, 1988, 95–96; author's interview with Clarence A. Tripp, Dec. 15, 1987, 18.
7 Wardell B. Pomeroy, Dr. Kinsey and the Institute for Sex Research (New York, 1972), 196.
8 Author's interview with Anon. B, Feb. 17, 1988, 15–16, 86.
9 Ibid., 86, 109, 108.

10   Ibid., 108, 111, 137, 80, 77–78, 138–39.
11   Ibid., 113, 128.
12   Author's interview with Paul H. Gebhard, Oct. 29, 1971, 24, IUOHP.
13   Author's interview with William Dellenback, Sept. 22, 1971, 2–3, IUOHP; author's joint interview with Dellenback and Clarence A. Tripp, Oct. 13, 1984, 26–30.
14   Author's joint interview with Dellenback and Tripp, Oct. 13, 1984, 14–15, 16–17.
15   Ibid., 17, 20, 15.
16   ACK to Dellenback, March 17, 1949, KIA.
17   Author's interview with Paul H. Gebhard, Oct. 14, 1984, 20.
18   Author's interview with Dellenback, Feb. 14, 1988, 5, 16.
19   Author's interview with Anon. B, Feb. 17, 1988, 109.
20   Author's interview with Clyde Martin, March 21, 1986, 25, 35.
21   Author's interview with Dellenback, Feb. 14, 1988, 20–21.
22   Author's conversation with Agnes West Gebhard, Oct. 15, 1984.
23   Author's interview with Dellenback, Feb. 14, 1988, 20–21.
24   Author's interview with Tripp, Dec. 15, 1987, 5–6.
25   Author's interview with Gebhard, Oct. 14, 1984, 24.
26   Author's interview with Dellenback, Feb. 14, 1988, 15.
27   Author's interview with Gebhard, Oct. 14, 1984, 7.
28   Author's interview with Dellenback, Feb. 14, 1988, 16–17, 34.
29   Author's interview with Gebhard, Oct. 14, 1984, 7.
30   Author's interview with Tripp, Dec. 15, 1987, 25.
31   Author's interview with Dellenback, Feb. 14, 1988, 8.
32   Author's interview with Anon. B, Feb. 17, 1988, 93.
33   Author's interview with Tripp, Dec. 15, 1987, 23, 24.
34   Quoted in Pomeroy, *Dr. Kinsey*, 196.
35   Author's interview with Tripp, Dec. 15, 1987, 83; author's interview with Anon. B, Feb. 17, 1988, 95.
36   Author's interview with Dellenback, Feb. 14, 1988, 9.
37   Ibid., 10.
38   Author's interview with Gebhard, Oct. 14, 1984, 7.
39   Pomeroy, *Dr. Kinsey*, 177.
40   Author's interview with Glenway Wescott, June 27, 1972, 11, 17, IUOHP.
41   Robert Phelps with Jerry Rosco, eds., *Continual Lessons: The Journals of Glenway Wescott, 1937–1955* (New York, 1990), 245.
42   Ibid., 245–46.
43   Author's conversation with Glenway Wescott, June 27, 1972. Wescott told this story off tape, stipulating that it could be used only after his death. The man's unique orgasm is also described by Pomeroy, though he, too, did not reveal the man's identity. See Pomeroy, *Dr. Kinsey*, 177–78.
44   Phelps with Rosco, eds., *Continual Lessons*, 298.
45   Author's interview with Anon. B, Feb. 17, 1988, 85.
46   Quoted in Samuel M. Steward, "Remembering Dr. Kinsey: Sexual Scientist and Investigator," *Advocate*, Nov. 13, 1980, 21.
47   Ibid.
48   Ibid., 22.
49   Ibid.
50   Author's interview with Gebhard, Oct. 14, 1984, 7.

51 Author's interview with Kenneth Anger, Oct. 13, 1990, 58.
52 Steward, "Remembering Dr. Kinsey," 22–23.
53 Author's interview with Clarence A. Tripp, Dec. 15, 1988, 11.
54 Anon. to ACK, April 25, 1954, KIA.
55 ACK to Anon., May 20, 1954, KIA.
56 Anon. to ACK, Oct. 31, 1955, KIA.
57 ACK to Anon., Dec. 15, 1955, KIA.
58 ACK to Anon., Aug. 12, 1948, KIA.
59 ACK to Anon., Nov. 12, 1949, KIA.
60 ACK to Anon., July 29, 1950, KIA.
61 ACK to Anon., June 2, 1955, KIA.
62 ACK to Anon., Jan. 24, 1949, KIA.
63 ACK to Anon., March 24, 1948, KIA.
64 ACK to Anon., Dec. 20, 1955, KIA.
65 Anon. to ACK, Jan. 19, 1951, KIA.
66 ACK to Anon., Jan. 23, 1951, KIA.
67 ACK to Dr. Adrien-Georges Gerard, Sept. 20, 1954, KIA.
68 Anon. to ACK, July 16, 1955, KIA.
69 ACK to Anon., July 16, 1955, KIA.
70 Anon. to ACK, Oct. 3, 1951, KIA.
71 ACK to Anon., Oct. 9, 1951, KIA.
72 Anon. to ACK, March 17, 1948, KIA.
73 ACK to Anon., March 21, 1948, KIA.
74 Anon. to ACK, April 22, 1948, KIA.
75 ACK to Anon., May 1, 1948, KIA.
76 ACK to Anon., June 28, 1948, KIA.
77 ACK to John O. Rinemann, Sept. 30, 1946, KIA.
78 ACK to R. A. Acher, March 18, 1949, KIA.
79 Anon. to ACK, May 21, 1952, KIA.
80 ACK to Anon., May 29, 1952, KIA.
81 ACK to Anon., Sept. 10, 1953, KIA.
82 ACK to Anon., Aug. 4, 1954, KIA.
83 ACK to Anon., Sept. 16, 1953, KIA.
84 ACK to Anon., May 5, 1951, KIA.
85 ACK to Anon., Oct. 10, 1955, KIA.
86 Anon. to ACK, Jan. 29, 1955, KIA.
87 ACK to Anon., Feb. 7, 1955, KIA.
88 Anon. to ACK, Oct. 26, 1951, KIA.
89 Anon. to Wardell B. Pomeroy, Feb. 16, 1949, KIA. "I would have written this to Prof. Kinsey, but his name is too well known for me to address an envelope to him," the man explained.
90 Anon. to ACK, April 12, 1948, KIA.
91 Anon. to ACK, Sept. 4, 1952, KIA.
92 ACK to Anon., Dec. 20, 1950, KIA.
93 ACK to Anon., Aug. 9, 1943, KIA.
94 ACK to Anon., Aug. 13, 1952, KIA.
95 ACK to Anon., Oct. 30, 1951, KIA.
96 ACK to Anon., Dec. 20, 1950, KIA.

97   ACK to Anon., Jan. 2, 1948, KIA.
98   ACK to Anon., Aug. 13, 1948, KIA.
99   ACK to Anon., Feb. 16, 1951, KIA.
100 Anon. to ACK, July 21, 1950, KIA.
101 ACK to Anon., July 25, 1950, KIA.
102 ACK to Anon., Jan. 19, 1948, KIA.
103 ACK to Anon., Aug. 13, 1948, KIA.
104 ACK to Anon., March 17, 1949, KIA.
105 ACK to O. Spurgeon English, June 13, 1952, KIA.
106 ACK to Anon., Jan. 19, 1948, KIA.
107 ACK to Anon., June 9, 1951, KIA.
108 ACK to Anon., Dec. 15, 1952, KIA.
109 ACK to Anon., April 4, 1949, KIA.
110 Henry Remak, "Dr. Kinsey," Aug. 28, 1956, KIA.
111 W. A. Higinbotham to ACK, Sept. 13, 1948, KIA.
112 ACK to W. A. Higinbotham, Oct. 15, 1948, KIA.
113 Quoted in George Chauncey, Jr., "The Postwar Sex Crime Panic," in *True Stories from the American Past,* ed., William Graebner (New York, 1993), 165, 170, 175. My discussion of the postwar moral panic in the United States draws heavily on Chauncey's excellent scholarship and incisive analysis.
114 Mrs. George A. Elder to ACK, Nov. 10, 1944, KIA.
115 Quoted in Chauncey, "Postwar Sex Crime Panic," 170.
116 Ibid., 171, 172.
117 S. William Henry to Alan Gregg, March 7, 1948, KIA. Kinsey received a copy of this letter from Gregg.
118 ACK to Anon., Feb. 4, 1956, KIA.
119 Morris L. Ernst to ACK, April 27, 1950, KIA.
120 ACK to Morris L. Ernst, May 1, 1950, KIA.
121 ACK to O. Spurgeon English, July 17, 1951, KIA.
122 ACK to "Sirs," July 9, 1942, KIA; J. Edgar Hoover to ACK, July 25, 1942, KIA.
123 Form No. 1, Philadelphia File No. 71-251, April 27, 1945, 100-343506-86, FBI Files. Some of the material on Kinsey was filed under the bureau's "100" designation, a file series for "Internal Security" and "Subversive Matter" inquiries. A great deal of material was filed under the "62" or "66" series, each labeled "Administrative Matters."
124 ACK to Edward Tamm, May 28, 1946, KIA; J. Edgar Hoover to ACK, June 4, 1946, KIA.
125 ACK to Morris L. Ernst, March 24, 1948, KIA.
126 Morris L. Ernst to J. Edgar Hoover, April 2, 1948, KIA. Ernst sent Kinsey a copy of the letter for the Institute's files.
127 ACK to Morris L. Ernst, April 13, 1948, KIA.
128 M. A. Jones to Mr. [L. B.] Nichols, April 8, 1948, "Dr. Alfred C. Kinsey," Office Memorandum, Serialization 62-87563-1, FBI Files.
129 M. A. Jones to Mr. [L. B.] Nichols, May 10, 1948, "Book Review 'Sexual Behavior in the Human Male,' by Alfred S. [*sic*] Kinsey et al.," Serialization 62-87562-3, FBI Files.
130 J. Edgar Hoover, "Must We Change Our Sex Standards?" *Reader's Digest,* June 1948, 6.

131 John D'Emilio, *Sexual Politics, Sexual Communities: The Making of a Homosexual Minority in the United States, 1940–1970* (Chicago, 1983), 46.

132 L. B. Nichols to Clyde Tolson, Jan. 5, 1950, 62-87563-5, FBI Files.

133 L. B. Nichols to Clyde Tolson, Jan. 11, 1950, 62-87563-6, FBI Files.

134 J. Edgar Hoover to ACK, Jan. 17, 1950, KIA.

135 ACK to J. Edgar Hoover, Jan. 21, 1950, KIA.

136 Curt Gentry, *J. Edgar Hoover: The Man and the Secrets* (New York, 1993). See also Richard Gid Powers, *Secrecy and Power: The Life of J. Edgar Hoover* (New York, 1987), 171–72, 185.

137 SAC, Indianapolis to Director, FBI, July 19, 1957, 62-10561-XI, FBI Files.

138 Wayne N. Aspinall to ACK, April 5, 1950, KIA.

139 ACK to Wayne N. Aspinall, April 11, 1950, KIA.

140 Wayne N. Aspinall to ACK, April 24, 1950, KIA.

Chapter 25: "THE OLD ATTITUDE ABOUT SEX"

1 Chester I. Barnard to Arthur Hays Sulzberger, Aug. 24, 1949, Series 200, Box 41, Folder 462, Rockefeller Archives.

2 W. Allen Wallis, "Statistics of the Kinsey Report," *Journal of the American Statistical Association* 44 (Dec. 1949): 466.

3 George W. Corner to Alan Gregg, Jan. 3, 1950, Series 200, Box 41, Folder 463, Rockefeller Archives.

4 Alan Gregg to George W. Corner, Jan. 12, 1950, ibid.

5 Warren Weaver to Chester I. Barnard, Feb. 24, 1950, Inter-Office Correspondence, ibid.

6 Gerald Jonas, *The Circuit Riders: Rockefeller Money and the Rise of Modern Science* (New York, 1989), 325. Jonas offers a vivid portrait of Weaver's long career at the Rockefeller Foundation.

7 Author's interview with Michael Gregg, Dec. 1, 1984, 9–11.

8 Chester I. Barnard, "Memorandum to Principal Officers: Responsibility of Officers to Trustees and of The Rockefeller Foundation to the Public," March 9, 1950, Record Group 61.6, Series 900 Pro-44, Box 1446, Rockefeller Archives.

9 Alan Gregg quoted ibid.

10 Chester I. Barnard, ibid.

11 Alan Gregg to George W. Corner, March 7, 1950, Series 200, Box 41, Folder 463, Rockefeller Archives.

12 George W. Corner to Alan Gregg, March 17, 1950, ibid.

13 Alan Gregg to George W. Corner, April 26, 1950, ibid.

14 ACK to George W. Corner, April 15, 1950, KIA.

15 George W. Corner to M. C. Winternitz, Sept. 12, 1950, CRPS Files, NRC Archives. Winternitz was the chairman of the NRC's Division of Medical Science.

16 ACK to Samuel S. Wilks, Aug. 28, 1950, KIA.

17 George W. Corner to Isadore Lubin, May 5, 1950, Series 200, Box 41, Folder 463, Rockefeller Archives. Corner sent copies of this letter to both Kinsey and Gregg.

18 George W. Corner to Isadore Lubin, May 5, 1950, CRPS Files, NRC Archives. Although it bears the same date, this was a separate letter from the one cited above.

19 Desk Diary of Warren Weaver, "Professor S. S. Wilks (Telephone)," May 22, 1950, Series 200, Box 41, Folder 463, Rockefeller Archives.

20 Isadore Lubin to George W. Corner, June 14, 1950, ibid. Gregg was copied on the letter.
21 Lois G. Bowen, "Memorandum for File," June 22, 1950, CRPS Files, NRC Archives.
22 Ibid.
23 Chester I. Barnard to Alan Gregg, June 16, 1950, Series 200, Box 41, Folder 463, Rockefeller Archives.
24 Desk Diary of Alan Gregg, July 7, 1950, ibid.
25 Ibid.
26 Ibid.
27 Ibid.
28 Samuel S. Wilks to ACK, Sept. 8, 1950, KIA.
29 ACK to Samuel S. Wilks, Sept. 12, 1950, KIA.
30 Alan Gregg to ACK, Oct. 9, 1950, Series 200, Box 41, Folder 463, Rockefeller Archives.
31 Author's interview with George W. Corner, Aug. 5, 1971, 27, IUOHP.
32 Author's interview with Frederick Mosteller, June 26, 1992, 23.
33 Ibid., 14–16.
34 Ibid., 15.
35 William G. Cochran, Frederick Mosteller, and John W. Tukey, "Statistical Problems of the Kinsey Report," *Journal of the American Statistical Association* 48 (Dec. 1953): 694, 693.
36 Author's interview with Mosteller, June 26, 1992, 16.
37 Author's interview with Mrs. ACK, Dec. 10, 1971, 32–33, IUOHP.
38 Author's interview with Paul H. Gebhard, Oct. 29, 1971, 48, IUOHP.
39 Author's interview with Mosteller, June 26, 1992, 13.
40 Author's interview with Clyde Martin, April 8, 1971, 25, IUOHP.
41 Author's interview with Clyde Martin, March 21, 1986, 29.
42 Author's interview with Martin, April 8, 1971, 25, 26.
43 Ibid., 25.
44 Author's interview with Martin, March 21, 1986, 30.
45 Ibid., 31.
46 Author's interview with Mosteller, June 26, 1992, 17.
47 ACK to Alan Gregg, Oct. 18, 1950, KIA.
48 ACK to George W. Corner, Oct. 18, 1950, KIA.
49 Author's interview with Mosteller, June 26, 1992, 8.
50 George W. Corner to Alan Gregg, Feb. 21, 1951, Series 200, Box 41, Folder 464, Rockefeller Archives.
51 Desk diary of Alan Gregg, March 1, 1951, Series 200, Box 39, Folder 446, Rockefeller Archives.
52 Alan Gregg to Warren Weaver, March 1, 1951, Inter-Office Correspondence, Series 200, Box 41, Folder 464, Rockefeller Archives.
53 Warren Weaver to Alan Gregg, March 8, 1951, ibid.
54 Ibid.
55 Warren Weaver to Alan Gregg, March 12, 1951, ibid.
56 Ibid.
57 "Statement," enclosed in William G. Cochran to Alan Gregg, March 22, 1951, ibid.
58 George W. Corner to ACK, March 27, 1951, KIA.
59 Gregg always prepared himself mentally for his presentations to the board, and he was never cooler than when he was under fire. "I can remember my mother saying, 'Your

dad is so remarkable. Even the days when he knows he has to present to the trustees, he's just as calm, cool and loving and wonderful as ever," recalled Gregg's son, Michael, many years later. See author's interview with Michael Gregg, Dec. 1, 1984, 12.

60 Ibid., 31.

61 Author's interview with Andrew J. Warren, March 24, 1972, 9, IUOHP.

62 This quotation was attributed to Robert Loeb by Michael Gregg, who remembered hearing it on medical rounds as a young intern under Loeb's supervision. "Bob hated John Foster Dulles, and he made it clear in our medical rounds," added Gregg. See author's interview with Michael Gregg, Dec. 1, 1984, 12–13.

63 Author's interview with Robert S. Morison, Oct. 18, 1971, IUOHP.

64 Author's interview with Andrew J. Warren, March 24, 1972, 12, IUOHP.

65 Thomas Parran to Dean Rusk, Oct. 15, 1953, Series 200, Box 41, Folder 464, Rockefeller Archives.

66 John Foster Dulles to Flora M. Rhind, April 24, 1951, ibid. Yerkes, who had followed the widening split within the Rockefeller Foundation's board of trustees for many years, was certain it boded ill for the future of sex research in the United States. Confiding to his diary, Yerkes later commented with sadness on "the shift of power (or influence) in its trustees from the medical sympathizers to the religionists Van Dusen, Dulles, Dodds, et al!" See diary of Robert Mearns Yerkes, Sept. 6, 1952, Box 176, Folder 2682, Yerkes Papers.

67 Warren Weaver to Chester I. Barnard, May 7, 1951, Series 200, Box 41, Folder 464, Rockefeller Archives.

68 Chester I. Barnard to Warren Weaver, June 21, 1951, ibid.

69 Ibid. Barnard summarized the conversations he had conducted with Gregg and Warren in this memorandum to Weaver.

70 Ibid.

71 Andrew J. Warren interview with George W. Corner, Sept. 24, 1951, Series 200, Box 39, Folder 446, Rockefeller Archives. The pertinent part of this entry reads, "Dr. Corner was passing through New York and came in to get acquainted. The Support for the Committee on Sex at the present time is derived entirely from grants from the RF. From a conference with Dr. Gregg in the spring, he [Corner] had correctly understood that support for Dr. Kinsey's work beyond the present commitments would not be continued by the RF."

72 Robert S. Morison interview with ACK, May 23, 1951, Series 200, Box 41, Folder 464, Rockefeller Archives.

73 Andrew J. Warren interview with ACK, May 23, 1951, ibid.

74 Morison interview with ACK, May 23, 1951.

75 George W. Corner to ACK, Feb. 4, 1952, KIA.

76 George W. Corner to ACK, Dec. 22, 1951, KIA.

77 ACK to George W. Corner, Jan. 8, 1952, KIA.

78 George W. Corner to Robert M. Yerkes, Jan. 4, 1952, Box 77, Folder 1462, Yerkes Papers.

79 William G. Cochran to George W. Corner, Jan. 3, 1952, CRPS Files, NRC Archives.

80 Comments on "Statisticians' Report on Institute for Sex Research," ACK to George W. Corner, Jan. 25, 1952, CRPS Files, NRC Archives.

81 ACK to Harold Davis, Jan. 25, 1952, KIA.

82 H. [Harold] T. Davis to ACK, Feb. 4, 1952, KIA.

83 ACK to Harold T. Davis, Feb. 8, 1952, KIA.

84 ACK to George Gallup, Jan. 18, 1952, KIA.

85 George Gallup to ACK, Jan. 23, 1952, KIA.

86 William A. Lydgate to ACK, Feb. 5, 1952, KIA.

87 ACK to George W. Corner, Feb. 16, 1952, KIA.

88 ACK to George W. Corner, Feb. 14, 1952, KIA. Corner also tried to persuade Yerkes, the retired chairman of the committee, to attend the meeting in Bloomington, but Yerkes declined. In his diary, Yerkes wrote, "I am eager to go, but my obligation is to the Y. L. P. B., not to the Committee for Research in Problems of Sex so I wrote George accordingly." See diary of Robert Mearns Yerkes, Feb. 8, 1952, Box 176, Folder 2682, Yerkes Papers.

89 Author's interview with Mosteller, June 26, 1992, 18–19.

90 Ibid., 19.

91 Desk diary of Warren Weaver, April 1, 1952, Series 200, Box 41, Folder 465, Rockefeller Archives.

92 William G. Cochran to George W. Corner, Feb. 25, 1952, CRPS Files, NRC Archives.

93 ACK to Albert Deutsch, Feb. 25, 1952, KIA.

94 ACK to Lawrence Saunders, Feb. 26, 1952, KIA.

95 Author's interview with George W. Corner, Aug. 5, 1971, 25–26, IUOHP.

96 Author's interview with Mosteller, June 26, 1992, 8.

97 Author's interview with Paul H. Gebhard, Oct. 29, 1971, 49, IUOHP.

98 Author's interview with Mosteller, June 26, 1992, 14.

99 Cochran, Mosteller, and Tukey, "Statistical Problems of the Kinsey Report," 674.

100 Ibid.

101 Ibid.

102 Ibid., 674–75.

103 Ibid., 675.

104 Ibid.

105 Ibid., 675, 676.

106 Ibid.

107 Ibid.

108 ACK to Willard M. Allen, Feb. 25, 1952, KIA.

109 ACK to George W. Corner, Feb. 25, 1952, KIA.

110 Author's interview with Martin, March 21, 1986, 32.

111 Author's interview with Gebhard, Oct. 29, 1971, 48–49.

112 Desk diary of Warren Weaver, April 1, 1952, Series 200, Box 41, Folder 465, Rockefeller Archives.

113 William A. Lydgate to ACK, March 6, 1952, KIA.

114 ACK to George W. Corner, March 17, 1952, KIA.

115 ACK to William G. Cochran, April 28, 1952, KIA.

116 William G. Cochran to ACK, May 3, 1952, KIA.

117 ACK to William G. Cochran, June 20, 1952, KIA. Kinsey outlined the sequence of events step-by-step in this letter.

118 George W. Corner's statement to the press, June 19, 1952, CRPS Files, NRC Archives.

119 Ibid.

120 Ibid.

121 George W. Corner to ACK, June 23, 1952, KIA.

122 William G. Cochran, Frederick Mosteller, and John W. Tukey, *Statistical Problems of the Kinsey Report* (Washington, D.C., 1954).

Chapter 26: "A VICTORIAN IMAGE OF FEMALE SEXUALITY"

1 ACK to Herman B Wells, Sept. 23, 1948, KIA.

2 ACK to Alan Gregg, June 22, 1949, KIA. Kinsey wrote, "We have done a good deal of field work this year, and by the end of the year we will be involved in the writing of the next volume, the female."

3 For example, he assured an official of the American Booksellers Association, "It will be sometime late next year or early in the year thereafter before our next book gets out." See ACK to Gilbert E. Goodkins, Sept. 24, 1949, KIA. Sounding less confident, Kinsey told another inquirer the following year, "Our present thinking is that it will be possible to get the volume on Sexual Behavior in the Human Female, off the press in 1951. However, I would not commit myself to you or to anyone else on that matter." See ACK to Clifford R. Adams, Sept. 25, 1950, KIA.

4 One of Kinsey's staff members recalled, "As was true of so many people, he had an infinite attention to detail and difficulty in honestly delegating authority to anyone else." See author's interview with William Dellenback, Sept. 22, 1971, 7, IUOHP.

5 Desk diary of Alan Gregg, July 7, 1950, Series 200, Box 41, Folder 463, Rockefeller Archives.

6 Author's interview with Paul H. Gebhard, Oct. 29, 1971, 42–43, IUOHP. Another staff member remembered that, when an important visitor came to the Institute, Kinsey "used all of his inherent public relations skills that he had for someone of that sort" and "that almost without exception the Institute stock went up a notch or two after a person had been here who had not been here before." See author's interview with Dellenback, Sept. 22, 1971, 10.

7 Author's interview with Gebhard, Oct. 29, 1971, 27.

8 "Progress Report, March 15, 1952," enclosed in ACK to Robert S. Morison (marked confidential), March 20, 1952, Series 200, Box 41, Folder 464, Rockefeller Archives.

9 Author's interview with Gebhard, Oct. 29, 1971, 27.

10 Ibid., 27–28.

11 Desk diary of Robert S. Morison, Nov. 16, 1955, Series 200, Box 39, Folder 449, Rockefeller Archives.

12 Desk diary of M. C. Balfour, May 3–4, 1951, Series 200, Box 41, Folder 464, Rockefeller Archives.

13 Desk diary of Alan Gregg, July 7, 1950, Series 200, Box 41, Folder 463, Rockefeller Archives.

14 Quoted in Kenneth R. Stevens, "United States v. 31 Photographs: Dr. Alfred C. Kinsey and Obscenity Law," *Indiana Magazine of History* 71 (Dec. 1975): 300. Unless otherwise indicated, my discussion of Kinsey's legal battles with the Customs Bureau relies on Stevens's excellent article.

15 Ibid.

16 ACK to Warren E. Cox, March 8, 1949, KIA.

17 Stevens, "United States v. 31 Photographs," 301. Kinsey blamed this development on the personnel change, telling a friend, "This is the result of the employment of a new inspector in our Indianapolis office who is inexperienced in regard to the rulings that

have come down from Washington." See ACK to Arnold Muirhead, Nov. 18, 1950, KIA.

18 Stevens, "United States v. 31 Photographs," 301.

19 Ibid., 303, 304, 305.

20 ACK to George W. Corner, Nov. 22, 1950, KIA.

21 Quoted in Stevens, "United States v. 31 Photographs," 303.

22 ACK to Corner, Nov. 22, 1950. Dr. Merril Davis of Marion, Indiana, was the physician who visited the library and then defended it to Governor Schricker. In a letter thanking Davis, Kinsey wrote, "I want to take the opportunity to express our appreciation of your understanding of what we are doing, and your splendid defense of the work both before the Trustees and before the Governor." See ACK to Merril Davis, Dec. 13, 1950, KIA.

23 "Institute for Sex Research," *Indiana Alumni Magazine,* March 1951, 9.

24 ACK to Herman B Wells, March 26, 1951, KIA.

25 Herman B Wells to ACK, April 18, 1951, KIA.

26 Hilda Henwood to Chester Barnard, March 27, 1951, Series 200, Box 41, Folder 464, Rockefeller Archives.

27 Recording his reaction to the piece, Yerkes wrote in his diary, "Particularly impressive and encouraging to me was a summary report about the Kinsey organization and the status of the project to which he has given most of his time for a dozen years and doubtless will devote the remainder of his life. It is an inspiring picture of research effort and progress which fills me with pride in the helpfulness of the N.R.C. Comm. For research in problems of sex. I must write Kinsey and his associates a letter of appreciation and cheer." Diary of Robert M. Yerkes, March 30, 1951, Box 175, Folder 2681, Yerkes Papers.

28 ACK to George W. Corner, Dec. 13, 1950, KIA. As usual, Kinsey was worried what effect his problems with the Customs Bureau would have on his relationship with the Rockefeller Foundation, telling Corner, "I should advise you that I have not heard anything from Dr. Gregg or the Rockefeller Foundation since this newspaper case developed, and I have not kept them informed of our present developments. I should think it appropriate to do so after we work out some final solution to the matter."

29 ACK to J. Rives Childs, Nov. 27, 1952, KIA.

30 Quoted in Stevens, "United States v. 31 Photographs," 308, 309. In 1950, the Customs Service did return to Kinsey approximately 80 percent of the material that it had seized.

31 An officer of the Rockefeller Foundation who visited Kinsey's new quarters in 1951 wrote in his diary, "[Kinsey] emphasized that the University now gives him priority treatment." See diary of M. C. Balfour, May 3–4, 1951, Series 200, Box 41, Folder 464, Rockefeller Archives. Kinsey, of course, knew who was responsible for the preferential treatment he received. "Let me thank you again, as we have in the report, for your long continued interest in the research, and this year especially for your arrangement that we get into new and more expanded quarters," Kinsey thanked Wells. See ACK to Herman B Wells, April 7, 1950, KIA.

32 Lawrence Saunders to Eleanor Roehr Gorman, Oct. 31, 1951, KIA. She responded, "I am afraid we have spoiled your fun in that direction because we have already become the possessor of a goodly number of strong, non-clattering wooden hangers. However, for whatever solace it may be to you: I'm not at all sure that it wasn't your chance remark that precipitated the purchase." See Eleanor Roehr Gorman to Lawrence Saunders, Nov. 2, 1951, KIA.

33 ACK to Frank A. Beach, Feb. 25, 1950, KIA.

34 ACK to Helen D'Amico, April 18, 1950, KIA.

35 Author's interview with Gebhard, Oct. 29, 1971, 18–19.

36 Author's interview with Paul H. Gebhard, Oct. 14, 1984, 18.

37 Author's interview with Dellenback, Sept. 22, 1971, 36.

38 Author's interview with Glenway Wescott, June 27, 1972, 47, IUOHP.

39 John D'Emilio, *Sexual Politics, Sexual Communities: The Making of a Homosexual Minority in the United States, 1940–1970* (Chicago, 1983), 58–74. Unless otherwise indicated, my discussion of the Mattachine Society is based on D'Emilio's excellent study.

40 ACK to Wallace Maxey, Feb. 5, 1953 (telegram), KIA.

41 ACK to Wallace Maxey, Feb. 6, 1953, KIA. In his reply, Maxey was the soul of contrition, declaring, "I have not now nor in the past mis-used your name in any way, nor will I in the future." See Wallace De Ortega Maxey to ACK, Feb. 11, 1953, KIA.

42 D'Emilio, *Sexual Politics,* 77.

43 Quoted in ibid., 76.

44 Ibid., 78–80.

45 Quoted in ibid., 81.

46 Kenneth Burns to ACK, Aug. 22, 1953, KIA.

47 ACK to Kenneth Burns, Sept. 18, 1953, KIA.

48 ACK to John Loy, Nov. 2, 1953, KIA.

49 E. M. Nickel to ACK, Feb. 18, 1953, KIA.

50 ACK to E. M. Nickel, April 14, 1953, KIA. "We got a nice group of histories of persons who had been in trouble with the law," wrote Kinsey.

51 Quoted in D'Emilio, *Sexual Politics,* 83–84.

52 For an excellent analysis of the political maneuvers that led to this change, see Ronald Bayer, *Homosexuality and American Psychiatry: The Politics of Diagnosis* (New York, 1981). In May 1955, the Mattachine Society bestowed its "Award of Merit" on the Institute for Sex Research, informing Kinsey, "We are very happy to present the award to your organization for the wonderful work you are doing in behalf of the sex-variant in the world." Dale C. Olson to ACK, May 18, 1955, KIA.

53 Author's interview with Paul H. Gebhard, Aug. 7, 1984, 1.

54 Paul Robinson, *The Modernization of Sex: Havelock Ellis, Alfred Kinsey, William Masters and Virginia Johnson* (New York, 1976), 70.

55 *SBHF,* 649–50, 669, 683, and 687.

56 Author's interview with Clarence A. Tripp, Dec. 15, 1987, 10.

57 Author's interview with William Dellenback, Feb. 14, 1988, 33.

58 "Kinsey Speaks Out," *Newsweek,* April 12, 1948, 51.

59 Anon. to ACK, April 26, 1948. Kinsey replied, "Females who are as highly responsive as you can contribute materially to our thinking on the volume we are to have on the female." ACK to Anon., May 26, 1948, KIA.

60 Natalie R. Hirschfeld to ACK, July 12, 1948, KIA.

61 Anon. to ACK, July 24, 1947, KIA.

62 ACK to Anon., Aug. 18, 1947, KIA.

63 ACK to David Riesman, April 19, 1956, KIA. Riesman replied, "What you say about the difficulty of getting a woman interviewer is very much to the point and is simply another indication of the subordinate status of women in our society." See David Riesman to ACK, April 29, 1956, KIA.

64 Author's interview with Anon. A, Dec. 15, 1987, 10.

65   Wardell B. Pomeroy, *Dr. Kinsey and the Institute for Sex Research* (New York, 1972), 330.
66   *SBHF,* 58–59.
67   ACK to George W. Corner, Sept. 13, 1950, KIA.
68   E. W. Palmer to Lawrence Saunders, Nov. 9, 1951, KIA.
69   Author's interview with Frederick Mosteller, June 26, 1992, 14, 10.
70   Frederick Mosteller to ACK, May 5, 1952, KIA.
71   ACK to Harold F. Dorn, July 20, 1952, KIA. Decades later, Gebhard acknowledged that they had made relatively few statistical changes in the female volume, but he firmly believed that they had done all that could reasonably be expected. Much of their effort involved the sample. "We excluded prison females," noted Gebhard. "In most cases we excluded lower social levels, and we tried to make our statements applicable only to middle- and upper-social-level females. Also, we didn't use standard deviation." Turning to what he considered the most important correction, Gebhard declared, "We tried to be careful not to exceed our data in what we said." Author's interview with Gebhard, Oct. 29, 1971, 53.
72   Harold F. Dorn to ACK, Aug. 7, 1952, KIA.
73   ACK to Harold F. Dorn, Oct. 15, 1952, KIA.
74   *SBHF,* 8.
75   Ibid.
76   Ibid., 9.
77   Ibid.
78   Ibid., 10.
79   Ibid., 10, 11.
80   Ibid., 11.
81   Ibid.
82   Ibid., 20, 21.
83   Ibid., 23–31.
84   Ibid., 46–52, 53, 57.
85   Ibid., 57.
86   Ibid., 103, 104, 106, 108, 115.
87   Ibid., 118, 120, 121.
88   Ibid., 121.
89   Ibid., 142, 196, 233, 286, 416, 454, 473, 505.
90   Ibid., 410, 412.
91   Ibid., 411.
92   Ibid., 326. Kinsey's inclusion of anthropological data also reflected Gebhard's input, as well as Kinsey's desire to protect himself from another round of attacks by anthropologists.
93   Ibid., 371–72, 386.
94   Ibid., 172, 385, 172 (for masturbation), 265 (for petting), 328 (for intercourse), 330.
95   Ibid., 316–17.
96   Ibid., 432–33.
97   Ibid., 433, 435–36.
98   Ibid., 434–35.
99   Ibid., 714–15.
100 Ibid., 574, 580.
101 ACK to Adrienne Sarti, March 27, 1950, KIA.
102 *SBHF,* 582.

103 Ibid., 380, 388, 390, 324.
104 Author's interview with Gebhard, Oct. 29, 1971, 99.
105 Kinsey's defensive strategy was evident when he asked Corner, "What would the NRC's Committee think of our publishing the names of the members of the present committee some place in the introductory pages to our volume—perhaps in the list of acknowledgments? If you and the committee would consider such a possibility, I think it would help satisfy people that we have had qualified persons supporting the project." See ACK to George W. Corner, July 12, 1952, KIA. After polling his committee, Corner agreed to this request. See George W. Corner to ACK, July 30, 1952, KIA. Delighted, Kinsey replied, "We are also greatly indebted to you and the rest of the committee for permission to publish the names of the NRC Committee. I think this is the finest sort of backing that your group could have given." See ACK to George W. Corner, Aug. 21, 1952, KIA. The names of the members of the CRPS were published (without explanation) in the female volume opposite the acknowledgments, on the back of the dedication page. See *SBHF* (unnumbered).
106 George W. Corner to ACK, June 23, 1953, KIA.
107 ACK to George W. Corner, June 30, 1952, KIA. For the formal invitation for Yerkes to join Corner, see ACK to Robert M. Yerkes, July 28, 1952, KIA. Yerkes, of course, was delighted to be asked and gladly accepted. See Robert M. Yerkes to ACK, Aug. 3, 1953, KIA.
108 George W. Corner to Robert M. Yerkes, July 30, 1952, Box 77, Folder 1460, Yerkes Papers.
109 Yerkes wrote a long diary entry about the preface, explaining that he had agreed to accept the assignment "because it is an opportunity to be helpful, and because Corner and I are in perfect agreement on essentials." See diary of Yerkes, Aug. 1, 1952, Box 176, Folder 2682, Yerkes Papers. Two days later, Yerkes confided to his diary, "I am eager to visit Kinsey and thus reestablish contacts with him and his staff. His remarkable project interests me as much as ever and I shall gladly join Corner in sponsoring this chapter of his report by trying to write an appropriate foreword." See diary of Yerkes, Aug. 3, 1952.
110 Diary of Yerkes, Sept. 12–13, 1953, ibid.
111 Diary of Yerkes, Sept. 15, 1952, ibid.
112 Diary of Yerkes, Sept. 24, 1952, ibid. Yerkes also recorded that Gregg "spoke freely of the disagreement which has appeared in his board and nearly defeated his last recommendation for support during another year beyond the present. It appears that two or three non-scientist opponents nearly defeated Alan. President Dodd of Princeton is one of the most influential dissenters, President Van Dusen is another—and no other was mentioned in our conversation, unless it be Dr. Warren Weaver, who evidently is unfriendly." See diary of Yerkes, Sept. 24–25, 1952, ibid.
113 Yerkes's labors on the preface can be traced in his diary, and many of the entries are quite touching, revealing an honest soul who felt a tremendous burden to discharge a duty he considered of historic importance. On Oct. 3, 1952, Yerkes wrote, "I am assembling my notes for the composition of the Preface and hope to write the first draft next week. I think I now have all the information I need or can use." On Oct. 7, he wrote, "To the composition of the Kinsey book preface. During a free hour or so I wrote the opening . . . and then rewrote it. Now that I have made the start I probably shall finish the initial draft this week. It should not prove a difficult task, as I am both interested and convinced that it is important." Oct. 8 found him complaining, "At my preface writing but without compulsion or enthusiasm, so progress was low

and I am not satisfied with any sentence written." On Oct. 10, he sounded more up-beat, noting, "With enthusiasm I wrote this morning the final paragraphs for a Kinsey book preface. In these I try to describe the setting within a period of revolutionary change, of the Kinsey project and the Institute for Sex Research. I featured Freud naturally, and dwell on the influence of woman's emancipation and of World War I on the climate of opinion and attitude toward matters of sex and reproduction. An astounding change has occurred in the last three or four decades. Kinsey stands out as the fact finding investigator." On Oct. 12, he wrote, "Bobby [his daughter] and her Mother have read and commented on my Kinsey preface ms. In its first draft. So I am encouraged and optimistic." On Oct. 14, Yerkes wrote, "After some hours of revision the preface ms. is ready for retyping where upon I shall mail it to Geo. Corner in Oxford, England to take a whack at it. I hope he can increase its value and improve the style. Largely because both Ada [his wife] and Bobby think well of my first attempt to write something appropriate I am encouraged to send it off hoping that it may have a like fate with Betsy [Corner's wife] and George, but I shall not be surprised or disappointed if he changes it radically, in case it should strike him as unsuitable. His responsibility is greater than mine because he is active instead of retired." On Oct. 24, Yerkes beamed, "At last I air-mailed the draft of 'preface' for Kinsey book with a letter about it to Geo. W. Corner in Oxford, England." On Nov. 17, Yerkes wrote, "This week-end's mail was heavy and full of interesting letters, among them one from Geo. Corner about the 'preface' ms. of which he thinks well. . . . He thinks it should be submitted to Kinsey for his reaction, before we attempt to revise it. And I agree." All citations from diary of Yerkes, ibid.

114 Recording his disappointment in his diary, Yerkes wrote, "From A. Kinsey comes back the Preface Ms., with the word that he is going to suggest ways of condensing it and making it more quotable. Evidently it does not please him or he would not have delayed so long in advising us. And now he says we shall hear from him again 'in some weeks.' I am sorry, but not surprised because his interests are not identical with those of the N.R.C. and our Committee." See diary of Yerkes, Dec. 2, 1952, ibid.

115 ACK, to "Sirs," *American Mercury,* May 13, 1953, KIA. Justifying this contract, Kinsey told one inquirer, "I hope you will also understand that while this appears to be a complicated legal document, that it has only one simple principle; namely, that of seeing that access is given equally to everyone who has a legitimate interest in seeing the material." In a less pious moment, Kinsey also noted, "We are interested in seeing that the maximum number of persons shall have the maximum opportunity to see our full report, and that, it seems to me, is an obligation to which any scientist is properly committed." See ACK to Seward Hiltner, May 28, 1953, KIA.

116 For the May 25–28 session, reporters came from *Colliers, Harpers, Life, McCall's, Mademoiselle, Redbook, Cosmopolitan,* and *Today's Woman;* for the June 1–4 session, *Ladies' Home Journal, Ebony, Parents', Look,* and *Newsweek;* and for the June 6–11 session, *Time,* Associated Press, *Pageant,* United Press, *Lifetime Living, Argosy,* and *Reader's Digest.*

117 Albert Deutsch, "How Kinsey Studies the Sexual Behavior of American Women," *Woman's Home Companion,* Aug. 1953, 54.

118 Clara Savage Littledale, "The Second Kinsey Report: What Has It to Say to Parents?" *Parents' Magazine,* Sept. 1953, 39.

119 "Medicine," *Time,* Aug. 24, 1953, 51.

120 Amram Scheinfeld, "A Social Scientist's Evaluation: Kinsey's Study of Female Sex Behavior," *Cosmopolitan,* Sept. 1953, 29.

121 *Bloomington Herald Telephone,* July 28, 1953, clipping files, KIA.
122 Eleanor L. Roehr to Alan J. Gould, July 17, 1953, KIA.
123 Author's interview with Gebhard, Oct. 29, 1971, 85.
124 Ibid., 88. Defending how they handled the press, Gebhard insisted, "But it wasn't wholly manipulation for self-aggrandizement or money. Part of it was an honest effort to try to give everybody an equal crack at the unpublished material."
125 ACK to George W. Corner, Feb. 19, 1953, KIA.
126 ACK to Robert S. Morison, March 12, 1953, KIA.
127 ACK to Fernandus Payne, June 19, 1953, KIA.
128 ACK to Herman B Wells, July 14, 1953, KIA.
129 *Indianapolis Star,* Aug. 15, 1953, clipping files, KIA.

Chapter 27: "DAMN THAT RUSK"

1 Amram Scheinfeld, "A Social Scientist's Evaluation: Kinsey's Study of Female Sexual Behavior," *Cosmopolitan,* Sept. 1953, 28.
2 Quoted in *Newsweek,* Aug. 31, 1953, 57.
3 Werner C. Michel to ACK, Sept. 5, 1953, KIA.
4 Bruce Bliven, "Hullabaloo on K-Day," *New Republic,* Nov. 9, 1953, 17.
5 "The Story Back of Kinsey: Sex Studies Yield Fame But Not Riches," *U.S. News & World Report,* Nov. 6, 1953, 40.
6 Orville Prescott, "Books of the Times," *New York Times,* Dec. 14, 1953, clipping files, KIA.
7 "5,940 Women," *Time,* Aug. 24, 1953, 53.
8 "Story Back of Kinsey," 42.
9 ACK to Irving Auerbach, Sept. 21, 1953, KIA.
10 "For Women Only: What Every Woman Should Know about Kinsey," *Look,* Sept. 8, 1953, 78.
11 "Story Back of Kinsey," 40.
12 "5,940 Women," 53. John Gunther, a writer for *Time,* wrote Kinsey privately, "Hearty congratulations on the masterful way you handled the prepublication details of the Female book, as well as the well-deserved success the book, itself, is having." See John Gunther to ACK, Oct. 14, 1953, KIA.
13 George Emerson, "How to Build a Best Seller," *Saturday Review of Literature,* Sept. 5, 1953, 21.
14 "The Female Sex," *New York Times,* Aug. 23, 1953, sec. 4, p. 2.
15 Review (unsigned) of *SBHF,* in *New Yorker,* Sept. 19, 1953, 120.
16 George Gallup, "Two American Institute of Public Opinion Surveys on the Kinsey Reports," reprinted in Jerome Himelhoch and Sylvia Fleis Fava, eds., *Sexual Behavior in American Society: An Appraisal of the First Two Kinsey Reports* (New York, 1955), 381–82.
17 Anon. to ACK, Aug. 11, 1953, KIA.
18 Anon. to ACK, Aug. 18, 1953, KIA.
19 Anon. to ACK, Aug. 21, 1953, KIA.
20 Anon. to ACK, Sept. 4, 1953, KIA.
21 Anon. to ACK, Sept. 17, 1953, KIA.
22 Anon. to ACK, Sept. 26, 1953, KIA.
23 Anon. to ACK, Sept. 1953 (n.d.), KIA.
24 Anon. to ACK, Sept. 10, 1953, KIA.

25 Anon. to ACK, July 23, 1954, KIA.

26 Anon. to ACK, Aug. 21, 1953, KIA. The woman revealed to Kinsey that she was not a virgin when she married, but insisted that her husband was the only man she had slept with before or after their marriage.

27 Anon. to ACK, Oct. 6, 1953, KIA.

28 Jane Stafford, "Kinsey's Data on Females," *Science News Letter,* Aug. 22, 1953, 120.

29 "5,940 Women," 58.

30 "Bombs, H and K," *Newsweek,* Aug. 31, 1953, 57.

31 Kathleen Norris, "Incredible," and Fannie Hurst, "Nourishing," *Life,* Aug. 24, 1953, 59–65.

32 Bliven, "Hullabaloo on K-Day," 18.

33 Unsigned review of *SBHF,* in *Freeman,* Oct. 19, 1953, 66.

34 My treatment of how Kinsey anticipated many of the arguments and concerns of feminists a decade later draws heavily on the analysis of Janice M. Irvine, *Disorders of Desire: Sex and Gender in Modern American Society* (Philadelphia, 1990), 63.

35 Jonathan Katz, *Gay American History: Lesbians and Gay Men in the U. S. A.* (New York, 1976), 336.

36 Quoted in Irvine, *Disorders of Desire,* 54.

37 *Indianapolis Star,* Aug. 21, 1953, 18.

38 "General Book Review," *New Yorker,* Sept. 19, 1953, 120.

39 Stafford, "Kinsey's Data on Females," 119.

40 Bliven, "Hullabaloo on K-Day," 18.

41 "All About Eve: Kinsey Reports on American Women," *Newsweek,* Aug. 24, 1953, 70.

42 Albert Deutsch, "How Kinsey Studies the Sexual Behavior of American Women," *Woman's Home Companion,* Aug. 1953, 36.

43 Scheinfeld, "Kinsey's Study," 28.

44 Ibid., 28–29. The *Chicago Tribune* assured its readers in an editorial, "The report should not be taken too seriously as the methods used in collecting the data have been questioned and its findings do not represent the actions of all women. Nor will the results alter our sexual behavior in the future." Quoted in *Indianapolis News,* Aug. 21, 1953, clipping files, KIA.

45 Scheinfeld, "Kinsey's Study," 29.

46 Ernest Havemann, "The Kinsey Report on Women," *Life,* Aug. 24, 1953, 56.

47 Bentley Glass, review of *SBHF,* in *Science,* April 30, 1954, 601–2.

48 Scheinfeld, "Kinsey's Study," 28.

49 "5,940 Women," 58.

50 Deutsch, "How Kinsey Studies," 54.

51 Clyde Kluckhohn, "The Complex Kinsey Study and What It Attempts to Do," review of *SBHF,* in *New York Times Book Review,* Sept. 13, 1953, sec. 7, p. 3.

52 "5,940 Women," 58.

53 *New York Journal American,* Aug. 25, 1953, clipping files, KIA. Less than two weeks following K-Day, a New York newspaper reported, "Radio networks last night banned all Kinsey songs." See ibid., Aug. 31, 1953, clipping files, KIA.

54 Ibid., Aug. 21, 1953, clipping files, KIA.

55 *Indianapolis Star,* Aug. 23, 1953, clipping files, KIA.

56 *Indianapolis News,* Aug. 20, 1953, clipping files, KIA.

57 *New York Journal American,* Sept. 14, 1953, clipping files, KIA. Sophie Tucker, the "red hot mamma" of the 1920s, was kinder. One of the few celebrities to say anything

positive, she exclaimed, "This is what I call a mark of progress." See *Indianapolis News,* Aug. 20, 1953, clipping files, KIA.

58 *New York World-Telegram and Sun,* Aug. 29, 1953, clipping files, KIA.

59 "Kinsey Releases Report on Women," *New York Times,* Aug. 21, 1953, 15.

60 *New York Journal American,* Aug. 21, 1953, clipping files, KIA. In his column "Television and Radio," Jack O'Brien also reported, "A TV magazine got the name on the cover this way: 'Absolutely no KINSEY REPORT' in this issue." Radio journalists were wise to tread softly. As late as 1954, the press reported, "New FCC Commissioner Doerfer vigorously and officially rapped a Memphis radio station for an uncommonly frank discussion of Dr. Kinsey's research." See ibid., June 12, 1954, clipping files, KIA.

61 "K-Day," *Time,* Aug. 31, 1953, 52.

62 "Bombs, H and K," 57.

63 "K-Day," 52.

64 *New York Post,* Aug. 30, 1953, clipping files, KIA.

65 *New York Times,* Aug. 30, 1953, 78. Looking on the bright side, one of Kinsey's friends predicted, "If the proposal of Representative Heller of Brooklyn to demand a postal ban on your book should become a reality, that would assure you a boost to at least a million copies, after the courts would have lifted the ban, as they surely would." See Werner C. Michel to ACK, Sept. 5, 1953, KIA.

66 *New York Post,* Sept. 2, 1953, clipping files, KIA.

67 *New York Times,* Sept. 2, 1953, 15. Kinsey did not fare as well with the Army. On Sept. 23, 1953, an announcement came from Heidelberg, Germany, the headquarters of the U.S. Army in Europe, that the Army had banned the female volume from its libraries in Europe. The official explanation was that the Army "does not intend to spend money on that kind of book." See ibid., Sept. 24, 1953, 10.

68 *Indianapolis News,* Aug. 20, 28, 1953, clipping files, KIA.

69 *Bloomington Herald-Telephone,* Aug. 20, Aug. 21, 1953, clipping files, KIA. A grateful Kinsey wrote Wells, "Let me assure you again, you have been most understanding and excellent in your support of the right of the scientist to investigate, and in your belief that increased knowledge can ultimately be of social benefit." See ACK to Herman B Wells, Sept. 18, 1953, KIA.

70 Mrs. Harold D. Brady and Mrs. Alfred C. Brown to Herman B Wells, Aug. 24, 1953, KIA. Wells sent a copy of this letter to Kinsey.

71 Herman B Wells to Mrs. Harold D. Brady, Sept. 2, 1953, KIA. Again, Wells sent a copy of his reply to Kinsey.

72 Ibid.

73 *Indianapolis News,* Oct. 6, Aug. 21, 1953, clipping files, KIA.

74 Herman B Wells to Robert S. Morison, Sept. 3, 1953, Series 200, Box 41, Folder 465, Rockefeller Archives.

75 Robert S. Morison to Herman B Wells, Sept. 10, 1953, ibid. Wells also sent Alan Gregg a copy of his press release. In his reply, Gregg called it "first rate in every way." See Alan Gregg to Herman B Wells, Sept. 2, 1953; an unsigned copy of the letter is located in the KIA.

76 Author's interview with Dean Rusk, April 13, 1972, 5, IUOHP.

77 For Dulles's appointments as chairman of the board and head of the presidential search committee, see Flora M. Rhind to John Foster Dulles, April 10, 1950, Box 49, John Foster Dulles Papers, Princeton University Library. Dulles's strong support for

Rusk comes through loud and clear in a letter Dulles wrote during the search. See John Foster Dulles to Lewis Douglas, Sept. 11, 1951, ibid.

78 Author's interview with Rusk, April 13, 1972, 13, 12.

79 Ibid., 12–13.

80 Hugh H. Smith to Dean Rusk, "Kinsey volume, 'Sexual Behavior in the Human Female,' " Inter-Office Correspondence, Aug. 13, 1953, Series 200, Box 41, Folder 465, Rockefeller Archives.

81 Hugh H. Smith to ACK, Aug. 13, 1953, ibid.

82 "Story Back of Kinsey," 40.

83 Hadley Cantril, "Sex without Love," *Nation,* Oct. 10, 1953, 294.

84 Beatrice Schapper, "Kinsey Interviews the Women," *Glamour,* Sept. 1953, 166.

85 Thomas Parran to Dean Rusk, Oct. 15, 1953, Series 200, Box 41, Folder 465, Rockefeller Archives.

86 William I. Myers to Dean Rusk, Oct. 19, 1953, ibid.

87 George W. Corner to Carl R. Moore, Feb. 11, 1953, CRPS Files, NRC Archives.

88 George W. Corner to Milton C. Winternitz, June 5, 1953, CRPS Files, NRC Archives. Winternitz was the chairman of the NRC's Division of Medical Science.

89 Referring both to the committee and to Kinsey, Warren's desk diary noted, "Dr. Corner and Dr. Cannon will prepare an argument and a proposal for continued foundation aid." See desk diary of Andrew J. Warren, Nov. 6, 1953, Series 200, Box 39, Folder 447, Rockefeller Archives. Nearly two decades later, I asked Weaver in an interview, "Now, do I understand you correctly, sir, that you in effect told Dr. Corner and Dr. Cannon that they could submit a budget for Dr. Kinsey or a budget which included Dr. Kinsey, but that you could not be optimistic that it would be passed?" Warren replied, "That is correct." I then followed up, "But you said nothing which would have prevented them from trying?" He answered, "I did not." See author's interview with Andrew J. Warren, March 24, 1972, 19, IUOHP.

90 George W. Corner to ACK, Dec. 2, 1953, KIA. In describing the meeting to Kinsey, Corner was candid. "They were very cautious in their remarks," he wrote. "They held out no certain prospect as to the continuation of the Committee's support, nor as to the size of a new grant from the Foundation, nor as to the attitude of their Board toward continued grants by the Committee to the Institute for Sex Research," continued Corner.

91 R. Keith Cannan to Andrew J. Warren, Nov. 27, 1953, CRPS Files, NRC Archives.

92 ACK to George C. Corner, Dec. 5, 1953, KIA.

93 Kluckhohn, "Complex Kinsey Study," 38. A distinguished anthropologist, Kluckhohn, the reader will recall, was one of Paul Gebhard's mentors at Harvard.

94 Joseph Zinkin, review of *SBHF,* in *Psychoanalytic Review* 41 (Oct. 1954): 403. Added Zinkin, "The author's ungrateful critics can now sit down and really make use of this quantitative spade work which Kinsey presents to us. . . . A veil of the curtain of our ignorance has been raised a little—psychodynamics notwithstanding. The private world of sex, known only to the individual and his psychiatrist (in infinitesimal samplings) is revealed more fully than ever before by some very courageous investigators and their equally courageous female collaborators."

95 Karl Menninger, "What the Girls Told," *Saturday Review,* Sept. 26, 1953, 21, 30.

96 Ibid., 30–31.

97 This interpretation draws heavily on the excellent analysis of Menninger's review in Lawrence J. Friedman's important study, *Menninger: The Family and the Clinic* (New York, 1990), 220–22.

98   ACK to Walter Alvarez, Sept. 10, 1953, KIA.

99   Billy Graham, "The Bible and Dr. Kinsey," *Moody Monthly,* Nov. 1953, 13.

100   Reinhold Niebuhr, "Sex and Religion in the Kinsey Report," *Christianity and Crisis,*
      Nov. 2, 1953, 138. In a letter to his editor who was compiling a book of essays on
      Kinsey, Niebuhr explained, "I have read the book and I want to make the chief bur-
      den of my chapter the failure of Kinsey to deal with people as persons, and therefore
      to deal with sexual relations as relations between persons." See Reinhold Niebuhr to
      Donald Porter Geddes, Sept. 21, 1953, Reinhold Niebuhr Papers, Box 16, Manuscript
      Division, Library of Congress.

101   Niebuhr, "Sex and Religion," 138, 140–41.

102   Ibid., 141. Privately, Niebuhr articulated his own views on sexuality. "All creatures are
      sexual," he declared. "Man's sexuality is related to all of his higher creativities. The free-
      dom seems to me not to be whether or not he 'makes love' but the indeterminate pos-
      sibilities in the sexual urge. In a sense man's creativity does not make him co-partner
      with God, 'if he wishes.' In some respects human creativity is a partnership in creation
      willy nilly." See Reinhold Niebuhr to Mrs. Jonathan Bingham, n.d. [Oct. 1953?],
      Reinhold Niebuhr Papers, Box 26, Manuscript Division, Library of Congress.
      Niebuhr was included among the critics who thought that Kinsey had inflated his
      numbers to make American women appear less moral. "Incidentally, the one point
      where I think Kinsey was completely wrong in formulating his statistics is that he in-
      corporated the statistics of premarital relations of those who had them with their fu-
      ture spouses in the general statistics of premarital sex relations," Niebuhr wrote a
      friend. "I personally think that these are completely in a different category, particularly
      if they occur between engagement and marriage." See Reinhold Niebuhr to June
      (Mrs. Jonathan) Bingham, Nov. 12, 1953, ibid. One of Niebuhr's friends rendered a
      perceptive reading of Kinsey. "I have been distressed at the ballyhoo preceding the
      publication of *Sexual Behavior in the Human Female,"* wrote the friend. "And now that
      I have read the book—or at any rate a good part of it—I am more disturbed than
      ever," the friend continued. "I am afraid that Kinsey's biological bias has led him to
      treat man merely as a more complicated mammal. One does not have to read very
      much between the lines to see that Kinsey would like to let the bars down pretty com-
      pletely, that is, to eliminate most, if not all, of the social rules restraining the expres-
      sion of human sexuality. He does not seem to have any comprehension of the
      conditions for the coexistence of people as opposed to the conditions for the realiza-
      tion of the desires of the individual. He does not grasp the sociological fact—tragic
      though it is—that community is purchased at the price of individual self-restraint." See
      Jackson Tolby to Reinhold Niebuhr, Sept. 13, 1953, ibid.

103   Henry P. Van Dusen to Warren Weaver, Nov. 11, 1953, Series 200, Box 41, Folder
      465, Rockefeller Archives.

104   Warren Weaver to Henry P. Van Dusen, Nov. 17, 1953, ibid.

105   Dean Rusk to Henry P. Van Dusen, Dec. 11, 1953, ibid.

106   For an overview of the Cox committee, see John Lankford, *Congress and the Founda-
      tions in the Twentieth Century* (River Falls, Wis., 1964), 33–53.

107   Author's interviews with Wayne L. Hays, May 5, 1971 and Aug. 4, 1971, 1, IUOHP.

108   Quoted in Lankford, *Congress and the Foundations,* 57.

109   Author's interview with Warren, March 24, 1972, 20.

110   Anon. to ACK, Oct. 21, 1953, KIA.

111   *Lincoln* (Nebraska) *State Journal,* Aug. 28, 1953, clipping files, KIA.

112   *Boston Traveler,* Sept. 8, 1953, clipping files, KIA.

113   *Indianapolis News,* April 18, 1953, clipping files, KIA.

114   These quotes from the *Indiana Catholic and Record* editorial were republished in the *Indiana Daily Student,* Feb. 17, 1954, clipping files, KIA. Calling the charge that Kinsey had promoted communism "the final straw," the *Indiana Daily Student* praised him for not answering his tormentors, "Patience, indeed, seems to be one of Dr. Alfred C. Kinsey's major virtues," declared the editors.

115   Edward J. Humphreys to Eleanor L. Roehr, Feb. 18, 1954, KIA. Humphreys was a physician who chaired the Commission on Religion and Health of the National Council of the Churches of Christ, and Roehr was Kinsey's private secretary.

116   Quoted in the *Indiana Daily Student,* Feb. 17, 1954, clipping files, KIA.

117   Quoted ibid., April 22, 1954, clipping files, KIA. Kinsey wrote a warm letter of thanks to the secretary of the Indiana University chapter of the American Association of University Professors. See ACK to Marsham Wattson, May 10, 1954, KIA.

118   *Bloomington Star Courier,* Jan. 8, 1954, clipping files, KIA.

119   Clipping from *Anniston* (Alabama) *Star,* Jan. 12, 1954, Record Group 11, Box 1, Folder 1, Rockefeller Archives.

120   *New York Times,* Jan. 7, 1954, 21.

121   Quoted in Lankford, *Congress and the Foundations,* 59.

122   Author's interview with Warren, March 24, 1972, 19–20.

123   Author's interview with Robert S. Morison, Oct. 18, 1971, 23, IUOHP.

124   Ibid., 21, 23, 25, 27.

125   Author's interview with George W. Corner, Aug. 5, 1971, 32, IUOHP.

126   Desk diary of Robert S. Morison, Jan. 18, 1954, Series 200, Box 39, Folder 448, Rockefeller Archives.

127   George W. Corner, "Memorandum for Sex Research Committee," Feb. 2, 1954, CRPS Files, NRC Archives.

128   Reflecting on the board's animus, Corner told an interviewer, "[A]t the bottom of all this was a stratum of Victorian reluctance to bring sex matters into the open." Astutely, he added that the trustees who felt this way were "fortified in their attitude by the criticisms of scientific method that came to them from some of the mathematicians, statisticians, and some psychologists." See author's interview with Corner, Aug. 5, 1971, 23.

129   Corner told his colleagues on the CRPS, "Informally and with the request that the details mentioned should be off the record, Dr. Morison explained to me that the attitude of the Rockefeller Foundation Board was very complicated, and that there were several different reasons why a majority vote could not be obtained for continuation of support to Kinsey." Corner continued, "I replied to Dr. Morison that I understood his personal embarrassment in having to transmit this message (which I believe does not represent his own best judgment)." See Corner, "Memorandum for Sex Research Committee."

130   Author's interview with Corner, Aug. 5, 1971, 32.

131   Author's interview with Morison, Oct. 18, 1971, 22, 23.

132   Corner, "Memorandum for Sex Research Committee."

133   George W. Corner to Robert M. Yerkes, Jan. 25, 1954, Box 77, Folder 1463, Yerkes Papers. Keith Cannan invited Morison to attend the committee meeting, but Morison declined, explaining, "All things considered, it seems better not to accept as my presence might hamper the free discussion which I am sure you ought to have." See Robert S. Morison to R. Keith Cannan, Feb. 1, 1954, Series 200, Box 39, Folder 448, Rockefeller Archives. Still, Morison did manage to testify for the record. In a long let-

ter to Corner, Morison admitted that some members of the committee might view the foundation's demands "as a reflection on the Committee's freedom of action," but he meant to explain how the support for Kinsey had "developed in such a way as, rightly or wrongly, to give our Board the feeling that the Foundation was much more closely identified with the various decisions than it was with those regarding any other beneficiaries of grants from the Committee for Research on Problems of Sex." This being the case, explained Morison, the board felt justified in declaring "its reluctance to include any allocation for Kinsey's work in any future grants to the Committee." Morison then proceeded to review the history of the relationship between the Rockefeller Foundation and Kinsey. Morison's main point was that a special relationship had developed between them, and for that reason the foundation felt free to terminate it. See Robert S. Morison to George W. Corner, Feb. 1, 1954, ibid.

134 Robert M. Yerkes to George W. Corner, Jan. 29, 1954, Box 77, Folder 1463, Yerkes Papers.

135 Filling in Yerkes on the deliberations, Corner wrote, "The Committee was unwilling to make a flat statement that it would not make further allocations to any group from money provided by the Foundation. It was almost unanimously felt that any such written undertaking would weaken the position of the Committee and of [the] NRC." See George W. Corner to Robert M. Yerkes, Feb. 3, 1954, ibid.

136 For the full text of the replacement paragraph, see ibid.

137 Ibid. As Corner explained to Yerkes, "The statement as passed was specifically drawn so that the Committee will not be prevented from making grants in response to the applications for specific projects that may originate in the Bloomington group, while clearly withdrawing from continued administration of a large sum earmarked for the Institute for Sex Research."

138 Robert M. Yerkes to George W. Corner, Feb. 8, 1954, Box 77, Folder 1463, Yerkes Papers.

139 Andrew J. Warren to R. Keith Cannan, Feb. 9, 1954, Series 200, Box 39, Folder 448, Rockefeller Archives.

140 R. Keith Cannan to Andrew J. Warren, Feb. 8, 1954, ibid.

141 R. Keith Cannan to Robert S. Morison, Feb. 8, 1954, ibid. Referring to the new application, Warren wrote, "As I indicated to you in our conversation last week, I shall plan to recommend favorable consideration of this item to our Board of Trustees at their annual meeting the first week of April."

142 George W. Corner to Robert M. Yerkes, Feb. 15, 1954, Box 77, Folder 1463, Yerkes Papers.

143 Robert M. Yerkes to George W. Corner, Feb. 19, 1954, ibid.

144 George W. Corner to ACK, Feb. 24, 1954, KIA.

145 Quoted in Wardell B. Pomeroy, *Dr. Kinsey and the Institute for Sex Research* (New York, 1972), 10.

146 ACK to Dean Rusk, March 3, 1954, KIA.

147 Author's interview with Rusk, April 13, 1972, 18, 14–15.

148 Norman Dodd to Dean Rusk, Feb. 19, 1954. A copy of this letter is housed in the CRPS Files, NRC Archives.

149 R. Keith Cannan, "Memorandum regarding interview with Mr. Karl Egmont Ettinger, 4 March 1954," CRPS Files, NRC Archives.

150 For Corner's request for the clippings, see Corner to ACK, Feb. 24, 1954; for the letter in which Kinsey sent the clippings to Rusk, see ACK to Dean Rusk, March 3, 1954, KIA.

151 Corner to Yerkes, Feb. 15, 1954. While he welcomed the opportunity to educate
     Rusk about the history of the relationship among Kinsey, the foundation, and the
     committee, Corner also hoped to gain a political advantage. As he told Yerkes, "This
     looks like a good opportunity to renew contact with the Foundation at a high level."

152 George W. Corner to Dean Rusk, Feb. 13, 1954, Series 200, Box 38, Folder 448,
     Rockefeller Archives.

153 George W. Corner to ACK, Feb. 24, 1954, KIA.

154 Author's interview with Corner, Aug. 5, 1971, 35–36.

155 Ibid., 36. Asked whether he thought Rusk was unnecessarily timid, Corner replied,
     "Yes, yes, I did." Queried if Rusk had stood up a little more he might have been able
     to defend Kinsey's research more successfully, Corner answered, "Yes, yes, I had that
     impression, definitely." Ibid., 37.

156 Author's interview with Morison, Oct. 18, 1971, 29. The man whose leadership
     Morison admired was Henry Allen Moe, the president of the Guggenheim Founda-
     tion. Morison thought that Moe did a good job of representing the foundations and
     standing up to Representative Reece. Ibid., 29, 34–35. Morison, however, was con-
     fused. The testimony he admired from Moe was delivered earlier before the Cox com-
     mittee. Moe did not testify before the Reece committee.

157 Author's interview with Warren, March 24, 1972, 16.

158 Lewis W. Douglas to John Foster Dulles, Sept. 19, 1951, John Foster Dulles Papers,
     Box 54, Princeton University Library.

159 George W. Corner to Robert M. Yerkes, March 11, 1954, Box 77, Folder 1463, Yerkes
     Papers.

160 Robert M. Yerkes to George W. Corner, March 19, 1954, ibid.

161 George W. Corner to Robert M. Yerkes, March 17, 1954, ibid. Corner wrote reas-
     suringly, "Unless you were quite anxious to take part personally, I think you would be
     fully justified in asking the Committee to leave to me the duty of speaking for the
     Committee."

162 Robert M. Yerkes to George W. Corner, March 22, 1954, ibid.

163 Kinsey wrote Rusk, "I regret that we have not had a chance to meet personally and I
     still hope you will be able to come here, as well as Dr. Warren and Dr. Morison, to
     visit in Bloomington and obtain a better idea of the research that we have under way.
     I regret that there has not been more personal contact with any of the people at the
     Rockefeller Foundation over the twelve years in which you have supported our re-
     search." Kinsey closed, "Is there any chance that we can get you out here to Bloom-
     ington some day?" See ACK to Rusk, March 3, 1954.

164 *Bloomington Herald-Telephone,* April 20, 1954, clipping files, KIA.

165 Desk diary of Robert S. Morison, April 19, 1954, Series 200, Box 39, Folder 448,
     Rockefeller Archives. Morison wrote Kinsey, "Please let me say that I think you struck
     just exactly the right note in your informal address last night. Let us hope that it had
     some effect on a couple of your neighbors at the head table." See Robert S. Morison
     to ACK, April 20, 1954, ibid.

166 *Louisville Times,* May 7, 1954, clipping files, Record Group 11, Series 2, Box 1, Folder
     1, Rockefeller Archives.

167 *Columbus Dispatch,* May 16, 1954, ibid.

168 This overview of current events was taken from Lankford, *Congress and the Founda-
     tions,* 60.

169 Ibid., 64.

170 Ibid., 70–71. Another witness before the committee, Kenneth Colegrove, a retired political science professor from Northwestern University, testified that he considered empiricism an affront to moral law and called for "more study of the healthy portions of American society rather than laying so much emphasis upon the pathological aspects." As examples of the latter, he cited the Kinsey studies, criminal studies, or examinations of "the Negro problem." See ibid., 77.

171 *Indiana Daily Student,* May 20, 1954, 1.

172 *New York Times,* May 20, 1954, 26.

173 Quoted in Lankford, *Congress and the Foundations,* 70.

174 *Indiana Daily Student,* May 20, 1954, 1. Gracie Bowers Pfost, Democrat, First District of Idaho, stated that she did not think it was relevant to the committee's purpose to investigate Kinsey's work. Reece replied, "What disturbs me is why foundations whose funds are made available by the people and by the government in foregoing taxes should be making grants for studies of this nature."

175 ACK to Ray H. Abrams, Dec. 30, 1955, KIA.

176 *Bristol* (Connecticut) *Press,* Aug. 6, 1954, Record Group 11, Series 2, Box 1, Folder 1, Rockefeller Archives.

177 Quoted in Lankford, *Congress and the Foundations,* 86, 89, 90.

178 Undated clippings from *Madison Capital Times, San Francisco Chronicle, Atlanta Constitution, San Antonio News, Washington Post and Times Herald,* and *Deseret News Telegram,* Series 900, Rockefeller Archives.

179 *New York Times,* Dec. 21, 1954, ibid.

180 Arthur Hays Sulzberger to Dean Rusk, Dec. 22, 1954, ibid.

181 Dean Rusk to W. H. Ferry, June 1, 1955, ibid.

182 *New York Times,* Aug. 24, 1954, 25.

Chapter 28: "UP AGAINST THE WALL"

1 ACK to Monroe Wheeler, June 10, 1954, KIA.

2 This episode was pieced together from a variety of sources. One interviewee related the story of Kinsey's self-torture in the basement of the Institute. Author's interview with Clarence A. Tripp, Dec. 15, 1987, 26–27. The location of the incident sets an outside time limit on this incident because the Institute was housed at this location only between 1951 and 1955. The massive pelvic infection discussed in the following paragraphs pinpoints the most likely time for this incident. Moreover, the timing I have posited was exactly when Albert Hoyt Hobbs attacked Kinsey before the Reece Committee, which upset Kinsey greatly. Finally, in this particular instance, Kinsey chose a classic means to attack himself. As Theodore Reik observed, "Being hung, or suspended from some contraption happens to be among the favorite masochistic practices." See Reik, *Masochism in Modern Man* (New York, 1941), 60.

3 ACK to F. S. Shields, Sept. 13, 1954, KIA. In a letter to another friend, Kinsey refined the diagnoses, declaring, "An infection, which we think may have been a strep throat, started a general pelvic infection which gave me a good five to six weeks of rest in Peru and now back here in Bloomington." See ACK to Earl Marsh, Oct. 7, 1954, KIA.

4 Harry H. Freilich to ACK, Sept. 29, 1954, KIA.

5 Author's interview with William Dellenback, Sept. 22, 1971, 27, IUOHP.

6 Robert Phelps, with Jerry Rosco, eds., *Continual Lessons: The Journals of Glenway Wescott, 1937–1955* (New York, 1990), 351.

7   ACK to Harriet Pilpel, Oct. 11, 1954, KIA.

8   Quoted in Cornelia V. Christenson, *Kinsey: A Biography* (Bloomington, 1971), 194.

9   Edgar Anderson, "Kinsey as I Knew Him" (unpublished notes, June 29, 1953). Gebhard, too, had vivid memories of the dramatic changes in Kinsey's appearance, noting he developed "a gray-pale hue to him, and his jowls would sort of sag." Added Gebhard, "He looked really like a very tired bloodhound or something." See author's interview with Paul H. Gebhard, Oct. 29, 1971, 19, IUOHP.

10   Quoted in Wardell B. Pomeroy, *Dr. Kinsey and the Institute for Sex Research* (New York, 1972), 438.

11   Author's interview with Margaret (Mrs. Frank K.) Edmondson, Nov. 9, 1971, 17, IUOHP.

12   Author's interview with Harry Benjamin, Aug. 23, 1971, 16, IUOHP.

13   Author's interview with Glenway Wescott, June 27, 1972, 41, IUOHP.

14   George W. Corner to Robert M. Yerkes, Jan. 11, 1955, Box 77, Folder 1463, Yerkes Papers.

15   Robert M. Yerkes to George W. Corner, Jan. 24, 1955, ibid.

16   George W. Corner to Robert M. Yerkes, Oct. 18, 1954, ibid.

17   Corner to Yerkes, Jan. 11, 1955.

18   "Interviews: Dean Rusk with President H. B. Wells," Jan. 12, 1955, Series 200, Box 39, Folder 449, Rockefeller Archives.

19   Robert M. Yerkes to George W. Corner, March 4, 1955, Box 77, Folder 1463, Yerkes Papers.

20   Pomeroy, *Dr. Kinsey,* 432–35.

21   Monroe Wheeler to ACK, April 26, 1955, KIA.

22   Author's interview with Wescott, June 27, 1972, 44, 21.

23   Ibid., 37. Wescott also cited Kinsey's relationship with Wells, noting, "I have never heard him express so much gratitude toward anyone as toward that man." Musing on Wells, Wescott added, "I always had great curiosity about him, even had great curiosity about his sexual nature and sexual reason, which needless to say I never got the remotest idea of, because I thought he was such a mysterious man. He was a magical man for Kinsey, because he loved the research, must have loved Kinsey in a curious way." Ibid., 37–38.

24   Ibid., 53.

25   Ibid., 38, 39.

26   Pomeroy, *Dr. Kinsey,* 432–33.

27   Ibid., 433.

28   Author's interview with Wescott, June 27, 1972, 42.

29   Author's interview with Gebhard, Oct. 29, 1971, 46–47.

30   Kinsey wrote one inquirer, "The Institute is primarily self-supporting, and our lecturing consumes such an amount of time as interferes with our getting material ready for publication which is our primary business in this research. Consequently, in order to justify the acceptance of further lectures, we have had to fix our fee for such lectures at $500.00 plus traveling expenses." See ACK to Larry Kretchmar, May 21, 1956, KIA.

31   Desk diary of Robert S. Morison, April 18, 1955, Series 200, Box 39, Folder 449, Rockefeller Archives.

32   ACK to Roger J. Williams, Oct. 20, 1953, KIA.

33   As Corner put it to a friend, "I broke through the door of the Ford Foundation, as you know, but was dismissed without action." See Corner to Yerkes, Jan. 11, 1955.

34 ACK to Walter C. Alvarez, April 19, 1956, KIA.
35 Author's interview with Gebhard, Oct. 29, 1971, 47.
36 Russell Yohn to Morris L. Ernst, Dec. 11, 1954, KIA.
37 ACK to Russell Yohn, Dec. 29, 1954, KIA.
38 ACK to George W. Corner, Feb. 9, 1955, KIA.
39 George W. Corner to ACK, March 2, 1955, KIA.
40 ACK to George W. Corner, March 8, 1955, KIA.
41 George W. Corner to ACK, May 20, 1955, KIA.
42 ACK to George W. Corner, May 18, 1955, KIA.
43 ACK to Herman B Wells, May 18, 1955, KIA.
44 Herman B Wells to ACK, May 23, 1955, KIA.
45 "Interoffice Correspondence from Morison to Rusk," May 20, 1955, Series 200, Box 39, Folder 449, Rockefeller Archives.
46 George W. Corner to ACK, June 10, 1955, KIA.
47 Robert S. Morison, notes on meeting, "Dr. Keith Cannon, Division of Medical Sciences, National Research Council," June 2, 1955, Series 200, Box 39, Folder 448, Rockefeller Archives. Morison's notes are quite extensive.
48 Ibid.
49 Ibid.
50 Ibid. This spelled the end for Corner. His days as the chairman of the CRPS were numbered. Two years later, he stepped down, and Frank Beach, the distinguished psychologist and expert on mammalian sexual behavior, replaced him. In the conservative and timid atmosphere of the 1950s, it was dangerous to be a Kinsey supporter.
51 Corner to ACK, June 10, 1955.
52 ACK to George W. Corner, June 14, 1955, KIA.
53 ACK, "Considerations for the Making of New Sex Law" (May 1952), KIA. This unpublished paper runs to nearly thirty pages and represents the fullest development of Kinsey's thought on the need to revise the sex offender codes. From beginning to end, Kinsey sought to rehabilitate the image of the sex offender, to dispute the need for criminalization of most sex acts, and to soften the public's condemnation of even the most despised sex offenses, including rape, incest, and child molestation.
54 ACK, "What I Believe" (unpublished, Dec. 1954), KIA.
55 Ibid.
56 Author's interview with Wescott, June 27, 1972, 47.
57 Ibid., 47–48.
58 Author's interview with Clarence A. Tripp, 80.
59 Pomeroy, Dr. Kinsey, 438.
60 Henry Remak, "Dr. Kinsey" (unpublished remembrance, Aug. 28, 1956), 11–12, KIA.
61 Pomeroy, Dr. Kinsey, 405. Drawing heavily on the notes Kinsey dictated on this trip after he returned to the United States, Pomeroy devoted an entire chapter to this topic.
62 ACK, "Notes on European Trip, 10–12/1955: Scandinavia, 10/9/55 Conference," 4, KIA.
63 ACK, "Notes on European Trip, England, 12-10-55," 11, KIA.
64 ACK, "Notes on European Trip, England, 12-12-[55]," 13–14, KIA.
65 Ibid., 15.
66 ACK, "Notes on European Trip, France, 12-12-55," 1, KIA.
67 Ibid., 2.

68 ACK, "Notes on European Trip, Italy, 12-16-55," 1, KIA.
69 Author's interview with Kenneth Anger, Oct. 13, 1990, 3–7, 9–10, 17–22.
70 Ibid., 54, 35.
71 ACK, "Notes on European Trip, Italy, 12-16-55," 9, 8, KIA.
72 Author's interview with Anger, Oct. 13, 1990, 39.
73 Ibid., 39, 41.
74 Ibid., 57, 41.
75 Ibid., 40, 41.
76 ACK, "Notes on European Trip, Spain, 12-17-55," 20, KIA.
77 Ibid. This observation appeared in the notes on Portugal, even though it dealt with what Kinsey had observed in Spain.
78 Ibid.
79 Ibid.
80 ACK to Eleanor Roehr, Nov. 27, 1955, KIA.
81 ACK to Sam Steward, Jan. 10, 1956, KIA.
82 ACK to Fosco Maraini, Jan. 20, 1956, KIA.
83 ACK to Georg K. Stürup, Jan. 24, 1956, KIA.
84 ACK to Eleanor Roehr, Nov. 1, 1955, KIA.
85 Christenson, *Kinsey,* 196.
86 Pomeroy, *Dr. Kinsey,* 430.

Chapter 29: "HE HELPED TO CHANGE THE TIMES"

1 *Indiana Daily Student,* March 13, 1956.
2 Author's interview with Paul H. Gebhard, Aug. 7, 1984, 11.
3 Author's interview with Dorothy Collins, Dec. 9, 1971, 11, IUOHP.
4 Ibid.
5 Author's interview with Paul H. Gebhard, Oct. 29, 1971, 68, IUOHP.
6 Ibid.
7 Ibid., 69. As it happened, Gebhard had a job offer around this time from the University of Southern Illinois. "Yes, I was tempted," he admitted many years later. "But then I felt that it would be very bad for the Institute if I left, and I had enough of an emotional investment in it by then that I just didn't want to see the thing go down the drain." Gebhard added, "I thought if I stayed I could perhaps prevent this." And that is what precisely what he did. Following Kinsey's death, Gebhard was named director of the Institute for Sex Research, and under his capable leadership the Institute developed into the nation's leading center for sex research.
8 Author's interview with Collins, Dec. 9, 1971, 24. Another fact that contributed to her decision to resign, Collins explained, was her concern that the position might be somewhat awkward for her husband, who was a senior administrator at Indiana University. "I should say, there was this element also that I felt some—it wasn't a ruling cause, but I did feel that my work in the Institute was somewhat of an embarrassment to my husband or to the administration, to have someone related to [the] administration working there."
9 Author's interview with Glenway Wescott, June 27, 1972, 58, IUOHP.
10 Author's interview with Gebhard, Oct. 29, 1971, 67.
11 ACK to Robert Winters, May 16, 1956, KIA.
12 ACK to Wentworth P. Johnson, May 11, 1956, KIA.

13   Wardell B. Pomeroy, *Dr. Kinsey and the Institute for Sex Research* (New York, 1972), 434–35.

14   Ibid., 435.

15   Quoted in Cornelia V. Christenson, *Kinsey: A Biography* (Bloomington, 1971), 199.

16   Ibid.

17   "Telephone Conversation, President Wells to Eleanor Roehr," June 5, 1956, Herman B Wells Papers, IUA.

18   Herman B Wells to ACK, June 6, 1956, KIA.

19   Quoted in Christenson, *Kinsey,* 200.

20   Osmond P. Breland to ACK, June 20, 1956, KIA.

21   Quoted in Christenson, *Kinsey,* 201.

22   Author's interview with Fernandus Payne, March 2, 1971, 9, IUOHP.

23   Author's interview with Theodore W. Torrey, Sept. 17, 1971, 22, IUOHP.

24   Quoted in ibid., 23.

25   ACK to Kenneth Anger, June 26, 1956, KIA.

26   ACK to Osmond P. Breland, July 5, 1956, KIA.

27   ACK to Kenneth Anger, July 10, 1956, KIA.

28   ACK to Hugo Gernsbach, July 9, 1956, KIA.

29   Henry Remak, "Dr. Kinsey," Aug. 28, 1956, KIA.

30   Kenneth R. Stevens, "United States v. 31 Photographs: Dr. Alfred C. Kinsey and Obscenity Law," *Indiana Magazine of History* 71 (Dec. 1975): 311, 313.

31   ACK, "The Right to Do Sex Research" (unpublished paper, Aug. 1956), KIA.

32   Quoted in Christenson, *Kinsey,* 199.

33   Stevens, "United States v. 31 Photographs," 310–11.

34   Author's interview with Herman B Wells, Dec. 3, 1971, 26, 27, IUOHP.

35   Quoted in ibid., 28–29.

36   Author's interview with Wescott, June 27, 1972, 38.

37   Quoted in Christenson, *Kinsey,* 294.

38   Author's telephone conversation with Paul H. Gebhard, Nov. 21, 1996.

39   Pomeroy, *Dr. Kinsey,* 435.

40   Author's interview with Gebhard, Oct. 29, 1971, 85.

41   Ibid., 79–80.

42   *Indianapolis News,* Aug. 27, 1956, clipping files, KIA.

43   *Indiana Catholic and Record,* Aug. 31, 1956, ibid.

44   *New York Times,* Aug. 27, 1956, 18.

45   See Stanley Elkin, "Alfred Kinsey: The Patron Saint of Sex," *Esquire,* Dec. 1983, 48–56.

46   See Judith A. Reisman and Edward W. Eichel, *Kinsey, Sex, and Fraud: The Indoctrination of a People* (Lafayette, La., 1990). The charges in this book were repeated by Patrick J. Buchanan, who aired them in his nationally syndicated newspaper column. See Buchanan, "Sex, Lies and Dr. Kinsey," *New York Post,* Oct. 20, 1990.

47   *Washington Post,* Dec. 8, 1995, F1, F4.

48   Lawrence S. Kubie to Robert S. Morison, April 10, 1956, Series 200, Box 39, Folder 449, Rockefeller Archives. See also Lawrence S. Kubie to Robert S. Morison, April 23, 1956, ibid.

49   Robert S. Morison to Lawrence S. Kubie, April 19, 1956, ibid.

50   Author's interview with Anon. A, 80–81.

51   Saul Bellow, "The Sealed Treasure," reprinted in Bellow, *It All Adds Up: From the Dim Past to the Uncertain Future* (New York, 1994), 62.

52 Author's interview with Mrs. ACK, Dec. 10, 1971, 45, IUOHP.
53 For the best explication and analysis of the importance of social and economic forces to changes in private behavior, see John D'Emilio and Estelle B. Freedman, *Intimate Matters: A History of Sexuality in America* (New York, 1988).
54 Author's interview with George W. Corner, Aug. 5, 1971, 48, IUOHP.

A NOTE ON SOURCES

PRIMARY SOURCES

Archival Collections. This biography draws heavily on primary sources. The most extensive materials on Kinsey's career as a sex researcher are housed in the Kinsey Institute Archives, located on the campus of Indiana University. Although many items appear to be missing, his correspondence approaches fifty thousand letters. The Institute also preserves memoranda of his meetings and telephone discussions with various figures, copies of his lectures notes in the marriage course, and numerous unpublished papers and articles. The collection contains a sprinkling of letters by Kinsey's staff, including Glenn V. Ramsey, Clyde E. Martin, Wardell B. Pomeroy, Vincent Nowlis, and Paul H. Gebhard. There are also more than forty brief reminiscences of Kinsey by various friends and associates written in the early 1960s at the request of Gebhard, who succeeded Kinsey as director. In addition, the Institute boasts a remarkable library, which houses books, periodicals, pamphlets, and other materials. Of particular interest to historians are the library's clipping files, which fill scores of volumes. The clippings chronicle the popular and professional responses to Kinsey, his staff, and the male and female volumes; and they include newspaper and magazine articles, letters to the editor, popular and scholarly reviews, cartoons, and the like. The Kinsey Institute's correspondence and clipping files are open to qualified scholars.

The records of three institutions are essential for explaining how Kinsey was able to conduct controversial research in an environment that ranged from skeptical to hostile. Records documenting the support for Kinsey's research provided by Herman B Wells and other university officials are housed in the Indiana University Archives. Glimpses of Kinsey's pre–sex research years at Indiana University are also afforded by letters and reports deposited in the Indiana University Archives. The Committee for Research in Problems of Sex Files, housed in the National Research Council Archives in Washington, D.C., are crucial for understanding Kinsey's rise to national prominence. These files (which fill six filing cabinet drawers) include the CRPS's unpublished annual reports, minutes of its regular and special meetings, letters exchanged by its members, correspondence with officials of the Bureau of Social Hygiene and the Rockefeller Foundation, and the correspondence between committee members and grantees. The committee also received letters from a number of outsiders who hoped to influence its policies. The Rockefeller Foundation's records, housed at the Rockefeller Archives Center, Hillcrest, Pocantico Hills, North Tarrytown, New York, are also essential to Kinsey's story. They include the correspondence and desk diaries of foundation officers, minutes of interviews and meetings, and a variety of materials pertaining to the trustees.

Materials on Kinsey's work and his place in the history of science and in popular culture must be gleaned from the papers of a variety of individuals and from the records of several institutions. In the course of preparing this biography, I consulted the following archives and collections:

Bowdoin College Archives, Brunswick, Maine
Columbia High School Archives, Maplewood, New Jersey
George W. Corner Papers and Raymond Pearl Papers, American Philosophical Society Archives, Philadelphia, Pennsylvania
Robert L. Dickinson Papers, Countway Library of Medicine, Harvard Medical School, Boston, Massachusetts
John Foster Dulles Papers, Princeton University Library, Princeton, New Jersey
Margaret Mead Papers and Reinhold Niebuhr Papers, Library of Congress, Washington, D.C.
New York Times Archive, New York, New York
South Orange Archive, South Orange, New Jersey
Stevens Institute of Technology Archives, Hoboken, New Jersey
Lewis M. Terman Papers, Stanford University Archives, Stanford, California
Lionel Trilling Papers, Butler Library, Columbia University, New York, New York
Henry P. Van Dusen Papers, Union Theological Seminary Archives, New York, New York
William M. Wheeler Papers, Pusey Library, Harvard University, Cambridge, Massachusetts
Robert M. Yerkes Papers, Sterling Library, Yale University, New Haven, Connecticut

Oral History. This biography could not have been written without oral history, and I drew, in some instances heavily, on the interviews I conducted with the following individuals:

Kenneth Anger, October 13, 1990
Anonymous B, February 17, 1988**
Hazel Phillips Balch, March 28, 1992
Frank A. Beach, August 20, 1971*
Harry Benjamin, August 23, 1971*
William R. Breneman, May 21, 1985
Robert E. Bugbee, October 19, 1971*
Dorothy Collins, December 9, 1971*
George W. Corner, August 5, 1971*
William Dellenback, September 21, 1971,* and February 14, 1988
William Dellenback and Clarence Tripp (joint interview), October 13, 1984
Frank K. Edmondson, November 8, 1971*
Margaret [Mrs. Frank K.] Edmondson, November 9, 1971*
Agnes West Gebhard, October 15, 1984
Paul H. Gebhard, October 29, 1971,* January 7, 1972,* July 30, 1982, August 7, 1984, and October 14, 1984
Lawrence E. Gichner, May 11, 1983
Michael Gregg, December 1, 1984
William Gury, March 28, 1992
Wayne L. Hays, August 4, 1971*
Edna Kinsey Higenbotham, November 28, 1984
Clara [Mrs. Alfred C.] Kinsey, December 10, 1971*
Robert Kroc, November 7, 1987, and October 13, 1990
Clyde E. Martin, April 8, 1971* and March 21, 1986

Robert S. Morison, October 18, 1971*
Frederick Mosteller, June 26, 1992
Kate Hevner Mueller, April 1, 1971*
Vincent Nowlis, January 18, 1988
Fernandus Payne, March 2, 1971*
Wardell B. Pomeroy, July 19, 1971*
Virginia Prince, February 11, 1971*
Homer T. Rainwater, May 30, 1990
Glenn V. Ramsey, March 15, 1972*
Joan Reid, February 14, 1972*
Eleanor Roehr, September 3, 1971*
Dean Rusk, April 13, 1972*
Edith B. Schuman, September 15, 1971*
Herman T. Spieth, February 18, 1988
Theodore W. Torrey, September 17, 1971*
Clarence A. Tripp, December 15, 1987
Cecilia [Mrs. Henry E.] Wahl, January 22, 1972*
Andrew J. Warren, March 24, 1971*
Herman B Wells, January 3, 1971*
Monroe Wheeler, January 20, 1988, and February 29, 1988
Mary G. Winther, March 11, 1971*
Glenway Wescott, June 27, 1972*
Frank Young, May 20, 1985

*A copy is on deposit with the Indiana University Oral History Project.

I also relied on three interviews by Thomas D. Clark in the Kinsey Institute Archives:

Clara [Mrs. Alfred C.] Kinsey, February 17, 1969
Fernandus Payne, October 8, 1968, October 12, 1968, October 15, 1968, and November 2, 1968
Herman B Wells, January 1968

Secondary Sources

The first book-length work on Kinsey was Cornelia V. Christenson, *Kinsey: A Biography* (Bloomington, 1971). A brief study written by a former member of Kinsey's staff, it offers the official version of his career and seldom gets below the surface. Still, it provides many useful details, largely because it was written with the cooperation of and considerable input from Clara Kinsey. At once longer and more entertaining is Wardell B. Pomeroy (with the assistance of John Tebbel), *Dr. Kinsey and the Institute for Sex Research* (New York, 1972). A staff member and a key figure in Kinsey's inner circle, Pomeroy was in an excellent position to move beyond the canonical Kinsey. Instead, his book is very much in the "I rode with the great man" genre. Although it contains a wealth of anecdotal material and a number of insights into Kinsey's complex personality, it conceals as much as it reveals about its subject.

Professionally trained historians have not produced a single biography or book-length study of Kinsey. Still, he has figured prominently in the work of several able scholars. Kinsey was discovered early by Sidney Ditzion, a pioneering social historian. In *Marriage, Morals, and Sex in America: A History of Ideas* (New York, 1953), Ditzion made a brave and remarkably successful attempt to place Kinsey in his cultural context. Paul Robinson, *The*

Modernization of Sex: Havelock Ellis, Alfred Kinsey, and William Masters and Virginia Johnson (New York, 1976), offers a brilliant analysis of the values and assumptions that run the length of Kinsey's work on human sexuality. In addition, Robinson gives an astute reading of Kinsey's conceptual strengths and weaknesses. Kinsey's place in the history of sexology is deftly assessed in Vern L. Bullough's important *Science in the Bedroom: A History of Sex Research* (New York, 1994). Also valuable is the provocative discussion of Kinsey's work in John D'Emilio and Estelle B. Freedman, *Intimate Matters: A History of Sexuality in America* (New York, 1988).

In the important *Disorders of Desire: Sex and Gender in Modern American Sexology* (Philadelphia, 1990), Janice M. Irvine, a sociologist, examined the rise and the cultural impact of sex research in the United States. She is especially strong in identifying the pleas for sexual liberation in Kinsey's work, and she shows how his agenda shaped large segments of the sexology movement that followed him.

Over the last fifteen years historians have produced a number of first-rate studies on the creation of gay communities and gay identity in the United States. The place to begin is with John D'Emilio, *Sexual Politics, Sexual Communities: The Making of a Homosexual Minority in the United States* (Chicago, 1983), an excellent study. No less valuable is Allan Berube, *Coming Out under Fire: The History of Gay Men and Women in World War II* (New York, 1990). George Chauncey, *Gay New York: Gender, Urban Culture, and the Making of the Gay Male World, 1890–1940,* is a work of impressive scholarship that applies theory to historical problems with great sophistication. A wealth of dearly arrived-at personal insight, joined to hard-biting social analysis, can be found in Martin Duberman's moving memoir, *Cures: A Gay Man's Odyssey* (New York, 1991).

INDEX

AAAS (American Association for the Advancement of Science), 226–27, 268–69, 424

Aarhus University, 754

abortion, 67, 669, 748, 749
  spontaneous, 350

academic freedom, 343, 406–7, 411–12, 472–73, 542, 557, 592, 633, 686, 713, 724

academic journals, peer reviews in, 552–54, 575

Academy of Natural Sciences of Philadelphia, 136

ACLU (American Civil Liberties Union), 713

acne, 624

Adams, Samuel, 104

Adler, Hermann, 144

adolescents:
  building character in, 41–42, 55, 86, 89, 118
  in college, 86
  legal system and, 43, 62–63
  masturbation and, 66, 69–75, 79–80, 82–83, 276, 300, 507, 510–12, 529
  molesting of, see pedophilia
  moral policing of, 63–65, 66, 258, 520, 772
  physical maturity of, 328
  sex education of, see sex education

sex histories collected from, 346–48, 376–77, 387, 398–99, 400, 429, 446, 469, 471–72, 483, 489, 491, 498, 513–16, 522, 552, 591, 592

sex segregation of, 66, 74

sexual banter of, 279, 285, 292

adrenal gland, 306

adultery, see marriage, sexual activity outside of

advertising, 291, 540–41, 542, 558–62

African Americans, 43, 494, 516, 626
  marriage and family among, 485
  sex histories collected from, 428–29, 434, 484–86

Agassiz, Louis, 103

Agassiz Museum, 135, 136, 144

age:
  sexual outlet and, 427, 522, 523–24, 579, 682, 695
  sexual partners and differences in, 619, 621; see also pedophilia

Agriculture Department, U.S., 47

AIDS, 773

Air Force, U.S., 474

alcohol, 43, 61–62, 64, 67, 68, 120, 137, 140, 150, 160, 178, 194, 292, 458

alcoholics, 429, 494

Copernicus, Nicolaus, 569, 685
Cornell University, 30, 47
Corner, George W., 431–37, 438,
    452, 456, 461–63, 464,
    584–85, 589, 596, 872n
    Kinsey supported by, 435–37,
    462–63, 557–58, 561, 582,
    590, 597–99, 636, 638, 639,
    642, 645, 646, 648, 653–54,
    655, 656, 658, 661, 662–65,
    671, 696–97, 699, 717–19,
    725–27, 728, 731, 732, 736,
    741–43, 747–51, 773
    sex history collected from,
    433–34, 436
Cornfield, Jerome, 683, 684
Coronet, 630
corporate trustees, 42
correlations, Kinsey's use of, 687
Correns, Carl, 130
corsets, 504
Cosmopolitan, 596, 571, 699, 701,
    709, 710
Court, Norman, 65
cousins, marriages between, 354,
    621
Cox, Eugene E., 722
Cox committee, 722
Craig, Margaret, 46
creationism, 188–89
"Criteria for a Hormonal
    Exploration of the
    Homosexual" (Kinsey), 425–26
CRPS, *see* Committee on Research
    in Problems of Sex, NRC
cruising, 379, 756
Cue, 567, 569
cultural anthropology, 302, 583
Customs Bureau, U.S., 670–72,
    750, 767
cytology, 182, 206, 264

dancing, 64–65, 68, 95, 120, 122,
    178, 292, 314

Darrow, Clarence, 188
Dartmouth College, 594
Darwin, Charles, 192, 305
    antiessentialism of, 145–46, 147
    common descent and, 223, 225
    Kinsey compared to, 147, 222,
    223, 225, 228, 367, 487, 517,
    569–70, 582, 704, 719, 733
    New Biology and, 130, 131,
    136
    religion and, 18, 189
dating, 65–66, 68, 96, 124, 140,
    163, 241, 292, 314
    sexual activity in, 169, 292; *see also*
    marriage, sexual activity outside
    of
Daughters of Bilitis (DOB), 708
Davis, Harold, 654
Davis, Katherine B., 306
deafness, 624
Dear Timothy, 790n
degeneration theory, 297
Dellenback, William "Bill," 605–11,
    613, 667, 674, 739, 759
Deming, William E., 654
Democratic Party, 722, 736
Denmark, 698, 754, 758
Denton, James Edgar "Jimmie D.,"
    9–10, 21, 94
depression, 319
Depression, Great, 243, 331,
    375–76
Deseret News Telegram, 736
De Voto, Bernard, 577
de Vries, Hugo, 130
Dewey, John, 31
diabetes, 237
*Diagnostic and Statistical Manual of
    Psychiatric Disorders,* 677
diaphragms, 330, 332, 356
Dickey, John S., 594
Dickinson, Robert Latou, 175, 270,
    291, 292, 293, 306, 331, 333,
    503–8, 603
    sex research of, 505, 506–8

safe sex, 773
Sage, Russell, 34
St. Louis, Mo., homosexual
subculture in, 388–89
St. Louis Globe-Democrat, 712
Salisbury, Don, 49
saliva, as lubricant, 332, 334
sampling, 184, 203, 206, 209–11,
294, 297–98, 300, 346–37,
372, 466, 578–79, 658
cluster, 636
random, 436, 579, 583, 641, 643,
654–55, 658, 659, 663, 683,
687
representativeness and, 636, 645,
646–47, 688, 709–10
stratified, 579
theory of, 210, 433, 577
San Antonio News, 736
San Francisco Chronicle, 736
San Francisco News, 711–12
Sanger, Margaret, 331, 503, 706
San Quentin, prison at, 673–74,
752
San Quentin News, 752
Saturday Night Club, 137
Saturday Review, 541, 703, 720
Saunders, Lawrence, 536–38, 547,
548, 552, 560, 672, 762
Saunders Company, *see* W. B.
Saunders Company
scarlet fever, 27
Schenectady Union-Star, 712
schools:
compulsory attendance of, 63
construction of, 29–30, 42
sex education in, 67–68, 69, 72,
120, 319–20, 321–36, 470–74,
527, 567
see also colleges and universities;
education
Schricker, Henry F., 671
Schulte, Paul C., 713
Schuman, Edith, 326, 398–99, 405
Schwartz, Charles, 256

science:
direct observation in, 46, 109,
134–35, 136, 144, 188, 205–6,
502–3, 507, 610–11, 660, 673,
720
essentialism in, 145–47, 221, 229,
365, 623
funding for, 417–18, 596, 742,
750–51, 769
heroism of, 522, 570, 575
incremental progress in, 596, 714,
771
moral neutrality and, 329, 513,
518–19, 595–96, 619, 720
practical value of, 188, 189–90,
304–5, 308–9, 421
prestige of, 152–53, 204, 586
questions in, 46, 107, 151, 204
religion and, 18, 126–27, 154,
189, 204, 294, 333, 336, 420,
466, 474, 520, 525, 586, 724
of sex and sexuality, *see* sexology
in sex education, 326, 328–29,
344, 424
social reform through, 328–29,
335–36, 374–75, 386, 396,
418–19, 423, 463, 466, 518,
520, 532–33, 580–81, 619,
623, 634, 649, 672, 684,
685–86, 704, 714, 750–51, 766
theory vs. facts in, 300
Science, 227, 710
Science Illustrated, 547, 549–50
Science News Letter, 706, 708–9
Science Progress, 226
Scientific Basis of Evolution, The
(Morgan), 224
scientific doubt, 300
scientific management, 99–100
Scientific Monthly, 153
Scientists Committee on Loyalty
Problems, 628
Scopes, John, 188–89
Scott, Will, 166
teaching skills of, 182–83

prurient interests and, 459, 476,
501–3, 568, 703, 744, 771
psychiatry and psychology in,
296–300, 324, 358, 366, 367,
383, 386, 418, 425–26, 439,
450, 453, 492, 495, 524, 529,
537, 541, 567, 575, 577, 582,
583, 594, 598, 625–26, 669,
682, 695, 703, 719, 771
rigor of, 359, 362–64, 426,
435–36
samples in, 294, 297–98, 300,
346–47, 358, 372–73, 375,
387, 427, 435, 436, 440, 446,
450, 452–53, 466, 473, 485,
506, 518, 521, 533, 565, 577,
578–79, 643–48, 655
sociology in, 386, 418, 439, 475,
529–30, 535, 537, 541, 575,
594, 682, 703
technology in, 429, 469–70
theories and assumptions of,
296–300, 365, 577, 587
sex organs, *see* reproductive organs
sex reversals, 306, 622
sexual activity:
abstaining from, 71, 72, 75, 79,
519, 523, 688, 691, 709–10
ambivalence about, 291, 293,
617–21
anonymous, 370, 379, 385,
496–97, 502
coercive, 511–12, 620, 691,
752–53, 772; *see also*
pedophilia; rape
collecting data on, 287, 306, 336,
346–68, 409, 503, 505, 507,
521–22, 685, 719, 733,
752–53, 763; *see also* sexology
control over, 4, 78–79, 258–59,
321, 328, 339, 422, 709
criminal, *see* sex offenders
denial of, 360, 362–65
emotional content of, 577, 579,
582, 587, 720

filming of, 605–14, 669, 684, 755
first experiences of, 383–84
frequency of, 470, 689–90
group, 271, 619
incidence of, 302–3, 425–26, 427
lack of response in, 350
life stages and, 427, 522, 523–24
marriage founded on, 290,
292–93, 297, 334–35, 359,
395–96, 504–5, 513–14, 516,
528, 691, 705, 707
of men vs. women, 679, 688,
689–90, 692, 693–96, 707–8
mismatches for, 274, 328,
334–36, 402, 504, 513, 516,
614
morality at odds with, 466, 565,
617–21, 689
of "natural man," 512
of other species, 302, 305, 307,
327, 329, 343, 439, 530
outside of marriage, 62, 66, 67,
69, 71, 169, 258, 260, 262,
290, 292, 300, 320–21, 331,
347, 349, 350, 351, 489, 501,
512, 513–14, 520, 525, 526,
527–28, 565, 574, 576, 608,
623, 624, 629, 689, 690–91,
692–93, 695, 707, 709, 712,
734
physical maturity and, 328
pleasure in, 81, 511, 519, 607
positions and techniques in, 270,
274, 276, 292, 293, 307, 328,
330, 334, 350, 356, 395, 526,
609, 705–6
procreation and, 70, 78, 231, 232,
290, 297, 331
romantic love and, 505, 577, 579,
733
subcultures of, 269, 364, 369–73,
378–83, 384–87, 388, 417,
484, 573, 763
sexual attraction, societies based on,
327